Contract Cases
and Materials

FOURTH EDITION

Robert Clark
&
Blanaid Clarke

GILL & MACMILLAN

Gill & Macmillan Ltd
Hume Avenue
Park West
Dublin 12
with associated companies throughout the world
www.gillmacmillan.ie

© Robert Clark and Blanaid Clarke 1994, 2000, 2004, 2008
978 07171 4378 8
Tables compiled by Cover to Cover
Design and print origination by Carrigboy Typesetting Services

The paper used in this book is made from the wood pulp of managed forests.
For every tree felled, at least one is planted, thereby renewing natural resources.

A catalogue record is available for this book from the British Library.

Contents

Preface to the First Edition

As law teachers charged with the task of instructing undergraduate students for whom contract law is a central element in the curriculum we have long felt the need for a collection of cases and materials which would give these students ready access to primary sources in this area. We hope that this casebook will provide teachers and students with much of the case-law and the academic commentary needed to give Irish students competence in what can be a difficult and complex area of law.

The materials compiled here are intended as a course book rather than a collection of indigenous Irish material. While acknowledging that a casebook restricted to Irish materials may be a worthy and justifiable tool (e.g. *McMahon and Binchy on Torts*), we prefer an intensive and comprehensive work that draws upon pertinent material from other jurisdictions. In the area of contract, many key issues are not covered in modern Irish case-law, and we believe that students should be aware of the nature of these issues and their potential solutions, even if the solutions presented are from other jurisdictions. This approach provides Irish students with a comparative analysis of common law contract law and with the opportunity to contrast competing approaches to universal problems.

While Irish contract law tends to follow the pattern set by the English common law there have always been points of divergence from, and differences in emphasis to, that jurisdiction. Irish law on unconscionability and the Statute of Frauds, for example, even prior to 1922, was often at different stages of development to the relevant English law. On the former, the wonderful judgment of Gavan Duffy J. in *Grealish v. Murphy* [1946] IR 35 stands both as a profound analysis of aspects of Irish law and society and as a literary gem. More recently, the development of promissory estoppel and legitimate expectation through *Webb* shows how judicial ingenuity in the area of contract continues to play an important cultural and historical role. In the main, we have set out the law in a way which, we hope, will enable the student to extract the conceptual and doctrinal lessons from the primary source.

The casebook is longer than we had planned and the problem was always rather what to discard than what to keep. Drawing on our experience of teaching in university law schools, we edited or omitted areas that are either shunned or are educationally incoherent (e.g. gaming contracts and infant contracts). Areas that we regard as of immense practical and academic interest were treated comprehensively (e.g. exemption clauses and damages). We hope that this selection process has not rendered the book too unbalanced.

The extracts are not laid out in a common format. Some judgments and some law reports include footnotes while others include references in the text. In general we have adhered to the layout of the primary source although we have tried to avoid duplication of references in order to preserve space. For similar reasons some footnotes have been omitted or abridged from certain primary materials. We accept responsibility for errors and omissions. We would be happy to hear from readers who wish to point these out or to castigate us for any infelicities detected in the book!

Robert Clark   Blanaid Clarke
Mount Merrion   Los Angeles

3 September 1994

Preface to the Second Edition

The publication of this collection of cases and materials in 1994 was met with a welcoming response by book reviewers and users. Any new venture of this kind is a source of anxiety and we were gratified by the willingness of Gill & Macmillan to consider the publication of a Second Edition soon after the initial launch of the book. As several reviewers have pointed out, the collection is, by and large, a traditional one which is intended to give students in particular a rather linear and chronological journey through substantive law topics. We have continued to adopt this approach.

The materials that made up the First Edition have been proved somewhat. The fact that as teachers we have been able to use the Casebook in class has led us to reorder some of the materials. This is particularly evident in the chapter on Illegal Contracts. We are grateful to colleagues who have made helpful suggestions about what works well in class and what is less successful. We have also sought to enhance the index to the cases by adding details about cases referred to in judgements, particularly the inclusion of the dates of the judgements or the law report.

In relation to the new material it should be said that new legislative developments have not been of primary concern. We have used the proposals for legislation and the Law Reform Commission Report on Gazumping to enhance the 'subject to contract' materials, and the EU Distance Contracts Directive and Proposed Directive on Electronic Commerce are also referred to. The chapter on Privity of Contract reproduces some of the UK Law Commission Report that was pivotal in shaping the Contracts (Rights of Third Parties) Act 1999. We hope that this may nudge the Oireachtas along the same path before too long.

New cases appear in just about every chapter. Highlights from Irish judicial decisions include *Hawberry Lane*, *Macken v. Wilde and Longin*, and *McCarson v. McCarson*, vis-à-vis issues of formation and proof. Significant case-law in the area of implied terms is included, particularly *Carna Foods*. The chapter on Illegality is enhanced by *Ennis v. Butterley* and *Fraser v. Buckle*, amongst others. We also include *Bolger v. Osbourne and the Turf Club*, a case that promises to do much to blur the boundary between judicial review of public/private law decision making bodies.

Of the English decisions included, particular attention should be paid to *Mahmud and Malik v. BCCI*, *Dartington BC v. Wittshier Northern Ltd*, *Ruxley Electronics* and the turmoil surrounding post *Barclay's Bank v. O'Brien* developments.

There are some omissions. We were unable to put the Supreme Court decision in *Carroll v. Carroll* into the chapter on undue influence and the judgement of Shanley J., upheld by the Supreme Court, is retained. We are glad that the Shanley J. judgment remains, for it is a masterful analysis of the law on undue influence and unconscionable bargain, serving also to remind us of just how great a loss the Irish legal community suffered when Peter Shanley was taken from us all too soon. Nor were we able to include the judgment of the Supreme Court in *Jodifern v. Fitzgerald*. Students of the law on frustration should be aware of the fascinating analysis of the judicial basis of frustration in Roderick Murphy J.'s judgment in *Quinton Zuphen and Others v. Kelly Technical Services (Ireland) Ltd.*, handed down on May 24, 2000.

While we have struggled to keep the new materials down to a minimum, there is no doubt that some of the Chapters will need to be reorganised somewhat if the Third Edition of this Casebook is to stay within manageable boundaries. With this future task in mind we would welcome comments and suggestions about the user-friendliness (or lack of same) of this Second Edition.

Everyone at Gill & Macmillan has been wonderful and supportive—and very patient!

Robert Clark   Blanaid Clarke
Mount Merrion   Barcelona

July 2000

Preface to the Third Edition

Since publication of the last edition in 2000, there have been a number of fundamental developments in the contract law area. Indeed a major challenge for us has been to include all the relevant material in the various areas while keeping the book within a manageable scale for publication.

New cases appear in every chapter of the book. Important Irish decisions included are: *O'Keeffe v Ryanair Holdings plc* on acceptance and consideration, *Carey v Independent Newspapers (Ireland) Ltd* on terms of a contract and damages, *Dakota Packaging Ltd v APH Manufacturing BV* on implied terms, *Supermacs Ireland Ltd. and McDonagh v Katesan (Naas) Ltd* on certainty, *Daly v Minister for the Marine* on legitimate expectation and *Coonan v AG* on legitimate expectation.

As always developments in the UK have proven a fruitful source of material. The chapter on mistake has benefited particularly in this respect. We have included the decision of the Court of Appeal in *Great Peace Shipping Ltd v Tsavliris Salvage (International) Ltd* which denies the existence of an equitable jurisdiction to set aside a contract on the grounds of common mistake as to quality. While this case has greatly clarified the theoretical base and the scope of the doctrine of mistake, it remains to be seen whether the House of Lords agree on the issue of discretionary relief for mistake and also whether the Irish courts would choose to follow it. A less satisfactory outcome is seen in *Shogun Finance Ltd v Hudson*. Following the decision of the Court of Appeal in 2001, it was hoped that the House of Lords would take the opportunity to clarify the effect of mistakes as to identity in regard to face to face dealings. Regrettably, its judgment in 2003 continues an injustice to innocent purchasers of dishonestly obtained goods. As the majority decided the matter largely on agency grounds, the dissenting judgment of Lord Nichols is included as the more illuminating analysis of the law and it is submitted as a better solution to the problem. He referred to the difficulty of maintaining a dividing line between transactions concluded face to face from those concluded in writing as, for instance, in situations where the contract is concluded over the telephone. The approach suggested was that in all cases of mistaken identity, where one party has misled the other and irrespective of whether the contract is oral or in writing, there would a presumption that there would be a contract, such contract being only voidable. Other UK cases included in this edition are *Hall v Woolston Hall Leisure Ltd* on illegalty, *The Queen on the Application of Factortame and Others v Secretary of State for Transport* on champertous contracts, *Gillett v Holt* on estoppel and *Alfred McAlpine Construction v Panatown* on damages in respect of third party's loss.

In addition to developments in caselaw, we have also included other recent relevant material. We were delighted to be able to include the *Company Law Review Group – First Report* (2000–2001) on Corporate Capacity and Authority in our capacity chapter with its useful analysis of the area and thoughtful suggestions for change. We have expanded the section on electronic contracting to include recent developments. We have included relevant extracts from the Electronic Commerce Directive, the Electronic Commerce Act 2000 and the European Communities (Directive 2000/31/EC) Regulations 2003. While these regulations explain when and where a person is deemed to be in receipt of an electronic communication and set out requirements in relation to acknowledging receipt of such orders, unfortunately they do not tell us whether the postal rule or the general rule applies. We must thus await further case law on this. In the area of electronic contracting, we have also included an extract from The European Communities (Protection of Consumers in Respect of Contracts Made By Means of Distance Communication) Regulations 2001 which gives effect to Directive 97/7/EC on the protection of consumers in respect of distant contracts.

While reviewing the last edition, we have also taken the opportunity to introduce a number of presentational changes to make the subject areas more comprehensible. For example cases such as *Boyle v Lee* and *Shirley Engineering* are analysed both in the chapter on formation and the chapter on formalities. Similarly, a new section in the chapter on express terms deals specifically with construction of a contract.

Particular thanks are due to everyone in Gill & Macmillan and most particularly Deirdre Nolan and Marion O'Brien for their assistance with the casebook. Special thanks also to our colleagues in the Law Library in University College Dublin and in particular Valerie Kendlin. Finally, as the majority of presentational changes introduced in this text arose as a consequence of our own experiences teaching contract law to students in University College Dublin, we owe a debt of gratitude to them for their helpful, if often direct, comments. As always we would welcome any comments from readers on this edition.

Robert Clark   Blanaid Clarke
Majorca   Mount Merrion

20 September 2004

Preface to the Fourth Edition

'Less is More'
(Ludwig Mies van der Rohe)

While this great German-born architect was explaining how he was able to arrange architectural elements in order to produce complex yet minimalist compositions (and we were merely required to re-edit and update a casebook), this aphorism helps to explain why the fourth edition includes additional materials while being 200 pages shorter than its predecessor. As law degrees become increasingly modular in structure, this puts greater pressure on teachers and students to cover a large syllabus in increasingly restricted timeframes. We have therefore tried to produce a casebook that takes a realistic perspective on what university contract courses may be expected to cover while at the same time facilitating students who use the casebook in Law Society and other professional examinations.

We have added a significant amount of new material in the chapters dealing with formation of contracts, mistake, privity of contract and damages. Even chapters that consider areas of contract law that do not change very much, such as illegality and contractual capacity, have been expanded. This, however, has created a need to re-edit existing materials in order to ensure that the book does not become completely unwieldy. We also decided to continue editing down the new case law and adding notes that summarised recent developments for the reader, rather than requiring the reader to plough through entire cases.

The expansion to update the text also required us to make space for this additional material. In the third edition we reduced the competition law materials following advice that few, if any, contract law teachers used this material in conjunction with the restraint of trade cases in that chapter.

Because we were told that few law teachers had the time to go into restitution other than on an 'in context' basis (i.e. in the context of mistake, duress and frustration, for instance) we culled the last chapter altogether.

Some old favourites have been deleted or edited down somewhat, but it is arguable that a further thinning down exercise would still be possible for the fifth edition, if such appears.

We have also attempted to make the text more user friendly by adding clarification on where the cases are going and what the reader may expect from the pages that follow. Apart from 'Notes' that provide additional information, several chapters ask students to 'consider' the impact or consequences of a decision or development, and most chapters contain exercises at the end to assist in revision and problem-solving. Most of the cases that have been added cite the neutral reference from either the Irish electronic version (IEHC for instance) or the relevant England and Wales data source (e.g. EWCA Civ). References to Canadian and Australian electronic sources have also been added. We acknowledge the excellent work that our colleagues in UCC do in maintaining the Bailii database as an invaluable (and free) resource to the Irish legal community.

We would be delighted to hear from anyone who has comments or suggestions about this book, either via the publishers or to us at UCD.

Our thanks go to the excellent staff at Gill and Macmillan for their support, patience and sheer professionalism.

Robert Clark   Blanaid Clarke

Warsaw   Mount Merrion

18 May 2008

Acknowledgments

For permission to use copyright material, grateful acknowledgment is made to the following:

Blackwell Publications for extracts from the *Modern Law Review*;

Butterworths (Australia) for extracts from the *Victoria Law Reports*;

Butterworths (UK) for extracts from the *All England Law Reports*;

Canada Law Book Inc. for extracts from the *Dominian Law Report*;

Carswell for extracts from the *British Columbia Law Reports*;

Clarendon Press for extracts from *Consideration: A Restatement* by P.S. Atiyah and *Remedies for Breach of Contract* by G.H. Treitel;

Columbia Law Review for extracts from the *Columbia Law Review*;

The Incorporated Council of Law Reporting for England and Wales for the use of case extracts from the *Weekly Law Reports*, *Queen's Bench*, *King's Bench*, *Appeal Courts*, *Industrial Case Reports*, all part of their series of English Law Reports;

The Incorporated Council of Law Reporting for Ireland for extracts from the *Irish Reports*;

The Incorporated Council of Law Reporting for Northern Ireland for extracts from the *Northern Ireland Law Reports*;

The Law Book Company Ltd for extracts from the *Commonwealth Law Reports* (Australia);

McGill-Queen's University Press for extracts from the *McGill-Queen's Law Journal*;

The Roundhall Press for extracts from the *Irish Law Reports Monthly* and the *Irish Law Times Journal*;

Sweet & Maxwell Ltd for the use of case extracts from the *Fleet Street Reports* (FSR), extracts from *Damages* by McGregor, *Exemption Clauses* by David Yates and *Contract Law in Ireland* by Robert Clark;

University of Queensland Press for extracts from *Consideration Reconsidered* by K.C.T. Sutton;

Yale University Press for extracts from the *Yale Law Journal*;

The Publishers, despite their best efforts, were unable to trace the remaining copyright holders. They will, however, make the usual and appropriate arrangements with any who contact them.

Table of Cases

Table of Statutes

Table of Articles of the Constitution

Table of EC/EU/US Legislation

Chapter One

Introduction to the Law of Contract

SECTION ONE—CONTRACT IN EARLY SOCIETIES

Max Weber, in his classic study, *On Law in Economy and Society* (ed. Rheinstein, New York: Clarion 1954) sought to develop the jurisprudential character of legal rights and privileges, one of which he identified as the legal privilege which grants a person the freedom to regulate relations with others by acts of volition or free will:

. . . Freedom of contract, for example, exists exactly to the extent to which such autonomy is recognised by the legal order. There exists, of course, an intimate connection between the expansion of the market and the expanding measure of contractual freedom or, in other words, the scope of arrangements which are guaranteed as valid by the legal order or, in again different terms, the relative significance within the total legal order of those rules which authorise such transactional dispositions. In an economy where self-sufficiency prevails and exchange is lacking, the function of the law will naturally be otherwise: it will mainly define and delimit a person's non-economic relations and privileges with regard to other persons in accordance, not with economic considerations, but with the person's origin, education, or social status.

Section 2. Development of Freedom of Contract—'Status Contracts' and 'Purposive Contracts'—The Historical Origin of Purposive Contracts
1. 'Freedom' in the legal sense means the possession of rights, actual and potential, which, however, in a marketless community naturally do not rest predominantly upon legal transactions but rather directly upon the prescriptive and prohibitory propositions of the law itself. Exchange, on the other hand, is, within the framework of a legal order, a 'legal transaction', *viz.* the acquisition, the transfer, the relinquishment or the fulfilment of a legal claim. With every extension of the market, these legal transactions become more numerous and more complex. However, in no legal order is freedom of contract unlimited in the sense that the law would place its guaranty of coercion at the disposal of all and every agreement regardless of its terms. A legal order can indeed be characterised by the agreements which it does or does not enforce. In this respect a decisive influence is exercised by diverse interest groups, which varies in accordance with differences in the economic structure. In an increasingly expanding market, those who have market interests constitute the most important group. Their influence predominates in determining which legal transactions the law should regulate by means of power granting norms.

That extensive contractual freedom which generally obtains today has, of course, *not always existed*; and even where freedom of contract did exist, it did not always prevail in the spheres in which it prevails today. Freedom of contract once existed indeed in spheres in which it is no longer prevalent or in which it is far less prevalent than it used to be. We shall survey the main stages of development in the following brief sketch.

In contrast to the older law, the most essential feature of modern substantive law, especially private law, is the greatly increased significance of legal *transactions*, particularly *contracts*, as a source of claims guaranteed by legal coercion. So very characteristic is this feature of private law that one can *a potiori* designate the contemporary type of society, to the extent that private law obtains, as a 'contractual' one.

Weber went on to examine certain legal phenomena that could be described as contract related, such as inheritance dispositions, public appointments by governments, and certain social arrangements within primitive societies which could loosely be described as contractual. These led Weber to conclude that a 'contract', in the sense of a voluntary agreement constituting the legal foundation of claims and obligations, has been widely diffused even in the earliest stages of legal history. He continued to develop this theme by examining the role of contract as an economic tool.

. . . however, the farther we go back in legal history, the less significant becomes contract as a device of economic acquisition in fields other than the law of the family and inheritance. The situation is vastly different today. The present-day significance of contract is primarily the result of the high degree to which our economic system is market-oriented and of the role played by money. The increased importance of the private law contract in general is thus the legal reflex of the market orientation of our economy. But contracts characteristic of a market economy are completely different from those contracts which in the spheres of public and family law once played a greater role than they do today. In accordance with this fundamental transformation of the general character of the voluntary agreement we shall call the more primitive type 'status contract' and that which is peculiar to the exchange or market economy 'purposive contract'.

The distinction is based on the fact that all those primitive contracts by which political or other personal associations, permanent or temporary, or family relations are created involve, substantially, a change in what may be called the total legal situation (the universal position) and the social status of the persons involved. To have this effect these contracts were originally either straightforward magical acts or at least acts having a magical significance. For a long time their symbolism retained traces of that character, and the majority of these contracts are 'fraternisation contracts'. By means of such a contract a person was to become somebody's child, father, wife, brother, master, slave, kin, comrade-in-arms, protector, client, follower, vassal, subject, friend, or, quite generally, comrade. To 'fraternise' with another person did not, however, mean that a certain performance of the contract, contributing to the attainment of some specific object, was reciprocally guaranteed or expected. Nor did it mean that the making of a promise to another would, as we might put it, have ushered in a new orientation in the relationship between the parties. The contract rather meant that the person would 'become' something different in quality (or status) from the quality he possessed before. For unless a person voluntarily assumed that new quality, his future conduct in his new role could hardly be believed to be possible at all. Each party must thus make a new 'soul' enter his body. At a rather late stage the symbolism required the mixing and imbibing of blood or spittle or the creation of a new soul by some animistic process or by some other magical rite.

One whose thinking is embedded in magic cannot imagine any other than a magical guaranty for the parties to conform, in their total behaviour, to the intention of the 'fraternisation' they contracted. But as the notion of the divinity gradually replaces animism, it is found necessary to place each party under the dominion of a supernatural power, which power constitutes not only their collective protection but also jointly and severally threatens them in case of antifraternal conduct. The *oath*, which originally appears as a person's conditional self-surrender to evil magical forces, subsequently assumes the character of a conditional self-curse, calling for the divine wrath to strike. Thus the oath remains even in later times one of the most universal forms of all fraternisation pacts. But its use is not so limited.

In contrast to the true magical forms of fraternisation, the oath is also technically suited to serve as a guaranty for purposive contracts, i.e. contracts neither affecting the status of the parties nor giving rise to new qualities of comradeship but aiming solely, as, for instance, barter, at some specific (especially economic) performance or result. This type of contract, however, does not appear in the most primitive society. In earliest times, *barter*, the archetype of all merely instrumental contracts, would seem to have been a general phenomenon among the comrades of an economic or political community only in the non-economic sphere, particularly as barter of women between exogamous sibs whose members seem to confront each other in the strange dual role of being partly comrades and partly strangers. In the state of exogamy barter appears also as an act of fraternisation; however much the woman may be regarded as a mere object, there will rarely be missing the concurrent idea of a change of status to be brought about by magical means. The peculiar duality in the relations between the exogamously cartelised sibs, created by the rise of regulated exogamy, may perhaps help to explain a much-discussed phenomenon, namely, the phenomenon that certain formalities were sometimes required for the marriage with a concubine while the marriage with the legitimate wife might be entered into without any formalities. It may be that the latter remained formless because it was the original and pre-exogamous type of marriage, while barter in pre-exogamous times did not yet have anything to do with fraternisation. It is more plausible, however, that fixed contractual formalities were necessitated by the need for special arrangements regarding the economic security of the concubine who lacked the generally fixed economic status of the legitimate wife.

Economic barter was always confined to transactions with persons who were not members of one's own 'house', especially with outsiders in the sense of non-kinsmen, non-'brothers'; in short, non-comrades. For precisely this reason barter also lacked in the form of 'silent' trade any trace of magical formalism. Only gradually did it acquire religious protection through the law of the market. Such protection, however, would not arise as a set of settled forms until a belief in gods had taken its place alongside those magical conceptions which had provided appropriate means of direct guaranty only for status contracts. Occasionally it would also happen that a barter transaction might be placed under the guaranty of the status contract through some special act of fraternisation or some equivalent. This would not generally happen, however, unless land were involved. Normally, barter enjoyed practically no guaranty, and the conception was non-existent that barter could mean the assumption of an 'obligation' which would not be the product of a natural or artificial all-inclusive fraternal relationship. As a result, barter at first took effect exclusively as a set of two simultaneous and reciprocal acts of immediate delivery of possession. Possession, however, is protected by the claim for vengeance on, and expiation by, the thief. Thus, the kind of 'legal protection' accorded to barter was not the protection of an obligation, but of possession. Where, at a later time, the obligation of warranty of title came to develop at all, it was protected only indirectly in the form of an action for theft against the seller who lacked title.

Formal legal construction of barter does not begin until certain goods, especially metals, have acquired a monetary function, i.e. where sale has arisen. This development does not depend upon the existence of chartal or even state money, but, as shown especially in Roman law, on mere pensatory means of payment. The transactions *per aes et libram* constitute one of the two original forms of legal transaction in ancient Roman *ius civile*. In the domain of Roman urban developments this form of cash purchase acquired an almost universal function for the most diverse classes of private legal transactions, regardless of whether they involved questions of family or inheritance law or of exchange proper. The agreements of fraternisation as well as other forms of status contract were oriented toward the total social status of the individual and his integration into an association comprehending his total personality. This form of contract, with its all-inclusive rights and duties and the special attitudinal qualities based thereon, thus appears in contrast to the money contract, which, as a specific, quantitatively delimited, qualityless, abstract, and usually economically conditioned agreement, represents the archetype of 'coercing contract' (*Zwangskontrakt*). The money contract, as such a coercing contract of ethical indifference, was the appropriate means for the elimination of the magical and sacramental elements from legal transactions and for the secularisation of the law. In Roman law, for example, the civil marriage form of *coemptio* thus came to confront the sacred marriage form of *confarreatio*. The money contract was, it is true, not the only suitable means, but it was the most suitable. Indeed, as a specific cash transaction it was of a rather conservative nature since, originally at least, it was completely devoid of any promissory elements oriented towards the future. For the effect of this transaction, too, was solely to provide secure possession as well as a guaranty that the goods were properly acquired; however, at any rate originally, the transaction did not constitute a guaranty that the promises involved in it would be fulfilled.

The concept of obligation through contract was entirely alien to primitive law; it knew but one form of obligation and claim, *viz.* that arising *ex delicto*. The amount of the claim of an injured party was rigorously fixed by the practice of composition and its attendant conventions. The *wergilt* debt as set by the judge was the most ancient true debt and all other forms of obligation have derived from it. Conversely it can be said that only such actions were cognisable by the courts as arose from an obligation. As regards disputes between members of different kinship groups, no formal procedure existed for the restitution of chattels or the surrender of immovables. Every complaint was necessarily based upon the argument that the defendant had personally done the plaintiff a wrong which would have to be expiated. Hence there was no place for an action *ex contractu* or for the recovery of a chattel or a piece of land or for actions to determine personal status.

The importance of contract in early Irish society is examined by Professor Neil McLeod in his book, *Early Irish Contract Law* (Sydney: Centre for Celtic Studies, 1993). Professor McLeod focused his attention on early Irish manuscripts in order to produce a statement of contractual principles to be found in seventh- and eighth-century Brehon law:

. . .

Early Irish law recognised the exchange of *féich*, 'obligations', as the basis of contract. The name given to each party to a contract, *féchem*, is itself an acknowledgment of the dominant role of such obligations in defining the contract relationship.

Berrad Airechta §49: Cid ara n-eperr féchem? Ní ansae, arindí dliges nó dligther de; ar is féchem cechtar n-aí.

Why is it that a contracting party (*féchem*) is so called? It is not difficult [to say], because of the fact that he is entitled to [something] or that [it] is owed from him; for each of them is a contracting party.

The obligation accepted by each contracting party is to render *folud*, 'consideration', to the other. The acceptance of this obligation in turn creates an entitlement (*dliged*) to the counter-consideration (*frithfolud*) promised by the other party.

In order to facilitate the enforcement of contracts, certain formal requirements are laid down in the laws; in particular the appointment of witnesses and sureties. The use of writing was limited and it was assumed that contracts would normally be made orally rather than in writing. In early Irish law there is no inherent distinction between the word *cor*, 'contract', and the fuller term *cor bél*, 'spoken contract'. In everyday usage *cor* had a wide range of meanings ('putting', 'throwing', 'casting') and *bél*, 'of the lips', simply indicated that the 'arrangement' meant was a contractual one.

In modern law, writing serves an important function in evidencing the terms of a contract. Early Irish law solved such problems of evidence by formally requiring the appointment of witnesses who were specifically charged with noting, and preserving in their memories, the terms of the agreement. The technical term of a contractual witness was *roach*, though often the more general term *fíadu*, 'eye-witness', is used in the law texts.

Under the canon law of the early Irish church, however, contracts were required to be in writing. While such a requirement did not spread to the secular law, the latter did accommodate church practice by recognising the validity of such written evidence as to the terms of a contract. Documents of this kind are referred to in the laws as *scríbend déodae*, 'holy writing', in acknowledgment of their ecclesiastical origin. But the use of writing was not a substitute for the appointment of witnesses; they were still required, as the canon law of the *Collectio Canonum Hibernensis* itself points out. While the native law accommodated the use of writing, a contract which had not yet been performed was unenforceable without witnesses.

As we shall see, the following passage neatly defines the role of sureties and witnesses in early Irish law.

Berrad Airechta §63: Báeth nech nad mbí naidm, na ráth, na fíadnaise fri cach cundrath fri forgell cuimne . . . Fir n-ambechtae cor cen ráith, cen fíadna, cen naidm. Ar is naidm do-boing, ráth gellas, fíadnaise con-oí la folta fíachu.

Senseless [is] anyone [for] whom there is not enforcing surety, nor paying surety, nor witnessing in regard to every bargain for the testimony of remembrance . . . An unprovable truth [is] a contract without a paying surety, without witnesses, without an enforcing surety. For in addition to considerations and obligations, it is the enforcing surety who exacts, paying surety who pledges, and the witnessing which preserves.

The institution of suretyship as a means of enforcing contracts was founded on the strength of personal bonds (of kinship and of patronage, for example). The sureties appointed by a party to a contract promised to safeguard the performance of the agreement much as a parent might guarantee a child's hire-purchase obligations today. The functional basis of suretyship was twofold. First, because of his superior social standing, the surety was more vulnerable to public disgrace, or more able to pay, than the party he secured. Second, the surety was in a better position to ensure adherence to the contract than the other party to it. The surety was often in the position of master in regard to the party whose contract he secured: a father would guarantee the contracts of his son, a lord those of his clients, an abbot the contracts of his monastic subordinates, a teacher those of his apprentices.

There were three types of surety invoked to support contracts. The first was the *naidm* (or *macc*), the 'enforcing surety'. The *naidm* promised on his honour that the party who had invoked him would not default on his duties under the contract, and that if he tried to the surety would force him to fulfil them. The *naidm* was entitled to use any means necessary to extract payment from the defaulter who had invoked him. Usually this meant the distraint of his cattle, but he could seize the defaulter himself, and even kill him without legal penalty. The *naidm* not only extracted the amount owed to the other party; he was, in addition, entitled to be paid his own honour-price as compensation for the injury to his honour caused by the default. Because of his status, the *naidm*'s honour-price would often be quite large and would in any event be at least as large as the original debt under the contract. Taken together with the close relationship that existed between the enforcing surety and the party he represented, the pressures on the latter to observe the contract are obvious enough. In addition, an enforcing surety who failed to compel compliance with the contract lost his honour, since he had pledged on his honour that he would ensure the contract was performed. To lose one's honour was to lose one's rights and position in society.

Most contractual obligations were secured by the appointment of both an enforcing surety (*naidm*) and a paying surety (*ráth*). The *ráth* was a 'paying surety' who guaranteed that he would make good from his own resources the debts of the party he represented, should that prove necessary. But he was only liable to do so if the efforts of the enforcing surety failed. In such cases the *ráth*, too, was entitled to his honour-price and to recover, with interest, the amount he had paid to satisfy the claims of the creditor.

A third type of surety, less well attested in regard to contracts, was the *aitire* or 'hostage-surety'. This type of surety may have been invoked when the parties to a contract were themselves of such high status that persons able to undertake the duty of forcing them to fulfil their respective obligations were not readily available. On the other hand, the hostage-surety is found being invoked where the breach of a contract would give rise to a right to exact physical retribution; namely in a contract to avoid a blood-feud and provide sick-maintenance for injuries inflicted by the party invoking the hostage-surety:

> *Críth Gablach* ll. 52–3: Tongair fri corp — anmain, — do-tét aitire ar fer feras in fuil, i córus n-othruso, i mboin.

> There is a swearing by body and soul, and [a man] offers himself as hostage-surety for the man who caused the bloodshed, in accordance with the system of sick-maintenance, in exchange for a cow.

If the obligations of 'the man who caused the bloodshed' were not met, the hostage-surety would become a ready target for the pursuit of the blood feud.

Upon default, the hostage had to submit himself to the aggrieved party. The defaulter had ten days to ransom the hostage by paying the amount due (including a surcharge for default). After the ten-day period the hostage was forfeit. His liberty and life were technically at the disposal of the party to whom he had given himself up. But he could redeem himself by paying over an amount equal to the valuation of a human body at Irish law (7 *cumals* = 21 milking cows). The hostage was entitled to recover this payment and his honour-price from the defaulter, who remained liable on the contract itself.

It appears that witnesses and sureties were entitled to be paid a fee for being invoked in support of a contract . . .

. . .

In general then, a contract was unenforceable if it was not supported by sureties. This is not to say that it was void, only that no action could be taken to compel its performance. A contract once executed was not rescindable merely because sureties had not been appointed; as we shall see, the law specifically contemplates that there may have been no sureties when it comes to deal with actions for defects in consideration paid.

Indeed, where a contract involved the instantaneous exchange of consideration by both sides, there would be little need for sureties. The size of fees commanded by sureties and witnesses may also have ruled them out in many minor contracts of a more promissory nature.

Furthermore, the rule that sureties ought to be invoked was only a general one to which there was quite an extensive list of exceptions.

Coibnes Uisci Thairidne §§6–7: Ar dí-chenglaither cach cor cen ráith la Féniu. Inge secht n-uasalchuru nadat assai do thaithbiuch neoch ma ro-látar . . .

For every contract without a paying surety is rendered non-binding according to Irish law. Except seven noble contracts which are not easy to dissolve if they have been made . . .

These exceptional contracts may be compared with the seven contracts made 'without an enforcing surety, without a paying surety' in *Heptad* 25. As usual, the 'heptads' are merely illustrative rather than exhaustive of their subject matter, as is shown by the fact that they only partially overlap and also by the much longer list given in *Berrad Airechta* §§1–15 and §34. The contracts covered in these sources consist mainly of service contracts, namely contracts of clientship, contracts to secure the care of the aged, contracts of fosterage and education, payments for the services of poets, lawyers and doctors, contracts for the services and craftsmen and contracts with messengers.

. . .

Berrad Airechta §§1, 5 and 6, *Coibnes Uisci Thairidne* §7 and *Heptad* 25 also state that alms and offerings to the church need not be secured by sureties. There are some grounds for arguing that these payments to the church should be seen as being in exchange for its services in much the same way as the *tuillem bathais*, 'baptism fee', mentioned in *Berrad Airechta* §1. *Córus Béscnai* tries to rationalise the church's rights to offerings, tithes and first fruits as being balanced by the laity's rights to baptism, communion, requiem and mass. Note that *Berrad Airechta* §§5 and 6 make it clear that offerings are not inviolable if the church to whom they are given has so strayed from orthodoxy in its religious functions as to no longer fit the definition of a church. But this appeal to the analogy of contracts for specific services as a rationale for the validity of unsecured offerings must in reality be seen as a legal fiction. That a church to whom an offering is made continues to function as it has always intended to function hardly amounts to consideration by way of the provision of services. (Note that *Córus Béscnai* elsewhere justifies such payments to the church rather on the basis that they are necessary to avert cosmic disorder.) In pragmatic terms at least, these payments are unilateral gifts to the church. Their inviolability is significant in that they cut across the interests of the donor's kin, and under ecclesiastical pressure appear to have been allowed in such a way that the donor need not turn to his kin either for permission or for the provision of sureties.

Most other promises of gifts are treated in early Irish law as normal contracts which must be secured by sureties in order to be enforceable. In modern law a contract only exists where it can be shown that each party has given consideration, i.e. (a promise of) something valuable, to the other. This modern definition of a contract cannot extend to gratuitous payments. Something quite different is the case in early Irish law. The explanation of the inclusion of gifts as contracts has as its starting-point a principle of law common to both ancient and modern Irish law. While both parties give 'something of value' to support their rights under the contract, it is not necessary for consideration to be evenly balanced. Modern law is only interested in the existence, not in the adequacy, of consideration. Consideration may be inadequate or minute, so long as it is tangible. But in early Irish law this principle was taken to its logical extreme: it was acknowledged that in some cases consideration may not be very one-sided but that it might even be totally so. In such cases the beneficiary, by doing what he has promised to do—namely nothing—easily 'fulfils' his obligations under the agreement and thereby creates an entitlement to the consideration promised him.
. . .

While an executed gift could not be reversed for want of consideration, not all gratuitous promises were binding as contracts. Except in the case of gifts to the church, the promise of a gift would need to be supported by sureties if it were to be enforceable. And all contracts were required to be made before formally appointed witnesses.

Sir Henry Maine, *Ancient Law* (Boston: Beacon (1864) (1963))

. . . The movement of the progressive societies has been uniform in one respect. Through all its course it has been distinguished by the gradual dissolution of family dependency, and the growth of individual obligation in its place. The individual is steadily substituted for the family, as the unit of which civil laws take account. The advance has been accomplished at varying rates of celerity, and there are societies not absolutely stationary in which the collapse of the ancient organisation can only be perceived by careful study of the phenomena they present. But, whatever its pace, the change has not been subject to reaction or recoil, and apparent retardations will be found to have been occasioned through the absorption of archaic ideas and customs from some entirely foreign source. Nor is it difficult to see what is the tie between man and man which replaces by degrees those forms of reciprocity in rights and duties which have their origin in the family. It is contract. Starting, as from one terminus of history, from a condition of society in which all the relations of persons are summed up in the relations of family, we seem to have steadily moved towards a phase of social order in which all these relations arise from the free agreement of individuals. In Western Europe the progress achieved in this direction has been considerable.

The word status may be usefully employed to construct a formula expressing the law of progress thus indicated, which, whatever be its value, seems to me to be sufficiently ascertained. All the forms of status taken notice of in the law of persons were derived from, and to some extent are still coloured by, the powers and privileges anciently residing in the family. If then we employ status, agreeably with the usage of the best writers, to signify these personal conditions only, and avoid applying the term to such conditions as are the immediate or remote result of agreement, we may say that the movement of the progressive societies has hitherto been a movement *from status to contract'*

Note

The development of the law of contract in Ireland under the influence of English law was shaped by a number of factors, the most significant of which were the expansion of the King's Courts over the private affairs of individuals, the standardisation of pleadings and remedies through the writ system, and the inevitable reaction against the inflexibility that resulted by virtue of equitable jurisdiction and equitable remedies. In English feudal society many of the areas that are seen as contractual now were conceived to be part of the law of tenure, a part of the law of real property. Actions in the King's Courts to protect such rights began to be possible if the right had been ceded by way of a formal instrument—a deed. The cause of action used to protect and vindicate such rights were actions in covenant and debt. Such deeds were used in relation to agreements to convey property, or grant a lease for years, although in the later mediaeval period the action in covenant could be used in proceedings relating to any non-observance of the terms of any deed under seal.

The enforceability of simple contracts, however, as distinct from contracts by specialty (verbal agreements as distinct from contracts under seal), evolved very slowly over the centuries. Actions in debt began to be entertained by the courts if the plaintiff, for example, had performed his part of the contract but the defendant had not. By the fifteenth century the limitations found in the writ system made it necessary to develop delictual or tortious causes of action if a wholly unperformed contract, broken by the defendant, could be capable of redress in the King's Courts. By forging an action from the action for trespass on the case and action in deceit, informal mutual promises could be enforceable, as where a doctor promised to cure a horse but did so negligently, thereby occasioning the death of the horse. The assumption of a duty by express or implied promise thus evolved into the action *in assumpsit*, available in cases of *misfeasance*, or a failure to correctly perform an assumed obligation. This action was, however, not available in cases of complete non-performance (*non feasance*) until 1602 when the Court of Exchequer Chamber decided *Slade's* case (1602) 4 Co. Rep. 91a. *Slade's* case marks the erosion of the older forms of action in covenant, debt and account, and the evolution of the principle that 'every contract executory imparts into itself an *assumpsit*, for when one agrees to pay money or to deliver anything, thereby he assumes or promises to pay or deliver it.'

For additional reading see Simpson, A *History of the Common Law of Contract* (OUP, 1975); Holdsworth, *History of English Law*, vol. III, ch. 3; Jackson (1937) 53 LQR 525.

SECTION TWO—THE CAUSES OF ACTION

A. CONTRACT AND TORT

The fact that contract emerged from the law of tort and the law of property does not mean that the causes of action are broadly concentric. In many respects the law of tort, in particular the law relating to negligence and actionable misrepresentation, seeks to achieve quite distinct goals. The law relating to third-party liability, the recoverability of non-economic loss and remoteness of damage, to mention just three elements, will produce different results depending on whether liability is established in contract or tort.

Finlay v Murtagh [1979] IR 249 SC

Henchy J.:

When a client complains that he has suffered loss because his solicitor has failed to show due care in the performance of his duty as solicitor, does the client's cause of action lie in contract or in the tort of the negligence? Or has he a choice? That is the problem presented in this appeal. The plaintiff client has founded his claim against the defendant solicitor in negligence, his case being (and it has not been denied) that the defendant did not, within the period fixed by the statute of limitations, bring an action for damages for personal injuries sustained by the plaintiff as a result of the alleged negligence of a third party. The plaintiff has served notice of trial against the defendant before a judge sitting with a jury, which he would be entitled to do if his cause of action lies, as has been pleaded, in tort. But the defendant contends that the cause of action is breach of contract, that is to say that it is founded on a breach of the implied term in the contract that he would carry out his duties as solicitor with due professional care and skill. If the defendant is correct in that contention, the notice of trial should have been for a judge sitting without a jury. So the defendant has moved in the High Court for an order setting aside the notice of trial which was served. Mr Justice D'Arcy refused to make that order as he held that the plaintiff's action lies in the tort of negligence. It is from that refusal that the present appeal has been brought by the defendant.

There has been no decision of this court on the point at issue but we have been referred to three decisions of the High Court. In *McGrath v Kiely*[1] the client sued his solicitor for negligence and, alternatively, for breach of contract in failing to show due professional care in the preparation of an action for damages for personal injuries. The claim was pursued in court as one for breach of contract and no effort was made to pursue the claim in negligence. The parties agreed to treat the solicitor's default as a breach of contract. Therefore, that case throws no light on the present problem.

The second case, *Liston v Munster and Leinster Bank*,[2] was an action by the personal representative of a customer of the bank against the bank for damages for negligence, for conversion, and for money had and received. The issue being whether the entire cause of action arose out of a contract, in which case notice of trial by a judge without a jury would be appropriate, or whether it lay partly in tort, in which case the notice of trial that had been served specifying trial by a judge with a jury would have been correct. In holding that the claim was partly for breach of contract and partly for conversion, O'Byrne J. applied the following test which had been laid down by Greer L.J. in *Jarvis v Moy, Davies, Smith, Vandervell & Co.*[3] at 405 of the report:

The distinction in the modern view, for this purpose, between contract and tort may be put thus: where the breach of duty alleged arises out of a liability independently of the personal obligation undertaken by contract, it is tort, and it may be tort even though there may happen to be a contract between the parties, if the duty in fact arises independently of that contract. Breach of contract occurs where that which is complained of is a breach of duty arising out of the obligations undertaken by the contract.

The third High Court case to which we were referred is *Somers v Erskine*.[4] There the question was whether an action commenced by a client against a solicitor for negligence, and sought to be continued against the solicitor's personal representative, had abated with the solicitor's death as an action in tort, or whether it survived his death as an action in contract. In an unreserved judgment Maguire P. applied the same test as was applied by O'Byrne J. in *Liston v Munster and Leinster Bank*, and held that the client's claim was essentially one in contract rather than in tort and that, therefore, the claim had survived the solicitor's death. In my opinion, the conclusion that an action by a client against a solicitor for damages for breach of his professional duty of care is necessarily and exclusively one in contract is incompatible with modern developments in the law of torts and should be overruled. In my view, the conclusion there reached does not follow from a correct application of the test laid down by Greer L.J. in the *Jarvis* case.

The claim made by the plaintiff in the *Jarvis* case was one by a client against stockbrokers 'for damages for breach of contract arising out of the defendants' relationship with the plaintiff as stockbrokers and client.' Therefore, it is clear that the action was one for breach of contract, at least in form. But the particulars given in the writ show that the substance of the complaint was that the stockbrokers had departed from the specific instructions given by the client. Therefore, the cause of action arose from the breach of a particular binding provision created by the parties, and not from any general obligation of care arising from the relationship of stockbroker and client. The nub of the matter was that the stockbrokers had defaulted on a special personal obligation which was imposed by the contract. They could not have been made liable otherwise than in contract and the court held correctly that the claim was 'founded on contract' in the words of the statute which was being applied.

The test adumbrated by Greer L.J., which commended itself to O'Byrne J. in *Liston v Munster and Leinster Bank* and to Maguire P. in *Somers v Erskine*, correctly draws a distinction between a claim arising out of an obligation deriving from, and owing its existence to, a personal obligation undertaken pursuant to a contract (in which case it is an action in contract) and a claim arising out of a liability created independently of a contract and not deriving from any special obligation imposed by a contract (in which case an action lies in tort). The action in tort derives from an obligation which is imposed by the general law and is applicable to all persons in a certain relationship to each other. The action in contract is founded on the special law which was created by a contract and which was designed to fit the particular relationship of that contract. As I understand it, therefore, the test propounded by Greer L.J. does not support the conclusion reached by Maguire P. that, because the contract of retainer implies a duty of professional care and skill and because a default in that duty has occurred, the cause of action lies exclusively in contract.

It has to be conceded that for over a hundred years there has been a divergence of judicial opinion as to whether a client who has engaged a solicitor to act for him, and who claims that the solicitor failed to show due professional care and skill, may sue in tort or whether he is confined to an action in contract. In *Somers v Erskine* (and in some

English cases) it was held that the sole cause of action was the solicitor's failure to observe the implied term in the contract of retainer that he would show due professional skill and care. It is undeniable that the client is entitled to sue in contract for breach of that implied term. But it does not follow that the client, because there is privity of contract between him and the solicitor and because he may sue the solicitor for breach of the contract, is debarred from suing also for the tort of negligence. Since the decision of the House of Lords in *Hedley Byrne & Co. Ltd v Heller & Partners Ltd*[5] and the cases following in its wake, it is clear that, whether a contractual relationship exists or not, once the circumstances are such that a defendant undertakes to show professional care and skill towards a person who may be expected to rely on such care and skill and who does so rely, then if he has been damnified by such default that person may sue the defendant in the tort of negligence for failure to show such care and skill. For the purpose of such an action, the existence of a contract is merely an incident of the relationship. If, on the one side, there is a proximity of relationship creating a general duty and, on the other, a reliance on that duty, it matters not whether the parties are bound together in contract. For instance, if the defendant in the present case had not been retained for reward but had merely volunteered his services to the plaintiff, his liability in negligence would be the same as if he was to be paid for his services. The coincidence that the defendant's conduct amounts to a breach of contract cannot affect either the duty of care or the common-law liability for its breach, for it is the general relationship, and not any particular manifestation such as a contract, that gives rise to the tortious liability in such a case: see per Lord Devlin in the *Hedley Byrne* case at 530 of the report.

A comprehensive survey of the law governing the liability of a solicitor to his client in negligence is to be found in the judgment of Oliver J. in *Midland Bank v Hett, Stubbs & Kemp*,[6] in which it was held that the solicitor's liability in tort exists independently of any liability in contract. That conclusion, which was reached at first instance and with which I agree, may be said to be reinforced by *dicta* in the judgments of the Court of Appeal in *Batty v Metropolitan Realisations Ltd*[7] and *Photo Production Ltd v Securicor Ltd*.[8]

On a consideration of those cases and of the authorities mentioned in them, I am satisfied that the general duty of care created by the relationship of solicitor and client entitles the client to sue in negligence if he has suffered damage because of the solicitor's failure to show due professional care and skill, notwithstanding that the client could sue alternatively in contract for breach of the implied term in the contract of retainer that the solicitor will deal with the matter in hand with due professional care and skill. The solicitor's liability in tort under the general duty of care extends not only to a client for rewards, but to any person for whom the solicitor undertakes to act professionally without reward, and also to those (such as beneficiaries under a will, persons entitled under an intestacy, or those entitled to benefits in circumstances such as a claim in respect of a fatal injury) with whom he has made no arrangement to act but who, as he knows or ought to know, will be relying on his professional care and skill. For the same default there should be the same cause of action. If others are entitled to sue in tort for the solicitor's want of care, so also should the client; that is so unless the solicitor's default arises not from a breach of the general duty of care arising from the relationship but from a breach of a particular and special term of the contract in respect of which the solicitor would not be liable if the contract had not contained such a term. Thus, if the client's instructions were that the solicitor was to issue proceedings within a specified time, or to close a sale by a particular date or, generally, to do or not to do some act, and the solicitor defaulted in that respect, any resulting right of action which the client might have would be in contract only unless the act or default complained of falls within the general duty of care owed by the solicitor.

The modern law of tort shows that the existence of a contractual relationship which impliedly deals with a particular act or omission is not, in itself, sufficient to rule out an action in tort in respect of that act or omission. For instance, in *Northern Bank Finance Corp. Ltd v Charlton*[9] it was unanimously held by this court that a customer of a bank can sue the bank for the tort of deceit where the deceit arises from fraudulent misrepresentation made by the bank in the course of carrying out the contract between the bank and the customer. The existence of a contract, for the breach of which he could have sued, did not oust the customer's cause of action in tort.

Therefore, I conclude that where, as in the instant case, the client's complaint is that he has been damnified by the solicitor's default in his general duty of care, the client is entitled to sue in negligence as well as for breach of contract. In the plaintiff's statement of claim, after reciting his accident and his retainer of the defendant as the solicitor to prosecute his claim for damages in respect of it, the plaintiff pleads that the defendant 'negligently failed to issue proceedings on behalf of the plaintiff in respect of the accident aforesaid within the time limited by the Statute of Limitations 1957.' That was intended to be, and is, a claim in negligence. Such being the case, by virtue of the provision of s. 94 of the Courts of Justice Act 1924, as amended, the plaintiff was entitled to serve notice of a trial by a judge and jury. Mr Justice D'Arcy was correct in refusing to set aside the notice of trial so served. I would dismiss this appeal.

Griffin J.:

On 10 March 1970, the plaintiff was injured in the course of his employment whilst he was engaged in lagging pipes at a factory premises in Cork. In May 1970, he retained the defendant as his solicitor to act for him in the prosecution of a claim for damages for negligence arising out of the accident. Proceedings were not issued on behalf of the plaintiff within the time limited by the Statute of Limitations 1957, with the result that the plaintiff's claims against his employer and against the occupier of the factory are now statute-barred. The plaintiff instituted proceedings against the defendant claiming damages for the negligence of the defendant in his conduct, as the plaintiff's solicitor, of business undertaken by the defendant on behalf of the plaintiff. In his defence the defendant has not denied his liability to the plaintiff, so that the only issue to be tried is that of damages.

The plaintiff served notice of a trial with a jury, and the defendant applied to the High Court to have the notice to trial set aside. The application was dismissed by Mr Justice D'Arcy. The defendant has now appealed to this court and the net issue for determination on the appeal is whether the action should be tried before a judge and jury or before a judge sitting without a jury.

A solicitor holds himself out to the client who has retained him as being possessed of adequate skill, knowledge and learning for the purpose of carrying out all business that he undertakes on behalf of his client. Once he has been retained to pursue a claim for damages for personal injuries, it is the duty of the solicitor to prepare and prosecute the claim with due professional skill and care. Therefore, he is liable to the client in damages if loss and damage are caused to the client owing to the want of such skill and care on the part of the solicitor as he ought to have exercised.

[Counsel], for the defendant, contends that the duty owed by a solicitor to his client under his retainer is a duty which arises *solely* from the contract and excludes any general duty in tort; he submits that this action is one founded upon contract, in which event the plaintiff would not be entitled to have the action tried by a jury. [Counsel], for the plaintiff, submits that, apart from the duty which arises from contract, there is a general duty to exercise skill and care on the part of the solicitor, for breach of which he would be liable in tort if damage is suffered by the client as a result of the want of such skill and care. He submits that, as one claiming damages for negligence, this action is properly a claim in tort, in which case the plaintiff is entitled as of right to have the action tried before a judge and jury pursuant to s. 94 of the Courts of Justice Act 1924, as amended.

There is abundant, if somewhat conflicting, authority on the question in England, and in argument we were referred also to two Irish cases in which the question arose.

In *Groom v Crocker*[10] the Court of Appeal in England had to consider whether the mutual rights and duties of a solicitor and his client were regulated by the contract of employment alone, and whether the solicitor was liable in tort. It was there held that the contract of employment regulated the relationship and that the solicitor was not liable in tort. In the course of his judgment, Sir Wilfred Greene M.R. said at 205 of the report: 'In my opinion, the cause of action is in contract and not in tort. The duty of the appellants was to conduct the case properly on behalf of the respondent as their client . . . The relationship of solicitor and client is a contractual one: *Davies v Lock*;[11] *Bean v Wade*.[12] It was by virtue of that relationship that the duty arose, and it had no existence apart from the relationship.'

Scott L.J. at p. 222, having set out the duty of a solicitor, said that the tie between the solicitor and the client is contractual and that no action lies in tort for the breach of such duties. MacKinnon L.J. put the position succinctly at 229 where he said: 'I am clear that this is a claim for damages for breach of contract . . .'

After that unanimous decision of the Court of Appeal, it was generally accepted in England, at least until very recently, that the liability of a solicitor to his client was contractual only and that he could not be sued in tort either in the alternative or cumulatively. The case has been almost universally followed and applied there since it was decided; see, for example, *Bailey v Bullock*;[13] and Hodson and Parker L.JJ. at pp. 447 and 481 respectively of the report of *Hall v Meyrick*;[14] *Cook v Swinfen*.[15] At 510 of the report of *Clark v Kirby-Smith*[16] Plowman J. said: 'A line of cases going back for nearly 150 years shows, I think, that the client's cause of action is in contract and not in tort: see, for example, *Howell v Young*[17] and *Groom v Crocker*'. In *Heywood v Wellers*[18] James L.J. said at 461 of the report: 'It is well known and settled law that an action by a client against a solicitor alleging negligence in the conduct of the client's affairs is an action for breach of contract: *Groom v Crocker*.' However, in that case Lord Denning did say at 459 that *Groom v Crocker* might have to be reconsidered, and in *Esso Petroleum v Mardon*[19] at 819 of the report he 'ventured to suggest' that that case, and cases which relied on it, are in conflict with other decisions of high authority which were not cited in them—decisions which show that, in the case of a professional man, the duty to use reasonable care arises not only in contract but is also imposed by the law apart from contract and is, therefore, actionable in tort; it is comparable to the duty of reasonable care which is owed by a master to his servant or vice versa; it can be put either in contract or in tort. In *Midland Bank v Hett, Stubbs & Kemp*, on which the plaintiff relied strongly, Oliver J., in a judgment in which he examined exhaustively all the leading cases on the subject of a solicitor's liability, held that a solicitor was liable in tort quite independently of any contractual liability.

In *Somers v Erskine* the client sued his solicitor for damages for negligence in the discharge of his professional duty to the client. The solicitor died after the action was commenced and one of the issues which then arose was whether or not the cause of action had survived against his executrix. It was held by Maguire P. that the action was in substance founded in contract and that, in considering whether an action is founded on contract or on tort, the court must look not merely at the form of the pleadings but at the substance of the action and decide whether it is founded on contract or tort. He adopted and applied the following passage from the judgment of Greer L.J. in *Jarvis v Moy, Davies, Smith, Vandervell and Co.* (a claim against a stockbroker) at 405 of the report:

> The distinction in the modern view, for this purpose, between contract and tort may be put thus: where the breach of duty alleged arises out of a liability independently of the personal obligation undertaken by contract, it is tort, and it may be tort even though there may happen to be a contract between the parties, if the duty in fact arises independently of that contract. Breach of contract occurs where that which is complained of is a breach of duty arising out of the obligations undertaken by the contract.

That passage had been accepted and approved by O'Byrne J. in *Liston v Munster and Leinster Bank*. Applying that test, the learned president held that the substance of the client's claim was the breach of a duty arising out of an obligation created by contract, and said that he found it difficult to dissociate that duty from the contract. Counsel for the defendant in that case had urged that the duty which was alleged to have been broken was merely the ordinary common-law duty, the breach of which constituted negligence, i.e. the duty to take reasonable care in the particular circumstances; but the president held that the duty arose out of a contractual obligation only.

I have had the advantage of reading in advance the judgment of Mr Justice Henchy and I agree with him that Maguire P. did not correctly apply the test laid down by Greer L.J. in the *Jarvis* case. I agree with the analysis made by Mr Justice Henchy of the passage quoted from the judgment of Lord Justice Greer.

The only other Irish case cited in argument was *McGrath v Kiely* in which the client sued a surgeon and a solicitor, founding her claim for damages on both negligence and breach of contract. In the course of the hearing before Mr Justice Henchy it was conceded on behalf of the client that the liability sought to be imposed on each of the defendants arose *ex contractu*, so that the question of the liability of the defendants in tort was not argued and did not fall to be decided.

In *Somers v Erskine*, the learned president was not prepared to accept that, in the case of a solicitor, there was a general duty to use reasonable care imposed by the law quite apart from contract. He took the view that because there was a contractual relationship between the solicitor and the client, and a liability in contract for breach of the duty owed to the client, there was no duty in tort. Counsel for the defendant had cited the passage in *Bevan on Negligence* (4th ed.) p. 1384 that states: 'A solicitor is liable for negligence both in contract and in tort. He is liable in contract where he fails to do some specific act to which he has bound himself. He is liable in tort where, having accepted a retainer, he fails in the performance of any duty which the relation of solicitor and client as defined by the retainer imposes on him.' Authorities to support that proposition were not cited; if they had been cited, it is likely that the president would have come to a different conclusion. The law is concisely and clearly summed up in a few sentences in the well-known passage in the speech of Viscount Haldane L.C. in *Nocton v Ashburton*[20] at 956 of the report: 'My Lords, the solicitor contracts with his client to be skilful and careful. For failure to perform his obligation he may be made liable at law in contract or even in tort, for negligence in breach of a duty imposed on him.' See also what was said by Tindal C.J. in *Boorman v Brown*[21] in the Court of Exchequer Chamber at 525 of the report and by Lord Campbell in the House of Lords at 44 of the report of the appeal. It is to be noted that these cases also were not cited in *Groom v Crocker*, or in the cases which followed it, and that the failure to do so led to the criticism of these cases by Lord Denning in *Esso Petroleum v Mardon*. In my opinion, the President was wrong in holding that the liability of the solicitor to the client was solely in contract. *Somers v Erskine* should not be followed.

Quite apart from the fact that *Somers v Erskine* was decided without the citation of relevant authorities and on an incorrect application of the test laid down by Greer L.J. in the *Jarvis* case, the decision is inconsistent with developments in the law of tort since the case was decided. It is now settled law that whenever a person possessed of a special knowledge or skill undertakes, quite irrespective of contract, to apply that skill for the assistance of another person who relies on such skill, a duty of care will arise: see the speech of Lord Morris of Borth-y-Gest at 502 of the report of *Hedley Byrne and Co. Ltd v Heller & Partners Ltd*. At 538 of the report Lord Pearce said: 'In terms of proximity one might say that they are in particularly close proximity to those who, as they know, are relying on their skill and care although the proximity is not contractual.' See also Lord Hodson at 510 and Lord Devlin at 530 of the report. Where damage has been suffered as a result of want of such skill and care, an action in tort lies against such person, and this applies whether a contractual relationship exists or not. This doctrine applies to such professional persons as solicitors, doctors, dentists, architects and accountants. Although in the *Hedley Byrne* case the aim was in respect of a non-contractual relationship, the statements of the Law Lords were general statements of principle, and it is clear from their speeches that they did not in any way mean to limit the general principle and that their statements were not to be confined to voluntary or non-contractual situations.

Therefore, where a solicitor is retained by a client to carry out legal business (such as litigation) on his behalf, a general relationship is established, and 'Where there is a general relationship of this sort, it is unnecessary to do more than prove its existence and the duty follows' per Lord Devlin at 530 of the report of the *Hedley Byrne* case. If, therefore, loss and damage is caused to a client owing to the want of such care and skill on the part of a solicitor as he ought to have exercised, there is liability in tort even though there would also be a liability in contract. Even if the relationship between the solicitor and the client was a non-contractual or voluntary one, the same liability in tort would follow.

In my opinion it is both reasonable and fair that, if the issues of fact are such that he would be entitled to succeed either in contract or in tort, the plaintiff should be entitled to pursue either or both remedies; there can be nothing wrong in permitting the plaintiff, who is the injured party, to elect or choose the remedy which to him appears to be that which will be most suitable and likely to attract the more favourable result.

In my judgment, the plaintiff in the instant case has a good cause of action in tort as well as in contract and is entitled to sue in respect of either or both remedies since he has suffered loss and damage as a result of the negligence of the defendant, as the plaintiff's solicitor, in failing to institute proceedings within the time limited by the Statute of Limitations 1957. Accordingly, the plaintiff is entitled as of right to have his action tried before a judge and jury, and Mr Justice D'Arcy was correct in so deciding. Accordingly, I would dismiss this appeal.

1. [1965] IR 497
2. [1940] IR 77
3. [1936] 1 KB 399
4. [1943] IR 348
5. [1964] AC 465
6. [1979] Ch. 384
7. [1978] QB 554
8. [1978] 1 WLR 856
9. [1979] IR 149
10. [1939] 1 KB 194
11. (1844) 3 LT (OS) 125
12. (1885) 2 TLR 157
13. [1950] 2 All ER 1167
14. [1957] 2 QB 455
15. [1967] 1 WLR 457
16. [1964] Ch. 506
17. (1826) 5 B & C 259
18. [1976] QB 446
19. [1976] QB 801
20. [1914] AC 932
21. (1842) 3 QB 511; (1844) 11 Cl. & Fin. 1

(O'Higgins C.J. and Kenny J. agreed.)

Note

1. The major losses experienced by members of Lloyds (names) during the late 1980s were the subject of substantial litigation in England in 1993 and 1994. The names sought compensation from underwriting agents alleging that these agents owed a duty of care in tort, and certain implied contractual duties, to the names in relation to the carrying out of their underwriting duties with care and skill.

In *Arbuthnott and Others v Fagan and Fettrim Underwriting Agencies Ltd and Others* TLR 26 July 1994, the House of Lords considered whether the names were owed concurrent duties in contract and tort and concluded that such duties, as a matter of principle, could subsist in the light of earlier cases that suggested that if liability was possible in tort and contract, the plaintiff should pursue his action in contract only.

Giving judgment for the House, Lord Goff rejected the view that there was any sound basis for a rule which confined the plaintiff to one cause of action only. Lord Goff observed that while the result may be untidy:

given that the tortious duty was imposed by the general law and the contractual duty was attributable to the will of the parties, it was not objectionable that the claimant might be entitled to take advantage of the remedy which was most advantageous to him, subject only to ascertaining whether the tortious duty was so inconsistent with the applicable contract that, in accordance with ordinary principle, the parties must be taken to have agreed that the tortious remedy was to be limited or excluded.

2. In cases of concurrent liability the plaintiff has a very good reason to seek to establish these alternative causes of action. Sometimes the alternative cause of action lengthens the period for which recovery of damages is possible or it revives an otherwise invalid cause of action. What happened in the *Arbuthnott* litigation as a result of their Lordships' decision?

3. For the importance of concurrent liability in damages, see, *inter alia*, the discussion at pages 1042–1044 below.

B. CONTRACT AND RESTITUTION

Beresford v Kennedy (1887) 21 ILTR 17

Beresford owned lands which adjoined the defendants' farmlands. The defendants' land was the subject of a boycott and fences and gates had not been maintained. The plaintiff's cattle wandered onto the defendants' land where they were seized by the local rate collector, the defendants owing some £25 in overdue rates. In order to obtain the release of his cattle the plaintiff paid the rates of £25 and then sued the defendants for this amount as being money paid for their use. The County Court Judge gave judgment in favour of the plaintiff saying it would be monstrous if the defendants could avoid payment of their lawful taxes as a result of a trifling trespass. The defendants appealed.

Andrews J.:

I am greatly indebted to the counsel on both sides for the assistance they have given me. It is not necessary for me to decide whether or not there was a deliberate act of trespass, on the part of the plaintiff Beresford, in driving his cattle on to defendants' land; but it was admitted by his counsel, that plaintiff's cattle were undoubtedly trespassing on defendants' land when they were seized, as they lawfully might be, by the collectors, the Miss Kennedys being the occupiers of the land, under the provisions of the Poor Rate and Grand Jury Acts. In all the cases in the books there has been something to create a privity between the parties in a case like this, and even if *England v Marsden* were not followed, I have enough materials to decide the case.

In *Exall v Partridge*, and that class of cases, the property seized was lawfully on the premises of the defendant, and there is no authority in the books to show that where property is unlawfully on defendants' premises, the wrongdoer can recover against the defendant, though, as I said, I don't hold that the trespass was wilful; but there is, in the facts before me, nothing from which there can be implied any request by defendant for the payment of the debt by plaintiff. I will not rely on *England v Marsden*, as I think that decision went too far; but I have carefully considered *Edmunds v Wallingford* and *Re Bishop*, and I can find nothing in them to warrant me in deciding in favour of the plaintiff, and, therefore, though I regret that I have to differ from the County Court Judge, I am obliged to reverse his decision, with costs; but I give defendants no costs of the hearing in the court below, as the case was one of much difficulty and importance.

Decree reversed.

C. CONTRACT AND PROMISSORY LIABILITY

The charitable subscriptions cases

Governors of Dalhousie College v Boutilier [1934] 3 DLR 593

Crocket J. gave judgment for the Supreme Court of Canada:

This appeal concerns a claim which was filed in the Probate Court for the County of Halifax, Nova Scotia, in the year 1931, by the appellant college against the respondent estate for $5,000, stated as having been 'subscribed to Dalhousie Campaign Fund (1920)', and attested by an affidavit of the college bursar, in which it was alleged that the stated amount was justly and truly owing to the college corporation.

The subscription, upon which the claim was founded, was obtained from the deceased on 4 June 1920, in the course of a canvass which was being conducted by a committee, known as the Dalhousie College Campaign Committee, for the raising of a fund to increase the general resources and usefulness of the institution and was in the following terms:

> For the purpose of enabling Dalhousie College to maintain and improve the efficiency of its teaching, to construct new buildings and otherwise to keep pace with the growing need of its constituency and in consideration of the subscription of others, I promise to pay to the Treasurer of Dalhousie College the sum of Five Thousand Dollars, payment as follows: Terms of payment as per letter from Mr Boutilier. A. 399.
> Name: Arthur Boutilier.

So far as the record discloses the subscription was not accompanied or followed by any letter from the deceased as to the terms of payment. He died on 29 October 1928, without making any payment on account. It appears that some time after he signed the subscription form he met with severe financial reverses which prevented him from honouring his pledge. That he desired and hoped to be able to do so is evidenced by a brief letter addressed by him to the President of the University on 12 April 1926, in reply to a communication from the latter, calling his attention to the subscription and the fact that no payments had been made upon it. The deceased's letter, acknowledging receipt of the president's communication, states: 'In reply I desire to advise that I have kept my promise to you in mind. As you are probably aware, since making my promise I suffered some rather severe reverses but I expect before too long to be able to redeem my pledge.'

. . .

There is, of course, no doubt that the deceased's subscription can be sustained as a binding promise only upon one basis, *viz.* as a contract, supported by a good and sufficient consideration. The whole controversy between the parties is as to whether such a consideration is to be found, either in the subscription paper itself or in the circumstances as disclosed by the evidence.

So far as the signed subscription itself is concerned, it is contended in behalf of the appellant that it shows upon its face a good and sufficient consideration for the deceased's promise in its statement that it was given in consideration of the subscription of others. As to this, it is first to be observed that the statement of such a consideration in the subscription paper is insufficient to support the promise if, in point of law, the subscriptions of others could not provide a valid consideration; therefore I concur in the opinion of Chisholm C.J., that the fact that others had signed separate subscription papers for the same common object or were expected so to do does not of itself constitute a legal consideration. Although there have been some cases in the United States in which a contrary opinion has been expressed, these decisions have been rejected as unsound in principle both by the Supreme Court of Massachusetts and the Court of Appeals of the State of New York. See *Cottage Street M. E. Church v Kendall* (1877), 121 Mass. 528; *Hamilton College v Stewart* (1848), 1 NY 581, and *Albany Presbyterian Church v Cooper* (1889), 112 NY 517. In the last mentioned case the defendant's intestate subscribed a paper with a number of others, by the terms of which they 'in consideration of one dollar' to each of them paid 'and of the agreements of each other' severally promised and agreed to and with the plaintiff's trustees to pay to said trustees the sums severally subscribed for the purpose of paying off a mortgage debt on the church edifice on the condition that the sum of $45,000 in the aggregate should be subscribed and paid in for such purpose within one year. The Court of Appeals held that it must reject the consideration, because it had no basis in fact, and the mutual promise between the subscribers, because there was no privity of contract between the plaintiff church and the various subscribers.

A perusal of the reasons for judgment of the Appeal Court of Manitoba, as delivered by Cameron J., in *Sargent v Nicholson*, already referred to, shows that that court also rejected the contention that it was a sufficient consideration that others were led to subscribe by the subscription of the defendant. In fact Cameron J.'s opinion quotes with approval a passage from the opinion of Gray C.J., in *Cottage St. M. E. Church v Kendall* that such a proposition appeared to the Massachusetts Supreme Court to be 'inconsistent with elementary principles'. The decision of the Appeal Court of British Columbia in *YMCA v Rankin* fully adopted the opinion of Cameron J., in *Sargent v Nicholson*, and is certainly no authority for the acceptance of other subscriptions as a binding consideration in such a case as the present one.

The doctrine of mutual promises was also put forward on the argument as a ground upon which the deceased's promise might be held to be binding. It was suggested that the statement in the subscription of the purpose for which it was made, *viz.*: 'of enabling Dalhousie College to maintain and improve the efficiency of its teaching, to construct new buildings and otherwise to keep pace with the growing need of its constituency' constituted an implied request on the part of the deceased to apply the promised subscription to this object and that the acceptance by the college of his promise created a contract between them, the consideration for the promise of the deceased to pay the money being the promise of the college to apply it to the purpose stated.

I cannot think that any such construction can fairly be placed upon the subscription paper and its acceptance by the college. It certainly contains no express request to the college either 'to maintain and improve the efficiency of its teaching' or 'to construct new buildings and otherwise to keep pace with the growing need of its constituency', but simply states that the promise to pay the $5,000 is made for the purpose of enabling the college to do so, leaving it perfectly free to pursue what had always been its aims in whatever manner its governors should choose. No statement is made as to the amount intended to be raised for all or any of the purposes stated. No buildings of any kind are described. The construction of new buildings is merely indicated as a means of the college keeping pace with the growing need of its constituency and apparently to be undertaken as and when the governors should in their unfettered discretion decide the erection of any one or more buildings for any purpose was necessary or desirable.

It seems to me difficult to conceive that, had the deceased actually paid the promised money, he could have safely relied upon the mere acceptance of his own promise, couched in such vague and uncertain terms regarding its purpose as the foundation of any action against the college corporation.

So far as I can discover, there is no English or Canadian case in which it has been authoritatively decided that a reciprocal promise on the part of the promisee may be implied from the mere fact of the acceptance by the promisee of such a subscription paper from the hands of the promisor to do the thing for which the subscription is promised. There is no doubt, of course, that an express agreement by the promisee to do certain acts in return for a subscription is a sufficient consideration for the promise of the subscriber. There may, too, be circumstances proved by evidence, outside the subscription paper itself, from which such a reciprocal promise on the part of the promisee may well be implied, but I have not been able to find any English or Canadian case where it has actually been so decided in the absence of proof that the subscriber has himself either expressly requested the promisee to undertake some definite project or personally taken such a part in connection with the projected enterprise that such a request might be inferred therefrom.

. . .

. . . the English decisions, give no countenance to the principle applied in *Sargent v Nicholson* and *YMCA v Rankin* and in the earlier American cases, as is so pointedly illustrated by the judgments of Pearson J., in *Re Hudson, Creed v Henderson* (1885), 33 WR 819, and Eve J., in *Re Cory, Kinnaird v Cory* (1912), 29 TLR 18. The headnote in *Re Hudson* states:

A. verbally promised to give £20,000 to the Jubilee Fund of the Congregational Union, and also filled up and signed a blank form of promise not addressed to anyone, but headed 'Congregational Union of England and Wales Jubilee Fund', whereby he promised to give £20,000, in five equal annual instalments of £4,000 each, for the liquidation of chapel debts. A. paid three instalments of £4,000 to the fund within three years from the date of his promise, and then died, leaving the remaining two instalments unpaid and unprovided for.

The Congregational Union claimed £8,000 from A.'s executors, on the ground that they had been led by A.'s promise to contribute larger sums to churches than they would otherwise have done; that money had been given and promised by other persons in consequence of A.'s promise; that grants from the Jubilee Fund had been promised to cases recommended by A.; and that churches to which promises had been made by the committee, and the committee themselves, had incurred liabilities in consequence of A.'s promise.

His Lordship held (33 WR, at p. 821) there was no consideration for the promise. 'There really is,' he said, 'in this matter, nothing whatever in the shape of a consideration which could form a contract between the parties.'

And he added:

I am bound to say that this is an attempt to turn a charity into something very different from a charity. I think it ought to fail, and I think it does fail. I do not know to what extent a contrary decision might open a new form of posthumous charity. Posthumous charity is already bad enough, and it is quite sufficiently protected by law without establishing a new principle which would extend the doctrine in its favour far more than it has been extended or ought to be extended.

In the *Cory* case a gift of 1,000 guineas was promised to a YMCA for the purpose of building a memorial hall. The sum required was £150,000, of which £85,000 had been promised or was available. The committee in charge decided not to commit themselves until they saw that their efforts to raise the whole fund were likely to prove successful. The testator, whose estate it was sought to charge, promised the 1,000 guineas and subsequently the committee felt justified in entering into a building contract,which they alleged they were largely induced to enter into by the testator's promise. Eve J., held there was no contractual obligation between the parties and therefore no legal debt due from the estate.

. . .

To hold otherwise would be to hold that a naked, voluntary promise may be converted into a binding legal contract by the subsequent action of the promisee alone without the consent, express or implied, of the promisor. There is no evidence here which in any way involves the deceased in the carrying out of the work for which the promised subscription was made other than the signing of the subscription paper itself.

. . .

The appeal, I think, should be dismissed with costs.

Contractual liability and conditional promises—'subject to contract' promises

Lowis v Wilson [1948] IR 347

By a document signed on 12 July 1948, the plaintiff, Muriel Lowis, Talbot Lodge, Blackrock, County Dublin, agreed to purchase from the defendant, James H. Wilson, Girley, Kells, County Meath, part of the lands of Girley, containing 76 acres, 2 roods, 30 perches, or thereabouts, statute measure, being the lands the subject of Folio No. 6959, County of Meath, held in fee simple subject to the revised annuity of £26, payable to the Irish Land Commission, for the sum of £6,000, together with five per cent auction fees, and to pay a deposit of £1,500 to the auctioneers on the signing of the agreement and the balance of the purchase money on 1 December 1948. The document contained a clause stating that 'this agreement is subject to the preparation of a formal contract to be prepared by W. O. Armstrong, Solicitor for the vendor, Kells, County Meath.' The defendant agreed to discharge all rent, rates and taxes up to 1 December 1948, upon which date possession was to be given to the plaintiff.

At the time of the signing of the said document, the plaintiff paid to the solicitor for the defendant, two sums, £1,500 and £300, respectively, representing the deposit and auction fees. Subsequently, the solicitor for the defendant drafted a formal contract for the sale of the lands and submitted it to the plaintiff for her approval. After negotiations between the parties the plaintiff intimated that she was not disposed to proceed with the purchase and, on 31 July 1948, her solicitor wrote to the solicitor for the defendant so informing him and requesting the return of the sums of £1,500 and £300 already paid as deposit and auction fees, respectively. In correspondence between the parties subsequently the plaintiff claimed that she had not entered into any binding contract for the purchase of the lands, on the ground that the document of 12 July 1948 was not a binding contract, but was merely an agreement for the preparation of a formal contract of sale; for the defendant it was contended that the document of 12 July 1948, was a binding contract for the sale of the lands, notwithstanding that it was a preliminary contract.

The defendant having failed to return the said sums of £1,500 and £300, as requested, the plaintiff by summary summons instituted proceedings for the return of the sum of £1,800.

Dixon J.:

If I had to deal with this matter on the basis of the principle stated (at p. 645) in *Chinnock v Marchioness of Ely*[1] and referred to, at p. 32, in *Winn v Bull*[2] and in later cases, I would have had some difficulty in deciding as to the proper application of this principle in the present case. It seems to me that it might have been arguable that the principle was not properly applied in all of the cases cited; but I have not now to consider any argument of that kind. [Counsel for the defendant's] argument was confined to a different question, possibly for the reason that the weight of all the cases from *Winn v Bull* onwards is that similar wording to that here was held to have had the effect of preventing an agreement, although it contained sufficient to satisfy the Statute of Frauds, from being a binding and enforceable agreement.

The reasons given in those cases were that the agreement was intended to be subject to the parties entering into a further agreement, and it was only when such further agreement had been entered into that the parties would have arrived at a firm and enforceable contract.

The progressive tendency in those cases in favour of regarding the original agreement as merely conditional culminated in *Chillingworth v Esche*.[3] In that case the position was put by two of the judges as being that, if an agreement to sell 'subject to contract' is entered into, it is not binding unless there are circumstances which would have the effect of inducing a court to take the opposite view. Although this statement of the position arrived at may represent a departure from, or advance on, the principle as originally formulated, the weight of authority would possibly have compelled me to adopt it.

I hold against the contention advanced by [counsel for the defendant], *viz.* that the document here was a final binding contract, subject to a condition which must be strictly and literally interpreted against the purchaser and that, on such interpretation, the condition has been fulfilled. That point is not dealt with in any of the cases referred to in the argument. Those cases dealt with the point whether the original agreement was a concluded one or merely an agreement to enter into an agreement.

The contention is that I am here dealing with a binding agreement subject to a condition subsequent for the 'preparation of a formal contract'. If that is a condition, then it may be divided into two parts, the first part being the preparation of the formal contract and the second part, that it should be prepared by the solicitor named. [Counsel for the defendant] says that this means what it says, *viz.* the preparation of a contract and that this condition has been fulfilled. I do not take the view that this is the meaning of the condition. It seems to me that the condition contemplates the completion between the parties of a contract and in that respect the use of the word, 'contract', is of importance. [The solicitor] could prepare a draft of a proposed contract, but he could not prepare a 'contract' as that would depend on the agreement of both parties evidenced by their signing or sealing the document.

I think that in view of the whole context of the agreement it is impossible to give it such a strictly literal meaning as [counsel for the defendant] contends for. In my view, the word, 'preparation', is used in a different sense to the words, 'to be prepared', unless the latter words are superfluous; and a literal interpretation would make the provision a futile and purposeless one. On the suggested interpretation I cannot see how either the condition or its fulfilment would advance the transaction in any way. There would, on such a view, be no necessity for the solicitor to do anything more than draft the document, and I refuse to accept the construction that the parties agreed to such an apparent futility.

I hold that the agreement comes into the category of the cases already cited, that is to say, that it is a contract to enter into a contract. It is a case where the parties had agreed up to a point, but were not fully agreed, and where the expression of their full agreement was to be embodied in a formal document. If my view is right, then it follows that the agreement is not enforceable and never was, and that the plaintiff has paid £1,800 without consideration and is entitled to recover that sum.

1. 4 De G. J. & S. 638.
2. 7 ChD 29.
3. [1924] 1 Ch. 97.

SECTION THREE—CONTRACT AND THE JUDICIAL PROCESS

Corbin, 'Conditions in the Law of Contract' (1919) 28 Yale LJ 739 at 740–1.

Interpretation and Construction of Contracts

The law of contract deals with those legal relations that arise because of mutual expressions of assent. The parties have expressed their intentions in words, or in other conduct that can be translated into words. The notion is not at all uncommon that legal relations called contractual cannot exist unless the parties intended them to exist, and that the sole function of the courts, therefore, is one of interpretation: What was the intention of the parties? This notion is far from correct. In almost all cases of contract, legal relations will exist, from the very moment of acceptance, that one or both of the parties never consciously expected would exist, and therefore cannot be said to have intended. Furthermore, the life history of any single contract may cover a long period of time, and new facts will occur after acceptance of the offer—facts that may gravely affect the existing legal relations and yet may have been utterly unforeseen by the parties. Many of these uncontemplated legal relations are invariably described as contractual. Therefore it appears that a necessary function of the courts is to determine the unintended legal relations as well as the intended ones.

The first step in this judicial process is the merely historical one of determining what the operative facts were. What did the parties say and do? What words did they use? Did they execute a document? This historical determination is made possible by evidence.

The next step is one of interpretation. In taking this step the court may put to itself two questions: first, what was the actual state of mind of the contracting parties, their meaning and intention at the time they said the words or performed the other acts to be interpreted; second, what meaning do the words and acts of the parties now express to a reasonable and disinterested third party? It is only in exceptional cases that these questions will be consciously considered by a court; usually the process of interpretation will involve rapid and unconscious shifts from the one aspect to the other.

Frequently the only way to arrive at an answer to the first question is to answer the second; in other cases the two may both be susceptible of answer and the two answers may not agree. If the actual intention of the parties is not the same as the meaning that is now conveyed to a reasonable man, it is the latter that will more often prevail. If, however, the parties clearly had a common meaning and intention, it will control irrespective of what a third person would have understood.

Often, however, the court cannot solve the problem before it by mere interpretation. The court's problem is to determine the jural relations of the parties as they are now; and these relations depend upon facts, both contemporaneous with the acceptance and subsequent thereto, which were not known or anticipated by the parties and as to which they made no provision that is capable of either sort of interpretation. The question now is, not what is the meaning of word, but what does the welfare of society require in view of these unknown or unanticipated circumstances? To answer this question the court must resort to general rules of law even though they were unknown by the parties, to rules of fairness and morality, to the prevailing *mores* of the time and place. This process may be called one of judicial construction. The line separating mere interpretation from *judicial construction*, although logically quite clear, will always be practically indistinct and difficult of determination, especially because the courts so frequently construct under the guise of mere interpretation.

Note

Corbin was not setting forward a view of the judicial process that characterised the essential nature of contract litigation as being mechanical in nature, rather he was emphasising the need to recognise that judicial techniques may be limited. The objectives behind the judicial process may differ.

As Duncan Kennedy wrote in 'Form and Substance in Private Law Adjudication' (1975) 89 Harv L Rev 1685 (footnotes omitted):

. . . The substantive and formal conflict in private law cannot be reduced to disagreement about how to apply some neutral calculus that will 'maximise the total satisfaction of human wants'. The opposed rhetorical modes lawyers use reflect a deeper level of contradiction. At this deeper level we are divided among ourselves and also within ourselves between irreconcilable visions of humanity, and society, and between radically different aspirations for our common future.

Considerations of space allow us to give just two examples of how perceptions may differ.

A. ETHICAL TENSIONS IN CONTRACT LAW

Terry, 'Unconscionable Contracts in NSW' (1982) 10 Aust B L Rev 311 at 313–6. (Footnotes omitted.)

Freedom and Sanctity of Contract

'If there is one thing which more than another public policy requires it is that men of full age and competent understanding shall have the utmost liberty of contracting, and that their contracts when entered into freely and voluntarily shall be held sacred and shall be enforced by the Courts of Justice. Therefore you have this paramount public policy to consider—that you are not lightly to interfere with freedom of contract'

Sir George Jessell's statement [above] of the principles of freedom of contract and sanctity of contract—that subject to the restraint of legality the parties are free to negotiate their contracts on their own terms and the terms mutually agreed upon will be enforced by the courts without interference on the ground of fairness—expresses the fundamental and underlying assumption of the law of contract. These principles offer little scope for relieving a party from the burden of an oppressive contract. Although it has been suggested that 'there is the vigilance of the common law which, while allowing freedom of contract, watches to see that it is not abused', there is weightier authority against a public policy placing the ideal of contractual fairness above the need for stability, certainty and predictability which the classical theory emphasises. Despite a 'mosaic of decisions' in which relief from unconscionable contracts has been granted in particular cases, the principles of freedom and sanctity have survived the vast economic and social changes of the last century more or less intact and still represent the cornerstone of the law of contract. That the classical theory is alive and well in Australia is readily illustrated by the recent decision of the High Court of Australia in *South Australia Rlys Commissioner v Egan*. Menzies J. regarded the contract as 'so outrageous that it is surprising that any contractor would undertake work for the Railways Commissioner upon its terms . . .'. His Honour commented that it was 'perhaps the most wordy, obscure and oppressive contract that I have ever come across . . .' from which 'not one oppressive provision which could have been found was omitted . . .'. the High Court made it clear that such provisions found little favour in modern eyes but nevertheless held that it was required to give legal effect to the provisions and was 'not to be deflected from that course because they appear unfair and one-sided'.

Criticism of the Classical Theory

The principles of freedom of contract and sanctity of contract developed in the context of a market place are very different from that of today. The classical theory was ideally suited to both the practical and the theoretical requirements of the time. Freedom of contract was a realistic approach to the unsophisticated market place of the nineteenth century and a policy of non-interference with contracts was in accordance with the prevailing philosophy of *laissez-faire*. However, the incredible social and economic changes since that time have rendered the application of the classical theory in its full vigour inappropriate. Freedom of contract is distorted in the market place by inequality of bargaining power and the common law and statutory inroads into the sanctity of contracts have recognised this fact.

The assumption underlying freedom of contract—that 'contracts are based always on mutual agreement and [arise] out of free choice unhampered by external control or interference'—is no longer valid. Advancing business technology, increasingly sophisticated marketing techniques, the growth of a massive credit industry and a tendency to bigger business all erode the consumer's influence in contracting. In particular, the widespread use of standard form contracts has restricted the consumer's freedom to negotiate the terms of a contract. Standard form contracts are the inevitable by-product of a standardised mass-production society and have distinct and undoubted virtues that are discussed later in this article. Nevertheless, they are often used to exploit and abuse superior bargaining power. In A. *Schroeder Music Publishing Co. Ltd v Macaulay* Lord Diplock expressed strong disapproval of standard form contracts containing terms which have not been the subject of negotiation but have been 'dictated' by the party whose superior bargaining power enables him to say: 'If you want these goods or services at all, these are the only terms on which they are obtainable. Take it or leave it.' The market place of today is characterised by inequality of bargaining power. Where there is gross disparity of bargaining power, as in the vast majority of consumer contracts, there is little actual freedom to negotiate terms and the party with superior bargaining power can impose the terms on the weaker party.

If freedom of contract does not exist in practice, a rigid adherence to sanctity of contract perpetuates a 'pathetic contrast' between the textbook approach to contract and the commercial reality. The principle of sanctity of contract follows from that of freedom of contract: contracts should be enforced by the courts no matter what their terms or effects because the parties have only themselves to blame if the contract was harsh or otherwise unsatisfactory. When freedom to contract does not represent the reality of the market place, sanctity of contract is no longer a logical conclusion. To suggest that the judiciary has not been aware of the pathetic contrast between the theory underlying the law of contract and its distortion in the real world, is to do the judges a grave injustice. For many years equity has protected those who are particularly susceptible to exploitation because of a special disadvantage such as illness, ignorance, impaired faculties, financial need or inexperience, but the categories where relief has been granted are isolated and exceptional and the jurisdiction is confined within narrow limits.

The equitable jurisdiction to grant relief from unconscionable contracts has depended [more] on a narrow allegation of misconduct than abuse of superior bargaining power. Nevertheless Lord Denning M.R. in *Lloyd's Bank Ltd v Bundy* regarded 'inequality of bargaining power' as the 'single thread' linking the exceptional equitable categories:

> Gathering all together, I would suggest that through all these instances there runs a single thread. They rest on 'inequality of bargaining power'. By virtue of it, the English law gives relief to one who, without independent advice, enters into a contract upon terms which are very unfair or transfers property for a consideration which is grossly inadequate, when his bargaining power is grievously impaired by reason of his own needs or desires, or by his own ignorance or infirmity, coupled with undue influences or pressures brought to bear on him by or for the benefit of the other. When I use the word 'undue' I do not mean to suggest that the principle depends on proof of any wrongdoing.

Lord Denning's proposition has received support in later cases and may one day be seen as the first step in the development of an abuse of bargaining power principle of general applications, but at this stage it has not matured into a principle of general application and, having regard to the support that sanctity of contract received from the High Court in *South Australian Rlys Commissioner v Egan*, its assimilation into Australian common law is not a strong possibility in the near future.

The common law's failure to develop an unconscionability doctrine of general application does not mean that sanctity of contract is inviolate. The courts pay lip service to the notion of absolute freedom of contract, yet relief from unfair or oppressive agreements is widely and frequently given by surreptitious means. The Peden Report was critical of the manner in which the courts have responded to changing needs and expectations in the community: they have 'developed a number of devices to subvert the doctrine of sanctity of contract in order to do justice in individual cases'. These devices may achieve justice in an individual case but do not make a frontal attack on the root cause of the problem and 'present a multitude of individual decisions which fail to accumulate experience or authority in marking out the minimal requirements of fairness'. The recognition that 'unfairness' is the basis of these individual decisions is, in the view of many commentators, an essential step in the development of the law and it is unfortunate that Lord Denning's principle of general application has not received wider support.

Although the common law developments '[fall] short of any quantum leap in doctrine' they have, in effect, subverted the principle of sanctity of contract by surreptitious means in response to the commercial reality of the modern market place. The legislature has also recognised that a rigid policy of non-interference in contractual rights and obligations is no longer appropriate. The mass of consumer protection legislation testifies to the fact that *caveat venditor* rather than *caveat emptor* is the appropriate description of the market place today. The regulations of the contents of consumer contracts is a necessary and proper function of a responsible legislature.

B. Contract and Economic Theory

Kronman and Posner, *The Economics of Contract Law* (Boston: Little, Brown & Co. 1979) 1–7. (Footnote omitted.)

The law of contracts regulates, among other kinds of transactions, the purchase and sale of goods (including real estate) and services. Since buying and selling—and related transactions, such as leasing and borrowing, which are also governed by contract law—are quintessentially economic activities, it would seem that economics should have something useful to say to students of contract law. For example, economics may be able to tell us why people make contracts and how contract law can facilitate the operation of markets. And to the extent that contract doctrines reflect judicial efforts, whether deliberate or unconscious, to achieve efficiency, economics may help toward an understanding of the meaning of the doctrines and their appropriate limits.

. . .

The fundamental economic principle with which we begin is that if voluntary exchanges are permitted—if, in other words, a market is allowed to operate—resources will gravitate toward their most valuable uses. If A owns a good that is worth only $100 to him but $150 to B, both will be made better off by an exchange of A's good for B's money at any price between $100 and $150; and if they realise this, they will make the exchange. By making both of them better off, the exchange will also increase the wealth of the society (of which they are members), assuming the exchange does not reduce the welfare of non-parties more than it increases A's and B's welfare. Before the exchange—which, let us say, takes place at a price of $125—A had a good worth $100 to him and B had $125 in cash, a total of $225. After the exchange, A has $125 in cash and B has a good worth $150 to him, a total of $275. The exchange has increased the wealth of society by $50 (ignoring, as we have done, any possible third-party effects).

The principle is the same whether we are speaking of the purchase of a string of pearls, a lawyer's time, a machine for making shoes or an ingot of aluminum. The existence of a market—a locus of opportunities for mutually advantageous exchanges—facilitates the allocation of the good or service in question to the use in which it is most valuable, thereby maximising the wealth of society.

This conclusion may be questioned on various grounds. For example, it may be argued that since 'value' in this analysis is measured by willingness to pay, which in turn is affected by the distribution of income and wealth (one cannot offer to buy a good without having money or the means to obtain it), the maximisation of value cannot be regarded as an uncontroversially proper goal for society to pursue.
. . .

The principle that voluntary exchange should be freely permitted in order to maximise value is frequently summarised in the concept (or slogan) of 'freedom of contract'. This is something of a misnomer, for the concept of *contract* typically plays an insignificant role in elucidations and critiques of the principle of voluntary exchange. Many value-maximising exchanges occur without contracts, or with contracts so rudimentary or transitory as to have little interest for economists studying the phenomenon of voluntary exchange. If A buys the *Chicago Tribune* from B, a news vendor, paying 20¢ for it on the spot, this is a value-maximising exchange; but it would be pretentious to speak of a contract between A and B, though technically there is one (if a section of the paper is missing, A can probably rescind the contract and get his 20¢ back). One can talk about the principle or system of voluntary exchange for quite some time before it becomes necessary to consider the role of contracts and contract law in facilitating the process.

In the newspaper example, the exchange is virtually (though not completely) instantaneous; and this provides a clue to the role of contracts in the process of voluntary exchange. It is true that, although money and good cross at the same moment, the actual *use* of the good—the reading of the newspaper—occurs after the exchange and takes some time; so really the process of exchange is not complete until the paper has been opened and inspected. Only then can the buyer be satisfied that he got what he paid for (that no pages are missing or illegible, etc.). Still, the time required to complete the exchange in the newspaper example is quite short. Where the time is long, contracts and contract law become important.

Suppose that A promises to build a house for B, construction to take six months to complete and B to pay either periodically or on completion. With construction so time-consuming, there is a significant likelihood that something will occur to frustrate the exchange—insolvency, changes in the price of inputs, labour troubles, etc. Nor is A's performance complete when construction of the house is finished. A durable good like a house by definition yields services to the purchaser over a period of time, a long one in the case of a house; and it is these services rather than the physical structure itself that the purchaser is hoping to acquire. If the house wears out long before the purchaser reasonably believed it would, the exchange will be effectively thwarted long after nominal completion of performance by the promisor.

Economists have pointed out that the cost of an undertaking tends to be inversely related to the time allowed for completion. Stated differently, it is costly to accelerate completion of a time-consuming task. It would also be costly to make goods less durable in order to compress the period in which the full exchange of the goods could be completed. These observations suggest that a system of contract rights, and not merely one of property rights, may be necessary to minimise the costs of production in a market system.

Thus far we have been attempting to elucidate the concept of a contract and explain its economic significance. We have said nothing about the economic function of contract *law*. Its basic function is to provide a sanction for reneging, which, in the absence of sanctions, is sometimes tempting where the parties' performance is not simultaneous. During the process of an extended exchange, a point may be reached where it is in the interest (though perhaps only the very narrow, short-run interest) of one of the parties to terminate performance. If A agrees to build a house for B and B pays him in advance, A can make himself better off, at least if loss of reputation (which, depending on A's particular situation, may be unimportant to him) is ignored, by pocketing B's money and not building the house. The problem arises because the non-simultaneous character of the exchange offers one of the parties a strategic advantage which he can use to obtain a transfer payment that utterly vitiates the advantages of the contract to the other party. Clearly, if such conduct were permitted, people would be reluctant to enter into contracts and the process of economic exchange would be retarded.

A non-instantaneous or extended exchange creates not only strategic opportunities that parties might try to exploit in the absence of legal sanction, but also uncertainty with regard to the conditions under which performance will occur. This uncertainty exposes the parties to the risk that the costs and benefits of their exchange will turn out to be different from what they expected. An important function of contract law is to enforce the parties' agreed-upon allocation of risk.

A related function is to reduce the costs of the exchange process by supplying a standard set of risk-allocation terms for use by contracting parties. Many substantive rules of contract law are simply specifications of the consequences of some contingency for which the contract makes no express provision. If the parties are satisfied with the way in which the rule allocates the risk of that contingency, they have no need to incur the expense of writing their own risk-allocation rule into the contract.

Besides (1) imposing costs on people who try to exploit the other party to the contract by refusing to abide by its terms and (2) providing a stock of standard contractual provisions, the law of contracts (3) imposes costs on, and thereby discourages, *careless* behaviour in the contracting process—behaviour that unnecessarily increases the costs of the process itself. Suppose A promises to give B a boat if B stops smoking, B complies with this condition (at some cost to himself), but A refuses to give him the boat. A proves that B misunderstood him—he never meant to promise him a boat. B in turn proves that he was reasonably induced by A's words and conduct to believe that A had indeed promised him the boat. If we believe that A did not in fact intend such a promise, then enforcement of the promise cannot be justified as necessary to prevent frustration of a value-maximising exchange; there is no basis for presuming that an exchange will make the parties better off if one of them never intended to make it. But we may still want to enforce the contract in order to give people in A's position an incentive to avoid carelessly inducing others to incur costs in reliance on the existence of a contract. This problem may seem to belong to the law of torts rather than contracts, since enforcement serves not to promote a mutually beneficial exchange but instead to deter careless behaviour. But enforcement does promote the contractual process by discouraging a costly form of carelessness that would tend to impede it.

The foregoing discussion suggests a resolution along economic lines of the old dispute in contract law over whether the basis of contract formation is a 'subjective' or 'objective' one—whether the law requires an actual meeting of minds or whether it is enough that the parties use words or conduct that would signify agreement to an impartial observer. Only a contract that involves an actual meeting of minds satisfies the economist's definition of a value-maximising exchange; but the economist allows a place for rules designed to prevent people from misleading others into thinking they have a contract with them; hence both the subjective and objective theories have a place in contract law.

The discussion to this point has emphasised the economic role of contract and has outlined the economic functions of contract law. It is, however, one thing to show that contract law *could* promote economic efficiency and another thing to prove that it *does*. A number of scholars in recent years have claimed that the common law, including the law of contracts, has an implicit economic logic—the purpose, or in any event the effect, of many common-law doctrines is, they believe, to increase economic efficiency. One of the points emphasised by those sceptical of this theory is the implausibility of supposing that judges have been able to work out the economics of legal obligations and liabilities correctly. To be sure, one observes business firms behaving 'correctly' from an economic standpoint (i.e. maximising profits by equating marginal revenue to marginal cost) without being conscious of, or at least articulate about, what they are doing. But this can be explained by the competitive process: firms that do not maximise profits will be unable to attract capital from competing demanders and so will eventually be driven out of business. The survivors, the firms we observe, are those that pursue, whether unwittingly or deliberately, profit-maximising strategies. But it is unclear what the mechanism is that drives judges to discover and apply correct microeconomic principles.

In the case of contract law, however, a competitive mechanism is at hand to explain why the rules of contract law might be expected to be generally efficient. As we have seen, many rules of contract law are designed simply to supply contract terms where the parties have not done so expressly. If prospective contracting parties do not like the terms supplied by contract law, normally they are free to supplant them with their own express terms. The parties will prefer efficient terms because those are the terms that minimise the costs of the transaction to them, and accordingly the tendency will be to contract around any inefficient rules of contract law. The efficient rules will survive; the inefficient will be progressively ignored and eventually forgotten.

This competitive or evolutionary process is reinforced by two other factors. The first is the willingness of the courts to honour the parties' designation of the law to be applied to resolve any dispute arising from a contract between them. The second is the right of contracting parties to agree to submit any disputes arising out of the contract to a private arbitrator. Because of these factors, courts that apply inefficient rules of contract law will tend to lose cases to tribunals that apply efficient rules. Even if a court system does not 'mind' losing contract business, one will observe a body of cases heavily concentrated in tribunals that apply efficient rules.

The foregoing discussion does not, of course, prove that the rules of contract law are efficient; it simply makes the idea a bit less shocking. It should be noted, however, that the relevance of economics to contract law does not depend on proving that the logic of that law is economics. Since efficiency is an important value in our society (we need not decide here how important), a critique of contract law based on efficiency is a potentially powerful tool of legal reform.

Chapter Two

Formation of a Contract

INTRODUCTION

The process whereby a contract is agreed is not standardised or uniform. The most straightforward transactions, such as buying a newspaper or contracting to travel to work in the morning by bus are in theory governed by the same rules on formation as the most complex share or property transaction. The parties, and the courts, must be able to decide when the preliminary inquiries as to terms have ended and when one party at least has been prepared, like the Earl of Kildare, to 'chance his arm' and make an offer. The courts must also try and guarantee some parity of fairness by negativing the prejudice this can induce, hence the counter-offer rule and perhaps judicial sensitivity on lock-out agreements. The rules governing acceptances are also designed to preclude unfair practices, such as the 'silence deemed acceptance' rule which is viewed with hostility by the courts and the Oireachtas. The acceptance rules must also provide practical and fair methods of determining whether, when and where the contract was concluded, while being consistent with the intentions of each party.

While the principle of private autonomy suggests that each party should be free to determine how long the negotiations should last, the cases suggest some constraints may be placed on 'free will'. Negotiations cannot be expected to go on forever, and the rules which decide whether an offer can be accepted or not impose limits. Conversely, the rules also allow concluded 'contracts' to be unravelled—the subject to contract cases—when commercial expediency and practice deems this appropriate, even though the results in individual cases can be patently unjust.

SECTION ONE—OFFER

An offer is 'a clear and unambiguous statement of the terms upon which the offeror is willing to contract, should the person or persons to whom the offer is addressed decide to accept.'
R. Clark, *Contract Law in Ireland* (5th ed. Dublin: Thompson RoundHall, 2005)

It is important to distinguish 'an offer' from other separate and distinct situations where a party makes a statement which resembles an offer, but which is not capable of being 'accepted', nor of giving rise to contractual obligations should the party to whom it is made assent to the terms proposed.

A. INVITATION TO TREAT

An invitation to treat invites the recipient to make an offer and sets out certain of the terms on which the recipient's offer is likely to be accepted. It does not amount to an offer which is itself capable of being accepted. Such invitations are commonly used in product advertisements, self-service displays, etc.

The Minister for Industry and Commerce *v* Pim Bros Ltd [1966] IR 154

The defendants displayed an advertisement attached to a coat indicating that the cash price of the coat was 24 guineas and that the weekly payments in respect thereof were 5s 10d.

The plaintiff claimed that this advertisement did not comply with certain provisions of the Hire-Purchase and Credit Sale (Advertising) Order 1961 in relation to 'goods offered or available for sale by way of hire-purchase or credit-sale agreement', and brought a prosecution against the defendant under that order.

Davitt P.:

Before one could determine whether the advertisement related to goods offered for sale by way of hire-purchase agreement or to goods offered for sale by way of credit-sale agreement one would have to decide whether it related to goods offered for sale at all; in other words, whether the advertisement constituted an offer by the defendants to sell the coat. In one sense it could be described as an offer to sell. In popular terms the coat could properly be said to be on offer to the public. In the strictly legal sense, however, the advertisement was merely a statement of the cash price at which the defendants were prepared to sell the goods, with an indication that certain credit facilities, the exact nature of which were unspecified, would be available. This would not constitute an offer to sell which could be made a contract of sale by acceptance: *Harvey v Facey* [1893] AC 552.

Consider:
What is the rationale for expressing an advertisement as an 'invitation to treat' rather than an offer?

A category of advertisement which does not constitute an invitation to treat is an offer which, if accepted, gives rise to a unilateral contract. (This is discussed at p.48 *et seq.*).

B. QUOTATIONS

In the process of negotiating a contract, it is not uncommon for statements to be made by one party which resemble offers but which lack the intention to create a binding legal arrangement in the event that the other party agrees. They are viewed merely as steps in negotiations.

Boyers & Co. *v* D. & R. Duke [1904] 2 IR 617

The plaintiffs, drapers, wrote to the defendants, linen manufacturers, asking for their lowest quotation to supply a quantity of canvas. The defendants replied stating their lowest price. The plaintiffs subsequently sent in an order at this price. On discovering that a clerical error had resulted in an excessively low quotation, the defendants refused to supply at the original price. The plaintiffs sued for breach of contract.

Lord O'Brien L.C.J:

The short question in this case is, whether these letters or documents which passed between the plaintiffs and the defendants constitute a completed contract—whether they amount to an offer and an acceptance of the offer, or to a quotation and an order? If they amount to the former, they constitute a contract; if to the latter, that is to say to a quotation and order, they do not constitute a contract. The action in which the question arises was brought by the plaintiffs against the defendants for alleged breach of contract for the supply of canvas. The controversy arises, as I have said, upon the construction of the documents. My brother Wright, who tried the case, held that they did not constitute a completed contract, and we are of opinion he was right in so holding.

What, then, are these documents? The first is dated 23 February 1904, from the plaintiffs to the defendants, and is in the following terms: 'Please give us your lowest quotation for 3,000 yards of canvas, 32¹/₂ inches wide, to the enclosed sample, or near, and your shortest time for delivery, and oblige,' &c. Now, this is expressly a request for a quotation. The reply is dated 24 February 1904, and is as follows: 'We enclose sample, No. B 3932, nearest we have to match yours, also enclosed. Lowest price, 32¹/₂ inches wide, is 4⁵/₈d per yard, 36 inches measure. Delivery of 3,000 yards in 5/6 weeks.' This, in my opinion, amounts only to a quotation. Certainly quantity, price and time of delivery are stated, but I think it is nothing more than a statement of their ability to turn out the subject-matter at a certain price at a certain time, and not an offer to sell it at the price, and to deliver it within the time mentioned. It amounted to nothing more, in my opinion, than a quotation in reply to a request for one.

Now comes the third and last letter, which is said by the plaintiffs to be an acceptance of an offer to sell on certain terms. It is dated 3 March. I shall read it: 'Messrs D. & R. Duke, Brechin, NB Gents, Please get made for us 3,000 yards of canvas, 32¹/₂ inches wide, as per your quotation, 24 February, at 4⁵/₈d per yard; deliver same as quickly as possible. Also please quote us for same, 52 inches wide, for quantity of about 20,000 yards annually. As we have not had the pleasure of doing business with you before, we give you as reference Messrs Baxter, Brothers, Dundee; Messrs Richards, Ltd, Aberdeen. Canvas No. B 3932. (Signed) Boyers & Co. Also please quote us for canvas to sample enclosed, 52 inches, and oblige, B. & Co.'

Is this an acceptance of an offer, or an order? In my opinion it is not the acceptance of an offer, because the letter to which it was a reply was a quotation and not an offer.

This letter is nothing more than it purports to be, namely, an order based on a quotation. The words are: 'Please get made for us 3,000 yards of canvas, 32¹/₂ inches wide, as per your quotation, 24 February.' The first letter, that is to say, the letter of 23 February, asked for a quotation; the letter of the twenty-fourth sent what was asked for; and the plaintiffs' letter of 3 March expressly refers to the letter of the twenty-fourth, as 'per your quotation, 24 February'.

Light is also thrown upon the true character of the letter of 3 March by the giving of references as therein, which is certainly far more compatible with the giving of an order, or offer to purchase, than with a completed contract. The words 'as quickly as possible' in the letter of 3 March would perhaps point to an uncompleted contract, but I think this criticism is so minute that much weight is not to be attached to it.

We are of opinion that my brother Wright's view was correct, and that judgment should be for the defendants.

Madden J.:

A quotation might be so expressed as to amount to an offer to provide a definite article, or to do a certain work, at a defined price. But the ideas of a quotation, and of an offer to sell, are radically different. The difference is well illustrated by the case of Harvey v Facey.[1] There, to a telegram in these terms, 'Will you sell us B. H. P.? Telegraph lowest cash price', the answer was returned, 'Lowest price for B. H. P., £900.' The inquirer telegraphed, 'We agree to buy B. H. P. for £900 asked by you.' An exceptionally strong judicial committee of the Privy Council, in a judgment delivered by Lord Morris, held that the statement, or quotation, of the lowest price at which a definite thing will be sold, does not import an offer to sell.

The principle on which this case was decided applies with a greater force to mercantile transactions than to an application for a statement of the price of a single parcel of land. It is a matter of common knowledge that quotations of prices are scatter broadcast among possible customers. Business could not be carried on if each recipient of a priced catalogue offering a desirable article—say a rare book—at an attractive price, were in a position to create a contract of sale by writing that he would buy at the price mentioned. The catalogue has probably reached many collectors. The order of one only can be honoured. Has each of the others who write for the book a right of action? Wholesale dealers have not in stock an unlimited supply of the articles the prices of which they quote to the public at large. This stock usually bears some proportion to the orders which they may reasonably expect to receive. Transactions of the kind under consideration are intelligible and business-like, if we bear in mind the distinction between a quotation, submitted as the basis of a possible order, and an offer to sell which, if accepted, creates a contract, for the breach of which damages may be recovered.

These observations seem to apply with special force to a quotation furnished by a manufacturer, in the position of the defendants, stating the terms on which he is prepared to work, as to price and time for completion. He may receive and comply with many applications for quotations on the same day. If his reply in each case can be turned into a contract by acceptance, his looms might be burdened with an amount of work which would render it impossible for him to meet his engagements. In my opinion, a merchant, dealer or manufacturer, by furnishing a quotation invites an offer which will be honoured or not according to the exigencies of his business. A quotation based on current prices usually holds good for a limited time. But it remains a quotation, on the basis of which an offer will not be entertained after a certain date. I have arrived at this conclusion irrespective of the terms of the letter of 3 March, as to which I will only say that it suggests to my mind that the writer knew well that he was giving an order, not accepting an offer for sale.

[1.] [1893] AC 552.

(Gibson J. also held that no concluded contract existed.)

Note

As the above case illustrates, the decision as to whether a proposal constitutes an offer or a mere quotation lacking contractual intent depends on the construction of the documentation and an examination of the circumstances of the negotiations.

C. AUCTION

Special rules regulate auction situations both at common law and under Statute.

Sale of Goods Act 1893 s. 58(2)

58. (2) In the case of a sale by auction:
(1) Where goods are put up for sale by auction in lots, each lot is prima facie deemed to be the subject of a separate contract of sale:
(2) A sale by auction is complete when the auctioneer announces its completion by the fall of the hammer, or in other customary manner. Until such announcement is made any bidder may retract his bid:
(3) Where a sale by auction is not notified to be subject to a right to bid on behalf of the seller, it shall not be lawful for the seller to bid himself or to employ any person to bid at such sale, or for the auctioneer knowingly to take any bid from the seller or any such person: Any sale contravening this rule may be treated as fraudulent by the buyer:
(4) A sale by auction may be notified to be subject to a reserve or upset price, and a right to bid may also be reserved expressly by or on behalf of the seller.

Where a right to bid is expressly reserved, but not otherwise, the seller, or any one person on his behalf, may bid at the auction.

In an auction situation, in addition to concluding a contract for the sale of property (the principal contract), a collateral contract may be formed to sell property without reserve. In such a case, an offer by the auctioneer to sell without reserve would be accepted by placing the highest bid.

Warlow *v* Harrison (1859) 1 E & E 309

An auctioneer advertised a sale of horses by auction 'without reserve'. Although the plaintiff was the highest bidder for a particular mare, the owner then made a higher bid which was accepted by the auctioneer. The plaintiff claimed that as the highest bona fide bidder, he was entitled to the mare.

Martin B.:

Upon the facts of the case, it seems to us that the plaintiff is entitled to recover. In a sale by auction there are three parties, *viz.* the owner of the property to be sold, the auctioneer and the portion of the public who attend to bid, which of course includes the highest bidder. In this, as in most cases of sales by auction, the owner's name was not disclosed: he was a concealed principal. The name of the auctioneers, of whom the defendant was one, alone was published; and the sale was announced by them to be 'without reserve'. This, according to all the cases both at law and equity, means that neither the vendor nor any person in his behalf shall bid at the auction, and that the property shall be sold to the highest bidder, whether the sum bid be equivalent to the real value or not; *Thornett v Haines*.[1] We cannot distinguish the case of an auctioneer putting up property for sale upon such a condition from the case of the loser of property offering a reward, or that of a railway company publishing a timetable stating the times when, and the places to which, the trains run. It has been decided that the person giving the information advertised for, or a passenger taking a ticket, may sue as upon a contract with him; *Denton v Great Northern Rly Co*.[2] Upon the same principle, it seems to us that the highest bona fide bidder at an auction may sue the auctioneer as upon a contract that the sale shall be without reserve. We think the auctioneer who puts the property up for sale upon such a condition pledges himself that the sale shall be without reserve; or, in other words, contracts that it shall be so; and that this contract is made with the highest bona fide bidder; and, in case of a breach of it, that he has a right of action against the auctioneer. The case is not at all affected by s. 17 of the Statute of Frauds, which relates only to direct sales, and not to contracts relating to or connected with them. Neither does it seem to us material whether the owner, or person on his behalf, bid with the knowledge or privity of the auctioneer. We think the auctioneer has contracted that the sale shall be without reserve; and that the contract is broken upon a bid being made by or on behalf of the owner, whether it be during the time when the property is under the hammer, or it be the last bid upon which the article is knocked down; in either case the sale is not 'without reserve', and the contract of the auctioneer is broken. We entertain no doubt that the owner may, at any time before the contract is legally complete, interfere and revoke the auctioneer's authority: but he does so at his peril; and, if the auctioneer has contracted any liability in consequence of his employment and the subsequent revocation or conduct of the owner, he is entitled to be indemnified.

[1]   15 M & W 367.   [2]   5 E & B 860.

Notes

1. Section 17 of the Statute of Frauds referred to above was similar to Section 58 of the Sale of Goods Act 1893 set out above.
2. In *Barry v Davies (t/a Heathcote Ball & Co. (Commercial Auctions) Ltd) and Others* [2000] 1 WLR 1962, the *Warlow* case was followed and a collateral contract was deemed by the Court of Appeal to exist between the auctioneer and the only bidder at the auction. In that case, the goods were withdrawn from the auction following the bid. See Meisel, 'What Price Auctions Without Reserve', 64(3) MLR 465 (2001).
3. In the *Warlow* case, Martin B. determined that the promise to sell without reserve was indistinguishable from a promise to pay a reward for the return of a lost item—a promise which gives rise to a unilateral contract. (This is discussed at p.48 *et seq*.)

Consider:

In a *Warlow* type scenario, when does a promise become a valid offer? Is it when the advertisement is published or when the item is put up for sale at the auction?

A collateral contract may also be formed on the basis of other promises made by the auctioneer.

Tully *v* The Irish Land Commission (1961) 97 ILTR 174

The defendants advertised that a certain piece of property would be sold at public auction. Clause 2 of the conditions of sale stated that: 'the highest bidder shall be the purchaser and if any dispute arises as to any bidding the property shall be again put up for sale at the last undisputed bidding. There will be a reserve price and the Irish Land Commission, the vendors or their agents shall be at liberty to bid . . .' Clause 3 provided that the purchaser should pay a deposit to the auctioneer immediately after the sale and subscribe his name and address to the memorandum of agreement. Following the auction, a dispute arose as to which party had made the final bid. The plaintiff demanded that the auctioneer put the property up for sale again. The auctioneer refused and the plaintiff sued for breach of clause 2 of the contract.

Kenny J.:

I think that clauses 2 and 3 of the conditions of sale were an offer which could be accepted by bidding at the auction and that they could constitute a contract between the Irish Land Commission and the highest bidder at the auction; this view seems to me to be in accord with legal principle and to be supported by the better authorities. Counsel have cited the views of some eminent writers of textbooks to establish that this view is incorrect; the passages cited shew some confusion between the two contracts which may be involved. When property is put up for sale, and is sold, a memorandum is signed by the purchaser, there is a contract for the sale of the property to the person who has signed the memorandum. The clauses of the conditions of sale which relate to what may happen before the purchaser signs the memorandum are capable of being an offer in connection with a different contract, a contract to which the Statute of Frauds does not apply and which may be accepted by bidding at the auction.

All the witnesses who gave evidence said that the conditions of sale were read before the bidding began; the bidding was clearly made on the terms of and by reference to them. When giving evidence, the plaintiff admitted that he did not attend the auction because of the conditions of sale, and he said that he would have gone in any event. It was argued by counsel for the Irish Land Commission that the plaintiff could not rely on the conditions of sale as an offer as he did not attend the auction because of them. But the conditions of sale were read before the bidding began and the biddings were made by reference to them and they were capable of being an offer.

It has also been argued that clause 2 of the conditions could not constitute an offer because the offeror (the vendor) cannot know the person who has accepted the bid and with whom the contract is made. This contention ignores the many cases in which it has been held that a person who had performed conditions published by another has thereby accepted the offer made by the publication even though his identity was not known. There is a contract when the conditions of a competition are published and somebody complies with the terms which entitles them to a prize. In most cases there is no difficulty about ascertaining the person who was the highest bidder and I do not see any ground, in principle, why it should be held that these conditions and the bidding at the auction were not capable of creating a contract between the Irish Land Commission and the person who made the highest bid. When conditions of sale are read, those relating to the conduct of the auction (such as clause 2) amount to an offer and the bidding is an acceptance. It has been suggested that this view leads to absurdity as it would have the result that the vendors were making an offer to everybody in this country, but the offer which is made by the reading of the conditions of sale and the making of bids is an offer made by the owner of the lands who puts them up for sale to those who attend the auction and bid. The view that these conditions were capable of being an offer gets support from the fact that the conditions of sale were prepared by the Irish Land Commission who now argue that clause 2 of these conditions was without legal effect. If words are without legal effect they should not be inserted in conditions of sale. Words such as this appear in the conditions of sale for most of the public auctions in this country and are to be found in all the recognised books of precedents in conveyancing matters. I do not view with favour an argument by those who have drafted legal documents that the words used are without legal effect.

This conclusion seems to me to be supported by all the better authorities. [Specific reference was made to *Warlow v Harrison* (1858) 1 E & E 295, In *re Agra & Masterman's Bank Ex parte Asiatic Banking Corp.* (1867) and *Carlill v Carbolic Smoke Ball Co.* [1893] 1 QB 256.]

I am therefore of opinion that clauses 2 and 3 of these conditions were an offer which could be accepted so as to create a contractual relation and that there was a contract between the Irish Land Commission and the highest bidder at the auction, the contract being that the highest bidder should be the purchaser and that if any dispute arose as to any bidding the property would be put up for sale at the last undisputed bidding.

Note

Not all advertisements of auctions give rise to collateral contracts. In *Harris v Nickerson* [1873] LR 8 QB 286 CA the defendant, an auctioneer, advertised a sale by auction of certain lots including office furniture on a certain day and the two following days. But the sale of furniture on the third day was withdrawn. The plaintiff attended the sale and claimed against the defendant for breach of contract in not holding the sale, seeking to recover his expenses in attending. The claim was rejected by the Court of Queen's Bench. Blackburn J. described the plaintiff's claim as 'a startling proposition' which would be 'excessively inconvenient' if correct. He opined: 'It amounts to saying that anyone who advertises a sale by publishing an advertisement becomes responsible to everybody who attends the sale for his cab hire or travelling expenses.'

Consider:

What distinguishes the *Warlow* case from the *Harris* case?

D. TENDERS

When an advertisement is placed seeking to invite tenders from prospective contractors—suppliers of goods or services over a period of time, perhaps—the advertisement is normally an invitation to treat. The tender form, setting out the terms upon which the contractors are prepared to contract, is normally an offer which can be accepted or rejected (*Spencer v Harding* (1870) LR 5 CP 561).

A collateral contractual obligation may, however, arise if the statement inviting tenders contains a promise such as a promise to accept the lowest figure or a promise to consider all bids. The existence of such a contract depends on the terms and conditions of the tender call and is independent of the principal contract which is entered into upon the acceptance of one of the tenders.

Blackpool and Fylde Aero Club Ltd *v* Blackpool Borough Council [1990] 3 All ER 25 (CA)

The Council sent invitations to tender for a concession to operate flights from its airport. The invitations stated that the tenders were to be submitted in the envelope provided to the council's post box and that tenders received after twelve noon on 17 March 1983 would not be considered. The club deposited its tender in the town hall letterbox at 11am on 17 March but the letterbox was not opened by council staff at noon that day as it should have been. The club's tender was only noticed the following morning when the post box was opened. It was deemed late and not considered. The club argued that the council had breached a warranty that if a tender was received in time, it would be considered. The trial judge held that the council had breached a warranty and the council appealed.

Bingham L. J.:

In attacking the judge's conclusion on this issue [counsel for the council] made four main submissions. First, he submitted that an invitation to tender in this form was well established to be no more than a proclamation of willingness to receive offers. Even without the first sentence of the council's invitation to tender in this case, the council would not have been bound to accept the highest or any tender. An invitation to tender in this form was an invitation to treat, and no contract of any kind would come into existence unless or until, if ever, the council chose to accept any tender or other offer. For these propositions reliance was placed on *Spencer v. Harding*[1] and *Harris v. Nickerson*.[2] Second, [counsel for the council] submitted that on a reasonable reading of this invitation to tender the council could not be understood to be undertaking to consider all timely tenders submitted. The statement that later tenders would not be considered did not mean that timely tenders would. If the council had meant that they could have said it. There was, although [counsel for the council] did not put it in these words, no *maxim exclusio unius, expressio alterius*. Third, the court should be no less rigorous when asked to imply a contract than when asked to imply a term in an existing contract or to find a collateral contract. A term would not be implied simply because it was reasonable to do so: *Liverpool City Council v Irwin*.[3] In order to establish collateral contracts, 'Not only the terms of such contracts but the existence of an *animus contrahendi* on the part of all the parties to them must be clearly shewn:' *Heilbut, Symons & Co. v. Buckleton*.[4] No lower standard was applicable here and the standard was not satisfied. Fourth, [counsel for the council] submitted that the warranty contended for by the club was simply a proposition 'tailor-made to produce the desired result' (per Lord Templeman in C.B.S. *Songs Ltd. v. Amstrad Consumer Electronics Plc*.[5]) on the facts of this particular case. There was a vital distinction between expectations, however reasonable, and contractual obligations: see per Diplock L.J. in *Lavarack v.*

Woods of Colchester Ltd.[6] The club here expected its tender to be considered. The council fully intended that it should be. It was in both parties' interests that the club's tender should be considered. There was thus no need for them to contract. The court should not subvert well-understood contractual principles by adopting a woolly pragmatic solution designed to remedy a perceived injustice on the unique facts of this particular case.

In defending the judge's decision [counsel for the club] accepted that an invitation to tender was normally no more than an offer to receive tenders. But it could, he submitted, in certain circumstances give rise to binding contractual obligations on the part of the invitor, either from the express words of the tender or from the circumstances surrounding the sending out of the invitation to tender or, as here, from both. The circumstances relied on here were that the council approached the club and the other invitees, all of them connected with the airport; that the club had held the concession for eight years, having successfully tendered on three previous occasions; that the council as a local authority was obliged to comply with its standing orders and owed a fiduciary duty to ratepayers to act with reasonable prudence in managing its financial affairs; and that there was a clear intention on the part of both parties that all timely tenders would be considered. If in these circumstances one asked of this invitation to tender the question posed by Bowen L.J. in *Carlill v. Carbolic Smoke Ball Co.*,[7] 'How would an ordinary person reading this document construe it?', the answer in [counsel's] submission was clear: the council might or might not accept any particular tender; it might accept no tender; it might decide not to award the concession at all; it would not consider any tender received after the advertised deadline; but if it did consider any tender received before the deadline and conforming with the advertised conditions it would consider all such tenders.

I found great force in the submissions made by [counsel for the council] and agree with much of what he said. Indeed, for much of the hearing I was of opinion that the judge's decision, although fully in accord with the merits as I see them, could not be sustained in principle. But I am in the end persuaded that [counsel for the council's] argument proves too much. During the hearing the questions were raised: what if, in a situation such as the present, the council had opened and thereupon accepted the first tender received, even though the deadline had not expired and other invitees had not yet responded? Or if the council had considered and accepted a tender admittedly received well after the deadline? [Counsel for the council] answered that although by so acting the council might breach its own standing orders, and might fairly be accused of discreditable conduct, it would not be in breach of any legal obligation because at that stage there would be none to breach. This is a conclusion I cannot accept. And if it were accepted there would in my view be an unacceptable discrepancy between the law of contract and the confident assumptions of commercial parties, both tenderers ... and invitors (as reflected in the immediate reaction of the council when the mishap came to light).

A tendering procedure of this kind is, in many respects, heavily weighted in favour of the invitor. He can invite tenders from as many or as few parties as he chooses. He need not tell any of them who else, or how many others, he has invited. The invitee may often, although not here, be put to considerable labour and expense in preparing a tender, ordinarily without recompense if he is unsuccessful. The invitation to tender may itself, in a complex case, although again not here, involve time and expense to prepare, but the invitor does not commit himself to proceed with the project, whatever it is; he need not accept the highest tender; he need not accept any tender; he need not give reasons to justify his acceptance or rejection of any tender received. The risk to which the tenderer is exposed does not end with the risk that his tender may not be the highest or, as the case may be, lowest. But where, as here, tenders are solicited from selected parties all of them known to the invitor, and where a local authority's invitation prescribes a clear, orderly and familiar procedure—draft contract conditions available for inspection and plainly not open to negotiation, a prescribed common form of tender, the supply of envelopes designed to preserve the absolute anonymity of tenderers and clearly to identify the tender in question, and an absolute deadline— the invitee is in my judgment protected at least to this extent: if he submits a conforming tender before the deadline he is entitled, not as a matter of mere expect- ation but of contractual right, to be sure that his tender will after the deadline be opened and considered in conjunction with all other conforming tenders or at least that his tender will be considered if others are. Had the club, before tendering, inquired of the council whether it could rely on any timely and conforming tender being considered along with others, I feel quite sure that the answer would have been 'of course'. The law would, I think, be defective if it did not give effect to that.

It is of course true that the invitation to tender does not explicitly state that the council will consider timely and conforming tenders. That is why one is concerned with implication. But the council do not either say that they do not bind themselves to do so, and in the context a reasonable invitee would understand the invitation to be saying, quite clearly, that if he submitted a timely and conforming tender it would be considered, at least if any other such tender were considered.

I readily accept that contracts are not to be lightly implied . . . In all the circum- stances of this case, and I say nothing about any other, I have no doubt that the parties did intend to create contractual relations to the limited extent contended for. Since it has never been the law that a person is only entitled to enforce his contractual rights in a reasonable way (*White and Carter (Councils) Ltd v. McGregor*,[8] per Lord Reid), [council for the club] was in my view right to contend for no more than a contractual duty to consider. I think it plain that the council's invitation to tender was, to this limited extent, an offer, and the club's submission of a timely and conforming tender an acceptance . . . I accordingly agree with the judge's conclusion on the contractual issue.

[Lord Justices Farquharson and Stocker agreed.]

1.	(1870) LR 5 CP 561.	5.	[1988] AC 1013, 1059F.
2.	(1873) LR 8 QB 286.	6.	[1967] 1 QB 278, 294.
3.	[1977] AC 239, 253h.	7.	[1893] 1 QB 256, 266.
4.	[1913] AC 30, 47.	8.	[1962] AC 413, 430A.

Consider:

Could the club have sought relief on the basis of a *quantum meruit* claim for the expenses they incurred in preparing the tender?

Howberry Lane Limited *v* Telecom Éireann, Radio Telefís Éireann, NTL Incorporated [1999] 2 ILRM 232

The first and second named defendants invited tenders for the purchase of Cablelink Ltd. In documents sent to bidders, it was expressly stated that the shareholders reserve the right to sell the company 'to any person at any time', that 'the shareholders are under no obligation to accept the highest bid offered or any bid at all', that they reserve the right 'to accept or reject any offer made irrespective of whether it is the highest offer' and the right 'not to accept any offer or to vary, amend or curtail the sale process at their discretion.' The plaintiff made the highest bid of £410 million and the third named defendant (NTL) made a referential bid of fifteen per cent more than the highest bid. The plaintiff subsequently sought an injunction preventing the first and second named defendants from selling the company to NTL and an order directing them to sell the company to itself.

Morris J.:

Counsel for the plaintiff has sought to rely upon a series of Canadian cases in which the courts have inserted an implied term into the contract which effectively overrides provisions similar to those herein before referred to so as to require the vendor to complete the transaction with the highest bidder. I am satisfied that in all of those cases special circumstances existed in which the courts saw it appropriate to introduce such an implied term. I am also satisfied that under no circumstances is such a term to be implied under the present law in this jurisdiction. *Sweeney v Duggan* 1997 2 IR is clear authority for the following proposition. 'Whether a term is implied pursuant to the presumed intention of the parties or as a legal incident of a definable category of contract, it must be not merely reasonable but also necessary. Clearly it cannot be implied if it is inconsistent with the express wording of the contract and furthermore it may be difficult to infer a term where it cannot be formulated with reasonable preciseness.'

In the present case such an implied term is not necessary and moreover it would be clearly inconsistent with the express wording of the contract.

Accordingly I do not accept the Canadian authorities as any indication of an emerging jurisprudence in this jurisdiction . . .

Counsel for the plaintiff has advanced an argument again based upon a series of Canadian authorities which, summarised, amount to this. It is submitted that upon submitting a bid in a transaction such as this the bidder enters into a contract, in the authorities referred to as contract A, and that under the terms of this contract, providing that his bid is otherwise satisfactory, for instance that he is the lowest bidder, he is entitled to enter into a second contract for the carrying out of the relevant work or provision of the relevant goods.

It is submitted by counsel that in the present case the plaintiff is entitled to regard himself as having entered into contract A with the first and second named defendant and that he is entitled to be offered contract B which will be the contract for the sale of the shares.

Even if, as counsel submits, this is a recognised emerging jurisprudence in Canada I do not accept it as representing the law in this jurisdiction. Moreover I am satisfied that it cannot apply to the circumstances of this case since the vendors have at all stages reserved for themselves the right to withdraw from the tendering procedure . . .

Accordingly I am not satisfied that the plaintiff has discharged the onus of proof of satisfying me that he has a fair case to make so as to entitle him to the injunctive relief sought.

Note

By contrast, in *Harvela Investments Ltd v Royal Trust Co. of Canada Ltd and Others* [1986] AC 207, the House of Lords held that on the construction of a tender invitation, the presumed intention of the vendor was to create a fixed bidding sale rather than an auction sale by means of referential bids. Thus it determined that the first defendant was not entitled to accept a referential bid. The *Harvela* case is discussed in the case below.

Smart Telecom Plc trading as Smart Telecom *v* Radio Telefís Éireann & Anor [2006] IEHC 176

RTÉ indicated that the weather forecast was available for sponsorship at a price of €1.25 million per annum for a minimum period of two years. Four parties indicated a willingness to sponsor the forecast on those terms and so RTÉ invited the parties to submit an offer in a sealed bid. The parties were asked to clearly state the price they would commit to for the contract and RTÉ indicated that the contract would be awarded to the highest bidder. The parties were also informed that in the event of more than one identical highest offer, RTÉ would enter into a second-round offer with these companies only. While Glanbia submitted a fixed offer of €1,595,500, Smart submitted both a fixed offer of €1,510,000 and a referential bid of '5% above the highest priced bid received by you'. The contract was awarded to Glanbia and Smart sought specific performance of the contract to award the sponsorship or alternatively damages.

Kelly J.

It is quite clear that nowhere in the RTÉ offer are referential bids expressly prohibited. Such being the case, I must construe the RTÉ offer so as to ascertain whether its provisions, read as a whole, permit of the making of referential bids. In attempting to ascertain the intention of RTÉ, I must do so by reference to the language used by it. I will carry out this exercise without reference to any of the authorities cited. They are of little value in attempting to ascertain the true intention of RTÉ. That must be done by a consideration of the words used by it in the RTÉ offer. Nonetheless, I will in due course consider relevant authorities insofar as they may have a bearing on the issue. The following elements of the RTÉ offer appear to me to be relevant.

1. The offer was made to a limited number of interested parties. Those parties were selected because they had each indicated a willingness to pay €1.25 million per year for the sponsorship.
2. The RTÉ offer was made in the interest of fairness and transparency and was described as a competition.
3. Each party was invited to submit its best offer.
4. The offer was to be in the form of a sealed bid which was to be opened at a specific time and in the presence of *inter alia* an RTÉ auditor.
5. The price was expressly required to be stated both as to its totality and per annum. Specific directions were given as to the way in which the best offer was to be quoted, namely as a gross figure inclusive of agency commission.
6. RTÉ undertook to award the sponsorship to the highest bidder. This is a matter of crucial importance and is of course the principal element of the RTÉ offer which translated it from being an invitation to treat into an offer with contractual consequences if properly accepted.
7. The offer anticipated more than 'one identical highest offer' in which case RTÉ undertook to 'enter into a second-round offer with these companies only'.

It is clear that a number of consequences flow from the above. First, RTÉ sought to extract the best price which each bidder was prepared to pay for the sponsorship. They were expressly asked to submit their 'best offer'. It is impossible to know whether a referential bid is the best offer which a bidder is prepared to make. Secondly, each bidder was asked to clearly state what price it would commit to per annum and in total for the two-year period. Not merely that, but the best offer was to be a gross figure inclusive of agency commission. This suggests to me that RTÉ wished to have actual figures quoted. This is entirely consistent with the idea that each bidder should make its best offer. Thirdly, the RTÉ offer was addressed solely to the four interested parties and envisaged that the bidding was to be on a confidential basis. Each bid had to be sealed. All of the bids were to be opened together in the presence of both the purchasing manager of RTÉ and an RTÉ auditor. All of the offers would therefore remain confidential until all of them were opened together at that meeting. Fourthly, RTÉ committed itself to accept the highest bid received. Fifthly, the RTÉ offer envisaged the possibility of more than one 'identical highest offer'. In such event a second-round offer was to be made. The reference to 'identical highest offer' in my view excludes referential bids, because, by their nature, they will always be higher than the highest price bid.

Finally, the RTÉ offer was made 'in the interest of fairness and transparency'. Only Smart ever had the opportunity to acquire the sponsorship with its referential bid. None of the other bidders had any prospect of securing the contract. Their bids would be used solely for the purposes of determining the price which Smart had to pay. In addition, Smart, through its subsidiary, Holdings, took the precaution of making a fixed bid thereby diminishing, if not obliterating, any risk which it would have.

All of these factors appear to me to indicate that it was never the intention of RTÉ that referential bids would be permissible. The terms which I have identified are inconsistent with the making of a referential bid. The matter can also be tested by reference to the following. It is clear that RTÉ were engaged in a serious business enterprise and wanted to obtain the best price for their product. They decided to go through a process which would produce that in a fair way and within a limited period of time. It is not to be inferred that they wished to engage in a process which would not give such a result or, worse, would produce absurdities. If the RTÉ offer permitted the making of referential bids, the ability to produce a good commercial result was diminished and the possibility of absurdities abounded. What, for example, would have been the result had all of the bidders made referential bids? The whole process would have been rendered nugatory. What if more than one had made referential bids? Confusion would ensue. These considerations further militate against the notion that referential bids were permissible.

In these circumstances I am of opinion that the terms of the RTÉ offer, when properly construed, did not permit of the making of a referential bid.

I now turn to a consideration of the relevant authorities with a view to testing whether my approach to the matter has been correct or not.

In my view the authority which comes closest to the facts of this case is the decision of the House of Lords in *Harvela Limited v Royal Trust Company*.[1]

In this case Royal Trust invited Harvela and Sir Leonard Outerbridge to submit offers by sealed tenders by a specified deadline to a named party who undertook not to disclose the sealed tenders before the deadline. The tenders were to be a single offer for all the shares of a company that were held by Royal Trust and were for sale. Royal Trust bound itself to accept the highest offer that complied with the terms of the invitation. Before the invitation expired, Harvela and Sir Leonard made the offers which resulted in the litigation. Harvela offered US$2,175,000. Sir Leonard offered

US$2,100,000 '*or* US$101,000 in excess of any other offer which Royal Trust may receive which is expressed as a fixed monetary amount, whichever is the higher'. Royal Trust purported to accept Sir Leonard's offer. Harvela challenged that decision. The case went to the House of Lords where the principal speech was that of Lord Templeman. His Lordship analysed the difference between a sale by auction and a sale by fixed bidding. He said:

> Where a vendor undertakes to sell to the highest bidder, the vendor may conduct the sale by auction or by fixed-bidding. In an auction sale each bidder may adjust his bid by reference to rival bids. In an auction sale the purchaser pays more than any other bidder is prepared to pay in order to secure the property. The purchaser does not necessarily pay as much as the purchaser was prepared to pay to secure the property. In an auction a purchaser who is prepared to pay US$2.5 million to secure a property will be able to purchase for US$2.2 million if no other bidder is prepared to offer as much as US$2.2 million.
>
> In a fixed-bidding sale, a bidder may not adjust his bid. Each bidder specifies a fixed amount which he hopes will be sufficient, but not more than sufficient, to exceed any other bid. The purchaser in a fixed-bidding sale does not necessarily pay as much as the purchaser was prepared to pay to secure the property. But any bidder who specifies less than his best price knowingly takes a risk of being outbid. In a fixed-bidding sale a purchaser who is prepared to pay $2.5 million to secure the property may be able to purchase for $2.2 million if the purchaser offers $2.2 million and no other bidder offers as much as $2.2 million. But if a bidder prepared to pay $2.5 million only offers $2.2 million he will run the risk of losing the property and will be mortified to lose the property if another bidder offers $2.3 million. Where there are two bidders with ample resources, each determined to secure the property and to prevent the other bidder from acquiring the property, the stronger will prevail in the fixed-bidding sale and may pay more than in an auction which is decided, not by the strength of the stronger, but by the weakness of the weaker of the two bidders. On the other hand, an open auction provides the stimulus of perceived bidding and compels each bidder, except the purchaser, to bid up to his maximum.
>
> Thus auction sales and fixed-bidding sales are liable to affect vendors and purchasers in different ways and to produce different results. The first question raised by this appeal, therefore, is whether Harvela and Sir Leonard were invited to participate in a fixed-bidding sale, which only invited fixed bids, or were invited to participate in an auction sale, which enabled the bid of each bidder to be adjusted by reference to the other bid. A vendor chooses between a fixed-bidding sale and an auction sale. A bidder can only choose to participate in the sale or to abstain from the sale. The ascertainment of the choice of the vendors in the present case between a fixed-bidding sale and an auction sale by means of referential bids depends on the presumed intention of the vendors. That presumed intention must be deduced from the terms of the invitation read as a whole.

The exercise prescribed in the latter part of this quotation is precisely the one which I have conducted. I have sought to deduce RTE's intention from the terms of the RTÉ offer read as a whole. Lord Templeman went on to identify three provisions which he said were only consistent with the presumed intention to create a fixed-bidding sale and which were inconsistent with any presumed intention to create an auction sale by means of referential bids. He said:

By the first significant provision, the vendors undertook to accept the highest offer; this shows that the vendors were anxious to ensure that a sale should result from the invitation. By the second provision, the vendors extended the same invitation to Harvela and Sir Leonard: this shows that the vendors were desirous that each of them, Harvela and Sir Leonard, and nobody else, should be given an equal opportunity to purchase the shares. By the third provision, the vendors insisted that offers must be confidential and must remain confidential until the time specified by the vendors for the submission of offers had elapsed; this shows that the vendors were desirous of provoking from Sir Leonard an offer of the best price he was prepared to pay in ignorance of the bid made by Harvela and equally provoking from Harvela the best price they were prepared to pay in ignorance of the bid made by Sir Leonard.

All of these elements have been identified by me as being present in the RTÉ offer. They point inexorably to the conclusion which I reached and which is fully supported by the same conclusion reached by Lord Templeman in the *Harvela* case.

Later in his speech Lord Templeman identified four consequences which might arise if referential bids had been permitted in the *Harvela* case. They are identified at pages 231 and 232 of his speech. They can be summarised as follows:

(a) If referential bids were permissible there was a danger, far from negligible, that the sale might be aborted. The shares could only be sold if at least one bidder submitted a fixed bid and the other bidder based his referential offer on that fixed bid.

(b) If referential bids were permissible, there was a possibility that one bidder would never have an opportunity to buy.

(c) The vendor's object of provoking the best price that Harvela and Sir Leonard were each prepared to offer in ignorance of the rival bid was frustrated.

(d) He said 'if referential bids were permissible by implication, without express provision in the invitation for that purpose, and without any indication in the invitation of the nature of the referential bids which would be acceptable, the results could have been bizarre'. He then gave an example of such bizarre results. It is not necessary to set it out here in detail save to comment that his Lordship was dealing with a two-bid process. The results would be even more complicated and potentially more bizarre in the case of a four-bid contest, as in the instant case.

These four consequences are similar, if not identical, to the ones which I have identified as ones which might occur if the RTÉ offer were construed as permitting referential bids.

It appears to me that the conclusions which I have reached concerning the inappropriateness of referential bids in the context of the RTÉ offer are supported by the unanimous views of the House of Lords in the *Harvela* case.

In explaining his conclusions Lord Templeman followed a number of other decisions which are worthy of mention. The first was *South Hetton Coal Co. v. Haswell Shotton and Easington Coal and Coke Co.*[2] In that case, the owner of a coalmine proposed to receive sealed tenders from two parties who were competing to purchase. The vendor undertook to accept the highest 'net money tender'. One of the competitors purported to offer 'such a sum as will exceed by £200 the amount . . . offered . . . by the other proposing purchaser'. That approach was rejected by the Court of Appeal. Lindley M.R. said:

Does the offer fairly answer the description of what the liquidator had bound himself to accept—in other words does it answer the description of being 'highest net money tender I receive'? It appears to me obviously not. Whether it was a tender at all depended . . . not upon the construction of that letter, but upon whether other people tendered. That is not what the liquidator wanted, and that is not what he bound himself to accept.

Lord Templeman said of this decision that it was 'decided by a powerful court, has stood unchallenged for over 80 years and was binding on the Court of Appeal in the present case'. He also cited with approval a decision of the New York Court of Appeals in SSI *Investors Limited v. Korea Tungsten Mining Co. Limited*.[3] He said as follows:

> The majority judgment at pages 174–175, succinctly and cogently summarised the reasons for rejecting referential bids as follows:-
> 'The very essence of sealed competitive bidding is the submission of independent, self-contained bids, to the fair compliance with which, not only the owner, but the other bidders are entitled . . . To give effect to this or any similar bidding practice in which the dollar amount of one bid was tied to the bid or bids of another or others in the same bidding would be to recognise means whereby effective sealed competitive bidding could be wholly frustrated. In the context of such bidding, therefore, a submission by one bidder of a bid dependant for its definition on the bids of others is invalid and unacceptable as inconsistent with and potentially destructive of the very bidding in which it is submitted.'

In my view those considerations are equally applicable in the present case.

I hold that on the true construction of the RTÉ offer, the making of a referential bid was impermissible. That finding is supported by reference to the wording of the offer itself and by high judicial authority from England and Wales and from New York. I find those authorities persuasive and in my view they are supportive of the conclusion which I have reached. Furthermore, I am of the view that there is much to be said for the opinion of Lord Templeman to the effect that where referential bids are sought there ought to be an express provision in the invitation permitting such bids to be made. Patent unfairness results unless that is done. Such unfairness would be inconsistent with the object which was sought to be achieved in the RTÉ offer . . . The referential bid submitted by Smart was not a valid bid in response to the RTÉ offer.

[1] [1986] AC 207.   [2] [1898] 1 Ch. 465.   [3] [1982] 449 NYS 2d173.

Notes

1. In MJB *Enterprises Ltd v Defence Construction* (1951) *Ltd* [1999] 1 SCR 619, the Supreme Court of Canada held that the inclusion of a privilege clause stating that the lowest of any tender would not necessarily be accepted did not allow the respondent to disregard the lowest compliant bid in favour of any other tender, including a non-compliant one. Iacobucci J. stated that: 'A review of the tender documents, including the privilege clause, and the testimony of the respondent's witnesses at trial, indicates that, on the basis of the presumed intentions of the parties, it is reasonable to find an implied obligation to accept only a compliant tender. I do not find that the privilege clause overrode the obligation to accept only

compliant bids, because on the contrary, there is a compatibility between the privilege clause and this obligation . . . however, the privilege clause is incompatible with an obligation to accept only the lowest compliant bid. With respect to this latter proposition, the privilege clause must prevail.' For further discussions of this case, see Craig, 'Developments in the Law of Tenders: Radical or Evolutionary Development' [2003] Con LJ 237 and Wallace, 'Tendering: Obligations of the Offeree' [1999] 115 LQR 583.

2. EU legislation and secondary legislation implementing EU Directives govern aspects of the tendering and award process in the various sectors. For example, two public procurement Directives regulate the purchase of goods and/or services by public bodies and entities operating in the utilities sector on the basis of special or exclusive rights granted by the state. These are Directive 2004/18/EC on the co-ordination of procedures for the award of public works contracts, public supply contracts and public service contracts and Directive 2004/17/EC, co-ordinating the procurement procedures of entities operating in the water, energy, transport and postal services sector.

Consider:

While the privilege clause means that the lowest bid does not have to be accepted, the Court in MJB held that it did not override the obligation to accept only a compliant bid. Is it possible to reconcile the decision in this regard with *Howberry Lane* above where Morris P. held that the existence of a privilege clause meant that the person inviting tenders was not obliged to sell to the plaintiff, even if the latter could establish that the only bid higher than its own was invalid? For a discussion of this point, see Paul McDermott, *Contract Law* (Butterworths, 2001), para.1.54.

E. UNILATERAL CONTRACTS AND ADVERTISEMENTS

Offers may take the form of a promise by one party, A, to perform some act (normally to pay a sum of money) for the other party, B, in return for B performing some act without making a promise to that effect. For example, A promises to pay B €500 if B gives A his car. Performance by B makes obligatory the promise by A, giving rise to a 'unilateral contract'. A contract is formed then when B presents his car to A. This is termed a 'unilateral contract' because at this stage, only one party, A, has an existing contractual obligation which is to pay B €500. A 'bilateral contract', by contrast, is one where both parties promise to perform mutual duties and both parties are bound.

As is clear from the *Carlill* case below, offers giving rise to unilateral contracts may be made to the world at large. An advertisement of a reward for the return of lost property is a further example of such an offer. Such offers are intended to be binding when a person acts upon them.

Carlill v Carbolic Smokeball Co. [1893] 1QB 256

The defendants manufactured a product called a 'carbolic smokeball', which was advertised as being so medicinally efficient that the defendants would pay £100 to any person who purchased a smokeball and used it as directed and contracted influenza. The advertisement stated that a sum of £1,000 had been deposited in the Alliance Bank, Regent Street as evidence of the manufacturer's sincerity. Mrs Carlill contracted influenza despite having purchased and used the smokeball as directed. She claimed to be entitled to £100.

Lindley L.J.:

We are dealing with an express promise to pay £100 in certain events . . . We must first consider whether this was intended to be a promise at all, or whether it was a mere puff which meant nothing. Was it a mere puff? My answer to that question is No, and I base my answer upon this passage: '£1,000 is deposited with the Alliance Bank, shewing our sincerity in the matter.' Now, for what was that money deposited or that statement made except to negative the suggestion that this was a mere puff and meant nothing at all? The deposit is called in aid by the advertiser as proof of his sincerity in the matter—that is, the sincerity of his promise to pay this £100 in the event which he has specified. I say this for the purpose of giving point to the observation that we are not inferring a promise; there is the promise, as plain as words can make it.

Then it is contended that it is not binding. In the first place, it is said that it is not made with anybody in particular. Now that point is common to the words of this advertisement and to the words of all other advertisements offering rewards. They are offers to anybody who performs the conditions named in the advertisement, and anybody who does perform the condition accepts the offer. In point of law this advertisement is an offer to pay £100 to anybody who will perform these conditions, and the performance of the conditions is the acceptance of the offer . . .

Bowen L.J.:

Was it intended that the £100 should, if the conditions were fulfilled, be paid? The advertisement says that £1,000 is lodged at the bank for the purpose. Therefore, it cannot be said that the statement that £100 would be paid was intended to be a mere puff. I think it was intended to be understood by the public as an offer which was to be acted upon.

But it was said there was no check on the part of the persons who issued the advertisement, and that it would be an insensate thing to promise £100 to a person who used the smokeball unless you could check or superintend his manner of using it. The answer to that argument seems to me to be that if a person chooses to make extravagant promises of this kind he probably does so because it pays him to make them, and, if he has made them, the extravagance of the promises is no reason in law why he should not be bound by them.

It was also said that the contract is made with all the world—that is, with everybody; and that you cannot contract with everybody. It is not a contract made with all the world. There is the fallacy of the argument. It is an offer made to all the world; and why should not an offer be made to all the world which is to ripen into a contract with anybody who comes forward and performs the condition? It is an offer to become liable to anyone who, before it is retracted, performs the condition, and, although the offer is made to the world, the contract is made with that limited portion of the public who come forward and perform the condition on the faith of the advertisement. It is not like cases in which you offer to negotiate, or you issue advertisements that you have got a stock of books to sell, or houses to let, in which case there is no offer to be bound by any contract. Such advertisements are offers to negotiate—offers to receive offers—offers to chaffer, as, I think, some learned judge in one of the cases has said. If this is an offer to be bound, then it is a contract the moment the person fulfils the condition.

Note

In *Kennedy v London Express Newspapers* [1931] IR 532, a unilateral contract arose as a result of an advertisement in its newspaper by the defendant in January 1929 of a free accident-insurance scheme for the benefit of 'registered readers'. To qualify as a registered reader a person had to be a postal subscriber to the paper or be registered in the books of the defendant as having placed a daily order with a registered newspaper and be receiving it daily. On 1 January 1930 the advertisement of the scheme was repeated for the year 1930. This advertisement stated that there was no need for readers already registered to re-register. The Supreme Court held inter alia that in January 1929, the offer contained in the newspaper was accepted by the placing of the order for delivery of the paper with the local newsagent in Clonmel and the posting in Clonmel of the coupon registration form. In January 1930, the offer contained in the newspaper was accepted by renewing or continuing the order with the local newsagent in Clonmel for daily delivery of the paper.

Billings *v* Arnott & Co. Ltd (1945) 80 ILTR 50 (HC)

The defendants posted a notice offering any of their employees who joined the Defence Forces one half of their salaries up to the sum of £2 per week. The plaintiff, an employee, informed the defendants that he intended to accept this offer. He was told that this would not be possible as another employee from his department had already joined and he could not be spared. Despite this the plaintiff joined the Defence Forces. The plaintiff later sued for salary due for three and a half years on foot of the notice.

Maguire J.:

There was an inducement to the employees to join the Defence Forces. The notice I find is unconditional, with no reservation to allow a refusal to release any employee. I cannot take the view that it was a mere declaration of intention. It is a clear expression of what the company would do. Acceptance was then completed when the plaintiff joined the Defence Forces and intimated his intention of so doing on 16 August 1940. On that view a contract was completed under which defendants undertook to pay the plaintiff the allowance. There was no provision in the notice published that the managing director had power to decide to whom the allowance was to be paid. I am satisfied that the money claimed is due and accordingly I give judgment for the plaintiff for the sum claimed, with costs.

Note

In *Wilson v Belfast Corporation* (1921) 55 ILTR 205, the defendants passed a resolution on 5 August 1914 agreeing to pay half wages to employees who joined the Defence Forces. This resolution was published in the press without the defendants' authority. At a further meeting on 23 September the defendants passed a second resolution limiting the offer to persons already in the council's service on 5 August. Subsequent to this second resolution Wilson entered the defendants' service and five months later joined the army. He notified the defendant of his claim to half pay. Wilson was later killed in action. His widow and child later sued to recover the amount claimed to be due as half pay from the date of enlistment to the date of death. The Irish Court of Appeal held that no contract had been made. It determined that there was no intention to make the resolution an offer. There was no communication as the reporting of the resolution was not authorised by the corporation and could not be prevented by it. Lord Justice O'Connor noted that 'Before Wilson joined the army a new resolution had been passed. Even if he saw the first resolution, and did not see the second, it makes no difference to him. He had no right to assume that the corporation's resolutions are unalterable: they may change from day to day. Therefore, no contract at all was made.'

Consider:

Explain the different outcomes in the *Billings* and *Wilson* cases.

Apicella *v* Scala (1931) 66 ILTR 33

The plaintiff sued the defendant, a UK resident who had purchased Irish sweepstake tickets as part of an alleged partnership agreement. The defendant had entered the names and addresses of subscribers on the counterfoil and returned these plus the appropriate payment to the Hospitals Trust Lmited. The latter then issued an acknowledgment of acceptance and an official receipt. The High Court held that the submission of the money with the counterfoil constituted an offer rather than an acceptance of an offer.

Meredith J.:

The Hospital Sweep tickets which the Hospitals Trust, Limited, scatter broadcast over the world are not to be regarded, in my opinion, as offers to each person into whose hands they may find their way to become a purchaser of the right to have the corresponding counterfoils included in the draw on forwarding the counterfoils and the price of the tickets. If a ticket coming into the hands of a person in England constituted such an offer, the posting in England of the counterfoil and the price of the ticket would constitute a binding contract, and a contract which would be made in England. The ticket is a very useful protection to the purchaser of certain rights, which are defined by reference to the number on the ticket, which corresponds with that on the counterfoil. The ticket is not an offer. It, with the attached counterfoil, is more like a proposal form, and an offer is first made by forwarding the counterfoil with the price of the ticket, the ticket being retained by the purchaser. If the offer is accepted the price of the ticket is retained and an official receipt is forwarded, the contract is thus concluded, and it is one made in Saorstát Éireann. But the offer might be refused. For instance, the number of tickets sold might so exceed expectations that it might be thought advisable not to accept any counterfoils after a date some days earlier than had been announced. Or, if the transmission of the counterfoils was illegal in a particular country, and if the encouragement of breaches of the law in that country were resented, the management committee might decide to refuse all counterfoils transmitted from that country. Also, the rights secured by the acceptance of the offer to subscribe, followed by success in the draw, are not secured by ownership of the ticket as a mere bit of paper, but by the purchaser as a subscriber, and the particular subscriber whose name appears on the counterfoil that has drawn a horse.

Notes

1. The *Apicella* case is also notable in that the Court decided not to apply the postal rule (set out at p.69) in that it would encourage breaches of law in the UK, where lotteries were at the time illegal.
2. In *Carroll v An Post National Lottery* [1996] 1 IR 443 Costello J. held that a lottery payslip constitutes an offer by the defendant company to sell lottery tickets to members of the public who complete their payslips in accordance with the prescribed rules. This offer, which is subject to the terms contained on the reverse, is accepted when the member of the public completes the payslip in accordance with the rules and tenders it to the lottery agent together with the price prescribed by the rules (see p.400).

Consider:

Why did the Court in *Carroll* take a different view to that of Meredith J. in the *Apicella* case?

A number of recent cases involving advertisements on the internet have challenged the traditional view that an advertisement is an invitation to treat. In 1999, the retail chain Argos displayed a price of £3 instead of the intended price of £300 for televisions. Customers who ordered the televisions automatically received an email confirming the order and argued that an enforceable contract existed. Argos refused to despatch the sets. Similarly in 2003, an advertisement on Thai Airways' website erroneously referred to free first-class tickets to Thailand subject to taxes of £55. More than 1,500 bookings were made for flights which should have cost £6,000. Despite automatic confirmations, the firm again refused to process the bookings.

In 2008 Aer Lingus sold transatlantic business fares for €5 to approximately 300 customers due to a technical error on its website. It subsequently agreed to honour these commitments but as economy fares (see further at p. 497)

SECTION TWO—ACCEPTANCE

'Acceptance may be defined as a final and unequivocal expression of agreement to the terms of an offer.' Clark (op.cit.)

A valid acceptance has two constituent parts. First, the fact of agreement must be proved. Such agreement may be inferred from the conduct of the parties or from the strict observance of the express terms. Second, the fact of acceptance must be communicated to the offeror.

A. FACT OF ACCEPTANCE

An acceptance must be an unqualified agreement to the terms of the offer.

In a unilateral contract, performance of the stipulated act constitutes acceptance. Thus in the *Carbolic Smokeball* case, Mrs Carlill accepted the offer by purchasing and using the smokeball in the manner indicated. No communication of her acceptance was required. Even in a bilateral framework, performance may be deemed to constitute acceptance, thus dispensing with the requirement to communicate acceptance. This would, however, be less usual.

Brennan v Lockyer and Others [1932] IR 100

On 27 March 1909, at the plaintiff's request, two members of the Postmen's Federation, Mr McGirt and Mr Hoare, sent a form to the Postmen's Federation Mutual Benefit Society ('the MBS') proposing the plaintiff for enrolment. At the same time the plaintiff, reciting that he was already a member of the MBS, purported to nominate his wife to receive all benefits and to propose her as a member. The plaintiff and his wife were elected as members on 29 March and a certificate of enrolment was sent to the plaintiff. A free certificate of membership was, in accordance with the rules, sent by the Federation's secretary from London to Dublin. The plaintiff contended that the contract of membership was not complete until the certificate had been communicated to him, and that as he received it in Dublin, the contract of membership was entered into in Dublin. This contention was rejected by the Supreme Court

Fitzgibbon J.:

There is, says Sir Frederick Pollock,[1] a material distinction, though it is not fully recognised in the language of our authorities, between the acceptance of an offer which asks for a promise, and of an offer which asks for an act, as the condition of the offer becoming a promise. When the acceptance is to consist of a promise, it must be communicated to the proposer. But when the acceptance is to consist of an act—as despatching goods ordered by post—it seems that no further communication of the acceptance is necessary than the performance of the proposed act, or at any rate the proposer may dispense with express communication, and an intention to dispense with it may be somewhat readily inferred from the nature of the transaction.

In the present case the plaintiff requested McGirt and Hoare to propose him 'for enrolment'. In the same document, reciting that he was already a member of the MBS, which he could not be until after the election and enrolment, he nominated his wife to receive all benefits, etc., and on the same day, by a separate document, again reciting that he was a member of the MBS, and purporting to exercise a privilege confined to members, he proposed his wife as a member of the branch.

These actions are in my opinion wholly inconsistent with an intention or belief on his part that he was not to become a member or possess any of the rights or privileges of membership unless and until the fact of his election had been communicated to him. If he had expressly said, 'I ask you to act on my request, and I waive all necessity for communication', there is no doubt that immediately upon enrolment he would have become a member of the benefit society, and in my opinion the nomination, and still more clearly the proposal for membership, of his wife, indicate a plain intention on his part to exercise the rights of membership at the earliest possible moment, and to dispense with any necessity for communicating his election to himself as a condition of his becoming a member. The rules of the society make liability to payment of levies depend upon the date of enrolment. 'All new members shall pay every levy announced after the date of their enrolment', and in my opinion a proposer who asked to be enrolled could not legally resist payment of a levy, announced after the date upon which he had in fact been enrolled, upon the ground that the fact of his enrolment had not come to his knowledge. It has been proved that Thomas Brennan was enrolled a member of the MBS upon 29 March, upon the proposal of McGirt, a member, and Hoare, the secretary, and that his wife, Sarah, was, upon the proposal of himself as a member and Hoare as secretary, enrolled as a member upon the same day. In my opinion the contract of membership was completed in London by the act of the management committee in accepting and acting upon the proposal of Thomas Brennan.

(Kennedy C.J. and Murnaghan J. concurred.)

[1.] *Pollock's Principles of Contract* (9th ed.), 36.

Notes

1. Similarly in *Saunders v Cramer* (1842) 5 Ir Eq R 12, a grandmother promised to leave upon her death £2,000 and a house to her granddaughter. This promise was made in anticipation of her granddaughter's imminent marriage. The Lord Chancellor held that the marriage of the granddaughter constituted 'solemn acceptance' of the grandmother's offer.
2. The idea of waiving an entitlement to communication of acceptance is an exception to the rule that acceptance must be communicated, discussed at p. 74 below.

Counter-offer

If the original terms in the offer are varied substantially it may be viewed as a counter-offer. Such a counter-offer may be accepted in turn by the original offeror. If no such acceptance occurs, no contract is formed.

Titus L. Swan v Miller, Son and Torrance, Ltd [1919] IR 151

The plaintiffs offered to buy an interest in property from the defendants for £4,750. The defendants wrote and telegraphed to accept £4,750 plus £50 ground rent. The question arose as to whether this gave rise to a concluded contract. Sir J. Campbell C noted that:

It was assumed by counsel on both sides that a vendor who, in purporting to accept the purchaser's offer, introduces a new term into the proposed contract is, in law and in fact, making a counter-offer, which the purchaser by accepting may convert into a contract; and this is stated to be the law in Halsbury's *Laws of England*, vol. vii, p. 350, para. 720. See *Lucas v James*[1] and *Honeyman v Marryat*.[2] In *Canning v Farquhar*[3] Lindley L.J. says that where a proposal for insurance does not state the premium to be paid, but is accepted by the company who state the premium, it amounts to a counter-offer by them, binding as a contract when the premium is paid.

On the facts of the case, the majority of the Court found no evidence that the counter-offer had been accepted.

[1] 7 Hare 410.   [2] 21 Beav 14.   [3] (16 QBD 727).

Wheeler & Co. Ltd *v* John Jeffrey & Co. [1921] IR 395

The defendants, a firm of Scottish brewers, entered into negotiations with the plaintiffs, aerated water manufacturers and exporters operating in Belfast. On 20 May 1911 the defendants wrote appointing the plaintiffs sole agents for their beers for the west coast of Africa. Following further correspondence the plaintiffs wrote on 10 June, 'We will agree to carry on your agency as from 1 July next on the terms and conditions specified in our joint correspondence.' Up to this time the date of commencement had not been mentioned. On 12 June the defendants wrote acknowledging this letter. The plaintiffs later sued for breach of contract and the question arose as to whether a contract came into existence in Scotland or in Northern Ireland. The Court of Appeal determined that it was the former.

Campbell C. (Court of Appeal):

[Referring to the plaintiff's letter of 10 June] If they had left out the words 'as from 1 July next', and had simply agreed to carry on the agency on the terms specified in the joint correspondence, the question then would have been what was a reasonable time in connection with the starting of the agency; and if the parties did not agree upon that, it would have to be determined by the court. In reply to [the plaintiff's] letter [the defendants] wrote: 'We are in receipt of your favour of 10 inst., and note with pleasure that you are agreeable to carry on the agency for our Lager, Pilsener and Munich beers for West Africa as from the 1 prox. on the terms and conditions stipulated in our joint correspondence.'

It is said that that was not an acceptance of the offer that the agency was to start from 1 July; that it was merely a notification in reference to an already completed agreement. I think it is impossible to construe it in that way, because it is admitted that it would have been open to Messrs Jeffrey to have said, 'No, we cannot agree; 1 July would not suit us.' And if it was open to them to reject, was it not a new and material term of the contract? The acceptance of that new and material term was by letter written in Scotland.

(Ronan and O'Connor L.JJ. concurred.)

Notes

1. A counter-offer also has the effect of rendering the original offer incapable of being accepted (*Hyde v Wrench* [1840] 3 Beav 334). However, care must be taken to distinguish a counter-offer from a mere request for

information. In *Stevenson, Jacques & Co. v McLean* (1880) 5 QBD 346 the defendant offered to sell iron at '40s nett cash per ton'. The plaintiffs sent a telegraph asking 'Please wire whether you would accept 40s for delivery over two months, or if not longest limit you would give.' As they received no reply they accepted the offer to sell at 40s cash. Meanwhile the defendant sold the iron to a third party. The plaintiffs were awarded damages for breach of contract as the court held that the plaintiffs had not made a counter-offer but rather 'a mere enquiry, which should have been answered and not treated as a rejection of the offer'. In *Lynch v St Vincent's Hospital* (HC), 31 July 1987, unrep,. the Court distinguished between the proposition of a new term which is a counter-offer and the expression of a previously agreed term which is not.

2. For a recent case, see *Covington Marine Corp v Xiamen Shipbuilding Industry Co Ltd* [2006] 1 Lloyd's Rep. 745, where after accepting that the question whether or not various letters constituted a binding agreement was one of law or mixed fact and law, the High Court sought to view an alleged offer and acceptance objectively but in their commercial context. In doing so, the Court identified a counter-offer whose acceptance led to the formation of a concluded contract.

Consider:

A offers to sell B a car for €4,000 and B replies stating that he accepts the offer and will pay by cheque. Is this an offer or a counter-offer?

Bridget Tansey *v* The College of Occupational Therapists Ltd (HC) 27 August 1986, unrep. (1983/3591P)

The plaintiff applied for admission to St Joseph's College, an independent college, to take a preparation course for the defendants' diploma examinations. She was granted a place on a course commencing in October 1978. The defendants published a manual providing details of the examination and stating that two retakes of each part of the examination were allowed. In April 1978 the defendant decided to amend their regulations and allow the students only one automatic retake. An erratum slip to this effect was included in only some of the copies of the manual handed out to new students in Autumn 1978. A notice of the amendment was dispatched by the defendants to St Joseph's in May 1978 and remained on the notice boards throughout 1978 and 1979. The amendment was also pointed out to students throughout the course. The plaintiff failed psychiatry in 1981 and again in the retake. An application to be allowed a second retake was denied. The plaintiff argued that she had a contractual right to two automatic retakes of each part of the defendants' examinations. She argued that the contract was made in November 1978 by the plaintiff offering herself as a student for the defendants' diploma course and the defendants by their agents, St Joseph's College, and their officials accepting her as a student and handing to the plaintiff the defendants' manual for the course. She argued that the acceptance of her offer was on the terms and conditions and subject to the regulations contained in the manual actually handed to the plaintiff and did not include any alterations thereof which were not at the time brought to her attention. As the contract was formed at this stage, the plaintiff argued that it was too late to introduce new terms without her consent [reference was made to *Olley v Marlborough Court Ltd* [1949] 1 KBD 532 in this regard].

Murphy J.

I am unable to accept that a contract between the defendants and the plaintiff came into existence at the time, in the manner or on the terms for which the plaintiff contends as aforesaid. One would like to think that a student in the plaintiff's position would have some guarantee that significant changes would not be made in the structure of the course which she was pursuing or the fundamental regulations governing it after she had embarked thereon. No doubt to some extent this is achieved by the sense of responsibility actually displayed by the defendants in the present case and hopefully exercised by similar bodies in other cases.

Contractual obligations derive from agreement made between two or more parties under which one promises or undertakes with the other the performance of some action. Ordinarily the existence of an agreement presupposes an offer by one party to perform the action on certain terms and the acceptance of that offer by the other. Logical analysis would suggest that the offer must be communicated to the person for whom it is intended and in turn his acceptance must likewise be communicated to the offerer. In the absence of such communication, whether expressed or implied, there would not be that meeting of minds which is implicit in the concept of any agreement. It must be recognised, however, that the innumerable authorities dealing with the law of contract and academic analyses of those decisions over many years reveal refinements of this analysis and apparent exceptions to it. Nevertheless, it seems to me that the case made on behalf of the plaintiff must be examined with a view to identifying the offer and acceptance constituting the alleged agreement.

The celebrated case of *Carlill v Carbolic Smoke Ball Co.* [1893] 1 QBD 256 is authority for the propositions first that an offer may be made to the world at large even though a contract can only be made with identified persons. Secondly that such an offer may be accepted by the performance of a particular condition prescribed in the offer and thirdly that as notification of acceptance is required for the benefit of the person who makes the offer he may, if he thinks it desirable to do so, dispense with such notice. Accordingly one could envisage circumstances in which an examining body might communicate to the public at large the terms in which they were offering a series of examinations and expressly or by implication inviting interested persons to accept that offer by undertaking a specified course of study. However that is not the present case. The plaintiff was not aware of any offer made by the defendants prior to the commencement of her studies and accordingly her application to St Joseph's and their admission of her as a student could not constitute acceptance of any offer by the defendants herein. Even if the position were otherwise this approach would be of no avail to the plaintiff—as her counsel fully recognised—because the terms and conditions on offer from the defendants at that time provided only for one automatic retake of failed examinations. Again it would not be sufficient for the plaintiff to argue that on her admission as a student of St Joseph's that the defendants thereby accepted an offer from her simply to take the exams which they proffered. To succeed in this case the plaintiff must establish the existence of a contract which incorporates the particular provision entitling her as of right to a second repeat of her examinations. In the circumstances of the present case it has to be contended either that the plaintiff should be seen as making an offer to take the defendants' course on such terms as they would prescribe and that the defendants accepted that offer by permitting or authorising St Joseph's College as their agents to hand to the plaintiff the manual containing the terms prescribed herein or, alternatively, that the presentation of the manual by St Joseph's to the plaintiff constituted an offer and that some conduct by the plaintiff—perhaps continuing with her course of studies—constituted acceptance of that offer. Counsel on behalf of the plaintiff did not pursue the second of these alternatives recognising, no doubt, the difficulty in establishing any action which could be interpreted as acceptance.

There are two formidable difficulties to be overcome in establishing the case on which the plaintiff does rely. First, it is difficult to conceive of an acceptance which would itself prescribe conditions. Ordinarily a communication in the course of negotiations leading to a contract which contains conditions not previously agreed by the party to whom the communication is addressed will fall to be treated as a new or counter-offer rather than an acceptance. Secondly the plaintiff's argument was criticised on the basis that if the offer permitted the defendants to establish the terms, conditions or regulations governing the contract that there was no justification for assuming that these provisions would not be subject to alteration. However perhaps the best way of presenting the defendants' counter argument is to say that the plaintiff did not prescribe the production of the manual as the means of accepting any offer made by her and there is no internal evidence in this manual and nothing in the conduct of the officials of St Joseph's College by whom it was distributed to suggest that the circulation of the manual amongst the students was intended to constitute acceptance of a contract either by St Joseph's College or by the defendants. I believe that this objection to the plaintiff's argument is well founded. The manual contains for the greater part a large body of information in relation to the medical and surgical conditions relevant to the study of occupational therapy. The information with regard to examinations is obviously important but there is nothing in its presentation to suggest that the communication of this information by the officials of a recognised college should constitute acceptance of an offer by potential students.

I am not to be taken as laying down any principle that conditions or regulations made by an examining body—be it the defendants or any such body—could not be made part of a legally binding contract. Indeed it is possible that a successful argument could have been made to the effect that the amended rules of the defendants did form part of such a contract. All that can be said in relation to the present case is that the plaintiff has not proved that the plaintiff offered or the defendants accepted any offer by the plaintiff to take the diploma course on terms which included and included only the regulations contained in the unamended 1977 manual.

In these circumstances it seems to me—not without some regret—that the plaintiff's claim must fail.

Battle of the Forms

Due to the prevalence of printed form contracts in modern business a problem described as 'the battle of the forms' has arisen. This involves one party A writing to another B offering to contract on the terms set out in a printed form. B responds purporting to accept on the terms set out in a second printed form. Often in the course of negotiations a series of forms will pass in this way between the parties. Finally, when a dispute arises as to the terms agreed, both parties claim to have contracted on the basis of their own printed forms. In the *Butler Machine Tool* case below, the majority of the Court of Appeal suggested a traditional analysis of offer, counter-offer and acceptance be applied. This involves attempting to match an offer with an acceptance at which stage a contract would be formed. This is called the 'mirror image rule'. In such a case where A accepts by performance a counter-offer proposed by B, the conditions set out in B's proposal are applicable as it was B who fired the last shot. This is also known as the 'last shot doctrine'. An alternative approach was suggested by Lord Denning MR which distinguished the formation of a contract from the determination of its content. This would involve determining whether the parties had reached agreement on all the material terms even though differences might remain between the forms and the conditions printed thereon.

Butler Machine Tool Co. Ltd *v* Ex-Cell-O Corp. (England) Ltd [1979] 1 WLR 401

Lord Denning M.R.:

This case is a 'battle of forms'. The plaintiffs, the Butler Machine Tool Co. Ltd, suppliers of a machine, on 23 May 1969, quoted a price for a machine tool of £75,535. Delivery was to be given in ten months. On the back of the quotation there were terms and conditions. One of them was a price variation clause. It provided for an increase in the price if there was an increase in the costs and so forth. The machine tool was not delivered until November 1970. By that time costs had increased so much that the sellers claimed an additional sum of £2,892 as due to them under the price variation clause.

The defendant buyers, Ex-Cell–O Corp. (England) Ltd, rejected the excess charge. They relied on their own terms and conditions. They said: 'We did not accept the sellers' quotation as it was. We gave an order for self-same machine at the self-same price, but on the back of our order we had our own terms and conditions. Our terms and conditions did not contain any price-variation clause.'

The judge held that the price variation clause in the sellers' form continued through the whole dealing and so the sellers were entitled to rely upon it. He was clearly influenced by a passage in Anson's *Law of Contract* (24th edn, 1975), 37 and 38, of which the editor is Professor Guest; and also by Treitel, *The Law of Contract* (4th edn, 1975), 15. The judge said that the sellers did all that was necessary and reasonable to bring the price variation clause to the notice of the buyers. He thought that the buyers would not 'browse over the conditions' of the sellers; and then, by printed words in their (the buyers') document, trap the sellers into a fixed-price contract.

I am afraid that I cannot agree with the suggestion that the buyers 'trapped' the sellers in any way. Neither party called any oral evidence before the judge. The case was decided on the documents alone. I propose therefore to go through them.

On 23 May 1969, the sellers offered to deliver one 'Butler' double column plane-miller for the total price of £75,535. Delivery ten months (subject to confirmation at time of ordering) other terms and conditions are on the reverse of this quotation. On the back there were sixteen conditions in small print starting with this general condition: 'All orders are accepted only upon and subject to the terms set out in our quotation and the following conditions. These terms and conditions shall prevail over any terms and conditions in the buyer's order.' Clause 3 was the price-variation clause. It said: 'Prices are based on present-day costs of manufacture and design and having regard to the delivery quoted and uncertainty as to the cost of labour, materials, etc. during the period of manufacture, we regret that we have no alternative but to make it a condition of acceptance of order that goods will be charged at prices ruling upon date of delivery.'

The buyers replied on 27 May 1969, giving an order in these words: 'Please supply on terms and conditions as below and overleaf.' Below there was a list of the goods ordered, but there were differences from the quotation of the sellers in these respects: (i) there was an additional item for the cost of installation, £3,100 and (ii) there was a different delivery date: instead of ten months, it was 10–11 months.

Overleaf there were different terms as to the cost of carriage: in that it was to be paid to the delivery address of the buyers: whereas the sellers' terms were ex warehouse. There were different terms as to the right to cancel for late delivery. The buyers in their conditions reserved the right to cancel if delivery was not made by the agreed date: whereas the sellers in their conditions said that cancellation of order due to late delivery would not be accepted.

On the foot of the buyers' order there was a tear-off slip headed: 'Acknowledgment: Please sign and return to Ex-Cell-O. We accept your order on the terms and conditions stated thereon—and undertake to deliver by _____ Date _____ signed.' In that slip the delivery date and signature were left blank, ready to be filled in by the sellers. On 5 June 1969, the sellers wrote this letter to the buyers: 'We have pleasure in acknowledging receipt of your official order dated 27 May covering the supply of one Butler Double Column Plane-Miller. This being delivered in accordance with our revised quotation of 23 May for delivery in 10/11 months, i.e. March/April 1970. We return herewith duly completed your acknowledgment of order form.' They enclosed the acknowledgment form duly filled in with the delivery date March/April 1970 and signed by the Butler Machine Tool Co.

No doubt a contract was then concluded. But on what terms? The sellers rely on their general conditions and on their last letter which said 'in accordance with our revised quotation of 23 May' (which had on the back the price-variation clause). The buyers rely on the acknowledgement signed by the sellers which accepted the buyer's order 'on the terms and conditions stated thereon' (which did not include a price-variation clause).

If those documents are analysed in our traditional method, the result would seem to me to be this: the quotation of 23 May 1969 was an offer by the sellers to the buyers containing the terms and conditions on the back. The order of 27 May 1969 purported to be an acceptance of that offer in that it was for the same machine at the same price, but it contained such additions as to cost of installation, date of delivery and so forth that it was in law a rejection of the offer and constituted a counter-offer. That is clear from *Hyde v Wrench* (1840) 3 Beav 334. As Megaw J. said in *Trollope & Colls Ltd v Atomic Power Constructions Ltd* [1963] 1 WLR 333, 337: ' . . . the counter-offer kills the original offer'. The letter of the sellers of 5 June 1969 was an acceptance of that counter-offer, as is shown by the acknowledgment which the sellers signed and returned to the buyers. The reference to the quotation of 23 May referred only to the price and identity of the machine.

To go on with the facts of the case. The important thing is that the sellers did not keep the contractual date of delivery which was March/April 1970. The machine was ready about September 1970 but by that time the buyers' production schedule had to be rearranged as they could not accept delivery until November 1970. Meanwhile the sellers had invoked the price-increase clause. They sought to charge the buyers an increase due to the rise in costs between 27 May 1969 (when the order was given) and 1 April 1970 (when the machine ought to have been delivered). It came to £2,892. The buyers rejected the claim. The judge held that the sellers were entitled to the sum of £2,892 under the price-variation clause. He did not apply the traditional method of analysis by way of offer and counter-offer. He said that in the quotation of 23 May 1969, 'one finds the price-variation clause appearing under a most emphatic heading stating that it is a term or condition that is to prevail.' So he held that it did prevail.

I have much sympathy with the judge's approach to this case. In many of these cases our traditional analysis of offer, counter-offer, rejection, acceptance and so forth is out of date. This was observed by Lord Wilberforce in *New Zealand Shipping* Co. Ltd v A. M. *Satterthwaite & Co. Ltd* [1975] AC 154, 167. The better way is to look at all the documents passing between the parties—and glean from them, or from the conduct of the parties, whether they have reached agreement on all material points—even though there may be differences between the forms and conditions printed on the back of them. As Lord Cairns said in *Brogden v Metropolitan Rly Co.* (1877) 2 App Cas 666, 672: '. . . there may be a consensus between the parties far short of a complete mode of expressing it, and that consensus may be discovered from letters or from other documents of an imperfect and incomplete description: . . .' Applying this guide, it will be found that in most cases when there is a 'battle of forms', there is a contract as soon as the last of the forms is sent and received without objection being taken to it. That is well observed in Benjamin's *Sale of Goods* (9th edn, 1974), 84. The difficulty is to decide which form, or which part of which form, is a term or condition of the contract. In some cases the battle is won by the man who fires the last shot. He is the man who puts forward the latest terms and conditions: and, if they are not objected to by the other party, he may be taken to have agreed to them. Such was *British Road Services Ltd v Arthur V. Crutchley & Co. Ltd* [1968] 1 Lloyd's Rep. 271, 281–282, per Lord Pearson; and the illustration given by Professor Guest in Anson's *Law of Contract* (24th edn), 37, 38 when he says that 'the terms of the contract consist of the terms of the offer subject to the modifications contained in the acceptance'. In some cases the battle is won by the man who gets the blow in first. If he offers to sell at a named price on the terms and conditions stated on the back, and the buyer orders the goods purporting to accept the offer—on an order form with his own different terms and conditions on the back— then if the difference is so material that it would affect the price, the buyer ought not to be allowed to take advantage of the difference unless he draws it specifically to the attention of the seller. There are yet other cases where the battle depends on the shots fired on both sides. There is a concluded contract but the forms vary. The terms and conditions of both parties are to be construed together. If they can be reconciled so as to give a harmonious result, all well and good. If differences are irreconcilable— so that they are mutually contradictory—then the conflicting terms may have to be scrapped and replaced by a reasonable implication.

In the present case the judge thought that the sellers in their original quotation got their blow in first: especially by the provision that 'these terms and conditions shall prevail over any terms and conditions in the buyer's order'. It was so emphatic that the price-variation clause continued through all the subsequent dealings and that the buyers must be taken to have agreed to it. I can understand that point of view. But I think that the documents have to be considered as a whole. And, as a matter of construction, I think the acknowledgment of 5 June 1969 is the decisive document. It makes it clear that the contract was on the buyers' terms and not on the sellers' terms: and the buyers' terms did not include a price-variation clause.

Note

Lawton L.J. and Bridge L.J. held that the buyers' counter-offer constituted the 'last shot' which was accepted by completing and returning the acknowledgment slip. It is clear from cases such as *Chichester Joinery v John Mowlem & Co* (1987) 42 BLR 100 that the battle of the forms is often won with a last shot in the form of a significant document viewed as a counter-offer and accepted by conduct. The traditional approach was also adhered to in the *Buchanan* case below.

Buchanan t/a Warnocks *v* Brook Walker and Co. Ltd [1988] NI 116

The defendant contracted to supply cloth to the plaintiff. In an action for breach of contract arising from a dispute over the cloth, the defendant attempted to rely on a jurisdiction clause which stated that the parties agreed to submit to the jurisdiction of the English courts. The plaintiff contended that this clause did not form part of the contract.

Carswell J.:

Although Lord Denning M.R. in *Butler Machine Tool Co. Ltd v Ex-Cell-O Corp. (England) Ltd* [1979] 1 All ER 965, 968 departed from the traditional analysis of offer and acceptance in a case of a complicated exchange of documents, I consider with respect that it is preferable to adhere to it where possible, as the other members of the court felt able to do. In my view the present case admits of such analysis. When the original order was sent on 29 September 1986 for twenty pieces, the colour had still to be decided, so that a material term remained to be agreed. The defendant on 3 October 1986 sent an order confirmation No. 716, containing some fresh terms, and on the principles set out in *Hyde v Wrench* (1840) 3 Beav 334 that document constituted a counter-offer. It was not, however, immediately capable of final acceptance, since the choice of colour was still outstanding. The plaintiff wrote on 11 December 1986 asking for lab. dye samples to match an enclosed sample, and stating that he required 1,000–1,500 metres of cloth, which was rather more than twenty pieces. When the samples were sent, he wrote on 14 January 1987 accepting colour 6303 and placing an order for 1,500 metres of HB quality cloth in dye shade 6303. The defendant replied on 21 January 1987 by a document entitled 'Confirmation of colouring instruction' No. 1293, for seventeen pieces of HB cloth in the colour blue 6303 at £6.35 per metre, and sent an additional order confirmation No. 879 for six pieces, which brought the total up to 1,500 metres. In offer and acceptance terms I consider that the plaintiff's order of 14 January 1987 was an acceptance of the defendant's offer to supply twenty pieces on the terms contained in its order confirmation No. 716, plus the additional term now agreed of the colour. It was also an offer to purchase an extra quantity of cloth to make the total amount up to 1,500 metres, which the plaintiff accepted by order confirmation No. 879. I do not consider that the fact the 'Confirmation of colouring instruction' document referring to seventeen pieces instead of twenty affects the analysis of agreement which I have set out.

The issue therefore is whether the plaintiff is to be taken to have agreed to accept the jurisdiction clause set out in the order confirmation documents. The defendant's case is that in sending the order confirmation No. 716 it propounded a number of terms set out on the reverse of the document, and that in finally placing the order on 14 January 1987 the plaintiff must be taken to have accepted those terms. In regard to the extra pieces ordered, the plaintiff must be taken to have offered to purchase them on the same terms as the original twenty pieces, so that when the defendant accepted the offer, all those terms, including the jurisdiction clause, became part of the contract. Whether the plaintiff is to be taken to have accepted the terms set out on the back of the order confirmation document is to be decided by considering whether the defendant did what was reasonably sufficient to give the plaintiff notice of those terms. In my judgment it did so. The order confirmation No. 716 contained on its face the statement that the order was subject to the conditions of sale on the back of the form. The sentence does not appear to have been emphasised or highlighted, but it was plain enough to be seen and not obscured by other matters of detail. This was a commercial document, containing a number of details of the order, and it was envisaged and intended that it should be read with care and checked by the recipient. That fact alone takes it out of the category of consumer contracts, where a customer might not ordinarily be expected to read the fine print on a ticket. The plaintiff did not at any stage raise any objection to the terms, for the simple reason, according to his affidavit, that he did not read them. I consider, nevertheless, that the defendant was entitled to and did assume on the facts of the case that the plaintiff accepted the terms contained in the order confirmation. I hold therefore that the jurisdiction clause formed part of the contract of sale and purchase of the cloth.

Although 'battle of the forms' cases generally involve disputes as to the terms of contracts agreed to have been formed, as the following case demonstrates, similar issues may arise in relation to the question of whether a contract has actually been formed.

G. Percy Trentham Ltd *v* Archital Luxfer Ltd and Others [1993] 1 Lloyd's Rep. 25

The plaintiff was a building contractor who had agreed to complete a project for a third party in two phases. The defendant agreed with the plaintiff to manufacture and supply windows for both phases and was paid by the plaintiff. Although no separate written contracts were agreed, there were oral and written exchanges. In negotiations, the defendant had referred to its preferred terms and queried the starting date. The plaintiff wrote reminding the defendant that its order was subject to the return of an acknowledgment slip. The plaintiff's site office also wrote confirming an oral agreement and confirming the date. When the plaintiff subsequently sued the defendant for breach of contract on the basis that the windows were defective, the defendant denied the existence of binding contracts between them. The trial judge found for the plaintiff.

Steyn L.J.:

It is necessary to consider the basis of the judge's decision that Trentham proved the formation of two valid sub-contracts. It is common ground that as between Trentham and Archital no integrated written sub-contracts ever came into existence. There was no orderly negotiation of terms. Rather the picture is one of the parties, jockeying for advantage, inching towards finalisation of the transaction. The case bears some superficial resemblance to cases that have become known as 'battle of the forms' cases where each party seeks to impose his standard conditions on the other in correspondence without there ever being any express resolution of that issue. In such cases it is usually common ground that there is a contract, but the issue is what set of standard conditions, if any, is applicable. Here the issue is one of contract formation. Moreover, the present case is different in the sense that Trentham's case was that the sub-contracts came into existence not simply by an exchange of correspondence but partly by reason of written exchanges, partly by oral discussions and partly by performance of the transactions...

Before I turn to the facts it is important to consider briefly the approach to be adopted to the issue of contract formation in this case. It seems to me that four matters are of importance. The first is the fact that English law generally adopts an objective theory of contract formation. That means that in practice our law generally ignores the subjective expectations and the unexpressed mental reservations of the parties. Instead the governing criterion is the reasonable expectations of honest men. And in the present case that means that the yardstick is the reasonable expectations of sensible businessmen. Secondly, it is true that the coincidence of offer and acceptance will in the vast majority of cases represent the mechanism of contract formation. It is so in the case of a contract alleged to have been made by an exchange of correspondence. But it is not necessarily so in the case of a contract alleged to have come into existence during and as a result of performance. See *Brogden v Metropolitan Rly* (1877) 2 AC 666; *New Zealand Shipping Co. Ltd v A.M. Satterthwaite & Co. Ltd* [1974] 1 Lloyd's Rep. 534 at p. 539, col. 1; [1975] AC 154 at p. 167 D-E; *Gibson v Manchester City Council* [1979] 1 WLR 294. The third matter is the impact of the fact that the transaction is executed rather than executory. It is a consideration of the first importance on a number of levels. See *British Bank for Foreign Trade Ltd v Novinex* [1949] 1 KB 628, at p. 630. The fact that the transaction was performed on both sides will often make it unrealistic to argue that there was no intention to enter into legal relations. It will often make it difficult to submit that the contract is void for vagueness or uncertainty. Specifically, the fact that the transaction is executed makes it easier to imply a term resolving any uncertainty, or, alternatively, it may make it possible to treat a matter not finalised in negotiations as inessential. In this case fully executed transactions are under consideration. Clearly, similar considerations may sometimes be relevant in partly executed transactions. Fourthly, if a contract only comes into existence during and as a result of performance of the transaction it will frequently be possible to hold that the contract impliedly and retrospectively covers pre-contractual performance. See *Trollope & Colls Ltd v Atomic Power Construction Ltd* [1963] 1 WLR 333 . . .

In a case where the transaction was fully performed the argument that there was no evidence upon which the judge could find that a contract was proved is implausible. A contract can be concluded by conduct. Thus in *Brogden v Metropolitan Rly*, the House of Lords concluded in a case where the parties had acted in accordance with an unsigned draft agreement for the delivery of consignments of coal that there was a contract on the basis of the draft. That inference was drawn from the performance in accordance with the terms of the draft agreement. In 1992 we ought not to yield to Victorian times in realism about the practical application of rules of contract formation. The argument that there was insufficient evidence to support a finding that a contract was concluded is wrong. But, in deference to counsel's submissions, I would go further.

One must not lose sight of the commercial character of the transaction. It involved the carrying out of work on one side in return for payment by the other side, the performance by both sides being subject to agreed qualifying stipulations. In the negotiations and during the performance of phase 1 of the work, all obstacles to the formation of a contract were removed. It is not a case where there was a continuing stipulation that a contract would only come into existence if a written agreement was concluded. Plainly the parties intended to enter into binding contractual relations. The only question is whether they succeeded in doing so. The contemporary exchanges, and the carrying out of what was agreed in those exchanges, support the view that there was a course of dealing which on Trentham's side created a right to performance of the work by Archital, and on Archital's side it created a right to be paid on an agreed basis. What the parties did in respect of phase 1 is only explicable on the basis of what they had agreed in respect of phase 1. The judge analysed the matter in terms of offer and acceptance. I agree with his conclusion. But I am, in any event, satisfied that in this fully executed transaction a contract came into existence during performance even if it cannot be precisely analysed in terms of offer and acceptance. And it does not matter that a contract came into existence after part of the work had been carried out and paid for. The conclusion must be that when the contract came into existence it impliedly governed pre-contractual performance. I would therefore hold that a binding contract was concluded in respect of phase 1.

(Gibson and Neill L.JJ. agreed.)

Note

The Uniform Commercial Code (UCC) in the US disapplies the last shot doctrine. CRS §4-2-207 creates a default provision whereby a final form that is not intended specifically as a counter-offer will act as an acceptance, even though it contains different or additional terms to those contained in the prior form. The additional terms are considered as proposals for additions to the contract and, as between merchants, become part of the contract, unless: (1) the offer expressly limits acceptance to the terms of the offer; (2) the terms materially alter the offer; or (3) notification of objection to the terms already has been given or is given within a reasonable time after notice has been received. The normal result thus under the UCC is to reverse the common-law presumption that the last form governs and replace it with the result that the second-to-last form usually governs. By contrast, Article 19(1) of the Vienna Convention, the Convention on the International Sale of Goods ('CISG') departs from the UCC approach and, instead, is consistent with the last shot doctrine. It states:

> 'A reply to an offer which purports to be an acceptance but contains material additions, limitations or other modifications is a rejection of the offer and constitutes a counter-offer.'

The concept of 'material' terms under the CISG include price, payment, quality and quantity of goods, place and time of delivery, extent of liability, and dispute resolution.

B. Communication of Acceptance

An acceptance is not effective until it is brought to the attention of the offerer by the offeree or any person authorised to convey this information.

The Guardians of the Navan Union *v* McLoughlin (1855) 4 ICLR 451

Monahan C.J.:

[Case law] establishes that where there are written communications between parties, it is not enough for one of them to accept the other's proposal in his own mind or in his own office, but he must by some act, binding on himself, communicate his acceptance to the other party.

A clause in the offer stating that silence will be deemed to be acceptance would not be enforced by an English or Irish court (*Felthouse v Bindley* (1862) 11 CB (NS) 869).

Sale of Goods and Supply of Services Act 1980. S. 47:

47. (1) Where:
- (a) unsolicited goods are sent to a person with a view in his acquiring them and are received by him, and
- (b) the recipient has neither agreed to acquire nor agreed to return them.
  and either:
  - (i) during the period of six months following the date of receipt of the goods the sender did not take possession of them and the recipient did not unreasonably refuse to permit the sender to do so, or
  - (ii) not less than 30 days before the expiration of that period the recipient gave notice to the sender and during the following 30 days the sender did not take possession of the goods and the recipient did not unreasonably refuse to permit the sender to do so.

then the recipient may treat the goods as if they were an unconditional gift to him and any right of the sender to the goods shall be extinguished . . .

Subsection (5) provides inter alia that 'unsolicited' means, in relation to goods sent to any person, that they are sent without any prior request by him or on his behalf.

Article 9 of the EU Distance Selling Directive (Directive 97/7/EC, [1997] OJ L 144/19)

Inertia selling
  Member States shall take the measures necessary to:
  - prohibit the supply of goods or services to a consumer without their being ordered by the consumer beforehand, where such supply involves a demand for payment,
  - exempt the consumer from the provision of any consideration in cases of unsolicited supply, the absence of a response not constituting consent.

In *Russell & Baird Ltd v Hoban* [1922] 2 IR 159 the plaintiffs sent a contract note to the defendant, a prospective purchaser of oatmeal with whom they had had discussions. The note concluded with the words 'If this sale note be retained beyond three days after this date, it will be held to have been accepted by the buyer.' Ronan L.J. held that 'No man can impose such conditions upon another. The document is conclusive evidence against the parties who sent it, that it was an offer which required acceptance.'

A recent case to examine the question of formation of contracts is *Commerce Commission v Telecom Mobile Limited* [2006] 1 NZLR 190. In that case, the defendant used telemarketers to cold call homeowners to market its mobile phone services. If the homeowner expressed interest, a credit check was carried out by the defendant. If approved, the consumer received a welcome letter, terms and conditions and a sealed box containing a telephone. Both the telemarketer on the initial call and the welcome letter made it clear to the prospective customer that once the seal was broken the telephone could not be returned. The seal on the box stated '[b]y breaking the seal on this phone box you agree that you have accepted this mobile phone . . .' The Court of Appeal was asked to determine whether the Door to Door Sales Act 1967 (akin to the Distance Marketing Directive) applied and thus whether a cooling-off period should have been allowed. As the Act only applied if the contract was 'made at a place other than appropriate trade premises', the key issue was whether the contract was made over the phone or at the buyer's home when the seal was broken. The defendant argued that the contract was completed during the phone conversation subject to the credit check as a condition subsequent to contract. However, the Court held that the discussions on the telephone were merely precursors to the completion of the contract as that was the only sensible way of explaining the documentation that accompanied the telephones. Accordingly, the agreements were subject to the Act and therefore unenforceable because a cooling-off period was not allowed.

The General Rule

The general rule, often referred to as the 'receipt rule', states that acceptance must be communicated to the offeror.

Carlill *v* Carbolic Smokeball Co. [1893] 1QB 256

Lindley L.J.:

Unquestionably, as a general proposition, when an offer is made, it is necessary in order to make a binding contract, not only that it should be accepted, but that the acceptance should be notified.

Bowen L.J.:

One cannot doubt that, as an ordinary rule of law, an acceptance of an offer made ought to be notified to the person who makes the offer, in order that the two minds may come together. Unless this is done the two minds may be apart, and there is not that consensus which is necessary according to the English law—I say nothing about the laws of other countries—to make a contract.

Notes

1. It follows from the receipt rule that if it is necessary to determine where a contract is formed, this is the place where acceptance is communicated to the offeror.

2. The above extract from Lindley L.J.'s judgment was cited with approval by the Supreme Court in *Embourg v Tyler* [1996] 3 IR 480.

In the case of a unilateral contract, acceptance involves performing a stipulated action. Thus no further communication is necessary.

Carlill *v* Carbolic Smokeball Co.

Lindley L.J.:

I apprehend that they are an exception to [the receipt rule], or if not an exception, they are open to the observation that the notification of the acceptance need not precede the performance. This offer is a continuing offer. It was never revoked; and if notice of acceptance is required—which I doubt very much, for I rather think the true view is that which was expressed and explained by Lord Blackburn in the case of *Brogden v Metropolitan Ry Co.*[1]—if notice of acceptance is required, the person who makes the offer gets the notice of acceptance contemporaneously with his notice of the performance of the condition. If he gets notice of the acceptance before his offer is revoked, that in principle is all you want. I, however, think that the true view, in a case of this kind, is that the person who makes the offer shews by his language and from the nature of the transaction that he does not expect and does not require notice of the acceptance apart from notice of the performance.

[1.] 2 App Cas 666.

Bowen L.J.:

Then it was said that there was no notification of the acceptance of the contract. ... there is this clear gloss to be made upon [the receipt rule], that as notification of acceptance is required for the benefit of the person who makes the offer, the person who makes the offer may dispense with notice to himself if he thinks it desirable to do so, and I suppose there can be no doubt that where a person in an offer made by him to another person, expressly or impliedly intimates a particular mode of acceptance as sufficient to make the bargain binding, it is only necessary for the other person to whom such offer is made to follow the indicated method of acceptance; and if the person making the offer expressly or impliedly intimates in his offer that it will be sufficient to act on the proposal without communicating acceptance of it to himself, performance of the condition is a sufficient acceptance without notification.

    That seems to me to be the principle which lies at the bottom of the acceptance cases, of which two instances are the well-known judgment of Mellish L.J., in Harris's *Case Law* Rep 7 Ch 587, and the very instructive judgment of Lord Blackburn in *Brogden v Metropolitan Ry Co.* in which he appears to me to take exactly the line I have indicated.

    Now, if that is the law, how are we to find out whether the person who makes the offer does intimate that notification of acceptance will not be necessary in order to constitute a binding bargain? In many cases you look to the offer itself. In many cases you extract from the character of the transaction that notification is not required, and in the advertisement cases it seems to me to follow as an inference to be drawn from the transaction itself that a person is not to notify his acceptance of the offer before he performs the condition, but that if he performs the condition notification is dispensed with. It seems to me that from the point of view of common sense no other idea could be entertained. If I advertise to the world that my dog is lost, and that anybody who brings the dog to a particular place will be paid some money, are all the police or other persons whose business it is to find lost dogs to be expected to sit down and write me a note saying that they have accepted my proposal? Why, of course, they at once look after the dog, and as soon as they find the dog they have performed the condition. The essence of the transaction is that the dog should be found, and it is not necessary under such circumstances, as it seems to me, that in order to make the contract binding there should be any notification of acceptance. It follows from the nature of the thing that the performance of the condition is sufficient acceptance without the notification of it, and a person who makes an offer in an advertisement of that kind makes an offer which must be read by the light of that common-sense reflection. He does, therefore, in his offer impliedly indicate that he does not require notification of the acceptance of the offer.

Consider:

Could an offer of a reward for a lost dog be accepted by a letter indicating that the offeree was agreeing to find the dog? Why would the offeree be unlikely to agree to do this?

Postal Rule

The postal rule, which was laid down in *Adams v Lindsell* (1818) 1 B & Ald 681 provides that if an acceptance is posted, unless otherwise stated, it becomes valid from the date of posting. Authority for the postal rule in Ireland can be found in *Sanderson v Cunningham* [1919] 2 IR 234 and *Dooley v Egan* (1938) 72 ILTR 155.

Although attempts have been made to justify the rule on the basis that the post office is deemed to be an agent of the offeror, it is generally agreed that the better explanation is based on commercial convenience.

Brinkibon Ltd v Stahag Stahl und Stahlwarenhandelsgesellschaft mbH [1983] 2 AC 34

Lord Wilberforce:

Then there is the case—very common—of communication at a distance, to meet which the so-called 'postal rule' has developed. I need not trace its history: it has firmly been in the law at least since *Adams v Lindsell* (1818) 1 B & Ald 681. The rationale for it, if left somewhat obscure by Lord Ellenborough C.J., has since been well explained. Mellish L.J. in *In re Imperial Land Co. of Marseilles* (Harris' case) (1872) LR 7 Ch App 587, 594 ascribed it to the extraordinary and mischievous consequences which would follow if it were held that an offer might be revoked at any time until the letter accepting it had been actually received: and its foundation in convenience was restated by Thesiger L.J. in *Household Fire and Carriage Accident Insurance Co. Ltd v Grant* (1879) 4 Ex D 216, 223. In these cases too it seems logical to say that the place, as well as the time, of acceptance should be where (as when) the acceptance is put into the charge of the post office.

Dooley *v* Egan (1938) 72 ILTR 155

The plaintiff sued the defendant for breach of a contract to pay for cabinets supplied. A dispute arose as to whether the contract was made in Dublin or Cork.

Meredith J.:

The defendant company carry on business in Cork as traders in and distributors of medical and surgical instruments and hospital equipment. It appears that in June 1937, the defendant company received enquiries as to their ability to supply medical instrument cabinets of the type described in the *Surgical Manufacturer Company's Catalogue*. The defendant company then made enquiries by a postcard, which is not forthcoming, as to the ability of the plaintiff to supply them, the defendant company, as distributors, with the articles specified under the title in the catalogue and in reply to this enquiry they received a quotation in the form of a letter dated 22 June 1937. The terms of this letter are important and are as follows:

John Dooley,
General Sheet Metal Works,
Garville Avenue, Rathgar, Dublin,
22 June 1937.

Messrs. T. L. Egan and Co. Ltd,
9 Lavitt's Quay,
Cork.

Quotation.

Dear Sir(s),

I thank you for your esteemed enquiry of the 18 inst. and I have much pleasure in submitting my quotation as follows:

Description.	Price.
Six Sterilising Drums as per Specification supplied	£3 17 6 each less 25%
One Instrument Cabinet similar to No. B9558 in the Surgical Manufacturer Company's Catalogue	£18 0 0 less 25%

Awaiting the favour of your valued order and assuring you of my best attention at all times,

I am, dear Sir(s),
Yours faithfully,
John G. Dooley.

Delivery 3–4 weeks. Terms Nett M/A.

All quotations for Copper, Monel Metal, Stainless Steel, Tin and Brass Goods are given subject to Market Fluctuations without notice. All quotations are for immediate acceptance only and are subject to change without notice. The delivery of all orders accepted by me shall be contingent upon strikes, fires, accidents, delays of carriers and other causes unavoidable or beyond my control. I will not be responsible for damages due to any delays whatever. Clerical errors are subject to correction. Orders accepted by me cannot be countermanded without my consent and upon terms which will indemnify me against all loss.

The sentence in the letter 'All quotations are made for immediate acceptance only and are subject to change without notice' is important and was largely dealt with in the argument. To this letter the defendant company replied immediately by letter dated 24 June in which they said:

'We enclose herewith order for two cabinets and trust that you can let us have delivery as soon as possible, if possible around 23 to 28 July. We have to cancel order for sterilising drum at the moment as we have to submit another quotation.

> Thanking you,
> Yours faithfully,
> T. L. Egan and Co. Ltd
> C. Egan, Secretary'

The Order referred to is in a printed form headed:

> 'T.L. Egan and Co. Ltd,
> Surgical Instruments, Appliances, Dressings, etc.,
> 9 Lavitt's Quay,
> Cork, 24 June 1937.'

It is directed to the plaintiff and simply specifies: '2 Instrument Cabinets similar to No. B9558, Surgical Manufacturing Company's catalogue at £18 0 0 each less 25%. C.E.' To this the plaintiff replied by letter dated 25 June 1937, which I will read later.

[Having determined that the letter of 22 June was a definite offer and that the order of 24 June was not an unqualified acceptance, but another offer, Meredith J found that that offer] was accepted by the plaintiff's letter of 25 June which said:

'Dear Sirs,
   I thank you for your valued order of the 24 inst., for two Instrument Cabinets, and have great pleasure in placing the work in hands immediately and shall let you have delivery as soon as possible. Again thanking you for your esteemed order and assuring you of our best attention at all times.

> I am,
> Yours faithfully,
> John G. Dooley.'

Therefore I am of opinion that this letter from Dublin was the acceptance of the offer and that therefore the contract was made in Dublin.

The postal rule is not, however, a universal rule.

Holwell Securities *v* Hughes [1974] 1 WLR 155

On 19 October 1971 the defendant agreed to grant the plaintiffs a six-month option to purchase certain freehold property. The terms of the agreement stated that the option would be exercisable 'by notice in writing to' the defendant. On 14 April 1972, just prior to expiry of the six-month period, the plaintiffs' solicitors sent a letter to the defendant's solicitors and a separate letter to the defendant purporting to exercise the option. The second letter was never delivered. The plaintiffs sued for specific performance of the sale agreement, claiming that they had validly exercised the option.

Lawton L.J.:

The issue in this appeal was clear. Did the plaintiffs exercise an option to purchase the premises known as 571, High Road, Wembley, by posting a letter to the defendant which he never received? The answer to this problem can be reached by two paths: the short one and the roundabout one. Both, in my judgment, are satisfactory but the roundabout one has some paths leading off it which can lead the traveller after legal truth astray. The plaintiffs, I think, took one of these paths.

I propose in this judgment to start by taking the short path and then to survey the other. It is a truism of the law relating to options that the grantee must comply strictly with the conditions stipulated for exercise: in *Hare v Nicholl* [1966] 2 QB 130. It follows that the first task of the court is to find out what was stipulated: the instrument of grant has to be construed. It is a formal document which must have been drafted by someone familiar with conveyancing practice. From its lay-out and content it is likely to have been based on a precedent in the *Encyclopaedia of Forms and Precedents*. It follows, so it seems to me, that the words and phrases in it should be given precise meanings whenever possible and that words which are in common use amongst conveyancers should be construed in the way they use such words.

The material parts of the option clause are as follows: 'The said option shall be exercisable by notice in writing to the intending vendor at any time within six months from the date hereof . . .'. In my judgment, the phrase 'notice in writing' is of importance in this context. Conveyancers are familiar with it and frequently use it. It occurs in many sections of the Law of Property Act 1925; for examples, see ss 36 (2), 136, 146 and 196. In the option clause under consideration the draftsman used the phrase in connection with the exercise of the option but in other parts of the agreement he was content to use such phrases as 'agreed in writing' (see clause 4) and 'if required in writing' (see clause 8 (a)). Should any inference be drawn from the use of the word 'notice'? In my judgment, yes. Its derivation is from the Latin word for knowing. A notice is a means of making something known. The *Shorter Oxford English Dictionary* gives as the primary meanings of the word: 'Intimation, information, intelligence, warning . . . Formal intimation or warning of something.' If a notice is to be of any value it must be an intimation to someone. A notice which cannot impinge on anyone's mind is not functioning as such.

Now in this case the 'notice in writing' was to be one 'to the intending vendor'. It was to be an intimation to him that the grantee had exercised the option; he was the one who was to be fixed with the information contained in the writing. He never was, because the letter carrying the information went astray. The plaintiffs were unable to do what the agreement said they were to do, namely, fix the defendant with knowledge that they had decided to buy his property. If this construction of the option clause is correct, there is no room for the application of any rule of law relating to the acceptance of offers by posting letters since the option agreement stipulated what had to be done to exercise the option. On this ground alone I would dismiss the appeal.

I turn now to what I have called the roundabout path to the same result. [Counsel] on behalf of the plaintiffs submitted that the option was exercised when the letter was posted, as the rule relating to the acceptance of offers by post did apply. The foundation of his argument was that the parties to this agreement must have contemplated that the option might be, and probably would be, exercised by means of a letter sent through the post. I agree. This, submitted [counsel], was enough to bring the rule into operation. I do not agree. In *Henthorn v Fraser* [1892] 2 Ch. 27, Lord Herschell stated the rule as follows, at p. 33: 'Where the circumstances are such that it must have been within the contemplation of the parties that, according to the ordinary usages of mankind, the post might be used as a means of communicating the acceptance of an offer, the acceptance is complete as soon as it is posted.'

It was applied by Farwell J. in *Bruner v Moore* [1904] 1 Ch. 305 to an option to purchase patent rights. The option agreement, which was in writing, was silent as to the manner in which it was to be exercised. The grantee purported to do so by a letter and a telegram.

Does the rule apply in all cases where one party makes an offer which both he and the person with whom he was dealing must have expected the post to be used as a means of accepting it? In my judgment, it does not. First, it does not apply when the express terms of the offer specify that the acceptance must reach the offeror. The public nowadays are familiar with this exception to the general rule through their handling of football pool coupons. Secondly, it probably does not operate if its application would produce manifest inconvenience and absurdity. This is the opinion set out in Cheshire and Fifoot, *Law of Contract* (3rd edn, 1952), 43. It was the opinion of Lord Bramwell as is seen by his judgment in *British & American Telegraph Co. v Colson* (1871) LR 6 Exch. 108, and his opinion is worthy of consideration even though the decision in that case was overruled by this court in *Household Fire and Carriage Accident Insurance Co. v Grant* (1879) 4 Ex D 216. The illustrations of inconvenience and absurdity which Lord Bramwell gave are as apt today as they were then. Is a stockbroker who is holding shares to the orders of his client liable in damages because he did not sell in a falling market in accordance with the instructions in a letter which was posted but never received? Before the passing of the Law Reform (Miscellaneous Provisions) Act 1970 (which abolished actions for breach of promise of marriage), would a young soldier ordered overseas have been bound in contract to marry a girl to whom he had proposed by letter, asking her to let him have an answer before he left and she had replied affirmatively in good time but the letter had never reached him? In my judgment, the factors of inconvenience and absurdity are but illustrations of a wider principle, namely, that the rule does not apply if, having regard to all the circumstances, including the nature of the subject matter under consideration, the negotiating parties cannot have intended that there should be a binding agreement until the party accepting an offer or exercising an option had in fact communicated the acceptance or exercise to the other. In my judgment, when this principle is applied to the facts of this case it becomes clear that the parties cannot have intended that the posting of a letter should constitute the exercise of the option.

The option agreement was one to which s. 196 of the Law of Property Act 1925 applied: see sub-s. (5), which is in these terms: 'The provisions of this section shall extend to notices required to be served by any instrument affecting property executed or coming into operation after the commencement of this Act unless a contrary intention appears.' The option agreement was an instrument affecting property. A notice in writing had to be given to exercise the option. Giving a notice means the same as serving a notice: see In re 88, *Berkeley Road*, N.W. 9 [1971] Ch. 648. The object of this subsection was to enable conveyancers to omit from instruments affecting property stipulations as to the giving of notices if they were prepared to accept the statutory ones. As there was nothing in the option agreement to a contrary effect, the statutory stipulations applied in this case. S. 196 (4) is in these terms:

> Any notice required or authorised by this Act to be served shall also be sufficiently served, if it is sent by post in a registered letter addressed to the lessee, lessor, mortgagee, mortgagor, or other person to be served, by name, at the aforesaid place of abode or business, office, or counting-house, and if that letter is not returned through the post office undelivered; and that service shall be deemed to be made at the time at which the registered letter would in the ordinary course be delivered.

The object of this subsection, as also of sub-s. (3), is to specify circumstances in which proof of actual knowledge may be dispensed with. This follows from the use of the phrase 'any notice . . . shall also be sufficiently served . . .' If [counsel's] submissions are well founded, a letter sent by ordinary post the evening before the option expired would have amounted to an exercise of it; but a registered letter posted at the same time and arriving in the ordinary course of post, which would have been after the expiration of the option, would not have been an exercise. The parties to the option agreement cannot have intended any such absurd result to follow. When the provisions of s. 196 (4) are read into the agreement, as they have to be, the only reasonable inference is that the parties intended that the vendor should be fixed with actual knowledge of the exercise of the option save in the circumstances envisaged in the subsection. This, in my judgment, was enough to exclude the rule.

     I would dismiss the appeal.

(Russell and Buckley L.JJ. agreed.)

Notes

1. In some cases the courts take the view that even if a method is apparently prescribed, e.g. a signature on an acceptance form, an equally efficacious method of acceptance may suffice. So, in *Staunton v St Laurence's Hospital Board and Ireland and the Attorney General* (HC) 31 July 1987, unrep. (1985/2383P) the plaintiff was held to have validly accepted an offer of employment by way of an oral response, notwithstanding that the offer included an attached form of acceptance. However, it is generally necessary to find that the method of acceptance selected by the offeree is not prejudicial to the interests of the offeror, otherwise the prescribed method will prevail.
2. The case of *Manchester Diocesan Council for Education v Commercial and General Investments Ltd.* [1969] 3 All ER 159 is authority for the fact that the offeror may waive his right to insist on the prescribed method of acceptance once this does not adversely affect the other party.
3. In certain other cases, the courts may also take the view that the postal rule should not be applied on public policy grounds. Contrast the approach taken in *Apicella v Scala* (1931) 66 ILTR 33 (see p.51) to that taken in *Stanhope v Hospitals Trust Ltd* (No. 2) [1936] Ir J Rep 25 (see p. 818) in relation to illegal contracts.

4. Blayney J in *Kelly v Cruise Catering Ltd & Another* [1994] 2 ILRM 3 stated 'It was contended by counsel . . . [that the postal rule] could on occasion cause injustice. It was possible, for example, that the acceptance might be lost in the post and in such cases it might be unjust to hold a party to a contract when he had never received the acceptance. That is no doubt correct but it is not a relevant consideration in the present case where the signed contract was received by the first-named defendant. There are no circumstances here calling for any divergence from the well-established rule.'

Instantaneous Communications

Entores Ltd *v* Miles Far East Corp. [1955] 2 QB 327

The plaintiffs, an English company, sent a message by telex from London to the defendants in Amsterdam offering to purchase a quantity of steel cathodes. The defendants accepted this offer by telex from Amsterdam. The plaintiffs applied to serve notice of a writ out of jurisdiction claiming damages for breach of a contract made in England.

Denning L.J.:

When a contract is made by post it is clear law throughout the common law countries that the acceptance is complete as soon as the letter is put into the post box, and that is the place where the contract is made. But there is no clear rule about contracts made by telephone or by telex. Communications by these means are virtually instantaneous and stand on a different footing.

The problem can only be solved by going in stages. Let me first consider a case where two people make a contract by word of mouth in the presence of one another. Suppose, for instance, that I shout an offer to a man across a river or a courtyard but I do not hear his reply because it is drowned by an aircraft flying overhead. There is no contract at that moment. If he wishes to make a contract, he must wait till the aircraft is gone and then shout back his acceptance so that I can hear what he says. Not until I have his answer am I bound . . .

Now take a case where two people make a contract by telephone. Suppose, for instance, that I make an offer to a man by telephone and, in the middle of his reply, the line goes 'dead' so that I do not hear his words of acceptance. There is no contract at that moment. The other man may not know the precise moment when the line failed. But he will know that the telephone conversation was abruptly broken off: because people usually say something to signify the end of the conversation. If he wishes to make a contract, he must therefore get through again so as to make sure that I heard. Suppose next, that the line does not go dead, but it is nevertheless so indistinct that I do not catch what he says and I ask him to repeat it. He then repeats it and I hear his acceptance. The contract is made, not on the first time when I do not hear, but only the second time when I do hear. If he does not repeat it, there is no contract. The contract is only complete when I have his answer accepting the offer.

Lastly, take the telex. Suppose a clerk in a London office taps out on the teleprinter an offer which is immediately recorded on a teleprinter in a Manchester office, and a clerk at that end taps out an acceptance. If the line goes dead in the middle of the sentence of acceptance, the teleprinter motor will stop. There is then obviously no contract. The clerk at Manchester must get through again and send his complete sentence. But it may happen that the line does not go dead, yet the message does not get through to London. Thus the clerk at Manchester may tap out his message of acceptance and it will not be recorded in London because the ink at the London end fails, or something of that kind. In that case, the Manchester clerk will not know of the failure but the London clerk will know of it and will immediately send back a message 'not receiving'. Then, when the fault is rectified, the Manchester clerk will repeat his message. Only then is there a contract. If he does not repeat it, there is no contract. It is not until his message is received that the contract is complete.

In all the instances I have taken so far, the man who sends the message of acceptance knows that he has not been received or he has reason to know it. So he must repeat it. But, suppose that he does not know that his message did not get home. He thinks it has. This may happen if the listener on the telephone does not catch the words of acceptance, but nevertheless does not trouble to ask for them to be repeated: or the ink on the teleprinter fails at the receiving end, but the clerk does not ask for the message to be repeated: so that the man who sends an acceptance reasonably believes that his message has been received. The offeror in such circumstances is clearly bound, because he will be estopped from saying that he did not receive the message of acceptance. It is his own fault that he did not get it. But if there should be a case where the offeror without any fault on his part does not receive the message of acceptance—yet the sender of it reasonably believes it has got home when it has not—then I think there is no contract.

My conclusion is, that the rule about instantaneous communications between the parties is different from the rule about the post. The contract is only complete when the acceptance is received by the offeror: and the contract is made at the place where the acceptance is received...

Applying the principles which I have stated, I think that the contract in this case was made in London where the acceptance was received. It was, therefore, a proper case for service out of the jurisdiction.

(Birkett and Parker L.JJ. concurred.)

Brinkibon Ltd *v* Stahag Stahl und Stahlwarenhandelsgesellschaft mbH [1983] 2 AC 34

Lord Wilberforce:

The general rule, it is hardly necessary to state, is that a contract is formed when acceptance of an offer is communicated by the offeree to the offeror. And if it is necessary to determine where a contract is formed (as to which I have already commented) it appears logical that this should be at the place where acceptance is communicated to the offeror. In the common case of contracts, whether oral or in writing inter praesentes, there is no difficulty; and again logic demands that even where there is not mutual presence at the same place and at the same time, if communication is instantaneous, for example by telephone or radio communication, the same result should follow.

Then there is the case—very common—of communication at a distance, to meet which the so-called 'postal rule' has developed . . . In these cases too it seems logical to say that the place, as well as the time, of acceptance should be where (as when) the acceptance is put into the charge of the post office.

In this situation, with a general rule covering instantaneous communication *inter praesentes*, or at a distance, with an exception applying to non-instantaneous communication at a distance, how should communications by telex be categorised? In *Entores Ltd v Miles Far East Corp.* [1955] 2 QB 327 the Court of Appeal classified them with instantaneous communications. Their ruling, which has passed into the textbooks, including *Williston on Contracts* (3rd edn, 1957), appears not to have caused either adverse comment, or any difficulty to business men. I would accept it as a general rule. Where the condition of simultaneity is met, and where it appears to be within the mutual intention of the parties that contractual exchanges should take place in this way, I think it a sound rule, but not necessarily a universal rule.

Since 1955 the use of telex communication has been greatly expanded, and there are many variants on it. The senders and recipients may not be the principals to the contemplated contract. They may be servants or agents with limited authority. The message may not reach, or be intended to reach, the designated recipient immediately: messages may be sent out of office hours, or at night, with the intention, or upon the assumption, that they will be read at a later time. There may be some error or default at the recipient's end which prevents receipt at the time contemplated and believed in by the sender. The message may have been sent and/or received through machines operated by third persons. And many other variations may occur. No universal rule can cover all such cases: they must be resolved by reference to the intentions of the parties, by sound business practice and in some cases by a judgment where the risks should lie: see *Household Fire and Carriage Accident Insurance Co. Ltd v Grant*, 4 Ex D 216, 227 per Baggallay L.J. *and Henthorn v Fraser* [1892] 2 Ch. 27 per Lord Herschell.

(Lord Brandon delivered a concurring judgment and Lords Russell and Bridge agreed.)

Lord Fraser:

. . . I have reached the opinion that, on balance, an acceptance sent by telex directly from the acceptor's office to the offeror's office should be treated as if it were an instantaneous communication between principals, like a telephone conversation. One reason is that the decision to that effect in *Entores v Miles Far East Corp.* [1955] 2 QB 327 seems to have worked without leading to serious difficulty or complaint from the business community. Secondly, once the message has been received on the offeror's telex machine, it is not unreasonable to treat it as delivered to the principal offeror, because it is his responsibility to arrange for prompt handling of messages within his own office. Thirdly, a party (the acceptor) who tries to send a message by telex can generally tell if his message has not been received on the other party's (the offeror's) machine, whereas the offeror, of course, will not know if an unsuccessful attempt has been made to send an acceptance to him. It is therefore convenient that the acceptor, being in the better position, should have the responsibility of ensuring that his message is received. For these reasons I think it is right that in the ordinary simple case, such as I take this to be, the general rule and not the postal rule should apply. But I agree with both my noble and learned friends that the general rule will not cover all the many variations that may occur with telex messages.

Note

While the *Brinkibon* case clearly covers telephones, advances in information technology and the increasing popularity of electronic communications have served to focus attention on the formation of contracts by electronic means. Although the Electronic Commerce Act

2000 allows for the formation of contracts electronically (s.19) and provides for the time and place of dispatch and receipt of electronic communications (s.21) and the European Communities (Directive 2000/31/EC) Regulations 2003 [S.I. No. 68 of 2003] provides for the placing of orders pursuant to electronic contracts (reg.14), no statutory provision answers the question when is an electronic contract deemed to have been complete. It is not clear whether the receipt rule or the postal rule applies to such a case.

SECTION THREE—TERMINATION OF AN OFFER

A. Revocation

Since *Payne v Cave* (1789) 3 Term Rep. 148 it has been established that an offeror is entitled to revoke an offer at any time up until the offer has been accepted. To be effective, however, this revocation must be brought to the attention of the offeree.

Henthorn *v* Fraser [1892] 2 Ch. 27

Lord Herschell:

I think a person who has made an offer must be considered as continuously making it until he has brought to the knowledge of the person to whom it was made that it was withdrawn.

Dickinson *v* Dodds (1876) 2 Ch D 463

The defendant offered to sell property to the plaintiff, indicating that the offer would be available until the following Friday at 9am. Before the plaintiff could accept this offer, he learned that the defendant had agreed to sell the property to someone else. The plaintiff later attempted to accept the offer. The Court of Appeal held that because the plaintiff was aware of the sale, the offer had in effect been revoked and was not capable of being accepted.

James L.J.:

But it is clear settled law, on one of the clearest principles of law, that this promise, being a mere *nudum pactum* was not binding, and that at any moment before a complete acceptance by Dickinson of the offer, Dodds was as free as Dickinson himself. Well, that being the state of things, it is said that the only mode in which Dodds could assert that freedom was by actually and distinctly saying to Dickinson, 'Now I withdraw my offer.' It appears to me that there is neither principle nor authority for the proposition that there must be an express and actual withdrawal of the offer, or what is called a retractation. It must, to constitute a contract, appear that the two minds were at one, at the same moment of time, that is, that there was an offer continuing up to the time of the acceptance. If there was not such a continuing offer, then the acceptance comes to nothing. Of course it may well be that the one man is bound in some way or other to let the other man know that his mind with regard to the offer has been changed; but in this case, beyond all question, the plaintiff knew that Dodds was no longer minded to sell the property to him as plainly and clearly as if Dodds had told him in so many words, 'I withdraw the offer.'

Mellish L.J.:

The question which arises is this—If an offer has been made for the sale of property, and before that offer is accepted, the person who has made the offer enters into a binding agreement to sell the property to somebody else, and the person to whom the offer was first made receives notice in some way that the property has been sold to another person, can he after that make a binding contract by the acceptance of the offer? I am of opinion that he cannot. The law may be right or wrong in saying that a person who has given to another a certain time within which to accept an offer is not bound by his promise to give that time; but, if he is not bound by that promise, and may still sell the property to someone else, and if it be the law that, in order to make a contract, the two minds must be in agreement at some one time, that is, at the time of the acceptance, how is it possible that when the person to whom the offer has been made knows that the person who has made the offer has sold the property to someone else, and that, in fact, he has not remained in the same mind to sell it to him, he can be at liberty to accept the offer and thereby make a binding contract? It seems to me that would be simply absurd. If a man makes an offer to sell a particular horse in his stable, and says, 'I will give you until the day after tomorrow to accept the offer', and the next day goes and sells the horse to somebody else, and receives the purchase-money from him, can the person to whom the offer was originally made then come and say, 'I accept', so as to make a binding contract, and so as to be entitled to recover damages for the non-delivery of the horse? If the rule of law is that a mere offer to sell property, which can be withdrawn at any time, and which is made dependent on the acceptance of the person to whom it is made, is a mere *nudum pactum*, how is it possible that the person to whom the offer has been made can by acceptance make a binding contract after he knows that the person who has made the offer has sold the property to someone else? It is admitted law that, if a man who makes an offer dies, the offer cannot be accepted after he is dead, and parting with the property has very much the same effect as the death of the owner, for it makes the performance of the offer impossible. I am clearly of opinion that, just as when a man who has made an offer dies before it is accepted it is impossible that it can then be accepted, so when once the person to whom the offer was made knows that the property has been sold to someone else, it is too late for him to accept the offer, and on that ground I am clearly of opinion that there was no binding contract for the sale of this property by Dodds to Dickinson . . .

(Baggallay J.A. concurred.)

Walker v Glass [1979] NI 129

The plaintiff entered into negotiations with the defendant to buy property owned by the defendant. The negotiations culminated in the defendant sending the plaintiff an offer on 27 February. This offer stated that the purchase price was £400,000 and the offer was to remain open until 13 March. Furthermore, it specified that unless the acceptance form annexed to the offer was delivered to the defendant's solicitors, together with a deposit of £40,000 before 5pm on 13 March, the offer would be deemed to have been withdrawn. The plaintiff signed the acceptance on 2 March and telephoned the defendant's solicitors to inform them of this fact. Later that day the plaintiff was informed by the defendant's solicitors that the offer was withdrawn. This fact was confirmed by a letter and telegram sent that same day. On 12 March the plaintiff left the signed acceptance form and the deposit with the defendant's solicitors.

The plaintiff sued for specific performance.

Lowry L.C.J.:

I start with the following propositions:

(1) An offer may be withdrawn at any time before it has been accepted. Provided no consideration has been given by the offeree, this is so even where the offer (as in this case) was expressed to be kept open for a specified period:
   Routledge v Grant (1828) 4 Bing. 653; 130 ER 920
   Dickinson v Dodds (1876) 2 ChD 463.
(2) If the offeror prescribes a particular mode of acceptance, no contract is created unless the offer is accepted in that mode or in a way which is a beneficial to the offeror:
   Chitty on Contract 24th ed. vol. 1, 38, para. 74;
   Manchester Diocesan Council v Commercial and General Investments Ltd [1969] 3 All ER 1593.
(3) Revocation of an offer is not effective on the posting of a letter of revocation or the dispatch of a telegram, but only when the offeree receives notice of the revocation:
   Henthorn v Fraser [1892] 2 Ch. 27.

In this case the question is whether the reference to delivery of the plaintiff's completed acceptance to the defendant's solicitors at their office together with £40,000 by way of deposit before 5 o'clock p.m. on 13 March 1979 merely conveyed the information that the defendant's offer should be deemed to have been withdrawn (without the need to withdraw it expressly) if these acts were not performed by the stated time or, on the other hand, prescribed a particular mode of acceptance. The plaintiff's counsel concede that, if the second view is correct, the plaintiff did not 'accept' the offer in a way which was as beneficial to the offeror as the prescribed mode.

The defendant, however, concedes that the delivery of a cheque on 12 March was as good as a payment in cash. There is also a third view, advanced on behalf of the plaintiff, namely that the need for payment by 13 March of a deposit of £40,000 (or such payment and also a signed acceptance) was an implied term of the contract.

On the first view there would be no need for a signed acceptance or a deposit by the offeree: the plaintiff could simply have telephoned his acceptance to Mr Murphy and the defendant, having made an offer in writing, would thereupon have become contractually bound to the plaintiff right up to the completion date (30 April 1979) and indeed up to such date (if later) as became the vital date when time was made of the essence. In the meantime, the defendant would have had no remedy against the plaintiff for non-performance and could not have withdrawn his offer before 13 March or had it deemed to be withdrawn thereafter. Nor could the defendant have insisted on a signed acceptance or a deposit at any time.

In face of the wording of the defendant's offer, one could not accept the proposition that he was not prescribing a mode of acceptance, because the consequences to the defendant of having his offer accepted by telephone would be unthinkable. The first view thus yields such an unlikely result that the plaintiff's counsel did not seriously support it. Instead, recognising that a signed acceptance was needed in order to put the parties on level terms and that a deposit would certainly be required by the vendor, he espoused the third view—that a deposit and probably a signed acceptance were required by necessary implication, but he argued that these requirements were satisfied, because there was evidence (if I believed it) that the acceptance of the offer was signed on 1 March and communicated to Mr Murphy on 1, or alternatively 2 March and it was agreed that the deposit was paid on 12 March. In other words, although the payment of the deposit by 13 March could be regarded as essential, the plaintiff, by writing and orally communicating his acceptance before the defendant withdrew, effectively froze the position (and thereby prevented the defendant from effectively withdrawing his offer) and then concluded the bargain by paying the deposit on 12 March (except for which payment the offer would have been deemed by 5.30 p.m. on 13 March to have been withdrawn).

The danger of this line from the plaintiff's point of view is that it concedes that a signed acceptance and payment of a £40,000 deposit are required, and thereby causes these two acts to assume the form of a prescribed mode of acceptance, but [counsel for the plaintiff] contends that the defendant was bound by the plaintiff's performance of one of the acts on 1 or 2 March, so that he could not withdraw his offer and had to give the plaintiff the chance to pay the £40,000 deposit at any time up to 5.30 p.m. on 13 March. He also makes the point that a purchaser who tells a vendor that he has signed the vendor's offer makes it possible for the vendor to give secondary evidence of the purchaser's having signed, if the signed offer is not produced by the purchaser at the trial of an action brought on the contract by the vendor. The practical difficulty, however, is that, in an action brought by the vendor, he (or his witness) might not be believed when he testifies that the purchaser had orally communicated the information that he had signed the offer.

The third view, as I have called it, ingeniously fits the facts, or alleged facts, in this case but I do not consider it to be sound. If the signing of the offer by the purchaser and the payment of a deposit constitute a prescribed mode of acceptance, one is driven to read the exact words by which the prescribed mode is expressed. They are found in the following sentence:

This offer shall remain open for acceptance until 13 March 1979 and if the acceptance annexed hereto duly completed by purchaser shall not be delivered to Messrs Murphy, Irwin & Co., Solicitors for the vendor at their office at 14 Victoria Street, Ballymoney, together with £40,000 by way of deposit before 5 o'clock p.m. on said date, this offer shall be deemed to have been withdrawn, and in this respect time shall be of the essence.

The form of the acceptance annexed to the offer is:

I hereby accept the above offer and:
(a) Tender herewith £40,000 for deposit,
(b) Agree to complete the purchase in accordance with the annexed conditions.

Dated this   day of   1979
. . . .

(The typed line is obviously meant to accommodate the purchaser's signature and that is the use to which it was in fact put.)

This means that the written and signed acceptance was to be delivered to Mr Murphy's office and to be accompanied by a deposit of £40,000. The close association of a signed acceptance and payment of a deposit in both the offer and the form of acceptance is, in my view an important pointer to the meaning of the contract. I now come back to the question whether what was done by 2 March was as beneficial to the offeror as the prescribed mode of acceptance and was sufficient to prevent effective revocation of the offer by the defendant. I consider that the answer to both questions is 'No'.

In the first place, as I have already stated, an oral communication to the vendor by a purchaser, saying that the latter has signed, does not put the vendor in as good a position as if the signed acceptance had been delivered to his solicitor. And in the second place, signature of the acceptance by the purchaser unaccompanied by payment of the deposit is not a complete performance of the prescribed mode of acceptance and does not put the vendor in as good a position as he demanded: if the purchaser does not go through with the contract a vendor who has not received the deposit is obviously in a worse position than a vendor who has received one. Indeed, [counsel for the plaintiff] frankly said that, if the written offer embodies a prescribed mode of acceptance, the vendor had not received as beneficial an acceptance as he demanded. In short, there is no good reason why the defendant here should have become and remained contractually bound from 1 to 12 March without having received a deposit from the plaintiff.

The defendant expressly withdrew his offer before he had received a written and signed acceptance and the deposit and in my opinion he was entitled to do so.

Accordingly I find, in favour of the defendant, that no binding contract existed before withdrawal of his offer.

Note

In the *Guardians of the Navan Union v McLoughlin* (1855) 4 ICLR 451, the plaintiffs placed an advertisement seeking tenders for the supply of certain articles. The defendant sent in a tender which was later accepted by the plaintiffs at a meeting of the Board of Guardians. Before the defendant was formally informed of his success, he learned from a third party that the plaintiffs were in debt and unlikely to be in a position to pay their suppliers. The defendant thus sent a letter to the plaintiffs stating that he had been informed that his tender was successful but demanding monthly payment of his bill. As he received no reply he refused to perform the contract. The plaintiffs sued for damages for breach of contract. The defendant was deemed to have revoked his offer as the plaintiffs had not validly accepted his offer at the time.

Unilateral contracts

As noted above, in a unilateral contract there is no acceptance of the contract until the offeree has fully performed the act required. For example: I offer a person €70 if he works for me for five hours. This contract is only complete when the offeree accepts, which he only does by working a full five hours. If the offeree works for four hours and I prevent him continuing, he has not fully performed and thus he has not accepted the contract. Therefore I am entitled to revoke my offer. In theory, thus, an offer to enter into a unilateral contract may be revoked at any time up until performance has been completed.

Errington v Errington [1952] 1 All ER 149

A father bought a house for his son and daughter-in-law in 1935. The consideration for the house was met partly by cash and partly by a building society loan repayable with interest by instalments. Although the house was in the father's name, he gave the building society book to his daughter-in-law and told her that if and when she and her husband had paid all the instalments the house would be their property. From that time, the daughter-in-law paid the instalments as they fell due. In 1945, the father died and the house was left in his will to his widow. As the son had left his wife, the widow took an action against her daughter-in-law for possession. The Court of Appeal determined that the son and daughter-in-law were entitled to remain in possession as long as they paid the instalments and the occupation of the house was not determinable by the widow.

Denning LJ.:

It is to be noted that the couple never bound themselves to pay the instalments to the building society, and I see no reason why any such obligation should be implied. It is clear law that the court is not to imply a term unless it is necessary, and I do not see that it is necessary here. Ample content is given to the whole arrangement by holding that the father promised that the house should belong to the couple as soon as they had paid off the mortgage. The parties did not discuss what was to happen if the couple failed to pay the instalments to the building society, but I should have thought it clear that, if they did fail to pay the instalments, the father would not be bound to transfer the house to them. The father's promise was a unilateral contract—a promise of the house in return for their act of paying the instalments. It could not be revoked by him once the couple entered on performance of the act, but it would cease to bind him if they left it incomplete and unperformed, which they have not done. If that was the position during the father's lifetime, so it must be after his death. If the daughter-in-law continues to pay all the building society instalments, the couple will be entitled to have the property transferred to them as soon as the mortgage is paid off, but if she does not do so, then the building society will claim the instalments from the father's estate and the estate will have to pay them. I cannot think that in those circumstances the estate would be bound to transfer the house to them, any more than the father himself would have been.

Note

In Luxor (Eastbourne) Ltd v Cooper [1941] AC 108, the House of Lords considered the revocation of an agreement by the owners of two cinemas to pay an agent £5,000 on the completion of the sale of those properties if the agent introduced the purchaser. It held that such an agreement did not tie the owner's hands and compel him to bind himself to sell to the agent's clients who offer the price sought. The Court refused to imply a term to the effect that the owners could not refuse to complete the sale as such a term would not be justified on the basis of the compulsion of some necessity.

Daulia v Four Millbank Nominees Ltd [1978] 2 All ER 557

Goff L.J.:

Whilst I think the true view of a unilateral contract must in general be that the offeror is entitled to require full performance of the condition which he has imposed and short of that he is not bound, that must be subject to one important qualification, which stems from the fact that there must be an implied obligation on the part of the offeror not to prevent the condition becoming satisfied, which obligation it seems to me must arise as soon as the offeree starts to perform. Until the offeror can revoke the whole thing, but once the offeree has embarked on performance it is too late for the offeror to revoke his offer.

Note

In *O'Connor v Sorohan* [1933] IR 591 the Irish Supreme Court followed *Offord v Davies* (1862) 12 CB (NS) 748 on this point. There is, however, no recent Irish decision on this issue.

B. Rejection

An offer will be terminated once it is rejected by the offeree. As noted above, a counter-offer by the original offeree will be viewed as a rejection of the original offer.

C. Lapse of Time

Whereas an offer will terminate upon the lapse of a reasonable period of time, what is reasonable in any given case will depend on the circumstances of the offer.

Commane v Walsh (HC) 3 May 1983, unrep.

By a standard form memorandum of agreement, the plaintiff agreed to buy property from the defendant for £60,000. The property comprised three parcels of land which when described in the memorandum amounted to a total area of 51 acres 3 roods. However, the final sentence of the memorandum noted that the total area being sold was 54.2 acres. The special conditions noted that 'No requisition or objection shall be raised as to the accuracy of the area in sale and purchaser shall be deemed to have inspected the property prior to completion of the contract.'

The vendor then wrote to say that due to a title problem with one of the parcels of land he suggested closing the sale in relation to the remaining two parcels and apportioning the purchase money accordingly.

In July the purchaser complained that the total acreage did not amount to 54.2 acres, and the vendor replied in August referring them to the Special Conditions. At some stage during the summer the purchaser entered on the land to cut and bale hay which was stored on the land. On 18 September he wrote to the vendors demanding completion on or before 19 October. On 30 September the vendors wrote back purporting to accept the offer previously made to complete the transfer of two parcels of the property. This was rejected by the purchaser on 1 October. Since the vendor was unable to establish title to one of the portions, the purchaser wrote on 20 October demanding the return of his deposit.

O'Hanlon J.:

I feel, however, that I should also consider whether . . . the agreement was validly rescinded because of unreasonable delay on the part of the vendor in completing the transfer of the lands.

I have no hesitation in finding that the vendor and her solicitors were extremely dilatory in the way the sale was dealt with between May and October 1981, but the correspondence does not suggest that the delay was a source of great annoyance or upset to the purchaser at the time. The offer was made in the month of May to close the sale in respect of the greater part of the lands, leaving over until later the transfer of the small parcel in Folio 13155, and this offer was never formally withdrawn until after the vendor's solicitors had written on 30 September 1981, expressing the vendor's willingness to put through the sale in this manner. The offer when made remained open until it was withdrawn, or until it would be unreasonable to hold the purchaser to it any longer because of the length of time which had elapsed without acceptance. What is a reasonable time is a question of fact depending on the circumstances of each particular case. See *Ramsgate Hotel Co. v Montefiore*, (1866) LR 1 Ex 109. In the present case, because of the rather casual approach adopted by both parties to the time for closing of the sale, and their early agreement that they would have to proceed on the basis of a good deal of delay in straightening out the title to Folio 13155, I would regard the offer to deal separately with this parcel of land as remaining open into the month of September 1981, and I do not consider that the letter of 19 September 1981, should be regarded as a revocation of the offer.

In this situation the vendor was willing to comply with her obligations under the Agreement for Sale, as varied by the special terms later arranged about Folio 13155, within the time which the purchaser sought to make of the essence of the contract. I think it very likely that the purchaser would have consented to the sale going through on this basis had he not become involved in a dispute about the acreage, when he asserted a claim which he was unable to enforce.

Consequently, if the matter had to be determined under the general law as to delay on completion and the entitlement of a purchaser in such circumstances to withdraw from his bargain, I would again hold that the contract had not been validly rescinded having regard to all the circumstances of the present case. The plaintiff's claim accordingly stands refused.

Note

In *Lynch v St Vincent's Hospital* (HC) 31 July 1987, unrep., the plaintiff, a hospital consultant, was offered a new contract with the hospital in February and again in September and finally accepted the offer in December. The Court noted that the forwarding to him by the hospital of a Department of Health circular reminding consultants of the final date for entering contracts of appointments confirmed the availability of the offer.

Earn *v* Kohut [2002] MBQB 84

The defendant pleaded guilty to a number of criminal charges involving an assault on the plaintiff and offered to settle the plaintiff's civil claim. Two and a half years later and subsequent to the expiry of the limitation period for taking such a civil action, the plaintiff purported to accept the offer. The Court of Queen's Bench of Manitoba, having determined that in the circumstances the offer was not revoked by the expiration of the limitation period, went on to consider whether two and a half years was an unreasonable length of time for the offer to remain open.

Beard J.:

The defendant questioned whether an acceptance some two and a half years after the date of the offer was an acceptance within a reasonable time. According to *Chitty on Contracts*, at pp. 129–30:

> Where the duration of an offer is not limited by its express terms, the offer comes to an end after the lapse of a reasonable time. What is a reasonable time depends on all the circumstances: for example on the nature of the subject-matter and on the means used to communicate the offer. An offer to sell a perishable thing, or a thing subject to violent price fluctuations, would terminate after a relatively short time; and this would often also be true of an offer made by telex or by telegram or by other equally speedy means of communication.

The law is similarly stated in Waddams, *The Law of Contracts* (3rd edn, Toronto: Canada Law Book Inc., 1993) at p. 74.

While two and a half years may seem like a long time to leave an offer open, I find that it was not unreasonable in this case. I have come to this conclusion for the following reasons:

There is no indication that the offer is limited and, in fact, the indication is quite the opposite. In his submissions on sentence, Mr Cuddy [the defendant's lawyer] is unequivocal about the defendant's intention to compensate the plaintiff. He stated as follows at pp. 47–8 of the transcript from the sentencing:

> He, as you can see in Dr Shane's report, feels a good deal of remorse about this matter and in fact I can advise you that Mr Kohut intends to compensate the complainant and in fact unilaterally has made an effort and as we have delivered to the complainant's lawyer, who's present here today, a consent to judgment in a substantial sum, which Mr Kohut hopes to be able to satisfy.

This is reinforced by the judge's comments on sentence that the defendant had arranged or at least consented to judgment for a sum of money which would compensate the plaintiff.

The offer was reinforced several months later when, at the end of April 1988, Mr Johannson [the plaintiff's lawyer] received a call from a lawyer on behalf of the defendant in which he repeated the defendant's intention to pay and asked for a letter from the plaintiff supporting his application for early parole.

As liability and quantum were never at issue, there would be no disadvantage to the defendant in giving an offer of extended duration to the plaintiff.

On 29 November 1988 the defendant was sentenced to three years in custody. The evidence is that he had no means, other than from his wages, to pay a judgment. As payment was always the issue, there was no urgency in resolving that question as the defendant would not have been in a position to propose any payments until he was released from jail and working again. Thus, Mr Johannson's letter to Mr Cuddy in January 1991 begins with the comment that he presumes that the defendant is out of jail and he inquires about settling the claim.

Based on these facts, I find that the offer was accepted within a reasonable time.

D. DEATH

Where the offer is an offer of personal service, obviously it terminates upon the offeror's death. However, in other circumstances the offer may subsist until the offeree becomes aware of the offeror's death.

In re Whelan deceased, Dodd *v* Whelan [1897] 1 IR 575

Whelan guaranteed the current account of the firm Whelan & Maher. Although Whelan died in April 1895, no notice of his death was given to the bank. In November 1895 the bank manager learned of Whelan's death in a casual conversation. However, the account was not closed until 1 January 1896.

The bank later claimed on foot of the guarantee for the balances due to them by the firm. The executors of Whelan's estate disputed their liability to any portion of the claim relating to advances after Whelan's death, or alternatively to the portion of the claim relating to advances made since the bank had knowledge of his death.

Chatterton V.C.:

I do not think that, having regard to the decision of the Court of Exchequer in *Bradbury v Morgan*[1] and the cases which have followed it, I can hold that the mere fact of the death of the guarantor, unknown to the creditor, terminated the operation of the guarantee. But the question arises whether mere knowledge of the death has that operation without formal notice being given by the executors to determine the guarantee. The nature of such guarantees and the right to determine them was carefully considered by Bowen J., in the case of *Coulthart v Clementson*[2] an action which was tried by him on circuit, when he reserved the case for his further consideration. It was argued before him subsequently, and he again took time for consideration, so that the questions there raised were fully deliberated on by that eminent judge, and his opinion is entitled to great weight. He put the case as one of contract, and refers to the decision of the Court of Common Pleas in *Offord v Davies*[3] and held that it was established by authority that such continuing guarantees can be withdrawn on notice during the lifetime of the guarantor, and that a limitation to that effect must be read, so to speak, into the contract. He then proceeded to consider the question of what is to happen on the death of the guarantor, and asks if the guarantee is then to become irrevocable and to go on for ever? He replies, and I think conclusively, that such a consequence of the death would be absurd. In this conclusion I entirely agree. He then proceeds to consider what notice should be deemed sufficient, and asks must the executor give special notice that the guarantee is withdrawn, or is it not enough that the creditor should be warned of the death of the guarantor and the devolution of his estate to others, and holds that, in the absence of special option to the personal representative to continue the guarantee, the notice of the death of the testator and of the existence of a will is constructive notice of the determination of the guarantee as to future advances. These words cannot be limited to cases where a will exists, and are *a fortiori* applicable to cases of intestacy, for such an option could only be given by a will, and if no will exists no such option can exist. In the absence of express authority from the deceased, whether he dies intestate or makes a will not giving such option, it would be equally outside the duty of the executor or of the administrator, as the case may be, to continue the course of dealing. Knowledge of the death therefore is, as considered by Bowen J., sufficient to put the creditor on inquiry whether there is any testamentary authority before making further advances. Nor is there any hardship upon or injustice to the creditor in so holding. His knowledge of the death should be enough to require him to hold his hand, and ascertain whether or not there is any option given to the personal representatives of the guarantor to continue the course of dealing, or rather to enter into a new contract of suretyship. The decision in *Coulthart v Clementson* is clear, that in case no such option exists, the course of dealing is determined by knowledge of the death.

The opinion of Mellish L.J., in *Harriss v Fawcett*,[4] a case referred to, not on this part of the question, by Bowen J., in *Coulthart v Clementson*, is quite in accordance with his views. The case of *Coulthart v Clementson* was commented on by Romer J., in *In re Silvester*,[5] but I cannot regard the *dicta* of the learned judge as sufficient to displace the decision of Bowen J., which was not appealed from and which I am prepared to follow. Of course, in the case of express provisions in the contract of guarantee, effect must be given to them, according to the true construction of the instrument; but there is not, in my opinion, anything in this letter of guarantee bearing upon the present question. I therefore hold that advances made by the bank subsequent to their having knowledge of the death of the testator are not covered by the guarantee, but that those made prior to this were so covered.

[1.] 1 H & C 249.   [4.] LR 8 Ch App 866.
[2.] 5 QBD 42.   [5.] [1895] 1 Ch. 573.
[3.] 12 CB (NS) 748.

Note

The death of the offeree before the offer has been accepted renders the offer incapable of being accepted. This is clear from *Reynolds v Atherton* (1921) 125 LT 690.

SECTION FOUR—CERTAINTY

An agreement which is either vague or incomplete will not constitute a legally binding contract. An agreement may be vague because it contains terms which are illusory, that is, lack promissory content, or are discretionary in nature, or are capable of interpretation in more than one way. Alternatively, agreement may not have been reached on certain important points.

Electricity Supply Board *v* Newman (1933) 67 ILTR 124

The defendant, Newman, entered into a contract with Dublin Corporation on 8 January 1927, which was in the following form: 'I, the undersigned, do hereby agree to indemnify the Dublin Corporation against any loss it may sustain by reason of the default of Mrs Betta Waddington, of No. 5 Lower Ormond Quay, in discharging the accounts for electricity supplied to her for a period not exceeding nine months at any time,' and was signed by the defendant.

During the period October 1929 to June 1930, electricity was supplied by the Electricity Supply Board to Mrs Betta Waddington at four different premises . . . *viz.* at 5 Lower Ormond Quay, to the amount of £10 8s 6d, 6 Lower Ormond Quay to the amount of £6 15s 10d, 87 Marlborough Street to the amount of £9 6s 9d, and 108 St Stephen's Green to the amount of 16s 4d. Default in payment having been made by Mrs Waddington, the plaintiffs sued Newman, the defendant, on foot of his contract of indemnity for the total sum of £27 7s 5d due by Mrs Waddington in respect of all four premises . . .

Judge Davitt held that the contract on the face of it was ambiguous, the word 'accounts' being capable of meaning either the periodic accounts in respect of the electricity supply to one set of premises or accounts due in respect of the supply to a number of premises. Accordingly, he had admitted oral evidence to explain the meaning of the contract. On the evidence of the defendant, he was satisfied that, in signing the contract, the defendant had had no intention of giving a 'drag-net' indemnity which would cover the supply of electricity to Mrs Waddington at any premises and any number of premises which she might occupy. He was satisfied that the contract of indemnity was intended to apply only to the periodic accounts for the supply of current to Mrs Waddington at the premises No. 5 Lower Ormond Quay alone.

Provincial Bank of Ireland Ltd *v* Donnell (1932) 67 ILTR 142

The defendant gave the plaintiffs a guarantee expressed to be made 'in consideration of advances heretofore made or that may hereafter be made from time to time' by the plaintiffs to the defendant's husband. When the defendant's husband defaulted on his payments, the plaintiffs sued the defendant for refusing to reimburse them under the guarantee.

Best L.J.:

The guarantee can, in my opinion, only be construed as an indication on the part of the plaintiffs that they might make further advances to the debtor, but there was no agreement binding them to do so and if, as is the case here, no advance was in fact made, the undertaking of the defendant fails for want of consideration and judgment should be in her favour.

Notes

1. In the *Provincial Bank* case, the Court also held that any promise made was unsupported by consideration. It was not possible to rely on advances already made as this would constitute past consideration. Furthermore, the court decided that as the plaintiffs had not threatened the defendant's husband with proceedings, there was no question of forebearance to sue which would have constituted good consideration. (See pp 133–138 below.)

2. See also *Central Meats v Carney* (1944) 10 Ir Jur Rep 34, where the Court found that an agreement by Dublin Boned Meat Ltd to supply as many cattle as possible to the plaintiffs, and to guarantee not to supply meat to any other canner without the plaintiff's consent, lacked certainty. Overend J noted:

> This would mean, no doubt, as many cattle as could be supplied, but there is nothing specific about the number, or the price, or the quality, and in my opinion, in the absence of these essential details, this letter cannot be regarded as a final offer. In addition, it is important to note that the capacity of the plaintiffs to purchase cattle is limited by law as a result of a Government quota.

Mackey v Wilde & Longin [1998] 1 ILRM 449

Mackey and Wilde were the owners of a joint fishery in County Donegal. Mackey claimed that they had agreed to limit the number of licences to twenty-five annual licences per side together with 'a few' day tickets. The trial judge held that there was a concluded agreement and interpreted 'a few' as meaning up to ten. The defendants appealed this decision, claiming that no concluded agreement had been reached.

Barron J.:

The remaining ground is one of law and is whether it is open to the court to give a precise meaning to the word 'few'. There have been many cases in which the full terms of the contract are not set out precisely, but which have been found to be valid binding agreements. Examples are where a term is implied, where there is a formula for determining the apparent uncertainty with precision or where the term is to be determined upon the basis of what is reasonable or by reference to custom or trade usage. Even in some cases, when none of these means can be operated, the agreement will still be upheld where the court is satisfied that the term which is still to be settled is a subsidiary one and the parties intended to be bound in any event by the main agreement.

The essential question is whether the parties have left over some matter to be determined which can only be determined by themselves. So an agreement to enter into an agreement is not a concluded contract.

In the instant case, the agreement was not capable of being saved by any of the means available to the court to which I have referred. The parties did not intend to be limited to twenty-five annual licences without any day tickets. Nor could the number be determined by what is reasonable. Reasonableness in law is an expression capable of certainty. But there can be no certainty here. The learned trial judge has held that the ten day tickets would be reasonable. But equally any other number between two and ten could have been said also to have been reasonable. When an apparently uncertain term is saved on the basis of what is reasonable, it is because this is imparting certainty, something which cannot be done by choosing which of several reasonable answers is the correct one. In other words, the court cannot make the agreement for the parties by saying this is reasonable. In the instant case what the parties have left over, what is meant by the word 'few', is something which only they can settle. It follows that there was no concluded agreement.

The following case sets out very clearly the steps to be followed in determining whether an agreement is sufficiently certain to constitute a legally binding agreement.

Pagnan SpA. *v* Feed Products Ltd [1987] 2 Lloyd's Rep. 601

The plaintiffs and defendants through an intermediary broker (Mr Pagnossin) entered into negotiations for the sale and purchase of corn pellets. On 1 February, following many telephone and telex exchanges, Mr Pagnossin sent telexes to both parties stating 'We confirm the following business today concluded through our intermediary' and setting out certain terms of the contract. The following day the defendants sent the plaintiffs a telex setting out the contract terms, not all of which corresponded with the previous telex. Certain of these terms proved unacceptable to the buyers and negotiations took place up to 8 February to sort out the differences. However, on 9 March Mr Pagnossin forwarded from the defendants the formal contract documents containing certain of the unacceptable terms. The plaintiffs claimed that no binding contract existed.

The trial judge determined that a binding contract was formed on 1 February.

Lloyd L.J.:

As to the law, the principles to be derived from the authorities, some of which I have already mentioned, can be summarised as follows:

(1) In order to determine whether a contract has been concluded in the course of correspondence, one must first look to the correspondence as a whole (see *Hussey v Horne-Payne* (1879) 4 App Cas 311).

(2) Even if the parties have reached agreement on all the terms of the proposed contract, nevertheless they may intend that the contract shall not become binding until some further condition has been fulfilled. That is the ordinary 'subject to contract' case.

(3) Alternatively, they may intend that the contract shall not become binding until some further term or terms have been agreed; see *Love and Stewart v Instone* (1917) 33 TLR 475, where the parties failed to agree the intended strike clause, and *Hussey v Horne-Payne*, where Lord Selborne said at p. 323:

. . . The observation has often been made, that a contract established by letters may sometimes bind parties who, when they wrote those letters, did not imagine that they were finally settling the terms of the agreement by which they were to be bound; and it appears to me that no such contract ought to be held established, even by letters which would otherwise be sufficient for the purpose, if it is clear, upon the facts, that there were other conditions of the intended contract, beyond and besides those expressed in the letters, which were still in a state of negotiation only, *and without the settlement of which the parties had no idea of concluding any agreement.* [My emphasis.]

(4) Conversely, the parties may intend to be bound forthwith even though there are further terms still to be agreed or some further formality to be fulfilled (see *Love and Stewart v Instone* per Lord Loreburn at p. 476).

(5) If the parties fail to reach agreement on such further terms, the existing contract is not invalidated unless the failure to reach agreement on such further terms renders the contract as a whole unworkable or void for uncertainty.

(6) It is sometimes said that the parties must agree on the essential terms and that it is only matters of detail which can be left over. This may be misleading, since the word 'essential' in that context is ambiguous. If by 'essential' one means a term without which the contract cannot be enforced then the statement is true: the law cannot enforce an incomplete contract. If by 'essential' one means a term which the parties have agreed to be essential for the formation of a binding contract, then the statement is tautologous. If by 'essential' one means only a term which the court regards as important as opposed to a term which the court regards as less important or a matter of detail, the statement is untrue. It is for the parties to decide whether they wish to be bound and, if so, by what terms, whether important or unimportant. It is the parties who are, in the memorable phrase coined by the judge, 'the masters of their contractual fate'. Of course the more important the term is the less likely it is that the parties will have left it for future decision. But there is no legal obstacle which stands in the way of the parties agreeing to be bound now while deferring important matters to be agreed later. It happens every day when parties enter into so-called 'heads of agreement'. [Counsel for the plaintiffs] submits that that is a special case, but I do not think it is.

[Counsel for the plaintiffs] relied heavily on the fact that the judge described the terms on which the parties had not yet agreed as 'terms of economic significance to these buyers'. If I am right in the propositions I have stated, and in particular propositions (4) and (6), the fact that the terms yet to be agreed were of economic significance would not prevent a contract coming into existence forthwith if that is what the parties intended. So I can find no error of law in the judge's approach.

Was the judge right to draw the inference which he did as to the parties' intentions? The matters upon which the judge relied are set out at p. 611 ante. I will not repeat them now. Among the more important are the following:

(1) Mr Pagnan told Mr Pagnossin on 1 February to book the business.
(2) Mr Pagnossin sent a confirmatory telex the same day referring to the business as:
    '. . . having been concluded through our intermediary.'
(3) Neither party raised any objection to the confirmatory telex.
(4) The plaintiffs thereafter headed their telexes 'Contract 1 February 1982'.
(5) There was no communication of any kind between 8 February, when the defendants agreed the loading rate, and 9 March, when Mr Pagnossin despatched the documents.

(6) The plaintiffs did not then react as one would have expected if there had been no question of a binding contract.

[Counsel for the plaintiffs] argued that the parties' reactions are as irrelevant as their beliefs. I agree of course that the test is objective and the reactions of the parties are not conclusive. But I cannot accept that they are irrelevant. As to the other matters relied on by the judge, some of the more important of which I have mentioned, [Counsel for the plaintiffs] submitted that the judge gave them altogether too much weight. As for the gap between 8 February and 9 March, [Counsel] said that there could be several explanations. To choose one rather than another would be mere speculation.

I cannot accept those submissions. The judge regarded the matters to which I have referred as being: '. . . very strong indications that the parties intended to, and did, make a binding contract on 1 February.'

In my view he was right. Indeed the only indication the other way is that the parties continued with their negotiations after the confirmatory telex of 1 February. But that is not really an indication at all. Once one accepts that the parties are in law capable of making what I will call an interim agreement, it was only to be expected that they would continue negotiating the terms that remained without delay. This is what they did. In my view the judge drew the right inference as to the parties' intentions. . .

For the reasons I have given I would dismiss the appeal.

(Stocker and O'Connor L.JJ. concurred.)

Note

In *Bryen & Langley Ltd v Boston* [2005] BLR 508, the Court of Appeal noted that the mere fact that two parties proposed that their agreement should be contained in a formal contract to be drawn and signed in the future did not preclude the conclusion that they had already informally contractually committed themselves on exactly the same terms.

Agreements to Sell Property

Many of the cases considered by the Courts in relation to certainty also give rise to questions as to compliance with formal requirements. For example, in the case of an agreement to sell land, the first question that arises is whether a complete agreement has been reached between the parties. The second question then is whether this agreement complies with the Statute of Frauds and is thus enforceable. As we will see in Chapter 5, this involves identifying a written memorandum which recognises the existence of this complete agreement. The three cases which follow will be examined both in this chapter and in Chapter 5 in relation to these separate issues.

The *Boyle v Lee* case below also introduces the important concept of a 'subject to contract' clause. These clauses are often used where the parties do not wish to commit to a sale without executing a formal contract. This is particularly likely in contracts for the sale of land or an interest in land. The purchaser may wish to allow sufficient time to check title, planning permission, compliance with environmental regulation, etc. The vendor may wish to keep his options open in order to allow higher offers be submitted. In such cases, there may be an oral statement that the agreement is subject to contract. The parties may also use the phrase to prevent the creation of an enforceable agreement by avoiding the creation of a memorandum for the purposes of the Statutes of Frauds. This will be examined in greater detail in Chapter 5.

Boyle v Lee and Goyns [1992] ILRM 65

The plaintiff, an experienced property developer, was negotiating to purchase a property from the defendant. The plaintiff argued that negotiations conducted with a Mr McManus of Lisney & Son auctioneers led to an agreement to purchase the property for £90,000. The plaintiff was aware that the development which had so far taken place in the premises had not got full planning permission and was prepared to waive any difficulty in that context. He was also prepared to accept whatever the nature of the existing tenancies were and to buy subject to them on a representation made by Mr McManus that none of them were protected tenancies. When the question of a deposit arose, the plaintiff claimed that Mr McManus told him that it was not necessary at that time and that this would be dealt with between the solicitors as part of the formalities afterwards. Furthermore, he claimed that no agreement was reached as to the specific date the sale would close because it was apparent to Mr McManus that he was anxious to close the sale as soon as possible. It was accepted on the evidence that when the offer of £90,000 was finally made by the plaintiff that Mr McManus got the express authority of his clients to accept that figure. It was also accepted that prior to 8 July 1988 the plaintiff satisfied himself as to the structural condition of the premises and arranged the entire finance for the immediate purchase of the premises. On 8 July 1988 Mr McManus wrote to Mr Walsh, solicitor for the vendors, confirming instructions from the vendors to accept the offer 'subject to contract' The letter, which was expressly stated to be 'for information purposes only', asked Mr. Walsh to prepare and forward the contract including the following terms which were stated to be agreed:

Proposed purchasers: Eoin Boyle & Susan Boyle, 165 Rathgar Road, Dublin 6.
Proposed purchase price: IR£90,000 subject to contract.
Proposed purchaser's solicitors: Patrick Clyne, Martin E. Marron & Co. 10 Northumberland Road, Dublin 4.
Contents: Contents of the apartments are included in the sale price.
Tenants: The property is being sold subject to, and with the benefits of the tenants.
Closing date: As soon as legal formalities can be completed.

Mr McManus gave evidence at the hearing in the High Court that it was a fixed policy of the firm not to purport to bind any client with regard to the sale of a property by any writing made by a member of the firm and that it was for that reason that he inserted the phrase 'subject to contract' into the letter. He stated that he believed he must have conveyed to Mr Boyle the fact that their negotiations were subject to contract, but he could not affirmatively state that he had used that particular expression. With regard to the question of a deposit, he stated that it was a fixed policy of his firm not under any circumstances to accept or fix the amount of a deposit in any sale and that it was for that reason that he informed the plaintiff that that would have to be arranged between the solicitors. He maintained that at all stages he did not intend to bind the vendors. The defendants appealed to the Supreme Court on the basis *inter alia* that the trial judge misdirected himself in law and on the facts in holding that the evidence supported or was capable of supporting a finding that prior to 8 July 1988 there was a concluded oral agreement for the sale of the premises at £90,000.

Finlay C.J.:

In the course of his judgment the learned trial judge stated that he believed both of the witnesses to be honest and candid in their evidence. His findings on the question as to whether an oral contract for sale had been made, and completely made, between the plaintiff and Mr McManus is based not, therefore, on the acceptance of the truth of one witness and the rejection of the truth or accuracy of another, but rather on inferences which he drew from the evidence. In particular, his finding that the failure of the parties to reach any agreement on the question of a deposit was irrelevant since it was of no importance in the contract, is a mixed finding of law and fact. In my view, this finding was in error. The amount of a deposit to be made, even if a purchaser is willing to make a deposit of the appropriate amount, or the usual amount then experienced in transactions in Dublin, is too important a part of a contract for the sale of land in the large sum of £90,000 to be omitted from a concluded and complete oral agreement unless the parties in such an agreement had agreed that no deposit would be paid. In this case the evidence irresistibly leads to the conclusion that both Mr Boyle and Mr McManus agreed that there had to be a deposit, but left it over to be agreed between the solicitors when the formal contract was being settled as to its amount and form. In my view, that evidence, which was not in contest, must lead to a conclusion that there was not a complete contract made orally between Mr Boyle and Mr McManus before 8 July 1988 . . .

(Hederman J. concurred).

McCarthy J.:

It is a feature of property transactions in Ireland that they are often made with a minimum of formality, the circumstances, including the venue, of such bargains not being always conducive to the 'dusty purlieus of the law' (see Tennyson, *In Memoriam*, lxxxix). If parties are agreed on the terms which they regard as essential, it is not for others to evaluate with a different result. Mr Boyle was prepared to accept the tenancies; so what did it matter to Mr McManus? Mr Boyle offered a substantial deposit but Mr McManus said that that was a matter that would be dealt with between the solicitors and there would have been no problem about it. So also, both parties were anxious to close the sale and that would have been taken care of by the solicitors. As Mr Boyle said (Q. 76), 'What he in fact said was, we had done a deal, and the solicitors would have to take care of the formalities.' The fact that one party says that there had been a deal would not make it so, if it were not in fact so. Equally, the fact that someone believes that no deal has been done would not make that necessarily so. In my view, Barrington J. was entitled to come to the conclusion that the parties had done a deal, the formalities to be cleared up by the solicitors. It may have been a highly informal deal; it may have omitted a variety of details that would be high in a lawyer's list of priorities, and Mr McManus may well have thought that there was no enforceable deal, but, in my judgment, there was a deal that contained all that the parties deemed essential . . .

O'Flaherty J.:

During the hearing of the appeal, we have had the benefit of elaborate arguments by both sides on the concept of 'subject to contract'. This incantation has no talismanic property.

Before examining this phrase at all, it is necessary to go back to the rudiments of the law of contract and find out whether there was an offer and acceptance and an intention to create legal relations. That there was an agreement on price, offer and acceptance, there is no doubt. But beyond that, in my judgment, there was much to be sorted out. For a start, the matter of the tenancies was not resolved. It was easy for Mr Boyle to say at the trial that he was prepared to take the property subject to the tenancies whatever kind they were—but one of his answers suggested that he might have had to engage in litigation because of what he felt was a misrepresentation in relation to a tenant who had, in effect, a six-year tenancy. It is common case that Mr McManus left him under the impression that they were all short tenancies, meaning thereby not more than one year. Then, there was no closing date agreed. Mr McManus expressly declined to take a deposit believing that that was a matter proper to be put into the formal contract. So, it appears to me, that there was no consensus ad idem. There was, at the most, an agreement to agree . . .

Egan J.:

It is submitted that certain terms remained outstanding and these would include the closing date, the deposit and final details in relation to the tenancies. It should be emphasised that I am now dealing only with the question as to whether or not there was a concluded oral agreement. The wording of the memorandum dated 8 July 1988 is irrelevant in relation to this question. I will deal with the terms which are alleged to be 'outstanding':

1. *The tenancies*
It is abundantly clear on the evidence that the plaintiff agreed to accept the tenancies as they stood even though he knew that they did not conform with the planning permission.

2. *The closing date*
The learned trial judge was satisfied on the evidence that the closing date was to be 'as speedily as the legal formalities have been completed' and that it did not appear in the circumstances of the case to be a term of any real significance. It has long been established that where no time for performance is agreed the law implies an undertaking by each party to perform his part of the contract within a time which is reasonable having regard to the circumstances of the case: *Simpson v Hughes*.[1]

Words such as 'as soon as possible' would also be construed by reference to what would be reasonable in the circumstances: *Hydraulic Engineering Co. Ltd v McHaffie Goslett & Co.*[2]

It is clear, therefore, that words which mean 'as speedily as the legal formalities have been completed' are not so uncertain in their meaning as to negative the existence of an oral agreement.

3. The *deposit*

In regard to this the learned trial judge stated that it was 'obvious that Mr Boyle was at all times prepared to pay a deposit, even a substantial deposit, had it been accepted from him and there was no problem in relation to the deposit'.

Again, in my view, the absence of specific agreement in relation to the payment of a deposit or the amount thereof does not negative the existence of an oral agreement. It is usual to have a deposit in the case of sales of land but it is not essential in law. In any event, having regard to the construction put on the evidence by the learned trial judge, it would be unrealistic to hold that failure to pinpoint a specific rate or sum for a deposit would, in the circumstances of this case, oblige the court to rule that there was no oral agreement.

Having regard to the foregoing matters, therefore, I am satisfied that the learned trial judge was justified in his finding that there had been a concluded oral agreement.

[1.] (1896) 66 LJ Ch. 143.
[2.] (1878) 4 QBD 670 (CA).

Notes

1. In *Boyle v Lee*, the Court's findings as to whether the letter dated 8 July 1988 from Lisney & Son to P. J. Walsh & Co. constituted a sufficient note or memorandum of an oral agreement to satisfy the Statute of Frauds (Ireland) 1695 is set out at p. 269.

2. In *Silver Wraith Ltd v Siúicre Éireann cpt* (HC) 8 June 1989, unrep., the Court was asked to determine *inter alia* whether a concluded agreement existed. In the course of negotiating a lease, the defendants indicated that certain terms were acceptable 'subject to full lease being agreed'. However, the term 'subject to contract' was not used. Keane J. stated as follows:

> If one leaves the legalities aside for the moment, I think that any lay person reading that correspondence would not have much difficulty in inferring from the phrase that Mr Gray was seeking to convey to his opposite number in these discussions that, while he was proceeding to set out terms which he (Mr Gray) understood were acceptable to both of them, he was conveying that in the normal course of events, if the parties were *ad idem* on the main features of the lease (the rent, the length of the term and when the term was to commence) the matter should go to their respective solicitors; that a full lease containing all the covenants and conditions that might be appropriate in such a lease would then be drawn up, considered by their solicitors, possibly amended between them and that eventually from discussions between the solicitors an agreed lease which both parties were prepared to execute would emerge. Mr Gray was seeking to convey to Mr Murray that until that time his principals would not in any contractual sense be bound . . . The phrase used must be carefully distinguished from the phrase 'subject to

contract' which is dealt with in the authorities here and in England. Those authorities have been concerned with situations where parties, usually lay parties or estate agents, had settled the terms of a purchase of property and then went to their solicitors and asked them to carry through the sale; and the solicitors, conscious of the fact that it might be dangerous for their clients to be bound by a purely oral contract, would write to their opposite number a letter headed 'subject to contract' and go on to say: 'We confirm the sale of this property, etc.' However, in this situation it is totally different. If these letters reflect (as I said at the outset, it is virtually agreed that they do) the actual state of mind of the parties at the time, then the coming into existence of a full lease is unquestionably a condition of the agreement and there is no question here of the phrase being subsequently inserted by a party in order to protect himself from an agreement already arrived at. That, I think, is the only inference that can be drawn from the use by Mr Gray in his letter of the phrase 'subject to full lease being agreed' because Mr Gray is the person concerned; he is a layman; he is not a solicitor coming into a deal which has already been concluded between others and saying: 'Well, I must protect these people because they have entered into an oral agreement. I will ensure that no note or memorandum comes into existence by heading the letter "subject to contract".' Here is a lay person writing his understanding of the situation as he sees it and he uses this phrase which in my opinion is only consistent with an intention to ensure that a contractual liability does not arise until a full lease has been agreed. That seems to me to be the weight that has to be attached to those words.

Keane J. held that this was fatal to the existence of a concluded contract.

However, that case should be compared to *Lark Developments v The Right Honourable the Lord Mayor Alderman and Burgesses of the City of Dublin* (HC), 10 February 1993, unrep., where the Court held that a concluded agreement had been reached. In this case, a formal document had been drafted, approved and executed by both parties and the defendants had informed the plaintiffs that the City Council had approved of the terms of the sale. Murphy J. stated that the fact that the defendants had stated that 'formal notification of this approval' would be issued in due course did not affect the validity of the defendants' acceptance of the plaintiffs' offer.

Shirley Engineering Ltd *v* Irish Telecommunications plc (HC) 2 December 1999

The plaintiff agreed to buy property for £780,000 from the defendant. The High Court held that in the circumstances of the case the failure to agree a deposit was fatal to the finding of a concluded contract and the plaintiff appealed to the Supreme Court.

Geoghegan J.:

It would have been unthinkable that the Defendant would enter into an agreement of this kind without insisting on a deposit. Mr Shirley fully accepts that he would have had to pay a deposit and he had no fixed views as to what the nature of the deposit would have been. My impression was that he was willing to pay any deposit within reason. It was not the policy of Jones Lang Wootton [Agents for the Sale] to agree the amount of a deposit and I am satisfied that it was clearly understood between Mr

Shirley and Jones Lang Wootton that the question of deposit was to be negotiated between the Solicitors. Now it may well be that in many types of sales or perhaps sales in particular areas, there would be a recognised percentage deposit which would invariably be inserted in the written contracts. In such a case there might be circumstances depending on the nature of the discussions where the Court would imply an agreement to pay the standard deposit. For reasons which I will explain, I do not think that the implication of such a term by the Court would be contrary to the views expressed by Finlay C.J. in *Boyle v Lee* [1992] 1 IR 555, quite apart from what the views of the majority of the Supreme Court in that case may have been. But this particular case is rather similar to *Boyle v Lee* in that there is no evidence to establish that there was a recognised standard percentage deposit. On the contrary, Mr Shirley indicated that he would not have known what the particular rate would be and that he was not concerned with it and furthermore it was understood that it would be negotiated between the Solicitors. It is true that witnesses called on behalf of the Defendant indicated that as far as Telecom was concerned a deposit of 10 per cent would have been acceptable. But as far as the oral discussions go all that emerged in relation to the deposit was a certain willingness on the part of the Plaintiff to pay any kind of deposit (though one must assume this was within reason). In those circumstances I do not see how a Court could imply a term that the deposit was to be 10 per cent. The deposit is a most important term in an agreement of this kind as it is a major weapon in the armoury of a vendor. Once there was no express or implied agreement as to the amount of the deposit there cannot be said to have been a concluded agreement. For that reason also therefore I hold that there was no concluded agreement in this case.

Before concluding this part of my judgment, however, in relation to whether there was a concluded agreement or not, I intend as I indicated to comment further on *Boyle v Lee* ... as it featured so prominently in the argument. What is particularly important to consider is what exactly did Finlay C.J. hold in relation to agreement on a deposit. [Geoghegan J. quoted from the passage of Finlay CJ's judgment cited above on p.95.] There are a number of important points to be drawn from this passage. The first is that the former Chief Justice was strongly disputing that the question of a deposit was so unimportant or minor that the absence of agreement on it did not prevent there being a concluded agreement. That of course was on the basis of the facts in that particular case. However, as I have already indicated, the facts in this case are remarkably similar. The same comment could therefore equally be made in this case. Secondly, the former Chief Justice was pointing out that this would be so in a contract of this kind even if a purchaser has expressed willingness to make a deposit of the appropriate amount or the usual amount then experienced in transactions in Dublin. The important words there are 'is willing to make'. A unilateral willingness cannot give rise to an implied agreement. There could only be an implied term that the usual deposit was to be paid if the words or conduct of both parties indicated that that is what was intended. The mere willingness on the part of one party to pay such a deposit could not give rise to an implied term. For that reason I do not think that *Boyle v Lee* is in any way an authority for the proposition that there can never be an implied term that the usual deposit will be paid. But neither in that case nor in this case is there the necessary surrounding evidence to give rise to such implication. Hederman J. agreed with the judgment of Finlay C.J. While there may be some ambiguity in the judgment of O'Flaherty J., I think that it is reasonably clear from his judgment that he considered that the deposit was of importance and that there had been no express or implied agreement in relation to its amount.

Supermacs Ireland Ltd and McDonagh *v* Katesan (Naas) Ltd and Sweeney [2000] 4 IR 273

The plaintiffs alleged that they entered into an agreement in November 1997 to buy several different premises from the defendants. The defendants argued *inter alia* that no concluded agreement had been reached in relation to this property, citing the failure to agree a deposit, a completion date or vacant possession. The defendants appealed to the Supreme Court against a refusal by the High Court to dismiss the plaintiffs' request for specific performance as unsustainable. Unlike *Boyle v Lee*, the term 'subject to contract' was not used by any of the parties in this case.

Hardiman J.:

[Having quoted from the passage of Finlay CJ's judgment cited above on p.95.] It seems clear that this passage, if and insofar as it suggested that one could never have a concluded agreement for the sale of land without agreement as to the payment of a deposit, represented a considerable development of what the position had previously been. Both *Barrett v Costello* (unrep. High Court, Kenny J. 13 July 1973) and *Black v Kavanagh* (1974) 108 ILTR 91, had stated that it is not essential for a concluded agreement that there should be a stipulation in relation to a deposit. In the latter case Gannon J. having held that neither party attached any importance to the matter of the payment of a deposit or its amount, said:

> The question whether or not a deposit should be paid was not considered by the parties to be material matter, and in my opinion is not an essential term of such a contract.

The plaintiffs' answer to the submission based on *Boyle v Lee* [1992] 1 IR 555 was first to distinguish that case on its facts and to contend that the evidence here was open to the interpretation that there was to be no deposit. This, counsel on behalf of the plaintiffs said, could be decided as a matter of interpretation of the words and conduct of the parties: there was no necessity for an express agreement that there would be no deposit. Secondly, the plaintiffs contended that it was not obvious (and they need go no further for the purpose of this motion) that the passage quoted above from Finlay C.J. represented the view of the majority. If it did, it would represent a substantial change in the pre-existing law: there was ample scope for argument, it was contended, that the judgment of O'Flaherty J. which was pivotal on the point having regard to the views expressed by McCarthy and Egan JJ., did not go as far as the Chief Justice on the question of deposit.

There is no doubt that an agreement in relation to deposit is usual in concluded agreements for the sale of land. But the cases prior to *Boyle v Lee* [1992] 1 IR 555 demonstrate that it is not invariable. The evidence on affidavit falls well short of certainty in relation to what if anything was agreed on this point and it must not be forgotten that the agreement was between franchisor and franchisee and involved the sale of assets other than real property in addition to the premises themselves. In such an agreement, I believe there is at least scope for contention that a deposit may not have been considered essential. It seems to me that the factual position will be a good deal clearer after discovery and, more importantly, oral evidence, and I could not say that I am confident that, no matter what transpired at the trial, the defendants would necessarily win.

Furthermore, since there is scope for the view that the parties agreed nothing whatever about a deposit, it seems to me at least arguable that *Boyle v Lee* [1992] 1 IR 555 is distinguishable in the present circumstances. The circumstances of that case were that there had been an express agreement that there would be a deposit. It is not manifestly clear that the judgment of the Chief Justice in that case was intended to apply to other circumstances. It is also in my view arguable that the judgment of Finlay C.J. did not represent the view of a majority. On a motion such as this it is neither necessary nor desirable to go further than saying that I am not convinced that the defendants must win no matter what happens at the trial. It is noteworthy that *Boyle v Lee* was itself a decision of this court after a full hearing in the High Court and Finlay C.J. was careful, at p. 563 of the report, to set out precisely what the oral evidence on this topic had been. In my view it would be necessary to hear the evidence in this case before a final decision could be made as to what if anything was agreed between the parties on this topic, what may be implied from what they did and from other facts and to hear legal argument based on that evidence.

Counsel on behalf of the defendants also contended that the absence of agreement as to completion date was a fatal defect in the proposition that there was a concluded agreement. In relation to the Naas premises there was a statement on affidavit that completion was to be after vacant possession had been obtained; there was no reference to a completion date at all in relation to the other five properties. He further submitted that there was no evidence on the basis on which a completion date could be implied.

In *Boyle v Lee* [1992] 1 IR 555, Egan J. at p. 593 stated that:

It has long been established that where no time for performance is agreed the law implies an undertaking by each party to perform his part. of the contract within a time which is reasonable having regard to the circumstances of the case: *Simpson v Hughes* (1896) 66 L.J. Ch. 143.

This is a long-standing and, to my knowledge, unchallenged statement of the law. Accordingly, it cannot be said with certainty that, if the other essentials of a concluded agreement are present, the plaintiff's case is bound to fail by reason of the non-specification of a completion date.

Counsel on behalf of the defendants contended that, in order to construe the November agreements as constituting a completed agreement for the sale of land, one had to construe the evidence as committing the defendants to getting vacant possession. This was nowhere stated. He further pointed out that the evidence was silent on the question of what was to happen if vacant possession were not obtained.

In para. 5 of his affidavit the mediator, Mr Chambers, said that the second defendant pointed out during discussions that the Naas property had a sitting tenant and that there was a court case pending in relation to that person's entitlements. He went on:

As a result of this difficulty and because of the fact that vacant possession was not available, a sum of money was agreed to accommodate the eventuality of allowing this property out of a deal. In other words figures were agreed for either five properties or alternatively six properties.

This is at variance with the defendants' contention that no provision was made about the eventuality that vacant possession was not obtained. It is unnecessary to go further than holding that there is clearly an evidential issue on this matter. There is also a legal issue which may arise as to the significance of the fact that vacant possession was, in fact, subsequently obtained. Furthermore, there is a distinction between the elements necessary to constitute a completed agreement on the one hand and the consequences of failure to honour such agreement in relation to vacant possession on the other. It is at least arguable that the parties' failure to reach any agreement (if that is found to have occurred) on the question of vacant possession would merely have exposed the defendants to a claim for damages, if vacant possession had not been obtained.

Geoghegan J.

[Having. quoted from the passage of Finlay CJ's judgment cited above on p.95.]

It is important to subject that passage to some analysis. First of all in holding that there had to be agreement on the deposit the former Chief Justice was dealing only with the question whether there was a concluded agreement and not in any way with the question of whether there was a sufficient note or memorandum to satisfy the Statute of Frauds. The passage therefore has no bearing on any question as to whether if a deposit is agreed the amount of it should be set out in the note or memorandum. Secondly, it is quite clear from the passage that Finlay C.J. was holding beyond doubt on the evidence that the amount of the deposit was still to be negotiated. If that was so that was clearly the end of the matter because if a term of agreement has still to be negotiated how can it be said that there is a concluded agreement? When read in that light the passage in the judgment is crystal clear. Confusion has arisen because of references both in the case law and in the textbooks to expressions such as 'material terms' or similar words in relation to the issue of whether there is a concluded agreement. That type of wording should have no place in that consideration. It is a wholly different matter when one comes to consider the sufficiency of a note of memorandum. Only the 'material terms' need be included in a note or memorandum for it to be sufficient but all the terms, whether they be important or unimportant, must be agreed before there can be said to be a concluded agreement. It follows therefore that if the evidence is that there is going to be a deposit but that the amount of it is still to be negotiated, there cannot be a concluded agreement. The third point which arises from the passage cited relates to the words 'even if a purchaser is willing to make a deposit of the appropriate amount, or the usual amount then experienced in transactions in Dublin.' Some interpret these words as meaning that there can never be an implied agreement as to the deposit. I cannot agree with that view. What the former Chief Justice is saying is that the mere fact that the purchaser was willing to make an appropriate deposit could not render the agreement a concluded agreement if the understanding was that the deposit was to be negotiated. If the evidence establishes that two proposed parties to an agreement intended that their agreement should contain an express term relating to a deposit there cannot then be an implied term. Finlay C.J. is merely pointing out that a unilateral willingness on the part of the purchaser to pay a reasonable deposit is irrelevant in the absence of an agreement by the other party to accept that amount.

[Geoghegan J. quoted the passage of O'Flaherty J.'s judgment cited above on p.96.]

It is clear from this passage that the evidence in the case must have been that Mr McManus as agent for the vendor had expressly declined to take a deposit on the basis that the deposit question was to be left to be put into the formal contract. There might be situations where that would not necessarily mean that there was not a concluded agreement as, for instance, where each side simply trusted the other to submit to reasonable arrangements which the solicitors might include in the contract relating to deposit and other matters etc. But it is obvious that on the transcript of evidence in *Boyle v Lee* [1992] 1 IR 555, both Finlay C.J. and O'Flaherty J. accepted that the question of the deposit was still to be negotiated and that it was intended to be a term of the agreement. In my view Finlay C.J.'s reference to the importance of a deposit in such a transaction was simply a comment on credibility. He was taking the view that once the deposit was still to be negotiated that meant there was an actual term of the contract still to be negotiated and therefore there was no concluded contract. The views of O'Flaherty J., although expressed differently, are not dissimilar.

Before considering the application of those principles to this case I think it appropriate briefly to review some other relevant authorities. In *Lynch v O'Meara* (unrep. Supreme Court, 8 May 1975) Henchy J. (with whom O'Higgins C.J. and Walsh J. concurred) had this to say at p. 4:

> In this court, counsel for the plaintiff contended that the first document and the second document should be read together and as such should be held to constitute the note or memorandum required by the Statute of Frauds. However, before one comes to the question of a note or memorandum it is necessary to see if an entire contract was concluded on Sunday 24 October, for it is only in that event that the statutory note or memorandum would be required. If the negotiations between the parties had not ripened into the fullness of an entire contract the plaintiff's claim for specific performance would fail, not for want of the statutory evidence necessary for the enforcement of a contract for the sale of lands, but simply in default of the existence of any such contract. There would be no contract to be specifically enforced.

I merely quote that passage because of its clarity as to the correct approach. There cannot be a concluded agreement unless everything intended to be covered by the agreement has been either expressly or impliedly agreed.

Black v Kavanagh [1974] 108 ILTR 91 would seem to be an example of a case where on the evidence of the judge (Gannon J.) took the view that the parties intended to reach a concluded agreement without dealing with the question of a deposit. It seems clear from the following passage in the judgment at p. 95:

> I am satisfied on the evidence that the plaintiff and the defendant entered into a firm agreement for the sale and purchase of the defendant's house at No. 1 Dodder Park Grove, Rathfarnham, and the specific contents identified by them before they went to their respective solicitors about the matter. At that stage each of them believed that he had entered into a binding agreement which he expected and intended would be legally enforceable by or against him subject only to an obligation to facilitate the other reasonably as to when possession would be given and received. I find that neither of them attached any importance to the matter of the payment of a deposit or as to its amount. On the evidence before me I am satisfied that neither of them gave any authority to his solicitor to enter into or negotiate the terms of a contract in any way at variance with the agreement they had already reached, and that on the unconcluded matter of the date of possession their final agreement would be communicated—but not decided—by their solicitors. Both of them recognised and accepted that legal formalities, which to them were no more than formalities, were necessary and that the procedures of such nature would be followed on their behalf by the named solicitors, and no further authority was given to either solicitor. They relied on their solicitors to prepare any documents necessary to give legal force and effect to their agreement,

and each was willing and expected to put his hand to whatever documents his solicitor required for that purpose whether it be called the contract, or a draft contract, or a memorandum of agreement.

In this respect it is clear that the evidence in *Black v Kavanagh* as to the status of the deposit was quite different from the evidence in *Boyle v Lee* [1992] 1 IR 555.

In *Barrett v Costello* (unrep. High Court, Kenny J., 13 July 1973) (noted in (1973) 107 ILTR 239) the plaintiff told his agent that he was prepared to pay £40,000 and auctioneer's fees in relation to a particular property but had stipulated that there was a deposit of ten per cent. The agent spoke to the vendor and told him of the offer but omitted to mention the stipulation about the deposit of ten per cent. The defendant approved the sale and although it had not been mentioned to him he would have agreed to the ten per cent deposit had it been mentioned. On the particular facts of the case and the evidence as to how the negotiations ran Kenny J. held that there was an oral concluded agreement without any express term relating to the deposit. But he went on to observe as follows:

> In former times a deposit of twenty-five per cent was usual but the evidence satisfies me that a deposit of ten per cent has become a common practice in property sales in Dublin. I do not accept the submission of the defendant's counsel that there was never a concluded contract between the parties.

While it is not entirely clear, I think that Kenny J. was effectively holding that there was an implied term as to a deposit of ten per cent rather than that there was no agreement of any kind relating to deposit. But it does not much matter because if Kenny J. was holding that there was neither an express nor implied term as to the deposit then effectively he was holding that there was a concluded agreement with both parties ignoring the question of a deposit and leaving it as something to be dealt with ultimately when the formal contracts were drawn up. In such a situation however if for some reason or other the solicitors drawing up the contract were unable to agree on a deposit, the original oral agreement would remain binding and there would be no contractual deposit. The underlying legal principle was referred to by Lavery J. in his dissenting judgment in *Godley v Power* (1961) 95 ILTR 135 at p. 147 where he quotes with approval what he described as 'the oft quoted and oft approved' passage from the judgment of Parker J. in *Van Hatzfedlt Wildenberg v Alexander* [1912] 1 Ch. 284 at p. 288. The passage reads as follows:

> It appears to be well settled by the authorities that if the documents or letters relied on as constituting a contract contemplate the execution of a further contract between the parties, it is a question of construction whether the execution of the further contract is a condition or term of the bargain or whether it is a mere expression of the desire of the parties as to the manner in which the transaction already agreed to will go through. In the former case there is no enforceable contract either because the condition is unfulfilled or because the law does not recognise a contract to enter into a contract. In the latter case there is a binding contract and the reference to the more formal document may be ignored.

Applying the above principles are enunciated in the case law to this particular case, it would seem that if this action goes to trial there may be a number of alternative arguments relating to the question of the deposit. I would list these as follows:

1. That it was always intended that the parties would be contractually bound by a particular deposit yet to be negotiated.
2. That having regard to the nature of the transaction in this case and in particular the fact there was a franchisor–franchisee relationship between the parties, it was not intended that there be a deposit.
3. That in all the circumstances of the case there would have been an implied term that a reasonable deposit would be paid.
4. That in all the circumstances there was an implied term that the standard deposit normally payable in transactions of this kind would be paid.
5. That it would never have occurred to any of the parties that there would be a problem about the deposit and that a concluded agreement was reached ignoring it with the assumption that the solicitors when drawing up formal contracts would agree a deposit.

If the trial judge held in favour of the first of those arguments the action would undoubtedly have to be dismissed because there would then have been no concluded agreement. But the action would not have to be dismissed if any of the remaining four arguments held good. At this stage of the proceedings it would be wrong and indeed it would not be possible for this court to hold that only the first argument was open. There can be no question therefore in my view of the proceedings being struck out at this stage on the basis that there was no concluded agreement as to deposits. Still less could this court hold at this stage that there was no concluded agreement because of there being no reference to a completion date. In many sets of circumstances the court implies a term that the agreement will be completed within a reasonable time. The evidence in this case suggests that a speedy completion date was desired but it was known to both parties that there were problems of vacant possession in relation to the actual property the subject matter of this action and at this stage it could not be said with certainty that there was not an implied term as to completion.

Nor is the absence of any stipulation about vacant possession in relation to the property the subject matter of the action fatal to the plaintiffs' claim. On the contrary the general rule would be that in the absence of any such stipulation an obligation to give vacant possession must be presumed. . . .

(Denham J. concurred.)

Note

See also *McGill Construction Limited v McKeon* (High Court, Finnegan P.) May 19, 2004.

Agreements to Negotiate

At an early stage of negotiations, the parties may reach agreement on certain terms and the question may arise whether an enforceable agreement has been reached. Despite early indications that these agreements might be enforceable, it now seems unlikely that this will be the case.

In *Guardians of Kells Union v Smith* (1917) 52 ILTR 65, the plaintiffs invited tenders for the weekly supply of meat. The advertisement stated that the accepted contractor would have to execute a contract under seal with the plaintiffs before a certain date. The defendants' tender was successful but the plaintiffs purported to withdraw the tender and refused to supply the meat. The defendants sued for damages for breach of contract. The court awarded nominal damages to the plaintiffs for a breach of a contract to enter into the formal contract.

Hillas & Co. Ltd *v* Arcos Ltd (1932) 147 LT 503
Lord Wright (*obiter*):

If, however, what is meant is that the parties agree to negotiate in the hope of affecting a valid contract . . . There is no bargain except to negotiate, and negotiations may be fruitless and end without a contract ensuing; yet even then, in strict theory, there is a contract (if there is good consideration) to negotiate, though in the event of repudiation by one party the damages may be nominal, unless the jury thinks that the opportunity to negotiate was of some appreciable value to the injured party.

Courtney & Fairbairn Ltd *v* Tolaini Brothers (Hotels) Ltd [1975] 1 All ER 716

The Court of Appeal determined that a contract to negotiate a building contract, even though supported by consideration, lacked sufficient certainty to be legally binding.

Lord Denning:

That tentative opinion by Lord Wright does not seem to me to be well founded. If the law does not recognise a contract to enter into a contract (when there is a fundamental term yet to be agreed) it seems to me it cannot recognise a contract to negotiate. The reason is because it is too uncertain to have any binding force. No court could estimate the damages because no one can tell whether the negotiations would be successful or would fall through; or if successful, what the result would be. It seems to me that a contract to negotiate, like a contract to enter into a contract, is not a contract known to the law . . . I think we must apply the general principle that when there is a fundamental matter left undecided and to be the subject of negotiation, there is no contract.

Notes

1. In *Cadbury Ireland Ltd v Kerry Co-op Creameries* [1982] ILRM 77 Barrington J. noted that a particular clause was not binding because it involved at best 'a commitment to enter into honest negotiations'. However, in *Bula Ltd & Others v Tara Mines Ltd* [1987] IR 95 Murphy J. noted that despite the decisions in *Courtney & Fairbairn v Tolaini Brothers (Hotels) Ltd* and *Cadbury Ireland Ltd v Kerry Co-op Creameries* consideration still had to be given to the observations of Lord Wright in *Hillas*.
2. In *Coal Cliff Collieries Pty Ltd v Sijehama Pty Ltd* (1991) 24 NSWLR 1, while the New South Wales Court of Appeal noted that the law will not enforce an agreement to agree, the majority of the court expressly rejected the view that every promise to negotiate in good faith is unenforceable. The majority agreed with Lord Wright's speech in *Hillas* 'that provided that there was consideration for the promise, in some circumstances a promise to negotiate in good faith will be enforceable depending on its precise terms.'

3. Section 205 of the Restatement (2d) of Contract [1981], states: 'Every contract imposes upon each party a duty of good faith and fair dealing in its performance and enforcement'. In *Channel Home Centers, Grace Retail v Grossman* 795 F.2d 291 (3rd Cir. 1986) the US Court of Appeal noted:

> Although no Pennsylvania court has considered whether an agreement to negotiate in good faith may meet these conditions, the jurisdictions that have considered the issue have held that such an agreement, if otherwise meeting the requisites of a contract, is an enforceable contract. See, e.g., *Thompson v Liquichimica of America, Inc.*, 481 F.Supp. 365, 366 (E.D.N.Y.1979); ('Unlike an agreement to agree, which does not constitute a closed proposition, an agreement to use best efforts [or to negotiate in good faith] is a closed proposition, discrete and actionable.'); *accord Repro-system, B.V. v SCM Corp.*, 727 F2d 257, 264 (2d Cir. 1984); *Chase v Consolidated Foods Corp.*, 744 F.2d 566, 571, (7th Cir. 1984) . . . We are satisfied that Pennsylvania would follow this rule . . .

Walford *v* Miles [1992] 2 WLR 174

Lord Ackner:

The reason why an agreement to negotiate, like an agreement to agree, is unenforceable is simply because it lacks the necessary certainty . . . How can a court be expected to decide whether, subjectively, a proper reason existed for the termination of negotiations? The answer suggested depends upon whether the negotiations have been determined 'in good faith'. However the concept of a duty to carry on negotiations in good faith is inherently repugnant to the adversarial position of the parties when involved in negotiations. Each party to the negotiations is entitled to pursue his (or her) own interest, so long as he avoids making misrepresentations. To advance that interest he must be entitled, if he thinks it appropriate, to threaten to withdraw from further negotiations or to withdraw in fact in the hope that the opposite party may seek to reopen the negotiations by offering him improved terms. [Counsel], of course, accepts that the agreement upon which he relies does not contain a duty to complete the negotiations. But that still leaves the vital question: how is a vendor ever to know that he is entitled to withdraw from further negotiations? How is the court to police such an 'agreement'? A duty to negotiate in good faith is as unworkable in practice as it is inherently inconsistent with the position of a negotiating party. It is here that the uncertainty lies. In my judgment, while negotiations are in existence either party is entitled to withdraw from those negotiations, at any time and for any reason. There can be thus no obligation to continue to negotiate until there is a 'proper reason' to withdraw. Accordingly, a bare agreement to negotiate has no legal content.

Consider

Do you agree that a duty to negotiate in good faith is inherently inconsistent with the position of a negotiating party? Is it possible to negotiate aggressively and still in good faith?

Mamidoil-Jetoil Greek Petroleum Company SA v Cross-Appeal Okta Crude Oil Refinery AD Cross [2001] 2 Lloyds Rep. 76

Lord Justice Rix:

In my judgment the following principles relevant to the present case can be deduced from [*May and Butcher v The King* [1934] 2 KB 17n, *Hillas and Co. Limited v Arcos Limited* [1932] 147 LT 503, *Courtney & Fairbairn Ltd v Tolaini Brothers (Hotels) Ltd* [1975] 1 WLR 297, *Walford v Miles* [1992] 2 AC 128, *Foley v Classique Coaches Limited* [1934] KB 1, *G Scammell & Nephew Ltd v Ouston* [1941] AC 251, *British Bank for Foreign Trade v Novinex* [1949] 1 KB 623, *F&G Sykes (Wessex) Ltd v Fine Fare Ltd* [1967] 1 Lloyds Rep 53, *Sudbrook Trading Estate Ltd v Eggleton* [1983] AC 444, and *G Percy Trentham v Archital Luxfer* [1993] 1 Lloyds Rep. 25], but this is not intended to be an exhaustive list.

   i) Each case must be decided on its own facts and on the construction of its own agreement. Subject to that,

  ii) Where no contract exists, the use of an expression such as 'to be agreed' in relation to an essential term is likely to prevent any contract coming into existence, on the ground of uncertainty. This may be summed up by the principle that 'you cannot agree to agree'.

 iii) Similarly, where no contract exists, the absence of agreement on essential terms of the agreement may prevent any contract coming into existence, again on the ground of uncertainty.

 iv) However, particularly in commercial dealings between parties who are familiar with the trade in question, and particularly where the parties have acted in the belief that they had a binding contract, the courts are willing to imply terms, where that is possible, to enable the contract to be carried out.

  v) Where a contract has once come into existence, even the expression 'to be agreed' in relation to future executory obligations is not necessarily fatal to its continued existence.

 vi) Particularly in the case of contracts for future performance over a period, where the parties may desire or need to leave matters to be adjusted in the working out of their contract, the courts will assist the parties to do so, so as to preserve rather than destroy bargains, on the basis that what can be made certain is itself certain. *Certum est quod certum reddi potest.*

 vii) This is particularly the case where one party has either already had the advantage of some performance which reflects the parties' agreement on a long-term relationship, or has had to make an investment premised on that agreement.

viii) For these purposes, an express stipulation for a reasonable or fair measure or price will be a sufficient criterion for the courts to act on. But even in the absence of express language, the courts are prepared to imply an obligation in terms of what is reasonable.

 ix) Such implications are reflected but not exhausted by the statutory provision for the implication of a reasonable price now to be found in section 8(2) of the Sale of Goods Act 1979 (and, in the case of services, in section 15(1) of the Supply of Goods and Services Act 1982).

  x) The presence of an arbitration clause may assist the courts to hold a contract to be sufficiently certain or to be capable of being rendered so, presumably as indicating a commercial and contractual mechanism, which can be operated with the assistance of experts in the field, by which the parties, in the absence of agreement, may resolve their dispute...

(Lord Justices Waterhouse and Schiemann agreed.)

Note

In *Willis Management (Isle of Man) Ltd v Cable & Wireless Plc* [2005] 2 Lloyd's Rep. 597, the Court of Appeal held that an agreement to agree an essential term or terms was not a binding legal agreement and the court could not make for the parties the agreement which they had not made for themselves. Rix L.J. noted, 'It is true that where a binding contract already exists, a provision that prices for future years are to be agreed is likely to remain a binding part of that contract: see *Mamidoil-Jetoil Greek Petroleum Co SA v Okta Crude Oil Refinery AD* [2001] 2 Lloyd's Rep 76, especially at 91, an authority relied on by the judge below. However, Mamidoil distinguished between a long-term contract which undoubtedly binds the parties initially and an agreement like the present where there is an issue from the very beginning as to whether it ever amounted to a contract at all.'

BBC Worldwide Ltd *v* Bee Load Ltd (t/a Archangel Ltd) [2007] EWHC 134

BBC Worldwide entered into contracts with Archangel Ltd concerning the intended commercial exploitation of recordings held by the BBC of performances of pop and rock music. One of the contracts was a profit-share agreement for the exploitation of certain recordings. Clause 15 provided: 'BBCW agrees to consider in good faith any request by Archangel to extend the scope of this Agreement.'

Toulson L.J.:

The agreement to consider in good faith any request by Archangel to extend the scope of the agreement is in my view unenforceable as a matter of English law on the principle of *Walford v Miles*.

[Counsel for Archangel Ltd] relied on observations of Longmore L.J. in *Petromec Inc v Petroleo Brasileiro SA Petrobus* [2005] EWCA Civ 891 at paragraphs 115 to 121. At paragraph 116 he said:

The traditional objections to enforcing an obligation to negotiate in good faith are (1) that the obligation is an agreement to agree and thus too uncertain to enforce, (2) that it is difficult, if not impossible, to say whether, if negotiations are brought to an end, the determination is brought about in good or in bad faith, and (3) that, since it can never be known whether good faith negotiations would have produced an agreement at all or what the terms of any agreement would have been if it would have been reached, it is impossible to asses any loss caused by breach of the obligation.

He went to say that he doubted whether any of those objections would be good reasons for saying that the obligation to negotiate in good faith contained in the clause with which the court was concerned in that particular case was unenforceable.

In that case Petromec agreed to carry out certain work to a vessel and Brasileiro SA agreed to pay to Petromec the reasonable cost of doing so. The relevant clause went on to say Brasileiro SA agreed to negotiate the costs with Petromec in good faith. (The clause was rather more complex, but that was the essence.) So there was a substantive obligation on the part of Brasileiro SA to pay Petromec's reasonable costs, and the agreement to negotiate them in good faith was a matter of machinery for quantifying them. Longmore L.J. observed that the cost to Petromec was comparatively easy to ascertain; that if agreement was not reached, the court would itself have to ascertain the reasonable cost; and that if the court was able to conduct the exercise of finding the reasonable cost, there should be no difficulty in deciding what the result of good faith negotiations was likely to have been. Unless there were special factors present, it was likely to be the same as the reasonable cost. By contrast, in the present case clause 15 cannot be regarded as machinery for determining the amount of a contractual liability. The clause provides no criteria by which a court could determine whether 'in good faith' any particular request for any particular form of extension should be considered favourably.

Agreements to use reasonable endeavours

An agreement to make reasonable endeavours to achieve a specified and fixed objective is deemed to be a binding contract.

Rooney v Byrne [1933] IR 609

O'Byrne J.:

This action arises out of a contract, dated 24 April 1931, for the sale of a house and premises. The consideration for such sale to the plaintiff was expressed to be the sum of £400, and the contract, which is in the form of a proposal and acceptance, then states: 'I now lodge the sum of £50 in the hands of your agents, Messrs Towers & Co., 11 Lower Abbey Street, being portion of such purchase money, and will pay the balance on the completion of the purchase.' There is a further stipulation in the contract that 'This proposal is subject to me getting an advance on the property.'

   The first question for determination arises out of the last mentioned stipulation. It is argued that this proposal must be taken at its face value and that it makes the contract conditional on an advance being in fact obtained. In my opinion the stipulation means something more than that. We have to consider what was in the minds of the parties at the time the contract was signed. It is fairly clear that, in the contemplation of the parties, the purchaser would require to get an advance for the purpose of providing the purchase money, and the object was to provide that, in the event of his failing to get such an advance, the contract also failed. But in my opinion it was equally con- templated that the purchaser should make an effort to secure the advance. [Counsel] contends that it was competent for the purchaser to elect whether he would get an advance or not, and that, if he elected not to do so, the contract failed, even though he could get such an advance on reasonable terms. That, in my opinion, was not the intention of the parties. In my view the purchaser was bound to make reasonable efforts to secure the necessary advance, and, if he failed after such reasonable efforts to secure an advance on reasonable terms, the contract was then at an end.

Notes

1. In the *Rooney* case, the relevant requirement to use reasonable endeavours to obtain finance could be viewed as a condition precedent not to the existence of a contract but to liability under an existing contract. Similarly, in *Donwin Productions v. EMI Films*, unrep., *The Times*, March 9, 1984, the Court implied a term that the parties would negotiate in good faith because an enforceable contract already existed, although certain other covenants existed which lacked precision. Pain J. said that the *Courtney* decision did not stop him implying such a term 'once a firm agreement has been made and a further agreement is in contemplation'.
2. In *Queensland Electricity Generating Board v New Hope Collieries Pty Ltd* [1989] 1 Lloyd's Rep. 205 the Privy Council implied an obligation 'to make reasonable endeavours' to agree the appropriate terms.
3. In *Rhodia International Holdings Ltd and another v Huntsman International LLC* [2007] EWHC 292, the High Court held that a contractual obligation to use 'reasonable endeavours' was less stringent than one to use 'best endeavours'.

Lock-out agreements

Agreements to negotiate are often accompanied by lock-out agreements. Whereas the former involves a positive duty to negotiate with the other party, the latter involves a prohibition on negotiating with any third party or parties.

Walford and Others *v* Miles and Others [1992] 2 WLR 174

The respondents entered into discussions with the appellants with a view to selling their beneficial interest in a company and its business premises. On 17 March the appellants orally agreed to provide a 'comfort letter' in return for the respondents agreeing to break off negotiations with any third party, and to deal with the appellants exclusively. The comfort letter was dispatched and a draft share-purchase agreement was sent to the respondents, but the respondents decided not to proceed with negotiations and later sold to a third party. The appellants sued for breach of contract. The trial judge found that the oral agreement of 17 March was a separate and collateral agreement which the respondents had repudiated. On appeal the Court of Appeal held that the collateral agreement was merely an agreement to negotiate and was thus unenforceable. The appellants appealed to the House of Lords.

Lord Ackner:

There is clearly no reason in the English contract law why A, for good consideration, should not achieve an enforceable agreement whereby B, agrees for a specified period of time, not to negotiate with anyone except A in relation to the sale of his property. There are often good commercial reasons why A should desire to obtain such an agreement from B. B's property, which A contemplates purchasing, may be such as to require the expenditure of not inconsiderable time and money before A is in a position to assess what he is prepared to offer for its purchase or whether he wishes to make any offer at all. A may well consider that he is not prepared to run the risk of expending such time and money unless there is a worthwhile prospect, should he desire to make an offer to purchase, of B, not only then still owning the property, but of being prepared to consider his offer. A may wish to guard against the risk that, while he is investigating the wisdom of offering to buy B's property, B may have already disposed of it or, alternatively, may be so advanced in negotiations with a third party as to be unwilling or for all practical purposes unable, to negotiate with A. But I stress that this is a negative agreement—B by agreeing not to negotiate for this fixed period with a third party, locks himself out of such negotiations. He has in no legal sense locked himself into negotiations with A. What A has achieved is an exclusive opportunity, for a fixed period, to try and come to terms with B, an opportunity for which he has, unless he makes his agreement under seal, to give good consideration. I therefore cannot accept [counsel's] proposition . . . that without a positive obligation on B to negotiate with A, the lock-out agreement would be futile.

The agreement . . . contains the essential characteristics of a basic valid lock-out agreement, save one. It does not specify for how long it is to last. Bingham L.J. sought to cure this deficiency by holding that the obligation upon Mr Miles and his wife not to deal with other parties should continue to bind them 'for such time as is reasonable in all the circumstances.' He said: 'the time would end once the parties acting in good faith had found themselves unable to come to mutually acceptable terms . . . the defendants could not . . . bring the reasonable time to an end by procuring a bogus impasse, since that would involve a breach of the duty of reasonable good faith which parties such as these must, I think, be taken to owe to each other.' However, as Bingham L.J. recognised, such a duty, if it existed, would indirectly impose upon the Miles a duty to negotiate in good faith. Such a duty, for the reasons which I have given above, cannot be imposed. . . .

(Goff, Jauncey and Browne-Wilkinson L.JJ. concurred.)

Note

See Neill, 'A Key to Lockout Agreements' vol. 108 LQR 405 (1992) and Davenport, 'Lockout Agreements' vol. 107 LQR 366 (1991).

Triatic Limited *v* Cork County Council [2006] IEHC 111

The plaintiff had been in negotiations with the defendants for a considerable period of time with a view to developing Fort Camden, a historical fort in Cork, as a tourist amenity. It argued *inter alia* that it had an agreement that negotiations would continue until a final binding agreement could be concluded. As a consequence, it objected *inter alia* to the defendant advertising for other purchasers of the site pending completion of negotiations with it. The defendant denied the existence of any such contract.

Laffoy J.

The authority primarily relied on by the defendant was the decision of the House of Lords in *Walford v. Miles* [1992] 2 AC 128 . . . The defendant cited an English authority in which a lock-out agreement was enforced: *Pitt v. PHH Asset Management Limited* [1993] 4 All ER 961. There, in a classic gazumping scenario, the Court of Appeal enforced against the defendant vendor an agreement by the defendant vendor to sell the property to the plaintiff for £200,000 and not to consider any further offers provided the plaintiff exchanged contracts within two weeks of receipt of a draft contract, in circumstances where the court considered the plaintiff had given consideration in withdrawing a threat to seek injunctive relief against the defendant and in committing to a time limit of two weeks for exchange of contracts.

In response to the defendant's submissions, counsel for the plaintiff submitted that the court should not regard the decision of the House of Lords in *Walford v. Miles* as a persuasive authority. In any event, it was suggested, it is distinguishable on the facts, in that in the instant case the court is not concerned with a bare agreement to negotiate; through the course of dealings between the parties, the matter has progressed beyond that stage. The plaintiff referred the court to the helpful commentary on good faith and fair dealing in a contractual context in McDermott on *Contract Law* (Butterworths, 2001) at paras. 7.41 to 7.44 inclusive. In particular, reference was made to the two Irish cases referred to in the commentary as examples of the Irish courts being prepared to enforce an express or implied obligation to use reasonable efforts to achieve some stipulated result: *Rooney v Byrne* [1933] I.R. 609; and *Fluid Power Technology Company v. Sperry (Ireland) Limited* (HC), 22 February 1985, unrep. In each of those cases, the court was concerned with a situation in which a contract existed. In the first, the contract was for the purchase of a house subject to the purchaser getting a mortgage. It was held that the purchaser was bound to make reasonable efforts to secure the necessary advance. The second concerned the exercise of a power to terminate a distributorship agreement in the context of an application for an interlocutory injunction. Costello J. held that the plaintiff, which was seeking the interlocutory injunction, had made out a fair case that there was an implied obligation to exercise the termination power in a bona fide manner, which he explained as meaning:

> ... that when they give reasons for termination these reasons must not be spurious ones, but it also means that if they honestly believe them to be valid, then even if they are subsequently proved to have been wrong the notice is valid. So, if honestly dissatisfied with the plaintiffs as distributors, this would mean that the notice of termination could be given.

A New Zealand authority, *Livingstone v Roskilly* [1992] 3 NZLR 230, in which Thomas J. stated that he would not 'exclude from our common law the concept that, in general, the parties to a contract must act in good faith in making and carrying out the contract', which is referred to in McDermott, was also relied on by counsel for the plaintiff. It was submitted that the court should apply that dictum rather than following the approach adopted in *Walford v Miles*. Like the Irish authorities cited by the plaintiff, that dictum is concerned with the implication of the concept of good faith and fair dealing on the part of the parties to an existing contractual relationship. No authority has been cited in which that concept was applied to negotiations, although McDermott does refer to extra-judicial and academic comment on the topic. Counsel for the plaintiff also referred the court to a decision of the Court of Appeal of England and Wales in which *Walford v Miles* was considered: *Petromec Inc. v Petroleo Brasileiro SA Petrobras* [2005] EWCA Civ 891. As was pointed out by Mance L.J. in his judgment in that case (at para. 120), the Court of Appeal was bound by the decision of the House of Lords for what it decided. He pointed out that the main distinction between *Walford v. Miles* and the *Petromec* case was that in the former there was no concluded agreement, since everything was 'subject to contract', and there was, moreover, no express agreement to negotiate in good faith. The comments of Mance L.J. in *Petromec*, which were clearly *obiter*, concerned the enforcement of an express provision in the contract under consideration, whereby the other contracting party agreed to negotiate certain extra costs with Petromec 'in good faith'. Having quoted Lord Ackner's view in *Walford v. Miles* [that 'while negotiations are in existence either party is entitled to withdraw from those negotiations, at any time and for any reason. There can be thus no obligation to continue to negotiate until there is a "proper reason" to withdraw. Accordingly a bare agreement to negotiate has no legal content.'], Mance L.J. stated as follows (at para. 121):

> That shows the difference from the present case. Clause 12.3 of the Supervision Agreement is not a bare agreement to negotiate. It is not irrelevant that it is an express obligation which is part of a complex agreement drafted by City of London solicitors . . . It would be a strong thing to declare unenforceable a clause into which the parties have deliberately and expressly entered. I have already observed that it is of comparatively narrow scope. To decide that it has 'no legal content' to use Lord Ackner's phrase would be for the law deliberately to defeat the reasonable expectations of honest men, to adapt slightly the title of Lord Steyn's . . . lecture delivered . . . on 24 October 1996 (113 LQR 433 (1977)). At p. 439 Lord Steyn hoped that the House of Lords might reconsider *Walford v. Miles* with the benefit of fuller argument.

For my part, I find the reasoning of Lord Ackner persuasive, particularly when applied to the facts of this case, in which the dealings and negotiations between the plaintiff and the defendant, the ultimate objective of which was to achieve agreement on terms for the development, subject to planning permission, and the acquisition by the plaintiff of Fort Camden, which the defendant could recommend to the elected members of the defendant, involved a considerably greater element of complexity, and, consequently, more scope for uncertainty than negotiations for the purchase of the shares of a company and a leasehold property or the purchase of a house . . . While the issue of what, if any, consideration was given by the plaintiff for that undertaking was not addressed, it can be assumed that consideration was given, in that the plaintiff was prepared to commit time and resources to preparing and submitting a development proposal. On that basis, I am prepared to find that between March 1995 and November 1996 there was a contractual relationship between the defendant and the plaintiff created by the letter of 10 March 1995 and the subsequent extensions of the exclusivity period. That agreement was in the nature of what Lord Ackner described as a 'lock-out' agreement. What the plaintiff achieved under it was an exclusive opportunity for the extended period to submit a comprehensive development proposal for Fort Camden. The defendant complied with its obligations under that agreement. It dealt exclusively with the plaintiff in relation to the development of Fort Camden up to the expiry of the exclusivity period. It accepted and considered the development proposal presented to it by the plaintiff. In my view, on the evidence, it did so in a bona fide manner. The defendant's contractual obligations terminated on the expiry of the exclusivity period.

What happened after November 1996 was that, while the defendant considered the development proposal submitted by the plaintiff to be inadequate, on the initiative of the defendant a new phase of negotiation commenced on 3 February 1997. In essence, the plaintiff's case is that there was an agreement to continue those negotiations until they would come to fruition in the form of a formal contract, which, as a matter of law, can only mean until the defendant's officials were prepared to recommend the agreed terms for the development, subject to planning permission, and the acquisition of Fort Camden by the plaintiff to the elected members. I have no doubt that, if a finding could be made on the evidence that there was such an agreement, it would be unenforceable for lack of certainty.

To take what, perhaps, would have been the simplest component of the trans-action, the acquisition price, as an example, one is entitled to ask how a court could be expected to decide the point at which the negotiations on that component had come to fruition. By September 1997 the point which had been reached in relation to the acquisition price was that the defendant had indicated an asking price of £500,000 some two years earlier. The plaintiff had neither indicated that the asking price was acceptable to it, nor had it made a counter-offer. Although very little was offered by way of analysis of this aspect of the case, what happened in 1997 is that the plaintiff had adopted the position that there had been an agreement, that the defendant was in breach, and that the plaintiff was entitled to elect to enforce the agreement or consider that it was discharged from further performance. It was only at the hearing that the plaintiff elected to terminate the alleged agreement. The breach alleged is that the defendant was not entitled to disengage other than for bona fide and valid reasons and none such existed. But, if the dealings between the parties had not taken the turn they took in September 1997 and negotiations had continued, and if the parties were unable to reach consensus on the acquisition price, how could it be said that one or other party could not withdraw? If the defendant persisted in an asking price of £500,000, and the plaintiff considered that the property was worth only half that price, would the plaintiff not have been entitled to withdraw? If there was to be a contract on the lines suggested by the plaintiff, both contracting parties would have to be locked into it. If either party withdrew because it considered the acquisition price proposed by the other to be unsatisfactory, to adopt the terminology of Lord Ackner, how could a court be expected to decide whether a proper reason existed for termination? Given that on the plaintiff's case an obligation to deal in good faith is to be implied in the alleged agreement, which must be assumed to bind both contracting parties, a subjective, rather than an objective, approach would be required in making that decision. In my view the court would be faced with an impossible task . . . Accordingly, I find that from February 1997 onwards the plaintiff and the defendant were merely in negotiations and no contractual relationship existed between them.

Notes

1. In *Triatic*, the extra judicial comment referred to was by Sir Anthony Mason, the former Chief Justice of Australia who stated (at (2000) 116 LQR 66) that 'the application of specific good faith and fair dealing duties, based on the reasonable expectations of the parties, might advance the interests of justice' and 'bring greater coherence and unity to the varied array of principles which are presently available in the area of contract performance'.
2. In *Pitt v PHH Asset Management Ltd* [1993] 4 All ER 961 referred to above, Bingham M.R. described the lock-out agreement as the prospective purchaser's 'one means of protection' against unscrupulous vendors engaging in gazumping. Such 'unprincipled' behaviour, he noted, was permitted by the rule that contracts for the sale and purchase of land must

be evidenced (or now made) in writing and the rule that terms agreed subject to contract do not give rise to a binding contract.

EXERCISES

1. Callan produces children's puzzle books and comics. He advertises in *The Irish Times* seeking a production designer to join his company. From the applications received, Callan interviews two candidates, Esme and James. Callan emails Esme on Monday 5 July and offers her the job. He stipulates that she must 'accept the job offer in writing by 9am the following Monday, 12 July'. As Esme's computer has been affected by a virus, she does not receive any emails. When she phones Callan's secretary on Friday 9 July to enquire about the position, she is informed that a job offer has been sent to her 'to be responded to by 9am this Monday morning'. No mention is made of a mode of response. That night, Esme phones Callan's direct line and leaves a message on his voice mail accepting the offer. On the Monday morning at 8.50am Esme also faxes a letter of acceptance into Callan's office. Although this letter arrives immediately, Callan's office does not open until 9am and it is only at 9.10am that his secretary checks the fax machine. Callan is not impressed by what he views as a lack of enthusiasm and he employs James instead. Esme announces her intention to sue for breach of contract. Advise Esme.

2. Bob places a note on a noticeboard in University College Galway offering to sell his car for €4,000 'on a first come, first served basis'. The note asks those interested in purchasing the car to 'email or fax me'. Trina emails Bob agreeing to pay €4,000 and asking 'if it is not too much trouble can you also deliver the car to my home in Limerick?' One day later, Liam faxes Bob asking 'would you accept €3,500?' Bob reads the fax but because of a fault on his computer cannot read the text of Trina's email. Bob faxes Liam back a note stating that 'we will split the difference and unless I hear from you in 24 hours, the car is yours for €3,750'. Liam is delighted to receive this note and tells all his friends of his new purchase. Advise Bob as to his contractual liability (if any) to Trina and Liam.

3. Arghus erroneously advertises new Sony playstations on its web site for €4.20 instead of the retail price of €42. Bill, Ben and Flower both place separate orders for ten units each. Flower receives no response. Bill and Ben receive automated order confirmations stating that €42 will be charged to their credit cards. Ben's credit card is subsequently charged but Bill's is not. Arghus subsequently contact Bill, Ben and Flower, refusing to proceed with the sale. Arghus asserts that no contract has been formed. Advise Bill, Ben and Flower.

4. Lucy reads an advertisement in her local paper for Everest Ltd, a new outdoor clothing manufacturing firm. The advertisement states that Everest Ltd is so confident about the heat-retaining capacity of its clothes that it promises '€5,000 plus a cup of hot tea to anyone who wears the new winter range to the top of Mount Everest and feels cold'. As she has

reserved a place on a team seeking to reach the summit of Mount Everest the following month, she buys an outfit from Everest Ltd and brings it with her. Everest Ltd subsequently publishes a notice purporting to withdraw any promises and/or offers made in respect of its clothing range. As Lucy has already left the country, she does not see this. Lucy successfully reaches the summit of Mount Everest while wearing her new outfit. On her return to base camp she is diagnosed with frostbite and informs everyone that she was indeed cold on the summit. She seeks to recover €5,000 from Everest Ltd, who argue that no contract exists. Advise Lucy.

5. Susan enters into a contract with Joe to purchase his house for 'market value' subject to obtaining a mortgage from Bank of Ireland. No deposit is agreed and the closing date is stated to be two days after the mortgage is obtained. Does a binding legal agreement exist?

6. Gail advertises her car for sale for '€5,000 or nearest offer'. Carrie agrees to pay her the full price when she gets paid the following week if Gail agrees not to sell to anyone else in the meantime. Carrie also enquires about Gail's roof rack. Gail promises that she will enter into a contract to sell that to Carrie the following week. If Gail sells the car and roof rack to someone else, can Carrie sue her for breach of contract?

Chapter Three

Contract as a Promised Exchange

AGREEMENTS UNDER SEAL

Common law recognises that a promise is enforceable if it is set out in a deed under seal. A seal may be affixed to the contract by using wax, a red sticker or simply by drawing a circle with 'LS' (*locus sigilli*) stamped on it. In many jurisdictions the requirement of sealing has been abolished by legislation. Treitel has suggested that the concept of a deed constitutes a recognition by law of 'a perfectly safe and relatively simple means of making gratuitous promises binding' (Treitel, *The Law of Contract* (12th edn) 2007 at p. 160).

Parsons v Romaine et al 205 (2001) DLR (4th) 320

The appellant's uncle Claude Romaine transferred the beneficial interest in certain property to the appellant and his wife by means of a letter of gift and declaration of trust ('the gift documents'). These documents stated that they were signed, sealed and delivered. A photocopy of the documents showed a black circle beside each signature which the parties accepted was a copy of a red 'wafer' seal which had been affixed to the documents by the lawyer who prepared them prior to their execution. The appellant subsequently attempted to enforce this agreement.

Levine J.A.:

In *Friedmann Equity Developments Inc. v Final Note Ltd* [2000] 1 SCR 842, 188 DLR (4th) 269, the Supreme Court [of Canada] unanimously confirmed the applicability of the sealed contract rule as part of the common law of Canada, rejecting the argument that it should be abolished as anachronistic and technical.

Bastarache J. for the court described the rule (at paras. 19–20) as follows:

The practice of sealing documents is one which is centuries old and which predates much of our modern legal history. Originally, it was used as a means of authenticating a document when most individuals were unable to sign their names. However, as time passed, the seal became a symbol of the solemnity of a promise and began to serve an evidentiary function. The seal rendered the terms of the underlying transaction indisputable, and thus rendered additional evidence unnecessary . . . A contract under seal derived, and still derives, its validity from the form of the document itself . . .

Because a contract under seal derives its validity from its form alone, there are several incidents of such a contract which differ from those of a simple contract.

The fundamental difference between contracts under seal and simple contracts is in relation to the doctrine of consideration. The law will enforce a contract under seal even without consideration. Therefore, a gratuitous promise which is expressed in an instrument under seal is enforceable.

In confirming the rule as part of the law of Canada, the court acknowledged that it is no longer applicable in other jurisdictions and has been criticised by academics and some courts in Canada (at para. 40). The court held (at paras. 47–8):

> The seal continues to serve a useful purpose in our law. It allows a promise to be enforced without evidence of consideration and, more importantly in the context of this case, grants parties to a contract a simple means of ensuring that they will not be liable to anyone but the parties named therein . . .

The effect of the sealed contract rule in this case, assuming all of its requirements have been met, is that the Gift Documents are given legal effect as a contract rather than as an *inter vivos* gift. The application of the sealed contract rule turns on Claude's intention when he executed the Gift Documents. The Supreme Court said in *Friedmann* (at para. 36):

> To create a sealed instrument, the application of the seal must be a conscious and deliberate act. At common law, then, the relevant question is whether the party intended to create an instrument under seal.

Friedmann concerned the rule that an undisclosed principal cannot sue or be sued on a contract under seal. The quoted portions of Bastarache J.'s reasons make it clear that the decision is equally applicable to the rule that a contract under seal does not require consideration. Furthermore, in *Friedmann*, the seal in question was that of a corporation and, as discussed by Bastarache J. at para. 37: 'Corporate seals have a different legal effect than the seal of an individual.' The question of the intention to create a sealed instrument arises, however, whether the party executing a document under seal is an individual or a corporation.

The Law Reform Commission of British Columbia, in its 'Report on Deeds and Seals' (Vancouver: 1988), helpfully summarised the law with respect to the execution of sealed documents (at p. 9):

> Whether a deed is binding on its maker depends upon whether he intended to execute and be bound by it as his deed. This he signifies by executing the document under seal, which raises the issue of what is a sufficient act of sealing.
>
> Affixing a seal does not in itself make an instrument a deed. That must be determined from the circumstances, such as the acts and words of the instrument's maker. It is useful to note the classic *dicta* of Blackburn J. [in *Xenos v Wickham* (1866), LR 2 HL 296]:
>
> > No particular technical form of words or acts is necessary to render an instrument the deed of the party sealing it. The mere affixing the seal does not render it a deed: but as soon as there are acts or words sufficient to show that it is intended by the party to be executed as deed presently binding on him, it is sufficient.
>
> It has been held that what constitutes a good seal is a question of law, while what constitutes a sufficient act of sealing is a question of fact. This is not a particularly useful distinction. Whether something constitutes a good seal invariably involves a consideration of the process of sealing. Ultimately, the issue becomes

whether the maker of the instrument *intended* to execute it under seal and make it a deed.

The footnote to the final sentence in this passage provides further insight into the issue of intent:

> From a practical perspective the tests are reconciled through an evidentiary presumption. If the seal is regular in form and material substance, a sufficient act of sealing is presumed: The more novel or unusual the form of the seal, such as a soot mark or finger impression, the more the enquiry becomes focused on the process of sealing to determine the maker's intention. See also David C. Hoath, 'The Sealing of Documents—Fact or Fiction,' (1980) 43 Mod. L. Rev. 415; *First National Securities Ltd v Jones*, [1978] 1 Ch. 109 (CA); *TCB Ltd v Gray*, [1986] 1 All ER 587 (Ch.).

The question then arises: what evidence is required to demonstrate that a person who signed a document on which a seal was affixed intended to make that document a deed, or a sealed document?

The Law Reform Commission Report draws a distinction between the 'form and material substance' of the seal and whether there was a 'sufficient act of sealing'.

Whether the seal is regular in 'form and material substance' relates to the physical form or appearance of the seal or the document. There are conflicting authorities about whether any physical representation of a seal must be present. . . . In British Columbia, a document was found to be sealed where it stated that it was 'Given under seal', but no wafer seals were affixed (*Hongkong Bank of Canada v New Age Graphic Design Inc.* [1996] BCJ No. 907 (QL) (SC); following *Canadian Imperial Bank of Commerce v Dene Mat Construction Ltd* [1988] 4 WWR 344 (NWTSC), where the document stated it was 'Given under seal' and the signature appeared beside a scrolled indication of a seal printed on the form before it was signed. In *872899 Ontario Inc. Iacovoni* (1998), 163 DLR (4th) 263 (Ont. CA); application for leave to appeal to SCC dismissed 11 February 1999, [1998] SCCA No. 476 (QL) [reported 167 DLR (4th) vi], the Court of Appeal held that a document was not sealed where it was stated to be 'signed, sealed and delivered', but there was no indication that any seal had been affixed opposite or near the signatures and there were no 'printed brackets or parentheses or the initials L.S., or a darkened spot resembling a photostatic copy of a law seal' (at para. 10).

In this case, the Gift Documents stated that they were 'signed, sealed and delivered' and the copies in evidence have the 'darkened spot resembling a photostatic copy of a law seal'. I have concluded that the lawyer who prepared them affixed wafers, which appear as darkened circles on the copies, before he gave them to Michael for Claude's signature. Lawyers know that under the sealed contract rule, gratuitous obligations are binding if made under seal and affix seals on transfers by gift for that reason. In my view, there is sufficient evidence to conclude that there were wafer seals on the Gift Documents when they were signed by Claude.

The presence of the wafer seals on the Gift Documents when they were signed satisfies the 'form and material substance' requirement.

Whether there was a 'sufficient act of sealing' relates to the procedure followed when the document was executed. There must be 'acts or words sufficient to show that it is intended by the party to be executed as his deed and presently binding upon him' (*Xenos v Wickam* (1866) LR 2 HL 296 at p. 312).

Traditionally, the executant placed his or her finger or thumb on the seal and at the same time uttered the words 'I deliver this as my act and deed'. There is no evidence that Claude did anything of the sort, or even that he knew there were seals on the Gift

Documents when he signed them. The Law Reform Commission suggests (at p. 12); 'Today, the signature, combined with whatever constitutes a seal in form and material substance is sufficient.' The rationale for that conclusion is 'that anyone signing a legal document, particularly if his signature is witnessed, understands that there will be legal consequences' (at p. 13).

Authority of this court supports that view. In *Ray v Gillmore* (1958), 26 WWR 138, 14 DLR. (2d) 572 (BCCA), this court found that a guarantee was enforceable as a sealed document although '[i]t is clear that neither party knew at the time the document was executed the effect or purpose of a seal' (at p. 141). The Court found from the form and words of the document that it was executed under seal (at p. 142). The Gift Documents contain similar wording. As to intent, the Court in Ray said (at p. 142):

> Construed in this way, there is then, a *testimonium* clause and an attestation clause and the seal being there when the document was signed, there is the presumption that the defendant intended to execute this as a sealed document and that presumption has not been rebutted.

On this authority, the conclusion that Claude signed a document on which a seal was present satisfies the requirement that he intended to make the Gift Documents sealed contracts. There is no evidence to the contrary. In modern law, the seal has become 'a symbol of the solemnity of a promise' (*Friedmann* at para. 19). Michael's evidence that following the signing of the Gift Documents, there was discussion among him, Claude and Ms Hoyd that 'it was sort of marked as a . . . milestone, in terms of passing the property over towards myself' indicates that they were aware of the significance of what they had signed.

From the evidence of the circumstances of the execution of the Gift Documents, I am satisfied that Claude understood and intended the Gift Documents to be legally binding on him.

I would give effect to the Gift Documents as sealed contracts.

CONSIDERATION

Because the common-law system of contract (save in cases where a promise is recorded under seal) has not imposed general requirements that promises be recorded in writing, or surrounded by other so-called requirements of form, the common-law has not been able to easily filter out promises that are contractual from other kinds of transaction, such as a gift promise. As we saw in Chapter 1, the classical means of doing this was through the evolution of consideration. (*Governors of Dalhousie College v Boutilier*, p.18 above.) What precisely is meant by consideration remains a matter of controversy, with scholars arguing about the differences between equitable and common-law perspectives as well as the internal features— promise *per se*, reliance or exchange. The orthodox view is that the exchange, or bargain theory, passed into the literature, and judicial utterances, as the paradigm, in the late nineteenth century, although even then the exceptions found in the case-law made this model neither a universal nor a reliable basis for predicting enforceability. As Sutton noted (below) 'a rigorous application of the bargain theory . . . would result in many decisions being found to be outside it.' Several lines of case-law appear to undermine the bargain theory. Furthermore, in Ireland, the recent cases on promissory estoppel and legitimate expectation make it clear that contract is only one way in which a promise, or a reasonably based belief or anticipated benefit, will be given legal substance by the judiciary.

SECTION ONE—BARGAIN

Atiyah, P. S., 'Consideration: A Restatement', *Essays on Contract* (Oxford: Clarendon Press, 1986)

1. *The Nature and Purposes of Consideration*

. . .

The truth is that the courts have never set out to create a doctrine of consideration. They have been concerned with the much more practical problem of deciding in the course of litigation whether a particular promise in a particular case should be enforced. Since it is unthinkable that any legal system could enforce *all* promises it has always been necessary for the courts to decide which promises they would enforce. When the courts found a sufficient reason for enforcing a promise they enforced it; and when they found that for one reason or another it was undesirable to enforce a promise, they did not enforce it. It seems highly probable that when the courts first used the word 'consideration' they meant no more than that there was a 'reason' for the enforcement of a promise. If the consideration was 'good', this meant that the court found sufficient reason for enforcing the promise. All this is not to suggest that the law was ever unprincipled, or that judges ever decided cases according to personal or idiosyncratic views of what promises it was desirable to enforce. As always in the common law, it was the collective view of the judges, based largely on the conditions and moral values of the community, which prevailed over a period of time. The doctrine of precedent, then as now, was always available as an aid to the courts in deciding what promises to enforce. . .

At a relatively early date it was established that the courts would enforce a promise if another promise or an act was given in return for it; and also that they would not normally enforce a promise if it was merely intended as a gift with no return of any kind. In the first class of case it came therefore to be said that there was good consideration; there were good reasons for enforcing the promise. In the second class there was no such reason, and therefore no consideration. But it also became clear from a very early time that the whole law could not be reduced to such very simple terms. There were some cases in which a promise was given in return for another promise or an act, in which for one reason or another it was felt unjust or inexpedient that the promise should be enforced. Such cases could be, and sometimes were explained by saying that there was no consideration for the promise; but as the nineteenth century wore on, an alternative approach began to manifest itself. This was to say that there was good consideration (though perhaps the word 'good' would more usually be omitted) but that nevertheless the promise was unenforceable for other reasons, for example, because it had been extorted by duress, or fraud, or because it was illegal. The last type of case was often dealt with by saying that the consideration was unlawful; a judge who formulated his reasons in this way would perhaps, if pressed, have said that there was no 'good' consideration . . .

More recently still, this alternative approach has hardened so that courts now find nothing inconsistent in holding that there is consideration for a promise, but nevertheless refusing to enforce it because the transaction is illegal. This approach also manifests itself in the relatively modern device of refusing to enforce a promise on the ground that the promisor did not 'intend' to create legal relations by his promise. Where this is done (as it usually is) in a case where there is no express disavowal of the intent to create legal relations, it appears to be merely a legal justification for refusing to enforce a promise which the courts think, for one reason or another, it is unjust or impolitic to enforce. There seems no doubt that a hundred years ago the courts would have dealt with these problems in terms of consideration ...

This change of approach is symptomatic of the change which has developed in the way lawyers think about consideration. It is no longer thought that consideration is a compendious word simply indicating whether there are good reasons for enforcing a promise; it is widely assumed that consideration is a technical requirement of the law which has little or nothing to do with the justice or desirability of enforcing a promise. Modern lawyers thus see nothing incongruous in asserting that a promise made for good consideration should nevertheless not be enforced ...

Exactly the same development has taken place with regard to those promises which are not normally enforced, that is the promise to make a gift with no return of any kind. Since the courts first decided that such promises were not enforceable, it came to be asserted that gratuitous promises were promises given without consideration. But in course of time, occasions arose when the courts found that there were sometimes very good reasons for enforcing gratuitous promises in certain cases, and they accordingly enforced them. When cases of this kind arose during the first part of the nineteenth century the natural approach of the courts was to say that there *was* consideration—which at that time seems merely to have meant that there were good reasons for enforcing the promise. But here again, as lawyers began to treat consideration as a 'doctrine' whose content was a set of fixed and rigid rules tailored to the typical case, these cases came to seem anomalous. It therefore became fashionable to deny that there was consideration; and yet such promises were and still are quite often enforced. Modern lawyers are thus forced to say that some promises may be enforceable even though there is no consideration for them.

However, this last proposition is one which lawyers have been much more reluctant to accept than the one previously discussed, that is that even promises supported by consideration may sometimes be unenforceable. There has seemed to be something almost akin to heresy in admitting that a promise may be enforced without consideration. This is fully borne out by the initial reactions to the *High Trees*[1] case which was originally looked on with great scepticism by the legal profession as an instance of Lord Denning's advanced and 'unsound' views.[2] But this is by no means the only instance of gratuitous promises being enforced by the courts. As will be seen below, many gratuitous promises are enforced by the courts, if the word 'gratuitous' is understood to mean a promise to make a gift, but the difference between most of these instances and the *High Trees* decision is that in the older cases it was traditionally asserted that there was in fact consideration ...

As will be apparent from the above discussion, there has gradually been a hardening of the attitude of the English common lawyer to the whole notion of consideration. From being merely a reason for the enforcement of a promise (or possibly a reason for the creation or recognition of an obligation), it has come to be regarded as a technical doctrine which has little to do with the justice or desirability of enforcing a promise, or recognising obligations. Thus a promise for consideration may be unenforceable; and a promise without consideration may be enforceable.

Interwoven with this development has been another which has also played a large part in leading to the conventional view of the law at the present day. This has been the persistent and apparently compulsive desire of lawyers to concentrate on the typical contractual promise and to draw conclusions of universal validity from that typical case. Thus, because it is often (or indeed usually) a good reason for enforcing a promise that the promisor has received a counter promise in return, lawyers appear to have convinced themselves that a wholly executory contract should always be enforceable, and that a counter promise is necessarily a benefit or a detriment, even before any performance or reliance. Because most contracts are bargains, lawyers have steadfastly refused to recognise the evidence under their very eyes, that courts often enforce promises which are not bargains, and that they do so for reasons of justice and good policy. Because a promise to make a gift is not usually recognised as a sufficient reason for its enforcement, lawyers have refused to acknowledge that in some circumstances it is particularly desirable to enforce a gratuitous promise and that the courts in fact do so. Because in most circumstances the consideration must in practice be supplied by the promisee, it was deduced (and even on one occasion stated by the House of Lords) that consideration must always move from the promisee; yet the courts in fact sometimes enforce promises in which the real ground for enforcing the promise is something done by a third party.

1. [1974] KB 130.
2. See e.g. Bennion, 'Want of Consideration' (1953), 16 MLR 441; Gordon [1963] Camb. LJ 222.

Defining Consideration

K.C.T. Sutton, *Consideration Reconsidered*, (University of Queensland Press 1974) ch. 2. (Footnotes abridged.)

Consideration and the Bargain Concept
The usual definition of consideration given by text writers and one which has received judicial approval on numerous occasions is that propounded by Lush J. in *Currie v Misa*.[1] 'A valuable consideration in the sense of the law may consist either in some right, interest, profit, or benefit accruing to the one party, or some forbearance, detriment, loss or responsibility given suffered or undertaken by the other.' The definition was itself based on a statement in Comyn's *Digest*,[2] which in turn relied upon cases decided at the close of the eighteenth century. However, the notion of defining consideration in terms of benefit or detriment goes back to at least 1588[3] and was explicable, as Ames has pointed out,[4] by the rise of the actions of *assumpsit* and *indebitatus assumpsit*.

But if the view put forward earlier is correct, and the doctrine of consideration is bound up with the concept of bargain which was inherent in it from the beginning, then the definition suggested by Lush J. is defective in that it does not emphasise this element. It is significant that Halsbury, in defining consideration, took the definition propounded in *Currie v Misa* but added the words 'at his [i.e. the promisor's] request' at the end, thus indicating that the detriment suffered by the promisee must be at the other party's behest.[5] It was this notion of reciprocity that suggested to some writers that the essence of consideration lay in the possible benefit or value to the promisor of what was given or promised in return, rather than the notion of detriment or burden to the promisee; but the answer to this view is that, if the doctrine of consideration is to be identified with the concept of bargain, any benefit to the promisor must necessarily be matched with a corresponding detriment to the promisee—with the one exception where the situation deals with the performance of a pre-existing contractual duty as in the *Shadwell v Shadwell* type of case.[6]

After the eighteenth century flirtation with notions of moral obligation and the like, the Victorian era saw a return to the orthodox view that the common law theory of enforcing simple contracts was one of giving effect to bargains.[7] Consideration came to be thought of as the price or agreed exchange for the promise, and increasing emphasis was laid on the necessity for an exchange reciprocally induced as an essential element. Hence, throughout the nineteenth century and persisting into the twentieth century, there is a hardening of the juristic attitude, with insistence being increasingly given to the notion of consideration as the price in return for which the promise is made.[8] Pollock in his *Contracts*[9] wrote that 'an act or forbearance of one party, or the promise thereof, is the price for which the promise of the other is bought, and the promise thus given for value is enforceable', and his description was adopted by Lord Dunedin in *Dunlop Pneumatic Tyre Co. Ltd v Selfridge & Co. Ltd*[10] and by the English Law Revision Committee in their report on the doctrine of consideration in 1937.[11]

When Holmes published *The Common Law* in 1881, he concluded that the same thing might be a consideration or not, according as it was dealt with by the parties. In his view, while consideration must not be confounded with motive, a consideration must still be given or accepted as the motive or inducement of the promise, and the promise must be made and accepted as the conventional motive or inducement for furnishing the consideration. The root of the whole matter lay in the relation of reciprocal conventional inducement, each for the other, between consideration and promise.[12] As Chief Justice of the Supreme Judicial Court of Massachusetts, Holmes declined to apply the 'reciprocal conventional inducement' theory rigorously in *Martin v Meles*[13] (which would have meant holding the promisor not bound by his promise) comforting himself with the reflection that 'courts have gone [to] very great lengths in discovering the implication of such an equivalence, sometimes perhaps even having found it in matters which would seem to be no more than conditions or natural consequences of the promise'.[14]

However, two years later, in delivering the opinion of the United States Supreme Court in *Wisconsin & Michigan Co. v Powers*[15] his Honour felt himself able to apply his 'conventional inducement' test to defeat the claim of the plaintiff company which had begun construction of a railway in reliance on a statute exempting any person who built such railway from taxation for ten years. The statute was later repealed and the plaintiff argued that the repealing Act was unconstitutional as impairing a contractual obligation. Holmes J. held that, while the building of the railway was a sufficient detriment to constitute consideration if other elements were present, yet in the absence of the element of conventional inducement the plaintiff's argument failed.

This case is somewhat reminiscent of the decision of the High Court of Australia in *Australian Woolen Mills Pty Ltd v Commonwealth*[16] where the plaintiff's claim, based on the existence of a contract between it and the defendant, was rejected on the ground that there was no such contract as alleged. The plaintiff relied on a statement by the Commonwealth Government that a subsidy would be paid to manufacturers of wool purchased and used for local manufacture, as a result of which it bought large quantities of wool and received certain subsidies. The claim was for subsidies payable in terms of the arrangement.

The High Court of Australia embraced the bargain theory of consideration with the comment that 'between the statement or announcement, which is put forward as an offer capable of acceptance by the doing of an act, and the act which is put forward as the executed consideration for the alleged promise, there must subsist, so to speak, the relation of a *quid pro quo*'.[17] Their Honours went on to endorse the proposition that the presence or absence of an implied request to do the act was a useful test for determining whether there was a true offer and acceptance or whether the offer was made to induce the doing of the act. In the result, the plaintiff's claim failed as there was no offer, no implied request that wool be bought, and no suggestion that promise of payment and purchase of wool were related so that one was consideration for the other.

It may be remarked at this point that it is a central thesis of this study that a rigorous application of the bargain theory, of the 'reciprocal conventional inducement' notion of consideration, would result in many decisions being found to be outside it. Street recognised this fact. He adopted Holmes' views but pointed out that while academic writers had embraced the bargain theory of consideration, its supremacy in the courts had never been complete. An element might be treated as consideration although the parties had not done so. The fact that the parties did not happen to treat an act of detriment as a consideration in a particular case was not conclusive that the act was not good consideration to support the promise.[18]

Corbin looked at another facet of the problem when he wrote that there were far too many decisions enforcing a promise where the only consideration was action by the promise in reliance on the promise, for the remarks of Holmes J. to be accepted without reserve.[19] Another American jurist, Langdell, likewise felt the difficulty of reconciling the bargain theory with its exceptions, but the exceptions he was concerned about were those bargains which the law did not regard as such and did not enforce. He defined consideration as the thing given or done by the promisee in exchange for the promise, and then had to enumerate a list of things which, if done by the promisee in exchange for the promise, would not be consideration therefore.[20] Finally, it should be noted that the American *Restatement of Contracts* first published in 1932, adopted the bargain theory of consideration,[21] but then felt constrained to introduce a new class of informal contracts which could not be brought within its framework.[22]

A thin veneer of rationalisation is usually given to the bargain theory by saying that certain acts given in exchange for a promise do not amount to consideration because they are of no value in the eye of the law. It was of course early realised that not every exchange could amount to consideration, and the test was evolved of according validity only to those exchanges which could be said to amount to a benefit to the promisor or a detriment to the promisee. In the prevailing climate of analytical historical juristic thinking in the nineteenth century, the theory became established that only an exchange which was a detriment to the promisee would be recognised by the law. Detriment to the promisee was the significant feature of consideration. The fact that the promisor received a benefit was merely incidental to the prime requirement of a bargained-for detriment to the promisee. This theory had the inestimable advantage that it met the demands of historical derivation from the action of *assumpsit*.

As a result, at the beginning of the twentieth century the view was widespread that the universal test of consideration was detriment to the promisee, and that the notion of benefit to the promisor was irrelevant and was a misconception due to the mistake of applying to *assumpsit* ideas which belonged exclusively to debt. There might be a benefit to the promisor and yet no consideration, as where the benefit did not come from the promisee, while on the other hand, detriment to the promisee was the all-embracing test.[23] However, this view was not accepted without question, and there were not wanting protagonists for the view that benefit to the promisor should be retained as an alternative test of consideration,[24] attention being drawn to the *Shadwell v Shadwell* type of case where there was said to be a benefit to the promisor without a corresponding detriment to the promisee in his right to have performed the pre-existing contractual duty owed by the promisee to a third party.

1. (1875) LR 10 Ex 153, 162.
2. 5th ed. (1822), vol. 1, 294.
3. See Coke *arguendo* in *Stone v Wythipol* (1588) Cro. Eliz. 126, and *Greenleaf v Barker* (1591) Cro. Eliz. 193.
4. 'The History of Assumpsit' in (1888) 2 Harv LR 1, 17.
5. *Laws of England* (2nd edn, ed. Hailsham 1932), vol. 7, 136.
6. (1860) 9 CBNS 159; 142 ER 62.
7. Sharp, 'Pacta Sunt Servanda' in (1941) 41 Col LR 783.
8. See e.g. Langdell, *Summary of Contracts*, s. 45.
9. See e.g. 8th edn, 175.
10. [1915] AC 847, 855.
11. Cmd. 5449, s. 17, 12.
12. See pp 289–95. See also Langdell, *Summary of Contracts*, ss. 66–8; and *Fire Insurance Assn. v Wickham* (1891) 141 US 564, 579; *McGovern v New York* (1923) 138 NE 26 (CANY); *Foster v Dawber* (1851) 6 Ex. 839, 849–50.
13. (1901) 60 NE 397.
14. Ibid. at p. 398.
15. (1903) 191 US 379, 386.
16. (1953–54) 92 CLR 424.
17. Ibid. at pp 456–7.
18. *Foundations of Legal Liability* (1901), vol. 2, 71, 81 et seq.
19. 'Does a Pre-existing Duty Defeat Consideration?' in (1918) 27 Yale LJ 362.
20. *Summary of Contracts*, ss 45 and 54.
21. S. 75.
22. Ss 85–90.
23. See Langdell, *Summary of Contracts*, s. 64.
24. See e.g. Bennett, 'Is Mere Gain to a Promisor a Good Consideration for His Promise?' in (1896) 10 Harv LR 257.

AG for England and Wales *v* R [2002] 2 NZLR 91

Keith J.:

The classic theory of consideration rests on a mutual exchange of benefits. A provides a benefit to B in return for the benefit which B provides to A. If B incurs a detriment it may qualify as consideration provided it is incurred at A's request or is otherwise of benefit to A. Detriment to B is often the logical corollary of the fact that B has conferred a benefit on A. By doing so B suffers the detriment of providing the benefit but receives in return the benefit of what A is providing under the contract.

Analysing consideration in terms of benefit and detriment is not always the most satisfactory way of addressing the topic. In this respect I agree with what Professor John Burrows says on the subject at para. 4.1.3 of *Cheshire and Fifot's Law of Contract* 8th NZ edn, 1997 (Burrows, Finn and Todd). It is often easier to speak in terms of each party having to pay a price for what the contract requires of the other. The result will be the same as that reached by the benefit/detriment analysis, but the difficulties sometimes encountered with that analysis, particularly in the area of detriment, are lessened. Sir Frederick Pollock adopted a price-based approach in his work on contracts (13th edn at p. 133). This was approved by the House of Lords in *Dunlop*

Pneumatic Tyre Co. Ltd v Selfridge & Co. Ltd [1915] AC 847 at p. 855. Sir Frederick's
summary of consideration was in these terms:

> An act or forbearance of one party, or the promise thereof, is the price for which the
> promise of the other is brought, and the promise thus given for value is
> enforceable.

Benefits may be conferred or, as I would prefer to put it, the necessary price can be
paid, either by a promise to do something or by actually doing it. Hence consideration
may be provided either by a promise or by an act. A promise confers a benefit in law
and an act provides a benefit in fact or a practical benefit, as it is sometimes called. An
exchange of promises may provide consideration and so may the exchange of an act
for a promise. In the latter case the act must be referable to or respond to the promise,
otherwise it will not constitute consideration in law. An act already done without
reference to a promise does not satisfy the concept of an exchange which underpins
the law of consideration. That is why past consideration, i.e. the conferring of a benefit
in the past, is no consideration in law. For an act to qualify as consideration for a
promise it must necessarily follow the promise unless the promise and the act can be
regarded as part of one and the same transaction in which case the sequence will not
be critical. The normal situation in which an act can respond to or be referable to a
promise is when the promissory expressly or implicitly requests the act as the price of
the promise.

A. PAST CONSIDERATION

Consideration may be executed or executory but it may not be past.

Pao On *v* Lau Yiu Long [1980] AC 614

The plaintiffs owned shares in a private company, Shing On, whose principal asset was a building under construction. The defendants were major
shareholders in a public company, Fu Chip, which wished to acquire the
building. It was agreed that the plaintiffs would transfer their shares to Fu
Chip in return for shares in Fu Chip. At the defendants' request the
plaintiffs agreed not to sell their Fu Chip shares for one year. Later the
defendants gave the plaintiffs a guarantee in which they promised to
indemnify the plaintiffs against any loss sustained if the Fu Chip share
price fell during that period. When the share price fell the defendants
refused to indemnify them, claiming *inter alia* that there was no
consideration for their promise.

This litigation took place before the courts of Hong Kong and was under
appeal to the Privy Council.

Lord Scarman:

The Board agrees with [counsel for the plaintiffs'] submission that the consideration
expressly stated in the written guarantee is sufficient in law to support the defendants'
promise of indemnity. An act done before the giving of a promise to make a payment
or to confer some other benefit can sometimes be consideration for the promise. The
act must have been done at the promisors' request: the parties must have understood

that the act was to be remunerated either by a payment or the conferment of some other benefit: and payment, or the conferment of a benefit, must have been legally enforceable had it been promised in advance. All three features are present in this case. The promise given to Fu Chip under the main agreement not to sell the shares for a year was at the first defendant's request. The parties understood at the time of the main agreement that the restriction on selling must be compensated for by the benefit of a guarantee against a drop in price: and such a guarantee would be legally enforceable. The agreed cancellation of the subsidiary agreement left, as the parties knew, the plaintiffs unprotected in a respect in which at the time of the main agreement all were agreed they should be protected.

[Counsel's] submission is based on *Lampleigh v Brathwait* (1615) Hobart 105. In that case the judges said, at p. 106: 'First . . . a meer voluntary courtesie will not have a consideration to uphold an assumpsit. But if that courtesie were moved by a suit or request of the party that gives the assumpsit, it will bind, for the promise, though it follows, yet it is not naked, but couples itself with the suit before, and the merits of the party procured by that suit, which is the difference.' The modern statement of the law is in the judgment of Bowen L.J. in *In re Casey's Patents* [1892] 1 Ch. 104, 115–116; Bowen L.J. said:

> Even if it were true, as some scientific students of law believe, that a past service cannot support a future promise, you must look at the document and see if the promise cannot receive a proper effect in some other way. Now, the fact of a past service raises an implication that at the time it was rendered it was to be paid for, and, if it was a service which was to be paid for, when you get in the subsequent document a promise to pay, that promise may be treated either as an admission which evidences or as a positive bargain which fixes the amount of that reasonable remuneration on the faith of which the service was originally rendered. So that here for past services there is ample justification for the promise to give the third share.

Conferring a benefit is, of course, an equivalent to payment: see *Chitty on Contracts*, (24th edn, 1977), vol. 1, para. 154.

[Counsel] for the defendants, does not dispute the existence of the rule but challenges its application to the facts of this case. He submits that it is not a necessary inference or implication from the terms of the written guarantee that any benefit or protection was to be given to the plaintiffs for their acceptance of the restriction on selling their shares. Their Lordships agree that the mere existence or recital of a prior request is not sufficient in itself to convert what is *prima facie* past consideration into sufficient consideration in law to support a promise: as they have indicated, it is only the first of three necessary preconditions. As for the second of those preconditions, whether the act done at the request of the promisor raises an implication of promised remuneration or other return is simply one of the construction of the words of the contract in the circumstances of its making. Once it is recognised, as the Board considers it inevitably must be, that the expressed consideration includes a reference to the plaintiffs' promise not to sell the shares before 30 April 1974—a promise to be performed in the future, though given in the past—it is not possible to treat the defendants' promise of indemnity as independent of the plaintiffs' antecedent promise, given at the first defendant's request, not to sell. The promise of indemnity was given because at the time of the main agreement the parties intended that the first defendant should confer upon the plaintiffs the benefit of his protection against a fall in price. When the subsidiary agreement was cancelled, all were well aware that the plaintiffs were still to have the benefit of his protection as consideration for the restriction on selling. It matters not whether the indemnity thus given be regarded as the best evidence of the benefit intended to be conferred in return for the promise not to sell, or as the positive bargain which fixes the benefit on the faith of which the promise was given—though where, as here, the subject is a written contract, the better analysis is probably that of the 'positive bargain'. Their Lordships, therefore, accept the submission that the contract itself states a valid consideration for the promise of indemnity.

Consider:

Is a guarantee given by an electrical store to a customer who has just bought a television supported by sufficient consideration?

B. SUFFICIENCY

Once consideration has been proven to exist, a court will not evaluate the comparative value of the promise given and the promise or act given in return. For this reason it is said the courts will not enquire as to the adequacy of consideration.

As Blackburn J. noted in *Bolton v Madden* (1873) LR 9 QB 55, 'The adequacy of consideration is for the parties to consider at the time of making the agreement not for the court when it is sought to be enforced.' Similarly, Ellis J. stated in *Kennedy v Kennedy* (HC) 12 January 1984, unrep., 'Once there is consideration, its adequacy in this sort of case is irrelevant to its validity and enforceability.'

However, consideration must be 'sufficient', i.e. it must be something which is of value in the eyes of the law. The following cases explain the view of the courts as to what is deemed valuable.

O'Neill v Murphy [1936] NI 16

The plaintiff sued for fees due for the performance of certain architectural and building work for the defendants. The defendants claimed that they had performed certain agreed services in return in the nature of prayers for the benefit of the plaintiff and his family. The court had to decide *inter alia* whether there was sufficient consideration in law for the alleged agreement.

Andrews L.J.:

In the first place the defendants have not satisfied me that the consideration relied upon in support of the alleged agreement is sufficient in law for that purpose. At the time that the plaintiff wrote the letter of 14 September 1926, to Father Murphy, a sum of £935 5s 0d, was due to him. In that letter he said: 'Now I think I will be well paid for anything I did if you can arrange with the Mother General to have daily prayers offered up for myself and family together with Mrs O'Neill and my brother J. K.' To this the Reverend Mothers replied on 18 September: 'The remuneration you ask for your gigantic work is indeed freely given. Daily prayers will be offered in every house of the Order for your intentions as a most generous benefactor.' A cheque for £200 was enclosed, which the plaintiff was asked to accept as a little favour and as a very small appreciation of the plaintiff's great work and generosity.

Now it is elementary law, which comes down to us from the Roman jurists, that to constitute an enforceable contract not under seal, there must be a good and valid consideration; and, whilst it is clear that courts will not interfere with the exercise of free will and judgment of the parties by inquiring into the adequacy of consideration, it is necessary that it should be sufficient in law. Thus, neither a mere voluntary courtesy nor some act already executed will suffice. So, too, a promise by a creditor to accept less than the full amount of his undisputed debt is not legally binding upon him. Such promise cannot be relied upon as a legal satisfaction, for there is no consideration for the relinquishment of the balance of the debt. *Cumber v Wane*,[1] and *Pinnel's* case,[2] are landmarks which are too firmly fixed in our law to be shaken; and, whilst it is true that the addition of some benefit or even of a legal possibility of benefit to a creditor will render the consideration sufficient to support an agreement, such benefit must, as pointed out by Lord Selborne in *Foakes v Beer*,[3] be an independent benefit of a kind which might in law be a good and valuable consideration for any other sort of agreement not under seal.

Now, whilst expressly disclaiming any opinion which might be construed as in the slightest degree derogatory of the real value and efficacy of prayer, I can only say that no case cited to us or which I have found, can properly be relied upon as an authority for the proposition that a mere promise by one person to say prayers or to cause prayers to be said for another amounts in law to a good and valuable consideration for a contract not under seal. If such be the law it should be laid down by our highest judicial tribunal—the House of Lords.

[1] 1 Sm. LC (13th ed.) 373.   [2] 5 Co. Rep. 117 (*a*).   [3] 9 AC 605, 614.

(Best L.J. decided the case on other grounds and thus found it unnecessary to deal with the issue of consideration.)

Note

Similarly, in *Re Wilson* [1933] IR 729, Johnson J held that an agreement by a father to transfer property to his son 'for natural love and affection' was not supported by consideration.

O'Keeffe *v* Ryanair Holdings plc [2002] 3 IR 228

The plaintiff purchased a ticket for a Ryanair flight and upon arrival at the airport was informed that she might be its millionth passenger. She was asked whether she would be prepared to participate in publicity exercises to mark the occasion and she agreed. She was then announced publicly as the millionth passenger and informed that she would have unlimited travel for herself and a chosen nominee for life. A number of years later, the defendant sought to restrict her flights and the plaintiff sued for breach of contract. In reaching his conclusion that an enforceable contract had been made which had been breached by the defendant, Kelly J. dealt with the issue of consideration.

Kelly J.:

The contention made by the defendant both in its pleadings and submissions is that there was no contract in existence between the plaintiff and the defendant. Rather it is said that the defendant conferred a gift on the plaintiff. Insofar as the terms of that gift are concerned the defendant appears to be in some considerable doubt. Five different alternatives are set forth in the defence and on the closing day of the trial leave was sought and granted even to amend those.

A gift is defined in the *Concise Oxford Dictionary* (7th ed.) as a 'voluntary transference of property without compensation'.

In the present case I am quite satisfied that on any reasonable view of what occurred in this case the entitlement given to the plaintiff to avail herself of free tickets on the defendant's flights was not gratuitous. The only basis upon which the defendant had any interest in the plaintiff arose from her agreement to participate in the public relations exercise which was undertaken by it. Had she not so consented, she would have had no entitlement to participate in the proposal which was put to her. The whole object of the exercise was to generate publicity for the defendant and the plaintiff's active participation was required in that. She gave her consent and it was on that basis that the entitlements in question were made available to her.

I am quite satisfied therefore that there is no question of a gift being involved here. The defendant had a very clear idea as to what it wanted from the plaintiff and it got it. It is trite law that in order for there to be a valid contract there must be agreement between the parties, consideration for such agreement and an intention to create legal relations.

In my view there was agreement between the parties that in consideration of the plaintiff consenting to participate in the publicity sought by the defendant she would be eligible for nomination as its millionth passenger. Should she be so nominated, she was to cooperate in the publicity being generated for the defendant's benefit. In return, she was entitled to unlimited travel on Ryanair routes for herself and a nominated person for the remainder of her natural life.

Under the doctrine of consideration a promise has no contractual force unless some value has been given for it. The court is not concerned with the adequacy of value: *Haigh v Brooks*[1]; *Wild v Tucker*[2]; *Midland Bank Trust Co. v Green*.[3] The consideration to support a contract must however be real, that is to say capable of estimation in terms of value. It must be of some value in the eyes of the law. *Thomas v Thomas*.[4] Certainly, the participation of the plaintiff in the publicity generated on the day in question was regarded as being of value by the defendant and I see no reason why the law should not regard it as likewise being of value. The surrender by the plaintiff of her anonymity and privacy and her active participation in the generation of the publicity that was created on the day in question in my view amounted to a real consideration and is sufficient to support a valid contract.

1. (1839) 10 A & E 309.   3. [1981] AC 513.
2. [1914] 3 KB 36.   4. (1842) 2 QB 851.

Note

A written promise made by a politican to the electorate not to introduce new taxes if elected was deemed by the Canadian Courts not to be supported by good consideration despite the favourable publicity generated. Rouleau J. noted that to deem such promises enforceable would render the current system of government 'dysfunctional' and would cause the Courts to 'hinder if not paralyse the Parliamentary system'. See *Canadian Taxpayers Federation v The Queen* (2004) 73 OR (3d) 621.

Consider:

Would an agreement to keep a lottery winner's name secret amount to good consideration?

C. COMPROMISE OF A CLAIM

Where a legal claim is made against a person, that person may dispute either the validity of the claim or the amount of the claim, but may agree, for various reasons, to settle the dispute for less than the amount claimed. This 'compromise' is deemed to be supported by sufficient consideration.

O'Donnell v O'Sullivan (1913) 47 ILTR 253

Palles L.C.B:

The action was brought on foot of a promissory note, and there is an admission here that this promissory note was given in respect of betting transactions. I have here the original document that shows the consideration for the £65. 'O'Donnell v O'Sullivan, £137 10s. I hereby consent to pay you £75–£10 in cash and promissory note for £65–in full payment of above. M. J. O'Sullivan, Hospital.' It is said that under these circumstance this is a good agreement for a compromise. This was an action which both parties knew could not succeed. The settlement of that is not good consideration for a compromise. I take it that it is settled law that unless there is a reasonable claim which is *bona fide* intended to be pursued, the settlement of that claim cannot be good consideration for a compromise. It lay then on the plaintiff to come forward and show that he had a reasonable claim against the defendant, and although this sum of £75 is in full payment of a gambling debt of £137 10s, that notwithstanding that there was new consideration for the agreement to pay the £75, and, to use the language of some of the cases, it was 'not to be taken as £75 on account of above, but for a sum equal to above.' He must come forward and prove that, in order to show that there is anything substantial in the nature of the compromise. If not, there was nothing to compromise. I doubt even if the new consideration would be sufficient, if part of the consideration was, as I think it was, this gambling debt of £137 10s, because that consideration is not made void, but illegal, and according to my recollection if part of the consideration is illegal it taints the whole. But my judgment is based on this, that the sum sued for is clearly for a gambling debt, and in order to make the agreement for a compromise a good contract there must be a reasonable claim *bona fide* intended to be pursued.

D. FORBEARANCE TO SUE AS CONSIDERATION

Where a legal claim is made against a person, instead of disputing the claim, the person may admit the claim but request more time to pay the debt. This forbearance may also constitute good consideration.

Fullerton v Provincial Bank of Ireland [1903] AC 309

In the spring of 1895 Colonel Stevenson, having overdrawn his account with the Provincial Bank of Ireland, was asked by the bank to reduce the debt. He wrote several letters to the manager in which he said that he was buying an estate and when he received the conveyance he would deposit the deed as a security for the overdraft. The Court was asked to determine whether there was good consideration for this promise.

Lord Macnaghten:

The other point on which the learned Solicitor General relied was that there was no proof of consideration. The promise, he said, if it was a definite promise, was *nudum pactum*—no doubt, he said, Colonel Stevenson had overdrawn his account, but there was no stipulation for forbearance for any definite time.

My Lords, this point seems to me to be settled by authority. In such a case as this it is not necessary that there should be an arrangement for forbearance for any definite or particular time. It is quite enough if you can infer from the surrounding circumstances that there was an implied request for forbearance for a time, and that forbearance for a reasonable time was in fact extended to the person who asked for it. That proposition seems to me to be established by the case of *Alliance Bank v Broom*,[1] to which my noble and learned friend Lord Lindley referred yesterday, and other cases, among which I may mention *Oldershaw v King*,[2] with the observations on that case and the case in Drewry and Smale, by Bowen L.J. in *Miles v New Zealand Alford Estate Co.*,[3] and I may add that the proposition seems to be good sense.

Lord Davey:

There can be no possible doubt that this promise was accepted by Mr Stuart on the part of the bank, but it is said that there was no consideration for it. Now in the letter of 18 May (that is the second letter) Colonel Stevenson writes to this effect, addressing Mr Stuart, 'All you require is a little patience and my account will be put on a satisfactory basis.' I think this means, 'Exercise patience and some forbearance and I will give you the required security and thus put my account in order.' The bank did exercise patience, and gave some forbearance by not demanding, as they might have done, immediate payment of the debt, and by giving Colonel Stevenson the required time to effect the security. I think that such forbearance in fact, although there was no agreement by the bank to forbear suing Colonel Stevenson for any definite period, was sufficient consideration to support his promise to give the security, on the principle stated by Kindersley V.C. in *Alliance Bank v Broom*. The Vice Chancellor's judgment in that case was quoted with approval by Lord Bowen in *Miles v New Zealand Alford Estate Co.*[4] as laying down a sound principle. In the case before Lord Bowen the question was whether a guarantee which had been given by the promoter of a company at a general meeting of the shareholders to guarantee a dividend of a certain amount for a certain time on the shares was given with or without consideration, and in referring to the case before him Lord Bowen said, after quoting the Vice Chancellor's judgment:

> So it will be sufficient here that the directors did forbear, if their forbearance was at the request expressed or implied of the guarantor and in consequence of his guarantee being given, and it seems to me there is no sort of necessity to discover language of any particular form, or writing of any particular character, embodying the resolution of the directors. We must treat the thing in a business way and draw an inference of fact as to what the real nature of the transaction was as between business men.

My Lords, that seems to me to be directly applicable to the present question. There can be no doubt that the forbearance was given in this case, and I think it is a just inference of fact that it was given at the request of Colonel Stevenson in consequence of his undertaking to secure the account and place it on what he describes as a satisfactory basis.

1. (1864) 2 Dr & S 289.
2. (1857) 2 H & N 517.
3. (1886) 32 ChD 289.
4. Ibid. 266, 290.

(Shand and Lindley L.JJ. agreed on this issue.)

Although, as the previous case demonstrates, there does not have to be an express promise to forbear, the next two cases emphasise that a forbearance is only good consideration for a promise which is induced by it.

Provincial Bank of Ireland Ltd v Donnell (1932) 67 ILTR 142
(Facts on p.89.)

Andrews L.J.:

In these circumstances the real defence urged before us by counsel for the defendant was that as the guarantee was not under seal it must, like other simple contracts, be supported by a valuable consideration. The mere existence of a debt is not sufficient to support the surety's promise to the creditor. A past or executed consideration, unless moved at the defendant's request, is not binding without some new consideration. It is true that an agreement by a creditor that he will forbear to sue the principal debtor for a past debt is a sufficient consideration for a person becoming a surety for the debt. So also is actual forbearance at the request, express or implied, of the defendant. But it is only by such agreement for forbearance or by actual forbearance to sue that a past consideration may be relied upon as a valuable consideration which will support the guarantee. It was to bring the present case within this principle that plaintiffs' counsel argued that the true meaning of the opening words of the guarantee sued upon is 'in consideration of your not suing my husband for advances already made to him.' The first difficulty, however, in upholding this construction is that, although such forbearance might have been easily expressed, this has not been done; and I am unable to put a forced and unnatural construction upon words which are in no way ambiguous merely to make the guarantee binding and enforceable by action. One ought to be slow in implying consideration in favour of the bank, whose document this guarantee is, especially when one remembers that when the guarantee was signed they did not stand to the defendant in the relationship of creditor and debtor.

The construction contended for becomes all the more difficult when it is remembered that as the Lord Chief Justice finds 'there was no talk about any agreement not to sue;' and, finally, the grammatical difficulties which arise from the reference to the past advances being immediately followed in the same sentence by a reference to the future advances compel me to reject the plaintiffs' contention without any hesitation. I leave the argument in reference to the consideration afforded by past advances by merely saying that if, apart from agreement, there was in fact a forbearance to sue there is not a particle of evidence to show, as is necessary, that such forbearance resulted from any request, express or implied, on the part of the defendant.

(Best L.J. concurred.)

The Commodity Broking Co. Ltd *v* Meehan [1985] IR 12

The defendant was the sole beneficial owner of the entire shareholding of Pistola Investments Ltd, a company which was heavily indebted to the plaintiff. In the course of a meeting between the two parties, the defendant intimated that the company was insolvent and agreed personally to pay off this debt by instalments. When the defendant defaulted in his payments, the plaintiff sued for breach of contract. The defendant pleaded an absence of consideration.

Barron J. (HC):

The consideration relied upon by the plaintiff is that it forbore to sue the company. In the *Alliance Bank Ltd v Broom*[1] the defendant who was a customer of the plaintiff bank was asked to give security for money which he owed to the bank. He agreed to hypothecate certain goods in favour of the bank. When he failed to do so, the bank sought to enforce his promise, which he pleaded was given without consideration. He failed in this plea. It was held that he had by implication asked the bank to forbear and that he had received a sufficient degree of forbearance to amount to consideration for his promise. The Vice Chancellor Sir D.R.E. Kindersley said at p. 292:

> It appears to me that, when the plaintiffs demanded payment of their debt, and, in consequence of that application the defendant agreed to give certain security, although there was no promise on the part of the plaintiffs to abstain for any certain time from suing for the debt, the effect was, that the plaintiffs did in effect give, and the defendant received, the benefit of some degree of forbearance; not, indeed, for any definite time, but, at all events, some extent of forbearance. If, on the application for security being made, the defendant had refused to give any security at all, the consequence certainly would have been that the creditor would have demanded payment of the debt, and have taken steps to enforce it. It is very true that, at any time after the promise, the creditor might have insisted on payment of his debt, and have brought an action; but the circumstances necessarily involve the benefit to the debtor of a certain amount of forbearance, which he would not have derived if he had not made the agreement.

In *Miles v New Zealand Alford Estate Co.*[2] a director and shareholder had sold certain property to the company. At a general meeting, several shareholders complained that the company had overpaid for the property. To still such criticisms, it was agreed that the company should pay a minimum dividend and that in any year in which it was not earned the vendor would make up the difference. He was subsequently sued on this agreement and it was contended that forbearance by the company to bring proceedings in relation to the sale was a sufficient consideration to make the agreement binding. Cotton L.J. at p. 283 in considering the proofs to establish consideration said:

> Now, what I understand to be the law is this, that if there is in fact a serious claim honestly made, the abandonment of the claim is a good 'consideration' for a contract; and if that is the law, what we really have to now consider is whether in the present case there is any evidence on which the court ought to find that there was a serious claim in fact made, and whether a contract to abandon that claim was the consideration for this letter of guarantee.

Having considered the evidence he said at p. 285:

> The conclusion at which I have arrived is, that there is no evidence on which we ought to rely that there was in fact a claim intended to be made against Grant (the vendor), and, in my opinion, on the evidence before us, we ought not to arrive at the conclusion that there was ever intended to be any contract by the company, much less that there was in fact any contract binding the company that that claim should not be prosecuted, and should be given up.

Fry L.J. accepted the same test and took the view that there was no intention by the company to abandon its claim. At p. 300 he said:

> I think the true result of the evidence is to show that there was an expectation in the mind of Mr Grant that if he gave this document no proceedings would be taken against him, that there was an expectation in the minds of many of those who were present, if they got this dividend they would take no proceedings; but it appears to me it is not right or competent for the court to turn an expectation into a contract, and that is what I think we should do if we gave effect to this as a valid contract.

Bowen L.J. dissented. He regarded consideration as being any forbearance to sue as a result of the express or implied request of the promissor. He regarded the decision of the trial judge 'as finding that proceedings had been threatened, that Mr Grant knew that they had been threatened, that he gave the guarantee in order to put an end to them, and that the proceedings were dropped in consequence of his giving that under-taking.' He regarded this as a finding that there has been consideration and in doing so he expressly followed *Alliance Bank Ltd v Broom*. The majority view that there should be an actual agreement to abandon threatened proceedings before there can be good consideration was not followed in later cases.

On similar facts, *Alliance Bank v Broom* was approved by the House of Lords in *Fullerton v Provincial Bank of Ireland*.[3] In the same case, the judgment of Bowen L.J. in *Miles v New Zealand Alford Estate Co.* was cited with approval by Lord Davey at p. 316. In *Combe v Combe*[4] the court had to consider whether there was consideration for a promise by a husband to pay permanent maintenance to his wife upon the dissolution of their marriage. The wife was not paid and after several years sued on the promise. It was held that there was no consideration since she had been entitled at all times to apply to the court for maintenance and such right would have been unaffected by her husband's promise. Accordingly there had been no request to forbear. At p. 771 Denning L.J. said: 'I cannot find any evidence of any intention by the husband that the wife should forbear from applying to the court for maintenance, or, in other words, any request by the husband, express or implied, that the wife should so forbear. Her forbearance was not intended by him, nor was it done at his request. It was, therefore, no consideration.' In the same case Asquith L.J. said at p. 774: 'Finally, I do not think an actual forbearance, as opposed to an agreement to forbear to approach the court, is a good consideration unless it proceeds from a request, express or implied, on the part of the promissor. If not moved by such a request, the forbearance is not in respect of the promise.'

In my view, these cases establish that the better view is that where a request express or implied to forbear from bringing proceedings induces such forbearance this amounts to good consideration. It is not necessary as the majority decided in *Miles v New Zealand Alford Estate Co.* that there should be an actual agreement not to sue.

The reality of the present case it that when the company was unable to meet its calls the plaintiff took steps to protect itself. So far as the plaintiff was concerned, the company was almost certainly unable to pay. Accordingly, every effort was made to ensure that a promise could be obtained from the defendant that he would pay instead. In the course of events, I can find no implied request by the defendant not to sue the company nor clearly any express request. Nor can I find that the defendant's promise to pay influenced the plaintiff's decision not to sue the company. The plaintiff did not deliberately refrain from suing the company. Had it seemed to it a sensible course to adopt, it would have done so. Its reason for not doing so was not the defendant's promise to pay, but the realisation that it would be a fruitless exercise. If it had been deliberately misled by the defendant, either as to the solvency of the company or into not suing the company by reason of the payments made, the matter might have been otherwise. But there is no evidence to suggest any such calculated conduct on the part of the defendant nor is such a case made. Reluctantly I must hold that no consideration was given for the defendant's promise. In the circumstances the plaintiff's claim must be dismissed.

1. (1864) 2 Dr and Sm 289.   3. [1903] AC 309.
2. (1886) 32 ChD 266.   4. [1951] 1 All ER 767.

Although forbearance to sue is the most common type of forbearance litigated, as the following cases demonstrate cases arise concerning different types of forbearance.

Hamer *v* Sidway (1891) 124 NY 538

An uncle promised his nephew that he would give him $5,000 when he was 21 if he refrained fom 'drinking alcohol, smoking, swearing, playing cards or playing billiards' until that time. The uncle's executor claimed before the New York Court of Appeals that the promise was unenforceable for lack of consideration.

Parker J.:

The defendant contends that the contract was without consideration to support it, and therefore invalid. He asserts that the promisee, by refraining from the use of liquor and tobacco, was not harmed, but benefited; that that which he did was best for him to do, independently of his uncle's promise—and insists that it follows that, unless the promisor was benefited, the contract was without consideration—a contention which, if well founded, would seem to leave open for controversy in many cases whether that which the promisee did or omitted to do was in fact of such benefit to him as to leave no consideration to support the enforcement of the promisor's agreement. Such a rule could not be tolerated, and is without foundation in the law . . . 'Consideration' means not so much that one party is profiting as that the other abandons some legal right in the present, or limits his legal freedom of action in the future, as an inducement for the promise of the first. Now, applying this rule to the facts before us, the promisee used tobacco, occasionally drank liquor, and he had a legal right to do so. That right he abandoned for a period of years upon the strength of the promise of the testator that for such forbearance he would give him $5,000. We need not speculate on the effort which may have been required to give up the use of those stimulants. It is sufficient that he restricted his lawful freedom of action within certain prescribed limits upon the faith of his uncle's agreement, and now, having fully performed the conditions imposed, it is of no moment whether such performance actually proved a benefit to the promisor, and the court will not inquire into it; but, were it a proper subject of inquiry, we see nothing in this record that would permit a determination that the uncle was not benefited in a legal sense.

Consider:

Why was there a different outcome in *White v Bluett* (1853) 23 LJ Ex 36 where a promise to a father to refrain from complaining was held not to constitute good consideration?

AG for England and Wales *v* R [2002] 2 NZLR 91

R, an SAS soldier, signed an agreement not to publish any information relating to his services in the Special Forces. Failure to sign would lead to the soldier being reported for review and ultimately transferred. After leaving the SAS, he sought to publish a book of his experiences in the first Gulf War and the appellant applied for an injunction to restrain publication on the basis that it would be in breach of contract. R argued *inter alia* that there was no consideration for his promise.

Keith J.:

The primary focus of R's argument was on the consideration specified in the contract. Parties are not, however, confined to the consideration so specified. If, for some reason, that proves insufficient it is open to the party seeking to uphold the contract to demonstrate that there was nevertheless sufficient consideration, albeit not that specified. The essential question is whether there was consideration which the law recognises. If there was, the fact that such consideration was not specified in the contract, or that some other insufficient consideration was so specified, is of no moment. It is for this reason that R's argument, based on the way the consideration was expressed in the contract, is too confined. While the specified consideration may, as R suggested, be analysed as a benefit to be enjoyed in the future (essentially therefore as a promise to provide that benefit) rather than as a forbearance to terminate an existing benefit (essentially an act), the way the matter is addressed in the contract is not decisive.

The key question is whether there was any act of forbearance by the Ministry which is sufficient consideration in law. R argued that there was not, whereas the appellant submitted the following analysis in support of the existence of sufficient consideration. It was first contended that R had not disputed the proposition that the Ministry had suffered a detriment amounting to valuable consideration. This contention was reinforced by the suggestion that R had failed to recognise that a detriment incurred by the promissory may be sufficient consideration. I regard R's submissions as putting in issue the sufficiency of the asserted act of forbearance, whether from the point of view of benefit to R as the effective promisee, or detriment to the Ministry as effective promissory. For present purposes I do not consider it matters whether one focuses on benefit or detriment. They are essentially opposite sides of the same coin, and in any event the question is more simply addressed by asking whether the Ministry paid any legally recognised price for R's promise of confidentiality.

The appellant's substantive contention was that the Ministry gave consideration for R's promise of confidentiality, not by means of a promise to continue his engagement, but rather by its 'continuing to give R a posting from 28 October 1996', that being the date when he signed the contract. No reliance is placed on the Ministry's forbearance from returning R to his parent unit up to the time he signed the contract. That is appropriate because such forbearance could not be regarded as having been in exchange for the promise which R gave by signing the contract. Until he signed, it was not known whether he would make a promise of confidentiality. The Ministry's earlier forbearance was past consideration as regards the promise made by R on 28 October 1966. . .

Did the Ministry pay a sufficient price for R's promise of confidentiality? No such price can have been paid by way of a promise of forbearance because, being unenforceable, such promise would not be of value in law and could not therefore constitute a legally recognised price. The question then is whether the Ministry performed any act referable to or in response to R's promise, which act was of value to R and thus constituted a sufficient price for his promise. As earlier noted, giving value in fact will qualify as consideration as well as giving value in law by making a promise capable of enforcement. The Ministry responded to R's promise of confidentiality by not returning him to unit. They forbore from doing so. The Ministry was not bound to forbear and, by doing something they were not already bound to do, they paid a price which the law recognises as sufficient.

There can be no doubt that when making his promise of confidentiality R was implicitly requesting the Ministry not to return him to unit. The Ministry's reciprocal act of forbearance constituted acceptance of R's request, in the sense of creating a contract based on that request and his associated promise of confidentiality. It also constituted consideration for such promise. The contract does not therefore fail for want of consideration.

[Keith J. cited the following cases in support of his analysis: *Alliance Bank Ltd v Broom* (1864) 2 Drew & Sm 289, *Miles v New Zealand Alford Estate Co.* (1886) 32 LR Ch. D 266 and *Williams v Roffey Bros & Nicholls (Contractors) Ltd* [1991] 1 QB 1.]

Note

In *Earn v Kohut* (2002) 164 Man. R. (20) 50 [for the facts see p.86], counsel for the defendant argued that following the expiration of the limitation period, there would be no consideration for the offer as the wronged party could no longer sue on the underlying claim. The Court held that 'while the consideration occurred before the acceptance, it was after the defendant's offer to pay, which predated the forbearance and, therefore, was valid consideration'.

E. CONSIDERATION MUST MOVE FROM THE PROMISEE

In *Tweddle v Atkinson* (1861) 1 B & Sm 393 Crompton J. stated that 'the consideration must move from the party entitled to sue upon the contract; it would be a monstrous proposition to say that a person was a party to the contract, for the purpose of suing upon it for his own advantage and not a party to it for the purpose of being sued.' This rule is closely related to the doctrine of privity of contract considered in Chapter 15.

McCoubray *v* Thompson (1868) 2 IRCL 226

Galwey owned a farm valued at £196 which he wished to divide equally between the plaintiff and the defendant. It was agreed that the farm would be transferred to the defendant who in turn promised to pay the plaintiff £98. Although the farm was transferred, the defendant refused to pay the plaintiff claiming (a) that no promise was alleged to have been paid (b) that no promise could be implied and (c) that no consideration moved from the plaintiff to support an express or implied promise by the defendant.

Monahan C.J.

The demurrer in this case must be allowed; no express promise is made to the plaintiff; and if a promise is to be implied, it would appear to be rather to A. Galwey, from whom the consideration moved. It is true that in the note to *Lampleigh v Braithwait* in *Smith's Leading Cases*, p. 142, it is stated that if the plaintiff have intervened in the agreement it is sufficient; but on examining *Tipper v Bicknell*[1], and the other cases which [counsel] has cited in support of that proposition, it will be found that in each of them something was done by the plaintiff, that some part of the consideration moved from him.

[1]. 3 Bing. NC 710.

Barry *v* Barry (1891) 28 LR (Ir.) 45

O'Brien J:

In this case the facts were that a farmer had two sons; and upon the marriage of one of them (the defendant), part of his farm, with part of his stock, was assigned to two persons in trust for the son. All the family lived together upon the lands till the father's death. By his will, taking no notice of the settlement, he bequeathed the whole lands to the same son, and bound him to pay certain legacies to his other children, amongst the rest £20 to the plaintiff. The terms of the will are considered sufficient either to create a charge of the legacies upon the farm or to amount to a gift of the lands upon the condition of paying them ... Afterwards the plaintiff asked the defendant to pay him, and he promised to pay him £12, after a certain fair where he would have cattle to sell ... Upon the question of law it was contended that there was no contract or consideration on which an action at law could be maintained at all, on the ground that there was no legal consideration at all, or that the plaintiff was a stranger to it.

I consider *Tweddle v* Atkinson,[1] and the other cases cited, really do not touch the point at all. But I am of opinion, if a person has a legacy upon land, and requires the devisee to pay it, and he promises to do so, that there is a consideration on which he can subject himself to liability in an action at law, and that that consideration is properly in the nature of forbearance, the person having the right and the power to enforce, as the plaintiff had, by means of a proceeding against the land or the assets, and it not being necessary, in my view, that the power should be actually used or referred to. There is another ground of consideration on which the plaintiff's claim was put. The assent of the executors to the defendant's possession of the whole of the lands was required, and without a positive act upon their part he was a trespasser. He must be presumed in law, therefore, to have taken possession by means of that positive act, and to that act the plaintiff was a party. In other words he was allowed by the executors, with the plaintiff's consent, to go into possession of property against which the plaintiff had a specific right, and the possession of the assets for a time however short was a benefit in law to the defendant, and might mean the whole loss of the plaintiff's remedy. The statement that he would 'possess' the lands might merely mean that the defendant would elect to take under the will, as against the settlement, but that, with his subsequent promises to pay, was evidence for the jury of a personal contract. For these reasons I consider that we do not, for the sake of honesty, trench upon any rule of law—nor are much affected as to anything but substantial right—in holding that the plaintiff was entitled to judgment.

Gibson J.:

In my opinion, apart from the fact of the defendant asking and getting time for payment, of which there was evidence, but which was not left to or found by the jury, the contract shows a valid consideration moving from the plaintiff, and is enforceable in law. The defendant got an advantage to which he was not entitled; and the plaintiff—who could have objected—might have been damnified by the defendant being then let into possession, and being enabled, with the consent of the executors, to deal with and dispose of the property bequeathed.

1.   1 B & S 393

(Holmes J. concurred.)

Notes

1. The *Barry* case indicates that the decision in *McCoubray v Thompson* would have been different if the plaintiff had some interest in the farm he had given up.
2. It has been suggested that in the case of joint promisees, only one of the promisees needs to provide consideration. See *McEvoy v The Belfast Banking Co. Ltd*, p.754. below.

F. Performance of Existing Duties

Performance of an existing duty imposed by a contract with a third party is good consideration.

Pao On v Lau Yiu Long [1980] AC 614
(Facts on p.128.)

Lord Scarman:

The extrinsic evidence in this case shows that the consideration for the promise of indemnity, while it included the cancellation of the subsidiary agreement, was primarily the promise given by the plaintiffs to the defendants, to perform their contract with Fu Chip, which included the undertaking not to sell sixty per cent of the shares allotted to them before 30 April 1974. Thus the real consideration for the indemnity was the promise to perform, or the performance of, the plaintiffs' pre-existing contractual obligations to Fu Chip. . . . Their Lordships do not doubt that a promise to perform, or the performance of, a pre-existing contractual obligation to a third party can be valid consideration. In *New Zealand Shipping Co. Ltd v A. M. Satterthwaite & Co. Ltd (The Eurymedon)*,[1] the rule and the reason for the rule were stated: 'An agreement to do an act which the promisor is under an existing obligation to a third party to do, may quite well amount to valid consideration . . . the promisee obtains the benefit of a direct obligation . . . This proposition is illustrated and supported by *Scotson v Pegg*[2] which their Lordships consider to be good law.' Unless, therefore the guarantee was void as having been made for an illegal consideration or voidable on the ground of economic duress, the extrinsic evidence establishes that it was supported by valid consideration.

1. [1975] AC 154; [1974] 1 Lloyd's Rep 534.
2. (1861) 6 H & N 295.

Performance of an existing public duty is generally determined to be good consideration where something more than is required is undertaken. For example, in *Ward v Byham* [1956] 2 All ER 318, a promise by a mother to exceed her statutory duty of caring for her child by agreeing to keep the child happy, was deemed by the Court to be supported by good consideration.

Williams *v* Williams [1957] 1 WLR 148

Following his desertion by his wife, a husband agreed to support her and pay her weekly maintenance. The wife later sued for sums due under this agreement.

Denning L.J.:

The husband relies on the fact that his wife deserted him. If there had been a separation by consent, he agrees that the agreement would have been enforceable. In that case the husband would still be under a duty to maintain, and the sum of 30s a week would be assumed to be a quantification of a reasonable sum for her maintenance having regard to her own earning capacity. The ascertainment of a specific sum in place of an unascertained sum has always been held to be good consideration. So long as circumstances remained unchanged, it would be treated by the courts as binding on her and she could not recover more from him: see *National Assistance Board v Parkes*.[1] But in the present case the husband says that, as the wife deserted him, he was under no obligation to maintain her and she was not entitled to pledge his credit in any way. Clause 2 therefore gives him nothing and is valueless to him. The husband says that *Goodinson v Goodinson*[2] is distinguishable because there was no finding in that case that the wife was in desertion, and moreover the wife promised to maintain the child as well as herself.

Now I agree that, in promising to maintain herself whilst she was in desertion, the wife was only promising to do that which she was already bound to do. Nevertheless, a promise to perform an existing duty is, I think, sufficient consideration to support a promise, so long as there is nothing in the transaction which is contrary to the public interest. Suppose that this agreement had never been made, and the wife had made no promise to maintain herself and did not do so. She might then have sought and received public assistance or have pledged her husband's credit with tradesmen: in which case the National Assistance Board might have summoned him before the magistrates, or the tradesmen might have sued him in the County Court. It is true that he would have an answer to those claims because she was in desertion, but nevertheless he would be put to all the trouble, worry and expense of defending himself against them. By paying her 30s a week and taking this promise from her that she will maintain herself and will not pledge his credit, he has an added safeguard to protect himself from all this worry, trouble and expense. That is a benefit to him which is good consideration for his promise to pay maintenance. That was the view which appealed to the County Court judge: and I must say that it appeals to me also.

There is another ground on which good consideration can be found. Although the wife was in desertion, nevertheless it must be remembered that desertion is never irrevocable. It was open to her to come back at any time. Her right to maintenance was not lost by the desertion. It was only suspended. If she made a genuine offer to return which he rejected, she would have been entitled to maintenance from him. She could apply to the magistrates or the High Court for an order in her favour. If she did so, however, whilst this agreement was in force, the 30s would be regarded as *prima facie* the correct figure. It is a benefit to the husband for it to be so regarded, and that is sufficient consideration to support his promise.

. . . I would dismiss the appeal accordingly.

[1.] [1955] 2 QB 506.   [2.] [1954] 2 QB 118.

(Hodson and Morris L.JJ. both dismissed the appeal on the grounds that the desertion acted only to suspend the wife's right to maintenance.)

Consider:

Would the protection from worry referred to in the *Williams* case be sufficient on its own without the 'trouble and expense' to constitute good consideration?

McKerring *v* The Minister for Agriculture [1989] ILRM 82

The plaintiff farmer applied for grant payments under the tuberculosis and brucellosis eradication schemes. The defendant refused payment, claiming first that the plaintiff had not complied with the necessary conditions of the schemes, and second that payment was made on a purely *ex gratia* basis, not as a matter of legal obligation.

O'Hanlon J.:

The conditions and provisions all convey to me the impression of a promise to pay, if they are duly complied with . . . and it appears to me that there is sufficient consideration involved in strict compliance with all the conditions, even though some of them may be a matter of legal obligation as well.

(O'Hanlon J. found, however, that the plaintiff by his failure to comply with the conditions of the scheme had disentitled himself to grant payments.)

Notes

1. The *McKerring* case may be deemed to be consistent with *Ward v Byham* on the basis that the plaintiff was agreeing to comply with certain obligations which were not legal binding on him.

2. In *McHugh v Kildare County Council* [2005] IEHC 356, unrep., the Court stated that the defendant conferred a benefit on the plaintiff by rezoning a portion of his lands and that this was good consideration for his promise to transfer certain land to it. Gilligan J. stated:

I take the view that the defendant clearly conferred a benefit on the plaintiff and that consideration moved from the defendants to the plaintiff. I adopt the rationale of Denning L.J. as expressed in *Ward v Byham* (1956) 2 AER 318 at p. 319 wherein he stated:

I have always thought that a promise to perform an existing duty or the performance of it should be regarded as good consideration because it is a benefit to the person to whom it is given.

The Court did not deal with the issue of consideration further and thus it is difficult to argue whether the defendant would be viewed as conferring some additional benefit in excess of his legal duty.

SECTION TWO—EXCEPTIONS TO BARGAIN

Although contracts are generally described as bargains, not all agreements can be viewed as bargains in the strict sense.

Atiyah (op. cit.). (Footnotes abridged.)

Consideration and Bargains

The third proposition which forms a central part of the orthodox doctrine is that the law enforces only bargains; that all contracts are bargains;[1] that consideration is not an artificial or accidental requirement of the law, but merely a recognition of the law's concern with bargains;[2] and that accordingly nothing can be consideration which is not regarded as such by the parties;[3] consideration, in short, is the 'price' of the promise.[4] It is my contention that this part of the orthodox doctrine, simply does not represent the law.

The American Restatement, Second (§3) defines a bargain as 'an agreement to exchange promises or to exchange a promise for a performance or to exchange performances', but Corbin adopts a narrower definition for the purposes of his great work. He regards a bargain as involving not merely an exchange, but an exchange of equivalents.[5] I think that Corbin's definition is nearer to the meaning of the term in ordinary usage, but whichever definition is adopted, I suggest that there are many contracts recognised and enforced by the courts which do not involve a bargain in either of these senses. I will refer to the Restatement's definition as the wider sense, and Corbin's as the narrower sense of the term. Both agree that the essential element of a bargain is that there should be an *exchange* of promise for promise, or promise for act. The consideration must be given *in return for* the promise. Now it cannot be doubted that most contracts are bargains, both in the narrow sense and the wide sense; but once again one sees here the apparent compulsion to generalise from the typical case. Because bargains are the most common form of contract, it is simply assumed, without examination of the evidence, that all contracts are bargains. Let us now examine the evidence, which in this context consists of the actual decisions of the courts. Naturally, there are more cases which do not fit the narrower sense than the wider sense.

Nominal consideration

A promise given for nominal consideration is perhaps a bargain in the wide sense, but not in the narrow sense. I doubt if the ordinary person would call such a contract a bargain which is one reason why the narrow definition of the term seems more accurate.

Collateral contracts

A collateral contract is sometimes a bargain in the wide sense, and perhaps arguably even in the narrow sense. For example, if a car dealer says to a prospective buyer, 'If you enter into a hire-purchase agreement to acquire this car from the X Finance Co., I promise to repair the brakes', or 'I warrant that the brakes are in good order', this is arguably a bargain even in the narrow sense. But even here it seems to stretch the meaning of the term to say that here is an exchange of *equivalents*, and I would prefer to regard this as a bargain only in the wider sense. But it must be recognised that there are a large number of collateral contracts which cannot possibly be regarded as bargains in either the narrow or the wide sense. An auctioneer promises to sell goods without reserve; this promise is enforceable by the highest bidder, his bid being treated as a sufficient consideration for the promise.[6] There is clearly no bargain here in any sense of the word; the auctioneer does not *exchange* his promise for the bid; the bid merely follows the promise in natural reliance thereon. Orthodox lawyers have indeed looked askance at the decision holding the auctioneer's promise binding,[7] but if we rid ourselves of the preconceived assumption that all considerations must fall within some predetermined pattern, is there any reason for doubting the decision? Orthodoxy finds difficulty in the decision because the consideration found in that case does not fit the typical pattern. But let us rephrase the issue facing the court in that case, and ask: Is there a sufficient reason for enforcing the auctioneer's promise? Can there be any doubt that the court's answer was correct?

Conditional gift promises

A whole range of cases in which promises are enforced though there is no bargain is to be found in those cases in which the courts have enforced conditional gift promises. This group of cases may come as a surprise to the orthodox lawyer because orthodoxy insists that a promise to make a gift is not enforceable as a contract at all. The fact that the promise is conditional does not, according to orthodox doctrine, render the promise enforceable; and it is in fact necessary to distinguish very carefully between a conditional gift promise and a contractual promise. Nevertheless, the fact is that many such contracts have been enforced; or have been refused enforcement only on other grounds than absence of consideration.

   One type of case in which a conditional gift promise may be enforced is exemplified by *Wyatt v Kreglinger*.[8] The plaintiff retires from the defendant's employment and the defendant promises to pay him a pension in consideration of a promise by the plaintiff not to compete or otherwise damage the defendant's interests. These promises are exchanged, but they are certainly not exchanged as equivalents; there is therefore a bargain in the wide sense, but none in the narrow sense. ...

   In other similar cases, orthodoxy seems to have been defied by the courts with less difficulty. For example, there are cases in which a person has desired to make a gift of a house to another, and has persuaded the donee to enter into a contract to buy the property from a third party on the strength of a definite promise that he will himself pay the price. Such promises have been enforced,[9] though they are plainly gift promises, and there is equally plainly no bargain in any sense of the term. Perhaps the courts have felt less difficulty about such a case because the promisee clearly incurs a detriment in reliance on the promise by entering into the contract to purchase and pay for the property. Orthodoxy thereby seems to be complied with in so far as detriment is present; but orthodoxy is not complied with inasmuch as no bargain is involved.

Then there is the well-known line of cases beginning with *Dillwyn v Llewellyn*,[10] and continuing up to the present day through *Inwards v Baker*[11] to *Pascoe v Turner*[12] and many similar cases, in which a person promises another to give him some land, and allows the promisee to build a property on the land in reliance on the promise.[13] Here again (need one repeat it?) there is plainly no bargain ...

The belief that all contracts are bargains has been unconscionably long in dying— indeed, it may be premature to say that it is dying even now, but it is certainly time that it was buried.

1. See e.g. Cheshire and Fifoot, *Law of Contract* (10th edn by M. P. Furmston, 1981), 60–61.
2. See Hamson's well-known article in 54 LQR 233.
3. A proposition stated by Holmes, *The Common Law*, 292.
4. Pollock's definition, adopted by Lord Dunedin in *Dunlop v Selfridge* [1915] AC at p. 855.
5. Op. cit., vol. i §10.
6. *Warlow v Harrison* (1859) 1 E & E 309.
7. See Slade, 68 LQR 238; cf. Gower, ibid., 457, and Slade's reply, 69 LQR 21.
8. [1933] 1 KB 793.
9. *Crosbie v M'Doual* (1806) 13 Ves Jr 148.
10. (1862) 4 De G F & J 517.
11. [1965] 2 QB 29.
12. [1979] 1 WLR 431.
14. See the analysis by S. Moriarty, 'Licences and Land Law: Legal Principles and Public Policy', 100 LQR 376 (1984).

Saunders *v* Cramer (1842) 5 Ir Eq R 12

In anticipation of a marriage between her granddaughter and the plaintiff, a grandmother stated her intention to leave upon her death £2,000 and a house to her granddaughter. The grandmother died shortly after the marriage of her granddaughter and the plaintiff and the plaintiff claimed to be entitled to the £2,000 and the property. The Lord Chancellor held that the plaintiff's marriage was 'the most valuable of all considerations' for the contract. The Lord Chancellor also held that the marriage constituted 'solemn acceptance' of the grandmother's offer.

Shadwell *v* Shadwell (1860) 9 CB (ns) 159

An uncle wrote to his nephew as follows: 'I am glad to hear of your intended marriage with Ellen Nicholl; and, as I promised to assist you at starting, I am happy to tell you that I will pay to you £150 yearly during my life and until your annual income derived from your profession of a chancery barrister shall amount to 600 guineas; of which your own admission will be the only evidence that I shall receive or require.' The nephew sued his uncle's executors for arrears of the annuity, claiming that as consideration for his uncle's promise he had married Ellen Nicholl.

Erle C.J.:

The question raised by the demurrer to the replication to the fourth plea is, whether there is a consideration which will support the action on the promise to pay the annuity of £150 per annum.

The circumstances are, that the plaintiff had made an engagement to marry one Ellen Nicholl, that his uncle had promised to assist him at starting—by which, as I understand the words, he meant on commencing his married life. Then the letter containing the promise declared on is sent, to specify what that assistance would be, namely, £150 per annum during the uncle's life, and until the plaintiff's professional income should be acknowledged by him to exceed 600 guineas per annum; and the declaration avers, that the plaintiff, relying on this promise, without any revocation on the part of the uncle, did marry Ellen Nicholl.

Now, do these facts shew that the promise was in consideration either of a loss to be sustained by the plaintiff or a benefit to be derived from the plaintiff to the uncle, at his, the uncle's request? My answer is in the affirmative.

First, do these facts shew a loss sustained by the plaintiff at his uncle's request? When I answer this in the affirmative, I am aware that a man's marriage with the woman of his choice is in one sense a boon, and in that sense the reverse of a loss: yet, as between the plaintiff and the party promising to supply an income to support the marriage, it may well be also a loss. The plaintiff may have made a most material change in his position, and induced the object of his affection to do the same, and may have incurred pecuniary liabilities resulting in embarrassments which would be in every sense a loss if the income which had been promised should be withheld; and, if the promise was made in order to induce the parties to marry, the promise so made would be in legal effect a request to marry.

Secondly, do these facts shew a benefit derived from the plaintiff to the uncle, at his request? In answering again in the affirmative, I am at liberty to consider the relation in which the parties stood and the interest in the settlement of his nephew which the uncle declares. The marriage primarily affects the parties thereto; but in a secondary degree it may be an object of interest to a near relative, and in that sense a benefit to him. This benefit is also derived from the plaintiff at the uncle's request. If the promise of the annuity was intended as an inducement to the marriage, and the averment that the plaintiff, relying on the promise, married, is an averment that the promise was one inducement to the marriage, this is the consideration averred in the declaration; and it appears to me to be expressed in the letter, construed with the surrounding circumstances.

No case shewing a strong analogy to the present was cited: but the importance of enforcing promises which have been made to induce parties to marry has been often recognised; and the cases cited, of *Montefiori v Montefiori*,[1] and *Bold v Hutchinson*,[2] are examples. I do not feel it necessary to advert to the numerous authorities referred to in the learned arguments addressed to us, because the decision turns upon the question of fact, whether the consideration for the promise is proved as pleaded. I think it is; and therefore my judgment on the first demurrer is for the plaintiff.

The second demurrer raises the question whether the plaintiff's continuance at the bar was made a condition precedent to the right to the annuity. I think not. The uncle promises to continue the annuity until the professional income exceeds the sum mentioned. I find no stipulation that the annuity shall cease if professional diligence ceases—no limitation except a defeasance in case of an amount of income from the other source. If the prospect of success at the bar had failed, a continuance to attend the courts might be an unreasonable expense. My judgment on this demurrer is also for the plaintiff.

The above is the judgment of my brother Keating and myself.

Byles J.:

I am of opinion that the defendant is entitled to the judgment of the court on the demurrer. The inquiry therefore narrows itself to this question—does the letter itself disclose any consideration for the promise? The consideration relied on by the plaintiff's counsel being the subsequent marriage of the plaintiff. I think the letter discloses no consideration. It is in these words: '11 August 1838. Gray's Inn. My dear Lancey—I am glad to hear of your intended marriage with Ellen Nicholl; and, as I promised to assist you at starting, I am happy to tell you that I will pay to you £150 yearly during my life and until your annual income derived from your profession of a chancery barrister shall amount to 600 guineas; of which your own admission will be the only evidence that I shall receive or require. Your ever affectionate uncle, Charles Shadwell.'

It is by no means clear that the words 'at starting' mean 'on marriage with Ellen Nicholl', or with any one else. The more natural meaning seems to me to be, 'at starting in the profession'; for, it will be observed that these words are used by testator in reciting a prior promise made when the testator had not heard of the proposed marriage with Ellen Nicholl, or, so far as appears, heard of any proposed marriage. This construction is fortified by the consideration that the annuity is not in terms made to begin from the marriage, but, as it should seem, from the date of the letter: neither is it in terms made defeasible if Ellen Nicholl should die before marriage.

But, even on the assumption that the words 'at starting' mean on marriage, I still think that no consideration appears, sufficient to sustain the promise. . .

1. 1 W Bl 363.   2. (1850) 20 Beavan 250.

Notes

1. It seems clear here that there is no element of a bargain in this case. Yet Erle C.J. went to great lengths to identify consideration in order to render the promise enforceable.
2. Under the Family Law Act 1981 it is no longer possible to sue for breach of a promise to marry.
3. In *M'Evoy v Moore* (1902) 36 ILTR 99, the plaintiff was requested by the defendant's head groom, without the knowledge of the defendant, to go to the defendant's residence and do work as a stableman. Nothing was said as to wages or period of employment. The plaintiff worked in the defendant's stable for some weeks, and was seen at work by the defendant on several occasions. He then brought the present Civil Bill for wages.

Barton J. held that when defendant's head groom employed plaintiff to do work for defendant, it might reasonably be presumed that he professed to do so on behalf of defendant, and although there was no contract as to time or rate of wages, an implied contract by the defendant to pay the plaintiff at the ordinary rate of wages arose by reason of the defendant having allowed the plaintiff to continue working for him after he became aware plaintiff was doing so.

Williams *v* Roffey Bros & Nicholls (Contractors) Ltd [1990] 1 All ER 512

Glidewell L.J.:

The facts
The plaintiff is a carpenter. The defendants are building contractors who in September 1985 had entered into a contract with Shepherd's Bush Housing Association Ltd to refurbish a block of flats called Twynholm Mansions, Lillie Road, London SW6. The defendants were the main contractors for the works. There are twenty eight flats in Twynholm Mansions, but the work of refurbishment was to be carried out in twenty seven of the flats.

The defendants engaged the plaintiff to carry out the carpentry work in the refurbishment of the twenty seven flats, including work to the structure of the roof. Originally, the plaintiff was engaged on three separate sub-contracts, but these were all superseded by a sub-contract in writing made on 21 January 1986 by which the plaintiff undertook to provide the labour for the carpentry work to the roof of the block and for the first and second fix carpentry work required in each of the twenty seven flats for a total price of £20,000.

The judge found that, though there was no express term providing for payment to be made in stages, the contract of 21 January 1986 was subject to an implied term that the defendants would make interim payments to the plaintiff, related to the amount of work done, at reasonable intervals.

The plaintiff and his men began work on 10 October 1985. The judge found that by 9 April 1986 the plaintiff had completed the work to the roof, had carried out the first fix to all twenty seven flats and had substantially completed the second fix to nine flats. By this date the defendants had made interim payments totalling £16,200.

It is common ground that by the end of March 1986 the plaintiff was in financial difficulty. The judge found that there were two reasons for this, namely: (i) that the agreed price of £20,000 was too low to enable the plaintiff to operate satisfactorily and at a profit. Mr Cottrell, a surveyor employed by the defendants, said in evidence that a reasonable price for the works would have been £23,783; (ii) that the plaintiff failed to supervise his workmen adequately.

The defendants, as they made clear, were concerned lest the plaintiff did not complete the carpentry work on time. The main contract contained a penalty clause. The judge found that on 9 April 1986 the defendants promised to pay the plaintiff the further sum of £10,300, in addition to the £20,000, to be paid at the rate of £575 for each flat in which the carpentry work was completed.

The plaintiff and his men continued work on the flats until the end of May 1986. By that date the defendants, after their promise on 9 April 1986, had made only one further payment of £1,500. At the end of May the plaintiff ceased work on the flats.

. . . the defendants engaged other carpenters to complete the work, but in the result incurred one week's time penalty in their contract with the building owners . . .

Was there consideration for the defendants' promise made on 9 April 1986 to pay an additional price at the rate of £575 per completed flat?

The judge made the following findings of fact which are relevant to this issue. (i) The sub-contract price agreed was too low to enable the plaintiff to operate satisfactorily and at a profit. Mr Cottrell, the defendants' surveyor, agreed that this was so. (ii) Mr Roffey, the managing director of the defendants, was persuaded by Mr Cottrell that the defendants should pay a bonus to the plaintiff. The figure agreed at the meeting on 9 April 1986 was £10,300.

The judge quoted and accepted the evidence of Mr Cottrell to the effect that a main contractor who agrees too low a price with a sub-contractor is acting contrary to his own interests. He will never get the job finished without paying more money.

The judge therefore concluded: 'In my view where the original sub-contract price is too low, and the parties subsequently agree that the additional moneys shall be paid to the sub-contractor, this agreement is in the interests of both parties. This is what happened in the present case, and in my opinion the agreement of 9 April 1986 does not fail for lack of consideration.' In his address to us counsel for the defendants outlined the benefits to the defendants which arose from their agreement to pay the additional £10,300 as (i) seeking to ensure that the plaintiff continued work and did not stop in breach of the sub-contract, (ii) avoiding the penalty for delay and (iii) avoiding the trouble and expense of engaging other people to complete the carpentry work.

However, counsel submits that, though the defendants may have derived, or hoped to derive, practical benefits from their agreement to pay the 'bonus', they derived no benefit in law, since the plaintiff was promising to do no more than he was already bound to do by his sub-contract, i.e. continue with the carpentry work and complete it on time. Thus there was no consideration for the agreement.

Counsel for the defendants relies on the principle of law which, traditionally, is based on the decision in *Stilk v Myrick*.[1] That was a decision at first instance of Lord Ellenborough C.J. On a voyage to the Baltic, two seamen deserted. The captain agreed with the rest of the crew that if they worked the ship back to London without the two seamen being replaced, he would divide between them the pay which would have been due to the two deserters. On arrival at London this extra pay was refused, and the plaintiff's action to recover his extra pay was dismissed. Counsel for the defendant argued that such an agreement was contrary to public policy, but Lord Ellenborough C.J.'s judgment (as reported in Campbell's Reports) was based on lack of consideration. It reads:

I think *Harris v Watson*[2] was rightly decided; but I doubt whether the ground of public policy, upon which Lord Kenyon is stated to have proceeded, be the true principle on which the decision is to be supported. Here, I say the agreement is void for want of consideration. There was no consideration for the ulterior pay promised to the mariners who remained with the ship. Before they sailed from London they had undertaken to do all they could under the emergencies of the voyage. They had sold all their services till the voyage should be completed. If they had been at liberty to quit the vessel at *Cronstadt*, the case would have been quite different; or if the captain had capriciously discharged the two men who were wanting, the others might not have been compellable to take the whole duty upon themselves, and their agreeing to do so might have been a sufficient consideration for the promise of an advance of wages. But the desertion of a part of the crew is to be considered an emergency of the voyage as much as their death; and those who remain are bound by the terms of their original contract to exert themselves to the utmost to bring the ship in safety to her destined port. Therefore, without looking to the policy of this agreement, I think it is void for want of consideration, and that the plaintiff can only recover at the rate of £5 a month.

In *North Ocean Shipping Co. Ltd v Hyundai Construction Co. Ltd, The Atlantic Baron*[3] Mocatta J. regarded the general principle of the decision in *Stilk v Myrick* as still being good law. He referred to two earlier decisions of this court, dealing with wholly different subjects, in which Denning L.J. sought to escape from the confines of the rule, but was not accompanied in this attempt by the other members of the court.

In *Ward v Byham*[4] the plaintiff and the defendant lived together unmarried for five years, during which time the plaintiff bore their child. After the parties ended their relationship, the defendant promised to pay the plaintiff £1 per week to maintain the child, provided that she was well looked after and happy. The defendant paid this sum for some months, but ceased to pay when the plaintiff married another man. On her suing for the amount due at £1 per week, he pleaded that there was no consideration for his agreement to pay for the plaintiff to maintain her child, since she was obliged by law to do so: see s. 42 of the National Assistance Act 1948. The County Court judge upheld the plaintiff mother's claim, and this court dismissed the defendant's appeal.

Denning L.J. said:

I approach the case, therefore, on the footing that, in looking after the child, the mother is only doing what she is legally bound to do. Even so, I think that there was sufficient consideration to support the promise. I have always thought that a promise to perform an existing duty, or the performance of it, should be regarded as good consideration, because it is a benefit to the person to whom it is given. Take this very case. It is as much a benefit for the father to have the child looked after by the mother as by a neighbour. If he gets the benefit for which he stipulated, he ought to honour his promise, and he ought not to avoid it by saying that the mother was herself under a duty to maintain the child. I regard the father's promise in this case as what is sometimes called a unilateral contract, a promise in return for an act, a promise by the father to pay £1 a week in return for the mother's looking after the child. Once the mother embarked on the task of looking after the child, there was a binding contract. So long as she looked after the child, she would be entitled to £1 a week. The case seems to me to be within the decision of *Hicks v Gregory*[5] on which the judge relied. I would dismiss the appeal.

However, Morris L.J. put it rather differently. He said:

Counsel for the father submits that there was a duty on the mother to support the child, that no affiliation proceedings were in prospect or were contemplated, and that the effect of the arrangement that followed the letter was that the father was merely agreeing to pay a bounty to the mother. It seems to me that the terms of the letter negative those submissions, for the father says: 'providing you can prove that [the child] will be well looked after and happy and also that she is allowed to decide for herself whether or not she wishes to come and live with you.' The father goes on to say that the child is then well and happy and looking much stronger than ever before. 'If you decide what to do let me know as soon as possible'. It seems to me, therefore, that the father was saying, in effect: Irrespective of what may be the strict legal position, what I am asking is that you shall prove that the child will be well looked after and happy, and also that you must agree that the child is to be allowed to decide for herself whether or not she wishes to come and live with you. If those conditions were fulfilled the father was agreeable to pay. On those terms, which in fact became operative, the father agreed to pay £1 a week. In my judgment, there was ample consideration there to be found for his promise, which I think was binding.

Parker L.J. agreed. As I read the judgment of Morris L.J., he and Parker L.J. held that, though in maintaining the child the plaintiff was doing no more than she was obliged to do by law, nevertheless her promise that the child would be well looked after and happy was a practical benefit to the father, which amounted to consideration for his promise.

In *Williams v Williams*,[6] a wife left her husband, and he promised to make her a weekly payment for her maintenance. On his failing to honour his promise, the wife claimed the arrears of payment, but her husband pleaded that, since the wife was guilty of desertion she was bound to maintain herself, and thus there was no consideration for his promise. Denning L.J. reiterated his view that: 'a promise to perform an existing duty is, I think, sufficient consideration to support a promise, so long as there is nothing in the transaction which is contrary to the public interest.'

However, the other members of the court (Hodson and Morris L.JJ.) declined to agree with this expression of view, though agreeing with Denning L.J. in finding that there was consideration because the wife's desertion might not have been permanent, and thus there was a benefit to the husband. . . .

There is, however, [a] legal concept of relatively recent development which is relevant, namely that of economic duress. Clearly, if a sub-contractor has agreed to undertake work at a fixed price, and before he has completed the work declines to continue with it unless the contractor agrees to pay an increased price, the sub-contractor may be held guilty of securing the contractor's promise by taking unfair advantage of the difficulties he will cause if he does not complete the work. In such a case an agreement to pay an increased price may well be voidable because it was entered into under duress. Thus this concept may provide another answer in law to the question of policy which has troubled the courts since before *Stilk v Myrick*, and no doubt led at the date of that decision to a rigid adherence to the doctrine of consideration.

This possible application of the concept of economic duress was referred to by Lord Scarman, delivering the judgment of the Judicial Committee of the Privy Council in *Pao On v Lau Yiu*.[7] He said:

Their Lordships do not doubt that a promise to perform, or the performance of, a pre-existing contractual obligation to a third party can be valid consideration. In *New Zealand Shipping Co. Ltd v A M Satterthwaite & Co. Ltd*[8] the rule and the reason for the rule were stated as follows: 'An agreement to do an act which the promisor is under an existing obligation to a third party to do, may quite well amount to valid consideration: . . . the promisee obtains the benefit of a direct obligation . . . This proposition is illustrated and supported by *Scotson v Pegg*[9] which their Lordships consider to be good law.' Unless, therefore, the guarantee was void as having been made for an illegal consideration or voidable on the ground of economic duress, the extrinsic evidence establishes that it was supported by valid consideration. Counsel for the defendants submits that the consideration is illegal as being against public policy. He submits that to secure a party's promise by a threat of repudiation of a pre-existing contractual obligation owed to another can be, and in the circumstances of this case was, an abuse of a dominant bargaining position and so contrary to public policy . . . This submission found favour with the majority in the Court of Appeal. Their Lordships, however, consider it misconceived . . .

It is true that *Pao On v Lau Yiu* is a case of a tripartite relationship, i.e. a promise by A to perform a pre-existing contractual obligation owed to B, in return for a promise of payment by C. But Lord Scarman's words seem to me to be of general application, equally applicable to a promise made by one of the original two parties to a contract.

Accordingly, following the view of the majority in *Ward v Byham* and of the whole court in *Williams v Williams* and that of the Privy Council in *Pao On v Lau Yiu* the present state of the law on this subject can be expressed in the following proposition: (i) if A has entered into a contract with B to do work for, or to supply goods or services to, B in return for payment by B and (ii) at some stage before A has completely performed his obligations under the contract B has reason to doubt whether A will, or will be able to, complete his side of the bargain and (iii) B thereupon promises A an additional payment in return for A's promise to perform his contractual obligations on time and (iv) as a result of giving his promise B obtains in practice a benefit, or obviates a dis-benefit, and (v) B's promise is not given as a result of economic duress or fraud on the part of A, then (vi) the benefit to B is capable of being consideration for B's promise, so that the promise will be legally binding.

As I have said, counsel for the defendants accepts that in the present case by promis-ing to pay the extra £10,300 the defendants secured benefits. There is no finding, and no suggestion, that in this case the promise was given as a result of fraud or duress.

If it be objected that the propositions above contravene the principle in *Stilk v Myrick*, I answer that in my view they do not: they refine and limit the application of that principle, but they leave the principle unscathed, e.g. where B secures no benefit by his promise. It is not in my view surprising that a principle enunciated in relation to the rigours of seafaring life during the Napoleonic wars should be subjected during the succeeding 180 years to a process of refinement and limitation in its application in the present day.

It is therefore my opinion that on his findings of fact in the present case, the judge was entitled to hold, as he did, that the defendants' promise to pay the extra £10,300 was supported by valuable consideration, and thus constituted an enforceable agreement.

As a subsidiary argument, counsel for the defendants submits that on the facts of the present case the consideration, even if otherwise good, did not 'move from the promisee'. This submission is based on the principle illustrated in the decision in *Tweddle v Atkinson*.[10]

My understanding of the meaning of the requirement that 'consideration must move from the promisee' is that such consideration must be provided by the promisee, or arise out of his contractual relationship with the promisor. It is consider-ation provided by somebody else, not a party to the contract, which does not 'move from the promisee'. This was the situation in *Tweddle v Atkinson*, but it is, of course, not the situation in the present case. Here the benefits to the defendants arose out of their agreement of 9 April 1986 with the plaintiff, the promisee. In this respect I would adopt the following passage from *Chitty on Contracts*,[11] and refer to the authorities there cited: 'The requirement that consideration must move from the promisee is most generally satisfied where some detriment is suffered by him: e.g. where he parts with money or goods, or renders services, in exchange for the promise. But the requirement may equally well be satisfied where the promisee confers a benefit on the promisor without *in fact* suffering any detriment.' (*Chitty's* emphasis.) That is the situation in this case.

I repeat, therefore, my opinion that the judge was, as a matter of law, entitled to hold that there was valid consideration to support the agreement under which the defendants promised to pay an additional £10,300 at the rate of £575 per flat.

For these reasons I would dismiss this appeal.

Russell L.J.:

In the late twentieth century I do not believe that the rigid approach to the concept of consideration to be found in *Stilk v Myrick* is either necessary or desirable. Consideration there must still be but in my judgment the courts nowadays should be more ready to find its existence so as to reflect the intention of the parties to the contract where the bargaining powers are not unequal and where the finding of consideration reflects the true intention of the parties.

What was the true intention of the parties when they arrived at the agreement pleaded by the defendants in para. 5 of the amended defence? The plaintiff had got into financial difficulties. The defendants, through their employee Mr Cottrell, recognised that the price that had been agreed originally with the plaintiff was less than what Mr Cottrell himself regarded as a reasonable price. There was a desire on Mr Cottrell's part to retain the services of the plaintiff so that the work could be completed without the need to employ another sub-contractor. There was further a need to replace what had hitherto been a haphazard method of payment by a more formalised scheme involving the payment of a specified sum on the completion of each flat. These were all advantages accruing to the defendants which can fairly be said to have been in consideration of their undertaking to pay the additional £10,300. True it was that the plaintiff did not undertake to do any work additional to that which he had originally undertaken to do but the terms on which he was to carry out the work were varied and, in my judgment, that variation was supported by consideration which a pragmatic approach to the true relationship between the parties readily demonstrates.

For my part I wish to make it plain that I do not base my judgment on any reservation as to the correctness of the law long ago enunciated in *Stilk v Myrick*. A gratuitous promise, pure and simple, remains unenforceable unless given under seal. But where, as in this case, a party undertakes to make a payment because by so doing it will gain an advantage arising out of the continuing relationship with the promisee the new bargain will not fail for want of consideration.

Purchas L.J.:

In my judgment, therefore, the rule in *Stilk v Myrick* remains valid as a matter of principle, namely that a contract not under seal must be supported by consideration. Thus, where the agreement on which reliance is placed provides that an extra payment is to be made for work to be done by the payee which he is already obliged to perform, then unless some other consideration is detected to support the agreement to pay the extra sum that agreement will not be enforceable, *Harris v Watson* and *Stilk v Myrick* involved circumstances of a very special nature, namely the extraordinary conditions existing at the turn of the eighteenth century under which seamen had to serve their contracts of employment on the high seas. There were strong public policy grounds at that time to protect the master and owners of a ship from being held to ransom by disaffected crews. Thus, the decision that the promise to pay extra wages even in the circumstances established in those cases was not supported by consideration is readily understandable. Of course, conditions today on the high seas have changed dramatically and it is at least questionable, counsel for the plaintiff submitted, whether these cases might not well have been decided differently if they were tried today. The modern cases tend to depend more on the defence of duress in a commercial context rather than lack of consideration for the second agreement. In the present case, the question of duress does not arise. The initiative in coming to the agreement of 9 April came from Mr Cottrell and not from the plaintiff. It would not, therefore, lie in the defendants' mouth to assert a defence of duress. Nevertheless, the court is more ready in the presence of this defence being available in the commercial context to look for mutual advantages which would amount to sufficient consideration to support the second agreement under which the extra money is paid. Although the passage cited below from the speech of Lord Hailsham L.C. in *Woodhouse AC Israel Cocoa Ltd SA v Nigerian Produce Marketing Co. Ltd*[12] at 757–758 was strictly *obiter dicta* I respectfully adopt it as an indication of the approach to be made in modern times. The case involved an agreement to vary the currency in which the buyer's obligation should be met, which was subsequently affected by a depreciation in the currency involved. The case was decided on an issue of estoppel but Lord Hailsham L.C. commented on the other issue, namely the variation of the original contract in the following terms:

> If the exchange letter was not variation, I believe it was nothing. The [buyers] asked for a variation in the mode of discharge of a contract of sale. If the proposal meant what they claimed, and was accepted and acted on, I venture to think that the [vendors] would have been bound by their acceptance at least until they gave reasonable notice to terminate, and I imagine that a modern court would have found no difficulty in discovering consideration for such a promise. Businessmen know their own business best even when they appear to grant an indulgence, and in the present case I do not think that there would have been insuperable difficulty in spelling out consideration from the earlier correspondence.

. . . The question must be posed: what consideration has moved from the plaintiff to support the promise to pay the extra £10,300 added to the lump sum provision? In the particular circumstances which I have outlined above, there was clearly a commercial advantage to both sides from a pragmatic point of view in reaching the agreement of 9 April. The defendants were on risk that as a result of the bargain they had struck the plaintiff would not or indeed possibly could not comply with his existing obligations without further finance. As a result of the agreement the defendants secured their position commercially. There was, however, no obligation added to the contractual duties imposed on the plaintiff under the original contract. *Prima facie* this would appear to be a classic *Stilk v Myrick* case. It was, however, open to the plaintiff to be in deliberate breach of the contract in order to 'cut his losses' commercially. In normal circumstances the suggestion that a contracting party can rely on his own breach to establish consideration is distinctly unattractive. In many cases it obviously would be and if there was any element of duress brought on the other contracting party under the modern development of this branch of the law the proposed breaker of the contract would not benefit. With some hesitation and comforted by the passage from the speech of Lord Hailsham L.C., to which I have referred, I consider that the modern approach to the question of consideration would be that where there were benefits derived by each party to a contract of variation even though one party did not suffer a detriment this would not be fatal to the establishing of sufficient consideration to support the agreement. If both parties benefit from an agreement it is not necessary that each also suffers a detriment. In my judgment, on the facts as found by the judge, he was entitled to reach the conclusion that consideration existed and in those circumstances I would not disturb that finding. . .

1.   (1809) 2 Camp. 317, 170 ER 1168.
2.   (1791) Peake 102, [1755–1802] All ER Rep 493.

3.   [1978] 3 All ER 1170, [1979] QB 705.
4.   [1956] 2 All ER 318, [1956] 1 WLR 496.
5.   (1849) 8 CB 378, 137 ER 556.
6.   [1957] 1 All ER 305, [1957] 1 WLR 148.
7.   [1979] 3 All ER 65 at 76, [1980] AC 614 at 632.
8.   [1974] 1 All ER 1015 at 1021, [1975] AC 154 at 168.
9.   (1861) 6 H & N 295, 158 ER 121.
10. (1861) 1 B & S 393, [1861–73] All ER 369.
11. (25th edn, 1983) para. 173.
12. [1972] 2 All ER 271 at 282, [1972] AC 741.

Notes

1. In the *Roffey Bros* case, all three judges emphasised the fact that the defendants obtained a practical benefit though they differed in describing the exact nature of the benefit.
2. The *Roffey Bros* case was applied by the English High Court in *Simon Container Machinery Ltd v Emba Machinery* [1998] 2 Lloyd's Rep. 429.

Consider:

None of the judges in the *Roffey Bros* case overrules *Stilk v Myrick*. Could it be argued that the captain in *Stilk v Myrick* obtained a practical benefit in return for his promise? Would that case be decided differently if heard today?

See Adams & Brownsword, 'Contract, Consideration and the Critical Path', (1990) vol. 53 MLR 536; the authors argue that the *Roffey Bros* decision is significant because it signals that the courts, in deciding whether or not to enforce a promise, may be guided less by technical questions of consideration than by questions of fairness, reasonableness and commercial utility. However, as the next case demonstrates, the decision has not been accepted completely without reserve.

South Caribbean Trading Ltd *v* Trafigura Beheer BV [2005] 1 Lloyd's Rep. 128

Colman J.

It was SCT's obligation to make delivery under contract 3053b. In promising to do so they were promising to perform an existing obligation. The authorities on this issue starting with *Stilk v Myrick*,[1] and developing more recently in *Syros Shipping Co. S.A. v Elaghill Trading Co. Ltd (The Proodos C)*,[2] and *Atlas Express Ltd v Kafco (Importers and Distributors) Ltd*,[3] indicate a firmly established rule of law that a promise to perform an enforceable obligation under a pre-existing contract between the same parties is incapable of amounting to sufficient consideration. The decision of the Court of Appeal in *Williams v Roffey Bros & Nicholls (Contractors) Ltd*[4] appears to have introduced some amelioration to the rigidity of this rule in cases where there has been refusal to perform not amounting to economic duress by the party who might otherwise be in breach of any existing contract and where the other party will derive a practical benefit from such performance.

. . . But for the fact that Williams v Roffey Bros was a decision of the Court of Appeal, I would not have followed it. That decision is inconsistent with the long-standing rule that consideration, being the price of the promise sued upon, must move *from* the promisee. The judgment of Lord Justice Glidewell was substantially based on *Pao On v Lau Yiu Long*,[5] in which the Judicial Committee of the Privy Council had held a promise by A to B to perform a contractual obligation owed by A to X could be sufficient consideration as against B. At p. 15 Lord Justice Glidewell regarded Lord Scarman's reasoning in relation to such tripartite relationship as applicable in principle to a bipartite relationship. But in the former case by the additional promise to B, consideration has moved from A because he has made himself liable to an additional party, whereas in the latter case he has not undertaken anything that he was not already obliged to do for the benefit of the same party. Lord Justice Glidewell substituted for the established rule as to consideration moving from the promisee a completely different principle—that the promisor must by his promise have conferred a benefit on the other party. Lord Justice Purchas at pp. 22–23 clearly saw the nonsequitur but was 'comforted' by observations from Lord Hailsham, L.C. in *Woodhouse AC Israel Cocoa Ltd v Nigerian Product Marketing Co. Ltd*,[6] at pp. 757–758. Investigation of the correspondence referred to in those observations shows that the latter are not authority for the proposition advanced 'with some hesitation' by Lord Justice Purchas.

However, seeing that Williams v Roffey Bros has not yet been held by the House of Lords to have been wrongly decided, and approaching the validity of consideration on the basis of mutuality of benefit, I would hold that SCT's threat of non-compliance with its delivery obligation under contract 3053b precluded its reliance on the benefit that its performance by effecting delivery would confer on Trafigura. This threat was analogous to economic duress as contemplated *in Williams v Roffey Bros, supra* because it was not based on any argument that SCT was discharged from its delivery obligation: reliance on cl. 7 of contract 5536 only came later.

1. (1809) 2 Camp. 317.
2. [1980] 2 Lloyd's Rep. 390.
3. [1989] 1 Q.B. 833.
4. [1991] 1 QB. 1.
5. [1980] A.C. 614.
6. [1972] A.C. 741.

A. Phang, 'Consideration at the Crossroads' (1991) 107 LQR 21

The second issue concerns (or, rather, questions) the very need for the doctrine of consideration in the first place. While the dispensation with the concept of legal benefit or detriment in Williams v Roffey Bros is desirable inasmuch as the concept entails 'an error of logic', serving, at any rate in bilateral contracts, to pull itself up by, as it were, its own bootstraps (see Goodhart, citing Corbin's views, in (1956) 72 LQR 490 at p. 492), it is submitted that the very doctrine itself needs re-examination, even in the formation of contract. It is, especially now that factual benefit and detriment have come to the fore, far too malleable. Further, despite the rejection of Lord Mansfield's gallant attempts at instituting a doctrine of 'moral' consideration, it looks very much as if we are back on the path towards it (witness, e.g. the reliance by the court in Williams v Roffey Bros on the judgments of the majority in Ward v Byham [1956] 1 WLR 496, the reasoning of which is not only vague, but, on one interpretation, also comes close to the borderline of 'moral' consideration).

In *The Alev*, Hobhouse J. observed ([1989] 1 Lloyd's Rep. 138 at p. 147): 'Now that there is a properly developed doctrine of . . . economic duress, there is no warrant for the court to fail to recognise the existence of some consideration even though it may be insignificant and even though there may have been no mutual bargain in any realistic use of that phrase.' A similar approach was adopted by Russell L.J. and Purchas L.J. in *Williams v Roffey Bros* (see [1990] 2 WLR 1153 at pp 1168 and 1170). Quite apart from the difficulties with economic duress mentioned earlier, this endorsement of technical consideration leads to at least one major problem. The doctrine would not aid in distinguishing between seriously intended agreements and gift arrangements, simply because (to paraphrase from para. 20 of the Law Revision Committee Report of 1937 (Cmd. 5449)) the well established rule that consideration need not be adequate entails the consequence that merely technical consideration will be enough, although the resulting transaction would, in substance, be a gift. Finally, the decisions of the courts, while true to the technicalities of the doctrine, often disregard business realities that could probably have been characterised as factual benefits or detriments had the court concerned been minded to do so.

Given the problems indicated above, it is submitted that serious thought ought to be given by both the legislature and the courts to a reappraisal of the doctrine of consideration. Complete abolition (advocated by Lord Wright as far back as 1936: see 49 Harv L Rev 1225) may be difficult to achieve except in the context of codification. The Law Commission could, perhaps, reconsider the 1937 proposal of the Law Revision Committee to the effect that consideration is merely evidence of a serious intention to contract, with the result that it should not be required where the promise itself is in writing. There are, of course, difficulties with that part of the proposal which emphasises the significance of writing. The experience in the US in this regard has not been altogether happy (see, e.g., von Mehren, (1959) 72 Harv L Rev 1009 at p. 1055). It has also been argued that writing can be just as casual and, consequently, produce just as unjust results as enforceable oral promises (see Patterson, (1958) 58 Col L Rev 929 at pp 958 and 963), although it is submitted that a process of education of the public could be initiated should this alternative criterion of writing be introduced. This proposed reform raises, in the final analysis, policy questions that are more appropriately within the province of Parliament.

It is suggested that, in the meantime, however, the courts ought to supplement the defects of consideration by a bolder development of the doctrine of promissory estoppel: indeed, there are signs that they are already moving towards doing so. This doctrine is grounded in the equitable rationale of unconscionability, and there is no reason in principle why it should not be employed even where to do so would incidentally override the rather technical requirements of consideration. Such an approach finds support in at least two first instance judgments: that of Oliver J. in *Taylors Fashions Ltd v Liverpool Victoria Trustees Co. Ltd* [1982] QB 133, especially at pp 151–152; and that of Robert Goff J. in *Amalgamated Investment & Pty Co. Ltd v Texas Commerce International Bank Ltd* [1982] QB 84, especially at pp 106–108 (although this liberal approach was limited by the Court of Appeal to the notion of 'estoppel by convention'). Indeed, in *Williams v Roffey Bros* itself, both Glidewell L.J. and Russell L.J. referred to a possible argument based upon promissory estoppel. The law relating to promissory estoppel has become more prominent since the recent High Court of Australia decision of *Waltons Stores (Interstate) Ltd v Maher*, (1988) 164 CLR 387—which, if accepted, gives the doctrine the effect of sword as well. There is no logical reason why promissory estoppel should not, if carefully developed, become a viable supplement to consideration. It need not, however, necessarily supersede consideration altogether; it is significant to note, in the context, that in the *Waltons Stores* case, at least one judge (Brennan J., at pp 423–4) indicated that given the various requirements of promissory estoppel, ' . . . the concern that a general application of the principle of equitable estoppel would make non-contractual promises enforceable as contractual promises can be allayed.'

Note

In 'Consideration and the Variation of Contracts' (2003) NZ Law Review 361, Coote criticises the view, found in *Williams v Roffey Bros*, that the consideration for an executory bilateral contract of variation consists in the hoped-for benefits that will or may result from performance. He argues that an executory bilateral contract to vary has to be formed like any other, and that, since consideration is essential to the existence of the contract, it has to be present in the exchange of promises by which the contract is formed. *Ex hypothesi*, the results of performance come too late. On this thesis, he argues that a promise to perform a duty already owed in contract to the promisee is a mere tautology. See also *Antons Trawling Co Ltd v Smith* [2003] 2 NZLR 23.

SECTION THREE—PART PAYMENT OF A DEBT

The doctrine as stated in *Pinnel's case* ((1603) 5 Rep. 117 a) is 'that payment of a lesser sum on the day in satisfaction of a greater cannot be any satisfaction for the whole, because it appears to the judges that by no possibility a lesser sum can be a satisfaction to the plaintiff for a greater sum.' This principle was affirmed by the House of Lords in *Foakes v Beer* [1884] 9 AC 605, where the court expressed the view that though the rule may be unwise it was too well established to overturn. In Ireland, the principle was accepted in *The Mayor, Aldermen and Burgesses of the Borough of Drogheda v Rev. Edward Fairtlough* (1858) 8 ICLR 98. Lefroy C.J. noted that 'payment of a less sum cannot be a satisfaction of a greater liquidated sum, unless there is some further advantage accompanying the payment, and that advantage must be a reasonable one, and must appear upon the face of the agreement'.

It was once considered that the pragmatic approach to identifying good consideration for a promise to perform an existing duty applied in the *Roffey Bros* case (see p.150) could also be applied to promises to accept lesser amounts in complete satisfaction of a greater debt. The following case dispelled this idea.

Re Selectmove Ltd [1995] 2 All ER 531
A company which owed the Revenue a substantial amount of income tax promised to pay its existing liability by instalments and also to pay future taxes as they fell due. Subsequently, the Revenue served a statutory demand and presented a winding-up petition.

Gibson J.:
There are two elements to the consideration which the company claims was provided by it to the Crown. One is the promise to pay off its existing liability by instalments from 1 February 1992. The other is the promise to pay future PAYE and NIC as they fell due . . . Accordingly, the second element is no more than a promise to pay that which

it was bound to pay under the fiscal legislation at the date at which it was bound to make such payment. If the first element is not good consideration, I do not see why the second element should be either.

The judge held that the case fell within the principle of *Foakes v Beer* (1884) 9 App Cas 605 [1881–5] All ER Rep 106 . . .

. . . it is clear that the House of Lords decided that a practical benefit of that nature is not good consideration in law.

[Counsel], however, submitted that an additional benefit to the Crown was conferred by the agreement in that the Crown stood to derive practical benefits therefrom: it was likely to recover more from not enforcing its debt against the company, which was known to be in financial difficulties, than from putting the company into liquidation. He pointed to the fact that the company did in fact pay its further PAYE and NIC liabilities and £7,000 of its arrears. He relied on the decision of this court in *Williams v Roffey Bros & Nicholls (Contractors) Ltd* [1990] 1 All ER 512 for the proposition that a promise to perform an existing obligation can amount to good consideration provided that there are practical benefits to the promisee. . .

[Counsel] submitted that although [in *Williams v Roffey Bros*] Glidewell L.J. in terms confined his remarks to a case where B is to do the work for or supply goods or services to A, the same principle must apply where B's obligation is to pay A, and he referred to an article by Adams and Brownsword 'Contract, Consideration and the Critical Path' (1990) 53 MLR 536 at 539–540 which suggests that *Foakes v Beer* might need reconsideration. I see the force of the argument, but the difficulty that I feel with it is that if the principle of Williams' case is to be extended to an obligation to make payment, it would in effect leave the principle in *Foakes v Beer* without any application. When a creditor and a debtor who are at arm's length reach agreement on the payment of the debt by instalments to accommodate the debtor, the creditor will no doubt always see a practical benefit to himself in so doing. In the absence of authority there would be much to be said for the enforceability of such a contract. But that was a matter expressly considered in *Foakes v Beer* yet held not to constitute good consideration in law. *Foakes v Beer* was not even referred to in Williams' case, and it is in my judgment impossible, consistently with the doctrine of precedent, for this court to extend the principle of Williams' case to any circumstances governed by the principle of *Foakes v Beer*. If that extension is to be made, it must be by the House of Lords or, perhaps even more appropriately, by Parliament after consideration by the Law Commission.

Notes

1. Re *Selectmove* was followed by Keane J. in *Truck & Machinery Sales Ltd v Marubeni Komatsu Ltd* (HC) 23 February 1996, unrep., and in *Corbern v Whatmusic Holdings Ltd* [2003] EWHC 2134. In the latter case, Corbern, a former director, had petitioned to have Whatmusic Holdings wound up on the basis of non-payment of his wages. Whatmusic Holdings argued that Corbern had agreed to forego payment until such time as the company had sufficient funds to meet its obligations. Whatmusic Holdings further argued that there had been consideration for Corbern's promise in the form of the benefits he would derive from its continued existence as a company as a result of his voluntary sacrifice. Hart J. in the High Court rejected this argument on the basis that such an attempted extension of the principle in *Roffey Bros* to a situation of the present kind 'would be

wholly to sterilise the effects of the decision of the House of Lords in
Foakes v Beer'.

2. In the Law Revision Committee's Sixth Interim Report (Cmd. 5449) the
abolition of the Rule in *Pinnel's case* was recommended.

A number of common-law exceptions to the Rule in *Pinnel's case* have arisen
which have gone some way towards ameliorating the injustice often
caused by the rule. These include an acceptance by a creditor of part
payment from a third party in full satisfaction of a debt and a compromise
with creditors. A further exception is the doctrine of estoppel considered
below.

SECTION FOUR – ESTOPPEL

Although, for ease of understanding, this section divides estoppel into a
number of different categories, it should be noted that there is no
consensus as to the exact number of estoppels, and indeed one of the
most controversial questions of estoppel is whether or not these different
estoppels should form part of one coherent doctrine adopted by the
Courts.

A. TRADITIONAL ESTOPPEL

Traditional estoppel or estoppel by representation involves one party
making a representation of existing fact to another party which is acted
upon by that other party to its detriment. In such a case the first party is
estopped from denying the truth of the representation.

M'Neill *v* Millen & Co. Ltd [1907] IR 328

The plaintiff left his car to be repaired in the defendants' garage. He
informed the defendants of his intention to take out an insurance policy to
cover his car against fire. The defendants said that this would be
unnecessary as they had themselves insured his car. As a result of this
statement the plaintiff refrained from insuring the car. When the car was
destroyed by a fire in the garage it materialised that the car was not
insured. The plaintiff sued for damages.

Lord O'Brien L.C.J.:

Now, putting out of consideration the earlier questions submitted to the jury, I apply
myself to findings 4, 5 and 6. Number 4 is this—'Did the defendants represent to the
plaintiff that the motor car was insured *for him*?' I emphasise the expression 'for him'; it
seems to have been deliberately inserted by the Lord Chief Baron. *Answer*: 'Yes.' No. 5.
'Was such representation made negligently, carelessly, and without due and proper
care?' *Answer*: 'Yes.' No. 6. 'Was it by reason of such representation that the plaintiff
refrained from insuring the said car?' *Answer*: 'Yes.' These are the material questions.
What do they amount to? That there was a representation made that a certain stage of

things existed in point of fact—*viz.* that the motor car was, in fact, insured *for him*, a distinction which is important, having regard to Lord Cranworth's judgment in *Jorden v Money*;[1] distinguishing the previous decisions. It was not a case of mere promise or statement of intention; it was a representation of a matter as actually existing.

I think it was the duty of the defendants in this business transaction to take reasonable care that the statement they made, that the car was insured, was true; and I am of opinion that, inasmuch as they did not discharge their duty in this respect, the action can be sustained on the fourth and fifth findings: see Lord Esher's statement of the law in *Seton v Lafone*.[2] This cause of action would rest on a breach of duty—the negligent omission to see that their statements, made in the course of business, in a business transaction, were well founded. This would be a cause of action irrespective of estoppel; but I own I prefer to rest my judgment on the ground of estoppel . . . and what is meant by the estoppel in this case is that the defendants were, having regard to the findings of the jury, estopped from denying that the evidence established the plaintiff's claim, as put forward in this amended paragraph. This is the way Lord Bowen, in the case cited (*Low v Bouverie*[3]), dealt with the topic of estoppel, as to estoppel not being in itself a cause of action, but merely a rule of evidence. On this question of estoppel all the findings of the jury are relevant, especially the sixth, to which, perhaps, an additional degree of importance should be attached; but I omit no one finding. The sixth finding is a finding that the representation made was the efficient cause, the *causa causans* of his not having insured himself. You have, then, in these findings a representation of fact plainly intended to be acted upon, as you have the representation in fact acted upon.

The leading case on this subject is *Freeman v Cooke*,[4] and it is there laid down that 'whatever a man's real meaning may be, if he so conducts himself that a reasonable man would take the representation to be true, and believe that it was meant that he should act upon it, and did act upon it as true, the party making the representation would be equally precluded from contesting its truth.' A host of other cases proceeded on the same lines; but there is a case which seems to be of considerable importance, *Carr v The London and North Western Rly Co.*[5]—of importance because this doctrine of estoppel or representation was gone into at great length. In that case the plaintiff received notice from the defendant railway company that they had three parcels of goods in their possession consigned to him. Thereupon, he instructed his broker to sell the three parcels. The three parcels were sold, and rent and charges due upon them were paid by the broker to the railway company. Only two parcels were, in fact, delivered to the railway company, and they discovered this two days after they had given the original notification to the plaintiff, but they did not correct the original advice, by stating that only two parcels had been in fact received, until after the sale and the payment of their charges. The plaintiff had to make good to his vendees the difference between the price of the third parcel and the price of the goods which they had to buy in substitution for it. It was held that the railway company were not estopped from showing that the goods had never reached their hands, and that they were not liable to the plaintiff for the difference.

In this case you have the very thing which was not in *Carr v London & North Western Rly Co.*, because you have here established that the efficient cause of his not insuring was the representation made by the defendants. Now, in *Carr v London & North Western Rly Co.* the court discussed at great length estoppel, and they laid down a number of propositions, amongst others this—'Another recognised proposition seems to be, that, if a man, either in express terms or by conduct, makes a representation to another of the existence of a certain state of facts which he intends to be acted upon in a certain way, and it be acted upon in that way in the belief of the existence of such a state of facts, to the damage of him who so believes and acts, the first is estopped from denying the existence of such a state of facts.' This is applicable to this case. A representation was made that the car was in fact insured for the benefit of the plaintiff, that there was a policy, portion of which had been placed opposite his car, and which in fact insured the money for him. It is clear that the person who made the representation intended it to be acted upon, and it was in fact acted upon, for, so to speak, the manner of acting was refraining from acting—refraining from insuring. The defendants must make good the representation that the insurance which existed was an insurance for the plaintiff's benefit, and that the money to be paid under it would be available for the plaintiff.

Madden J.:

I concur with the Lord Chief Justice in holding that the defendants are estopped from denying that the motor car was not only insured, but insured for the plaintiff. The defendants' counsel have contended that estoppel is not sufficient to support the plaintiff's action. Estoppel, they say, is only a rule of evidence, and cannot of itself be the foundation of an action. The thing the defendants are estopped from denying is, they contend, *nudum pactum*, inasmuch as they were not bound to insure the car for the plaintiff. I am not to be taken as deciding that there was no consideration for the insuring of the car, having regard to the agreement between the parties. But the answers of the jury to the fifth and sixth questions render it unnecessary to consider that question. The defendants may not have been under a legal obligation to insure the car. But there was, in my opinion, a duty cast upon them to take reasonable care that a statement made in the course of business, likely from its nature to affect conduct, was in accordance with fact. In the words of Lord Esher, M.R.: 'If a man, in the course of business, volunteers to make a statement on which it is probable that, in the course of business, another will act, there is a duty which arises towards the person to whom he makes that statement. There is clearly a duty not to state a thing which is false to his knowledge, and further than that, I think there is a duty to take reasonable care that the statement shall be correct': *Seton v Lafone*. The jury have found that the representation that the car was insured for the plaintiff was made negligently, carelessly, and without due and proper care, and further that it was by reason of such representation that the plaintiff refrained from insuring his car. The fact that the plaintiff has, as a consequence of the representation, altered his position to his loss, brings into operation the principle of representation. The defendants are bound to make good the representation thus acted upon, apart from any consideration in regard to the original action of the defendants in insuring the car.

1. 5 HL Cas 185.
2. 19 QBD at p. 72.
3. [1891] 3 Ch. at p. 105.
4. 2 Ex. 654.
5. LR 10 CP 307.

(Wright J. concurred.)

Note

In the M'Neill case, the defendant's appeal to the Court of Appeal was dismissed. However, the Court of Appeal stated that the ground of legal liability was contract.

B. PROMISSORY ESTOPPEL

Promissory estoppel involves reliance on promises rather than statements of existing fact. As an acknowledgment of its roots, the doctrine is also termed 'equitable estoppel' or 'High Trees estoppel'.

Central London Pty Trust Ltd *v* High Trees House Ltd [1947] KB 130

In 1937 the plaintiffs leased to the defendants (a subsidiary of the plaintiffs) a block of flats for a term of ninety-nine years at a ground rent of £2,500. In early 1940, owing to war conditions, only a few of the flats were let and the plaintiffs agreed that the ground rent for the premises would be reduced to £1,250 as from the commencement of the lease. By the beginning of 1945 all the flats were let. In September 1945, the plaintiffs wrote to the defendants claiming that rent was payable at the rate of £2,500 and, subsequently, in order to determine the legal position, they initiated friendly proceedings in which they claimed the difference between rent at the rate of £2,500 and £1,250 for the last two quarters of 1945. By their defence the defendants claimed that the agreement for the rent reduction operated during the whole term of the lease and, as alternatives, that the plaintiffs were estopped from demanding rent at the higher rate or had waived their right to do so.

Denning J.:

If I were to consider this matter without regard to recent developments in the law, there is no doubt that had the plaintiffs claimed it, they would have been entitled to recover ground rent at the rate of £2,500 a year from the beginning of the term, since the lease under which it was payable was a lease under seal which, according to the old common law, could not be varied by an agreement by parol (whether in writing or not), but only by deed. Equity, however stepped in, and said that if there has been a variation of a deed by a simple contract (which in the case of a lease required to be in writing would have to be evidenced by writing), the courts may give effect to it as is shown in *Berry v Berry*.[1] That equitable doctrine, however, could hardly apply in the present case because the variation here might be said to have been made without consideration. With regard to estoppel, the representation made in relation to reducing the rent, was not a representation of an existing fact. It was a representation, in effect, as to the future, namely, that payment of the rent would not be enforced at the full rate but only at the reduced rate. Such a representation would not give rise to an estoppel, because, as was said in *Jorden v Money*,[2] a representation as to the future must be embodied as a contract or be nothing.

But what is the position in view of developments in the law in recent years? The law has not been standing still since *Jorden v Money*. There has been a series of decisions over the last fifty years which, although they are said to be cases of estoppel are not really such. They are cases in which a promise was made which was intended to create legal relations and which, to the knowledge of the person making the promise, was going to be acted on by the person to whom it was made, and which was in fact so acted on. In such cases the courts have said that the promise must be honoured. The cases to which I particularly desire to refer are: *Fenner v Blake*,[3] *In re Wickham*,[4] *Re William Porter & Co. Ltd*[5] and *Buttery v Pickard*.[6] As I have said they are not cases of estoppel in the strict sense. They are really promises—promises intended to be binding, intended to be acted on, and in fact acted on. *Jorden v Money* can be distinguished, because there the promisor made it clear that she did not intend to be legally bound, whereas in the cases to which I refer the proper inference was that the promisor did intend to be bound. In each case the court held the promise to be binding on the party making it, even though under the old common law it might be difficult to find any consideration for it. The courts have not gone so far as to give a cause of action in damages for the breach of such a promise, but they have refused to allow the party making it to act inconsistently with it. It is in that sense, and that sense only, that such a promise gives rise to an estoppel. The decisions are a natural result of the fusion of law and equity: for the cases of *Hughes v Metropolitan Rly Co.*,[7] *Birmingham and District Land Co. v London & North Western Rly Co.*[8] and *Salisbury (Marquess) v Gilmore*,[9] afford a sufficient basis for saying that a party would not be allowed in equity to go back on such a promise. In my opinion, the time has now come for the validity of such a promise to be recognised. The logical consequence, no doubt is that a promise to accept a smaller sum in discharge of a larger sum, if acted upon, is binding notwithstanding the absence of consideration: and if the fusion of law and equity leads to this result, so much the better. That aspect was not considered in *Foakes v Beer*.[10] At this time of day however, when law and equity have been joined together for over seventy years, principles must be reconsidered in the light of their combined effect. It is to be noticed that in the Sixth Interim Report of the Law Revision Committee, paras 35, 40, it is recommended that such a promise as that to which I have referred, should be enforceable in law even though no consideration for it has been given by the promisee. It seems to me that, to the extent I have mentioned, that result has now been achieved by the decisions of the courts.

I am satisfied that a promise such as that to which I have referred is binding and the only question remaining for my consideration is the scope of the promise in the present case. I am satisfied on all the evidence that the promise here was that the ground rent should be reduced to £1,250 a year as a temporary expedient while the block of flats was not fully, or substantially fully let, owing to the conditions prevailing. That means that the reduction in the rent applied throughout the years down to the end of 1944, but early in 1945 it is plain that the flats were fully let, and, indeed the rents received from them (many of them not being affected by the Rent Restrictions Acts), were increased beyond the figure at which it was originally contemplated that they would be let. At all events the rent from them must have been very considerable. I find that the conditions prevailing at the time when the reduction in rent was made, had completely passed away by the early months of 1945. I am satisfied that the promise was understood by all parties only to apply under the conditions prevailing at the time when it was made, namely, when the flats were only partially let, and that it did not extend any further than that. When the flats became fully let, early in 1945, the reduction ceased to apply.

In those circumstances, under the law as I hold it, it seems to me that rent is payable at the full rate for the quarters ending 29 September and 25 December 1945.

If the case had been one of estoppel, it might be said that in any event the estoppel would cease when the conditions to which the representation applied came to an end, or it also might be said that it would only come to an end on notice. In either case it is only a way of ascertaining what is the scope of the representation. I prefer to apply the principle that a promise intended to be binding, intended to be acted on and in fact acted on, is binding so far as its terms properly apply. Here it was binding as covering the period down to the early part of 1945, and as from that time full rent is payable.

I therefore give judgment for the plaintiff company for the amount claimed.

1. [1929] 2 KB 316.
2. (1854) 5 HLC 185.
3. [1900] 1 QB 426.
4. (1917) 34 TLR 158.
5. [1937] 2 All ER 361.

6. [1946] WN 25.
7. (1877) 2 App Cas 439, 448.
8. (1888) 40 ChD 268, 286.
9. [1942] 2 KB 38, 51.
10. (1884) 9 App Cas 605.

Kenny v Kelly (HC) 27 July 1988, unrep.

The applicant was offered a place in Arts in UCD in September 1986. On 29 or 30 September, the applicant's father met an administrative officer in the Admissions Office who discussed the possibility of deferral with the Senior Administrative Officer, a Miss O'Connor. The applicant's father claimed that he was told that his daughter could defer her place but that she would have to write setting out her reasons for requiring the deferral. The respondent claimed that no deferral was granted. Although the applicant wrote on 10 November, Miss O'Connor wrote to the applicant's father on 30 October stating that it was too late to consider requests for deferral. The applicant was not offered a place the following year as the entry points rose. The applicant instituted judicial review proceedings claiming to be entitled to a place in Arts in 1987.

Barron J.:

The applicant's case depends upon the proper construction to be placed upon what occurred when her father called to the Admissions Office on either 29 or 30 September 1986. His evidence is that he spoke to Miss O'Connor on the telephone that morning and explained to her the reasons for the application and the need for an immediate decision. He was told that the matter could not be dealt with over the telephone and that he should come to the office. This he did in the early afternoon. He again made the same points. The official with whom he spoke went into the inner office and when she returned told him that he could have the deferral but that his daughter would have to write in to confirm the reasons which had already been given. This she did.

No one has been called to give evidence of any conversation with the applicant's father at the Admissions Office on 29 or 30 September 1986. The evidence for the respondent however accepts that he was there and made his application and I accept his evidence that he was told that his daughter could have her deferral. It is clear that the Admissions Office did not regard whatever occurred as amounting to the grant of a deferral. Otherwise the place would have been re-offered. But it is not a question of mistake or misrepresentation. Miss O'Connor to whom the request must have been put in the inner office did not intend to authorise a deferral. The official who communicated her instructions clearly misconstrued them. Nevertheless, this was not known to the applicant's father who was entitled to rely upon what she told him. As between them, there was no mistake. If she did misrepresent her instructions, this does not entitle the respondent to deny her apparent authority to bind the respondent.

The applicant seeks to rely upon the doctrine of 'legitimate expectation' as approved in *Webb v Ireland*, an unreported decision of the Supreme Court delivered on 16 December 1987. In that case, the plaintiffs, having found treasure trove, very properly handed it over to the National Museum. When doing so, they had been assured that they would be treated honourably. It was held that such assurance was an integral part of the transaction whereby the find was handed over and was enforceable. The principles of promissory estoppel upon which this decision was based apply equally in the present case. The applicant had already accepted her place and paid the deposit towards her fees. If she wanted to attend as a student in that year, she had to pay the balance of her fees and to register. If she did not do so, she would have lost her rights to attend subsequently and would also have lost her deposit. The promise of a deferral was in effect a promise not to require the applicant to register and pay the balance of her fees in 1986 but a promise to permit her to do so instead in 1987.

Such a promise to delay the enforcement of legal rights is of the essence of the doctrine of promissory estoppel as it has developed. In *Birmingham and District Land Co. v London and North Western Rly* (1888) 40 ChD 268, Bowen L.J. said at p. 286:

> It seems to me to amount to this, that if persons who have contractual rights against others induce by their conduct those against whom they have such rights to believe that such rights will either not be enforced or will be kept in suspense or abeyance for some particular time, those persons will not be allowed by a court of equity to enforce the rights until such time has elapsed, without at all events placing the parties in the same position as they were before.

In *Central London Pty Trust Co. v High Trees House Ltd*, the essence of promissory estoppel was said to be a promise intended to be binding, intended to be acted upon and in fact acted upon. In my view, the facts of the present case come within these principles. Each of the elements necessary to establish the estoppel is present.

Since the applicant could, if no promise had been made to her, have cancelled her acceptance and obtained a return of her deposit, then it may be argued that there was consideration for the grant of the deferral giving it contractual status. Whichever legal approach is adopted, the applicant is entitled to a declaration that she was entitled to a place in the Arts School in University College Dublin in 1987.

Limitations—Need for an Independent Cause of Action

The doctrine of promissory estoppel is limited in the sense that it is essentially defensive in nature. It cannot be used as an independent cause of action. The rationale for this is that to do so would be contrary to the doctrine of consideration.

Combe v Combe [1951] 1 All ER 767

Following their divorce, the defendant agreed to make the plaintiff an allowance of £100 a year. The defendant did not make any of the agreed payments, but the plaintiff did not apply to the court for an order for permanent maintenance. It was proved as a matter of fact that the plaintiff earned more than the defendant. Nearly seven years later the plaintiff sued for arrears.

Denning L.J.:

Byrne J. held that the first three quarterly instalments of £25 were barred by the Limitation Act, 1939, but he gave judgment for £600 in respect of the instalments which accrued within the six years before the action was brought. He held, on the authority of *Gaisberg v Storr*,[1] that there was no consideration for the husband's promise to pay his wife £100, but, nevertheless, he held that the promise was enforceable on the principle stated in *Central London Pty Trust Ltd v High Trees House Ltd*[2] and *Robertson v Minister of Pensions*,[3] because it was an unequivocal acceptance of liability, intended to be binding, intended to be acted on, and, in fact, acted on.

Much as I am inclined to favour the principle of the *High Trees* case, it is important that it should not be stretched too far lest it should be endangered. It does not create new causes of action where none existed before. It only prevents a party from insisting on his strict legal rights when it would be unjust to allow him to do so, having regard to the dealings which have taken place between the parties. That is the way it was put in the case in the House of Lords which first stated the principle—*Hughes v Metropolitan Rly Co.*[4]—and in the case in the Court of Appeal which enlarged it—*Birmingham and District Land Co. v London & North Western Rly Co.*[5] It is also implicit in all the modern cases in which the principle has been developed. Sometimes it is a plaintiff who is not allowed to insist on his strict legal rights. Thus, a creditor is not allowed to enforce a debt which he has deliberately agreed to waive if the debtor has carried on business or in some other way changed his position in reliance on the waiver: *Re Porter (William) & Co. Ltd*,[6] *Buttery v Pickard*,[7] *Central London Pty Trust Ltd v High Trees House Ltd*, *Ledingham v Bermejo Estancia Co. Ltd*, *Agar v Bermejo Estancia Co. Ltd*.[8] A landlord who has told his tenant that he can live in his cottage rent free for the rest of his life is not allowed to go back on it if the tenant stays in the house on that footing: *Foster v Robinson*.[9] Sometimes it is a defendant who is not allowed to insist on his strict legal rights. His conduct may be such as to debar him from relying on some condition, denying some allegation, or taking some other point in answer to the claim. Thus, a government department, who had accepted a disease as due to war service, were not allowed afterwards to say it was not, when the soldier, in reliance on the assurance, had abstained from getting further evidence about it: *Roberston v Minister of Pensions*. A buyer who had waived the contract date for delivery was not allowed afterwards to set up the stipulated time as an answer to the seller: *Charles Rickards Ltd v Oppenheim*.[10] A tenant who had encroached on an adjoining building, asserting that it was comprised in the lease, was not allowed afterwards to say that it was not included in the lease: J. F. *Perrott & Co. Ltd v Cohen*.[11] A tenant who had lived in a house rent free by permission of his landlord, thereby asserting that his original tenancy had ended, was not afterwards allowed to say that his original tenancy continued: *Foster v Robinson*. In none of these cases was the defendant sued on the promise, assurance, or assertion as a cause of action in itself. He was sued for some other cause, for example, a pension or a breach of contract, or possession, and the promise, assurance, or assertion only played a supplementary role, though, no doubt, an important one. That is, I think, its true function. It may be part of a cause of action, but not a cause of action in itself. The principle, as I understand it, is that where one party has, by his words or conduct, made to the other a promise or assurance which was intended to affect the legal relations between them and to be acted on accordingly, then, once the other party has taken him at his word and acted on it, the one who gave the promise or assurance cannot afterwards be allowed to revert to the previous legal relations as if no such promise or assurance had been made by him, but he must accept their legal relations subject to the qualification which he himself has so introduced, even though it is not supported in point of law by any consideration, but only by his word.

Seeing that the principle never stands alone as giving a cause of action in itself, it can never do away with the necessity of consideration when that is an essential part of the cause of action. The doctrine of consideration is too firmly fixed to be overthrown by a side-wind. Its ill effects have been largely mitigated of late, but it still remains a cardinal necessity of the formation of a contract, although not of its modification or discharge. I fear that it was my failure to make this clear in *Central London Pty Trust Ltd v High Trees House Ltd* which misled Byrne J. in the present case. He held that the wife could sue on the husband's promise as a separate and independent cause of action by itself, although, as he held, there was no consideration for it. That is not correct. The wife can only enforce the promise if there was consideration for it. That is, therefore, the real question in the case: Was there sufficient consideration to support the promise?

If it were suggested that, in return for the husband's promise, the wife expressly or impliedly promised to forbear from applying to the court for maintenance—that is, a promise in return for a promise—there would clearly be no consideration because the wife's promise would not be binding on her and, therefore, would be worth nothing. Notwithstanding her promise, she could always apply to the divorce court for maintenance—perhaps, only with leave—but nevertheless she could apply. No agreement by her could take away that right: *Hyman v Hyman*,[12] as interpreted by this court in *Gaisberg v Storr*. There was, however, clearly no promise by the wife, express or implied, to forbear from applying to the court. All that happened was that she did, in fact, forbear—that is, she did an act in return for a promise. Is that sufficient consideration? Unilateral promises of this kind have long been enforced so long as the act or forbearance is done on the faith of the promise and at the request of the promisor, express or implied. The act done is then in itself sufficient consideration for the promise, even though it arises *ex post facto*, as Parker J. pointed out in *Wigan v English and Scottish Law Life Assurance Assoc.*[13] ([1909] 1 Ch. 298). If the findings of Byrne J. are accepted, they are sufficient to bring this principle into play. His finding that the husband's promise was intended to be binding, intended to be acted on, and was, in fact, acted on—although expressed to be a finding on the principle of the *High Trees House* case—is equivalent to a finding that there was consideration within this long settled rule, because it comes to the same thing expressed in different words: see *Oliver v Davis*.[14] My difficulty, however, is to accept the findings of Byrne J. that the promise was 'intended to be acted on'. I cannot find any evidence of any intention by the husband that the wife should forbear from applying to the court for maintenance, or, in other words, any request by the husband, express or implied, that the wife should so forbear. He left her to apply, if she wished to do so. She did not do so, and I am not surprised, because it is very unlikely that the divorce court would have made any order in her favour, since she had a bigger income than her husband. Her forbearance was not intended by him, nor was it done at his request. It was, therefore, no consideration.

Birkett L.J.:

I think the description which was given by counsel for the husband in this court, namely, that the doctrine there enunciated was, so to speak, a doctrine which would enable a person to use it as a shield and not as a sword, is a very vivid way of stating what, I think, is the principle underlying both those cases. Denning J. in *Central London Pty Trust Ltd v High Trees House Ltd* concluded his judgment with these words ([1947] KB 136): 'I prefer to apply the principle that a promise intended to be binding, intended to be acted on and in fact acted on, is binding so far as its terms properly apply.' If a husband who had entered into an agreement of this kind was to try to take advantage of it, I think the doctrine would then apply, but, so far as the wife is concerned, her right to apply to the court for maintenance is still, theoretically, in full force . . .

Asquith L.J.:

The learned judge decided that while the husband's promise was unsupported by any valid consideration, yet the principle in *Central London Pty Trust Ltd v High Trees House Ltd* entitled the wife to succeed. It is unnecessary to express any view as to the correctness of the decision in the *High Trees* case, although I certainly must not be taken to be questioning it. I would, however, remark in passing that it seems to me a complete misconception to suppose that it struck at the roots of the doctrine of consideration. Assuming, without deciding, that it is good law, I do not think it helps the wife at all. What that case decides is that when a promise is given which (i) is intended to create legal relations, (ii) is intended to be acted on by the promisee, and (iii) is, in fact, so acted on, the promisor cannot bring an action against the promisee which involves the repudiation of his promise or is inconsistent with it. It does not, as I read it, decide that a promisee can sue on the promise. Denning J. expressly states the contrary. . .

Finally, I do not think an actual forbearance, as opposed to an agreement to forbear to approach the court, is a good consideration unless it proceeds from a request, express or implied, on the part of the promisor.

1. [1949] 2 All ER 411; [1950] 1 KB 107; 2nd Digest. Supp.
2. [1947] KB 130; [1947] LJR 77; 175 LT 332; 2nd Digest Supp.
3. [1948] 2 All ER 767; [1949] 1 KB 227; [1949] LJR 323; 2nd Digest Supp.
4. (1877), 2 App Cas 439; 46 LJQB 583; 36 LT 932; 42 JP 421; 21 Digest 310, 1137.
5. (1888), 40 ChD 268; 60 LT 527; 11 Digest 214, 990.
6. [1937] 2 All ER 361; Digest Supp.
7. (1946), 174 LT 144; 2nd Digest Supp.
8. [1947] 1 All ER 749; 2nd Digest Supp.
9. [1950] 2 All ER 342; [1951] 1 KB 149.
10. [1950] 1 All ER 420; [1950] 1 KB 616.
11. [1950] 2 All ER 939.
12. [1929] AC 601; 98 LJP 81; 141 LT 329; 93 JP 209; Digest Supp.
13. [1909] 1 Ch. 291; 78 LJ Ch. 120; 100 LT 34; 12 Digest 212, 1701.
14. [1949] 2 All ER 353; [1949] 2 KB 727; [1949] LJR 1661; 2nd Digest Supp.

Chartered Trust Ireland Ltd *v* Thomas Healy and John Commins (HC) 10 December 1985, unrep.

The first defendant agreed to acquire a lorry from Fleming, who, unknown to the first defendant, had illegally imported it into this jurisdiction, passing it off as another lorry which had a proper and valid registration here. The purchase was financed by the plaintiffs under a hire-purchase agreement. Fleming furnished the plaintiffs with an invoice from a Mr Commins. It subsequently materialised that this invoice had been obtained illicitly. The first defendant used this lorry for one year before handing it back to Fleming to regularise a tax problem. Fleming disappeared with the lorry and the first defendant later ceased paying the hire-purchase instalments. The plaintiffs sued for the balance due on foot of the agreement.

Barron J.:

The defendant's defence to the plaintiff's claim is that the hire-purchase agreement was not made in compliance with the provisions of the Hire-Purchase Act 1946. Secondly, the defendant maintains that since he did not receive the vehicle set out in the hire-purchase agreement that the entire was a nullity and that he is entitled to damages from the plaintiff for his failure to deliver to him the correct vehicle. He then counterclaims for all the sums paid on foot of the agreement since he says that he got no consideration for the sums paid. In defence to this counterclaim the plaintiffs say that the defendant is estopped from making this allegation. They then say that if he is entitled to claim damages from them that they are entitled to an indemnity from John Commins. John Commins' defence to this claim for an indemnity is that he knew nothing at all about the transaction, and is not responsible for the action of his secretary who wrote out the invoice since it was done to his prejudice.

The first question to be determined is whether or not there was a valid hire-purchase agreement. The arrangements for the purchase of the lorry were made by the plaintiff with either Fleming or his agent. Whichever it was, it is clear that the latter was aware that the lorry which he had for sale was not the lorry registered under the number 889 OZA. Such person was also aware that the plaintiff did not know this and was entering into the contract to purchase the lorry in the mistaken belief that it was. I am also satisfied that such person must have known that the plaintiff would not have entered into such a contract if it had been aware of the mistake it was making. In my view, the mistake made by the plaintiff to the knowledge of Fleming or his agent was such that the contract became null and void. In the result, the plaintiff never became the owner of the lorry delivered to the defendant. It follows that the plaintiff was not the owner of the lorry in respect of which it purported to make the hire-purchase agreement. Such agreement was accordingly a nullity. Nevertheless the plaintiff contends that it is entitled to sue on foot of this agreement since the defendant is estopped from denying its validity. It has been said many times that an estoppel does not operate as a sword, but only as a shield. Accordingly, there is no agreement upon which the plaintiff is entitled to sue and its claim accordingly fails.

This rule as to the effect of an estoppel does not prevent the plaintiff from relying upon an estoppel as a defence to the defendant's counterclaim. In my view, the defendant must be taken by virtue of the fact that he signed the hire-purchase agreement and saw the invoice upon which it was based to have known that the details contained in the hire-purchase agreement and in the invoice were incorrect. However, there is no suggestion on the evidence that the defendant was aware that the lorry which he was receiving was not the lorry registered number 889 OZA. Accordingly, it seems to me that while the defendant would be estopped from denying the existence of a trade-in, and from denying the fact that the dealer was the third party in these proceedings, he is not estopped from denying the title of the plaintiff to the lorry which he received. It may well be that the plaintiff would have a cause of action against the defendant for misrepresenting the name of the dealer and the existence of a trade-in but any such cause of action must be the subject matter of separate proceedings. Since the defendant is not estopped from denying the plaintiff's title to the lorry, it follows that his counterclaim must succeed. There has been a total failure of consideration.

Notes

1. See also *Traynor v Fegan* [1985] IR 586.
2. In *The Brantford General Hospital Foundation v The Canada Trust Company* (2003) 67 OR (3d) 432, it was held that the claimant could not argue that the executors of the estate of a taxpayer who had pledged to donate $1 million to it was estopped from completing the payment as they had no independent cause of action. The pledge was deemed to be unsupported by consideration.

Consider:

In the following two examples, will Bill be able to rely on the doctrine of promissory estoppel?

1. Sara promises to give Bill money to allow him buy computer software. Bill orders the software and Sara refuses to pay him. Bill sues her.
2. Bill enters into a contract to supply computer software to Sara. Under the contract Bill must deliver the goods before 1 May. Sara tells Bill that as she has no immediate need for them he may deliver them at his convenience. Bill delivers the goods in April. Sara refuses to pay for them and Bill sues her.

The principle that promissory estoppel does not create legal rights is closely linked to the principle that there must be a pre-existing legal relationship between the parties. The exact nature of this relationship has been the subject of judicial consideration.

The Revenue Commissioners *v* Moroney [1972] IR 372

In order to avoid estate duty at a later stage, the defendants' father agreed to transfer his licensed business to the defendants. The transfer took place by way of a sale of the property to the defendants for £16,000. None of this money was ever paid nor did any of the parties to the transaction expect that it would be paid. The plaintiffs later claimed that part of the £16,000 was an asset of the father and that duty was thus payable on it.

Kenny J. (HC):

In the course of the hearing I asked whether the sons could succeed on a plea that the parent was estopped from claiming any part of the 'purchase' money. Counsel for the defendants did not show any enthusiasm for this point and so I did not have the advantage of hearing counsel for the plaintiffs on it. Despite this, I think that in an action by the parent against the sons they would succeed on what is now called promissory estoppel.

This doctrine first appeared in *Hughes v Metropolitan Rly Co.*[1] which was a claim that a lease be forfeited on the ground that the lessee was in breach of a covenant to effect certain required repairs within six months from the date on which the lessee received from the lessor a notice specifying the defects. The landlord gave notice of the breaches on 22 October 1874, and the tenant's solicitors wrote that the repairs would be commenced immediately but that they proposed to postpone them until they heard whether the landlord wished to purchase the tenant's interest. The landlord's solicitors replied asking whether the tenant was the owner of other adjoining property and was willing to give immediate possession of it and stating that, when they had this information, their client would consider whether he would acquire the tenant's interest. The attempt to negotiate a settlement broke down on 31 December and the question in the case was whether the six months ran from that date or from 22 October, for the repairs had been carried out within the period of six months from 31 December. The case was decided before the law was altered by s. 14 of the Conveyancing Act, 1881. In the course of his speech the Lord Chancellor, Lord Cairns, said at p. 448 of the report:

. . . it is the first principle upon which all courts of equity proceed, that if parties who have entered into definite and distinct terms involving certain legal results— certain penalties or legal forfeiture—afterwards by their own act or with their own consent enter upon a course of negotiation which has the effect of leading one of the parties to suppose that the strict rights arising under the contract will not be enforced, or will be kept in suspense, or held in abeyance, the person who otherwise might have enforced those rights will not be allowed to enforce them where it would be inequitable having regard to the dealings which have thus taken place between the parties.

Lord Justice Bowen in *Birmingham & District Land Co. v London & North Western Rly Co.*[2] showed that the principle was not confined to forfeiture cases but was of general application; at p. 286 of the report he said: '. . . if persons who have contractual rights against others induce by their conduct those against whom they have such rights to believe that such rights will either not be enforced or will be kept in suspense or abeyance for some particular time, those persons will not be allowed by a court of equity to enforce the rights until such time has elapsed, without at all events placing the parties in the same position as they were before.'

The doctrine got little attention in the textbooks until it was revived in striking fashion by Mr Justice Denning (as he then was) in *Central London Pty Trust Ltd v High Trees House Ltd.*[3] . . . In *Combe v Combe*[4] the same judge said that the doctrine 'only prevents a party from insisting upon his strict legal rights, when it would be unjust to allow him to enforce them, having regard to the dealings which have taken place between the parties.' These cases were discussed by Viscount Simonds in *Tool Metal Manufacturing Co. Ltd v Tungsten Electric Co. Ltd*[5] in which he said at p. 764 that the gist of the equity lies in the fact that one party has by his conduct led the other to alter his position; this aspect was emphasised by Mr Justice McVeigh in *Morrow v Carty;*[6] see also *Cullen v Cullen*[7] and *Inwards v Baker.*[8]

In *Ajayi v R. T. Briscoe (Nig.) Ltd*[9] the advice of the Privy Council, given by Lord Hodson, was that the doctrine is confined to cases where the representation relates to existing contractual rights. At p. 1330 of the report Lord Hodson said:

> Their Lordships are of opinion that the principle of law as defined by Bowen L.J. has been confirmed by the House of Lords in the case of *Tool Metal Manufacturing Co. Ltd v Tungsten Electric Co. Ltd* where the authorities were reviewed and no encouragement was given to the view that the principle was capable of extension so as to create rights in the promisee for which he had given no consideration. The principle, which has been described as quasi estoppel and perhaps more aptly as promissory estoppel, is that when one party to a contract in the absence of fresh consideration agrees not to enforce his rights an equity will be raised in favour of the other party. This equity is, however, subject to the qualifications (1) that the other party has altered his position, (2) that the promissor can resile from his promise on giving reasonable notice, which need not be a formal notice, giving the promisee a reasonable opportunity of resuming his position, (3) the promise only becomes final and irrevocable if the promisee cannot resume his position.

This, if correct, would conclude this case in favour of the plaintiffs as any promissory estoppel arises here because the parent before the deed was signed represented by his conduct and by what he said to his sons that he would not require payment of any part of the 'purchase' price. Until the deed was signed, there were no legal relations to be effected.

In my view there is no reason in principle why the doctrine of promissory estoppel should be confined to cases where the representation related to existing contractual rights. It includes cases where there is a representation by one person to another that rights which will come into existence under a contract to be entered into will not be enforced. This is the way in which the doctrine is stated at p. 627 of *Snell's Principles of Equity* (26th edn 1966) which has the considerable authority of having had Mr Megarry (as he then was) as one of its co-editors: 'Where by his words or conduct one party to a transaction makes to the other a promise or assurance which is intended to affect the legal relations between them, and the other party acts upon it, altering his position to his detriment, the party making the promise or assurance will not be permitted to act inconsistently with it.' It seems to me that the parent represented to his sons that he would never seek payment of any part of the consideration of £16,000 and that they acted on this by signing the assignment. Each of them altered his position to his detriment because by signing each took on a legal liability to pay two thirds of the consideration which they would not otherwise have assumed. Although they got the benefit of the interest in the joint tenancy, it seems to me to be probable that if they had refused to sign the deed in the form in which it was they would have got this without payment. The assumption of the legal liability created by the deed was in my opinion sufficient to raise the equity against the parent and the representation has become final because the sons cannot be restored to their original position unless the view is taken that there never was a debt. This equity does not affect the rights of other parties who would be entitled to rely on the deed, but this does not assist the plaintiffs. Their claim can succeed only if the parent would have succeeded in a claim against his sons.

In my view the plaintiffs' claim fails because the parent would not have got judgment against the sons for any part of the 'purchase' price if he had sued them for it.

1. (1877) 2 App Cas 439.
2. (1888) 40 ChD 268.
3. [1947] KB 130.
4. [1951] 2 KB 215, 219.
5. [1955] 1 WLR 761.
6. [1957] NI 174, 181.
7. [1962] IR 268, 292.
8. [1965] 2 QB 29.
9. [1964] 1 WLR 1326.

Notes

1. In *Durham Fancy Goods Limited v Michael Jackson (Fancy Goods) Limited* [1968] 2 QB 839 at p.847, Donaldson J. opined that it was sufficient that 'there is a pre-existing legal relationship which could in certain circumstances give rise to liabilities and penalties' without the relationship being contractual.
2. In *Moroney*, the plaintiffs appealed to the Supreme Court. There the Court held that the evidence established that the defendants were never indebted at any time to their father in respect of the £16,000. As the doctrine of promissory estoppel arises only when there is liability in law to pay the money, it was deemed unnecessary to express any view on the applicability of the doctrine.
3. In *Moroney*, evidence that the £16,000 was never intended to be paid was admitted despite the Parol Evidence Rule. This was because the rule does not apply to the statement of the consideration in the deed because 'the statement of the consideration forms no part of the terms of the deed, but is only a statement contained in the deed of an antecedent fact'.
4. In *Moroney*, the defendants' counsel argued that if the father had sued the sons could have successfully counterclaimed for rectification. This argument did not succeed because 'the court could have rectified the deed

only if there was a mutual mistake so that the deed did not express the transaction between the parties or if there was fraud by the parent because he, knowing that there was a mistake and that his sons did not realise this, allowed them to execute the deed in the form in which it was.' Furthermore, 'a deed cannot be rectified because it has consequences which the parties did not foresee if the transaction which they intended finds expression in the document which it sought to rectify.'

Limitations—the Nature of the Representation

In *Keegan & Roberts Ltd v Comhairle Chontae Átha Cliath* (HC) 12 March 1981, unrep., Ellis J. applied the test set out in *Woodhouse AC Israel Cocoa Ltd SA v Nigerian Produce Marketing Co. Ltd* [1972] AC 741 that to be effective 'an estoppel has to be clear and unequivocal and be understood in the sense required as a question of construction in all the surrounding circumstances'.

In *Folens and Co. Ltd v The Minister for Education, Ireland and the Attorney General* [1984] ILRM 265 McWilliam J. made it clear that in order to claim promissory estoppel there should be 'a definite commitment or representation'.

Limitations—Reliance

In the matter of J.R., a Ward of Court [1993] ILRM 657

Costello J.:

Since 1990 the ward has been living in a psychiatric hospital, unable to manage his own affairs. The ward's committee now wants to sell the dwelling house in which he formerly lived because it has fallen into a dilapidated state. The ward is unmarried but his committee has ascertained that since 1978 he had been living in the dwelling house with a lady who still resides in it and who now claims rights in relation to it. This lady has been named as the respondent to this motion, a motion seeking an order for sale. As will appear later, it is obviously in the interests of the proper management of the ward's estate that this be done, but the court is of course bound by any rights affecting the property and the court's power of sale may be restricted by rights which may have been created by the ward. The issues now for determination are the nature of the rights, if any, to which the respondent is entitled in the property, and the proper order to be made in the circumstances.

The ward is now aged seventy-three years. He was admitted to a psychiatric hospital in Dublin on 19 July 1990 for investigation of a depressed mood, weight loss and inability to take care of himself. He was then depressed and disorientated, with decreased concentration and some short-term and some long-term loss of memory. It was established on assessment that he could not live on his own and that he required help with dressing, bathing, toileting and even with sorting out his own possessions. A diagnosis of multiple infarct dementia having been made, he was transferred to a psycho-geriatric unit. Since then his mood has fluctuated and at times he is regarded as a suicide risk. In February of this year he became very agitated but a change in medication seemed to bring about an improvement for a limited time. His cognitive functions cannot improve but there is a possibility, but it is only a possibility, that his depression may improve. His life expectation is quite good, but he will need full-time institutional care for the rest of his life. I am quite satisfied that he will never be able to return to live in his former dwelling house. He made a will in 1988 and I think it is extremely unlikely that he will ever be capable of making another will.

When taken into wardship on 8 October 1990, the General Solicitor was appointed committee of his person and his estate. There is presently standing to the credit of his account the sum of £39,205.61. In addition he is the owner of a dwelling house the subject of these proceedings.

The respondent to this motion was born on 2 November 1944 so that she is now nearly forty-eight years of age. She married in 1965 but her husband left her in September 1971 and she has not heard from him since. There were two children of the marriage, a son born in July 1968 and a daughter born in February 1970 but as the respondent was unable to look after them they were brought up by her mother. In 1968 she suffered a brain tumour. The operation to remove it was successful and thereafter for some years she was able to work as a tailoress. But in 1977 a second brain tumour developed and although it was successfully removed she has since been disabled; her leg is permanently weakened so that she has to use a stick, and one of her arms is almost powerless. She has been unable to work and has had only a small disability pension on which to live. She has suffered from depression. This was so severe that in 1978 she required hospitalisation in a Dublin hospital. There she met the ward. He too was undergoing psychiatric treatment. They struck up a friendship which developed into a deeper relationship and resulted in his asking her to go to live with him in the dwelling which is the subject of these proceedings. They lived together as man and wife until 1990 when the ward had to be taken into hospital because of the illnesses to which I have referred. When they lived together the ward maintained the respondent out of his resources, and in addition gave her a small allowance to augment her disability pension.

The respondent's claim to a legal interest in the ward's dwelling is based on the following facts. She says that when she went to live with him that he represented to her that he would look after her, and that she would be sure of a home for the rest of her life. She says that he continued to make these representations to her and she acted on them. Furthermore, on 2 November 1988 the ward made a will. By it he bequeathed: 'all my property of every nature and kind whatsoever both real and personal including my residence at . . . to my great friend . . . [the respondent] for her own use and benefit absolutely . . .' and he appointed the respondent executrix of his will. The evidence establishes that the will was validly executed, and that the ward was of sound mind, memory and understanding when he executed it. 2 November was the respondent's birthday. On that day he handed her a folder which contained his will and said to her, 'it is not my house now, it's our house and eventually it will be your house'. It will be recalled that the ward was then sixty-nine years of age, and that the respondent was forty-four.

The ward's dwelling is now in a very dilapidated state, as appears from an architect's report of 31 July 1991. Urgent repairs are needed to the roof and the rear wall, the house timbers need to be checked and because of damp penetration their replacement may be necessary. The cost of making the house structurally sound is estimated at £34,000. The ward's only money is a sum of £39,205 and out of this liabilities will have to be discharged including (a) such sums that may be due to the hospital, (b) the cost of future maintenance, (c) costs of the committee (past and future), (d) the possibility of future specialist nursing for the ward and (e) eventually his funeral expenses. The respondent agrees that the dwelling is in need of repairs but has obtained a contractor's estimate that urgent repairs could be carried out at a cost of £3,000.

The claims advanced on behalf of the respondent are based (a) on the representations made to her at the time she went to live with the ward and subsequently and (b) the representations made on 2 November 1988. She relies on the principles of the law of estoppel. For present purposes I will use the classification which is now generally accepted (see *Snell's Principles of Equity* (28th edn), 554 and *Halsbury's Laws of England* (4th edn), vol. 16, 1071, 1072) and refer to (i) promissory estoppel and (ii) proprietary estoppel. A promissory estoppel will arise where by words or conduct a person makes an unambiguous representation as to his future conduct, intending that the representation will be relied on, and to affect the legal relations between the parties and the representee acts on it or alters his or her position to his or her detriment the representor will not be permitted to act inconsistently with it (see *Snell's Principles of Equity* (28th edn), 556). If the subject matter of the representation is land, no right or interest in the land results from this estoppel—a personal right is vested in the representee which will preclude the representor from enforcing a title to the land. A proprietary estoppel is different in a number of ways. When it relates to land it may result in the creation of rights in or over the land. It has been explained as follows: 'Where one person (A) has acted to his detriment on the faith of a belief, which was known to and encouraged by another person (B), that he either has or is going to be given a right in or over B's property, B cannot insist on his strict legal rights if to do so would be inconsistent with A's belief. (See In re *Basham* [1987] 1 All ER 405 at 410).' *Maharaj v Chand* [1986] AC 898 illustrates the operation of the law relating to promissory estoppel. This was a case which originated in Fiji and was eventually decided by the Privy Council. The plaintiff and the defendant were living as man and wife (but unmarried) when the plaintiff applied to the housing authority for a lease to enable him to build a house. With the approval of the Native Land Trust Board he obtained a sub-lease and erected a house on the land demised to him. In reliance on a representation made by the plaintiff to her that it would be a permanent home for her and her children the defendant left her flat and went to live with the plaintiff. Their relationship later broke down. The plaintiff left the house, giving the defendant permission to remain in it. Later he revoked the permission and instituted ejectment proceedings against her. The trial judge dismissed the claim on the ground that the plaintiff was estopped from evicting her. On appeal the plaintiff succeeded on the ground that the licence he gave the defendant was an unlawful 'dealing' within the meaning of s. 12 of the Native Land Trust Act. The Privy Council allowed the defendant's appeal and restored the order of the trial judge.

In reaching its conclusions the Privy Council firstly held that s. 12 did not apply as the right on which the defendant relied was a purely personal right and no 'dealing' with the land in breach of the section had occurred. Its opinion was that it might have been possible, but for the provisions of that section, to have made out an entitlement to an equitable interest in the land but this had not been claimed. The claim advanced was a more modest one, namely that the requirements of a promissory estoppel existed. It was pointed out that the plaintiff had represented to the defendant that the house would be a permanent home for herself and her children, that in reasonable reliance on this representation she acted to her detriment by giving up her flat, that it was not possible to restore her to her former position. In these circumstances it would be 'plainly inequitable', the court concluded, for the plaintiff to evict her and held that she had permission to reside permanently in the house, that this was a personal right which did not amount to a property interest diminishing the right of the plaintiff's lessor or mortgagee.

Greasley v Cooke [1980] 1 WLR 1306 is an example of proprietary estoppel. It was a case in which the owners by inheritance of a dwelling house took ejectment proceedings against an occupier whose defence was that she had reasonably believed and was encouraged by members of the family of the deceased owner so to believe that she could regard the property as her home for the rest of her life and that she was entitled to a declaration to that effect. The evidence established that in 1938 at the age of 16 she went to the house as a maid servant of the deceased, that from 1946 she had co-habited in it with one of the deceased's sons, that after the owner's death she remained in the house and looked after it and also cared for the deceased's mentally ill daughter, that she received no payment, that she had been assured by members of the family that she could regard the house as her home for the rest of her life. It was held by the Court of Appeal that once it was shown that the defendant had relied on the assurances given to her then the burden of proving that she had acted to her detriment in staying on to look after the house without payment did not rest on her and that in the absence of proof to the contrary the court could infer that her conduct was induced by the assurances given to her, that expenditure of money was not a necessary element to establish proprietary estoppel, and that it was for the courts to decide in what way the equity established by the evidence should be satisfied.

Another example of the operation of the doctrine of proprietary estoppel is to be found in *In re Basham* [1987] 1 All ER 405. The plaintiff's mother married a second time when the plaintiff was aged fifteen. The plaintiff worked for her stepfather without payment for many years, helping him to run various public houses and a service station. After she had herself married she considered moving elsewhere but she was dissuaded by her stepfather from doing so. After the death of her mother she looked after her stepfather. He owned a cottage and on many occasions he indicated to her that she would get the cottage on his death in return for what she had been doing for him and also his estate. But he died intestate and two nieces were his next of kin. The plaintiff instituted these proceedings claiming a declaration that she was entitled to the deceased's entire estate because the deceased had induced and encouraged in her the expectation or belief that she would receive the estate on his death and because she had acted to her detriment in reliance on that expectation a proprietary estoppel arose in her favour. She succeeded in her claim.

Having stated the principle of proprietary estoppel already quoted, the court pointed out that although the principle is commonly known as proprietary estoppel where the belief is that A is going to be given a right in the future it may properly be regarded as giving rise to a species of constructive trust, the concept employed by a court of equity to prevent a person from relying on his legal rights when it would be unconscionable for him to do so. The court held that a proprietary estoppel could be raised when an expectation exists that future rights would be given over a person's residuary estate. As the plaintiff's belief that she would inherit the estate had been encouraged by the deceased and as the plaintiff had acted to her detriment in subordinating her own interests to the wishes of the deceased in reliance on her belief that she would inherit, she had established a proprietary estoppel and was entitled to the estate. The court considered how effect should be given to the equity which had arisen in the plaintiff's favour. It held that the extent of the equity was to have made good, as far as could fairly be done between the parties, the expectations which the deceased had encouraged. It followed from this that the plaintiff was entitled to a declaration that the personal representatives held the whole of the net estate in trust for the plaintiff.

Conclusions
In the light of the facts and the applicable legal principles, I have come to the following conclusions:

(1) The uncontradicted evidence is that at the time that the respondent went to live with the ward and thereafter he represented to her that he would look after her and that she could be sure of a home in his dwelling house for the rest of her life. I think the respondent acted on this representation and that she did so to her detriment. The law relating to the nature of detriment suffered by a representee has been clarified by a number of recent cases. As was shown in *Maharaj v Chand* detriment may exist when a representee leaves a permanent home on the faith of a representation that another will be offered in its place. Whilst I have no evidence of where the respondent was living in 1978, I think I am entitled to assume that she had a house or a flat which she gave up to go live with the respondent and that accordingly she has made out a case of promissory estoppel as she acted on the representation made to her. It would be plainly inequitable for the ward now to deny that she has a right to live in his house and it seems to me that she has an equity which entitles her to stay in the house rent free for as long as she wishes to which the court must give effect.

(2) I do not think that any further or additional rights were conferred by the events of 2 November 1988. When on 2 November 1988 the ward handed the respondent a folder and said 'it's not my house now, it's our house and eventually will be yours' I think he was intending by those words to give a gift of an interest in the house to the respondent. But the respondent cannot claim any enforceable rights from this fact, because the gift was an imperfect one which the courts cannot enforce. I do not think that by using those words and handing her the executed will the ward thereby conferred on the respondent an immediate beneficial interest under a constructive trust—the ward intended that she would have (a) a right to reside in the house during his life and (b) ownership of it after his death, but he did not intend that she would have an immediate beneficial interest in it—if he had so intended he would have arranged to transfer the property either to her alone or jointly with him. And the respondent cannot rely on the doctrine of estoppel because she cannot show that she acted in any way to her detriment arising from the representation which was made to her on 2 November.

In cases such as this the court must (a) ascertain the nature of the equity to which a representee is entitled and (b) decide in what way the equity may be satisfied (see Denning M.R. in *Greasley v Cooke, op. cit.*, p. 1312). The equity which the respondent has been able to establish is a right to reside in the ward's dwelling house for her life and normally such a right would be satisfied by an order refusing to evict the representee or where the representor is a ward of court refusing to sell the dwelling house. But there are special circumstances in this case. The house is in a very serious state of dilapidation. Major work needs to be done on it. There has been severe damp penetration which has caused the timbers to rot. There is rising damp in the basement walls, the plumbing and electrical wiring need to be replaced. The cost of doing the work was estimated last year as being £34,000 approximately. It is quite a large three-storey house and the respondent no longer uses the basement. It is not reasonable to spend the ward's limited resources in attempting to repair it and the respondent herself has no money to do so and no doubt it is declining in value all the time. The respondent's equity can be satisfied by selling the house and buying another smaller one suitable for the respondent's needs. It should be bought in the ward's name but I will declare that the respondent has a right to reside in it for as long as she wishes. This will not of course prejudice in any way the rights she will have should the ward predecease her (as would normally be expected) and should he not revoke his will (a most remote eventuality).

In order to satisfy the equity the new house should meet the respondent's reasonable needs for accommodation as a single person. It should be purchased in consultation with the respondent and should any difference arise this motion can be re-entered. The committee should take expert advice as to when to sell and when to purchase the new property.

I will therefore order that the premises be sold provided that there is made available to the respondent suitable alternative accommodation in a dwelling to be purchased in the ward's name, and I will declare that the respondent has a right to live in the newly acquired dwelling for as long as she may wish.

Consider:

If the respondent had painted her room and bought new furniture on foot of the second promise, do you think the decision of the Court in J.R. would have been different?

Daly *v* Minister for the Marine [2001] 3 IR 513

In 1991, the applicant was offered a new sea fishing boat licence restricting him to aquaculture and denying him the right to use his tonnage for replacement. The applicant, having agreed to comply with these conditions, then received a licence which omitted these conditions. Having been advised that the Minister was not entitled to restrict his fishing as he was exempt from licensing, the applicant continued to fish for demersal fish. In 1993, the applicant received a letter from the Department of the Marine allowing him to fish for demersal fish and allowing his boat to be used for replacement capacity purposes contrary to the 1991 letter. As this letter confirmed his existing understanding, the applicant continued as before. Subsequently the Department informed him that ships licensed for aquaculture were ineligible to be used as replacement tonnage to facilitate the entry of another vessel into the fishing fleet. The applicant claimed that the Minister was estopped from preventing him using his tonnage in this way and also that he had a legitimate expectation that he could use it in this manner. The Supreme Court determined that an application based on the doctrine of promissory estoppel failed as there was no detrimental reliance.

Fennelly J.:

The applicant relied at the hearing of the appeal also on the doctrine of promissory estoppel, though without citing any of the relevant authorities other than the well-known passage from the judgment of Finlay C.J. (Webb) treating legitimate expectation as an 'aspect of the well-recognised equitable concept of promissory estoppel (which has frequently been applied by our courts) whereby a promise or representation as to intention may in certain circumstances be held binding on the representor or promisor' (p. 384).

[Counsel] contended that this was either an exceptionally generous application of promissory estoppel or a new doctrine of promissory estoppel. In either event he contended that he did not have to point to any act of reliance on the promise which formed the basis of his case. It is not unfair to characterise that as a daring submission, striking, as it does, at the root of the concept of equitable estoppel. The passage cited was clearly not intended to convey that the doctrine of legitimate expectation is co-extensive with promissory estoppel. It clearly is not. The learned Chief Justice, in the passage in question cited, as authority a judgment of Denning M.R. which proceeded precisely from the fact that the parties had 'conducted the dealings between them . . .' on foot of an underlying assumption. It is the fact that it would be unconscionable for one party to be permitted to depart from a position, statement or representation, upon which the other party has acted to his detriment, that justifies the courts in intervening to restrain him from doing so. If the recipient of a promise of representation, is to be dispensed from any obligation to demonstrate reliance, the doctrine would be more than exceptionally generous. It would be a virtually ungovernable new force affecting potentially not only equity but the laws of contract and property and, as here, the exercise of administrative powers.

This court explained the doctrine of promissory estoppel very clearly in *Doran v Thompson* [1978] IR 222, where Griffin J. said (at p. 230):

> Where one party has, by his words or conduct, made to the other a clear and unambiguous promise or assurance which was intended to affect the legal relations between them and to be acted on accordingly, and the other party has acted on it by *altering his position to his detriment*, it is well settled that the one who gave the promise or assurance cannot afterwards be allowed to revert to their previous legal relations as if no such promise or assurance had been made by him, and that he may be restrained in equity from acting inconsistently with such promise or assurance.

Kenny J. at p. 233, cited as being correct the statement of the law on promissory estoppel at p. 563 of the 27th edition (1973) of *Snell's Principles of Equity* which reads:

> Where by his words or conduct one party to a transaction makes to the other an unambiguous promise or assurance which is intended to affect the legal relations between them (whether contractual or otherwise) and the other party acts upon it, *altering his position to his detriment*, the party making the promise or assurance will not be permitted to act inconsistently with it. [emphasis added in each case]

Turning to the facts of the present case, I think the letter of 1 October 1993 is well capable of qualifying as the type of unambiguous promise or assurance contemplated by the doctrine of promissory estoppel. It told the applicant simply and directly that his vessel would be acceptable for replacement purposes. The applicant does not, however, satisfy the second requirement. The facts to which I have referred in rejecting his claim based on legitimate expectations apply with greater force in the present context.

The applicant frankly accepted at all stages that he had not acted on foot of this letter. He did not change his position in any material way. It was not inequitable, therefore, for the Minister to withdraw the offer contained in that letter to treat the applicant as being part of the demersal sector and entitled to use his tonnage for replacement.

It would accordingly dismiss the appeal.

Note

The American Law Institute Restatement Contracts (2d) S. 90(1) states: 'A promise which the promisor should reasonably expect to induce action or forbearance of a definite and substantial character on the part of the promisee and which does induce such action or forbearance is binding if injustice can be avoided only by enforcement of the promise.' In *Walton Stores (Interstate) Ltd v Maher* (1988) 164 CLR 406 Mason C.J. and Wilson J. in the High Court of Australia pointed out that while in the US, as in Australia, promissory estoppel tends 'to occupy ground left vacant due to the constraints affecting consideration', this statement seems to reflect a closer connection with the general law of contract than the doctrine of promissory estoppel would allow.

C. Proprietary Estoppel

Proprietary estoppel is a species of estoppel which operates when one party acts to his detriment on a belief that he has or will be granted an interest in or over the property of another. Unlike promissory estoppel, it may give rise to a cause of action. The J.R. case above sets out some of the relevant principles to be applied and also makes it clear that one single representation may give rise to a claim both in promissory estoppel and equitable estoppel.

Cullen *v* Cullen and Cullen [1962] IR 268

The plaintiff owned a grocery shop, bar and 60 acres of land in Adamstown, County Waterford. The relationship between the plaintiff and his wife and children (including the defendants) was poor. The plaintiff was diagnosed as suffering from a paranoid illness. In order to avoid removal to a mental institution under an arrest order, the plaintiff left his home and business in Adamstown and went to Dublin. Mr Lawton, an accountant, was authorised to inform Mrs Cullen that the plaintiff was prepared to make over to her the place at Adamstown. Although the plaintiff intended this transfer to be conditional upon the withdrawal of the arrest order, this fact was not communicated to Mrs Cullen. The plaintiff brought an action claiming an injunction to restrain his two sons from interfering in the family business and from trespassing on the property at Adamstown. Martin Cullen counterclaimed that he was entitled to a site on the property upon which he had constructed his house.

Kenny J.:

The plaintiff authorised Father Kavanagh to tell Mr Lawton that he was going to transfer to Mrs Cullen the place at Adamstown and every blade of grass on it and everything except the cattle on the lands and Mr Lawton told her of this. It seems to me that this was a statement of intention by the plaintiff of what he proposed to do. He offered to do this because he wanted to retain his liberty and to avoid arrest under the order made under the Mental Treatment Act, 1945. Mr Matheson has relied on the decision in *Dillwyn v Llewelyn*[1] as an authority for the proposition that the court should now compel the plaintiff to transfer the lands and premises at Adamstown to Mrs Cullen. The case is an authority for the proposition that a person claiming under a voluntary agreement will not be assisted by a court of equity but that the subsequent acts of the donor may give the donee a ground of claim which he did not acquire from the original gift. In that case a father had told his son (the plaintiff) that he should live near him and had offered him a farm in order that the plaintiff might build a house: there was a written memo in which the father confirmed that it was his wish that his widow should give the lands to his son so that he would have a house. The plaintiff expended a large sum of money in building a house on the lands. Lord Westbury held that the making of the promise to give the lands coupled with the knowledge that the plaintiff had spent a considerable sum of money in building the house on the lands gave the plaintiff an equity to call on those claiming through the father to complete the gift. In this case, however, the only act relied on by Mrs Cullen to create the equity is the putting of £403 into the business on Mr Lawton's suggestion; she has, however, been in receipt of the profits of the business since 6 June 1959, and these are considerably more than the sum which she paid in. Moreover, the balance sheet of the business as at 31 December 1960, shows a sum of £680 16s 2d to the credit of the bank account (I assume that this is the bank account in her name) and she could at any time since January 1960, have repaid out of the profits of the business the monies advanced by her. The equity referred to by Lord Westbury is a discretionary one and when I consider the circumstances in which the plaintiff made the statement that he was about to transfer the property at Adamstown to his wife and that he made it because he believed that it was the only way by which he could remain free, I have no doubt whatever that it would be grossly inequitable to regard Mrs Cullen as being entitled to a transfer of the property at Adamstown or as having acquired any proprietary interest, legal or equitable, in the property as a result of what was said. The use by Mrs Cullen of her own monies for the running of the business, particularly when she could have repaid this advance at any time, does not, in my opinion, create any claim in conscience or in equity which the court should enforce or give any ground for disregarding the general principle that equity will not aid an imperfect gift. As Mrs Cullen has no proprietary interest in the property the defendants cannot shelter behind her permission to them or her employment of them in the business. A further ground relied on was that the plaintiff made no provision for Mrs Cullen when he left, that she had to run the business to provide maintenance for herself and that she was accordingly entitled to employ the defendants and to license them to reside in the premises. In the circumstances I think that she was entitled to conduct the business when the plaintiff left, but she had no authority to employ either of the defendants in the business or to license them to reside in the premises after the letters of 14 September . . .

I come now to deal with the ownership of the site on which the house, won by Mrs Cullen in the competition in the *Sunday Press*, had been erected. However unfortunate the Cullens may have been in their domestic relations, they have been singularly fortunate in competitions; Seán had won a substantial prize in the Hospitals Sweepstake and in March or April, 1959, Mrs Cullen had won a fully furnished portable house. She gave this house to Martin and the plaintiff knew this in April 1959. Martin intended to erect the house on his lands at Coolnagreine and, when representatives from the *Sunday Press* visited Adamstown in April 1959, a site on his farm at Coolnagreine was selected. Shortly after this, Martin began to prepare the site for the house and did some work on the foundations. He had offered the house to his father before 6 June 1959, as he thought that his father did not approve of the position selected for it, but the offer was not accepted. When the plaintiff left Adamstown on 6 June, Mrs Cullen decided that she would like to have the house erected on the farm at Adamstown and, when she was speaking to Mr Lawton, she told him this and sought her husband's permission for it. Mr Lawton said that he did not see why the permission was necessary as the property at Adamstown would be transferred to her; she persisted and Mr Lawton undertook that he would write to Father Kavanagh and would telephone to her when he got a reply. A few days afterwards Mr Lawton wrote to Father Kavanagh who discussed the matter with the plaintiff. The plaintiff told him that it was not necessary to discuss the matter because he was making over the place at Adamstown to Mrs Cullen and that she could put the house where she liked. This discussion took place on 13 or 14 June. Father Kavanagh gave this information to Mr Lawton who then telephoned Mrs Cullen and told her that she could go ahead with 'the project as mentioned' and put the house up wherever she liked. Mrs Cullen sent a message to Martin that he was not to go on with the preparation of the site on his farm and was to put up the house on the lands at Adamstown. He then stopped the preparation of the site on his own lands and began to work on a site for the house at Adamstown. He employed a man to work with him and spent about £200 in installing a water supply and building the foundations. The house arrived at the end of July and was assembled and erected in August. Some time after it was erected Martin heard that his father objected to its being placed at Adamstown and in August 1960, Martin, who was about to get married, wrote to his father asking him to attend the wedding, and added: 'I am hoping that you will give me the site the bungalow is on and your blessing.'

I am satisfied that Martin would have erected the house on his own lands if the plaintiff had not given Mrs Cullen permission to put up the house at Adamstown and that he erected the house on the lands at Adamstown because he relied on the permission given. I am convinced that the plaintiff knew at all times that Mrs Cullen had given the house to Martin and that the house was being erected for Martin to live in. It would cost £700 at least to take it down now and to lay foundations for it elsewhere; the cost of the decoration of the house which would be made necessary by its removal would be an additional £100. It has been submitted on the authority of *Ramsden v Dyson*[2] that Martin Cullen has acquired a right to compel the plaintiff to transfer to him the site on which the house now stands. That case decides that if a stranger begins to build on land which he thinks is his and the real owner, seeing the mistake, abstains from correcting it and leaves him to continue, equity will not afterwards allow the real owner to assert his title to the land: but that if a stranger builds on land knowing it to be the property of another, equity will not prevent the real owner from claiming the lands afterwards. In this case, however, Martin knew that the land belonged to the plaintiff and his letter written in August 1960, supports this view. In my opinion the argument based on *Ramsden v Dyson* is incorrect.

I am of opinion, however, that the plaintiff is estopped by his conduct in giving consent to the erection of the house at Adamstown when he knew that the house had been given to Martin and that the plaintiff cannot now assert any title to the site on which the house has been erected. There was a representation by him that he consented to this and that representation was acted on by Martin who spent £200 at least in erecting the house and gave a considerable amount of his time to this work. It seems to me that the principle stated by Denning J. in *Central London Pty Trust Ltd v High Trees House Ltd*[3] and affirmed by the same judge when he was a Lord Justice of Appeal in *Lyle-Meller v Lewis & Co. (Westminster) Ltd*[4] applies to this aspect of the case and that the plaintiff cannot withdraw the permission which he gave for the erection of the house on the lands at Adamstown and cannot now assert a title to the site on which the house stands or to the house. While the estoppel created by the plaintiff's conduct prevents him asserting a title to the site, it does not give Martin a right to require the plaintiff to transfer the site to him: if I had jurisdiction to make such an order I would do so, but I do not think I have. However, neither the plaintiff nor any person claiming through him can now successfully assert a title to the lands on which the house is built by any proceedings and, at the end of the twelve year period from the date when the erection of the bungalow commenced, Martin will be able to bring a successful application under s. 52 of the Registration of Title Act, 1891, for his registration as owner. If this case goes further, I hope that it will be held that I was wrong in deciding that I had no power to order the plaintiff to transfer the site to Martin. There is a claim in the pleadings that Martin has acquired a lien on the lands but this was not argued. I must accordingly dismiss the counterclaim.

1. (1862) 4 De G F & J 517.   3. [1947] KB 130.
2. (1866) LR 1 HL 129.   4. [1956] 1 All ER 247.

Notes

1. In *Cullen*, as in *J.R., a Ward of Court*, promissory estoppel was used successfully by the claimants when claims in proprietary estoppel were denied. In both cases, the Courts suggested practical ways of avoiding the drawbacks of the rule that promissory estoppel is essentially defensive in nature.

2. In *McCarron v McCarron* (SC) 13 February 1997, Murphy referred to the Cullen case but noted *obiter* that:

> In principle I see no reason why the doctrine should be confined to the expenditure of money or the erection of premises on the lands of another. In a suitable case it may well be argued that a plaintiff suffers as severe a loss or detriment by providing his own labours or services in relation to the lands of another and accordingly should equally qualify for recognition in equity.

The following cases indicate that unlike promissory estoppel, proprietary estoppel may be used as a cause of action and also that it may be available where there is something less than a clear and unequivocal agreement.

Crabb *v* Arun District Council [1975] 3 All ER 865

Lord Denning M.R.:

[I]t is commonly supposed that estoppel is not itself a cause of action. But that is because there are estoppels and estoppels. Some do give rise to a cause of action. Some do not. In the species of estoppel called proprietary estoppel, it does give rise to a cause of action . . . The new rights and interests, so created by estoppel, in or over land, will be protected by the courts and in this way give rise to a cause of action. This was pointed out in Spencer Bower and Turner on *Estoppel by Representation*.

    The basis of this proprietary estoppel—as indeed of promissory estoppel—is the interposition of equity. Equity comes in, true to form, to mitigate the rigours of strict law. The early cases did not speak of it as 'estoppel'. They spoke of it as 'raising an equity' . . . What then are the dealings which will preclude him from insisting on his strict legal rights? If he makes a binding contract that he will not insist on the strict legal position, a court of equity will hold him to his contract. Short of a binding contract, if he makes a promise that he will not insist on his strict legal rights—even though that promise may be unenforceable in point of law for want of consideration or want of writing—and if he makes the promise knowing or intending that the other will act on it, and he does act on it, then again a court of equity will not allow him to go back on that promise: see *Central London Pty Trust v High Trees House, Charles Rickards v Oppenheim*. Short of an actual promise, if he, by his words or conduct, so behaves as to lead another to believe that he will not insist on his strict legal rights—knowing or intending that the other will act on that belief—and he does so act, that again will raise an equity in favour of the other, and it is for a court of equity to say in what way the equity may be satisfied. The cases show that this equity does not depend on agreement but on words or conduct. In *Ramsden v Dyson* Lord Kingsdown spoke of a verbal agreement 'or what amounts to the same thing, an expectation, created or encouraged'. In *Birmingham Land Co. v London and North Western Rly* Cotton L.J. said that '. . . what passed did not make a new agreement but what took place . . . raised an equity against him'. And it was the Privy Council who said that 'the court must look at the circumstances in each case to decide in what way the equity can be satisfied', giving instances: see *Plimmer v Mayor of Wellington*.

Scarman L.J.:

I think the law has developed so that today it is to be considered as correctly stated by Lord Kingsdown in his dissenting speech in *Ramsden v Dyson* . . .

> The rule of law applicable to the case appears to me to be this: If a man, under a verbal agreement with a landlord for a certain interest in land, or what amounts to the same thing, *under an expectation, created or encouraged by the landlord* [my italics], that he shall have a certain interest, takes possession of such land, with the consent of the landlord, and upon the faith of such promise or expectation, with the knowledge of the landlord, and without objection by him, lays out money upon the land, a court of equity will compel the landlord to give effect to such promise or expectation.

Smyth v Halpin [1997] 2 ILRM 38

The plaintiff's father owned a house and farm in Meath which he had agreed to leave to his son. Following his engagement, the plaintiff asked his father for a site on the farm upon which to build a house. The plaintiff was told that that would be unnecessary as, 'This place is yours after your mother's day.' The plaintiff acted upon his father's suggestion that the plaintiff build an extension onto the family home on the basis that one day the entire house would be his. When he died, the plaintiff's father left the house to his wife for life and then to his daughter absolutely. The plaintiff instituted proceedings seeking a declaration that he was entitled to the reversionary interest following the life interest in favour of his mother.

Geoghegan J.:

The plaintiff does not and indeed cannot ground his action upon contract. He does not suggest that there was any agreement on his part to confer any benefit on his father in return for making over the dwelling house. The fact that the plaintiff has not tried to make that very convenient case is to his overall credit in my view when assessing the credibility of his evidence. It might have been easy for him to have suggested that the father indicated that it would suit him if the plaintiff could look after him and his wife in their old age and that in return for that he would allow him build an extension to the house for immediate living in and give him the entire house in due course along with the land. Although such an agreement would not have been in writing or indeed evidenced by writing, it might have been quite a simple matter to establish it through acts of part performance. However, none of that arises. The plaintiff does not suggest that there was a contract. His claim to have the reversionary interest transferred to him is an equitable claim based on the principle of proprietary estoppel. The question I have had to consider therefore is whether in the light of the authorities on proprietary estoppel the facts of this case give rise to a proper recourse to that principle and if so, whether the application of the principle of proprietary estoppel in this case actually requires that this court make an order directing a transfer of the reversionary interest. The granting of the latter remedy would effectively involve permitting the estoppel to be used as a sword and not merely a shield and would also be an exceptional inroad into the well-established principle that equity will not complete an uncompleted gift.

The kind of proprietary estoppel invoked in this case has its origins in *Dillwyn v Llewelyn* (1862) 4 De GF & J 517. In that case a father had placed a son in possession of land and at the same time signed a document which was intended to be a conveyance of the land to him but proved not to be sufficient for the purpose. The son, with the full approval of the father, built a house on the land and occupied it as his own residence. After the father's death, he claimed and obtained a court declaration that he was beneficially entitled to the land and an order requiring the trustee to whom the father had devised the land under his will to convey it to him. Two important principles emerged from that case. First of all the extent of the estate to be handed over was determined not by what was in the document but by the nature of the transaction and the entitlement then to that estate arose by reason of the expenditure acquiescence. The same principle has been applied in a number of other English cases. In *Inwards v Baker* [1965] 1 All ER 446, for instance, the Court of Appeal held that in a case where a father had suggested to his son that he build on his land which the son then did largely at his own expense, the son had an equity to remain in the house for the rest of his life notwithstanding that the father in fact left all his property to a lady with whom he had lived for some years and the two children he had by her. The son who lived in the house in that case was unmarried and the court took the view that a life interest was sufficient. The following passage from the judgment of Lord Denning MR at p. 449 illustrates the position:

> In this case, it is quite plain that the father allowed an expectation to be created in the defendant's mind that this bungalow was to be his home. It was to be his home for his life or, at all events, his home as long as he wished it to remain his home. It seems to me that, in the light of that equity, the father could not in 1932 have turned to the defendant and said 'You're to go, it is my land and my house'. Nor could he at any time thereafter so long as the defendant wanted it as his home.
>
> Counsel for the plaintiffs put the case of a purchaser. He suggested that the father could sell the land to a purchaser who would get the defendant out but I think that any purchaser who took with notice would clearly be bound by the equity. So here, too, the plaintiffs, the successors in title of the father, are clearly themselves bound by this equity. It is an equity well recognised in law. It arises from the expenditure of money by a person in actual occupation of land when he is

led to believe that, as a result of that expenditure he will be allowed to remain there. It is for the court to say in what way the equity can be satisfied. I am quite clear in this case that it can be satisfied by holding that the defendant can remain there as long as he desires to use it as his home.

The important sentence in that passage is:

It is for the court to say in what way the equity can be satisfied.

As I understand the authorities, the court is at large as to how best it will protect the equity and of course it has to consider what the equity is. In this case the clear expectation on the part of Mr Smyth was that he would have a fee simple in the entire house. The protection of the equity arising from the expenditure therefore requires in this case that an order be made by this court directing a conveyance of that interest to him. The same principle is well enunciated in the judgment of Cumming-Bruce LJ. in *Pascoe v Turner* [1979] 2 All ER 945 at p. 950 where the following passage appears:

So the principle to be applied is that the court should consider all the circum-stances and the counter-claimant having at law no perfected gift or licence other than a licence revocable at will, the court must decide what is the minimum equity to do justice to her, having regard to the way in which she changed her position for the worse, by reason of the acquiescence and encouragement of the legal owner. The defendant submits that the only appropriate way in which the equity can here be satisfied is by perfecting the imperfect gift as was done in *Dillwyn v Llewelyn*.

Later on in the judgment at p. 951, Cumming-Bruce L.J. had this to say:

We are satisfied that the problem of remedy on the facts resolves itself into a choice between two alternatives: should the equity be satisfied by a licence to the defendant to occupy the house for her lifetime or should there be a transfer to her of the fee simple?

The main consideration pointing to a licence for her lifetime is that she did not, by her case at the hearing, seek to establish that she had spent more money or done more work in the house than she would have done had she believed that she had only a licence to live there for her lifetime. But the court must be cautious about drawing any inference from what she did not give in evidence as the hypothesis put is one that manifestly never occurred to her. Then it may be reasonably held that her expenditure and effort can hardly be regarded as comparable to the change of position of those who have constructed buildings on land over which they had no legal rights.

The court went on to take the view that the equity established in that case could only be satisfied by granting a remedy which ensured to the defendants security of tenure and quiet enjoyment. The court therefore ordered that the gift be perfected by the execution of the appropriate conveyance.

In my view, the plaintiff has clearly established that he falls within these principles.

Gillett *v* Holt [2000] 3 WLR 815

The claimant worked for nearly forty years in the defendant's farming business in reliance on a number of assurances that he would be left the bulk of the defendant's estate. These included a statement that it was unnecessary to have a written confirmation that his residence, a farm-house (The Beeches) owned by the defendant's company (KAHL), would be his as it was 'all' going to be his anyway. The two parties had been close friends since the claimant was a teenager and the defendant had even considered adopting him at one stage. When this relationship broke down, the defendant excluded the claimant from his will and the latter claimed that the defendant had become subject to an obligation based on proprietary estoppel to bequeath substantially the whole of his estate to the claimant. This claim was rejected at first instance by Mr Justice Carnwath.

Robert Walker L.J.:

In the course of the oral argument in this court it repeatedly became apparent that the quality of the relevant assurances may influence the issue of reliance, that reliance and detriment are often intertwined, and that whether there is a distinct need for a 'mutual understanding' may depend on how the other elements are formulated and understood. Moreover the fundamental principle that equity is concerned to prevent unconscionable conduct permeates all the elements of the doctrine. In the end the court must look at the matter in the round.

In his discussion of the law the judge took as his starting point the decision of Mr Edward/Nugee QC in In re Basham decd. [1986] 1 WLR 1498. In that case the claimant and her husband had helped her mother and her stepfather in all sorts of ways throughout the claimant's adult life. She received no remuneration but understood that she would inherit her stepfather's property when he died. After her mother's death in 1976, and until her stepfather's death in 1982, she and her husband lived near the cottage to which her stepfather had moved (but never lived in the cottage). The claimant was told by her stepfather that 'she would lose nothing' by her help and (a few days before his death) that she was to have the cottage. The deputy judge held that she was entitled, by proprietary estoppel, to the whole of the estate of her stepfather (who died intestate). He rejected the submission that the principle could not extend beyond cases where the claimant already had enjoyed of an identified item of property: see pp. 1509–10. In that context he referred to the well-known judgment of Oliver J. in *Taylors Fashions Ltd v Liverpool Victoria Trustees Co. Ltd* (Note) (1979) [1982] QB 133. That judgment has been described as 'a watershed in the development of proprietary estoppel'—see Gray, *Elements of Land Law*, 2nd edn (1993), p. 324. In it Oliver J. stated that in the light of the more recent cases the principle, at pp. 151–2:

> . . . requires a very much broader approach which is directed rather at ascertaining whether, in particular individual circumstances, it would be unconscionable for a party to be permitted to deny that which, knowingly, or unknowingly, he has allowed or encouraged another to assume to his detriment than to inquiring whether the circumstances can be fitted within the confines of some preconceived formula serving as a universal yardstick for every form of unconscionable behaviour.

In re Basham may be difficult to reconcile with the decision of Scott J. in *Layton v Martin* [1986] 2 FLR 227, which was not cited in In re Basham and may not have been reported at the time when Mr Nugee heard the case. Nevertheless In re Basham has been referred to at least twice in this court without its correctness being challenged. In *Jones v Watkins* (unrep.) 26 November 1987; Court of Appeal (Civil Division) Transcript No.

1200 of 1987, Slade L.J. referred to it as containing a helpful statement of the principle. Slade L.J.'s judgment also contains some important observations about the possibility of proprietary estoppel (unlike promissory estoppel) arising even from an equivocal representation:

> At first sight, it may be surprising that a promise to confer an interest in property which is so equivocal in its terms that it would be incapable of giving rise to a binding contract may be capable of conferring on the promisee a right in equity to a transfer of the whole property. However, I think that [counsel] must be right in describing this as simply one instance of equity supplementing the law. The equivocal nature of the promises found by the judge is clearly one relevant factor when considering whether or not it would be unconscionable to permit the administrators to rely on their strict legal title, having regard to any detriment suffered by the plaintiff in reliance on them.

The other case in which In re Basham has been referred to in this court is *Wayling v Jones* (1993) 69 P & CR 170. It concerned an assurance ('It'll all be yours one day') given by the elder partner in a male homosexual relationship to his younger partner. Balcombe L.J. cited Mr Nugee's statement of principle in In re Basham decd. [1986] 1 WLR 1498, 1503 as having been accepted by the parties:

> The plaintiff relies on proprietary estoppel, the principle of which, in its broadest form, may be stated as follows: where one person, A, has acted to his detriment on the faith of a belief, which was known to and encouraged by another person, B, that he either has or is going to be given a right in or over B's property, B cannot insist on his strict legal rights if to do so would be inconsistent with A's belief.'

Balcombe L.J. went on to state the relevant principles as to reliance and detriment, at p. 173:

(1) There must be sufficient link between the promises relied upon and the conduct which constitutes the detriment—see *Eves v Eves* [1975] 1 WLR 1338, 1345c-f, in particular per Brightman J. *Grant v Edwards* (1986) Ch. 638, 648–9, 655–7, 656g–h, per Nourse L.J. and per Browne-Wilkinson V-C and in particular the passage where he equates the principles applicable in cases of constructive trust to those of proprietary estoppel.
(2) The promises relied upon do not have to be the sole inducement for the conduct: it is sufficient if they are an inducement—*Amalgamated Property Co. v Texas Bank* [982] QB 84, 104–5.
(3) Once it has been established that promises were made, and that there has been conduct by the plaintiff of such a nature that inducement may be inferred then the burden of proof shifts to the defendants to establish that he did not rely on the promises—*Greasley v Cooke* [1980] 1 WLR 1306; *Grant v Edwards* [1980] Ch. 638, 657.

Irrevocability of Assurances
The judge referred to these authorities and then to the decision of Judge Weeks QC in *Taylor v Dickens* [1998] 1 FLR 806 (which has since been compromised on appeal). That was the case of the elderly lady who said that she would leave her estate to the gardener and did so, but then changed her mind (without telling him) after he had stopped charging her for his help with gardening and odd jobs. Judge Weeks rejected the claim and, at p. 821, criticised In re Basham in two respects. The first criticism was

that Mr Nugee's judgment omitted the requirement of unconscionability. That criticism seems misplaced: see [1986] 1 WLR 1498, 1504a–b and 1509a–c. The second criticism was [1998] 1 FLR 806, 821:

> . . . it is not sufficient for A to believe that he is going to be given a right over B's property if he knows that B has reserved the right to change his mind. In that case, A must show that B created or encouraged a belief on A's part. that B would not exercise that right.

For that proposition Judge Weeks referred to the decision of the Privy Council in *Attorney General of Hong Kong v Humphreys Estate (Queen's Gardens) Ltd* [1987] AC 144. *Taylor v Dickens* has itself attracted a good deal of criticism: see, for instance, Professor M.P. Thompson, 'Emasculating Estoppel' [1998] Conv. 210, and William Swadling [1998] RLR 220; but compare the contrary view in M. Dixon, 'Estoppel: A panacea for all wills?' [1999] Conv. 39, 46. Mr Swadling's comment is short and pithy.

> This decision is clearly wrong, for the judge seems to have forgotten that the whole point of estoppel claims is that they concern promises which, since they are unsupported by consideration, are initially revocable. What later makes them binding, and therefore irrevocable, is the promisee's detrimental reliance on them. Once that occurs, there is simply no question of the promisor changing his or her mind.

Mr McDonnell [acting for the claimant] has added his voice to the criticism. In his skeleton argument he has submitted that *Taylor v Dickens* is 'simply wrong'. Mr Martin [acting for the defendant], while reminding the court that it is not hearing an appeal in *Taylor v Dickens*, has not given the case whole-hearted support. He has been inclined to concede that Judge Weeks should have focused on the promise which was made and whether it was an irrevocable character, instead of looking for a second promise not to revoke a testamentary disposition.

In my judgment these criticisms of *Taylor v Dickens* are well founded. The actual result in the case may be justified on the other ground on which it was put (no unconscionability on the facts); or (as Mr Swadling suggests later in his note) the gardener's unremunerated services might have merited some modest restitutionary relief. But the inherent revocability of testamentary dispositions (even if well understood by the parties, as Mr Gillett candidly accepted that it was by him) is irrelevant to a promise or assurance that 'all this will be yours' . . . Even when the promise or assurance is in terms linked to the making of a will . . . the circumstances may make clear that the assurance is more than a mere statement of present (revocable) intention, and is tantamount to a promise. *Attorney General of Hong Kong v Humphreys Estate (Queen's Gardens) Ltd* [1987] AC 114, on which Judge Weeks relied, is essentially an example of a purchaser taking the risk, with his eyes open, of going into possession and spending money while his purchase remains expressly subject to contract. Carnwath J. observed that the advice to the claimant in *Taylor v Dickens*, 'not to count his chickens before they were hatched' is [1998] 3 All ER 917, 929:

> . . . an apt statement of how, in normal circumstances, and in the absence of a specific promise, any reasonable person would regard—and should be expected by the law to regard—a representation by a living person as to his intentions for his will.

In the generality of cases that is no doubt correct, and it is notorious that some elderly persons of means derive enjoyment from the possession of testamentary power, and from dropping hints as to their intentions, without any question of an estoppel arising. But in this case Mr Holt's assurances were repeated over a long period, usually before the assembled company on special family occasions, and some of them (such as 'it was all going to be ours anyway' on the occasion of The Beeches incident) were completely unambiguous. With all respect to the judge, I cannot accept the conclusion which he reached on this point. The judge attached weight to The Beeches incident in reaching his conclusion. To my mind it is highly significant, but its significance goes the other way. I find it wholly understandable that Mr and Mrs Gillett, then ten years married and with two young sons, may have been worried about their home and their future depending on no more than oral assurances, however emphatic, from Mr Holt. The bitterly fought and ruinously expensive litigation which has ensued shows how right they would have been to be worried. But Mr Gillett, after discussing the matter with his wife and his parents, decided to rely on Mr Holt's assurances because 'Ken was a man of his word.' Plainly the assurances given on this occasion were intended to be relied on, and were in fact relied on. In any event reliance would be presumed: see *Greasley v Cooke* [1980] 1 WLR 1306; Mr Martin accepted that, while challenging the suggestion that that case also supported any presumption of detriment.

It may be that the judge, having gone deeply and correctly into the law of mutual wills in *In re Goodchild decd.* [1996] 1 WLR 694 (affirmed by this court [1997] 1 WLR 1216) went too far in seeking a parallel between those principles and those of proprietory estoppel. Mr Nugee also discerned a parallel in *In re Basham decd.* [1986] 1 WLR 1498, 1504. But although both doctrines show equity intervening to prevent unconscionable conduct, the special feature of the mutual wills and secret trust cases is that they involve not two parties but three. In mutual wills cases they are (typically) a testator (A), a testatrix (B) and an intended beneficiary or class of beneficiaries (C). In secret trust cases they are the testator (A), the secret trustee (B) and the beneficiary (C). There must be an agreement between A and B as to conferring a benefit on C because it is the agreement (and not C's moral claims) which would make it unconscionable for B to resile from his agreement. The judge did make clear [1998] 3 All ER 917, 929, and again at p. 930, that he was well aware of the differences between mutual wills and proprietary estoppel as regards the need for a binding contract. But whether or not he was influenced in that way, I differ from his conclusion that Mr Holt's assurances were incapable of forming the foundation for an enforceable claim based on proprietary estoppel. In my judgment they were well capable of doing so.

Mr Martin has in two spirited passages of his oral submissions supported the judge's paragraph headed 'Conclusion', at p. 932, as containing findings of fact which the judge reached after seeing and hearing the witnesses (in particular, Mr Gillett, who was cross-examined for the best part of three days). Mr Martin forthrightly submitted that it was not open to this court to disregard or disturb these findings of fact made by the judge. That submission calls for serious consideration and it has led to some close textual analysis of the paragraph in question. When the judge stated, at p. 932:

> What I am unable to find in the representations reviewed above is anything which could reasonably be construed as an irrevocable promise that the Gilletts would inherit, regardless of any change in circumstances . . .

. . . he must, it seems to me, have been exaggerating the degree to which a promise of this sort must be expressly made irrevocable if it is to found an estoppel. As already noted, it is the other party's detrimental reliance on the promise which makes it irrevocable. To that extent the judge seems to have misdirected himself as to what he was looking for in the facts. Mr Gillett was cross-examined at length about some increasingly improbable eventualities: that Mr Hold would marry his housekeeper, that he would have children, that his elderly sister would suddenly lose all her investments and turn to him for help. Mr Gillett naturally enough conceded that in those circumstances Mr Hold could or would have made some provision for these moral obligations. But, in giving evidence, he stuck resolutely to the promises made to him:

> I am aware that promises were made by Mr Holt to me and I continued through forty years of my life on the basis of those promises . . . This was a partnership arrangement effectively between Ken and [me] over many, many years and hypothetical situations like that are inappropriate I would have thought.

The last two sentences of the 'Conclusion' paragraph begin [1998] 3 All ER 917, 932: 'No doubt it was because of this insecurity . . .' and 'He must have been well aware . . .' Neither of these sentences can readily be described as a simple finding of primary fact. Moreover the second sentence does, with great respect to the judge, beg the whole question, because Mr Gillett was not in the witness box to take part in a seminar on the elements of proprietary estoppel (although parts of his cross-examination suggest otherwise). He was there to give evidence, which was largely unchallenged and which the judge accepted, about the assurances made to him and his detrimental reliance on them. Whether those assurances put his expectations on a legally enforceable foundation was not a question for him. But unfortunately he was right in his instinct that his lack of success in getting Mr Holt to give him anything more formal might lead to tears . . .

Mutual Understandings and Reliance
The judge's approach seems also to have been influenced by the need to find what he called, at p. 929: 'a mutual understanding—which may be express or inferred from conduct—between promisor and promisee, both as to the content of the promise and as to what the promisee is doing, or may be expected to do, in reliance on it.' Similarly he set out his view that, at p. 932, 'the *In re Basham* principle requires some 'mutual' understanding as to the *quid pro quo*' i.e. the consideration—'for the promise . . .' Here again I think that the judge may have been too influenced by the cases on mutual wills in which a definite agreement is an essential part of the doctrine. There is of course a kernel of truth, indeed a considerable nugget of truth in this approach, because (as Balcombe L.J. said in *Wayling v Jones* (1993) 69 P & CR 170, and other distinguished judges said in the earlier cases which he cited) there must be a sufficient link between the promises relied on and the conduct which constitutes the detriment. In cases where the detriment involves the claimant moving house (as in *Watts v Story* (unrep.) 14 July 1983; Court of Appeal (Civil Division) Transcript No. 319 of 1983), or otherwise taking some particular course of action at the other party's request, the link is, in the nature of things, going to have some resemblance to the process of offer and acceptance leading to a mutual understanding. But in other cases well within the mainstream of proprietary estoppel, such as *Inwards v Baker* [1965] 2 QB 29 and the nineteenth-century decisions which this court applied in that case, there is nothing like a bargain as to what particular interest is to be granted, or when it is to be granted, or by what type of disposition it is to be granted. The link is provided by the bare fact of A encouraging B to incur expenditure on A's land. The judge seems to have recognised this point when he said, at p. 930:

It may be easier to infer a fixed intent when the subject matter is a particular property, which the plaintiff has been allowed to enjoy in return for services, than in relation to a whole estate.

But when he got to his conclusion he was taking too restricted a view of the first essential element of this very flexible doctrine. If it had been necessary to find a mutual understanding in this case, the judge might readily have found it in Mr Holt promising to reward Mr Gillett for his past, present and future loyalty and hard work which (backed up by that of Mrs Gillett) made Mr Holt's life more pleasant and prosperous. That seems to have been the general theme of the speech which Mr Holt made on the occasion of his seventieth birthday party in 1984. It also seems to be reflected in an exchange in Mr Martin's cross-examination of Mr Gillett:

> [Question:] Let us take an example, you say, as I understand it, that Ken's promises were not a one-way street. You had obligations too. You were obliged to provide companionship and keep on working for him? [Answer:] Yes, that's fair.

But particular findings of that sort were not necessary because Mr Gillett had abandoned his claim in contract.

Detriment
It is therefore necessary to go on to consider detriment. The judge would have decided the case against Mr Gillett on this point also, as he indicated at the end of his judgment in the main action [1998] 3 All ER 917, 932–6. The judge devoted almost all of this part of his judgment to an analysis of whether Mr Gillett was substantially underpaid between 1965 and 1995. He dealt with the other matters relied on as detriment in a manner which Mr McDonnell has described as perfunctory . . .

Both sides agree that the element of detriment is an essential ingredient of proprietary estoppel. There is one passage in the judgment of Lord Denning M.R. in *Greasley v Cooke* [1980] 1 WLR 1306, 1311 which suggests that any action in reliance on an assurance is sufficient, whether or not the action is detrimental. In *Watts v Story*, 14 July 1983, Dunn L.J. (who was a party to the decision in *Greasley v Cooke*) explained Lord Denning M.R.'s observations as follows:

> Nor, if that passage from Lord Denning M.R.'s judgment is read as a whole, was he stating any new proposition of law. As the judge said, it matters not whether one talks in terms of detriment or whether one talks in terms of it being unjust or inequitable for the party giving the assurance to go back on it. It is difficult to envisage circumstances in which it would be inequitable for the party giving an assurance alleged to give rise to a proprietary estoppel, i.e. an estoppel concerned with the positive acquisition of rights and interests in the land of another, unless the person to whom the assurance was given had suffered some prejudice or detriment.

The overwhelming weight of authority shows that detriment is required. But the authorities also show that it is not a narrow or technical concept. The detriment need not consist of the expenditure of money or other quantifiable financial detriment, as long as it is something substantial. The requirement must be approached as part of a broad inquiry as to whether repudiation of an assurance is or is not unconscionable in all circumstances.

There are some helpful observations about the requirement for detriment in the judgment of Slade L.J. in *Jones v Watkins*, 26 November 1987. There must be sufficient causal link between the assurance relied on and the detriment asserted. The issue of detriment must be judged at the moment when the person who has given the assurance seeks to go back on it. Whether the detriment is sufficiently substantial is to be tested by whether it would be unjust or inequitable to allow the assurance to be disregarded—that is, again, the essential test of unconscionability. The detriment alleged must be pleaded and proved.

As authority for the second of these observations Slade L.J. referred to Spencer Bower & Turner in *Estoppel by Representation*, 3rd edn (1977), p. 110, which in turn cites the judgment of Dixon J. in *Grundt v Great Boulder Pty Gold Mines Ltd* (1938) 59 CLR 641, 674–5 (High Court of Australia):

> One condition appears always to be indispensable. The other must have so acted or abstained from acting upon the footing of the state of affairs assumed that he would suffer a detriment if the opposite party were afterwards allowed to set up rights against him inconsistent with the assumption. In stating this essential condition, particularly where the estoppel flows from representation it is often said simply that the party asserting the estoppel must have been induced to act to his detriment. Although substantially such a statement is correct and leads to no misunderstanding, it does not bring out clearly the basal purpose of the doctrine. That purpose is to avoid or prevent a detriment to the party asserting the estoppel by compelling the opposite party to adhere to the assumption upon which the former acted or abstained from acting. This means that the real detriment or harm from which the law seeks to give protection is that which would flow from the change of position if the assumption were deserted that led to it. So long as the assumption is adhered to, the party who altered his situation upon the faith of it cannot complain. His complaint is that when afterwards the other party makes a different state of affairs the basis of an assertion of right against him then, if it is allowed, his own original change of position will operate as a detriment. His action or inaction must be such that, if the assumption upon which he proceeded were shown to be wrong, and an inconsistent state of affairs were accepted as the foundation of the rights and duties of himself and the opposite party, the consequence would be to make his original act or failure to act a source of prejudice.

This passage was not directed specifically to proprietary estoppel, but Slade L.J. was right, in my respectful view, to treat it as applicable to proprietary estoppel as well as to other forms of estoppel.

The point made in the passage may be thought obvious, but sometimes it is useful to spell out even basic points. If in a situation like that in *Inwards v Baker* [1965] 2 QB 29, a man is encouraged to build a bungalow on his father's land and does so, the question of detriment is, so long as no dispute arises, equivocal. Viewed from one angle (which ignores the assurance implicit in the encouragement) the son suffers the detriment of spending his own money in improving land which he does not own. But viewed from another angle (which takes account of the assurance) he is getting the benefit of a free building plot. If and when the father (or his personal representative) decides to go back on the assurance and assert an adverse claim then, as Dixon J. put it in the passage just quoted from *Grundt v Great Boulder Pty Gold Mines Ltd*, 'if [the assertion] is allowed, his own original change of position will operate as a detriment'. The matters which Mr Gillett pleaded as detriment, and on which he adduced evidence of detriment, included, apart from the level of his remuneration, (i) his continuing in Mr Holt's employment (through KAHL) and not seeking or accepting offers of employment elsewhere, or going into business on his own; (ii) carrying out tasks and spending time beyond the normal scope of an employee's duty; (iii) taking no substantial steps to secure his future wealth, either by larger pension contributions or otherwise; and (iv) expenditure on improving The Beeches farmhouse which was Mr Gillett said, barely habitable when it was first acquired by KAHL in 1971. The company paid for some structural work, with a local authority improvement grant, but Mr Gillett paid for new fittings and materials and carried out a good deal of the work himself. . . .

After listening to lengthy submissions about the judgment, and after reading much of Mr Gillett's evidence both in his witness statement and under cross-examination, I am left with the feeling that the judge, despite his very clear and careful judgment, did not stand back and look at the matter in the round. Had he done so I think he would have recognised that Mr Gillett's case on detriment (on the facts found by the judge, and on Mr Gillett's uncontradicted evidence) was an unusually compelling one.

In my judgment the cumulative effect of the judge's findings and of the undisputed evidence is that by 1975 (the year of The Beeches incident) Mr Gillett had an exceptionally strong claim on Mr Holt's conscience. Mr Gillett was then thirty-five. He had left school before he was sixteen, without taking any of the examinations which might otherwise have given him academic qualifications, against the advice of his headmaster and in the face of his parents' doubts, in order to work for and live with a 42-year-old bachelor who was socially superior to, and very much wealthier than, his own parents. Mr Holt seriously raised the possibility of adopting him. Mr Holt's influence extended to Mr Gillett's social and private life and it seems to have been only through the diplomacy of Miss Sally Wingate (as she then was) that Mr Holt came to tolerate, and then accept, the notion of Mr Gillett having a girlfriend. Mr Holt had said that he would arrange for Mr Gillett to go to agricultural college but then did not arrange it, and it was only through Mr Gillett's own hard work and determination that he learned additional skills at evening classes. He proved himself by getting in the harvest in 1964 when Mr Holt was away fishing. All these matters preceded the first of the seven assurances on which Mr Gillett relied, so they are in a sense no more than background. But they are very important background because they refute Mr Martin's suggestion (placed in the forefront of his skeleton argument) that Mr Gillett's claim should be regarded as a 'startling' claim by someone who was no more than an employee. On the contrary, Mr McDonnell was not putting it too high when he said that for thirty years Mr and Mrs Gillett and their sons provided Mr Holt with a sort of surrogate family.

However, a surrogate family of that sort is not the same as a birth family, and it is clear that Mr Gillett and his wife must often have been aware of the ambivalence of their position. Mr Holt was generous but it was the generosity of the patron; his will prevailed; Mr and Mrs Gillett were expected to, and did, subordinate their wishes to his: compare *In re Basham decd.* [1986] 1 WLR 1498, 1505. One telling example of this was over the education of their sons. Mr Holt decided that he would like to pay for the Gillett's elder son, Robert to go to Mr Holt's old school (Greshams in Norfolk). The offer did not extend to their younger son, Andrew, and the Gilletts not unnaturally felt that if one boy was to go to boarding school then both should go. In the end Robert went to Greshams and Andrew to a less well-known boarding school at Grimsby, and Mr and Mrs Gillett used some maturing short-term endowment policies and increased their overdraft in order to bear half the combined cost of the school fees and extras. Mr Gillett also incurred substantial expenditure on the farmhouse at The Beeches, most of it after the clear assurance which Mr Holt gave him when, in 1975, he ventured to ask for something in writing: 'that was not necessary as it was all going to be ours anyway'. This was after the Gilletts had sold their own small house at Thimbleby and so had stepped off the property-owning ladder which they had got on to in 1964.

It is entirely a matter of conjecture what the future might have held for the Gilletts if in 1975 Mr Hold had (instead of what he actually said) told the Gilletts frankly that his present intention was to make a will in their favour, but that he was not bound by that and that they should not count their chickens before they were hatched. Had they decided to move on, they might have done no better. They might, as Mr Martin urged on us, have found themselves working for a less generous employer. The fact is that they relied on Mr Holt's assurance, because they thought he was a man of his word, and so they deprived themselves of the opportunity of trying to better themselves in other ways. Although the judge's view, after seeing and hearing Mr and Mrs Gillett, was that detriment was not established, I find myself driven to the conclusion that it was amply established. I think that the judge must have taken too narrowly financial a view of the requirement of detriment, as his reference [1998] 3 All ER 917, 936 to 'the balance of advantage and disadvantage' suggests. Mr Gillett and his wife devoted the best years of their lives to working for Mr Holt and his company, showing loyalty and devotion to his business interests, his social life and his personal wishes, on the strength of clear and repeated assurances of testamentary benefits. They received (in 1983) twenty per cent of the shares in KAHL, which must be regarded as received in anticipation of, and on account of, such benefits. Then in 1995 they had the bitter humiliation of summary dismissal and a police investigation of alleged dishonesty which the defendants called no evidence to justify at trial. I do not find Mr Gillett's claim startling. Like Hoffman L.J. in *Walton v Walton* (unrep.) 14 April 1994; Court of Appeal (Civil Division) Transcript No 479 of 1994, I would find it startling if the law did not give a remedy in such circumstances.

[The Court found that the 'minimum equity to do justice' required allowing the applicant the freehold of the Beeches plus £100,000 to compensate for his exclusion from all the rest of the farming business.]

Note

In the recent case of *Thorner v Curtis* [2007] EWHC 2422 (Ch), where the claimant, like Mr Gillet, had worked for approximately thirty years without remuneration on a farm on the understanding that he would inherit the farm, the High Court determined the 'minimum equity' that was necessary to do justice by reference to the claimant's expectation. It was held that it would not be disproportionate or unjust to give the farm worth £2.4m plus other farming assets worth £650,000. The claimant's right was found to be based not only on his contribution but also the impact that this had had on the farm's survival. The Court noted that attempting to put a monetary value on the contribution would be virtually impossible.

Consider:

Why can proprietary estoppel create a cause of action when traditional or promissory estoppel cannot?

D. Estoppel by Convention

This type of estoppel is founded not on a representation by one party to another, but on an agreed assumption between parties as to the existence of a state of facts or as to the true construction of a document which forms the basis of the transaction. Once the parties have acted in their transaction upon this assumption, the parties are precluded from denying the truth of that assumption if it would be inequitable to allow them (or one of them) to go back on it.

Amalgamated Investment and Pty Co. Ltd *v* Texas Commerce International Bank Ltd [1982] QB 84

In this case the plaintiff requested that the defendant would advance money to ANPP (a subsidiary of the plaintiff) in the Bahamas and covenanted to pay on demand any money owed by ANPP to the defendant. To avoid certain Bahamian trading restrictions, the money was directed from the defendants to a Bahamian bank which then lent the same to ANPP. As a result of this no money was advanced directly from the defendant to ANPP. Both parties, however, believed that the guarantee was binding. Later the plaintiff claimed that it was under no liability to the defendants under the guarantee.

Robert Goff J.:

It is not, therefore, surprising to discover a tendency in the more recent authorities to reject any rigid classification of equitable estoppel into exclusive and defined categories. The authorities on the subject have recently been reviewed by Oliver J. in his judgment in two related actions, *Taylors Fashions Ltd v Liverpool Victoria Trustees Co. Ltd* and *Old & Campbell Ltd v Liverpool Victoria Friendly Society*; and on the basis of his analysis of the cases, which I gratefully adopt, he rejected an argument founded upon rigid categorisation. The argument was that a clear distinction must be drawn between cases of proprietary estoppel and estoppel by representation (whether express or by conduct) on the other; and that in the former class of cases it was essential that the party alleged to be estopped himself knew the true position (that is, that he knew that the other party was acting under a mistake as to his rights), the fourth of the five criteria laid down by Fry J. in *Willmott v Barber*, 15 ChD 96, as necessary to establish estoppel by acquiescence. Oliver J., however, while recognising that the strict *Willmott v Barber* criteria may be necessary requirements in cases where all that has happened is that the party alleged to be estopped has stood by without protest while his rights have been infringed, concluded that the recent authorities supported a much wider jurisdiction to interfere in cases where the assertion of strict legal rights is found by the court to be unconscionable. The cases before him were concerned with a situation where both parties had proceeded on the same mistaken assumption; and he concluded that the inquiry which he had to make was simply whether, in all the circumstances of the cases before him, it was unconscionable for the defendants to seek to take advantage of the mistake which, at the material time, all parties shared.

In my judgment, in the case before me, the inquiry which I have to make is precisely the same. But before I turn to consider the facts of the case before me, there are certain general observations which I wish to make.

First, the case advanced before me by the bank is not one of simple acquiescence by the plaintiffs in the mistaken belief of the bank; it is founded upon active encouragement by the plaintiffs or representations by the plaintiffs—encouragement and representations which I have already found were in fact given and made by the plaintiffs to the bank. Now, in my judgment, where an estoppel is alleged to be founded upon encouragement or representation, it can only be unconscionable for the encourager or representor to enforce his strict legal rights if the other party's conduct has been influenced by the encouragement or representation.

Second, it is, in my judgment, no bar to a conclusion that the other party's conduct was so influenced, that his conduct did not derive its origin only from the encouragement or representation of the first party. There may be cases where the representee has proceeded initially on the basis of a belief derived from some other source independent of the representor, but his belief has subsequently been confirmed by the encouragement or representation of the representor. . . .

Third, it is in my judgment not of itself a bar to an estoppel that its effect may be to enable a party to enforce a cause of action which, without the estoppel, would not exist. It is sometimes said that an estoppel cannot create a cause of action, or that an estoppel can only act as a shield, not as a sword. In a sense this is true—in the sense that estoppel is not, as a contract is, a source of legal obligation. But, as Lord Denning M.R. pointed out in *Crabb v Arun District Council* [1976] Ch. 179, 187, an estoppel may have the effect that a party can enforce a cause of action which, without the estoppel, he would not be able to do. This is not, of course, true of all estoppels. Thus a promissory estoppel derived from *Hughes v Metropolitan Rly Co.*, 1 App Cas 439, is concerned with a representation by a party that he will not enforce his strict legal rights; of its very nature such an estoppel cannot enable a party to enforce a cause of action. But in other cases an estoppel may do so, as, for example, in cases of estoppel by acquiescence. Moreover (subject to one limitation, to which I shall shortly refer) I can see no reason, in logic or in authority, why such a cause of action should not consist of a contractual right . . .

Fourth, however, what I have just said has to be reconciled with the general principle that a purely gratuitous promise is unenforceable at law or in equity. In law and in equity, generally speaking a promise is only enforceable as a contractual obligation if it is supported by consideration; and neither law nor equity will perfect an imperfect gift. Furthermore, even if a purely gratuitous promise is acted upon by the promisee, generally speaking such conduct will not of itself give rise to an estoppel against the promissor; such an estoppel would be inconsistent with the general principle that purely gratuitous promises will not be enforced: see *Combe v Combe* [1951] 2 KB 215. It was suggested to me that that case provided authority that no cause of action in contract could be created by an estoppel. But that, in my judgment, is too sweeping a proposition; . . .

Indeed, there are at least three groups of cases where estoppels may be enforced despite infringement of this general principle, and I do not suggest that this list is exhaustive. The basis of all these groups of cases appears to be the same—that it would, despite the general principle, be unconscionable in all the circumstances for the encourager or representor not to give effect to his encouragement or representation. The first group concerns cases where equity would regard it as fraudulent for the party against whom the estoppel is alleged not to give effect to his encouragement or representation; an example of such a case is where, on the principle stated by Lord Kingsdown in *Ramsden v Dyson*, LR 1 HL 129, a party has encouraged another in the expectation that he shall have an interest in the encourager's land, and the other party has, on the faith of that encouragement, expended money on that land. The second group consists of cases concerned with promissory estoppel, in which one party represents to another that he will not enforce his strict legal rights under a legal relationship between the parties. The representation may be no more than a gratuitous promise; but it may nevertheless be unconscionable for the representor to go back upon it, because a representee may reasonably be expected to act in reliance upon such a forbearance, without going to the extent of requiring a contractual variation. The third group concerns cases where one party has represented to the other that a transaction between them has an effect which in law it does not have. In such a case, it may, in the circumstances, be unconscionable for the representor to go back on his representation, despite the fact that the effect is to reduce his rights or to enlarge his obligations and so give effect to what is in fact a gratuitous promise; for the effect of the representation may be to cause or contribute to the representee's error or continued error as to his true legal rights, or to deprive him of an opportunity to re-negotiate the transaction to render it legally enforceable in terms of the representation. . . .

My fifth observation is this. Where, as in cases of promissory estoppel, the estoppel is founded upon a representation by a party that he will not enforce his legal rights, it is of course a prerequisite of the estoppel that there should be an existing legal relationship between the parties. But where, for example, the estoppel relates to the legal effect of a transaction between the parties, it does not necessarily follow that the underlying transaction should constitute a binding legal relationship. In such a case the representation may well, as I have already indicated, give rise to an estoppel although the effect is to enlarge the obligations of the representor; and I can see no reason in principle why this should not be so, even if the underlying transaction would, but for the estoppel, be devoid of legal effect. Certainly the doctrine of consideration cannot of itself provide any insurmountable obstacle to this conclusion; for, whether the representation consists (as in the case of a promissory estoppel) of a forbearance, or consists of a representation as to the legal effect of a transaction, it will in any event constitute an inroad upon that doctrine.

Note

The Court of Appeal agreed with this whilst also taking the view that as a matter of construction the guarantee did cover the loan.

E. A UNIFIED DOCTRINE

An academic debate exists as to whether a general principle should be established which could unify the various estoppels—based perhaps on a test of unconscionability. As the following judgment indicates, this question has also been considered in the Courts.

Amalgamated Investment and Pty Co. Ltd *v* Texas Commerce International Bank Ltd [1982] QB 84

Denning M.R.:

The doctrine of estoppel is one of the most flexible and useful in the armoury of the law. But it has become overloaded with cases. That is why I have not gone through them all in this judgment. It has evolved during the last 150 years in a sequence of separate developments: proprietary estoppel, estoppel by representation of fact, estoppel by acquiescence, and promissory estoppel. At the same time it has been sought to be limited by a series of maxims: estoppel is only a rule of evidence, estoppel cannot give rise to a cause of action, estoppel cannot do away with the need for consideration, and so forth. All these can now be seen to merge into one general principle shorn of limitations. When the parties to a transaction proceed on the basis of an underlying assumption—either of fact or of law—whether due to misrepresentation or mistake makes no difference—on which they have conducted the dealings between them—neither of them will be allowed to go back on that assumption when it would be unfair or unjust to allow him to do so. If one of them does seek to go back on it, the courts will give the other such remedy as the equity of the case demands. That general principle applies to this case.

However, not all judges share this view. In *First National Bank v Thompson* [1996] Ch 231 at p.236, Millett L.J. noted that:

> the attempt . . . to demonstrate that all estoppels . . . are now subsumed in the single and all-embracing estoppel by representation and that they are all governed by the same requirements has never won general acceptance. Historically unsound, it has been repudiated by academic writers and is unsupported by authorities.

Similarly, in *Johnson v Gore Wood & Co.* (No. 1) [2002] 2 AC 1, Lord Goff, having quoted the above passage from Lord Denning's judgment, stated:

> This broad statement of law is most appealing. I yield to nobody in my admiration for Lord Denning; but it has to be said that his attempt in this passage to identify a common criterion for the existence of various forms of estoppel—he refers in particular to proprietary estoppel, estoppel by representation of fact, estoppel by acquiescence, and promissory estoppel—is characteristically bold; and that the criterion which he chooses, *viz.* that the parties to a transaction should have proceeded on the basis of an underlying assumption, was previously thought to be relevant only in certain cases (for example, it was adopted by Oliver J. (as he then was) in his important judgment in *Taylors Fashions v Liverpool Victoria Trustees Co. Ltd*) and, in particular, in the case of estoppel by convention, a species of estoppel which Lord Denning does not mention.

Referring to the 'separate requirements and different terrains of application' between the various forms of estoppel, Lord Goff concluded:

> In the end, I am inclined to think that the many circumstances capable of giving rise to an estoppel cannot be accommodated within a single formula, and that it is unconscionability which provides the link between them. In other words, acknowledging the abstract relationship is acceptable, but attempting to formulate a general principle to replace them is not.

Note

See Mee, J., 'Lost in the Big House: Where Stands Irish Law on Equitable Estoppel' (1998) 33 Ir Jur 187.

Consider:

What would be the advantages and disadvantages to unifying the various forms of estoppels?

SECTION FIVE—DOCTRINE OF LEGITIMATE EXPECTATION

'Legitimate, or reasonable, expectation may arise either from an express promise given on behalf of a public authority or from the existence of a regular practice which the claimant can reasonably expect to continue.' Per Lord Fraser in *Council of Civil Service Unions v Minister for the Civil Service* [1985] AC 374.

As the following cases indicate, the relationship between legitimate expectation and promissory estoppel has been the subject of some debate in the Courts. In particular, the High Court in *Coonan* appears to obscure the distinction between the doctrines somewhat.

Webb and Webb *v* Ireland and the Attorney General [1988] IR 353

The plaintiffs used a metal detector to find a number of valuable antique items near Derrynaflan Abbey which they delivered to the National Museum. Upon receiving the items, the museum's director informed the plaintiffs that they would be honourably treated. The plaintiffs were subsequently offered £10,000 and in response sought to have the items returned.

Finlay C.J.:

The plaintiffs' alternative claim for the enforcement by this court of a right of reward in respect of so much of the hoard as constituted treasure trove is based on an assertion that a combination of the practices both of the British Treasury prior to 1922 and the State through the agency of the National Museum since that time and the particular conversations and conduct of the officials of the National Museum acting as agents for the State after the finding of this hoard gave to the plaintiffs a 'legitimate expectation' of the making to them of a substantial reward by the State which they are entitled to enforce in the courts.

In support of the assertion that they are entitled to rely on a 'legitimate expectation' the plaintiffs point to the evidence which was adduced, some of it undoubtedly being hearsay but apparently without objection, as to the rewards which had been paid in the past by the museum in respect of the finding of antique objects and in respect of interdepartmental or administrative minutes and decisions made with regard to the general approach to such rewards. In particular, of course, they rely on the statement already noted in this judgment and accepted by the learned trial judge, made by the director of the National Museum at the very first interview with the first plaintiff that he would be treated honourably.

It would appear that the doctrine of 'legitimate expectation' sometimes described as 'reasonable expectation', has not in those terms been the subject matter of any decision of our courts. However, the doctrine connoted by such expressions is but an aspect of the well recognised equitable concept of promissory estoppel (which has been frequently applied in our courts), whereby a promise or representation as to intention may in certain circumstances be held binding on the representor or promisor. The nature and extent of that doctrine in circumstances such as those of this case has been expressed as follows by Lord Denning M.R. in *Amalgamated Pty Co. v Texas Bank* [1982] QB 84, 122:

> When the parties to a transaction proceed on the basis of an underlying assumption—either of fact or of law—whether due to misrepresentation or mistake makes no difference—on which they have conducted the dealings between them—neither of them will be allowed to go back on that assumption when it would be unfair or unjust to allow him to do so. If one of them does seek to go back on it, the courts will give the other such remedy as the equity of the case demands.

Applying the law as there stated, which seems to me to accord with fundamental equitable principles, I am satisfied that the unqualified assurance given to the first plaintiff by the director of the National Museum that he (Mr Webb) would be honourably treated was an integral part of the transaction under which the hoard was deposited in the museum and accepted on behalf of the State, and that the State cannot now go back on the assurance. It must be given effect to in the form of a monetary award of an amount which is reasonable in the light of all the relevant circumstances.

It is not necessary to rule on the submission made on behalf of the plaintiffs that, regardless of any specific assurance given on behalf of the State, the plaintiffs are entitled as of right, as finders, to appropriate monetary payment for the treasure trove acquired by the State. As I have indicated, the right to treasure trove asserted by the State in this case is essentially the right vested in the State by reason of its sovereign nature bearing the characteristics attached to it by the common law prior to 1922. Prior to 1922 it appears to have been the practice in this country to give monetary rewards to finders of treasure trove. The defendants contend that such rewards were mere *honoraria* given as a matter of grace and not on foot of any legal liability to give them. The plaintiffs on the other hand contend that the giving of rewards to finders of treasure trove was so well established and regular that the expectation of a reward in this case was so well founded that the courts should give effect to it.

It is not necessary for the resolution of this case to choose between those two submissions. In my opinion the plaintiffs' claim for compensation rests solidly on the fact that the assurance given to Mr Webb that he would be honourably treated (which should be held to mean that he would be reasonably rewarded) was an integral part of the transaction whereby he deposited the hoard in the National Museum. It would be inequitable and unjust if the State were to be allowed to repudiate that assurance and give only a meagre and disproportionate award. For the State to avoid giving the plaintiffs a reasonable reward would not be to treat them honourably. . . .

It is not possible at this stage and in the absence of specific legislation to set out in any exhaustive detail the factors which might or should, as a matter of policy cover the assessment of what is a proper or reasonable reward for the finding of objects of treasure trove. . . .

It would appear to me that factors which would be certainly of relevance are the general value and importance of the objects found; the circumstances of their finding; and the nature and extent of rewards granted in other instances of treasure trove. Lastly, and of very considerable importance, is the attitude and conduct of the finders of the objects after they have been found and the alacrity with which their finding is disclosed and their possession is surrendered to the appropriate authorities. Consideration must also, in my view, be given to a situation where objects are found by an act of trespass, even though that may be not of any flagrant type and even though that may not, as on the facts of this case, disentitle the finders to their reward. . . .

Having regard to all the considerations which I have set out above, I would assess a sum of £50,000 as a reward to the finders of this hoard to be divided equally between the two plaintiffs.

(Walsh, McCarthy, Henchy and Griffin JJ. concurred.)

Notes

1. It is interesting to note that the plaintiffs' acts in reliance (i.e. handing over the hoard to the museum) occurred before the museum director's representation. How does Finlay C.J. circumvent this?

2. In *Garda Representative Association v Ireland* [1989] IR 193, Murphy J. noted that the *Webb* decision demonstrated a reluctance to recognise the doctrine as a new or separate concept within the legal system.

3. One of the policy considerations that underpins the imaginative or creative features of the *Webb* case is the need to create some kind of incentive whereby persons who discover valuable items which form part of the Irish cultural heritage will come forward and declare them to the relevant authorities. For example, Walsh J. in his judgment noted 'I fully recognise that as a matter of prudence and indeed as a way of safe-guarding similar such objects as may in the future be found that it could well be regarded as expedient on the part of the State, not merely to reward such persons but generously to reward them for the sake of ensuring, or assisting in ensuring, that the objects will be disclosed to the State . . . for the benefit of the common good.' S. 10 of the National Monuments (Amendment) Act 1994 now puts the payment of a reward to persons who find an archaeological object onto a statutory footing.

4. The *Webb* case was distinguished on one important issue in *Re 'La Lavia'* [1996] ILRM 194. In that case, the plaintiffs were members of a private exploration group which discovered a number of Spanish Armada wrecks. Barr J. in the High Court held that the plaintiffs were entitled to a reward from the State on the basis of a long-standing practice and also on the ground that negotiations between the group and the State organisers had created a legitimate expectation in the finders' minds that they would receive a fair reward. In the Supreme Court, having referred to the unqualified assurance given to one of the plaintiffs by the director of the National Museum in *Webb*, O'Flaherty J. stated:

> I cannot find that anything in the nature of a promise was held out to the respondents at any time by the servants of the State in such a manner as would bind the State. Indeed, the whole idea of a promise is that it has to make an impression on the mind of the promisee. The evidence in this case is to the contrary because it is clear that from the outset the respondents claimed to be salvors in possession of the wrecks and they maintained that position at the trial in the High Court. Further, they did not recognise any entitlement of the State to the ownership or possession of the wrecks until the start of the case in the High Court. To adopt the position that they were entitled to either ownership or to salvage of the wrecks in question is inconsistent with the concept that they should be regarded as having a legitimate expectation of a reward from the State in the sense described by Finlay CJ. in the *Webb* case as entitling the finders in that case to an award.

The Supreme Court determined that the matter of a reward was a decision for the Commissioners for Public Works, not for the Courts.

Abrahamson & Others *v* The Law Society of Ireland and the Attorney General [1996] 2 ILRM 481

Following the removal by the Law Society of regulations allowing exemptions to students who had obtained law degrees in certain specified universities, the applicants, who were pursuing courses for law degrees at these universities, insisted on action. They claimed *inter alia* that they had a legitimate expectation that they would be considered according to the regulations which, before they commenced their law courses, they were told they were told would be in force.

McCracken J.:

[Referring to the comment of Finlay C.J. in *Webb v Ireland* [1988] IR 353, [1988] ILRM 565 that legitimate expectation is but an aspect of the equitable concept of promissory estoppel.] While there is no doubt that the doctrine of legitimate expectation is similar to and probably founded upon the equitable concept of promissory estoppel, I would respectfully suggest that it has in fact been extended well beyond the bounds of that doctrine. Promissory estoppel is largely defensive in its nature, and has been described as 'a shield and not a sword'. Its use is basically to ensure that a person who has made a representation that they will not exercise some legitimate right is in fact bound by that expectation, and cannot exercise the right. Furthermore, it is usually, although not exclusively, related to matters of private law rather than public law.

The case of *Duggan v An Taoiseach* [1989] ILRM 710 appears to go considerably further than the *Webb* case. It concerned certain Land Commission inspectors who were made Farm Tax Commissioners to administer the Farm Tax Act 1985. The applicants were told that their appointment would be temporary, and they would be returned to their previous grading as inspectors, but the Farm Tax Act itself clearly implied that its provisions would last at least for a period of five years. In fact, a government decision was made some eighteen months later to cease collecting farm tax and the appointments of the applicants were terminated, and they reverted to their previous position as Land Commission inspectors. They sought declarations that the government decision to cease to collect farm tax and to terminate their appointments was void, and further claimed damages. It was held that they had a legitimate expectation that their appointment would only be terminated in accordance with the Farm Tax Act, or would last until the Act had been repealed. In considering their right to a substantive benefit, Hamilton P., as he then was, said at p. 727:

> The doctrine of legitimate or reasonable expectation being in accord with equitable principles, is recognised by the courts and if a person establishes that he has a legitimate expectation of receiving a benefit or privilege, the courts will protect his expectation by judicial review as a matter of public law.

He then considered that on the facts of the case the applicants did not have a legitimate expectation to permanent employment, but continued at the bottom of p. 727:

> I am, however, satisfied that the applicants herein and each of them had a reasonable and legitimate expectation that they and each of them would be continued in the post to which they had been appointed in an acting capacity until

the work of the farm tax office as set forth in the Farm Tax Act 1985 had been completed or until the work of the farm tax office upon which they were engaged was terminated in accordance with law. I am further satisfied that this legitimate expectation was frustrated by the decision of the respondents (other than the last named respondent) and the direction of the third named respondent given to the last named respondent to discontinue the classification of land which was being carried out in accordance with the provisions of s. 4 of the Farm Tax Act 1985.

While that case may be distinguished from the present one, in that it was held that the decision to discontinue collecting the farm tax was unlawful, nevertheless it does establish a principle that, unlike promissory estoppel, a legitimate expectation may give rise to a cause of action in respect of which the court will award damages.

This principle was supported by the decision of Costello J., as he then was, in *Phillips v Medical Council* [1991] 2 IR 115. This case bears a considerable resemblance to the present case in that it concerned regulations made by a statutory body regulating a profession. The plaintiff had applied to the Medical Council for full registration as a medical doctor, following a period of some six years in which he practised under a temporary registration. When he sought full registration he was sent a copy of rules which had been made pursuant to s. 27 of the Medical Practitioners Act 1978, which were dated September 1980. Under those rules he was eligible for full registration and he made a formal application on 12 July 1987. He was subsequently told that the council had adopted new rules which rules were in fact adopted before his application was considered. Under these rules, the plaintiff would not have been eligible for full registration. It was held that the Medical Council was bound to consider and determine his application in accordance with the 1980 rules, and it was further held that he was entitled to damages because of the delay which had taken place between his original application and the hearing. After considering the *Webb* case and the *Duggan* case, Costello J. said at p. 138:

> The parties in this case had treated the September 1980 rules as those governing the plaintiff's application. The plaintiff had a reasonable expectation that his application would be determined in accordance with them. It would, to my mind, be grossly unfair to allow the council to rescind the rules when an application was pending under them and adopt new ones which effectively made it impossible for the plaintiff to be registered.

This would seem to me to be the high point of the applicants' case on the authorities. It must be considered in the light of certain other decisions in which the courts have refused to interfere with the exercise of a statutory discretion. For example, in *Wiley v Revenue Commissioners* [1994] 2 IR 160, [1993] ILRM 482, Finlay CJ. said at pp. 166/488:

> An additional feature, however, in my view, also arises in this case which would independently defeat the plaintiff's claim. The Revenue Commissioners are a statutory body who can only act pursuant to the statutory powers vested in them. As of 1987 they did not have any statutory power to grant repayments by way of concession of excise duties, otherwise than in accordance with the scheme which they had put in operation and which had received, one presumes, the consent of the Minister for Finance. For them to repay excise duty on a motor car to a person who is disabled but who did not come within the approved scheme, would be ultra vires and a breach of their statutory obligation to collect excise duties, except where they were validly exempted or avoided. . . . I am satisfied that quite indepen-

dently of the more generally applicable principle of legitimate expectation and the limit it may impose on the doctrine, that this applicant could not pursue on the basis of expectation a remedy which would involve the carrying out by the statutory authority, the Revenue Commissioners, of activities which they were not empowered to carry out, and the payment or repayment of monies which they were not empowered to pay or repay.

There was a somewhat similar decision in *Hempenstall v Minister for the Environment* [1994] 2 IR 20, [1993] ILRM 318, where the plaintiffs sought to challenge regulations made by the minister relating to the issue of new hackney licences on the grounds, *inter alia*, that it was alleged that the making of the regulations was contrary to a verbal assurance given by the minister that there would be a moratorium on granting new licences, and that they had a legitimate expectation that no regulations of this nature would be made. It was submitted on behalf of the minister that no estoppel could arise to prevent the discharge by a minister of a statutory duty, and when considering the matter, Costello J. refused the relief sought. He clearly differentiated between procedural relief and substantive relief and said at pp. 32/328:

> The assurance or representation which it is alleged the minister gave was to the effect that he would defer making regulations for an indeterminate period and did not relate to the procedures he would adopt when making them, and it seems to me that in this case I must apply the principle to which I have been referred and hold that the minister cannot be estopped from making the regulation.

Similarly, in *Tara Prospecting Ltd v Minister for Energy* [1993] ILRM 771 Costello J. said at p. 783:

> It is unnecessary to examine here how legitimate expectations may be created. What is important to stress is that the case law developed in England has established that a duty to afford a hearing may be imposed when such expectations are created by public authorities. The correlative right thus arising is therefore a procedural one. And it is important also to recognise that the claim I am now considering is a very different one. It is not that the legitimate expectations which the applicants held entitled them to a fair hearing (such a right arising from constitutional and well established common law principles I have already considered), but that they created a right to the benefit itself which should be enforced by an order of mandamus.

He then referred to the Australian case of *Attorney General for New South Wales v Quin* (1990) 170 CLR 1, to which I have also been referred. In relation to that case he said at p. 785:

> The applicant for judicial review was a former stipendiary magistrate who claimed that the attorney's decision not to recommend his appointment was invalid. The applicant claimed that he had a legitimate expectation that his application for appointment would be dealt with in a certain way and because it was not the impugned decision was invalid. The claim in effect was not that he had the right to procedural fairness but that he had the right to have his expectation fulfilled. It was helpfully analysed by Brennan J. He began by asking the question:
>> When an administrative power is conferred by the legislature on the executive and its lawful exercise is apt to disappoint the expectations of an individual, what

is the jurisdiction of the courts to protect that individual's legitimate expectation against adverse exercise of the power?

He answered this question by saying:

> I have no doubt that the answer is, 'None', adding 'Judicial review provides no remedies to protect interests falling short of enforceable rights, which are apt to be affected by the lawful exercise of executive or administrative power.' The point being made, and it is one with which I would respectfully agree, is that the fact that an applicant for a benefit has a legitimate expectation that he will receive it does not in itself confer any enforceable legal right.

I find it very difficult to reconcile some of these decisions, although it is only to be expected that in an evolving concept there will be contradictory judgments. As I see it, the following principles are now established:

(1)   It is now well established in our law that the courts will, as a general rule, strive to protect the interests of persons or bodies who have a legitimate expectation that a public body will act in a certain way.
(2)   In protecting those interests, the courts will ensure that, where that expectation relates to a procedural matter, the expected procedures will be followed.
(3)   Where the legitimate expectation is that a benefit will be secured, the courts will endeavour to obtain that benefit or to compensate the applicant, whether by way of an order of mandamus or by an award of damages, provided that to do so is lawful.
(4)   Where a minister or a public body is given by statute or statutory instrument a discretion or a power to make regulations for the good of the public or of a specific section of the public, the court will not interfere with the exercise of such discretion or power, as to do so would be tantamount to the court usurping that discretion or power to itself, and would be an undue interference by the court in the affairs of the persons or bodies to whom or to which such discretion or power was given by the legislature . . .

To return to the facts of the present case, it is undeniable that representations were made to the applicants that certain exemptions would be given by the society to graduates who fulfilled certain conditions. In so far as it may be necessary for the applicants to show that they relied on these representations, and I think it is questionable whether reliance is necessary, I am also satisfied that these representations would be a matter which persons wishing to become solicitors would have taken into account when deciding what courses to study, and indeed, in which universities they would be studied. As these representations were made to students at the start of their third level studies, I think it would be reasonable to imply that the regulations would remain in being for long enough for them to be taken advantage of by first year students. I would, therefore, hold that the applicants had a legitimate expectation that the regulations would remain in force, and that they would be able to benefit from them.

Daly *v* Minister for the Marine [2001] 3 IR 513
[Facts on p.181.]

Fennelly J.:

The learned trial judge decided the case essentially on the facts. The applicant did not, he held, have an expectation which it was reasonable or legitimate for him to have. The very name of the doctrine demonstrates, in my view, that this approach is correct. If authority were need for this self-evident proposition, it is to be found in express terms in the judgments of this Court *in Wiley v The Revenue Commissioners* [1994] 2 IR, 160. Blayney J. in the High Court and both Finlay C.J. and McCarthy J. accepted that the plaintiff, a disabled person, expected, as a fact, that he would be granted a refund of excise tax on a new motor car under a scheme designed to benefit disabled drivers. He had received a refund on previous occasions, but the Minister altered the terms of the scheme so as to require medical evidence that the applicant possesses the disability described in the scheme. He did not, however, in the view of the Court, have an expectation which was legitimate.

The Minister relied upon the following passage from the judgment of Barr J. in *Cannon v Minister for the Marine* [1991] 1 IR 82, which seems to me to distil the essence of the doctrine which is fairness:

> . . . the concept of legitimate expectation, being derived from an equitable doctrine, must be reviewed in the light of equitable principles. The test is whether in all the circumstances it would be unfair or unjust to allow a party to resile from a position created or adopted by him which at that time gave rise to a legitimate expectation in the mind of another that that situation would continue and might be acted upon by him to his advantage.

. . .

The licensing of sea-fishing boats was and is a statutory scheme. Fishing without a licence was rendered unlawful, but the Minister had full discretion to grant or refuse a licence. He was entitled, in the exercise of this statutory discretion, to adopt a policy relevant to the attainment of a balance between the available fish stocks and fishing capacity in the form of boats, and to alter that policy from time to time. The replacement tonnage policy was designed to ensure that additional fishing capacity would not be added to the fleet: a new licence would be granted only upon it being shown to the satisfaction of the Minister that equivalent existing capacity would be eliminated. Aquaculture or mussel fishing was, as we have seen, outside the scope of this policy. In *Murphy v Minister for the Marine and others* [1997] 1 ILRM 523, Shanley J. fully considered the replacement-tonnage policy and held that the Minister was fully entitled to have regard to it in exercising his discretion to grant or refuse sea-fishing licences . . .

The central plank of the applicant's case is not, as he has accepted at all times, the letter of 1 October 1993, but his claim that everything changed in August 1991, when as he put it, 'it all unravelled.' Firstly, the licence, when issued did not repeat the conditions contained in the letter, restricting him to aquaculture and denying him the right to use his tonnage for replacement. At the same time, he was informed, apparently by BIM that the Minister could not restrict his fishing. Furthermore, he was issued with logbooks to enable him to record his catches. This was done although he would not in fact be required to make returns, but he was told that it would be useful to keep records for his own benefit. He did, in fact, fish for what he calls demersal species even before the issue of the licence. In that respect, I have noted that, prior to 1994, his fishing other than mussel fishing, consisted of fishing for lobster and shrimp. These are not normally classed as demersal, though they are so treated by the Department of the Marine for tonnage replacement. The applicant also received the benefit of a scheme of assistance for loss of lobster pots. He says this further confirmed his understanding that he was allowed to fish in the demersal sector.

I can find no basis in fact, whatever the quality of promise required to justify a legitimate expectation, in the so-called unravelling events, formed on any objective or reasonable basis, that the Minister had departed from what he had consistently stated, and that he was, on the contrary, now implicitly promising that he would allow the applicant to use his tonnage for replacement. The silence of the licence on the topic was perfectly consistent with the view that the Minister had no power to restrict the applicant's fishing, since he was exempt from licensing. Nor can the applicant rely on his fishing, in fact, for demersal species or the apparent tolerance of this fact by officers of the Department of the Marine. This fishing was perfectly lawful. Insofar as the applicant was told by officials of BIM that the Minister could not impose conditions on his licence, this was also consistent with this fact. In evaluating the reasonableness of an expectation, it will usually be easier to establish that an authority has bound itself when its actions are consistent with and imply the continued effectiveness of a position already communicated. Promise by implication is no doubt conceivable, but is not easy to establish where it flies in the face of the authority's stated position.

On the face of it, the letter of 1 October 1993, furnishes a much more robust material for a legitimate expectation by the applicant. However, that, strangely, is not the applicant's case. So far as he was concerned, that letter changed nothing. It merely confirmed his existing understanding . . .

Any expectation he had prior to receipt of that letter, which contains an explicit recognition of the essentials of his claim, could not be considered legitimate. He, however, attaches little or no importance to the letter, claiming that it represented the Minister's position as he already (incorrectly, in my view) understood it to be.

Furthermore, the applicant accepted in evidence without demur that he had done nothing on foot of the letter to alter his position to his detriment. Counsel for the applicant argued strenuously in response to questions from the Court that the doctrine of legitimate expectations contains no requirement that the claimant show that he has so acted; that is relevant only to the alternative claim based on promissory estoppel . . .

I would accept that there is a distinction between the doctrine of legitimate expectations and promissory estoppel. Legitimate expectations constitutes an accepted part of the principles of administrative law applied by our courts through the vehicle of Judicial Review. It is concerned essentially to see that administrative powers are not used unfairly. An expectation may be legitimate and cognisable by the courts even in the absence of the sort of action to the claimant's detriment that forms part of the law of estoppel. On the other hand, I would not accept that the mere fact of an expectation can suffice without some context relevant to fairness in the exercise of legal or administrative powers. Those who come within the ambit of an administrative or regulatory regime may be able to establish that it would be unfair, discriminatory or unjust to permit the body exercising a power to change a policy or a set of existing rules, or depart from an undertaking or promise without taking account of the legitimate expectations created by them. However, the very notion of fairness has within it an idea that there is an existing relationship which it would be unfair to alter. The existing relationship between the applicant and the Minister was that created in 1991. The letter of 1 October 1993 did not tend to alter that to the disadvantage of the applicant. On the contrary, it constituted a gratuitous or fortuitous and uncovenanted benefit. This is not the sort of interest that the doctrine is designed to protect.

One further point is the change from 1 January 1995 in the licensing rules. From that date, the applicant was no longer exempt. He said in evidence that he was unaware of this change. It emerged in evidence that the Department of the Marine, at least in their internal records, treated the applicant as being licensed but only for aquaculture i.e. 'specific'. The applicant did not apply for or receive any licence. However, insofar as he fished for demersal species after 1 January 1995, his fishing was unlawful. It is abundantly clear that such illegal action could not form the basis of any legitimate expectation, nor could any act of the Minister permit it to do so. . . .

Coonan v AG [2002] 1 ILRM 295

The plaintiff was appointed as State Solicitor for North Kildare. While his contract stated that he was entitled to hold this office until he reached the age of 65, it provided for its extension by the Attorney General until he reached the age of 70. It was accepted that it was the practice for a year-to-year extension to be granted to any State Solicitor who applied for it up to the age of 70. The plaintiff, however, was refused such an extension as a result of a general change in policy. The plaintiff sought a declaration that he was entitled to continue as State Solicitor and also sought damages for breach of contract.

Murphy J.:

Nor can I see any basis on which the ill-defined and inadequately explored doctrine of legitimate expectations could be invoked so as to prevent successive attorneys general exercising or declining to exercise the discretion expressly reserved to them simply because a practice or pattern could be identified which indicated that for many years the discretion had in fact been exercised one way rather than another. Even in that context the question would arise 'What was it that the office holder was led to expect?' [Murphy J. then cited Finlay C.J.'s statement in *Webb* that legitimate expectation is but an aspect of the equitable concept of promissory estoppel.] It was in that context that Finlay C.J. quoted with approval certain passages from the judgment of Lord Denning M.R. in *Amalgamated Property Co. Ltd v Texas Commerce International Bank* [1982] QB 84 on which considerable reliance was placed by counsel on behalf of Mr Coonan. In his judgment in *Wiley v Revenue Commissioners* [1994] 2 IR 160; [1993] ILRM 482 O'Flaherty J. repeated the observations which I have quoted from the judgment of Finlay C.J. in the *Webb* case and went on to analyse the evolution of the doctrine of legitimate expectations. In concluding that it had no application to the claim of the plaintiff to the repayment of excise duty in accordance with certain representations made to him O'Flaherty J. said (at pp. 174–494):

> The appellant is not concerned with seeking fair procedures in the sense of submitting that he should have been heard by the Revenue Commissioners before they changed their evidentiary requirements in relation to the granting of a refund. Rather does he submit that he should continue to have conferred on him a sub-stantive benefit by way of exemption in the circumstances that he was not informed in advance of the more stringent requirements the Revenue Commissioners had put in place to satisfy themselves so that they could properly discharge their duty in accordance with the scheme they had set up under the relevant legislation. It will be clear immediately that acceptance of this admission would involve a radical enlargement of the scope of legitimate expectation. It would involve the courts saying to the administration that it was not entitled to set more stringent standards, so that it might discharge its statutory obligations, without giving notice

to anyone who might have benefited in the past from a more relaxed set of rules. Stated thus, I believe it would involve the courts in an unwarranted interference with the actions of the administrators. Our constitutional system is based on the separation of powers and just as the judicial organ of state requires the respect of the legislative and executive branches of government, so must the courts exercise proper judicial restraint.

Even if the relationship between the Attorney General (or the Director of Public Prosecutions) and a state solicitor is to be seen as a matter of public law to which the doctrine of legitimate expectation applied, it would seem to me that the judgment of O'Flaherty J. would preclude Mr Coonan from obtaining any substantive benefit.

Geoghegan J.: (Fennelly J. concurring.)

Carroll J. in her judgment, chose not to analyse what exactly the contractual terms were but preferred to base her decision on estoppel arising out of the manner in which the Attorney General, over many, had exercised his contractual discretion. At p. 10 of her judgment she said the following:

> This case seems to me to fit four square within the doctrine expressed by Lord Denning M.R. in *Amalgamated Investment Property Co. Ltd v Texas Commerce International Bank* [1982] QB 84 and referred to by Finlay C.J. in *Webb v Ireland* [1988] IR 353:
>
> > Where the parties to a transaction proceed on the basis of an underlying assumption either of fact or law, whether due to misrepresentation or mistake makes no difference, on which they have conducted the dealings between them neither of them will be allowed to go back on that assumption when it would be unfair or unjust to allow them to do. If one of them does seek to go back on it the court will give the other such remedy as the equity of the case demands.

Counsel for the Attorney General, Mr McDonagh SC, argued very forcefully by reference to case law that the doctrine of legitimate expectation had no place in private law but only in public law. But in view of the fact that the *Amalgamated Property Co. Ltd v Texas Commerce International Bank* was a private law case and not a public law case, I do not think that this issue really arises. It would seem that it was more on the basis of estoppel than legitimate expectation that the learned trial judge came to her decision. . . .

The question of whether legitimate expectation should be confined to procedural rather than substantive rights has been discussed by the Courts.

Kavanagh v The Governor of Mountjoy Prison and others [2002] 3 IR 96

Fennelly J.:

. . . the doctrine of legitimate expectation does not, in the normal course of events, guarantee anything more than procedural fairness. Mason C.J. and Deane J. in their joint judgment in *Minister for State for Immigration and Ethnic Affairs v Teoh* (1994–5) 183 CLR 273, at p. 291:

> The existence of a legitimate expectation that a decision-maker will act in a particular way does not necessarily compel him or her to act in that way. That is the

difference between a legitimate expectation and a binding rule of law. To regard a legitimate expectation as requiring the decision-maker to act in a particular way is tantamount to treating it as a rule of law.

Depending on circumstances, it is conceivable that application of the doctrine will have the effect of conferring substantive rights, but that will necessarily be an indirect consequence. The decision-maker, confronted with the duty to take created expectations into account may find it difficult or even impossible credibly to reject an application for a particular result.

Note

Fennelly J. then went on to explain that there could be no legitimate expectation of a substantive right which would conflict with the statute law of the State or the Constitution or with the well-established principles of the common law.

Power & Others *v* The Minister for Social and Family Affairs [2007] 1 ILRM 109

In September 2002, Mr Power was accepted on a non-statutory scheme which provided payments for persons in receipt of social-welfare payments who decide to return to education. The published booklet indicated that payments would be made during the course dates and the holiday periods. In March 2003, Mr Power was notified that with effect from summer 2003, the allowance will not be payable for the summer holiday period between the academic years. Mr Murphy claimed *inter alia* that he had a legitimate expectation that the scheme would remain as advertised pending the completion of his course.

MacMenamin J.:

In *Glencar Exploration plc v Mayo County Council* [2002] 1 IR 84 Fennelly J. made the following observations on the issue of legitimate expectation.

In order to succeed in a claim based on a failure of a public authority to respect legitimate expectations, it seems to me to be necessary to establish three matters. Because of the essentially provisional nature of these remarks, I would emphasise that these propositions cannot be regarded as definitive. Firstly the public authority must have made a statement or adopted a position amounting to a promise or representation, express or implied, as to how it will act in respect of an identifiable area of its activity. I will call this the representation. Secondly, the representation must be addressed or conveyed either directly or indirectly to an identifiable person or group of persons, affected actually or potentially, in such a way that it forms part of a transaction definitively entered into or a relationship between that person and group and the public authority or that the person or group has acted on the faith of the representation. Thirdly, it must be such as to create an expectation, reasonably entertained by the person or group, that the public authority will abide by the representation to the extent that it would be unjust to permit the public authority to resile from it. Refinements or extensions of

these propositions are obviously possible. Equally there are qualified by considerations of the public interest including the principle that freedom to exercise
properly a statutory bar is to be respected. However, the propositions I have
endeavoured to formulate seem to me to be preconditions for the right to invoke
the doctrine ((2002) 1 IR 84 p.162–163).

Two questions then arise for consideration. The first of these is as to whether or not
the first-named applicant can rely upon the doctrine of legitimate expectation in order
to obtain the relief sought in these proceedings, there, in addition, having been no
such evidence relating to the other applicants. The second question is, if so, has that
applicant satisfied the preconditions described by Fennelly J.? In answering these
questions it is necessary first to advert to the fact that the scheme in this case is not a
statutory scheme. It is an administrative non-statutory scheme approved by
government decision only.

[MacMenamin J] then cited Finlay C.J.'s statement in *Webb* that legitimate
expectation is but an aspect of the equitable concept of promissory estoppel and the
four principles enunciated by McCracken J in *Abrahamson* set out above.] It is true that
non-statutory rules are more easily changed than statutory rules in order to meet
changing circumstances and increased knowledge of the matters with which the rules
deal . . . Counsel [for the respondent] submits that the conventions of statutory
drafting do not apply to non-statutory rules so that they can be more loosely worded.
He points to certain variations in wording in the explanatory booklets issued by the
respondent in the succeeding years of 1999, 2001 and 2002. He submits that this
emphasises that they were not a legal interpretation and that some fluidity unfettered
by legal obligation must be permitted. However, insofar as relates to the representation in question, the wording is clear and unequivocal. Nowhere in the booklet
do I find any indication that the terms and conditions of the scheme may be liable to
change without notice especially to persons who had already embarked, at significant
sacrifice, on the scheme and were thereby pursuing an undergraduate course in third-
level education. As is pointed out in Cane, *Administrative Law* (4th edn, 2004) at p. 205:

> The very nature of a discretionary power requires that its holder be given
> considerable freedom in deciding what to do in exercise of it; and this includes a
> power, in suitable circumstances of changing direction and replacing existing
> policies with new ones; in *Re Findlay* 1985 AC 318 338. Professor Cane points out
> that provided there is good enough reason for the change of published policy it will
> not be held to be unfair or illegal.

Counsel for the respondent adopts in argument a quotation from Professor Cane's
work at p. 205–206.

At first sight there might seem to be a conflict between the principle in *British
Oxygen Company Limited v Minister of Technology* [1971] AC 610 [where the courts and
House of Lords refused to overrule a particular grant-giving policy] and the
doctrine of legitimate expectation: does the latter not allow in effect a fettering of
the decision-maker's discretion? Two points need to be made. The first is that a
legitimate expectation will arise only if the court thinks that there is no good
reason of public policy why it should not. That is why the word 'legitimate' is used
rather than the word 'reasonable'. The matter is not to be judged just from the
claimant's point of view. The interest to the claimant in being treated in the way

expected has to be balanced against the public interest in the unfettered exercise of the decision-maker's discretion; and it is the court which must ultimately do this balancing. Secondly, the *British Oxygen* principle is concerned with ensuring that policies are properly applicable to the particular case in hand, where as the legitimate expectation principle is designed to prevent the alteration of a policy which the citizen accepts as applicable.

The first point which must be made is that what was in issue here is a non-statutory discretionary power. Secondly the statement that a legitimate expectation will arise *only* if the court thinks that there is no good reason of public policy why it should not is certainly applicable in the instance of a discretion or power made pursuant to a statue or statutory instrument which is exercisable for the good of the public or a specific section thereof. Thirdly it is clear that the court must ultimately carry out a balancing exercise between the interest to the claimant and the public interest in the unfettered exercise of the decision-maker's discretion. Finally the applicant here is seeking the application to himself of a principle already enunciated and clearly applicable to his particular situation and to a well-defined and categorisable group. The booklet in its terms cannot be seen as a mere general statement of policy, particularly so when taken in conjunction with the application form which creates an individualised clear and unequivocal relationship between the applicant and the respondent; thus, having regard to the circumstances, it is fair to see that the relationship created in the instant case is more akin to an individualised promise and representation rather than the mere enunciation of a general policy. Thus the facts of the instant case are distinguishable from a number of authorities cited by the respondent in the course of submission see R. *v Secretary of State for Education and Employment ex parte Begbie* [2000] 1 WLR 1115 ; R. *v Secretary of State for the Home Department ex parte Hargreaves* [1997] 1 WLR 906 ; R. *v Secretary of State for Health, ex parte United States Tobacco International Inc.* [1992] QB 353 *United States Tobacco (Ireland) Ltd v Ireland* [1993] 1 I.R. 241.

It is clear that the expectation in this case relates to a benefit rather than to a procedure. In *Glencar* the Supreme Court expressly declined to rule upon the point as to whether the doctrine of legitimate expectation can always be successfully relied upon in order to obtain a benefit sought in a particular case. However, on the basis of the third test in *Abrahamson* outlined above, it seems to me that the issue has been decided in this jurisdiction where (as here) public authorities are carrying out functions of an administrative or non-statutory nature regarding a clearly defined category of persons who avail of a scheme on an individualised basis by way of application form analogous to contract.

The point is illustrated in the case of R. *v North and East Devon H.A. ex parte Coughlan* [2001] QB 213 where the respondent had guaranteed a 'home for life' to the applicant who suffered from disabilities in a residential home. The subsequent decision to close that home was quashed by the Court of Appeal on *certiorari*. In so doing that court held that where a public body acted to induce a legitimate expectation of a substantive benefit, to frustrate that benefit would be so unfair that it would amount to an abuse of power. In such circumstances the court had to determine whether there were such overriding interests to justify a departure from the promise. It further considered that the fact that the consequence to the public authority of honouring the expectation was financial only was not a relevant factor.

In *Coughlan* Lord Wolfe M.R. described three categories of expectation, the third of which was described as follows:

Where the court considers that a lawful promise or practice has induced a legitimate expectation of a benefit which is substantive, not simply procedural, authority now establishes that hereto the court will in a proper case decide whether to frustrate the expectation is so unfair that to take a new and different course will amount to an abuse of power. Here, once the legitimacy of the expectation is established, the court will have the task of weighing the requirements of fairness against any overriding interest relied upon a change of policy. [2000] 2 WLR 622 at 645.

Where the promise is induced in expectation of a substantive benefit, the Court of Appeal found that its task was to 'determine whether there is a sufficient overriding interest to justify departure from what has being previously promised.' I do not consider that the evidence which has been adduced in this case is sufficient to justify removing the benefit of the scheme from the first-named applicant. While the change took place as a result of a budgetary constraint, no 'sufficient overriding interest' has been established. On the evidence the respondent has not demonstrated the existence of any overriding public interest, insofar as relates to the category a person to whom the first-named applicant belongs to justify the change in the application of the scheme to him as a person who, on specific representations, had been admitted to third-level education and who was participating in the scheme; as opposed to any person seeking to benefit from the modified scheme in the future. In this connection the court notes no such change took place at post-graduate level or to certain other categories of persons of limited means.

One turns then to the issue of the representation. Here the applicant relies on the decision of *Keogh v The Criminal Assets Bureau* [2002] 1 IR 84; in the course of that judgment Keane C.J. stated:

In the many cases which have subsequently come before the High Court and this court dealing with applications for refugee status, it has been generally accepted that the applicants in such cases are entitled to have their applications dealt with under the Von Arnim procedure, later replaced by the 'Hope Hanlon' procedure. The judgments I have cited indicate some divergence of views to whether that approach is properly regarded as an application of the doctrine of legitimate expectation or (as McCarthy J. preferred to put it) simply the recognition of the duty on the Minister to observe the procedures he had undertaken to apply. This may reflect the fact, noted by Fennelly J. in his judgment in this case in *Glencar Exploration plc v Mayo County Council* (No. 2), that the doctrine of legitimate expectation is a developing one and that its legal parameters cannot be regarded as having being definitely established as yet. For the purposes of this judgment it is sufficient to say that the respondents, having acknowledged that fair procedures require the furnishing to all the tax payers with whom they had dealings of full accurate and timely information failed to observe those requirements in the case of the applicant . . . It is undoubtedly the case that documents such as the 'Charter of Rights' in the consideration of the present case, whether so described or called a 'mission statement' or given some other title, frequently contain what are no more than praiseworthy statements of an aspirational nature designed to encourage the members of the organisation concerned to meet acceptable standards of behaviour in their dealings with the public and to give the latter some form of assurance that complaints as to discourtesy or other shortcomings on the part of the former will be seriously entertained. Some at least of the undertakings of the taxpayers' charter of rights would fall in to that category. The statements of that nature would not normally give rise to causes of action based on an legitimate expectation doctrine . . .

In this case we are concerned with the *specific* undertaking to give taxpayers full timely and accurate information as to the provisions of a notoriously opaque and difficult code . . .

In a manner analogous to that in *Keogh*, I consider that the respondent herein issued a statement or adopted a position amounting to a specific promise or representation, express or implied, as to how it would act in respect of an identifiable area of its activity. Furthermore, through the booklet and other material exhibited, the representation was conveyed to an identifiable group of persons, namely those individuals who had entered, obtained the benefit of the scheme, and who were in third-level education by the time the decision challenged in these proceedings was adopted. The representation formed part of the transaction definitively entered into by persons who commenced third-level education on the basis of representations contained in the booklet. It was reasonable for the first-named applicant to conclude that the respondent would abide by the representation to the extent that it would be unjust to permit the respondent to resile therefrom. One need only go as far as the statement in the booklet, referred to earlier, that 'the allowance is payable for the duration of the course, including all holiday periods. It is not means tested so you may also work without affecting your payment.' The first-named applicant, as a beneficiary of the scheme, came within a category of persons who were prevented from otherwise obtaining educational benefit by reason of their socio-economic status. On that basis I consider that it would be unjust to permit the respondent to alter the applicant's circumstances once he had committed himself to following a course of third-level education on foot of the respondent's representations . . .

I am satisfied, however, that the applicant herein is entitled to a declaration that the decision of the respondent to implement the said changes was contrary to his legitimate expectation. He is entitled to restitution, that is to be placed in the same financial position as he would have been in had the decision not been made.

Note

For an interesting discussion of the *Power* case and its possible implications, see Delaney, 'Legitimate Expectations and Substantive Effect: Recent Developments' (2007) 29 DULJ 413.
Consider:

In what way can the doctrine of legitimate expectation be viewed 'as an aspect' of the doctrine of promissory estoppel?

EXERCISES

1. Hugh notices that his sister-in-law Caroline has resumed smoking. He writes to her stating, 'I am worried for your health and have become so concerned about the detrimental effect on all your family that I cannot sleep. I will give you a cheque for €10,000 if you agree not to smoke for six months. I hope you will agree that you need to quit.' Hugh receives a letter from Caroline accepting the offer and noting. 'I feel so much better and am grateful to you for encouraging me to do something I should have done months ago.' Has Caroline provided consideration for Hugh's promise?

2. Bill enters into a contract with David to refurbish a block of apartments for David by 30 December 2004. The fee agreed is €1.5million. Unfortunately, Bill experiences financial problems and indicates that the work will not be completed on time. David agrees to pay Bill an additional €250,000 if he meets the December deadline. Although Bill's work is completed on time, David refuses to pay him the additional sum of money on the grounds that its promise to Bill is unenforceable. Advise David as to whether an enforceable contract exists to pay the additional money.

3. In June 2005, Rob enters into a contract with Else to build a new house for her at a cost of €1,200,000. The contract states that this sum is due upon completion and a completion date of 30 June 2006 is specified. Rob completes the project by the agreed date and requests payment of €1,200,000. By November 2006, Else still has not paid and Rob is in desperate financial straits. He explains his predicament to her but finds her unsympathetic. She explains that he may have to wait six months for his money as she only has a part of it in her bank account at present. Rob requests that Else pay him €750,000 immediately 'in full settlement' of their account. Although Else pays him this amount immediately, Rob subsequently sues Else for the outstanding balance plus interest. Else argues that Rob is estopped from making such a claim but Rob insists that his promise to accept €750,000 in full settlement of the debt is unenforceable. Advise Rob.

4. Ben repairs the gymnasium roof of his local primary school. Ben is on the school board and feels that it is his duty as a parent to ensure that the school is properly maintained. On the last day of work, the school principal promises Ben that he will be paid for the cost of the materials used in repairing the roof. Subsequently, the school refuses to pay him anything. Has Ben an enforceable contract?

5. Jay agrees to build a clubhouse for his local tennis club without charge. It is agreed that the building will be renamed the Jay Moore Club House. Is this agreement binding?

6. Karen offers to let her friend Katie have a plot on her property. She tells Katie that she should go ahead and apply for planning permission to build a house on the site. Katie spends €25,000 on architectural fees, surveyor fees, etc. in preparation for the development. She tells Karen that she 'cannot believe my luck' and that 'it is unimaginable that I will soon have a place to call my own'. Karen then changes her mind and informs Katie that she will not transfer the land. Having pleaded with her to reconsider and give her the land, Katie asks your advice on taking an action in estoppel against Karen.

7. Explain the relationship between the doctrines of consideration and promissory estoppel.

8. Explain what is meant by the statement, 'Promissory estoppel may be used as a shield but not a sword' and the rationale for applying this principle. In what sense has the decision in *Williams v Roffey Bros* [1991] QB 1 opened up a debate on the future of this limitation?

220   *Contract as a Promised Exchange*

9. BFD National University accept you onto their three-year LLB course. In your first year, repeat examinations are offered in August for students failing courses in May examinations. At the start of your second year, you are informed that from the following May, repeat examinations will not be offered and students who fail will have to wait twelve months until the next May sitting. What considerations need to be taken into account in determining whether you have a legitimate expectation to repeat examinations in August?

Chapter Four

Intention to Create Legal Relations

INTRODUCTION

Despite the fact that consideration is supposed to filter out unenforceable promises from those that are truly contractual, there are residual lines of judicial decision which deny apparent exchanges the status of a contract. At one end of the spectrum are transactions which the judiciary do not traditionally regard as contracts because the parties are thought not to wish their promises to be 'legal' in nature, most often husband and wife agreements reached during the currency of a viable and subsisting marriage. This hostility to judicial enforcement also surfaces within the context of contracts which are contrary to public policy, but the increasing use of pre- or post-nuptial contracts will force a reconsideration of both these lines of case-law. The other end of the spectrum is presented by commercial or market-based transactions where, save in the case of ambiguity or compelling proof to the contrary, the external manifestations of the bargain will lead to enforcement *qua* contract.

'In the case of agreements regulating business arrangements it follows, almost as a matter of course, that the parties intend legal consequences to follow. In the case of arrangements requiring social arrangements it equally follows, also as a matter of course, that the parties do not intend legal consequences to follow.' Per Banks L.J. in *Rose & Frank Co. v Crompton* [1923] 2 KB 261 and approved by the House of Lords at [1925] AC 445

SECTION ONE—DOMESTIC AND SOCIAL AGREEMENTS

Mere social or domestic arrangements do not usually give rise to legal relations. As Atkin L.J. noted in *Balfour v Balfour* [1919] 2 KB 571 where two parties agree to take a walk together or where arrangements are made between a husband and wife 'nobody would suggest in ordinary circumstances that those agreements result in what we know as a contract'. This presumption may however be rebutted.

Jones v Padavatton [1969] 1 WLR 328

A mother suggested that if her daughter gave up her job in the United States and returned to England to study for the bar, the mother would provide her with a maintenance of $200 a month. The daughter returned in November 1962 and commenced her studies and received £42 a month (the equivalent of West Indian $200 a month). In 1964 the mother agreed to provide a house in which her daughter could reside, and let out rooms to tenants, their rents providing maintenance in place of the £42 per month. In 1967 the mother claimed possession of the house. This was refused by the court at first instance and the mother appealed.

Dankwerts L.J.:

. . .

Before us a great deal of time was spent on discussions as to what were the terms of the arrangements between the parties, . . . two questions emerged for argument: (1) Were the arrangements (such as they were) intended to produce legally binding agreements, or were they simply family arrangements depending for their fulfilment on good faith and trust, and not legally enforceable by legal proceedings? (2) Were the arrangements made so obscure and uncertain that, though intended to be legally binding, a court could not enforce them?

. . . . .

   Of course, there is no difficulty, if they so intend, in members of families entering into legally binding contracts in regard to family affairs. A competent equity draftsman would, if properly instructed, have no difficulty in drafting such a contract. But there is possibly in family affairs a presumption against such an intention (which, of course, can be rebutted). I would refer to Atkin L.J.'s magnificent exposition of the situation in regard to such arrangements in *Balfour v Balfour* [1919] 2 KB 571, 578–580.

   There is no doubt that this case is a most difficult one, but I have reached a conclusion that the present case is one of those family arrangements which depend on the good faith of the promises which are made and are not intended to be rigid, binding agreements. *Balfour v Balfour* was a case of husband and wife, but there is no doubt that the same principles apply to dealings between other relations, such as father and son and daughter and mother. This, indeed, seems to me a compelling case. Mrs Jones and her daughter seem to have been on very good terms before 1967. The mother was arranging for a career for her daughter which she hoped would lead to success. This involved a visit to England in conditions which could not be wholly foreseen. What was required was an arrangement which was to be financed by the mother, and was such as would be adaptable to circumstances, as it in fact was. The operation about the house was, in my view, not a completely fresh arrangement, but an adaptation of the mother's financial assistance to her daughter due to the situation which was found to exist in England. It was not a stiff contractual operation any more than the original arrangement.

   In the result, of course, on this view, the daughter cannot resist her mother's rights as the owner of the house to the possession of which the mother is entitled.

Salmon L.J.:

I agree with the conclusion at which my Lord has arrived, but I have reached it by a different route. The first point to be decided is whether or not there was ever a legally binding agreement between the mother and daughter in relation to the daughter's reading for the bar in England. The daughter alleges that there was such an agreement, and the mother denies it. She says that there was nothing but a loose family arrangement which had no legal effect. The onus is clearly on the daughter. There is no dispute that the parties entered into some sort of arrangement. It really depends upon (a) whether the parties intended it to be legally binding, and (b) if so, whether it was sufficiently certain to be enforceable.

Did the parties intend the arrangement to be legally binding? This question has to be solved by applying what is sometimes (although perhaps unfortunately) called an objective test. The court has to consider what the parties said and wrote in the light of all the surrounding circumstances, and then decide whether the true inference is that the ordinary men and women, speaking or writing thus in such circumstances, would have intended to create a legally binding agreement.

. . . as a rule when arrangements are made between close relations, for example, between husband and wife, parent and child or uncle and nephew in relation to an allowance, there is a presumption against an intention of creating any legal relationship. This is not a presumption of law, but of fact. It derives from experience of life and human nature which shows that in such circumstances men and women usually do not intend to create legal rights and obligations, but intend to rely solely on family ties of mutual trust and affection. This has all been explained by Atkin L.J. in his celebrated judgment in *Balfour v Balfour*. There may, however, be circumstances in which this presumption, like all other presumptions of fact, can be rebutted.

. . .

On the facts as found by the County Court judge this was entirely different from the ordinary case of a mother promising her daughter an allowance whilst the daughter read for the bar, or a father promising his son an allowance at university if the son passed the necessary examinations to gain admission. The daughter here was thirty-four years of age in 1962. She had left Trinidad and settled in Washington as long ago as 1949. In Washington she had a comfortable flat and was employed as an assistant accountant in the Indian Embassy at a salary of $500 a month (over £2,000 a year). This employment carried a pension. She had a son of seven years of age who was an American citizen, and had, of course, already begun his education. There were obviously solid reasons for her staying where she was.

. . .

In the very special circumstances of this case, I consider that the true inference must be that neither the mother nor the daughter could have intended that the daughter should have no legal right to receive, and the mother no legal obligation to pay, the allowance of $200 a month.

. . .

Then again it is said that the duration of the agreement was not specified. No doubt, but I see no difficulty in implying the usual term that it was to last for a reasonable time. The parties cannot have contemplated that the daughter should go on studying for the bar and draw the allowance until she was seventy, nor on the other hand that the mother could have discontinued the allowance if the daughter did not pass her examinations within, say, eighteen months. The promise was to pay the allowance until the daughter's studies were completed, and to my mind there was a clear implication that they were to be completed within a reasonable time. Studies are completed either by the student being called to the bar or giving up the unequal struggle against the examiners.

. . .

I cannot think that a reasonable time could possibly exceed five years from November 1962, the date when she began her studies.

It follows, therefore, that on no view can she now in November 1968 be entitled to anything further under the contract . . .

Fenton Atkinson L.J.:

...

The first question in this most unhappy case is whether the arrangement made between mother and daughter in August 1962 was intended to create a legally enforceable contract between them, or was merely one of those family or domestic arrangements where the parties at the time had no thought or intention of invoking the assistance of the courts should the arrangement not be honoured.

Was the mother legally binding herself to support the daughter at the rate of £500 a year for a wholly uncertain length of time whatever changes might come about in their respective circumstances? Was the daughter assuming a contractual obligation to pursue her legal studies to successful completion whatever the difficulties she experienced, and whatever attractive alternatives might appear, such as possible marriage or well paid employment?

If the test were the giving of consideration by the daughter, the answer would be simple. She gave up well paid work and good living accommodation, and removed herself and her son to England, where she began her studies in November 1962. But the giving of consideration by the daughter cannot decide the question whether the parties intended to make a binding contract. Aktin L.J. in *Balfour v Balfour* at p. 578 of the report put it in this way:

> To my mind those agreements, or many of them, do not result in contracts at all, and they do not result in contracts even though there may be what as between other parties would constitute consideration for the agreement. The consideration, as we know, may consist either in some right, interest, profit or benefit accruing to one party, or some forbearance, detriment, loss or responsibility given, suffered or undertaken by the other. That is a well known definition, and it constantly happens, I think, that such arrangements made between husband and wife are arrangements in which there are mutual promises, or in which there is consideration in form within the definition that I have mentioned. Nevertheless they are not contracts, and they are not contracts because the parties did not intend that they should be attended by legal consequences.

On the other hand, I do not think that the lack of formality and precision in expressing the arrangement is necessarily an indication that no contract was intended having regard to what the court knows of the parties and their relationship. The problem is, in my view, a difficult one, because though one would tend to regard a promise by a parent to pay an allowance to a child during a course of study as no more than a family arrangement, on the facts of this case this particular daughter undoubtedly gave up a great deal on the strength of the mother's promise.

In my judgment it is the subsequent history which gives the best guide to the parties' intention at the material time. There are three matters which seem to me important: (1) The daughter thought that her mother was promising her US $200, or £70 a month, which she regarded as the minimum necessary for her support. The mother promised $200, but she had in mind British West Indian $200, £42 a month, and that was what she in fact paid from November 1962 to December 1964. Those payments were accepted by the daughter without any sort of suggestion at any stage that the mother had legally contracted for the larger sum. (2) When the arrangements for the purchase of No. 181, Highbury Quadrant were being discussed, and the new arrangement was made for maintenance to come out of the rents, many material matters were left open: how much accommodation was the daughter to occupy; how much money was she to have out of the rents; if the rents fell below expectation, was the mother to make up the difference below £42, or £42 less the sum saved by the daughter in rent; for how long was the arrangement to continue, and so on. The whole arrangement was, in my view, far too vague and uncertain to be itself enforceable as a contract; but at no stage did the daughter bring into the discussions her alleged legal right to £42 per month until her studies were completed, and how that right was to be affected by the new arrangement. (3) It is perhaps not without relevance to look at the daughter's evidence in cross-examination. She was asked about the occasion when her mother visited the house, and she, knowing perfectly well that her mother was there, refused for some hours to open the door. She said: 'I didn't open the door because a normal mother doesn't sue her daughter in court. Anybody with normal feelings would feel upset by what was happening.' Those answers and the daughter's conduct on that occasion provide a strong indication that she had never for a moment contemplated the possibility of her mother or herself going to court to enforce legal obligations, and that she felt it quite intolerable that a purely family arrangement should become the subject of proceedings in a court of law.

At the time when the first arrangement was made, mother and daughter were, and always had been, to use the daughter's own words, 'very close'. I am satisfied that neither party at that time intended to enter into a legally binding contract, either then or later when the house was bought. The daughter was prepared to trust her mother to honour her promise of support, just as the mother no doubt trusted her daughter to study for the bar with diligence, and to get through her examinations as early as she could.

It follows that in my view the mother's claim for possession succeeds, and her appeal should be allowed.

Rogers *v* Smith (SC) 16 July 1970, unrep.

The plaintiff's father carried on a money-lending business. The business was handed over to the plaintiff upon an express agreement that the plaintiff should retain £4 a week himself from the business profits and that he should also pay his mother's housekeeping expenses and the rent, rates and other sundry expenses from the business profits. Although the plaintiff paid his mother's bills he never retained the weekly sum stipulated. After the plaintiff's father died a hospital bill was furnished for £300. The plaintiff's mother suggested that the plaintiff should pay this bill himself and noted 'when I am dead and gone you will be able to claim anything you may have spent on me.' When his mother died the plaintiff claimed money owed to him against her estate.

O'Dalaigh C.J.:

. . .

Counsel for Mrs Smith has, moreover, urged on the court that in family relations, and particularly in regard to agreements entered into between son and mother, the court will readily imply that such arrangements were not intended to give rise to legal relations. Scrutton L.J. in *Rose and Frank Co. v Crompton & Bros Ltd*[1] took this point in the following language:

> Now it is quite possible for parties to come to an agreement by accepting a proposal with the result that the agreement concluded does not give rise to legal relations. The reason of this is that the parties do not intend that their agreement

shall give rise to legal relations. This intention may be implied from the subject matter of the agreement, but it may also be expressed by the parties. In social and family relations such an intention is readily implied, while in business matters the opposite result would ordinarily follow. But I can see no reason why, even in business matters, the parties should not intend to rely on each other's good faith and honour, and to exclude all idea of settling disputes by any outside intervention, with the accompanying necessity of expressing themselves so precisely that outsiders may have no difficulty in understanding what they mean. If they clearly express such an intention I can see no reason in public policy why effect should not be given to their intention.

Scrutton L.J. in the course of his judgment, on the same page, called attention to *Balfour v Balfour*[2] where the court declined to recognise relations of contract as flowing from an agreement between a husband and wife that he should send her £30 a month for her maintenance. There Atkin L.J. speaking of agreements and arrangements between husband and wife involving mutual promises and consideration in form, said 'They are not contracts, because the parties did not intend that they should be attended by legal consequences.'
. . .

The plaintiff's evidence, in my opinion, is much too uncertain and obscure to be acted upon. There is also the general background that the payments after John Rogers' death in 1960 were a continuation of payments which commenced six years earlier in 1954, and the post-1960 payments were treated in exactly the same way as the earlier payments. Even if the arrangement relied upon were free from the uncertainty and obscurity to which I have called attention, the court, before inferring an intention that the arrangement should have legal consequences, should have clear and unambiguous evidence. In my opinion there is in this case an absence of such evidence.

Budd J.:
. . .

It was further submitted that the matter of the intention of the parties to the alleged contract requires particular attention in this case. These parties were mother and son, and if an agreement can be spelt out of the conversations between them, it was contended that the surrounding circumstances and the words used lead to the conclusion that the parties did not intend that any agreement, which could be said to have been come to, was to have legal consequences and to be enforceable but was rather of a purely family nature not intended to have such consequences. The learned Chief Justice in the course of his judgment has referred to passages from the judgments of Scrutton L.J. in *Rose and Frank Co. v J.R. Crompton & Bros Ltd* and Atkin L.J. in *Balfour v Balfour* which are highly relevant on this point. It clearly emerges from these passages that in social and family matters agreements may be come to which do not give rise to legal relations because such a consequence is not the intention of the parties, and in family matters, an intention *to remain free of legal obligation* will be readily implied whereas in business matters the opposite result would ordinarily follow.
. . .

Having regard to the background to the conversations between the plaintiff and his mother and the indefiniteness of the evidence both as to the making of any binding agreement and as to its terms the plaintiff has, in my view, failed to establish his case.

There is also, in my view, no sufficient evidence of the intention of the parties to enter into a contract having legal consequences.

FitzGerald J.:

. . .

[Counsel] relied upon *Rose & Frank Co. v Crompton & Bros Ltd.*[4] This was an action for breach of a commercial contract relating to the sale of goods and the facts do not require further recital here. [Counsel], however, placed reliance on passage from the judgments in the Court of Appeal and in particular from the judgment of Lord Justice Banks, reported at p. 282, which is as follows: 'In the case of agreements regulating business arrangements it follows, almost as a matter of course, that the parties intend legal consequences to follow. In the case of arrangements requiring social engagements it equally follows, also as a matter of course, that the parties do not intend legal consequences to follow.' While I accept this as a general proposition, the question of whether an enforceable legal contract has been entered into or not must depend upon the evidence in the particular case. In the case of family arrangements it would be quite unreasonable to expect that the arrangement would be come to with all the particularity which one would expect to find in relation to a commercial contract, either formal or informal. It appears to me that the proper approach is to see whether obligations were undertaken with the mutual intention that the obligations should be carried out by one party and whether there was a consideration from the other party in return and whether, finally, those matters can be established with certainty. In the present case I am satisfied that the evidence of [the son], having been accepted by the trial judge, the true position was that [the son] had undertaken the obligation of paying the weekly amount to his mother during her lifetime and also of paying the outgoings in respect of the house which she occupied and that the consideration for his undertaking these obligations was that he should be repaid out of his mother's estate after her death. This appears to me to be a contract between them in which the terms are certain and which the parties must be taken to have intended that the agreement should be carried out which necessarily involves legal consequences.

1. [1923] 2 KB 261 at 288.
2. [1919] 1 KB 571.
3. 8 App Cas 467.
4. [1923] 2 KB 261 and [1925] AC 445.

Courtney v Courtney (1923) 57 ILTR 42

Due to the respondent's acts of cruelty the petitioner was forced to leave their home. The petitioner later returned her wedding ring and a watch and in May 1921, before the local parish priest, the respondent agreed to pay her £150 'in discharge of all claims of every nature and kind'. The petitioner later filed a petition for divorce *a mensa et thora* on the ground of cruelty. The respondent contended that because of the agreement the petitioner was estopped from bringing proceedings.

At first instance the jury stated that the agreement was not a good one and the trial judge opined that the agreement did not operate as a bar to the petition. The respondent appealed to the High Court.

Dodd J. (delivering the judgment of the court):

. . .

It is to be borne in mind that there must be a contract. A contract consists of a promise and a consideration. The agreement to refrain from taking proceedings was held to be a good consideration in *Wilson v Wilson*. Mutual promises would not seem to be enough (see the judgment of Atkin L.J. in *Balfour v Balfour*, [1919] 2 KB 571). Having given a definition of what is consideration in general law, he says, at p. 578: 'It constantly happens that such arrangements made between husband and wife are arrangements in which there are mutual promises, or in which there is consideration given in form within the definition I have mentioned, nevertheless they are not contracts, and they are not contracts because the parties did not intend that they should be attended by legal consequences.' Warrington L.J. and Duke L.J. say the same, but the words of Atkin L.J. are of crystal clearness. . . . The law being as I think clear, and the cases cited giving a guide in applying it, the sole question of fact is on the plea which the learned judge at the trial allowed to be pleaded, and on which he framed question 5: 'Did the wife and the husband in May 1921, mutually agree to live separate and not to molest each other in consideration of the husband paying to his wife £150, she giving him her ring and watch?' To which the jury's answer is 'Yes.' They added a rider: 'We do not believe the agreement of May 1921, a good one,' and there being no evidence of consideration. It is not clear whether the words 'and there being no evidence of consideration' were part of the rider, or were added by the judge. That is not material, it is for the Court to say now whether there was evidence of consideration moving from the wife. It is on this that the weighty words of the judges in the cases cited become applicable. In *Wilson v Wilson*, Shadwell V.C., whose judgment was upheld in the Lords, decided that the promises of the wife not to bring proceedings in the Ecclesiastical Court, which the husband was most anxious to avoid, was a sufficient consideration. In *Besant v Wood* we have Sir Geo. Jessel's judgment that a compromise of a matrimonial quarrel before proceedings were taken was a good consideration for a contract. We also have the concluding words of the Chief Baron's judgment in *MacMahon v MacMahon*: 'Can it be the policy of the law that the spouses cannot be free to contract that they will not co-habit?' And Lord Justice Bowen's words: 'All that is required is that there shall be evidence of a contract into which the wife entered with her eyes open, and under which she has received benefits.' When this contract was entered into the wife was in a position in which she could have sued her husband. What relief could she get in a suit? A separation from bed and board, and an allowance from the court from the husband's means for alimony. The alimony would have been in the usual practice granted as an annual payment. That it was arranged for between the parties to be granted at once as a lump sum in this case throws light upon the intention of the parties. It was to be given once for all—no further dealings. The consideration from the wife was that if the husband agreed to the terms she would abstain from bringing any proceedings for separation or for alimony. She got the money—for what? It was not damages for a prior assault: it was in settlement of all claims. The handing back of the ring was a most significant matter. The husband stipulated for that. The wife at first refused. The watch, too, seems to have had some sentimental significance, if sentiment could be attributed to such a pair. But the husband's view, apparently, was to terminate, once and for all, all matrimonial relations. The wife professed she had lost the watch. Finally it was settled that pending the return of the watch £10 should be deducted from the £150 and retained by Father Courtney. The husband got the ring; the wife bought a new ring, and the priest blessed it. Was this merely an agreement between spouses, such as Atkin L.J. referred to? Or was it a bargain? Was it intended to be a bargain? Could she, next day, have brought a matrimonial suit? The priest thought the lady ought to have got more.

The jury also thought so. But did she conclude the contract with her eyes open—can she keep the £150 and still sue? It is said that there is no covenant not to sue, no express contract not to sue. But if parties who are free to contract do in fact contract for the settlement of an action, or for the settlement of proceedings which might but for the settlement terminate in legal proceedings, can it be contended that the settlement having been entered into and completed by one party complying with it, the other party can keep the money and go on with an action? The contract need not be under seal, nor take the form of a covenant. Nor need it be necessarily in writing, though it is hardly conceivable that there should not be some documentary evidence forthcoming in such an issue. Nor need the bargain that no proceedings are to be taken but put in express words—though here again caution is required to ascertain the real nature of the transaction. A matrimonial tribunal must bring to the consideration of such a case great circumspection, and must not lightly sanction the severance of the marriage tie. But when all this is said, and the tribunal is satisfied that the transaction was a binding contract, the parties to it who so agree to settle a matrimonial controversy must be taken to contract that they will not go behind the settlement, and cannot be listened to saying they did not make an express bargain that they would not sue. This decision must be kept within its legitimate bounds, and is not to be taken to extend to contracts that are against public policy.

SECTION TWO—COMMERCIAL AGREEMENTS

In commercial agreements it will be presumed that the parties intended to create legally binding contracts. This presumption may, however, be rebutted, for example an express statement by the parties of their intention not to form a contract.

In *The Commodity Broking Co. Ltd v Meehan* [1985] IR 12 (p. 148) the presumption applied by Barron J. was that the defendant intended a promise in respect of a commercial transaction to have legal effect.

In *The Cunard Steam Ship Co. Ltd v The Revenue Commissioners* [1931] IR 297 the presumption was rebutted when a booking arrangement was held not to be a contract because it was intended that a subsequent contract be made. A similar finding was reached in *Cadbury Ireland Ltd v Kerry Co-operative Creameries Ltd* [1982] ILRM 77 (see p. 781 below).

Sadler v Reynolds [2005] EWHC 309

The plaintiff was an experienced sports journalist who had ghost-written a number of autobiographies. He proposed to write the autobiography of the defendant, a reformed criminal and successful businessman, and while it was apparent that some agreement had been reached, and that the plaintiff had acted upon that belief by seeking to negotiate a publishing contract, a number of factual issues had to be resolved by Deputy High Court Judge Slade QC. One of them was the issue of legal intent. Judge Slade QC observed:

The approach of the courts to contractual intention has regard to:

- The nature of the relationship between the parties,
- The context in which agreement was reached, and
- Any express declaration of intent.

(*Chitty on Contracts*, 29th edn., vol 1 paras 2–175, 2–159, 2–157).

Contractual intention is normally judged objectively.

> In the absence of . . . an expression [of the absence of contractual intention] . . . the legal *effect* of an agreement which is clearly intended to give rise to some legal relations is not determined by the subjective intentions of the parties or of one of them (*Chitty* para. 2–156).

[Counsel] drew attention to *Hadley and others v Kemp and another* [1999] EMLR 589 in which Park J. held that on the facts of that case he was not satisfied that an intention to create legal relations had been established. In my judgement, the case is simply an illustration of the general principles referred to above.

In my judgment, the only other issue of law which arises for consideration in this case is whether any duty of confidence in relation to the title of the autobiography and the idea for the first chapter can give rise to a cause of action independently of the claim in breach of contract. Confidentiality in original ideas is pleaded as an implied term of the contract between the parties. A cause of action in breach of confidence is asserted additionally or alternatively to the implied term.

The facts of this case place the agreement between the parties somewhere between an obviously commercial transaction and a social exchange. In my judgment, the onus is on John Sadler to establish an intention to create legal relations, albeit that the onus is a less heavy one than that which would be required to establish such an intent in the context of a purely social relationship.

I have found that John Sadler has established that by 2 May 2001 an oral agreement had been entered into between him and George Reynolds giving John Sadler the right to write George Reynolds' autobiography. It was, *inter alia*, an express term of the agreement that Mr Sadler would obtain a reputable publisher for the book and negotiate suitable terms for the publishing agreement and that all earnings from the book under any publishing agreement would be shared by Mr Sadler and Mr Reynolds on a 50–50 basis.

In my judgment John Sadler has established an intention to create legal relations. He was an experienced journalist who met and dealt with George Reynolds in that context. Mr Reynolds was well aware that Mr Sadler had made money from his previous ghost-writing. On the evidence, George Reynolds, too, hoped to make money from the autobiography.

In paragraph 5.3 of the Defence served on behalf of Mr Reynolds it is pleaded that

> The Defendant did not, at any time, agree that the Claimant should be involved in writing such a book.

I have found that such an agreement was entered into. Although the contention is not raised in the pleaded Defence served on behalf of Mr Reynolds, because of his observation in evidence that 'A verbal contract is new to me', I have considered whether it could be said that it was the intention of the parties that the agreement was not intended to be binding until it was reduced to writing. In my view the evidence does not support such a contention. Nothing is alleged to have been said to that effect nor do the circumstances of the oral agreement indicate that it was not intended to have legal effect unless and until reduced to writing.

Accordingly I hold that by 2 May 2000 the parties had entered into a contract for John Sadler to ghost-write the autobiography of George Reynolds.

A. Legal Intent and Uncertainty of Terms

Sometimes the courts are forced to confront the twin problems of lack of legal intent and lack of clarity over what is promised. Judicial opinions will differ on the inferences to be drawn, as the following case illustrates.

Bowerman and Another *v* Association of British Travel Agents Ltd. The Times, 24 November 1995

Summary: There was a direct contractual relationship between a customer of a failed ABTA tour operator and ABTA themselves under their well-known scheme of protection against such failure.

The Court of Appeal so held by a majority, Lord Justice Hirst dissenting, in allowing an appeal by Miss Emma Bowerman and Mr Stephen Wallace from the dismissal by Mr Justice Mitchell on 11 March 1994 of their claim for reimbursement of £10 holiday insurance deducted from a claim paid by ABTA in respect of a holiday cancelled through the insolvency of the operator. Lord Justice Hirst said that Miss Bowerman was a pupil who had booked a skiing holiday and Mr Wallace was the teacher who had made the actual booking. The arrangements had to be cancelled owing to the insolvency of the ABTA tour operator and in making a reimbursement ABTA had deducted the sum of £10 in respect of holiday insurance and that sum formed the subject matter of the appeal, which turned entirely on the construction of a notice which each ABTA tour operator was required to display prominently in its office.

The appellants' case was that that notice constituted a contractual offer to the public at large to protect them financially in the various con-tingencies there specified and that each customer accepted that offer when he booked his holiday with the relevant ABTA agent. Strong reliance was placed on *Carlill v Carbolic Smoke Ball Company* [1893] 1 QB 256, where the Court of Appeal had held that an advertisement by the defendants, who were the proprietors and vendors of a medical preparation, costituted an offer to anybody who accepted it by performing the conditions named in the advertisement. It was submitted that that was comparable with the ABTA notice and his Lordship accepted that if the words of that notice were truly promissory in character it would be capable of constituting a contractual offer to the public in general. First, it was essential to give full weight to the main heading to which his Lordship attached great importance, namely: 'Notice describing ABTA's scheme of protection against the financial failure of ABTA's members'. That was an accurate epitome of the terms of the notice as a whole, which was descriptive rather than contractual in character. Nowhere in the first five paragraphs was there found any specific words of promise or any firm commitment and nothing in the last four paragraphs headed 'Limitation' pointed in a different direction. By contrast the crisp wording of the advertisement in the *Carlill* case, '£100 reward will be paid', was essentially promissory in character and highlighted the shortcomings, from the appellants' point of view, of the wording in the ABTA notice.

Lord Justice Waite said that in the end the case depended, as with so many questions involving construction of a document, upon impression; in this instance an impression gained by the court at one remove through the eyes of the hypothetical member of the public. The issue was not an easy one, as evidenced by the fact that Lord Justice Hirst and Lord Justice Hobhouse had each reached different conclusions on it for persuasive reasons. His Lordship's own view was that the notice, notwithstanding the bewildering miscellany it contained of information, promise, disclaimer and reassurance, would be understood by the ordinary member of the public as importing an intention to create legal relations with customers of ABTA members. The words that were crucial to the present case: 'Where holidays or other travel arrangements have not yet commenced at the time of failure, ABTA arranges for you to be reimbursed the money you have paid in respect of your holiday arrangements' would be understood by the ordinary reader as words of clear promise which did not lose their significance or their promissory character through being associated in the same context with words connoting a lesser degree of commitment.

Lord Justice Hobhouse said that the document was intended to be read and would reasonably be read by a member of the public as containing an offer of a promise which the customer was entitled to accept by choosing to do business with an ABTA member. A member of the public would not analyse his situation in legal terms but he would clearly understand that the notice would only apply to him if he should choose to do business with an ABTA member and he would also understand that if he did so he would be entitled to hold ABTA to what he understood ABTA to be promising. In his Lordship's judgment it satisfied the criteria for a unilateral contract and contained promises which were sufficiently clear to be capable of legal enforcement. The principles established in the *Carbolic Smoke Ball* case applied. The plaintiffs were entitled to enforce the right of reimbursement given to them in the notice. That conclusion also covered the question of the intention to create legal relations. The document as reasonably read by a member of the public would be taken to be an offer of a legally enforceable promise.

Given that that was the effect of the document which ABTA had chosen to publish, it did not advance ABTA's case to say that ABTA privately did not intend to expose themselves to any legal liability. It sufficed that ABTA intentionally published a document which had that effect.

Note

The National Lottery has provoked a considerable volume of litigation between individuals who have claimed entitlement to all or part of a lottery win vis-a-vis a person who has either possession of the winning ticket or the proceeds. In one High Court action a two-person syndicate had allegedly been formed, one of the syndicate collecting a winning half share in a lottery payout of £500,000 without informing the other. O'Neill J. ordered the holder of the monies to disclose the whereabouts of the payout. See 'Widow ordered to disclose where Lotto money is': *The Irish Times* 2 February 2000. 'Syndicate man seeks share of Lotto win': *The Irish Times* 22 October 2002. The leading English case is *Simpkins v Pays* [1955] 3 All ER 10 in which it was established that informal syndicates created in order to enter competition and the like may be enforceable contracts.

In December 2004 Clarke J. awarded Martin Horan a one-fifth share of a €2 million lottery jackpot on the basis that while his involvement in a syndicate had been irregular in certain respects, the other members of the syndicate had not terminated the arrangement prior to the purchase of the winning ticket; while an appeal to the Supreme Court was lodged (see *The Irish Times* 7 January 2005, 'Ruling on Lotto winnings row goes to Supreme Court') proceedings have apparently been settled.

The courts in the UK have also had a significant volume of employment case-law testing the questions whether religious ministers who undertake vocational callings do so in circumstances where the arrangements are struck with intention to create legal relations and the resultant contract is a contract of employment: see *Percy v Church of Scotland* [2006] 2AC28 and *New Testament Church of God v Stewart* [2007] EWCA Civ 1004 for the most recent decisions.

B. Letters of Comfort

Kleinwort Benson Ltd *v* Malaysia Mining Corp. Bhd [1989] 1 All ER 785

The plaintiff bank entered into negotiations with the defendants to make a loan facility available to MMC Metals, a subsidiary of the defendants. The defendants issued a 'comfort letter', para. 3 of which stated *inter alia*: 'It is our policy to ensure that the business of MMC Metals Ltd is at all times in a position to meet its liabilities to you under the above arrangements.'

When MMC Metals went into liquidation, the plaintiffs called on the defendants to ensure payment. When they refused, the plaintiffs sued.

At first instance Hirst J. awarded the plaintiffs damages arising from breach of a warranty and/or a representation.

Gibson L.J.:

. . .

The central question in this case, in my judgment, is that considered in *Esso Petroleum Co. Ltd v Mardon* [1976] 2 All ER 5, [1976] QB 801, on which counsel for the plaintiffs relied in this court but which was not cited to Hirst J. That question is whether the words of para. 3, considered in their context, are to be treated as a warranty of contractual promise. Para. 3 contains no express words of promise. Para. 3 is in its terms a statement of present fact and not a promise as to future conduct. I agree with the submission of counsel for the defendants that, in this regard, the words of para. 3 are in sharp contrast with the words of para. 2 of the letter: 'We confirm that we will not' etc. The force of this point is not limited, as Hirst J. stated it, to the absence from para. 3 of the words 'We confirm'. The real contrast is between the words of promise, namely 'We will not' in para. 2, and the words of statement of fact, 'It is our policy' in para. 3. Hirst J. held that, by the words of para. 3, the defendants gave an undertaking that now and at all times in the future, so long as Metals should be under any liability to the plaintiffs under the facility arrangements, it is *and will be* the defendants' policy to ensure that Metals is in a position to meet their liabilities. To derive that meaning from the words it is necessary to add the words emphasised, namely 'and will be', which do not appear in para. 3. In short, the words of promise as to the future conduct of the defendants were held by Hirst J. to be part of the necessary meaning of the words used in para. 3. The question is whether that view of the words can be upheld.

The absence of express words of warranty as to present facts or the absence of express words of promise as to future conduct does not conclusively exclude a statement from the status of warranty or promise. According to the well known dictum of Holt C.J., ' . . . an affirmation can only be a warranty provided it appears on evidence to have been so intended': see Ormrod L.J. in *Esso Petroleum Co. Ltd v Mardon*, citing Viscount Haldane L.C. in *Heilbut Symons & Co. v Buckleton* [1913] AC 30 at 38, [1911–13] All ER Rep 83 at 86.

. . .

The evidence does not show that the words used in para. 3 were intended to be a promise as to the future conduct of the defendants but, in my judgment, it shows the contrary.

The concept of a comfort letter was, as counsel for the defendants acknowledged, not shown to have acquired any particular meaning at the time of the negotiations in this case with reference to the limits of any legal liability to be assumed under its terms by a parent company. A letter, which the parties might have referred to at some stage as a letter of comfort, might, after negotiation, have emerged containing in para. 3 in express terms the words used by Hirst J. to state the meaning which he gave to para. 3. The court would not, merely because the parties had referred to the document as a comfort letter, refuse to give effect to the meaning of the words used. But in this case it is clear, in my judgment, that the concept of a comfort letter, to which the parties had resort when the defendants refused to assume joint and several liability or to give a guarantee, was known by both sides at least to extend to or to include a document under which the defendants would give comfort to the plaintiffs by assuming, not a legal liability to ensure repayment of the liabilities of its subsidiary, but a moral responsibility only. Thus, when the defendants by Mr John Green in June 1984 told the plaintiffs that Mr Green would recommend that credit lines for Metals be covered by a letter of comfort rather than by guarantee, the response of Mr Irwin, before any draft of a comfort letter had been prepared, was ' . . . that a letter of comfort would not be a problem, but that [he] would probably have to charge a higher rate'. The comfort letter was drafted in terms which in para. 3 do not express any contractual promise and which are consistent with being no more than a representation of fact. If they are treated as no more than a representation of fact, they are in that meaning consistent with the comfort letter containing no more than the assumption of moral responsibility by the defendants in respect of the debts of Metals. There is nothing in the evidence to show that, as a matter of commercial probability or common sense, the parties must have intended para. 3 to be a contractual promise, which is not expressly stated, rather than a mere representation of fact which is so stated.

Next, the first draft of the comfort letter was produced by the plaintiffs. Para. 1 contained confirmation that the defendants knew of and approved of the granting of the facilities in question by the plaintiffs to Metals, and para. 2 contained the express confirmation that the defendants would not reduce their current financial interest in Metals until (in effect) facilities had been paid or the plaintiffs consented. Both are relevant to the present and future moral responsibility of the defendants. If the words of para. 3 are to be treated as intended to express a contractual promise by the defendants as to their future policy, which Hirst J. held the words to contain, then the recitation of the plaintiff's approval and the promise not to reduce their current financial interest in Metals, would be of no significance. If the defendants have promised that at all times in the future it will be the defendants' policy to ensure that Metals is in a position to meet its liabilities to the plaintiffs under the facility, it would not matter whether they had approved or disapproved, or whether they had disposed of their shares in Metals. Contracts may, of course, contain statements or promises which are caused to be of no separate commercial importance by the width of a later promise in the same document. Where, however, the court is examining a statement which is by its express words no more than a representation of fact, in order to consider whether it is shown to have been intended to be of the nature of a contractual promise or warranty, it seems to me to be a fact suggesting at least the absence of such intention if, as in this case, to read the statement as a contractual promise is to reduce to no significance two paragraphs included in the plaintiffs' draft, both of which have significance if the statement is read as a representation of fact only.

That point can be made more plainly thus: if para. 3 in its original or in its final form was intended to contain a binding legal promise by the defendants to ensure the ability of Metals to pay the sums due under the facility, there was no apparent need or purpose for the plaintiffs, as bankers, to waste ink on paras 1 and 2.

As I have said, the absence of express words of promise does not by itself prevent a statement from being treated as a contractual promise. The example given in argument by counsel for the plaintiffs, namely of the shop stating by a notice that it is its policy to accept, within fourteen days of purchase, the return in good condition of any goods bought and to refund the price without question, seems to me to be a case in which a court would be likely to hold that the notice imported a promise that the policy would continue over the fourteen day period. It would be difficult on those facts to find any sensible commercial explanation for the notice other than a contractual promise not to change the policy over the fourteen day period. It would not be satisfactory or convincing to regard the notice as no more than the assumption of a moral responsibility by the shop giving such a notice to its customers. In such a case, and in the absence of any relevant factual context indicating otherwise, it seems to me that the court would probably hold that the statement was shown to have been intended to be a contractual promise.

In this case, however, the opposite seems to me to be clear.

...

But the evidence of the refusal by the defendants to assume legal responsibility for the liabilities of Metals to the plaintiffs in the normal form of joint and several liability or of a gaurantee, and the consequent resort by the parties to what they described as a comfort letter substantially in the terms submitted by the plaintiffs to the defendants, is, in my judgment, admissible on the question whether, for the purposes of the test applied by the court in *Esso Petroleum Co. Ltd v Mardon*, the defendants' affirmation in para. 3 appears on the evidence to have been intended as a warranty or contractual promise.

With that evidence before the court I find it impossible to hold that the words in para. 3 were intended to have any effect between the parties other than in accordance with the express words used. For this purpose it seems to me that the onus of demonstrating that the affirmation appears on evidence to have been intended as a contractual promise must lie on the party asserting that it does, but I do not rest my conclusion on failure by the plaintiffs to discharge any onus. I think it is clear that the words of para. 3 cannot be regarded as intended to contain a contractual promise as to the future policy of the defendants.

. . .

If my view of this case is correct, the plaintiffs have suffered grave financial loss as a result of the collapse of the tin market and the following decision by the defendant company not to honour a moral responsibility which it assumed in order to gain for its subsidiary the finance necessary for the trading operations which the defendants wished that subsidiary to pursue. The defendants have demonstrated, in my judgment, that they made no relevant contractual promise to the plaintiffs which could support the judgment in favour of the plaintiffs. The consequences of the decision of the defendants to repudiate their moral responsibility are not matters for this court.

I would allow this appeal.

The other Lord Justices concurred with Gibson LJ.

Note

1. See Reynolds (1988) 104 LQR 353, and *Orion Insurance Co. plc v Sphere Drake Insurance plc* [1990] 1 Lloyd's Rep. 465.
2. If the letter constitutes an acceptance of a prior offer, then irrespective of its description, or cautionary language, a legally binding contract will result. See *Wilson Smithett & Cape (Sugar) Ltd v Bangladesh Sugar and Food Industries Corp.* [1986] 1 Lloyd's Rep. 378.
3. The TEAM Aer Lingus Letters of Comfort
The most highly publicised instance of letters of comfort in an Irish context relate to the transfer of Aer Lingus personnel to the aircraft maintenance company TEAM, a statutory company set up in 1990. Lawyers acting for ICTU, the TEAM unions and Aer Lingus drew up a set of guarantees that were approved in 1990 by the then Minister for Transport. These guarantees were:

1. Each Aer Lingus employee who will work within the new maintenance company will remain a member of Aer Lingus staff.
2. All working conditions, rights and privileges, including ID Cards, pension entitlements, seniority and other benefits will be preserved for each Aer Lingus employee working within the new company.
3. Each individual's seniority and service with Aer Lingus will continue and accumulate in the new company.
4. Promotion within the new company will not affect the guaranteed Aer Lingus status of each individual working within the new company.
5. The agreement will provide that the guarantees given will become part of the individual's contract of employment and will be enforceable by each such individual employee.
6. No change in the terms of the agreement can take place without the individual consent of each employee affected.

The last two clauses give every TEAM employee with a letter—about 1,200 of the 1,600 currently working in the company—the right to sue Aer Lingus for breach of contract if it attempts to transfer them to another employer.

The company also provides guarantees that it will retain at least 51 per cent of TEAM in perpetuity. And any new investors would not have 'any influence on the application, use or investment of pension fund contributions or assets'.

These letters of comfort were in turn 'repurchased' by Aer Lingus when TEAM was sold off in 1998. For litigation surrounding these arrangements see *King v Aer Lingus* [2005] 4 IR 310.

SECTION THREE—INDUSTRIAL CONFLICT AND LEGAL INTENT

In contrast to the well-known English case of *Ford v AEF* [1969] 1 All ER 339, Irish case-law tends to favour the enforcement, via contract, of no-strike clauses in industrial relations law.

Goulding Chemicals *v* Bolger [1977] IR 211

In anticipation of the closure of their manufacturing company, the plaintiffs reached agreement with the trade unions in regard to the manner of the closure and the amounts of the redundancy payments to be paid to the employees. All of the employees were then dismissed in accordance with the agreement. The defendants were former employees of the plaintiffs, and trade union members who refused to accept the terms of the agreement. The plaintiffs claimed an injunction to prevent the defendants picketing their premises.

O'Higgins C.J.:

The second ground of appeal put forward by the plaintiffs was based on the acceptance by all the unions concerned (including ITGWU of which the defendants are members) of the plaintiffs' proposals for the closing of their plant. These proposals were designed to ensure that the closing would be accepted by the unions as being in the circumstances unavoidable and that satisfactory monetary compensation would be paid to all employees. It was of course implicit in the proposals and in their acceptance by the unions that there would be no trade dispute and, of course, no picketing. The six-point proposal or statement from the plaintiffs which was accepted by the unions was a business-like document and had all the appearances of being intended to create legal relations between the unions which accepted and the plaintiffs who proposed. I would regard the agreement resulting from the acceptance of these proposals as being similar in effect to that dealt with in *Edwards v Skyways Ltd*[1] and, there being nothing to suggest the contrary, in my view a valid contract was thereby created between these unions and the plaintiffs. However, this is not the point of this ground of appeal.

The plaintiffs' contention is that this valid enforceable agreement has the effect of binding the defendants who are all members of one of the unions involved. This submission must be considered in the light of the evidence, which was uncontradicted, that the defendants at all times opposed the conclusion of any agreement with regard to the closing of the plant and made it abundantly clear, both inside the union and to the plaintiffs, that they would not accept any agreement to this effect. I find it hard to accept that in such circumstances the defendants can be bound by an agreement which they have expressly repudiated and opposed. It seems to me that to hold them bound would be contrary to all principle. The only basis put forward for suggesting that they should be bound was that they did not resign and continued to be members of their union. The rules of the union were not put in evidence but I would find it very difficult to accept that membership of an association like a union could bind all members individually in respect of union contracts merely because such had been made by the union. I cannot accept for these reasons that this ground of appeal is well founded.

Kenny J.:

The defendants contended that the six-point statement and its acceptance by the unions did not constitute an enforceable agreement. An agreement between parties is enforceable by the law unless the agreement itself or the surrounding circumstances show that the parties did not intend to enter into legal relations (*Rose and Frank Co. v J. R. Crompton & Bros Ltd*[2]) and reliance was placed on the decision of Lane J. in *Ford Motor Co. Ltd v A.E.F.*[3] where it was held that two collective agreements did not, having regard to their background, constitute a legally enforceable agreement. In *Edwards v Skyways Ltd*[4] Megaw J. held that an agreement by the defendants to make *ex gratia* payments to their employees whom they were dismissing created an enforceable agreement. I have considerable doubts about the correctness of the decision in the *Ford Motor Co.* case particularly as Lane J. did not say anything about the decision in *Edwards v Skyways Ltd* although it was cited to him. It seems to me that the six-point agreement was intended to create legal relations and was intended to be a contract between the plaintiffs and the unions engaged in the negotiations. I think that Megaw J. was right when he said that when an apparent agreement in relation to business relations is entered into, the onus on the party who asserts that it was not intended to have legal effect is a heavy one. In my opinion the six-point statement and its acceptance created a valid enforceable contract between the plaintiffs and the unions who took part in the negotiations.

The plaintiffs then argued that if the six-point statement and its acceptance by the unions created a contract the defendants, as members of the union, were bound by it because the majority of their co-members had accepted it. No authority to support this argument was cited and the rules of the union, which would show the authority of the majority, were not referred to or proved. I think that the contention is wrong in principle and that all the reported cases on this matter are against it. Membership of a corporate body or of an association does not have the consequence that every agreement made by that corporate body or association binds every member of it. None of the defendants are parties to the agreement and as they consistently opposed it, no question of their being bound by acquiescence can arise. . . .

[1] [1964] 1 WLR 349.   [2] [1923] 2 KB 261.   [3] [1969] 2 QB 303

(Henchy, Griffith and Parke JJ. agreed and the appeal was dismissed.)

Even where the agreement seems to be vague or aspirational, the courts will incline towards enforceability.

O'Rourke & Others v Talbot (Ireland) Ltd [1984] ILRM 587

Barrington J.:

. . . The defendant is a well-known firm, formerly engaged in the assembly, and now engaged in the importation and distribution, of motor cars. The plaintiffs are nine foremen formerly employed by the defendants in their motor assembly business. All were senior men with from 12 to 28 years service when they were made redundant by the defendant on 26 September 1980. A strike which attracted considerable public notoriety took place at the defendant's premises in the year 1981 so that it may be worthwhile to mention that this case has nothing to do with that strike, all of the plaintiffs having been made redundant in the previous year.

In their proceedings the plaintiffs claim a declaration that the defendant company is bound by a certain agreement dated 21 June 1979 as amended by another agreement dated 25 July 1979 whereby they allege the defendant company gave a guarantee that the plaintiffs would not be made redundant prior to 1984. The defendant, in its substantial defence to the proceedings argued before me, did not deny the existence of the said alleged agreements but pleaded that the said alleged agreements or agreement did not contemplate legal relations and do not entitle the plaintiffs to any relief in a court of law. . . .

The agreement

In 1979 the defendant company was running into difficulties. Costs were rising and sales and production were falling. Under these circumstances management were anxious to secure the agreement of the plaintiffs that foremen who had left car assembly, or were being redeployed elsewhere in the defendants' business, would not be replaced. The plaintiffs, on the other hand, were worried about their own jobs but were prepared to go along with management's proposals provided they got some security in return.

A meeting was held between management and the foremen's representatives on 20 June 1979, Mr Gould, Mr Power and Mr Oakes represented management while Mr O'Rourke, Mr Myler and Mr Coleman represented the foremen. The following extract from a memorandum from Mr Oakes, the personnel manager, to Mr Ronayne, the managing director of the defendant company, gives some insight into the problem with which management and foremen were concerned just prior to the meeting of 20 June. The memorandum is headed 'Foremen' and is dated 15 June 1979. It reads, in part, as follows:

> At the foremen's request Jim [i.e. Mr Power the production manager] and I met them on Wednesday to discuss problems which have a direct bearing on their attitudes and ultimately their behaviour.
>
> They expressed grave concern on the future of the plant and ultimately on employment levels. This has been brought to a head by the departure of John Ryan (foreman) and the company indicating that there will be no replacement.
>
> We explained in answer to their question, that for the level of production of sixteen cars a day we had surplus foremen, a fact that we had indicated some time ago.

There is very little conflict about what happened at the meeting. The foremen's representatives appeared to be of the opinion that virtually all issues were agreed, at least in principle, at the meeting of 20 June whereas the management representatives appeared to think that it took a number of meetings to reach agreement. Be that as it may I am quite satisfied that by the end of July the foremen and the management were in agreement on all outstanding points and that the foremen, in return for what they took to be a guarantee of job security, agreed that production foremen who retired or were transferred would not be replaced on the assembly line and that the remaining foremen would fill in for those who left and would work at any job to which they were assigned by management, including security work, provided they suffered no loss in pay. I am quite satisfied that the foremen, in return for agreeing to the management's plans for the redeployment of supervisory staff, asked for an assurance that their jobs would be secure and asked to have this assurance, in writing, on company notepaper.

It is not clear whether a draft of the proposed assurance was produced at the meeting of 20 June but, on the following day, the foremen received a document on company notepaper signed by Mr Gould, Mr Power and Mr Oakes and which read as follows: 'The company gives an assurance that compulsory redundancy will not be introduced among production supervisory grades should the market situation and other conditions affecting the company's performance necessitate a realignment of manning and staffing arrangements.' It will be noticed that this document contemplates changes in the 'market situation and other conditions affecting the company's performance'. Should such factors necessitate 'a realignment of manning and staffing arrangements' the company still gives an assurance that compulsory redundancy will not be introduced among production supervisory grades.

The foremen discussed this document either on the twenty first or some later date and were not satisfied with it. They wanted something that would bind the company legally. Some of the foremen—and in particular Mr Coleman—did not like the word 'assurance'. They wished to substitute the word guarantee' which they considered to be a better word from the legal point of view. They were also familiar with the term 'guarantee', in the sense of a legally binding warranty as to fitness, in the motor trade. I am quite satisfied—and indeed there is no controversy about it—that at some stage the foremen asked for a 'guarantee' instead of the 'assurance' contained in the document of 21 June. I am quite satisfied also that management created no difficulty about giving the guarantee. A meeting was held between representatives of management and representatives of the foremen on 25 July 1979. At some stage before this meeting draft minutes of the meeting were shown to the foremen's representatives and agreed to by them. These minutes contain the following paragraphs:

> The company gave a guarantee of no compulsory redundancy prior to 1984 and that surplus supervisors would be redeployed.
>
> On re-location a supervisor would retain all his benefits as a 'no worse off' condition.

So far as the representatives of management were concerned I am quite satisfied that they negotiated with the foremen's representatives in good faith. They were, at least, equally concerned about the future of the plant. They recognised that the foremen were senior men who had given the company loyal service They always envisaged that if a particular foreman's job became outdated that it would be possible to redeploy him in some other part of the company's business. They acknowledged that the foremen had agreed to work in any capacity and that, as senior men, they should be secure on the principle of first in last out. But things did not work out that way. The company's business deteriorated in 1980. They were five unions in the plant and it was not practicable to sack one man and replace him by a man from a different union. Neither was it practicable to have two men receiving different rates of pay for the one job. In September 1980 the company felt that it had to let all the plaintiffs go.

I think the truth of the matter is that the representatives of management did not think that they were entering into a legally binding arrangement with the foremen at all. They felt that they were entering into a productivity agreement of a kind binding in honour but not in law. Mr John Kane the secretary of the No. 2 Branch of the Irish Transport and General Workers' Union, who give evidence in the case, acknowledged that many agreements negotiated between employers and trade unions were regarded as falling into this category. Moreover, management were probably more conscious than the man of the importance of market forces and felt that no matter what was decided in negotiations, market forces would ultimately decide what would happen to the plant and to the men's jobs.

I am satisfied, however, that not only were the men looking for something which was legally binding but that management knew this. Mr Oakes admitted in cross-examination that he knew the foremen were very happy with the assurance and guarantee because they appeared to feel that their jobs were protected. They were no longer relying on the general arrangements made between the motor assemblers and the government which, while designed to maintain employment levels in the motor assembly industry, did not guarantee the particular job of any one man. They now had a further assurance which applied specifically to their jobs with the defendant company. He knew that the foremen thought they were getting more than other workers with the defendant company. The management company knew that the foremen were not getting more but did not consider it necessary to tell them.

The law

The agreement in the present case was a commercial agreement. It is clear from the internal memo sent by Mr Oakes to Mr Ronayne that management knew that an offer of job security would influence the men's attitude towards the scheme of redeployment in the company. It is also clear that the assurance given did influence their attitude and that the scheme of redeployment was implemented with the men's agreement and co-operation because of the assurance given. It therefore appears to me that the presumption of law is that the parties intended to create legal relations. In these circumstances as Megaw J. said in *Edwards v Skyways Ltd* [1964] 1 WLR 349, the onus is on the party who asserts that no legal effect was intended, and the onus is a heavy one.

In that case the plaintiff was an aircraft pilot employed by the defendant. At a meeting held between representatives of the defendant company and the plaintiff's trade association it had been agreed that pilots declared redundant when leaving the defendant company would be given 'an *ex gratia* payment' equivalent to the defendant's contributions to the pension fund. The plaintiff having retired, the defendant refused to make the '*ex gratia* payment'. Megaw J. held that the agreement was a binding one and that the term *ex gratia* related to the position prevailing before the plaintiff carried out his end of the agreement and not afterwards.

The decision in *Edwards v Skyways Ltd* was cited with approval by the Chief Justice in a passage which appears at p. 231 of the report in *Gouldings Chemicals Ltd v Bolger* [1977] IR 211. But one of the matters which influenced the Chief Justice in the view he expressed in the passage quoted was that the document under discussion in that case, though negotiated between employers and a trade union, was 'a business-like document and had all the appearances of being intended to create legal relations'.

[Counsel for the defendant] says that the minute of the meeting of 25 July 1979 which contains, at para. 3, the guarantee of no compulsory redundancy prior to 1984, does not look like a business-like document or one intended to create legal relations. He points, for instance, to para. 2 which is as follows: 'The company cannot anticipate plant lay-out or supervising requirements should diversification take place but supervising ratios will be fully discussed before implementation.'

[Counsel] relies strongly on the case of *Ford Motors Co. Ltd v* A.E.F. [1969] 2 QB 303 where it was held that collective agreements negotiated between a large industrial company and various trade unions and containing many 'aspirational' clauses, were not intended to create legal relations. In the course of his judgment in that case (at p. 496) Lane J. (as he then was) put the matter as follows: 'Agreements such as these, composed largely of optimistic aspirations, presenting grave practical problems of enforcement and reached against a background of opinion adverse to enforceability, are, in my judgment, not contracts in the legal sense and are not enforceable at law.'

In *Goulding Chemicals Ltd v Bolger* Kenny J., at p. 237 of the report, expressed some reservations as to the correctness of the decision in the *Ford Motor Co. Ltd* case but I do not consider it necessary to go into these matters for three reasons. Firstly, we are not here dealing with a trade union or a group of trade unions negotiating on behalf of all the men employed in a vast concern or a particular industry but with three foremen negotiating on behalf of not more than seventeen of their peers and referring back to their peers and getting authority from time to time. Secondly, a productivity agreement which might not be legally enforceable in all its terms can still amend particular provisions in a worker's contract of employment e.g. his rate of pay. In the present case I have no doubt that the foremen made quite clear that they were looking for an alteration in their terms of employment. Finally, the plaintiffs in the present case carried out their side of the bargain and are standing over the authority of the agents who negotiated the agreement on their behalf.

CODES OF PRACTICE

Wandsworth London Borough Council (Respondents/Appellants) *v* D'Silva and other (applicants/respondents) [1998] ILIR 193

Wandsworth Borough Council had in place a code of practice, which set out procedures for monitoring and reviewing staff absenteeism. The code distinguished between short-term and long-term absences and absences due to different circumstances. The code itself set out the need for 'some flexibility of approach' in relation to patterns and durations of absences. Wandsworth Borough Council sought to amend the code so as to add another 'review' event in the case of short-term absences and to reduce the period of continuous absence that could trigger a long-term review from twelve months to six months. The staff objected to these changes on the ground that the code was a contractual document, which could not be altered unilaterally. Both the industrial tribunal and the EAT held that the code of practice was contractually binding and could not be varied by the employer. The employer appealed to the Court of Appeal. Lord Woolf M.R. (Millett and Walker L.JJ. concurring) allowed the appeal.

Lord Woolf M.R.:

On the first issue the outcome of the appeal therefore turns on whether, on the proper interpretation of the code, the relevant paragraphs are to be construed as conferring rights on the employee or as setting out no more than good practice which the council's officers were intended to follow.

The industrial tribunal were aware that this was an issue they were required to tackle. They understandably found it difficult to identify any:

. . . very clear yardstick by which to divine what provisions which govern the relationship between the employer/employee are properly to be described as 'contractual terms and conditions' and what yardstick should apply to some kind of lesser mutual obligation which could be described as 'code', 'policy' or 'statement of intent'.

In relation to this code the industrial tribunal spoke good sense when they stated a general approach to codes of this sort in these terms:

It is, we believe, from our industrial experience eminently desirable that an employer's approach to dealing with ill-health absence should not run the risk of being viewed by management and staff in the same manner as misconduct disciplinary procedures. It is very much an area which we as a tribunal would wish to see covered by negotiated codes and policy statements and staff agreements with that kind of spirit and effect than by being treated as part of the contractually binding obligations of the employer and employee. As a matter of good industrial practice we believe that ill-health absence should be treated with much more flexibility compassion and common sense than many other aspects of the employment relationship. There is a case for saying that a young man who takes one day off allegedly for a cold but is seen shopping in the town centre should be treated much more severely than, say, someone with long-term asthma difficulties and a number of days' absence.

However, the industrial tribunal went on to indicate that they could not 'legitimately find that the terms which the applicants argue are so far away from the centre of the contract of employment that they may properly be included within the wide range of day-to-day instructions which any large employer must be free to issue.' However, the tribunal declined to come to a conclusion about the code as a whole. They took the view that many of the provisions sit very much more easily within a definition such as 'guidance' or 'policy' than contractual terms. In relation to the suggested amendments, however, the conclusion was that the existing provisions constituted:

A clear statement by the employer that in a certain situation of days or months of absence certain consequences will follow.

This they went on to say led to 'a complementary right in the employee that where the absence in question does not reach the number of days or months so specified that employee is thus not at risk for the consequences which otherwise might follow'.

In addition, the tribunal basing itself upon the judgment of Mr Justice Hobhouse in *Alexander v Standard Telephones and Cables Ltd* (No. 2) [1991] IRLR 286 decided that the terms which were subject of the proposed amendment, were 'apt' to be regarded as terms of a contract.

In the *Alexander* case, Hobhouse J. was concerned with contracts of employment where employees had been given written particulars and there was a collective agreement. The issue was whether the collective agreement had, or had not been incorporated into the contracts of employment or not. In his judgment Hobhouse J. having referred to the case of *National Coal Board v National Union of Mineworkers* (1986) IRLR 439, where Scott J. had indicated that it was unlikely that a collective agreement was intended to be legally enforceable at the behest of the employee, went on to say:

> Therefore, even in a case which involved wide express words of incorporation the court considered it necessary to look at the content and character of the relevant parts of the collective agreement in order to decide whether or not they were incorporated into the individual contracts of employment.
>
> The principles to be applied can therefore be summarised. The relevant contract is that between the individual employee and the employer; it is the contractual intention of those two parties which must be ascertained. In so far as that intention is to be found in a written document, that document must be construed on ordinary contractual principles. In so far as there is no such document or that document is not complete or conclusive, their contractual intention has to be ascertained by inference from other available material including collective agreements. The fact that another document is not itself contractual does not prevent it from being incorporated in the contract if that intention is shown as between the employer and the individual employee. Where a document is expressly incorporated by general words it is still necessary to consider in conjunction with the words of incorporation, whether any particular part of that document is apt to be a term of the contract; if it is inapt, the correct construction of the contract may be that it is not a term of the contract. Where it is not a case of express incorporation, but a matter of inferring contractual intent, the character of the document and the relevant part of it and whether it is apt to form part of the individual contract is central to the decision whether or not the inference should be drawn.

Those views of Hobhouse J. do provide a valuable guide as to the solution of this issue on this appeal. They can, however, be supplemented in this context by asking a question, identified by Millett L.J. in the course of argument of this case. That question is whether the code should properly be regarded as conferring a right on the employees not to have the short- or long-term procedures contained in the code invoked without the triggering event having happened? This is a question which the tribunal did consider and having done so came to a conclusion in favour of the employees. The appeal tribunal came to the same conclusion. Their conclusions were however as to the legal effect of the relevant parts of the code. However, although their decisions involve deciding a question of law, on an appeal to this court, the fact that the tribunals are expert bodies will not be ignored by this court. Nonetheless, this court will intervene if it is satisfied that the industrial tribunal has come to a decisions which is wrong in law.

In this case this court can have less reservations about interfering because the tribunal itself said that the changes which the council wish to introduce were 'eminently reasonable'. Here the decision which the industrial tribunal came to on the first issue is not sustainable. If the language of the provisions which are to be amended are examined in the context of the scheme as a whole, they are not an appropriate foundation upon which to base contractual rights. If what was being triggered was a disciplinary or an appeal procedure, the position would probably be different. Both in the case of the short- and the long-term absentees, the code is doing no more than providing guidance for both the supervisors and the employees as to what is expected to happen. The code does not set out what is contractually required to happen. The whole process in the initial stages is sensibly designed to be flexible and informal in a way which is inconsistent with contractual rights being created. At later stages of the process proposed the employees' arguments would have much more force. The appeal should therefore be allowed.

EXERCISES

1. Tom and Geraldine have just announced their engagement. Geraldine is told by Tom that if she gives up her job and 'project manages' the restoration of a house that the couple have just bought, Tom will pay Geraldine 'an allowance' of €3,000 per month. Geraldine wants to know if this promise is legally enforceable. What would you advise Geraldine to do (she has yet to resign from her job)?

2. Pippa has just started work in Bebo Boxes. On day two she asks Bill, the car-park attendant, if there is anywhere for her to park her car. Bill says she can have space no. 57. She leaves her car in that space for three weeks, but Bill has told Pippa that as from tomorrow she cannot use that space (or any other space) because Alice, the marketing manager, is coming back from a month's holiday. Pippa claims that her contract of employment with Bebo Boxes now contains an obligation on Bebo Box to allow her to park on the premises. Do you agree?

3. Brian has registered to cycle from New York to San Francisco on a sponsored charity event. The charity required Brian to pay an airfare and accommodation charges of €1,000 as well as raise €5,000 in sponsorship. Brian has been training and paid €6,000 to the charity, but he has been told that, due to rising fuel and accommodation costs, he has to pay an extra €200 and raise an additional €3,000 in sponsorship if he is to be allowed to participate in the even. Brian thinks the charity is acting in breach of contract. Do you agree?

Chapter Five

Legal Form

INTRODUCTION

Certain contracts, in order to be enforceable, must be in the form pre-scribed by law. Some contracts must be under seal, some in writing and some evidenced in writing. Common law dictates that contracts unsupported by consideration must be under seal.

Similarly, many pieces of domestic legislation require contracts to be written. For example, hire-purchase agreements under the Consumer Credit Act 1995 and arbitration agreements under the Arbitration Acts 1954–1998 must be recorded in writing. In recent years, complying with our obligations under the various EU directives has led to a substantial increase in consumer protection legislation prescribing formal requirements for contracts. For example, the substantial growth in 'distance contracts' (i.e. contracts made by the supplier with a consumer making exclusive use of means of distant communications such as the phone, electronic mail, mail order, catalogues, etc.) gave rise to Directive 97/7/EC on the Protection of Consumers in Respect of Distant Contracts. This was implemented into Irish law by means of the European Communities (Protection of Consumers in Respect of Contracts Made By Means of Distance Communication) Regulations, 2001 [S.I. No. 207 of 2001] and requires certain specified information to be made available prior to the formation of the contract. It also requires subsequent written confirmation or 'confirmation in another durable medium available and accessible to him or her' of that information. The information includes: information on conditions and procedures for exercising a right of cancellation, the geographical address of the place of business of the supplier to which the consumer may address any complaints, information on after-sales services and guarantees which exist, and conditions for cancelling the contract in the event that it is of unspecified duration or its duration exceeds one year.

Finally, section 2 of the Statute of Frauds (Ireland) 1695 lists a number of contracts which must be evidenced in writing:

No action shall be brought . . . whereby to charge the defendant upon any special promise to answer for the debt, default or miscarriage of another person, or to charge any person upon any agreement made upon consideration of marriage, or upon any contract of sale of lands, tenements or hereditaments or any interest in or concerning them, or upon any agreement that is not to be formed within the space of one year from the making thereof, unless the agreement upon which such action shall be brought, or some memorandum or note thereof, shall be in writing, and signed by the party to be charged therewith, or some other person thereunto by him lawfully authorised.

It should be noted that agreements made in consideration of marriage, though common at one stage, are relatively rare today. Section 13 of the Statute of Frauds (Ireland) 1695 also requires a memorandum for contracts for the sale of goods in excess of [€12.70] unless the buyer accepts and receives part of the goods sold, gives something in earnest to bind the bargain or makes part payment. This section appears to have been impliedly repealed and these agreements are now regulated by section 4 of the Sale of Goods Act 1893 which provides:

(1) A contract for the sale of any goods of the value of [€12.70] or upwards shall not be enforceable by action unless the buyer shall accept part of the goods so sold, and actually receive the same, or give something in earnest to bind the contract, or in part payment, or unless some note or memorandum in writing of the contract be made and signed by the party to be charged or his agent in that behalf.
(2) The provisions of this section apply to every such contract, notwithstanding that the goods may be intended to be delivered at some future time, or may not at the time of such contract be actually made, procured, or provided, or fit or ready for delivery, or some act may be requisite for the making or completing thereof, or rendering the same fit for delivery.
(3) There is an acceptance of goods within the meaning of this section when the buyer does any act in relation to the goods which recognises a pre-existing contract of sale whether there be an acceptance in performance of the contract or not.

In the UK, the majority of section 4 of the Statute of Frauds 1677, which was similar to our section 2, was repealed and the only category remaining is promises to answer for the debt of another. The UK Law of Property (Miscellaneous Provisions) Act 1989 now requires contracts for the sale of land or other dispositions of an interest in land to be in writing.

SECTION ONE—FORMAL REQUIREMENTS

A. Contracts to Which the Statute of Frauds Applies

The reference in the Statute to 'contracts to answer for the debt of another' involves Contracts of Guarantee, not contracts of indemnity. A guarantee is an undertaking which is conditional on the default of the debtor. Both the debtor and the promisor are liable to the creditor. An indemnity is an undertaking to be liable irrespective of whether the debtor defaults. In such a case, only the promisor is liable. The following case explains the rationale behind the distinction in the Statute.

Actionstrength Ltd (t/a Vital Resources) *v* International Glass Engineering Inglen SpA and others [2003] 2 WLR 1060

Lord Bingham of Cornhill:

Actionstrength agreed with Inglen to supply labour to enable Inglen (the main contractor chosen by St-Gobain) to build a factory for St-Gobain. Inglen's deficiencies as a contractor led to Actionstrength being drawn, more closely than would be normal for a labour-only subcontractor, into the oversight of Inglen's performance. From an early date Actionstrength had difficulty obtaining payment by Inglen and considerable arrears built up. Actionstrength was contractually entitled to terminate its contract with Inglen on thirty days' notice if duly approved invoices had not been paid within thirty days and remained unpaid. Such termination would have been seriously prejudicial to St-Gobain, whose interest was to take expeditious possession of a completed factory. Actionstrength threatened to withdraw its labour. St-Gobain induced it not to do so by promising that, if Inglen did not pay Actionstrength any sums which were or became owing, it (St-Gobain) would do so. On that undertaking Actionstrength forebore to withdraw its labour and continued to supply labour to Inglen, whose indebtedness to Actionstrength increased fivefold over the weeks that followed. St-Gobain received the benefit of the work done by the labour which Actionstrength supplied. When Actionstrength, unable to obtain payment by Inglen, sought to enforce the agreement against St-Gobain, that company relied on the absence of a written memorandum or note of the agreement to defeat Actionstrength's claim.

While section 4 of the Statute of Frauds has been repealed or replaced in its application to the other four classes of contract originally specified, it has been retained in relation to guarantees. In 1937 the Law Revision Committee (in its Sixth Interim Report, *Statute of Frauds and the Doctrine of Consideration*, Cmd 5449, paragraph 16) recommended the repeal of so much as remained of section 4. But a minority headed by Goddard J. dissented in relation to guarantees, on the grounds:

(1) that there was a real danger of inexperienced people being led into undertaking obligations which they did not fully understand, and that opportunities would be given to the unscrupulous to assert that credit was given on the faith of a guarantee which the alleged surety had had no intention of giving;
(2) that a guarantee was a special class of contract, being generally one-sided and disinterested as far as the surety was concerned, and the necessity of writing would give the proposed surety an opportunity for thought;
(3) that the requirement of writing would ensure that the terms of the guarantee were settled and recorded;
(4) that Parliament had imposed a requirement of writing in other contractual contexts;
(5) that judges and juries were not infallible on questions of fact, and in the vast majority of cases the surety was getting nothing out of the bargain;
(6) that it was desirable to protect the small man; and
(7) that the necessity for guarantees to be in writing was generally understood.

No action was taken on the 1937 report. In 1953 the Law Reform Committee (First Report, *Statute of Frauds and Section 4 of the Sale of Goods Act 1893*, Cmd 8809) endorsed the recommendation of its predecessor that section 4 of the Statute of Frauds should be largely repealed but, agreeing with those who had earlier dissented, unanimously recommended that the section should continue to apply to guarantees. Effect was given to this report by enactment of the 1954 Act. Whatever the strength of the reasons given by the dissenting minority for retaining the old rule in relation to conventional consumer guarantees, it will be apparent that those reasons have little bearing on cases where the facts are such as those to be assumed here. It was not a bargain struck between inexperienced people, liable to misunderstand what they were doing. St-Gobain, as surety, had a very clear incentive to keep the Actionstrength workforce on site and, on the assumed facts, had an opportunity to think again. There is assumed to be no issue about the terms of the guarantee. English contract law does not ordinarily require writing as a condition of enforceability. It is not obvious why judges are more fallible when ruling on guarantees than other forms of oral contract. These were not small men in need of paternalist protection. While the familiar form of bank guarantee is well understood, it must be at least doubtful whether those who made the assumed agreement in this case appreciated that it was in law a guarantee. The judge at first instance was doubtful whether it was or not. The Court of Appeal reached the view that it was, but regarded the point as interesting and not entirely easy: [2002] 1 WLR 566, 568, [2001] EWCA Civ 1477, paragraph 2. Two members of the court discussed the question at a little length, with detailed reference to authority.

It may be questionable whether, in relation to contracts of guarantee, the mischief at which section 4 was originally aimed, is not now outweighed, at least in some classes of case, by the mischief to which it can give rise in a case such as the present, however unusual such cases may be. But that is not a question for the House in its judicial capacity. Sitting judicially, the House must of course give effect to the law of the land of which (in England and Wales) section 4 is part. As Mr McGhee for Actionstrength correctly recognised, that section is fatal to his client's claim unless St-Gobain can be shown to be estopped from relying on the section.

(Lord Hoffmann, Lord Walker of Gestingthorp, Lord Woolf and Lord Clyde concurred.)

Notes

1. It has been noted that this case emphasises the importance of determining whether or not an 'understanding' can be classified as a 'guarantee'. It appears that if the overall effect of any such arrangement is on all fours with a guarantee, it will be treated as such. (See 'Guarantees: need for writing' PLB 2003, 24(1), 3.)
2. A further claim that St-Gobain should be estopped from relying on section 4 is considered at p.293.

Consider:

What is the rationale for including guarantees in the Statute of Frauds?

The requirement that contracts for the sale of goods in excess of €12.70 be evidenced in writing has been severely criticised (Stephen and Pollock (1885) 1 LQR 1) and often ignored in practice. No attempt has been made to increase the paltry figure involved to keep apace with inflation. Although the exceptions provided for have been utilised, for example in *Tradax (Ireland) Ltd v Irish Grain Board Ltd* [1984] IR 1, there has been an element of unpredictability in the case-law.

Consider:

Should section 4 of the Sale of Goods Act 1893 be repealed or amended in any way?

To come within the category of contracts not to be performed within the year, evidence must demonstrate that at the time the contract was made the parties did not intend to perform it within one year.

Hynes *v* Hynes (HC) 21 December 1984, unrep.

When the plaintiff's business got into financial difficulties, he entered into a verbal agreement with the defendant, his brother, whereby the latter agreed to form two new companies to complete the plaintiff's outstanding contracts and to be his successor in business. The plaintiff maintains that it was also agreed that all the profits of the new companies would, in the first instance, be used to discharge the plaintiff's debts, and thereafter to be split between the parties. The defendant claimed *inter alia* that there was no memorandum in writing sufficient for the purposes of the Statute of Frauds.

Barrington J:

The defendant maintains that the alleged agreement between him and Tom, being a contract not to be performed within the space of one year from the making thereof, required to be evidenced by a memorandum in writing and that there is no such memorandum in existence . . .

[T]he plaintiff's principal submission is that the alleged agreement was not governed by the Statute of Frauds at all. In deciding whether an agreement was an agreement 'not to be performed within the spaces of one year from the making thereof' one looks at the situation which prevailed at the time when the agreement was made and at the intentions of the parties. There was no intention that the agreement should not be completed within the space of one year. It would appear that the intention was that the implementation of the agreement should commence immediately and that the completion of the agreement should take place as soon as possible.

The evidence of Mr Edmund Burke throws some light on the intention of the parties about the time of the making of the agreement. At the meeting in Jury's Hotel with John and Tom at about the time of Tom's bankruptcy Mr Burke understood that there was some scheme to pay off Tom's bankruptcy. Witness enquired how long it would take to which Tom replied that he thought it would take a year or so for him 'to come back'.

I am satisfied that there was no intention that the agreement should not be performed within the space of one year from the making thereof and I am satisfied also that it was not an agreement which, from its nature, precluded such performance. I am satisfied therefore that it was not an agreement 'not to be performed within the space of one year from the making thereof' and that the Statute of Frauds does not apply to it.

Notes

1. In this case the defendant also claimed that the alleged agreement was not intended to constitute a binding agreement between the parties. Barrington J. held that in the circumstances the agreement was enforceable.

2. In a probate case, *In the goods of Leslie Good, decd* (HC) 14 July 1986 unrep., an agreement by a couple to leave property to their children 'on the death of either' was held to be an agreement 'that is not to be performed within the space of one year from the making thereof'. See also *Naughton v Limestone Land Co. Ltd* [1952] in JR 18.

Contracts for the sale of lands or interest therein form the most common category of contracts under the statute. All but one of the remaining cases in this chapter fall under this heading.

B. CONTENTS OF A MEMORANDUM

In order to satisfy the Statute of Frauds, a memorandum must include the names of the parties involved in the transaction, a description of the property to be transferred and the consideration. In addition the memorandum must include any additional terms viewed as essential by the parties. As noted in Chapter 2 and in the following cases, a distinction must be drawn between material terms for the purpose of concluding an agreement and material terms for the purposes of inclusion in the memorandum. As Geoghegan J. explained in the *Supermacs* case (p.102) 'only the "material terms" need be included in a note or memorandum for it to be sufficient but all the terms, whether they be important or unimportant, must be agreed before there can be said to be a concluded agreement.'

Godley *v* Power (1961) 95 ILTR 135

The plaintiff entered into an oral agreement to sell a licensed premises to the defendant. This was confirmed by the defendant's letter which stated the purchase price, the liability of the vendor to pay half the auctioneer's fees and asked to have an enclosed inventory included in the Agreement for Sale. When the defendant attempted to withdraw from the sale, the plaintiff sued for specific performance or, in the alternative, damages for breach of contract.

   The High Court dismissed the plaintiff's claim and the plaintiff appealed.

Kingsmill Moore J.:

It was next contended that the memorandum was defective, in that it did not set out correctly the terms of the contract, and did not contain all the terms of the contract.

   A memorandum must contain all essential terms. The parties, the property, and the consideration must always be ascertainable from it, but it need not contain any terms which the general law would imply. The letter of 14 September contains the parties, an adequate description of the property and—apparently—the consideration. It was however objected by the defendant's counsel that it was inaccurate, in as much as it did not show the tenure of the property to be leasehold, and insufficient, in as much as it made no reference to, what was alleged to be part of the consideration for the bargain, an agreement to take over the stock in trade at cost price.

An agreement to sell land implies that the whole of the vendor's interest in the land is to be sold; *Bower v Cooper* 2 Hare 408, and, in the absence of anything to lead to a contrary view, the interest is implied by law to be a fee simple. If, however, a purchaser has notice that the vendor is only a lessee such an implication does not arise, and the contract will have reference only to the leasehold title which the vendor possesses. . . . The question therefore arises whether the purchaser, Mr Power, had notice that the vendor could only offer a leasehold title. There is not direct evidence of this, but I think there is an irresistible inference.

. . .

The next objection was that the memorandum was incomplete, because it made no mention of an alleged agreement that the purchase should take over the balance of stock left on completion at invoice figures. . . .

Assuming however that such an agreement had been come to would its absence from the memorandum render the memorandum invalid? A memorandum under the Statute of Frauds is only required of a contract or sale of lands. If it could be shown clearly that the agreement for the taking over of the stock was part of the consideration for the sale of the lands then the memorandum would be defective, because it did not fully set out the consideration. But it seems more likely that any such agreement was a collateral and subsidiary contract. Its execution, indeed, depended on the completion of the contract for the sale of the lands, for it was only on completion that the stock could be ascertained and its value discovered; but it appears to me to be a reversal of probability to suggest that the sale of the lands was in any way contingent on the disposal of the residue of the stock. . . .

In argument this letter was sometimes referred to and relied on as if it was part of the formation of the contract, an acceptance of an offer, and it was urged that such acceptance was only conditional or preliminary because of the words—'Kindly let me have agreement for sale. Purchaser would like to have the enclosed inventory included in the agreement.' I do not read the letter in this way. It does not purport to be an *acceptance* of an offer. It is a formal *confirmation* of an agreement which had been already completed at an earlier period, and the terms of which it purports to set out, 'I wish to confirm that my client *has* agreed with your client to purchase from him the above premises on the following terms.' There is not the slightest suggestion that this pre-existing contract was subject to the preparation of a written agreement, or that the terms as set out were not the complete terms. The letter is evidence of what the contract was, and provides a memorandum of the contract. It is not an instrument making the contract. If the contract had already been made orally, without the incorporation of a condition requiring a written agreement, the subsequent desire or request of the purchaser to have a written agreement could not in any way affect the validity of the existing oral agreement or its enforceability, once a memorandum came into existence. This letter seems to be direct evidence that a contract containing all the necessary terms had already been concluded.

(O'Daly and Maguire JJ. agreed. Maguire C.J. dissented on the grounds that there was no sufficient memorandum as the letter did not describe the premises or the title nor did it mention a deposit, or completion times. Lavery J. also dissented.)

Note

In *Kearns v Manning* [1935] IR 869 Murnaghan J. in the Supreme Court stated that 'the date of the commencement of the term is a material part of an agreement for a lease'.

Guardian Builders Ltd *v* Patrick Kelly and Park Avenue Ltd (HC) 31 March 1981, unrep.

The defendant owned a site which he wished to sell, and for this purpose an agent, Mr O'Brien, was appointed. An oral agreement was concluded with the plaintiff and the area of land to be sold was marked on a site map. The parties also agreed that the plaintiff would obtain possession within three months. Mr O'Brien stated that he would ask the defendant's solicitor to prepare a contract. Mr O'Brien then wrote a letter, which was typed by his secretary and dated 26 April. A dispute later arose as to the existence of an agreement evidenced by a sufficient memorandum.

Costello J.:

The first point that [counsel for the defendant] propounds is that Mr O'Brien had no authority to sign the memorandum. It is well established that an express authority need not be given to authorise an agent to sign a memorandum which is sufficient to satisfy the statute, and I refer to *Godley v Power*, 95 ILTR, 135. So the question arises as to whether or not Mr O'Brien had authority, either express or implied, to sign the memorandum. Now it is true that Mr Kelly did not say to Mr O'Brien: 'You're to sign a contract which is to satisfy the Statute of Frauds.' What he did was to authorise him to find a purchaser for the site. I agree with the submission of [counsel for the plaintiff] that in the circumstances of this case Mr O'Brien had an implied authority to write the letter of 26 April.

In addition to that implied authority, which arose from the relationship Mr O'Brien had with the defendant, there is the fact that Mr O'Brien stated expressly at the meeting that he was going to write a letter. It seems there is authority to be obtained from the fact that, having said this, he was not told not to write the letter; in fact, I think he obtained authority to write asking for a contract and so impliedly to write a letter to indicate that an oral agreement had been reached. I am satisfied, therefore, that Mr O'Brien had authority to sign the letter of 26 April.

What this case then turns on is whether or not this memorandum was sufficient to satisfy the statute. The first point made by [counsel for the defendant] is that the portion of the lands given in the memorandum is insufficient. The letter is headed 'The Nurseries, Park Avenue' and it states that a sale had been concluded of 'Half of the above site' and that the site area was as agreed between the plaintiff and the defendant. The parties had agreed the site area. They had marked it on a map and agreed it and in my opinion this is sufficient description to satisfy the Statute of Frauds. The test is that the property so described has to be readily identifiable. It can be identifiable on the oral evidence which produces the map agreed between the parties as being the site.

It is also suggested that the parties were not identified. I think they were. Although referred to by individual name in the case of Mr Kelly, it is nonetheless sufficient, and the error in the name of the plaintiff company does not invalidate the identity of the parties. Again the test is whether the parties can be readily identifiable, and I think they can. On this point the memorandum is adequate.

This brings me to the submission made by [counsel for the defendant] that material terms of the agreement were omitted from the memorandum and so the memorandum does not satisfy the statue. It was firstly suggested that there had been agreement in relation to possession, which is not in the memorandum, that possession would be given before six weeks of the portion of the site not claimed by Mrs Jameson. I agree that there was discussion at the meeting in relation to this part of the transaction. I do not think it was made a term of the contract that in four to six weeks the plaintiff was to be entitled to obtain possession of the site, it was merely a discussion; and even if it was a term of the contract it was not a material term because it is clear that the parties did not envisage that Mr Molloy would be able to develop the site for a year after the contract was signed.

It is said that there was agreement in relation to the building of a road by Mr Kelly. Again, I am satisfied that there was discussion about this but that it was not a material term of the contract.

It was also suggested that there was a problem in relation to rights-of-way because of the particular position of the site. There was certainly no discussion between the parties as to rights-of-way. The parties were practical businessmen and were not concerned with the legal problems which would arise, which they would leave to their solicitors to iron out. In my view there was no discussion about rights-of-way and no material term was omitted in this connection from the memorandum. I have already indicated that there was no term agreed in relation to the open spaces to be included on the site which the plaintiff was purchasing and so there was no material term omitted in this connection from the contract.

It was finally urged by [counsel] that questions of title had been discussed and that a material term in this connection was omitted from the contract in this connection, but I am quite satisfied that title was not discussed at the meeting.

I conclude, therefore, that there was an oral agreement and that there is a memorandum of this agreement sufficient to satisfy the statute. The plaintiff is entitled to the relief claimed.

Supermacs Ireland Ltd and McDonagh *v* Katesan (Naas) Ltd and Sweeney [2000] 4 IR 273
(See facts on p.100.)

Geoghegan J.:

If, notwithstanding the absence of any express reference to a deposit, the court should ultimately hold that there was a concluded agreement the absence of any reference to the deposit in the alleged note or memorandum would not necessarily be fatal. If there was an implied term as to the deposit, it is well established that there is no need for such implied term to be expressed in the note or memorandum. If, on the other hand, the question of the deposit was to be left to the solicitors but that there was nevertheless a concluded agreement reached beforehand then the absence of any mention of the deposit in the memorandum is irrelevant. Even if there had been, which there was not, an express agreement as to the amount of the deposit, there would still be plenty of room for argument that it does not have to be referred to in the note or memorandum as it might not all in the circumstances of the case be regarded as a 'material term'.

In addition to setting out the material terms, the memorandum must be signed by the party to be charged. The purpose of this is to authenticate the document and affirm its contents. The concept of a signature has been given a broad interpretation by the Courts. In *Casey v Irish Intercontinental Bank Ltd* [1979] IR 364, the Supreme Court accepted that printed names on headed notepaper could constitute a sufficient signature for the purposes of the Statute of Frauds. In *Clipper Maritime Ltd v Shirlstar Container Transport Ltd* [1987] 1 Lloyd's Reports 546, an answer back of a telex machine was deemed to constitute a signature. Similarly, in *Re a Debtor* (No.2021 of 1995) [1996] 2 All ER 345, a computer-scanned signature sent by fax was deemed to be signed by the author. The use of electronic signatures appears to have been approved by the Electronic Commerce Act 2000. For example, section 13(1) provides that, with exceptions, a signature provided electronically must be recognised in law as a signature which can satisfy any legal requirement that a signature be provided. However, the Act deals with general principles and does not deal with specific issues such as email signatures. Such a signature was considered in the case below.

Mehta *v* J Pereira Fernandes SA [2006] EWHC 813 (Ch)

A guarantee was sent by Mr Mehta's employee in an email which was not signed and which omitted Mr Mehta's name or initials in the body of the email. The High Court was asked to determine whether the signature was sufficient for the purposes of section 4 of the Statute of Frauds 1677 on the basis that Mr Mehta's email address was automatically included in the email header. The trial judge had concluded that the email document had amounted to a guarantee sufficient to satisfy section 4 and that the presence of the email address on the copy of the email received constituted a sufficient signature for the purposes of the Act.

Pelling J.:

The purpose of the statute of frauds is to protect people from being held liable on informal communications because they may be made without sufficient consideration or expressed ambiguously or because such a communication might be fraudulently alleged against the party to be charged. That being so, the logic underlying the authorities I have referred to would appear to be that where (as in this case) there is an offer in writing made by the party to be bound which contains the essential terms of what is offered *and* the party to be bound accepts that his offer has been accepted unconditionally, albeit orally, there is a sufficient note or memorandum to satisfy section 4 . . .

The email . . . is not signed by anyone in a conventional sense. Mr Mehta's name or initials do not appear at the end of the email or, indeed, anywhere else in the body of the email. Inevitably, therefore, JPF must contend that the presence of the email address at the top of the email constitutes a signature sufficient to satisfy the requirements of section 4. As is well known to anyone who uses email on a regular basis, what is relied upon is not inserted by the sender of the email in any active sense. It is inserted automatically. My knowledge of the technicalities of email is not sufficiently detailed to enable me to know whether it is inserted by the ISP with whom the sender or the recipient has his email account. However, I accept [counsel for the respondent's] submission that as a matter of obvious inference, if it is inserted by the latter it can only be from information supplied by the former . . .

It is submitted on behalf of JPF that the appearance of the sender's address at the top of the document constitutes a signature either by the sender or by '. . . some other person thereunto by him lawfully authorised . . .' because it is well known to all users of email that the recipient of the email will always be told the email address of the email account from which the email is sent in the form it appears on the email . . . That being so, it is submitted that by authorising an agent to send an email, using the sender's email account, to a third party the sender knows that his, her or its email address will appear on the recipient's copy and that is sufficient for it to be held to be a signature for the purposes of section 4. It was submitted by [counsel for the respondent] that intention was irrelevant—all that was required was a document that constituted a sufficient memorandum (which, as I have held, the email was) and the signature somewhere on the note or memorandum of either the person to be bound or his duly authorised agent. In support of this contention, [counsel] relied on the decision of the House of Lords in *Elpis Maritime Co. Ltd v Marti Chartering Co. Inc.* [1991] 2 Lloyd's Rep 311. The facts of that case were very different to the facts of this case. There was no dispute in that case that the party to be charged had signed the document. The dispute in that case concerned whether or not the fact that the party to be bound signed the relevant document as agent made any difference given that there was a clause within the document that purported to create a guarantee by the party purporting to sign only as agent. It had been contended that if such was the case then the fact the agreement contained a clause under which the signing party personally agreed to guarantee certain obligations was not relevant. It was this last argument that was rejected by the House of Lords by reference to *In re Hoyle* [1893] 1 Ch 84 in which A. L. Smith L.J. said: 'The question is not what is the intention of the person signing the memorandum but is one of fact, *viz* is there a note or memorandum of the promise signed by the party to be charged?' It is because this is so that in other cases the courts have accepted letters to third parties, instructions to telegraph companies signed by the sender, and affidavits in unconnected actions as being a sufficient memorandum providing they are signed by the parties to be bound. It was this that led the House of Lords to conclude that it was irrelevant in what capacity or with what intention the document there being considered was signed. In my judgment, the issue that arises in this case is not the issue that the House of Lords considered in *Elpis Maritime* . Here the issue is not with what intention or with what capacity did Mr Mehta or his employee sign the relevant document—rather the issue is whether it has been signed at all.

What is relied upon is an email address. It is the email equivalent of a fax or telex number. It is well known that the recipient of a fax will usually receive a copy that has the name and/or number of the sender automatically printed at the top together with a transmission time. Can it sensibly be suggested that the automatically generated name and fax number of the sender of a fax on a faxed document that is otherwise a section 4 note or memorandum would constitute a signature for these purposes? If [counsel for the respondent] is right then the answer depends solely upon whether the sender (or the sender's principal where the sender was an agent) knew that the number or address would appear on the recipient's copy.

[Counsel for the respondent] relies on *Evans v Hoare* [1892] 1 QB 593 in support of this argument. The issue in that case was whether the defendant was bound by the relevant document. The evidence in that case established that the relevant document had been drawn up by a duly authorised agent of the defendants. The document was in the form of a letter from the plaintiff and the words 'Messrs Hoare, Marr & Co, 26, 29 Budge Row, London EC' appeared after the plaintiff's address at the head of the letter. The question was whether these words constituted a signature of '. . . some person . . . thereunto lawfully authorised . . .' by the defendants. It was argued on behalf of the plaintiff in that case that the appearance of the defendant's name in the letter tendered to the plaintiff for signature on behalf of the defendant was sufficiently signed on behalf of the defendant because the defendant's name had been '. . . written . . . with the defendant's authority, with the intention of designating the party to be charged, and for the purpose of making a contract which should be binding on the Plaintiff'—see pages 594–595 of the reported argument. It was this argument that succeeded. Cave J. said:

> I am of opinion that the principle to be derived from the decisions is this. In the first place, there must be a memorandum of a contract, not merely a memorandum of a proposal; and secondly, there must be in the memorandum, somewhere or other, the name of the party to be charged, signed by him or by his authorised agent. Whether the name occurs in the body of the memorandum, or at the beginning, or at the end, *if it is intended for a signature* there is a memorandum of the agreement within the meaning of the statute. [Emphasis supplied]

As was emphasised by Cave J, the appearance of the name of the party to be bound must be 'intended for a signature'. It is noteworthy that this case was cited to the House of Lords in *Elpis Maritime* but was not disapproved by Lord Brandon. I do not think it can be said (and, in any event, there is no evidence) that either Mr Mehta's employee or the ISP either sending or receiving the email intended Mr Mehta's email address to be a signature in the sense identified above.

There are *dicta* that support the approach of Cave J. in *Caton v Caton* (1867) LR 2 HL 127. In that case, the House was concerned with a document that started by referring to 'the under-mentioned parties' and then referred to the parties in question by name in relation to various promises. Neither party signed the document and the question was whether the document constituted a sufficient note or memorandum signed by the parties to be bound within section 4. The House of Lords held that it was not. In arriving at this conclusion, Lord Chelmsford C. said at 139–140:

> The cases on this point . . . establish that the mere circumstances of the name of a party being written by himself in the body of a memorandum of agreement will not of itself constitute a signature. It must be inserted in the writing in such a manner as to have the effect of 'authenticating the instrument' or 'so as to govern the whole instrument' . . . The name of the party, and its application to the whole of the instrument, can alone satisfy the requisites of a signature.

Lord Westbury said (page 143) that what is alleged to constitute the signature must

> . . . be so placed as to show that it was intended to relate and refer to, and that in fact it does relate and refer to, every part of the instrument . . . It must govern every part of the instrument. It must shew that every part of the instrument emanates from the individual so signing, and that the signature was intended to have that effect. It *follows that if a signature be found in an instrument incidentally only*, or having relation and reference only to a portion of the instrument, *the signature cannot have legal effect and force which it must have in order to comply with the statute, and to give authenticity to the whole of the memorandum* . [Emphasis supplied]

In the light of the *dicta* cited above, it seems to me that a party can sign a document for the purposes of section 4 by using his full name or his last name prefixed by some or all of his initials or using his initials, and possibly by using a pseudonym or a combination of letters and numbers (as can happen for example with a Lloyd's slip scratch, providing always that whatever was used was inserted into the document in order to give, and with the intention of giving, authenticity to it. Its inclusion must have been intended as a signature for these purposes. I agree with [counsel for the respondent's] analysis . . . that in Caton the names were included in the document under consideration to describe intended performance. I also accept his submission . . . that the meaning of 'incidental' in this context means ' . . . where the signature or name just happens to appear somewhere'. I do not accept his submissions that *Godwin v Francis* (1870) LR 5 CP 295 or *McBlain v Cross* (1871) 25 LT 804 have relevance to the issue I have to decide. *Godwin* plainly involved a section 9 note or memorandum in the form of instructions to a telegraph company signed by the party to be charged on whose behalf the telegram concerned was sent. Bovill C.J. then proceeded to consider the position in the event that this was wrong and concluded that ' . . . the mere telegram written out and signed in the way indicated by the telegram clerk, if done with the authority of the vendors, would have been a sufficient signature'. This is not this case—no name or signature or any sort appears in the body of the email. McBlain takes the issue no further because the telegram in that case stated that it came from the sender and did so with his express authority. That is not this case. I have no doubt that if a party creates and sends an electronically-created document then he will be treated as having signed it to the same extent that he would in law be treated as having signed a hard copy of the same document. The fact that the document is created electronically as opposed to as a hard copy can make no difference. However, that is not the issue in this case. Here the issue is whether the automatic insertion of a person's email address after the document has been transmitted by either the sending and/or receiving ISP constitutes a signature for the purposes of section 4. In my judgment the inclusion of an email address in such circumstances is a clear example of the inclusion of a name which is incidental in the sense identified by Lord Westbury in the absence of evidence of a contrary intention. Its appearance, divorced from the main body of the text of the message, emphasises this to be so. Absent evidence to the contrary, in my view it is not possible to hold that the automatic insertion of an email address is, to use Cave J.'s language, ' . . . intended for a signature . . .' To conclude that the automatic insertion of an email address in the circumstances I have described constituted a signature for the purposes of section 4 would I think undermine or potentially undermine what I understand to be the Act's purpose, would be contrary to the underlying principle to be derived from the cases to which I have referred and would have widespread and wholly unintended legal and commercial effects. In those circumstances, I conclude that the email referred did not bear a signature sufficient to satisfy the requirements of section 4.

C. JOINDER OF DOCUMENTS

A memorandum may consist of two or more documents read together.

McQuaid *v* Lynam and Lynam [1965] IR 564

The plaintiff inspected a house at 1 Kinvara Road belonging to the defendants. On telephoning the defendants he was told the price of the house was £2,800. On 4 September the plaintiff called to the defendants' office, informed them that he liked the house and paid a deposit of £800. He was given a receipt in these terms: 'Received from Mr Michael McQuaid the sum of £800 being deposit on no. 1 Kinvara Road.' The name 'E. & J. Lynam' was put on the receipt with a rubber stamp and, underneath this, the signature of the second defendant.

The plaintiff filled in one half of a building society loan application form at this meeting and on a later date the plaintiff completed the form. The plaintiff then signed the form and dated it 27 September. This form contained a description of the property, a statement that it was freehold, that it was vacant, and that it was being purchased for £2,800 and gave E. & J. Lynam as the name of the builder. This form was then lodged with the building society. In November the plaintiff decided to reduce the amount required from the building society and, on 4 November 1963, he went to the office of the defendants, paid them an additional £500, and got a receipt which read: 'Received from Mr Michael McQuaid the sum of £500 re no. 1 Kinvara Road,' which was signed by the second-named defendant. Before the plaintiff paid this sum he was told by one of the defendants that the property would not be sold to him as freehold but would be leased to him and that the price would be reduced by £100; the plaintiff agreed to this. The defendant later refused to complete the agreement and the plaintiff sued for damages.

Kenny J.:

The first submission by the plaintiff's counsel in connection with the Statute of Frauds was that the application to the building society which was written by the second-named defendant was a sufficient memorandum or note of the oral contract. The application contains all the terms of the oral contract which was made on 4 September 1963, and the name of the defendants but it was not signed by them or either of them unless the writing in of 'E. J. Lynam' opposite the printed words, 'name of builder', was a signature. It is settled law that the memorandum or note required by the Statute of Frauds may consist of a document which was not intended to be such a note or memorandum but it must, however, be signed by the party to be charged and the signature must have been intended to authenticate the whole document of which it forms a part. This was emphasised by Lord Westbury in *Caton v Caton*[1] when he said:

> Now, what constitutes a sufficient signature has been described by different judges in different words. In the original case upon this subject, though not quite the original case, but the case most frequently referred to as of the earliest date, that of *Stokes v Moore*,[2] the language of the learned judge is, that the signature must authenticate every part of the instrument; or again, that it must give authenticity to every part of the instrument. . . . Probably the phrases 'authentic' and 'authenticity' are not quite felicitous, but their meaning is plainly this, that the signature must be so placed as to show that it was intended to relate and refer to, and that in fact it does relate and refer to, every part of the instrument. The language of Sir William Grant in *Ogilvie v Foljambe*[3] is (as his method was) much more felicitous. He says it must govern every part of the instrument. It must show that every part of the instrument emanates from the individual so signing, and that the signature was intended to have that effect. It follows, therefore, that if a signature be found in an

instrument incidentally only, or having relation and reference only to a portion of the instrument, the signature cannot have that legal effect and force which it must have in order to comply with the statute, and to give authenticity to the whole of the memorandum.

The writing of 'E. J. Lynam' by the second-named defendant on the application to the building society was not a signature of that document by the defendants or by either of them as it was not intended to give authenticity to any part of it. The document was intended to be—and was—signed by the plaintiff and the writing of the name of the defendants was intended to give information to the building society. The application is not therefore a memorandum or note in writing of the contract.

The next issue is whether the receipt of 4 September 1963, and the application to the building society, dated 27 September 1963, together constitute such a memorandum or note. The receipt refers to '£800 being the deposit on no. 1 Kinvara Road.' The application to the building society has the figure £800 opposite the query, 'Amount of cash applicant is prepared to pay down?' This figure of £800 written in ink is crossed out in pencil and the figure of £1,500 was subsequently written in at this space by an official of the building society on the instructions of the plaintiff but the figure of £800 is legible. I have already stated that the application to the building society gives the address of the property to be mortgaged as 1, Kinvara Road. . . .

The many cases on the issue whether a number of documents read together can constitute such a memorandum or note in writing show a progressively liberal approach by the courts to this question. I think that the modern cases (*Long v Millar*,[4] *Stokes v Whicher*[5] and *Timmins v Moreland Street Pty Co.*[6]) establish that a number of documents may together constitute a note or memorandum in writing if they have come into existence in connection with the same transaction or if they contain internal references which connect them with each other. But as the memorandum or note considered as a whole must be signed, it would seem to follow that the document which is signed must be the last of the documents in point of time, for it would be absurd to hold that a person who signed a document could be regarded as having signed another document which was not in existence when he signed the first. I think that the correct view on this difficult matter is that stated in the judgment of Romer L.J. in *Timmins v Moreland Street Pty Co.*, at p. 278. One of the matters discussed in that case was whether a cheque and a receipt read together constituted a valid memorandum or note and it was argued that the two documents could not unless the document signed by the party to be charged was the later one. On this matter, Romer L.J. said:

The next point which counsel for the defendant company took was whether the cheque and receipt taken together could form a memorandum having regard to the order in which they were signed. His argument as to that was that although two separate documents can together constitute a memorandum for the purposes of s. 40 [Law of Property Act 1925], the party to be charged must have signed the second of the two; that is to say, if the defendant had signed a document, the plaintiff cannot rely on it in conjunction with a later document signed by himself. This in general must be true. A defendant cannot be bound by a document which he has not signed unless he has in effect incorporated it in the document which he had signed, in which case he would be regarded as having notionally signed both documents; but as he cannot be taken to have incorporated or signed a document which does not exist, the theory is inapplicable except where the defendant has signed the second of two documents on which the plaintiff relies as together constituting a memorandum. If, however, on the same occasion and as part of one and the same transaction—for example, as here, the payment of a deposit under an oral agreement for sale—a vendor and purchaser sit down at a table and respectively write out a receipt and a cheque, then, assuming that these documents between them sufficiently evidence the terms of the bargain, it would be going too far to say that the vendor could not rely on them as constituting a memorandum if the purchaser signed his cheque a few seconds before the vendor signed the receipt. I think it is enough to say that the documents relied on were brought into being more or less contemporaneously for the purpose of furthering a bargain which the party had made . . .

and in the same case Jenkins L.J. said (at p. 272):

. . . but I am, on the whole, of opinion that where two documents relied on as a memorandum are signed and exchanged at one and the same meeting as part of the same transaction, so that they may fairly be said to have been to all intents and purposes contemporaneously signed, the document signed by the party to be charged should not be treated as incapable of referring to the other document merely because the latter, on a minute investigation of the order of events at the meeting, is found to have come second in the order of preparation and signing.

The evidence is that on 4 September one half of the application to the building society was filled in by the second-named defendant immediately after the payment of the £800. The remaining half was completed at a subsequent date (probably 27 September). Thus, one half of the application to the building society and the receipt were contemporaneous: in my view, the receipt of 4 September and the whole of the application to the building society should be regarded as having come into existence in such circumstances that the signature to the receipt authenticates the building society application.

The next question is whether the receipt of 4 September and the building society application can be treated together as a memorandum or note. In my view, the reference to the deposit and 1 Kinvara Road and the close connection in time between the two documents enables me to read the documents together. The true principle on this matter was, I think, stated by Jenkins L.J. in *Timmins v Moreland Street Pty Co.*, when he said:

. . . I think it is still indispensably necessary, in order to justify the reading of documents together for this purpose [the provision of a memorandum or note in writing for the purposes of Statute of Frauds], that there should be a document signed by the party to be charged which, while not containing in itself all the necessary ingredients of the required memorandum, does contain some reference, express or implied, to some other document or transaction. Where any such reference can be spelt out of a document so signed, then parol evidence may be given to identify the other document referred to, or, as the case may be, to explain the other transaction, and to identify any document relating to it. If by this process a document is brought to light which contains in writing all the terms of the bargain so far as not contained in the document signed by the party to be charged, then the two documents can be read together so as to constitute a sufficient memorandum for the purposes of s. 40 of the Law of Property Act 1925. The laying of documents side by side may no doubt lead to the conclusion as a matter of *res ipsa loquitur* that the two are connected; but before a document signed by the party to be charged can be laid alongside another document to see if between them they constitute a sufficient memorandum, there must, I conceive, be found in the document signed by the party to be charged some reference to some other document or transaction.

If therefore the issue in the case be whether there was a sufficient memorandum or note in writing signed by the party to be charged of the agreement made on 4 September, I am of opinion that the plaintiff would succeed. But the agreement made on 4 September was varied by mutual consent on 4 November when the plaintiff and the defendants agreed that the plaintiff would purchase the house by way of lease and that the purchase money would be reduced by £100 and there is no memorandum or note in writing of this variation. . . .

The real problem I think is whether the defendants can successfully contend that the contract of 4 September was varied by mutual agreement when there is a memorandum or note in writing of the contract of 4 September but not of the variation. In any discussion of this problem it is essential to distinguish between the case in which the parties to an agreement intend that agreement to find expression in a written contract and that in which the parties make an oral contract which is intended to be binding. If in the latter case a memorandum or note in writing is required by the Statute of Frauds, that memorandum or note does not become the contract. This distinction appears in s. 2 of the Statute of Frauds which so far as material provided: 'No action shall be brought . . . upon any contract or sale of lands, tenements or hereditaments, or any interest in or concerning them . . . unless the agreement upon which such action shall be brought, or some memorandum or note thereof, shall be in writing and signed by the party to be charged therewith or some other person thereunto by him lawfully authorised.' The same distinction was emphasised in *Thompson v The King*[7] and in *Law and Another v Robert Roberts and Co.*[8] In the first type of case, that is, where the parties intend their agreement to find expression in a written document, a subsequent oral variation of the contract is not effective unless it is evidenced by a memorandum or note in writing (see *Goss v Nugent*[9] and the speech of Lord Atkinson in *British and Beningtons Ltd v N. W. Cachar Tea Co. and Others*.[10] But in the other type of case, where the oral agreement is intended to be the contract, evidence may be given of an agreed variation even if there is a memorandum or note of the contract but not of the variation. This view is supported by the decision of the Court of Appeal in England in *Beckett v Nurse*.[11] In that case the plaintiff claimed specific performance of an alleged agreement for the sale of land and relied on a receipt as the memorandum or note in writing. The Court of Appeal held that the receipt was not the contract and that as the plaintiff was relying on an oral agreement for sale, the defendant was entitled to show that the real bargain between the parties was different from that contained in the memorandum.

In this case the evidence establishes that the oral contract made on 4 September was varied by mutual agreement on a subsequent date. The variation was that the defendants were to sell to the plaintiff not a freehold interest but a leasehold interest, but the amount of the rent to be paid and the date of the commencement of the lease were not agreed: as these were not agreed, there was never a valid contract to sell the property by lease or to grant a lease (see the judgment of the Supreme Court delivered by Mr Justice James Murnaghan in *Kerns v Manning*[12]).

Counsel for the plaintiff has also contended that the payment of £500 on 4 November was an act of part performance and that the Statute of Frauds is not therefore an answer to the plaintiff's claim. As there was not a valid contract between the parties, the question of part performance does not arise.

1. (1867) LR 2 HL 127.
2. 1 Cox 219.
3. 3 Mer. 53.
4. (1879) 4 CPD 459.
5. [1920] 1 Ch. 411.
6. [1937] 3 All ER 265.
7. [1957] 3 All ER 263, at p. 276.
8. [1920] 2 IR 365; [1921] 2 IR 438.
9. [1964] IR 292.
10. (1833) 5 B. & Ad. 58.
11. [1923] AC 48.
12. [1948] 1 All ER 81.

Notes

1. In *Kelly v Ross & Ross* (HC) 29 April 1980, unrep. McWilliam J. also referred to the case of *Timmins v Moreland Street Pty Co. Ltd* [1957] 3 All ER 265 in holding that nine documents could not jointly constitute a memorandum for the purposes of the Statute as the signed documents did not refer to the other documents.

2. In *Tradax (Ireland) Ltd v Irish Grain Board Ltd* [1984] IR 1 a majority of the Supreme Court held that a telex and a letter sent by the defendants with the object of cancelling the contracts constituted a sufficient note or memorandum for the purposes of s.4 of the Sale of Goods Act 1893. It was also noted in this case that even if no memorandum existed, the acceptance and receipt by the plaintiffs of part of the goods would have made the absence immaterial to the question of enforceability.

3. In *Keller v Crowe* (HC) 6 August 1999, unrep. an exchange of correspondence between the purchaser and the defendant's auctioneer and signed by the latter was deemed to constitute a sufficient memorandum for the purposes of the Statute.

D. SUBJECT TO CONTRACT

It is common for agreements for the sale of land by private treaty to contain the term 'subject to contract'. Often parties will wish to ensure that the agreement will not be binding until a formal contract is signed by both parties. Much debate has occurred both in England and Ireland as to the precise effect of this phrase. The *Mulhall* case below is particularly helpful in setting out the early history of the treatment of this phrase in the UK and Irish courts.

Mulhall v Haren [1981] IR 364

An oral agreement was concluded between the plaintiffs and an auctioneer authorised by the defendants to sell their family home. The plaintiffs' solicitor later wrote to the auctioneer requesting a contract 'as the sale is subject to contract'. When the defendants refused to proceed with the sale the plaintiffs instituted an action claiming specific performance of the sale agreement.

Keane J.:

One of the earliest statements of the principle that the use of the phrase 'subject to contract' normally indicates that neither party to an agreement intends to be bound by the terms of the arrangement until they are embodied in a form of contract is to be found in *Winn v Bull*.

At p. 32 Jessel M.R. said:

It comes, therefore, to this, that where you have a proposal or agreement made in writing expressed to be subject to a formal contract being prepared, it means what it says; it is subject to and is dependent upon a formal contract being prepared.

When it is not expressly stated to be subject to a formal contract it becomes a question of construction, whether the parties intended that the terms agreed on should merely be put into form, or whether they should be subject to a new agreement the terms of which are not expressed in detail. The result is, that I must hold that there is no binding contract in this case, and there must therefore be judgment for the defendant.

The latter passage was cited by Molony C.J. in the leading Irish case: *Thompson v The King*.[1] In that case, the words used were 'subject contract' and it was held that the agreement came within what might be called the 'subject to contract' line of authorities as distinct from the line of authorities applied in *Law v Robert Roberts & Co.* Accordingly, the agreement was held to be unenforceable. Gibson J. put the matter thus at p. 390 of the report: '2. Did the expression "subject contract" defer contractual obligation till a formal contract was settled, accepted, and executed; or does it mean that the purchase terms having been fully and finally settled, a further contract was only contemplated for the purpose of putting the bargain into legal shape, without substantial additions or alterations? I adopt the former construction.' . . .

But while the law on this topic had the advantages of reasonable certainty, it was also capable of producing results which appeared harsh and unjust. The extraordinary volatile market in land which developed in England and Ireland during the 1970s also led to a practice as unattractive as its name which is 'gazumping'. A vendor of land who had shaken hands on a deal frequently found himself with a substantially more attractive offer for the property within days, or even hours. There were many vendors who, whatever the temptations, refused to resile from bargains freely entered into, whether they were legally enforceable or not. But there were also some who either accepted the higher offer or went back to their original purchaser and attempted to squeeze more money out of him. Where no shadow of a memorandum in writing existed, even the most resourceful of lawyers or courts were powerless to redress such inequities unless, indeed, the doctrine of part performance could be successfully invoked. But where anything which could conceivably be regarded as a memorandum existed, considerable ingenuity was naturally expended upon bringing about the downfall of the 'gazumper'. It was perhaps to be expected that, in this context, some attempt would be made to dislodge the well entrenched 'subject to contract' rule.

The first bridgehead was effected in *Griffiths v Young*.[2] . . .

It was argued on behalf of the plaintiff that the phrase 'subject to contract' was not a term of the contract but merely referred to a 'suspensive condition' which had been subsequently waived and could, accordingly, be ignored for the purpose of determining whether there was a sufficient memorandum or note of the agreement actually concluded. Widgery L.J., as he then was, thought the point a difficult one; but he appears to have accepted the general principle that a memorandum which, on its face, asserted that agreement had not been reached, could not be a memorandum for the purpose of s. 40. He accepted the submission made on behalf of the plaintiff that this principle had no application where the only defect in the memorandum was a reference to a 'suspensive provision' which had subsequently been waived. The other members of the court (Russell and Cross L.JJ.) came to the same conclusion, but neither of them appear to have experienced the same difficulty which troubled Widgery L.J. They were both satisfied that the subsequent oral waiver of the 'suspensive condition' cured any defect in the memorandum.

The far-reaching implications of the decision in *Griffiths v Young* soon became apparent when *Law v Jones* came before the same court—this time composed of Russell, Buckley and Orr L.JJ. . . .

So far as the applicable law is concerned, the crucial passage from the judgment of Buckley L.J. appears at p. 124 of the report: 'But it is not, in my judgment, necessary that the note or memorandum should acknowledge the existence of a contract. It is not the fact of agreement but the terms agreed upon that must be found recorded in writing.' ...

In the words of Lord Denning M.R. at p. 159 of the report of *Tiverton Ltd v Wearwell Ltd*, the decision in *Law v Jones* 'sounded an alarm bell' in the offices of every solicitor in England. I recall the decision being greeted with equal consternation in Ireland. In England, it prompted a leading article in the Solicitor's Journal (117 Sol J 293) and a lengthy correspondence from solicitors in the same periodical. The earliest possible opportunity was taken of questioning the correctness of the decision. The appeal from the order of Goulding J. in *Tiverton Ltd v Wearwell Ltd* was heard by the Court of Appeal (Lord Denning M.R., Stamp and Scarman L.JJ.) as a matter of urgency within a few months. ...

Lord Denning, after a detailed review of the authorities, summed up his view of the law as follows at p. 160 of the report: 'I cannot myself see any difference between a writing which—(i) denies there was any contract; (ii) does not admit there was any contract; (iii) says that the parties are in negotiation; or (iv) says that there was an agreement 'subject to contract', for that comes to the same thing. The reason why none of those writings satisfies the statute is because none of them contains any recognition or admission of the existence of a contract.' ...

Since the other members of the court did not share the view of Lord Denning that the Court of Appeal in England had jurisdiction to overrule its earlier decisions, the position in theory in England is that there are at least two conflicting decisions of the Court of Appeal and that the law in that jurisdiction cannot be regarded as certain beyond doubt. However, I think that it is more sensible to regard the forceful judgments of Lord Denning and Stamp L.J. as representing the view of the law generally now held in England. ...

It appears to me that the wording of s. 2 of the Statute of 1695 plainly envisages a writing which is evidence of a contract entered into by the party sought to be charged, and that this is not met by a writing which uses language inconsistent with the existence of a concluded contract. It also appears to me that a long line of authorities has clearly established that the use of the words 'subject to contract' is inconsistent with the existence of a concluded agreement, save in the most exceptional cases. The post–1970 Irish decisions commence with *Arnold v Veale*. ...

I take that decision as accepting, at least by implication, the principle that the writing relied on must acknowledge the existence of a concluded contract.

The next decision to which reference must be made is *Kelly v Park Hall School*.[3] In that case the trial judge (Mr Justice Hamilton) found that there was a concluded oral contract for the sale of the land. Two documents were relied upon as constituting a sufficient memorandum. The first was a letter dated 19 December 1977, from the auctioneers acting on behalf of the defendant vendors to the vendors' property adviser in the following terms:

Hall School—Lands at Rere

Dear Michael,
Further to our telephone conversation this morning, I confirm that we have agreed terms, subject to contract, for the sale of these lands to Mr Paddy Kelly of Berkeley Homes Ltd who were purchasers of the front lands. The principal terms to be included in the contract for sale are as follows:

Proposed purchaser: Hickey, Beauchamp, Kirwan & O'Reilly (in trust).
Proposed price: £175,000.

A non-refundable deposit of £35,000 to be paid on exchange of contracts, the balance to be paid not later than six months thereafter with interest at twelve per cent from the contract date until the closing date. I am sending a copy of this letter to Mr Haugh of A. & L. Goodbody and perhaps you could kindly confirm instructions to him on behalf of the Committee.

The second writing relied on was a letter from the defendants' solicitors to the plaintiffs' solicitors dated 13 January 1978, which enclosed a draft contract and concluded with the following sentence: 'On the instructions of our clients, this offer remains open for acceptance by your clients for a period of seven days only from the date of this letter and we are instructed that, if the contract is not back with us within the said period of time, duly executed, the offer is deemed to be withdrawn.' In the High Court Mr Justice Hamilton held that this latter document was a sufficient memorandum, since it enclosed a draft contract containing all the material terms. On appeal to the Supreme Court (Mr Justice Henchy, Mr Justice Kenny and Mr Justice Parke) it was held that the letter from the auctioneers dated 19 December 1977, was a sufficient memorandum, and the appeal was dismissed. Mr Justice Henchy said at p. 352 of the report:

The case hangs on whether the letter of 19 December 1977, which I have quoted, constitutes a sufficient memorandum for the purpose of the Statute of Frauds. In my opinion it does. *It contains not only all the essential terms of the contract but also a recognition that a contract had been made.* It says: ' . . . we have agreed terms, subject to contract . . .' Since the judge, having heard oral evidence, held that the oral agreement recorded in the letter was a completed agreement in the sense that nothing further was left to be negotiated, the words 'we have agreed terms, subject to contract' must be taken to mean that a contract had been made, subject to its being formalised in writing. Therefore, it constitutes a sufficient memorandum.

The words which I have reproduced in italics appear to indicate an acceptance by Mr Justice Henchy of the proposition that the memorandum must recognise the existence of a concluded contract. Moreover, if the situation were otherwise, I consider it inevitable that the Supreme Court in that case would have expressed their disapproval of the decision in the *Tiverton* case. It is noteworthy that Mr Justice Henchy appears not to have shared the view of the High Court judge that the letter of 13 January 1978, was a sufficient memorandum—presumably because he did not consider that that letter recognised the existence of a concluded contract. I am fortified in arriving at this conclusion on the effect of the decision in the *Park Hall* case by the fact that a similar view of its effect was taken by Mr Justice Hamilton in *McInerney Properties Ltd v Roper*.[4]

While the decision in the *Park Hall* case seems to have proceeded on the basis that the memorandum must contain a recognition that a contract has been made, it might on first reading appear to lend support to the proposition that the words 'subject to contract' are not inconsistent with the existence of a concluded contract. If that were the effect of the decision, it would mean that the Supreme Court, by necessary implication, was disapproving of the decision in the *Tiverton* case and, also by implication, was overruling or disapproving of the long line of authority on the 'subject to contract' topic to which I have already referred. I doubt very much whether the Supreme Court intended to disapprove of the decision in the *Tiverton* case or to disturb the authorities in question. Had that been their intention, I think it would have been made clear in the judgment of Mr Justice Henchy. It may be significant that the plaintiff in the *Park Hall* case had already purchased the adjoining lands of the defendant and that, therefore, the title to the property being sold had been fully investigated by the plaintiff, so that the necessity for a formal contract had been significantly reduced. The actual wording used ('we have agreed terms, subject to contract') was also treated as being of importance. I think that the *Park Hall* case should properly be regarded as a special one decided on particular facts which do not arise in the present case and, as such, to be more akin to the *St Saviour's* case[5] . . .

The next case is *Casey v Irish Intercontinental Bank*.[6] In that case also the High Court found that there had been a concluded oral contract for the sale of the lands and that, as in the *Tiverton* case, the oral agreement had not been made expressly 'subject to contract'. However, the writing relied on as a memorandum, so far as material, was in the following terms: 'I, Patrick Casey, Gurrane House, Donoughmore, agree to purchase Park House and lands for £110,000 subject to contract and title. I agree to pay £25,250 as deposit.' Mr Justice Costello found in favour of the plaintiff. I believe that he did so in a written judgment but, as the text is not available in the Central Office, I cannot say what his reasons were for arriving at this conclusion. On appeal his decision was upheld by the Supreme Court (Mr Justice Henchy, Mr Justice Kenny and Mr Justice Parke). The main judgment in the Supreme Court (with which the other two judges agreed) was delivered by Mr Justice Kenny. The greater part of that judgment is taken up with a point which does not arise in the present case. The only reference to the fact that the writing relied on had used the phrase 'subject to contract and title' is in the following passage from the judgment of Mr Justice Kenny at p. 368 of the report:

The words 'subject to contract and title' were not introduced into the transaction until 2 February when an oral contract for sale had already been made. Even if the reference to the contract and title is regarded as being incorporated in the contract, it does not make the execution of a contract a term of the agreement or a condition precedent to any contractual liability arising. I have already discussed this matter in the judgment which I gave, when I was a judge of the High Court, in *Law v Robert Roberts & Co.* That decision was affirmed by the Supreme Court and I do not intend to repeat what I said there.

Before preparing this judgment I read with the utmost care the judgment delivered by Mr Justice Kenny in *Law v Robert Roberts & Co.* In none of the letters to which reference is made in the statement of facts taken from that judgment (and appearing at pp 293–6 of the report) does the phrase 'subject to contract' or 'subject to contract and title' appear. Not merely are the letters in that case perfectly consistent with the existence of a concluded contract, but they go further. In his letter of 7 November 1960, Mr Hamilton, who was the auctioneer acting on behalf of the defendant vendors, said: 'We confirm herewith that acting on the instructions of our clients, Messrs Robert Roberts, we have accepted your offer of £4,750 and fees at 2? per cent for the above property . . .'. *Law v Robert Roberts & Co.* is in no sense a decision on the meaning of the words 'subject to contract'. Nor is it an authority on the question as to whether a writing which does not acknowledge the existence of a concluded contract can be a sufficient memorandum. As the letter of 7 November 1960 (and the other letters referred to in the judgment) recognised in the plainest terms the existence of a concluded contract, that question did not arise. In these circumstances, I confess to finding some difficulty in understanding the reference to the *Roberts* case in the above passage from the judgment of Mr Justice Kenny in *Casey's* case.

In the course of argument counsel suggested that Mr Justice Kenny, in delivering judgment in *Casey's* case, must have overlooked the fact that the *Roberts* case was not an authority on the 'subject to contract' issue. Whether that be so or not, I must apply the law as stated by the Supreme Court. If this passage has the effect contended for by counsel for the plaintiffs, then, however that conclusion may have been arrived at, I am bound to apply the principle of law laid down. But it is stretching credibility too far for me to suppose that in this brief passage Mr Justice Kenny intended to overrule *Winn v Bull* and the other pre-1921 decisions on the 'subject to contract' point, *Thompson v The King* and *Lowis v Wilson*; and to express his disapproval of the numerous English authorities since 1921 on the same topic, culminating in the *Tiverton* case. Since *Casey*'s case has not yet been reported, I do not know what arguments may have been advanced or what concessions made in the course of argument on either side. In these circumstances, I have come to the conclusion that I should not treat the decision as laying down any general principle of the nature contended for by counsel for the plaintiffs.

The last Irish case is *McInerney Properties Ltd v Roper*. In this case again the High Court (Mr Justice Hamilton) found as a fact that there was a concluded oral contract for the sale of the land. The writings relied on by the plaintiff as constituting a sufficient memorandum were two letters (each being headed 'subject to contract') dated 23 March and 17 April 1978, from the defendant's solicitors, and a draft contract which, it was claimed, was incorporated therewith. Mr Justice Hamilton, having considered the authorities and, in particular, *Law v Jones*, the *Tiverton* case and the *Park Hall* case, came to the conclusion that the letters were a sufficient memorandum. He summarised his conclusion as to the effect of the *Tiverton* case as follows: 'Consequently, it appears to me that the decision in *Tiverton Estates Ltd v Wearwell Ltd* was based not on the fact that the words "subject to contract" were used but that the writings sought to be relied upon as a sufficient note or memorandum did not contain an admission or a recognition that a contract had in fact been entered into.' That is a view which, with respect, I do not share. On the contrary, it seems to me that Lord Denning was at pains to emphasise that it was precisely the use of the words 'subject to contract' which prevented the writings from constituting an acknowledgement of the existence of a contract.

From this analysis of the authorities, I think that the following conclusions emerge:

1. A memorandum or note cannot satisfy the Statute of Frauds if, when it is read alone or with other documents which can properly be read with it, it does not contain a recognition, express or implied, of the existence of the oral contract sought to be enforced.
2. A letter, which expressly states that a transaction is 'subject to contract' cannot be a sufficient note or memorandum, since the use of those words is normally inconsistent with the existence of a concluded contract. It is only in certain rare and exceptional circumstances such as arose in *Kelly v Park Hall School* and *Michael Richards Properties v St Saviour's Parish* that the words 'subject to contract' can be treated as being of no effect.
3. In applying the two foregoing principles, it is immaterial whether the writing relied on itself contains the words 'subject to contract' or is part of a chain of correspondence initiated by a letter which makes it clear that any oral agreement already arrived at is 'subject to contract'.

It seems to me that the application of those principles to the present case is sufficient to dispose of the contention that the letters referred to can be treated as a sufficient note or memorandum. . . .

One cannot help feeling considerable sympathy for the plaintiffs in this case; but sympathy cannot determine the legal rights of the parties. I must apply the law as it appears to me to have been stated by courts of the highest authority in this country and in England. It follows that I must dismiss the plaintiffs' claim for specific performance.

1. [1920] 2 IR 365.	4.	(HC 31 July 1979).
2. [1970] Ch, 675.	5.	[1973] 3 All ER 416.
3. [1979] IR 340.	6.	[1979] IR 364.

Note

During the course of the arguments the plaintiffs claimed that the words 'subject to contract' had been inserted by their solicitor without their authority. Keane J. held, however, that the solicitor had implied authority to include this phrase. Although a solicitor may not alter the terms of an oral agreement already entered into by a client ('the unauthorised variation theory'), or indulge in further negotiations, he is bound to 'embody the bargain already concluded in a formal contract which gives his client the maximum protection consistent with the bargain'.

Boyle v Lee & Goyns [1992] ILRM 65
(See facts on p.94.)

Finlay C.J.:

I have carefully considered this section [section 2 of the Statute of Frauds of 1695], and leaving aside for the moment the strength or weakness of contending decisions, it appears clear that the section required that the *agreement* with which the person concerned was to be charged, had either to be in writing and signed by the party to be charged, or to be evidenced by some memorandum or note in writing, signed by the party to be charged. This must, it seems to me, inevitably lead to the conclusion that such of the decisions as speak of the necessity for the terms to be evidenced by a note or memorandum, or for the important terms, or necessary terms, to be so evidenced are, strictly speaking, incorrect.

It is obvious that in certain instances a total recital of all the necessary ingredients of a contract for the sale of land, that is to say, the names of the purchaser and the vendor, the exact description of the property and such other terms as would be considered essential, namely, the price, deposit, closing date, resume of the title, etc., could without any other expression indicating an acknowledgment of a binding or completed contract, necessarily imply the existence of such a contract.

Where, however, on the other hand, a document which contains a recital of certain terms, obviously relevant to a purchase and sale of land, purports to deny the existence of a completed or concluded contract, or makes use of expressions specially adapted to exclude the existence of a completed or concluded contract, it does not seem to me that as a matter of first principle the terms of s. 2 of the Act of 1695 could be complied with.

The argument largely put against this strict interpretation, which is, of course, an acceptance of the broad statement of principle to which I have already referred, and which is contained in the judgment of Keane J. in *Mulhall v Haren*, is that a party to an orally concluded agreement which is complete and intended to be complete, should not be permitted by the unilateral insertion into a note or memorandum in writing which he makes of the terms of that agreement, of a denial of it, or of a provision such as the phrase 'subject to contract' which is inconsistent with it, to escape on his own behalf or on behalf of this principal, from the enforcement of the contract.

To advance that argument is, of course, attractive but, in my view, it necessarily involves the precise mischief which the Statute of Frauds of 1695 was intended to avoid, and that is that it invites the court to amend by deletion, or by ignoring one of its terms, the note or memorandum relied upon by the plaintiff and signed by the defendant, such amendment or deletion depending on the finding by the court on oral evidence as to what was the agreement between the parties.

Such a principle clearly puts the oral evidence as superseding the only written evidence that is available. In broad terms, it is the clearest possible purpose of the Statute of Frauds 1695 to put the written evidence as dominant and superseding any oral evidence.

It is possible, without much difficulty, to see on consideration of the cases to which we have been referred, that the many instances which occurred of the making of contracts orally for the sale of land the existence of which and the complete nature of which is not even denied in subsequent litigation, has led courts to view with considerable disfavour the defence of non-enforceability due to a want of sufficient note or memorandum under the Statute of Frauds. It does not seem to me, however, that it can be justified, having regard to the obligation of the courts in the implementation of a plain statutory provision, to introduce into the interpretation of s. 2 of the Act of 1695 clauses or provisos which are not consistent with its plain meaning. Furthermore, all one's experience of the massive losses and inconvenience which can be suffered by prospective purchasers or vendors of land from non-completion of what they believe to be a contract, and the subsequent delays and difficulties arising from complicated litigation concerning it, indicates that the requirements of justice are that the law applicable to the formation of contracts for the purchase of land should be as certain as it is possible to make it. In modern times, probably the most important legal transaction a great number of people make in their lifetimes is the purchase or sale of their home. The avoidance of doubt and, therefore, the avoidance of litigation concerning such a transaction must be a well worthwhile social objective, as far as the law is concerned. To that end, certainty in the question of what is or is not a sufficient note or memorandum is a desirable aim. In my view, the very definite statement that a note or memorandum of a contract made orally is not sufficient to satisfy the Statute of Frauds unless it directly or by very necessary implication recognises, not only the terms to be enforced, but also the existence of a concluded contract between the parties, and the corresponding principle that no such note or memorandum which contains any term or expression, such as 'subject to contract' can be sufficient, even if it can be established by oral evidence that such term or expression did not form part of the originally orally concluded agreement achieves that certainty. The existence of such a rule or provision would not, in my view, allow for the 'exceptional cases' mentioned by Keane J. in the decision in *Mulhall v Haren*.

The decision in *Kelly v Park Hall School Ltd*, in so far as it appears to amend by deletion the note or memorandum in writing, signed on behalf of the vendor, by reference to the evidence of the oral agreements which had previously been arrived at between the parties, with great reluctance, is not a decision which I think this court can and should follow.

Similar considerations may, it seems to me, apply to the decision of this court in *Casey v Irish Intercontinental Bank*, though a decision on the validity of the concept of oral waiver of a suspensory condition in the writings which were part of the formation of the contract, is not a question at issue in this case. I would, therefore, allow this appeal . . .

(Hederman J. concurred.)

McCarthy J.:

[Section 2 of the Statute of Frauds of 1695] came to be construed as liberally as possible—seeking to 'find' the necessary evidence once the bargain was proved until, as appears to me to be the case, a note or memorandum which necessarily denied the existence of a bargain became itself evidence to support its enforcement. In my judgment, that is what happened here. Mr McManus wrote a letter to his client's solicitors, sending a copy to each of his clients, the vendors, recounting his instructions to accept the offer of £90,000 'subject to contract', a phrase repeated in the context of the proposed purchase price. He went on to say 'in the meantime, you will appreciate that this letter is for information purposes only, and does not by itself, constitute part of the binding contract.' It identified the agreed terms including price, 'the benefits of the tenants [sic]' and a closing date such as I have instanced. It made no reference to a deposit, because there was no agreement as to deposit save that there might be one. Mr McManus had no intention of evidencing an agreement; it was contrary to the fixed policy of his firm. If the letter to the solicitors is to be held to provide the required compliance with s. 2 of the statute, it means that the note itself has to be disregarded wherever it conflicts with the findings of fact made in respect of the oral agreement, and yet be used as the necessary evidence to support an action to enforce that agreement. In short, it means that the words 'subject to contract' do not mean what they say. In *Mulhall v Haren*, Keane J. made an exhaustive analysis of the Irish and English case law and concluded that *Tiverton Estates Ltd v Wearwell Ltd* correctly represented the law of England and should be followed unless it had been disapproved of in Ireland. ..

In *Mulhall*, Keane J. sought to distinguish *Kelly v Park Hall School* and *Casey v Irish Intercontinental Bank*, the one as being a special case decided on particular facts and the other as not laying down any general principle in support of using a 'subject to contract' note as sufficient for the statute. I find it difficult so to distinguish these two cases. No particular set of facts surrounding the making of the contract itself can relieve a plaintiff from giving the necessary evidence in writing; I find it impossible not to read *Casey's* case as other than holding that the words 'subject to contract' in the memorandum did not mean what they said. It follows that in my view neither case should be followed. It may well be thought that this rigidity of construction will result in genuine bargains not being enforced and that a court should, as I believe it has in the past 'to do a great right, do a little wrong' (see *Merchant of Venice*, IV i, 215). It is reasonable to assume that the writing requirement is well known to owners and buyers of land; Portia's rule of construction is the preferred alternative. . .

It follows that part of the deal between the parties was that the deal itself was subject to contract; in that sense, the deal was incomplete. As I understand it, the law does not recognise as enforceable a contract to enter into a contract. In any event, whatever be the exact nature of the deal, the terms of Mr McManus' letter cannot be used to meet the requirements of the Statute of Frauds.

O'Flaherty J.:

And so I turn to a consideration of the 'subject to contract' cases. The phrase is used twice in the letter of 8 July and, in addition, Mr McManus made clear that the letter was written for information purposes only and did not by itself constitute part of a binding contract.

I cannot conceive of any language that could more clearly express the denial of the existence of a binding contract short of saying: 'Existence of contract denied'.

The historic purpose of the phrase 'subject to contract' or some similar phrase, was to keep negotiations in train and to allow either party to resile from the agreement made. That was the position for over a hundred years until in the 1970s property prices both in England and here became volatile. This led to the practice of 'gazumping' and since it is regarded as an odious thing, in the spirit of examining anything that may be said in defence of it, I put forward the views of Farrand, *Contract and Conveyance* (4th ed. 1980) 17:

> This established ability to resile led eventually to the imaginatively named and much maligned sub-practice of 'gazumping' i.e. of potential vendors increasing the agreed price of property (especially houses) sold 'subject to contract' and the ignominy seems to extend also to selling at an increased price to a different purchaser. The original prospective purchaser will nowadays have a tendency to flaunt his disappointment and indignation, for one thing he will likely enough have been hit in the pocket (e.g. surveyor's fees) and for another he may not be willing or able to pay more. Is the potential vendor to be blamed? It is true that most solicitors and many clients will say that they regard an agreement 'subject to contract' as morally, if not legally, binding (see, e.g. *Pimms Ltd v Tallow Chandlers in the City of London* [1964] 2 QB 547 at p. 552). Yet much more worthy of notice is Sachs J.'s penetrating judgment on:
>
>> this hybrid type of 'subject to contract' transaction which is so often referred to as a gentleman's agreement but which experience shows is only too often a transaction in which each side hopes the other will act like a gentleman and neither intends so to act if it is against his material interests (*Goding v Frazer* [1967] 1 WLR 286, at p. 293).

. . .

The foundation case on this topic is *Chinnock v Marchioness of Ely* (1865) 4 De G. J. & S. 638. . . .

. . . Lord Westbury L.C. said at pp 645–6:

> I entirely accept the doctrine contended for by the plaintiff's counsel . . . that if there had been a final agreement, and the terms of it are evidenced in a manner to satisfy the Statute of Frauds, the agreement shall be binding although the parties may have declared that the writing is to serve only as instructions for a formal agreement, or although it may be an express term that a formal agreement shall be prepared and signed by the parties. As soon as the fact is established of the final mutual assent of the parties to certain terms, and those terms are evidenced by any writing signed by the party to be charged or his agent lawfully authorised, there exist all the materials, which this court requires, to make a legally binding contract. But if to a proposal or offer an assent be given subject to a provision as to a contract, then the stipulation as to the contract is a term of the assent, and there is no agreement independent of this stipulation.
>
> That decision was followed in *Winn v Bull* (1877) 7 ChD 29. . . .

. . .

In the House of Lords decision of *Rossiter v Miller* (1878) 3 App Cas 1124 Lord Cairns L.C. at p. 1139 said in relation to Lord Westbury's judgment:

> . . . I entirely acquiesce in what he says, that if you find, not an unqualified acceptance of a contract, but an acceptance subject to the condition that an agreement is to be prepared and agreed upon between the parties, and until that

condition is fulfilled no contract is to arise, then undoubtedly you cannot, upon a correspondence of that kind, find a concluded contract.

Now it is important to recall, I think, that most of these 'subject to contract' cases deal with correspondence passing *inter partes*. We have not that here. All that we have here is a letter sent by the estate agent to the clients' solicitor informing him, in broad outline, what had been agreed, but making clear that no *binding agreement* had been entered into . . .

In the circumstances, I do not think it necessary to traverse the ground that was so ably covered by Keane J. in the course of his judgment in *Mulhall v Haren*. While I appreciate that it would be possible to confine my judgment within a narrow ambit, out of deference to the elaborate arguments that were advanced before us, I feel I should give my conclusions as fully as possible. They are:

(1) The letter of 8 July 1988 does not satisfy the Statute of Frauds in that it makes clear that while there has been a measure of agreement reached, matters remain in a state of suspension pending the execution of a formal contract; in other words the negotiations have not been concluded. In addition, as I have already pointed out, the letter did not contain all the terms that the parties intended should be part of their bargain and which they intended would find expression in the formal contract.

(2) In order to satisfy the Statute of Frauds, the actual contract must be in writing or there must be some memorandum or note thereof. The agreement must be one where there is an intention to create legal relations and the writing must contain all the essential terms which had been agreed.

(3) The expression 'subject to contract' or 'subject to a formal contract being drawn up' or the like is *prima facie* a strong declaration that a concluded agreement does not exist. I would hold that there must be cogent evidence of a contrary intention before such a phrase is put to one side. I would equate it to 'existence of contract denied'. In this regard, the decisions of this Court in *Kelly v Park Hall School* and *Casey v Irish Intercontinental Bank* must be regarded as exceptional and confined to the peculiar facts found in each case and as properly confined to the era in which they were decided. I do not regard them as reversing the principles laid down in the nineteenth century decisions to which I have referred.

(4) Even if an oral agreement is concluded, and it is not itself made 'subject to contract' or the like nevertheless if the initiating correspondence thereafter contains that or a similar phrase, this involves that there is not a recognition, express or implied, of the existence of an oral agreement in the sense of one meant to be a binding contract.

(5) The 'written offer accepted orally' position is anomalous but is explained, I think, by the fact that once there is an oral acceptance of a written offer it is at that moment that a contract comes into existence and, therefore, the note or memorandum becomes relevant. See *Colgrave v Upcot* 5 Vin Abr 527 and *Reuss v Picksley* (1886) LR 1 Ex 342 and the discussion of this topic in the cases of *Law v Jones* [1974] Ch. 112; *Tiverton Estates Ltd v Wearwell Ltd* [1975] Ch. 146 and *Daulia Ltd v Four Millbank Nominees Ltd* [1978] 2 WLR 621. See, too, *Mulhall v Haren* p. 383 et seq.

. . .

In the circumstances, I would answer the questions posed: that there was no concluded oral agreement in the month of July 1988, and, even if there were, that the memorandum or note thereof relied upon is not sufficient to satisfy the Statute of Frauds.

Egan J.:

[referring to section 2] The agreement itself need not be in writing. A 'note or memorandum' of it is sufficient, provided that it contains all the material terms of the contract.
The circumstances of each case need to be examined to discover if any individual term
has been deemed material by the parties; and, if so, it must be included in the
memorandum: *Hawkins v Price* [1947] Ch. 645; *Schott v Bradley* [1971] Ch. 850.

Can it be said that all material terms of the oral agreement were included in the
letter of 8 July 1988? The closing date is described as 'as soon as legal formalities can be
completed' and this represents fairly what was agreed to. There is no mention of the
requirement of a deposit but, there was no definite parol agreement and, in the circumstances of this case, the parties did not regard the question of a deposit as being of any
significant or necessary materiality: see *Black v Kavanagh* (1974) 108 ILTR 91.

A more serious matter arises in relation to the tenancies. The evidence disclosed
that there was a breach of planning permission and that it was a continuing breach.
Mr Boyle gave evidence to the effect that he would accept the tenancies as they stood,
even though there was a breach. In my opinion, this was an important and material
term. It meant that if the sale went through he could be compelled by the Corporation
to take steps to remedy the breach and that these steps might be difficult and costly.
He was prepared to face up to this position but there was nothing in the note or
memorandum to exonerate the vendors from any liability towards the purchasers in
this event. For this reason alone, I hold that the note or memorandum was not
sufficient to satisfy the requirements of the statute.

Having regard to the foregoing, it is not strictly necessary for me to deal with the
legal effect of the words 'subject to contract' which are included twice in the memorandum relied upon and also the sentence which reads: 'In the meantime you will
appreciate that this letter is for information purposes only and does not by itself
constitute part of a binding contract'. Nothing could be clearer than the intention of
the writer and the meaning, in particular, of the sentence quoted. Is this an answer to
the problem in the sense of meaning that there can be no binding contract until a
formal contract is entered into? It is consistent with the plain view of one of the
parties but not necessarily of the other party. If the words are to be construed with
reference to the parol agreement it could be argued that a finding to the effect that
there had been a concluded agreement should mean that one party could not
unilaterally negative the existence of such agreement. It has been held that the court,
in determining whether a document is a sufficient memorandum is not 'in quest of the
intention of the parties, but only of evidence under the hand of one of the parties to it,
that he has entered into it': *In re Hoyle* [1893] 1 Ch. 84.

In England the balance of authority suggests that any alleged memorandum which
purports to deny the existence of a contract cannot constitute a sufficient note or
memorandum for the purpose of the Statute of Frauds, even though the parties themselves have actually reached a concluded agreement and parol evidence can be
produced to prove this: *Tiverton Estates Ltd v Wearwell Ltd* [1975] Ch. 146.

The entire history of the law in relation to the expression 'subject to contract' was
reviewed exhaustively by Keane J. in *Mulhall v Haren* [1981] IR 364 in which he held *inter
alia* that a letter which expressly states that a transaction is 'subject to contract' cannot
be a sufficient note or memorandum, since the use of those words is normally
inconsistent with the existence of a concluded contract. He held that it was only in
certain rare and exceptional circumstances such as arose in *Kelly v Park Hall School Ltd*
[1979] IR 340 and *Michael Richards Properties Ltd v Corporation of Wardens of St Saviour's Parish*
[1975] 3 All ER 416 that the words 'subject to contract' could be treated as being of no

effect. It is true that the *Park Hall* decision was that of the Supreme Court but the qualification or explanation of it given by Keane J. was subsequently accepted by Henchy J. in *McCarthy v O'Neill* [1981] ILRM 443 when he impliedly approved of the decision in *Mulhall v Haren*. I similarly approve. I would allow the appeal.

Notes

1. As the majority of the Supreme Court had found that no concluded agreement existed (see Chapter 2, p. 94), their comments on the enforceability of the agreement are *obiter*.
2. In *Jodifern Ltd v Fitzgerald and Fitzgerald* [2000] 3 IR 321, the decision in *Boyle* was confirmed. There, the plaintiff sought specific performance of an agreement to sell property for £2 million. Although written agreements were executed, correspondence between the parties' solicitors which followed was headed 'subject to contract/contract denied'. Barron J. stated:

> The question of the sufficiency of a memorandum in writing arises whenever the evidence shows that the parties reached a concluded oral agreement. If a party or his agent wishes to negotiate in correspondence but does not at the same time wish to enter into an enforceable contract, this can be avoided by heading the letter or, if appropriate, any other form of writing with the form of words which says and can be understood to mean 'there is not as yet any concluded agreement'. The expression which has legal sanction and which is normally used is 'subject to contract'.
>
> It is important to realise that this expression has such a meaning when placed at the head of the letter or other writing so as to govern the entire. If not so contained, but contained in the body of the document it is a matter of construction of the writing as a whole whether it is intended to deny the existence of a concluded agreement.

Hamilton C.J.; Keane, Murphy and Murray JJ. concurred.

3. As the *Shirley* case below indicates, however, the principle established in the *Boyle* case has been the subject of a certain degree of judical speculation.

Shirley Engineering Ltd *v* Irish Telecommunications plc (HC) 2 December 1999

Geoghegan J.:

[I]t is not entirely clear to me that in his comments on the adequacy of the note or memorandum in *Boyle v Lee*, Finlay C.J. addressed the question of whether every term or only the essential terms in an orally concluded agreement had to be included in the note or memorandum. What the former Chief Justice seems to have been addressing were two different points. One is whether the note or memorandum must either expressly or by implication acknowledge the existence of a concluded agreement and he, like the other members of the Court held that it must, thereby agreeing with the views already expressed by Keane J. in *Mulhall v Haren* [1981] IR 364. His reference to 'the price, deposit, closing date, resume of title etc.' is in that particular context and not in any other context. He is suggesting that if those matters were clearly set out in a document that would be an implied acknowledgement of an agreement. Secondly, he was again agreeing with the views of Keane J. in *Mulhall v Haren* that any words in the memorandum which indicated a denial of a contract prevented the memorandum itself from being sufficient for the purposes of the statute. I have already held that there was no implied term in the relevant negotiations in this case that a so-called usual deposit would be paid and I have also held that the deposit was an important term. But that was entirely in the context of whether there was a concluded agreement or not. Once the deposit had still to be agreed there was no concluded agreement. It does not follow from that that the amount of a deposit expressly or by implication agreed upon would have to be set out in the note or memorandum to satisfy the Statute of Frauds. The authorities seem to establish that only the essential terms need be included in the note or memorandum and by that I mean the kind of terms that would always be regarded as essential, together with any special added terms which the parties in the particular case regarded as essential. I do not think that the amount of the deposit is an essential term in that sense, that is to say in the sense that it would have to be included in the note or memorandum. Mr John Farrell, S.C., in his book *Irish Law of Specific Performance* says the following:

> Questions may arise whether every term agreed by the parties must be in that memorandum. The case law makes it clear that some terms are always 'essential' or 'material' in contracts for the sale of land. These are the parties, the property and the consideration so these must be ascertainable from the memorandum relied on.

He goes on to cite a passage from Lord McDermott, L.C.J., in *Stinson v Owens* unreported judgment but noted in 107 ILTSJ 239:

> . . . that a memorandum may satisfy the requirements of the statute without mentioning every term that has been agreed between the parties, but that to be good it must mention all the terms which are essential or material. And I am further of the opinion that for the purposes of this requirement what is material or essential must be considered, at any rate primarily, from the point of view of the parties themselves.

Similar views were expressed by the Supreme Court in the form of the leading judgment by Maguire C.J. in *Godley v Power* [1961] 95 ILTR 135 at 145, the relevant passage is as follows:

> A memorandum must contain all essential terms. The parties, the property, and the consideration must always be ascertainable from it, but it need not contain any terms which the general law would imply. . . .

Note

See Maddox & Canny, 'Agreements for the Sale of an Interest in Land: Have the Irish Courts Retreated from *Boyle v Lee and Goyns*?' (2005) 12 CLP 3.

Consider:

Would a phrase such as 'conditional on tidying these terms up and getting our lawyers to prepare a formal document' have the same effect as 'subject to contract'?

E. Gazumping

A private member's Bill, the House Purchasers (Anti-Gazumping) Bill, 1988 was introduced with the objective of preventing vendors of residential property who had agreed to sell property at a specified price and who had accepted a booking deposit from selling the property to a third party at an increased price within an unreasonably short time after receipt of the deposit. The Bill, which sought to make gazumping a criminal offence, was defeated at Second Stage on the basis that it was potentially unconstitutional and its provisions would be unworkable and ineffective in practice. It was noted, for example, that it would cut across many fundamental principles of contract law and would represent an unacceptable attempt to interfere with the basic rights of buyers and sellers to freely enter into contracts. Furthermore, it was noted that it would penalise home purchasers as well as vendors (494 Dáil Debates, 7 October 1998).

In October 1999, the Law Reform Commission published a report on gazumping (LCR 59-1999). This report identified a number of limitations to both the IHBA code and the proposed legislation

Summary of Recommendations and Conclusions

6.01 Gazumping can occur during the stage of negotiations for the sale of land, before a concluded agreement on all relevant terms has been reached, even though the parties have informally settled the price. It is also possible where an oral agreement has been concluded, but the evidence required by law (i.e. a note or memorandum of the essential terms of the agreement, which does not deny the existence of a contract) is not available. In short, gazumping can take place at any stage before the parties enter into an enforceable contract for the sale of land. During this time, the vendor is free to accept other offers.

6.02 The reader may well query why there is a need for any delay between the conclusion of negotiations and the payment of a booking deposit and, on the other hand, the making of a formal contract. The brief answer is that it is usually in the purchaser's interest that there should be a delay to facilitate the arranging of finance or to ascertain if there are legal difficulties. The non-legal character of the relationship between the parties is preserved by the use of the term 'subject to contract', as is explained in chapter 2. In the case of houses in the course of construction, this period of delay is sometimes unduly long and, in chapter 4, we consider non-legally binding codes of practice which attempt to reduce it. It seems to the Commission that in view of the unusual character of 'subject to contract' agreements such codes of practice may present the best avenue to reform.

6.03 A number of possible reforms of the existing laws are considered in chapter 3. Among these are proposals for legislation which would deem the payment of a booking deposit as creating either a binding contract for sale or an option to buy for the purchaser. Another option was to make compensation payable by a gazumping vendor to a purchaser, either for the purchaser's out-of-pocket expenses, or for his loss of expectation. While these proposals are initially attractive, for a variety of reasons, none of them can be recommended.

6.04 Our conclusion is that the only practicable reforms, are to take steps to inform purchasers and, in that way, to protect them; and also to regulate the terms according to which booking deposits are paid and accepted. These recommendations, which are summarised below, are set out at paragraphs 5.08–5.28.

6.05 In making these recommendations, the Commission is conscious that they are of limited usefulness, and that they do not in any way alter the legal framework within which gazumping occurs. However, the Commission is also conscious that gazumping is a temporary problem which is related to the present rapid rise in the price of houses and—most important of all—that our empirical research has shown that it occurs rather seldom, despite the high publicity, which surrounds the few cases which occur. Moreover, the laws and practices relating to house purchases do not give rise to gazumping in a stable market, and in a falling market, the gap provided by the necessary delays in proceeding to a formal contract may be exploited by purchasers.

6.06 Accordingly, we recommend the following reforms. First, legislation should be enacted requiring that a receipt, in the form prescribed by law, be issued to a purchaser on the payment of a booking deposit. The receipt should include at least the following information:

   (i) a statement that the receipt is one which merely confirms the payment and receipt of a booking deposit and does not of itself create a contract;

   (ii) the name of the person paying the deposit;

   (iii) the name of the person receiving the deposit;

   (iv) the amount of the deposit;

   (v) reference to the property concerned;

   (vi) a statement that the deposit is refundable in full in the event that the parties do not enter into any contract;

   (vii) a statement that the purchaser will not be entitled to reimbursement of any expenses incurred should the parties fail to proceed to a formal contract;

   (viii) such further matters as may be prescribed by law. For example, it might be desirable to require the payee to identify those organisations of which he is a member, e.g. the IHBA.

6.07 The obligation to issue a receipt in the required form should be enforced by the criminal sanction deemed appropriate by the Oireachtas.

6.08 The duty should be imposed on the person who actually receives the money, or their employee, and will therefore apply to estate agents and auctioneers as well as to the builder or other vendors acting in the course of business.

6.09 Next, we recommend that legislation be enacted regulating the advertisement of the sale of houses in new housing developments. Such legislation would, *inter alia*, provide for the following matters:

• that any advertisement be required to specify the number of houses offered for sale at each price level as well as the period for which these prices are fixed;

• that a criminal penalty be imposed on any person who fails to provide the required information, or fails to comply with the terms of the advertisement and dishonours the commitment which it implies.

6.10 Finally, it is recommended that legislation, again backed by criminal penalties for non-observance, be enacted to prevent the taking of booking deposits of more than 0.5% of the purchase price. Secondly, we recommend that legislation be enacted to provide that the entire amount of the booking deposit, without any deduction, be refunded to the purchaser in any case where the parties do not proceed to a contract.

Consider:

Should gazumping be prohibited? Is this practical?

SECTION TWO—EQUITABLE MEANS OF ENFORCING THE CONTRACT

A. PART PERFORMANCE

'The principle upon which the rule in cases of part performance was engrafted on the Statute of Frauds is, that it would be a fraud on the part of the person who had entered into an agreement by parol for a lease or sale, and had allowed expenditure to be made upon the faith of it, afterwards to turn around and say that it did not legally exist.' Per Vice-Chancellor Chatterton in *Hope v Lord Cloncurry* (1874) IR 8 Eq 555.

Where an agreement is not enforceable as a result of its non-compliance with the Statute of Frauds, the doctrine of part performance may afford the claimant some relief and facilitate an action for specific performance. This doctrine will only apply where a concluded agreement has been reached. However, it is not now considered necessary that the acts of part performance relate unequivocally to the actual agreement.

Lowry v Reid [1927] NI 142

The plaintiff's mother undertook to leave her property to the plaintiff, if he transferred his own farm together with £200 to his brother. The plaintiff did this and went to live with his mother. Although his mother made a will giving effect to their agreement, she later revoked it, leaving the plaintiff only a life interest in her property. The plaintiff sought specific performance of the agreement. Wilson J. at first instance held that making a will and allowing the plaintiff to bring his wife to live on the property was not part performance by his mother.

Moore L.C.J.:

Counsel for the respondents have attempted to put the case on a different ground based on certain dicta in the judgment of Lord Selborne in *Maddison v Alderson*.[1] They say that evidence of the parol contract cannot be admitted unless it is first established that the alleged acts of part performance unequivocally establish the existence of some such contract. If I have correctly stated this proposition, I can only say that I do not accept it. I think it is an inversion of the principle which should obtain. In my opinion, we must at some stage consider the contract and its effect, before we are in a position to judge, whether or not the acts relied on to take the case out of the statute are acts of part performance of the contract.

If such acts are not unequivocally referable to the performance of the contract, in whole or part, then the evidence as to them is irrelevant and the necessary proof of part performance fails. Lord Selborne's speech in *Maddison v Alderson* lays it down that 'the doctrine of part performance is applicable to any case in which a court of equity would before the statute have decreed specific performance.'. . .

Now has there been such part performance of that contract as would entitle William to succeed in equity in a suit for specific performance? Would it be a fraud on the part of Mary Lowry to take advantage of the fact that there was no contract in writing pursuant to the statute? . . .

In my judgment there is relief for him, because on the facts of the case, having given up his own property to his own detriment, on the faith of his mother's representation, this is a parol contract for the specific performance of which he is entitled in equity to a decree to carry those representations into execution, and if he is entitled to such a decree, he is equally entitled to rely on the doctrine of part performance to take the case out of the statute.

Andrews L.J.:

. . . Wilson J. held that it was necessary that there should also be a part performance of the contract by Mary Lowry, and that the making of the will of 19 April 1916, and her allowing William to bring his wife to live at Drumhirk did not amount to such part performance. When one considers the principle upon which the doctrine of part performance is based, it becomes, in my opinion, clear that no such performance on her part is required. In *Bond v Hopkins*,[2] Lord Redesdale said: 'The Statute of Frauds says that no action or suit shall be maintained on an agreement relating to lands which is not in writing, signed by the party to be charged with it; and yet the court is in the daily habit of relieving, where the party seeking relief has been put into a situation which makes it against conscience in the other party to insist on the want of writing so signed, as a bar to his relief.' Thus the doctrine is a purely equitable one. Its underlying principle is, that the court will not allow a statute which was passed to prevent fraud to be made itself an instrument of fraud. In other words, the court disregards the absence of that formality which the statute requires when insistence upon it would render it a means of effecting, instead of a means of averting, fraud. The question in each case is, whether the plaintiff has an equity arising from part performance which is so affixed upon the conscience of the defendant that it would amount to a fraud on his part to take advantage of the fact that the contract is not in writing. The right to relief rests not so much on the contract as on what has been done in pursuance or in execution of it. Under the statute the note or memorandum of the contract must be signed by the party to be charged. Under the doctrine of part performance the equity must be possessed, not by the party to be charged, but by the plaintiff—the person who seeks relief; and this equity arises from his part performance of the contract. . . .

I see no reason in principle, nor has any authority been cited to us to show, why a party who seeks contractual relief in regard to certain lands cannot rely as acts of part performance upon his own acts to other lands in furtherance of the same contract. . . . and, in my opinion, there could be no foundation for the suggestion that the doctrine does not apply to contracts for the exchange of lands, as in my judgment the doctrine applies to all contracts of which, before the Judicature Act, a court of equity would have granted specific performance if the alleged contract had been in writing; and these are not confined to contracts for the sale of land. . . . I would add that I can find no authority to support [counsel for the defendant's] contention that it is not permissible even to consider the terms of the parol agreement until it is clearly established that the acts of part performance refer unequivocally to the contract relied upon, and to that alone. Indeed, it would be, in my opinion, impossible to apply the proposition as so stated in practice; for how, I ask, could it be said that the acts of part performance referred unequivocally to an agreement the terms of which were *ex hypothesi* not known, unless, indeed, they were acts of such a clear, cogent, and conclusive character that they embodied and themselves proved the actual terms of the agreement, in which case it would be wholly unnecessary for the plaintiff to make any reference to or to rely in any way upon the parol agreement. In support of his contention [counsel] referred us to a passage in Lord O'Hagan's judgment in *Maddison v Alderson*, where he said:

> Next, assuming that the action must be considered maintainable, if at all, for the purpose of enforcing a parol contract, partly performed, the course of the argument appears to me to have been further erroneous in this, that, instead of seeking to establish primarily such a performance as must necessarily imply the existence of the contract, and then proceeding to ascertain its terms, it reversed the order of the contention. The court was asked, from the findings of the jury and the testimony supporting them, to say there was a contract; and then to discover in the conduct of the parties acts of performance sufficient to validate the bargain so previously ascertained.

If these words are to be taken literally, and to be construed as deciding that the acts of performance must in themselves necessarily imply the existence of *the* contract, that is, the precise contract pleaded, I am not prepared to accept them as containing a correct statement of the law, being, as they are, at variance with the terms of the classical judgment of the Earl of Selborne C. in the same case, and, indeed, as it seems to me, with other passages of Lord O'Hagan's own judgment. . . .

I have referred to the Earl of Selborne's judgment, from which I shall only make two extracts—the first, the passage at p. 476, to which [counsel for the plaintiff] referred us in his very forcible reply:

> It is not arbitrary or unreasonable to hold that when the statute says that no action is to be brought to charge any person upon a contract concerning land, it has in view the simple case in which he is charged upon the contract only, and not that in which there are equities resulting from *res gestae* subsequent to and arising out of the contract. So long as the connexion of those *res gestae* with the alleged contract does not depend upon mere parol testimony, but is reasonably to be inferred from the *res gestae* themselves, justice seems to require some such limitation of the scope of the statute.

The second passage is taken from p. 479, where the learned Lord Chancellor summarises the effect of the cases in the following terms: 'All the authorities show that the acts relied upon as part performance must be unequivocally and in their own nature referable to some such agreement as that alleged.' These words 'some such agreement' are also adopted as his own by Lord Fitzgerald in his judgment in the same case at p. 491.

I would like to refer to one other case of recognised authority, *Morphett v Jones*,[3] where Sir T. Plumer, referring to the equitable doctrine, says that 'Admission into possession, having unequivocal reference to the contract, has always been considered an act of part performance. The acknowledged possession of a stranger in the land of another is not explicable except on the supposition of an agreement, and has, therefore, constantly been received as evidence of an antecedent contract, and as sufficient to authorise an inquiry into the terms.' In the opinion, therefore, of this eminent authority the sole requisite preliminary to inquiry into and proof of the terms of the parol agreement is the establishment of an act which is only explicable on the basis of the existence of some contract.

I make no apology for citing, in conclusion, as a correct summary of the law a passage from *Fry on Specific Performance* (5th edn) 292, where the editor states that the true principle of the operation of acts of part performance seems only to require that the acts in question be such as must be referred to some contract, and may be referred to the alleged one; that they prove the existence of some contract, and are consistent with the contract alleged.

[1] 8 AC 457.   [2] 1 Sch. & L., 413 at 433.   [3] 1 Swanston, 181.

(Best L.J. concurred and the appeal was allowed.)

Jodifern Ltd *v* Fitzgerald and Fitzgerald (HC) 28 July 1999 Unreported
(Facts on p.275)

McCracken J.:

There is one further matter which was raised, although not pursued with any vigour, on behalf of the plaintiff, namely that there was part performance of the contract. This of course assumes that there was an oral contract. I am quite satisfied that nothing was done by or on behalf of the plaintiffs which could possibly be construed as part performance. They attempted to survey the land, and were prevented from doing so by the defendants, and subsequently acknowledged that they would not apply for planning permission without the defendants' consent. They certainly applied for finance, but I do not accept that negotiating a loan with the bank could be construed as part performance of a contract for the sale of land any more than the payment of the deposit is part performance.

Consider:

What is the difference, if any, between part performance and reliance?

There was some debate in the Courts as to whether the payment of money alone could constitute sufficient acts of part performance. In the following case, the High Court held that it could.

Howlin *v* Thomas Power (Dublin) Ltd (HC) 5 May 1978, unrep.

The defendant entered into an oral agreement to surrender a leasehold interest to the plaintiff. The plaintiff paid £200 as part of the purchase price. The defendant then refused to complete the agreement and tendered repayment of the £200. Although the agreement was not evidenced by a written memorandum, the plaintiff claimed that his actions in negotiating a new tenancy and/or paying the £200 constituted sufficient acts of part performance. The plaintiff thus sought specific performance of the oral agreement.

McWilliam J.:

The plaintiff then relies on acts of part performance as taking the case out of the statute. To take the first of these. The plaintiff has given evidence that he made an arrangement with an agent to let the premises to a building society with vacant possession of 1 February 1977, at the yearly rent of £2,500.00 and rates. It does not appear that there was any contract in writing with the building society and, in cross-examination, the plaintiff stated that he had had negotiations about letting in December, towards the end of that month, and that he wrote to the estate agent that he would have vacant possession on 31 January. On this aspect of part performance I have been referred to the following cases:

Lowry v Reid [1927] NI 142, Brough v Nettleton [1921] 2 Ch. 25, Broughton v Snook [1938] 1 Ch. 505, Daniels v Trefusis [1914] 1 Ch. 788, Estate of Earl of Longford 5 LR (Ir.) 99.

I have also read the case of Crowley v Sullivan [1900] 2 IR 478 cited in the case of Lowry v Reid. In each of these cases the plaintiff had taken some conclusive or irrevocable or prejudicial step in pursuance of the contract, such as conveying land to a third party, entering into occupation of premises agreed to be let or sold to him, ejecting tenants at the request of the other party or commencing to carry on a business in partnership in pursuance of an agreement to do so. The principle established by these and other cases appears to be that, where the party seeking relief in proceedings has taken some step in pursuance of the contract which has left him in such a position that it would amount to a fraud or be inequitable on the part of the other party to rely on the fact that there was no sufficient memorandum of the contract, the case is taken out of the statute and the court will enforce the contract. With regard to negotiating a tenancy in the present case, the plaintiff does not appear to have prejudiced himself in any way by reason of the contract with the defendant or left himself in a position where he could be required to perform any act which he was not able to do. He merely appears to have consulted or instructed estate agents with regard to negotiating a letting and to have discussed terms with them and with a possible tenant but without entering into any binding contract. Accordingly, apart from causing him disappointment at the loss of his bargain, I cannot see that there is, on these facts, any special equity to take the case out of the statute.

With regard to the payment and acceptance of the sum of £200.00 as part of the purchase price, I have been referred to the cases of Steadman v Steadman [1976] AC 536 and Re. Gonin decd, [1977] 2 All ER 720. It is urged, on the authority of the former case, that, if the payment of the money is referable only to the contract alleged, it is a sufficient act of part performance. Until this case was brought to my attention, I had accepted the proposition that the mere payment of money could not constitute a sufficient act of part performance. Four of the five judges in the House of Lords and two of the three judges in the Court of Appeal refused, in Steadman's case, to accept that this proposition was well founded and, in the unusual circumstances of that case, held that the payment of £100 by a husband to his wife was a sufficient act of part performance of a contract containing four provisions for the compromise of matrimonial proceedings. I cannot disagree with the reasoning of the majority of the judges in that case but, accepting that the decision is correct on the question of the mere payment of money constituting an act of part performance sufficient to take the case out of the statute, I must keep before my mind that the statute does provide that a contract for the sale of land shall not be enforceable unless there is a sufficient note or memorandum thereof in writing and that the application of the doctrine of part performance is still confined to cases in which it would be fraudulent or inequitable for a defendant to rely on the statute because a plaintiff has prejudiced himself in some way by reason of the contract. As I have stated, this is not shown to have occurred in the present case and the following passage from the judgment of Lord Reid in Steadman's case at p. 541 appears to me to be relevant. It is as follows:

Normally the consideration for the purchase of land is a sum of money and there are statements that a sum of money can never be treated as part performance. Such statements would be reasonable if the person pleading the statute tendered repayment of any part of the price which he had received and was thus able to make *restitutio in integrum*. That would remove any 'fraud' or any equity on which the purchaser could properly rely. But to make a general rule that payment of money can never be part performance would seem to me to defeat the whole purpose of the doctrine and I do not think that we are compelled to do that.

Here, not only was the sum of money paid comparatively small, but it was actually tendered in repayment to the plaintiff. Accordingly, I do not accept that this payment was sufficient to take the case out of the statute.

Note

In *Silver Wraith Ltd v Siuicre Éireann*, 8 June 1989 (see p.97) Keane J. noted *obiter* that 'as a matter of probability' the plaintiff failed to establish that the expenditure incurred was unequivocally referable to the type of contract alleged. Therefore a plea of part performance was unsuccessful.

Consistent with the equitable nature of the doctrine, an element of unconscionability will raise an equity in favour of the claimant.

McCarron v McCarron (SC) 13 February 1997 unreported

The plaintiff worked continuously over a sixteen-year period with Mr McKenna, a relation of his, on the latter's farm. The plaintiff claimed that Mr McKenna, an elderly and infirm bachelor, had agreed to devise all his property to the plaintiff in remuneration for all his work. When Mr McKenna died, the plaintiff sought specific performance of this agreement.

Murphy J.

The actual discussions which took place between the plaintiff and the deceased in relation to remunerating the plaintiff for the work which he had done or was to do were extremely limited. It would seem that the first discussion of any sort took place in 1980. The deceased was quoted by the Plaintiff as saying:

'I suppose you are wondering about some compensation for your work.'

To which the plaintiff replied:

'I suppose I will not be forgotten.'

And then the deceased responded:

'Well you will be a rich man after my day.'

A further discussion took place at a later date in the following brief terms:

'Kevin,' said Mr McKenna 'my pain is getting no better. I will soon be in a wheelchair and I want you to look after me and take your father up and we will draw up some class of an agreement.'

To that the plaintiff replied:

   'I will not put you out of house or home, George.'

The conversation then concluded with the sentence:

   'Right (said Mr McKenna) we will leave it at that.'

The other and perhaps more significant conversation took place in 1984 . . .

   . . . [where the deceased] said 'You'll be a rich man some day, Kevin, this is all yours.'. . .

What is noticeable from the transcript and in particular the evidence of the plaintiff was that natural courtesy (which John Millington Synge associated with the west of Ireland) which often results in an unwillingness to pursue discussion to a logical and perhaps harshly expressed commercial conclusion. In other parts of Ireland the concept of a person working long hours over a period of four years before any discussion takes place in relation to remuneration or reward might be unthinkable. Even less likely would be agreement or an expression of satisfaction at that stage that the question of compensation would not be overlooked. I would merely conclude that in some, particularly rural areas, a meeting of minds can be achieved without as detailed a discussion as might be necessary elsewhere. . . .

   [S]tatute law has required for many centuries that a contractual claim to land cannot be sustained unless evidenced by an appropriate note or memorandum in writing (see the Statute of Frauds Ireland 1695 section 2) or supported by acts of part performance by the plaintiff referable to some such contract (see Lowry v Reid 1927 NI 142). Indeed frequently the issue in such claims relates to the existence or adequacy of alleged acts of part performance. However every case must be examined on its own special facts. The facts of which the plaintiff in particular gave evidence established that the plaintiff worked on the farms of the deceased over a period of sixteen years— and that for long hours—without reward. Furthermore I would attach importance to the fact that the deceased was a relatively young and very active man in the early years of the plaintiff's service with him. This was never a case in which it might have been suggested that work was done or humanitarian services provided on a purely neigh-bourly or charitable basis for some person in need. Nor does it seem to me that the help and assistance provided by the plaintiff was undertaken and continued in the vague hope that Mr McKenna might in his discretion remember his kindness if and when he came to make a will. Apart from any other consideration the fact that both parties might well have anticipated that the arrangement—whatever it may have been— could have continued another ten or twenty years makes such an interpretation extremely unlikely. Considering expressions used in that context and in the light of what each of them knew about the deceased's holdings of land, I think it is reasonably clear that the deceased was agreeing in consideration of work that had been done and which was to be done by the plaintiff to give him 'the home place' and 'the outside place' with the result that the plaintiff would be a rich man after the deceased's 'day'.

   In these circumstances I am satisfied that the learned trial judge was correct in holding that there was evidence of a sufficient degree of certainty of a contract between the plaintiff and the deceased by which the latter agreed to devise his farms to the plaintiff and it was appropriate for the court to grant specific performance of that contract. . . .

Note

A claim on the basis of proprietary estoppel was not determined by Murphy J. because of his finding as to the existence of a contract.

Mackey v Wilde & Longin [1998] 1 ILRM 449

Despite having determined that no concluded agreement existed, Barron J. proceeded to consider the doctrine of part performance. (Facts stated on p.90.)

Barron J.:

The doctrine is based upon principles of equity. There are three things to be considered:
(1) The acts on the part of the plaintiff said to have been in part performance or of concluded agreement;
(2) the involvement of the defendant with respect to such acts;
(3) the oral agreement itself.

It is obvious that these considerations only relate to a contract of a type which the courts will decree ought to be specifically performed. Each of the three elements is essential. In my view, it does not matter in which order they are considered. Ultimately what is essential is that
(1) there was a concluded oral contract;
(2) that the plaintiff acted in such a way that showed an intention to perform that contract;
(3) that the defendant induced such acts or stood by while they were being performed; and
(4) it would be unconscionable and a breach of good faith to allow the defendant to rely upon the terms of the Statute of Frauds to prevent performance of the contract.

If the terms of the contract cannot be considered until the acts of the plaintiff have been found capable of being acts of part performance, there is the possibility, admittedly not a very strong one, that the acts might well have been inconsistent with the terms of a contract and in fact not carried out in pursuance of it, but for a different reason. I do not suggest that in such circumstances, the court would still accept that there had been part performance. But it does show that it is more logical to find out what the parties agreed since, in the absence of a concluded agreement, there is no point in seeking to find acts of part performance. The court can only then begin its determination whether the behaviour of the parties justifies the application of the equitable doctrine to modify the legal rule.

In the result it seems to me that while the passage from Fry on specific performance cited by Andrews LJ. in *Lowry v Reid* expresses the law, the different approach requires the statement of principle to be altered. It would then read: What is required is that the acts relied upon as being acts of part performance be such that on examination of the contract which has been found to have been concluded and to which they are alleged to refer show an intention to perform that contract.

In all the earlier cases, it was assumed that the acts of part performance must necessarily relate to and affect land: see the judgment of Lord Fitzgerald in *Maddison v Alderson* at p. 491. Nothing which I have said should be taken to suggest a modification of that position.

There is no evidence in the instant case that the plaintiff issued any more or any less licences than he had the previous year or that the defendant was aware of how many he was issuing. The plaintiff had never complained during the season that too many tickets were being issued by the defendant and in that regard there was nothing different in his behaviour as between 1985 and 1986. The detriment to the plaintiff which is alleged is presumably the lessening in value of the fishery by over-fishing. But the detriment to the plaintiff must be the result of what the plaintiff does with the defendant standing by and not detriment to the plaintiff as a result of what the defendant does with the plaintiff standing by. There was nothing in what was alleged which would in any way be a breaking of faith by the defendant with the plaintiff for the defendant to plead the statute. Even if there had been a concluded oral agreement as claimed, there were no acts on the part of the plaintiff which show an intention to perform that contract.

Notes

1. In *Sheridan v The Louis Fitzgerald Group Ltd & Anor* [2006] IEHC 125, referring to *Mackey v Wilde* and *Manus v Cook* [1887] 35 Ch. D 681, Clarke J stated:

> It is clear, therefore, that the mere allowance of a person, who is already in possession, to continue in possession cannot amount to an act of part performance. On the other hand, allowing someone who was not in possession to go into possession can, in an appropriate case, amount to such an act of part performance. The circumstances of this case are, undoubtedly, complicated. . . . It would therefore seem to be the case that Mr Sheridan was let into possession in a personal capacity on 20th December, being the date upon which he contends that he entered into an agreement with Fitzgerald for the grant of a lease. The case is not as clear as a simple one where a person who was wholly out of possession goes into possession immediately after the conclusion of an oral agreement. In practical (as opposed to legal) terms there would seem to have been very little different about the possession of the property on 20th December as opposed to the 19th. Mr Sheridan may well, in those circumstances, have a significant further hurdle to climb in order to persuade the court at trial that an act of part performance sufficient to obviate the necessity for a written agreement between the parties can be said to exist. I am not, however, prepared to hold, at this stage, that there is no fair issue to be tried on this ground either.

2. In the Law Reform Commission Report on Gazumping (LCR 59–1999 at paras 2.055–2.057), the *Mackey* case was described as a move away from the traditional approach which asked whether the acts alleged to be acts of part performance could only be explained by the existence of a contract such as the one alleged. If that was so the Courts would then consider the oral evidence as to the terms of the precise contract alleged. The Commission notes, however, that the traditional doctrine is upheld to some degree, in the clear statements that the doctrine noted based on the equities raised and not on the need to provide alternative evidence of the contract.

3. While the doctrine of part performance has been applied almost exclusively to contracts for the sale or other disposition of interests in land, it is a moot point to suggest, as Barron J. does, that it must relate to and affect land.

4. Even if a claim of part performance is not successful, the plaintiff may use a *quantum meruit* plea to obtain the return of wasted expenditure or the value of services rendered: *Deglman v Guarantee Trust* [1954] 3 DLR 785.
5. The limits of part performance are uncertain. Contrast the US model.

American Law Institute Restatement Contracts (2d) S. 139
Enforcement by Virtue of Action in Reliance
(1) A promise which the promisor should reasonably expect to induce action or forbearance on the part of the promisee or a third person and which does induce the action or forbearance is enforceable notwithstanding the Statute of Frauds if injustice can be avoided only by enforcement of the promise. The remedy granted for breach is to be limited as justice requires.
(2) In determining whether injustice can be avoided only by enforcement of the promise, the following circumstances are significant:
  (a) the availability and adequacy of other remedies, particularly cancellation and restitution;
  (b) the definite and substantial character of the action of forbearance in relation to the remedy sought;
  (c) the extent to which the action or forbearance corroborates evidence of the making and terms of the promise, or the making and terms are otherwise established by clear and convincing evidence;
  (d) the reasonableness of the action or forbearance;
  (e) the extent to which the action or forbearance was foreseeable by the promisor.

B. OTHER EQUITABLE DEVICES

Even where there has been a failure to satisfy the Statute of Frauds or the doctrine of part performance, the courts may avail of other equitable devices to provide relief to the claimant.

Avoiding the Perpetration of a Fraud
In *The McGillycuddy of the Reeks v David Joy and William Joy* [1959] IR 189 Budd J. expressly approved the *dicta* of Lindley L.J. in *Rochefoucauld v Boustead* [1897] 1 Ch. 196 where the latter states:

It is further established . . . that the Statute of Frauds does not prevent the proof of a fraud; and that it is a fraud on the part of a person to whom land is conveyed as a trustee, and who knows it was so conveyed, to deny the trust and claim the land himself. Consequently, notwithstanding the statute, it is competent for a person claiming land conveyed to another to prove by parol evidence that it was so conveyed upon trust for the claimant, and that the grantee, knowing the facts, is denying the trust and relying upon the form of conveyance and the statute, in order to keep the land himself.

Doherty v Gallagher (HC) 9 June 1975, unrep.

The plaintiff agreed to buy certain property from the defendant for £3,500 and gave him a cheque for £500 as a deposit. The property to be sold was described on the face of the cheque. The parties agreed that the defendant would be allowed keep his cattle on the property until he had a reasonable opportunity to sell them. The defendant endorsed and cashed the cheque, but later refused to complete the contract and returned the £500.When the plaintiff sued for specific performance the defendant claimed *inter alia* that the cheque was not a sufficient note or memorandum for the purposes of the Statute of Frauds because it omitted any reference to the agreement to allow the defendant graze his cattle for a time on the property.

Finlay P.:

In general I am satisfied that there must be in this context a much greater danger of permitting injustice and in that sense encouraging a fraud by a strict application of the Statute of Frauds than by a liberal application. It seems to me that where the term alleged to have been omitted from the note or memorandum relied on applies solely to the question of the date for completion of the transaction or for the giving over of vacant possession and certainly where that term was never expressed by the parties at the time of the making of the contract in a precise or definite fashion and where the party seeking to enforce the contract has before the institution of proceedings allowed an ample reasonable time for the vendor to complete his contract that it would be an injustice to refuse an order for specific performance on the grounds that what can only be considered a vague assurance of reasonable time or even of ample time was not set out in the note or memorandum.
. . .
    The object of the Statute of Frauds is to prevent the mischief arising or likely to arise from proof by parol evidence of the contract or its terms.
    I cannot see any logical basis for a contention that such a mischief could arise where the only alleged term of the contract not evidenced by an appropriate memorandum in writing is a vague assurance of ample time and where what can only be described as ample time is allowed to elapse before the defendant is firmly called upon to perform the contract.
    In this case on the evidence before me I am satisfied that it is quite improbable that had the defendant not changed his mind for other reasons or . . . for family reasons and refused to proceed with this sale that any term would have been written into any subsequent legal contract providing for the grazing of the cattle or the time for selling them off. I think it much more probable that the easy going dealing and general goodwill of two neighbours both of whom knew each other over a long period of time in agreement about the sale of land would have been sufficient to carry out the sort of assurance that had been given.
    I am therefore satisfied that the absence of a reference to this assurance in the note or memorandum consisting of the cheque which is otherwise complete is not fatal to its compliance with the Statute of Frauds and that this defence also fails. I am therefore satisfied that the plaintiff is entitled to an order for specific performance.

Black *v* Grealy (HC) 10 November 1977, unrep.

The plaintiff entered into an agreement with Mr Finnegan, the defendant's agent, to buy property from the defendant for £46,000. Mr Finnegan arranged for the plaintiff to pay the defendant £6,000 in advance and the memorandum noted a price of £40,000. When the plaintiff queried why the memorandum did not reflect the agreement, Mr Finnegan promised that matters would be organised. As a result the plaintiff signed the memorandum. When the defendant refused to complete the sale, the plaintiff sued for specific performance.

Costello J.:

It will . . . be noted that in the circumstances of the present case the document relied on does not omit the consideration—it contains a figure for the consideration for the sale which the evidence establishes is the balance of the purchase price. Nor is it a case in which an omission arose by mistake so that the jurisdiction of the court to rectify the memorandum and order specific performance of the oral agreement (see: *United States of America and Another v Motor Trucks Ltd*, [1924] AC 196 and *Nolan v Graves and Another*, [1946] IR 376) arises. This is a case in which the parties (through their agents) entered into an oral agreement for the sale of land and as part of the agreement decided that the full purchase price would not be disclosed, but that the balance after the payment of the deposit would be treated as the purchase price in the written memorandum which it was agreed should be signed by the purchaser. It is not apt to describe the resultant written document as a memorandum 'of' the parties' oral agreement (as it does not properly state the full consideration for the sale); rather it is a memorandum which is 'in accordance with' one of the stipulations of the oral agreement—which is not quite the same thing. I do not think therefore that this memorandum satisfies the statute. But the statute cannot be used as an instrument of fraud, and it would in my opinion be a fraudulent use of the statute if the court permitted the defendant to avoid liability on foot of the oral agreement on the ground that the memorandum of it, which was prepared expressly in accordance with his wishes and for his benefit, was inadequate because it treated the balance of the purchase price as the purchase price. It follows, therefore, that the plea of the statute fails and that the plaintiff is entitled to have the oral agreement specifically enforced.

Waiver

Where the memorandum does not comply with the statute as a result of its failure to set out certain terms of the agreement, it may be possible for those terms to be waived and the agreement to be enforced as evidenced by the memorandum.

Healy v Healy (HC) 3 December 1973, unrep.

Kenny J.:

On principle it seems to me that when a clause in a contract (whether it is a condition or a term) is inserted solely for the benefit of one party and is severable from the other clauses and when the other party on completion will get everything that he contracted for, the party for whose benefit the clause was inserted may waive performance of the clause and insist on completion despite the non-performance of the condition or term.

Anom Engineering Ltd v Thornton (HC) 1 February 1983, unrep.

The defendants entered into an oral agreement to sell the plaintiffs a parcel of property. The defendants' solicitors later sent the plaintiffs a draft contract and documents of title. No agreement was reached at this stage as to the power and water services and the discharge of effluent into the defendants' water course. When the defendants refused to complete the agreement, the plaintiffs sued for specific performance. The defendants claimed that no memorandum existed to evidence the oral agreement.

Costello J.:

It is urged on the plaintiffs' behalf that if I were to hold that no sufficient memorandum existed relating to the terms of:

(a) the water and power supply and/or
(b) the effluent and storm water discharge

that the plaintiffs were entitled to waive the benefit of those terms and were entitled to seek the specific performance of the contract as evidenced by the memorandum of 8 May or any other memorandum contained in the correspondence. The principle of law to be applied on this aspect of the law of specific performance has been stated by Kenny J. as follows:

> My view is that when parties conclude an oral contract which contains a term wholly for the benefit of one of them and there is a written memorandum which does not contain any reference to that term the party for whose benefit the term was inserted may waive it and sue successfully on the contract of which there is a memorandum. The note in writing for the purpose of the Statute of Frauds has to be of the contract sued on not the contract made and the plaintiff may waive a term which is wholly in his favour and which is not referred to in the memorandum. (See *Barrett v Costello* quoted in Wiley *Irish Conveyancing Law* para. 9.007 and also *Tiernan Homes Ltd v Fagan and Others* (SC) 23 July 1981, unrep.).

Applying the waiver principle to this case it seems to me that the express agreement relating to the right to connect at agreed points on the defendants' land to obtain a supply of power and water was a stipulation in the agreement entirely for the benefit of the plaintiffs and that they can waive this express stipulation and obtain specific performance of the rest of the agreed terms because they were evidenced in writing.

Black v Grealy (HC) 10 November 1977, unrep.
(Facts on p.289.)

Costello J.:

The plaintiff's counsel relied on a further submission to defeat the plea of the statute. It is one which I accept and is a further reason why the order sought should in my opinion be granted. This submission was based on the principle applied in *Scott v Bradley* ([1971] 1 All ER 583) which was stated in Williams *Vendor and Purchaser* (4th edn) vol. 1, 4, as follows:

> It is essential, however, whether the writing given in evidence is of a formal or informal nature, that the terms of the agreement sought to be proved thereby shall be sufficiently ascertained therein. The parties to the contract and the property sold

must therefore be sufficiently described, and the price, or the means of ascertaining it, be stated; and any other terms of the bargain (except, of course, such as are implied by law, as that a good title should be shown) must be defined. It appears, however, that if a stipulation which is to the detriment or for the benefit of one of the parties exclusively is omitted from the memorandum, that party may submit to perform it or waive the benefit of it (as the case may require) and may with such submission or waiver specifically enforce the contract as stated in the memorandum.

Martin v Pycroft (1852 2 De GM & G 785) is one of the cases relied on by the author to justify the principle which I have quoted. That was a case in which a tenant sought specific performance of a written agreement for a lease. The tenant had agreed to pay a premium of £200, but this term was omitted from the written agreement. In the course of the proceedings he offered to pay this sum, and as a result a decree for specific performance was made and a plea of the statute failed. Part of the judgment of Knight Bruce L.J. reads as follows:

> And our opinion is that, where persons sign a written agreement upon a subject, obnoxious or not to the statute which has been so particularly referred to, and there has been no circumvention, no fraud, nor (in the sense in which the term 'mistake' must be considered as used for this purpose) mistake, the written agreement binds at law and in equity, according to its terms, although verbally a provision was agreed to, which has not been inserted in the document; subject to this, that either of the parties sued in equity upon it may perhaps be entitled in general to ask the court to be neutral, unless the plaintiff will consent to the performance of the omitted term.

Martin v Pycroft was quoted with approval in *North v Loomes* ([1919] 1 Ch. 378) in which the plaintiff obtained an order for specific performance when he waived a term in the oral agreement which was solely to his benefit but which was omitted from the written memorandum. In *Scott v Bradley* the court was concerned with the omission from a memorandum of a term of an oral agreement which provided that the plaintiff would pay half the defendants' legal costs of the sale. Plowman J. held that this term was in fact a material term of the agreement, but notwithstanding this fact and its absence from the written memorandum of the contract a decree for specific performance was granted, on the plaintiff submitting to be bound by the missing term.

In the present case the term that is missing from the memorandum is one which is to the detriment of the plaintiff. From the memorandum of 6 October 1976 it would seem that the purchase price of the property was £40,000, but in fact the oral agreement provided that the purchase price was to be £46,000. What is missing from the memorandum are terms of the oral agreement which can be paraphrased as follows: 'the purchase price of the property is £46,000; of which £6,000 will be paid forthwith, the parties treating the balance as the purchase price in any written memorandum of the agreement which may be drawn up'. The plaintiff, through his counsel accepts that the purchase price was £46,000 has submitted to be bound by this term, accordingly the plaintiff is entitled to an order for specific performance of the oral agreement.

Estoppel

In certain cases, the doctrine of estoppel may be used to prevent a party relying on non-compliance with the Statute of Frauds where they have previously agreed to accept the adequacy of the memorandum.

Actionstrength Ltd (t/a Vital Resources) v International Glass Engineering Inglen SpA and others [2003] 2 WLR 1060
(See facts on p.248.)

Lord Bingham of Cornhill:

Neither party suggested, nor could it be suggested, that the ordinary rules of estoppel are inapplicable to guarantees. The well-known case of *Amalgamated Investment & Property Co. Ltd (In Liquidation) v Texas Commerce International Bank Ltd* [1982] QB 84 is one in which a party was held to be estopped from disputing the assumed effect of a guarantee. But the same approach should be followed as in other cases. On the facts of this case that involves asking three questions: (1) What is the assumption which Actionstrength made? (2) Did St-Gobain induce or encourage the making of that assumption? (3) Is it in all the circumstances unconscionable for St-Gobain to place reliance on section 4? It would, as Mr Soole QC for St-Gobain submitted, be wrong in principle to ask the third question before both of the first two.

It is implicit in the assumed facts that Actionstrength believed itself to be the beneficiary of an effective guarantee. Its difficulty, in my view insuperable, arises with the second question. For in seeking to show inducement or encouragement Actionstrength can rely on nothing beyond the oral agreement of St-Gobain which, in the absence of writing, is rendered unenforceable by section 4. There was no representation by St-Gobain that it would honour the agreement despite the absence of writing, or that it was not a contract of guarantee, or that it would confirm the agreement in writing. Nor did St-Gobain make any payment direct to Actionstrength which could arguably be relied on as affirming the oral agreement or inducing Actionstrength to go on supplying labour. If St-Gobain were held to be estopped in this case it is hard to see why any oral guarantor, where credit was extended to a debtor on the strength of a guarantee, would not be similarly estopped. The result would be to render nugatory a provision which, despite its age, Parliament has deliberately chosen to retain.

Lord Hoffmann:

Very soon after the statute of 1677, the courts introduced the doctrine of part performance to restrict its application to sales of land. It was held that a contract, initially unenforceable because of the statute, could become enforceable by virtue of acts which the plaintiff did afterwards. The doctrine was justified by a combination to two reasons. The first was a form of estoppel: as Lord Reid said in *Steadman v Steadman* [1976] AC 536, 540:

> If one party to an agreement stands by and lets the other party incur expense or prejudice his position on the faith of the agreement being valid he will not then be allowed to turn round and assert that the agreement is unenforceable.

The second reason was that the acts done by the plaintiff could in themselves prove the existence of the contract in a way which could be an acceptable substitute for the note or memorandum required by the statute. These two reasons did not cover the same ground: acts which satisfied the first might fail to satisfy the second. In Steadman's case the House of Lords gave priority to the first reason and relaxed the need for the acts of part performance to be probative of the contract. It was however still possible to adhere to the reconciliation of the statute and the part performance doctrine which the Earl of Selborne L.C. gave in *Maddison v Alderson* (1883) 8 App. Cas. 467, 475–6:

> In a suit founded on . . . part performance, the defendant is really 'charged' upon the equities resulting from the acts done in execution of the contract, and not (within the meaning of the statute) upon the contract itself . . . The matter has advanced beyond the stage of contract; and the equities which arise out of the stage which it has reached cannot be administered unless the contract is regarded.

The reconciliation thus draws a distinction between the executory contract, not performed on either side, and the effect of subsequent acts of performance by the plaintiff. The former attracted the full force of the statute while the latter could create an equitable rather than purely contractual right to performance. The statute and the doctrine of part performance could co-exist in this way because contracts for the sale of land almost always start by being executory on both sides and usually remain executory until completed by mutual performance.

What Mr McGhee [for Actionstrength] submits in this case is that the estoppel principle which partly underpins the doctrine of part performance is wide enough to be applied to contracts of guarantee. On the facts presently alleged, it is also the case that, in Lord Reid's words, St-Gobain stood by and let Actionstrength prejudice its position, by extending credit to Inglen, on the faith of the guarantee being valid. There is authority for saying that estoppel is a principle of broad, not to say protean, application: see, for example *Taylors Fashions Ltd v Liverpool Victoria Trustees Co. Ltd (Note)* [1982] QB 133. Although he cited no case in any jurisdiction in which estoppel had been applied to avoid the application of the statute to a guarantee, Mr McGhee says that there is no argument of principle against it.

The difficulty which faces this submission is that while the nature of a sale of land is such that the contract and part performance can co-exist in their respective domains, no such co-existence is possible between the statute and the estoppel for which Mr McGhee contends. It is in the nature of a contract of guarantee that the party seeking to enforce it will always have performed first. Unless he has advanced credit or forborne from withdrawing credit, there will be no guaranteed debt for which he can sue. It will always be the case that the creditor will have acted to his prejudice on the faith of the guarantor's promise. To admit an estoppel on these grounds would be to repeal the statute.

Mr McGhee argues that the estoppel need not apply in every case. What makes this case different, he says, is that (a) Actionstrength continued to supply Inglen only because of St-Gobain's encouragement, (b) St-Gobain knew that without such encouragement Actionstrength would not continue to perform its contract with Inglen, (c) St-Gobain stood to suffer loss and delay if Actionstrength did not continue to perform and gave the guarantee to avoid this, and (d) St-Gobain knew that if Actionstrength continued to perform, there was a real prospect that it would suffer substantial loss unless the guarantee was honoured.

In my opinion none of these features are different from those which attend the giving of every guarantee. If a creditor or prospective creditor asks for a guarantee, it is always a reasonable inference that without the guarantee he would not have extended or continued to extend credit. The guarantor may reasonably be expected to know this. It is frequently in the interest of the guarantor to give the guarantee; for example, when it secures the indebtedness of a company he controls, a business associate or even a spouse. And it must be obvious that the creditor may suffer loss if the guarantee is not honoured. No doubt in each case there will be differences in degree, but no distinctions that could be drawn without throwing the law into total confusion.

It is not necessary to consider whether circumstances may arise in which a guarantor may be estopped from relying upon the statute. It is sufficient that in my opinion the estoppel which Actionstrength seeks to rely upon in this case would be inconsistent with the provisions of the statute. I would therefore dismiss the appeal.

(Lord Walker of Gestingthorp, Lord Woolf and Lord Clyde concurred.)

Notes

1. This case suggests that the requirement in the Statute affecting guarantees cannot be subject to estoppel equivalent to that developed in relation to contracts for the sale of land. Estoppel cannot arise from the promise which constitutes the guarantee. Lord Clyde accepted that the defendants' reliance on the Statute was unfair but was reluctant to have recourse to 'the underlying idea of unconscionable conduct in the particular circumstances' in the absence of 'some recognisable structural framework'.

2. In *Kinane v Mackie-Conteh* [2005] EWCA Civ 45, Mr Mackie-Conteh relied on *Actionstrength* stating that estoppel could not be used to effectively validate a contract otherwise invalid under section 2 of the 1989 Act as this would be to defeat the policy of the Act. Arden L.J. in the Court of Appeal noted that in *Actionstrength* there was no equivalent saving for 'constructive trusts' that could come to the aid of the claimant and, second, that while it was true that the mere fact of an invalid agreement could not found an estoppel because this would be to defeat the policy of the 1989 Act, it was important to assess whether the claimant was seeking to rely on the invalid agreement or, rather, the unconscionable conduct of the defendant connected to that agreement. Arden L.J. concluded: '. . . reliance on the unenforceable agreement only takes the claimant part of the way: he must still prove all the other components of proprietary estoppel. In particular, the requirement that the defendant encouraged or permitted the claimant in his erroneous belief is not satisfied simply by the admission of the invalid agreement in evidence. In this sort of case, the claimant has to show that the defendant represented to the claimant, by his words or conduct, including conduct in the provision or delivery of the agreement, that the agreement created an enforceable obligation. The cause of action in proprietary estoppel is thus not founded on the unenforceable agreement but upon the defendant's conduct which, when viewed in all relevant aspects, is unconscionable.' In *Kinane*, the respondent was allowed to rely on a constructive trust. Neuberger L.J. explained '. . . the essential difference between a proprietary estoppel which does not also give rise to a constructive trust, and one that does, is the element of agreement, or least expression of common understanding, exchanged between the parties, as to the existence, or intended existence, of a proprietary interest, in the latter type of case.' See McFarlane, 'Proprietary

Estoppel ad Failed Contractual Negotiations' Conv. (2005) 501–523 for a critical analysis of these cases.

3. In *Black v Grealy* (HC) 10 November 1977, unrep. (facts on p.289), Costello J. noted that:

I should add that the question of an estoppel arising in the circumstances of the present case was not argued before me and so I refrain from basing my decision on this ground. I should, however, point out that there may well be cases (and this could be one of them) where a party, expressly agreeing to accept the adequacy of a memorandum of an oral agreement, is in subsequent proceedings estopped from alleging its inadequacy.

Debate on Reform

Boyle *v* Lee and Goyns [1992] ILRM 65
(Facts on p.94.)

O'Flaherty J.:

The Statute of Frauds was enacted to prevent perjury and subornation of perjury as well as other fraudulent practices. In due course, equity made sure that the invocation of the statute should not be used to bring about fraud and, thus, was developed the doctrine of part performance. However, it seems to me that equity has now done its work and the statute should be looked at again because what it is now necessary to prevent is the burgeoning of actions based on subtleties and niceties to get around the clear wording of the statute. For my part, I would advocate that the statute should be amended so as to provide that all contracts for the sale of land should be in writing. This is because life has not got any less complicated over the intervening centuries; nowadays, as this very case illustrates, there are often planning aspects to a sale; there is finance to be arranged; there is the tax end of matters to be sorted out (in this case there was the question of certain furnishings being part of the sale and no apportionment had been made in relation to them); family law legislation may often have some relevance, and, further, there is the fact that the boundaries of negligence in relation to people involved in the buying and selling of property have been widened over the last number of decades. In these circumstances, I would rather the occasional gazumper go unbound than that people should be involved in needless uncertainty leading often to long drawn out litigation.

I think such a law would accord with the view the average person—not versed in the mysteries of conveyancing law—would take who knows that when he buys a dwelling house or other property in the normal course of events it is necessary to have a proper contract executed to bind both parties.

EXERCISES

1. Polly enters into an agreement to guarantee her sister's debts with the bank. She subsequently tries to avoid the contract on the basis that it does not comply with the Statute of Frauds. The written document comprises an email with an automatic signature at the bottom. She claims that it is not signed for the purposes of the Statute. Advise the bank.

2. Anna agrees to refurbish Fred's house. The parties do not discuss the length of time this will take. Eleven months later, the job is complete apart from painting the shoe closet. Fred delays choosing the paint colour for six weeks. He then claims that as performance took more than twelve months the contract is unenforceable and he refuses to pay. Advise Anna.

3. Frank is approached by Kate with a view to selling his house. Frank agrees a price of €650,000 and a deposit of 15 per cent payable within one month. Frank writes to Kate setting out the terms that they have agreed and he marks the letter 'Subject to Contract'. Kate replies, noting that she is in agreement on all the terms except the deposit which, upon reflection, she considers excessive. Kate's letter is not marked 'Subject to Contract'. Subsequently Frank informs Kate that he does not intend to proceed with the sale. Advise Kate.

4. Should the Irish courts look behind the phrase 'subject to contract' in a memorandum?

5. Rachel agrees to buy a house from Gary for €590,000. Gary allows Rachel take measurements of all the windows and she purchases new curtains for €5,000. As no memorandum exists, Rachel claims that her actions constitute part performance. Is she correct?

6. Compare and contrast the doctrines of part performance and estoppel (Chapter 3).

Chapter Six

Express Terms

INTRODUCTION

It is an essential feature of a contract that the boundaries of the contract be capable of clear delineation. In Chapter 2 we saw that if contractual terms are ambiguous or uncertain the court may be compelled to hold the contract void for uncertainty. A number of contrasting, or indeed contradictory, statements may have been made during negotiations, and it is not unreasonable for a judge to decide that if the parties have troubled themselves to write down their agreement, they intended that document to be their agreement to the exclusion of all else. While this approach retains some vitality, the ultimate consideration is whether the contract gives effect to the intention of the parties, and it is increasingly likely that a contract may be a mixture of verbal promises, standardised clauses and custom-made documents. Indeed, the use of printed conditions is closely scrutinised by the judiciary for unfair contract practices under both the common law and under statutory fiat—see Chapter 8.

In section one of this chapter, the reader is introduced to the methods whereby contractual and non-contractual representations are identified. For representations classified as non-contractual, Chapter 10 explores the broad range of remedies which apply where they are untrue. For representations classified as contractual, Chapters 18 and 19 consider the effects of their breach. These effects will depend in part on the further classification of these contractual terms, and section 2 of this chapter deals with this. The final sections of the chapter set out various rules of construction.

SECTION ONE—DISTINGUISHING TERMS OF A CONTRACT FROM MERE REPRESENTATIONS

It is essential to distinguish a term of a contract, a breach of which will give rise to contractual liability and in particular liability in damages, from a mere representation, which will not.

Oscar Chess Ltd *v* Williams [1957] 1 WLR 370

The defendant agreed to exchange his Morris car with the plaintiff car dealer for a new car. Both parties believed the Morris to be a 1948 model, as evidenced by its registration book. It materialised later that the car was a 1939 model. The plaintiffs sued for damages for breach of a condition or, alternatively, a warranty. At first instance damages were awarded. The defendant appealed.

Denning L.J.:

The effect of such a mistake is this: It does not make the contract a nullity from the beginning, but it does in some circumstances enable the contract to be set aside in equity. If the buyer had come promptly, he might have succeeded in getting the whole transaction set aside in equity on the ground of this mistake: see *Solle v Butcher*;[1] but he did not do so and it is now too late for him to do it; see *Leaf v International Galleries*.[2] His only remedy is in damages, and to recover these he must prove a warranty.

In saying that he must prove a warranty, I use the word 'warranty' in its ordinary English meaning to denote a binding promise. Everyone knows what a man means when he says 'I guarantee it' or 'I warrant it' or 'I give you my word on it.' He means that he binds himself to it. That is the meaning it has borne in English law for 300 years from the leading case of *Chandelor v Lopus*[3] onwards. During the last fifty years, however, some lawyers have come to use the word 'warranty' in another sense. They use it to denote a subsidiary term in a contract as distinct from a vital term which they call a 'condition'. In so doing they depart from the ordinary meaning, not only of the word 'warranty' but also of the word 'condition'. There is no harm in their doing this, so long as they confine this technical use to its proper sphere, namely to distinguish between a vital term, the breach of which gives the right to treat the contract as at an end, and a subsidiary term which does not. But the trouble comes when one person uses the word 'warranty' in its ordinary meaning and another uses it in its technical meaning. When Holt C.J., in *Crosse v Gardner*[4] and *Medina v Stoughton*,[5] made his famous ruling that an affirmation at the time of a sale is a warranty, provided it appears on evidence to be so intended, he used the word 'warranty' in its ordinary English meaning of a binding promise; and when Lord Haldane L.C. and Lord Moulton in 1913 in *Heilbut, Symons & Co. v Buckleton*,[6] adopted his ruling, they used it likewise in its ordinary meaning. These different uses of the word seem to have been the source of confusion in the present case. The judge did not ask himself, 'Was the representation (that it was a 1948 Morris) intended to be a warranty?' He asked himself, 'Was it fundamental to the contract?' He answered it by saying that it was fundamental; and therefore it was a condition and not a warranty. By concentrating on whether it was fundamental, he seems to me to have missed the crucial point in the case which is whether it was a term of the contract at all. The crucial question is: was it a binding promise or only an innocent misrepresentation? The technical distinction between a 'condition' and a 'warranty' is quite immaterial in this case, because it is far too late for the buyer to reject the car. He can at best only claim damages. The material distinction here is between a statement which is a term of the contract and a statement which is only an innocent misrepresentation. This distinction is best expressed by the ruling of Lord Holt: Was it intended as a warranty or not? using the word warranty there in its ordinary English meaning: because it gives the exact shade of meaning that is required. It is something to which a man must be taken to bind himself.

In applying Lord Holt's test, however, some misunderstanding has arisen by the use of the word 'intended'. It is sometimes supposed that the tribunal must look into the minds of the parties to see what they themselves intended. That is a mistake. Lord Moulton made it quite clear that 'The intention of the parties can only be deduced from the totality of the evidence.' The question whether a warranty was intended depends on the conduct of the parties, on their words and behaviour, rather than on their thoughts. If an intelligent bystander would reasonably infer that a warranty was intended, that will suffice. And this, when the facts are not in dispute, is a question of law. . . .

What is the proper inference from the known facts? It must have been obvious to both that the seller had himself no personal knowledge of the year when the car was made. He only became owner after a great number of changes. He must have been relying on the registration book. It is unlikely that such a person would warrant the year of manufacture. The most he would do would be to state his belief, and then produce the registration book in verification of it. In these circumstances the intelligent bystander would, I suggest, say that the seller did not intend to bind himself so as to warrant that it was a 1948 model. If the seller was asked to pledge himself to it, he would at once have said 'I cannot do that. I have only the log book to go by, the same as you.'. . .

One final word: It seems to me clear that the motor dealers who bought the car relied on the year stated in the log book. If they had wished to make sure of it, they could have checked it then and there, by taking the engine number and chassis number and writing to the makers. They did not do so at the time, but only eight months later. They are experts, and, not having made that check at the time, I do not think they should now be allowed to recover against the innocent seller who produced to them all the evidence he had, namely, the registration book. I agree that it is hard on the dealers to have paid more than the car is worth; but it would be equally hard on the seller to make him pay the difference. . . .

1. [1950] 1 KB 671; 66 TLR (Pt. 1) 448; [1949] 2 All ER 1107.
2. [1950] 2 KB 86; 66 TLR (Pt 1) 1031; [1950] 1 All ER 693.
3. (1603) Cro. Jac. 4.
4. (1689) Carth. 90, as glossed by Buller J. in *Pasley v Freeman* (1789) 3 Term Rep. 51, 57.
5. (1699) 1 Salk. 210.
6. [1913] AC 30, 38, 50, 51.

(Hodson L.J. concurred.)

Note

In *Dick Bentley Productions Ltd v Harold Smith (Motors) Ltd* [1965] 1 WLR the *Oscar Chess* case was distinguished. There, a dealer sold a car to a private individual and the Court of Appeal held that a statement by the dealer as to the mileage of the car constituted a warranty binding on the seller. Denning L.J. stated that the dealer was in a better position than the other party to verify the truth of the statement. Both cases were considered in the following case.

The Governor and Company of the Bank of Ireland *v* Smith [1966] IR 646

An advertisement of land for sale erroneously stated that a portion of the lands was sown with barley and undersown with permanent pasture. This statement was made honestly but mistakenly by the vendor's agents. The purchaser discovered the mistake, and sued for damages for breach of a warranty.

Kenny J.:

The next argument was that the statement in the advertisement about the under-sowing of the barley was a warranty and not an innocent misrepresentation. Counsel for the defendants said that the statement was not a warranty and that the matter was concluded by the speech of Lord Moulton in *Heilbut, Symons & Co. v Buckleton*.[1] Lord Moulton, who quoted the much praised remark of Holt C.J., 'An affirmation at the time of the sale is a warranty, provided it appear on evidence to be so intended' (a statement which contains at least two ambiguities), went on to say:

> It is . . . of the greatest importance, in my opinion, that this House should maintain in its full integrity the principle that a person is not liable in damages for an innocent misrepresentation, no matter in what way or under what form the attack is made. In the present case the statement was made in answer to an inquiry for information. There is nothing which can by any possibility be taken as evidence of an intention on the part of either or both of the parties that there should be a contractual liability in respect of the accuracy of the statement. It is a representation as to a specific thing and nothing more. The judge, therefore, ought not to have left the question of warranty to the jury, and if, as a matter of prudence, he did so in order to obtain their opinion in case of an appeal, he ought then to have entered judgment for the defendants notwithstanding the verdict.

In an earlier part of his speech he had said:

> It is evident, both on principle and on authority, that there may be a contract the consideration for which is the making of some other contract. 'If you will make such and such a contract I will give you £100,' is in every sense of the word a complete legal contract. It is collateral to the main contract, but each has an independent existence, and they do not differ in respect of their possessing to the full the character and status of a contract. But such collateral contracts must from their very nature be rare. . . . Such collateral contracts, the sole effect of which is to vary or add to the terms of the principal contract, are therefore viewed with suspicion by the law.

See also the decision in *Gilchester Properties v Gomm*,[2] in which an innocent misrepresentation made in connection with a sale was held not to be a warranty and not to entitle the purchaser to damages.

The modern cases, however, show a welcome tendency to treat a representation made in connection with a sale as being a warranty, unless the person who made it can show that he was innocent of fault in connection with it. The rule that an innocent misrepresentation causing loss does not entitle a person to recover damages for its falsity produces injustice in many cases. In *Oscar Chess Ltd v Williams*,[3] Denning L.J., having referred to the famous ruling of Holt C.J., said: 'The question whether a warranty was intended depends on the conduct of the parties, on their words and behaviour rather than on their thoughts. If an intelligent bystander would reasonably infer that a warranty was intended, that will suffice,' and in *Dick Bentley Productions Ltd v Smith (Motors) Ltd*[4] the same judge said:

> It seems to me that if a representation is made in the course of dealings for a contract for the very purpose of inducing the other party to act on it, and it actually induces him to act on it by entering into the contract, that is *prima facie* ground for inferring that the representation was intended as a warranty. It is not necessary to speak of it as being collateral. Suffice it that the representation was intended to be

acted upon and was in fact acted on. But the maker of the representation can rebut this inference if he can show that it really was an innocent misrepresentation, in that he was in fact innocent of fault in making it, and that it would not be reasonable in the circumstances for him to be bound by it.

I have not had the advantage of hearing counsel on these two cases but I believe that they express the true rule.

The statement in the advertisement was a representation and was made with the intention of inducing a purchaser to act on it: the purchaser was induced to enter into the contract by it. The representation was incorrect, but was made innocently and honestly. . . . it would be against conscience that the vendor in a court sale should not be bound by a representation made by his agent in connection with that sale.

It follows, in my opinion, that the purchaser is entitled to recover damages for breach of warranty relating to the undersowing of 40 acres.

[1] [1913] AC 30.
[2] [1948] 1 All ER 493.
[3] [1957] 1 All ER 325.
[4] [1965] 2 All ER 65.

Note

In *Schawel v Reade* (1) [1913] 2 IR 64 the House of Lords held that a statement to a prospective purchaser: 'You need not look at anything; the horse is perfectly sound. If there was anything the matter with the horse I would tell you' was an express warranty made for the purposes of the sale.

Consider:

Why does the principle of *caveat emptor* not apply to these cases?

Inntrepreneur Pub Co. v East Crown Ltd [2002] 2 Lloyd's 611

Lightman J.:

It is unnecessary . . . to decide whether the alleged collateral warranty was ever given. Indeed it is, as I have said, the whole purpose of the entire agreement clause that this further exercise should not have to be undertaken. But, as this is a test case, I have decided that I should consider this question.

The relevant legal principles regarding the recognition of pre-contractual promises or assurances as collateral warranties may be stated as follows:

(1) a pre-contractual statement will only be treated as having contractual effect if the evidence shows that parties intended this to be the case. Intention is a question of fact to be decided by looking at the totality of the evidence;

(2) the test is the ordinary objective test for the formation of a contract: what is relevant is not the subjective thought of one party but what a reasonable outside observer would infer from all the circumstances;

(3) in deciding the question of intention, one important consideration will be whether the statement is followed by further negotiations and a written contract not containing any term corresponding to the statement. In such a case, it will be harder to infer that the statement was intended to have contractual effect because

the *prima facie* assumption will be that the written contract includes all the terms the parties wanted to be binding between them;

(4) a further important factor will be the lapse of time between the statement and the making of the formal contract. The longer the interval, the greater the presumption must be that the parties did not intend the statement to have contractual effect in relation to a subsequent deal;

(5) a representation of fact is much more likely intended to have contractual effect than a statement of future fact or a future forecast.

Crown challenged (3) and (4) above relying on a dictum of Lord Denning, M.R. in J. *Evans & Son (Portsmouth) v Andrea Merzario Ltd* [1976] 2 Lloyd's Rep., 165 at p. 168 . . . to this effect: 'When a person gives a promise or assurance to another, intending that he should act on it by entering into a contract, and he does act on it by entering into the contract, we hold that it is binding.' It may be noted that Lord Denning M.R. cited in support of this proposition his judgment in *Dick Bentley Productions Ltd. v Harold Smith (Motors) Ltd*, [1965] 1 WLR 623, where (at p. 627) he was more guarded in his language: 'it seems to me that if a representation is made in the course of dealings for a contract for the very purpose of inducing the other party to act upon it, and actually inducing him to act upon it, by entering into the contract, that is *prima facie* ground for inferring that it was intended as a warranty.' Whether the inference should be made depends on all the facts of the case. The task in all cases is to consider the representation or assurance in the context of the totality of the facts, and the question to be addressed is whether reliance on the inducement afforded by the representation or promise should be understood as intended to continue and extend to the contract subsequently concluded. For this purpose factors referred to in propositions (3) and (4) are of critical importance.

Note

The test set out in the *Inntrepreneur* case was applied in *Business Environment Bow Lane Ltd v Deanwater Estates Ltd* [2007] L&TR 26 by the Court of Appeal. Three of the five propositions set out above indicated that no collateral contract existed. In that case, although the landlord had given the tenant, during the course of negotiations for a new lease, an assurance in writing that it would not serve a terminal schedule of dilapidations, this assurance was followed by further negotiations and a subsequent amendment to the lease. Taken as a whole, the correspondence did not show objectively the existence of a collateral contract at the date of execution of the new lease, preventing the landlord from relying on the terms of the new lease.

Carey *v* Independent Newspapers (Ireland) Ltd (2005) 15 ELR 45

The plaintiff was headhunted by Mr Drury, the editor of the *Evening Herald*, and recruited as political correspondent of the newspaper, leaving a secure post to take up this appointment. As the plaintiff's domestic obligations made it impossible to attend the *Herald* offices before 9.30am, it was agreed that her duties would be discharged at those times by working at home. Shortly after the plaintiff's contract of employment had commenced, a new editor was appointed who insisted that the plaintiff attend editorial meetings before 9.30am. When the plaintiff refused, her employment was terminated summarily. The plaintiff sought (1) damages for breach of contract and/or wrongful dismissal, (2) general damages for negligent misstatement/representation. The defendants disputed that a warranty or misrepresentation of any kind had been given in relation to the plaintiff's starting time.

Gilligan J.:

Not every statement or representation of fact made by parties in pre-contractual negotiations will form part of any concluded contract: such statements may be in the interests of extracting the best possible bargain from the give and take nature of negotiations. Further, any potential for contractual effect such statements may have could be negated by the express intentions of the parties. However, there is a tension between such situations and situations where (for one party at least) the contractual incorporation of a matter ventilated in negotiations may be of fundamental importance: circumstances could leave a question mark hovering over whether such matters were in fact mutually understood as having contractual effect. Given the need to define the boundaries of any contractual arrangement, the common law has drawn a distinction between representations having no contractual effect and those having such contractual effect: the textbooks classify the former as 'mere representations' and the latter as 'warranties' (for example, see McDermott, *Contract Law*, p. 269). Broadly, 'warranty' means a term having contractual effect: more narrowly, it denotes a contractual term any breach of which will give rise to an entitlement to damages.

The manner in which the courts will approach the question of whether a representation constitutes a warranty or a matter having no contractual effect is outlined in *Scales v Scanlan* (1843) 6 ILRCL 423 by Lefroy B. at p. 457 of the report:

> To make a warranty it is not necessary that the word 'warrant' or 'warranty' should be used. There was a time in law when it was otherwise . . . but it has long since been well settled, that words of affirmation, affirming a matter of fact, on the faith of which the party contracts, are as competent to make a warranty as any strict technical term.

[Gilligan J. then referred to the extract of Denning M.R.'s judgment in the *Dick Bentley Productions Ltd* case quoted in the *Smith* case above.]

This statement of principle was approved and applied in the employment context by the Queen's Bench Division of Northern Ireland in *Gill v Cape Contracts Ltd* [1985] ILR 49. In that case, the defendant company required around forty insulation engineers to complete a contract in the Shetland Islands. The defendant company contacted their representatives in Northern Ireland who passed word among the insulation engineers employed by Harland and Wolff (which included the plaintiffs). The plaintiffs, who were married men in the main, were informed that they would receive a much higher wage than they were earning at Harland and Wolff to compensate for the difficult conditions working in the Shetlands would entail. They were told that the job would last for at least six months: as a result of the assurances they received, the plaintiffs applied for employment with the defendants. When the plaintiffs were informed that they were acceptable, they gave notice to Harland. Wolff which, irked at losing workers in this way, told the plaintiffs that they would not be employed there again. The opportunity in the Shetlands fell through due to industrial relations problems and the plaintiffs sued for damages. O'Donnell L.J. held that the plaintiffs were entitled to damages for breach of a warranty by the defendants as the defendants failed to honour a representation to the plaintiffs forming a collateral contract that if they gave up their existing employment, they would be employed by the defendant company in the Shetlands for approximately six months at wages considerably in excess of their existing earnings. The court again affirmed the basic principle that if a representation is made in the knowledge and intention that the representee will act on it, it constitutes a warranty. In *Gill*, the court characterised the representations made by the defendants as representations which the defendant intended the plaintiff to act upon and upon which the plaintiffs did act. With regard to the role of the representations in the plaintiffs' decision to switch their employment from Harland and Wolff to the defendant, the court remarked at p. 51:

> The plaintiffs were in the main married men, in steady employment. To give up such employment on the mere expectation of obtaining employment at Sullum Voe, albeit with vastly increased wages, would have been foolhardy in the extreme. Both parties were aware of this and it appears to me that negotiations never proceeded on this basis. I do not believe that the plaintiffs would have terminated their employment with Messrs Harland & Wolff, had they been offered no more than a reasonable expectation of obtaining employment.

Accordingly, the court awarded damages for loss of bargain. . . .

I take the view that the agreement as regards the morning working conditions was a fundamental term of the agreement reached between Mr Drury and the plaintiff and that it constituted a warranty and an inducement to the plaintiff to give up her contractual arrangement with *Ireland on Sunday*. Furthermore, I am satisfied that the plaintiff left her job with *Ireland on Sunday* to join the *Evening Herald* as a result of the representation made by Mr Drury that the plaintiff could work from home for the first edition of the *Evening Herald*. I am also satisfied on the evidence as a matter of probability that without the assurance on the morning working arrangements, the plaintiff would not have taken up employment with the defendants. I fully accept that due to unforeseen circumstances, namely the departure of Mr Drury as editor of the *Evening Herald*, the agreed working conditions were immediately in jeopardy, leading to the termination of the plaintiff's employment on April 17, 2000. I take the view that no blame attaches in this regard to the plaintiff and in any event there does not appear to me to have been any way open to the plaintiff to check on the accuracy of the representation which was made to her by Mr Drury and she simply trusted him and relied on what he said. Accordingly, I come to the conclusion that the plaintiff is entitled to damages for breach of warranty as against the defendants.

[Damages were also awarded for negligent misrepresentation. See p. 1035]

Entire Contract Clauses

In the course of negotiations to complete a contract, representations and assurances may be made by one party in order to encourage the other party to reach an agreement. As is clear from the above cases, such representations may take effect as one of the terms of the concluded contract and be enforceable as a 'collateral warranty'. In order to avoid a representation becoming legally binding, the representor may seek to include a clause in the concluded contract emphasising that the written agreement constituted 'the whole agreement and understanding between the parties with respect to all matters therein referred to'. Such a clause constitutes a binding agreement between the parties that the full contractual terms are to be found in the document containing the clause and not elsewhere. This means that any promises or assurances made in the course of the negotiations, which but for the clause might have had effect as a collateral warranty, will have no effect, save to the extent they are reflected and given effect in the document. These clauses are referred to as 'entire contract clauses' or 'whole agreement clauses'.

Inntrepreneur Pub Co. v East Crown Ltd [2002] 2 Lloyd's 611

Inntrepreneur leased a public house to East Crown on the foot of a 1996 lease which obliged East Crown to purchase a range of specified beers from Inntrepreneur. East Crown took supplies of beer from other brewers, in breach of the covenant. In an action to enforce the covenant, East Crown asserted that they had been given a collateral warranty, verbally communicated by Inntrepreneur to Hickey, a director of East Crown, that the tie would not be enforced after 28 March 1988. Inntrepreneur denied that any such warranty had been given, referring also to clause 14 of the 1996 lease, known to contact draftspersons as an entire agreement clause. Clause 14.1 provided.

> Any variations of this agreement which are agreed in correspondence shall be incorporated in this agreement where that correspondence makes express reference to this clause and the parties acknowledge that this agreement (with the incorporation of any such variations) constitutes the entire agreement between the parties.

Lightman J.:

The purpose of an entire agreement clause is to preclude a party to a written agreement from threshing through the undergrowth and finding in the course of negotiations some (chance) remark or statement (often long forgotten or difficult to recall or explain) on which to found a claim such as the present to the existence of a collateral warranty. The entire agreement clause obviates the occasion for any such search and the peril to the contracting parties posed by the need which may arise in its absence to conduct such a search. For such a clause constitutes a binding agreement between the parties that the full contractual terms are to be found in the document containing the clause and not elsewhere, and that accordingly any promises or assurances made in the course of the negotiations (which in the absence of such a clause might have effect as a collateral warranty) shall have no contractual force, save insofar as they are reflected and given effect in that document. The operation of the clause is not to render evidence of the collateral warranty inadmissible in evidence as is suggested in *Chitty on Contract*, 28th edn, vol. 1, paras. 12–102: it is to denude what would otherwise constitute a collateral warranty of legal effect.

Entire agreement clauses come in different forms. In the leading case of *Deepak v Imperial Chemical Industries plc*, [1998] Lloyd's Rep. 139, affirmed [1999] 1 Lloyd's Rep. 387, the clause read as follows:

10.16 Entirety of Agreement
This contract comprises the entire agreement between the PARTIES . . . and there are not any agreements, understandings, promises or conditions, oral or written, express or implied, concerning the subject matter which are not merged into this CONTRACT and superseded thereby . . .

Mr Justice Rix and the Court of Appeal held in that case (in particular focusing on the words 'promises or conditions') that this language was apt to exclude all liability for a collateral warranty. In *Alman & Benson v Associated Newspapers Group Ltd*, 20 June 1980 (cited by Mr Justice Rix at p. 168), Mr Justice Browne-Wilkinson reached the same conclusion where the clause provided that the written contract 'constituted the entire agreement and understanding between the parties with respect to all matters therein referred to' focusing on the word 'understanding'. In neither case was it necessary to decide whether the clause would have been sufficient if it had been worded merely to state that the agreement containing it comprised or constituted the entire agreement between the parties. That is the question raised in this case, where the formula of words used in the clause is abbreviated to an acknowledgement by the parties that the agreement constitutes the entire agreement between them. In my judgment that formula is sufficient, for it constitutes an agreement that the full contractual terms to which the parties agree to bind themselves are to be found in the agreement and nowhere else and that what might otherwise constitute a side agreement or collateral warranty shall be void of legal effect. That can be the only purpose of the provision. This view is entirely in accord with the judgment of Mr John Chadwick, QC (as he then was) sitting as a deputy High Court Judge in *McGrath v Shah* (1987) P & CR 452.

An entire agreement provision does not preclude a claim in misrepresentation, for the denial of contractual force to a statement cannot affect the status of the statement as a misrepresentation. The same clause in an agreement may contain both an entire agreement provision and a further provision designed to exclude liability, e.g. for misrepresentation or breach of duty. As an example, cl. 14 in this case, after setting out in cl.14.1 the entire agreement clause, in cl.14.2 sets out to exclude liability for misrepresentation and breach of duty. Whether this latter provision is legally effective for this purpose may turn on the question of its reasonableness as required by s. 3 of the Misrepresentation Act, 1967: see e.g. *Inntrepreneur Estates* (CPC) *v Worth*, [1996] 1 EGLR 84. But (contrary to the contentions of Crown) s. 3 has no application to an entire agreement clause provision defining where the contractual terms between the parties are to be found: see *McGrath v Shah*. It seems to me therefore that cl. 14.1 of the agreement provides in law a complete answer to any claim by Crown based on the alleged collateral warranty.

Note

In *Ravennavi SpA v New Century Shipbuilding Co Ltd* [2006] 2 Lloyd's Rep. 280, the High Court applied the principle in *Inntrepreneur* to determine that an entire agreement clause, when read together with the express provisions relating to delivery and payment dates in a shipbuilding contract, had the effect of replacing the provisions of the option agreement or depriving them of legal effect.

Consider:

Would an entire agreement clause prevent a party taking an action for fraudulent misrepresentation?

SECTION TWO—CATEGORIES OF TERMS

A. CONDITIONS, WARRANTIES AND INNOMINATE TERMS

Prior to 1962 only two categories of terms were identified: conditions and warranties. A Condition is a major term of a contract regarded by the parties as essential. Any breach of this term allows the innocent party not only to sue for damages but to terminate the contract. By contrast a Warranty is a term of the contract regarded by the parties as a minor term, i.e. ancillary to the main thrust of the contract. A breach allows the innocent party to claim only damages. These common-law definitions are mirrored in the statutory definitions. Thus section 11(2) of the Sale of Goods Act 1893 (as amended by the Sale of Goods and Supply of Services Act 1980) states:

Whether a stipulation in a contract of sale is a condition, the breach of which may give rise to a right to treat the contract as repudiated, or a warranty, the breach of which may give rise to a claim for damages but not to a right to reject the goods and treat the contract as repudiated, depends in each case on the construction of the contract. A stipulation may be a condition though called a warranty in the contract.

Section 62 of the Sale of Goods Act 1893 defines a warranty for the purposes of the Act as:

an agreement with reference to goods which are the subject of a contract of sale, but collateral to the main purpose of such contract, the breach of which gives rise to a claim for damages, but not to a right to reject the goods and treat the contract as repudiated.

In distinguishing between the two categories of term, Bowen L.J.'s judgment in *Bentsen v Taylor* [1893] 2 QB 274 is useful. At p. 281, he opined:

There is no way of deciding that question except by looking at the contract in the light of the surrounding circumstances, and then making up one's mind whether the intention of the parties, as gathered from the instrument itself, will best be carried out by treating the promise as a warranty sounding only in damages, or as a condition precedent by the failure to perform which the other party is relieved of his liability.

However, since the decision of the Court of Appeal in the Hong Kong Fir Shipping case below, a further category of term was identified which could not immediately be classified as either a condition or a warranty. The effect of breaching one of these 'innominate terms' would only become apparent when the breach actually occurred.

Hong Kong Fir Shipping Co. Ltd *v* Kawasaki Kisen Kaisha Ltd [1962] 2 QB 26

Charterers hired a ship for a period of twenty-four months ' . . . she being in every way fitted for ordinary cargo service . . . ' A clause in the charterparty provided that the ship's owners should ' . . . maintain her in a thoroughly efficient state in hull and machinery during service . . .'. The ship was delivered on 13 February 1957 and sailed on that day from Liverpool to Virginia to collect cargo and carry it to Osaka, Japan. Because the ship was twenty-six years old, she required careful handling by competent and adequate staff. As the chief engineer was inefficient and the number of engine room staff insufficient, the ship broke down on numerous occasions throughout the journey. By the time the ship reached Japan on 25 May she had been off hire for about five weeks and had incurred repair expenses of £21,400. A further period of about fifteen weeks and expenses of £37,500 were then required to make her seaworthy. In June the charterers repudiated the charterparty. They sued for damages for wrongful repudiation, claiming *inter alia* that the owners had broken their obligation to deliver a seaworthy vessel. At first instance, Salmon J. held that although the owners were in breach of their duty to supply a seaworthy vessel, seaworthiness was not a condition precedent to their rights and thus the owners were entitled to damages. The charterers appealed.

Upjohn L.J.:

Why is this apparently basic and underlying condition of seaworthiness not, in fact, treated as a condition? It is for the simple reason that the seaworthiness clause is breached by the slightest failure to be fitted 'in every way' for service. Thus, to take examples from the judgments in some of the cases I have mentioned if a nail is missing from one of the timbers of a wooden vessel or if proper medical supplies or two anchors are not on board at the time of sailing, the owners are in breach of the seaworthiness stipulation. It is contrary to common sense to suppose that in such circumstances the parties contemplated that the charterer should at once be entitled to treat the contract as at an end for such trifling breaches. . . .

It is open to the parties to a contract to make it clear either expressly or by necessary implication that a particular stipulation is to be regarded as a condition which goes to the root of the contract, so that it is clear that the parties contemplate that any breach of it entitles the other party at once to treat the contract as at an end. That matter has to be determined as a question of the proper interpretation of the contract. Bramwell B. in *Tarrabochia v Hickie*[1] has warned against the dangers of too ready an implication of such a condition. He said . . . 'No doubt it is competent for the parties, if they think fit, to declare in express terms that any matter shall be a condition precedent, but when they have not so expressed themselves, it is necessary for those who construe the instrument to see whether they intended to do it. Since, however, they could have done it, those who construe the instrument should be chary in doing for them that which they might, but have not done for themselves.' Where, however, upon the true construction of the contract, the parties have not made a particular stipulation a condition, it would in my judgment be unsound and misleading to conclude that, being a warranty, damages is necessarily a sufficient remedy.

In my judgment the remedies open to the innocent party for breach of a stipulation which is not a condition strictly so called, depend entirely upon the nature of the breach and its foreseeable consequences. Breaches of stipulation fall, naturally, into two classes. First there is the case where the owner by his conduct indicates that he considers himself no longer bound to perform his part of the contract; in that case, of course, the charterer may accept the repudiation and treat the contract as at an end. The second class of case is, of course, the more usual one and that is where, due to misfortune such as the perils of the sea, engine failures, incompetence of the crew and so on, the owner is unable to perform a particular stipulation precisely in accordance with the terms of the contract try he never so hard to remedy it. In that case the question to be answered is, does the breach of the stipulation go so much to the root of the contract that it makes further commercial performance of the contract impossible, or in other words is the whole contract frustrated? If yea, the innocent party may treat the contract as at an end. If nay, his claim sounds in damages only.

If I have correctly stated the principles, then as the stipulation as to the seaworthiness is not a condition in the strict sense the question to be answered is, did the initial unseaworthiness as found by the judge, and from which there has been no appeal, go so much to the root of the contract that the charterers were then and there entitled to treat the charterparty as at an end. The only unseaworthiness alleged, serious though it was, was the insufficiency and incompetence of the crew, but that surely cannot be treated as going to the root of the contract for the parties must have contemplated that in such an event the crew could be changed and augmented. In my judgment on this part of his case [counsel for the charterers] necessarily fails.

Diplock L.J.:

Every synallagmatic contract contains in it the seeds of the problem: in what event will a party be relieved of his undertaking to do that which he has agreed to do but has not yet done? The contract may itself expressly define some of these events, as in the cancellation clause in a charterparty; but, human prescience being limited, it seldom does so exhaustively and often fails to do so at all. In some classes of contracts such as sale of goods, marine insurance, contracts of affreightment evidenced by bills of lading and those between parties to bills of exchange, Parliament has defined by statute some of the events not provided for expressly in individual contracts of that class; but where an event occurs the occurrence of which neither the parties nor Parliament have expressly stated will discharge one of the parties from further performance of his undertakings, it is for the court to determine whether the event has this effect or not.

The test whether an event has this effect or not has been stated in a number of metaphors all of which I think amount to the same thing: does the occurrence of the event deprive the party who has further undertakings still to perform of substantially the whole benefit which it was the intention of the parties as expressed in the contract that he should obtain as the consideration for performing those undertakings?

This test is applicable whether or not the event occurs as a result of the default of one of the parties to the contract, but the consequences of the event are different in the two cases. Where the event occurs as a result of the default of one party, the party in default cannot rely upon it as relieving himself of the performance of any further undertakings on his part, and the innocent party, although entitled to, need not treat the event as relieving him of the further performance of his own undertakings. This is only a specific application of the fundamental legal and moral rule that a man should not be allowed to take advantage of his own wrong. Where the event occurs as a result of the default of neither party, each is relieved of the further performance of his own undertakings. . . .

It was early recognised that contractual undertakings were of two different kinds: those collateral to the main purpose of the parties as expressed in the contract and those which were mutually dependent so that the non-performance by one party of an undertaking of this class was an event which excused the other party from the performance of his corresponding undertaking. . . .

The fact that the emphasis in the earlier cases was upon the breach by one party to the contract of his contractual undertakings, for this was the commonest circumstance in which the question arose, tended to obscure the fact that it was really the event resulting from the breach which relieved the other party of further performance of his obligations. . . .

Once it is appreciated that it is the event and not the fact that the event is a result of a breach of contract which relieves the party not in default of further performance of his obligations, two consequences follow. (1) The test whether the event relied upon has this consequence is the same whether the event is the result of the other party's breach of contract or not, as Devlin J. pointed out in *Universal Cargo Carriers Corp. v Citati*.[2] (2) The question whether an event which is the result of the other party's breach of contract has this consequence cannot be answered by treating all contractual undertakings as falling into one of two separate categories: 'conditions' the breach of which gives rise to an event which relieves the party not in default of further performance of his obligations, and 'warranties' the breach of which does not give rise to such an event.

Lawyers tend to speak of this classification as if it were comprehensive, partly for the historical reasons which I have already mentioned and partly because Parliament itself adopted it in the Sale of Goods Act, 1893, as respects a number of implied terms in contracts for the sale of goods and has in that Act used the expressions 'condition' and 'warranty' in that meaning. But it is by no means true of contractual undertakings in general at common law.

No doubt there are many simple contractual undertakings, sometimes express but more often because of their very simplicity ('It goes without saying') to be implied, of which it can be predicated that every breach of such an undertaking must give rise to an event which will deprive the party not in default of substantially the whole benefit which it was intended that he should obtain from the contract. And such a stipulation, unless the parties have agreed that breach of it shall not entitle the non-defaulting party to treat the contract as repudiated, is a 'condition'. So too there may be other simple contractual undertakings of which it can be predicated that *no* breach can give rise to an event which will deprive the party not in default of substantially the whole benefit which it was intended that he should obtain from the contract; and such a stipulation, unless the parties have agreed that breach of it shall entitle the non-defaulting party to treat the contract as repudiated, is a 'warranty'.

There are, however, many contractual undertakings of a more complex character which cannot be categorised as being 'conditions' or 'warranties', if the late nineteenth century meaning adopted in the Sale of Goods Act, 1893, and used by Bowen L.J. in *Bentsen v Taylor, Sons & Co.*[3] be given to those terms. Of such undertakings all that can be predicated is that some breaches will and others will not give rise to an event which will deprive the party not in default of substantially the whole benefit which it was intended that he should obtain from the contract; and the legal consequences of a breach of such an undertaking, unless provided for expressly in the contract, depend upon the nature of the event to which the breach gives rise and do not follow automatically from a prior classification of the undertaking as a 'condition' or a 'warranty'. For instance, to take Bramwell B.'s example in *Jackson v Union Marine Insurance Co. Ltd*[4] itself, breach of an undertaking by a shipowner to sail with all possible dispatch to a named port does not necessarily relieve the charterer of further performance of his obligation under the charterparty, but if the breach is so prolonged that the contemplated voyage is frustrated it does have this effect. . . .

As my brethren have already pointed out, the shipowners' undertaking to tender a seaworthy ship has, as a result of numerous decisions as to what can amount to 'unseaworthiness', become one of the most complex of contractual undertakings. It embraces obligations with respect to every part of the hull and machinery, stores and equipment and the crew itself. It can be broken by the presence of trivial defects easily and rapidly remediable as well as by defects which must inevitably result in a total loss of the vessel.

Consequently the problem in this case is, in my view, neither solved nor soluble by debating whether the shipowner's express or implied undertaking to tender a seaworthy ship is a 'condition' or a 'warranty'. It is like so many other contractual terms, an undertaking one breach of which may give rise to an event which relieves the charterer of further performance of his undertakings if he so elects and another breach of which may not give rise to such an event but entitle him only to monetary compensation in the form of damages.

. . .

What the judge had to do in the present case, as in any other case where one party to a contract relies upon a breach by the other party as giving him a right to elect to rescind the contract, and the contract itself makes no express provision as to this, was to look at the events which had occurred as a result of the breach at the time at which the charterers purported to rescind the charterparty and to decide whether the occurrence of those events deprived the charterers of substantially the whole benefit which it was the intention of the parties as expressed in the charterparty that the charterers should obtain from the further performance of their own contractual undertakings. . . .

The question which the judge had to ask himself was, as he rightly decided, whether or not at the date when the charterers purported to rescind the contract, namely, 6 June 1957, or when the shipowners purported to accept such rescission, namely, 8 August 1957, the delay which had already occurred as a result of the incompetence of the engine-room staff, and the delay which was likely to occur in repairing the engines of the vessel and the conduct of the shipowners by that date in taking steps to remedy these two matters, were, when taken together, such as to deprive the charterers of substantially the whole benefit which it was the intention of the parties they should obtain from further use of the vessel under the charterparty.

In my view, in his judgment—on which I would not seek to improve—the judge took into account and gave due weight to all the relevant considerations and arrived at the right answer for the right reasons.

1. 1 H. & N. 183.   3. [1893] 2 QB 274, 280, 9 TLR 552, CA.
2. [1957] 2 QB 401, 434.   4. LR 10 CP 125, 142.

(Sellers L.J. held that the maintenance clause was merely a warranty.)

Consider:

Compare and contrast the approach of Diplock L.J. and Upjohn L.J. to the problem. How many categories of term does each allow for?

Note

In *Cehave NV v Bremer Handelsgesellschaft mbH, The Hansa Nord* [1975] 3 All ER 739 the Court of Appeal applied the *Hongkong Fir Shipping* case. In that case it was Upjohn L.J.'s approach rather than Diplock L.J.'s approach which was followed.

As the next case demonstrates, the classification of a term as a condition, warranty or innominate term involves the Court in a delicate interpretative exercise.

BS&N Ltd (BVI) *v* Micado Shipping Ltd (Malta) (The Seaflower) (No. 1) [2001] 1 Lloyd's Rep. 341

Clause 46 of a charterparty required the owners to guarantee to obtain approval of the vessel by an oil company, Exxon, within sixty days. This was in addition to the approval of forty other companies, which had already been obtained. Clause 46 read as follows:

If for any reason, during the time-charter period. Owners would loose (sic) even one of such acceptances they must advise charterers at once and they must reinstate same within 30 (thirty) days from such occurance (sic) failing which charterers will be at liberty to cancel charterparty or to maintain same at reduced rate as stipulated above. Hire rate will be reinstated once Owners will show written evidence of approvals from Major Oil Companies.

The charterers argued that this term was a condition of the charterparty, breach of which amounted to repudiatory conduct. The owners argued that it was an intermediate term and the charterers' sole remedy for breach was by way of damages unless the consequences of the breach were such as to justify an entitlement to terminate the charterparty. The High Court accepted the owner's classification and the charterers appealed.

Waller L.J.:

There was cited to us *Bunge Corporation v Tradax Export SA* [1981] 2 Lloyd's Rep 1. [Counsel for the charterers] relied on the passage in the speech of Lord Wilberforce at pp. 5–6 and in particular the passage where Lord Wilberforce said:

It remains true, as Lord Roskill has pointed out in *Cehave* NV *v Bremer Handelsgesellschaft m.b.*H. [1975] 2 Lloyd's Rep. 445; [1976] 1 QB 44, that the Courts should not be too ready to interpret contractual clauses as conditions. And I have myself commended, and continue to commend, the greater flexibility in the law of contracts to which *Hong Kong Fir* points the way (*Reardon Smith Line Ltd v Hansen-Tangen*, [1976] 2 Lloyd's Rep 621; [1976] 1 WLR 989 at pp. 627 and 998). But I do not doubt that, in suitable cases, the Courts should not be reluctant, if the intentions of the parties as shown by the contract so indicate, to hold that an obligation has the force of a condition, and that indeed they should usually do so in the case of time clauses in mercantile contracts. To such cases the 'gravity of the breach' approach of *Hong Kong Fir* would be unsuitable. I need only add on this point that the word 'expressly' used by Lord Justice Diplock at pp. 494 and 70 of his judgment in *Hong Kong Fir* should not be read as requiring the actual use of the word 'condition': any term or terms of the contract, which, fairly read, have the effect indicated, are sufficient.

He relied also on Lord Roskill's speech from pp. 12–13.

[Counsel for the owners] relied on passages in Lord Lowry's speech at p. 8 and on the passage in Lord Roskill's speech at p. 15 where he said that:

> The most important single factor in favour of [the term being a condition in that case] is that until the requirement of the 15-day consecutive notice was fulfilled, the respondents could not nominate . . . as the loading port.

He further relied on the famous passage in Bowen L.J.'s judgment in *Bentsen v Taylor* [1893] 2 QB 274 at p. 281 cited by Lord Roskill in *Bunge* at p. 12:

> There is no way of deciding that question except by looking at the contract in the light of the surrounding circumstances, and then making up one's mind whether the intention of the parties, as gathered from the instrument itself, will best be carried out by treating the promise as a warranty sounding only in damages, or as a condition precedent by the failure to perform which the other party is relieved of his liability . . .

Paragraph 12–040 from *Chitty on Contracts*, 28th ed., seems to me to provide a neat summary of the principles. Having discussed the numerous authorities on the point, including the authorities cited to us, the editors say this:

> The conclusion to be drawn from these cases is that a term of a contract will be held to be a condition:
>
> (i)   if it is expressly so provided by statute;
>
> (ii) if it has been so categorised as the result of previous judicial decision (although it has been said that some of the decisions on this matter are excessively technical and are open to re-examination by the House of Lords);
>
> (iii) if it is so designated in the contract or if the consequences of its breach, that is, the right of the innocent party to treat himself as discharged, are provided for expressly in the contract; or
>
> (iv) if the nature of the contract or the subject-matter or the circumstances of the case lead to the conclusion that the parties must, by necessary implication, have intended that the innocent party would be discharged from further performance of his obligations in the event that the term was not fully and precisely complied with.
>
> Otherwise a term of a contract will be considered to be an intermediate term. Failure to perform such a term will ordinarily entitle the party not in default to treat himself as discharged only if the effect of breach of the term deprives him of substantially the whole benefit which it was intended that he should obtain from the contract.

The problem with clause 46 is that on a strict construction of the language there would appear to be an inconsistency about the situations in which the clause would contemplate that a failure to have or obtain a major's approval should be considered as of great importance, and indeed of such importance that the charterers should have a right to cancel. . . .

It seems to me that the parties should be assumed to have intended to be consistent about the importance of the obtaining and maintaining of majors' approvals. Only if the language drives one to inconsistency should the clause be construed so as to provide for that inconsistency. What is more it seems to me that they should not be taken to have intended to be inconsistent about the absence of 'even' one major's approval, nor to be contemplating a distinction between having the approval in the first place and losing the approval after commencement of the charter period. . . .

It would be surprising if the loss of one major and failure to reinstate within thirty days provided a right to cancellation, if the failure in effect to reinstate Exxon within sixty days did not do so.

In my view the word guarantee is the pointer that demonstrates that it was intended that sixty days was to be the outside limit for the obtaining of the approval of Exxon. If I ask myself whether the nature of the contract leads to the conclusion that the parties must by necessary implication have intended that the charterers would be entitled to cancel i.e. accept a repudiation if the Exxon approval was not obtained within sixty days, the answer I would give would be 'yes'. That, as it seems to me, achieves consistency in relation to the importance of the obtaining and maintaining of the majors' approvals, and that is what I suggest the contract intended.

I would accordingly allow the appeal.

(Jonathan Parker L.J. and Rix L.J. agreed.)

Note

The difficulty with the courts engaging in an interpretative exercise is that it can lead to a lack of predictability, which is not good in the context of a commercial contract.

B. Conditions Precedent and Conditions Subsequent

A further means of classifying terms is required where a contingency is provided for in the contract. In such a case, the contingent condition may be defined as either a condition precedent or a condition subsequent. A condition precedent is a condition which must be satisfied before any legally binding contract comes into operation. A condition may also be precedent to liability under a contract. In such a case the contract will be deemed to have come into existence and the parties will not be free to withdraw. However, their obligations will depend on the fulfilment of the condition. A condition subsequent provides that an existing binding contract will determine on the occurence of some event.

Re Application of Butler [1970] IR 45

The applicant was involved in an accident on 24 June 1963. A condition of his policy required the applicant to give written notice to the company 'as soon as practicable' after any accident. As he had been informed that the insurance company was insolvent, notice of the accident was not given until a year later. Fulfilment of the conditions in the policy was stated to be 'conditions precedent to any liability'. Damages were later awarded against the applicant as a result of the accident. A special fund was set up to meet the claims of policyholders of the insurance company and the applicant sought indemnification. The Supreme Court held that no sum was due to the applicant as there had been a breach of the conditions of the policy. The applicant's belief in the futility of giving notice immediately after the accident was irrelevant.

Dorene Ltd *v* Suedes (Ireland) Ltd [1981] IR 312

The plaintiffs entered into negotiations to lease premises owned by the defendants. On 18 July the plaintiffs made a conditional offer to take the lease. They expressly made the offer subject to final agreement on a commencement date and a rent-free period, and subject to the approval of grant aid from the IDA and to the approval of the board of its parent company. This conditional offer was conditionally accepted by the defendants who emphasised that neither party was to be bound until the lease was executed. The conditions were not fulfilled and the defendants refused to proceed with the letting. The plaintiffs sued for specific performance in the High Court.

Costello J.:

It was suggested on Dorene's behalf in counsel's closing submissions that a concluded bargain had been reached between the parties. It was urged that Dorene had not pressed for the rent-free period as required in the letter of 18 July and that agreement on the commencement date of the lease had been reached. As to the other conditions laid down by Dorene in the letter of 18 July (i.e. the approval of IDA and the approval of Doreen Holdings), it was said that these should be regarded as conditions subsequent in a concluded contract. It is, of course, important to make a distinction between a condition which must be satisfied before any legally binding contract comes into operation (a condition precedent) and a condition which is a part of a legally binding contract which, if not fulfilled, can result in the contract ceasing to be binding (a condition subsequent): see Wylie's *Irish Conveyancing Law*—para. 9.069 at pp 383–4. Dorene's counsel suggested that these conditions were conditions subsequent and were analogous to a case in which a purchaser agrees to buy a house 'subject to me getting an advance on the property'—a condition which did not prevent a binding contract for sale coming into operation in *Rooney v Byrne* [1933] IR 609. He also suggested, as an alternative argument, that in any event the evidence established that these conditions had been waived by Dorene. He said that Dorene could enforce the concluded bargain which the parties had made even though the final terms of the lease had not been agreed, as the court would itself fix them in default of agreement. I find myself unable to agree with these propositions. Dorene, as I have said, made an offer to take a lease but made the offer subject to certain conditions which had to be fulfilled before they could be legally bound. The situation was in no way similar to that of a purchaser who agrees to buy a property but safeguards himself by providing that he may avoid the bargain if, for example, he fails to obtain a loan or fails to obtain planning permissions. Even if the condition relating to the date of commencement was agreed and the condition relating to the rent-free period tacitly dropped, and even if the conditions relating to grant aid from IDA and main-board approval had been waived, there still remains an insurmountable obstacle in the way of specific performance proceedings because Suedes had made it abundantly clear that they too wished to keep their options open and because their acceptance of Dorene's offer was on the basis that Suedes would not be contractually bound to grant a lease until its terms had been finally agreed. This never happened. On 9 October 1979, the parties were still in negotiation. Therefore, it seems to me that there was no legally binding agreement to grant a lease when Dorene's proceedings were launched and, in my opinion, they were instituted without reasonable or probable cause.

Note

It is important to note that although the main obligations may be inoperative in such cases until the relevant condition is fulfilled, subsidiary obligations may arise and be enforceable relating to the fulfilment of the condition. For example, in *Rooney v Byrne* referred to above, a duty to use reasonable efforts to bring about the fulfilment of the contract was implied. Similarly, in *Smith v Pisani* [2001] SASC 21, the Supreme Court of South Australia held that the purchaser under a contract 'subject to finance' is obliged to act honestly and reasonably in seeking finance and cannot escape the contract by unreasonably refusing to take advantage of available sources of finance falling within the terms of the contract. The Court followed *Meehan v Jones* (1982)149 CLR 571, a decision of the High Court of Australia, in this regard.

Consider:

How will parties distinguish between a condition precedent to the formation of a contract or a condition precedent to liability under a contract?

The idea of waiving compliance with a condition precedent was discussed in the following case.

In the Matter of the Arbitration Act 1954, and of an Arbitration between Gaelcrann Teoranta and Michael Payne and others, Underwriters at Lloyds [1985] ILRM 109

Underwriters refused to indemnify a company against claims made by an employee on the grounds that the company had failed to comply with a condition in the policy which provided as follows: 'The assured shall give . . . immediate notice in writing, with full particulars of the happening of any occurrence which could give rise to a claim under this insurance, or of the receipt by the assured of notice of any claim and of the institution of any proceedings against the assured.' The policy also stated 'All conditions are precedent to liability under this assurance.' Although the company notified the underwriters of the two claims and sent them the two plenary summonses, it did not furnish written particulars of the happening of an event which could give rise to a claim. At arbitration the arbitrator stated the case for the opinion of the court on the correct interpretation of the clause.

Gannon J.:

[T]the interpretation which I advise should be applied in relation to the obligations imposed on the insured is that:

(1) In every instance in which to the knowledge of the assured an occurrence happens which he recognises could give rise to a claim under the policy he must give to the nominated agent of the underwriters immediate notice in writing of the happening of such occurrence, or alternatively give them the like immediate notice of his receipt of the claim if such be made;

(2) In the event of a claim being made or received which arises from no identifiable occurrence as a happening, or of the happening of which the assured was unaware, he must give the nominated agent of the underwriters immediate notice in writing of his receipt of notice of such claim;

(3) In every case he must give to the nominated agent of the underwriters immediate notice in writing of the institution of proceedings . . .

It was recognised in the course of argument that a distinction must be made between a condition expressed in a contract to be a condition precedent and one which is not so described in the contract. Counsel referred to *In Re Coleman's Depositories Ltd* [1907] 2 KB 798 and in particular to the judgment of Fletcher Moulton L.J. from which it would appear that upon non-compliance with the condition that is stated to be a condition precedent performance of the obligations of the contract cannot be enforced by the party in default. Nevertheless, Fletcher Moulton L.J. says in reference to what he calls a trifling default at p. 807 of the report: 'The courts have not always considered that they are bound to interpret provisions of this kind with unreasonable strictness, and although the word 'immediate' is no doubt a strong epithet I think that it might be fairly construed as meaning with all reasonable speed considering the circumstances of the case.' In the event of non-compliance with a condition not described as a condition precedent the party in default may be able to establish a right to the benefit of the contract subject to an assessment in damages for the consequences of the default or may be unable to enforce the contract. It was also accepted in the course of argument that compliance with a condition expressed in either form could be waived by the party to benefit by it either expressly or impliedly from conduct. But a difficulty has been created by some observations of Lord Justice Denning M.R. in his judgment in *Lickiss v Milestone Motor Policies at Lloyd's* [1966] 2 All ER 972 also reported as *Barrett Bros (Taxis) Ltd v Davies* [1966] 1 WLR 1354. In that judgment Denning M.R. stated at p. 975 of the All ER report:

> First, it was unnecessary for the motor cyclist to send the documents to the insurers. They had all the relevant facts, and that absolved the motor cyclist from doing more. The police headquarters at Blackpool by their letter of 18 January 1964 gave to the insurers all the material information. The insurers would be entitled, if they so wished, to send their own representative to the Magistrates' Court and watch the proceedings or, indeed, to take such other steps if any as they were entitled to take. Seeing that they had received the information from the police, it would be a futile thing to require the motor cyclist himself to give them the self-same information. The law never compels a person to do that which is useless and unnecessary.

In that case the motor cyclist was obliged under the terms of his policy to notify immediately the insurers of intended prosecution and had failed to do so. Towards

the end of his judgment Lord Denning adds the following observation at p. 976:
'Condition 1 was inserted in the policy so as to afford a protection to the insurers so
that they should know in good time about the accident and any proceedings
consequent on it. If they obtain all the material knowledge from another source so
that they are not prejudiced at all by the failure of the insured himself to tell them,
then they cannot rely on the condition to defeat the claim.' When a similar point was
taken before McKenna J. in *Farrell v Federated Employers Ltd* |1970| 1 All ER 360 those
observations of Denning M.R. were cited to him. In his judgment McKenna J. says at p.
363 of the report:

> Counsel for the plaintiff in his able argument contended that there could be no
> breach of a condition entitling the insurers to repudiate liability unless the breach
> had caused actual prejudice to the insurers. For this surprising proposition he cited
> *Lickiss v Milestone Motor Policies at Lloyd's* |1966| 2 All ER 972. In that case the insurers
> relied on a failure of the insured to inform them of the receipt by the insured of a
> notice of intended prosecution. The insurers had received information of this
> matter from the police. There was also some evidence that they had waived the
> condition entitling them to such notice.

McKenna J., then quotes the passage which I have quoted above from the judgment of
Lord Denning M.R. in the cited case, McKenna J. then went on at p. 364:

> I distinguish that case from the present. There the insurers had contemporary
> knowledge from another reliable source of the matter which the insured failed to
> notify. Here the insurers had no knowledge from any source of the issue of the writ
> until they received the letter of 2 March 1966. I do not regard Lord Denning M.R.'s
> judgment as authority for the wider proposition that an insurer cannot rely on a
> breach of condition unless he has suffered actual prejudice.

An appeal from the decision of McKenna J. came before the Court of Appeal in England
over which Lord Denning M.R. presided. That court in upholding unanimously the
decision of McKenna J., carefully avoided expressing any approval or acceptance of the
proposition advanced by Lord Denning M.R. in 1966. To the extent that any of the
observations of Lord Denning M.R. as stated in the 1966 case seem to be at variance
with the statements of the law as expressed by Fletcher Moulton L.J. *In Re Coleman's
Depositories Ltd* I would not be prepared to adopt them.

In the policy under consideration by the arbitrator condition 5 is expressed to be a
condition precedent to liability under the policy. Non-compliance with the provisions
of that condition, if such there be, may be waived by the underwriters or they, the
underwriters, may be found to have waived impliedly their right to rely on non-
compliance. If they were found to have led the assured by their conduct to believe that
their right to rely on the non-compliance was being waived by them the matter of
prejudice might possibly arise for consideration. Save in the investigation of such
matters of fact it seems to me there is no onus on the underwriters to show that they
are prejudiced by a non-compliance with condition 5. That is to say in the absence of
waiver the underwriters are entitled without the obligation of proof of prejudice to
their position to rely on non-compliance with condition 5 as releasing them from
liability to meet a claim under the policy.

In the following case, the Supreme Court confirmed the principles that
apply in bringing to an end a conditional contract for the sale of land. In

doing so, the usefulness of distinguishing between a condition precedent and a condition subsequent was discussed.

O'Connor v Coady [2005] 1 ILRM 256

On 31 May 2001, the appellant agreed to sell property in Meath to the respondent subject to certain conditions. These conditions provided, *inter alia*, that the contract was subject to the purchaser obtaining a final grant of planning permission for the residential development of the property within four months, and that the closing date of the sale be seven days after the date of issue of the final grant. Planning permission was not obtained within the prescribed four-month period. On 23 August 2001 the appellant's solicitor inquired about the status of the planning application. No further correspondence took place until 3 September 2002, when the respondent's solicitor wrote seeking replies to requisitions on title in order to complete the sale. The appellant's solicitor responded in a letter of 12 September 2002 headed 'Subject to contract/contract denied' expressing surprise at the respondent's letter and stating his belief that the contract had lapsed.

McCracken J.:

. . . Both before the learned trial judge and at the hearing of this appeal there was considerable discussion as to whether the condition relating to planning permission was a condition precedent or a condition subsequent. The distinction may at times be of considerable importance, in that if there is a condition precedent, then no contract comes into existence unless the condition is fulfilled, while if there is a condition subsequent, there is a valid contract in being, but it is not enforceable unless the condition is fulfilled. However, the distinction does not seem to me to be relevant in the present case. The real issue in this case is not whether a contract ever existed, but whether the terms of the contract can be enforced once the time for compliance with the condition has passed. . . .

The important features of this condition are, firstly that it relates to a planning application which was already in existence, secondly there was a fixed period for compliance with the condition and thirdly time was not made of the essence of the contract in relation to that period. The general principles relating to conditional contracts were laid down expressly and succinctly by Lord Jenkins giving the judgment of the Privy Council in *Aberfoyle Plantations Ltd v Cheng* [1960] AC 115. After pointing out that the intention of the parties as expressed in the contract ought to be implied from the language used therein was all important, he said at p.124:

But, subject to this overriding consideration, their Lordships would adopt as warranted by authority and manifestly reasonable in themselves, the following general principles: (I) Where a conditional contract of sale fixes a date for the completion of the sale, then the condition must be fulfilled by that date; (II) Where a conditional contract of sale fixes no date for completion of the sale, then the condition must be fulfilled within a reasonable time; (III) Where a conditional contract of sale fixes (whether specifically or by reference to the date fixed for completion) the date by which the condition is to be fulfilled, then the date so fixed must be strictly adhered to, and the time allowed is not to be extended by reference to equitable principles.

While that case did not refer to a planning condition, nevertheless the principles enunciated have since been adopted as being applicable to planning conditions. The condition in the present case clearly comes within the principles set out at (III) cited above.

In an earlier case, cited in the *Aberfoyle Plantations Ltd* case, somewhat similar views were expressed by Maugham J. In *In re Sandwell Park Colliery Company* [1929] 1 Ch. 277, a contract was subject to what was admittedly clearly a condition precedent, namely the approval of the court. At p.282 Maugham J. stated as a general principle:

> Courts of equity, in dealing with actions for specific performance relating to land, have been accustomed to give effect to the real intention rather than to the precise words fixing the date for completion. The effect is that a clause fixing the date for completion is equivalent to a clause stating that completion shall be on that date or within a reasonable time thereafter. But there is no ground for a similar construction in the case of a condition upon which the validity of the contract as one of sale depends. The distinction is obvious. In the first case both parties are bound, and a moderate delay in completion is thought not to injure either. In the latter, the very existence of the mutual obligations is dependent on the performance of the condition. The purchasers do not know in the first instance if their purchase money will ever be required. In general, and in the present case, there is no promise or undertaking by the vendor that the condition will be fulfilled. Equity has, I think, never applied its liberal views as to time to such a condition. If a date is mentioned, the condition must be exactly complied with. If a date is not mentioned, the condition must be fulfilled within a reasonable time; there is no difference between the views of law and equity in considering what is a reasonable time, and the uncertain position of the purchaser must be borne in mind.

While that case concerned a condition precedent and concerned a condition to be performed by the vendor rather than the purchaser, in my view the same principles apply to the present case. Whether this is a condition precedent or a condition subsequent, the existence of the mutual obligations, or their enforcement, is dependent on the performance of the condition. There is no undertaking by the purchaser in this case that the condition will be fulfilled, and the vendor does not know whether he will ever get his money.

The effect of a conditional contract has been considered in several Irish cases since the *Aberfoyle Plantations Ltd* case. In *O'Mullane v Riordan* [1978] ILRM 73, McWilliam J. implicitly refused to accept that a planning condition was a condition precedent to the coming into operation of a contract, and said at p.77:

> The fact that a contract is subject to a condition has the effect of making it unenforceable until the condition is fulfilled, but it does not mean that there is no contract at all and the case cited (the *Aberfoyle Plantations Ltd* case) decided that the purchaser was entitled to recover his deposit under a term in the agreement. A conditional contract is one which becomes enforceable provided the condition is fulfilled within the time provided by the contract or, if no time is provided, within a reasonable time.

Similarly in *Maloney v Elf Investments Ltd*, unreported, High Court, McWilliam J., 7 December 1979, McWilliam J. expressly rejected the argument that by analogy with the date fixed for closing, the time fixed in a contract for performance of a condition in relation to planning should be regarded in equity as the date fixed in the contract or a reasonable time thereafter unless time had been made of the essence of the contract. He expressly approved the third proposition in the Aberfoyle Plantations Ltd case. . . . [McCracken J. makes reference to *Sepia Ltd v M & P Hanlon Ltd* [1979] ILRM 11 and *McKillop v McMullen* [1979] NI 85 where the *Aberfoyle Plantations Ltd* case was expressly approved.] Strangely enough, there does not appear to be any case in which the *Aberfoyle Plantations Ltd* decision was considered by this court. However, it has been approved and followed in England, Australia and New Zealand. It appears to me to be a correct analysis of the legal position of conditions inserted in a contract which postpone the enforceability of the contract, be they conditions precedent or conditions subsequent. These propositions are clearly particularly applicable to conditions relating to the obtaining of planning permission, and indeed to any condition to where the time required for its performance is uncertain. Particularly in contracts for the sale of land, certainty is important to both parties. I am quite satisfied that the effect of the contract in the present case is that at the expiration of the four-month period for obtaining planning permission the condition had not been fulfilled and the time allowed for its fulfilment could not be extended by reference to equitable principles.

Somewhat surprisingly the appellant has not sought to argue that the contract came to an end immediately on the expiration of the four-month period allowed for fulfilment of the condition. Indeed, the wording of the questions in the summons seems to make it clear that the appellant considers that the failure to comply with the condition rendered the contract voidable rather than void. In my view there is certainly an argument to be made that where there is a fixed date by which there must be completion of a condition, the contract automatically becomes void on the failure to comply with the time limit. However, that is not an argument which this court has been asked to consider, nor is it one raised on the pleadings, and accordingly, expressly without deciding the point, for the purposes of this decision I am assuming that the contract became voidable.

The letter of September 12, 2002 from the vendor's solicitors did not opt to avoid the contract in express terms. It did state, rightly or wrongly, the belief and contention of the appellant's solicitor at the time that the contract had lapsed 'and is at an end'. It offered to enter into negotiations for a new contract and it purported to return the deposit. Perhaps more importantly it was headed 'Subject to Contract/Contract Denied'. In my view this letter in unequivocal terms notified the respondent solicitor that the appellant was treating the contract as being at an end. In the absence of any express contractual provision, the rescission of a voidable contract does not have to be in any particular form. What is required is a clear notification that the relevant party is treating the contract as at an end. In my view this letter clearly complies with that requirement.

The only question, therefore, is whether the appellant's right to avoid the contract became lost due to the passage of time, either by reason of the appellant's delay in taking any action or by reason of the waiver of the condition by the appellant. There is no doubt that there are many cases of this nature in which a condition inserted for the benefit of one party, in this case the respondent, can be waived by that party, but that requires some positive act by that party. The fact that the respondent in the present case continued his planning application and made no attempt to notify the appellant that he was prepared to complete without the condition being fulfilled, seems to me to make it quite clear that the respondent always considered that the condition remained. Indeed, the respondent's solicitor's letter of September 3, which brought matters to a head, was written on the basis that the condition remained, but was shortly going to be complied with. Accordingly, in my view no question of waiver can arise.

The question of the appellant's delay might have been very serious had she done anything to encourage the respondent to believe that she was not going to enforce the time limit attached to the condition. It could then possibly be argued that the situation amounted to an estoppel. However, there is no suggestion of anything of that nature in the present case. The appellant simply did nothing until the respondent notified her solicitor that the planning permission was shortly going to issue. The most that could be said is that her solicitor held the deposit, which of course belonged to the respondent. On the other hand, the respondent never requested the return of the deposit, and there is no suggestion that the appellant personally benefited in any way from it being held by her solicitor. In those circumstances, I do not consider that the delay in any way affected the appellant's right to avoid the contract.

In the circumstances of this case I would allow the appeal. I am doing so on the basis that the contract became voidable on the expiration of the four-month period for compliance with the planning condition, that the letter of September 12, 2002 constituted a valid rescission of the contract, and that this rescission took place before the planning condition had been fulfilled and in the absence of any waiver on the part of the respondent.

Geoghegan J.:

It is important, however, to note that whatever answers may be arrived at by this court to the questions raised in the summons it does not necessarily follow that they can be transported to some other future case in which a planning permission condition or some similar condition is inserted. In every case, as to what is to happen in the event of a condition not being fulfilled is first and foremost a matter for agreement between the parties. The courts will uphold any lawful agreement in this connection. Such agreement may be expressed or implied. If, however, there are no express provisions and if there are no concrete outside circumstances which would raise particular implications there are principles which a court can lay down as applicable in interpreting what the implied agreement of the parties is. The important principles in this connection were in fact laid down by the Privy Council in *Aberfoyle Plantations Ltd v Cheng* cited above, principles which in whole or in part have been referred to in Irish cases as well as Australian, New Zealand, Northern Ireland and other English cases. [Geoghegan J quoted the abstract from *Aberfoyle* quoted in McCracken's judgment above.]

The decision of the Privy Council in *Aberfoyle* has always been controversial but only in one respect. On one interpretation of the opinion delivered by Lord Jenkins (I put it this way because there are hugely varying interpretations as to what he did in fact mean) the condition in that case was treated as a condition precedent in the sense of a condition precedent to the coming into existence of the contract. But as far as I can understand from the case-law both in this jurisdiction, in Northern Ireland, in England, in Australia and New Zealand, there is no judicial controversy as to the principle that if a time limit is specified in such a condition, then, in the absence of agreement to the contrary, it is nonextendable. Not only was this principle accepted by Costello J. in *Sepia* . . . but it was also acknowledged by McWilliam J. in *Maloney v Elf Investments Ltd*, unreported, High Court, McWilliam J., 7 December 1979. Speaking in the context of waiver of the condition which of course does not apply here, McWilliam J. at p.8 of the judgment said that he was of opinion that 'in the absence of any other authority, that the decision in the *Aberfoyle* case as to the necessity for exact compliance with the date mentioned in the condition means that there can be no question of waiver after that date has passed'. Again in reliance on *Aberfoyle* Murray J. in the Northern Ireland case of *McKillop v McMullan* [1979] NI 85 at 92 appears to endorse the view that where there was a specified completion date and the contract was subject to planning permission, that date had to be adhered to for fulfilment of the condition. In this non-controversial respect *Aberfoyle* has been followed also in judgments delivered in the High Court of Australia in *Perri v Coolangatta Investments Property Ltd* (1982) 149 CLR 537. In relation to all aspects of this case I have gained considerable assistance from the judgments in that Australian case and I will be returning to them. It is of some passing interest to note that the five-judge court comprised three judges, all of whom are now former Chief Justices of the High Court of Australia, and each of whom delivered written judgments. The court consisted of Gibbs C.J., Stephen, Mason, Wilson and Brennan JJ.

The judgment of Kenny J. in *Healy v Healy*, unreported, High Court, 3 December 1973 deals with the question of waiver and is not of any real assistance in this case except that by way of *obiter dicta*. Kenny J. throws out the suggestion that where, as in this case, the closing date is fixed by reference to the grant of the planning permission under the condition and where no planning permission has in fact issued by the date, the so-called contract without the obligation to comply with the condition might be void for uncertainty. It would seem to me that a court would be slow to come to that conclusion unless it was absolutely compelled to do so. Fortunately the question does not arise to be determined on this vendor and purchaser summons.

I am of the view, for the reasons which I have indicated, that once the date mentioned in the condition had passed without the planning permission being available there was an entitlement to bring the contract to an end. I put it that way because I do not accept . . . . that the contract automatically came to an end. It was capable of being brought to an end by notification from one party to the other. . . . . There is no doubt that the condition was not fulfilled within the prescribed time but the question is, did the appellant effectively bring the contract to an end?

. . . A number of points are worth noting from this letter [of 12 September]. First of all it is not a letter expressly purporting to rescind the contract. On the face of it, it is simply expressing surprise on the basis that the contract had lapsed once the date on the condition had passed. It is necessary, however, to look at the substance and not the mere form of the letter. There is no doubt that the letter is making clear that the vendor does not regard herself as bound by the contract. The denial of contract at the head of the letter copperfastens that view. Once the condition was not fulfilled within the correct time, either party was entitled to treat the contract as at an end but was bound to notify the other party that he or she was so treating it. Once such notification in whatever form took place there was no longer a contract unless the party purporting to treat the contract as at an end had in fact expressly or impliedly affirmed the contract. Mere lapse of time would not necessarily constitute such affirmation; there would have to be some positive indication that the party otherwise entitled to rescind was treating the contract as still in being. Although time was allowed to elapse in this case, no such affirmation took place and, therefore, this voidable contract was effectively avoided or rescinded by the letter of September 12, 2002.

As I have already pointed out, counsel for the appellant has not argued in either court that the contract automatically came to an end. On one view this concession was surprising in the light of the terms of the letter of September 12, 2002 in which the case of automatic lapse was made. I agree with the views of McCracken J. that the issue of automatic lapse does not arise but, for reasons which I will be indicating, my present view at any rate would be that such a conditional contract is voidable and not void on the non-fulfilment of the condition.

The second point to be noted from the letter of September 12, 2002 is the phrase 'in order to finalise matters' preceding a statement that they were returning the deposit. The deposit was not in fact enclosed. However, as McCracken J. points out in his judgment it appears to be accepted that this was an oversight. The non-return of the deposit therefore is not inconsistent with the rescission.

If I am right in my view that the time limit on the condition would not be self-executing and that an act of rescission would be required, the basis for such requirement must be considered as flowing from the implied agreement of the parties. Obviously such rescission cannot be effective after a positive affirmation of the contract.

In fairness to the parties on both sides of this case and their legal advisers, the questions raised are not without difficulty and have not really been considered before by the Irish courts. Analogous questions, however, have been considered in the Australian case of *Perri* referred to above. I do not intend to go into the facts of that case in too much detail. The condition involved was not a planning permission condition though other Australian cases involving such a condition are considered throughout the judgments in the context of their relevance. The condition in the *Perri* case was that the contract was being entered into subject to the purchasers completing a sale of certain other properties. No express time limit was fixed for the performance of the condition but it was held, as would be held in these courts, that it had to be complied with within a reasonable time. Nor was there an express completion date. Despite the differences in the factual background the observations of the judges were in many instances highly relevant to this case. First of all, a number of the judgments dealt with the distinction between condition precedent and condition subsequent. Both counsel in this case and, I think by implication, the learned trial judge considered that distinction relevant. But the Australian judgments and references to other cases and articles contained therein dealing with that distinction have convinced me that it is not really a helpful one. On the hearing of the appeal before this court, counsel for the appellant, Mr Dwyer SC and counsel for the respondent, Mr Ralston SC seemed to assume that the expression 'condition precedent' necessarily and exclusively refers to a condition the effect of non-compliance with which means that no contract of any kind comes into existence. They seemed to take the view that every other kind of a condition that might be said to render the contract 'conditional' was a condition subsequent. Gibbs C.J. in the *Perri* case considered that the completion of the sale of the other property was a 'condition precedent to the performance of certain of the obligations of the parties under the contract including the obligation of the respondent to complete the sale'. He goes on to make the following observation:

> It has sometimes proved difficult to decide whether a particular condition of a contract should be classified as a condition precedent or a condition subsequent, and as Professor Stoljar has pointed out in 'The Contractual Concept of Condition', Law Quarterly Review Volume 69 (1953) 485 at p. 506 if the words 'precedent' and 'subsequent' are to make sense they must be connected with a definite point of reference since they express a relationship in time, the question which must be asked is 'precedent to what? Subsequent to what?'. However, provided the effect of a condition is clearly understood, its classification may be merely a matter of words. *The condition in the present case was not a condition precedent to the formation of a binding contract* (my emphasis). It is clear that a binding contract came into existence immediately upon signature, and that the parties to it were from that moment subject to certain obligations.

Referring to a passage in a judgment of Isaacs J. in another Australian case *Maynard v Goode* (1926) 37 CLR 529 at 540 he agrees with Isaacs J. in pointing out that:

> In one sense the stipulation might be a condition precedent to the performance of a particular term of the contract, while in another sense it was a condition subsequent in relation to the whole contract, since the failure of the stipulation would have entitled the vendor to retire from the transaction altogether.

He goes on to refer to other cases in which it was pointed out the problems of making any relevant distinction between condition precedent and condition subsequent. Mason J. deals with the topic in similar vein in his judgment. He points out that generally speaking the court will tend to favour the construction which leads to the conclusion that a particular stipulation is a condition precedent to performance as against that which leads to the conclusion that the stipulation is a condition precedent to the formation or existence of the contract. He points out that in most cases it is artificial to say in the face of the details settled upon by the parties that there is no binding contract unless the event in question happens. This view exactly corresponds with the view expressed by McWilliam J. in *O'Mullane v Riordan* [1978] ILRM 73 at 77 where he said the following:

> The price of the land has increased astronomically since May 1972 and it has been argued that, as this contract was subject to a condition (i.e. the obtaining of planning permission) there was no contract until the planning permission had been obtained and that this is the time at which I have to ascertain the value of the land for the purpose of establishing the fairness of the bargain. I was referred in this context to the case of *Aberfoyle Plantations Ltd v Kajw Bien Cheng* [1960] AC 115. I cannot accept this argument. The fact that a contract is subject to a condition has the effect of making it unenforceable until the condition is fulfilled, but it does not mean that there is no contract at all and the case cited decided that the purchaser was entitled to recover his deposit under a term of the agreement. A conditional contract is one which becomes enforceable provided the condition is fulfilled within the time provided by the contract or if no time is provided within a reasonable time.

I think that this was the view adopted also by Murray J. in the Northern Ireland case of *McKillop* cited above notwithstanding the adverse views on that case expressed by the learned High Court judge.

Returning to the *Perri* case and moving to the judgment of Wilson J., he refers to a passage in the judgment of the well-known New Zealand judge, Cooke J. , in a case called *Hunt v Wilson* [1978] 2 NZLR 261 at 267 in which that judge said the following:

> I venture to think that the ambiguous labels precedent and subsequent when applied to conditions are seldom of real help in solving issues in this branch of contract law. Certainly they can be positively misleading unless the meaning of what has been said is made specific by explaining to what the condition in question is seen as precedent or subsequent.

Wilson J. goes on to agree with that view and to point out that the special condition in the *Perri* case could be described with accuracy as either a condition subsequent to the formation of the contract or as a condition precedent to an obligation in either party to proceed to completion. These views as to the respective meanings of 'condition precedent' and 'condition subsequent' and as to their frequent overlap were endorsed in the judgment of Brennan J. with which Stephen J. agreed.

In my view, the more helpful terminology is the distinction between a 'conditional contract' and an 'unconditional contract'. As we all know, by a strange quirk of the law, ordinary terms of an unconditional contract, if they are of sufficient importance, will themselves be described as 'conditions' but that does not mean that the contract is conditional. Normally, a conditional contract will not mean a contract which only comes into existence upon fulfilment of the condition but rather a contract which can only be enforced upon fulfilment of the condition. That is what this contract was.

As I have explained, it has already been conceded that the contract did not automatically lapse upon the breach of condition. Although not all of the views of the judges in the *Perri* case on this point fully coincided, I think that the case can be read as supporting that concession. But if the contract does not automatically 'lapse' to use the terminology contained in the letter from the solicitors for the appellant, how does it come to an end? That is the question which now has to be explored in more detail and on that question also there was no real assistance to be gained from any of the authorities in the book of authorities but I did find assistance from the judgments in the *Perri* case. Gibbs C.J. in paragraph 10 of his judgment said the following:

> For these reasons I consider that when the time has elapsed for performance of a condition which is not a promissory condition, but a condition precedent to the obligation to complete a contract of sale, either party, if not in default, can elect to treat the contract as at an end if the condition has not been fulfilled or waived and that it is not necessary first to give a notice calling on the party in default to complete the contract or fulfil the condition.

Later in the same paragraph the same judge says the following:

> Although in *Aberfoyle Plantations Ltd v Cheng* . . . an erroneous view may have been taken of the nature of the condition there considered, nevertheless, in my respectful opinion, it was correct to hold that the time fixed by the contract for performance of the condition was not to be extended by reference to equitable principles . . .

But in paragraph 11 the same judge also observes:

> In the view that I have formed, it was then open to the respondent to avoid the contract without first giving any notice limiting a reasonable time for completion. By instituting the proceedings before the condition had been either fulfilled or waived, the respondent sufficiently evidenced its election to avoid the contract.

I should point out that these views expressed by Gibbs C.J. were in the context of his approving similar views expressed in other Australian cases and in particular the following passage expressed in a case of *Gange v Sullivan* (1966) 116 CLR 418, 441:

> Whilst the effect of a condition must in every case depend upon the language in which it is expressed and a decision upon the meaning of one condition cannot

determine the meaning of a different condition, the authorities cited do show a disposition on the part of the courts to treat non-fulfilment of a condition such as that here under consideration as rendering a contract voidable rather than void in order to forestall a party to a contract from gaining some advantage from his own conduct in securing or contributing to the non-fulfilment of a condition bringing the contract to an end. Accordingly . . . we are prepared to treat the non-fulfilment of the condition as rendering the contract voidable rather than void.

Mason J. also makes it clear that, in his view, the time clause would not be self-executing and that the party relying on it would have to rescind. Indeed, that appears to have been the view of all the judges. As there is no authority requiring this court to hold otherwise, I have likewise taken the same view as the Australian courts endorsed in English cases also that non-fulfilment of the condition within the time stipulated renders the contract voidable rather than void. This would seem to me to be especially sensible in the Irish context. I think that two Irish solicitors dealing with each other on a sale would naturally assume that if one was going to treat the contract as at an end because of the breach of the condition he would so inform the other and that it is reasonable to imply such an obligation. This observation is necessarily *obiter* as the question was not argued in the light of counsel's concession. I would allow the appeal. I would answer the questions in the manner suggested by McCracken J. in his judgment.

(McGuiness J. concurring)

SECTION THREE—CONSTRUCTION OF CONTRACTS

As the cases in section 1 indicate, the objective when construing a contract is to determine the intention of the parties. There are two basic approaches to interpreting contracts in order to ascertain this intention: the literal interpretation and the factual matrix approach.

LAC Minerals Ltd *v* Chevron Mineral Corp. of Ireland (CMCI) and Ivernia West plc (HC) 6 August 1993, unrep.

CMCI entered into an agreement with Ivernia to develop mineral deposits. A pre-emption clause provided that if either party wished to sell their interest to a third party, they were required to offer the interest first to the other party. Clause 15.3.1.4 required that the notice must state that the offer would be open for acceptance for a period of fifty-five days after receipt of the offer by the offeree. Clause 15.3.2 provided that the offeree would have the 'right and option' for a period of sixty days after receipt of the offer to accept. CMCI offered their interest to Ivernia who accepted within sixty days but after forty-five days. LAC who had an agreement to buy the interest in the event of Ivernia not accepting claimed that such acceptance was not valid. LAC claimed *inter alia* that parol evidence should be admitted to explain the inconsistency between the time period allowed in the two clauses.

Keane J.:

The legal principles applicable in determining the construction of a disputed term in a contract were stated by Lord Wilberforce in *Reardon Smith Line v Hansen-Tangen*, ((1976), 3 All ER 570 at pp 574–575) as follows:

> When one speaks of the intention of the parties to the contract, one is speaking objectively—the parties cannot themselves give direct evidence of what their intention was—and what must be ascertained is what is to be taken as the intention which reasonable people would have if placed in the situation of the parties. Similarly, when one is speaking of the aim, or object, or commercial purpose, one is speaking objectively of what reasonable persons would have had in mind in the situation of the parties. . . . What the court must do is to place itself in thought in the same factual matrix as that in which the parties were.

That statement of the law was expressly approved of by Griffin J. in *Rohan Construction v ICI* (1988) ILRM 373.

The extent to which a court should take into account the surrounding circumstances in construing a contract was again the subject of some observation by Lord Wilberforce in *Prenn v Simmonds* ((1971) 1 WLR 1381). He said:

> The time has long passed when agreements, even those under seal, were isolated from the matrix of facts in which they were set and interpreted purely on internal linguistic considerations. There is no need to appeal here to any modern, anti-literal, tendencies, for Lord Blackburn's well known Judgment in *River Wear Commissioners v Adamson* (1877) 2 App Cas 743, provides ample warrant for a liberal approach. We must, as he said, enquire beyond the language and see what the circumstances were with reference to which the words were used, and the object, appearing from those circumstances, which the person using them had in view.

If, however, a term of a contract is unambiguous and can only have one meaning, the court cannot go beyond that unambiguous meaning so as to seek to interpret the intention of the parties: see *Marathon Petroleum (Ireland) Ltd v Bord Gáis Éireann* (SC) 31 July 1986, unrep.

The law applicable when there are inconsistent or repugnant clauses in a contract is stated as follows in *Chitty on Contract*, para. 833 as follows:

> Where the different parts of an instrument are inconsistent, effect must be given to that part which is calculated to carry into effect the real intention of the parties as gathered from the instrument as a whole, and that part which would defeat it must be rejected. The old rule was, in such a case, the earlier clause was to be received and the latter rejected, but this rule was a mere rule of thumb, totally unscientific, and out of keeping with the modern construction of documents. To be inconsistent, a term must contradict another term or be in conflict with it, such that effect cannot fairly be given to both clauses. A term may also be rejected if it is repugnant to the intention of the parties as it appears from the document. However, an effort should be made to give effect to every clause in the agreement and not to reject a clause unless it is manifestly inconsistent with or repugnant to the rest of the agreement.

It has also been said that it is not possible to look at the antecedent negotiations, where there is such an inconsistency, in order to determine the true intention of the parties: see *Prenn v Simmons*, above. Nor, it would seem, are prior drafts admissible in aid of the interpretation of the contract. As to the admissibility of evidence to explain a patent ambiguity, the law is thus stated in *Chitty*, at para. 875:

> *Patent Ambiguity*. In the case of a patent ambiguity, that is to say, a defect or ambiguity appearing on the face of the document which renders the words used unintelligible or meaningless, a rule is said to exist that any reference to matter dehors the document is forbidden. It is doubtful, however, whether such a rule applies today in respect of written contracts, except possibly in the case of total blanks in a document, although evidence will not be admitted to show what the author himself intended to say.

It is also clear that it is not legitimate to use as an aid in the construction of the contract anything which the parties said or did after it was made: see *Re Wogans Ltd*, (SC) 10 April 1992, unrep. . . .

[I]t would seem clear that there is on the face of the document an inconsistency between the provisions of clause 15.3. 1.4, under which the notice must state that the offer is open for acceptance for a period of forty five days after receipt of the offer by the offeree, and clause 15.3.2 which provides that the offeree is to have the 'right and option' for a period of sixty days after receipt of the offer, unless enlarged in the specified circumstances, to accept. . . .

In the light of the legal principles to which I have already referred, it is obvious that, if this action proceeds to a hearing, the court would be in a position to conduct a full investigation into the circumstances surrounding the execution of the JVA Agreement in order to ascertain whether this apparent inconsistency can be reconciled. The result of that investigation may lend support to the contentions advanced on behalf of LAC or it may not. The necessary materials for such an investigation may emerge from the process of discovery or they may not. The court may be assisted in arriving at a resolution of the difficulty by the oral evidence adduced at the hearing or it may not. It appears to me that, in these circumstances, it is not possible to say with the degree of confidence which the authorities suggest should be present in the mind of the judge when deciding an application of this nature that, no matter what may emerge on discovery or at the trial of the action, the inconsistency will be resolved only in a manner which will be fatal to the plaintiff's contentions.

In this context, I think there is a clear distinction to be drawn at this stage between the clause in *Marathon Petroleum v Bord Gais*, the subject of the decision of the Supreme Court which was much discussed during the course of the argument, and the clause in the present case. In that case, not merely was the clause in plain and unambiguous language: Finlay C.J. rejected the submission that it made no sense, saying:

> It was urged, as I have indicated, on behalf of the plaintiff that there was no meaning or sense in the parties reaching an agreement with regard to a currency exchange rate and confining it to a period of ten years with the knowledge and in the expectation that for up to four years of that period it would be inoperable and irrelevant. I do not see this as being a consideration which renders unreasonable or illogical the construction which I would put upon the clause on the basis of the actual words used in it. . . . There would be no illogicality in (the parties) deciding that they were not prepared to permit of an exchange rate fluctuation into a period beyond ten years from the time at which they were making the contract and viewing the likely movements of currency insofar as they could be prophesised.

No such reasonable or logical explanation has been put forward on behalf of the defendants of the inconsistencies in the clause in this case. . . .

I am satisfied that, having regard to the unexplained—and it may be inexplicable—inconsistency in the wording of clauses 15.3. 1.4 and 15.3.2 of the JVA Agreement, the court of trial may well be in position where it will think it proper to admit evidence of the factual matrix, to use Lord Wilberforce's words, in which the agreement was set, and which may assist the court in arriving at a construction of the clause. In these circumstances, I am satisfied that the first issue which I have posed must be resolved in favour of LAC.

Consider:

In the LAC *Minerals Ltd* case, why did the plaintiff not seek to have the agreement rectified to include the correct time period in the second clause?

Investors' Compensation Scheme *v* West Bromwich Building Society [1998] 1 All ER 98

Lord Hoffmann:

[S]ome general remarks about the principles by which contractual documents are nowadays construed. I do not think that the fundamental change which has overtaken this branch of the law, particularly as a result of the speeches of Lord Wilberforce in *Prenn v Simmonds* [1971] 1 WLR 1381, 1384–6 and *Reardon Smith Line v Hansen-Tangen* [1976] 1 WLR 989, is always sufficiently appreciated. The result has been, subject to one important exception, to assimilate the way in which such documents are interpreted by judges to the common sense principles by which any serious utterance would be interpreted in ordinary life. Almost all the old intellectual baggage of 'legal' interpretation has been discarded. The principles may be summarised as follows:

(1) Interpretation is the ascertainment of the meaning which the document would convey to a reasonable person having all the background knowledge which would reasonably have been available to the parties in the situation in which they were at the time of the contract.

(2) The background was famously referred to by Lord Wilberforce as the 'matrix of fact', but this phrase is, if anything, an understated description of what the background may include. Subject to the requirement that it should have been reasonably available to the parties and to the exception to be mentioned next, it includes absolutely anything which would have affected the way in which the language of the document would have been understood by a reasonable man.

(3) The law excludes from the admissible background the previous negotiations of the parties and their declarations of subjective intent. They are admissible only in an action for rectification. The law makes this distinction for reasons of practical policy and, in this respect only, legal interpretation differs from the way we would interpret utterances in ordinary life. The boundaries of this exception are in some respects unclear. But this is not the occasion on which to explore them.

(4) The meaning which a document (or any other utterance) would convey to a reasonable man is not the same thing as the meaning of its words. The meaning of words is a matter of dictionaries and grammars; the meaning of the document

is what the parties using those words against the relevant background would reasonably have been understood to mean. The background may not merely enable the reasonable man to choose between the possible meanings of words which are ambiguous but even (as occasionally happens in ordinary life) to conclude that the parties must, for whatever reason, have used the wrong words or syntax. (see *Mannai Investments Co. Ltd v Eagle Star Life Assurance Co. Ltd* [1997] 2 WLR 945.

(5) The 'rule' that words should be given their 'natural and ordinary meaning' reflects the common sense proposition that we do not easily accept that people have made linguistic mistakes, particularly in formal documents. On the other hand, if one would nevertheless conclude from the background that something must have gone wrong with the language, the law does not require judges to attribute to the parties an intention which they plainly could not have had. Lord Diplock made this point more vigorously when he said in *The Antaios Compania Neviera SA v Salen Rederierna A.B.* 19851 AC 191, 201:

. . . if detailed semantic and syntactical analysis of words in a commercial contract is going to lead to a conclusion that flouts business common sense, it must be made to yield to business common sense.

Note

The *Investors Compensation Scheme* case has been widely praised as adopting a pragmatic approach to understanding words within their factual context (See for example Kramer 23 OJLS 173) and widely applied by the Courts. However, it was distinguished in LT&R *Vowles (Parent) Ltd v Aston* [2005] EWHC (1459). Patten J. in the High Court accepted that sometimes the Court may give words which are ambiguous, whatever meaning best fits the commercial purpose of the transaction, so far as that is evident from the admissible background facts, and that this method of construction enables the court to go so far as to give words a meaning which it is not easy to find even in the dictionary. Specific reference was made to points (4) and (5) in the judgment above. However, on the facts, the Court found that it was not necessary to go that far and an assignment was construed solely by reference to its internal provisions and other material that could be objectively inferred in relation to the background to the transaction.

Igote Ltd *v* Badsey Ltd [2001] 4 IR 511

The plaintiff claimed that the defendant owed it £40,000 on foot of Clause 4.3 of a share subscription agreement which provided that the defendant shall 'distribute' at least £40,000 between the plaintiff and another share-holder of the defendant. The plaintiff argued that the agreement required an annual payment, whereas the defendant maintained that the agreement only amounted to an obligation to pay the sum by way of dividend, if available.

Murphy J.:

The issue between the parties concerns the proper construction of the share sub-scription agreement. The purpose of construing a document entered into between two or more persons is to ascertain their common intention. What 'intention' in that context means and how it is ascertained has been the subject matter of much judicial authority in respect of which no real controversy arises in the present case. Perhaps a convenient explanation of the word 'intention' in this context was provided by Lord Shaw in *Great Western Railway v Bristol Corporation* (1918) 87 LJ Ch. 414 when he said at p. 424:

> . . . one hears much use of the word 'intention', but courts of law when on the work of interpretation are not engaged upon the task of study of what parties intended to do, but of what the language which they employed shows that they did: in other words, they are not constructing a contract on the lines of what may be thought to have been what the parties intended, but they are construing the words and expressions used by the parties themselves. What do these mean? That, when ascertained, is the meaning to be given effect to, the meaning of the contract by which the parties are bound. The suggestion of an intention of parties different from the meaning conveyed by the words employed is no part of interpretation, but is mere confusion.

Lord Wright expressed the same view in not dissimilar terms in *Inland Revenue Commissioners v Raphael* [1935] AC 96 when he said at p. 142:

> It must be remembered at the outset that the court, while it seeks to give effect to the intention of the parties, must give effect to that intention as expressed, that is, it must ascertain the meaning of the words actually used. There is often an ambiguity in the use of the word 'intention' in cases of this character. The word is constantly used as meaning motive, purpose, desire, as a state of mind, and not as meaning intention as expressed.

There are numerous maxims and rules which have evolved over the years which may provide assistance in what can be the difficult task in ascertaining the intention of the parties. The plaintiff placed particular reliance on one such rule. It may be described as 'the factual matrix rule'. That rule is frequently identified with Lord Wilberforce and the speeches made by him in *Prenn v Simmonds* [1971] 1 WLR 1381 and *Reardon Smith Line v Hansen-Tangen* [1976] 1 WLR 989. In *Prenn v Simmonds* Lord Wilberforce said at p. 1383:

> The time has long passed when agreements, even those under seal, were isolated from the matrix of facts in which they were set and interpreted purely on internal linguistic considerations . . . We must . . . inquire beyond the language and see what the circumstances were with reference to which the words were used, and the object appearing from those circumstances, which the person using them had in view.

Lord Wilberforce then continued at p. 1385 in terms to the later part. of which particular attention was directed by counsel on behalf of the plaintiff, namely:

> In my opinion, then, evidence of negotiations, or of the parties intentions, and, a fortiori, of Dr Simmonds' intentions, ought not to be received, and evidence should be restricted to evidence of the factual background known to the parties at or before the date of the contract, including evidence of the 'genesis' and objectively the 'aim' of the transaction.

In *Reardon Smith Line v Hansen-Tangen* [1976] WLR 989, Lord Wilberforce repeated his views at p. 995 in these terms:

> No contracts made are in a vacuum; there is always a setting in which they have to be placed. The nature of what is legitimate to have regard to is usually described as 'the surrounding circumstances' but this phrase is imprecise: it can be illustrated but hardly defined. In commercial contract it is certainly right that the court should know the commercial purpose of the contract and this in turn presupposes knowledge of the genesis of the transaction, the background, the context, the market in which the parties are operating.

The dangers involved in exploring the background or surrounding circumstances to a document under construction and the limitations which must be placed upon the factual matrix rule were referred to in *Plum Brothers v Dolmac (Agriculture) Ltd* [1984] 271 EG 373 by May L.J. when he said at p. 374:

> There has grown up a tendency to speak about construing documents in or against what is described as the 'factual matrix' in which the contract or documents first saw the light of day. In truth that is only, I think, a modern way of saying what has always been a rule for a long time that, in construing a document, one must look at all of the circumstances surrounding the making of the contract at the time it was made. There is the danger, if one stresses reference to the 'factual matrix' that one may be influenced by what is in truth a finding of the subjective intention of the parties at the relevant time, instead of carrying out what I understand to be the correct exercise, namely, determining objectively the intent of the parties from the words of the documents themselves in the light of the circumstances surrounding the transaction. It is not permissible, I think, to take into account the find of fact about what the parties intended the document to achieve when one is faced with the problem some five, ten or many years later of construing it. In deciding what the document did in fact achieve, all that one can look at are the general circumstances surrounding the making of the document and in which it was made, and deduce the intention of the parties from the actual words of the document itself. The contract between the parties is what they said in the relevant document. It is not for this or any court to make a contract for the parties different from the words that the documents actually use merely because it may be that the parties intended something different.

In *Rohan Construction Ltd v Insurance Corporation of Ireland* [1988] ILRM 373 this court, in a judgment delivered by Griffin J., did apply the principles enunciated by Lord Wilberforce in *Reardon Smith Line v Hansen-Tangen* [1976] 1 WLR 989, but the warning note sounded by May L.J. must be equally applicable in this jurisdiction. At the end of the day the rule as to construction and the context in which it is to be achieved is most succinctly expressed in the judgment of Keane J. (as he then was) in *Kramer v Arnold* [1997] 3 IR 43 at p. 55 when he said:

> In this case, as in any case where the parties are in disagreement as to what a particular provision of a contract means, the task of the court is to decide what the intention of the parties was, having regard to the language used in the contract itself and the surrounding circumstances.
>
> . . . In my view the complicated background to the share subscription agreement is at best of a very limited value in construing the concluded agreement. At worst it

provides the temptation, foreseen by May L.J., of seeking to extract the subjective intention or motivation of one or other, or even both, of the parties from the history rather than construe it in the context of that history. . . .

In my view the judge erred in ascertaining the intentions of the parties from the evidence heard by him as well as the [change in terminology from the heads of agreement] and documents prepared in the course of the negotiations. The intention of the parties may be gleaned only from the document ultimately concluded by them, albeit construing it in the light of surrounding circumstances but not ascertaining their intentions from such circumstances. Such a process would be justified only where one or other of the parties claimed rectification of the document executed by him: that is not the present case.

Reading and rereading the share subscription agreement as a whole and in particular art. 4.3 thereof and having regard to the surrounding circumstances insofar as they are material, I am satisfied that the obligation of the defendant under art. 5.3 was to distribute the sum of £40,000 by way of dividend and that the shareholders, the plaintiff and Baggrave Ltd had a comparable obligation to ensure that such a dividend was paid if, but only if, such a dividend could be lawfully paid. The trial judge expressed the view that the ordinary and natural meaning of the word 'distribute' as used in the paragraph in question was 'pay'. I would respectfully disagree with that view. *The Shorter Oxford Dictionary* gives the primary definition of 'distribute' as 'to deal out or bestow in proportions or shares amongst many; to allot or apportion as his share to each'.

Accordingly the use of the word 'distribute' suggests the payment of a dividend rather than the discharge of a particular commercial indebtedness. . . .

However, it seems to me that the proper interpretation of the clause is put beyond doubt by the final sentence thereof which provides:

> The first subscriber and the second subscriber will execute any dividend waiver necessary to implement the above, and will arrange where possible to pay such distributions by way of interim dividends as agreed.

That sentence clearly recognises that the £40,000 to be paid to the plaintiff in priority to the claims of the second subscriber was a dividend which, *prima facie*, would be payable to all of the shareholders of the same class in proportion to their shareholdings and could be dealt with otherwise only by agreement between the parties. The final words of the sentence resolve any possible doubt by requiring arrangements to be made to make the annual payments, not by lump sum, but by 'interim dividend'.

The only other clause of the share subscription agreement which throws any light on the matter is clause 5.8. That clause is headed 'Dividends' and in the first sentence thereof provides:

> Subject as hereinafter provided and to clause 4.3 the dividend policy of the company shall be determined by the Board from time to time.

The expression confirms that clause 4.3 was in fact dealing with dividends and is at the very least consistent with the view that the sums of £40,000 payable to the plaintiff and second subscriber were indeed dividends, but payable in a manner which differed from the routine procedure and required—as provided—the express agreement or waiver of the shareholders concerned.

Unhappily, it would seem to me that the effort to place the agreement in the context in which it was made evolved into an impermissible investigation of the subjective intentions of the parties in entering into the agreement. I have no doubt that the agreement and in particular clause 4.3 thereof properly construed requires the defendant and the other parties thereto to procure the payment of the sums of £40,000 by way of dividend subject to the necessary qualification that such sums may only be paid when profits are available for that purpose.

In those circumstances I would allow the appeal, set aside the order of the High Court and substitute an order dismissing the plaintiff's claim.

(Denham J. and Keane C.J. concurred.)

Notes

1. In *Boyle v Whitvale Ltd and Hurley* (HC) [2003] IEHC 61 24 July 2003 unreported, the factual matrix approach was used by the Court in construing a development contract and Ms Justice Finlay Geoghegan affirmed the principles stated by Keane J. in *Kramer v Arnold* [1997] 3 IR 43 in this respect.
2. In *Irish Pensions Trust Ltd v Central Remedial Clinic and Others* [2005] IEHC 87, 2005 unreported, Kelly J. considered the principles applicable to the construction of pension documents and cited with approval the approach taken by Millett J. in *Re Courage Pension Schemes* [1987] 1 WLR 495 and Warner J. in *Mettoy Pension Trustees Ltd v Evans* [1990] 1 WLR 157. These principles were subsequently applied by Finlay Geoghegan J. in *Boliden Tara Mines Ltd v Frank Cosgrove & Others* [2007] IEHC 60, and summarised as follows.

There are no special rules of construction which apply to Pension Scheme Documents. Nevertheless where possible they should be construed so as to give reasonable and practical effect to the *Pension Scheme*. This is particularly so where the documents are ones intended to have legal effect but couched in very general terms. The construction should be practical and purposive rather than detached and literal. In construing the documents the court should take into account the factual background and surrounding circumstances (i.e. 'the factual matrix').

Consider:

What are the disadvantages to employing the factual matrix approach?

SECTION FOUR—PAROL EVIDENCE RULE

'Parol testimony cannot be received to contradict, vary, add to or subtract from the terms of a written contract or the terms in which the parties have deliberately agreed to record any part of their contract.' Per Lord Morris in *Bank of Australasia v Palmer* [1897] AC 540.

EXCEPTIONS

(a) *To establish that no contract exists*

Parol evidence is admissible to show that what appears to be a valid contract is in fact no contract at all or that there were two distinct contracts. See *Godley v Power* (1961) 95 ILTR 135 p.251 above.

(*b*) To establish consideration

See Black *v* Grealy 10 November 1977 p.289 above.

(*c*) To explain the circumstances surrounding the agreement

Parol evidence is admissible to prove the true nature of the agreement or the legal relationship of the parties.

Revenue Commissioners *v* Moroney [1972] IR 372
(Facts on p.173.)

Kenny J.

Counsel for the plaintiffs has objected to the admission of the affidavit and declaration because, he says, no evidence of extrinsic circumstances is admissible to add to, contradict, vary or alter the terms of a deed; he referred to the statement of this rule in Norton's *Treatise on Deeds* (2nd edn, 1928) 135. This rule however does not apply to the statement of the consideration in the deed (Ibid. p. 140) because 'the statement of the consideration forms no part of the terms of the deed, but is only a statement contained in the deed of an antecedent fact.' Moreover, if no evidence was admissible to contradict, vary or alter the terms of the deed, the Revenue claim would fail because there is a receipt for the consideration in the deed. It is not necessary to give authority for the proposition that evidence may be given to show that, despite the receipt, the consideration was not paid. Similarly, evidence is admissible when it is relevant to explain the circumstances in which the deed was executed and to establish that the parties did not intend that the purchase price mentioned in the deed should ever be paid.

O'Neill *v* Ryan [1991] ILRM 672

The plaintiff instituted contemporaneously two sets of proceedings, a petition seeking relief under s. 205 of the Companies Act 1963 and a plenary action claiming damages for *inter alia* fraudulent misrepresentation. The defendants brought a motion to consolidate the two actions and to be permitted to make a joint lodgment to all the claims in the consolidated action. Blayney J. refused to order consolidation but agreed that the two actions could be tried together. On 24 May the defendants wrote to the plaintiff's solicitors offering to settle proceedings. The plaintiff accepted this. Later the defendants claimed that the settlement related to both proceedings. The plaintiff denied this and sued for specific performance of the settlement agreement. The defendants resisted the order on the grounds that the agreement had been entered into by mistake.

Costello J. in the High Court granted specific performance. After dealing with the issue of mistake, Costello J. considered the admissibility of parol evidence as to the intentions of the defendants.

Costello J.:

By way of alternative it was urged that the rules of evidence relating to the construction of written documents permit the court to consider the evidence of the intention of the authors of the letter of 24 May 1990, as part of the surrounding circumstances in which the letter was written and that in the light of this evidence the offer which was made was an offer to settle the two sets of proceedings, and that as the plaintiff's solicitor intended to settle on the s. 205 proceedings the parties were not *ad idem*. In support of this submission I was referred to the passages in *Chitty on Contracts* dealing with the admissibility of extrinsic evidence to interpret and explain written agreements (26th edn) para. 867 et seq. and *Phipson on Evidence* (12th edn) para. 196 et seq. to *Prenn v Simmonds* [1971] 1 WLR 1381, 1383–4. The passage of *Prenn* (approved by O'Hanlon J. in *British Leyland Exports v Brittain Manufacturing Ltd* [1981] IR 335 at 346) to which I was referred is as follows:

> The time has long passed when agreements, even those under seal, were isolated from the matrix of facts in which they were set and interpreted purely on internal linguistic considerations. There is no need to appeal here to any modern, anti-literal, tendencies, for Lord Blackburn's well known judgment in *River Wear Commissioners v Adamson* (1877) 2 App Cas 743, 763 provides ample warrant for a liberal approach. We must, as he said, inquire beyond the language and see what the circumstances were with reference to which the words were used, and the object, appearing from those circumstances, which the person using them had in view.

This judgment affords justification for hearing extrinsic evidence of the general circumstances in which the offer of settlement was made and accepted, including the pleadings in the two sets of proceedings, the motion to consolidate, what transpired at its hearing and the judgment on it, as an aid to construe the written contract contained in the two letters. It is not however an authority for the proposition that the parties can adduce evidence as to their intention in entering the written agreement. In *Prenn v Simmonds* [1971] 1 WLR 1381 the court was concerned with the construction of a written contract. Counsel for the defendant, Dr Simmonds, had argued that in considering it prior negotiations could be looked at as an aid to construction. Rejecting this submission Lord Wilberforce said at p. 1385 of the report: 'In my opinion, then, evidence of negotiations, or of the parties' intentions, and *a fortiori* of Dr Simmonds' intention, ought not to be received, and evidence should be restricted to evidence of the factual background known to the parties at or before the date of the contract, including evidence of the "genesis" and objectively the "aim" of the transaction.' And I do not think that the passages in *Chitty on Contracts* relating to the admissibility of extrinsic evidence to which I was referred must be taken as in some way modifying the earlier passages on the law of mistake, nor do those general principles on the same subject in *Phipson on Evidence* allow the defendant to adduce evidence which in effect contradicts the reasonable construction of the words used in the written agreement.

Finally it was submitted that the objective test as set out in *Chitty on Contracts* must be read in the light of the Supreme Court decision in *Mespil Ltd v Capaldi* [1986] ILRM 373 and that *Mespil* is authority for the proposition that in considering whether parties are *ad idem* the court is not bound by the construction of the words used in the written document but may take into account the subjective intent of the offeror when writing them.

I do not think that *Mespil Ltd v Capaldi* [1986] ILRM 373 supports this view. That was a case in which a settlement of an action had been negotiated by counsel for the plaintiff and counsel for the defendant. The result of their negotiations was reduced into writing and was headed 'Full and final settlement of all matters and acts in dispute between the parties in these proceedings.' A dispute arose as to the terms of the settlement and proceedings were instituted. Evidence was given at the trial by the plaintiff's counsel to the effect that the words did not mean that an existing dispute unrelated to the proceedings between the parties about the user of the premises was settled, whilst counsel for the defendants gave evidence that the words meant that all matters in dispute (including the user dispute) between the parties and not just those referred to in the two actions were settled. The Supreme Court held, at p. 376, that it was clear that the form of the written consent, viewed in terms of its wording and of the negotiations leading up to it, was capable of justifying the opinion of counsel for the defendant, but that it could also be said that on an objective consideration of the relevant circumstances that the plaintiff's counsel's construction was justified. There was therefore a latent ambiguity and a mutual misunderstanding which meant that in fact there was no agreement.

Mespil Ltd v Capaldi [1986] ILRM 373 is an example of a case where, looking at the words used by the parties, the court could come to the conclusion that, objectively speaking, they suffered from such ambiguity that it was impossible to conclude that the parties had reached an agreement. That is not, in my judgment, the situation which pertains in this case. In my view the words used by the defendant's solicitors could only be construed as an offer to settle the s. 205 proceedings only. This was the sense in which they were understood by the plaintiff's solicitor, and accepted by him.

(Affirmed by the Supreme Court on appeal.)

Note

See also *Re Richardson v National Trust* [1988] NI 86.

(d) Where the written agreement is not the whole agreement

Howden Bros v Ulster Bank Ltd [1924] IR 117

A firm of shipbuilders orally agreed to build a boat for the plaintiffs. A letter was sent by the plaintiffs confirming the order to build the boat. Instalments of the price agreed were paid by the plaintiffs, but before the boat was completed the company went into liquidation, and a receiver was appointed by the defendants, debenture holders. The defendants detained the boat and the plaintiffs sued for damages, claiming the boat to be their property.

Wilson J.:

I do not doubt or impugn the settled rule of evidence, that parol evidence is not admissible to add to, vary, or contradict a written agreement or any transaction in writing: *Meres v Ansell*;[1] but in this case I have come to the conclusion that the letters are not a written agreement and do not contain or purport to contain the whole transaction, and in allowing the evidence I follow the law laid down in Roscoe's *Nisi Prius Evidence* (18th edn), 17; and *Allen v Pink*,[2] which decided that parol evidence of a verbal transaction is not excluded by the fact that a writing was made concerning or relating to it unless such writing was in fact the transaction itself and not merely a note or memorandum of it or portion of the transaction; and the judgment therein of Lord Abinger C.B., concurred in by Bolland and Alderson B.B.:

The general principle is quite true that if there has been a parol agreement, which is afterwards reduced by the parties into writing, that writing alone must be looked to to ascertain the terms of the contract; but the principle does not apply here; there was no evidence of any agreement by the plaintiff that the whole contract should be reduced into writing by the defendant; the contract is first concluded by parol and afterwards the paper is drawn up, which appears to have been meant merely as a memorandum of the transaction or an informal receipt for the money, not as containing the terms of the contract itself.

. . . Again in *Hutton v Warren*[3] Baron Parke says that the principle on which extensive evidence is admissible to annex incidents to written contracts is a presumption that the parties did not mean to express in writing the whole of the contract by which they intended to be bound. In *Angell v Duke*[4] Blackburne J. says: 'It is a most important rule of law that people should not add to or vary a written contract, which is the record of all the terms relating to the same matter agreed upon between the parties.'

It is because it was alleged that the letters in this case on their face were not intended to be the record of all the terms agreed on between the parties that I admitted the parol evidence. . . .

There is enough in this case, in the verbal contract, in the conduct of the parties, and in the circumstances to show that the agreement and intention of the parties was that the property in the boat should pass to the plaintiffs as she was constructed.

1. 3 Wilson, KB 276.
2. 4 M. & W. 140.
3. 1 M. & W. 466.
4. 23 WR 548.

Notes

1. In *Clayton Love & Sons (Dublin) Ltd v British and Irish Steam Packet Co. Ltd* (1970) 104 ILTR 157 the defendants contracted to carry the plaintiffs' frozen food from Dublin to Liverpool. An agent of the plaintiffs telephoned the defendants prior to the shipments to explain the nature of the cargo and to request that it be shipped at a sub-zero temperature. The food was damaged because the loading was conducted at atmospheric temperature and the plaintiffs sued. Evidence of the telephone conversation was admitted as the court found that the terms of the contract were to be found in the written contract and the additional terms agreed to in the telephone conversation.

2. Proving the existence of a collateral contract will not involve varying or adding to the original agreement because it will be totally separate and independent from it. (See *Mitchelstown Co-operative Society Ltd v Societé des Produits Nestlé SA, Chambourcy Food Company Ltd and Nestlé (Ire) Ltd* [1989] ILRM 582, where the Supreme Court held that the Co-op had established an arguable case for the existence of a collateral contract.) In *Heilbut, Synoms & Co. v Buckleton* [1913] AC 30, Lord Moulton stated:

It is evident . . . that there may be a contract the consideration for which is the making of some other contract. 'If you will make such and such a contract I will give you one hundred pounds,' is in every sense of the word a complete legal contract. It is collateral to the main contract, but each has an independent existence, and they do not differ in respect of their possessing to the full the character or status of a contract.

For this reason, Murphy J. in *Cotter v Minister for Agriculture* (HC) 15 November 1991 unreported, stated that where a collateral contract exists, 'it is hardly an exception at all' to the parol evidence rule. See also Wedderburn 'Collateral Contracts' (1959) 17 CLJ 58.

(e) To identify the subject matter of the contract

Ulster Bank v Synnott (1871) 5 IR Eq 595

The defendant, being indebted to the plaintiff, deposited debentures certificates with the plaintiff, accompanied by a letter stating that they were so deposited 'against acceptances made' on the defendant's account. The court had to determine *inter alia* whether the expression 'acceptances made' was clear or whether parol evidence was admissible to aid construction.

Chatterton V.C.:

The defendant contends that the word *made*, being a past participle, grammatically excludes future acceptances, and that there is no ambiguity to warrant me in admitting parol evidence to explain it. I do not concur in this view—first, because I think that in every such case it is necessary to learn, by parol evidence, the circumstances under which the document was written, so as to enable the court to ascertain what it was with which the parties were dealing; and, also, because I think that the word *made* is capable of two different significations. That it refers to past acceptances is plain, but the question is, when past? Whether past at the time at which it was written, or past when it should afterwards come to be acted on. The expression 'against acceptances made' &c., requires to be expanded, and means, 'to be held by the bank as a security for the repayment of the sums which shall become due on foot of the acceptance made by the London and Westminster Bank on my account, and through you.' The word *made* may be read either as, which have been heretofore made, or, which shall have been made during the continuance of the security. The latter is neither a forced nor an unusual meaning, and instances of the use of the past participle with reference to future events are common. . .

The expression being therefore ambiguous, parol evidence of the surrounding circumstances is clearly admissible to aid the construction.

(Evidence showed that the expression meant 'acceptances which shall have been made during the continuance of the security'.)

Chambers v Kelly (1873) 7 IRCL 231

The plaintiff entered into an agreement to sell the defendant oaks growing on certain land 'together with all other trees growing through the oak plantation and mixed with the oak'. A dispute arose as to correct interpretation of this agreement.

Fitzgerald B.:

It appears plain, at least I think, that the term 'oak plantations', in the agreement in question does not mean plantations in which there was nothing but oak, because in the agreement itself, trees of another kind are described as being mixed up with oak, and as growing through these 'oak plantations'; and, on the other hand, that it does not mean plantations in which there was any oak at all, because otherwise there would have been no necessity whatever for the introduction of the description 'oak plantations'.

That being so, it was necessary to go outside the written agreement to ascertain the subject matter in this respect, that is to say, 'oak plantations'. I am of opinion that, for this purpose, evidence of what passed, leading, in the words of the learned judge who tried the case, 'up to' the agreement, could not be excluded.

Macklin and McDonald *v* Graecen and Co. Ltd [1983] IR 61

The defendants agreed to sell a licence attached to a certain public house to the plaintiffs 'provided the sale of the premises to the Northern Bank Ltd is completed'. The public house had been demolished prior to the date of this agreement. The plaintiffs sued for specific performance of this agreement.

Griffin J.:

When (as in this case) a transaction has been reduced to writing by agreement of the parties, no evidence may be given to prove the terms of the transaction except the document itself, and extrinsic evidence is not admissible to vary the terms of the document. I agree with the learned trial judge that, in an appropriate case, an agreement made by the holder of a licence for its extinguishment is enforceable; indeed, such agreements are frequently made. Such an agreement would be more elaborate in form and would (*inter alia*) recite such matters as the agreement of the parties, that the licensee holds the licence, that the licence is subsisting and will be kept in force, the intended application to the court for a new licence, the description of the premises to which it is attached, and the agreement to consent to the extinguishment of the licence. But this is not such a case. Here, the plaintiffs' claim is, and remains, one for specific performance of an agreement to sell the licence. It is not and cannot be treated as a claim seeking rectification of the document, in which case parol evidence would be admissible in support of such a claim.

Therefore, the plaintiffs' claim must be confined to the terms of the agreement and, unquestionably, those terms make the agreement one for the sale of the licence. . .

It follows that, as the licence is inalienable, on this ground alone the plaintiffs are not entitled to enforce the agreement of 29 August 1975, or to obtain specific performance of it.

Notes

1. In *Bula Ltd v Tara Mines* (SC), 15 January 1999, unrep., Keane J. explained that the parol evidence rule 'is subject to the qualification that oral evidence may be received as to the factual matrix in which a written arrangement was concluded (examined in section 3 above) so as to explain and to interpret the terms of the agreement'. It was emphasised, however, that this does not mean that evidence of negotiations and of the parties' subjective intentions is admissible but that 'what is permissible is evidence of the factual context in which the parties came to terms'.

2. See also BCT *Software Solutions Ltd v Arnold Laver & Co. Ltd* [2002] 2 All ER (Comm) 85.

(f) *To explain a custom*

In *Wilson and Strain v Pinkerton* (1897) 31 ILTR 86 parol evidence was admitted as an aid to construction in relation to a particular custom in contracts between bakeries and their employees.

(g) To show that the document should be rectified because the agreed terms which were intended to be reduced to writing were not accurately recorded or the contract document contains a mistake.

O'Neill *v* Ryan [1991] ILRM 672
(Facts on p.337)

Costello J.:

The court will also grant relief by way of rectification where the parties have reached an agreement but where an error is made in giving effect to the parties' common intention in a written agreement. The general rule is that where this is a common shared mistake in that the written agreement fails to record the intention of both parties the court will order its rectification. Rectification may also be ordered when a party has entered into a written agreement by mistake, if he establishes that the other party with knowledge of the mistake concluded that agreement.

Note

The English Law Commission, in report No. 154, a study of the Parol Evidence Rule, concluded that the rule does not have the effect of excluding evidence which ought to be admitted if justice is to be done between the parties. Evidence will only be excluded, the Commission felt, when its reception would be inconsistent with the intention of the parties. Legislation in this area would not be helpful as it would require reference to the rule by name or a description of the rule. The Law Commission stated:

> Naming the rule would not be possible because, the same name is used for more than one rule of law. Describing the rule might seem to leave more scope for the production of a plausible provision. But we could not avoid the conclusion that any description consistent with our analysis of the rule would be circular, so that any purported abolition would plainly appear to be beating the air. We considered the possibility of legislation which would enact the opposite of the rule, instead of abolishing it. But this approach involved the same problem—if on a true analysis the rule cannot be said to have legal effect, nor can its opposite. [Footnotes omitted.]

EXERCISES

1. Suzie operates a garage and car-sales business. She advertises to sell 'a 1999 sports model BMW'. When trying to sell the car to Adele, who comes to view it, she notes that it seems to be 'a terrific car' from an excellent and reliable manufacturer. Suzie mentions that the car has just arrived in the showroom and that they have not yet had time to service it. Adele is an amateur rally driver and impressed by the price. Adele buys the car and subsequently discovers that it is a 1990 model. Furthermore, the engine is seriously defective and in need of expensive repair. She sues for breach of contract.

2. Richard is a motor dealer who specialises in classic cars. Thomas, a collector of miniature cars, sees a full size Aston Martin car in Richard's showrooms. The logbook indicates that the car was manufactured in 1960. Richard tells him that the car is in 'excellent condition' and that 'this DB5 model is particularly sought after by collectors as it was the model used in the James Bond movie *Goldfinger*'. Thomas agrees to buy the car immediately, declining Richard's offer to 'take it home, show it to your friends, see what they think'. Two days later, the car breaks down and Thomas's mechanic tells him that the car is virtually unrepairable. He also tells him that the car is not a DB5 model as production of these models only commenced in 1963. Advise Thomas.

3. An auctioneer informs potential bidders that a horse he is currently selling in the ring is in perfect health. This comment is made to encourage bidding and without checking with Jim, its owner. When a veterinary inspection subsequently reveals health problems, the purchaser claims that this 'term' has been broken and that he wishes to get his money back. Advise Jim.

4. Helen buys a car from Molly who promises that it is 'roadworthy'. When the car is delivered, one wheel is loose. Helen argues that she is entitled to repudiate the contract on this ground. Advise Molly.

5. What balance should be struck between deeming contracts void for uncertainty and admitting parol evidence to explain them further?

Chapter Seven

Implied Terms

INTRODUCTION

Contracting parties do not generally have the time, the expertise or the opportunity to agree or draft all the terms which they wish to include in their bargain. Few contracting parties are omniscient; fewer still are able to envisage how future developments will influence their bargain or their expectations of it. In these circumstances the express terms of the contract, whether written or verbal, will cast little or no light on how the contract should be interpreted or performed. It is at this stage that gaps in the contract will be filled, by reference to so-called implied terms. This is an important process which is intended to allow the parties to proceed towards completion of their contractual venture, often at the cost of some modification in the expectations of one or other of the parties, but in general this is viewed as preferable to a judicial declaration that the contract is void for uncertainty, invalid due to mistake, or discharged by operation of law (see Chapters 2, 9 and 18 respectively).

SECTION ONE—TERMS IMPLIED AT COMMON LAW

A. TERMS IMPLIED IN FACT

Terms will be implied into a contract where necessary to give effect to the presumed intentions of the parties. Two formulations of this test have been suggested: the 'business efficacy' test and the 'officious bystander' test:

> An implied warranty, or as it is called a covenant at law, as distinguished from an express contract or express warranty, really is in every instance founded on the presumed intention of the parties and upon reason. It is the implication which the law draws from what must obviously have been the intention of the parties, an implication which the law draws with the object of giving efficacy to the transaction and preventing such a failure of consideration as cannot have been within the contemplation of either of the parties.

Per Bowen L.J. in the *Moorcock* [1886–90] All ER 530.

> *Prima facie* that which in any contract is left to be implied and need not be expressed is something so obvious that it goes without saying; so that, if, while the parties were making their bargain, an officious bystander were to suggest some express provision for it in their agreement, they would testily suppress him with a common 'Oh, of course!'

Per MacKinnon L.J. in *Shirlaw v Southern Foundries Ltd* [1939] 2 All ER 113.

Butler v McAlpine [1904] 2 IR 445

The defendants hired a barge from the plaintiff to carry goods to a wharf which they had leased. The barge was damaged when it grounded on a block of hardened cement whose existence was unknown to the defendants. The plaintiff sued for damages for negligence. The defendants appealed against a decision of the King's Bench Division granting the plaintiff damages for breach of an implied duty to take reasonable care to ascertain that the berth was reasonably safe.

Fitzgibbon L.J.:

The defendants have contended that the *ratio decidendi* in *The Moorcock*[1] was that the defendant was a wharfinger, in the sense of a person who hires a wharf to a shipowner. With all respect, it is only necessary to read the case to see, as the Lords expressly said in *The Calliope*,[2] that the liability rested upon the fact that for good consideration the defendants had *invited* the plaintiff to moor his ship in the place where it was injured, under circumstances which, in the ordinary course of business and in reason, raised the implication that the defendants had at least undertaken to use reasonable care to *see* that the berth was safe; the wider undertaking to *make* it safe, or to *keep* it safe, was there, more than here, qualified by the evidence as to the control of the place in question. But the distinction is immaterial, because even if the lesser duty only—to see that the berth was safe—existed, the defendants here are liable for its breach.
. . .

In *The Moorcock* the defendants were held liable for injuries caused by a hardened ridge left on the natural bottom of the Thames by the weight of a previous occupant of the berth, which did not strip at low water; here the mischief was done by a bag of the defendants' cement, which either fell off their wharf, where it was in charge of their servant, or dropped overboard from a barge while unloading at their quay under the superintendence of the same servant. In addition, their general manager stated that it was the storekeeper's duty to see that the berth was clear, and he had on other occasions known bags of cement to fall into the berth, and had taken them out for the defendants.

Lord Esher said that *The Moorcock* decision went a step beyond any of the cases cited, which were not all wharfingers' cases. This case falls far short of *The Moorcock* upon the facts.

Bowen L.J. based the implied contract on the presumed intention of the parties and on reason; he held that both parties must have known that unless the ground was safe the ship would be simply 'buying an opportunity of danger' in grounding at the jetty, and although the defendants had no duty, by statute or at common law, to repair the bed of the river, and had 'no power to interfere with it unless under the license of the conservators,' he said:

The law will not imply that the persons who have not control of the place have taken reasonable care to make it good, but it does not follow that they are relieved from all responsibility; they are on the spot; they must know that the jetty cannot be used unless reasonable care is taken, if not to make it safe, at all events to see whether it is safe. No one can tell whether reasonable safety has been secured except themselves, and if they let out their jetty for use, they at all events imply that they have taken reasonable care to see whether the berth, which is the essential part of the use of the jetty, is safe; and if it is not safe, and if they have not taken such reasonable care, it is their duty to warn persons with whom they have dealings that they have not done so.

. . .

The Calliope was decided in favour of the defendants, because the Lords took a view of the facts different from that taken by the Court of Appeal. But they described the state of facts in which the defendants would have been liable in words precisely applicable to this case; and they rested the liability upon a principle not peculiar to navigation, or to wharfingers, but directly applicable to the defendants here.

Lord Halsbury said:

If the vessel had been invited to a berth at which it was unfit for a vessel under any circumstances to lie [words appropriate to a berth occupied by a bag of hardened cement], and that by reason of the inequality and unfitness of the berth, the vessel being brought there was injured, he certainly entertained no doubt that the law, as laid down in the case of *The Moorcock*, would have been applicable to that state of things.

He extends the limit of the duty, where it exists, to a reasonable distance from the wharf; and refers particularly, as distinguishing the case of *The Moorcock*, to the fact that there was no evidence in the case of *The Calliope* that the alleged obstruction was not 'the normal condition of the bank.'

. . .

Seeing that the facts here are stronger against the defendants than were the facts in *The Moorcock*, and applying the decision in *The Moorcock* and the statements of law by the Lords in *The Calliope* to these facts, I am clearly of opinion that the appeal must be dismissed with costs.

[1] 14 PD 64.   [2] 14 PD 138; [1891] AC 11.

(Walker L.J. concurred. Holmes L.J. dissented on the ground that unlike the *Moorcock* case the bargemen in this case had the opportunity to examine the berth.)

Sweeney v Duggan [1997] 2 ILRM 211

The plaintiff, a former employee of a quarrying company, had been injured whilst operating a drill in the company's quarry and, in separate proceedings, was awarded damages against the company. At the time of the award the company was in voluntary liquidation, and was unable to pay even its preferential creditors in full. The defendant was the managing director and effectively the only shareholder of the quarrying company. He also held the post of quarry manager and as such was, by virtue of s. 23 of the Mines and Quarries Act 1965, under a duty to ensure that the Act's provisions concerning the safety, health and physical welfare of persons in quarrying operations were observed. The plaintiff instituted proceedings against the defendant claiming that the defendant personally had a duty to ensure that the company, as the plaintiff's employer, procured employer's liability insurance to meet any claims for damages for personal injuries, or alternatively, to ensure that the company warned the plaintiff that no such policy of insurance was in existence. The plaintiff submitted that such a duty derived primarily from the contract of employment. Such a term was to be implied having regard to the exceptionally dangerous nature of the business of quarrying, the precarious state of the company's finances at the time of the accident, and the fact that the plaintiff had insured himself to a small extent against loss in connection with injuries sustained in the course of his employment.

In the High Court Barron J. dismissed the plaintiff's claim. The plaintiff appealed.

Murphy J. gave judgment on behalf of the Supreme Court.

Murphy J.:

...

There are at least two situations where the courts will, independently of statutory requirement, imply a term which has not been expressly agreed by the parties to a contract. The first of these situations was identified in the well-known *Moorcock* case (1889) 14 PD 64 where a term not expressly agreed upon by the parties was inferred on the basis of the presumed intention of the parties. The basis for such a presumption was explained by MacKinnon LJ. in *Shirlaw v. Southern Foundries* (1926) *Ltd* [1939] 2 KB 206 at p. 227 in an expression, equally memorable, in the following terms:

> *Prima facie* that which in any contract is left to be implied and need not be expressed is something so obvious that it goes without saying; so that, if while the parties were making their bargain, an officious bystander were to suggest some express provision for it in their agreement, they would testily suppress him with a common, 'Oh, of course.'

Whether a term is implied pursuant to the presumed intention of the parties or as a legal incident of a definable category of contract it must be not merely reasonable but also necessary. Clearly it cannot be implied if it is inconsistent with the express wording of the contract and furthermore it may be difficult to infer a term where it cannot be formulated with reasonable precision.

It seems to me clear that the contention that a term as to insurance by the company of its risk for liability to the plaintiff as its employee or an obligation to warn him of the absence of such insurance could not be implied in pursuance of the *Moorcock* doctrine. The contract of employment would and did operate effectively without any such term and if one postulated an inquiry by the ubiquitous and officious bystander as to whether such a term should be included I anticipate that it might have well been rejected and certainly would not have been accepted without considerable negotiation and discussion a result which would negative the existence of an implied term. In *Spring v National Amalgamated Stevedores & Dockers Society* [1956] 1 WLR 585 the defendant trade union sought to expel the plaintiff from its membership and in doing so relied upon what they alleged was implied in the contract between the plaintiff and them. The term which it was said should be implied arose from an agreement which had been reached at Bridlington in 1939 and regulated the transfer of members from one union to another. That agreement was, in trade union circles, referred to as 'the Bridlington Agreement'. What, therefore, the defendants sought to incorporate by implication in their agreement with the plaintiff was a provision that the plaintiff should comply with 'the Bridlington Agreement'. In his judgment the Vice Chancellor Sir Leonard Stone postulated the *Moorcock* test in the following terms (at p. 599):

> If that test were to be applied to the facts of the present case and the bystander had asked the plaintiff at the time he paid his five shillings and signed the Acceptance form, 'Won't you put into it some reference tot he Bridlington Agreement?' I think (indeed, I have no doubt) the plaintiff would have answered 'What's that?' In my judgment, that is sufficient to dispose of this case ...

Clearly the plaintiff in the present case would have little difficulty in appreciating the general concept of employer's liability insurance but so far from an immediate acquiescence to any proposals in relation to such insurance I think it is reasonable to anticipate that a debate would have arisen as to the value of such insurance to the employee seeing that such insurance is primarily for the benefit of the employer and, if it were explained how it might also benefit the employee, further and useful discussion might well follow as to whether the interests of the plaintiff would not be better secured by some other arrangement which would be of immediate and direct benefit to the plaintiff. The parties to the negotiations might recognise (as did their counsel) that a contractual obligation by the company to insure would add little protection to the plaintiff as default by the company would merely duplicate the plaintiff's right to recover a judgment against the company with no greater prospect of recovering thereon. I would reject the contention that the term for which the plaintiff contends could be implied on the basis of the *Moorcock* doctrine.

Ward *v* Spivack Ltd; Fagan *v* Spivack Ltd [1957] IR 40

Ward and Fagan were sales agents for the defendant company. Both operated within a defined area on a commission basis. Their contracts made no reference to the payment of commission on the termination of their agencies. Therefore when the defendant terminated their agencies they sought a declaration that there should be implied into the contracts a term that commission was to continue to be paid on all orders from customers in their respective areas who did business with the company during the period of their agencies.

Davitt P.:

Should a term then be implied with regard to it? The test is, I think, as I suggested to [counsel for the plaintiffs] during the hearing. Let us envisage the parties at the moment they have agreed on the expressed terms of their contract. Then imagine one of them saying, with regard to the term sought to be implied: 'Of course such and such is understood?' If the probability is that the other would say, 'Of course!', then the term may be implied. If the probability is that he would say, 'Certainly not, I will agree to nothing of the kind,' then clearly the term cannot be implied no matter how desirable or reasonable it may seem, as the court cannot make a contract for the parties; it can only determine what they agreed on, either expressly or impliedly. Let us apply the test here. If after the terms already mentioned had been agreed on Fagan had said: 'Of course, it is understood that in the event of my ceasing to be your agent commission will still continue to be payable to me and after my death to my executors on all business subsequently done with any customer in my territory whether introduced by me or not,' I am quite sure that Spivack would have said, 'Certainly not; I am not going to agree on commission being paid on that basis.' I must also look at it the other way round. If Spivack had said: 'Of course, it is understood that in the event of your agency coming to an end you will cease to draw any commission except on orders still to be completed; and I will continue to reap the benefit of your work and receive orders from customers introduced by you without paying you anything,' I cannot imagine Fagan entering into the contract at all.

Another way of looking at the matter is this. Consider the ordinary case of a house agent whom I employ to secure a purchaser to buy my house at a certain price. The agent produces a purchaser who is suitable and willing to pay their price, and a deal is made. I am not entitled to terminate his agency before concluding the deal so as to deprive him of his commission which he has earned.

I do therefore hold that I should imply a term to the effect that if Fagan's agency were determined he would be entitled to draw continuing commission on all orders from customers which had been introduced by him. In Ward's case I come to similar conclusions of fact and imply the same term in his contract.

The defendants appealed to the Supreme Court.

Maguire C.J.:

It is settled law that a term may be implied in a contract to repair what *Cheshire and Fifoot*, (3rd ed., 1952), 127 calls 'an intrinsic failure of expression.' Where there has been such a failure the judge may supply the further terms which will implement their (the parties') presumed intention and in a hallowed phrase give 'business efficacy' to the contract. 'In doing this he purports at least to do merely what the parties would have done themselves had they thought of the matter. The existence of this judicial power was asserted and justified in *The Moorcock*.'[1] In that case Bowen L.J. explained the nature of the implication in all the cases; he says where they were implied 'the law is raising an implication from the presumed intention of the parties, with the object of giving to the transaction such efficacy as both parties must have intended that at all events it should have.' The test to be applied by the court has been stated by several judges in much the same language: see Scrutton L.J. in *Reigate v Union Manufacturing Co. (Ramsbottom)*;[2] and MacKinnon L.J. in *Shirlaw v Southern Foundries (1926), Ltd.*[3]

It will be seen from the language used in so stating the tests that something more is required than the *probability* of which the president speaks that the parties must have agreed to the term to be implied had the matter been mentioned. There must be something approaching certainty or as put by Jenkins L.J. in *Sethia (1944) Ltd v Partabmull Rameshwar*[4] it must be 'clear beyond a peradventure that both parties intended a given term to operate, although they did not include it in so many words.'

. . .

. . . although it might have been a reasonable thing for Mr Spivack to have agreed to continue to pay commission on orders from customers introduced by the plaintiffs at least for some time after the termination of the agency I am quite unable to hold as the president does that had the matter been raised Mr Spivack must have agreed. To read such a term into the contract would in my view not be to make clear the intention of the parties unexpressed at the time but would be to make a new contract.

I have been authorised by the other members of the court to say that they agree with the foregoing judgment.

[1.] (1889) 14 PD 64.
[2.] [1918] 1 KB 592, at 605.
[3.] [1939] 3 KB 206.
[4.] [1950] 1 All ER 51.

Murphy Buckley & Keogh v Pye (Ireland) [1971] IR 57

The defendants appointed the plaintiffs to be their sole agents for the purpose of procuring a purchaser for their factory. It was agreed that a commission would be paid to the plaintiffs if they succeeded in effecting a sale. The defendants then proceeded to negotiate a sale with a third party who had approached them directly before the plaintiff's appointment. The plaintiffs sued for commission.

Henchy J.:

The plaintiffs' case for commission, therefore, stands or falls on the submission that once they had been appointed sole selling agents commission at the agreed rate became payable when the defendants themselves sold during the currency of the sole agency. In answer to this submission, the defendants relied primarily on the decision of McCardie J. in *Bentall, Horsley and Baldry v Vicary*.[1] The headnote of that case reads as follows:

> The defendant, the owner of property, appointed the plaintiffs, who were estate agents, his sole agents for the sale of the property for a stipulated period, it being agreed that, if the plaintiffs introduced a purchaser, they should receive a commission of five per cent on the purchase price. During the period of the agency the defendant negotiated personally and quite apart from the plaintiffs with a purchaser who had never had any communication with the plaintiffs and whom the plaintiffs did not know. The result of the negotiations was that the property was sold to this purchaser. The plaintiffs thereupon claimed from the defendant damages for breach of contract on the ground that, in selling the property direct to the purchaser, he had acted in breach of his contract with them and had thereby deprived them of their commission: Held, that the plaintiffs were not entitled to damages, as the contract contained no express prohibition against a sale by the defendant himself, and the implication of such a prohibition was not necessary to give business efficacy to the transaction. Held further, on the terms of the contract, that the plaintiffs could not recover commission at the agreed rate on the purchase price received by the defendant, as they had failed to introduce the purchaser, nor could they recover on a *quantum meruit*.

. . .

Commenting on the form of the contract, McCardie J. said at p. 258 of the report:

> In the contract now before me I see nothing to prevent the business efficacy of the document by reason of the circumstance that the defendant was himself entitled to sell. If the plaintiffs had got a purchaser within the six months and before the defendant had himself sold, then they would have gained their full commission together with their right to advertisement expenses. It is to be noted that the contract contains no express words at all indicating a prohibition against a sale by the defendant himself. If the parties intended such a prohibition nothing would have been easier than to insert the appropriate words. It is also to be noted that the defendant does not say by the contract: 'I give you the sole right to sell.' He says only: 'I appoint you sole agents for the sale', which is, in my opinion, quite a different thing.

It seems to me that these observations are fully applicable to the present case. Insofar as I have been able to ascertain the terms of the contract from the conversations that led up to it, and from the correspondence and the conduct of the parties, there was nothing in the contract which gave the plaintiffs the sole right to sell; they were merely appointed sole agents to find a purchaser who would be ready to complete at a price acceptable to the defendants, and the defendants were to have the right to revoke the agency. It is clear that the contract precluded the defendants from selling through another agent during the currency of the plaintiffs' agency; it is equally clear that the contract contained no express term which precluded the defendants themselves from selling. If I am correct in thinking that, in this respect, the contract in the present case is indistinguishable from that in the *Bentall* case, then under authority of the latter case it is not possible to read into the contract in the present case an implied term precluding the defendants from selling.

In *Luxor* (*Eastbourne*) *Ltd v Cooper*[2] it was held in the House of Lords, according to the head-note, that 'where an agent is promised a commission only if he brings about the sale which he is endeavouring to effect there is no room for an implied term that the principal will not dispose of the property himself or through other channels or otherwise act so as to prevent the agent earning his commission.' Viscount Simon L.C., having stressed the dangers of formulating general propositions as to contracts with agents for commission which depend in each case on the precise terms of the contract under consideration, said at p. 120 of the report: '. . . in contracts made with commission agents there is no justification for introducing an implied term unless it is necessary to do so for the purpose of giving to the contract the business effect which both parties to it intended it should have.'

Viscount Simon then continued as follows:

It may be useful to point out that contracts under which an agent may be occupied in endeavouring to dispose of the property of a principal fall into several obvious classes. There is the class in which the agent is promised a commission by his principal if he succeeds in introducing to his principal a person who makes an adequate offer, usually an offer of not less than the stipulated amount. If that is all that is needed in order to earn his reward, it is obvious that he is entitled to be paid when this has been done, whether his principal accepts the offer and carries through the bargain or not. No implied term is needed to secure this result. There is another class of case in which the property is put into the hands of the agent to dispose of for the owner, and the agent accepts the employment and, it may be, expends money and time in endeavouring to carry it out. Such a form of contract may well imply the term that the principal will not withdraw the authority he has given after the agent has incurred substantial outlay, or, at any rate, after he has succeeded in finding a possible purchaser . . . But there is a third class of case (to which the present instance belongs) where, by the express language of the contract, the agent is promised his commission only upon completion of the transaction which he is endeavouring to bring about between the offeror and his principal. As I have already said, there seems to me to be no room for the suggested implied term in such a case. The agent is promised a reward in return for an event, and the event has not happened. He runs the risk of disappointment, but if he is not willing to run the risk he should introduce into the express terms of the contract the clause which protects him.

It seems to me that the contract in the present case falls into the third category of cases outlined by Viscount Simon in that passage. The contract made between the plaintiffs and the defendants was one under which the owner of the property appointed an estate agent to be the owners' sole agent for the purpose of finding a purchaser, and agreed that, if the agent through his activities was instrumental in bringing about an actual sale, the agent would be remunerated at a fixed percentage of the purchase money. In such a case it was held by McCardie J. in the *Bentall* case that there was no room for an implied term that the owner will not himself sell and thereby deprive the agent of commission; and that decision was expressly approved in the Court of Appeal in *George Trollope & Sons v Martyn Bros*[3] by Scrutton, Greer and Maugham L.JJ., and in the House of Lords in the *Luxor* case by Viscount Simon L.C. at p. 117 of the report and by Lord Wright at p. 145 of the report. . . . The result is that in my judgment, the plaintiffs are not entitled to any part of the sum claimed as being equivalent to commission.

[1.] [1931] 1 KB 253.   [2.] [1941] AC 108.   [3.] [1984] 2 KB 486.

Notes

1. In *Irish Welding v Philips Electrical (Ireland) Ltd* (HC) 8 October 1976, unrep. Finlay J. implied a term into an agency agreement to the effect that reasonable notice should be given before either party terminated the agreement.
2. In *Fluid Power Technology Company v Sperry (Ireland) Ltd* (HC) 22 February 1985, the power to terminate a distributorship agreement was held by Costello J. to require the party exercising this power to demonstrate substantial cause and an honest belief in the validity of those reasons. 'Lock-out' clauses, that is, agreements under which a party to negotiations agrees to negotiate with one person only for a defined period, have also been held to be enforceable *within the context of a pre-existing agreement* as an implied term to negotiate in good faith on the grounds that, absent on agreed duration or some contractual agreement underpinning the negotiation, such an agreement lacks certainty: see Lord Ackner in *Walford v Miles and Others* [1992] 1 All ER 453, at 461, applied by Laffoy J. in *Triatic Ltd v Cork County Council* [2006] IEHC 111.

Paragon Finance plc *v* Nash and another [2002] 1 WLR 685

Paragon Finance entered into mortgage agreements with Mr and Mrs Nash in 1987 and 1990 respectively. Both mortgagors were in arrears but challenged Paragon's right to possession for breach of the agreement on the ground, *inter alia*, that the loan agreement contained certain implied terms that limited the power of the lender to vary interest rates without restriction. At trial of the action the recorder refused to allow the defendants to amend their pleadings in the light of *Lombard Tricity Finance Limited v Paton* [1989] 1 All ER 918. A study revealed that 'ordinary' mortgagors like the defendants had gradually been charged higher rates of mortgage than certain 'blue chip' Paragon mortgagers.

The defendants appealed against the decision not to allow them to amend their pleadings. The decision of the Court of Appeal (Dyson L.J., Astill and Thorpe L.JJ.) favoured the implied term argument but held that Paragon Finance had not acted in breach of the implied term contended for by the defendants.

Dyson L.J. at p. 694–8.

It was also pleaded that, upon the true construction of the variation of rate clause, the claimant was bound to exercise its discretion to vary the interest rate 'fairly as between both parties to the contract, and not arbitrarily, capriciously or unreasonably.' The recorder rejected this construction of the contract, but said that his decision would be different if the defendants had sought to achieve the same result by way of an implied term. Encouraged by this remark, the defendants in both proceedings applied to the recorder for permission to amend their defences and counterclaims. The implied term was formulated in accordance with the recorder's suggestion. Permission was, however, refused on the grounds that the pleadings gave insufficient particulars of breach.

Mr Malek for *Paragon*, submits that, in a case such as this, a term will only be implied if the strict test of necessity has been satisfied: see, for example, per Lord Steyn in *Equitable Life Assurance Society v Hyman* [2000] 3 WLR 529, 539. He submits that this test is not satisfied in this case for a number of reasons. First, commercial considerations require a lender to behave sensibly when fixing interest rates. Market forces dictate that the interest rate must be competitive and comparable with other available interest rates since, if it is not, the borrowers will simply go elsewhere. Secondly, the regulatory framework is relevant. The Director General of Fair Trading has considerably regulatory powers, including the power to grant or withhold licences under section 25 of the 1974 Act. Thirdly, neither the Nash nor the Staunton agreements prevented the borrowers from redeeming their mortgages and remortgaging elsewhere, although they did contain certain penalty provisions in the event of early redemption.

Fourthly, Mr Malek submits that it is inherently unlikely that, at the date of the making of a variable interest loan agreement, a lender would agree to restrict the rates to 'reasonable' rates. There are problems of determining the yardstick of by reference to which reasonableness is to be judged. There are different types of loans and mortgages suitable for different kinds of borrowers. Moreover, there are different types of lending institution ranging from high street banks and building societies to so-called 'tertiary' or 'non-status lenders'. The latter carry out the most limited checks of the proposed borrower's financial circumstances, and they often deal with borrowers who have a poor credit rating. Mr Malek also makes the point that if the lender were precluded from demanding 'unreasonable' interest rates there would be endless disputes as to what was payable, and it is most unlikely that the lender would have agreed to a term which had that consequence.

I cannot accept the submission of Mr Malek that the power given to the claimant by these loan agreements to set the interest rates from time to time is completely unfettered. If that were so, it would mean that the claimant would be completely free, in theory at least, to specify interest rates at the most exorbitant level. It is true that in the case of the Nash agreement clause 3.3 provides that the rate charged is that which applies to the category of business to which the claimant considers the mortgage belongs. That prevents the claimant from treating the Nashes differently from other borrowers in the same category. But it does not protect borrowers in that category from being treated in a capricious manner, or, for example, being subjected to very high rates of interest in order to force them into arrears with a view to obtaining possession of their properties.

The Stauntons do not even have the limited protection that is afforded by clause 3.3 of the Nash agreement. In the absence of an implied term, there would be nothing to prevent the claimant from raising the rate demanded of the Stauntons to exorbitant levels, or raising the rate to a level higher than that required of other similar borrowers for some improper purpose or capricious reason. An example of an improper purpose would be where the lender decided that the borrower was a nuisance (but had not been in breach of the terms of the agreement) and, wishing to get rid of him, raised the rate of interest to a level that it knew he could not afford to pay. An example of a capricious reason would be where the lender decided to raise the rate of interest because its manager did not like the colour of the borrower's hair.

It seems to me that the commercial considerations relied on by Mr Malek are not sufficient to exclude an implied term that the discretion to vary interest rates should not be exercised dishonestly, for an improper purpose, capriciously or arbitrarily. I shall come shortly to the question whether the discretion should also not be exercised unreasonably. But, before doing so, I should explain in a little more detail why I would reject Mr Malek's submission that there is no need for an implied term at all.

Of course I accept as a general proposition that a lender must have an eye to the market when it sets its rate of interest. To do otherwise is bound ultimately to lead to commercial disaster. But commercial considerations of that kind will not necessarily deter a lender from acting improperly in all situations. They may not deter a lender from unfair discrimination against an individual borrower. They may not even avail a class of borrowers. Take the present cases. The defendants borrowed from the claimant, which withdrew from the lending business in 1991. The rates of interest offered by Paragon are highly competitive. But the history of the interest rates demanded by the claimant in the late 1990s demonstrates how limited the deterrent argument is. The proof of the pudding is in the eating. Between 1989 and 1992 the difference between the claimant's standard rate and the rate demanded by the Halifax Building Society was approximately two percentage points. By 1997 the gap was in excess of four points. In March 1999 it rose to 5.14%, when the claimant's rate was 12.09% and the Halifax rate was 6.95%.

The argument based on the existence of the regulatory powers of the Director General of Fair Trading is in my view not sufficient to deny the implied term. I note that in the *Lombard* case [1989] 1 All ER 918, 923 the court said that if a lender capriciously treated old borrowers unfavourably 'one would hope that the Director General of Fair Trading would consider whether he should still have a licence under the 1974 Act' (my emphasis). One would indeed have such a hope, but that does not seem to me to be a secure basis on which to decide that there is no need for an implied term that a lender will not exercise the discretion to set rates of interest capriciously. There are two strands to the argument that found favour with the court in the *Lombard* case: (a) it is implicitly accepted that the lender should not act capriciously; but (b) there is no need to impose an obligation on the lender not to act capriciously, because there is no realistic possibility that he will do so. I can see that there may be no need to impose such an obligation on a lender where it would be impossible for him to act in breach of it. But it is *inter alia* for the very reason that lenders can act unfairly and improperly that the Director General has the power to withdraw licences from those who provide credit to customers. In my judgment, the existence of the Director General and the fact that he has certain regulatory powers is not a good reason for holding that the power to set rates of interest is absolutely unfettered.

Finally, I must consider whether the fact that the borrowers can redeem their mortgages and seek loans from another source if the rates are set capriciously etc. is a sufficient reason for acceding to Mr Malek's argument. In my view, it is not. As with the last point, this is not so much an argument against the need to imply a term as an argument that it is unlikely to be broken because the lender will be aware that it is open to the borrower to go elsewhere. But it seems to me to be obvious that there may be circumstances in which the lender will act capriciously towards an individual borrower knowing that it might compel the borrower to redeem the mortgage and go elsewhere. Indeed, the lender may have decided to increase the rate of interest for that very reason. But why should the lender be able capriciously to compel the borrower to find another lender with impunity? The borrower may find it difficult to find another lender, especially if he has fallen into arrears with the first lender as a result of that lender's interest rate policy. His employment status may have changed adversely since he entered into the first loan agreement. The process of remortgaging is costly. The new lender will probably require a survey. There will be lawyer's fees. And there may be a penalty for early redemption.

It follows that I do not agree with the *obiter dicta* expressed by this court in the *Lombard* case in the passage that I have cited. I would hold that there were terms to be implied in both agreements that the rates of interest would not be set dishonestly, for an improper purpose, capriciously or arbitrarily. I have no doubt that such an implied term is necessary in order to give effect to the reasonable expectations of the parties. I am equally in no doubt that such an implied term is one of which it could be said that 'it goes without saying'. If asked at the time of the making of the agreements whether it accepted that the discretion to fix rates of interest could be exercised dishonestly, for an improper purpose, capriciously or arbitrarily, I have no doubt that the claimant would have said 'of course not'.

I come, therefore, to question whether the implied term should also extend to 'unreasonably'.

In *Abu Dhabi National Tank Co. v Product Star Shipping Ltd* (No 2) [1993] I Lloyd's Rep 397 Leggatt L.J. said that, where A and B contract with each other to confer a discretion on A, the discretion must be exercised honestly and in good faith, and not 'arbitrarily, capriciously or unreasonably'. In that case, the judge held the owner acted unreasonably in the sense that there was no material on which a reasonable owner could reasonably have exercised the discretion in the way that he did. Leggatt L.J. (with whom the other two members of the court agreed) found that various factors called into question the owners' good faith and strongly suggested that their decision was arbitrary. He also upheld the judge's approach to the question of reasonableness. Thus the word 'unreasonably' in the passage at p. 404 must be understood in a sense analogous to unreasonably in the *Wednesbury* sense: *Associated Provincial Picture Houses Ltd v Wednesbury Corpn* [1948] I KB 223.

This question whether an apparently unfettered discretion is subject to an implied limitation that it must be exercised reasonably has been considered in other context. They were helpfully reviewed by Mance L.J. in *Gan Insurance Co. Ltd v Tai Ping Insurance Co. Ltd* (No 2) [2001] 2 ALL ER (Comm) 299. That case concerned a reinsurance contract which contained a clause which provided that no settlement or compromise of a claim could be made or liability admitted by the insured without the prior approval of the reinsurers. One of the questions that arose was whether the right to withhold approval was subject to any (and if so what) restriction. The judge held that the reinsurers could not withhold approval unless there were reasonable grounds for doing so. Mance L.J. (with whom Latham L.J. agreed) decided that the right to with-hold consent was less restricted. Having reviewed a number of previous authorities, Mance L.J. said, at p. 323, para. 64, that what was proscribed in all of them was 'unreasonableness in the sense of conduct or a decision to which no reasonable person having the relevant discretion could have subscribed.'

So here, too, we find a somewhat reluctant extension of the implied term to include reasonableness that is analogous to *Wednesbury* unreasonableness. I entirely accept that the scope of an implied term will depend on the circumstances of the particular contract. But I find the analogy of the Gan Insurance case and the cases considered in the judgment of Mance L.J. helpful. It is one thing to imply a term that a lender will not exercise his discretion in a way that no reasonable lender, acting reasonably, would do. It is unlikely that a lender who was acting in that way would not also be acting either dishonestly, for an improper purpose, capriciously or arbitrarily. It is quite another matter to imply a term that the lender would not impose unreasonable rates. It could be said that as soon as the difference between the claimant's standard rates and the Halifax rates started to exceed about two percentage points the claimant was charging unreasonable rates. From the defendants' point of view, that was undoubtedly true. But, from the claimant's point of view, it charged these rates because it was commercially necessary, and therefore reasonable, for it to do so.

I conclude therefore that there was an implied term of both agreements that the claimant would not set rates of interest unreasonably in the limited sense that I have described. Such an implied term is necessary in order to give effect to the reasonable expectations of the parties.

Karim Aga Khan *v* Firestone [1992] ILRM 31

The plaintiff entered into negotiations with the defendant with a view to purchasing a stud farm and certain company shares owned by the defendant. The plaintiff claimed that the property was offered to him for the sum of $14.2 million and he accepted. The agreement was to be confirmed in writing and was confirmed in two letters from the defendants' lawyers to the plaintiff's lawyer on 1 and 4 December 1989 setting out all the terms agreed. The defendants later claimed that there were only discussions and that no valid contract existed. The plaintiff sought specific performance of the agreement.

Morris J.:

Counsel for Mr and Mrs Firestone next argues that the circumstances of the case are such that there clearly was an implied term of the contract that the transaction would be carried through by means of a formal contract to be executed by the parties. More specifically that such a term should be implied into the contract on the basis of the principle in *The Moorcock* (1889) 14 PD 64. He is in effect saying, as Bowen L.J. said in *The Moorcock*, that I should presume that it was the intention of the parties that this provision should be in the contract 'with the object of giving the transaction such efficacy as both parties must have intended that at all events it should have'. In reply counsel for the Aga Khan has pointed out, in my view correctly, that the effect of making such an assumption or implying the existence of such a term would be to destroy the contract and far from giving efficacy to it, would in effect prevent its operation. I am satisfied that *The Moorcock* principle only applies where, through mischance, such a term as is sought to be implied has been omitted from the contract and is necessary in order to give the contract efficacy and to prevent the failure of the contract. To imply such a term into this contract would have the contrary effect. It would be to defeat it. It cannot in my view be logical to ask the court to imply into a contract a term so as to give it business efficacy when it would have the contrary effect. I do not accept this argument.

(An order for specific performance was granted.)

Carna Foods Ltd *v* Eagle Star Insurance [1997] 2 ILRM 99

The facts of this case, taken from the headnote were as follows:

Both plaintiffs had insurance policies with the defendant covering several premises and the businesses carried on therein. The second named plaintiff was the managing director of the first named plaintiff. On 24 August 1993 the defendant wrote to the plaintiffs stating that it would not be renewing three of the policies. Similar letters on the same day cancelled two other policies which were not up for renewal. The plaintiffs demanded that the defendant should give reasons for their letters of 24 August 1993, but the defendant declined to do so. The plaintiffs then instituted proceedings seeking a declaration that the defendant was wrong in failing to disclose the reasons for the cancellation of policies and they sought to direct the defendant to disclose the reasons.

Lynch J. gave the leading judgment for the Supreme Court.

Lynch J.:

. . .

The plaintiffs say that one must imply a term into the policies of insurance issued by the defendant to the plaintiffs in this case to the effect that if a policy is cancelled or its renewal is declined the defendant must give its reasons for so doing. Apart from cases where the law implies some terms into certain kinds of contract, whether by statute or by common law (for example sale of goods, hire purchase, landlord and tenant, sale of lands etc.) one can imply a term into a contract only when the implied term gives effect to the true intentions of all the parties to the contract who might be affected by such implied term. The learned trial judge in his judgment in this case which is now reported in [1995] 1 IR 526, [1995] 2 ILRM 474 quoted from the well known dictum of MacKinnon LJ. in *Shirlaw v Southern Foundries* (1926) Ltd [1939] 2 KB 206 at p. 227 and I also quote that dictum here:

> *Prima facie* that which in any contract is left to be implied and need not be expressed is something so obvious that it goes without saying: so that if while the parties were making their bargain an officious bystander were to suggest some express provisions for it in their agreement, they would testily suppress him with a common 'Oh of course.'

Here the evidence before the learned trial judge is quite clearly to the effect that if such a term were sought to be included in the insurance policies at the time when the plaintiffs were seeking insurance the defendant would not have contracted with the plaintiffs at all. If the officious bystander had interrupted in relation to condition 13 of the policies and had asked the defendant 'If you do cancel, will you give your reasons for cancelling?' The defendant's answer would have been an emphatic 'No' whereas to imply such a term into the policies the answer would have to be by both parties 'Yes, of course' expressed rather testily to discourage the officious bystander from further interrupting.

It is also helpful to quote what Lord Pearson said in 1973 in the case of *Trollope and Colls Ltd v. North West Metropolitan Regional Hospital Board* [1973] 2 All ER 260 at p. 268:

An unexpressed term can be implied if and only if the court finds that the parties must have intended that term to form part of their contract: it is not enough for the court to find that such a term would have been adopted by the parties as reasonable men if it had been suggested to them; it must have been a term that went without saying, a term necessary to give business efficacy to the contract, a term which although tacit, formed part of the contract which the parties made for themselves.

These basic principles of law preclude the implication of a term into the policies to the effect that in the event of a declinature or cancellation the defendant must state its reasons therefor.

Specifically in relation to insurance law this question of an obligation to give reasons has long since been decided in the case of *Sun Fire Office v. Hart* referred to above. The relevant clause in that case read:

If by reason of such change, or from any other cause whatever, the society or its agents should desire to terminate the insurance effected by the said policy, it shall be lawful for the society or its agents so to do, by notice to the insured or to the authorised representatives of the insured and to require the policy to be given up for the purpose of being cancelled; provided that in any such case the society shall refund to the insured a rateable proportion for the unexpired term thereof of the premium received for the insurance.

A question arose as to whether the words 'or from any other cause whatever' were governed and restricted by the reference to 'such change' which had been described earlier in the clause. It was decided that they were not so governed or restricted and stood on their own. At p. 103 of the report of the judgment of Lord Watson he states as follows:

The condition does not involve the avoidance of the policy *ab initio*, or forfeiture of the premium paid to the insured. There may be many circumstances calculated to beget, in the mind of a fair and reasonable insurer, a strong desire to terminate the policy, which it would be inconvenient to state and difficult to prove; and it must not be forgotten that the whole business of fire insurance offices consists in the issue of policies, and they have no inducement, and are not likely to curtail their business, without sufficient cause. On the other hand the insured gets all the protection which he pays for, and when the policy is determined, can protect his own interests by effecting another insurance.

Of course the plaintiffs in this case say that having been refused renewal of three policies and had another two policies cancelled and not being aware of what the reasons are for such an attitude by the defendant it is not possible for them to effect alternative insurance. A curious feature of the case of course is that no effort was made either by the plaintiffs themselves or by their insurance brokers to negotiate with an alternative insurer with a view to getting insurance cover again. Undoubtedly it makes it more difficult to get alternative cover when policies have not been renewed or have been cancelled but that would have been so to some extent at any rate at the time of the *Sun Fire Office* case just as it is today.

If the court were to imply such a term into the contracts of insurance the consequences would be very far reaching. Supposing for example that in the present case the defendant although not having evidence to support its suspicions in fact genuinely believes that the fire in the abattoir and the meat factory at Castleblayney was a case of arson committed by or at the behest of the plaintiffs and that that is the real reason for its rejecting the plaintiffs as insured parties. This appears to be what the plaintiffs themselves are suggesting at question 187 of the transcript of 31 May and question 29 of the transcript of 1 June 1995. If the defendant is bound to give reasons it must do so truthfully. One can scarcely imagine the litigation that such a situation would spawn especially when one recalls the plaintiffs' solicitors' suggestion in their letter of 19 April 1994 that the defendant's mere silence was defamatory of the plaintiffs.

For all the foregoing reasons I would reject the claim by the plaintiffs that a term that the defendant should give its reasons for a declinature and/or cancellation should be implied in the policies of insurance.

It is also claimed that the defendant in addition to stating reasons should have an implied obligation to put the plaintiffs back into the same position that the plaintiffs enjoyed regarding obtaining insurance cover before they entered into the contracts of insurance with the defendant. This is an impossibility. The fact is that the plaintiffs did contract with the defendant as its insurers and that the defendant cancelled two of the policies and declined to renew the other three policies and that will always be the position. One recalls the often quoted lines of the poet Edward Fitzgerald:

> The moving finger writes: and having writ,
> moves on: nor all thy piety nor wit
> shall lure it back to cancel half a line,
> nor all thy tears wash out a word of it.

I reject therefore the submission that such a term should be implied into the contracts between the parties.

B. Terms Implied in Law

Many terms are implied in a contract as a result of rules of law. In such cases it is not necessary to refer the terms to the subjective intentions of the parties. The terms generally arise out of certain types of contracts where policy considerations are paramount.

Brown *v* Norton and Norton; Burgess *v* Same; O'Connor *v* Same [1954] IR 34

The plaintiffs sued the defendants claiming damages for breach of contract in selling them houses with structural defects. The plaintiffs had purchased houses which were in the course of erection.

Davitt P.:

. . .

. . . each plaintiff pleads that his purchase agreement was an agreement for the purchase of a house in the course of erection; that the defendants impliedly agreed that they would complete the erection of his house and that it would be completed of sound and suitable materials and in a proper and workmanlike manner, and when complete would be fit for human habitation. Each alleges a breach of the implied agreement as subsequently described in his evidence.

. . .

The plaintiffs rested their cases almost entirely upon the authority of the decision in *Miller v Cannon Hill Estates Ltd*[1] as accepted and applied in this country. It is sufficient at this stage to say that I consider that that case is an authority for the proposition that where a building contractor agrees to sell to a purchaser a dwelling house which is in the course of erection, and both parties understand that the purchaser is buying for the purpose of occupying it as a residence as soon as it is completed, a court may, in the absence of any circumstances negativing such an implication, hold that the vendor impliedly agrees that he will complete the house, and will do so in such a way that when complete it will be reasonably fit for immediate occupation as a residence. In this sense I believe that the decision has been readily accepted and applied during the last twenty years by the High Court and the Circuit Court in this country. . . .

I think that the law which I have to apply in these cases may be stated thus: where there is an agreement to purchase a house in the course of erection, and it is clearly understood by the parties that what the purchaser is contracting to buy and the vendor is contracting to sell is a dwelling house in which the purchaser can live as soon as it is completed by the vendor, the court may hold, in the absence of any circumstances negativing such an implication, that the vendor impliedly agrees (1) that he will complete the building of the house; (2) that as regards what has already been done at the date of the agreement the quality of the work and materials *is* such, and as regards what then remains to be done the quality *will be* such, that the house when completed will be reasonably fit for immediate occupation as a residence; and (3) that as regards what then remains to be done the work will be carried out in a good and workmanlike manner and with sound and suitable materials. The expressions, 'completed house' and 'house in course of erection', so frequently used in cases of this kind are not, of course, to be treated as if they were expressions used in an enactment of the legislature. In no case has it been sought to define them nor would it be advisable to make an attempt at definition.

1. [1931] 2 KB 113.

(Davitt P. awarded damages for breach of contract to the first two defendants, but not to the third defendant as his house was found to be complete at the time of the agreement.)

Liverpool City Council *v* Irwin and Another [1976] 2 All ER 39

The tenants of a council maisonette on the ninth and tenth floors of a fifteen-storey tower block refused to pay rent, and sought damages claiming that the council were in breach of their duty to repair and maintain the common parts of the building of which they retained control.

The Court of Appeal allowed an appeal from the court of first instance where the tenants were awarded damages. The tenants appealed to the House of Lords, reported at [1977] AC 239.

Lord Wilberforce:

We have then a contract which is partly, but not wholly, stated in writing. In order to complete it, in particular to give it a bilateral character, it is necessary to take account of the actions of the parties and the circumstances. As actions of the parties, we must note the granting of possession by the landlords and reservation by them of the 'common parts'—stairs, lifts, chutes, etc. As circumstances we must include the nature of the premises, *viz.*, a maisonette for family use on the ninth floor of a high block, one which is occupied by a large number of other tenants, all using the common parts and dependent upon them, none of them having any expressed obligation to maintain or repair them.

To say that the construction of a complete contract out of these elements involves a process of 'implication' may be correct; it would be so if implication means the supplying of what is not expressed. But there are varieties of implications which the courts think fit to make and they do not necessarily involve the same process. Where there is, on the face of it, a complete, bilateral contract, the courts are sometimes willing to add terms to it, as implied terms: this is very common in mercantile contracts where there is an established usage: in that case the courts are spelling out what both parties know and would, if asked, unhesitatingly agree to be part of the bargain. In other cases, where there is an apparently complete bargain, the courts are willing to add a term on the ground that without it the contract will not work—this is the case, if not of *The Moorcock* (1889) 14 PD 64 itself on its facts, at least of the doctrine of *The Moorcock* as usually applied. This is, as was pointed out by the majority in the Court of Appeal, a strict test—though the degree of strictness seems to vary with the current legal trend—and I think that they were right not to accept it as applicable here. There is a third variety of implication, that which I think Lord Denning M.R. favours, or at least did favour in this case, and that is the implication of reasonable terms. But though I agree with many of his instances, which in fact fall under one or other of the preceding heads, I cannot go so far as to endorse his principle; indeed, it seems to me, with respect, to extend a long, and undesirable, way beyond sound authority.

The present case, in my opinion, represents a fourth category, or I would rather say a fourth shade on a continuous spectrum. The court here is simply concerned to establish what the contract is, the parties not having themselves fully stated the terms. In this sense the court is searching for what must be implied.

. . .

There can be no doubt that there must be implied (i) an easement for the tenants and their licensees to use the stairs, (ii) a right in the nature of an easement to use the lifts, (iii) an easement to use the rubbish chutes.

But are these easements to be accompanied by any obligation upon the landlord, and what obligation?

. . .

In my opinion such obligation should be read into the contract as the nature of the contract itself implicitly requires, no more, no less: a test, in other words, of necessity. . . . To leave the landlord free of contractual obligation as regards these matters, and subject only to administrative or political pressure, is, in my opinion, inconsistent totally with the nature of this relationship. The subject matter of the lease (high rise blocks) and the relationship created by the tenancy demand, of their nature, some contractual obligation on the landlord.

I do not think that this approach involves any innovation as regards the law of contract. The necessity to have regard to the inherent nature of a contract and of the relationship thereby established was stated in this House in *Lister v Romford Ice and Cold Storage Co. Ltd* [1957] AC 555. That was a case between master and servant and of a search for an 'implied term'. Viscount Simonds, at p. 579, makes a clear distinction between a search for an implied term such as might be necessary to give 'business efficacy' to the particular contract and a search, based on wider considerations, for such a term as the nature of the contract might call for, or as a legal incident of this kind of contract. If the search were for the former, he says, ' . . . I should lose myself in the attempt to formulate it with the necessary precision.' (p. 576).

. . .

I accept, of course, the argument that a mere grant of an easement does not carry with it any obligation on the part of the servient owner to maintain the subject matter. The dominant owner must spend the necessary money, for example in repairing a drive leading to his house. And the same principle may apply when a landlord lets an upper floor with access by a staircase: responsibility for maintenance may well rest on the tenant. But there is a difference between that case and the case where there is an essential means of access, retained in the landlord's occupation, to units in a building of multi-occupation, for unless the obligation to maintain is, in a defined manner, placed upon the tenants, individually or collectively, the nature of the contract, and the circumstances, require that it be placed on the landlord.

It remains to define the standard. My Lords, if, as I think, the test of the existence of the term is necessity the standard must surely not exceed what is necessary having regard to the circumstances. To imply an absolute obligation to repair would go beyond what is a necessary legal incident and would indeed be unreasonable. An obligation to take reasonable care to keep in reasonable repair and usability is what fits the requirements of the case.

. . .

And in agreement, I believe, with your Lordships I would hold that it has not been shown in this case that there was any breach of that obligation. On the main point therefore I would hold that the appeal fails.

Lord Cross of Chelsea:

When it implies a term in a contract the court is sometimes laying down a general rule that in all contracts of a certain type—sale of goods, master and servant, landlord and tenant and so on—some provision is to be implied unless the parties have expressly excluded it. In deciding whether or not to lay down such a *prima facie* rule the court will naturally ask itself whether in the general run of such cases the term in question would be one which it would be reasonable to insert. Sometimes, however, there is no question of laying down any *prima facie* rule applicable to all cases of a defined type but what the court is being in effect asked to do is to rectify a particular—often a very detailed—contract by inserting in it a term which the parties have not expressed. Here it is not enough for the court to say that the suggested term is a reasonable one the presence of which would make the contract a better or fairer one; it must be able to say that the insertion of the term is necessary to give—as it is put—'business efficacy' to the contract and that if its absence had been pointed out at the time both parties— assuming them to have been reasonable men—would have agreed without hesitation to its insertion. The distinction between the two types of case was pointed out by Viscount Simonds and Lord Tucker in their speeches in *Lister v Romford Ice and Cold Storage Co. Ltd* [1957] AC 555, 579, 594, but I think that Lord Denning M.R. in proceeding—albeit with some trepidation—to 'kill off' Mackinnon L.J.'s 'officious bystander' (*Shirlaw v Southern Foundries* (1926) Ltd [1939] 2 KB 206, 227) must have overlooked it. Counsel for the appellant did not in fact rely on this passage in the speech of Lord Denning. His main argument was that when a landlord lets a number of flats or offices to a number of different tenants giving all of them rights to use the staircases, corridors and lifts there is to be implied, in the absence of any provision to the contrary, an obligation on the land- lord to keep the 'common parts' in repair and the lifts in working order. But, for good measure, he also submitted that he could succeed on the 'officious bystander' test.

I have no hesitation in rejecting this alternative submission. We are not here dealing with an ordinary commercial contract by which a property company is letting one of its flats for profit. The respondent council is a public body charged by law with the duty of providing housing for members of the public selected because of their need for it at rents which are subsidised by the general body of ratepayers. Moreover the officials in the council's housing department would know very well that some of the tenants in any given block might subject the chutes and lifts to rough treatment and that there was an ever present danger of deliberate damage by young 'vandals'— some of whom might in fact be children of the tenants in that or neighbouring blocks. In these circumstances, if at the time when the respondents were granted their tenancy one of them had said to the council's representative: 'I suppose that the council will be under a legal liability to us to keep the chutes and the lifts in working order and the staircases properly lighted,' the answer might well have been—indeed I think, as Roskill L.J. thought [1976] QB 319, 338, in all probability would have been—'Certainly not.'

(Lord Salmon, Lord Edmund-Davies and Lord Fraser of Tullybelton concurred and the appeal was dismissed.)

Note

In relation to the third category of implication referred to by Lord Wilberforce in this case, see *Sepes Establishment v K.S.K. Enter. Ltd* [1993] ILRM 46 where O'Hanlon expressly approved of the following dicta of Roskill J. in *Bandar Pty Holdings Ltd v J. S. Darwen (Successors) Ltd* [1968] 2 All ER 305:

It is axiomatic that a court will not imply a term which has not been expressed merely because, had the parties thought of the possibility of expressing that term it would have been reasonable for them to have done so. Before a term which has not been expressed can be implied it has got to be shown not only that it would be reasonable to make that implication, but that it is necessary in order to make the contract work that such a term should be implied. It has sometimes been expressed as 'necessary for the business efficacy of the contract'.

Siney *v* The Right Honorable the Lord Mayor, Aldermen and Burgesses of Dublin [1980] IR 400

The defendant corporation was a housing authority obliged by the Housing Act 1966 to provide for the housing needs of the inhabitants of a functional area. The plaintiff was let a flat in one of the defendants' blocks of flats. Within two months water appeared under the floor covering of the bedroom and a fungus spread over the walls. Eventually the plaintiff and his family were forced to leave. In the Circuit Court the plaintiff claimed damages from the defendants for breach of contract, breach of statutory duty and negligence. Certain questions of law were referred by way of case stated to the Supreme Court. The first question asked if the facts constituted a breach by the defendants of their contract with the plaintiff.

O'Higgins C.J.:

The first question involves a consideration as to whether, in the particular letting of this flat to the plaintiff, a warranty can be implied as to its fitness or suitability for habitation by the plaintiff and his family. This is so because the document which was signed on 23 August 1973, contains thirty two conditions which either define the rights of the defendants or specify the obligations of the plaintiff tenant. There is no express warranty on the part of the defendants as to the suitability of the flat for any particular purpose, nor is such a warranty expressly excluded. Therefore, it becomes a question as to whether such a warranty can be implied in this particular letting in the circumstances. The law as to the circumstances under which a warranty may be implied in a contract was stated many years ago by Bowen L.J. in this well known passage from p. 68 of his judgment in *The Moorcock*[1]:

> Now, an implied warranty, or, as it is called, a covenant in law, as distinguished from an express contract or express warranty, really is in all cases founded on the presumed intention of the parties, and upon reason. The implication which the law draws from what must obviously have been the intention of the parties, the law draws with the object of giving efficacy to the transaction and preventing such a failure of consideration as cannot have been within the contemplation of either side; and I believe if one were to take all the cases, and they are many, of implied warranties or covenants in law, it will be found that in all of them the law is raising an implication from the presumed intention of the parties with the object of giving to the transaction such efficacy as both parties must have intended that at all events it should have.

At once the question arises as to whether this principle of law has any application or relevance in a case such as the present. Counsel for the defendants submit very strongly that it has not. As this was a letting of an unfurnished flat or dwelling, they assert that no such warranty can be implied. In this respect they rely on a long line of authorities as illustrated by *Sutton v Temple*;[2] *Hart v Windsor*;[3] *Brown v Norton*[4] and *Chambers v Cork Corporation*.[5] Those authorities established the proposition that the mere letting of land, with or without an unfurnished dwelling house upon it, carried no such implication of a warranty with regard to fitness for any particular purpose. Those cases applied the rule of *caveat emptor* to all lettings of land, with or without a house thereon, in the same way as it was applied to contracts for the sale of land.

An exception, which is not relevant to this case, was recognised where a furnished house was let for occupation; in such a case a covenant on the part of the landlord that the premises would be fit for such occupation at the commencement of the tenancy is implied: *Smith v Marrable*;[6] *Wilson v Finch Hatton*;[7] *Collins v Hopkins*[8] and *Brown v Norton*. A further exception was recognised where a lessor sold by way of lease a house under construction; in such circumstances terms could be implied with regard to the completion of the house, the suitability of the materials used, the quality of the workmanship and its fitness for habitation: *Norris v Staps*;[9] *Pearce v Tucker*;[10] G. H. Myers & Co. v Brent Cross Service Co.*;[11] *Hall v Burke*[12] and *Brown v Norton*.

There can be no doubt that the authorities mentioned (and others which are too numerous to cite) do establish the proposition that a mere letting of land, with or without an unfurnished house thereon, carried with it no implication that either the land or the house would be fit for any particular purpose. This rule probably developed when the main subject of conveyances and leases was land, and when buildings and houses were often of secondary importance in a society that was thinly urbanised. To-day the application of such a rule in a society which is becoming more and more urbanised, and in which the building and sale of houses has become a major industry, may appear somewhat harsh and inappropriate. However, whether the rule has or has not survived changes in society is not in issue in this case. The issue is whether it can be applied, or ought to be applied, in the particular circumstances of this letting by the defendants to the plaintiff.

To answer this question, regard must be had to the Housing Act, 1966, under which this letting was made, and to the position, powers and obligations of the defendants under that Act. The Act of 1966 is a major piece of social legislation which is aimed at dealing with the distressing problem of families that are unable to provide for themselves and being either homeless or living in overcrowded, unhealthy and unfit houses. The Act sought to establish administrative machinery under which such conditions could be eliminated gradually throughout the country, and by means of which new and suitable dwellings could be provided for those in need. Under its provisions the defendant corporation became a housing authority.

. . .

Generally, it may be said that under the Act of 1966 the defendant corporation, as a housing authority, was charged with the task, in respect of its own functional area, of ending overcrowding and of eliminating substandard and unsuitable housing for poor people. The defendants were also empowered, and obliged, to let such housing accommodation as they were able to provide, on a priority basis, to people released from these conditions. In short, the aim of the Act of 1966 was to bring into existence decent housing which, in each functional area, would be introduced by the housing authority and the standards of which would be maintained by that authority. It is now necessary to consider the particular letting made to the plaintiff.

This letting was expressed to be a letting of a 'dwelling provided by the corporation under the Housing Act, 1966.' Moreover, it was a letting of one of a number of newly-built flats. Therefore, it was a letting made by the defendant corporation of a dwelling provided under its building programme and let by it in accordance with its scheme of priority for, *inter alia*, the ending of overcrowding and the elimination of houses unfit in any respect for human habitation. Under these circumstances, can it be said that such a letting carried no implication that the accommodation thereby provided for a necessitous family would be fit for habitation by them? It seems to me that to not imply such a condition or warranty would be to assume that the defendant corporation was entitled to disregard, and was disregarding, the responsibilities cast upon it by the very Act which authorised the building and letting of the accommodation in question.

. . .

Accordingly, I have come to the conclusion that the letting made to the plaintiff by the defendants did include an implied warranty that the premises let would be reasonably fit for human habitation and, therefore, I would answer affirmatively the first question in the case stated. In my view the plaintiff is entitled to damages on this account.

Henchy J.:

To determine what is implied in such a letting, it is the powers and duties of the housing authority under the Act that must be examined and, as I hope I have shown, these necessarily require the housing authority to ensure that the dwelling, when let, is fit for human habitation.

I do not find it necessary or desirable to express an opinion as to the wider question whether there should be held to be implied a condition as to habitability in the letting of every kind of dwelling house.

As I construe the law, the plaintiff is entitled to succeed in contract for the particular reason that this flat was provided under the Act of 1966. Therefore, it is academic to consider whether he would be entitled to succeed if the flat had not been provided under the Act. Whether in such circumstances he would be entitled to sue on an implied condition as to habitability is a point on which this court has never pronounced. Were it necessary to decide the point, it is not unlikely that the Chief Justice would consider it necessary to convene a full court for that purpose, for there are long-standing judicial authorities which hold that a condition as to habitability is not to be implied in the letting of an unfurnished dwelling house. If those authorities are to be set aside, it would probably be better to do so by statute, with prospective effect, rather than by judicial decision with its necessarily retrospective effect.

1. (1889) 14 PD 64.

2. (1843) 12 M. & W. 52.

3. (1843) 12 M. & W. 68.

4. [1954] IR 34.

5. (1958) 93 ILTR 45.

6. (1843) 11 M. & W. 5.

7. (1877) 2 ExD 336.

8. [1923] 2KB 617.

9. (1616) Hob. 210.

10. (1862) 3 F. & F. 136.

11. [1934] 1 KB 46.

12. (1886) 3 TLR 165.

(Kenny J. concurred.)

Notes

1. The court also found that in the special circumstances the defendant had owed the plaintiff a duty to take reasonable care to ensure that the flat was fit for human habitation based on the principles in *Donoghue v Stevenson* [1932] AC 562 and *Anns v Merton London Borough* [1978] AC 728. There was said, however, to be no cause of action for breach of a statutory duty based on an interpretation of the Act.

2. Counsel for the defendants in this case argued that a term which is not expressed in a contract cannot be held to be implied merely because its implication would be reasonable. They suggested that based on the decision in *Liverpool City Council v Irwin*, such a term can be inserted by implication only if its implied insertion is necessary to make the contract work. Furthermore they claimed that the liability of the landlord in *Liverpool City Council v Irwin* related to structures which were ancillary to the demised premises and which had never passed out of the landlord's control.

3. In *Burke (a minor), Tinkler, Hickey and Wade v The Right Honourable The Lord Mayor, Aldermen and Burgesses of Dublin* [1991] IR 341 the Supreme Court held that the implied warranty that premises were habitable acknowledged in *Siney* applied equally to the letting of a house which was not new as to a flat. The warranty was also held to apply to a transfer under the same Act to a person entitled under the Act to be housed by the housing authority.

4. *R (M) v R (T) and Others* [2006] 3 IR 499. In 2002 the plaintiff underwent fertility treatment and at that time she and her husband signed a number of consent forms, including a form that permitted the transfer of embryos into the uterus of the plaintiff. At this time six frozen embryos were created and three were transplanted, this resulting in the birth of a child. Later, the marriage between the plaintiff and her husband broke up; the plaintiff sought to have the three remaining frozen embryos transplanted. The plaintiff's estranged husband objected to this and McGovern J. had to consider, first, whether the husband's consent to this course of action had been given under the express terms of the contract. After finding that express consent was absent, McGovern J. went on to consider whether the consent forms contained implied consent, either as a matter of presumed intent or by virtue of the contract itself. In relation to the presumed intent

test, McGovern J. held that the evidence indicated that the latter three embryos were retained for use should the first implantation process be unsuccessful (which it was not). As such, the officious bystander test was not satisfied in light of the fact that the first implantation had led to the birth of a daughter and the subsequent separation of the parties. On the argument that the agreement itself required the three remaining embryos to be implanted into the plaintiff's uterus, McGovern J. held that such a term did not pass the necessity test and the implied term contended for could not be formulated with the necessary degree of precision. Nor could it be said that both parties would have agreed to the term if it had been suggested at the time of the contract, applying *Carna Foods* and *Sweeney v Duggan*.

Note

Treitel argues that in the *Moorcock* case itself Bowen L.J was not exclusively concerned with the actual intention of the parties but rather concentrated on objective criteria of reasonableness. (Treitel, *The Law of Contract*, (11th ed.), 211–212).

C. Contracts of Employment

Terms may be implied into contracts of employment by operation of law.

Carvill v Irish Industrial Bank Ltd [1968] IR 325. The plaintiff sued for wrongful dismissal from his post as managing director of the defendant company. He had been dismissed on grounds of misconduct without any notice.

O'Keeffe J.:

I think the plaintiff must be regarded as employed under a contract from year to year as managing director, and that it must be implied also that such contract could not be determined without such notice as is appropriate to an engagement of the kind mentioned. . . . In the circumstances I see no reason for disturbing the finding of the trial judge that the appropriate period of notice was a year.

(O'Dalaigh C.J., Lavery, Haugh and Walsh JJ. concurred. Damages were thus awarded.)

Imperial Group Pension Trust Ltd and Others *v* Imperial Tobacco Ltd and Others [1991] 2 All ER 597

Browne-Wilkinson V.C.:

. . .

In every contract of employment there is an implied term: 'that the employers will not, without reasonable and proper cause, conduct themselves in a manner calculated or likely to destroy or seriously damage the relationship of confidence and trust between employer and employee . . . ' (See *Woods v WM Car Services (Peterborough) Ltd* [1981] ICR

666 at 670, approved by the Court of Appeal in *Lewis v Motorworld Garages Ltd* |1986| ICR 157.) I will call this implied term 'the implied obligation of good faith'. In my judgment, that obligation of an employer applies as much to the exercise of his rights and powers under a pension scheme as they do to the other rights and powers of an employer. Say, in purported exercise of its right to give or withhold consent, the company were to say, capriciously, that it would consent to an increase in the pension benefits of members of union A but not of the members of union B. In my judgment, the members of union B would have a good claim in contract for breach of the implied obligation of good faith: see *Mihlenstedt's* case |1989| IRLR 522 at 525, 531–532 (paras 12, 64, 70).

Note

In *Scally v Southern Health and Social Services Board* |1992| 1 AC 294 the House of Lords decided that where a contract of employment negotiated between employers and a representative body contained a particular term conferring on an employer pension rights of the benefit of which he could not be expected to be aware unless the term was brought to his attention, there was an implied obligation on the employer to take reasonable steps to publicise that term. Lord Bridge of Harwich drew a clear distinction between 'the search for an implied term necessary to give business efficacy to a particular contract and the search, based on wider considerations, for a term which the law will imply as a necessary incident of a definable category of contractual relationship.'

Lord Bridge also referred to the difficulty which would arise if the implied term 'must necessarily be too wide in its ambit to be acceptable as of general application'. He suggested that 'this difficulty is surmounted if the category of contractual relationship in which the implication will arise is defined with sufficient precision'.

The *Scally* case was relied upon in *Spring v Guardian Assurances plc and Others* |1994| 3 All ER 129. The majority of the House of Lords accepted that if a reference is given by an employer, an implied obligation arises to take reasonable care in giving the reference. Reference was also made to the sentence in Lord Edmund-Davies' judgment in *Liverpool City Council v Irwin* |1977| AC 239 to the effect that 'the touchstone is always necessity and not merely reasonableness'.

Lord Woolf:

. . .

. . . As I understand *Scally*, it recognises that, just as in the earlier authorities the courts were prepared to imply by necessary implication a term imposing a duty on an employer to exercise due care for the physical well-being of his employees, so in the appropriate circumstances would the court imply a like duty as to his economic well-being, the duty as to his economic well-being giving rise to an action for damages if it is breached.

Here, it is also possible to specify circumstances which would enable a term to be implied. The circumstances are:

(i) The existence of the contract of employment or services.
(ii) The fact that the contract relates to an engagement of a class where it is the normal practice to require a reference from a previous employer before employment is offered.

(iii) The fact that the employee cannot be expected to enter into that class of employment except on the basis that his employer will, on the request of another prospective employer made not later than a reasonable time after the termination of a former employment, provide a full and frank reference as to the employee.

This being the nature of the engagement, it is necessary to imply a term into the contract that the employer would, during the continuance of the engagement or within a reasonable time thereafter, provide a reference at the request of a prospective employer which was based on facts revealed after making those reasonably careful inquiries which, in the circumstances, a reasonable employer would make.

The Supreme Court, in *Sweeney v. Duggan* [1997] 2 ILRM 211 endorsed the reasoning in *Scally*. Lynch J. on this point observed:

Lynch J.:

In his judgment with which all of their Lordships were in agreement, Lord Bridge in fact concluded that the term for which the plaintiffs contended should be implied in the contract between them and their employers. His analysis of the circumstances in which the term was implied is . . . in the following terms:

> . . . Here there is no doubt whatever that the terms of the superannuation scheme as laid down in the regulations in force from time to time were embodied in the terms of the contract of employment of each plaintiff. Since the relevant board was in each case the employer upon whom, although acting as agent for the department, all liabilities were imposed by paragraph 2 of schedule 1 to the Order of 1972, it seems to me beyond question that the legal obligation, if there was one, to notify the plaintiffs of their rights in relation to the purchase of added years rested in each case on the board, not on the department.
>
> Will the law then imply a term in the contract of employment imposing such an obligation on the employer? The implication cannot, of course, be justified as necessary to give business efficacy to the contract of employment as a whole. I think there is force in the submission, that since the employee's entitlement to enhance his pension rights by the purchase of added years is of no effect unless he is aware of it and since he cannot be expected to become aware of it unless it is drawn to his attention, it is necessary to imply an obligation on the employer to bring it to his attention to render efficacious the very benefit which the contractual right to purchase added years was intended to confer.

I agree that a term may be implied independently of the intention of the parties where it is necessary as a matter of law and logic to enable the provisions of the agreement to have operative effect. No such necessity exists in the present case. The decision is also relevant in setting out the principles, with which I fully agree, which establish that the obligation as between the employer and employee in a case such as the present are to be found in contract and not in tort.

Mahmud and Malik *v* Bank of Credit and Commerce International SA [1998] AC 20

The defendant (BCCI) ceased business in the summer of 1991 when financial irregularities and illegal business practices came to light. Thousands of depositors lost their money and several hundred employees in the UK lost their jobs. Further, many employees claimed that such was the depth of corruption within BCCI that they found it very difficult to find work because they were tainted by their association with BCCI. During the BCCI winding up, Mr Mahmud, who had worked in a key post for 16 years with BCCI, and Mr Malik, another senior employee with 12 years' service, sought damages for their loss in not securing alternative employment—so-called 'stigma' damages. While both the trial judge and the Court of Appeal held that the plaintiffs' pleadings did not disclose a reasonable cause of action, the House of Lords disagreed.

This case is a very important one in relation to the concept of implied terms in employment law and in relation to the availability of damages arising out of breach of the contract of employment. We deal with the first issue at this juncture and the second below.

Lord Nicholls of Birkenhead:

Before this House, as in the courts below, the issue is being decided on the basis of an agreed set of facts. The liquidators do not admit the accuracy of these facts, but for the purpose of this preliminary issue it is being assumed that the bank operated in a corrupt and dishonest manner, that Mr Mahmud and Mr Malik were innocent of any involvement, that following the collapse of BCCI. its corruption and dishonesty became widely known, that in consequence Mr Mahmud and Mr Malik were at a handicap on the labour market because they were stigmatised by reason of their previous employment by BCCI, and that they suffered loss in consequence.

In the Court of Appeal and in your Lordships' House the parties were agreed that the contracts of employment of these two former employees each contained an implied term to the effect that the bank would not, without reasonable and proper cause, conduct itself in a manner likely to destroy or seriously damage the relationship of confidence and trust between employer and employee. Argument proceeded on this footing, and ranged round the type of conduct and other circumstances which could or could not constitute a breach of this implied term. The submissions embraced questions such as the following: whether the trust-destroying conduct must be directed at the employee, either individually or as part of a group; whether an employee must know of the employer's trust-destroying conduct while still employed; and whether the employee's trust must actually be undermined. Furthermore, and at the heart of this case, the submissions raised an important question on the damages recoverable for breach of the implied term, with particular reference to the decisions in *Addis v. Gramophone Co. Ltd* [1909] AC 488 and *Withers v. General Theatre Corporation Ltd* [1933] 2 KB 536.

A *dishonest and corrupt business*

These questions are best approached by focusing first on the particular conduct of which complaint is made. The bank operated its business dishonestly and corruptly. On the assumed facts, this was not a case where one or two individuals, however senior, were behaving dishonestly. Matters had gone beyond this. They had reached the point where the bank itself could properly be identified with the dishonesty. This was a dishonest business, a corrupt business.

It is against this background that the position of an innocent employee has to be considered. In my view, when an innocent employee of the bank learned the true nature of the bank's business, from whatever source, he was entitled to say: 'I wish to have nothing more to do with this organisation. I am not prepared to help this business, by working for it. I am leaving at once.' This is my intuitive response in the case of all innocent employees of the business, from the most senior to the most junior, from the most long serving to the most recently joined. No one could be expected to have to continue to work with and for such a company against his wish.

This intuitive response is no more than a reflection of what goes without saying in any ordinary contract of employment, namely, that in agreeing to work for an employer the employee, whatever his status, cannot be taken to have agreed to work in furtherance of a dishonest business. This is as much true of a doorkeeper or cleaner as a senior executive or branch manager.

An *implied obligation*

Two points can be noted here. First, as a matter of legal analysis, the innocent employee's entitlement to leave at once must derive from the bank being in breach of a term of the contract of employment which the employee is entitled to treat as a repudiation by the bank of its contractual obligations. That is the source of his right to step away from the contract forthwith.

In other words, and this is the necessary corollary of the employee's right to leave at once, the bank was under an implied obligation to its employees not to conduct a dishonest or corrupt business. This implied obligation is no more than one particular aspect of the portmanteau, general obligation not to engage in conduct likely to undermine the trust and confidence required if the employment relationship is to continue in the manner the employment contract implicitly envisages.

Second, I do not accept the liquidators' submission that the conduct of which complaint is made must be targeted in some way at the employee or a group of employees. No doubt that will often be the position, perhaps usually so. But there is no reason in principle why this must always be so. The trust and confidence required in the employment relationship can be undermined by an employer, or indeed an employee, in many different ways. I can see no justification for the law giving the employee a remedy if the unjustified trust-destroying conduct occurs in some ways but refusing a remedy if it occurs in others. The conduct must, of course, impinge on the relationship in the sense that, looked at objectively, it is likely to destroy or seriously damage the degree of trust and confidence the employee is reasonably entitled to have in his employer. That requires one to look at all the circumstances.

Breach

The objective standard just mentioned provides the answer to the liquidators' submission that unless the employee's confidence is actually undermined there is no breach. A breach occurs when the proscribed conduct takes place: here, operating a dishonest and corrupt business. Proof of a subjective loss of confidence in the employer is not an essential element of the breach, although the time when the employee learns of the misconduct and his response to it may affect his remedy.

...

Lord Steyn:

The implied term of mutual trust and confidence

The applicants do not rely on a term implied in fact. They do not therefore rely on an individualised term to be implied from the particular provisions of their employment contracts considered against their specific contextual setting. Instead they rely on a standardised term implied by law, that is, on a term which is said to be an incident of all contracts of employment: *Scally v. Southern Health and Social Services Board* [1992] 1 AC 294, 307B. Such implied terms operate as default rules. The parties are free to exclude or modify them. But it is common ground that in the present case the particular terms of the contracts of employment of the two applicants could not affect an implied obligation of mutual trust and confidence.

The employer's primary case is based on a formulation of the implied term that has been applied at first instance and in the Court of Appeal. It imposes reciprocal duties on the employer and employee. Given that this case is concerned with alleged obligations of an employer I will concentrate on its effect on the position of employers. For convenience I will set out the term again. It is expressed to impose an obligation that the employer shall not:

'without reasonable and proper cause, conduct itself in a manner calculated and likely to destroy or seriously damage the relationship of confidence and trust between employer and employee': see *Woods v W. M. Car Services (Peterborough) Ltd.* [1981] ICR 666, 670 (Browne-Wilkinson J.), approved in *Lewis v. Motorworld Garages Ltd* [1986] ICR 157 and *Imperial Group Pension Trust Ltd. v Imperial Tobacco Ltd.* [1991] 1 WLR 589.

The evolution of the implied term of trust and confidence is a fact. It has not yet been endorsed by your Lordships' House. It has proved a workable principle in practice. It has not been the subject of adverse criticism in any decided cases and it has been welcomed in academic writings. I regard the emergence of the implied obligation of mutual trust and confidence as a sound development.

Given the shape of the appeal my preceding observations may appear unnecessary. But I have felt it necessary to deal briefly with the existence of the implied term for two reasons. First, the implied obligation involves a question of pure law and your Lordships' House is not bound by any agreement of the parties on it or by the acceptance of the obligation by the judge or the Court of Appeal. Secondly, in response to a question counsel for the bank said that his acceptance of the implied obligation is subject to three limitations: (1) that the conduct complained of must be conduct involving the treatment of the employee in question; (2) that the employee must be aware of such conduct while he is an employee; (3) that such conduct must be calculated to destroy or seriously damage the trust between the employer and employee.

In order to place these suggested limitations in context it seemed necessary to explain briefly the origin, nature and scope of the implied obligation. But subject to examining the merits of the suggested limitations, I am content to accept the implied obligation of trust and confidences as established.

. . .

Notes

1. The *Mahmud* case has been endorsed by the Irish High Court. In *Cronin v Eircom Ltd* [2006] IEHC 380 Laffoy J. observed that, 'as a matter of principle, a contractual term of mutual trust and confidence which was recognised by the House of Lords; the Mahmud Case should be implied into each contract of employment in this jurisdiction by operation of law'. Ms Cronin had been seconded abroad and upon her return to Ireland she was not assimilated back into the workplace. Laffoy J. held that under an implied term in her contract 'her employer was under a contractual obligation, beyond the payment of her salary, to provide her with work so that she would have an opportunity to gain experience, pursue promotion in her job and advance her career . . . under an implied term in the plaintiff's contract of employment, whether as a facet of the obligation to maintain mutual trust or confidence or otherwise'. See also *Berber v Dunnes Stores* [2006] IEHC 327.

2. While the implied duty of trust and confidence that the employer owes to an employee must be recognised as of general application after *Malik*, the scope of the duty must remain to be teased out in future litigation. In *Bank of Credit and Commerce International SA (in liquidation) v Ali and Others* [1999] 2 All ER 1005 Lightman J. held that the implied term does not require an employer to disclose the fact that the employer is guilty of wrongdoing. Nor does the duty extend to a positive duty to provide advice to an employee about that person's optimum position *vis-à-vis* pension entitlements when other means of ascertaining those entitlements are available to the employee: *University of Nottingham v. Eyett and Another (No. 1)* [1999] 2 All ER 437.

SECTION TWO—TERMS IMPLIED IN CUSTOM

Relevant customs of a particular market, trade, profession or region may be implied into a contract.

O'Reilly v The Irish Press Ltd (1937) 71 ILTR 194

The plaintiff, chief sub-editor of a paper owned by the defendants, claimed damages for wrongful dismissal on the basis that custom entitled him to six months' notice.

Maguire P.:

As was said, ... a custom or usage of any kind is a difficult thing to establish. Before a usage such as is contended for here can be held to be established it must be proved by persons whose position in the world of journalism entitles them to speak with certainty and knowledge of its existence. I have to be satisfied that it is so notorious, well known and acquiesced in that in the absence of agreement in writing it is to be taken as one of the terms of the contract between the parties.

. . .

The absence of evidence of actual instances to show the length of notice given to or by chief sub-editors does not surprise me. Having regard to the relatively small number of such posts it was natural that instances of dismissal or resignation of chief sub-editors should be exceedingly rare. A chief sub-editor generally goes higher and seldom goes down or out.

. . .

The absence of actual instances of the usage in practice would not, however, preclude me from holding that the usage existed if I were satisfied that it was well known and universally recognised.

As I have already stated, it is necessary in order to establish a custom of the kind claimed that it be shown that it was so generally known that anyone concerned should have known of it, or could easily have become aware of it.

With some hesitation and considerable regret I must hold that the evidence before me has not established such notoriety or general acquiescence for the usage as to enable me to hold it established. I say 'with considerable regret' because I would be glad to decide the case on usage. Apparently a usage with regard to dismissal of sub-editors and editors can be established. As regards chief sub-editors, notwithstanding the fact that several witnesses knew of the existence of a usage in certain circles governing the length of notice to be given I have come to the conclusion that there was not that universality of acceptance of the usage in the newspaper world in general that is required to establish it as a usage.

Notes

1. In *O'Conaill v The Gaelic Echo* (1958) 92 ILTR 156 Hannan J. in the District Court accepted that the customary period of notice in the absence of express agreement to dismiss newspaper reporters in the Dublin City area was one month.

2. It may be necessary for the Court to 'interpret' the scope of the implied custom. In *Carroll v Dublin Bus* [2006] IEHC 278 the plaintiff was a bus driver who had returned to work following illness. The plaintiff complained that upon his return to work he was rostered unfairly and that there was a custom and practice within Dublin Bus (amounting to a contractual entitlement) that drivers not fully able to carry out duties would be assigned to less onerous or rehabilitative routes. Clarke J. narrowed down the entitlement to cases where:

1. the Chief Medical Officer had recommended the driver as being suitable to a route,
2. there was such a route available,
3. there was no good reason why the driver should not be assigned to such a route.

The 'entitlement' was limited to a reasonable period so as to facilitate rehabilitation, the decision on this being a matter for the Chief Medical Officer.

SECTION THREE—TERMS IMPLIED BY STATUTE

Many terms that are implied in law have been incorporated into statutes.

For example ss 12–15 of the Sale of Goods Act 1893, as amended by the Sale of Goods & Supply of Services Act 1980, in addition to s. 39 of the 1980 Act, imply terms into contracts for goods and services with the object of protecting the consumer.

12. (1) In every contract of sale, other than one to which subsection (2) applies, there is:

    (*a*) an implied condition on the part of the seller that, in the case of a sale, he has a right to sell the goods and, in the case of an agreement to sell, he will have a right to sell the goods at the time when the property is to pass, and

    (*b*) an implied warranty that the goods are free, and will remain free until the time when the property is to pass, from any charge or encumbrance not disclosed to the buyer before the contract is made and that the buyer will enjoy quiet possession of the goods except so far as it may be disturbed by the owner or other person entitled to the benefit of any charge or encumbrance so disclosed.

(2) In a contract of sale, in the case of which there appears from the contract or is to be inferred from the circumstances of the contract an intention that the seller should transfer only such title as he or a third person may have, there is:

    (*a*) an implied warranty that all charges or encumbrances known to the seller have been disclosed to the buyer before the contract is made, and

    (*b*) an implied warranty that neither:

        (i) the seller, nor

        (ii) in a case where the parties to the contract intend that the seller should transfer only such title as a third person may have, that person, nor

        (iii) anyone claiming through or under the seller or that third person otherwise than under a charge or encumbrance disclosed to the buyer before the contract is made.

    will disturb the buyer's quiet possession of the goods.

13. (1) Where there is a contract for the sale of goods by description, there is an implied condition that the goods shall correspond with the description; and if the sale be by sample as well as by description, it is not sufficient that the bulk of the goods corresponds with the sample if the goods do not also correspond with the description.

(2) A sale of goods shall not be prevented from being a sale by description by reason only that, being exposed for sale, they are selected by the buyer.

(3) A reference to goods on a label or other descriptive matter accompanying goods exposed for sale may constitute or form part of a description.

14. (1) Subject to the provisions of this Act and of any statute in that behalf, there is no implied condition or warranty as to the quality or fitness for any particular purpose of goods supplied under a contract of sale.

(2) Where the seller sells goods in the course of a business there is an implied condition that the goods supplied under the contract are of merchantable quality, except that there is no such condition:

(*a*) as regards defects specifically drawn to the buyer's attention before the contract is made, or

(*b*) if the buyer examines the goods before the contract is made, as regards defects which that examination ought to have revealed.

(3) Goods are of merchantable quality if they are as fit for the purpose or purposes for which goods of that kind are commonly bought and as durable as it is reasonable to expect having regard to any description applied to them, the price (if relevant) and all the other relevant circumstances, and any reference in this Act to unmerchantable goods shall be construed accordingly.

(4) Where the seller sells goods in the course of a business and the buyer, expressly or by implication, makes known to the seller any particular purpose for which the goods are being bought, there is an implied condition that the goods supplied under the contract are reasonably fit for that purpose, whether or not that is a purpose for which such goods are commonly supplied except where the circumstances show that the buyer does not rely, or that it is unreasonable for him to rely, on the seller's skill or judgement.

(5) An implied condition or warranty as to quality or fitness for a particular purpose may be annexed to a contract of sale by usage.

(6) The foregoing provisions of this section apply to a sale by a person who in the course of a business is acting as agent for another as they apply to a sale by a principal in the course of a business, except where that other is not selling in the course of a business and either the buyer knows that fact or reasonable steps are taken to bring it to the notice of the buyer before the contract is made.

Sale by sample

15. (1) A contract of sale is a contract for sale by sample where there is a term in the contract, express or implied, to that effect.

(2) In the case of a contract for sale by sample:

(*a*) There is an implied condition that the bulk shall correspond with the sample in quality;

(*b*) There is an implied condition that the buyer shall have a reasonable opportunity of comparing the bulk with the sample;

(*c*) There is an implied condition that the goods shall be free from any defect, rendering them unmerchantable, which would not be apparent on reasonable examination of the sample.

39. Subject to section 40, in every contract for the supply of a service where the supplier is acting in the course of a business, the following terms are implied:

(*a*) that the supplier has the necessary skill to render the service.

(*b*) that he will supply the service with due skill, care and diligence,

(*c*) that, where materials are used, they will be sound and reasonably fit for the purpose for which they are required, and

(*d*) that, where goods are supplied under the contract, they will be of merchantable quality within the meaning of section 14(3) of the Act of 1893 (inserted by section 10 of this Act).

Notes

1. Under a headline of 'Court awards €10,000 over porn images', *The Irish Times* reported on 14 December 2002:

> A family exposed to lurid pornographic pictures on their computer after it came back from a repair shop in Dublin was awarded €10,000 damages for mental distress.
>
> Mr Ronan Dolan, counsel for the parents and their two young children from Blanchardstown, Co. Dublin told the Circuit Civil Court yesterday that when the repaired computer was switched on, pornographic images appeared on the screen.
>
> Judge Alison Lindsay heard that just before Christmas 1999, the parents had bought a computer to help with their children's education from Time Computer Systems in the Blanchardstown Shopping Centre.
>
> When it had been set up, the screen was not operating properly and it had been sent back to the shop for repair.
>
> It had come back with pornographic images and they had been seen by the couple's 15-year-old daughter.
>
> Mr Dolan said that when the father brought it back to the store a second time, a manager had suggested to him that the pictures must have been downloaded from the internet.
>
> 'The family computer did not have an internet link-up at the time and the suggestion caused the parents distress' Mr Dolan said.
>
> Later the store discovered the images had been downloaded while it was in for repair.
>
> Mr Dolan said the store had apologised for its error and had conceded liability.

This is an interesting set of facts and the court reporter viewed this as being of interest for both the circumstances and the damages for mental distress. While the defendants conceded liability, what causes of action do you think the plaintiff would have relied upon? Express or implied terms? It is likely that section 39 would have been very important in establishing the plaintiff's case.

2. However, the scope of these implied terms will often depend upon the question whether the seller is acting 'in the course of a business' or not. A private sale of a motor vehicle does not bring the seller within the scope of these implied duties while the sale by a motor dealer will attract these implied terms. Intermediate situations can arise. For example, should a solicitor decide to sell off a redundant typewriter which has been used for business purposes, does the solicitor sell those goods 'in the course of business'? See Sealy (1999) CLJ 276. The Court of Appeal, in *Stevenson v. Rogers* [1999] 1 All ER 613 has given an affirmative answer. It should be noted, when reading this case, that section 14(2) of the UK Sale of Goods Act 1979 is the same as section 14(2) of the Sale of Goods Act 1893, as amended in Ireland in the 1980 Act. The UK legislature in 1994 changed the terminology from 'merchantable quality' to 'satisfactory quality'.

SECTION FOUR—TERMS IMPLIED UNDER THE CONSTITUTION

Principles of constitutional and national justice may impose upon a contracting party certain 'good faith' obligations. This is particularly so where one party seeks to terminate a contractual relationship. There may be a duty to provide some form of inquiry or hearing before one party purports to terminate the contract because of an alleged breach of contract by the other party or under an express term afforded by the contract.

The leading case is *Glover v. BLN Ltd* [1973] IR 388. In *Fagan v. General Accident Fire and Life Assurance Corporation plc*, 14 October 1998 the Supreme Court held that insurance contracts contain mutual obligations of good faith but that constitutional justice does not require the insurer to conduct a kind of mini-trial before purporting to exercise a contractual right to disclaim an insurance contract. However in this case the insured was given an opportunity to respond to allegations prior to termination of this contract.

Where, however, the contractual relationship is essentially a private law relationship, implied good faith obligations will not be allowed to take on the full rigour of natural and constitutional justice principles and it will be enough if the party who is challenging the conduct of the other contracting party is afforded a right to challenge that other party—a right to a fair hearing as a matter of implied contract. This position has been reaffirmed in *Barry v Medical Defence Union* [2005] IESC 41. On the other hand, where a regulatory body can be said to exercise a combination of public law and private law junctions, private law and constitutional law implied obligations may overlap. The Irish Courts are currently being deluged by Judicial Review applications which are testing the resolve of the judiciary to resist invitations to hold that a diverse number of companies and agencies must observe principles of natural and constitutional justice; see, for example, *Bolger v Osborne and Others and the Turf Club* [2000] 1 ILRM 250. In this case a finding by the Turf Club that a trainer had infringed Turf Club rules was held to be improper and irrational when the inquiry conducted under the rules of the Turf Club failed to disclose any wrongdoing by the trainer. Macken J. held that in the absence of strict or vicarious liability, a finding of fault against the plaintiff constituted both a breach of contract and breach of the constitutional right to a fair and proper hearing.

Dooley v Great Southern Hotels Ltd [2001] ELR 340

The plaintiff had been engaged as a hotel manager for less than one year but had been employed in a managerial capacity for several years prior to that. His performance was regarded as unsatisfactory, but matters came to a head when he failed to carry out an instruction to try to persuade a key employee from leaving employment. A disciplinary hearing was called and one issue was whether fair procedures had been followed.

McCracken J.:

The law

I have already referred to *Pepper v Webb* and *Brewster v Burke*. I would point out that both those cases were decided over twenty years ago, and it could certainly be argued that they do not represent the law as of today. Employment law has developed very considerably over those years.

There is no doubt that some at least of the principles of natural justice must apply to a situation where an employee is being dismissed for misconduct. In *Glover v BLN Ltd* [1973] IR 288 Walsh J. said at p. 425:

> The plaintiff was neither told of the charges against him nor was he given any opportunity of dealing with them before the Board of Directors arrived at its decision to dismiss him. In my view this procedure was a breach of the implied term of the contract that the procedure should be fair, as it cannot be disputed, in the light of so much authority on the point, that failure to allow a person to meet the charges against him and to afford him an adequate opportunity of answering them is a violation of an obligation to proceed fairly.

In the present case there was no procedure laid down for the conduct of any disciplinary procedures against the plaintiff, although there were quite detailed procedures in relation to more junior members of the staff. The situation was addressed by the Supreme Court in *Mooney v An Post* [1998] ELR 238, where Barrington J. giving the judgment of the court said at p. 247:

> If the contract or the statute governing a person's employment contains a procedure whereby the employment may be terminated it usually will be sufficient for the employer to show that he has complied with this procedure. If the contract or the statute contains a provision whereby an employee is entitled to a hearing before an independent board or arbitrator before he can be dismissed then clearly that independent board or arbitrator must conduct the relevant proceedings with due respect to the principles of natural and constitutional justice. If however the contract (or the statute) provides that the employee may be dismissed for misconduct without specifying any procedure to be followed the position may be more difficult. Certainly the employee is entitled to the benefit of fair procedures but what these demand will depend upon the terms of his employment and the circumstances surrounding his proposed dismissal. Certainly the minimum he is entitled to is to be informed of the charge against him and to be given an opportunity to answer it and to make submissions.

Finally, there is authority that a claim that employment is permanent in the sense of being continuous for life or until a pensionable age is not sustainable at common law and that in those circumstances the plaintiff's employment is permanent only in the sense of being for an indefinite period terminable by reasonable notice (*Walsh v Dublin Health Board* 98 ILTR 82).

McCracken J. held that fair procedures had been followed but upheld Dooley's entitlement to damages for insufficient notice of termination.

Tierney *v* An Post [2000] 2 ILRM 214

Tierney applied for orders of *certiorari* and prohibition in respect of a purported termination of his contract with respondents as a sub-postmaster.

Alleged irregularities in the way in which the applicant's duties had been performed were investigated and Tierney's contract was terminated. The Supreme Court had to determine if there was a basis for implying certain constitutional rights into the contract of service.

Keane J.: (Hamilton C.J. and Lynch J. concurring.)

There remains the question as to whether the contract, although a contract for services, should be construed as containing an implied term that the respondent was obliged to conduct the disciplinary machinery provided for in the contract in accordance with fair procedures.

Giving the judgment of the majority of this court in *Glover v BLN Ltd* [1973] IR 388, Walsh J. said at p. 425:

> This court in *In re Haughey* [1971] IR 217 held that [Article 40.3] of the Constitution was a guarantee of fair procedures. It is not, in my opinion, necessary to discuss the full effect of this article in the realm of private law or indeed of public law. It is sufficient to say that public policy and the dictates of constitutional justice require that statutes, regulations or agreements setting up machinery for taking decisions which may affect rights or impose liability should be construed as providing for fair procedures. It is unnecessary to decide to what extent the contrary can be provided for by agreement between the parties.

That statement of the law is not confined to contracts of service. It is in accordance with the general principle laid down by the same learned judge in *Meskell v* CIE [1973] IR 121, that constitutional rights may be protected or enforced in proceedings between private citizens and not merely in proceedings against the state.

In the present case, the contract, although not a contract of service, provided a machinery for taking a decision which could result, and did in this case result, in the determination of the applicant's tenure of the office of sub-postmaster. It is not in dispute that it had financial consequences for the applicant which could fairly be equated to those resulting from a dismissal from a particular employment.

As was pointed out by Barrington J. giving the judgment of this court in *Mooney v An Post* [1998] 4 IR 288, the two central maxims traditionally associated with the concept of natural justice—*nemo judex in causa sua* and *audi alteram partem*—are not necessarily capable of application where an employer dismisses an employee. Similar considerations would apply to a contract for services of the nature now under consideration. But where, as here, the contract provides a disciplinary machinery which is invoked to determine whether the person should retain the office of sub-postmaster or be visited with a lesser sanction, the reasoning in the passage I have cited from *Glover v BLN* is, in my view, fully applicable.

It is true that the disciplinary machinery provided under the Postmaster's Manual does not expressly provide for an oral hearing. Where, however, the respondent by implication accepts, as it did here, that the matter was sufficiently serious to warrant an oral hearing, it follows inevitably that the applicant was entitled to fair procedures in the conduct of that oral hearing and the determination arrived at by the respondent following the hearing.

Unfortunately, as found by the learned High Court judge, such fair procedures were not observed in the present case.

Chapter Eight

Risk Allocation and Consumer Protection

INTRODUCTION

The use of express contractual terms to order and regulate commercial transactions is an indispensable part of the free market system. The ability of the parties to create or transfer liability, should certain stated events occur, is an important aspect of all contract regimes and an essential feature of the principle of freedom of contract. In the Industrial Age the movement towards concluding agreements by reference to standard conditions of contract became the norm in a number of specific areas such as banking, insurance and the carriage of goods and persons. The use of standardised contracts, in contradistinction to individualised bargaining, was explored by several distinguished American commentators, most notably perhaps Professor Karl Llewellyn:

Review of Prausnitz, O. *The Standardization of Commercial Contracts in English and Continental Law* (1937) in (1939) 52 Harv L Rev 700.

. . . when contract ceases to be a matter of dicker, bargain by bargain, and item by item, and becomes in any field or any outfit's business or any trade's practice a matter of mass production of bargains, with the background (apart from price, quantity and the like) filled in not by the general law but by standard clauses and terms, prepared often by one of the parties only—then what? One 'what' is clear: the presuppositions of our general law no longer maintain in such a situation. Those presuppositions can be stated somewhat as follows: (1) The general law is adequately specialised, and is detailed and balanced to fill in with moderate adequacy any gaps which parties leave open in their bargaining. (2) Any particular or specialised terms the parties are interested in they will bargain about. (3) Almost any particular clause included in a deal represents the parties' joint judgment as to what they want; and this alone is ground enough for letting it, for the deal in hand, displace and replace the general law. But when contracts are produced by the printing press, with the fountain pen used not for recording thought but for authentication, the adequacy of the general law for filling gaps in the conscious bargain is flatly negatived, in the view of the party preparing and ordering the form pads. And, commonly, that party is in this in good part right: specialisation of rule *is* then needed. And contracts which incorporate by reference the full 'rules' of some association stand in this on like footing. In neither case, it is to be remembered, are the individual variations from the general law bargained about. The contract is a block-contract, for one side (or both) to take or leave. If for goods, then description, quantity, delivery date, price, perhaps credit terms, may be open for actual

bargain, and these are all that at least one bargainor is in fact thinking about. Meanwhile the rest descends upon him: passage of risk, warranty, inspection requirements, exemption of seller for this or that contingency—such as strike, fire, shortage of raws or of transportation facilities—incidence of taxation, insurance, revocation of credit terms, special limitation of buyers' remedies in case of short or defective deliveries, exclusion of oral warranty or other modification, privilege of seller in the event shipping instructions are not received or goods are rejected, provision for arbitration or waiver of procedural rights—all such matters are covered *in toto* in the form or rules, to leave or to take, in block—and, commonly, to take without knowledge.
. . .

'The general law' is much too general. It needs tailoring to trades and to lines of trading. Nothing can approach in speed and sanity of readaptation the machinery of standard forms of a trade and for a line of trade, built to meet the particular needs of that trade. They save trouble in bargaining. They save time in bargaining. They infinitely simplify the task of internal administration of a business unit, of keeping tabs on transactions, of knowing where one is at, of arranging orderly expectation, orderly fulfilment, orderly planning. They ease administration by concentrating the need for discretion and decision in such personnel as can be trusted to be discreet. This reduces human wear and tear, it cheapens administration, it serves the ultimate consumer. Standardising contracts is in this a counterpart of standardising goods and production processes, as well as a device for adjustment of law to need. Prausnitz adds that such contracts, by limiting loss possibilities, can ease provision against risk (reminding us of Holmes' observation that the price paid for a contract commonly negates expectation of unusual risk). He adds, too, that it advantages a customer outfit to know that all *their* competitors are getting the same terms.

What worries Prausnitz is the combination of mass production of bargains with *one-sided* control of their detailed terms. The virtue of the 'general law', despite all inexpertness of the judges and sometimes of their formalism, has lain and does lie in a drive toward fairness, toward sane balance.
. . .

Our own concept of 'public policy' has a much more restricted field of operation. Our courts are loath indeed to throw out a contract clause under the plain justification that it is contrary to public policy, that it is such a clause as 'private' parties *cannot* make legally effective in the circumstance. Once we admit that it *is* a contract clause, and admit that it does mean what it says, we tend to regret, but to let the clause stand. And it may be that the English go even further in this than we; certainly some of the cases Prausnitz collects teach justice to shiver and shake.[1] But lacking ready recourse to *gute Sitten* or that near-equivalent in contract law, *l'ordre public* plus the *bonnes mœurs*, we have developed a whole series of semi-covert techniques for somewhat balancing these bargains. A court can 'construe' language into patently not meaning what the language is patently trying to say. It can find inconsistencies between clauses and throw out the troublesome one. It can even reject a clause as counter to the whole purpose of the transaction. It can reject enforcement by one side for want of 'mutuality', though allowing enforcement by the weaker side because 'consideration' in some other sense is present. Indeed, the law of agreeing can be subjected to divers modes of employment, to make the whole bargain or a particular clause stick or not stick according to the status of the party claiming under it: as when, in the interest of the lesser party, the whole contract is conditioned on some presupposition which is held to have failed.[2] The difficulty with these techniques of ours is threefold. First, since they all rest on the admission that the clauses in question are permissible in purpose and content, they invite the draftsman to recur to the attack. Give him time, and he will make the grade. Second, since they do not face the issue, they fail to accumulate either experience or authority in the needed direction: that of marking out for any given type of transaction what the *minimum decencies* are which a court will insist upon as essential to an enforceable bargain of a given type, or as being inherent in a bargain of that type. Third, since they purport to construe, and do not really construe, nor are intended to, but are instead tools of intentional and creative misconstruction, they seriously embarrass later efforts at true construction, later efforts to get at the true meaning of those wholly legitimate contracts and clauses which call for their meaning to be got at instead of avoided. The net effect is unnecessary confusion and unpredictability, together with inadequate remedy, and evil persisting that calls for remedy. Covert tools are never reliable tools. And the reason why Prausnitz's presentation itself rests still partly in confusion is because he does not clearly sever for separate discussion and comparison the two bodies of doctrine which run side by side in the English cases. There are, first, the doctrinal techniques of avoidance, or of misconstruction and remodelling. There are, second, the doctrinal techniques of really reading or supplementing an agreement according to its true purpose and meaning. English and American adjudication are not to be truly and fully compared with the French and German, save on the latter branch; for French and German law have the technical wherewithal for *always* trying to read accurately, and then for openly discarding objectionable clauses. Their courts have not fully grasped the opportunity, as Prausnitz's review of their decisions shows; but it is along this line that they have developed a somewhat greater clarity than have ours.[3]

1. *Hollis Bros & Co., Ltd v White Sea Timber Trust, Ltd* [1936] 3 All Eng 895 (KB) ('subject to seller's making necessary chartering arrangements' held to confer an option on seller to deliver or not at choice); *L'Estrange v F. Graucob, Ltd*, [1934] 2 KB 394 (small print clause: the writing includes 'All the terms and conditions under which I agree to purchase the machine specified above, and any express or implied condition, statement, or warranty, statutory or otherwise, not stated herein is hereby excluded,' stymies Scrutton himself in regard to unfitness of a slot machine for its purpose: café proprietor against manufacturer and seller; judgment on counterclaim for full unpaid price).

2. In such cases it is not to be expected that 'the whole contract' fails if the lesser party is claiming under it, on which Prausnitz's view of English law would be misleading if applied to American. But the further problem he raises is a fascinating one: whether, with a given clause or condition knocked out, the dominant bargainor would have entered on the deal at all. Fascinating, and hardly soluble. The practical answer lies in disregard of the problem: the type of deal was meant; the court in knocking out the clause is knocking out an inadmissible incident to that type of deal: e.g. *re* clogging an equity of redemption, or voiding usurious interest.

3. This is not to say that continental doctrine at large is clear. The questions surrounding the concept of contracts 'of adhesion' to which one party more affixes itself turn attention too much to the type of matter discussed by us under reality of consent; if one must take or leave in block, and needs to take, has he 'assented'? It is with a sound instinct that many writers have been impelled to answer: Yes. But that merely sets the problem. You take or leave your marriage agreement, pretty much in block; you 'adhere', you do not 'bargain'. The point is that when that is the type of choice and the only type of choice really available, it has been and still is the law's business, and in a case-law system, the judges', to see that the block to which you are indeed *assenting as a transaction* is carved into some approximation of decent balance in its detail. The 'mass' aspect properly stressed by Prausnitz goes to social importance, but it goes even more to evidencing the presence of a block of terms which is not individualised to the bargainors, and which needs re-establishment of the type of balance provided by the general 'law of sales' or 'of partnership', etc., for those who assent in block.

Note

Problems of contractual fairness and abuse of freedom of contract become particularly acute when there is a contractual imbalance as between the parties, or where one party enjoys a statutory or *de facto* monopoly. For a thoughtful analysis see H.B. Sales, 'Standard Form Contracts' (1953) 16 MLR 318.

F. Kessler 'The Contract of Adhesion' (1943) Col L Rev 629

The development of large scale enterprise with its mass production and mass distribution made a new type of contract inevitable—the standardised mass contract.[1] A standardised contract, once its contents have been formulated by a business firm, is used in every bargain dealing with the same product or service. The individuality of the parties which so frequently gave colour to the old type contract has disappeared. The stereotyped contract of today reflects the impersonality of the market. It has reached its greatest perfection in the different types of contracts used on the various exchanges. Once the usefulness of these contracts was discovered and perfected in the transportation, insurance, and banking business, their use spread into all other fields of large scale enterprise, into international as well as national trade, and into labour relations. It is to be noted that uniformity of terms of contracts typically recurring in a business enterprise is an important factor in the exact calculation of risks. Risks which are difficult to calculate can be excluded altogether. Unforseeable contingencies affecting performance, such as strikes, fire, and transportation difficulties can be taken care of.[2] The standard clauses in insurance policies are the most striking illustrations of successful attempts on the part of business enterprises to select and control risks assumed under a contract. The insurance business probably deserves credit also for having first realised the full importance of the so-called 'juridical risk', the danger that a court or jury may be swayed by 'irrational factors' to decide against a powerful defendant. Ingenious clauses have been the result.[3] Once their practical utility was proven, they were made use of in other lines of business. It is highly probable that the desire to avoid juridical risks has been a motivating factor in the widespread use of warranty clauses in the machine industry limiting the common law remedies of the buyer to breach of an implied warranty of quality and particularly excluding his right to claim damages.[4] The same is true for arbitration clauses in international trade. Standardised contracts have thus become an important means of excluding or controlling the 'irrational factor' in litigation. In this respect they are a true reflection of the spirit of our time with its hostility to irrational factors in the judicial process, and they belong in the same category as codifications and restatements.

Insofar as the reduction of costs of production and distribution thus achieved is reflected in reduced prices, society as a whole ultimately benefits from the use of standard contracts. And there can be no doubt that this has been the case to a considerable extent. The use of standard contracts has, however, another aspect which has become increasingly important. Standard contracts are typically used by enterprises with strong bargaining power. The weaker party, in need of the goods or services, is frequently not in a position to shop around for better terms, either because the author of the standard contract has a monopoly (natural or artificial) or because all competitors use the same clauses. His contractual intention is but a subjection more or less voluntary to terms dictated by the stronger party, terms whose consequences are often understood only in a vague way, if at all. Thus, standardised contracts are frequently contracts of adhesion; they are *à prendre ou à laisser*.[5] Not infrequently the weaker party to a prospective contract even agrees in advance not to retract his offer while the offeree reserves for himself the power to accept or refuse;[6] or he submits to terms or change of terms which will be communicated to him later. To be sure, the latter type of clauses regularly provide for a power to disaffirm,[7] but as a practical matter they are acquiesced in frequently, thus becoming part of the 'living law'. Lastly, standardised contracts have also been used to control and regulate the distribution of goods from producer all the way down to the ultimate consumer. They have become one of the many devices to build up and strengthen industrial empires.

And yet the tremendous economic importance of contracts of adhesion is hardly reflected in the great texts on contracts or in the Restatement. As a matter of fact, the term 'contract of adhesion' or a similar symbol has not even found general recognition in our legal vocabulary. This will not do any harm if we remain fully aware that the use of the word 'contract' does not commit us to an indiscriminate extension of the ordinary contract rules to all contracts. But apparently the realisation of the deepgoing antin-omies in the structure of our system of contracts is too painful an experience to be permitted to rise to the full level of our consciousness. Consequently, courts have made great efforts to protect the weaker contracting party and still keep 'the elementary rules' of the law of contracts intact. As a result, our common law of standardised contracts is highly contradictory and confusing, and the potentialities inherent in the common law system for coping with contracts of adhesion have not been fully developed.

[1.] Pausnitz, *The Standardization of Commercial Contracts in English and Continental Law* (1937) reviewed by Llewellyn (1939) 52 Harv L Rev 700; Llewellyn, *'What Price Contract—An Essay in Perspective'* (1931) 40 Yale LJ 704; Issacs, *'The Standardising of Contracts'* (1917) 27 Yale LJ 34; Raiser, *Das Recht der Allgemeinen Geschäftsbedingungen* (1936).

[2.] For a far reaching clause in a sales contract see *Hollis Bros. & Co. Ltd v White Sea Timber Trust, Ltd,* 3 All ER 895 (1936). Here the seller of timber from a port in the Arctic Circle open for navigation only about twenty one days stipulated 'this contract is subject to sellers making necessary chartering arrangements for the expedition and sold subject to shipments any goods not shipped to be cancelled.'

[3.] Patterson, *Essentials of Insurance Law* (1935) 282 *et seq.*

[4.] For an effort of the legislature to protect the interests of the buyer of agricultural machinery see North Dakota Laws (1919) c. 238, construed in *Palaniuk v Allis Chalmers Mfg Co.,* 57 ND 199, 220 NW 638 (1928).

[5.] The word 'contract of adhesion' has been introduced into the legal vocabulary by Patterson, *'The Delivery of a Life Insurance Policy'* (1919) 33 Harv L Rev 198, 222.

[6.] *Cole, McIntyre, Norfleet Co. v Hollaway,* 141 Tenn. 679, 214 SW 817 (1919) discussed by Corbin in (1920) 29 Yale LJ 441.

[7.] See the standard form of an application for a life insurance policy, reprinted in Patterson, *Cases and Other Materials on the Law of Insurance* (1932) 819; *Robinson v US Benevolent Society,* 132 Mich. 695 (1903).

SECTION ONE—UNCONSCIONABLE BARGAIN

Schroeder Music Publishing Co. *v* Macauley [1974] 3 All ER 616

A young and inexperienced songwriter signed a music publishing contract which bound him for up to ten years while at the same time giving copy-right in the songs written by him to the publisher without creating a corresponding obligation to publish all or any of these songs. The contract was standard within the music publishing industry.

The House of Lords held the contract, insofar as it was not performed, to be unenforceable.

Lord Diplock:

My Lords, the contract under consideration in this appeal is one whereby the respondent accepted restrictions on the way in which he would exploit his earning power as a song-writer for the next ten years. Because this can be classified as a contract in restraint of trade the restrictions that the respondent accepted fell within one of those limited categories of contractual promises in respect of which the courts still retain the power to relieve the promisor of his legal duty to fulfil them. In order to determine whether this case is one in which that power ought to be exercised, what your Lordships have in fact been doing has been to assess the relative bargaining power of the publisher and the song-writer at the time the contract was made and to decide whether the publisher had used his superior bargaining power to exact from the song-writer promises that were unfairly onerous to him. Your Lordships have not been concerned to enquire whether the public have in fact been deprived of the fruit of the song-writer's talents by reason of the restrictions, nor to assess the likelihood that they would be so deprived in the future if the contract were permitted to run its full course.

It is, in my view, salutory to acknowledge that in refusing to enforce provisions of a contract whereby one party agrees for the benefit of the other party to exploit or to refrain from exploiting his own earning power, the public policy which the court is implementing is not some nineteenth century economic theory about the benefit to the general public of freedom of trade, but the protection of those whose bargaining power is weak against being forced by those whose bargaining power is stronger to enter into bargains that are unconscionable. Under the influence of Bentham and of *laissez-faire* the courts in the nineteenth century abandoned the practice of applying the public policy against unconscionable bargains to contracts generally, as they had formerly done to any contract considered to be usurious; but the policy survived in its application to penalty clauses and to relief against forfeiture and also to the special category of contracts in restraint of trade. If one looks at the reasoning of nineteenth century judges in cases about contracts in restraint of trade one finds lip service paid to current economic theories but if one looks at what they said in the light of what they did, one finds that they struck down a bargain if they thought it was uncon-scionable as between the parties to it, and upheld it if they thought that it was not.

So I would hold that the question to be answered as respects a contract in restraint of trade of the kind with which this appeal is concerned is: was the bargain fair? The test of fairness is, no doubt, whether the restrictions are both reasonably necessary for the protection of the legitimate interest of the promisee and commensurate with the benefits secured to the promisor under the contract. For the purpose of this test all the provisions of the contract must be taken into consideration.

My Lords, the provisions of the contract have already been sufficiently stated by my noble and learned friend, Lord Reid. I agree with his analysis of them and with his conclusion that the contract is unenforceable. It does not satisfy the test of fairness as I have endeavoured to state it. I will accordingly content myself with adding some observations directed to the argument that because the contract was in a 'standard form' in common use between music publishers and song-writers, the restraints that it imposes on the song-writer's liberty to exploit his talents must be presumed to be fair and reasonable.

Standard forms of contracts are of two kinds. The first, of very ancient origin, are those which set out the terms on which mercantile transactions of common occurrence are to be carried out. Examples are bills of lading, charterparties, policies of insurance, contracts of sale in the commodity markets. The standard clauses in these contracts have been settled over the years by negotiation by representatives of the commercial interests involved and have been widely adopted because experience has shown that they facilitate the conduct of trade. Contracts of these kinds affect not only the actual parties to them but also others who may have a commercial interest in the transactions to which they relate, as buyers or sellers, charterers or shipowners, insurers or bankers. If fairness or reasonableness were relevant to their enforceability the fact that they are widely used by parties whose bargaining power is fairly matched would raise a strong presumption that their terms are fair and reasonable.

The same presumption, however, does not apply to the other kind of standard form of contract. This is of comparatively modern origin. It is the result of the concentration of particular kinds of business in relatively few hands. The ticket cases in the nineteenth century provide what are probably the first examples. The terms of this kind of standard form of contract have not been the subject of negotiation between the parties to it, or approved by any organisation representing the interests of the weaker party. They have been dictated by that party whose bargaining power, either exercised alone or in conjunction with another providing similar goods or services, enables him to say: 'If you want these goods or services at all, these are the only terms on which they are obtainable. Take it or leave it.'

To be in a position to adopt this attitude towards a party desirous of entering into a contract to obtain goods or services provides a classic instance of superior bargaining power. It is not without significance that on the evidence in the present case, music publishers in negotiating with song-writers whose success has been already established do not insist on adhering to a contract in the standard form they offered to the respondent. The fact that the appellants' bargaining power *vis-à-vis* the respondent was strong enough to enable them to adopt this take-it-or-leave it attitude raises no presumption that they used it to drive an unconscionable bargain with him, but in the field of restraint of trade it calls for vigilance on the part of the court to see that they did not.

McCord v ESB [1980] ILRM 153

O'Higgins C.J.:

The appellant is a statutory board established by s. 2 of the Electricity (Supply) Act, 1927. In accordance with the provisions of this Act it is armed with certain powers and charged with certain duties in relation to the provision of electric power throughout the country. In particular, by s. 19 it is charged with a duty to distribute, sell and promote the use of electricity and to control, co-ordinate and improve the supply of electricity generally. Over the years since its establishment the appellant has carried out these statutory functions with regard both to the supply and control of electricity to such an extent that it now exercises a virtual monopoly in relation to this essential source of energy and power. As the appellant is charged with the duty of selling electricity it is implicit, and envisaged by the Act, that it should have the power to enter into contracts with individual consumers providing for the sale of supply of electricity and for matters connected therewith. The appellant in fact does this by operating what are termed 'General Conditions relating to Supply'. These are a set of conditions, fifteen in number, which the appellant enforces throughout the country as governing the supply by it of electricity to its consumers. Every applicant for a supply of electricity is required to sign a document agreeing that such is 'to be connected, supplied and charged for in accordance with the board's general conditions relating to electrical supply.' The document contains a further acknowledgment on behalf of the applicant that he has seen and carefully read these general conditions and 'all such further or amended conditions and regulations as may be made from time to time by the board as to conditions, price or otherwise, in as full a manner as if the same were in force at the date hereof.' A postscript is added at the bottom of this document of application to the effect:

> *Important*—The board's general conditions relating to electricity supply are on display at the board's offices and showrooms, and copies are available on request. The board has the right to amend, alter or vary these conditions from time to time, and the condition of supply as so amended, altered or varied shall, while in force, be *ipso facto* binding upon the consumer.

While the ensuing relationship between the appellant and the successful applicant for a supply of electricity is termed contractual it is quite clear that it is a contract into which the person seeking a supply has no option but to enter. Not only is this so but it is one which is subject to unilateral alteration which must be accepted by the consumer if supply is to be continued. The true nature and effect of these general conditions are not in issue in this case nor has their validity been called into question. For the purpose of this case it is agreed that the relationship existing between the appellant and its consumers is based on contract and that the terms of this contract are those contained in these general conditions. I would also add, however, that these general conditions emanating as they do exclusively from the appellant must be construed strictly and must be operated fairly and reasonably.

The respondent in this appeal was and is one of the appellant's consumers. He was supplied with electricity in connection with his house at 166 Arthur Griffith Park, Lucan, in October 1973. He occupied this house with his wife and family. On 10 May 1978 one of the appellant's meter inspectors, on visiting the respondent's house, discovered that the appellant's meter therein installed had been tampered with. This meter had been opened, interfered with, and a false seal had been attached to conceal what had been done. The result was that the actual amount of electricity consumed by the household was not recorded and a considerable amount of electricity so consumed was neither charged to nor paid for by the respondent. When this was discovered the respondent and his wife disclaimed all responsibility for or knowledge of what had occurred. In ensuing interviews with representatives of the appellant the respondent was asked and required to sign a statement to the effect that while disclaiming responsibility in the manner he had indicated, he nevertheless acknowledged that the interference had taken place while the meter was in his custody and undertaking to pay for the electricity which had not been accounted for. The respondent refused to do so. Eventually and because of his attitude the appellant cut off the supply of electricity to his house. This took place on 23 May 1978. On 20 December 1978 the respondent commenced these proceedings by plenary summons claiming against the appellant damages for breach of contract and an order providing for the reconnection of supply. As a result and pending the trial of the action supply was recommenced to the respondent's house on 28 February 1979. In his statement of claim, subsequently furnished, the respondent claimed damages for the inconvenience and loss suffered by him and his family in the period in which the supply of electricity was withdrawn.

The respondent's action was tried in the High Court by the late Butler J. He came to the conclusion and so stated in his spoken judgment that the appellant was not entitled, whether for the purpose of enforcing payment of sums due or for the purpose of enforcing other terms of the contract, to cut off supply to a consumer without an order of the court. For this reason he held that the appellant had acted unreasonably and in breach of contract. However, he also held that the respondent and his wife had acted unreasonably in refusing to co-operate with the appellant's representatives and in refusing to do what was asked. He held that if the respondents had agreed to the reasonable request made of him to sign the suggested agreement and undertaking the supply of electricity would not have been cut off and none of the suffering and inconvenience which was subsequently caused would have resulted. For this reason he awarded the plaintiff only £50 damages.

The appellant brings this appeal to call into question the view expressed by Butler J. that it was not entitled to terminate or cut off supply to a consumer without first having obtained an order of the court enabling it to do so. A cross-appeal has been served by the respondent complaining that the damages awarded were inadequate.

On the hearing of the appeal, as already indicated, it was agreed that the rights of the parties depended on the contract as contained in the general conditions. The respondent did not seek to support the trial judge's view that the appellant could not act, in a situation covered by these conditions, without an order of the court. The appeal, therefore, resolved itself into a question as to whether the appellant's action, in the circumstances, was justified under the general conditions. The appellant conceded that, if not so justified, the action taken was without authority and, therefore in breach of contract. At this stage I think it proper to say that not only do these general conditions empower the appellant to cut off electricity in particular circumstances but also, that such a power is expressly given to the appellant by s. 99 of the Electricity (Supply) Act, 1927, in the circumstances to which that section applies. The question which now arises on this appeal is whether the circumstances of this particular case justified the appellant in doing what it did. In my view, these circumstances do not justify the action taken.

Counsel for the appellant rested justification for the action taken on the provisions of clause 13 of the general conditions taken in conjunction with those of clause 10. Clause 13 provides as follows:

13. Power to disconnect supply and/or terminate agreement
     The board may disconnect supply without prior notice to the consumer:

   (a) If the consumer fails to pay on demand any account issued for electricity supplied by the board, including any estimated account or any statutory charges arising in connection therewith or any other sum due to the board on foot of a contract for the supply of electricity.
   (b) If the consumer commits any breach or fails to comply with any of these terms and conditions.
   (c) To make alterations or repairs.

     The board may also disconnect from its supply mains any installation where, in the opinion of the board, such use of the energy is made as to interfere with the satisfactory distribution of electricity or where in the opinion of the board such installation interfered with the quality of supply to other consumers or where the board considers the installation to be in a dangerous condition. The board may also disconnect supply and/or terminate agreement at any time upon giving forty eight hours notice to the consumer, such notice to be left at or sent by post to the premises supplied. If the notice is sent by post it shall be deemed to have been received on the week day following the day of posting.

The particular provisions of this clause relied on was sub-clause (b). It was contended that in this case there was a breach or failure by the respondent to comply with a term or condition and that this justified the appellant in exercising its power to disconnect. The term or condition which it was contended had not been complied with or broken was that contained in clause 10. This clause reads as follows:

10. Liability of consumer for damage to board apparatus

The consumer shall be held responsible by the board for the safe keeping of all meters and other electrical apparatus, service lines and fittings belonging to the board and placed on his premises, and should any damage or injury be caused by fire, water, accident or other cause for which the board or its officers, servants or agents are not responsible, the consumer must pay to the board on demand, the cost of making good and repairing any such damage or injury.

What does this condition mean? It provides that the consumer is to be held responsible for the safe keeping of meters and other electrical apparatus placed on his premises and that this responsibility is to be discharged by paying for the cost of making good any damage caused other than damage caused by the board's servants. How can it be suggested that this clause has not been observed or will not be observed by the respondent? It was never suggested to him that he should pay for the repair of the meter nor was he required to do so. He was required to sign a statement, already indicated, which was quite a different matter. It is true, as Butler J. held, that he acted unreasonably in refusing to do so. This, however, did not constitute a breach or non-compliance with a clause which the appellant never brought to his notice or sought to enforce against him. On the contrary, at an early stage of these proceedings the appellant sought to justify the action taken by reliance on another clause, clause 7 (g). This clause is as follows:

(g) No person except an official of the board shall fix, connect or disconnect, remove or otherwise interfere with any such meter, main fuse box or other apparatus, the property of the board all of which will be sealed by the Board and such seals must on no account be broken except by Board officials. Breach of this regulation may expose the offender to prosecution. The Board reserves the right to remove any meter or meters at any time.

As, of course, there was no evidence that the respondent so interfered or caused any other person to interfere with the meter, reliance on this clause was discontinued. I am, therefore, of the opinion that there was, on the facts of this case, no evidence that the respondent has been in breach of the clause relied upon and that accordingly the appellant's action was not justified under the general conditions and was accordingly in breach of contract.

As to damages this court is bound by the finding of fact made by the learned trial judge that the appellant would not have cut off supply had the respondent co-operated in the manner already indicated. In this respect the appellant relies on the provisions of s. 34(1) of the Civil Liability Act, 1961. In the circumstances of this case, in my view, unreasonable conduct by the respondent without regard to the comfort and convenience of his family and household can fairly be regarded as contributory negligence or want of care within the meaning of the section. It cannot, however, justify an action which was unlawful and in breach of contract. The sanction which the section provides for is that the damages recoverable in respect of the wrong complained of, shall, where such damage was caused partly by the sufferer's negligence or want of care, be reduced by such amount as the court thinks just and equitable. The section authorises the reduction, not the negativing or annulment of such damage. Here the appellant was seeking to enforce its own general conditions. It cannot, in my view, seek to avoid all responsibility for an action not authorised because, through ignorance or fear or for any other reason, the threatened consumer behaved without due care and responsibility. It seems to me having regard to what was suffered by the plaintiff and his family that the award of £50 damages made by the trial judge was a reduction in damages which in the circumstances was just and equitable. I would not interfere with this award of damages.

Henchy J.:

. . . it is important to point out that the contract made between the plaintiff and board (incorporating the general conditions relating to supply) is what is nowadays called a contract of adhesion: it is a standardised mass contract which must be entered into, on a take it or leave it basis, by the occupier of every premises in which electricity is to be used. The would-be consumer has no standing to ask that a single iota of the draft contract presented to him be changed before he signs it. He must lump it or leave it. But, because for reasons that are too obvious to enumerate, he cannot do without electricity, he is invariably forced by necessity into signing the contract, regardless of the fact that he may consider some of its terms arbitrary, or oppressive, or demonstrably unfair. He is compelled, from a position of weakness and necessity *vis-à-vis* a monopolist supplier of a vital commodity, to enter into what falls into the classification of a contract and which, as such, according to the theory of the common law which was evolved in the *laissez-faire* atmosphere of the nineteenth century, is to be treated by the courts as if it had emerged by choice from the forces of the market place, at the behest of parties who were at arm's length and had freedom of choice. The real facts show that such an approach is largely based on legal fictions. When a monopoly supplier of a vital public utility—which is what the board is—forces on all its consumers a common form of contract, reserving to itself sweeping powers, including the power to vary the document unilaterally as it may think fit, such an instrument has less affinity with a freely negotiated interpersonal contract than with a set of bye-laws or with any other form of autonomic legislation. As such, its terms may have to be construed not simply as contractual elements but as components of a piece of delegated legislation, the validity of which will depend on whether it has kept within the express or implied confines of the statutory delegation and, even if it has, whether the delegation granted or assumed is now consistent with the provisions of the Constitution of 1937.

(Kenny, Griffin and Parke JJ. concurred.)

Note

The *Irish Times* of 26 February 1985 carried the following account of a District Court case under the heading 'Bord Telecom's powers almost draconian—judge':

A District Justice yesterday said that people were 'almost dragooned' into paying telephone bills because of the near draconian powers given to Bord Telecom under the legislation.

    In the Dublin District Court, District Justice McMenamin suggested that the Oireachtas, in granting monopoly powers to the telephone authorities, should have provided a 'built-in system where the customer would have some rights to protest, some very quick way of appealing to someone, some independent or quasi-independent person to examine a dispute over an account, without having his telephone cut off.

'But be that as it may I am not here to make law, I'm here to apply law,' he said.

Counsel for the board later pointed out that the Ombudsman will be empowered to deal with telephone complaints from 1 April next.

Dismissing a case brought against Bord Telecom for overcharging and abuse of personal rights under the common law of contract, the District Justice said the case had raised some interesting points of law 'but the law is clear that any constitutional issues must begin in the High Court, and only in the High Court'.

The case had been brought by Mr Garret Hooper, of Clarinda Park West, Dun Laoghaire, whose telephone was cut off in November 1980. Mr Hooper had argued that certain terms of the telephone contract were contrary to common law, and that it was therefore null and void, and that the telephone authorities had been in breach of common law duty in relation to supply of services and proper account keeping. He asked the court to state a case to the High Court as to whether common law had indeed been breached.

In particular he argued that the minister's blanket powers under the telephone regulations to determine the time and duration of calls and the amount owing in cases of dispute were such that they were prejudicial to the administration of justice and tended to promote corruption in public life.

Counsel for the board, however, replied that the state frequently limited the rights of contract such as by fixing maximum period and drink prices, and noted that the revenue commissioners and to some extent the gardai had discretionary powers to waive or amend penalties or charges.

District Justice McMenamin noted that Mr Hooper had admitted under cross-examination that during the period when the alleged overcharging had occurred, he had allowed another person to use his telephone 'to make telephone calls to exotic places like Bangkok'. Mr Hooper was not therefore on strong ground in challenging the authenticity of the telephone account.

Concluding that 'both the law and the facts are against Mr Hooper', the District Justice awarded costs to Bord Telecom.

A. DUTY TO READ

I. Calamari 'Duty to Read—A Changing Concept', (1974) 43 Fordham L Rev 1 341, 351–8

The Modern View—Contracts of Adhesion

There has been a tendency, particularly in recent years, to treat contracts of adhesion or standard form contracts differently from other contracts.[1] This is particularly true with respect to the duty to read.[2] There is a growing body of case law which subverts the traditional duty to read concept either upon a theory that there was not true assent to a particular term, or that, even if there was assent, the term is to be excised from the contract because it contravenes public policy or is unconscionable.[3] At times, the same decision may employ all three rationales. This modern approach to the problem and the meaning of true assent may be shown best by a brief examination of three of the leading cases on the subject.

Perhaps the most significant case is *Weaver v American Oil Co.*,[4] which considered a lease by an oil company to an individual. The lessee signed without reading the lease under which he agreed, *inter alia*, to indemnify the lessor as a result of damages caused by the lessor's negligence. The majority opinion first stated that the duty to read rule had no application to the case because *'the clause was in fine print and contained no title heading . . .'*[5]

This conclusion would have ended the matter under the rules discussed above, but the court seemed anxious to break new ground for it hastened to add:

> When a party show[s] that the contract, which is . . . to be enforced, was . . . an unconscionable one, due to a prodigious amount of bargaining power on behalf of the stronger party, which is used to the stronger party's advantage and is unknown to the lesser party, the contract provision, or the contract as a whole, if the provision is not separable, should not be enforceable on the grounds that the provision is contrary to public policy. The party seeking to enforce such a contract has the burden of showing that the provisions were explained to the other party and *came to his knowledge* and there was in fact *a real and voluntary meeting of the minds and not merely an objective meeting.*[6]

Although the above quotation combines three different concepts (unconscionability, violation of public policy, and lack of true assent),[7] the court's ultimate approach appears to be that the contract is unconscionable because an objective assent which flows from a duty to read is not sufficient (despite the objective theory of contracts) to bind a party to clauses which are unusual or unfair unless the clauses are at least brought to his attention and explained.[8] The theory is that since such clauses impose a great hardship or risk on the weaker party, who is otherwise unable to protect himself, an informed and voluntary consent should be required.[9]

The same approach was employed by the court in the well known case of *Henningsen v Bloomfield Motors, Inc.*[10] which arose under the Uniform Sales Act rather than the Uniform Commercial Code.[11] In *Henningsen*, a consumer brought an action for personal injuries against both the vendor and manufacturer of his automobile. Relying upon a provision in the contract of sale that an express warranty contained therein was in lieu of all other warranties express or implied, the defendants argued that the plaintiff's action should be limited to a claim for defective parts. The heart of the *Henningsen* decision appears in a paragraph near the end of the opinion:

> True, the Sales Act authorises agreements between buyer and seller qualifying the warranty obligations. But quite obviously the legislature contemplated lawful stipulations (which are determined by the circumstances of a particular case) arrived at freely by parties of relatively equal bargaining strength. The lawmakers did not authorise the automobile manufacturer to use its grossly disproportionate bargaining power to relieve itself from liability and to impose on the ordinary buyer, who in effect has no real freedom of choice, the grave danger of injury to himself and others that attends the sale of such a dangerous instrumentality as a defectively made automobile. In the framework of this case, illuminated as it is by the facts and the many decisions noted, we are of the opinion that Chrysler's attempted disclaimer of an implied warranty of merchantability and of the obligations arising therefrom is so inimical to the public good as to compel an adjudication of its invalidity.[12]

Although there was some discussion about mutual assent, the ultimate holding was based upon the conclusion that such a clause, under the circumstances of the case (clause on reverse side, small print, disparity of bargaining power, clause on a take-it-or-leave-it basis and included by all major car manufacturers), was invalid as being contrary to public policy. This was made clear when the court further stated that it was not required to consider whether a particular charge which related to mutual assent was correct because 'the disclaimer is void as a matter of law'.[13]

Another leading case illustrating the same approach is *Williams v Walker-Thomas Furniture Co.*[14] There, an instalment sales agreement had a provision which resulted in 'a balance due on every item purchased until the balance due on all items, whenever purchased, was liquidated.'[15] As a result, in the event of a default on any one item, all items could be repossessed. The court in concluding that the fairness of the clause needed to be tested at trial stated:

> Ordinarily, one who signs an agreement without full knowledge of its terms might be held to assume the risk that he has entered a one-sided bargain. But when a party of little bargaining power, and hence little real choice, signs a commercially unreasonable contract with little or no knowledge of its terms, it is hardly likely that his consent, or even an objective manifestation of his consent, was ever given to all the terms. In such a case the usual rule that the terms of the agreement are not to be questioned should be abandoned and the court should consider whether the terms of the contract are so unfair that enforcement should be withheld.[16]

The three cases discussed above do not expunge the duty to read rule, but create an exception thereto if the terms (or a term) of the contract are unfair under the circumstances. In such a case, the ordinary manifestation of assent implicit in a signature or acceptance of a document is insufficient because the assent is not reasoned and knowing. Such consent involves an understanding of the clause in question[17] and a reasonable opportunity to accept or decline.[18] Even then, if the clause is sufficiently odious, it will be struck down as unconscionable or contrary to public policy.

[1.] Kessler, 'Contracts of Adhesion—Some Thoughts About Freedom of Contract', 43 Col L Rev 629 (1943). Patterson, 'The Delivery of a Life Insurance Policy', 33 Harv L Rev 198, 222 (1919) (origin of the term 'adhesion contract'). In the Kessler article, as here, the terms contract of adhesion and standardised contract are used interchangeably. But the two concepts are not always treated as coextensive. See Sheldon, 'Consumer Protection and Standard Contracts: The Swedish Experiment in Administration Control', 22 Am J Comp L 17, 18 (1974).

[2.] Ehrenzweig, 'Adhesion Contracts in the Conflict of Laws', 53 Col L Rev 1072 (1953); Note, 'Contract Clauses in Fine Print', 63 Harv L Rev 494 (1950); see Wilson, 'Freedom of Contract and Adhesion Contracts', 14 Int'l & Comp L Q 172 (1965).

[3.] The notion of condemning clauses as illegal or contrary to public policy is hardly new. However, it is being used today more often and in a wider variety of circumstances. See, e.g. von Hippel, 'The Control of Exemption Clauses—A Comparative Study', 16 Int'l & Comp L Q 591 (1967). Unconscionability is discussed in note 8 infra.

[4.] 257 Ind. 458, 276 N.E.2d 144 (1971); Annot., 49 ALR.3d 306 (1973). See also *Frame v. Merrill Lynch, Pierce, Fenner & Smith, Inc.*, 20 Cal App 3d 668, 97 Cal Rptr 811 (1st Dist. 1971).

[5.] 257 Ind. at 462, 276 NE 2d at 147.

[6.] Ibid. at 464, 276 NE 2d at 148.

[7.] The Weaver opinion also proceeded upon a warranty analogy when it stated: 'The burden should be on the party submitting such 'a package' in printed form to show that the other party had knowledge of any unusual or unconscionable terms contained therein. The principle should be the same as that applicable to implied warranties, namely, that a package of goods sold to a purchaser is fit for the purposes intended and contains no harmful materials other than that represented.' Ibid., 276 NE 2d at 147–48.

[8.] The relationship of unconscionability to true assent and violation of public policy is interesting. Leff, in his article, 'Unconscionability and the Code—The Emperor's New Clause', 115 U Pa L Rev 485 (1967), distinguishes between substantive and procedural unconscionability. Procedural unconscionability exists where there is unfair surprise—which may be another way of saying that there was not a true, informed and voluntary mutual assent. Substantive unconscionability exists where a particular clause is unfair and oppressive. This is akin to a clause which is contrary to public policy. In the latter situation (theoretically at least) questions of true assent are unimportant. Very often, the two categories overlap. Professor Murray prefers to restrict the notion of unconscionability to questions of mutual assent. See Murray, 'Unconscionability: Unconscionability', 31 U Pitt L Rev 1 (1969). Although unconscionability clearly is related to the duty to read concept, it has other aspects, and so is treated here only incidentally. The literature on the subject is voluminous. In addition to the articles cited above see. e.g. Braucher, 'The Unconscionable Contract or Term', 31 U Pitt L Rev 337 (1970); Ellinghaus, 'In Defence of Unconscionability', 78 Yale LJ 757 (1969); Leff, 'Unconscionability and the Crowd—Consumers and the Common Law Tradition', 31 U Pitt L Rev 349 (1970); Spanogle, 'Analysing Unconscionability Problems', 117 U Pa L Rev 931 (1969); Speidel, 'Unconscionability, Assent and Consumer Protection', 31 U Pitt L Rev 359 (1970).

9. A party might be considered to be otherwise able to protect himself if he has a bargaining power relatively equal to that of the other party, or if he were able to obtain insurance at a reasonable rate to protect against a known risk being imposed upon him. See, e.g. *Vitex Mfg Corp. v Caribtex Corp.*, 377 F 2d 795, 799–800 (3d Cir. 1967); Johnston, 'The Control of Exemption Clauses: A Comment', 17 Int'l & Comp L Q 232 (1968).

10. 32 NJ 358, 161 A 2d 69 (1960), Annot., 75 ALR 2d 39 (1961).

11. If the case had arisen under the UCC, the court could have noted the provision that, in the case of a disclaimer of the warranty of merchantability, the word merchantability must be used and the disclaimer conspicuous. UCC § 2–316(2). The term 'conspicuous' is defined in ibid. §1–201(10). What is or is not conspicuous still appears to be a matter of controversy. A disclaimer in the smallest type preceded by the word 'Note' printed in the largest type was held to be conspicuous in *Velez v Craine & Clark Lumber Corp*, 41 App Div 2d 747, 341 NYS 2d 248 (2d Dep't), rev'd on other grounds, 33 NY 2d 117, 305 NE 2d 750, 350 NYS 2d 617 (1973). But see *Tennessee Carolina Transp., Inc. v Strick Corp*, 283 NC 423, 196 SE 2d 711 (1973). Even more to the point is UCC §2–719(3) which provides: 'Consequential damages may be limited or excluded unless the limitation or exclusion is unconscionable. Limitation of consequential damages for injury to the person in the case of consumer goods is *prima facie* unconscionable but limitation of damages where the loss is commercial is not.' See also UCC §§2–316(1), –718, –719(1) & (2).

Professor Murray takes the position that even if the disclaimer is conspicuous it must, in addition, be negotiated, and comprehensible to the buyer. See Murray, 'Unconscionability: Unconscionability', 31 U Pitt L Rev 1, 48–49 (1969). Contra, Leff, 'Unconscionability and the Code—The Emperor's New Clause', 115 U Pa L Rev 485, 523–24 (1967). There are, as usual, cases which support each position. Compare *Belden-Stark Brick Corp. v Morris Rosen & Sons, Inc.*, 39 App Div 2d 534, 331 NYS.2d 59 (1st Dep't), aff'd, 31 NY.2d 884, 292 NE 2d 321, 340 NYS 2d 185 (1972) (mem.) with *Dobias v Western Farmers Ass'n*, 6 Wash App 194, 491 P 2d 1346 (3d Div. 1971). Professor Broude suggests that under §§2–202 and 2–316 printed form disclaimers of warranties, even though they are contained in an integration, should not be considered to be part of the agreement because they are not truly assented to. Broude, 'The Consumer and the Parol Evidence Rule: Section 2–202 of the Uniform Commercial Code', 1970 Duke LJ 881.

12. 32 NJ at 404, 161 A 2d at 95.

13. Ibid. at 405, 161 A 2d at 95.
14. 350 F 2d 445 (DC Cir 1965), noted in 79 Harv L Rev 1299 (1966).
15. 350 F 2d at 447. See also 'Uniform Consumer Credit Code' §3.302; UCC §9–204.
16. 350 F 2d at 449–50 (footnotes omitted).
17. See, e.g. *Henningsen v Bloomfield Motors, Inc.*, 32 NJ 358 (1960).
18. Ibid. at 390, 161 A 2d at 87. But what is the choice being discussed? In the *Henningsen* case it was clear that a person could not buy a new car from a major manufacturer without submitting to the clause in question. But in *Weaver* there was no evidence that the lessee could not have obtained a similar lease from another oil company without the offending clause. How important should this be on the issue of true assent?

By now it should be clear that the assent discussed in Parts II and III hereof is not the same type of assent being discussed here under the label 'true assent'.

Interfoto Picture Library Ltd *v* Stiletto Visual Programmes Ltd [1988] 1 All ER 349

Dillon L.J.:

The defendants appeal against a decision of his Honour Judge Pearce QC given in the Lambeth County Court at the trial of this action on 11 March 1987 whereby the judge awarded the plaintiffs judgment against the defendants in the sum of £3,783.50 with interest and costs. The judge described the case as an interesting case, and in that I agree with him.

The plaintiffs run a library of photographic transparencies. The defendants are engaged in advertising. On 5 March 1984 Mr Beeching, a director of the defendants, wanting photographs for a presentation for a client, telephoned the plaintiffs, whom the defendants had never dealt with before. He spoke to a Miss Fraser of the plaintiffs and asked her whether the plaintiffs had any photographs of the 1950s which might be suitable for the defendants' presentation. Miss Fraser said that she would research his request, and a little later on the same day she sent round by hand to the defendants forty seven transparencies packed in a jiffy bag. Also packed in the bag, among the transparencies, was a delivery note which she had typed out, and to which I shall have to refer later.

Having received the transparencies, Mr Beeching telephoned the plaintiffs at about 3.10 on the afternoon of 5 March, and told Miss Fraser, according to a contemporary note which the judge accepted, that he was very impressed with the plaintiffs' fast service, that one or two of the transparencies could be of interest, and that he would get back to the plaintiffs.

Unfortunately he did not get back on to the plaintiffs and the transparencies seem to have been put on one side and overlooked by the defendants. The plaintiffs tried to telephone Mr Beeching on 20 March and again on 23 March, but only spoke to his secretary. In the upshot the transparencies, which the defendants did not use for their presentation, were not returned to the plaintiffs until 2 April.

The plaintiffs thereupon sent an invoice to the defendants for £3,783.50 as a holding charge for the transparencies. The invoice was rejected by the defendants, and accordingly in May 1984 the plaintiffs started this action claiming the £3,783.50, the amount of the invoice. That is the sum for which the judge awarded the plaintiffs judgment by his order now under appeal.

The plaintiffs' claim is based on conditions printed on their delivery note, which I have briefly mentioned, and must now describe in greater detail.

It is addressed to Mr Beeching of the defendants at the defendants' address and in the body of it the forty seven transparencies are listed by number. In the top right-hand corner the date of dispatch is given as 5 March 1984 and the date for return is clearly specified as 19 March. Across the bottom, under the heading 'Conditions' fairly prominently printed in capitals, there are set out nine conditions, printed in four columns. Of these the important one is no. 2 in the first column, which reads as follows: 'All transparencies must be returned to us within fourteen days from the date of posting/delivery/collection. A holding fee of £5.00 plus VAT per day will be charged for each transparency which is retained by you longer than the said period of fourteen days save where a copyright licence is granted or we agree a longer period in writing with you.' Condition 8 provides: 'When sent by post/delivered/collected the above conditions are understood to have been accepted unless the package is returned to us immediately by registered mail or by hand containing all the transparencies whole and undefaced and these conditions shall apply to all transparencies submitted to you whether or not you have completed a request form.'

The conditions purport to be merely the conditions of the bailment of transparencies to a customer. If the customer wishes to make use of transparencies so submitted to him, a fresh contract has to be agreed with the plaintiffs, but, as that did not happen so far as the defendants are concerned, it is unnecessary to consider that aspect further.

The sum of £3,783.50 is calculated by the plaintiffs in strict accordance with condition 2 as the fee for the retention of forty seven transparencies from 19 March to 2 April 1984. It is of course important to the plaintiffs to get their transparencies back reasonably quickly, if they are not wanted, since if a transparency is out with one customer it cannot be offered to another customer, should occasion arise. It has to be said, however, that the holding fee charged by the plaintiffs by condition 2 is extremely high, and in my view exorbitant. The judge held that on a *quantum meruit* a reasonable charge would have been £3.50 per transparency per week, and not £5 per day, and he had evidence before him of the terms charged by some ten other photographic libraries, most of which charged less than £3.50 per week and only one of which charged more (£4 per transparency per week). It would seem therefore that the defendants would have had a strong case for saying that condition 2 was void and unenforceable as a penalty clause; but that point was not taken in the court below or in the notice of appeal.

The primary point taken in the court below was that condition 2 was not part of the contract between the parties because the delivery note was never supplied to the defendants at all. That the judge rejected on the facts; he found that the delivery note was supplied in the same jiffy bag with the transparencies, and that finding is not challenged in this court. He made no finding however that Mr Beeching or any other representative of the defendants read condition 2 or any of the other printed conditions, and it is overwhelmingly probable that they did not.

An alternative argument for the defendants, in this court as below, was to the effect that any contract between the parties was made before the defendants knew of the existence of the delivery note, *viz.* either in the course of the preliminary telephone conversation between Mr Beeching and Miss Fraser or when the jiffy bag containing the transparencies was received in the defendants' premises but before the bag was opened. I regard these submissions as unrealistic and unarguable. The original telephone call was merely a preliminary inquiry and did not give rise to any contract. But the contract came into existence when the plaintiffs sent the transparencies to the defendants and the defendants, after opening the bag, accepted them by Mr Beeching's phone call to the plaintiffs at 3.10 on 5 March. The question is whether condition 2 was a term of that contract.

There was never any oral discussion of terms between the parties before the contract was made. In particular there was no discussion whatever of terms in the original telephone conversation when Mr Beeching made his preliminary inquiry. The question is therefore whether condition 2 was sufficiently brought to the defendants' attention to make it a term of the contract which was only concluded after the defendants had received, and must have known that they had received the transparencies *and* the delivery note.

This sort of question was posed, in relation to printed conditions, in the ticket cases, such *Parker v South Eastern Rly Co.* (1877) 2 CPD 416, [1874–80] All ER Rep 166, in the last century. At that stage the printed conditions were looked at as a whole and the question considered by the courts was whether the printed conditions as a whole had been sufficiently drawn to a customer's attention to make the whole set of conditions part of the contract; if so the customer was bound by the printed conditions even though he never read them.

More recently the question has been discussed whether it is enough to look at a set of printed conditions as a whole. When for instance one condition in a set is particularly onerous does something special need to be done to draw customers' attention to that particular condition? In an *obiter dictum* in J. *Spurling Ltd v Bradshaw* [1956] 2 All ER 121 at 125, [1956] 1 WLR 461 at 466 (cited in *Chitty on Contracts* (25th ed., 1983) vol 1, para. 742, 408) Denning L.J. stated: 'Some clauses which I have seen would need to be printed in red ink on the face of the document with a red hand pointing to it before the notice could be held to be sufficient.'

Then in *Thornton v Shoe Lane Parking Ltd* [1971] 1 All ER 686, [1971] 2 QB 163 both Lord Denning M.R. and Megaw L.J. held as one of their grounds of decision, as I read their judgments, that where a condition is particularly onerous or unusual the party seeking to enforce it must show that that condition, or an unusual condition of that particular nature, was fairly brought to the notice of the other party. Lord Denning restated and applied what he had said in the *Spurling* case, and held that the court should not hold any man bound by such a condition unless it was drawn to his attention in the most explicit way (see [1971] 1 All ER 686 at 689–90, [1971] 2 QB 163 at 169–70).

. . .

Counsel for the plaintiffs submits that *Thornton v Shoe Lane Parking Ltd* was a case of an exemption clause and that what their Lordships said must be read as limited to exemption clauses and in particular exemption clauses which would deprive the party on whom they are imposed of statutory rights. But what their Lordships said was said by way of interpretation and application of the general statement of the law by Mellish L.J. in *Parker v South Eastern Rly Co.* and the logic of it is applicable to any particularly onerous clause in a printed set of conditions of the one contracting party which would not be generally known to the other party.

Condition 2 of these plaintiffs' conditions is in my judgment a very onerous clause. The defendants could not conceivably have known, if their attention was not drawn to the clause, that the plaintiffs were proposing to charge a 'holding fee' for the retention of the transparencies at such a very high and exorbitant rate.

At the time of the ticket cases in the last century it was notorious that people hardly ever troubled to read printed conditions on a ticket or delivery note or similar document. That remains the case now. In the intervening years the printed conditions have tended to become more and more complicated and more and more one-sided in favour of the party who is imposing them, but the other parties, if they notice that there are printed conditions at all, generally still tend to assume that such conditions are only concerned with ancillary matters of form and are not of importance. In the ticket cases the courts held that the common law required that reasonable steps be taken to draw the other parties' attention to the printed conditions or they would not be part of the contract. It is in my judgment a logical development of the common law into modern conditions that it should be held, as it was in *Thornton v Shoe Lane Parking Ltd*, that, if one condition in a set of printed conditions is particularly onerous or unusual, the party seeking to enforce it must show that that particular condition was fairly brought to the attention of the other party.

In the present case, nothing whatever was done by the plaintiffs to draw the defendants' attention particularly to condition 2; it was merely one of four columns' width of conditions printed across the foot of the delivery note. Consequently condition 2 never, in my judgment, became part of the contract between the parties.

I would therefore allow this appeal and reduce the amount of the judgment which the judge awarded against the defendants to the amount which he would have awarded on a *quantum meruit* on his alternative findings, i.e. the reasonable charge of £3.50 per transparency per week for the retention of the transparencies beyond a reasonable period, which he fixed at fourteen days from the date of their receipt by the defendants.

(Bingham L.J. agreed.)

Carroll *v* An Post National Lottery Co. [1996] 1 IR 443

Costello J.:

The following are the relevant facts established at the hearing of this action.

(1) The plaintiff is a mechanic and carries on a car repair business in Capel Street close to the Capel Street Post Office in the City of Dublin. The proprietor of the Post Office (Mrs McKay) is a Lotto agent. The plaintiff does not regularly purchase Lotto tickets but he had done so on several occasions prior to 9 January 1993. On the morning of that day the plaintiff went into the Post Office and whilst there filled in a 'Scratch Card' (a game organised by the National Lottery) and became entitled to a prize of £2.00. He also obtained four playslips for the draw to be held on that evening by the National Lottery. He brought them back to his premises and filled in all eight panels on each of the playslips. Later he returned to the Post Office, at approximately 12.45, and handed the playslips to a member of the staff in the Post Office (who happened to be the Lotto agent's husband) together with £14 and asked him to add to this sum the £2 he had earlier won on the scratch card to pay for 16 plays. The member of the staff took the four playslips and the money and handed him back four tickets as well as the four playslips the plaintiff had completed. The plaintiff put these in his pocket and he left both the tickets and the playslips in his premises over the weekend. On the following Monday, 11 January, he checked the playslips and found that on one he had chosen six numbers which had been the winning jackpot numbers drawn on the evening of the previous Saturday. He then ascertained that he had not obtained a ticket in respect of this playslip but that due to an error he had obtained two tickets in respect of one playslip. He went to the Post Office and there met Mr McKay and explained to him what had happened. Mr McKay sent him to the headquarters of the company in Abbey Street. He was there told that he was too late to make a claim as he should have checked the tickets after they had been given to him. Later that day he went to a solicitor and subsequently these proceedings were instituted.

(2) The plaintiff did not verify that the tickets corresponded to the playslip when he received them on 9 January as he was required to do under Rule 4(5)(a).

(3) The defendants are not in a position to deny that the error of which the plaintiff complained took place and the evidence established that Mr McKay failed to obtain

from the computer terminal a ticket for the plaintiff in respect of one of the playslips given to him by the plaintiff.

(4) There was no notice in the Post Office displaying the rules of the National Lottery. However the Lotto agent had on her premises at the time the Lotto rules and these were available for inspection should the plaintiff or any other player have requested to see them. The plaintiff made no such request and such requests are seldom, if ever, made.

(5) The plaintiff said that he did not read the rules printed on the back of the playslip on 9 January and I accept that evidence. He also said that he was not aware that there were rules on the back of the playslip. I cannot accept that evidence. The plaintiff agreed that he was aware that there were rules regulating the National Lottery. He must have seen on each of the playslips the words 'See instructions on Reverse Side.' On the reverse side the words in capital letters 'Rules and Regulations' headed two paragraphs. I cannot accept that he never looked at the back of the playslip. From even the most cursory glance he would have seen those words and I am satisfied that even if he never read the two paragraphs under the capital letters he must have been aware, either from a perusal of the reverse side of the playslips on 9 January or on a previous occasion when he purchased Lotto tickets that there were rules printed on it.

(6) The playslip which Mr McKay had failed to enter into the terminal on which the winning numbers had been entered would not have been accepted by the terminal because one panel on it had seven numbers marked on it and so he would not have received a ticket for it. It is now a matter of speculation what the plaintiff would have done had Mr McKay inserted the playslip into the terminal and had it then been rejected. The playslip could have been amended and then re-entered and the plaintiff's opinion is that that is what he would have done had the error of which he complained been discovered and had he requested it to be rectified.

(7) There was one winner of the jackpot which, on the draw held on 9 January 1993, amounted to £506,000.00. Had the plaintiff's playslip been entered into the terminal correctly he would have received a ticket with the winning numbers printed on it and he would have been entitled to a half share in the jackpot, namely £253,000.00.

. . .

The plaintiff has alternatively claimed damages for breach of contract. I will firstly consider the plaintiff's claim that damages are recoverable because of a breach of a term implied in the parties' contract by the Sale of Goods and Supply of Services Act 1980, and in particular ss 3, 39 and 40 of the Act.

(i) The Sale of Goods and Supply of Services Act 1980

Section 39 of the Act provides that, subject to s. 40 'every contract for the supply of a service where the supplier is acting in the course of a business' is subject to an implied term that the supplier 'will supply the service with due skill, care and diligence.' Section 40 provides that a term implied by s. 39 may be negatived by an express term of the contract 'except that where the recipient of the service deals as a consumer it must be shown that the express term is fair and reasonable and has been specifically brought to his attention'. The plaintiff contends (a) that the contract between him and the defendant company was 'for the supply of a service' and (b) that the term implied in their contract to use skill and care was not negatived by either of the express terms on which the defendant company relies because neither was brought to his attention, and (c) as there was a breach by the defendant company of the terms implied by the Act the plaintiff is entitled to damages for the loss claimed.

For reasons already explained the contract between the plaintiff and the defendant company was not for the supply of services by the company to the plaintiff but for the sale of a lottery ticket by the defendant company and accordingly there was no term implied into the parties' contract by virtue of the Act of 1980. Furthermore, I am of the opinion that the exemption printed on the playslip to the effect that the Lotto agent at the time was the player's agent was brought to the plaintiff's attention and as required by s. 40 the implied term on which the plaintiff relies had been lawfully negatived in this case.

(ii) The implication of a term in the contract by the court

The plaintiff pleaded that there is an express or, alternatively, an implied condition in his contract with the defendant company that the counterhand would use reasonable skill and care in entering his plays into the Lotto draw. Quite clearly there was no express term in that behalf in the parties' contract. I am of the opinion that the court cannot imply such a term into the contract for two reasons. The [National Lottery] Act of 1986 provides that the National Lottery is to be held in accordance with rules approved by the Minister for Finance (s. 28) and the rules so approved have an express condition that the National Lottery shall not in any circumstances be liable to a player for any acts or omissions by the Lotto agents (Rule 4(3)(f)). The court cannot properly imply into the parties' contract a term which not only is not contained in the rules but which would be directly contrary to an express term in the rules as approved by the minister. Secondly the court will only imply a term in a contract if it is necessary to do so in order to give effect to the intention of the parties. In this case the defendant company quite clearly expressed the intention that it would not be liable for the negligence of its Lotto agents and so the court cannot imply a term which is contrary to the clear intention of one of the parties.

As the plaintiff has no cause of action based on an alleged breach of a term in the contract implied by the Act of 1980, or on the alleged breach of a term which the court should imply into the contract, and as the defendant company is not vicariously liable for the Lotto agent's negligence (assuming in the plaintiff's favour that Mr McKay was acting as the defendant company's agent at the time the negligent act was performed), this means that the plaintiff's claim must fail. However, as the parties may wish to have my decision on all the issues that have been raised I will consider whether or not the defendant company can rely on the exemption clauses in the contract, assuming that it is vicariously liable for the negligence of the Lotto agents and their staff and three other issues raised by the defendant company.

The exemption clauses

I can summarise the plaintiff's submissions on this part of the case as follows:

(1) The court is required to interpret the terms and conditions of play. And in so doing, because they are not free from doubt, the *contra proferentem* rule should apply and the exemption clauses should be construed against the defendant company if they are ambiguous (as it is said they are).

(2) It is accepted that if the plaintiff had read the back of the playslip and read the rules then he is bound by the conditions printed thereon, subject to the *contra proferentem* rule. If the court decides that the plaintiff did not read the conditions then it is submitted the court has to decide whether the defendant company took sufficient steps to give reasonable notice of the conditions on the back of the ticket. In this case the exemption terms relied on should have been particularly drawn to the attention of

the player by some signs or highlighting the terms in heavy type. The failure to give adequate or reasonable notice of the onerous terms imposed by the conditions means that as a matter of law the court will not enforce them.

(3) In support of these submissions the plaintiff in particular relied on *Chitty on Contract*, 27th Ed., paragraph 12.007 to 12.013 and to *Parker v South Eastern Railway Company* (1877) 2 CPD 416, *Thornton v Shoe Lane Parking Ltd* [1971] 2 QB 163, *Olley v Marlborough Court Ltd* [1949] 1 KB 532, *Interfoto Picture Library Ltd v Stiletto Visual Programmes Ltd* [1989] QB 433.

(4) The exemption relied on which was printed on the reverse side of the playslip contained an acknowledgment by the players that Lotto agents 'are acting in their behalf on entering plays into the National Lottery computer system.' It is submitted that as the act of negligence relied on in this case occurred when the playslip was not being entered into the computer system this exemption does not apply and is ineffective as a defence to the plaintiff's claim.

Applicable legal principles and conclusions

There is a large body of case law on the subject of standard form contracts and the binding effect of exemption clauses they may contain. In the present case the plaintiff accepts that a contractual relationship arose between himself and the defendant company and has, as I understand the submissions made on his behalf, accepted that the contract arose when he filled in the playslip, paid the applicable charge, and received a ticket from the computer terminal. Dispute, however, arises as to the terms on which the parties contracted. I have found as a fact that the plaintiff knew that there were rules printed on the reverse side of the playslip and that he did not read them. This finding means that, subject to certain qualifications to which I will refer in a moment, the plaintiff is bound by them (see *Parker v South Eastern Railway Co. Ltd* (1877) 2 CPD 416 at p. 423) and they are enforceable terms of the parties' contract. And this applies both to the term printed on the reverse side of the playslip by which a player accepted that the Lotto agents acted on their behalf in entering plays into the National Lottery computer system and also to the Rule 4 (3)(f) incorporated into the contract by the term on the reverse side (see *Thompson v London Midland and Scottish Railway Company* [1930] 1 KB 41). This means that, in principle, the term printed on the reverse of the playslip which I have just quoted had contractual effect as did Rule 4 (3)(f) of the rules (which provided that the National Lottery would not in any circumstances be liable to a player for any act or omission by Lotto agents), and will be enforced by the courts.

The qualifications to which I have referred are as follows. When it is generally known that tickets and other documents which contain conditions are not read by those to whom they are given then there is an implied understanding that there is no condition included in them which is unreasonable to the knowledge of the party tendering them. (See *Parker v South Eastern Railway Co.* (1877) 2 CPD 416, 428, and *Thompson v London Midland and Scottish Railway Co. Ltd* [1930] 1 KB 41, at p. 50.) So, if it can be shown in this case that either of the exemption clauses on which the defendant company relies was unreasonable the plaintiff is not bound by it. But there is a further qualification. The party receiving a document which forms part of a contract between him and the party tendering it may know that it contains conditions which he does not take the trouble to read. But if the condition relied on by the party tendering the document is particularly onerous or unusual that party must show that it has been fairly and reasonably brought to the other party's attention. If he cannot do so, then he cannot rely on it. This proposition is illustrated by the following cases:

Spurling v Bradshaw [1956] 3 All ER 121 was a case in which the defendant sent to the plaintiff, who carried on a business as a warehouseman, eight barrels of orange juice which due to his negligence were badly damaged. The plaintiff sued for his charges and in answer to the defendant's counterclaim for damages pleaded a clause in a 'landing account' which he had delivered to the plaintiff which exempted him from liability for any loss howsoever, whensoever, and wheresoever even if occasioned by his servants or agents. In the course of his judgment, Denning LJ. expressed the opinion that he should consider the plaintiff had given sufficient notice of this condition to the defendant and only if he had would the claim be enforceable. In holding that this had been done he observed that the more unreasonable the clause, the greater the notice which must be given of it adding:

> some clauses which I have seen would need to be printed in red ink on the face of the document with a red hand pointing to it before the notice could be held to be sufficient (p. 125).

Thornton v. Shoe Lane Parking Ltd [1971] 2 QB 163 was a case in which the proprietors of a car park sought to avoid liability for severe personal injuries which the plaintiff sustained, by relying on an exemption clause in a set of printed conditions which were displayed on the premises. The ticket issued to the plaintiff had the following words printed on them: 'This ticket is issued subject to the conditions of issue displayed on the premises.'

The Court of Appeal held that the car park proprietors could not rely on them. Counsel for the defendant had in fact admitted that the defendant had not done what was reasonably necessary to give the plaintiff notice of the exempting condition, and Denning M.R. (at p. 690) stated:

> I do not pause to enquire whether the exempting condition is void for unreasonableness. All I say is that it is so wide and so destructive of rights that the court could not hold any man bound by it unless it is drawn to his attention in the most explicit way.
> . . .

The basis for the refusal of the courts to permit a party to rely on certain contractual terms is a two-fold one. Firstly, by the application of the law of contract; secondly, by the application of the concept of fair dealing in the particular circumstances (see Bingham *Interfoto Picture Library Ltd v Stiletto Visual Programmes Ltd* [1989] QB 433 at p. 439). If a party does not do what is reasonably necessary to draw attention to the fact that the document (including a ticket) being tendered contains conditions of a contractual nature and the other party does not know this fact, then he/she has not given consent to the conditions (see Mellish, LJ in *Parker v South Eastern Railway Company* (1877) 2 C.P.D. 416 at page 423). If the document being tendered contains conditions of an unusual or particularly onerous nature the party tendering it must take reasonable steps to draw attention to such conditions in order to establish that the other party has agreed to it. The refusal to enforce the conditions is also justified if it can be shown that in all the circumstances of the case it would not be fair or reasonable to hold the other party bound by it. As Bingham LJ. stated at page 445:

> The tendency of the English authorities has, I think, been to look at the nature of the transaction in question and the character of the parties to it; to consider what notice the party alleged to be bound was given of the particular condition said to bind him; and to resolve whether in all the circumstances it is fair to hold him

bound by the condition in question. This may yield a result not very different from the civil law principle of good faith, at any rate so far as the formation of the contract is concerned.

Turning, then, to the two exemption terms in this case it seems to me that both pass the test of reasonableness in all the circumstances. Firstly, as to the incorporated exemption, by exempting the defendant company from vicarious liability for the negligent acts of Lotto agents Rule 4 (3)(f) is merely declaratory of the existing legal position, and is therefore reasonable.

Secondly, as to the playslip exemption I think that the agency agreement must be construed as meaning that the Lotto agent is acting as the *company's* agent (not the *player's* agent) when receiving playslips and entering them into the terminal. This means that the contractual term of the agreement contained in the playslip exemption is not declaratory of the existing agency relationship—rather it draws attention and gives effect to the rule by which the company is not liable for the agent's negligence. But the playslip exemption is declaratory of the existing legal position for another reason—it gives recognition to the legal relationship arising from the rules authorised by the minister.

Both the playslip exemption and the incorporated exemption contained in Rule 4 (3)(f) can be justified as being reasonable on another ground, as follows.

The risks involved in holding the National Lottery in the absence of such exemptions would leave the defendant company open to fraudulent claims and the defendant company is entitled to reasonable protection from such claims. As can be seen from the circumstances of this case a malefactor could complete two duplicate playslips and after the draw complete another playslip with the winning number on it and then claim fraudulently that the Lotto agent had negligently failed to enter the playslip into the computer and deliver him a ticket. This fraud would not be easy to detect. Indeed it seems to me that the absence of a protective exemption clause might make the whole National Lottery unworkable.

I am also of the opinion that neither of the terms relied on is particularly onerous or unusual. Of course, every exemption clause which limits the liability of one party imposes some detriment on the other. The court must look at all the surrounding circumstances to see whether an unduly burdensome and therefore unenforceable term was imposed. In doing so in this case, bearing in mind the risk of fraudulent claims to which I have referred, it cannot be said that either of these terms is exceptionally onerous. It is to be noted that the exemption is not a general one in that it does not exempt the defendant company from liability for the negligence of its own servants and employees—its ambit, therefore, is comparatively limited. It is also to be noted that the two exempting clauses are not by any means unusual in that it is not uncommon for one party to include an exempting term in a contract by which its possible vicarious liability for at least some of the acts of its agents is excluded.

I conclude, therefore, that as the plaintiff knew there were rules printed on the back of the playslip (but did not bother to read them) the defendant company can rely on both exemption terms because it was not required to give special notice of these particular terms to the purchasers of Lotto tickets. If I am wrong in this conclusion it seems to me that the defendant company had, in all the circumstances, done what was reasonably necessary to bring to the notice of purchasers of Lotto tickets the exempting term relating to the status of the agent printed on the back of the playslips by drawing the attention of purchasers to 'instructions' on the rear of the playslip and by printing the exempting term in such a way as to make it readily accessible to, and understandable by, readers of the matter printed on the reverse side of the playslip.

This conclusion also means that had the Act of 1980 applied to this transaction (because the defendant company was delivering a 'service') that there had been compliance with s. 40 of the Act of 1980 in that the term was fair and reasonable and had been specifically brought to the plaintiff's attention.

SECTION TWO—THE EXEMPTION CLAUSE

D. Yates *Exemption Clauses* (2nd edn, London: Sweet & Maxwell, 1982), 33–8

D. *Types of Exclusion Clauses*

1. *Exemption from liability for breach*

Some clauses may be in a form which purports to excuse the defendant from any liability incurred as a result of his breach; others may appear to limit or define the circumstances in which the *proferens* will be bound under the contract. . . . The flavour of the problem may, perhaps, be gleaned from the following exclusion found in an engineering company's 'back-of-order' terms:

> The company's liability under any order is limited to replacement or remedial work undertaken under these conditions of sale, to the entire exclusion of any other remedy which, but for this condition, the buyer might have. Any representation, condition, warranty or other undertaking in relation to the contract whether express or implied by statute, common law, custom or otherwise and whether made or given before or after the date of order or acceptance thereof, is hereby excluded for all purposes. Save as provided in these conditions, the company shall be under no liability of any sort (however arising) and shall not in any circumstances be liable for any damage, injury, direct consequential or other loss or loss of profits or costs, charges and expenses, howsoever arising.

2. *Limitations of liability or remedies*

These will be provisions in the contract that restrict the exercise of a right or remedy arising out of the breach of any obligation, express or implied, in the contract. So, for example, a term commonly found in building and civil engineering contracts that the contractor's liability for failure to complete on the due date shall not exceed a specified figure, is such a clause. Similar clauses are found in contracts of carriage. The following example is contained in clause 12 of the standard conditions of carriage issued by the Road Haulage Association.

> Subject to these conditions the liability of the carrier in respect of any one consignment shall in any case be limited:
>
> (1) where the loss or damage however sustained is in respect of the whole of the consignment to a sum at the rate of £800 per ton on either the gross weight of the consignment as computed for the purpose of charges under clause 9 hereof [the provisions for calculating carriage charges by weight] or where no such computation has been made, the actual gross weight;
>
> (2) where loss or damage however sustained is in respect of part of a consignment to the proportion of the sum ascertained in accordance with (1) of this condition which the actual value of that part of the consignment bears to the actual value of the whole of the consignment.

Provided that:

(a) nothing in this clause shall limit the carrier's liability below the sum of £10 in respect of any one consignment;

(b) the carrier shall not in any case be liable for indirect or consequential damages or for loss of a particular market whether held daily or at intervals;

(c) the carrier shall be entitled to require proof of the value of the whole of the consignment . . .

. . .

Some clauses may go further and purport to exclude the right to damages or the right to reject altogether. It could be argued that excluding the right to damages altogether is rather different in effect from simply limiting damages. By denying the remedy of damages the promisor is depriving his promise of any contractual content. This is not the case with a clause denying the promisee the right to repudiate, since it leaves the remedy of damages intact.

3. Time limit clauses

These clauses are generally designed to limit the time within which suit must be brought. They can be of two kinds. A clause may impose a time limit shorter than that fixed by the general law for the enforcement of a right or remedy, or alternatively it may impose a time limit on action necessary (e.g. notification of claims) before any right, remedy, duty or liability arises. The purpose of a time limit clause may not always be immediately apparent. Thus, a clause whereby 'the carrier . . . shall be discharged from all liability . . . unless suit is brought within one year' was held not merely to bar the remedy but extinguished the claim. An example of a time limit clause may again be cited from the conditions of carriage of the Road Haulage Association:

The carrier shall not be liable:

(1) (a) for loss from a package or from an unpacked consignment; or,
    (b) for damage, deviation, misdelivery, delay or detention;
unless he is advised thereof in writing otherwise than upon a consignment note or delivery document within three days and the claim be made in writing within seven days after the termination of transit;
    (2) for loss or non-delivery of the whole of the consignment or of any separate package forming part of the consignment;
unless he is advised of the loss or non-delivery in writing (other than upon a consignment note or delivery document) within twenty eight days and the claim be made in writing within forty two days after the commencement of transit.

4. Controls on evidence

Some limitation clauses may attempt to affect the question of how certain items of evidence are to be treated in the event of any claim being made against the *proferens*. It may purport to alter the onus of proof of matters under the contract, or provide that one matter is to be treated as conclusive evidence of another. An old case that provides a clause combining the effect of a time limit clause and a clause affecting evidentiary matters is that of *Buchanan v Parnshaw* (1788) 2 Term Rep. 745. In that case a horse sold at auction was warranted to be six years old and sound. It was a term of the sale that, if the horse were unsound, it should be returned within two days, otherwise it should be deemed sound. The failure to return within two days was, therefore, made conclusive evidence of soundness.

5. Indemnity clauses

Any clause which requires the promisee to indemnify another as a consequence of the promisee having exercised a right or remedy under the contract can have the same effect as a straightforward exclusion clause . . .

6. Arbitration clauses

An arbitration clause would seem to be only procedural in that a provision whereby the parties agree that any disputes should be submitted to arbitration does not exclude or limit rights or remedies but simply provides a procedure under which the parties may settle their grievance. The courts have held that such a clause is not an exclusion clause proper and the parties are free, such a clause notwithstanding, to pursue their claims in the courts (see *Doleman & Sons v Ossett Corp.* [1912] 3 KB 257) subject to the right of the court to grant a stay of proceedings. However, one type of arbitration can have substantive effect in that it can make the obligation to perform contingent upon the happening of an event. This clause is the so-called *Scott v Avery* clause (see (1856) LJ Ex. 308), under which the parties agree that no action shall be brought upon the contract until the arbitrator's award has been made, or that the promisor's liability shall be to pay only such sum as an arbitrator shall award. However, notwithstanding the difference between these clauses and the more normal type of arbitration clause, the courts have still been reluctant to treat them as exclusion clauses . . .

7. Liquidated damages clauses

A liquidated damages clause, unlike a clause that simply fixes a maximum limit on the amount of damages recoverable, is a genuine attempt at a pre-estimate of damages (see *Dunlop Pneumatic Tyre Co. Ltd v New Garage & Motor Co. Ltd* [1915] AC 79).

Kenyon Son and Craven *v* Baxter Hoare & Co. Ltd [1971] 2 All ER 708

Donaldson J.:

The plaintiffs are the makers of K.P. salted peanuts and similar commodities. The defendants are both warehousemen. Between July 1965, and May 1966, the first defendants took delivery from ocean carriers of nine parcels of shelled groundnuts in bags. Three of these parcels were warehoused by the second defendants and six by the first defendants. The nuts were eventually delivered to the plaintiffs in a damaged condition, the damage having occurred during the period of warehousing. Hence this action. The second defendants have admitted liability, although issues of *quantum* remain. The first defendants deny liability and agree with the plaintiffs that all issues of *quantum* shall be deferred until after the question of liability has been settled.

Liability turns upon the facts found and the true construction of two of Baxter, Hoare & Co. Ltd's conditions of business which are, I am told, not exclusive to them but are widely used by shipping and forwarding agents. The first of these conditions is: '11. The company shall not be liable for loss of or damage to goods unless such loss or damage occurs whilst the goods are in the actual custody of the company and under its actual control and unless such loss or damage is due to the wilful neglect or default of the company or its own servants.'

It is agreed that at all material times the goods were in the actual custody of the first defendants to whom I will refer hereafter as 'the defendants', and under their actual control.

The primary issue which arises is whether the damage was due to the wilful neglect or default of the company or its servants, the burden of proving that this was not the case being upon the defendants.

. . .

The second condition is: '13. In no case shall the liability of the company exceed the value of the goods or a sum at the rate of £50 per ton of 20 cwt. of goods lost or damaged, whichever shall be the smaller. . . .'

. . .

The quantity of nuts was very considerable—over 5000 bags weighing at least 250 tons. They were stored in the defendants' warehouse at Field Lane, Bootle, the first two parcels being received in September and October 1965, and the remainder in the months of February, March, April and May 1966. When received the nuts were in apparent good order and condition, but a few bags were slack or burst. When the nuts were redelivered to the plaintiffs in January 1967, they were so seriously damaged both quantitatively and qualitatively that special procedures had to be devised and operated in order to sort the nuts into categories of those which could be used after cleaning and those which were valueless. The damage alleged exceeds twenty per cent of the value of the nuts.

The effective cause of the damage was rats which ate the bags, thereby releasing the contents, ate some of the nuts and contaminated part of the remainder with urine and droppings. The plaintiffs also complained of contamination by Cellaton powder which was stored in the same warehouse, but I am quite satisfied that this powder, which is used as a filtration substance, is quite harmless and did no more damage to the nuts than would inevitably have been done by dust in the atmosphere. It, like the ordinary atmospheric dust, could easily have been removed by washing.

Before considering the history of the storage of these nuts, it may be useful to consider what was the defendants' duty in relation to them and for what breaches of that duty they would be liable on the true construction of condition 11 of their standard terms of business. The defendants were bailees for reward and as such it was their duty to redeliver the nuts in the like good order and condition as when received, subject only to such loss or damage as might arise despite the exercise of all reasonable skill and care in their preservation and custody. I put it this way rather than that simply it was the defendants' duty to exercise all reasonable skill and care in the preservation and custody of the nuts because it better reflects the burden of proof. The plaintiffs need only prove redelivery in a condition worse than when the goods were delivered to the defendants and it is then for the defendants to show that the damage arose despite the exercise of all reasonable skill and care. I doubt, however, whether it matters which way round the duty is expressed save in relation to the burden of proof.

Protective conditions are of three distinct types, namely, first, those which limit or reduce what would otherwise be the defendant's duty; second, those which exclude the defendant's liability for breach of specified aspects of that duty and third, those which limit the extent to which the defendant is bound to indemnify the plaintiff in respect of the consequences of breaches of that duty.

A condition which provided that a warehouseman should be under no obligation to take greater care of perishable goods than was appropriate to imperishable goods, would constitute a good example of the first category of protective conditions. Another example, in a different field, is provided by the well known clauses which exclude the conditions implied by the Sale of Goods Act, 1893. If, in such a case, the warehouseman takes such care of perishable goods as would be appropriate had they been imperishable and damage results, he will escape liability not because the clause exempts him from liability for breach of contract (whether fundamental or otherwise), but because there has been no breach of contract.

A. Incorporation of the Exemption Clause

The signature rule

Duff *v* Great Northern Rly Co. (1878) 4 LR (Ir.) 178

Palles C.B.:

It was admitted that a contract was made between the plaintiff and the defendants for the carriage by the defendants of certain cattle of the plaintiff's from Dundalk to St Ives. The terms of this contract were reduced to writing, and were signed by the plaintiff. The terms to which the plaintiff's name is attached are as follows:

> It is hereby agreed between the undersigned and Great Northern and Manchester, Sheffield, and Lincolnshire Joint Railway Companies, that the animals named on the other side are to be conveyed only *upon the conditions mentioned upon the back of the invoice*, handed to the undersigned by the company's agent, and in consideration of the reduced rate charged, at the owner's sole risk in connexion with the sea part of the transit.
>
> (Signed) James Duff, *Owner*.

An invoice was handed to the plaintiff by the defendants' agent, at the time of his signing these terms, having on the back certain conditions, which are therein called conditions of carriage. One of these conditions is in the following words: 'That as a drover is allowed to attend the cattle during transit, they (i.e. the defendants) will allow such drover to travel free of charge upon condition that he so travel at his own risk.'

I think it unnecessary to discuss cases which have been put during the argument, as to the effect of conditions wholly foreign to the carriage of cattle being endorsed on the invoice. It seems to me to be clear that the conditions on the invoice, including that which I have read, are the conditions referred to in the document signed by the plaintiff, and that that document must be read as if the conditions were in terms stated therein. The agreement then is to carry the cattle on the terms (*inter alia*) that the owner's drover may not only attend them during transit, but (if he elect to travel at his own risk) need not pay the ordinary fare of a passenger. The plaintiff was not bound to travel on these terms, but unless he did so he was bound to pay his fare, and an election to travel free under this contract was an election to travel at his own risk.

Now it is admitted upon the evidence that the plaintiff did elect to travel under the contract. He himself states he travelled free, and the free pass proved is identified by the figures on it with the contract for carriage of the cattle. This appears to me to conclude the case. It reduces the question from one of fact—what was the contract under which plaintiff travelled—to matter of law, what is the legal effect and validity of the particular contract under which he shows as matter of fact he did travel? This latter question admits of no doubt. Under the contract the plaintiff is without remedy against the defendants for negligence during the journey, and such a contract (being for the conveyance of a passenger, and outside the 17 & 18 Vict. c. 31, and the statutes extending the same), is valid.

I do not think it necessary to refer in detail to any of the cases relied upon for the plaintiff. In all of them the contracts were by parol, and the question was what was the contract.

In *Henderson v Stevenson*,[1] Lord Cairns distinguishes between those cases and one such as the present, in which the terms of the contract have been reduced to writing. 'There were,' he says, 'a considerable number of other cases in which, for the conveyance of animals or of goods, a ticket or paper had been *actually signed* by the owner of the animals, or by the owner of the goods. With regard again to those cases, there might indeed be a question what was the construction of the contract, or how far the contract was valid. But there could be no question whatever that the contract, such as it was, was assented to, and entered into by the person who read the ticket.'

For those reasons, I am of opinion that the defendants were entitled to have had a verdict directed for them upon the claim for personal injuries. I desire, however, to observe that my judgment is based upon the fact that the person who actually travelled as drover was the person who signed the contract. Had he been a different person, the connection of the drover with the contract might have involved a question of fact, and this might have been for the jury.

The verdict on the claim for personal injuries will be entered for the defendants, and there will be judgment accordingly.

Dowse B.:

I am of the same opinion. Suppose this was a case in which the railway company proposed in writing to carry for the plaintiff forty-two head of cattle on the following terms, namely, that the plaintiff should be at liberty to travel with the cattle free, provided he did so at his own risk. If the plaintiff had signed this and had travelled free, could he recover a verdict against the defendants for personal injuries sustained during the journey? . . .

[1]. 2 Sc App 470, 474.

(Fitzgerald B. concurred.)

L'Estrange *v* F. Graucob Ltd [1934] 2 KB 394

Scrutton L.J.:

In this case the plaintiff commenced proceedings against the defendants in the County Court, her claim being for £9 1s as money received by the defendants to the use of the plaintiff as part of the consideration for the delivery of an automatic slot machine pursuant to a contract in writing dated 7 February 1933, which consideration was alleged to have wholly failed by reason of the fact that the machine was delivered in a condition unfit for the purpose for which it was intended. The only document which corresponds to the contract there mentioned is a long document on brown paper headed 'Sales Agreement'. By their defence the defendants denied that the machine was delivered in a condition unfit for the purpose intended, and denied that the sum claimed was payable to the plaintiff; and they counterclaimed for the balance of the price of the machine. Just before the trial the plaintiff amended her claim by adding a count for breach of an implied warranty that the machine was reasonably fit for the purpose for which it was sold; though she still claimed only £9 1s. There the pleadings stopped. At the trial, as the judge has stated in his judgment, the plaintiff's claim was put in three different ways: total failure of consideration; breach of implied conditions going to the root of the contract; and breach of warranty. The defendants pleaded: no total failure of consideration; no implied conditions; and that no action would lie for breach of implied warranty, as the agreement expressly provided for the exclusion of all implied warranties. To this last defence the plaintiff contended that she was induced to sign the contract by the misrepresentation that it was an order form, and that at the time when she signed she knew nothing of the conditions.

The County Court Judge has given judgment for the plaintiff for £70, though there is no claim by the plaintiff for that sum; and he has given judgment for the defendants on the counterclaim for £71 18s 6d, the balance of the price.

As to the defence that no action would lie for breach of implied warranty, the defendants relied upon the following clause in the contract: 'This agreement contains all the terms and conditions under which I agree to purchase the machine specified above and any express or implied condition, statement, or warranty, statutory or otherwise not stated herein is hereby excluded.' A clause of that sort has been before the courts for some time. The first reported case in which it made its appearance seems to be *Wallis, Son & Wells v Pratt & Haynes*,[1] where the exclusion clause mentioned only 'warranty' and it was held that it did not exclude conditions. In the more recent case of *Andrews Bros (Bournemouth) Ltd v Singer & Co.*,[2] where the draftsman had put into the contract of sale a clause which excluded only implied conditions, warranties and liabilities, it was held that the clause did not apply to an express term describing the article, and did not exempt the seller from liability where he delivered an article of a different description. The clause here in question would seem to have been intended to go further than any of the previous clauses and to include all terms denoting collateral stipulations, in order to avoid the result of these decisions.

The main question raised in the present case is whether that clause formed part of the contract. If it did, it clearly excluded any condition or warranty.

In the course of the argument in the County Court reference was made to the railway passenger and cloak-room ticket cases, such as *Richardson, Spence & Co. v Rowntree*.[3] In that case Lord Herschell L.C. laid down the law applicable to these cases and stated the three questions which should there be left to the jury. In the present case the learned judge asked himself the three questions appropriate to these cases, and in answering them has found as facts: (i) that the plaintiff knew that there was printed material on the document which she signed, (ii) that she did not know that the document contained conditions relating to the contract, and (iii) that the defendants did not do what was reasonably sufficient to bring these conditions to the notice of the plaintiff.

The present case is not a ticket case, and it is distinguishable from the ticket cases. In *Parker v South Eastern Rly Co.*[4] Mellish L.J. laid down in a few sentences the law which is applicable to this case. He there said: 'In an ordinary case, where an action is brought on a written agreement which is signed by the defendant, the agreement is proved by proving his signature, and, in the absence of fraud, it is wholly immaterial that he has not read the agreement and does not know its contents.' Having said that, he goes on to deal with the ticket cases, where there is no signature to the contractual document, the document being simply handed by the one party to the other: 'The parties may, however, reduce their agreement into writing, so that the writing constitutes the sole evidence of the agreement, without signing it; but in that case there must be evidence independently of the agreement itself to prove that the defendant has assented to it. In that case, also, if it is proved that the defendant has assented to the writing constituting the agreement between the parties, it is, in the absence of fraud, immaterial that the defendant had not read the agreement and did not know its contents.' In cases in which the contract is contained in a railway ticket or other unsigned document, it is necessary to prove that an alleged party was aware, or ought to have been aware, of its terms and conditions. These cases have no application when the document has been signed. When a document containing contractual terms is signed, then, in the absence of fraud, or, I will add, misrepresentation, the party signing it is bound, and it is wholly immaterial whether he has read the document or not.

The plaintiff contended at the trial that she was induced by misrepresentation to sign the contract without knowing its terms, and that on that ground they are not binding upon her. The learned judge in his judgment makes no mention of that contention of the plaintiff, and he pronounces no finding as to the alleged misrepresentation. There is a further difficulty. Fraud is not mentioned in the pleadings, and I strongly object to deal with allegations of fraud where fraud is not expressly pleaded. I have read the evidence with care, and it contains no material upon which fraud could be found. The plaintiff no doubt alleged that the defendants' agent represented to her that the document which was given her to be signed was an order form, but according to the defendants' evidence no such statement was made to her by the agent. Moreover, whether the plaintiff was or was not told that the document was an order form, it was in fact an order form, and an order form is a contractual document. It may be either an acceptance or a proposal which may be accepted, but it always contains some contractual terms. There is no evidence that the plaintiff was induced to sign the contract by misrepresentation.

In this case the plaintiff has signed a document headed 'Sales Agreement', which she admits had to do with an intended purchase, and which contained a clause excluding all conditions and warranties. That being so, the plaintiff, having put her signature to the document and not having been induced to do so by any fraud or misrepresentation, cannot be heard to say that she is not bound by the terms of the document because she has not read them.

The County Court Judge has given judgment for the defendants on the counterclaim for the balance of the price, £71 18s 6d. I do not see how he could have done that unless he found that the contract included the clause in small print providing that, if any instalment of the price should not be duly paid, all the remaining instalments should fall due for immediate payment. That judgment on the counterclaim must stand. As to the claim, judgment was given for the plaintiff for £70 for breach of an implied warranty, though only £9 1s was claimed. Such a judgment could not have been given even in the High Court without an amendment of the claim. But even if there had been an amendment, the further difficulty would have remained that the signed document contained a clause excluding any implied condition or warranty. If the view which I have expressed as to the effect of a signed document is correct, the plaintiff has no ground of claim, and the judgment in her favour cannot stand. In my opinion, the judgment for the plaintiff on the claim should be set aside and judgment entered for the defendants on the claim; and the judgment for the defendants on the counterclaim should stand.

Maugham L.J.:

I regret the decision to which I have come, but I am bound by legal rules and cannot decide the case on other considerations.

. . .

In this case it is, in my view, an irrelevant circumstance that the plaintiff did not read, or hear of, the parts of the sales document which are in small print, and that document should have effect according to its terms. I may add, however, that I could wish that the contract had been in a simpler and more usual form. It is unfortunate that the important clause excluding conditions and warranties is in such small print. I also think that the order confirmation form should have contained an express statement to the effect that it was exclusive of all conditions and warranties.

I agree that the appeal should be allowed.

1. [1911] AC 394.   3. [1894] AC 217.
2. [1934] 1 KB 17.   4. 2 CPD 416.

Note

The signature rule has been strongly endorsed by the High Court of Australia in *Toll* (FGCT) *Pty v Alphapharm* [2004] HCA 52 and, in the absence of fraud or misrepresentation, the effectiveness of a signature in indicating assent to the terms proposed, as well as allowing other persons to rely on the signor's apparent signature, was said in *Toll* to be effective across the contractual landscape and not just confined to exemption clauses.

Even if the document is not signed, the following case indicates that standard terms may still form the basis of a contract, once performance has commenced.

Slattery *v* C.I.E. (1968) 106 ILTR 71

The plaintiff's action was for breach of contract occasioned by the negligent loading of three yearlings, one of which was injured as a result. The only issue was whether the contract was concluded on the basis of the defendants' standard conditions of carriage.

Teevan J.:

In the civil bill action in the Circuit Court giving rise to this appeal the plaintiff alleged negligence in the handling of a race horse by the defendant's servant on the occasion of the carriage of the horse by the defendants from the plaintiff's residence at Milltown, near Clonmel, to Ballsbridge. The plaintiff is a breeder of bloodstock. He decided to engage the defendants to transport three unbroken yearling thoroughbred horses by road to the bloodstock sales at Ballsbridge on 8 August 1967. He made the arrangements for transport by telephone from his house to the defendants' Waterford office. The defendants accepted the business and it was agreed that one of their road horse boxes would arrive at the plaintiff's residence at 8 a.m. on 8 August 1967. No terms of contract were then arranged and nothing on either side was said about rates of charges, or conditions of carriage.

The defendants' box arrived at the plaintiff's residence as arranged. The box had been driven from Dublin that morning having left Dublin at 3 a.m. The operation of loading the horses was commenced, the loading being done by the plaintiff assisted by one of his men and the defendants' driver, Mr Peter Murphy. Mr Murphy has some twenty-two years experience of this work and it is customary for him to assist in loading the stock to be carried. Again nothing was said about rates or conditions of carriage. Mr Murphy had with him the usual combined form of consignment note and delivery sheet on which is printed in bold type: 'It is the responsibility of drivers to see that the attention of hirers or their agents . . . is drawn to the conditions on back of sheet and that their signatures are inscribed in the appropriate spaces.' There are in fact two spaces for signatures of assignor or his agent. The first of these is under the consign-ment note portion of the document which reads (so far as material): 'Receive and forward the undermentioned horses subject to the regulations and conditions shown on the back hereof . . .'. Then follows the space for consignor's signature. The particulars

of the transaction including the charge for the carriage and the plaintiff's name and address were already inserted on this form. This should properly be signed at the commencement of carriage. This was not done nor was the plaintiff at that stage shown or informed of the terms and conditions of carriage printed on the back of the sheet. . . .
. . .
I now have to go back on the history of this contract. I have already said that the consignment note had not been signed by the plaintiff at the initiation of the carriage; neither was his attention called to the defendants' terms of carriage. If the consignment note had been signed at the commencement of the business it would of course have constituted the terms of contract and of carriage. What happened was this: on reaching the end of the journey and on off-loading the horses the driver presented the consignment note for the plaintiff's signature. The plaintiff signed both in the space acknowledging receipt of the horses (for in this case he was consignee as well as consignor) and also in the space acknowledging the regulations and conditions printed on the back of the sheet. (There was also a third signature relating to permission to him to travel personally in the box during the transit but this is of no present materiality). The plaintiff signed without demur, without reading the conditions and without making any point about holding the company liable for the horse's injury. There are two rates of carriage charges; one for owner's risk carriage and a higher rate for carriage at the carrier's risk. Even in the latter case the company's liability for loss or damage due to negligence is limited to £100 per horse unless a higher value be declared at time of delivery of the horse to the company for carriage. The charge inserted in the consignment note was at the lower rate; i.e. at the rate appropriate to 'owner's risk' carriage.

In fact the consignment note signed by the plaintiff is headed in large heavy black print 'Consignment note and delivery sheet for horses to be carried . . . at owner's risk.' The plaintiff's signature stands about two inches or three inches below that heading. The plaintiff did not read the terms: he signed because, according to his evidence, he thought he was only signing a receipt or acknowledgment of completion of the carriage and did not know that he was signing a memorandum of the contract.

If the consignment note as so signed is binding on the plaintiff; that is to say if it fixes the terms of his contract, that is the end of his case. It is contended, however, that as the document was signed after completion by the defendants of the contract on their part it cannot be read as constituting terms not previously agreed upon or to bind the plaintiff by the conditions exempting liability of the defendants. The question is whether the plaintiff can be heard to deny that the conditions set out in the consignment note signed by him form part of the contract? 'The best way of proving [the terms of a contract] is by a written document signed by the party to be bound' (per Denning L.J. in Olley v Marlborough Court Ltd [1949] 1 KB 532 p. 549). Here we have such a document but the argument is that it must be ignored because it was signed after delivery of the horses, in other words after completion of the defendants' part of the transaction. The plaintiff could have refused to sign the document particularly as it was not shown or its terms otherwise made known to him at the inception of carriage: the fact is that he signed it. Before signing it he was aware, needless to say, of the damage to his horse but he did not then know that the injury was likely to result in loss. In his very candid and honourable evidence in cross-examination he admitted that he was aware that the defendants had two rates of charges; that the higher rate involved the carrier's liability and that the lesser was an owner's risk rate. He said he thought the charges entered on the consignment note (£27 5s) were as he put it 'the company's rate—fully insured' but admitted that he did not look to see whether such was the case. On being asked 'Isn't it in fact at the owner's risk rate?' he replied: 'It turned out to be that but I thought it would be the 'board rate'. Had I been asked which I would prefer and if the 'board rate' had been the higher I would have taken that rate.' ('board's risk rates' is the term used to denote carriage at the defendant carrier's risk.) While the plaintiff cannot be exculpated for his own carelessness the defendants are open to criticism; in the interest of their customers they should in fairness bring the choice of rates and the consequences attending the disparity to the customer's notice at the commencement particularly where, as in this case, the conditions are lengthy complicated and set up in small type following the worst in railway tradition. If it is too much to expect that the casual as distinct from the regular customer will read and follow this complex mass of conditions, nevertheless I must repeat that the actual consignment note was headed '. . . horses to be carried . . . at owner's risk' almost immediately above each of the spaces where the plaintiff put his signature.

If the plaintiff had declined to sign the delivery note at Ballsbridge he could not be compelled to do so nor in my opinion could he be held bound by the pleaded conditions, which could not be unilaterally imposed. He could then take the stand that he sought to take in this case: that the contract was simply on the defendants' part to carry the horses and on his part to pay for the service. It has been argued that the latter was in fact the contract agreed upon by and within the intention of the parties.

The defendants relied on *Knox v Great Northern Rly*, 29 ILTR 47; [1896] 2 IR 632. That case resembles the present case in that the terms of contract were agreed upon by the parties after the carriage had commenced, although in *Knox's* case this was done immediately after boxing and before departure of the horse on its journey: it differs in that the owner's agent consciously or with deliberation elected between the choice of rates. (This does not appear in the statement of facts but the judgments appear to proceed on that basis: see for instance Johnson J. at p. 636, '[the booking clerk] offered Creighton his choice of the two rates and Creighton with the knowledge that the horse was injured, elected to take the reduced rate with the liability incident to it.') *Knox's* case differs from the present in another respect; if Creighton, the plaintiff's agent, had refused to sign the formal contract with one effect or the other, the railway company could have refused to continue the carriage, while the defendants' driver in the case before me had effectively removed that lever by delaying to have his contract signed until journey's end had been reached. It cannot be said that Mr Slattery was in the dilemma which confronted Creighton the groom in *Knox's* case. I do not mean it to be inferred that this distinction is of any conclusive worth but at least it illustrates the present plaintiff's freedom of action. Be that as it may he signed the contract and no authority has been cited to me and no convincing argument presented to avoid the plaintiff's assent to its terms, or to support assertion that having been signed on delivery it cannot be read as the contract the parties entered into. In the words of Holmes J. in *Knox's* case in the Queen's Bench Division (p. 639): 'It is neither illegal, unreasonable, nor unusual, for the terms of a contract to be reduced to writing after the performance of the services contracted for has been begun'. To my mind the case is no different from what might have happened if in the course of the journey to Dublin, the driver had bethought himself that he had neglected to have the form of contract signed and had asked the plaintiff to sign it then. If on such an occasion the plaintiff agreed to and did sign it, I cannot see how he could escape the consequences and I fail to see any distinction between such a situation and that in which, in fact, the contract was signed at Ballsbridge. The contract was not even then wholly performed; the plaintiff had not carried out his part of it, namely to pay the carriage charge. Furthermore the signing of the contract at the lower rate put it beyond the power of the carriers to recover the higher rate for their services. [Counsel for the plaintiff] sought to distinguish the present case from *Knox's* case, on the submitted ground that the latter had to

Section 2: The Exemption Clause

do with conditions laid down by statute and did not rest in contract. It is clear, on the contrary, that the judgments rest on the contract concluded between the parties.

I must hold that the plaintiff bound himself by the conditions on signing the contract note. It amounts to a declaration by the plaintiff of what the terms of the contract were. [Counsel] referred me to Anson (9th ed.) at p. 159 et seq., wherein the learned author discusses cases of standard conditions on a take-it-or-leave-it method of business, allowing of no variation. The present case materially differs from those in which the aggrieved parties were held not bound by such conditions by reason of the failure of the parties prescribing the conditions to bring the same effectively to their customers' notice. Having regard to the very prominent manner in which the defendants have called attention, almost at the very place where the plaintiff placed his signature, to the carriage being at owner's risk and subject to the condition over-leaf, the plaintiff has only himself to blame for failing to notice this.

Accordingly I must regretfully find for the defendants and dismiss the claim. I say regretfully because as a matter of fair dealing these stringent conditions and the purpose or implication of the varying rates should be brought to the customer's notice at the time of engagement, unless to the knowledge of the company's officers, the customer by reason of frequency of dealing may be taken as already aware of them. The choice of rates should be left to the customer's election. Nothing could be simpler than an enquiry by the defendants' agent when the business was being placed with him, whether the customer required the service at company's, or his own risk and to make known the differential in rates and the limits of liability in the former case unless on declaration of higher value than the pre-ordained values in the standard conditions.

B. Incorporation by Reasonable Notice

If no condition is used or pleaded, common law or statutory liability will result.

Roche v Cork Blackrock and Passage Rly Co. (1889) 24 LR (Ir.) 250

Gibson J.:

The plaintiff deposited in the defendants' cloakroom a Gladstone bag, locked with an ordinary lock, and containing the sum of £10. He received a ticket in the usual way. The ticket contained no conditions in any way limiting liability. The plaintiff did not apprise the defendants that the bag contained money or valuables. On the plaintiff applying for his bag at the cloakroom he received it; but on unlocking it (which he found some difficulty in doing), he discovered the money had been abstracted. The servant in charge of the cloakroom was not examined. The plaintiff claimed the £10 against the defendants, as having been lost by their negligence.
. . .

Why this company should have omitted to protect themselves by conditions, as other railways have done for years past, I do not know. They are fortunate in having now been taught their mistake and danger at so small a cost.

Ryan v Great Southern and Western Rly Co. (1898) 12 ILTR 108

Gibson J.:

The plaintiff took from the defendants a return excursion ticket to Ennistymon, beyond the defendants' line, and the luggage was lost, not by the defendants, but by one of the other companies. On the face of the ticket there was printed in minute type a reference to the regulations and conditions of the defendants as binding the passenger, and by such conditions, if incorporated into the contract, the defendants were exonerated from liability for loss occurring beyond their own railway. The plaintiff did not read the printed matter, and could not have learned the condition, which was not disclosed on the ticket, without special inquiry. The company relied on *Zunz's* case, LR 4 QB 539. As the point seemed of some importance, I offered the company a case stated on terms which they declined to accept. The plaintiff having taken and paid the defendants for a through return ticket was *prima facie* entitled to treat them as the contracting carriers. The defendants failed to do what was reasonably sufficient to give the plaintiff notice of the restriction of liability (*Rowntree's* case, 1894, AC 217). The case is quite different from *Zunz's* case and *Burke's* case, 5 CPD 1, in each of which there was a book with express printed conditions. Where the passenger is an experienced traveller and the company have done all that is reasonably possible to bring home to him the terms on which the ticket is issued, he may not be able to better his position by the allegation of voluntary ignorance. The facts of the present case do not bring the plaintiff within any such principle. The appeal must, therefore, be allowed, and a decree given for the amount claimed, with costs.

Note

Even if the plaintiff could not, in a specific case, have seen or consented to the terms relied upon, the rule about reasonable notice will still prevail. Under earlier cases the nature of the risk run did not appear to affect the level of reasonableness.

Early *v* Great Southern Rly Co. [1940] IR 414

Sullivan C.J.:

I am of opinion that this appeal must be dismissed.

The material facts can be summarised in a few sentences. On the 12 April 1936, Easter Sunday, a special train was run by the defendant company from Arigna to Mohill, returning to Arigna that evening. In ordinary circumstances no train runs on this line on Sunday, and for this special train return tickets were issued at a reduced price. The plaintiff, with some companions, joined the train at a 'halt' at Fenagh and travelled to Mohill to take part in a demonstration there. Return tickets from Fenagh to Mohill had been purchased at Fenagh. Late in the evening the train with the plaintiff and his companions on board left Mohill on its return journey to Arigna, and, shortly after it had started, the tickets were taken up by the ticket collector. When the train arrived at Fenagh the plaintiff should have alighted, as his ticket was not available for any further journey, but he decided to remain in the train until it got to Cornabrone. No one except the plaintiff and his companions was aware that he should have alighted at Fenagh. When the train reached Cornabrone the accident happened in respect of which damages are claimed by the plaintiff. The question whether that accident was caused by negligence on the part of the defendants' servants was not determined at the trial and does not arise on this appeal.

The case made on behalf of the plaintiff was:

1. That he had got no reasonable notice of the conditions on which his ticket was issued, and therefore was not bound by them.

2. That if those conditions were binding upon him they were so only during the journey for which his ticket was available and were no longer operative when he travelled beyond Fenagh on the return journey.

At Fenagh, where the plaintiff purchased his ticket, there was a poster advertising the excursion to Mohill, which stated that excursion tickets and tickets issued at less than ordinary fares are issued subject to the notices and conditions shown in the company's time tables. The ticket purchased by the plaintiff bore on its face the words: 'Special train—available for day of issue only—not transferable. See back.' On the back was printed—'Issued subject to the conditions and regulations in the company's time tables, books, bills and notices.' One of those conditions was that the holder of a ticket issued at a fare less than the ordinary fare should not have any right of action against the company in respect of injury, fatal or otherwise. No copy of the time table or of any document containing those conditions was available for inspection by intending passengers at Fenagh 'halt'. The plaintiff, however, made no inquiry about them.

The learned trial judge held: (1) That the defendants had taken reasonable steps to bring to the plaintiff's notice the conditions upon which he was accepted as a passenger. (2) That the plaintiff was bound by those conditions so long as he continued to be a passenger in the train.

If the accident to the plaintiff had happened during the journey for which his ticket was available this case would be governed by the principles stated in the cases to which the learned judge referred—*Grand Trunk Rly Co. of Canada v Robinson*,[1] and *Thompson v London, Midland and Scottish Rly Co.*[2] In the former case Lord Haldane L.C. in delivering the opinion of the Privy Council said (at p. 747):

> If a passenger has entered a train on a mere invitation or permission from a railway company without more, and he receives injury in an accident caused by the negligence of its servants, the company is liable for damages for breach of a general duty to exercise care. Such a breach can be regarded as one either of an implied contract, or of a duty imposed by the general law, and in the latter case as in form a tort. But in either view this general duty may, subject to such statutory restrictions as exist in Canada and in England in different ways, be superseded by a specific contract, which may either enlarge, diminish, or exclude it. If the law authorises it, such a contract cannot be pronounced to be unreasonable by a court of justice. The specific contract, with its incidents either expressed or attached by law, becomes in such a case the only measure of the duties between the parties, and the plaintiff cannot by any device of form get more than the contract allows him.

Again, at p. 748:

> The only right to be carried will be one which arises under the terms of the contract itself, and these terms must be accepted in their entirety. The company owes the passenger no duty which the contract is expressed on the face of it to exclude, and if he has approbated that contract by travelling under it he cannot afterwards reprobate it by claiming a right inconsistent with it. For the only footing on which he has been accepted as a passenger is simply that which the contract has defined.

In *Thompson v London, Midland and Scottish Rly Co.*, the ticket held by the plaintiff bore on its face the words: 'Excursion, for conditions see back,' and on the back: 'Issued subject to the conditions and regulations in the company's time tables and notices and excursion and other bills.' In the course of his judgment Lord Hanworth M.R. says (p. 47):

> It appears to me that the right way of considering such notices is put by Swift J. in *Nunan v Southern Rly Co.*[3] After referring to a number of cases which have been dealt with in the courts he says: 'I am of opinion that the proper method of considering such a matter is to proceed upon the assumption that where a contract is made by the delivery, by one of the contracting parties to the other, of a document in common form stating the terms upon which the person delivering it will enter into the proposed contract, such a form constitutes the offer of the party who tenders it, and if the form is accepted without objection by the person to whom it is tendered this person is as a general rule bound by its contents and his act amounts to an acceptance of the offer to him whether he reads the document or otherwise informs himself of its contents or not, and the conditions contained in the document are binding upon him.'

In a later passage Lord Hanworth says:

> It is, however, argued that it is a question of fact for the jury, whether or not sufficient notice was given of these conditions, and whether or not, therefore, the plaintiff ought to be held bound by the conditions; for it is said that the conditions are, I will not say past finding out, but difficult to ascertain. The learned commissioner who tried the case appreciated that the verdict of the jury was based probably on the fact that you have to make a considerable search before you find out the conditions. I think he is right in saying that in the line of cases, and there are many, under which this case falls, it has not ever been held that the mere circuity which has to be followed to find the actual condition prevents the passenger having notice that there was a condition.

The judgments of Lawrence L.J. and Sankey L.J. are to the same effect.

The only remaining question is whether the plaintiff, when he travelled beyond Fenagh on the return journey, was travelling subject to the special conditions or as an ordinary passenger. This was a special train on which no ordinary passengers were carried, all the passengers were carried on special terms at a reduced rate. When the plaintiff remained on the train after passing Fenagh he was, in my opinion, being carried not as an ordinary passenger but on the special conditions on which his ticket had been issued.

In my opinion the learned judge was right in holding that the defendants had taken all reasonable steps to bring to the notice of the plaintiff the conditions on which he would be carried as a passenger, and that the plaintiff was bound by those conditions at the time when he sustained the injury for which he claims damages. I do not think that the jury could properly find otherwise, and it follows that the direction given by the learned judge was right.

Murnaghan J.:

I agree, but, as this case is of some importance, I think it is right that I should give my reasons.

A contract to carry, once it is entered upon, imports a condition to carry safely; this obligation may, however, be excluded by special agreement. A passenger on a railway obtains a ticket as a receipt for payment, but the company uses that ticket to convey to the passenger that the ordinary terms of the contract have been altered.

A great number of cases have been decided on the question whether or not notice has been reasonably brought to the knowledge of the passenger. If not, the passenger is not bound by the attempted alteration. In this case the front of the ticket bears the words: 'See back', and on the back is printed: 'Issued subject to the conditions and regulations in the company's time tables, books, bills and notices.'

The point that is new in this case is that the time tables were not available at Fenagh where the ticket was issued. The plaintiff did not ask for the time tables, but he would be entitled to rely on the fact if it were the law that the absence of the time tables from the booking office amounted to a failure to give him notice of the condition. I personally sympathise with a person making a contract when the terms to which he is asked to assent are not put before him, but the law is that a document may incorporate conditions which are not expressed in it but in some other document. *Thompson's* case, was very similar to this and the court held in that case that the regulations were incorporated by the ticket.

In my opinion Hanna J., was right. I have no doubt that the principle of the law is as stated by him, and the only remedy for the present legal position would be legislation.

1. [1915] AC 740.   2. [1930] 1 KB 41.   3. [1923] 2 KB 703, at p. 707.

(Geoghegan J. agreed.)

Note

The nature of the risk being displaced or excluded can now considerably influence the standard of reasonableness required before the clause will be held to have been incorporated.

Thornton *v* Shoe Lane Parking Ltd [1971] 2 QB 163

Lord Denning M.R.:

In 1964 Mr Thornton, the plaintiff, who was a free-lance trumpeter of the highest quality, had an engagement with the BBC at Farringdon Hall. He drove to the city in his motor car and went to park it at a multi-storey automatic car park. It had only been open a few months. He had never gone there before. There was a notice on the outside headed 'Shoe Lane Parking'. It gave the parking charges: '5s for two hours; 7s 6d for three hours', and so forth; and at the bottom: 'All Cars Parked At Owner's Risk'. Mr Thornton drove up to the entrance. There was not a man in attendance. There was a traffic light which showed red. As he drove in and got to the appropriate place, the traffic light turned green and a ticket was pushed out from the machine. Mr Thornton took it. He drove on into the garage. The motor car was taken up by mechanical means to a floor above. Mr Thornton left it there and went off to keep his appointment with the BBC. Three hours later Mr Thornton came back. He went to the office and paid the charge for the time the car was there. His car was brought down from the upper floor. He went to put his belongings into the boot of the car. But unfortunately there was an accident. Mr Thornton was severely injured. The judge has found it was half his own fault, but half the fault of Shoe Lane Parking Ltd, the defendants. The judge awarded him £3,637 6s 11d.

On this appeal the garage company do not contest the judge's findings about the accident. They acknowledge that they were at fault, but they claim that they are protected by some exempting conditions. They rely on the ticket which was issued to Mr Thornton by the machine. They say that it was a contractual document and that it incorporated a condition which exempts them from liability to him. The ticket was headed 'Shoe Lane Parking'. Just below there was a 'box' in which was automatically recorded the time when the car went into the garage. There was a notice alongside: 'Please present this ticket to cashier to claim your car.' Just below the time, there was some small print in the left hand corner which said: 'The ticket is issued subject to the conditions of issue as displayed on the premises.' That is all.

Mr Thornton says he looked at the ticket to see the time on it, and put it in his pocket. He could see there was printing on the ticket, but he did not read it. He only read the time. He did not read the words which said that the ticket was issued subject to the conditions as displayed on the premises.

If Mr Thornton had read those words on the ticket and had looked round the premises to see where the conditions were displayed, he would have had to have driven his car on into the garage and walked round. Then he would have found, on a pillar opposite the ticket machine, a set of printed conditions in a panel. He would also have found, in the paying office (to be visited when coming back for the car) two more panels containing the printed conditions. If he had the time to read the conditions—it would take him a very considerable time—he would read:

Conditions

The following are the conditions upon which alone motor vehicles are accepted for parking:

1. The customer agrees to pay the charges of Shoe Lane Parking Developments Ltd. . . .
2. The customer is deemed to be fully insured at all times against all risks (including, without prejudice to the generality of the foregoing, fire, damage and theft, whether due to the negligence of others or not) and the company shall not be responsible or liable for any loss or misdelivery of or damage of whatever kind to the customer's motor vehicle, or any articles carried therein or thereon or of or to any accessories carried thereon or therein *or injury to the customer* or *any other person occurring when the customer's motor vehicle is in the parking building howsoever that loss, misdelivery, damage or injury shall be caused*; and it is agreed and understood that the customer's motor vehicle is parked and permitted by the company to be parked in the parking building in accordance with this licence entirely at the customer's risk. . . .

There is a lot more. I have only read about one-tenth of the conditions. The important thing to notice is that the company seek by this condition to exempt themselves from liability, not only for damage to the car, but also for injury to the customer howsoever caused. The condition talks about insurance. It is well known that the customer is usually insured against damage to the car. But he is not insured against damage to himself. If the condition is incorporated into the contract of parking, it means that Mr Thornton will be unable to recover any damages for his personal injuries which were caused by the negligence of the company.

We have been referred to the ticket cases of former times from *Parker v South Eastern Rly Co.* (1877) 2 CPD 416 to *McCutcheon v David MacBrayne Ltd* [1964] 1 WLR 125. They were concerned with railways, steamships and cloakrooms where booking clerks issued tickets to customers who took them away without reading them. In those cases the issue of the ticket was regarded as an *offer* by the company. If the customer took it and retained it without objection, his act was regarded as an acceptance of the offer: *Watkins v Rymill* (1833) 10 QBD 178, 188 and *Thompson v London, Midland and Scottish Rly Co.* [1930] 1 KB 41, 47. These cases were based on the theory that the customer, on being handed the ticket, could refuse it and decline to enter into a contract on those terms.

He could ask for his money back. That theory was, of course, a fiction. No customer in a thousand ever read the conditions. If he had stopped to do so, he would have missed the train or the boat.

None of those cases has any application to a ticket which is issued by an automatic machine. The customer pays his money and gets a ticket. He cannot refuse it. He cannot get his money back. He may protest to the machine, even swear at it. But it will remain unmoved. He is committed beyond recall. He was committed at the very moment when he put his money into the machine. The contract was concluded at that time. It can be translated into offer and acceptance in this way: the offer is made when the proprietor of the machine holds it out as being ready to receive the money. The acceptance takes place when the customer puts his money into the slot. The terms of the offer are contained in the notice placed on or near the machine stating what is offered for the money. The customer is bound by those terms as long as they are sufficiently brought to his notice beforehand, but not otherwise. He is not bound by the terms printed on the ticket if they differ from the notice, because the ticket comes too late. The contract has already been made: see *Olley v Marlborough Court Ltd* [1949] 1 KB 532. The ticket is no more than a voucher or receipt for the money that has been paid (as in the deckchair case, *Chapelton v Barry Urban District Council* [1940] 1 KB 532) on terms which have been offered and accepted before the ticket is issued.

In the present case the offer was contained in the notice at the entrance giving the charges for garaging and saying 'at owner's risk', i.e. at the risk of the owner so far as damage to the car was concerned. The offer was accepted when Mr Thornton drove up to the entrance and, by the movement of his car, turned the light from red to green, and the ticket was thrust at him. The contract was then concluded, and it could not be altered by any words printed on the ticket itself. In particular, it could not be altered so as to exempt the company from liability for personal injury due to their negligence.

Assuming, however, that an automatic machine is a booking clerk in disguise—so that the old fashioned ticket cases still apply to it. We then have to go back to the three questions put by Mellish L.J. in *Parker v South Eastern Rly Co.*, subject to this qualification: Mellish L.J. used the word 'conditions' in the plural, whereas it would be more apt to use the word 'condition' in the singular, as indeed the Lord Justice himself did on the next page. After all, the only condition that matters for this purpose is the exempting condition. It is no use telling the customer that the ticket is issued subject to some 'conditions' or other, without more: for he may reasonably regard 'conditions' in general as merely regulatory, and not as taking away his rights, unless the exempting condition is drawn specifically to his attention. (Alternatively, if the plural 'conditions' is used, it would be better prefaced with the word 'exempting', because the exempting conditions are the only conditions that matter for this purpose.) Telescoping the three questions, they come to this: the customer is bound by the exempting condition if he knows that the ticket is issued subject to it; or, if the company did what was reasonably sufficient to give him notice of it.

[Counsel for the defendant] admitted here that the company did not do what was reasonably sufficient to give Mr Thornton notice of the exempting condition. That admission was properly made. I do not pause to inquire whether the exempting condition is void for unreasonableness. All I say is that it is so wide and so destructive of rights that the court should not hold any man bound by it unless it is drawn to his attention in the most explicit way. It is an instance of what I had in mind in J. *Spurling Ltd v Bradshaw* [1956] 1 WLR 461, 466. In order to give sufficient notice, it would need to be printed in red ink with a red hand pointing to it—or something equally startling.

But, although reasonable notice of it was not given, [counsel] said that this case came within the second question propounded by Mellish L.J., namely that Mr Thornton 'knew or believed that the writing contained conditions.' There was no finding to that effect. The burden was on the company to prove it, and they did not do so. Certainly there was no evidence that Mr Thornton knew of this exempting condition. He is not, therefore, bound by it.

Mr Machin relied on a case in this court last year—*Mendelssohn v Normand Ltd* [1970] 1 QB 177. Mr Mendelssohn parked his car in the Cumberland Garage at Marble Arch, and was given a ticket which contained an exempting condition. There was no discussion as to whether the condition formed part of the contract. It was conceded that it did. That is shown by the report in the Law Reports at p. 180. Yet the garage company were not entitled to rely on the exempting condition for the reasons there given.

That case does not touch the present, where the whole question is whether the exempting condition formed part of the contract. I do not think it did. Mr Thornton did not know of the condition, and the company did not do what was reasonably sufficient to give him notice of it.

I do not think the garage company can escape liability by reason of the exemption condition. I would, therefore, dismiss the appeal.

(Megaw L.J. and Wilmer J. gave judgments to the same effect.)

Western Meats Ltd *v* National Ice and Cold Storage Co. Ltd [1982] ILRM 99

Barrington J.:

The plaintiffs are a limited liability company with a registered office at Bridge Street, Longford. They operate meat factories at Dromond, County Leitrim and at Charleville, County Cork.

The defendants are two limited liability companies associated together and jointly trading under the name 'Frigoscandia'. Among their activities they maintain a cold storage freezing plant and depot at Midleton, Co. Cork.

In 1969 the plaintiffs had recently taken over a meat factory at Charleville, County Cork and had embarked on a policy which was greatly to expand the turnover and the work force in that factory. They were approached by the defendants who solicited their business, and offered them the facilities of the cold storage plant which the defendants operated at Midleton, County Cork. In September 1969 the defendants' representatives met with Mr William Lyons, who is a director of the plaintiff company, and followed up this meeting with a letter dated 22 September 1969 in which they stated:

> Our group are the largest operators of public cold stores in Europe and from their years of experience have worked out the most efficient and economical way to store customers' products. We operate a total of 7 million cubic feet of controlled temperature storage in England, with stores at Stratford, London and Kings Lynn, Norfolk. Our store at Stratford, being adjacent to the Smithfield Market, handles a high tonnage of carcass meat, boneless beef and offals. The Midleton store, which is the most modern cold store in Ireland, can offer you . . . .

The letter then proceeds to describe the facilities which the Midleton store can provide.

These facilities appeared to the plaintiffs to meet their business requirements and a mutually satisfactory business relationship commenced between the parties and continued for many years. On 21 December 1973 the defendants' Mr W. S. Stephen wrote a letter to the plaintiffs which concluded in the following terms: 'Finally, I would like to take this opportunity of thanking you for your co-operation and the good business relationships that existed between our two companies in 1973. I look forward to these conditions continuing during 1974.'

Unfortunately, the difficulties which gave rise to the present action arose during the year 1974. Among the meats which the plaintiff deposited with the defendants for cold storage were various forms of pig meat including ham, bacon, pork and offals. The plaintiffs, in the course of the year, sold various forms of pig meat in the home market, and, through the Pigs and Bacon Commission, in the export market. They stored their surplus produce with the defendants in the confident expectation that they could withdraw this as and when required, and in particular for the Christmas trade. Coming up to Christmas 1974 I am satisfied that the plaintiffs had stored with the defendants very considerable quantities of gammons and other forms of pig meat and that they attempted to withdraw these to meet the Christmas demand, but were unable to do so.

I am satisfied that the reason why the plaintiffs were unable to withdraw their meat from cold storage was that the defendants, during the year 1974, had accepted into cold storage more meat than they could cope with or keep track of. I am satisfied also, that in the weeks coming up to Christmas in 1974, the plaintiffs sought to withdraw all their meat from cold storage to meet the Christmas demand but they were unable to do so simply because the defendants could not locate it and deliver it to them. The situation was so chaotic that the plaintiffs, instead of stipulating various quantities of meat which they wished to withdraw, had to resort to the device of sending their lorry to the defendants' store and giving the lorry driver a blank order book and authorising him to give a receipt for such meat as he could obtain from the defendants. I am satisfied also that the plaintiffs, being unable to withdraw their meat from cold storage, were forced in an effort to meet their customers' demands, to buy in, and slaughter, pigs in order to make available to their customers, for the Christmas trade, gammons which were in fact in cold storage and ought to have been readily available to the plaintiffs. I am quite satisfied that the reason why they were not so available, and could not be found, was that the defendants, during the year 1974, had taken into cold storage more meat than they could efficiently cope with or trace.

Under these circumstances it appears to me that, *prima facie*, the defendants, as bailees for reward, are liable for their failures to produce the plaintiffs' meat on demand and are also liable for consequential loss which befell the plaintiffs as a result of this failure.

To the plaintiffs' claim the defendants have two principal defences. The first is based on their standard conditions of trade and the second is based on the defendants' assertion that the plaintiffs were negligent in labelling, depositing, and withdrawing their goods and are consequently, at least in part, the authors of their own misfortune.

The conditions of trade, if part of the contract between the parties, appear to me to be a complete answer to the plaintiffs' claim.

Clause I of the conditions of storage provides that all goods are stored at the owner's risk. Clause II provides that the company will not be answerable for any delay, loss or damage arising (*inter alia*) from maintaining too high or too low a temperature in the stores, failure of machinery or plant, negligence, thefts, including theft by the company's servants, 'or any other cause whatsoever'.

There is no doubt that it was competent for the parties to include such clauses in their contract if they wished to do so. We are not here dealing with a monopoly providing a necessary service for an ignorant and unwary public. We are dealing with two commercial concerns one of which is providing a specialist service for the other and each of which is competent to protect its own interests. So far as this aspect of the case is concerned the relevant principles would appear to be those laid down in the House of Lords in *Photo Production Ltd v Securicor Transport Ltd* [1980] AC 827.

But the primary question is whether the plaintiffs were given reasonable notice of these conditions. Mr William Lyons says he was not aware of them an there is no evidence that they were ever expressly brought to his attention.

In later years these conditions appeared on the back of the defendants' notepaper and also on the back of many of their storage documents. We only have a photostat copy of the original letter passing between the parties dated 22 September 1969. The conditions do not appear on the back of this copy though they may have been on the back of the original.

However, in the text of the letter itself there is no reference to the conditions, though certain terms are set out in the letter. I am satisfied that the terms were never expressly brought to Mr Lyons' attention and I accept his word that he was not aware of them. I am satisfied that he is a man who carries on business by personal contact and on the telephone and that he relies greatly on his assessment of the men he is dealing with. Indeed, in the present case, even the defendants' managers do not appear to have been particularly conscious of the standard conditions. When disputes arose between the parties over the years, prior to the present dispute, these were resolved as between businessmen and, even in the present case, there was no reference to the standard conditions until the matter reached the hands of the lawyers.

It appears to me to be important that this is a case in which the defendants initially solicited the plaintiffs' business. Had they, the initial negotiators, expressly drawn to Mr Lyons' attention not only the excellence of their services but also the fact that they accepted no responsibility whatsoever for the manner in which they would handle his goods, Mr Lyons' decision of whether to retain them might well have been different. In all the circumstances of this case it appears to me that the defendants did not give the plaintiffs reasonable notice of the contents of the standard conditions. It appears to me also that a businessman, offering a specialist service, but accepting no responsibility for it, must bring home clearly to the party dealing with him that he accepts no such responsibility. In all the circumstances I think, that in the present case, the defendants were guilty of negligence and breach of contract.

Note

Recent English case-law has demonstrated that the courts are prepared to consider whether the clause in question is customary or standard on the one hand, or unprecedented or unique on the other. How the term is classified is relevant to both the question of incorporation and whether the term is fair and reasonable. See HIH *Casualty & General Insurance v New Hampshire* [2001] 2 Lloyds Reports 161; *Shepherd Homes Ltd v Encia Remediation Ltd and Others* [2007] EWHC 70 (TCC), discussing *Stiletto* in particular.

C. Incorporation Through a Course of Dealing

J. Spurling Ltd *v* Bradshaw [1956] 1 WLR 461

The owner of barrels of orange juice left them with the plaintiff under a contract of bailment. The goods were damaged or destroyed. The plaintiff brought an action for the contracted sums. The defendant refused to pay and counterclaimed for damages. On several previous occasions the defendant had left goods with the plaintiff and had been given receipts which contained exemption clauses. At trial of the action the counterclaim was held to be defeated by these clauses. The defendant appealed.

Denning L.J.:

This brings me to the question whether this clause was part of the contract. [Counsel for the defendant] urged us to hold that the warehousemen did not do what was reasonably sufficient to give notice of the conditions within *Parker v South Eastern Rly Co.*[1] I quite agree that the more unreasonable a clause is, the greater the notice which must be given of it. Some clauses which I have seen would need to be printed in red ink on the face of the document with a red hand pointing to it before the notice could be held to be sufficient. The clause in this case, however, in my judgment, does not call for such exceptional treatment, especially when it is construed, as it should be, subject to the proviso that it only applies when the warehouseman is carrying out his contract, and not when he is deviating from it or breaking it in a radical respect. So construed, the judge was, I think, entitled to find that sufficient notice was given. It is to be noticed that the landing account on its face told Mr Bradshaw that the goods would be insured if he gave instructions; otherwise they were not insured. The invoice, on its face, told him they were warehoused 'at owner's risk'. The printed conditions, when read subject to the proviso which I have mentioned, added little or nothing to those explicit statements taken together.

Next it was said that the landing account and invoice were issued after the goods had been received and could not, therefore, be part of the contract of bailment: but Mr Bradshaw admitted that he had received many landing accounts before. True he had not troubled to read them. On receiving this landing account, he took no objection to it, left the goods there, and went on paying the warehouse rent for months afterwards. It seems to me that by the course of business and conduct of the parties, these conditions were part of the contract.

In these circumstances, the warehousemen were entitled to rely on this exempting condition. I think, therefore, that the counterclaim was properly dismissed, and this appeal also should be dismissed.

[1] (1877) 2 CPD 416, [1874–80] All ER Rep 166.

(Morris L.J. concurred.)

SECTION THREE—CONSTRUCTION

A. INTERPRETATION CONTRA PROFERENS

American Law Institute Restatement Contracts (2d) S. 206
Interpretation Against the Draftsman

In choosing among the reasonable meanings of a promise or agreement or a term thereof, that meaning is generally preferred which operates against the party who supplies the words or from whom a writing otherwise proceeds.

Comment:

a. *Rationale.* Where one party chooses the terms of a contract, he is likely to provide more carefully for the protection of his own interests than for those of the other party. He is also more likely than the other party to have reason to know of uncertainties of meaning. Indeed, he may leave meaning deliberately obscure, intending to decide at a later date what meaning to assert. In cases of doubt, therefore, so long as other factors are not decisive, there is substantial reason for preferring the meaning of the other party. The rule is often invoked in cases of standardised contracts and in cases where the drafting party has the stronger bargaining position, but it is not limited to such cases. It is in strictness a rule of legal effect, sometimes called construction, as well as interpretation: its operation depends on the positions of the parties as they appear in litigation, and sometimes the result is hard to distinguish from a denial of effect to an unconscionable clause.

Andrews Bros (Bournemouth) Ltd *v* Singer and Co. Ltd [1934] 1 KB 17

Scrutton L.J.:

This is an appeal from a judgment of Goddard J. in an action by the plaintiffs, a company carrying on business at Bournemouth, who in the agreement between them and the defendants out of which the dispute has arisen are called agents for manufacturers, which is quite a misleading term inasmuch as they are really purchasers of motor cars which they intend to sell. They brought their action against Singer & Co. alleging that the latter delivered a car which did not comply with the terms of the contract.

The facts which are fully set out in the careful judgment of Goddard J. may be shortly summarised: the description of the kind of car the plaintiffs wanted could have been satisfied by delivery to them of a new car; but the particular car which Singer & Co. tendered to them was in this position. Another agent, who thought he had in view a purchaser for the car, had it sent to Darlington and thence it was driven some distance further to show to the prospective customer, but as that person did not like it the agent returned it to Singer & Co., the result being that it had run a very considerable mileage with the consequence no doubt that certain changes had taken place in it. When the car was tendered to the plaintiffs' representative he noticed or suspected that it had run a considerable distance, but he took it, doing nothing, however, so far as I can see, to abandon any claim for damages on the ground that it was not a new car.

At the trial two points arose: First, the plaintiffs said that the car was not a new car as that term was understood in the trade. The defendants on the other hand said it was. Goddard J. came to the conclusion that it was not a new car, and in this court his decision on that point has not been questioned and I therefore proceed on the assumption that the defendants, who were bound to supply a new car, tendered a car which was not a new one. The defendants contended secondly that they are exempted from liability by reason of clause 5 of the agreement entered into. That clause reads as follows: 'All cars sold by the company are subject to the terms of the warranty set out in schedule no. 3 of this agreement and all conditions, warranties and liabilities implied by statute, common law or otherwise are excluded.' The defendants say that their obligation to supply a car complying with the description in the contract is a condition implied by statute, and as the plaintiffs accepted the car under the agreement containing clause 5 they cannot bring an action in respect of the supplying of a car which was not a new one. Clause 5 is, I take it, a sequel to *Wallis, Son & Wells v Pratt & Haynes.*[1] In that case the subject matter of the sale was 'common English sainfoin', and the contract contained this clause: 'Sellers give no warranty express or implied as to growth, description or any other matters.' What in fact was sold under the contract was not 'common English sainfoin' but something quite different, namely, 'giant sainfoin'. On discovering this the purchasers sued for damages, to which claim the sellers replied that they gave no warranty express or implied as to description. The Court of Appeal (Moulton L.J. dissenting) took the view that the clause excluded any liability even though the seed supplied was not of the description contracted to be supplied. The House of Lords adopted Moulton L.J.'s judgment and said that the goods tendered should comply with the description in the contract, which description was not a warranty but a condition, and as the clause relied on did not include 'condition' it did not operate to protect the sellers. Those advising the present defendants in preparing this agreement appear to have thought that by the inclusion of the word 'conditions' in the relevant clause liability would be excluded, although what was supplied did not comply with the description. The question therefore is whether the defendants have succeeded in excluding liability in this case—whether they can tender under the contract goods not complying with the description in the contract and say that the plaintiffs having accepted the car cannot now sue for breach of contract.

In my opinion this was a contract for the sale of a new Singer car. The contract continually uses the phrase 'new Singer cars'. At the end of the agreement I find this: 'In the event of the dealer having purchased from the company during the period of this agreement 250 new cars of current season's models'; and in the very beginning of the agreement I find this: 'The company hereby appoint the dealer their sole dealer for the sale of new Singer cars.' The same phrase also occurs in other parts of the agreement, and the subject matter is therefore expressly stated to be 'new Singer cars'. The judge has found, and his view is not now contested, that the car tendered in this case was not a new Singer car. Does then clause 5 prevent the vendors being liable in damages for having tendered and supplied a car which is not within the express terms of the contract? Clause 5 says this: 'All conditions, warranties and liabilities implied by statute, common law or otherwise are excluded.' There are well known obligations in various classes of contracts which are not expressly mentioned but are implied. During the argument Greer L.J. mentioned an apt illustration, namely, where an agent contracts on behalf of A he warrants that he has authority to make the contract on behalf of A although no such warranty is expressed in the contract. Mr Pritt relied on s. 13 of the Sale of Goods Act, 1893, which provides that 'where there is a contract for the sale of goods by description, there is an implied condition that the goods shall correspond with the description . . . ,' and from that he says it follows that this particular condition comes within the words employed by the section. That, I think, is putting a very strained meaning on the word 'implied' in the section. Where goods are expressly described in the contract and do not comply with that description, it is quite inaccurate to say that there is an implied term; the term is expressed in the contract. Suppose the contract is for the supply of a car of 1932 manufacture, and a car is supplied which is of 1930 manufacture, there has not been a breach of an implied term; there has been a breach of an express term of the contract. It leads to a very startling result if it can be said that clause 5 allows a vendor to supply to a purchaser an article which does not comply with the express description of the article in the contract, and then, though the purchaser did not know of the matter which prevented the article supplied from complying with the express terms of the contract, to say, 'We are under no liability to you because this is a condition implied by statute and we have excluded such liability.'

In my view there has been in this case a breach of an express term of the contract. If a vendor desires to protect himself from liability in such a case he must do so by much clearer language than this, which, in my opinion, does not exempt the defendants from liability where they have failed to comply with the express term of the contract. For these reasons I think Goddard J. came to a correct conclusion, and this appeal therefore fails.

[1] [1910] 2 KB 1003; [1911] AC 394.

(Greer L.J. and Eve J. concurred.)

Notes

1. L'*Estrange v F. Graucob Ltd* (p. 411 above) finally closes this drafting loop-hole. Re-read Llewellyn (above p. 382) in order to understand how limited these techniques of 'misreading' a clause can be.

2. The two following cases illustrate graphically the pressure on the courts to construe clauses narrowly. The *Ailsa Craig* case (below), however, cautions against fanciful results but that case was decided after statutory controls of abusive exemption clauses were in place.

O'Connor *v* McCowen and Sons Ltd (1943) 77 ILTR 64

Overend J.:

. . . The plaintiff was a farmer, and was ill at the time of the transaction. He sent his son John to Tralee to buy the seed. The son went into the shop and saw Mr Scanlan, who was in charge of the seed department. He told Mr Scanlan of his requirements, and a discussion arose as to the amount of seed that would be sufficient. There was no doubt that the nature of the purchase was clear. The amount having been arrived at, Mr Scanlan told the assistant to fill out 14 lbs. Blue Top turnip seed, and Mr Scanlan made the entry on the blue paper. This transaction was sale by description. The purchaser had no opportunity of examining the seed and if he had it would be no use for him. When he had filled up the blue docket, and before O'Connor had signed it, Mr Scanlan told John O'Connor that they had not get their seeds from their usual suppliers and could not guarantee them. These words were not sufficient to warn the buyer that the seeds might not be turnip seeds at all, and contained nothing to indicate that they would not produce turnips. If purchasers were to be precluded, when they purchased articles by description and got different goods, then the very clearest words must be used by the seller, such as: 'You may be purchasing seeds that are not turnip seeds at all.'

Mr Scanlan then asked O'Connor to sign the conditions of sale—the usual conditions which Messrs McCowen had on their dockets for a considerable time. At the time of the sale it had not entered into Mr Scanlan's head that what he was selling was not turnip seed at all. The buyer, however, got something that was not turnip seed, and, quite apart from the Sale of Goods Act [1893], he had a cause of action. [Counsel for the defendant] had put forward the proposition that in the conditions of sale all the risk was covered. But it was not. The conditions said that they selected their seeds with the greatest care. These conditions were not applicable to the case where Messrs McCowen had not selected their goods with the greatest care, which in this case they had not, as they took what they could get.

Under the circumstances (said his Lordship) he had to decide that the defendants were liable. It was a serious case for both the plaintiff and the defendants. One of two innocent parties would suffer, but since the plaintiff did not get what he bought, the defendants, though not morally liable, were legally so, and accordingly he must affirm the decree of the Circuit Court.

Ailsa Craig Fishing Ltd *v* Malvern Fishing Ltd [1983] 1 WLR 964

Lord Fraser of Tullybelton:

My Lords, the only surviving issue in these appeals is whether the respondents ('Securicor') have succeeded in limiting their liability under a contract between themselves and the Aberdeen Fishing Vessel Owners' Association Ltd ('the association') who were acting on behalf a number of owners of fishing vessels, including the appellants. Nothing turns upon the fact that the appellants were not themselves a party to the contract and I shall proceed as if the contract had been made with them.

The appellants were the owners of the fishing vessel *Strathallan* which sank while berthed in Aberdeen Harbour on 31 December 1971, at a time when Securicor were bound, under the contract with the association, to provide security cover in the harbour. Her gallows fouled the vessel moored next to her on the starboard side, called the *George Craig*, which also sank. Both vessels became total losses. Two actions were then raised. In one the appellants claimed damages from the owners of the *George Craig* as first defenders and from Securicor as second defenders. In the other the owners of the *George Craig* claimed damages from the appellants, who brought in Securicor as a third party. The Lord Ordinary (Lord Wylie) held that the loss of both vessels had been caused by breach of contract and negligence on the part of Securicor. He found them liable to the appellants in damages for the loss of the *Strathallan*, and found them liable to relieve the appellants of their full liability to the owners of the *George Craig* for the loss of that vessel. He assessed the damages in each case at a little over £55,000. The Lord Ordinary rejected arguments on behalf of Securicor to the effect that their liability was either wholly excluded, or limited in amount, by the terms of their contract. Securicor reclaimed against the Lord Ordinary's judgment but they did not contest his findings of breach of contract and negligence. Their contention on the reclaiming motion was solely that their liability had been either excluded or limited by the terms of the contract. The First Division of the Court of Session (the Lord President, Lord Cameron and Lord Dunpark) allowed the reclaiming motion in part, holding that liability had been limited in amount but that it had not been excluded. The appellants now appeal to your Lordships' House against that decision in so far as it held that liability had been limited.

In order to appreciate the contentions of the parties, it is necessary to refer briefly to the circumstances in which the contract came to be made. Until 31 December 1971, Securicor had for some months been providing a security service for vessels of owners represented by the association. They did so under a contract dated 12 May 1971, under which the service was limited to vessels berthed at the Albert Quay in Aberdeen Harbour, and operated only during the nights and at weekends. The main object was to prevent intruders from boarding unmanned vessels and damaging them or stealing from them. Early on 31 December an official of the association realised that the service would not be adequate for the New Year period, partly because there were many more vessels than usual in the harbour and partly because they would be remaining there for several days. Owing to the unusual number of vessels they could not all be berthed at Albert Quay, where the security patrols were already provided during certain hours, and some of them would have to be berthed at the Fish Market/Commercial Quay ('the Fish Market area'). The quay in the Fish Market area was of open structure, and there was a special risk that vessels might slide under the deck of the quay and become caught or 'snubbed' by the bow. The risk arose especially on a rising tide. That was just what happened to the appellants' vessel the *Strathallan*, during the evening of 31 December 1971, and caused her to sink taking the *George Craig* with her. As Securicor accept the Lord Ordinary's findings of fault against them, it is unnecessary to refer in greater detail to the events of that evening. Securicor also accept the decision of the First Division that the liability was not wholly excluded by the contract.

The question whether Securicor's liability has been limited falls to be answered by construing the terms of the contract in accordance with the ordinary principles applicable to contracts of this kind. The argument for limitation depends upon certain special conditions attached to the contract prepared on behalf of Securicor and put forward in their interest. There is no doubt that such conditions must be construed strictly against the *proferens*, in this case Securicor, and that in order to be effective they must be 'most clearly and unambiguously expressed': see W & S *Pollock & Co. v Macrae*, 1922 SC (HL) 192, 199 per Lord Dunedin. *Pollock* was a decision on an exclusion clause but insofar as it emphasised the need for clarity in clauses to be construed *contra proferentem* it is in my opinion relevant to the present case also. It has sometimes apparently been regarded as laying down, as a proposition of law, that a clause excluding liability can never have any application where there has been a total breach of contract, but I respectfully agree with the Lord President who said in his opinion in the present case that that was a misunderstanding of *Pollock*. *Pollock* was followed by the Second Division in *Mechans Ltd v Highland Marine Charters Ltd*, 1964 SC 48 and there are passages in the judgments in that case which might seem to treat *Pollock* as having laid down some such general proposition of law, although it is not clear that they were so intended. If they were I would regard them as being erroneous. *Mechans* appears to have been relied upon by counsel for the appellants before the Second Division, but was not relied on in this house.

There are later authorities which lay down very strict principles to be applied when considering the effect of clauses of exclusion or of indemnity: see particularly the Privy Council case of *Canada Steamship Lines Ltd. v The King* [1952] AC 192, 208, where Lord Morton of Henryton, delivering the advice of the board, summarised the principles in terms which have recently been applied by this house in *Smith v U.M.B. Chrysler (Scotland) Ltd*, 1978 SC (HL) 1. In my opinion these principles are not applicable in their full rigour when considering the effect of clauses merely limiting liability. Such clauses will of course be read *contra proferentem* and must be clearly expressed, but there is no reason why they should be judged by the specially exacting standards which are applied to exclusion and indemnity clauses. The reason for imposing such standards on these clauses is the inherent improbability that the other party to a contract including such a clause intended to release the *proferens* from a liability that would otherwise fall upon him. But there is no such high degree of improbability that he would agree to a limitation of the liability of the *proferens*, especially when, as explained in condition 4 (i) of the present contract, the potential losses that might be caused by the negligence of the *proferens* or its servants are so great in proportion to the sums that can reasonably be charged for the services contracted for. It is enough in the present case that the clause must be clear and unambiguous.

The contract was arranged during the morning of 31 December 1971, in some haste. It is set out on a form partly printed and partly filled in in ink, which is headed 'Temporary Contract or Contract Change Request' and in which the association 'request Securicor Ltd to carry out the services detailed below subject to the special conditions printed overleaf.' The form requested 'continuous security cover for your [sic] vessels from 1900 hours on 31 December 1971 until 07.00 hours on 5 January 1972' and stated that the area covered was to be extended to include the Fish Market area. Nothing turns upon that part of the contract but I should mention that the appellants contended that this temporary contract, so long as it was in operation, entirely superseded the contract of 12 May 1971, and was the sole measure of parties' rights and obligations to one another. Having regard to condition 8 of the special conditions, I see no reason to question that contention.

The 'special conditions of contract' were elaborate and are applied to services of several types. So far as this appeal is concerned, the part which is most directly applicable is condition 2, and especially clause (f) of that condition. Condition 2 (f) is in the following terms: [His Lordship read clause (f) and continued:] On behalf of the appellants it was argued that that clause, even if apparently clear in its own terms, is not applicable when read in the context of the contract as a whole, where there has been a total failure to perform the services contracted for or what is sometimes called a total failure of contract, and that this was such a case. It was said that clause 2 (f) must be qualified by the opening words of condition 2 and of clause (a) of that condition which show that liability can only arise for some fault in the course of providing the services contracted for, and not where there has been a total failure to provide the service. I cannot accept that submission, because clause 2 (f) expressly states that it applies to liability arising out of 'the provision of, or purported provision of, or failure in provision of' the services contracted for. If this submission had not been so persuasively presented, I would have thought it to be unarguable in face of the provisions of clause (f).

The learned judge of the First Division found that this was a case of total failure or total breach of contract, in the sense of Lord Dunedin's speech in *Pollock*, 1922 SC (HL) 192. As that is the finding most favourable to the appellants on this part of the case it is not now material to consider whether this is strictly a case of total failure. If the question had been material at this stage I would have wished to give it further consideration, because there is no suggestion that the security cover was not duly maintained during the evening of 31 December 1971, in the Albert Dock area, which was part of the area covered by the temporary contract, and I think there is much to be said for the view that the contract was performed in part. But it is not necessary to come to a decision on that point.

A further argument for the appellants was that clause (f) of condition 2 applied only to liability which arose 'pursuant to' the provisions of the contract, and that pursuant to meant 'in accordance with the express provisions of the contract.' This meaning was said to be emphasised by the first sentence of clause 4 (iii). But that argument fails, in my opinion, if for no other reason than that clause (f) itself proclaims unambiguously that it applies to liability which shall arise under the 'express or implied' terms of the contract. Next, the appellants argued that there is an inconsistency between clause (a) of condition 2 which purports to exclude liability altogether and clause (f) which purports to limit the amount of liability in certain cases. The existence of that inconsistency was one of the reasons for the First Division's decision that the exclusion clause was lacking in clarity, and counsel sought to apply the same argument in reverse to the limitation clause. But the argument is in my opinion unsound. It is one thing to say, as the First Division did, that when you find a provision for limiting liability coming after a provision which is capable of being read as excluding liability altogether, the limitation provision casts doubt on the meaning of the earlier one. But it is quite a different thing to say that the inconsistency casts doubt on the meaning of the limitation clause. If the exclusion clause had succeeded in its purpose, the limitation might have been unnecessary, but its meaning as a sort of long stop is in my opinion clear and is not affected by the existence of the exclusion clause.

A separate argument was advanced to the effect that clause (f) was confused and uncertain in itself because the provisions of sub-paras (i) (a) and (b) did not make it clear whether the limit of liability in any particular case was £1,000 or £10,000. Perhaps the intention of subparas (a) and (b) may not be immediately clear on first reading to a person unfamiliar with provisions of this sort, but a very little consideration is enough to show, in my opinion, that the meaning is that explained by the learned judges of the First Division. Sub-para. (*a*) relates to any *claim* arising in any of the ways there mentioned and it limits the liability of Securicor to £1,000 for each claim. Sub-para. (*b*) relates to any one *incident* and limits their liability to £10,000 in respect of each incident. The two provisions overlap but they are in no way inconsistent. For example, in the present case the owner of each of the vessels has a separate claim which, if the clause is applicable, will be limited to £1,000. But both claims arise out of one incident, and if there had been more than ten claims for £1,000 each arising out of the same incident, the total liability of Securicor would have been limited to £10,000. That meaning is in my view clear and unambiguous and I reject this argument.

Having considered these particular criticisms of clause (*f*) the question remains whether in its context it is sufficiently clear and unambiguous to receive effect in limiting the liability of Securicor for its own negligence or that of its employees. in my opinion it is. It applies to any liability 'whether under the express or implied terms of this contract, or at common law, or in any other way.' Liability at common law is undoubtedly wide enough to cover liability including the negligence of the *proferens* itself, so that even without relying on the final words 'any other way', I am clearly of opinion that the negligence of Securicor is covered.

For these reasons I would refuse the appeal. The respondents must have their costs in this house.

B. The Main Purpose Rule of Construction

Glynn *v* Margetson & Co. [1893] AC 351

Oranges were shipped on board a vessel from Malaga to Liverpool. The bill of loading contained a 'liberty to deviate' clause which gave the master the power to proceed to Liverpool via any ports in the Mediterranean, Levant, Black Sea, Coasts of Africa, etc. The vessel left Malaga, proceeded east to another Spanish port, and then rejoined the usual route to Liverpool. The oranges were damaged when they reached Liverpool.

Lord Herschell L.C.:

. . .

My Lords, the main object and intent, as I have said, of this charterparty is the carriage of oranges from Malaga to Liverpool. That is the matter with which the shipper is concerned; and it seems to me that it would be to defeat what is the manifest object and intention of such a contract to hold that it was entered into with a power to the shipowner to proceed anywhere that he pleased, to trade in any manner that he pleased, and to arrive at the port at which the oranges were to be delivered when he pleased.

Then is there any rule of law which compels the construction contended for? I think there is not. Where general words are used in a printed form which are obviously intended to apply, so far as they are applicable, to the circumstances of a particular contract, which particular contract is to be embodied in or introduced into that printed form, I think you are justified in looking at the main object and intent of the contract and in limiting the general words used, having in view that object and intent. Therefore, it seems to me that the construction contended for would be an unreasonable one, and there is no difficulty in construing this clause to apply to a liberty in the performance of the stipulated voyage to call at a particular port or ports in the course of the voyage. That port or those ports would differ according to what the stipulated voyage was, inasmuch as at the time when this document was framed the parties who framed it did not know what the particular voyage would be, and intended it to be equally used whatever that voyage is. The ports a visit to which would be justified under this contract would, no doubt, differ according to the particular voyage stipulated for between the shipper and the shipowner; but it must, in my view, be a liberty consistent with the main object of the contract—a liberty only to proceed to and stay at the ports which are in the course of the voyage.

Lord Halsbury L.C.:

My Lords, I am entirely of the same opinion. It seems to me that in construing this document, which is a contract of carriage between the parties, one must in the first instance look at the whole of the instrument and not at one part of it only. Looking at the whole of the instrument, and seeing what one must regard, for a reason which I will give in a moment, as its main purpose, one must reject words, indeed whole provisions, if they are inconsistent with what one assumes to be the main purpose of the contract. The main purpose of the contract was to take on board at one port and to deliver at another port a perishable cargo. I do not think the learned counsel who argued this case on the part of the appellants gave sufficient effect in the argument which he addressed to your Lordships to the difference between the ordinary and formal parts of the document which are to be found in print and the written parts— indeed I gathered from him at one time that he rather contested the legitimacy of considering the difference whether the words were in print or in writing; he appeared to intimate that that doubt was justified by the terms of this particular document, because that, in the ordinary construction of a commercial document, such a principle as I have mentioned has been adopted certainly for something like a century cannot be a matter of doubt, and the reason for it appears to me to be very cogent and relevant to the case before your Lordships.

C. CONSTRUCTION OF A CONTRACT

Is *liability in negligence covered*?

Regan *v* RIAC [1990] 1 IR 278

Lynch J.:

This action arises out of an unfortunate accident which happened about 4 p.m. on Saturday 14 September 1985, in the course of a motor race being lawfully held in the Phoenix Park, Dublin. The plaintiff was officiating at the race as a flag marshal and was injured when a competing motor racing car went out of control, left the track and knocked down the plaintiff causing serious injuries to her.

The plaintiff has sued the defendants as the organisers and controllers of the race and the race-track alleging negligence against them particularly in regard to an alleged lack of protection for the flag marshals including the plaintiff at the flag marshals' post to which the plaintiff had been assigned.

The evidence established to my satisfaction that the plaintiff and other officials camped in the Phoenix Park on the night of 13/14 September 1985, and reported for duty to an administration caravan between 6 a.m. and 7 a.m. on the morning of Saturday 14 September 1985. There the plaintiff and the other intending officials signed a form proffered to them by the clerical officer in charge of the administration caravan. The form contained the following passage:

I agree to act in an official capacity at this meeting and in consideration of the organising club(s) having effected for my benefit a personal accident policy for death or benefits as prescribed more specifically by RIAC requirements, I agree to absolve all persons having any connection with the promotion and/or organisation and/or conduct of the meeting including the [RIAC] the promoting club(s) the owner of the land, entrants and drivers and owners of vehicles from liability arising out of accidents howsoever caused, resulting in damage and/or personal injury to my person and/or property.

The evidence further established that an insurance policy such as is referred to in the form had been obtained and was in existence at the time when the plaintiff signed the form although the precise amounts payable thereunder were not clearly established. This imprecision does not seem to me to be material however. The plaintiff did not know the details of the insurance policy taken out by the defendants for the benefit of officials at races but she did know that some such provision had been made and she also knew what was in the document she signed to the extent at least that it contained an exemption clause which purported to restrict her rights to compensation in the event of an accident causing injury to her.

Para. 9 of the defence as impliedly denied raises the question of the construction of the terms of the form signed by the plaintiff before officiating at the motor race meeting and the really relevant portion of that form that falls for construction is the second half of the paragraph already quoted that is to say: 'I agree to absolve all persons having any connection with the promotion and/or organisation and/or conduct of the meeting including the [RIAC] the promoting club(s) the owner of the land entrants and drivers and owners of vehicles from liability arising out of accidents howsoever caused, resulting in damage and/or personal injury to my person and/or property.' Counsel for the defendants (the moving party in the issue) conceded that the form did not expressly refer to negligence but submitted that it necessarily extended to and included negligence. He cited the following authorities: *O'Hanlon v Electricity Supply Board* [1969] IR 75; *Chitty on Contract* (24th ed.) para. 818; and *Smith v South Wales Swithchgear* [1978] 1 WLR 165.

Counsel for the plaintiff submitted that in the absence of an express reference to negligence and in the light of the rule of law that the contract should be construed strictly against the person who drafted and proffered it, the document should be construed as referring only to accidents without negligence. He submitted that such accidents could readily happen at such an event as a motor race and he cited the following authorities: *Charlesworth on Negligence*; *Wilks v Cheltenham Cycle Club* [1971] 1 WLR 668; and *Clayton Love & Sons (Dublin) Ltd v British & Irish Steam Packet Co. Ltd* (1966) 104 ILTR 157.

I am satisfied that it is not fanciful or unreal to envisage accidents happening without negligence on the part of anyone at an event such as that at which the plaintiff was officiating. Therefore while accidents usually occur due to some carelessness or other on the part of someone and a reference to 'accidents' would usually imply and include negligent accidents the mere reference to accidents in this case would not necessarily imply negligent accidents. However I have to give effect to the words used and the word 'accidents' is not left unqualified. It is qualified by the words 'howsoever caused' and these words are obviously wide enough to embrace negligent accidents for which someone is responsible in law as well as pure accidents for which no one is responsible in law. In addition the use of the word 'liability' presupposes some form of wrong. A pure accident for which no one is responsible would create no liability in anyone and therefore the reference to liability necessarily brings within the ambit of the clause accidents resulting from the wrongful or negligent conduct of others.

It follows that my decision on the preliminary issue actually referred to me by the order of 27 February 1989, is that the plaintiff agreed for valuable consideration to absolve the defendants from liability in respect of the accident which in fact happened to her and further that the plaintiff before the accident complained of agreed to waive her legal rights as against the defendants in respect of it. Accordingly I rule that, subject to the issue as to whether there was a fundamental breach of contract by the defendants and is so the effect thereof, the plaintiff is barred from maintaining these proceedings against the defendants.

If for the purposes of the issues raised by para. 5 of the reply I were to assume that all the allegations made by the plaintiff before me were established nevertheless my view would be that those allegations do not amount to such a fundamental breach of agreement on the part of the defendants in this case as to disentitle them from relying on the exemption clause in the form signed by the plaintiff. Moreover I am not to be taken as either accepting or rejecting the proposition that a fundamental breach of contract will necessarily have the results submitted on behalf of the plaintiff having regard to cases decided since the decision in *Clayton Love & Sons (Dublin) Ltd v British & Irish Steam Packet Co. Ltd* (1966) 104 ILTR 157.

D. THE DEVELOPMENT OF THE FUNDAMENTAL BREACH DOCTRINE

Note

There are isolated instances where the courts have developed exceptions to the general view that the application of an exemption clause depends entirely on its construction or interpretation. Most notable are the deviation cases which hold that if a contracting party seeks to rely on an exemption clause, or another defence to liability such as an act of God, it must be shown that the party invoking the defence was performing the contract in its essential respects. These cases originated in common carrier cases and eventually found their way into ordinary contracts of bailment.

Lilley v Doubleday (1881) 7 QBD 510

The facts

The action was to recover the value of certain drapery goods warehoused by the defendant for the plaintiff, which were destroyed by fire. The contract was that the goods should be deposited at the defendant's repository at Kingsland Road, but a portion of them were deposited by the defendant elsewhere, and a fire occurring they were destroyed. The plaintiff had insured the goods, giving Kingsland Road as the place where they were deposited, and in consequence lost the benefit of the insurance.

Grove J.:

I think the plaintiff is entitled to judgment. It seems to me impossible to get over this point, that by the finding of the jury there has been a breach of contract. The defendant was entrusted with the goods for a particular purpose and to keep them in a particular place. He took them to another, and must be responsible for what took place there. The only exception I see to this general rule is where the destruction of the goods must take place as inevitably at one place as at the other. If a bailee elects to deal with the property entrusted to him in a way not authorised by the bailor, he takes upon himself the risks of so doing, except where the risk is independent of his acts and inherent in the property itself. That proposition is fully supported by the case of Davis v Garrett,[1] which contains very little that is not applicable to this case. It was argued that that case was decided on the ground that the defendant was a common carrier, but that is not the ground of the judgment of Tindal C.J., who decided that as the loss had happened while the wrongful act of the defendant was in operation and was attributable to his wrongful act, he could not set up as an answer to the action the bare possibility of the loss if his wrongful act had never been done, and he illustrated the case by saying that a defendant who had by mistake forwarded a parcel by the wrong conveyance, if a loss had thereby ensued, would undoubtedly be liable. I do not give any opinion whether what was done here amounted to a conversion, but I base my judgment on the fact that the defendant broke his contract, by dealing with the subject matter in a manner different from that in which he contracted to deal with it. . . .

Lindley J.:

I am of the same opinion. The plaintiff gave his goods to the defendant to be warehoused at a particular place, the defendant warehoused them elsewhere, where, without any particular negligence on his part, they were destroyed. The consequence is that the plaintiff has a cause of action and is entitled to damages. . . .

[1] 6 Bing. 716.

(Stephen J. concurred.)

Note

These carrier cases, as extended into bailment contracts, then formed the basis of a general rule of law which found its way into sales law, the law relating to hire purchase and contracts for the provision of services.

Karsales Harrow Ltd v Wallis [1956] 1 WLR 936

The facts

In this case the defendant took a used Buick car on hire purchase, the contract containing a clause that 'no condition or warranty that the vehicle is roadworthy, or as to its age, condition or fitness for any purpose is given by the owner or implied herein.' On delivery the car was in a deplorable state and the defendant refused to make any payments under the contract.

Denning L.J.:

[Counsel] on behalf of the defendant, says that he agreed to take on hire-purchase terms a Buick motor car which he had seen a week or two before he had signed these documents. He says that it was the duty of the finance company to see that there was delivered to the defendant a motor car which corresponded to the car he had seen. He says that, owing to its condition on delivery, there was a fundamental breach by the finance company and that they cannot recover the instalments. In answer, [counsel for the plaintiff] says that there was delivered to the defendant a Buick motor car of the registration number specified in the agreement, and that they are in no way responsible for its condition on delivery. They rely on clause 3 (g) of the hire-purchase agreement:

'No condition or warranty that the vehicle is roadworthy, or as to its age, condition or fitness for any purpose is given by the owner or implied herein.' The judge held that that clause in this document meant that the hire-purchase company were not responsible in any way for the condition of this car when it was delivered, and that although it was in this deplorable condition, they could still recover the instalments due under the agreement; and that, even though the car was rejected by the defendant, they could still recover them.

In my opinion, under a hire-purchase agreement of this kind, when the hirer has himself previously seen and examined the motor car and made application for hire-purchase on the basis of his inspection of it, there is an obligation on the lender to deliver the car in substantially the same condition as when it was seen. It makes no difference that the lender is a finance company which has bought the car in the interval without seeing it. The lender must know, from the ordinary course of business, that the hirer applies on the faith of his inspection and on the understanding that the car will be delivered in substantially the same condition: and it is an implied term of the agreement that pending delivery the car will be kept in suitable order and repair for the purposes of the bailment. This is supported by *Story on Bailment*, articles 383 to 385, and *Robertson v Amazon Tug and Lighterage Co.*[1]

The plaintiffs say that there can be no such implication in this case in view of the express terms of clause 3 (g): but the law about exempting clauses has been much developed in recent years, at any rate about printed exempting clauses, which so often pass unread. Notwithstanding earlier cases which might suggest the contrary, it is now settled that exempting clauses of this kind, no matter how widely they are expressed, only avail the party when he is carrying out his contract in its essential respects. He is not allowed to use them as a cover for misconduct or indifference or to enable him to turn a blind eye to his obligations. They do not avail him when he is guilty of a breach which goes to the root of the contract. The thing to do is to look at the contract apart from the exempting clauses and see what are the terms, express or implied, which impose an obligation on the party. If he has been guilty of a breach of those obligations in a respect which goes to the very root of the contract, he cannot rely on the exempting clauses. I would refer in this regard to what was said by Roche J. in the 'copra cake' case (*Pinnock Brothers v Lewis & Peat Ltd*[2]) and the judgments of Devlin J. in *Alexander v Rly Executive*[3] and *Smeaton Hanscomb & Co. Ltd v Sassoon I. Setty, Son & Co. (No. 1)*,[4] and the recent case in this court of *J. Spurling Ltd v Bradshaw*,[5] and the cases there mentioned. The principle is sometimes said to be that the party cannot rely on an exempting clause when he delivers something 'different in kind' from that contracted for, or has broken a 'fundamental term' or a 'fundamental contractual obligation', but these are, I think, all comprehended by the general principle that a breach which goes to the root of the contract disentitles the party from relying on the exempting clause. In the present case the lender was in breach of the implied obligation that I have mentioned. When the defendant inspected the car before signing the application form, the car was in excellent condition and would go: whereas the car which was subsequently delivered to him was no doubt the same car, but it was in a deplorable state and would not go. That breach went, I think, to the root of the contract and disentitles the lender from relying on the exempting clause.

The only real difficulty that I have felt in the case is whether this point is put with sufficient clarity in the pleadings. It is not put as clearly as one could wish.

[1] (1881) 7 QBD 598.
[2] [1923] 1 KB 690, 695, 39.
[3] [1951] 2 KB 882.
[4] [1953] 1 WLR 1468; [1953] 2 All ER 1471.
[5] [1956] 1 WLR 461; [1956] 2 All ER 121.

(Birkett and Parker L.JJ. concurred.)

Clayton Love v B & I Transport (1966) 104 ILTR 157

(Facts on p. 340.)

Clark R., (op. cit) pp 190–1 explains the case thus:

. . . The parties contracted to transport deep frozen scampi from Dublin to Liverpool. The loading was conducted at atmospheric temperature and this led to the scampi deteriorating to the extent that it was condemned when it arrived in Liverpool. The plaintiffs sued but were met by two exemption clauses, one of which was drafted widely enough to protect the defendants from liability. The second clause obliged the plaintiffs to claim within three days, otherwise the claim would be absolutely barred. Davitt P. at first instance relied on the substantive rule of law and dicta in two English cases, *Spurling Ltd v Bradshaw*[1] and *Smeaton Hanscomb & Co. Ltd v Sassoon I. Setty*[2] and refused to apply the first limiting clause. It is symptomatic of the confusion and complexity of this doctrine that Davitt P. then shifted ground and applied the second clause by holding that 'it was intended to, and does in fact cover the case of a clause arising from the breach of a fundamental term of the contract.' This reasoning seems to be unsatisfactory because Davitt P. applied a rule of law to the first clause and a rule of interpretation to the other limiting clause. The Supreme Court eliminated this inconsistency by holding that the rule of law must apply to the second limiting clause, regardless of the intention of the *proferens*. A better approach to the problem in *Clayton Love* would have been to ask if the contract had been freely negotiated; did the shipper have a choice of terms upon which he could ship his goods (as in *Slattery v* CIE). Most importantly, did the shipper know and consent to loading of such delicate frozen goods at atmospheric temperatures and did he know of the existence of this sweeping clause? It is probable that the Supreme Court would have still found in favour of the plaintiffs but they would have addressed the issues of freedom of contract and consent, factors that were not always considered by pro-fundamental breach judges.

[1] [1956] 1 WLR 461.   [2] [1953] 1 WLR 1468.

Note

While the Supreme Court has not had occasion to reconsider the *Clayton Love* decision, it is generally recognised that the jurisprudential basis upon which it rests is in doubt.

Suisse Atlantique [1967] AC 361

Suisse Atlantique [1967] AC 361, *obiter*, disapproved of the 'fundamental breach as a rule of law' approach. Lord Reid in particular was critical of Devlin J.'s judgment in *Smeaton Hanscomb*, the basis of *Clayton Love* itself. He continued:

. . .

If this new rule of law is to be adopted, how far does it go? In its simplest form it would be that a party is not permitted to contract out of common law liability for a fundamental breach. If that were right then a demurrage clause could not stand as limiting liability for loss resulting from a fundamental breach; and the same would apply to any clause providing for liquidated damages. I do not suppose that anyone has intended that this rule should go quite so far as that. But I would find it difficult to say just where the line would have to be drawn.

In my view no such rule of law ought to be adopted. I do not take that view merely because any such rule is new or because it goes beyond what can be done by developing or adapting existing principles. Courts have often introduced new rules when, in their view, they were required by public policy. In former times when Parliament seldom amended the common law, that could hardly have been avoided. And there are recent examples although, for reasons which I gave in *Shaw v Director of Public Prosecutions*, I think that this power ought now to be used sparingly. But my main reason is that this rule would not be a satisfactory solution of the problem which undoubtedly exists.

Exemption clauses differ greatly in many respects. Probably the most objectionable are found in the complex standard conditions which are now so common. In the ordinary way the customer has no time to read them, and if he did read them he would probably not understand them. And if he did understand and object to any of them, he would generally be told he could take it or leave it. And if he then went to another supplier the result would be the same. Freedom to contract must surely imply some choice or room for bargaining.

At the other extreme is the case where parties are bargaining on terms of equality and a stringent exemption clause is accepted by a *quid pro quo* or other good reason. But this rule appears to treat all cases alike. There is no indication in the recent cases that the courts are to consider whether the exemption is fair in all the circumstances or is harsh and unconscionable or whether it was freely agreed by the customer. And it does not seem to me to be satisfactory that the decision must always go one way if, e.g. defects in a car or other goods are just sufficient to make the breach of contract a fundamental breach, but must always go the other way if the defects fall just short of that. This is a complex problem which intimately affects millions of people and it appears to me that its solution should be left to Parliament. If your Lordships reject this new rule there will certainly be a need for urgent legislative action but that is not beyond reasonable expectation.

Note

The doctrine of fundamental breach lived on for another fourteen years, despite the admonitions of the House of Lords in *Suisse Atlantique*.

In **Photo Production Ltd *v* Securicor Transport Ltd [1980] 2 WLR 283** the House of Lords overruled the doctrine. Although Lord Diplock's judgment in that case gives an excellent jurisprudential analysis of the nature of an exemption clause, the judgment of Lord Wilberforce examines the policy issues with great clarity.

Lord Wilberforce:

My Lords, this appeal arises from the destruction by fire of the respondents' factory involving loss and damage agreed to amount to £615,000. The question is whether the appellant is liable to the respondents for this sum.

The appellant is a company which provides security services. In 1968 it entered into a contract with the respondents by which for a charge of £8 15s 0d (old currency) per week it agreed to 'provide their night patrol service whereby four visits per night shall be made seven nights per week and two visits shall be made during the afternoon of Saturday and four visits shall be made during the day of Sunday.' The contract incorporated printed standard conditions which, in some circumstances, might exclude or limit the appellant's liability. The questions in this appeal are (i) whether these conditions can be invoked at all in the events which happened and (ii) if so, whether either the exclusion provision, or a provision limiting liability, can be applied on the facts. The trial judge (MacKenna J.) decided these issues in favour of the appellant. The Court of Appeal decided issue (i) in the respondents' favour invoking the doctrine of fundamental breach. Waller L.J. in addition would have decided for the respondents on issue (ii).

What happened was that on a Sunday night the duty employee of the appellant was one Musgrove. It was not suggested that he was unsuitable for the job or that the appellant was negligent in employing him. He visited the factory at the correct time, but when inside he deliberately started a fire by throwing a match on to some cartons. The fire got out of control and a large part of the premises was burnt down. Though what he did was deliberate, it was not established that he intended to destroy the factory. The judge's finding was in these words: 'Whether Musgrove intended to light only a small fire (which was the very least he meant to do) or whether he intended to cause much more serious damage, and, in either case, what was the reason for his act, are mysteries I am unable to solve.' This, and it is important to bear it in mind when considering the judgments in the Court of Appeal, falls short of a finding that Musgrove deliberately burnt or intended to burn the respondents' factory.

The condition upon which the appellant relies reads, relevantly, as follows:

> Under no circumstances shall the company [Securicor] be responsible for any injurious act or default by any employee of the company unless such act or default could have been foreseen and avoided by the exercise of due diligence on the part of the company as his employer; nor, in any event, shall the company be held responsible for (a) any loss suffered by the customer through burglary, theft fire or any other cause, except insofar as such loss is solely attributable to the negligence of the company's employees acting within the course of their employment. . . .

There are further provisions limiting to stated amounts the liability of the appellant upon which it relies in the alternative if held not to be totally exempt.

It is first necessary to decide upon the correct approach to a case such as this where it is sought to invoke an exception or limitation clause in the contract. The approach of Lord Denning M.R. in the Court of Appeal was to consider first whether the breach was 'fundamental'. If so, he said, the court itself deprives the party of the benefit of an exemption or limitation clause ([1978] 1 WLR 856, 863). Shaw and Waller L.JJ. substantially followed him in this argument.

Lord Denning M.R. in this was following the earlier decision of the Court of Appeal, and in particular his own judgment in *Harbutts 'Plasticine' Ltd v Wayne Tank & Pump Co. Ltd* [1970] 1 QB 447. In that case Lord Denning M.R. distinguished two cases (a) the case where as the result of a breach of contract the innocent party has, and exercises, the right to bring the contract to an end, (b) the case where the breach automatically brings the contract to an end, without the innocent party having to make an election whether to terminate the contract or to continue it. In the first case the Master of the Rolls, purportedly applying this House's decision in *Suisse Atlantique Société d'Armement Maritime S.A. v N.V. Rotterdamsche Kolen Centrale* [1967] 1 AC 361, but in effect two citations from two of their Lordships' speeches, extracted a rule of law that the 'termination' of the contract brings it, and with it the exclusion clause, to an end. The *Suisse Atlantique* case in his view 'affirms the long line of cases in this court that when one party has been guilty of a fundamental breach of the contract . . . and the other side accepts it, so that the contract comes to an end . . . then the guilty party cannot rely on an exception or limitation clause to escape from his liability for the breach' (*Harbutt's* case [1970] 1 QB 447, 467). He then applied the same principle on the second case.

My Lords, whatever the intrinsic merit of this doctrine, as to which I shall have something to say later, it is clear to me that so far from following this House's decision in the *Suisse Atlantique* it is directly opposed to it and that the whole purpose and tenor of the *Suisse Atlantique* was to repudiate it. The lengthy, and perhaps I may say some-times indigestible speeches of their Lordships, are correctly summarised in the head-note—holding No. 3 [1967] 1 AC 361, 362—'That the question whether an exceptions clause was applicable where there was a fundamental breach of contract was one of the true construction of the contract.' That there was any rule of law by which exceptions clauses are eliminated, or deprived of effect, regardless of their terms, was clearly not the view of Viscount Dilhorne, Lord Hodson, or of myself. The passages invoked for the contrary view of a rule of law consist only of short extracts from two of the speeches—on any view a minority. But the case for the doctrine does not even go so far as that. Lord Reid, in my respectful opinion, and I recognise that I may not be the best judge of this matter, in his speech read as a whole, cannot be claimed as a supporter of a rule of law. Indeed he expressly disagreed with the Master of the Rolls' observations in two previous cases (*Karsales (Harrow) Ltd v Wallis* [1956] 1 WLR 936 and U.G.S. *Finance Ltd v National Mortgage Bank of Greece and National Bank of Greece* S.A. [1964] 1 Lloyd's Rep. 446 in which he had put forward the 'rule of law' doctrine. In order to show how close the disapproved doctrine is to that sought to be revived in *Harbutt's* case I shall quote one passage from *Karsales* [1956] 1 WLR 936, 940:

> Notwithstanding earlier cases which might suggest the contrary, it is now settled that exempting clauses of this kind, no matter how widely they are expressed, only avail the party when he is carrying out his contract in its essential respects. He is not allowed to use them as a cover for misconduct or indifference or to enable him to turn a blind eye to his obligations. They do not avail him when he is guilty of a breach which goes to the root of the contract.

Lord Reid comments at p. 401 as to this that he could not deduce from the authorities cited in *Karsales* that the proposition stated in the judgments could be regarded as in any way 'settled law'. His conclusion is stated on p. 405: 'In my view no such rule of law ought to be adopted'—adding that there is room for legislative reform.

My Lords, in the light of this, the passage cited by Lord Denning M.R. [1970] 1 QB 447, 465 had to be considered. For convenience I restate it:

> If fundamental breach is established the next question is what effect, if any, that has on the applicability of other terms of the contract. This question has often arisen with regard to clauses excluding liability, in whole or in part, of the party in breach. I do not think that there is generally much difficulty where the innocent party has elected to treat the breach as a repudiation, bring the contract to an end and sue for damages. Then the whole contract has ceased to exist including the exclusion clause, and I do not see how that clause can then be used to exclude an action for loss which will be suffered by the innocent party after it has ceased to exist, such as loss of the profit which would have accrued if the contract had run its full term. (*Suisse Atlantique* [1967] 1 AC 361, 398).

It is with the utmost reluctance that, not forgetting the 'beams' that may exist elsewhere, I have to detect here a note of ambiguity or perhaps even of inconsistency. What is referred to is 'loss which will be suffered by the innocent party after [the contract] has ceased to exist' and I venture to think that all that is being said, rather elliptically, relates only to what is to happen in the future, and is not a proposition as to the immediate consequences caused by the breach: if it were that would be inconsistent with the full and reasoned discussion which follows.

It is only because of Lord Reid's great authority in the law that I have found it necessary to embark on what in the end may be superfluous analysis. For I am convinced that, with the possible exception of Lord Upjohn whose critical passage, when read in full, is somewhat ambiguous, their Lordships, fairly read, can only be taken to have rejected those suggestions for a rule of law which had appeared in the Court of Appeal and to have firmly stated that the question is one of construction not merely of course of the exclusion clause alone, but of the whole contract.

Much has been written about the *Suisse Atlantique* case. Each speech has been subjected to various degrees of analysis and criticism, much of it constructive. Speaking for myself I am conscious of imperfections of terminology, though sometimes in good company. But I do not think that I should be conducing to the clarity of the law by adding to what was already too ample a discussion a further analysis which in turn would have to be interpreted. I have no second thoughts as to the main proposition that the question whether, and to what extent, an exclusion clause is to be applied to a fundamental breach, or a breach of a fundamental term, or indeed to any breach of contract, is a matter of construction of the contract. Many difficult questions arise and will continue to arise in the infinitely varied situations in which contracts come to be breached—by repudiatory breaches, accepted or not, by anticipatory breaches, by breaches of conditions or of various terms and whether by negligent, or deliberate action or otherwise. But there are ample resources in the normal rules of contract law for dealing with these without the superimposition of a judicially invented rule of law. I am content to leave the matter there with some supplementary observations.

1. The doctrine of 'fundamental breach' in spite of its imperfections and doubtful parentage has served a useful purpose. There was a large number of problems, productive of injustice, in which it was worse than unsatisfactory to leave exception clauses to operate. Lord Reid referred to these in the *Suisse Atlantique* case [1967] 1 AC 361, 406, pointing out at the same time that the doctrine of fundamental breach was a dubious specific. But since then Parliament has taken a hand: it has passed the Unfair Contract Terms Act 1977. This Act applies to consumer contracts and those based on standard terms and enables exception clauses to be applied with regard to what is just and reasonable. It is significant that Parliament refrained from legislating over the whole field of contract. After this Act, in commercial matters generally, when the parties are not of unequal bargaining power, and when risks are normally borne by insurance, not only is the case for judicial intervention undemonstrated, but there is everything to be said, and this seems to have been Parliament's intention, for leaving the parties free to apportion the risks as they think fit and for respecting their decisions.

At the stage of negotiation as to the consequences of a breach, there is everything to be said for allowing the parties to estimate their respective claims according to the contractual provisions they have themselves made, rather than for facing them with a legal complex so uncertain as the doctrine of fundamental breach must be. What, for example, would have been the position of the respondents' factory if instead of being destroyed it had been damaged, slightly or moderately or severely? At what point does the doctrine (with what logical justification I have not understood) decide, *ex post facto*, that the breach was (factually) fundamental before going on to ask whether legally it is to be regarded as fundamental? How is the date of 'termination' to be fixed? Is it the date of the incident causing the damage, or the date of the innocent party's election, or some other date? All these difficulties arise from the doctrine and are left unsolved by it.

Note

Later Irish cases show that judges are unwilling to apply fundamental breach, notwithstanding the fact that the Supreme Court has not had occasion to review Clayton Love: see the extract at the end of *Regan v* RIAC at p. 437 above. The English High Court has recently declined Counsel's invitation to re-instate the fundamental breach doctrine: *Decoma* UK *v Haden Drysys International* [2005] EWHCC 2948(TCC). In contrast, the Canadian Courts have retained a fundamental breach doctrine in cases where the contracting parties do not possess parity of knowledge or superior bargaining power is abused: *Hunter Engineering Co. v Syncrude Canada Ltd* [1989] 57 DLR (4th) 321; *Prairie Petroleum Products Ltd v Husky Oil Ltd* [2006] 11 WWR 606.

SECTION FOUR—CONSUMER SALE TRANSACTIONS

A. STATUTORY CONTROL OF EXEMPTION CLAUSES

Note

In the area of railway transport, parliamentary regulation of the use of limiting clauses occurred in 1854 by way of the Railway and Canal Traffic Act of that year—see *Boland v Waterford, Limerick and Western Rly Co.* (1897) 31 ILTR 62. However, this legislation, which gave the courts the power to either declare contractual conditions *per se* invalid, and subject other clauses to scrutiny, by reference to whether they were unjust or unreasonable or not, was the exception that proved the rule. As Andrews J. said in *Devitt v The Glasgow, Dublin and Londonderry Steampacket Co.* (1894) 29 ILTR 30, 'Railway companies and other carriers by land are more restricted than carriers by sea; the latter may, in the absence of fraud inducing the shipper to enter the contract, make almost any conceivable contract.'

In sale of goods law, the Sale of Goods Act 1893 initially reinforced and improved the common-law rights of the buyer by implying into every contract for the sale of goods certain statutory conditions and warranties. However, these implied terms could be displaced by a properly worded exemption clause—see *Andrews Bros (Bournemouth) Ltd v Singer and Co. Ltd* (p. 428 above).

The implied conditions and warranties found in the Sale of Goods and Supply of Services Act 1980 however (pp 376–7 above) cannot be excluded by an exemption clause as a matter of course. Consumer sale transactions, as defined in s. 3, are subject to s. 22 which provides that exemption clauses in these contracts are void. The crucial issue is whether the buyer deals as consumer.

O'Callaghan *v* Hamilton Leasing (Ireland) Ltd [1984] ILRM 146

McWilliam J.:

The plaintiff owned and operated a take away food shop known as The Magnet Take Away Foods at Main Street, Dunleer, Co. Louth. The shop sold chips, hamburgers, ice-cream, minerals and other similar types of food. There was a cigarette vending machine in the premises. In March 1982 the plaintiff purchased from the second-named defendant (Access Refrigeration) a machine known as a 'Slush Puppy Iced Drink Dispensing Machine' for use in his shop. This machine produced fruit drinks containing crushed ice.

The plaintiff himself dispensed them from the machine before serving them to his customers. The purchase was financed on foot of a leasing agreement concluded between the plaintiff and the first-named defendant (Hamilton Leasing) dated 12 March 1982. The plaintiff signed this agreement 'T/A The Magnet'. On foot of the agreement, the plaintiff leased from the first-named defendant for a period of sixty months the said machine at a quarterly rent of £210.00 plus VAT. The machine proved to be defective and after the plaintiff had made the first two quarterly payments he instituted proceedings in the Circuit Court claiming a refund of the monies paid by him to the first-named defendant, as well as damages for loss of profits. The second-named defendant was later joined as a co-defendant and on 7 July 1983 Judge Roe held that the plaintiff was entitled to succeed and entered judgment against both defendants in the sum of £1,112.50. He also ordered that the first-named defendant be indemnified against the decree by the second-named defendant. The first-named defendant appealed the decision but no Appeal was filed by the second-named defendant. At the hearing of the Appeal the first-named defendant did not contest the Circuit Court finding that the machine was defective or the damages decree. It disputed the Circuit Court finding against it, solely on the basis that the plaintiff, in entering into the said leasing agreement, was not dealing as a consumer within the meaning of s. 3 of the Sale of Goods and Supply of Services Act, 1980 and that, in consequence, was not entitled to succeed against the first-named defendant, either under ss 14 or 38 of the said Act. Mr Justice McWilliam heard evidence from the plaintiff as to the nature of his business and the circumstances surrounding the conclusion of the leasing agreement. He also heard evidence from a representative of the first-named defendant, to the effect that it was its policy to only conclude leasing agreements with firms, companies or persons carrying on business.

S. 3 of the Sale of Goods and Supply of Services Act, 1980 provides as follows:

> (1) In the Act of 1893 and this Act the party to a contract is said to deal as consumer in relation to another party if:
>
>> (a) he neither makes the contract in the course of a business nor holds himself out as doing so, and
>> (b) the other party does make the contract in the course of a business, and
>> (c) the goods or services supplied under or in pursuance of the contract are of a type ordinarily supplied for private use or consumption.
>
> (2) On:
>
>> (a) a sale by competitive tender, or
>> (b) a sale by auction:
>>
>>> (i) of goods of a type, or
>>> (ii) by or on behalf of a person of a class
>>
>> defined by the Minister by Order,
>
> the buyer is not in any circumstances to be regarded as dealing as consumer.
>
> (3) Subject to this, it is for those claiming that a party does not deal as consumer to show that he does not.

The defendant, Hamilton Leasing (Ireland) Ltd can only be liable to the plaintiff under s. 14 of the Sale of Goods and Supply of Services Act, 1980 if the plaintiff was a buyer dealing as a consumer within the meaning of sub-s. (1) of s. 3 of the Act.

It seems to me that this contract was made in the course of the plaintiff's business. It was certainly made for the purposes of his business although I appreciate the point made on behalf of the plaintiff that this business does not in any way include a re-sale or further dealing with the goods dealt with by the contract before me.

In order to interpret the words of s. 3 otherwise I would have to amend para. (a) of sub-s. (1) by reading it as though it provided 'in the course of a business which includes a further dealing with the goods' or some words of that sort.

I cannot depart from the clear words of a statute and try to construe it in accordance with my view of an unexpressed intention of the legislature although I suspect the legislature was more concerned with the business of engaging in further dealings with the goods.

With regard to para. (c) of the subsection, I am of opinion that the expression 'ordinarily supplied for private use or consumption' should be contrasted with use for the purposes of a business rather than contrasted with use for the purpose of re-sale of or further dealings with the goods. These goods were supplied for the purpose of a business and it has not been suggested that they would ever be supplied for use other than for the purpose of a business.

Accordingly, although these goods were supplied for the personal use of the plaintiff and he is the consumer in the ordinarily accepted meaning of the word, I must hold that, in this transaction, he did not 'deal as consumer' within the meaning of the Act.

Judge McWilliam then varied the Order of the Circuit Court by allowing the first-named defendant's appeal and dismissing the plaintiff's claim against it. He allowed the first-named defendant its costs in both courts but directed that the plaintiff be indemnified against same by the second-named defendant.

Cunningham *v* Woodchester Investments Ltd (HC) 16 November 1984, unrep.

McWilliam J.:

The defendant, Woodchester Investments Ltd [trading as Hamilton Executive Services] (hereinafter called Hamilton) agreed to lease to the plaintiff a telephone system which it had been agreed would be supplied to the plaintiff by the defendant, Inter-Call Limited (hereinafter called Inter-Call). The plaintiff was then the bursar of the Salesian Agricultural College at Warrenstown, Co. Meath, which, at the time of the agreement, had a manual telephone system with fifteen extensions. Eight more were required and it was decided, on the recommendation of Inter-Call, to install a complete new electronic system as being more efficient for the purposes of the college.

The installation was not completed by Inter-Call and what was installed was most unsatisfactory. This was not contested by Hamilton.

Inter-Call did not enter an appearance or contest the claim and judgment was given in the Circuit Court against both defendants on 11 June 1984. Hamilton at all times denied liability and has appealed the judgment against it.

The plaintiff stated that the college is a non-profit-making venture but, in addition to training students in agriculture, the college sells very considerable quantities of farm produce, including cattle, pigs, vegetables, mushrooms and eggs, with a turnover approaching £1,000,000. The plaintiff stated that all money earned was put back into the farm.

Condition 2 of the leasing agreement provided as follows: 'The lessee's acceptance of delivery of the equipment shall be conclusive evidence that the lessee has examined the equipment and found it to be complete, in accordance with the description overleaf, in good order and condition, fit for the purpose for which it may be required, and in every way satisfactory.'

The plaintiff relies on the provisions of s. 14 of the Sale of Goods and Supply of Services Act, 1980, which provides as follows:

> Where goods are sold to a buyer dealing as consumer and in relation to the sale an agreement is entered into by the buyer with another person acting in the course of a business (in this section referred to as a finance house) for the repayment to the finance house of money paid by the finance house to the seller in respect of the price of the goods, the finance house shall be deemed to be a party to the sale and the finance house and the seller shall, jointly and severally, be answerable to the buyer for breach of the contract of sale and for any misrepresentations made by the seller with regard to the goods.

The plaintiff was the buyer within the section and, to benefit from its provisions, must have been buying as consumer within the meaning of the Act. 'Consumer' is construed at s. 3 of the Act. This section provides:

(1) In the Act of 1893 and this Act, a party to a contract is said to deal as consumer in relation to another party if:
   (a) he neither makes the contract in the course of a business nor holds himself out as doing so, and
   (b) the other party does make the contract in the course of a business, and
   (c) the goods or services supplied under or in pursuance of the contract are of a type ordinarily supplied for private use or consumption.

Hamilton relied on the provisions of condition 2 of the leasing agreement and also on the contention that the plaintiff was not a 'consumer' within the meaning of the Act. I was referred to my own decision in *O'Callaghan v Hamilton Leasing (Ireland) Ltd* [1984] 4 ILRM 146.

I do not accept that condition 2 can apply where only a part of the equipment was delivered. An argument advanced on behalf of the plaintiff that this condition should not be enforceable unless it was fair and reasonable seems to depend on the provisions of s. 31 which, under the provisions of s. 38, appear to apply only to lettings to a person dealing with a consumer, which is the situation arising under s. 14.

Whatever may be done with the profits accruing from the extensive agricultural activities carried on at Warrenstown, I do not see how it can be said that engaging in these activities with a turnover of the amount indicated does not constitute carrying on a business. The evidence indicated that the equipment to be supplied was mainly or largely to be used in the course of the farming activities, although I am sure it was also to be used for other purposes of the college as well. Furthermore, the equipment was quite clearly not of a type ordinarily supplied for private use or consumption.

No argument has been advanced in this case which persuades me that I should alter the view I formed in *O'Callaghan's* case.

Finally, it was suggested on behalf of the plaintiff that he was entitled to succeed at common law on the grounds that he did not get what was agreed to be supplied, that the equipment was not merchantable or fit for the purpose for which it was supplied and that what was delivered was not complete. This may be correct as against Inter-Call but, with regard to Hamilton, I was not referred to any authorities and I am not satisfied that there is any liability on a finance house in circumstances such as these.

Accordingly, I must, somewhat reluctantly, reverse the decision of the Circuit Court.

B. Is the Implied Term Broken?

If the buyer cannot be in any sense considered to purchase goods in the course of a business, the seller must seek to plead that the term has not been broken.

Two contrasting cases illustrate the tendency of Irish judges to find for the purchaser. The first is a Northern Ireland decision on the 'traditional' implied terms.

Lutton v Saville Tractors (Belfast) Ltd [1986] NI 327

Carswell J.:

This appeal from the County Court for the Division of Ards concerns defects found to exist in a secondhand car bought by the plaintiff and the remedies which he seeks to obtain because of their existence, but its apparent simplicity masks quite a considerable degree of complexity in the points of law involved and difficulty in determining the issues.

The plaintiff never found this car satisfactory and returned it constantly with lists of complaints. I did receive the impression that he was an owner who liked everything to be in as near perfect order as possible and that he had demanding standards for the performance and condition of his cars. I do not think, however, that his complaints were unfounded, and the fact that he regarded minor defects as requiring attention where less particular owners might have overlooked them does not necessarily make his complaints unreasonable. They have to be considered in the light of the type, age and cost of the car, and the fact that a three month warranty had been given with it. There was not a great deal of evidence before me about what a reasonable purchaser should expect to find when he buys a secondhand car like this one. It was established, however, that it was intended to be a car giving better than ordinary performance, and in modern conditions I think that a purchaser of a three year old car of a dependable make with a mileage of 32,000 at the price agreed could reasonably expect to find it performing well and free from minor defects, even if he is incautious enough to buy it without the opportunity of a road test or an expert's inspection.

The plaintiff's claim, as presented on the appeal before me, was based upon misrepresentation and breach of the conditions implied by statute in a sale of goods. He sought rescission of the sale and the return of the instalment paid and the value of the car which he traded in, together with damages. If he were not granted rescission, he sought damages by misrepresentation and breach of contract. I shall deal with these issues in turn.

I turn then to consideration of the terms as to quality and fitness implied by the law into contracts of hire-purchase where it is appropriate on the facts to do so. The plaintiff relied first upon s. 14(2) of the Sale of Goods Act 1979, which reads as follows:

> Where the seller sells goods in the course of a business, there is an implied condition that the goods supplied under the contract are of merchantable quality, except that there is no such condition:
>
> (a) as regards defects specifically drawn to the buyer's attention before the contract is made; or
> (b) if the buyer examines the goods before the contract is made, as regards defects which that examination ought to reveal.

Except for the fact that the battery was obviously flat, the provisos do not apply to this transaction. There was no evidence that any defect was drawn to the plaintiff's attention, and none of the defects of which he complains could have been revealed by any examination which he could have carried out.

'Merchantable quality' is defined by s. 14(6) in the following terms: 'Goods of any kind are of merchantable quality within the meaning of sub-s. (2) above if they are as fit for the purpose or purposes for which goods of that kind are commonly bought as it is reasonable to expect having regard to any description applied to them, the price (if relevant) and all the other relevant circumstances.' Much judicial ink has been spilled in explaining the meaning of the concept of merchantable quality, which did not have a statutory definition until the 1973 Act was passed. It is just as important not to modify a clear definition contained in a statute by incorporating inconsistent statements from previous judicial decisions as it is to avoid treating judicial observations made in the context of the facts and issues in particular cases as complete definitions. The statutory definition is generally regarded, however, as an attempt to codify the definitions advanced in the decided cases. In a case of the present nature I think that I derive most assistance from the test laid down by Dixon J. in the High Court of Australia in *Australian Knitting Mills Ltd v Grant* (1933) 50 CLR 387, 413, which was approved by several members of the House of Lords in *Henry Kendall & Sons v William Lillico & Sons Ltd* [1967] 2 AC 31: 'The condition that goods are of merchantable quality requires that they should be in such an actual state that a buyer fully acquainted with the facts and, therefore, knowing what hidden defects existed, and not being limited to their apparent condition would buy them without abatement of the price obtainable for such goods if in reasonably sound order and condition and without special terms.' This requires one qualification in particular, that the goods will only be unmerchantable where the price which would be paid by a buyer knowing of the defects is substantially lower than the contract price: see B. S. *Brown & Son Ltd v Craiks Ltd* [1970] 1 All ER 823.

Professor Atiyah points out in his book *The Sale of Goods*, (7th edn), 133, that the tests are somewhat circular in their reliance upon reasonableness and suggests that they are somewhat vacuous in practice and give little guidance as to what kind of defects or damage will render goods unmerchantable. Lord Denning M.R. stated, however, with his customary directness in *Cehave N. V. v Bremer Handelsgesellschaft* mbH [1976] QB 44, 62, that it is as well to remember that one is dealing with a condition breach of which entitles the buyer to reject the goods. He went on to say: 'In these circumstances I should have thought a fair way of testing merchantability would be to ask a commercial man: was the breach such that the buyer should be able to reject the goods?' In answering that he would have regard to the matters mentioned in the statutory definition, the purpose for which the goods are bought, the description applied to them and the price.

As so often, it is easier to state the law than to apply it to a specific case or type of cases. When one is dealing with secondhand goods which have defects not known to the buyer at the time of sale, it is particularly difficult to apply it. Defects which might entitle a buyer to reject a new car may not be sufficient to make a secondhand car unmerchantable—although even in the case of a new car the existence of a manufacturer's warranty may mean that a buyer cannot reject it over a minor repairable defect: see, e.g. *Millars of Falkirk Ltd v Turpie* [1976] SLT 66. On the other hand, I would venture to express some doubt whether it is necessary in every case of a sale of a secondhand car to go so far as to find that it is unsafe to be put on the road, which might appear from the tenor of the judgments in *Lee v York Coach & Marine* [1977] RTR 35. The English Court of Appeal has regularly held that a secondhand car must not be regarded as being of unmerchantable quality merely because it has a string of defects, and before this can be found it must be shown to be unroadworthy or even unsafe: see *Porter v General Guarantee Corp. Ltd* [1982] RTR 384, 393, per Kilner Brown J. A clear statement of this approach appears in the judgment of Lord Denning M.R. in *Bartlett v Sidney Marcus Ltd* [1965] 2 All ER 753, 755: 'A buyer should realise that, when he buys a secondhand car, defects may appear sooner or later; and, in the absence of an express warranty, he has no redress. Even when he buys from a dealer the most that he can require is that it should be reasonably fit for the purpose of being driven along the road.' As always, the context is vital, and his statement has to be read in that context. I should myself respectfully suggest that it is not universally valid in sales of second-hand cars, nor would Lord Denning have intended it to be. At the end of the day a decision whether a car is of merchantable quality is a matter of fact and degree, and it is essential to take account of the factors specified in the statutory definition.

It seems to me of critical importance to preserve a proper balance between the legitimate interests of vendors and purchasers in such sales. It would not make commercial sense that a buyer of a secondhand car should be entitled to return it and claim his money back if one or more minor faults developed, and applying Lord Denning's test in the *Cehave* case one is readily brought to the conclusion that this is not intended by the concept of merchantability. By the same token, I cannot think it right that the buyer should have to endure the burden of ownership of a car with a series of defects which are commercially intolerable in a car of the type and condition which he has bought, and should have to keep getting it repaired, restricting his claim to damages. At one end of the scale is the purchase of a seven year old family car with a high mileage at a low price. A buyer of such a car would not ordinarily expect that vehicle to be free of potentially troublesome defects, and if some developed during the first weeks after his purchase he would be unlikely to be able to return the car. At the other end is a transaction concerning a luxury car, a few months old and with a small mileage, for which the price is correspondingly high. The development of defects in such a car on a scale which the buyer would have to tolerate in the case of the elderly model might well be sufficient cause for rescission of the sale, because the parties contemplated that the car would give high performance and trouble-free motoring, and these characteristics were necessary to make it of merchantable quality in the circumstances of that transaction. In between these extremes it is a matter of fact and degree on which side of the line the case falls, but it is salutary nevertheless to bear in mind the warning issued by Lord Denning M.R. in *Bartlett v Sidney Marcus Ltd*.

The car which Mr Lutton bought was three years old, and at that age and with a mileage of some 32,000 it would in my view have been reasonable for him to expect some of the mechanical and electrical parts would be worn and would need replacement or repair. It may not have been realistic to expect the performance of the engine to be up to the standard of a new one. Nevertheless, I consider that such a car, sold at such price, should still be reliable and capable of giving good service and fair performance. I think that the giving of a three month warranty, which I believe to be common in sales by reputable dealers of the better type of secondhand car, is a relevant factor. It demonstrates that the parties to the transaction regard the car as one which ought to be expected to give a period of trouble-free motoring. It is also a safeguard to both parties, in that if minor faults develop the purchaser does not have to bear the cost of repair, but the vendor can discharge his obligations by carrying out the repairs without being expected to rescind the transaction and take the car back.

In my judgment the number and seriousness of the faults which were present or developed in the car the subject of this case were such that it was not of merchantable quality. I consider that the plaintiff was entitled to expect that it would be in much better condition on the purchase of a car of this age, type and mileage at the price he agreed. I do not think that he should be required to rely solely on having these faults repaired under the warranty, faithfully though Saville Motors observed its terms.

The other implied term upon which the plaintiff relied is contained in s. 14(3) of the Sale of Goods Act 1979, the material portion of which reads as follows:

Where the seller sells goods in the course of a business and the buyer, expressly or
by implication, makes known
(a) to the seller . . .
any particular purpose for which the goods are being bought, there is an implied
condition that the goods supplied under the contract are reasonably fit for that
purpose, whether or not that is a purpose for which such goods are commonly
supplied, except where the circumstances show that the buyer does not rely, or that
it is unreasonable for him to rely, on the skill or judgment of the seller or credit-
broker.

In view of my finding under s. 14(2) it is not strictly necessary for me to reach a decision
under s. 14(3), but since the issue was argued before me, and it is likely to arise fairly
regularly, I shall express my conclusions under it.

It may be seen that this sub-section removes the need for the purchaser to prove *in
limine* that he relied upon the seller's skill and judgment (see s. 14(1) of the Sale of
Goods Act, 1893). It is now reduced to a matter upon which the seller may rely by way
of defence, as an exception to the liability which may be imposed on him as a seller of
goods in the course of a business. One may dispose of it shortly by saying that it does
not arise in the present case, since the plaintiff was unusually dependent on the salesman in the circumstances, and it was not suggested to him in cross-examination that
he formed his own independent judgment and relied solely upon it.

Under the decisions given on s. 14(1) of the Sale of Goods Act 1893, it was well
settled that the word 'particular' was used in the sense 'specified' rather than in contradistinction to 'general'; *Henry Kendall & Sons v William Lillico Sons Ltd* [1969] 2 AC 31, 123,
per Lord Wilberforce. The purpose may in fact be a very general purpose, for example, a
car to drive on the road: Atiyah, (op. cit.), p. 141. It has also been held that the phrase
'particular purpose' would apply even if the goods could only be used for one purpose
in the ordinary way. As Lord Wright said in *Grant v Australian Knitting Mills Ltd* [1936] AC
84, 99: 'There is no need to specify in terms the particular purpose for which the buyer
requires the goods, which is nonetheless the particular purpose within the meaning of
the section, because it is the only purpose for which anyone would ordinarily want the
goods.' The change of wording from 'the particular purpose' in the 1893 Act to 'any
particular purpose' in the 1979 Act seems to me to confirm the effect of those decisions.

I consider that the plaintiff impliedly made known to the dealers his purpose in
taking the car, which was the only purpose for which anyone would ordinarily want it,
viz. to have a means of transport which was reasonably suitable to drive. I would express
it in these terms rather than the narrower purpose stated by Lord Denning M.R. in
Bartlett v Sidney Marcus Ltd, as 'a motor car to drive along the road'. Even under that
narrower definition, however, I think that the present car fell short of the required
standard of being reasonably fit for the purpose, and *a fortiori* if one defines the
purpose as I have done. It is clear from Lord Reid's speech in *Henry Kendall & Sons v
William Lillico & Sons Ltd* that the statutory condition covers not only defects which the
seller or dealer ought to have detected but also defects which are latent in the sense
that even the utmost skill and judgment on the part of the seller would not have
detected them. I therefore hold that there was in the present case a breach of both
s. 14(2) and s. 14(3) of the Sale of Goods Act 1979.

Each of the implied terms which I have discussed ranks as a condition, with the
concomitant right on the part of the purchaser to reject the goods for breach of
condition and obtain the return of his money.

Note

The implied terms pleaded in *Lutton* are substantially identical to those found in the Sale of Goods and Supply of Services Act 1980. However, s. 13 of that Act adds a further implied condition that a motor vehicle supplied under a contract will be free from any defect that would render the vehicle a danger to members of the public, including those travelling within the vehicle.

Glorney v O'Brien (HC) 14 November 1988, unrep. decided that liability in damages will extend to even the most venerable or decrepit motor vehicle and that the court will not readily accept a plea that the vehicle was sold for spare parts rather than use on the road.

C. THE FAIR AND REASONABLE TEST

If the buyer of goods, or the hirer of goods under a contract of hire-purchase, does not deal as consumer, an exclusion clause may operate if the clause is fair and reasonable within the Schedule of the 1980 Act. This legislative provision was modelled upon the UK Supply of Goods (Implied Terms) Act 1973.

The leading case on that Act is **George Mitchell (Chesterhall) Ltd v Finney Lock Seeds [1983] 2 AC 805.**

Lord Bridge of Harwich:

My Lords, the appellants are seed merchants. The respondents are farmers in East Lothian. In December 1973 the respondents ordered from the appellants 30lb of Dutch winter white cabbage seeds. The seeds supplied were invoiced as 'Finney's Late Dutch Special'. The price was £201.60. 'Finney's Late Dutch Special' was the variety required by the respondents. It is a Dutch winter white cabbage which grows particularly well in the area of East Lothian where the respondents farm, and can be harvested and sold at a favourable price in the spring. The respondents planted some 63 acres of their land with seedlings grown from the seeds supplied by the appellants to produce their cabbage crop for the spring of 1975. In the event, the crop proved to be worthless and had to be ploughed in. This was for two reasons. First, the seeds supplied were not 'Finney's Late Dutch Special' or any other variety of Dutch winter white cabbage, but a variety of autumn cabbage. Secondly, even as autumn cabbage the seeds were of very inferior quality.

The issues in the appeal arise from three sentences in the conditions of sale endorsed on the appellants' invoice and admittedly embodied in the terms on which the appellants contracted. For ease of reference it will be convenient to number the sentences. Omitting immaterial words they read as follows:

1. In the event of any seeds or plants sold or agreed to be sold by us not complying with the express terms of the contract of sale . . . or any seeds or plants proving defective in varietal purity we will, at our option, replace the defective seeds or plants, free of charge to the buyer or will refund all payments made to us by the buyer in respect of the defective seeds or plants and this shall be the limit of our obligation.

2. We hereby exclude all liability for any loss or damage arising from the use of any seeds or plants supplied by us and for any consequential loss or damage arising out of such use or any failure in the performance of or any defect in any seeds or plants supplied by us or for any other loss or damage whatsoever save for, at our option, liability for any such replacement or refund as aforesaid.

3. In accordance with the established custom of the seed trade any express or implied condition, statement or warranty, statutory or otherwise, not stated in these conditions is hereby excluded.

I will refer to the whole as 'the relevant condition' and to the parts as 'clauses 1, 2 and 3' of the relevant condition.

The first issue is whether the relevant condition, on its true construction in the context of the contract as a whole, is effective to limit the appellants' liability to a refund of £201.60, the price of the seeds ('the common law issue'). The second issue is whether, if the common law issue is decided in the appellants' favour, they should nevertheless be precluded from reliance on this limitation of liability pursuant to the provisions of the modified s. 55 of the Sale of Goods Act 1979 which is set out in para. 11 of Schedule 1 to the Act and which applies to contracts made between 18 May 1973, and 1 February 1978 ('the statutory issue').

The learned trial judge, Parker J. [1981] 1 Lloyd's Rep. 476, 480, on the basis of evidence that the seeds supplied were incapable of producing a commercially saleable crop, decided the common law issue against the appellants on the ground that 'what was supplied . . . . was in no commercial sense vegetable seed at all' but was 'the delivery of something wholly different in kind from that which was ordered and which the defendants had agreed to supply.' He accordingly found it unnecessary to decide the statutory issue, but helpfully made some important findings of fact, which are very relevant if that issue falls to be decided. He gave judgment in favour of the respondents for £61,513.78 damages and £30,756.00 interest. Nothing now turns on these figures, but it is perhaps significant to point out that the damages awarded do not represent merely 'loss of anticipated profit', as was erroneously suggested in the appelants' printed case. The figure includes, as [counsel] very properly accepted, all the costs incurred by the respondents in the cultivation of the worthless crop as well as the profit they would have expected to make from a successful crop if the proper seeds had been supplied.

In the Court of Appeal, the common law issue was decided in favour of the appellants by Lord Denning M.R. [1983] QB 284, 296 who said: 'On the natural interpretation, I think the condition is sufficient to limit the seed merchants to a refund of the price paid or replacement of the seeds.' Oliver L.J. [1983] QB 284, 305, 306, decided the common law issue against the appellants primarily on a ground akin to that of Parker J., albeit somewhat differently expressed. Fastening on the words 'agreed to be sold' in clause 1 of the relevant condition, he held that the clause could not be construed to mean 'in the event of the seeds sold or agreed to be sold by us not being the seeds agreed to be sold by us.' Clause 2 of the relevant condition he held to be 'merely a supplement' to clause 1. He thus arrived at the conclusion that the appellants had only succeeded in limiting their liability arising from the supply of seeds which were correctly described as 'Finney's Late Dutch Special' but were defective in quality. As the seeds supplied were not 'Finney's Late Dutch Special', the relevant condition gave them no protection. Kerr L.J. [1983] QB 284, 313, in whose reasoning Oliver L.J. also concurred, decided the common law issue against the appellants on the ground that the relevant condition was ineffective to limit the appellants' liability for a breach of contract which could not have occurred without negligence on the appellants' part, and that the supply of the wrong variety of seeds was such a breach.

The Court of Appeal, however, were unanimous in deciding the statutory issue against the appellants.

In his judgment, Lord Denning M.R. traces, in his uniquely colourful and graphic style, the history of the courts' approach to contractual clauses excluding or limiting liability, culminating in the intervention of the legislature, first by the Supply of Goods (Implied Terms) Act 1973, secondly, by the Unfair Contract Terms Act 1977. My Lords, in considering the common law issue, I will resist the temptation to follow that fascinating trail, but will content myself with references to the two recent decisions of your Lordships' House commonly called the two *Securicor* cases: *Photo Production Ltd v Securicor Transport Ltd* [1980] AC 827 ('*Securicor 1*') and *Ailsa Craig Fishing Co. Ltd v Malvern Fishing Co. Ltd* [1983] 1 WLR 964 ('*Securicor 2*').

Securicor 1 gave the final quietus to the doctrine that a 'fundamental breach' of contract deprived the party in breach of the benefit of clauses in the contract excluding or limiting his liability. *Securicor 2* drew an important distinction between exclusion and limitation clauses. This is clearly stated by Lord Fraser of Tullybelton, at p. 105:

> There are later authorities which lay down very strict principles to be applied when considering the effect of clauses of exclusion or of indemnity: see particularly the Privy Council case of *Canada Steamship Lines Ltd v The King* [1952] AC 192, 208, where Lord Morton, delivering the advice of the board, summarised the principles in terms which have recently been applied by this House in *Smith v U.M.B. Chrysler (Scotland) Ltd*, 1978 SC (HL) 1. In my opinion these principles are not applicable in their full rigour when considering the effect of conditions merely limiting liability. Such conditions will of course be read *contra proferentem* and must be clearly expressed, but there is no reason why they should be judged by the specially exacting standards which are applied to exclusion and indemnity clauses.

My Lords, it seems to me, with all due deference, that the judgments of the learned trial judge and of Oliver L.J. on the common law issue come dangerously near to re-introducing by the back door the doctrine of 'fundamental breach' which this House in *Securicor 1* [1980] AC 827, had so forcibly evicted by the front. The learned judge discusses what I may call the 'peas and beans' or 'chalk and cheese' cases, sc. those in which it has been held that exemption clauses do not apply where there has been a contract to sell one thing, e.g a motor car, and the seller has supplied quite another thing, e.g. a bicycle. I hasten to add that the judge can in no way be criticised for adopting this approach since counsel appearing for the appellants at the trial had conceded 'that if what had been delivered had been beetroot seed or carrot seed, he would not be able to rely upon the clause': [1981] 1 Lloyd's Rep. 476, 479. Different counsel appeared for the appellants in the Court of Appeal, where that concession was withdrawn.

In my opinion, this is not a 'peas and beans' case at all. The relevant condition applies to 'seeds'. Clause 1 refers to seeds 'sold' and 'seeds agreed to be sold'. Clause 2 refers to 'seeds supplied'. As I have pointed out, Oliver L.J. concentrates his attention on the phrase 'seeds agreed to be sold'. I can see no justification, with respect, for allowing this phrase alone to dictate the interpretation of the relevant condition, still less for treating clause 2 as 'merely a supplement' to clause 1. Clause 2 is perfectly clear and unambiguous. The reference to 'seeds agreed to be sold' as well as to 'seeds sold' in clause 1 reflects the same dichotomy as the definition of 'sale' in the Sale of Goods Act 1979 as including a bargain and sale as well as a sale and delivery. The defective seeds in this case were seeds sold and delivered, just as clearly as they were seeds supplied, by the appellants to the respondents. The relevant condition, read as a whole, unambiguously limits the appellants' liability to replacement of the seeds or refund of the price. It is only possible to read an ambiguity into it by the process of strained construction which was deprecated by Lord Diplock in *Securicor* 1 and by Lord Wilberforce in *Securicor* 2.

In holding that the relevant condition was ineffective to limit the appellants' liability for a breach of contract caused by their negligence, Kerr L.J. applied the principles stated by Lord Morton of Henryton giving the judgment of the Privy Council in *Canada Steamship Lines Ltd v The King* [1952] AC 192, 208. The learned Lord Justice stated correctly that this case was also referred to by Lord Fraser of Tullybelton in *Securicor* 2. He omitted, however, to notice that, as appears from the passage from Lord Fraser's speech which I have already cited the whole point of Lord Fraser's reference was to express his opinion that the very strict principles laid down in the *Canada Steamship Lines* case as applicable to exclusion and indemnity clauses cannot be applied in their full rigour to limitation clauses. Lord Wilberforce's speech contains a passage to the like effect, and Lord Elwyn-Jones, Lord Salmon and Lord Lowry agreed with both speeches. Having once reached a conclusion in the instant case that the relevant condition unambiguously limited the appellants' liability, I know of no principle of construction which can properly be applied to confine the effect of the limitation to breaches of contract arising without negligence on the part of the appellants. In agreement with Lord Denning M.R., I would decide the common law issue in the appellants' favour.

The statutory issue turns, as already indicated, on the application of the provisions of the modified s. 55 of the Sale of Goods Act 1979, as set out in paragraph 11 of Schedule 1 of the Act. The Act of 1979 is a pure consolidation. The purpose of the modified s. 55 is to preserve the law as it stood from 18 May 1973, to 1 February 1978, in relation to contracts made between those two dates. The significance of the dates is that the first was the date when the Supply of Goods (Implied Terms) Act 1973 came into force containing the provision now re-enacted by the modified s. 55, the second was the date when the Unfair Contract Terms Act 1977 came into force and super-seded the relevant provisions of the Act of 1973 by more radical and far-reaching provisions in relation to contracts made thereafter.

The relevant subsections of the modified s. 55 provide as follows:

(1) Where a right, duty or liability would arise under a contract of sale of goods by implication of law, it may be negatived or varied by express agreement . . . but the preceding provision has effect subject to the following provisions of this section. . . .
(4) In the case of a contract of sale of goods, any term of that or any other contract exempting from all or any of the provisions of ss 13, 14 or 15 above is void in the case of a consumer sale and is, in any other case, not enforceable to the extent that it is shown that it would not be fair or reasonable to allow reliance on the term. (5) In determining for the purposes of sub-s. (4) above whether or not reliance on any such term would be fair or reasonable regard shall be had to all the circumstances of the case and in particular to the following matters—(a) the strength of the bargaining positions of the seller and buyer relative to each other, taking into account, among other things, the availability of suitable alternative products and sources of supply; (b) whether the buyer received an inducement to agree to the term or in accepting it had an opportunity of buying the goods or suitable altern-atives without it from any source of supply; (c) whether the buyer knew or ought reasonably to have known of the existence and extent of the term (having regard, among other things, to any custom of the trade and any previous course of dealing between the parties); (d) where the term exempts from all or any of the provisions of

ss 13, 14 or 15 above if some condition is not complied with, whether it was reasonable at the time of the contract to expect that compliance with that condition would be practicable; (e) whether the goods were manufactured, processed, or adapted to the special order of the buyer. . . . (9) Any reference in this section to a term exempting from all or any of the provisions of any section of this Act is a reference to a term which purports to exclude or restrict, or has the effect of excluding or restricting, the operation of all or any of the provisions of that section, or the exercise of a right conferred by any provision of that section, or any liability of the seller for breach of a condition or warranty implied by any provision of that section.

The contract between the appellants and the respondents was not a 'consumer sale', as defined for the purpose of these provisions. The effect of clause 3 of the relevant condition is to exclude, *inter alia*, the terms implied by ss 13 and 14 of the Act that the seeds sold by description should correspond to the description and be of merchantable quality and to substitute therefore the express but limited obligations undertaken by the appellants under clauses 1 and 2. The statutory issue, therefore, turns on the words in sub-s. (4) 'to the extent that it is shown that it would not be fair or reasonable to allow reliance on' this restriction of the appellants' liabilities, having regard to the matters referred to in sub-s. (5).

This is the first time your Lordships' House has had to consider a modern statutory provision giving the court power to override contractual terms excluding or restricting liability, which depends on the court's view of what is 'fair and reasonable'. The particular provision of the modified s. 55 of the Act of 1979 which applies in the instant case is of limited and diminishing importance. But the several provisions of the Unfair Contract Terms Act 1977 which depend on 'the requirement of reasonableness', defined in s. 11 by reference to what is 'fair and reasonable', albeit in a different context, are likely to come before the courts with increasing frequency. It may, therefore, be appropriate to consider how an original decision as to what is 'fair and reasonable' made in the application of any of these provisions should be approached by an appellate court. It would not be accurate to describe such a decision as an exercise of discretion. But a decision under any of the provisions referred to will have this in common with the exercise of a discretion, that, in having regard to the various matters to which the modified s. 55 (5) of the Act of 1979, or s. 11 of the Act of 1977 direct attention, the court must entertain a whole range of considerations, put them in the scales on one side or the other, and decide at the end of the day on which side the balance comes down. There will sometimes be room for a legitimate difference of judicial opinion as to what the answer should be, where it will be impossible to say that one view is demonstrably wrong and the other demonstrably right. It must follow, in my view, that, when asked to review such a decision on appeal, the appellate court should treat the original decision with the utmost respect and refrain from interference with it unless satisfied that it proceeded upon some erroneous principle or was plainly and obviously wrong.

Turning back to the modified s. 55 of the Act of 1979, it is common ground that the onus was on the respondents to show that it would not be fair or reasonable to allow the appellants to rely on the relevant condition as limiting their liability. It was argued for the appellants that the court must have regard to the circumstances as at the date of the contract, not after the breach. The basis of the argument was that this was the effect of s. 11 of the Act of 1977 and that it would be wrong to construe the modified s. 55 of the Act as having a different effect. Assuming the premise is correct, the conclusion does not follow. The provisions of the Act of 1977 cannot be considered in construing the prior enactment now embodied in the modified s. 55 of the Act of 1979.

But, in any event, the language of sub-ss (4) and (5) of that section is clear and unambiguous. The question whether it is fair or reasonable to allow reliance on a term excluding or limiting liability for a breach of contract can only arise after the breach. The nature of the breach and the circumstances in which it occurred cannot possibly be excluded from 'all the circumstances of the case' to which regard must be had.

The only other question of construction debated in the course of the argument was the meaning to be attached to the words 'to the extent that' in sub-s. (4) and, in particular, whether they permit the court to hold that it would be fair and reasonable to allow partial reliance on a limitation clause and, for example, to decide in the instant case that the respondents should recover, say, half their consequential damage. I incline to the view that, in their context, the words are equivalent to 'insofar as' or 'in circumstances in which' and do not permit the kind of judgment of Solomon illustrated by the example. But for the purpose of deciding this appeal I find it unnecessary to express a concluded view on this question.

My Lords, at long last I turn to the application of the statutory language to the circumstances of the case. Of the particular matters to which attention is directed by paras (a) to (e) of s. 55 (5), only those in (a) to (c) are relevant. As to para. (c), the respondents admittedly knew of the relevant condition (they had dealt with the appellants for many years) and, if they had read it, particularly clause 2, they would, I think, as laymen rather than lawyers, have had no difficulty in understanding what it said. This and the magnitude of the damages claimed in proportion to the price of the seeds sold are factors which weigh in the scales in the appellants' favour.

The question of relative bargaining strength under para. (a) and of the opportunity to buy seeds without a limitation of the seedsman's liability under para. (b) were interrelated. The evidence was that a similar limitation of liability was universally embodied in the terms of trade betwen seedsmen and farmers and had been so for very many years. The limitation had never been negotiated between representative bodies but, on the other hand, had not been the subject of any protest by the National Farmers' Union. These factors, if considered in isolation, might have been equivocal. The decisive factor, however, appears from the evidence of four witnesses called for the appellants, two independent seedsmen, the chairman of the appellant company, and a director of a sister company (both being wholly-owned subsidiaries of the same parent). They said that it had always been their practice, unsuccessfully attempted in the instant case, to negotiate settlements of farmers' claims for damages in excess of the price of the seeds, if they thought that the claims were 'genuine' and 'justified'. This evidence indicated a clear recognition by seedsmen in general, and the appellants in particular, that reliance on the limitation of liability imposed by the relevant condition would not be fair or reasonable.

Two further factors, if more were needed, weight the scales in favour of the respondents. The supply of autumn, instead of winter, cabbage seeds was due to the negligence of the appellants' sister company. Irrespective of its quality, the autumn variety supplied could not, according to the appellants' own evidence, be grown commercially in East Lothian. Finally, as the trial judge found, seedsmen could insure against the risk of crop failure caused by supplying the wrong variety of seeds without materially increasing the price of seeds.

My Lords, even if I felt doubts about the statutory issue, I should not, for the reasons explained earlier, think it right to interfere with the unanimous original decision of that issue by the Court of Appeal. As it is, I feel no such doubts. If I were making the original decision, I should conclude without hesitation that it would not be fair or reasonable to allow the appellants to rely on the contractual limitation of their liability.

I would dismiss the appeal.

(Brightman, Diplock, Scarman and Roskill L.JJ. concurred.)

The only Irish case decided on the fair and reasonable test is **McCarthy v Joe Walsh Tours [1991] ILRM 813**

Carroll J.:

The McCarthy family are the plaintiffs in this action. They booked a holiday with the defendants, Joe Walsh Tours Ltd, on 17 July 1989. The question before this court is whether their Circuit Court action claiming damages for breach of contract should be stayed under s. 5 of the Arbitration Act 1980, on the basis that there is an arbitration clause in the standard form contract signed by Mr McCarthy on behalf of the family when he booked the holiday.

Different reasons have been advanced on behalf of the plaintiffs as to why this court should refuse to stay their Circuit Court proceedings.

First, Mr McCarthy says that the contract was concluded only after he had already agreed details of the holiday with the defendants' representative in their office in Patrick Street, Cork. He considered the contract to be an oral contract. He says in his affidavit that when he was asked to sign a document he did so and paid the deposit and it was never indicated to him that the document contained any terms other than those which had been agreed and that he had no reason to suppose that the defendants were to introduce new terms into the written contract. He said that he was not offered any opportunity to read the document and that a copy of the document was not provided either before or after he signed it. The booking form which he signed contains a box for a signature which states:

> The terms and conditions (see over) of this booking form have been brought to my attention and have been read, understood and fully agreed to and accepted by me, both on behalf of all persons included herein and on my own behalf. I warrant and represent that all the information herein is true and accurate and that I have been duly authorised by all persons included on this form to execute this agreement on their behalf and accordingly I sign my name on their behalf and on my own.

I consider that it was not reasonable for Mr McCarthy to suppose that the contract which he had made was an oral one and that by signing the document he had added nothing to the oral agreement. There is no suggestion that he could not have taken time to read what he had signed or that he was prevented in any way from doing so. In my opinion, this booking form constituted the written agreement between the parties.

The second argument is that the contract and the arbitration clause is affected by Part IV of the Sale of Goods and Supply of Services Act 1980. The arbitration clause reads as follows:

> 15(c)(1) If any dispute or difference should arise out of or in respect of the agreement between the parties and or in respect of any matter, or thing, directly or indirectly touching, concerning or otherwise connected with the holiday transaction between the parties, the same shall be referred to arbitration with the arbitrator being the independent arbitrator for the time being under, and with such arbitration being in accordance with the rules, provisions of the ITAA arbitration scheme. This scheme, *inter alia*, limits the liability of the company, with specific provisions about costs, and places a time limit on invoking an arbitration. Details of the scheme are available at and from the ITAA offices. Please ask for a copy. It is hereby agreed

between the parties that such arbitration shall be a condition precedent to the commencement of any action of law.

S. 39 of the Sale of Goods and Supply of Services Act 1980, provides:

> Subject to s. 40, in every contract for the supply of a service where the supplier is acting in the course of a business, the following terms are implied:
>
> (a) that the supplier has the necessary skill to render the service,
> (b) that he will supply the service with due skill, care and diligence. . . .

S. 40(1) of that Act provides that any term of a contract implied by virtue of s. 39 may be 'negatived or varied', *inter alia*, by an express term of the contract 'except that where the recipient of the service deals as consumer it must be shown that the express term is fair and reasonable and has been specifically brought to his attention'. S. 40(3) explains the meaning of 'negative' and 'vary' in s. 40(1). S. 40(3) provides: 'The reference in subs. (1) to a term negativing or varying a term implied by s. 39 is a reference to a term which purports to exclude or restrict, or has the effect of excluding or restricting, the operation of any provision of that section, or the exercise of a right conferred by any provision of that section, or any liability of the supplier for breach of a term implied by any provision of that section.'

S. 40(2) adds to the definition of 'negative' by providing that 'an express term does not negative a term implied by this part unless inconsistent therewith'. The ITAA scheme itself limits liability of £5,000 for any claim. In addition, it excludes recovery in respect of personal injury although the latter exclusion is not relevant in the context of the present case as any allegation of personal injury is not substantiated by the pleadings. These limitations amount to provisions which restrict liability of the supplier for a breach of a term implied by s. 39 and are, therefore, a term 'varying' the terms implied by virtue of s. 39 into this contract. To be effective in a consumer contract such a term must be fair and reasonable and have been specifically brought to the consumer's attention. If the provisions restricting liability were contained in the general conditions of the contract then the arbitrator himself could decide whether or not the terms implied by s. 39 had been effectively negatived or varied. This would involve deciding whether the terms were fair and reasonable and had been specifically brought to the consumers' attention. However, in the present case the position is different. In this case it is the arbitration clause itself which incorporates the provisions of the ITAA scheme and an arbitrator appointed to administer that scheme could not enter into a deliberation going to his competence and enquire whether he was legally entitled to disregard the provisions of that scheme and, for example, award more than £5,000 for damages or award damages for personal injury. Therefore, since the arbitration clause is a term varying (within the meaning of s. 40 of the Act of 1980) the defendants' liability under the implied terms of s. 39 of the Act of 1980, it can only be effective in a consumer contract if it was 'fair and reasonable' and had been specifically brought to the attention of the plaintiffs.

Mr McCarthy, the first-named plaintiff, says in his affidavit, that at no time during or after negotiations was any mention made to him concerning what would happen if he was dissatisfied with the holiday or that any dispute between himself and the defendants would have to be referred to arbitration. That stands as an uncontested fact. To mention, as was done in the present case, the arbitration clause in general terms in the box for signature in the booking form is only giving general information. In order that the arbitration clause should be specifically brought to the attention of a consumer it would be necessary, in my opinion, that the consumer should be informed of the extent of the monetary limit of liability and any other limits on the defendants' liability. Accordingly, it is unnecessary for me to decide whether the arbitration term is 'fair and reasonable' as it is an uncontested fact that the arbitration clause was not specifically brought to the attention of the plaintiffs. Since this was not done, the arbitrator cannot apply the scheme.

I will therefore, make an order under s. 5 of the Arbitration Act 1980, refusing to refer the plaintiffs' action to arbitration on the ground that the arbitration clause in question is inoperative and incapable of being performed.

Note

In the US two 'statutory' solutions to problems of abuse of power have been suggested. The first, s. 2–302 of the Uniform Commercial Code, adopts a legislative position which empowers a court to rule on whether a clause is unconscionable or not. It was the product of Professor Llewellyn and critics of this approach argue that it is vague and difficult to apply consistently—see Leff (1967) 115 U.Pa L Rev. 485; contrast Ellinghaus, (1969) 78 Yale LJ 757.

The second approach is found in the **American Law Institute Restatement (2d) Contracts s. 208:**

Unconscionable Contract or Term

If a contract or term thereof is unconscionable at the time the contract is made a court may refuse to enforce the contract, or may enforce the remainder of the contract without the unconscionable term, or may so limit the application of any unconscionable term as to avoid any unconscionable result.

Comment:

a. *Scope*. Like the obligation of good faith and fair dealing (§205), the policy against unconscionable contracts or terms applies to a wide variety of types of conduct. The determination that a contract or term is or is not unconscionable is made in the light of its setting, purpose and effect. Relevant factors include weaknesses in the contracting process like those involved in more specific rules as to contractual capacity, fraud, and other invalidating causes; the policy also overlaps with rules which render particular bargains or terms unenforceable on grounds of public policy. Policing against unconscionable contracts or terms has sometimes been accomplished 'by adverse construction of language, by manipulation of the rules of offer and acceptance or by determinations that the clause is contrary to public policy or to the dominant purpose of the contract.' Uniform Commercial Code §2–302 Comment 1.

D. EUROPEAN COMMUNITY INITIATIVES

The European Communities have acted on many occasions by promoting legislation to protect consumers against improper bargaining techniques or pressurised sales techniques. Witness the so-called doorstep directive which provides cancellation rights in respect of contracts concluded away from business premises: see the European Communities (Cancellation of

Contracts Negotiated away from Business Premises) Regulations 1989 (SI No. 224 of 1989). In the area of package travel, the Travel Directive 90/314/EEC also provides protection to consumers who would otherwise be subject to broad exempting provisions, but this Directive has yet to be transposed into Irish law. Further proposed legislation includes community-wide protection for persons pressured into entering into holiday time-share contracts.

The Unfair Terms Directive, however, is the most important measure proposed to date. For an analysis see (1993) 56 MLR 581 (Dean).

Council Directive 93/13/EEC of 5 April 1993 on Unfair Terms in Consumer Contracts

THE COUNCIL OF THE EUROPEAN COMMUNITIES,

Having regard to the Treaty establishing the European Economic Community, and in particular Article 100 A thereof,

Having regard to the proposal from the Commission,[1]

In cooperation with the European Parliament,[2]

Having regard to the opinion of the Economic and Social Committee,[3]

Whereas it is necessary to adopt measures with the aim of progressively establishing the internal market before 31 December 1992; whereas the internal market comprises an area without internal frontiers in which goods, persons, services and capital move freely;

Whereas the laws of Member States relating to the terms of contract between the seller of goods or supplier of services, on the one hand, and the consumer to them, on the other hand, show many disparities, with the result that the national markets for the sale of goods and services to consumers differ from each other and that distortions of competition may arise amongst the sellers and suppliers, notably when they sell and supply in other Member States;

Whereas, in particular, the laws of Member States relating to unfair terms in consumer contracts show marked divergences;

Whereas it is the responsibility of the Member States to ensure that contracts concluded with consumers do not contain unfair terms;

Whereas, generally speaking, consumers do not know the rules of law which, in Member States other than their own, govern contracts for the sale of goods or services; whereas this lack of awareness may deter them from direct transactions for the purchase of goods or services in another Member State;

Whereas, in order to facilitate the establishment of the internal market and to safeguard the citizen in his role as consumer when acquiring goods and services under contracts which are governed by the laws of Member States other than his own, it is essential to remove unfair terms from those contracts;

Whereas sellers of goods and suppliers of services will thereby be helped in their task of selling goods and supplying services, both at home and throughout the internal market; whereas competition will thus be stimulated, so contributing to increased choice for Community citizens as consumers;

Whereas the two Community programmes for a consumer protection and information policy[4] underlined the importance of safeguarding consumers in the matter of unfair terms of contract; whereas this protection ought to be provided by laws and regulations which are either harmonised at Community level or adopted directly at that level;

Whereas in accordance with the principle laid down under the heading 'Protection of the economic interests of the consumers', as stated in those programmes: 'acquirers of goods and services should be protected against the abuse of power by the seller or supplier, in particular against one-sided standard contracts and the unfair exclusion of essential rights in contracts';

Whereas more effective protection of the consumer can be achieved by adopting uniform rules of law in the matter of unfair terms; whereas those rules should apply to all contracts concluded between sellers or suppliers and consumers; whereas as a result *inter alia* contracts relating to employment, contracts relating to rights under family law and contracts relating to the incorporation and organisation of companies or partnership agreements must be excluded from this Directive;

Whereas the consumer must receive equal protection under contracts concluded by word of mouth and written contracts regardless, in the latter case, of whether the terms of the contract are contained in one or more documents;

Whereas, however, as they now stand, national laws allow only partial harmonisation to be envisaged; whereas, in particular, only contractual terms which have not been individually negotiated are covered by this Directive; whereas Member States should have the option, with due regard for the Treaty, to afford consumers a higher level of protection through national provisions that are more stringent than those of this Directive;

Whereas the statutory or regulatory provisions of the Member States which directly or indirectly determine the terms of consumer contracts are presumed not to contain unfair terms; whereas, therefore, it does not appear to be necessary to subject the terms which reflect mandatory statutory or regulatory provisions and the principles or provisions of international conventions to which the Member States or the Community are party; whereas in that respect the wording 'mandatory statutory or regulatory provisions' in Article 1 (2) also covers rules which, according to the law, shall apply between the contracting parties provided that no other arrangements have been established;

Whereas Member States must however ensure that unfair terms are not included, particularly because this Directive also applies to trades, business or professions of a public nature;

Whereas it is necessary to fix in a general way the criteria for assessing the unfair character of contract terms;

Whereas the assessment, according to the general criteria chosen, of the unfair character of terms, in particular in sale or supply activities of a public nature providing collective services which take account of solidarity among users, must be supplemented by a means of making an overall evaluation of the different interests involved; whereas this constitutes the requirement of good faith; whereas, in making an assessment of good faith, particular regard shall be had to the strength of the bargaining positions of the parties, whether the consumer had an inducement to agree to the term and whether the goods or services were sold or supplied to the special order of the consumer; whereas the requirement of good faith may be satisfied by the seller or supplier where he deals fairly and equitably with the other party whose legitimate interests he has to take into account;

Whereas, for the purposes of this Directive, the annexed list of terms can be of indicative value only and, because of the cause of the minimal character of the Directive, the scope of these terms may be the subject of amplification or more restrictive editing by the Member States in their national laws;

Whereas the nature of goods or services should have an influence on assessing the unfairness of contractual terms;

Whereas, for the purposes of this Directive, assessment of unfair character shall not be made of terms which describe the main subject matter of the contract nor the quality/price ratio of the goods or services supplied; whereas the main subject matter of the contract and the price/quality ratio may nevertheless be taken into account in assessing the fairness of other terms; whereas it follows, *inter alia*, that in insurance contracts, the terms which clearly define or circumscribe the insured risk and the insurer's liability shall not be subject to such assessment since these restrictions are taken into account in calculating the premium paid by the consumer;

Whereas contracts should be drafted in plain, intelligible language, the consumer should actually be given an opportunity to examine all the terms and, if in doubt, the interpretation most favourable to the consumer should prevail;

Whereas Member States should ensure that unfair terms are not used in contracts concluded with consumers by a seller or supplier and that if, nevertheless, such terms are so used, they will not bind the consumer, and the contract will continue to bind the parties upon those terms if it is capable of continuing in existence without the unfair provisions;

Whereas there is a risk that, in certain cases, the consumer may be deprived of protection under this Directive by designating the law of a non-Member country as the law applicable to the contract; whereas provisions should therefore be included in this Directive designed to avert this risk;

Whereas persons or organisations, if regarded under the law of a Member State as having a legitimate interest in the matter, must have facilities for initiating proceedings concerning terms of contract drawn up for general use in contracts concluded with consumers, and in particular unfair terms, either before a court or before an administrative authority competent to decide upon complaints or to initiate appropriate legal proceedings; whereas this possibility does not, however, entail prior verification of the general conditions obtaining in individual economic sectors;

Whereas the courts or administrative authorities of the Member States must have at their disposal adequate and effective means of preventing the continued application of unfair terms in consumer contracts,

HAS ADOPTED THIS DIRECTIVE:

Article 1

1. The purpose of this Directive is to approximate the laws, regulations and administrative provisions of the Member States relating to unfair terms in contracts concluded between a seller or supplier and a consumer.

2. The contractual terms which reflect mandatory statutory or regulatory provisions and the provisions or principles of international conventions to which the Member States or the Community are party, particularly in the transport area, shall not be subject to the provisions of this Directive.

Article 2

For the purposes of this Directive:

(a) 'unfair terms' means the contractual terms defined in Article 3;
(b) 'consumer' means any natural person who, in contracts covered by this Directive, is acting for purposes which are outside his trade, business or profession;
(c) 'seller or supplier' means any natural or legal person who, in contracts covered by this Directive, is acting for purposes relating to his trade, business or profession, whether publicly owned or privately owned.

Article 3

1. A contractual term which has not been individually negotiated shall be regarded as unfair if, contrary to the requirement of good faith, it causes a significant imbalance in the parties' rights and obligations arising under the contract, to the detriment of the consumer.

2. A term shall always be regarded as not individually negotiated where it has been drafted in advance and the consumer has therefore not been able to influence the substance of the term, particularly in the context of a pre-formulated standard contract.

The fact that certain aspects of a term or one specific term have been individually negotiated shall not exclude the application of this Article to the rest of a contract if an overall assessment of the contract indicates that it is nevertheless a pre-formulated standard contract.

Where any seller or supplier claims that a standard term has been individually negotiated, the burden of proof in this respect shall be incumbent on him.

3. The Annex shall contain an indicative and non-exhaustive list of the terms which may be regarded as unfair.

Article 4

1. Without prejudice to Article 7, the unfairness of a contractual term shall be assessed, taking into account the nature of the goods or services for which the contract was concluded and by referring, at the time of conclusion of the contract, to all the circumstances attending the conclusion of the contract and to all the other terms of the contract or of another contract on which it is dependent.

2. Assessment of the unfair nature of the terms shall relate neither to the definition of the main subject matter of the contract nor to the adequacy of the price and remuneration, on the one hand, as against the services or goods supplied in exchange, on the other, in so far as these terms are in plain intelligible language.

Article 5

In the case of contracts where all or certain terms offered to the consumer are in writing, these terms must always be drafted in plain, intelligible language. Where there is doubt about the meaning of a term, the interpretation most favourable to the consumer shall prevail. This rule on interpretation shall not apply in the context of the procedures laid down in Article 7 (2).

Article 6

1. Member States shall lay down that unfair terms used in a contract concluded with a consumer by a seller or supplier shall, as provided for under their national law, not be binding on the consumer and that the contract shall continue to bind the parties upon those terms if it is capable of continuing in existence without the unfair terms.

2. Member States shall take the necessary measures to ensure that the consumer does not lose the protection granted by this Directive by virtue of the choice of the law of a non-Member country as the law applicable to the contract if the latter has a close connection with the territory of the Member States.

Article 7

1. Member States shall ensure that, in the interests of consumers and of competitors, adequate and effective means exist to prevent the continued use of unfair terms in contracts concluded with consumers by sellers or suppliers.

2. The means referred to in paragraph 1 shall include provisions whereby persons or organisations, having a legitimate interest under national law in protecting consumers, may take action according to the national law concerned before the courts or before competent administrative bodies for a decision as to whether contractual terms drawn up for general use are unfair, so that they can apply appropriate and effective means to prevent the continued use of such terms.

3. With due regard for national laws, the legal remedies referred to in paragraph 2 may be directed separately or jointly against a number of sellers or suppliers from the same economic sector or their associations which use or recommend the use of the same general contractual terms or similar terms.

Article 8

Member States may adopt or retain the most stringent provisions compatible with the Treaty in the area covered by this Directive, to ensure a maximum degree of protection for the consumer.

Article 9

The Commission shall present a report to the European Parliament and to the Council concerning the application of this Directive five years at the latest after the date in Article 10 (1).

Article 10

1. Member States shall bring into force the laws, regulations and administrative provisions necessary to comply with this Directive no later than 31 December 1994. They shall forthwith inform the Commission thereof.

These provisions shall be applicable to all contracts concluded after 31 December 1994.

2. When Member States adopt these measures, they shall contain a reference to this Directive or shall be accompanied by such reference on the occasion of their official publication. The methods of making such a reference shall be laid down by the Member States.

3. Member States shall communicate the main provisions of national law which they adopt in the field covered by this Directive to the Commission.

Article 11

This Directive is addressed to the Member States.

Done at Luxembourg, 5 April 1993

> *For the Council*
> *The President*
> N. Helveg Petersen

ANNEX

TERMS REFERRED TO IN ARTICLE 3 (3)

1. *Terms which have the object or effect of:*

(a) excluding or limiting the legal liability of a seller or supplier in the event of the death of a consumer or personal injury to the latter resulting from an act or omission of that seller or supplier;

(b) inappropriately excluding or limiting the legal rights of the consumer *vis-à-vis* the seller or supplier or another party in the event of total or partial non-performance or inadequate performance by the seller or supplier of any of the contractual obligations, including the option of offsetting a debt owed to the seller or supplier against any claim which the consumer may have against him;

(c) making an agreement binding on the consumer whereas provision of services by the seller or supplier is subject to a condition whose realisation depends on his own will alone;

(d) permitting the seller or supplier to retain sums paid by the consumer where the latter decides not to conclude or perform the contract, without providing for the consumer to receive compensation of an equivalent amount from the seller or supplier where the latter is the party cancelling the contract;

(e) requiring any consumer who fails to fulfil his obligation to pay a disproportionately high sum in compensation;

(f) authorising the seller or supplier to dissolve the contract on a discretionary basis where the same facility is not granted to the consumer, or permitting the seller or supplier to retain the sums paid for services not yet supplied by him where it is the seller or supplier himself who dissolves the contract;

(g) enabling the seller or supplier to terminate a contract of indeterminate duration without reasonable notice except where there are serious grounds for doing so;

(h) automatically extending a contract of fixed duration where the consumer does not indicate otherwise, when the deadline fixed for the consumer to express this desire not to extend the contract is unreasonably early;

(i) irrevocably binding the consumer to terms with which he had no real opportunity of becoming acquainted before the conclusion of the contract;

(j) enabling the seller or supplier to alter the terms of the contract unilaterally without a valid reason which is specified in the contract;

(k) enabling the seller or supplier to alter unilaterally without a valid reason any characteristics of the product or service to be provided;

(l) providing for the price of goods to be determined at the time of delivery or allowing a seller of goods or supplier of services to increase their price without in both cases giving the consumer the corresponding right to cancel the contract if the final price is too high in relation to the price agreed when the contract was concluded;

(m) giving the seller or supplier the right to determine whether the goods or services supplied are in conformity with the contract, or giving him the exclusive right to interpret any term of the contract;

(n) limiting the seller's or supplier's obligation to respect commitments undertaken by his agents or making his commitments subject to compliance with a particular formality;

(o) obliging the consumer to fulfil all his obligations where the seller or supplier does not perform his;

(p) giving the seller or supplier the possibility of transferring his rights and obligations under the contract, where this may serve to reduce the guarantees for the consumer, without the latter's agreement;

(q) excluding or hindering the consumer's right to take legal action or exercise any other legal remedy, particularly by requiring the consumer to take disputes exclusively to arbitration not covered by legal provisions, unduly restricting the evidence available to him or imposing on him a burden of proof which, according to the applicable law, should lie with another party to the contract.

2. *Scope of subparagraphs (g), (j) and (l)*

(a) Subparagraph (g) is without hindrance to terms by which a supplier of financial services reserves the right to terminate unilaterally a contract of indeterminate duration without notice where there is a valid reason, provided that the supplier is required to inform the other contracting party or parties thereof immediately.

(b) Subparagraph (j) is without hindrance to terms under which a supplier of financial services reserves the right to alter the rate of interest payable by the consumer or due to the latter, or the amount of other charges for financial services without notice where there is a valid reason, provided that the supplier is required to inform the other contracting party or parties thereof at the earliest opportunity and that the latter are free to dissolve the contract immediately.

Subparagraph (j) is also without hindrance to terms under which a seller or supplier reserves the right to alter unilaterally the conditions of a contract of indeterminate duration, provided that he is required to inform the consumer with reasonable notice and that the consumer is free to dissolve the contract.

(c) Subparagraphs (g), (j) and (l) do not apply to:

- transactions in transferable securities, financial instruments and other products or services where the price is linked to fluctuations in a stock exchange quotation or index or a financial market rate that the seller or supplier does not control;
- contracts for the purchase or sale of foreign currency, traveller's cheques or international money orders denominated in foreign currency;

(d) Subparagraph (l) is without hindrance to price-indexation clauses, where lawful, provided that the method by which prices vary is explicitly described.

1. OJ No C 73, 24 March 1992, p. 7.
2. OJ No C 326, 16 December 1991, p. 108 and OJ No C 21, 25 January 1993
3. OJ No C 159, 17 June 1991, p. 34
4. OJ No C 92, 25 April 1975, p. 1 and OJ No C 133, 3 June 1981, p. 1.

Note

1. The Directive has been transposed into Irish domestic law, on a word-for-word basis, by S.I. No. 27 of 1995. While Irish case-law is limited (see the High Court action which resulted in a number of standard terms in home construction contracts being declared invalid, Dorgan [2002] *Law Society Gazette* 12) on this Directive, English case-law tends to regard the Directive as having a significant overlap with the UK Unfair Contract Terms Act 1977: see *Scheps v Fine Art Logistic Ltd* [2007] EWHC 541(QB). Litigation is not the most effective way of counteracting these instances where an industry tends to use unfair terms against consumers. Consumer protection agencies have a good record of challenging industries such as banking and financial services, leasing and construction, as well as mobile phone companies who tie consumers into onerous contracts. A recent example of this is found in relation to standard contracts used by gyms: the National Consumer Agency has issued draft guidelines which seek to press for discontinuance of some standard terms by fitness centres: see '"Unfair" gym terms prompt guidelines', *The Irish Times* 31 October 2007. See also *Marshall v Capital Holdings* [2006] IEHC 271.

2. Directive 1999/44/EC affords consumers a distinct set of remedies should goods supplied under a contract not be in conformity with the contract, including the new rights to have the goods brought into conformity by repair or alteration. See the European Communities (Certain Aspects of the Sale of Consumer Goods and Associated Guarantees) Regulations 2003 (S.I. No.11 of 2003).

3. The most recent consumer protection measure that the European Commission has promoted is Directive 2005/29/EC, the Unfair Commercial Practices Directive. This has been transposed by the Consumer Protection Act 2007, with effect from 1 January 1 2008. Where a consumer is influenced by an unfair commercial practice which affects decisions on whether to purchase a product, or the freedom of choice the consumer may exercise in relation thereto, the contract will be unfair, and criminal

liability may be imposed for misleading or aggressive commercial practices—sections 47 and 54. This legislation creates positive obligations to provide information so as to allow consumers to make an informed choice as well as making obvious misrepresentations about the origins, characteristics and effectiveness of a product.

4. The European Commission has also sponsored two recent initiatives that suggest both a more coordinated approach to consumer law and a more ambitious contract-reform agenda in the years ahead. The first initiative is *The Green Paper on the Review of the Consumer Acquis* (Brussels, 08.02.2007, COM(2006) 744 final). This Review concludes that Community Directives to protect consumers have adopted a fragmented approach which in turn has led to significant differences in transposition in member states. The European Commission clearly favours a new legislative instrument as a framework text. The second initiative builds upon earlier research on European contract law (e.g. *Lando and Beale*) and seeks to establish a set of principles, definitions and model rules for lawyers, legislators and the community lawmakers. The Joint Network of European Private Law, established in 2005, has presented a *Draft Proposal for a Common Frame of Reference on Contract Law* (6 March 2008). While this proposal has rowed back from being a draft European Contract Code, it will clearly have a significant impact on future legislative changes in Ireland.

EXERCISES

1. Last week Joe took his only suit to Zippo dry cleaners. This is Joe's third visit to Zippo. On the first occasion, three years ago, he signed a 'receipt' acknowledging that the cleaning was 'at customer's risk'. On the second occasion, and at the time of his most recent visit, he was given the same receipt but was not asked to sign it. At no time did Joe read the receipt. Joe went to collect his suit today, but was told it had been destroyed when the cleaning machine went on fire. Zippo have refused to compensate Joe. Is the 'at customer's risk' provision part of the contract? What do the 1980 Act and the 1995 Regulations do to assist Joe?

2. Would your answer to (1) above be different if the garments that Joe had left with Zippo were a set or curtains that Joe, a medical practitioner, used in his consulting rooms?

3. Why are limitation clauses not subjected to the same level of hostile treatment as are exemption clauses?

4. Barney has downloaded a Spanish-language tuition course from Lingo Language Tools. Barney paid €50 for the course. Barney has discovered that the tuition course is the Latin American course in Spanish and is unsuitable for his needs. Consider whether he has any redress from Lingo. Is the contract between Barney and Lingo one for goods or services? How does this affect Barney's chances of success (see *St Alban's City and District Council v International Computer* [1986] 4 All ER 481.

Chapter Nine

Mistake

INTRODUCTION

When a contract is concluded it may later be evident that one (or both) of the parties entered into the agreement under a mistaken belief about some circumstance, fact or consequence which perhaps induced that person to enter the contract. The range and variety of such mistakes is infinite: the error may relate to the actual terms of the contract or to the results that follow (e.g. the value of the thing bought or sold). The error may be induced by the fraud of the other party or be completely self-induced. The mistake may or may not be known by the other contracting party. The financial consequences of the error will vary in their effect, and the error in question may be a 'one-off' event that could not have been envisaged or a predictable commercial risk.

The resolution of disputes where one party pleads mistake as a factor which should vitiate or modify the contract does not generally take place within any uniform conceptual framework; agreements are not *per se* void or voidable simply because a mistake is shown to have occurred. Rather, the courts tend to confine pleas of mistake within narrow boundaries in order to avoid an apparent contract from falling apart, to encourage the parties to make provision for such errors in their contract, and to avoid having to readjust the interests of the parties if the contract has in part been performed.

Nonetheless, pleas of mistake are successful in a wide variety of situations, where the contractual subject matter never existed or has perished, where the agreement is laced with latent ambiguity and the court cannot identify what has been agreed, or where the error relates to the actual terms of an executed contract and the error of one party is known to the other. Additionally, the courts do resolve disputes by reference to important matters of principle and justice such as the objective behaviour of the parties, which of the parties, if any, was responsible for the mistake, and whether either party could have avoided or mitigated the situation.

Students should pay particular attention to issues of fact; for example, are both parties mistaken or is the mistake made by one party only? The jurisdictional aspect is also relevant—is the plaintiff invoking common law or equitable principles? Finally, the remedy sought is all important: the bases upon which rectification and rescission will be awarded, for example, differ substantially, as indeed does the nature of the relief itself.

471

SECTION ONE—MISTAKE OF LAW

At common law, the traditional rule was that a mistake of law had no effect on the basis that ignorance of the law is no excuse. This was applied in O'*Loghlen v O'Callaghan* (1874) IR 8 Cl 116. Whiteside C.J. noted that:

> It was the business of the gentlemen who settled their accounts to make themselves acquainted with that law, and to act accordingly. It is well argued, and it is not unsound in principle, that if one man gets hold of money which he ought not to get, he ought to be obliged to pay it back to the party who has paid it to him in his own wrong. But the question here is whether money paid under the circumstances of this case can be recovered back by compulsion of law, and we think it cannot. Our judgment rests on the principle that the money was paid in mistake of law.

As the next case indicates, however, relief may be available in equity through the law of restitution.

Rogers *v* Louth County Council [1981] ILRM 144

The plaintiff claimed the return of a sum of money overpaid to the defendant in redeeming an annuity in respect of a cottage under s. 99 of the Housing Act 1966. The Circuit Court Judge stated a case for the opinion of the Supreme Court as to whether payment by mistake of law was recoverable.

Griffin J.:

The general rule is usually stated to be that where money is paid under the influence of a mistake, and the mistake is one of fact, an action will lie to recover it back; but that to entitle the plaintiff to recover, the mistake upon which he has acted must be one of fact, not of law. Thus in *Pollock on Contracts* (13th edn, edited by Professor Winfield), it is stated at p. 378 that 'money paid under a mistake of law cannot in any case be recovered'. Similar statements are to be found in many textbooks. However, the Judicial Committee of the Privy Council held in *Kiriri Cotton Co. Ltd v Dewani* [1960] 2 WLR 127 that a plaintiff may recover money paid on a mistake of law provided that he is not in *pari delicto* with the defendant in mistaking the law. Delivering the advice of the Privy Council, Lord Denning said at p. 133:

> Nor is it correct to say that money paid under a mistake of law can never be recovered back. The true proposition is that money paid under a mistake of law, by itself and without more, cannot be recovered back. James L.J. pointed that out in *Rogers v Ingham*. If there is something more in addition to a mistake of law—if there is something in the defendant's conduct which shows that, of the two of them, he is the one primarily responsible for the mistake—then it may be recovered back. Thus, if as between the two of them the duty of observing the law is placed on the shoulders of the one rather than the other—it being imposed on him specially for the protection of the other—then they are not in *pari delicto* and the money can be recovered back; see *Browning v Morris*, by Lord Mansfield. Likewise, if the responsibility for the mistake lies more on the one than the other because he has misled the other when he ought to know better—then again they are not in *pari delicto* and the money can be recovered back.

This passage was cited with approval by Kenny J. in *Dolan v Neligan* [1967] IR 247, at 260. Again, even where there has been no mistake of fact, a plaintiff may still recover monies so paid in an action for money had and received upon proof that the monies were paid by him involuntarily, that is, as the result of some extortion, coercion or compulsion in the legal sense—see per Windeyer J. in *Mason v New South Wales*, 102 CLR 108, 180. He cannot recover if the payment was made voluntarily. A payment may be said to be voluntary, in this instant, when the payer makes it deliberately with a knowledge of all relevant facts, and either being indifferent to whether or not he is liable in law, or knowing, or having reason to think, himself not liable, yet intending finally to close the transaction—see per Windeyer J. ibid. at 143. Whether the payment has been voluntary in this sense may also be deduced from the relationship of the parties. As Abott C.J. said in *Morgan v Palmer*, 2 B & C 729 at 734:

> It has been well argued that the payment having been voluntary, it cannot be recovered back in an action for money had and received. I agree that such a consequence would have followed had the parties been on equal terms. But if one party has the power of saying to the other, 'That which you require shall not be done except upon the conditions I choose to impose', no person can contend that they stand upon anything like an equal footing.

In such a case, the payment is by no means to be considered to be voluntary—see per McTiernan J. in *Bell v Shire of Serpentine* (1969) 121 CLR 137.

Applying these principles to the present case, the plaintiff is in my judgment entitled to recover the overpayment of £935.53 made by her. The payment of £1,163 made by the plaintiff was not 'voluntary' in the context aforesaid. The parties were not on equal terms; the defendants had the power, if they thought fit, to withhold permission for the redemption of the annuity; they were however prepared to allow the plaintiff to redeem it, but only on the conditions imposed by them, which included exacting a payment in excess of that permitted by the statute. The plaintiff was not in possession of all the relevant facts, and did not know, nor had she reason to think, that she was not liable to pay the sum demanded by the defendants for the redemption of the annuity. The defendants were in my view primarily responsible for the mistake and the parties were accordingly not in *pari delicto*.

(O'Higgins C.J. and Kenny J. concurred.)

Notes

1. As was emphasised by the Court in *Great Peace Shipping Ltd v Tsauliris Salvage (International) Ltd* [2002] 4 All ER 689 (p. 478 below), in equity a distinction may be drawn between a mistake as to public law and a mistake as to private law.

2. In *Kleinwort Benson v Lincoln City Council* [1998] 4 All ER 513, the House of Lords abolished the bar on recovering money paid under a mistake in law. Lord Goff stated that:

> The present rule, under which in general money is not recoverable in restitution on the ground that it has been paid under a mistake of law, should no longer be maintained as part of English law . . . It is no defence to a claim in English law for

restitution of money paid . . . under a mistake of law that the defendant honestly believed when he learnt of the payment or transfer, that he was entitled to retain the money . . . .

In *Deutsche Morgan Grenfell Group plc v Inland Revenue Commissioners* [2007] 1 All ER 449, having considered the *Kleinwort Benson* case, the House of Lords held that there was no reason in principle why the right to restitution of payments made by mistake of law should not apply to payments of tax. However, despite the decision in *Kleinwort Benson*, uncertainty still exists as to the operation of claims for mistake in practice. Thus in *Nurdin & Peacock plc v DB Ramsden & Co. Ltd* [1999] 1 All ER 941, the High Court held that to establish a claim for recovery of money paid under a mistake of law, it was sufficient for the payer to show that the payment would not have been made but for the mistake. Neuberger J. opined that any claim for money paid under a mistake of fact or law was based on restitution, and it was almost as illogical for recovery to turn on the precise nature of the mistake of law as it was for it to turn on whether the mistake was one of fact or law.

SECTION TWO—COMMON MISTAKE

A common mistake involves the parties reaching agreement on the basis of a common misunderstanding. A common mistake will not affect the formation of a contract since the parties are genuinely *ad idem*. However, if it later materialises that they have reached agreement on the basis of some fundamental underlying assumption which is false, consent may be nullified. The doctrine applies to situations where the subject matter of the contract no longer exists (*res extincta*), and situations where performance of the contract is impossible because of some physical or legal impossibility (*res sua*). It seems clear, however, that the doctrine has a wider operation than this.

In *Bell v Lever Brothers* [1932] AC 161, Lord Atkin suggested that a mistake as to the quality of the subject matter would affect assent if it were 'the mistake of both parties, and is as to the existence of some quality which makes the thing without the quality essentially different from the thing as it was believed to be'. In such a case, the contract would be void. While the UK courts in cases such as *Leaf v International Galleries* [1950] 2 KB 86 adopted a very narrow view of such mistakes, as cases such as *Western Potato Co-operative* below indicate, the Irish Courts have adopted a more liberal interpretation.

It should also be noted that common mistake arises in equity too and may render the contract voidable. For example, in *Solle v Butcher* [1950] 1 KB 671 a lease agreed at the time the parties believed the property was subject to rent-restriction legislation was deemed voidable. A question has arisen as to whether a court may, in the exercise of its equitable jurisdiction, set aside an agreement which would not be void at common law. The *Great Peace* case below indicates that at present at least the UK and Irish Courts differ in this respect.

Western Potato Co-operative Ltd v Durnan [1985] ILRM 5

The plaintiff contracted to supply seed potatoes to the defendant in order to produce eighty tons of potatoes which were then to be resold to the plaintiff. Clarke J. stated that since the seed potatoes were not capable of producing the crop because of physical defects in their genetic structure, both parties entered the contract on the basis of a mistaken assumption.

. . . Mistake as to the existence of a fact at the root of the contract or on the basis of an assumption which subsequently proves to be false is dealt with in Anson's Law of Contract (25th ed.), in the light of the House of Lords decision in Bell v Lever Bros Ltd [1932] AC 161, stated to be the leading case on the subject; and, in interpreting the decision, citing Denning L.J. in Solle v Butcher [1950] 1 KB 671, at p. 691: 'The correct interpretation of that case, to my mind, is that, once a contract has been made, that is to say, once the parties, whatever their inmost states of mind, have to all outward appearances agreed with sufficient certainty in the same terms on the same subject matter, then the contract is good unless and until it is set aside for failure of some condition on which the existence of the contract depends, or for fraud, or on some equitable ground . . .' And Anson notes at p. 287, fn.: 'Mistake can be regarded as a type of 'pre-contractual frustration''. Pursuing the implications of Bell v Lever Bros. Ltd in the matter of mistake as to the quality of the thing contracted for, Anson at p. 292 cites from Lord Atkin's speech [1932] AC 161, at p. 218 that: 'Mistake as to quality of the thing contracted for raises more difficult questions. In such a case mistake will not affect assent unless it is the mistake of both parties, and is as to the existence of some quality which makes the thing without the quality essentially different from the thing as it was believed to be.' And, under the heading of 'A False and Fundamental assumption', Anson at p. 296 states:

Where the parties contract under a false and fundamental assumption, going to the root of the contract, and which both of them must be taken to have in mind at the time they entered into it as the basis of their agreement, the contract is void. This should not be regarded as a category separate and distinct from those categories of mistake already mentioned, but rather as a more compendious statement of the type of error required. . . . It is not surprising that the strictness of this test has resulted in a dearth of cases on the subject of fundamental mistake.

It seems to me that on the facts of the present case this strict test is fulfilled.

(The contract was held to be void.)

Consider:

Would the outcome have been different if the seeds produced the crop desired but in substantially reduced numbers such that production for market was not viable?

O'Neill v Ryan [1991] ILRM 672

Costello J.:

There is a category of cases in which it is accepted that there was an offer and acceptance and agreement reached between the parties but in which it is claimed that the parties shared a common mistake which has resulted in the agreement being void. For example where both parties agree on the purchase and sale of a painting believing it to be a Gainsborough and it is subsequently established that this is not so, or where both parties agree on the sale of tenanted property and both believe that the tenant is protected by the Rent Restriction Acts and subsequently ascertain that this is not so, the existence of a valid offer and acceptance is not in doubt and what is in issue is the effect on the parties' contract on what I call a shared common mistake. . . .

There were a number of earlier cases in which a shared common mistake as to the existence of the subject matter of the contract, enabled the court to declare the contract to be void. Thus an assignment of a life assurance policy was held to be void where it was shown that at its date the person whose life was assured was wrongly assumed by both parties to have been alive (*Scott v Coulson* [1903] 2 Ch. 249), and a separation deed was declared a nullity because it was made by the common and shared mistake that the parties were married to each other (*Galloway v Galloway* (1914) 30 TLR 531). But later cases have shown that the circumstances in which a shared common mistake will nullify a contract are extremely limited. *Solle v Butcher* [1950] 1 KB 671 was a case of a shared common mistake, both parties believing that a flat had been so extensively reconstructed that it was no longer controlled by the Rent Restrictions Acts as a result of which a rent was agreed that was higher than that which would have been payable had the true position been known. But the tenant failed in his claim to recover the rent he had overpaid on the ground of the common mistake. The law on the subject was stated by Denning L.J. in terms which were approved in a later case as follows at p. 691:

> . . . Once a contract has been made, that is to say, once the parties, whatever their inmost states of mind, have to all outward appearances agreed with sufficient certainty in the same terms on the same subject matter, then the contract is good unless and until it is set aside for failure of some condition on which the existence of the contract depends, or for fraud, or on some equitable ground. Neither party can rely on his own mistake to say it was a nullity from the beginning, no matter that it was a mistake which to his mind was fundamental, and no matter that the other party knew that he was under a mistake. A *fortiori*, if the other party did not know of the mistake, but shared it.

In most cases, then, a shared common mistake will not result in a void contract. This does not mean however that an injured party is without a remedy. As *Solle v Butcher* showed the court may in the exercise of equitable jurisdiction set aside an agreement even though it is not avoided by the common shared mistake. Lord Denning expressed the court's equitable jurisdiction as follows at p. 693: 'A contract is also liable in equity to be *set aside* if the parties were under a common misapprehension either as to facts or as to their relative and respective rights, provided that the misapprehension was fundamental and that the party seeking to set it aside was not himself at fault.'

And in that case the Court of Appeal set aside the lease on terms, the tenant being allowed to surrender the lease entirely or to remain in possession at the rent payable under the Rent Restriction Acts. The court will also grant relief by way of *rectification* where the parties have reached an agreement but where an error is made in giving effect to the parties' common intention in its written agreement. The general rule is that where there is a common shared mistake in that the written agreement fails to record the intention of both parties the court will order its rectification. *Rectification* may also be ordered when a party has entered into a written agreement by mistake if he establishes that the other party with knowledge of the mistake concluded that agreement (see *Irish Life Assurance Co. Ltd v Dublin Land Securities Ltd* [1989] IR 253, 260 and *Monaghan County Council v Vaughan* [1948] IR 306, 312). And in the exercise of its discretion the court may refuse to make an order for *specific performance* in cases of common shared mistakes. *Grist v Bailey* [1967] Ch. 532 was a case in which both the vendor and purchaser of a tenanted house contracted in the same mistaken belief that the tenancy was protected. When the mistake was ascertained the vendor tried to avoid the contract. The court held that the contract was a valid one but that in the exercise of its discretion it would refuse the purchaser's claim for specific performance and allow the defendant's counterclaim for rescission.

Note

Costello J.'s exposition of the effect of mistake in contracts was affirmed by the Supreme Court on appeal. See [1992] 1 IR 166.

In the Matter of the Estate of Patrick Brennan Deceased between James Fitzsimons and Christopher Fitzsimons *v* Christopher O'Hanlon and Paul O'Hanlon (HC) 29 June 1999

The plaintiffs were cousins of Patrick Brennan, who died unmarried and intestate. Believing themselves to be the deceased's next of kin, the plaintiffs instructed solicitors to ascertain the deceased's assets. Subsequently, the defendants who claimed to be the deceased's non-marital children issued an application for a declaration to this effect. Although the plaintiffs originally opposed the application, they subsequently reached a compromise with the defendants. It was agreed that a payment of £60,500 plus costs would be paid to the plaintiffs in return for their withdrawing their opposition to the declaration of parentage. When a further deposit in the deceased's name was discovered in a building society, the plaintiffs sought a share of it. They contended that the compromise had been reached on the basis of a mutual mistake as to the value of the deceased's estate.

Budd J.:

[Following consideration of *O'Neill v Ryan* [1991] ILRM 672 and *Kennedy v Panama New Zealand & Australian Royal Mail Company* [1867] LR 2 QB 580] It was foreseeable in this case that further assets might be found. The plaintiffs were aware of the search for the whereabouts of the assets having been diligently carried out by Miss O'Reilly on their behalf. They must have known from her inquiries that Patrick Brennan had been discreet, perhaps even secretive, about the whereabouts of his assets. The fact that a party pleading mutual mistake has failed to anticipate the event of further assets being found may well be a factor which militates against setting aside the contract. . . . While a fundamental mistaken assumption can nullify consent so as to make a contract void this rule is confined within very narrow limits. It is in the interest of commercial convenience that, in general, apparent contracts should be enforced.

In this case the parties all bona fide believed that all the assets had been located and their approximate value ascertained. There was no mistake as to what assets were included in the estate at the time when the compromise was reached in consideration of which the plaintiffs withdrew their opposition to the declaration of paternity. The fact of the further fund in the Building Society which came to light subsequently, while an important factor, did not destroy the identity of the subject matter of the agreement as it was when the contract was made and accordingly the contract was not void. This principle is explained in *Bell & Snelling v Lever Bros Limited* [1932] AC 161. Lever Brothers had terminated the five year contracts of Bell and Snelling and had paid them £50,000 for loss of office. Lever Bros were not aware that Bell and Snelling had broken their service contracts in a way which would have justified dismissal without compensation. However, Bell & Snelling were found to be not guilty of fraudulent concealment about this. Lever Bros had paid £50,000 when they might have got rid of Bell & Snelling for nothing. The Court of Appeal held that the compensation agreements were void as Lever Bros had made them under a fundamental mistake. The House of Lords reversed this decision holding that the mistake related only to a quality of the service contracts and was not fundamental. Lord Atkin said: *'the contract released is the identical contract in both cases, and the party paying for release gets exactly what he bargained for'*. Furthermore, mistake even as to a fundamental quality was of no effect unless it related to a mistaken assumption which both parties regarded as essential. By analogy, since I accept Mr Doyle's account in the present case, there is a dearth of evidence that there was a mistake as to subject matter which related to something which *both must necessarily have accepted in their minds as an essential and integral element of the subject matter*. (My italics.).

The situation can be viewed from an alternative standpoint. There was no mistake that the compromise on the basis of withdrawal of opposition to the declaration was to be rewarded by a substantial sum of money from the estate. Both sides were mistaken as to the quality of the consideration, in this instance being the pecuniary amount available in the estate eventually. This does not make the contract void. . . .

The following case is important not just for its discussion of the nature of common mistake but also for its consideration of the relationship between a mistake at common law and a mistake in equity.

Great Peace Shipping Ltd *v* Tsavliris Salvage (International) Ltd [2002] 4 All ER 689

The defendants entered into a contract to hire the claimant's vessel *Great Peace* to escort and stand-by a second ship, *Cape Providence*, which was sinking. Both parties mistakenly believed the ships to be in close proximity. When *Cape Providence* was rescued by another closer ship a few hours later, the defendants cancelled the contract but refused to make any payment despite the provision in the contract of a five-day cancellation fee.

Lord Phillips M.R.:

It is generally accepted that the principles of the law of common mistake expounded by Lord Atkin in *Bell v Lever Brothers* were based on the common law. The issue raised by [counsel for the defendant's] submissions is whether there subsists a separate doctrine of common mistake founded in equity which enables the court to intervene in circumstances where the mistake does not render the contract void under the common law principles. The first step is to identify the nature of the common law doctrine of mistake that was identified, or established, by *Bell v Lever Brothers*.

Lord Atkin and Lord Thankerton were breaking no new ground in holding void a contract where, unknown to the parties, the subject matter of the contract no longer existed at the time that the contract was concluded. The Sale of Goods Act 1893 was a statute which set out to codify the common law. Section 6, to which Atkin J. referred, provided:

> When there is a contract for the sale of specific goods, and the goods without the knowledge of the seller have perished at the time when the contract is made, the contract is void.

Judge Chalmers, the draftsman of the Act, commented in the first edition of his book on the Act, published in 1894:

> The rule may be based on the ground of mutual mistake, or on the ground of impossibility of performance.

. . . Where that which is expressly identified as the subject of a contract does not exist, the contract will necessarily be one which cannot be performed. Such a situation can readily be identified. The position is very different where there is 'a mistake as to the existence of some quality of the subject matter which makes the thing without the quality essentially different from the thing as it was believed to be'. In such a situation it may be possible to perform the letter of the contract. In support of the proposition that a contract is void in such circumstances, Lord Atkin cited two authorities, in which he said that the principles to be applied were to be found. The first was *Kennedy v Panama etc. Mail Co.* (1867) LR 2 QB 580 . . . [and the second] was *Smith v Hughes* (1871) LR 6 QB 597. On no view did that difficult case deal with common mistake and . . . We conclude that the two authorities . . . provided an insubstantial basis for his formulation of the test of common mistake in relation to the quality of the subject matter of a contract. Lord Atkin advanced an alternative basis for his test: the implication of a term of the same nature as that which was applied under the doctrine of frustration, as it was then understood. In so doing he adopted the analysis of Scrutton L.J. in the Court of Appeal. It seems to us that this was a more solid jurisprudential basis for the test of common mistake that Lord Atkin was proposing. At the time of *Bell v Lever Brothers* the law of frustration and common mistake had advanced hand in hand on the foundation of a common principle. Thereafter frustration proved a more fertile ground for the development of this principle than common mistake, and consideration of the development of the law of frustration assists with the analysis of the law of common mistake. . . .

[Lord Phillips then considered the following cases: *Taylor v Caldwell* (1863) 3 B & S 826, *Jackson v Union Marine Insurance Co. Ltd* (1874) LR 10 CP 125, *Hobson v Pattenden & Co.* (1903) 19 TLR 186, *Clark v Lindsay* (1903) 19 TLR 202, *Griffith v Brymer* (1903) 19 TLR 434, *Krell v Henry*, *Tamplin Steamship Co. Ltd v Anglo-Mexican Petroleum Products Company Ltd* [1916] 2 AC 397, *National Carriers v Panalpina* [1981] AC 675, *Davis Contractors Ltd v Fareham UDC* [1956] AC 696 and the *Fibrosa* case [1943] AC 32.]

What do these developments in the law of frustration have to tell us about the law of common mistake? First that the theory of the implied term is as unrealistic when considering common mistake as when considering frustration. Where a fundamental assumption upon which an agreement is founded proves to be mistaken, it is not realistic to ask whether the parties impliedly agreed that in those circumstances the contract would not be binding. The avoidance of a contract on the ground of common mistake results from a rule of law under which, if it transpires that one or both of the parties have agreed to do something which it is impossible to perform, no obligation arises out of that agreement.

In considering whether performance of the contract is impossible, it is necessary to identify what it is that the parties agreed would be performed. This involves looking not only at the express terms, but at any implications that may arise out of the surrounding circumstances. In some cases it will be possible to identify details of the 'contractual adventure' which go beyond the terms that are expressly spelt out, in others it will not. Just as the doctrine of frustration only applies if the contract contains no provision that covers the situation, the same should be true of common mistake. If, on true construction of the contract, a party warrants that the subject matter of the contract exists, or that it will be possible to perform the contract, there will be no scope to hold the contract void on the ground of common mistake.

If one applies the [principles set out by Lord Alverstone C.J. in *Hobson v Pattenden*] to a case of common mistake, it suggests that the following elements must be present if common mistake is to avoid a contract: (i) there must be a common assumption as to the existence of a state of affairs; (ii) there must be no warranty by either party that that state of affairs exists; (iii) the non-existence of the state of affairs must not be attributable to the fault of either party; (iv) the non-existence of the state of affairs must render performance of the contract impossible; (v) the state of affairs may be the existence, or a vital attribute, of the consideration to be provided or circumstances which must subsist if performance of the contractual adventure is to be possible.

The second and third of these elements are well exemplified by the decision of the High Court of Australia in *McRae v Commonwealth Disposals Commission* (1951) 84 CLR 377. The Commission invited tenders for the purchase of 'an oil tanker lying on the Jourmaund Reef . . . said to contain oil'. The plaintiff tendered successfully for the purchase, fitted out a salvage expedition at great expense and proceeded to the reef. No tanker was to be found—it had never existed. The plaintiff claimed damages for breach of contract. The Commission argued that the contract was void because of a common mistake as to the existence of the tanker. In the leading judgment Dixon and Fullagar JJ. expressed doubt as to the existence of a doctrine of common mistake in contract. They considered that whether impossibility of performance discharged obligations, be the impossibility existing at the time of the contract or supervening thereafter, depended solely upon the construction of the contract. They went on, however, to consider the position if this were not correct. They observed that the common assumption that the tanker existed was one that was created by the Commission, without any reasonable grounds for believing that it was true. . . . They held . . . that, on its proper construction the contract included a promise by the Commission that the tanker existed in the position specified. Alternatively, they held that if the doctrine of mistake fell to be applied:

> The agreement was made on the supposition by both parties that nothing had happened which made performance impossible. This was a missupposition of the state of facts which went to the whole root of the matter. The contract was therefore void, and the plaintiff was entitled to recover his £100.

This seems, if we may say so, an entirely satisfactory conclusion and one that can be reconciled with the English doctrine of mistake. That doctrine fills a gap in the contract where it transpires that it is impossible of performance without the fault of either party and the parties have not, expressly or by implication, dealt with their rights and obligations in that eventuality.

. . . Thus, while we do not consider that the doctrine of common mistake can be satisfactorily explained by an implied term, an allegation that a contract is void for common mistake will often raise important issues of construction. Where it is possible to perform the letter of the contract, but it is alleged that there was a common mistake in relation to a fundamental assumption which renders performance of the essence of the obligation impossible, it will be necessary, by construing the contract in the light of all the material circumstances, to decide whether this is indeed the case. . . . Once the court determines that unforeseen circumstances have, indeed, resulted in the contract being impossible of performance, it is next necessary to determine whether, on true construction of the contract, one or other party has undertaken responsibility for the subsistence of the assumed state of affairs. This is another way of asking whether one or other party has undertaken the risk that it may not prove possible to perform the contract, and the answer to this question may well be the same as the answer to the question of whether the impossibility of performance is attributable to the fault of one or other of the parties.

Circumstances where a contract is void as a result of common mistake are likely to be less common than instances of frustration. Supervening events which defeat the contractual adventure will frequently not be the responsibility of either party. Where, however, the parties agree that something shall be done which is impossible at the time of making the agreement, it is much more likely that, on true construction of the agreement, one or other will have undertaken responsibility for the mistaken state of affairs. This may well explain why cases where contracts have been found to be void in consequence of common mistake are few and far between. Lord Atkin himself gave no examples of cases where a contract was rendered void because of a mistake as to quality which made 'the thing without the quality essentially different from the thing as it was believed to be'. He gave a number of examples of mistakes which did not satisfy this test, which served to demonstrate just how narrow he considered the test to be. Indeed this is further demonstrated by the result reached on the facts of *Bell v Lever Brothers* itself.

[I]n *Japanese Bank v Credit du Nord* [1989] 1 WLR 257, [t]he plaintiff bank entered into an agreement with a rogue under which he purported to sell and lease back four specific machines. The defendant bank agreed with the plaintiff bank to guarantee the rogue's payments under the lease-back agreement. The machines did not, in fact, exist. The rogue defaulted on his payments and the plaintiffs called on the guarantee. The defendants alleged (1) that on true construction of the agreement it was subject to an express condition precedent that the four machines existed; if this was not correct: (2) that the agreement was void at law for common mistake; if this was not correct the agreement was voidable in equity on the ground of mistake and had been avoided. . . . After reviewing the authorities on common mistake, [Steyn J] reached the following formulation of the law:

> The first imperative must be that the law ought to uphold rather than destroy apparent contracts. Secondly, the common law rules as to a mistake regarding the quality of the subject matter, like the common law rules regarding commercial frustration, are designed to cope with the impact of unexpected and wholly exceptional circumstances on apparent contracts. Thirdly, such a mistake in order to attract legal consequences must substantially be shared by both parties, and must relate to facts as they existed at the time the contract was made. Fourthly,

and this is the point established by *Bell v Lever Brothers Ltd* [1932] AC 161, the mistake must render the subject matter of the contract essentially and radically different from the subject matter which the parties believed to exist. While the civilian distinction between the substance and attributes of the subject matter of a contract has played a role in the development of our law (and was cited in speeches in *Bell v Lever Brothers Ltd*), the principle enunciated in *Bell v Lever Brothers Ltd* is markedly narrower in scope than the civilian doctrine. It is therefore no longer useful to invoke the civilian distinction. The principles enunciated by Lord Atkin and Lord Thankerton represent the *ratio decidendi* of *Bell v Lever Brothers Ltd*. Fifthly, there is a requirement which was not specifically discussed in *Bell v Lever Brothers Ltd*. What happens if the party, who is seeking to rely on the mistake, had no reasonable grounds for his belief? An extreme example is that of the man who makes a contract with minimal knowledge of the facts to which the mistake relates but is content that it is a good speculative risk. In my judgment a party cannot be allowed to rely on a common mistake where the mistake consists of a belief which is entertained by him without any reasonable grounds for such belief: cf *McRae v Commonwealth Disposals Commission* (1951) 84 CLR 377, 408. That is not because principles such as estoppel or negligence require it, but simply because policy and good sense dictate that the positive rules regarding common mistake should be so qualified.

The detailed analysis that we have carried out leads us to concur in this summary, subject to the proviso that the result in *McRae* can, we believe, be explained on the basis of construction, as demonstrated above. In agreeing with the analysis of Steyn J., we recognise that it is at odds with comments that Lord Denning made on more than one occasion about *Bell v Lever Brothers Ltd* to the effect that 'a common mistake, even on a most fundamental matter, does not make a contract void at law'. As to this Steyn J. said at p. 267:

> With the profoundest respect to the former Master of the Rolls I am constrained to say that in my view his interpretation of *Bell v Lever Brothers Ltd* does not do justice to the speeches of the majority.

. . . We share both the respect and the conclusion. . . . Steyn J. held that the test of common mistake was satisfied . . . We agree with [Toulson J.] that, on the facts of the present case, the issue in relation to common mistake turns on the question of whether the mistake as to the distance apart of the two vessels had the effect that the services that the *Great Peace* was in a position to provide were something essentially different from that to which the parties had agreed. We shall defer answering that question until we have considered whether principles of equity provide a second string to the defendants' bow.

Mistake in equity
In the House of Lords [in *Bell v Lever Brothers*] the report shows that the appellants relied on both common law authorities and *Cooper v Phibbs* in support of the submission that a common mistake had to be as to the existence of the subject matter of the contract if it was to render it void. The respondents do not appear to have suggested that equity might provide relief where common law would not. . . . Lord Blanesborough, when considering the pleadings, remarked at p. 190:

. . . the claim made by the heads of claim is for rescission of the agreements of settlement, relief properly consequent upon a case of voidability either for fraud or unilateral mistake induced by fraud. But if the allegation, even alternative, was that the agreements were entered into under mutual mistake of fact, then these agreements were not voidable but void *ab initio*, and no order on that footing is even hinted at in the relief sought.

Lord Warrington, who was for dismissing the appeal, does not appear to have believed that there was a significant difference between the situation where the common law would declare a contract void and that where equity would grant rescission on the ground of common mistake. . . . Lord Atkin at p. 218 cited *Cooper v Phibbs* as an example of mistake as to the subject matter of the contract:

This is the case of *Cooper v Phibbs*, where A agreed to take a lease of a fishery from B, though contrary to the belief of both parties at the time A was tenant for life of the fishery and B appears to have had no title at all. To such a case Lord Westbury applied the principle that if parties contract under a mutual mistake and misapprehension as to their relative and respective rights the result is that the agreement is liable to be set aside as having proceeded upon a common mistake. Applied to the context the statement is only subject to the criticism that the agreement would appear to be void rather than voidable.

Lord Thankerton at p. 235, when considering the type of mistaken assumption that would render a contract void in the light of a number of common law authorities, added:

The phrase 'underlying assumption by the parties', as applied to the subject matter of a contract, may be too widely interpreted so as to include something which one of the parties had not necessarily in his mind at the time of the contract: in my opinion it can only properly relate to something which both must necessarily have accepted in their minds as an essential and integral element of the subject matter. In the present case, however probable it may be, we are not necessarily forced to that assumption. *Cooper v Phibbs* (1) is a good illustration, for both parties must necessarily have proceeded on the mistaken assumption that the lessor had the right to grant the lease and that the lessee required a lease.

These passages demonstrate that the House of Lords in *Bell v Lever Brothers* considered that the intervention of equity, as demonstrated in *Cooper v Phibbs*, took place in circumstances where the common law would have ruled the contract void for mistake. We do not find it conceivable that the House of Lords overlooked an equitable right in *Lever Brothers* to rescind the agreement, notwithstanding that the agreement was not void for mistake at common law. The jurisprudence established no such right. Lord Atkin's test for common mistake that avoided a contract, while narrow, broadly reflected the circumstances where equity had intervened to excuse performance of a contract assumed to be binding in law.

Having considered the effect of *Solle v Butcher*, Lord Phillips then stated:

A number of cases, albeit a small number, in the course of the last fifty years have purported to follow *Solle v Butcher*, yet none of them defines the test of mistake that gives rise to the equitable jurisdiction to rescind in a manner that distinguishes this from the test of a mistake that renders a contract void in law, as identified in *Bell v Lever Brothers*. This is, perhaps, not surprising, for Lord Denning, the author of the test in *Solle v Butcher*, set *Bell v Lever Brothers* at nought. It is possible to reconcile *Solle v Butcher* and *Magee v Pennine Insurance* [1969] 2 QB 507 with *Bell v Lever Brothers* only by postulating that there are two categories of mistake, one that renders a contract void at law and one that renders it voidable in equity. Although later cases have proceeded on this basis, it is not possible to identify that proposition in the judgment of any of the three Lords Justice, Denning, Bucknill or Fenton Atkinson, who participated in the majority decisions in the former two cases. Nor, over fifty years, has it proved possible to define satisfactorily two different qualities of mistake, one operating in law and one in equity.

In *Solle v Butcher* Denning L.J. identified the requirement of a common misapprehension that was 'fundamental', and that adjective has been used to describe the mistakes in those cases which have followed *Solle v Butcher*. We do not find it possible to distinguish, by a process of definition, a mistake which is 'fundamental' from Lord Atkin's mistake as to quality which 'makes the thing contracted for essentially different from the thing that it was believed to be'. A common factor in *Solle v Butcher* and the cases which have followed it can be identified. The effect of the mistake has been to make the contract a particularly bad bargain for one of the parties. Is there a principle of equity which justifies the court in rescinding a contract where a common mistake has produced this result? . . .

[T]he premise of equity's intrusion into the effects of the common law is that the common law rule in question is seen in the particular case to work injustice, and for some reason the common law cannot cure itself. But it is difficult to see how that can apply here. Cases of fraud and misrepresentation, and undue influence, are all catered for under other existing and uncontentious equitable rules. We are only concerned with the question whether relief might be given for common mistake in circumstances wider than those stipulated in *Bell v Lever Brothers*. But that, surely, is a question as to where the common law should draw the line; not whether, given the common law rule, it needs to be mitigated by application of some other doctrine. The common law has drawn the line in *Bell v Lever Brothers*. The effect of *Solle v Butcher* is not to supplement or mitigate the common law; it is to say that *Bell v Lever Brothers* was wrongly decided.

Our conclusion is that it is impossible to reconcile *Solle v Butcher* with *Bell v Lever Brothers*. The jurisdiction asserted in the former case has not developed. It has been a fertile source of academic debate, but in practice it has given rise to a handful of cases that have merely emphasised the confusion of this area of our jurisprudence. . . . If coherence is to be restored to this area of our law, it can only be by declaring that there is no jurisdiction to grant rescission of a contract on the ground of common mistake where that contract is valid and enforceable on ordinary principles of contract law . . . We have been in some doubt as to whether this line of authority goes far enough to permit us to hold that *Solle v Butcher* is not good law. We are very conscious that we are not only scrutinising the reasoning of Lord Denning in *Solle v Butcher* and in *Magee v Pennine Insurance Co*, but are also faced with a number of later decisions in which Lord Denning's approach has been approved and followed. Further, a Division of this Court has made it clear in *West Sussex Properties Ltd v Chichester DC* that they felt bound by *Solle's* case. However, it is to be noticed that while junior counsel in the court below in *West Sussex* had sought to challenge the correctness of *Solle*, in the Court of Appeal leading counsel accepted that it was good law unless and until overturned by their Lordships' House. In this case we have heard full argument, which has provided what we believe has been the first opportunity in this court for a full and mature consideration of the relation between *Bell v Lever Brothers Ltd* and *Solle v Butcher*. In the light of that consideration we can see no way that *Solle v Butcher* can stand with *Bell v Lever Brothers*. In these circumstances we can see no option but so to hold.

We can understand why the decision in *Bell v Lever Brothers Ltd* did not find favour with Lord Denning. An equitable jurisdiction to grant rescission on terms where a common fundamental mistake has induced a contract gives greater flexibility than a doctrine of common law which holds the contract void in such circumstances. Just as the Law Reform (Frustrated Contracts) Act 1943 was needed to temper the effect of the common law doctrine of frustration, so there is scope for legislation to give greater flexibility to our law of mistake than the common law allows.

The result in this case
We revert to the question that we left unanswered [above]. It was unquestionably a common assumption of both parties when the contract was concluded that the two vessels were in sufficiently close proximity to enable the *Great Peace* to carry out the service that she was engaged to perform. Was the distance between the two vessels so great as to confound that assumption and to render the contractual adventure impossible of performance? If so, the appellants would have an arguable case that the contract was void under the principle in *Bell v Lever Brothers Ltd*. Toulson J. addressed this issue in the following paragraph:

> Was the *Great Peace* so far away from the *Cape Providence* at the time of the contract as to defeat the contractual purpose—or in other words to turn it into something essentially different from that for which the parties bargained? This is a question of fact and degree, but in my view the answer is 'no'. If it had been thought really necessary, the *Cape Providence* could have altered course so that both vessels were heading toward each other. At a closing speed of nineteen knots, it would have taken them about twenty-two hours to meet. A telling point is the reaction of the defendants on learning the true positions of the vessels. They did not want to cancel the agreement until they knew if they could find a nearer vessel to assist. Evidently the defendants did not regard the contract as devoid of purpose, or they would have cancelled at once.

[Counsel for the defendants] has attacked this paragraph on a number of grounds. He has submitted that the suggestion that the *Cape Providence* should have turned and steamed toward the *Great Peace* is unreal. We agree. The appellants were sending a tug from Singapore in an attempt to salvage the *Cape Providence*. The *Great Peace* was engaged by the appellants to act as a stand-by vessel to save human life, should this prove necessary, as an ancillary aspect of the salvage service. . . . Next [counsel for the defendants] submitted that it was not legitimate for the Judge to have regard to the fact that the appellants did not want to cancel the agreement with the *Great Peace* until they knew whether they could get a nearer vessel to assist. We do not agree. This reaction was a telling indication that the fact that the vessels were considerably further apart than the appellants had believed did not mean that the services that the *Great Peace* was in a position to provide were essentially different from those which the parties had envisaged when the contract was concluded. The *Great Peace* would arrive in time to provide several days of escort service. The appellants would have wished the contract to be performed but for the adventitious arrival on the scene of a vessel prepared to perform the same services. The fact that the vessels were further apart than both parties had appreciated did not mean that it was impossible to perform the contractual adventure. The parties entered into a binding contract for the hire of the *Great Peace*. That contract gave the appellants an express right to cancel the contract subject to the obligation to pay the 'cancellation fee' of five days hire. When they engaged the *Nordfarer* they cancelled the *Great Peace*. They became liable in consequence to pay the cancellation fee. There is no injustice in this result.

For the reasons that we have given, we would dismiss this appeal.

Notes

1. In A.Chandler, J.Devenney and J.Poole 'Common Mistake: Theoretical Justification and Remedial Inflexibility' [2004] JBL 34, the authors argue that although by denying the existence of an equitable jurisdiction to grant relief the Court of Appeal removed the need to reconcile the meaning of 'fundamental mistake' at common law and in equity, it has posed a dilemma for future courts by removing remedial flexibility almost in its entirety. The authors suggest that this is likely to result in a greater willingness by the courts to adopt a position on the contractual allocation of risk or to conclude that the contractual performance is not impossible or essentially different, and thereby avoid the limitations of a narrow doctrine of common mistake.

2. The question whether the equitable jurisdiction to set contracts aside for unilateral mistakes has survived the *Great Peace* decision has not been decided in the UK courts, although its continued existence has been assumed (see *Huyton SA v Distribuidora Internacional de Productos Agricolas SA de CV* [2003] 2 Lloyd's Rep. 780 and *Harrison v Halliwell Landau* [2004] EWHC 1316 (QB)). In 'Great Peace: A Distant Disturbance' 121 L.Q.R. 393 (2005), Yeo examines the decision of the Singapore Court of Appeal in *Chwee Kin Keong v Digilandmall.com Pte Ltd* [2005] 1 SLR 502 on this point. In that case, the court answered in the affirmative and further hinted that, even in respect of common mistakes, it may not follow *Great Peace*. It criticised *Great Peace* for putting too much weight on the lack of definition of the equitable jurisdiction as a reason for overruling *Solle v Butcher* and found that there was no logic to the denial of existence of this equitable jurisdiction. In the *Chwee Kin Keong* case, the defendant mistakenly offered a laser printer worth S$4,000 for sale on a website at S$66. Six individuals acting in concert ordered 1,606 printers and subsequently sued the defendant for refusing to honour the contract. The Court held that only actual knowledge of another's mistake would render a contract void at common law. It also held that the court had equitable jurisdiction to rescind a contract for unilateral mistake, but emphasised that there must be an element of impropriety or 'sharp practice' involved before the jurisdiction could be invoked. In such a case, it was not enough to show constructive knowledge; it had to be shown what advantage had been taken with the constructive knowledge. Thus it held that even if the claimants did not have actual knowledge, the sharp practice involved would have provided justification for rescission in equity.

3. While the view of the Irish Courts is not yet clear, there have been no indications to date of an intention to overturn *Solle v Butcher*.

Consider:

Should the Irish courts follow *Great Peace*?

Intrum Justitia Bv *v* Legal and Trade Financial Services Limited [2005] IEHC 190

The plaintiff agreed to purchase the entire issued share capital of an Irish subsidiary of the defendant for €2.15 million, of which 90 per cent was paid on closing. Prior to entering into the agreement the plaintiff had conducted a comprehensive due diligence process. The agreement provided for delivery of the completion accounts no later than four weeks following the completion date. During this period, the defendant discovered that the plaintiff's financial director had embezzled approximately €453,000 from the company. One of the issues before the High Court was whether the plaintiff was entitled to recission on the basis of mistake. It held that it was not entitled either at common law or in equity as the fraud did not essentially change the subject matter of the contract.

O'Sullivan J.:

The parties entered into an agreement which contains warranties by the defendant as vendor as to the accuracy and reliability of the financial information known to the parties at the time. These warranties are numerous and comprehensive and it is clear that they are wide enough to cover the situation that has arisen in the present case. Both parties clearly thought at the time that the accounts and financial information presented a true picture, and in that sense, of course, were mistaken as to the actual situation, but they also included by agreement warranties from the defendant intended to deal with a situation where their view of the account might not turn out to be the case. They acknowledged, in other words, that their current state of knowledge might be incomplete or inaccurate and came to an agreement as to which of them should bear the consequences if such should prove to be the case. Mistake in contract law concerns a situation where the parties think they know the true facts and proceed upon the basis of their erroneous assumption without even suspecting that their assumptions might be wrong, quite a different thing from the situation of the parties in the present case who thought they knew the true financial circumstances of the company but contemplated at the same time that their information may be misleading and proceeded to agree what was to happen if that should prove to be the case. Nobody suggests a contract of insurance is based on a mistake just because the parties cannot identify the event which it is intended to deal with.

Furthermore if, contrary to the above, it is correct to subject the circumstances of the present case to an analysis driven by the traditional law of mistake in contract cases, and that this analysis could, therefore, result in a conclusion that the plaintiff company is entitled to rescission, by reason of the fact that the parties did not appreciate the true financial picture, then in my view such a result would be anomalous given the situation that the same parties have addressed the possibility that the accounts might not present a true picture and in arranging what is to happen in such an event have agreed that rescission would not be available to the plaintiff. . .

Having considered such evidence as is available in my opinion, the effect of the fraud does not mean that the subject matter of the share-purchase agreement is essentially different from the one contracted for. Accordingly the plaintiff would not be entitled on the basis of mistake to rescission under common law as identified in *Bell v Lever Bros* [1932] AC 161. Nor is this a case where the misapprehension (to the effect that there had been no embezzlement) was fundamental to the agreement (which included the wide-ranging warranties already discussed and an agreement that their breach would not give rise to rescission). Accordingly the plaintiff would not be entitled to rescission in equity as identified in *Solle v Butcher* [1950] 1 KB 671 and as applied in this country by Costello J. (as he then was) in *O'Neill v Ryan* [1992] 1 IR 166 672 at p. 185.

Of course I acknowledge that the plaintiff company's witnesses said that if they had known in advance of the embezzlement, they would not have entered the agreement. This does not prove, however, that therefore the effect of the embezzlement was fundamental, anymore than an insured driver's assertion that he would not have driven on the day of the accident had he known of it beforehand means that he did not need insurance. This was an agreement to buy shares in a company with specific objectives in mind and the plaintiff company's evidence referred to has to be seen in context. The evidence is that the 'drivers' for the purchase of these shares were the plaintiff company's desire to acquire the very good client base including some blue-chip clients of the defendant, and its good employees and in particular, John Cahill the Managing Director, to improve the company's position in the Irish market and to receive the disclosed revenue stream, enhanced by the synergies that would become operative when the two companies were merged together. It is also clear from the evidence that the merging process has been put on hold since the discovery of Colin Thorpe's embezzlement but that notwithstanding this the revenue stream has remained as predicted, and that John Cahill remains employed at the Ashtown Gate premises albeit not as Managing Director. One or two clients have transferred from the Ashtown Gate (erstwhile defendant) company's business to the plaintiff's own English subsidiary business at Park West and the one or two clients who have ceased doing business have done so for reasons other than those related to the embezzlement. Of course it is true that the embezzlement has not become public knowledge and that when it does many clients may become concerned as has happened apparently in England to a subsidiary of the plaintiff company's where a non-fraudulent discrepancy was discovered and which caused considerable upset and loss to that company. There was further evidence that the clients, particularly the blue-chip clients such as banks, of a company engaged in debt collection on behalf of those clients, will be particularly sensitive to the publication of financial impropriety within the debt-collecting company. They can only be reassured, it is said, by a full forensic audit which establishes that none of their own monies were taken, that none of their clients had complained about being asked to discharge bills already paid and that there was a clear and reliable identification of the extent of the embezzlement. Nobody suggested that such an exercise is impossible but there has been widely divergent views as to the cost of such an audit and indeed the specific scope involved. Once again in this context I am left in the situation where no such audit has taken place and accordingly I must deal with the evidence produced without speculating beyond it. Given, therefore, that the likelihood is that the extent of the audit is limited to some four hundred and fifty-seven thousand euro and that a forensic exercise can be done which will establish with reasonable certainty such extent and can satisfy clients including blue-chip clients of the defendant company, and bearing in mind the 'drivers' which motivated the plaintiff in acquiring the defendant's company shares, I do not think that what the plaintiff got in their share-purchase agreement was so different from what they contracted for as to qualify for the descriptions in the authorities which justify an entitlement to rescission either at common law or in equity. In other words this is not one of those exceptional circumstances which are extremely limited where rescission as distinct from damages will be granted by a court as identified by Costello J. (as he then was) in *O'Neill v Ryan*.

Note

The above case demonstrates that despite the acknowledgment of a doctrine of common mistake as to the terms of an agreement, in practice it is very difficult to establish the necessary radical difference required to invalidate the contract. This point is borne out by the recent decision of the Court of Appeal in *Kyle Bay Ltd (t/a Astons Nightclub) v Underwriters* [2007] Lloyd's Rep. IR 460. In that case, the Court applied the test in *Associated Japanese Bank* and deemed that the mistake made by the parties in the case before it did not render what the parties believed to be the subject matter of the agreement 'essentially and radically different' from what it was. The case involved an insurance policy on a nightclub. The parties correctly believed that they were settling a business interruption claim resulting from a fire at the nightclub and they agreed the period of interruption and the nature of the cover. The only mistake related to the assumption that the policy was on a gross-profits basis rather than on the declaration-linked basis. In commercial terms, this led to the plaintiff receiving 33 per cent less than it should have received. Neuberger L.J. held that the difference between the actual and assumed subject matter of the agreement could be characterised as significant, but was not an 'essential and radical' difference. The mistake was deemed thus to relate to a detail and did not go to the validity of the policy.

Consider:

Does a broad doctrine of common mistake allow a purchaser to abdicate responsibility from engaging in a proper verification exercise?

SECTION THREE—MUTUAL MISTAKE

A mutual mistake occurs where each party is mistaken as to the other's intention. For example, a vendor owning two cars intends to sell his 1980 model Porsche. Unknown to him the purchaser believes the vendor to be selling his 1990 model Porsche. The parties are thus bargaining at cross purposes. The general rule is that parties are bound by their apparent agreements, in the interests of certainty and commercial convenience.

Smith v Hughes (1871) LR 2 QB 597

The plaintiff offered to sell oats to the defendant, a racehorse trainer. He exhibited a sample which the defendants kept for two days before accepting the offer. The defendant later refused to accept the oats on the ground that they were new and he believed he was buying old oats. The plaintiff sued for damages for breach of contract.

Cockburn C.J.:

I take the true rule to be, that where a specific article is offered for sale, without express warranty, or without circumstances from which the law will imply a warranty—as where, for instance, an article is ordered for a specific purpose—and the buyer has full opportunity of inspecting and forming his own judgment, if he chooses to act on his own judgment, the rule *caveat emptor* applies. If he gets the article he contracted to buy, and that article corresponds with what it was sold as, he gets all he is entitled to, and is bound by the contract. Here the defendant agreed to buy a specific parcel of oats. The oats were what they were sold as, namely, good oats according to the sample. The buyer persuaded himself they were old oats, when they were not so; but the seller neither said nor did anything to contribute to his deception. He has himself to blame. . . .

It only remains to deal with an argument which was pressed upon us, that the defendant in the present case intended to buy old oats, and the plaintiff to sell new, so the two minds were not *ad idem*; and that consequently there was no contract. This argument proceeds on the fallacy of confounding what was merely a motive operating on the buyer to induce him to buy with one of the essential conditions of the contract. Both parties were agreed as to the sale and purchase of this particular parcel of oats. The defendant believed the oats to be old, and was thus induced to agree to buy them, but he omitted to make their age a condition of the contract. All that can be said is, that the two minds were not *ad idem* as to the age of the oats; they certainly were *ad idem* as to the sale and purchase of them. Suppose a person to buy a horse without a warranty, believing him to be sound, and the horse turns out unsound, could it be contended that it would be open to him to say that, as he had intended to buy a sound horse, and the seller to sell an unsound one, the contract was void, because the seller must have known from the price the buyer was willing to give, or from his general habits as a buyer of horses, that he thought the horse was sound? The cases are exactly parallel.

In *Smith v Hughes* (1871) LR 2 QB 597, Blackburn J. stated:

I apprehend that if one of the parties intends to make a contract on one set of terms, and the other intends to make a contract on another set of terms, or, as it is sometimes expressed, if the parties are not *ad idem*, there is no contract, unless the circumstances are such as to preclude one of the parties from denying that he has agreed to the terms of the other. The rule of law is that stated in *Freeman v Cooke* 2 Ex at p.663. If, whatever a man's real intention may be, he so conducts himself that a reasonable man would believe that he was assenting to the terms proposed by the other party, and that other party upon that belief enters into the contract with him, the man thus conducting himself would be equally bound as if he had intended to agree to the other party's terms.

However, if there is a degree of ambiguity which makes it impossible to say objectively that the parties intended to be bound by one set of terms or another, the contract will be invalid because the offer and acceptance will not coincide and no agreement will have been reached. Such was the case in *Raffles v Wichelhaus* 2 H & C 906, *Scriven Bros v Hindley & Co* [1913] 3 KB 564 and the *Mespil* case below.

The important question for the Courts is whether there has been a fundamental mistake as to the basis of the contract or merely a mistake as to motive, i.e. the quality of the item being sold. The latter will not affect the validity of the contract.

Mespil Ltd and Aramaic Ltd *v* Capaldi and Bowes [1986] ILRM 373

Certain actions brought by the plaintiffs against the defendants were purported to be settled by their respective counsel. The scope of the written settlement was later disputed by the parties, the defendants believing that the settlement covered all acts in dispute between the parties, and the plaintiffs believing that it covered merely the matters in issue in the proceedings in question.

Henchy J.:

Having regard to the evidence given in the High Court, I am satisfied that the finding of mutual mistake was fully justified. No blame is to be attributed to the two able and experienced counsel in question who, in the limited time available to them on the morning of the hearing, sought to achieve a binding settlement in accordance with their respective instructions. But, not having time to reduce the terms of settlement to full and unambiguous written expression, the heads of settlement which they authenticated with their signatures were not sufficiently specific to exclude ambiguity. The result was that the two counsel left court that day, each with a genuine but opposite belief as to what the settlement had achieved.

Notwithstanding the finding of mutual mistake, the judge held that the defendants were bound by the terms of the settlement to the extent of having to pay the £21,000 outstanding. This conclusion was reached on the basis of cases which have decided that when a person enters into an agreement, giving the other person the impression that he understands the nature and effect of the agreement, the general rule is that he will not be allowed to say later that he should not be bound by the agreement because he did not at the time understand its import or effect. That is undoubtedly correct law. Business relations would be thrown into undesirable uncertainty if a party to an agreement, who at the time gave no indication that he did not understand what he was doing, could later renounce the agreement on subjective considerations. If he freely and competently entered into the agreement, he will not normally escape being bound by it by saying that he misunderstood its effect.

The position is essentially different when, as is the case here, there was mutual or bilateral mistake as to the true nature of the agreement. Different and more fundamental principles of the law of contract come to be applied in such circumstances.

It is of the essence of an enforceable simple contract that there be a *consensus ad idem*, expressed in an offer and an acceptance. Such a consensus cannot be said to exist unless there is a correspondence between the offer and the acceptance. If the offer made is accepted by the other person in a fundamentally different sense from that in which it was tendered by the offeror, and the circumstances are objectively such as to justify such an acceptance, there cannot be said to be the meeting of minds which is essential for an enforceable contract. In such circumstances the alleged contract is a nullity.

Applying those basic principles to the present case, it is clear that the form of the written consent, viewed in terms of its wording and of the negotiations leading up to it, was capable of justifying the opinion of counsel for the defendants that the settlement was adequate to cover all outstanding complaints between the parties. It is also to be said, on an objective consideration of the relevant circumstances, that counsel for the plaintiffs was justified in thinking that the settlement was limited to the matters in dispute in the two actions then being settled. In those circumstances of latent ambiguity and mutual misunderstanding, it must be held that there was no real agreement between the parties. The two counsel who negotiated the settlement were understandably at cross purposes. The result was that the seeming agreement expressed in the written consent was in fact no agreement. There was a fundamental misunderstanding as to the basis of the settlement. It is clear that the defendants would not have agreed to make the payments required by the settlement if they knew that the plaintiffs could seek to oust them from the premises by means of other proceedings. It is equally clear that counsel for the plaintiffs would not have signed the settlement if he knew it would be treated by the defendants as an absolution of them from all complaints by the plaintiffs. Objectively viewed, the situation justified the misapprehension on each side. The result is that, for want of correspondence between offer and acceptance, no enforceable contract was made. The alleged settlement, whether in the interpretation of the plaintiffs or in that of the defendants, must be held to be nullity.

O'Neill v Ryan [1991] ILRM 672.
(For the facts see p. 337)

Costello J.:

I come now to the category of mistake which it is said operated in this case, that is one in which each party is mistaken as to the other's intention, although neither appreciates that he is misunderstood. This can arise, and has here arisen the defendants submit, where one party makes an offer which the other party accepts in a fundamentally different sense from that intended by the offeror. The legal principles to be applied in such cases have been long established and I adopt the following passages of *Chitty on Contracts* (1989 ed.) vol. 1 paras 351 and 352 as a correct statement of the law:

> The intention of the parties is, as a general rule, to be construed objectively. The language used by one party, whatever his real intention may be, is to be construed in the sense in which it would be reasonably understood by the other, or at least in the sense in which a reasonable person would construe it. Nevertheless cases may occur in which the terms of the offer and acceptance suffer from such latent ambiguity that it is impossible reasonably to impute any agreement between them; or it may happen that one party knowingly accepts a promise in different terms from those intended by the other. In such circumstances the mistake may render the contract void.
>
> In most cases the application of the objective test will preclude a party who has entered into a contract under a mistake from setting up his mistake as a defence to an action against him for breach of contract. If a reasonable man would have understood the contract in a certain sense, then despite his mistake, the court will hold that the mistaken party is bound. But where parties are genuinely at cross purposes as to the subject matter of the contract and the terms of the offer and acceptance are so ambiguous that it is not possible to point to one or other of the interpretations as the more probable, the court must necessarily hold that no contract exists.

It is the principle of law thus formulated that I applied earlier in this judgment. It required me to consider the words used by the defendants' solicitors in their letter of 24 May 1990 and to construe them objectively in the sense in which they would reasonably be understood. In doing so I concluded that they would be reasonably understood as an offer to settle the s. 205 [Companies Act 1963] proceedings only and not as an offer to settle those proceedings and the plenary action. It was in this sense that the offer was accepted by the letter of 30 May 1990. The defence of mistake therefore fails as I cannot take into account that the authors of the letter may have intended to make an offer of settlement different to that which a reasonable construction of the words they used disclosed.

There are a number of reasons why the court should adopt this rule. As explained by the Supreme Court:

> . . . when a person enters into an agreement, giving the other person the impression that he understands the nature and effect of the agreement, the general rule is that he will not be allowed to say later that he should not be bound by the agreement because he did not at the time understand its import or effect. That is undoubtedly correct law. Business relations would be thrown into undesirable uncertainty if a party to an agreement, who at the time gave no indication that he did not understand what he was doing, could later renounce the agreement on subjective considerations. If he freely and competently entered into the agreement, he will not normally escape being bound by saying that he misunderstood its effect. (*Mespil Ltd v Capaldi* [1986] ILRM 373, 376.)

In addition to the reason there given the rule is required for the proper administration of justice. As explained, a considerable time ago, in *Fry on Specific Performance*, (5th ed.), 765: 'It seems on general principle clear that one party to a contract can never defend himself against it by setting up a misunderstanding on his part as to the real meaning and effect of the contract, or any of the terms in which it is expressed. To permit such a defence would be to open the door to perjury and to destroy the security of contracts (quoted with approval in *Eastes v Russ* [1914] 1 Ch. 468, 480.)'

Furthermore it seems to me that an estoppel arises which precludes an offeror adducing evidence of intention. If an offeror intends his offer in one sense but fails to convey that sense in the words he uses (as objectively determined) and the offeree accepts it in the sense in which the words could reasonably be construed it seems to me that the offeror is estopped from relying on his own error if detriment would thereby be suffered by the offeree. As quite clearly detriment would be suffered by the plaintiff if the defendants for the purpose of showing the parties were not *ad idem* were at liberty to adduce evidence to contradict the sense in which the words in the letter of 24 May 1990 can reasonably be construed, the law should not permit such evidence to be adduced. . . .

There is another aspect of the principles enunciated in the quotation from *Chitty* to which I should refer. If one party knows that a mistake is made by the offeror in the offer and accepts it with this knowledge the mistaken party may give evidence of what his intention was and the fact that the parties were at cross purposes will mean that the contract was void. This principle is illustrated by *Hartog v Colin and Shields* [1939] 3 All ER 566. That was a case dealing with the sale of hare skins by the defendant to the plaintiff. In pre-contract negotiations the parties bargained on the basis of the skins being sold at a price per piece. By mistake the defendant eventually offered them at a price based on their *weight*, an offer which the plaintiff accepted. When the defendant ascertained his mistake and refused to deliver the skins he was sued by the purchaser for damages for non-delivery. It was held that the objective test did not apply because the plaintiff must have known that the offer did not reflect the defendant's true intention and that the contract was void. I draw attention to this principle because it was relevant to know whether the plaintiff's solicitor knew that the defendants had made an error in their letter of 24 May 1990. Had he known that they intended to make an offer to settle both sets of proceedings then the objective test would not apply and the apparent agreement would be declared void. His evidence was therefore relevant to the issues I had to consider and I do not think that by tendering it the plaintiff thereby is precluded from objecting to the relevance of the evidence of the intention of the defendant's solicitors. As he clearly did not know of their intention and could not reasonably have known it the objective test applies.

[Having concluded that a valid enforceable came into existence, Costello J. made an order for specific performance.]

Ferguson *v* Merchant Banking Ltd [1993] ILRM 136

The plaintiff agreed to sell the defendant lands contained in certain folios consisting of ground rental properties. Unknown to the defendant the folios also included a valuable vacant site. The plaintiff's principal was aware of this error but did not believe the vacant site to be of significant value. When the error was discovered the defendant refused to complete the contract and the plaintiff sued for specific performance. The defendant counterclaimed seeking rectification or alternatively rescission of the contract to give effect to what were claimed to be the true intentions of the parties. The High Court granted specific performance.

Murphy J.:

[Having referred to *Dore v Stephenson*, (HC) 24 April 1980, unreported, *Mespil Ltd v Capaldi* [1986] ILRM 373 and *Magee v Pennine Insurance Co. Ltd* [1969] 2 All ER 891] Whether the matter is viewed as fundamental mistake or absence of consensus it seems to me that the defendants in the present case are not entitled to deprive the plaintiff of the benefit of the contract into which he entered. In my view there is no fundamental error and no absence of agreement on any fundamental term. The liquidator of the defendant company agreed to sell the property which was clearly defined in the legal documents executed by him. There was no material provision overlooked or neglected in that documentation. There was no want of consensus and no mistake as to what in substance was being sold. An error or misunderstanding may have arisen as to the extent of the undeveloped property and certainly an error on the part of the vendor as to the potential value thereof. These are not considerations which would give rise to a right of rescission in law or in equity in the absence of some abuse or sharp practice on the part of the vendor.

SECTION FOUR—UNILATERAL MISTAKE

A unilateral mistake arises where one party is aware of the other party's mistake. This mistake may relate either to the terms of the agreement or the identity of one of the parties.

(a) Mistake as to terms of the agreement.

In this context the nature of the mistake made by one of the parties, i.e. as to the basis of the contract or the motivation of the party entering the contract, is again crucial. The following extract from *Anson's Law of Contract* (28th edn), pp. 324–5 usefully illustrates the different approaches to mutual and unilateral mistake.

A sells X a piece of china.
1. X thinks that it is Dresden china. A thinks it is not. Each takes his chance. X may get a better thing than A intended to sell, or a worse thing than he himself intended to buy; in neither case is the validity of the contract affected.
2. X thinks that it is Dresden china. A knows that X thinks so, and knows that it is not. The contract holds, A must do nothing to deceive X, but he is not bound to prevent X from deceiving himself as to the *quality* of the thing sold. X's error is one of motive alone, and although it is known to A, it is insufficient.
3. X thinks that it is Dresden china and thinks that A intends to contract to sell it as Dresden china; and A knows that it is not Dresden china, but does not know that X thinks that he is contracting to sell it as Dresden china. A reasonably believes that X is assenting to a sale of china in general terms.

The contract holds. The misapprehension by X of the extent of A's promise, *if unknown to A*, has no effect, unless, as in *Scriven Bros & Co. v Hindley & Co.*, A has caused or contributed to X's misapprehension.

4. X thinks it is Dresden china, and thinks that A intends to contract to sell it as Dresden china. A knows that X *thinks he is contracting to sell it as Dresden china*, but does not mean to, and in fact does not offer more than china in general terms. There is no contract to sell the particular piece of china. X's error was not one of judgment as to the quality of the china, as in 2., but was an error as to the nature of A's promise, and A, knowing that his promise was misunderstood, nevertheless allowed the mistake to continue. The apparent agreement is not a contract if A knows that X has accepted his offer in terms different from those in which it was in fact made.

These propositions can be illustrated by two cases. The first is *Smith v Hughes*. The second case in which the same rule was applied in slightly different circumstances is *Hartog v Colin and Shields*.

The *Hartog* case is explained by Costello J. in *O'Neill v Ryan* above at p. 493.

Smith v Hughes (1871) LR 2 QB 597
(facts on p. 490)

Cockburn C.J.:

[W]e must assume that nothing was said on the subject of the defendant's manager desiring to buy old oats, nor of the oats having been said to be old; while, on the other hand, we must assume that the defendant's manager believed the oats to be *old* oats, and that the plaintiff was conscious of the existence of such belief, but did nothing, directly or indirectly, to bring it about, simply offering his oats and exhibiting his sample, remaining perfectly passive as to what was passing in the mind of the other party. The question is whether, under such circumstances, the passive acquiescence of the seller in the self-deception of the buyer will entitle the latter to avoid the contract. I am of opinion that it will not . . .

If, indeed, the buyer, instead of acting on his own opinion, had asked the question whether the oats were old or new, or had said anything which intimated his understanding that the seller was selling the oats as old oats, the case would have been wholly different; or even if he had said anything which shewed that he was not acting on his own inspection and judgment, but assumed as the foundation of the contract that the oats were old, the silence of the seller, as a means of misleading him, might have amounted to a fraudulent concealment, such as would have entitled the buyer to avoid the contract. Here, however, nothing of the sort occurs. The buyer in no way refers to the seller, but acts entirely on his own judgment.

Blackburn J.:

In this case I agree that on the sale of a specific article, unless there be a warranty making it part of the bargain that it possesses some particular quality, the purchaser must take the article he has bought though it does not possess that quality. And I agree that even if the vendor was aware that the purchaser thought that the article possessed that quality, and would not have entered into the contract unless he had so thought, still the purchaser is bound, unless the vendor was guilty of some fraud or deceit upon him, and that a mere abstinence from disabusing the purchaser of that impression is not fraud or deceit; for, whatever may be the case in a court of morals, there is no legal obligation on the vendor to inform the purchaser that he is under a mistake, not induced by the act of the vendor.

Notes

1. McMahon J. in *Reen v Bank of Ireland Finance and Luceys Garage* (*Mallow*) *Ltd* [1983] ILRM 507 relied on the above statement of Blackburn J. in considering a claim for unilateral mistake. In that case, an offer to settle action for breach of contract was made to the plaintiff. Unknown to the plaintiff the settlement did not include provision for all the legal costs involved. Although the defendant's solicitor was aware of this at the time the agreement was made, he did not notify the other party of its mistake. McMahon J. opined that 'The [the defendant's solicitor] must have recognised that there was a possibility that [the plaintiff's solicitor] was making a mistake in overlooking the matter of his client's liability for the bank's costs but in the absence of any mistake as to the terms of the agreement [the defendant's solicitor] in my view had no duty to enquire of [the plaintiff's solicitor] whether the bank's costs had been dealt with.'

2. It is clear from the case of *Stapleton v Prudential Assurance Co. Ltd* (1928) 62 ILTR 56 (see p. 608 below) that a self-induced mistake will not ground relief. There, a life assurance contract was valid though the plaintiff entered it under a mistake as to the nature of its terms.

Gill *v* McDowell [1903] 2 IR 463

A hermaphrodite animal, as well as a bullock and a heifer, were sold together by the defendant to the plaintiff at a fair. Although no warranty was given as to the sex of the hermaphrodite animal, the plaintiff bought it in the belief that it was either a bullock or a heifer.

Lord O'Brien L.C.J.:

[I]n my opinion there is evidence that the defendant believed the plaintiff believed that he (the defendant) was contracting to sell two heifers and a bullock, and if the plaintiff did so believe, the case comes, in my opinion, within the doctrine laid down in *Smith v Hughes*, and the defendant is responsible.

Gibson J.:

Where the seller knows that the buyer is under a mistake as to the subject matter contracted to be sold there is no enforceable contract. The plaintiff bought what he thought the defendant was professing to sell as a heifer. If the plaintiff had expressed his meaning in words, and defendant said nothing, or if the defendant had expressly sold the beast as a heifer, unquestionably there would have been no valid sale. Where nothing is said on either side, if the vendor knows that the purchaser intends a different contract from what he himself contemplates, he cannot by silence impose on the purchaser a contract which he knows the latter never intended to make. Does the principle apply here? Nothing was said as to warranty or description; the animal was there to be examined, and its defect on careful examination would have been ascertained. Does this exclude the application of the principle? I think not. The rule depends on the necessity of intelligent consent to the same contract; and it does not cease to be applicable because the buyer is guilty of some oversight or want of care. The vendor cannot force on the purchaser an article which he knows the latter never proposed to buy. The principle does not conflict with the maxim *caveat emptor*, or with the legal right of the vendor to acquiesce in the silent self-deception of the purchaser, where he is under no duty to set him right. It only applies where the parties are not *ad idem* as to the contract proper. The distinction is clearly pointed out in the judgments in *Smith v Hughes* and in the text-books to which I have referred. . . . The determining fact in the case is that the animal did not answer the description of bullock or heifer under which description, as part of the contract, the defendant knew the plaintiff was proposing to buy. It was not a case of the animal being a bullock or a heifer with a sexual malformation or deficiency. I hold that there was no effectual contract. . . .

Notes

1. In this case the majority of the Court also held that there was evidence of deceit on the part of the defendant. As a result the defendant was held liable in damages to the plaintiff.
2. In 2008, Aer Lingus advertised transatlantic business fares worth €1,175 on its website for €5. Aer Lingus subsequently claimed that this was caused by a technical error and it notified approximately 300 customers who had booked flights at this price that it was cancelling the bookings and not providing compensation. Initially an Aer Lingus representative stated that anyone booking these tickets should have realised that there had been a mistake. Subsequently, however, Aer Lingus agreed to honour the flights (as economy fares) on the basis that its investigation had indicated that customers might genuinely have believed they were making a booking in economy class.

MISTAKE AS TO IDENTITY

A unilateral mistake as to identity arises where a person sell goods to one person believing that they are a particular person. Often the mistake only comes to light when the rogue who has acquired goods on credit sells them on to an innocent purchaser and the original owner seeks to recover the goods. In such a case it becomes important to determine whether the rogue acquired title to the goods. If the contract with the original owner is deemed void for mistake no such title is acquired but if the title is merely voidable, section 23 of the Sale of Goods Act 1893 allows a *bona fide* purchaser for value without notice to acquire title. In determining the consequences of a mistake as to identity, the courts have drawn a distinction between face-to-face transactions and transactions concluded by post.

Cundy v Lindsay (1978) 3 AC 459

The respondents were linen manufacturers in Belfast. A rogue, Alfred Blenkarn, living at 37 Wood Street, Cheapside, ordered goods from the plaintiffs signing his name to look like 'Blenkiron & Co'. The respondents, believing themselves to be dealing with a highly respected firm called 'W. Blenkiron & Son' which actually operated from premises at 123 Wood Street, dispatched the goods addressed to 'Blenkiron & Co' at 37 Wood Street. The goods were later sold to the appellants who were without knowledge of the fraud. The appellants appealed against a decision of the Court of Appeal (overturning Queen's Bench) that no valid contract existed.

Lord Cairns:

[H]ow is it possible to imagine that in that state of things any contract could have arisen between the respondents and Blenkarn, the dishonest man? Of him they knew nothing, and of him they never thought. With him they never intended to deal. Their minds never, even for an instant of time rested upon him, and as between him and them there was no consensus of mind which could lead to any agreement or any contract whatever. As between him and them there was merely the one side to a contract, where, in order to produce a contract, two sides would be required. With the firm of Blenkiron & Co. of course there was no contract, for as to them the matter was entirely unknown, and therefore the pretence of a contract was a failure.

   The result, therefore, my Lords, is this, that your Lordships have not here to deal with one of those cases in which there is *de facto* a contract made which may afterwards be impeached and set aside, on the ground of fraud; but you have to deal with a case which ranges itself under a completely different chapter of law, the case namely in which the contract never comes into existence. My Lords, that being so, it is idle to talk of the property passing. The property remained, as it originally had been, the property of the respondents, and the title which was attempted to be given to the appellants was a title which could not be given to them.

Note

This case was distinguished in the case of *King's Norton Metal Co. Ltd v Eldridge, Merrett & Co.* (1897) 14 TLR 98 where a contract was said to exist. In that case a rogue obtained goods by purporting to be a successful business. The court held that unlike *Cundy v Lindsay* the plaintiffs had not confused the rogue's company with any other existing company.

Phillips *v* Brooks Ltd [1919] 2 KB 243

A rogue entered the plaintiff's jewellery shop and offered to purchase certain items of jewellery. He wrote a cheque for the sum due, saying 'You see who I am, I am Sir George Bullough', and he gave an address in St James' Square. The plaintiff knew that such a person existed and verified in a directory that the address was correct. The plaintiff allowed the rogue to take a ring with him. Later the cheque was dishonoured. In the meantime the ring was pledged to the defendants, a firm of pawnbrokers who advanced money upon it in good faith.

Horridge J.:

I have carefully considered the evidence of the plaintiff, and have come to the conclusion that, although he believed the person to whom he was handing the ring was Sir George Bullough, he in fact contracted to sell and deliver it to the person who came into his shop, and who was not Sir George Bullough, but a man of the name of North, who obtained the sale and delivery by means of the false pretence that he was Sir George Bullough. It is quite true the plaintiff in re-examination said he had no intention of making any contract with any other person than Sir George Bullough; but I think I have myself to decide what is the proper inference to draw where a verbal contract is made and an article delivered to an individual describing himself as somebody else. . . .

The question, therefore, in this case is whether or not the property had so passed to the swindler as to entitle him to give a good title to any person who gave value and acted *bona fide* without notice. This question seems to have been decided in an American case of *Edmunds v Merchants' Despatch Transportation Co.*[1] . . . The following expressions used in the judgment of Morton C.J. seem to me to fit the facts in this case:

> The minds of the parties met and agreed upon all the terms of the sale, the thing sold, the price and time of payment, the person selling and the person buying. The fact that the seller was induced to sell by fraud of the buyer made the sale voidable, but not void. He could not have supposed that he was selling to any other person; his intention was to sell to the person present, and identified by sight and hearing; it does not defeat the sale because the buyer assumed a false name or practised any other deceit to induce the vendor to sell.

Further on, Morton C.J. says: 'In the cases before us, there was a *de facto* contract, purporting, and by which the plaintiffs intended, to pass the property and possession of the goods to the person buying them; and we are of opinion that the property did pass to the swindler who bought the goods.' . . .

It was argued before me that the principle quoted from Pothier (Traité des Obligations, §19), in *Smith v Wheatcroft*,[2] namely, 'Whenever the consideration of the person with whom I am willing to contract enters as an element into the contract which I am willing to make, error with regard to the person destroys my consent and consequently annuls the contract' applies. I do not think, however, that that passage governs this case, because I think the seller intended to contract with the person present, and there was no error as to the person with whom he contracted, although the plaintiff would not have made the contract if there had not been a fraudulent misrepresentation. Moreover, the case of *Smith v Wheatcroft* was an action for specific performance, and was between the parties to the contract, and had no relation to rights acquired by third parties innocently under the contract, and misrepresentation would have been an answer to the enforcement of the contract. In this case, I think, there was a passing of the property and the purchaser had a good title, and there must be judgment for the defendants with costs.

[1.] 135 Mass. 283.   [2.] 9 ChD 223.

Ingram *v* Little [1960] 3 All ER 332

The plaintiffs advertised their car for sale and a rogue viewed it and agreed to purchase it for £717. When the plaintiffs refused to accept a cheque, the rogue claimed to be a Mr P.G.M. Hutchinson of Stanstead House, Caterham. Having checked the telephone book and ascertained that such a person did exist, the plaintiffs accepted the cheque. The cheque was dishonoured and the car was later sold to the defendant, a *bona fide* purchaser. The plaintiffs' action for conversion succeeded and the defendant appealed.

Sellers L.J.:

Where two parties are negotiating together and there is no question of one or the other purporting to act as agent for another and an agreement is reached, the normal and obvious conclusion would no doubt be that they are the contracting parties. A contrary finding would not be justified unless very clear evidence demanded it. The unfortunate position of the defendant in this case illustrates how third parties who deal in good faith with the fraudulent person may be prejudiced. The mere presence of an individual cannot, however, be conclusive that an apparent bargain which he may make is made with him. If he were disguised in appearance and in dress to represent someone else and the other party, deceived by the disguise, dealt with him on the basis that he was that person and would not have contracted had he known the truth, then, it seems clear, there would be no contract established. If words are substituted for outward disguise so as to depict a different person from the one physically present, in what circumstances would the result be different?

Whether the person portrayed, by disguise or words, is known to the other party or not is important in considering whether the identity of the person is of any moment or whether it is a matter of indifference . . . It would seem that there is an area of fact in cases of the type under consideration where a fraudulent person is present purporting to make a bargain with another and that the circumstances may justify a finding that, notwithstanding some fraud and deceit, the correct view may be that a bargain was struck with the person present or on the other hand they may equally justify, as here, a finding the other way . . .

The question in each case should be solved in my opinion by applying the test which Slade J. applied: 'How ought the promisee to have interpreted the promise?'

Devlin L.J. (dissenting):

. . . The presumption that a person is intending to contract with the person to whom he is actually addressing the words of contract seems to me to be a simple and sensible one and supported by some good authority. It is adopted in *Benjamin on Sale* (8th ed.), 102, where two decisions in the US are referred to, *Edmunds v Merchants' Despatch Transportation Co.*[1] and *Phelps v McQuade*.[2] . . . What seems plain to me is that the presumption cannot in the present case be rebutted by piling up the evidence to show that Miss Ingram would never have contracted with Hutchinson unless she had thought him to be Mr P. G. M. Hutchinson. That fact is conceded and, whether it is proved *simpliciter* or proved to the hilt, it does not go any further than to show that she was the victim of fraud. With great respect to the learned judge, the question that he propounded as the test is not calculated to show any more than that. He said: 'Is it to be seriously suggested that they were willing to accept the cheque of the rogue other than in the belief, created by the rogue himself, that he, the rogue, was in fact the honest Mr P. G. M. Hutchinson of the address in Caterham with the telephone number which they had verified?' In my judgment there is everything to show that Miss Ingram would never have accepted Hutchinson's offer if she had known the truth, but nothing to rebut the ordinary presumption that she was addressing her acceptance, in law as well as in fact, to the person to whom she was speaking. I think therefore that there was offer and acceptance in form.

On my view of the law, it therefore becomes necessary to consider next whether there has been a mistake that vitiates the contract. . . . In my judgment there has been no such mistake. I shall assume without argument what I take to be the widest view of mistake that is to be found in the authorities; and that is that a mistake avoids the contract if at the time when it is made there exists some state of fact which, as assumed, is the basis of the contract and, as it is in truth, frustrates its object. . . . The fact that Miss Ingram refused to contract with Hutchinson until his supposed name and address had been 'verified' goes to show that she regarded his identity as fundamental. In this she was misguided. She should have concerned herself with credit-worthiness rather than with identity. The fact that Hutchinson gave Mr P. G. M. Hutchinson's address in the directory was no proof that he was Mr P. G. M. Hutchinson; and, if he had been, that fact alone was no proof that his cheque would be met. Identity therefore did not really matter. Nevertheless, it may truly be said that to Miss Ingram, as she looked at it, it did. In my judgment Miss Ingram's state of mind is immaterial to this question. When the law avoids a contract *ab initio*, it does so irrespective of the intentions or opinions or wishes of the parties themselves.

[1]. (1883), 135 Mass. Rep. 283.
[2]. (1917), 220 N.Y. 232.

Consider:

Is it possible to reconcile the cases of *Ingram* and *Phillips*? Why do you think different outcomes resulted?

Lewis v Averay [1971] 3 All ER 907

A rogue arranged to view a car advertised for sale by the plaintiff in a newspaper. The rogue tested the car that evening, introducing himself as 'Richard Green', a well-known actor. He then offered to buy the car and a price was agreed. The rogue then wrote a cheque intending to take the car immediately. When the plaintiff asked for proof of identity, he was shown a special stamped admission pass to Pinewood Studios bearing a photograph of the rogue and the name 'Richard A. Green'. Satisfied, the plaintiff allowed the rogue take the car away. Later the cheque was proved to be worthless. In the meantime the defendant had purchased the car in good faith from the rogue. The plaintiff brought an action against the defendant for conversion.

Lord Denning M.R.:

What is the effect of this mistake? There are two cases in our books which cannot to my mind, be reconciled the one with the other. One of them is *Philips v Brooks*[1] where a jeweller had a ring for sale. The other is *Ingram v Little*,[2] where two ladies had a car for sale . . . It seems to me that the material facts in each case are quite indistinguishable the one from the other. In each case there was, to all outward appearance, a contract but there was a mistake by the seller as to the identity of the buyer. This mistake was fundamental. In each case it led to the handing over of the goods. Without it the seller would not have parted with them. . . . in *Ingram v Little* the majority of the court suggested that the difference between *Phillips v Brooks* and *Ingram v Little* was that in *Phillips v Brooks* the contract of sale was concluded (so as to pass the property to the rogue) before the rogue made the fraudulent misrepresentation, whereas in *Ingram v Little* the rogue made the fraudulent misrepresentation before the contract was concluded. My own view is that in each case the property in the goods did not pass until the seller let the rogue have the goods.

Again it has been suggested that a mistake as to the identity of a person is one thing; and a mistake as to his attributes is another. A mistake as to identity, it is said, avoids a contract; whereas a mistake as to attributes does not. But this is a distinction without a difference. A man's very name is one of his attributes. It is also a key to his identity. If then, he gives a false name, is it a mistake as to his identity? or a mistake as to his attributes? These fine distinctions do no good to the law.

As I listened to the argument in this case, I felt it wrong that an innocent purchaser (who knew nothing of what passed between the seller and the rogue) should have his title depend on such refinements. After all, he has acted with complete circumspection and in entire good faith; whereas it was the seller who let the rogue have the goods and thus enabled him to commit the fraud. I do not, therefore, accept the theory that a mistake as to identity renders a contract void.

I think the true principle is that which underlies the decision of this court in *King's Norton Metal Co. Ltd v Eldridge, Merrett & Co. Ltd*[3] and of Horridge J. in *Phillips v Brooks Ltd* which has stood for these last fifty years. It is this: when two parties have come to a contract—or rather what appears, on the face of it, to be a contract—the fact that one party is mistaken as to the identity of the other does not mean that there is no contract, or that the contract is a nullity and void from the beginning. It only means that the contract is voidable, that is, liable to be set aside at the instance of the mistaken person, so long as he does so before third parties have in good faith acquired rights under it.

Applied to the cases such as the present, this principle is in full accord with the presumption stated by Pearce L.J. and also by Devlin L.J. in *Ingram v Little*. When dealing is had between a seller like Mr Lewis and a person who is actually there present before him, then the presumption in law is that there is a contract, even though there is a fraudulent impersonation by the buyer representing himself as a different man than he is. There is a contract made with the very person there, who is present in person. It is liable no doubt to be avoided for fraud but it is still a good contract under which title will pass unless and until it is avoided. In support of that presumption, Devlin L.J. quoted, not only the English case of *Phillips v Brooks*, but other cases in the US where:[4] 'The courts hold that if A appeared in person before B, impersonating C, an innocent purchaser from A gets the property in the goods against B.' It seems to me to be right in principle in this country also.

In this case Mr Lewis made a contract of sale with the very man, the rogue, who came to the flat. I say that he 'made a contract' because in this regard we do not look into his intentions, or into his mind to know what he was thinking or into the mind of the rogue. We look to the outward appearances. On the face of the dealing Mr Lewis made a contract under which he sold the car to the rogue, delivered the car and the log book to him, and took a cheque in return. The contract is evidenced by the receipts which were signed. It was, of course, induced by fraud. The rogue made false representations as to his identity. But it was still a contract though voidable for fraud. It was a contract under which this property passed to the rogue, and in due course passed from the rogue to Mr Averay, before the contract was avoided.

Although I very much regret that either of these good and reliable gentleman should suffer, in my judgment it is Mr Lewis who should do so. I think the appeal should be allowed and judgment entered for the defendant.

[1] [1919] 2 KB 243, [1918–19] All ER Rep 246
[2] [1960] 3 All ER 332, [1961] 1 QB 31
[3] (1897) 14 TLR 98
[4] This quotation is from *Corbin on Contracts*, vol. 3, s. 602

Papas v Bianca Investments [2002] SASC 190

The plaintiff's son advertised to sell the plaintiff's car. He agreed to sell it to a fraudster who purported to be a Mr Cherrington for $12,500 to be paid in cash or by a bank cheque. The fraudster subsequently showed him a driving licence in the name of Cherrington which did not contain a photograph and he accepted a cheque in that name. The fraudster passed the car on to the defendant, a pawnbroker who accepted it as security for a $7,000 loan.

Doyle C.J.:

The cases bearing on the effect of such a mistake are few in number, are difficult to reconcile, and do not yield a clear principle. The main cases are English cases. They are *Phillips v Brooks Ltd* [1919] 2 KB 243; *Lake v Simmons* [1927] AC 487; *Ingram v Little* [1961] 1 QB 31 and *Lewis v Averay* [1972] 1 QB 198. . . . [Doyle CJ indicated a preference for the approach of Lord Denning to the other judges in *Lewis*.] However, that is not to say that the relevant principle is as unqualified as his statement would suggest.

In the present case the identity of the purchaser was immaterial to Mr Papas and to his son. They were willing to sell the motor car to any person who provided cash or a good bank cheque. The inquiry as to the identity of the purchaser was probably made with a view to keeping an appropriate record of the transaction, with a view to complying with requirements of the Registrar of Motor Vehicles, and as some kind of protection against fraud. But there is no reason to think that it mattered to the plaintiff who the purchaser was. All that mattered was that the plaintiff would receive cash or, what the plaintiff thought was equally good, a bank cheque. In the present case there was the appearance of a contract. The purchaser misrepresented his identity and knowingly tendered a bad cheque. The plaintiff was certainly entitled to rescind the contract on the basis of these misrepresentations, and possibly on the basis of the former alone. But, in my opinion, there is no reason to treat the plaintiff's mistake as to the identity and creditworthiness of the purchaser as preventing any contract at all coming into existence. This was not a case in which the plaintiff was willing to sell only to Mr Cherrington. I consider that all three judgments in *Lewis v Averay* support the magistrate's conclusion, even though the reasoning in each judgment is slightly different.

I agree generally with the approach taken to this issue by Carter and Harland, *Contract Law in Australia* (4th edn, 2002) at [1244]:

> The cases are impossible to reconcile, but it is suggested that since it is the victim's apparent intention to contract with the person physically present, there exists a sufficient element of assent on which a contract can come into being, albeit a contract voidable at the instance of the representee.
>
> A starting point for analysis of these cases is the undoubted presumption that where parties appear to contract, there is a contract between the parties. In order for that presumption to be rebutted there must be admissible evidence that there was no such intention.

In the present case there is no evidence that the plaintiff was not prepared to contract with any person willing to provide cash or a bank cheque to the appropriate amount, and no evidence that the plaintiff contracted with Mr Cherrington because of the plaintiff's belief as to his identity, as distinct from the plaintiff's belief that he was providing a bank cheque . . .

In the following paragraph [of *Halsbury's Laws of England*, vol. 9(1), (4th ed. Reissue, 1998] the editor makes the point that when the parties are dealing face to face:

> . . . there is a presumption that each party intends to deal with the person in front of him; but it is clear that this presumption may be rebutted. (Footnotes omitted.)

Even applying this approach, I am not satisfied that the presumption that the plaintiff intended to deal with the person physically present has been rebutted. The plaintiff was willing to deal with that person. The plaintiff was misled as to that person's identity, but that was not a material matter. The plaintiff was misled as to the bank cheque, but that does not mean that the plaintiff was not willing to deal with the person present.

I have examined a number of textbooks, both English and Australian. The writers generally comment on the difficulty of identifying a clear principle from the case law. But generally they focus on a presumed but rebuttable intention to deal with a person who is actually present when the contract is made, whoever that person may be. They also emphasise that a mistake as to creditworthiness of that person, or a mistake which arises from a representation about creditworthiness linked to identity, will not usually render a contract void. In my own researches I did not find any Australian case which is of binding or persuasive authority. In *Porter v Latec Finance (Qld) Pty Ltd* (1964) 111 CLR 177 at 194–5, Kitto J. and Windeyer J. at 200–201 made remarks in passing which might be seen as supporting a more subjective approach than I have taken. I mean an approach which gives more emphasis to the fact of a mistake as to identity, as distinct from an emphasis on an outward appearance of agreement on subject matter and terms, and on the absence of any reason to regard the identity of the party dealt with as material, except to the extent that that reflects an interest in credit-worthiness. But these remarks were made in the context of a case dealing with interests in land, and in a context far removed from the present one. Pointing the other way are remarks made by Mason A.C.J., Murphy and Deane JJ. in *Taylor v Johnson* (1983) 151 CLR 422 at 428–30, where their Honours said that the clear trend of late has been toward an objective theory in relation to the impact of mistake on the formation of a contract. They refer to an approach under which the emphasis is on an outward appearance of agreement of terms and subject matter. In the present case there was an outward appearance of agreement on terms and subject matter, and there is nothing to suggest that the plaintiff was unwilling to deal with the purchaser, whoever the purchaser might be, as long as that purchaser paid by cash or bank cheque. I recognise that the law in this area is in a somewhat unsatisfactory state, but my conclusion is that a contract did come into existence, although the plaintiff had a right to rescind.

What is the effect of the tender of the forged bank cheque, and the implied representation that it was a good cheque? The cases do not suggest that this mistake by the plaintiff makes the contract void. In *Lewis v Averay* the plaintiff thought that the cheque was the cheque of a well-known actor, a person of substance. In *Phillips v Brooks* the plaintiff thought the cheque tendered to him was the cheque of Sir George Bullough, a person of substance of whom the plaintiff was aware. In neither case was it suggested that this distinct mistake prevented a contract coming into existence. For all those reasons I agree with the magistrate that the contract was valid, liable to be rescinded for misrepresentation, but not rescinded until after the defendant acquired its interest in the motor car.

(On the facts, the Court found that the defendant acted *bona fide* in acquiring its interest and thus the plaintiff was not entitled to possession.)

Shogun Finance Ltd *v* Hudson [2004] 1 AC 919

A motor dealer agreed to sell a car to a fraudster who purported to be a Mr Patel and who produced a stolen driving licence as proof of his identity. The claimant finance company completed a satisfactory credit check on the person named in the licence, verified that the signatures on the hire-purchase application form and the licence matched and approved the sale. The fraudster paid the deposit partly in cash and partly by cheque and drove away with the vehicle selling it to the defendant, a *bona fide* purchaser, the following day.

The majority of the Court of Appeal held that there was no contract between the finance company and the fraudster as the former only intended to deal with the person the fraudster claimed to be. Sedley L.J. dissented on the basis that the finance company, using the dealer as its agent, had in law contracted face to face with the fraudster in circumstances insufficient to rebut the presumption that it was with him, and not with the person he claimed to be, that the company was contracting. The majority of the House of Lords concluded that, as the contract was a written document, the identity of the hirer should be ascertained by construing that document. This may be said to be based on the parol evidence rule. Such an analysis indicated that the finance company was willing to do business not with anyone but with a person who had identified himself in the way required by the written document so as to enable it to check before it enters into any contractual relationship that he meets its credit requirements. Mr Patel was such an identified person and met its credit requirements so it was willing to do business with him. Adopting that approach, the hirer was, or more accurately purported to be, Mr Patel. As he had not authorised the conclusion of the contract, it was void. This approach has been criticised (Hare, 'Identity Mistakes: A Missed Opportunity' (2004) 67 MLR 993) and the dissenting judgments generally preferred. Lord Nicholls of Birkenhead and Lord Millett in their dissenting judgments focused on the nature of the mistake made and they suggested that the distinction between face-to-face transactions and written correspondence was arbitrary and advocated applying the face-to-face principle more generally.

Lord Nicholls of Birkenhead (Dissenting):

This appeal raises a difficult problem about the effect of fraudulent misrepresentation on the formation of a contract. If a crook (C) fraudulently represents to the owner of goods (O) that he is another identifiable person (X) and on that basis O parts with goods to C by way of sale, is there in law a contract between O and C? Does the answer to this question differ according to whether O and C communicated face to face, or by correspondence, or over the telephone, or by e-mail? The law on cases involving this type of fraudulent conduct, euphemistically described as cases of 'mistaken identity', is notoriously unsatisfactory. The reported decisions are few in number and they are not reconcilable. In the present case Sedley L.J. said the law has tied itself into a Gordian knot. Brooke L.J. said the law is in a 'sorry condition' which only Parliament or your Lordships' House can remedy: see [2002] QB 834, 847, 855.

. . . In cases of face to face dealings the law, as declared by the preponderance of authority, is tolerably clear. The owner of the goods believes the person in front of him is X, and in that belief he contracts with the person in front of him. The fraudulent misrepresentation by the crook C regarding his identity no more negatives O's intention to contract with C than, in my earlier example, the seller's misrepresentation about the identity of the proffered goods negatives the buyer's intention to buy the proffered goods. In each case the relevant intention is to be ascertained by looking at the position which, as a result of the misrepresentation, the other party believes to exist. On that footing there is consensus, in the relevant respect, between the parties. O believes C, the person in front of him, to be X *and he deals with C in that belief*. The fraud entitles O to avoid the contract, but it does not negative the formation of a contract with C. [Reference to *Phillips v Brooks Ltd* [1919] 2 KB 243] . . .

But what of the case where a fraudulent misrepresentation is made in writing but O and C do not meet each other? . . . In his dealings with O the crook C represented that he was X, and O proceeded to *deal with him* (C) in that belief. When this feature is kept in mind it readily becomes apparent that in principle cases of this type are no different from cases of face to face dealings. The existence of physical immediacy in one case, and the absence of it in the other, is immaterial. The physical immediacy of C in face-to-face cases tends to emphasise O's intention to deal with the person in front of him. With other forms of communication such as the telephone or correspondence this physical immediacy is lacking. But in each case, whatever the mode of communication, what matters is *whether* O agreed to sell his goods to the person with whom he was dealing, not *why* he did so or under what name. The latter is relevant to remedy, not to formation of a contract.

In this regard mention must be made of reasoning sometimes advanced here, along the lines that the identity of the person to whom a written offer is made is a question solely of construction of the document. The offer, it is said, is made to the person identified in the document and no one else. A written offer made by O to X is not capable of acceptance by C. Hence, it is said that, whatever the position in face-to-face dealings, in cases of written contracts or contracts made by correspondence there can be no contract between O and C, contradicting as this would the terms of the document. The flaw in this reasoning is that it begs the crucial question: to whom was the offer made? The reasoning assumes this is a straightforward case of an offer made to the person named. Indeed the person named is X. But that is only part of the picture. O believes that X, the person to whom he is writing and to whom he addressed the offer, is one and the same person as the person with whom he is dealing. In fact he is not dealing with X. He is dealing with C. O's misapprehension in this regard, induced by C's fraud, is no different in principle from a case where C's misrepresentation is made orally in the course of the face-to-face meeting. The legal problem is the same in both cases. The presence or absence of writing does not constitute a principled ground of distinction.

Thus, when Lindsay & Co. supplied linen handkerchiefs in response to a written order [in *Cundy v Lindsay*] they were under a misapprehension regarding the identity of the person placing the order in the same way as the jeweller in the shop was under a misapprehension regarding the identity of his customer ('I am Sir George Bullough') in *Phillips v Brooks Ltd* [1919] 2 KB 243. If the approach adopted in *Phillips v Brooks* is correct, Lindsay's misapprehension no more negatived the formation of a contract with the person placing the written order for handkerchiefs than did the like misapprehension by the jeweller in the case of *Phillips v Brooks*. The jeweller parted with his ring to the customer in his shop. Lindsay parted with their linen by sending it to the address supplied by the crook. On what terms? The answer must be, on the terms agreed between Lindsay and the person with whom they were dealing. That was a contract Lindsay could enforce, should they have wished, or repudiate on the grounds of fraudulent misrepresentation.

In *Cundy v Lindsay* (1878) 3 App. Cas. 459 the House reached the contrary conclusion. The reasoning of all their Lordships was to the same effect. Lord Cairns LC encapsulated this reasoning, at p. 465:

> Of [the crook Blenkarn] [Lindsay] knew nothing, and of him they never thought. With him they never intended to deal. Their minds never, even for an instant of time, rested upon him, and as between him and them there was no consensus of mind which could lead to any arrangement or any contract whatever.

Lord Hatherley and Lord Penzance left open what the position would be had the crook come into personal contact with Lindsay . . . In my view this decision is not reconcilable with *Phillips v Brooks Ltd* [1919] 2 KB 243 or with *Lewis v Averay* [1972] 1 QB 198 or with the starting point 'presumption' formulated by Devlin L.J. in *Ingram v Little* [1961] 1 QB 31.

The legal principle applicable in these cases cannot sensibly differ according to whether the transaction is negotiated face to face, or by letter, or by fax, or by e-mail, or over the telephone or by video link or video telephone. Typically today a purchaser pays for goods with a credit or debit card. He produces the card in person in a shop or provides details of the card over the telephone or by e-mail or by fax. When a credit or debit card is fraudulently misused in this way the essence of the transaction is the same in each case. It does not differ from one means of communication to the next. The essence of the transaction in each case is that the owner of the goods agrees to part with his goods on the basis of a fraudulent misrepresentation made by the other regarding his identity. Since the essence of the transaction is the same in each case, the law in its response should apply the same principle in each case, irrespective of the precise mode of communication of offer and acceptance.

Accordingly, if the law of contract is to be coherent and rescued from its present unsatisfactory and unprincipled state, the House has to make a choice: either to uphold the approach adopted in *Cundy v Lindsay* and overrule the decisions in *Phillips v Brooks Ltd* and *Lewis v Averay*, or to prefer these later decisions to *Cundy v Lindsay*.

I consider the latter course is the right one, for a combination of reasons. It is in line with the direction in which, under the more recent decisions, the law has now been moving for some time. It accords better with basic principle regarding the effect of fraud on the formation of a contract. It seems preferable as a matter of legal policy. As between two innocent persons the loss is more appropriately borne by the person who takes the risks inherent in parting with his goods without receiving payment. This approach fits comfortably with the intention of Parliament in enacting the limited statutory exceptions to the proprietary principle of *nemo dat non quod habet*. Thus, by section 23 of the Sale of Goods Act 1979 Parliament protected an innocent buyer from a seller with a voidable title. The classic instance of a person with a voidable title is a person who acquired the goods by fraud: see Bramwell L.J. in *Babcock v Lawson* (1880) 5 QBD 284, 286. Further, this course is supported by writers of the distinction of Sir Jack Beatson: see *Anson's Law of Contract*, 28th ed., p. 332. It is consistent with the approach adopted elsewhere in the common law world, notably in the United States of America in the *Uniform Commercial Code*, 14th ed., section 2–403. And this course makes practical sense. In a case such as the present the owner of goods has no interest in the identity of the buyer. He is interested only in creditworthiness. It is little short of absurd that a subsequent purchaser's rights depend on the precise manner in which the crook seeks to persuade the owner of his creditworthiness and permit him to take the goods away with him. This ought not to be so. The purchaser's rights should not depend upon the precise form the crook's misrepresentation takes.

Cundy v Lindsay has stood for a long time. But I see no reason to fear that adopting this conclusion will unsettle the law of contract. In practice the problems surrounding *Cundy v Lindsay* arise only when third parties' rights are in issue. To bring the law here into line with the law already existing in 'face-to-face' cases will rid the law of an anomaly. Devlin L.J.'s starting point presumption is a workable foundation which should apply in all cases. A person is presumed to intend to contract with the person with whom he is actually dealing, whatever be the mode of communication.

Although expressed by Devlin L.J. as a presumption, it is not easy to think of practical circumstances where, once in point, the presumption will be displaced. The factual postulate necessary to bring the presumption into operation is that a person (O) believes that the person with whom he is dealing is the person the latter has represented himself to be. Evidence that the other's identity was of importance to O, and evidence of the steps taken to check the other's identity, will lead nowhere if the transaction proceeds on the basis of the underlying factual postulate. . . . It follows that I would allow this appeal. The principles applicable to the formation of a contract of sale are equally applicable to the formation of a hire-purchase agreement. The document submitted to Shogun Finance, and signed by the crook in the name of Mr Patel, does of course refer unequivocally to Mr Patel. The document identifies him with some particularity: his full name and address, his date of birth, his driving licence number, and his employer's name and address. These details were of prime importance to Shogun Finance because they identified the person whose credit rating it had checked and approved. The company intended to contract with this person. But it is clear from the evidence that Shogun Finance, as much as the dealer in the car showroom, thought this was one and the same person as the individual in the showroom. Shogun Finance proceeded in this (fraud-induced) belief.

This is manifest because Shogun Finance authorised the dealer to hand over the car to the person in the showroom, he being (as the finance company knew) the person who had signed the agreement and he being (so the finance company believed) the person whose credit rating it had checked. Shogun Finance believed he was Mr Patel, in the same way as the jeweller in *Phillips v Brooks* believed the customer in his shop was Sir George Bullough. In the belief that the person in the dealer's showroom was Mr Patel, Shogun Finance intended to hire the car to *that person*. That is what the finance company intended to do by the written hire-purchase agreement, and that is what it thought it had done. Had this not been so it would not have released the car to him. Shogun Finance was mistaken in its belief about the identity of the person in the showroom, in the same way as the jeweller was mistaken in his belief about the identity of the person in his shop. But that mistaken belief, induced by the crook's fraudulent misrepresentation, did not negative the finance company's intention to let the car on hire to the person in the showroom on the terms set out in the hire-purchase agreement.

Note

Shogun was considered in *Dumford Trading* AG *v OAO Atlantrybflot* [2004] 2 Lloyd's Rep. 157. In that case the High Court admitted extrinsic evidence to identify the guarantor in a contract of guarantee where there was sufficient uncertainty on the face of the document.

Consider:

Is the identity of the purchaser relevant to a large car sales company?

SECTION FIVE—MISTAKE IN EXECUTING A DEED

A. MISSTATED TERM

A situation may arise where parties reach agreement but at the time of the execution of the contract one of the parties realises that the terms have been incorrectly stated to that party's advantage. In such a case, rectification is likely to be granted.

Nolan v Graves and Hamilton [1946] IR 376

The plaintiff's bid of £5,550 for the first defendant's property at an auction was accepted. However, due to a mistake on the part of the auctioneer, the contract stated the price to be £4,550 and the plaintiff paid a deposit and auctioneer's fees calculated as percentages of this sum. When the vendor refused to complete except at the higher price, the plaintiff sued to recover her deposit and fees. The vendor then counterclaimed to have the memorandum rectified and this new memorandum specifically enforced.

Haugh J:

In my view, on the facts of this case, an innocent and very careless mistake was made by the auctioneer's servants in the conduct of this sale. The plaintiff immediately realised that a mistake had been made and attempted to take an immediate advantage of it. . . . The jurisdiction of the court as regards both rectification and specific performance is a delicate jurisdiction, and it is clear, from the mass of decisions cited before me, that it must be exercised with discretion and care. . . . Mr Graves had done everything, rightly and properly, as far as he was concerned and as far as he and the plaintiff were concerned. True it is that his agent, or one of his agents, acting for these parties made a careless mistake, and, of course, if that careless mistake in any way contributed to causing her to do anything to her prejudice, I, for one moment, would not let it weigh against her. Of course I do not take that view at all. My view is that the mistake contributed nothing to her misfortunes, because it immediately lay in her power, the moment she saw it, to say to Mr Comyn, or whatever the name of the gentleman was: 'You are mistaken there. That is wrong. It is down as £4,550; it should be £5,550. That is what I bid; ask Mr Hamilton; ask any of the others.' That was the remedy of a person dealing *bona fide* and honestly. I want to make that clear. I do not think this mistake was a cause over which she had no control in respect of the subsequent controversy or the present proceedings. She (and in fact at that time she alone) had that control, because, as I have said, she, of course, knew what the price was and, in a word, could have put Mr Richardson right. . . . I cannot see that rescission in itself will afford Mr Graves any remedy or redress for the wrong done to him. It is clear that he could have had that, on the plaintiff's submission, without ever coming into court, or without ever making a counterclaim, by simply handing back her money and having another auction on some other day by Mr Hamilton. I cannot and do not, from his point of view, regard rescission of the contract even at £4,550 without rectification, or by rectifying it to the higher figure and then rescinding it, as being a real remedy at all to the vendor, Mr Graves, though plaintiff's counsel say that that is his only right.

A great number of cases have been cited, some of which conflict. The case of *Craddock Bros v Hunt*[1] decided by the Court of Appeal in England and the case of *The United States of America v Motor Trucks, Ltd*[2] were cited by counsel for the defendants as establishing from their point of view, the principles upon which I should act. Now, these cases have been referred to over and over again; and Dr Baker points out that in *Craddock's* case the contract was an executed contract. It was a case in which the parties had gone into possession of the respective premises, portion of one of which was in dispute, and in which the persons who later became plaintiffs, actually received the rent of the yard in dispute for some years; and it was only when they sent out an architect for some building purpose who measured the yard and compared it with the parcels shown on the plaintiffs' deeds and plans and found that the plaintiffs, Craddock Bros, had never, in fact, under their conveyance got this yard, that the defendant on his part for the first time realised that it was in the conveyance to him, and immediately and for the first time sought to take advantage of what he knew he never got at the sale. He took advantage of the actual conveyance to him and refused any relief, by way of rectification or otherwise, to the plaintiffs who had paid for the yard in question. Dr Baker, with some force, pointed out that that was a case in which, if the court did not rectify the transaction the man who had bought and paid for the disputed plot could not get any other form of relief; and the defendant, who had got possession of the disputed plot, could have retained it, although he was dishonestly in possession of it, and dishonestly making claim to it, even though he knew at the auction that he never got it and only found he had got it when he examined his conveyance. The difference between that case and this case is that there is no similar conclusion between the parties. There has been no conveyance here; no parting by Mr Graves with his houses to the plaintiff, Mrs Nolan. At most there is only a contract made pursuant to the Statute of Frauds and in anticipation of the actual conveyance. For all one knows, this present contract might have broken down through some answers to the requisitions on title, as they sometimes do. I see the difference between the altered position of the parties in *Craddock's* case against what I might call the unaltered position of the parties in this case. At p. 151 of the report, the Master of the Rolls said: 'I think I am at liberty, at any rate since the Judicature Act, 1873, to express my opinion that rectification can be granted of a written agreement on parol evidence of mutual mistake, although that agreement is complete in itself, and has been carried out by a more formal document based upon it.' Well, in this case I have a written agreement complete in itself, the parties' names are there; it recites the auction, and contains all that it should. . . .

I cannot, in equity at least, see why he should be in any weaker position by reason of the fact that her conduct is worse than that of making a mere mistake. Why should the principle stated by the Master of the Rolls in *Craddock's* case which I have just quoted, not apply here? Lord Warrington, at p. 159 of the report in *Craddock's* case says, 'The jurisdiction of courts of equity in this respect is to bring the written document executed in pursuance of an antecedent agreement into conformity with that agreement.' Now, that is the jurisdiction—to bring a written document, executed in pursuance of an antecedent agreement into conformity with that agreement. Translate that passage in reference to this case: 'The jurisdiction of courts of equity in this respect is to bring' the memorandum, 'executed in pursuance of' the bidding, 'into conformity with' the bidding. Lord Warrington goes on: 'The conditions to its exercise are that there must be an antecedent contract.' Well, the condition to the exercise of that jurisdiction in this case is that there must have been an antecedent agreement— antecedent to the memorandum. There is an offer to pay £5,500 and the acceptance of that offer. That is the antecedent agreement here. 'And the common intention of embodying or giving effect to the whole of that contract by the writing.' I am satisfied, as I have said before, that the plaintiff's bid was one of £5,550; I am satisfied that her conversation with Mr Houlihan was on the basis of such an offer. I am satisfied that it was the common intention of Mr Richardson, representing the vendor, and of the plaintiff, 'to bring the document into conformity with that agreement' (in the words of the learned Lord Justice in *Craddock's* case); they had 'the common intention of embodying or giving effect to the whole of that contract by the writing.' To put it shortly, these two parties came together with the common intention of reducing to writing a sale at £5,550, 'and', as Lord Warrington continued, 'there must be clear evidence that the document, by common mistake, failed to embody such contract and either contained provisions not agreed upon or omitted something that was agreed upon, or otherwise departed from its terms.' There is cogent, clear and preponderating evidence in this case that this document failed to embody the contract, because the price is different. It contains a provision that has a lower price which is not agreed upon and omits something agreed upon, that is the higher price, and in that respect it departs from its terms. I can only repeat that I do not see why this lady, who is in a worse position than that of making a mistake in common with the defendant, should not be at least in the same position as if common mistake and common mistake only, was the cause of this incorrect document being executed.

The case of the *United States of America v Motor Trucks Ltd*, has been referred to already. That was a case brought by the US government against Motor Trucks Ltd, who were a firm who, during the last war, agreed to make munitions for the American government, subject to hostilities ceasing, when the contract could be terminated. Some time after the armistice the US government did serve notice of termination and certain accounts had to be taken as to what amount of money the US government owed to the defendant company. A sum of $1.5 million was agreed upon, which included the sum of $376,000, being the amount which the company claimed in respect of certain lands and buildings which had been erected by them following their activities as munition makers. After deducting large sums from the above total, which the government had already advanced to the appellants, it was agreed that the sum of $637,812 was due. Now, one has to bear in mind that the sum included the $376,000 for the premises, and it was agreed that a contract should be drawn up. It was drawn up between the parties and the schedule to the contract failed to include those buildings in the conveyance although the government of the US paid for them; . . . The trial judge and the Privy Council later, in effect, ordered rectification and specific performance of the agreement. The learned judge who delivered the judgment of the Privy Council, with clarity, put his views as to the position between the parties in passages which I do not intend to read fully but some of which I shall quote. He says (at p. 200 of the report): 'And indeed the power of the court to rectify mutual mistake implies that this power may be exercised notwithstanding that the true agreement of the parties has not been expressed in writing. Nor does the rule make any inroad upon another principle, that the plaintiff must show first, that there was an actually concluded agreement antecedent to the instrument which is sought to be rectified.' (In this case the antecedent agreement is the bidding.) 'And secondly, that such agreement has been inaccurately represented in the instrument.' (I have found that it has been.) 'When this is proved either party' (be it vendor or purchaser, in the capacity of plaintiff or defendant), 'may claim, in spite of the Statute of Frauds, that the instrument on which the other insists does not represent the real agreement.'

I am satisfied from my reading of these cases that I have jurisdiction to rectify, and ought to rectify, the memorandum in such a way that it will represent the actual contract, voluntarily entered into between the plaintiff and the defendants. The mistake was one over which the plaintiff had full power to remedy, every opportunity and chance of remedying, and it in no way prejudiced her; but she knowingly sought to take advantage of it for the reasons I have stated. . . . . I shall decree rectification and order that the first figure be changed to the higher sum of £5,550 and any consequential figures that may follow in respect of the deposit and auctioneer's fees. I shall also decree that the balance at the bottom shall be changed from £3,412 to the correct figure that follows from the purchase price being £5,550.

After rectification, there arises the question of the specific performance of the agreement. I rather think that under the circumstances I cannot give specific performance of this agreement because it is my view that the document has been rectified as against the written memorandum. It is only now that it becomes effective as an instrument required by the Statute of Frauds. From now on, at least from the time my order is made up, it remains for the plaintiff to elect whether she will, or will not, perform the sale at the price that she has contracted to buy the premises for.

However, I am satisfied on the document that I rectify that the vendor will have the ordinary rights that accrue to him under what I now call the contract that correctly represents the intention of the parties, and for the same reasons I will not decree forfeiture of the deposit.

1. [1923] 2 Ch. 136.   2. [1924] AC 196.

Nolan v Nolan (1954) 92 ILTR 94

A separation deed provided that the plaintiff should pay the defendant 'such sum as will after the deduction of income tax at the standard rate amount to the sum of £15 per week.' The phrase 'at the standard rate' was inserted at the defendant's request in the belief that that it would entitle her to retain refunds of income tax on the sums paid to her. The plaintiff later sought to have the deed rectified claiming that it did not reflect a prior agreement to the effect that any tax refunds would be his property.

Dixon J.:

It had been submitted on behalf of the wife that it was not a case of mutual mistake, susceptible of rectification, and that seemed to be so in a limited sense, in as much as no case of rectification could really be regarded as a case of mutual mistake; if it were there would be no contest, for the parties could rectify the instrument themselves. The whole question whether a mistake was mutual or unilateral was largely one of phrase-ology. The present position was analogous to that with which his Lordship had to deal in *Monaghan County Council v Vaughan* [1948] IR 306 and also, although expressed in a different and probably better way, in the passage quoted by counsel from Kerr on the *Law of Fraud and Mistake*. The basis of the decision in *Monaghan County Council v Vaughan* was that if there were a mistake in a document, in that it did not express the agreement between the parties and one party was not aware of that circumstance while the other party was aware of it, then that was a case of mutual mistake. The party who knew that the expression of the agreement was incorrect could not allege that there was not a mutual mistake because the other party was not aware of that mistake. What happened here came close to misrepresentation or estoppel. Mrs Nolan knew what the agreement was between herself and her husband and what was intended to be recorded in the separation deed. She knew when the alteration was made that the deed might not then correctly express the agreement, nevertheless she decided that she would have the alteration made and, if she could, take advantage of the legal consequences. In those circumstances she could not now be heard to say that there was not a mutual mistake. To hold otherwise would come close to permitting fraud.

Accordingly, his Lordship was of opinion that the plaintiff, the husband, was entitled to have the deed rectified to express what his Lordship was satisfied was the agreement between the parties, and which the husband was under the impression it did record, while the defendant, the wife, knew or suspected that it did not.

B. ERROR IN THE PREPARATION

A situation may exist where, subsequent to the execution of a contract, one of the parties claims that the written contract does not adequately reflect the bargain struck.

In *Peter Cremer GmbH & Co. v Co-operative Molasses Traders Ltd* [1985] ILRM 564 Costello J. noted: 'Once the terms actually agreed have been established I do not think that an error in the preparation of a formal contract affects the legal consequences.'

Fallon *v* Robins (1865) IR Ch R 422

The respondent agreed to let property to the petitioner for several years. Although the petitioner alleged that it was agreed that only he should have a right to determine the tenancy at the end of any third year, the memorandum was ambiguously worded.

Smith M.R.:

So far as the petition seeks to reform the agreement, in case the court should consider that the respondent's construction of the clause authorising the determination of the tenancy by the six months' notice therein mentioned is right, I am of opinion that I can make no such decree. The case of *Fowler v Fowler*[1] is a very important case on this subject. The authorities are collected in Lord St Leonards' work on *Vendors and Purchasers* (14th edn), 171. A deed which agrees with the intention of one of the parties, although under a mistake as to the other, cannot be rectified.

I am also of opinion (if the petitioner's construction of the agreement be right) that the defence set up by the respondent's counsel during the argument, founded on the case of *Townsend v Stangroom* 6 Ves. 328, and other cases referred to by Lord St Leonards in his work on *Vendors and Purchasers*, p. 160, is not sustainable. A respondent may no doubt insist, in a suit for specific performance, that a term of the agreement was omitted when reducing it to writing; but such a defence must be clearly established. I do not think, having regard to the evidence on both sides, that it has been established that a term in the agreement was omitted.

The affidavit of the petitioner and that of the respondent are in direct conflict. I do not see what right I have to decide, on the conflicting testimony in the case, what the agreement was. That is to be decided by reference to the agreement itself.

[1] 4 De G. & J., 273.

(According to the construction of the clause, Smith M.R. decided that the respondent had no right to determine the term.)

Young *v* Halahan (1875) 9 IR Eq 70

The plaintiff possessed a leasehold interest in certain land which he purported to sell at auction. Because of a mistake the plaintiff failed to notify the purchaser that a portion of the land had already been assigned to a railway company. However, any person viewing the land would have noticed the works constructed by the railway company. The plaintiff sought to have the deed of conveyance rectified to except the property owned by the railway company.

Chatterton V.C.:

. . . The general rule of this court in reference to the rectification of deeds is that, where it is satisfactorily proved by mutual mistake a deed as executed does not express the real contract of the parties, the court will reform it, and make it conformable to the contract. For this purpose, it is necessary that the mistake should be mutual, the principle on which the equity proceeds being that the parties are to be placed in that position in which both believed that they were placed by the deed. If one party only were under a mistake, while the other without fraud knew what the operation of the deed was, and intended that it should be so, the court cannot interfere, for otherwise it would be forcing on the latter a contract he never entered into, or depriving him of a benefit he had *bona fide* acquired by an executed deed. This rule is not confined to, though probably it originated in, cases upon marriage settlements made in pursuance of previous agreements. It is one, from its nature, of general application.

(Rectification was allowed.)

Consider:

Is there any overlap between rectification and estoppel?

Irish Life Assurance Co. Ltd v Dublin Land Securities Ltd [1989] IR 253

The defendants offered to buy a large portfolio of ground rents owned by the plaintiffs. Due to a mistake by the plaintiff's legal department, certain property in Palmerstown also owned by the plaintiffs was included in the portfolio. Although the auctioneer was aware that the land in Palmerstown was not included, the defendant was not informed of this. The defendants refused to alter the contract when the mistake was discovered. The plaintiff sought rectification of the contract claiming that the contract was signed under a mutual mistake of fact. The defendant counterclaimed for an order of specific performance. The High Court dismissed the plaintiff's claim on the grounds that there was no common intention between the parties to exclude the property in Palmerstown. The plaintiff appealed to the Supreme Court.

Griffin J.:

It should be emphasised that the claim of the appellant in this case is solely for rectification of the contract for sale. There is no claim for rescission although it is quite clear, and the learned judge so held, that it was at all times the intention of the appellant to exclude the lands in question. In *Monaghan County Council v Vaughan* [1948] IR 306 at p. 312, Dixon J., in contrasting rescission and rectification, stated that where the parties contract under a mutual mistake of fact the agreement is liable to be rescinded at the instance of either party, since in such a case no contract came into being; likewise, where there is a unilateral mistake, and one of two or more parties is not *ad idem* with the other party or parties, there is no real agreement between them and rescission may also be appropriate. During the course of the hearing of this appeal the court indicated to counsel for the appellant that, even at this late stage, it would consider an application to amend the pleadings to include a claim for rescission of the agreement if the appellant wished to apply for such amendment, in case it should transpire that this was a more appropriate remedy when all the matters in issue were being considered. The appellant however steadfastly refused to apply for any such amendment, as it did not seek nor did it want rescission of the agreement. The appellant's attitude is readily understandable having regard to its reasons for selling the rent roll in the first instance. The appellant was supported in this attitude by the respondent, so that neither party wished to contemplate rescission of the agreement. In these circumstances, this court is solely concerned with the issue of rectification, upon which the claim of the appellant must stand or fall, and I would express no view on the question as to whether the remedy of rescission is appropriate or otherwise.

Rectification is concerned with defects in the recording, not in the making, of an agreement. 'Courts of equity do not rectify contracts; they may and do rectify instruments purporting to have been made in pursuance of terms of contracts', per James V.C. in *Mackenzie v Coulson* (1869) LR 8 Eq. 368 at p. 375.

As a general rule, the courts only rectify an agreement in writing where there has been mutual mistake—i.e. where it fails to record the intention of *both* parties. Although that was the original conception of reformation of an instrument by rectification, nowadays a party who has entered into a written agreement by mistake will also be entitled to rectification if he establishes by convincing evidence that the other party, with knowledge of such intention and mistake, nevertheless concluded the agreement—see Kenny J. in *Lucey v Laurel Construction Co. Ltd* (HC), 18 December 1970, unrep.; *Roberts and Co. Ltd v Leicestershire County Council* [1961] Ch. 555; *Riverlate Properties Ltd v Paul* [1975] 1 Ch. 133. In the last case it was considered by the Court of Appeal that the knowledge of such other party must be such as to involve him in a degree of sharp practice . . .

It was formerly considered that the court could not rectify a document in writing unless it was preceded by a concluded oral contract. In taking this view, Kenny J. in *Lucey v Laurel Construction Co. Ltd* cited with approval what was said by Denning L.J. (as he then was) in *Rose v Pim* [1953] 2 QB 450 at p. 461:

> Rectification is concerned with contracts and documents, not with intentions. In order to get rectification it is necessary to show that the parties were in complete agreement on the terms of their contract, but by an error wrote them down wrongly; and in this regard, in order to ascertain the terms of their contract, you do not look into the inner minds of the parties—into their intentions—any more than you do in the formation of any other contract. You look at their outward acts, that is, at what they said or wrote to one another in coming to their agreement, and then compare it with the document which they have signed. If you can predicate with certainty what their contract was, and that it is, by a common mistake, wrongly expressed in the document, then you rectify the document; but nothing less will suffice. [It is not necessary that all the formalities of the contract should have been executed so as to make it enforceable at law (see *Shipley Urban District Council v Bradford Corporation* [1936] Ch. 375) but, formalities apart, there must have been a concluded contract]. There is a passage in *Crane v Hegeman-Harris Co. Inc.* [1939] 1 All ER 662, 664 which suggests that a continuing common intention alone will suffice; but I am clearly of opinion that a continuing common intention is not sufficient unless it has found expression in outward agreement. There could be no certainty at all in business transactions if a party who had entered into a firm contract could afterwards turn around and claim to have it rectified on the ground that the parties intended something different. He is allowed to prove, if he can, that *they agreed something different*: see *Lovell & Christmas v Wall*, per Lord Cozens-Hardy M.R., and per Buckley L.J. (1911) 104 LT 85, 88, 93, but not that they *intended* something different.

Two things need to be noted—the emphasis was Denning L.J.'s; and the sentence inside square brackets was inadvertently omitted from the quotation by Kenny J., presumably in transcription. Kenny J. does not appear to have been referred to *Joscelyne v Nissen* [1970] 2 QB 86, a decision of the Court of Appeal reported some months before *Lucey v Laurel Construction Ltd*. In *Joscelyne v Nissen* the judgment was delivered by Russell L.J. and was the judgment of the court. In giving judgment he reviewed what he himself described as 'the train of this undoubtedly formidable array of judicial opinion' from the decision of *MacKenzie v Coulson* (one hundred years earlier) onwards. Amongst the cases considered was *Crane v Hegeman-Harris Co. Inc.* [1939] 1 All ER 662 decided by Simonds J. Buckley L.J. at p. 95 (*inter alia*) cited the following passage from the judgment of Simonds J. at p. 664:

> I am clear that I must follow the decision of Clauson J., as he then was, in *Shipley Urban District Council v Bradford Corporation* [1936] 1 Ch. 375, the point of which is that, in order that this court may exercise its jurisdiction to rectify a written instrument, it is not necessary to find a concluded and binding contract between the parties antecedent to the agreement which it is sought to rectify. The judge held, and I respectfully concur with his reasoning and his conclusion, that it is sufficient to find a common continuing intention in regard to a particular provision or aspect of the agreement. If one finds that, in regard to a particular point, the parties were in agreement up to the moment when they executed their formal instrument, and the formal instrument does not conform with the common agreement, then this court has jurisdiction to rectify, although it may be that there was, until the formal instrument was executed, no concluded and binding contract between the parties . . .
>
> Secondly, I want to say this upon the principle of the jurisdiction. It is a jurisdiction which is to be exercised only upon convincing proof that the concluded instrument does not represent the common intention of the parties. That is particularly the case where one finds prolonged negotiations between the parties eventually assuming the shape of a formal instrument in which they have been advised by their respective skilled legal advisers. The assumption is very strong in such a case that the instrument does represent their real intention, and it must be only upon proof which Lord Eldon, I think, in a somewhat picturesque phrase described as 'irrefragable' that the court can act, I would rather, I think say that the court can only act if it is satisfied beyond all reasonable doubt that the instrument does not represent their common intention, and is further satisfied as to what their common intention was. For let it be clear that it is not sufficient to show that the written instrument does not represent their common intention unless positively also one can show what their common intention was.

In *Joscelyne v Nissen* Russell L.J. in considering what was said in *Rose v Pim* said at p. 97: 'The decision in our judgment does not assert or reinstate the view that an antecedent complete concluded contract is required for rectification: it only shows that prior accord on a term or the meaning of a phrase to be used must have been outwardly expressed or communicated between the parties.' He then referred to the passage from the judgment of Denning L.J. already cited, and said: 'Insofar as this passage might be taken to suggest that an antecedent complete concluded contract is necessary it would be in conflict with the views of both courts in *Crane v Hegeman-Harris* and is not supported by the other judgments' (those of Singleton L.J. and Morris L.J. who were the other members of the court in *Rose v Pim*). And at p. 98 he said:

In our judgment the law is as expounded by Simonds J. in *Crane's* case with the qualification that some outward expression of accord is required. We do not wish to attempt to state in any different phrase that with which we entirely agree, except to say that it is our view better to use only the phrase 'convincing proof' without echoing an old fashioned word such as 'irrefragable' and without importing from the criminal law the phrase 'beyond all reasonable doubt'.

In *Rooney and McParland Ltd v Carlin* [1981] NI 138 at p. 146 Lord Lowry L.C.J. summarised the principles clarified by Russell L.J. in the following terms:

1. There must be a concluded agreement antecedent to the instrument which is sought to be rectified; but
2. The antecedent agreement need not be binding in law (for example, it need not be under seal if made by a public authority or in writing and signed by the party if relating to a sale of land) nor need it be in writing: such incidents merely help to discharge the heavy burden of proof; and
3. A complete antecedent concluded contract is not required, so long as there was prior accord on a term of a proposed agreement, outwardly expressed and communicated between the parties, as in *Joscelyne v Nissen*.

Like the learned trial judge, I would adopt what was said by Russell L.J. and Lord Lowry L.C.J. as representing the law on the subject in question in this jurisdiction. Applying those principles to the facts of this case, and bearing in mind the heavy burden of proof that lies on those seeking rectification, the question to be addressed is whether there was convincing proof, reflected in some outward expression of accord, that the contract in writing did not represent the common continuing intention of the parties on which the court can act, and whether the plaintiff can positively show what that common intention was in relation to the provisions which the appellant says were intended to exclude the vacant lands at Palmerstown . . . . Like the learned trial judge, I am quite satisfied that the instant case is one of unilateral mistake and not of common or mutual mistake.

[Rectification was thus refused.]

Notes

1. In *Michael McMahon v Patrick O'Loughlin* (HC) 9 June 2005 unreported, the plaintiff was negotiating to buy property from the defendant and the latter claimed that as part of this agreement the plaintiff was required to enter into a supply agreement with Irish Shell. The plaintiff argued that there was a mistake in that the defendant understood that the plaintiff knew and had accepted the Shell agreement. Although the plaintiff was aware, and was put on notice of the defendant's view, his solicitor made inquiries and was satisfied that the Shell agreement did not affect the sale. Thus he could not be said to have relied on the mistake, or indeed sought to benefit from it. Murphy J. applied the *Dublin Land Securities* case and determined that such a mistake was not one which would entitle the defendant to rescind or disentitle the plaintiff to seek specific performance.
2. Where the party pleading mistake shows that, despite the apparent assent of both parties to the written terms of the agreement, the document does

not carry into effect 'the contract formula', rectification may be allowed. This is clear from the case of *Coleen Bros v The County Council of the City of Dublin* [1908] 1 IR 503.

SECTION SIX—NON EST FACTUM—'IT IS NOT MY DEED'

While this plea was originally confined to cases where blind or illiterate persons signed contracts whose contents had been misrepresented, it is now available to persons who sign instruments which turn out to be different documents to those they believed they were signing.

The Governors and Company of the Bank of Ireland *v* McManamy and Others [1916] 2 IR 161

The defendants signed a bank guarantee of the liabilities of Boyle Co-operative in the genuine belief that it was a receipt for goods purchased, milk supplied or dividends received. They subsequently sought to avoid their obligations under the guarantee on the basis of *non est factum*. At trial, in response to the trial judge's questions, the jury determined that the document was signed by them in the honest belief that it was one of an entirely different character from what it really was, and that it was signed by them without negligence on their part. However, the jury disagreed as to whether fraud had been present. When the trial judge found for the defendants, the plaintiff sought a new trial on the basis of this failure to find fraud. Cherry L.C.J. refused on the basis that it was not necessary to find fraud.

Cherry L.C.J.:

The principle of law which the learned judge evidently had in his mind when framing the questions for the jury, was that laid down by Byles J., in delivering the judgment of the court in the well-known case of *Foster v McKinnon* LR 4 CP 704, namely this: That where a party signs a document under a fundamental mistake as to its nature and character, and that mistake is not due to negligence on his part, he is not bound by his signature, upon the ground that there is, in reality, no contact at all binding him on his part. It is true that in *Foster v McKinnon*, and I think also in nearly all the cases which have followed it, the cause of the error has been fraud on the part of some person, but this is due to the fact that such error as to the nature of the document can scarcely ever exist without fraud on somebody's part. The principle of the cases is not, however, that fraud vitiates consent, but rather that there is an entire absence of consent. That the mind of the party who signs under a fundamental error does not go with the act of signing, and that there is consequently no contract at all in fact. The defendant, if he succeeds, does so upon the issue *non est factum*, not upon the issue of fraud, though fraud, as I have said, is usually present, and is generally found by the jury to have existed. The following passage, frequently quoted with approval from the judgment of Byles J. in *Foster v McKinnon*, at p. 711, clearly lays down the principle in that way:

It seems plain, on principle and on authority, that if a blind man, or a man who cannot read, or who for some reason (not implying negligence) forbears to read, has a written contract falsely read over to him the reader misreading to such a degree that the written contract is of a nature altogether different from the contract pretended to be read from the paper which the blind or illiterate man afterwards signs; then, at least if there be no negligence, the signature so obtained is of no force. And it is invalid not merely on the ground of fraud, where fraud exists, but on the ground that the mind of the signer did not accompany the signature; in other words, that he never intended to sign, and, therefore, in contemplation of law never did sign, the contract to which his name is appended.

This passage plainly indicates that the fundamental error as to the nature of the document which vitiates the contract need not necessarily have been induced by fraud, though in the great majority of such cases fraud is present, and is the cause of the error.

In the recent case of *Carlisle and Cumberland Co. v Bragg* [1911] 1 KB 489, where the defendant was induced by the fraud of a third party to sign a guarantee to the plaintiff company in entire ignorance of the nature of the document, the decision of the Court of Appeal in England was based upon the same principle. This most clearly appears from the judgment of Kennedy L.J.: 'I entirely assent,' he says, 'to the exposition which has been given of the law with regard to *non est factum* as a defence. The principle involved, as I understand it, is that a consenting mind is essential to the making of a contract, and that in such a case as this there was really no consensus, because there was no intention to make a contract of the kind in question.'

It is important to note that the doctrine will not be available merely to provide relief to a party who was careless in verifying the nature of a contract being entered. This is clear from the following cases.

Saunders *v* Anglia Building Society [1971] AC 1004
[On appeal from *Gallie v Lee*]

Lord Reid:

The plea of *non est factum* obviously applies when the person sought to be held liable did not in fact sign the document. But at least since the sixteenth century it has also been held to apply in certain cases so as to enable a person who in fact signed a document to say that it is not his deed. Obviously any such extension must be kept within narrow limits if it is not to shake the confidence of those who habitually and rightly rely on signatures when there is no obvious reason to doubt their validity. Originally this extension appears to have been made in favour of those who were unable to read owing to blindness or illiteracy and who therefore had to trust someone to tell them what they were signing. I think it must also apply in favour of those who are permanently or temporarily unable through no fault of their own to have without explanation any real understanding of the purport of a particular document, whether that be from defective education, illness or innate incapacity.

But that does not excuse them from taking such precautions as they reasonably can. The matter generally arises where an innocent third party has relied on a signed document in ignorance of the circumstances in which it was signed, and where he will suffer loss if the maker of the document is allowed to have it declared a nullity. So there must be a heavy burden of proof on the person who seeks to invoke this remedy. He must prove all the circumstances necessary to justify its being granted to him, and that necessarily involves his proving that he took all reasonable precautions in the circumstances. I do not say that the remedy can never be available to a man of full capacity. But that could only be in very exceptional circumstances: certainly not where his reason for not scrutinising the document before signing it was that he was too busy or too lazy. In general I do not think he can be heard to say that he signed in reliance on someone he trusted. But, particularly when he was led to believe that the document which he signed was not one which affected his legal rights, there may be cases where this plea can properly be applied in favour of a man of full capacity.

The plea cannot be available to anyone who was content to sign without taking the trouble to try to find out at least the general effect of the document. Many people do frequently sign documents put before them for signature by their solicitor or other trusted advisers without making any inquiry as to their purpose or effect. But the essence of the plea *non est factum* is that the person signing believed that the document he signed had one character or one effect whereas in fact its character or effect was quite different. He could not have such a belief unless he had taken steps or been given information which gave him some grounds for his belief. The amount of information he must have and the sufficiency of the particularity of his belief must depend on the circumstances of each case.

Further, the plea cannot be available to a person whose mistake was really a mistake as to the legal effect of the document, whether that was his own mistake or that of his adviser. . . . Finally, there is the question as to what extent or in what way must there be a difference between that which in fact he signed and that which he believed he was signing . . . There must, I think, be a radical difference between what he signed and what he thought he was signing—or one could use the words 'fundamental' or 'serious' or 'very substantial'. But what amounts to a radical difference will depend on all the circumstances.

Lord Hodson:

The plea of *non est factum* requires clear and positive evidence before it can be established. As Donovan L.J. said, delivering the judgment of the Court of Appeal in *Muskham Finance Ltd v Howard* [1963] 1 QB 904, 912: 'The plea of *non est factum* is a plea which must necessarily be kept within narrow limits.' To take an example, the man who in the course of his business signs a pile of documents without checking them takes the responsibility for them by appending his signature. It would be surprising if he was allowed to repudiate one of those documents on the ground of *non est factum*. . . . Want of care on the part of the person who signs a document which he afterwards seeks to disown is relevant. The burden of proving *non est factum* is on the party disowning his signature; this includes proof that he or she took care. There is no burden on the opposite party to prove want of care. The word 'negligence' in this connection does not involve the proposition that want of care is irrelevant unless there can be found a specific duty to the opposite party to take care.

Lord Wilberforce:

How, then, ought the principle, on which a plea of *non est factum* is admissible, to be stated? In my opinion, a document should be held to be void (as opposed to voidable) only when the element of consent to it is totally lacking, that is, more concretely, when the transaction which the document purports to effect is essentially different in substance or in kind from the transaction intended . . . To this general test it is necessary to add certain amplifications. First, there is the case of fraud. The law as to this is best stated in the words of the judgment in *Foster v Mackinnon* (1869) LR 4 CP 704, 711 where it is said that a signature obtained by fraud 'is invalid not merely on the ground of fraud, where fraud exists, but on the ground that the mind of the signer did not accompany the signature; in other words, that he never intended to sign, and therefore in contemplation of law never did sign, the contract to which his name is appended.' In other words, it is the lack of consent that matters, not the means by which this result was brought about. Fraud by itself may do no more than make the contract voidable.

Secondly, a man cannot escape from the consequences, as regards innocent third parties, of signing a document if, being a man of ordinary education and competence, he chooses to sign it without informing himself of its purport and effect. This principle is sometimes found expressed in the language that he is 'doing something with his estate' (*Hunter v Walters* (1871) LR 7 Ch App 75, 88, *Howatson v Webb* [1907] 1 Ch. 537, 547) but it really reflects a rule of common sense on the exigency of busy lives.

Thirdly, there is the case where the signer has been careless in not taking ordinary precautions against being deceived. . . .

In my opinion, the correct rule is that, leaving aside negotiable instruments to which special rules may apply, a person who signs a document, and parts with it so that it may come into other hands, has a responsibility, that of the normal man of prudence, to take care what he signs, which, if neglected, prevents him from denying his liability under the document according to its tenor. I would add that the onus of proof in this matter rests upon him, i.e. to prove that he acted carefully, and not upon the third party to prove the contrary. . . . The preceding paragraphs contemplate persons who are adult and literate: the conclusion as to such persons is that, while there are cases in which they may successfully plead *non est factum* these cases will, in modern times, be rare. As to persons who are illiterate, or blind, or lacking in understanding, the law is in a dilemma. On the one hand, the law is traditionally, and rightly, ready to relieve them against hardship and imposition. On the other hand, regard has to be paid to the position of innocent third parties who cannot be expected, and often would have no means, to know the condition or status of the signer. I do not think that a defined solution can be provided for all cases. The law ought, in my opinion, to give relief if satisfied that consent was truly lacking but will require of signers even in this class that they act responsibly and carefully according to their circumstances in putting their signature to legal documents.

Note

This case was relied on by Morris J. in *Ted Castle McCormack & Co. v McCrystal* (HC) 15 March 1999, stating that the following factual matters require to be established in order that the Defence be proven:
1. That there was a radical or fundamental difference between what was signed and what it was thought was being signed.
2. That the mistake was as to the general character of the document as opposed to its legal effect.
3. That there was a lack of negligence. That is, that the person concerned took all reasonable precautions in the circumstances to find out what the document was.

In that case Morris J. held that where the defendant was physically and mentally unwell, signing a document without caring what that document was, he nevertheless was able to show 'a fair or reasonable probability of his having a real or *bona fide* defence'.

United Dominions Trust Ltd *v* Western B.S. Romanay [1976] 1 QB 513

The defendant agreed to acquire a car on hire purchase from a firm of car dealers. He signed the plaintiff finance company's standard form in blank, leaving the dealers to fill in the form. The dealers later inserted false figures.

Megaw L.J.:

For the defendant appellant in this case [counsel], to whose argument I would like to pay tribute, has submitted—and this really is the essence of his submission—that there is a material distinction, for the purpose of the doctrine of *non est factum*, between, on the one hand, the careless signing of a document which is complete when it is signed, as in *Gallie v Lee* [1971] AC 1004 and, on the other hand, the sort of situation that arose in this case, the careless signature of a document in blank; where it is left to somebody (not being an agent of the other party) who is trusted to fill it in in a particular way but who, perhaps from fraud (as it would seem to have been in this case), or perhaps from mistake, in fact fills it in in some different way. [Counsel] argues that the principles which apply to the former type of case do not apply to the latter. With great respect to [counsel's] argument, I am unable to see either that that is right on authority or that it would be acceptable to common sense. Why should a careless act which results in the opposite party being misled as to one's contractual intentions be of less legal significance and effect than a careless act of not reading, or failing to understand, an existing completed document which is put before one to sign?
. . . On the principle of *Gallie v Lee* [1971] AC 1004 the onus was on the defendant to show that in permitting the intended contractual document to be filled in by the dealer he acted carefully. He wholly failed to do so.

Lloyds Bank plc *v* Waterhouse [1991] Fam Law 23

The defendant guaranteed his son's loan in the belief that he was doing no more than guaranteeing enough money to enable his son to buy a farm and that his position would be protected by the sale of the land if necessary. In fact the guarantee was in respect of all monies advanced to his son. The defendant was illiterate although the plaintiff was not aware of this. The plaintiff later sued the defendant on foot of the guarantee.

Purchas L.J.:

For the defence of *non est factum* to succeed the father must establish three things: (a) that he was under a disability, in the present case, illiteracy. There was no challenge to that as an existing fact and for that purpose it was irrelevant that the bank was not aware of the disability; (b) that the document which the father signed was 'fundamentally different' or 'totally different' or 'radically different' from the document which he thought he was signing; and (c) that he was not careless or that he did not fail to take proper precautions to ascertain the contents or significance of the document he was signing (see *Saunders* (*Execution of the will of Rose Maude Gallie, decd*) v *Anglia Building Society* [1971] AC 1004).

The first requirement above was not in dispute. As regards (b) it was submitted for the father that an 'all monies' guarantee was a fundamentally different document from a guarantee restricted to the money borrowed for the purpose of purchasing the land and that the court ought to accept the father's evidence that he would never guarantee an overdraft, unlimited apart from the overall limit of the guarantee, whether for his son or any other person. In considering that requirement of the defence one must look at the respective liabilities which each type of document would have imposed on the person seeking to take advantage of the defence, rather than what in fact happened subsequently. In his Lordship's judgment the father had established his incapacity and the document which he had signed was different within the concept of *non est factum* from the document which he thought he was signing.

The third aspect of the defence had given his Lordship the greatest difficulty, but after a careful review of the position he had formed the conclusion that there was ample evidence before the judge which would discharge the onus of proof, strict as it was in those particular circumstances, imposed upon the father in order to establish his defence of *non est factum*. Having made exhaustive inquiries of the bank's representatives, and having received answers which gave no hint of any liability beyond guaranteeing the son's indebtedness arising out of the purchase of the farmland and farmhouse, the father was excused from making any specific inquiry about the contents of the guarantee which had been the sole object of his earlier inquiries.

The defence of negligence or breach of duty relied essentially on the answer given by the bank's representative in the context of the father's inquiries about the extent of his guarantee, to the effect that the reason why the bank required a guarantee over and above the value of the land was that it was a matter of the bank's standard practice to obtain security greater than the value of the land being purchased. Even if the defence of *non est factum* were to fail his Lordship would consider that in the conduct of the bank's negotiations with the father, the father was misled by that answer. The father had established, *vis-à-vis* the bank, a defence of negligent misrepresentation and a defence of *non est factum* and, therefore, the appeal should be allowed.

[Woolf L.J. and Everleigh allowed the appeal on the grounds of misrepresentation and mistake respectively.]

Bank of Ireland v McCabe and McCabe (HC) 23 March 1993

The defendants gave a joint and several guarantee of the obligation of Ballybay Meat Exports Limited to the plaintiffs. When the plaintiffs sought to enforce the guarantee, the defendants claimed that the guarantee came into existence for the purpose of securing the bank in respect of a single transaction, or series of transactions, whereby the bank released a specific load of stored meat, over which the bank had rights, to the defendants to enable its sale. They argued that it was not intended to be a guarantee of a continuing situation.

Flood J.:

The reality of that submission is that the said written guarantee was intended to be a wholly different document, namely, a guarantee of a single transaction as distinct from a guarantee of a continuing situation. It involves a material alteration, not only in the words used but in the import of the words used. It is pointed out to me that this is in fact a document under seal. It effectively amounts to a contention that the defendants had been misled into executing a deed or signing a document essentially different from that which they intended to execute or sign and that the writing is wholly void. In short a plea of non est factum. It should, however, be noted that that case is not pleaded. In most cases in which 'non est factum' has been successfully pleaded a mistake has been induced by fraud. I am quite satisfied that as far as the bank and its agent is concerned there is no question of fraud.Even in circumstances where it is clearly established that the person relying on the doctrine did not understand the particular purport of the particular document, such person must establish that they took such precautions as they reasonably could to have the document explained to them and to acquire knowledge of the import of the document. See *Saunders v Anglia Building Society* (1970) 3 All ER 963. There is no such evidence in this case.

Notes

1. The doctrine was not applied in AIB *Group* (UK) *plc v Martin* (2000) 97(28) LSG 34. In that case, AIB drew up a mortgage deed consolidating a number of loan accounts, some of which were sole accounts of Martin and some of which were joint accounts of Martin and his partner Gold. Having agreed to the consolidation and signed the facility letter without reading it, Gold subsequently realised that AIB had wrongly designated some of Martin's sole acounts as joint accounts, including one that had a debt of almost £800,000. The documents had in effect already been checked by his solicitor, who was aware of the provisions of the mortgage deed, and although the solicitor failed to notice the error in the consolidation of the accounts, his assistant knew the full extent of the proposed liability. That knowledge was imputed to Gold by way of the solicitor/client relationship.
2. Similarly, in *Adm Londis plc v Arman Retail Ltd and others* [2006] IEHC 309, the *Ted Castle* case was relied on to reject a claim of *non est factum*. The parties claimed to have signed a guarantee without a true understanding of the document. Clarke J held that the document was 'clearly, on its face, a guarantee' and that in these circumstances 'even a cursory reading of the document would have brought to the Defendants' attention the fact that they were signing a guarantee'.

EXERCISES

1. Ronan enters into a contract to sell his car to Catherine. Unknown to either, the car has just been set on fire. Although the fire brigade is called, there is substantial damage to the interior although the engine is still intact. Catherine argues that the contract is void for common mistake. Is she correct?
2. Karen visits Chuck's art gallery and agrees to buy one of the paintings on display. Although the painting is unsigned, Karen believes that it is an

early Graham Knuttel piece and is delighted when Chuck agrees to sell it for €10,000 (at least 50 per cent below the average price for a work by this artist). Chuck recognises Karen as a collector of Knuttel works but does not tell her that an amateur painter, an admirer of Knuttel, deliberately copying Knuttel's style, produced the picture. Karen thanks Chuck for selling the painting to her and notes that this will be 'a marvellous addition to my collection'. Subsequently Karen discovers the error and argues that the contract is void because of this substantial mistake. Advise Chuck.

3. Callan designs a sophisticated computer mouse which is more flexible than an ordinary mouse and which operates merely by pointing it at the screen. He manufactures two thousand of them and decides to market them himself. He puts an advertisement in *The Irish Times* offering a 'Designer Mouse for Sale' for €1,000. Due to a clerical error, Callan's advertisement is placed in the 'Pets' section rather than the 'Computers' section of the classified advertisements. Biddie, a lottery winner, is setting up a small zoo and telephones Callan offering to buy 'the cute mouse'. Callan accepts the offer. When Biddie asks what age the mouse is, Callan suspects that Biddie is slightly confused but he tells her that they are brand new. Biddie sends Callan a cheque and is astonished to receive a piece of computer equipment. She argues that their contract is void as a result of this mistake.

4. Kevin advertises in the paper the sale of his family silver. The advertisement states a price of '€3,000 or nearest offer for the lot'. He receives a response from Carrie in New York who claims to be his second cousin-once-removed. Carrie writes a passionate letter explaining that she wants to 'get in touch with her roots' and is anxious to acquire all the silver. She indicates her willingness to pay €3,000 and informs him that she will collect it on her forthcoming visit to Ireland. Despite a number of other offers, Kevin agrees to sell the silver to her but when Carrie arrives at his door, she asks whether he will take a cheque. Reluctantly, but on the basis that she looks like his aunt, Kevin takes the cheque. It subsequently turns out that Carrie is not a relation of his at all. She absconds and the cheque is rejected by the bank. Kevin discovers that she has sold the silver to an antique dealer. He seeks your advice about his chances of getting the silver back.

5. Wendy is blind. She normally gets her solicitor to check everything she signs. However, seeking to reduce her legal bills, she signs what she believes to be a contract to let a room in her house without asking anyone to look at it for her. It transpires that the document is instead a contract to sell her house. Can she rely on the doctrine of *non est factum*?

Chapter Ten

Misrepresentation

INTRODUCTION

The law relating to pre-contractual misrepresentation, that is, the law which controls the range of reliefs available to a person who has entered into a contract following upon a misstatement made to that person, involves a complex network of common-law and contract rules, tortious causes of action and equitable and statutory rules and principles. In this chapter it is hoped to introduce the student to this area of the law. It is essential for the student to grasp that the range of options available to the misrepresentee traverses the broad expanse of civil liability and is not purely contract related.

In general, there have been a significant number of developments within the law of misrepresentation. New tortious (*Hedley Byrne*) and statutory (s. 45 (1) of the 1980 Act) causes of action have become available to the misrepresentee. Several obstacles to the granting of certain remedies such as rescission have been removed either by way of practical decision or under the 1980 legislation. The courts, both in England and Ireland, have made considerable efforts to reinterpret the boundary between actionable misrepresentation and non-actionable bare representation (*Dick Bentley*, and the *Bank of Ireland* cases respectively) and the judicial trend is towards creating overlapping or concurrent liability in contract and tort. These trends make good contract drafting more (not less) important, than ever.

SECTION ONE—REPRESENTATION

A. EXISTING FACT

In order to claim relief, the general rule is that a representation of existing fact must have been made by one party to induce the other party to enter into a contract.

Esso Petroleum Co. Ltd *v* Mardon [1976] 1 QB 801

The defendant entered into a tenancy agreement with the plaintiffs in respect of a filling station on the basis of a representation made by one of the plaintiffs' agents. This agent, a man with forty years' experience of the trade, calculated that the potential throughput was likely to reach 200,000 gallons by the third year of operation. This figure proved to be over-optimistic because planning restrictions had been overlooked by the agent

527

and the defendant lost his business. He claimed damages for breach of the warranty as to the potential throughput, or alternatively for negligent misrepresentation.

Lord Denning M.R.:

. . .

Now I would quite agree with [counsel for the plaintiff] that it was not a warranty—in this sense—that it did not *guarantee* that the throughput *would be* 200,000 gallons. But, nevertheless, it was a forecast made by a party—Esso—who had special knowledge and skill. It was the yardstick (the e.a.c.) by which they measured the worth of a filling station. They knew the facts. They knew the traffic in the town. They knew the through-put of comparable stations. They had much experience and expertise at their disposal. They were in a much better position than Mr Mardon to make a forecast. It seems to me that if such a person makes a forecast, intending that the other should act upon it—and he does act upon it, it can well be interpreted as a warranty that the forecast is sound and reliable in the sense that they made it with reasonable care and skill. It is just as if Esso said to Mr Mardon: 'Our forecast of throughput is 200,000 gallons. You can rely upon it as being a sound forecast of what the service station should do. The rent is calculated on that footing.' If the forecast turned out to be an unsound forecast such as no person of skill or experience should have made, there is a breach of warranty. Just as there is a breach of warranty when a forecast is made—'expected to load' by a certain date—if the maker has no reasonable grounds for it: see *Samuel Sanday and Co. v Keighley, Maxted and Co.* (1922) 27 Com Cas 296; or bunkers 'expected 600/700 tons': see E*fploia Shipping Corp. Ltd v Canadian Transport Co. Ltd (The Pantanassa)* [1958] 2 Lloyd's Rep. 449, 455–7 by Diplock J. It is very different from the New Zealand case where the land had never been used as a sheep farm and both parties were equally able to form an opinion as to its carrying capacity: see particularly *Bisset v Wilkinson* [1927] AC 177, 183–4.

In the present case it seems to me that there was a warranty that the forecast was sound, that is, Esso made it with reasonable care and skill. That warranty was broken. Most negligently Esso made a 'fatal error' in the forecast they stated to Mr Mardon, and on which he took the tenancy. For this they are liable in damages.

. . .

. . . It seems to me that *Hedley Byrne & Co. Ltd v Heller & Partners Ltd* [1964] AC 465, properly understood, covers this particular proposition: if a man, who has or professes to have special knowledge or skill, makes a representation by virtue thereof to another— be it advice, information or opinion—with the intention of inducing him to enter into a contract with him, he is under a duty to use reasonable care to see that the represent-ation is correct, and that the advice, information or opinion is reliable. If he negligently gives unsound advice or misleading information or expresses an erroneous opinion, and thereby induces the other side to enter into a contract with him, he is liable in damages.

Notes

1. This case was distinguished in the Canadian case of *447927 Ontario Inc. v Pizza Pizza Ltd* (1987) 44 DLR (4th) 366 affd. (1990) 64 DLR (4th) 160. The plaintiff claimed to have entered a franchise agreement with the defendant franchisor, on the basis of representations made by the defendant's agent to the effect that, properly managed, the franchise could enjoy possibly average sales. When sales fell below average the plaintiff sought damages for *inter alia* misrepresentation and breach of warranty.

Anderson J.:

...

Based on E*sso* and H*edley Byrne*, I am prepared to conclude that, the defendant having held itself out as having special expertise in the operation of such franchise business as those with which the action is concerned, the relationship between the defendant and the plaintiff in the pre-contractual negotiations was such as to give rise to a duty of care. I am also prepared to conclude that the representation made by Davis as to the potential of the site was an inducement to the plaintiff in entering into the franchise agreement. I think what was said by Davis bears a reasonable analogy to what was said by the plaintiff's representative in E*sso*. In E*sso* the phrases 'negligent representation' and 'negligent misrepresentation' are used as though they were interchangeable. With great deference to the learned judges of the Court of Appeal, I think that speaking precisely the appropriate phrase is 'negligent misrepresentation', in other words, the proper connotation is that the words spoken were not true. There then remains the further question of whether they were spoken negligently. In my view, the plaintiff in the case at bar has difficulty in both aspects.

... I could not find on the evidence that, when Davis said what he did say in May and June of 1980, that what he said was untrue.

In view of that conclusion, it may not be essential, but I consider it appropriate to consider whether there was negligence. It is in this area that there is a conspicuous variance between the facts in E*sso* and the facts in the case at bar.

To return to E*sso* for the moment, and to consider the facts in that case, the potential throughput for the station had been estimated by its representatives predicated upon a certain anticipated design. As events developed, the planning authorities would not permit construction according to that design, and the final layout was such that the potential of the station was materially reduced. No new calculation was made by E*sso* based on the altered design. This was described by the trial judge, Lawson J. ([1975] QB 819), as a 'fatal error'. On this point a paragraph from the judgment of Lord Denning M.R., at pp 814–5, is appropriate:

Now at this point Esso made an error which the judge described as a 'fatal error'. They did not revise their original estimate which they had made in 1961. They still assessed the e.a.c. (estimated annual consumption) of petrol at 200,000 gallons. Whereas they should have made a re-appraisal in the light of the building being now 'back to front'. This adversely affected the site's potential: because passing traffic could not see the station. It would reduce the throughput greatly. The judge found that this 'fatal error' was due to want of care on the part of Esso. There can be no doubt about it.

There is simply no such error demonstrated on the evidence in the case at bar.

In my view, the plaintiff has failed to establish misrepresentation and has failed to establish negligence.

...

The agreement contains an exclusionary clause in the following terms:

22. No Warranty
The franchisor makes and has made no warranties, inducements, promises or representations to the franchisee respecting the subject matter of this agreement, except as may be expressly stated in this agreement, or is otherwise stated in writing in a document executed by the franchisor and the franchisee and has made

no representations to the franchisee in respect of income or profit to be derived by the franchisee pursuant to this agreement.

This clause must be considered in deciding whether a warranty should be found (quite apart from any result the clause might have upon the right to enforce a warranty, if one were found). It seems to me more difficult to conclude that a collateral oral warranty was intended, when, after it was alleged to have been made, a formal written agreement was submitted for consideration by the plaintiff, was negotiated and amended, and ultimately executed, containing a clause flatly asserting that no warranty had been made. It is significant that in *Esso* the agreement contained no such clause.

2. However, should the evidence disclose that industry practice is not to verify a factual assertion that has induced a contract, then a disclaimer may not be effective. In *Walsh v Jones Lang Lasalle* [2007] IEHC 28 the plaintiff purchased an investment property stated to have a total floor area of 23,057 square feet. After completion it was discovered that the floor area was 21,248 square feet. The misrepresentation, contained in the defendant's brochure, was qualified by a clause stating that 'Whilst every care has been taken in the preparation of these particulars, and they are believed to be correct, they are not warranted and intending purchasers/lessees should satisfy themselves as to the correctness of the information given.' Quirke J., in an action based on negligent mistatement, found for the purchaser on the basis that every care had not been taken and that custom and practice of investors was to rely on the apparently precise measurements in brochures rather than undertake a pre-contractual measuring exercise. Quirke J. said:

If the defendant wished to reserve to itself the right, (a) to publish within its sales brochure precise measurements which were in fact grossly inaccurate and, (b) to relieve itself of liability to the category of persons to whom the brochure and its contents were directed, then there was an obligation upon the defendant to draw to the attention of the plaintiff and other prospective purchasers the fact that the seemingly precise measurements published were likely to be wholly unreliable and should not be relied upon in any circumstances.

By including within its brochure an enigmatic sentence in small print claiming to have taken particular care in the preparation of all of the particulars within the brochure but advising prospective purchasers to *'satisfy themselves as to the correctness of the information given'* the defendant failed to discharge that obligation.

On the evidence of the practice adopted by buyers and sellers of commercial property in Dublin at the relevant time the defendant's 'disclaimer' was a quite inadequate means of notifying prospective purchasers that the seemingly precise measurements of the floor areas so prominently published within the sales brochure were wholly unreliable.

Smyth v Lynn (1954) 85 ILTR 57

A property which was advertised as being 'in excellent structural and decorative repair' was auctioned. The plaintiff was successful in the auction outbidding the defendant. Six weeks later the plaintiff advertised the property for sale by auction again, using the same advertisement. This time the property was knocked down to the defendant. Upon inspecting the house the defendant discovered extensive woodworm infestation, and refused to complete. The plaintiff sued for specific performance.

Curran J.:

The principles underlying the contentions of counsel and what are the relevant inquiries in a case such as the present are discussed in the judgment of the Privy Council in the case of *Bisset v Wilkinson & Anor*, [1927] AC 177, in which a vendor of land in New Zealand brought an action to recover under the contract. The purchaser claimed to rescind the contract on the ground of the falseness of a statement as to the carrying capacity of the land for sheep. The headnote of this case contains the following proposition: '. . . When it is sought to rescind a contract on the ground of the falseness of a statement of opinion by which it was induced, it must be enquired what was the meaning of the statement made, and whether it was true. Relevant to those inquiries are, the material facts of the transaction, the knowledge of the parties, the words used, and the actual condition of the subject matter.'

It was held, on the evidence, applying the above considerations, that the statement was merely of an opinion which the vendor honestly held; and accordingly that the defence failed, and the judgment of the Court of Appeal was reversed.

The learned judge who tried the action, (Sim J.) based his judgment in favour of the appellant upon the conclusions at which he arrived upon his examination of the evidence, firstly, that the representation made by the plaintiff was a representation only of his opinion of the capacity of the farm, not a representation of what that capacity in fact was; and secondly, that this representation of opinion was honestly made by the appellant. By these conclusions the whole case of misrepresentation was disposed of and the charge of fraud was specifically negatived. At p. 181 Lord Merivale says:

> In an action for rescission, as in an action for specific performance of an executory contract, when misrepresentation repudiates the contract, it is, of course, essential to ascertain whether that which is relied upon is representation of fact, or a statement of opinion, since an erroneous opinion stated by the party affirming the contract, though it may have been relied upon and induced the contract on the part of the party who seeks rescission, gives no title to relief unless fraud is established.

The learned judge then cited *Karberg's* case [1892] 3 Ch. 1. and *Smith v Land and House Property Corp.* (1884) 28 ChD 7. In *Karberg's* case the test used to ascertain whether a representation was one of opinion or belief, was: 'Was the statement of expectation a statement of things not really expected?' In *Smith v Land and House Property Corp.* a tenant was described as 'a most desirable tenant'. This description was held by the Court of Appeal to be a misrepresentation of fact, which, without proof of fraud, disentitled the vendor to specific performance of the contract. In *Smith v Chadwick* (1884) 9 App Cas 187; (1882) 20 ChD 27, the words under consideration involved an inquiry in relation to the sale of an industrial concern. The question was, was a statement of 'the present value of the turnover or output' a statement of fact that the produce of the works was of the amount mentioned or a statement that the productive power of the works was estimated at so much. The words were held to be capable of the second of these meanings. The decisive enquiries came to be: what meaning was actually conveyed to the party complaining; was he deceived, and, as the action was based on a charge of fraud, was the statement in question made fraudulently?

I now proceed to consider the application of the foregoing principles to the present case. The advertisement contains statements which are undoubtedly statements of fact such as 'the property is brick-built, pebble-dashed and slated.' No question of standard or degree enters into these statements. When the advertisement goes on, however, to state that the property is 'in excellent structural and decorative repair and ready for immediate owner occupation' one is forced with the question 'What standard has the person making these statements applied?'

It is my view that the statements referred to are expressions of opinion, and that the opinions expressed are erroneous. Was the position of the parties such that, nevertheless, those expressions of opinion constituted statements of fact? Both parties inspected the premises prior to the auction on 11 March 1949, when the plaintiff purchased the property. It is clear that neither of them had discovered the woodworm infestation before that date. It is suggested that the plaintiff either personally or by her agents had discovered the woodworm infestation after the first and before the second sale. On the evidence before me I find it difficult to believe that the plaintiff had discovered the woodworm prior to the execution of the assignment of 2 April, or prior to the payment of the purchase money on 11 or 12 April.

It is not my view that the words used in the advertisement were apt to describe the actual condition of the premises. The law gives no special sanctity to statements contained in an advertisement for the sale of property. They may, for example, be made the subject of proceedings based upon misrepresentation or may be relied upon as grounds for rescission of a contract or in answer to a claim for specific performance—provided the necessary elements are present. Such advertisements, however, must be looked at in their true perspective. They do not purport to be detailed reports by experts as to the condition of the property to be sold. It is common knowledge that the purpose of such advertisements is to draw attention to the good points of the property, and that one usually finds in such advertisements rather flourishing statements.

In my opinion the defendant is not the type of person to rely on 'Auctioneers' encomiums.' There is something to be said for the contention that the defendant placed more reliance upon the description of the property in the second advertisement by reason of the fact that the plaintiff was reselling the property so soon after she had purchased it. I am inclined to the view that the statement in the advertisement assumed a more positive importance in the defendant's mind after his discovery of the woodworm and when he came to consider with his advisers what grounds he had for getting out of his contract.

On the evidence I am satisfied that the statements complained of did not in any positive sense induce the defendant to purchase or contribute to the inducement of the defendant. If I were satisfied that the defendant was so induced or if I had a reasonable doubt as to whether he was so induced or not I would find it necessary to give further consideration to the question as to whether specific performance of the contract should be granted. In all the circumstances of the case the plaintiff is entitled to specific performance of the contract. This may be a hardship to the defendant, but that, by itself, is not a ground for refusing the enforcement of the contract.

Note

In *Doolan v Murray, Murray, Murray Cheevers, Aziz and Dun Laoghaire Corporation* (HC), 21 December 1993, unrep., considered in detail at p. 550 below, Keane J. further expanded on the scope of a permissible plea of misrepresentation.

It is also to be borne in mind—and this is of obvious relevance in the present case—that the representation, to give rise to legal consequences, must normally be a representation of fact and not of law. While the leading cases on this aspect of the law, such as *Cooper v Phibbs* (1867) LR 2 HL 149 concern cases of mistake, I think Dr Robert

Clark, in *Contract Law in Ireland*, (3rd ed.), 229, is correct in stating that that principle also applies to misrepresentation cases. (A similar view seems to be taken by the learned editors of *Chitty on Contracts*, (26th ed.) vol I, 274. That law, as demonstrated by the decision in *Cooper v Phibbs*, draws a distinction between mistakes as to the law in general as distinct from mistakes as to private rights. Thus, a misrepresentation as to private rights may still afford a cause of action.

B. RELIANCE

Reliance on the representation is essential. Thus a representation will not be actionable if it did not come to the attention of the other party, or if the other party already knew the truth, or took a deliberate risk as to the truth, or if the other party relied on their own information. The effect of signature where one party signs a document that transfers risk to the signor will generally be to bind that person, even if he or she does not read the document: *Toll FGCT Pty Ltd v Alphapharm* [2004] HCA 52; *Peekay Intermark Ltd v Australia and* N. Z. *Banking Group* [2006] EWCA Civ 386. It will be necessary to invoke a vitiating factor such as misrepresentation, duress or undue influence if such apparent consent is to be overturned.

Phelps *v* White (1881) 5 LR (Ir.) 318

The plaintiff agreed to purchase property from the defendant. The agreement of sale represented in substance that the timber on the estate was reserved to the vendor and formed part of the property to be sold. However, an examination of the contents of the abstract of title which was delivered to the plaintiff would have indicated that the vendor had no title to the timber. Upon discovering the error the plaintiff sought compensation.

The Vice Chancellor held that the plaintiff entered the contract on the basis of a material misrepresentation. He then continued:

. . .

. . . The real question here has throughout appeared to me to be, what is the effect which the possession of those means of knowledge should have upon the plaintiff's right to compensation? If the defendant had brought home actual knowledge of the fact that the timber was not the defendant's to convey, the case would wear a different aspect; for if the plaintiff, knowing that this was the case, had proceeded to complete his purchase without objection, he could scarcely be entitled afterwards to claim rescission or compensation. But as I believe, from the evidence, that the defendant had not by himself or his agent such actual knowledge till after completion, and that he went on with his purchase believing the timber was to be his, the question is, whether his neglect to avail himself of the information afforded him debars him from relief? I find negligence on the one hand, but legal fraud on the other. Assuming that the defendant had not discovered the error in his rental, which is far the more favourable view for him, I cannot see how he can rely on the plaintiff's failure to discover the mistake. It was the defendant's duty to have discovered it, and at once called the plaintiff's attention expressly to it. The plaintiff has the excuse of relying on the defendant's express and unequivocal representation of that which it was his duty to the plaintiff to know and to remember, and to represent truly. The plaintiff had no duty towards the defendant to discover the defendant's mistake. He cannot, as has more than once been well observed, complain of the plaintiff's having relied too implicitly on the truth of what he has himself stated. The critical time, too, at which this misrepresentation operated on the plaintiff's mind was that when he estimated the price he should offer, and made his offer. That offer was accepted, and upon this basis the whole of the subsequent dealings took place. During all those dealings the error was never pointed out to him, and I believe he never discovered it. His neglect was, therefore, innocent as compared with the fraudulent negligence of the defendant.

Reliance on the misrepresentation may also be negatived by evidence that the misrepresentee undertook parallel investigations into the subject matter of the contract. In *Intrum Justitia BV v Legal and Trade Financial Services Ltd* [2005] IEHC 190, the seller of shares in a company misrepresented that the target company 'had no skeletons in its cupboard' but it was held that this statement did not of itself invalidate the share-purchase agreement: O'Sullivan J. said that the misrepresentation:

. . . must be part of the underlying basis upon which the representee proceeds. This was not satisfied in this case since although told that no due diligence was necessary the plaintiff continued with his investigations following the representation and did not allow it to affect his conduct in any way . . . In the present case it is clear that the plaintiff relied on the financial information thrown up by its own thorough and rigorous due-diligence process for the purpose of informing itself as to the financial situation of the defendant company.

The leading Irish case is *Gahan v Boland*, Unreported, High Court, Murphy J., 21 January 1983 affirmed by the Supreme Court in 1984.

Gahan *v* Boland and Wendy Boland (SC) 20 January 1984, unrep.

Henchy J.:

The defendants Maurice and Wendy Boland are husband and wife. In February 1981 they had on offer for sale the property known as Glencarrig, situate at Bride's Glen, Loughlinstown, Co. Dublin. That property consists of a dwelling house and some 3 ¼ acres of land.

The plaintiff, who is a solicitor, entered into a written contract on Monday 16 February 1981 for the purchase of the property for £135,000. In the present proceedings he has sought an order for the rescission of that contract. When his case came for hearing before Murphy J. in the High Court he succeeded in getting that order. The defendants now appeal.

The order for rescission was made as a result of certain events which are said to have taken place on Friday 13 February 1981. On that day the plaintiff visited the defendants at Glencarrig. The purpose of the visit was to inspect the property and to make certain inquiries about it. The plaintiff says that amongst the inquiries he made was one as to whether a projected motorway connecting Dublin and Wicklow would affect the Glencarrig property. His evidence was that Mr Boland assured him that the property would not be affected by the proposed motorway and that this assurance led him to enter into a written contract on the following Monday for the purchase of the property. It seems to be common case that the proposed motorway is in fact routed to pass through the Glencarrig property. That is something the plaintiff did not discover until after he had signed the contract.

There was a conflict of evidence as to what representation, if any, was made as to the motorway. The judge, however, having reviewed the evidence was of the clear opinion that an innocent but false representation was made by Mr Boland to the effect that the property would not be affected by the motorway, if and when it came to be constructed; that this representation was a material one made with the intention of inducing the plaintiff to act on it; and that it was one of the factors that induced the plaintiff to enter into the written contract on the following Monday to purchase the property.

Having perused the transcript of the evidence, I am satisfied that there was ample evidence to support those findings as to the misrepresentation relied on by the plaintiff for rescission of the contract. Once there was evidence to support the judge's findings in that respect, the defendants' main ground of appeal, namely that the findings as to misrepresentation are unsustainable, must be held to fail. This court cannot set aside primary facts of that nature found by the judge and supported by evidence.

The alternative or secondary ground of appeal argued was that, even if the defendants' argument as to the misrepresentation fails, the claim for rescission should have been rejected because the plaintiff should be held to have had constructive notice of the true position as to the route of the proposed motorway. It was suggested that the plaintiff, a solicitor and an intending purchaser, having made inquiries of the vendors as to whether the property would be affected by the motorway, was required, by the application of the doctrine of constructive notice, to pursue those inquiries in quarters where he would have been reliably informed as to the true position. For that reason, it is submitted, he should be held disentitled, for the purposes of rescission, to rely on the misrepresentation made and should be deemed to have constructive notice of the true position as to the route of the motorway.

I was unable to accept this argument. I consider it to be well settled law that the only knowledge that will debar a purchaser from repudiating a contract he has been induced into by the vendor's misrepresentation is actual and complete knowledge of the true situation. It does not lie with a vendor, who has by his misrepresentation induced the purchaser to enter into a contract to purchase, to have his misrepresentation excused or overlooked and to have the purchaser deprived of a right to rescind because he did not ignore the misrepresentation and pursue matters further so as to establish the truth of what was misrepresented. That would be unconscionable and unfair. The doctrine of constructive notice, as it arises under s. 3 of the Conveyancing Act, 1882 and as it was applied by this court in *Somers v W* 1979 IR 94, has no application to the facts of this case.

I would dismiss this appeal.

Note

The situation will be different if the representee can be proven to be actually aware of the truth. For example in *Grafton Court Ltd v Wadson Sales Ltd* (HC) 17 February 1975, unrep., the defendant claimed to have leased a unit in a shopping complex on the basis of representations by the lessor that the other tenants would be 'of high-quality retail type'. The court stated that since the majority of the other units were occupied at the time of the lease, the defendant knew the quality and nature of those tenants and was not thus relying on any representations made.

S. Pearson & Son Ltd *v* Lord Mayor & C. of Dublin [1907] AC 351

Agents for Dublin Corporation furnished the appellants with plans, drawings and specifications as a result of which the appellants contracted to execute certain work. In the plans representations were made as to the position of a certain wall:

... In the contract (clauses 43, 46, 47, 48) it was stipulated that the contractor should satisfy himself as to the dimensions, levels and nature of all existing works and other things connected with the contract works; that the corporation did not hold itself responsible for the accuracy of the information as to the sections or foundations of existing walls and works; and that no charges for extra work or otherwise would be allowed in consequence of incorrect information or inaccuracies in the drawings or specifications. The appellants performed the contract, and brought an action of deceit against the corporation, claiming damages for false representations as to the position, dimensions and foundations of the wall, whereby the appellants were compelled to execute more costly works than would otherwise have been required.

Palles C.B. refused to leave any question to the jury, and entered judgment for the respondents on the ground that the contractors were bound by their contracts to verify for themselves all the information contained in the plans.

Lord Loreburn L.C.:

...

... Inasmuch as I am about to propose that the case be remitted for a new trial, it is desirable that I should say no more than is necessary to explain my view.

The plaintiffs' case is that they were induced to enter into a contract for the construction of certain sewage works by statements made by and on behalf of the defendants as to the existence to a depth of nine feet below ordnance datum of an old wall. Undoubtedly evidence was adduced at the trial from which the jury might, if they thought right, conclude that the plaintiffs were so induced by statements made on behalf of the defendants. Also, there was evidence for the jury that those statements were made either with a knowledge of their falsity, or (which is the same thing) with a reckless indifference whether they were true or false, on the part of the engineers employed by the defendants to make the plans which were submitted to plaintiffs as the basis of the tender. And had the case rested there I gather that the Chief Baron would have left the case to the jury, and that the learned judges who subsequently had this litigation before them would have approved this course.

But another feature of the case was considered fatal to the plaintiffs' claim. The contract contained clauses, which I need not cite at length, to the effect that the contractors must not rely on any representation made in plans or elsewhere, but must ascertain and judge of the facts for themselves. And, therefore, the Chief Baron withdrew the case from the jury. As I understand it, the view he held, in substance confirmed by the Court of Appeal, was that the plaintiffs, so forewarned, had no right to rely on any representation, and could not be heard to say they were induced by statements on which by contract they were not to rely. Or, at all events, it was said that the defendants, being themselves innocent, are protected by such clauses against the consequence of contractors acting on false statements made by defendants' agents, however fraudulent those agents might be.

Now it seems clear that no one can escape liability for his own fraudulent statements by inserting in a contract a clause that the other party shall not rely upon them. I will not say that a man himself innocent may not under any circumstances, however peculiar, guard himself by apt and express clauses from liability for the fraud of his own agents. It suffices to say that in my opinion the clauses before us do not admit of such a construction. They contemplate honesty on both sides and protect only against honest mistakes. The principal and the agent are one, and it does not signify which of them made the incriminated statement or which of them possessed the guilty knowledge.

Lord Ashbourne:

. . . I cannot think that in face of the evidence in the case this clause 43 could be regarded as establishing a defence. Such a clause might in some cases be part of a fraud, and might advance and disguise a fraud, and I cannot think that on the facts and circumstances of this case it can have such a wide and perilous application as was contended for. Such a clause may be appropriate and fairly apply to errors, inaccuracies, and mistakes, but not to cases like the present.

(The Earl of Halsbury and Lord James of Hereford delivered concurring judgments. Lord Macnaghten and Lord Collins agreed.)

Note

1. In *Dublin Port and Docks Board v Brittania Dredging Co. Ltd* [1968] IR 136 Lord Loreburn's observations were noted but as the misrepresentations in that case were innocent, a clause avoiding liability for misrepresentation or lack of information was deemed effective.
2. It is clear from the case of *Sargent v Irish Multiwheel Ltd* (1955) 21–22 Ir Jur *Rep* 42 that it is not necessary for a representee to inform the representor that he or she is relying on the representation. Contrast with *Walsh v Jones Lang Lasalle* [2007] IEHC 28.
3. S. 46 of the Sale of Goods and Supply of Services Act 1980 regulates the extent to which an express clause can exclude or limit the right of a misrepresentee to bring an action in respect of an otherwise actionable, non-fraudulent misrepresentation. Such clauses are permissible if they pass the 'fair and reasonable' test. For English cases on the same statutory provision in English law see *Walker v Boyle* [1982] 1 WLR 495 and *South Western General Pty Co. v Marton* (1982) 263 EG 1090

C. Is the Clause in the Contract an Exemption Clause?

Inntrepreneur Pub Co. *v* East Crown Ltd [2000] 2 Lloyd's 611
(The facts on p. 306 above)

Clause 14.1 of a lease contained an entire agreement clause. Clause 14.2 of the contract sought to exclude liability in respect of any pre-contractual misrepresentations in the following terms:

14.2 Before executing this Agreement the Tenant and Guarantor have:
    14.2.1 received independent professional advice about its terms, or

14.2.2 been advised of the wisdom of taking independent professional advice
but have chosen not to do so and accordingly they have not relied upon any
advice or statement of the Company or its solicitors.

Lightman J. held that the entire agreement clause had the effect of
precluding any argument that there had been a collateral warranty given at
the time of negotiation of the agreement. The learned judge went on to
consider the effect of the above clauses in the context of section 3 of the
Misrepresentation Act 1967 (drafted in the same terms as section 46 of the
Sale of Goods and Supply of Terms Act 1980).

Lightman J.:

An entire agreement provision does not preclude a claim in misrepresentation, for the
denial of contractual force to a statement cannot affect the status of the statement as a
misrepresentation. The same clause in an agreement may contain both an entire agreement provision and a further provision designed to exclude liability e.g. for misrepresentation or breach of duty. As an example cl. 14 in this case, after setting out in cl. 14.1 the
entire agreement clause, in cl. 4.2 sets out to exclude liability for misrepresentation and
breach of duty. Whether this latter provision is legally effective for this purpose may turn
on the question of its reasonableness as required by s. 3 of the Misrepresentation Act
1967: see e.g. *Inntrepreneur Estates* (CPC) *v Worth* [1996] 1 EGLR 84. But (contrary to the contentions of Crown) s. 3 has no application to an entire agreement clause provision defining where the contractual terms between the parties are to be found: see *McGrath v Shah*.

While section 46 of the 1980 Act will not affect the contractual cause of
action, it has been held that where the contract contains a non-reliance or
no-misrepresentation statement, and the misrepresentee brings a claim in
tort (e.g. fraudulent misrepresentation or negligent misstatement) then
the fair and reasonable test in section 46 may be called into play. See
Leofelis SA v Lonsdale Sports Ltd [2007] EWHC 451 (Ch).

SECTION TWO—MISREPRESENTATION AND TORT

A. FRAUDULENT MISREPRESENTATION

Delany v Keogh [1905] 2 IR 267

The facts

The defendant, an auctioneer, was employed by Bradley, a solicitor, to sell
the latter's interest in leasehold property. The conditions of sale stated
that although the annual rent was £25, a rent of £18 had been accepted for
several years. Prior to the auction, the defendant was informed that the
landlord was insisting on a rent of £25 *per annum*. Bradley opined however
that the landlord would be estopped from such an action. The conditions
of sale were read out at the auction, and the plaintiff purchased the
leasehold interest. He was later obliged to pay full rent, and sued the

defendant for deceit. The majority of the King's Bench Division entered judgment for the defendant.

Johnson J.:

To succeed in this action, the plaintiff must prove fraud by the defendant, and damage to the plaintiff thereby induced to act on fraud—nothing short of that will be sufficient to maintain the action. Proof of damage without proof of fraud will not suffice. The plaintiff's case is that he sustained damage by having been induced by the defendant's false and fraudulent misrepresentations and false and fraudulent concealment of facts known to the defendant to purchase a leasehold public house and 3 acres of land at a public auction for a price larger than he would otherwise have given.

For the purpose of the present action, I dismiss from consideration the class of authorities in which equity relieves from contracts on the ground of misrepresent-ation—to which some of the cases cited in argument apply. There is a distinct cleavage between that class of authorities and those by which the case in hand is now to be determined, and in which, as I understand the law, the authorities establish that the alleged fraud must be such as would sustain an action for deceit, *viz. mala fides*—intentional deceit to deceive the plaintiff, which is a question of fact on the evidence, and is of the very essence of the alleged cause of action. A statement untrue in fact, but made without *mala fides*, and in the honest belief that it is true, is not evidence of fraud, although made through want of care or even through negligent carelessness or without reasonable grounds for belief in its truth, provided always it is made without *mala fides* and in honest belief of its truth. Of course it is not sufficient for a person making a representation to induce another to act on it, and who does act on it, to say I honestly believed what I said was true. The grounds on which the honest belief is really entertained and *mala fides* is absent necessarily depend on the facts of the particular case; and it is obviously of the last importance to investigate and ascertain whether on the evidence the person making the representation has really such honest belief. The authorities supply some tests.

For instance, if a person states what he knows to be false to induce another to act on that statement, it is plain that he has no honest belief in his statement; if he wilfully shuts his eyes to the facts, or purposely abstains from inquiry into them, no reasonable person would in such circumstances infer he had any honest belief in the matter. For the present purpose it is not necessary to multiply illustrations. False and fraudulent misrepresentation to induce another to act on it may be effectuated by *mala fide* active concealment (so to speak) with intent to deceive as by actual *mala fide* false statement. The same principles are equally applicable to such cases, whether the con-cealment is of a fact, or part of a fact, or by apparent disclosure of a fact, while there is *mala fide* concealment of that which, if disclosed, would put a wholly different complex-ion on the disclosure, and show what only is disclosed is false, and fraudulent, and dishonest, because it was not the whole truth.

> A lie which is all a lie may be met and fought with outright;
> But a lie which is part a truth is a harder matter to fight.

In all such cases the question is whether the representation is effected by actual statement or actual concealment; whether it was made dishonestly and intentionally to deceive another, and with intent that the other shall act on it, and so to induce him to act on it; or whether it was made *bona fide* in the honest belief of its truth; and the solution of this question depends on the evidence in the particular case in which it lies on the plaintiff to prove the alleged fraud and damage.

. . .

. . . The defendant, who was not a lawyer, *bona fide* inquired from Bradley, the solicitor who employed him, and who was the best source of information accessible to him, what he ought to do in the circumstances. This was the defendant's reasonable and proper course to pursue. Bradley was a solicitor, and personally acquainted with all the facts. Bradley, as a lawyer, gave the defendant his opinion that no more than £18 a year could be recovered, and directed him to proceed with the auction under the published advertisements and particulars and conditions of sale. The defendant states: 'I believed Bradley's statement, and acted on his opinion. I thought the rent was £18 a year and no more, outgoings 11s weekly, on the basis that the rent was only £18.' The defendant also says that no authority was given him to alter the particulars, and he sold the premises by Bradley's orders under the published particulars and conditions of sale, which he read then at the auction, without comment or alteration. He believed they truly represented the state and condition of the subject matter of the sale, and Mr Justice Wright, who saw and heard all the witnesses, with his experience at the bar and on the bench, believed the defendant. I think the decision of the House of Lords in *Derry v Peek*,[1] both on the facts of the case and in law, practically covers the present case.

The defendant knew nothing of the correspondence between Tench and Bradley, and it is not evidence against him.

I fail, on the facts, to discover any intention on the part of the defendant to deceive any person, either before or at the auction; he appears to me to have been honest and straightforward in the matter.

[1] 14 AC 337.

Holmes L.J. in the Court of Appeal:

. . . There is no doubt that to sustain an action for misrepresentation, there must be proof of fraud on the part of the defendant. It is, I think, equally certain that fraud is proved when it is shown that the defendant made the misrepresentation, knowing it to be false. To use the words of Lord Herschell, in *Derry v Peek*: 'To prevent a false statement being fraudulent, there must always be an honest belief in its truth.' To these propositions I add another, suggested by the peculiar facts of the present case. It is not necessary that the misrepresentation which will sustain an action of deceit should be made in actual terms. Words may be used in such circumstances, and in such a connection, as to convey to the person to whom they are addressed a meaning or inference beyond what is expressed; and if it appears that the person employing them knew this, and also knew that such meaning or inference was false, there is sufficient proof of fraud.

Of course whether the misstatement be express or implied, the plaintiff must show that he has suffered loss by acting on it; . . .

. . .

. . . The statement was not made for the purpose of informing a would-be purchaser of a past incident with which he was not concerned. It was intended that he should draw the inference that the reduction hitherto made would probably be continued, and, in my opinion, it clearly implied a representation that the vendor had no reason to believe that it would be discontinued. . . .

The question is whether, in the foregoing circumstances, the particulars of sale, taken in connection with the suppression of the contents of the landlord's letter, showed fraud of the kind that entitles the plaintiff to recover in an action of deceit such damages, if any, as he sustained therefrom?

Let me present the case in a way suggested by [counsel for the respondent]. Let me assume that the defendant, after he received the particulars from Mr Bradley, but before he made them public, had ascertained from the landlord that he would insist on the full rent for the future, would it not have been manifestly dishonest to frame the advertisement as he did? His doing so would be an example of the trick described by Lord Blackburn in *Smith v Chadwick*:[2]

> If, with intent to lead the plaintiff to act upon it, they [i.e. the defendants] put forth a statement which they know may bear two meanings, one of which is false to their knowledge, and thereby the plaintiff, putting that meaning on it, is misled, I do not think they can escape by saying he ought to have put the other. If they palter with him in a double sense, it may be that they lie *like* truth; but I think they lie, and it is a fraud. Indeed, as a question of casuistry, I am inclined to think the fraud is aggravated by a shabby attempt to get the benefit of a fraud without incurring the responsibility.

But the information, which would have made the statement fraudulent if it had been obtained before the advertisement was issued, reached the defendant in time to enable him to prevent persons attending the auction from being misled; and the fact that the landlord communicated with him as auctioneer ought to have impressed, and I am sure did impress, him with the importance of correcting the false inference which his language was calculated and intended to convey. All that was necessary for Mr Keogh to do was, after reading the particulars at the auction, to have added, that since they had been prepared the landlord had expressed his intention to insist on the rent of £25, but that the vendor's solicitor was of opinion that he was legally estopped from obtaining more than £18. He did not do this. He allowed the sale to proceed on the basis that the reduced rent might be voluntarily received in the future as in the past, or, at least, that he knew nothing to the contrary.

How does the defendant himself account for this? His evidence on this point is clear: 'The conditions were Bradley's. I did not get authority to make any change. I was selling under Bradley's orders. I acted on Bradley's directions to me to go on with the sale.' In other words, an intelligent auctioneer, who admits that 'it would have been material to have let those at the auction know of Tench's determination to enforce the higher rent', kept back this information, because the solicitor under whose orders he was acting did not authorise him to disclose it or make any change in the particulars. In matters of truth and falsehood, of honesty and dishonesty, our law requires a man to judge for himself, and will not allow him to escape responsibility by pleading that he was carrying out the directions of another. Knowing that he could not thus free himself from liability, his counsel relied on his belief in the soundness of Mr Bradley's legal opinion. I accept Mr Keogh's statement that he believed what he was told by the solicitor, although this was not his reason for suppressing Tench's letter, and although the solicitor himself had not ventured to state it in the particulars of sale; but the defendant must have understood the difference between a landlord accepting voluntarily an abated rent, and a tenant being forced to fight for the abatement in a doubtful lawsuit. I do not understand either the legal or ethical aspect of [counsel's] argument on this point.

I have observed, not for the first time, in the discussion of this case the prevalence of an idea that *Derry v Peek* has laid down a new rule in actions of deceit, and has given a latitude to falsehood that did not previously exist. This seems to me to be a great mistake. The directors of a Tramway Co. that had authority to use steam power with the consent of the Board of Trade, believing that this consent would be given as a matter of course, issued a prospectus in which it was stated that they had the right to use steam power without reference to any condition. It was held that this was not actionable, inasmuch as the statement was made in the honest belief that it was true.

This is, I think, old law; but if the directors had known, before they issued the prospectus, that the Board of Trade had refused to consent, or had announced its intention to refuse, the case would have been like this, and the directors would have had no defence; nor in such case would their position have been improved if their solicitor had assured them that there would be no difficulty in obtaining from Parliament an amending Act removing the condition.

I am satisfied that when the defendant read in his auction mart to the assembled bidders the particulars of sale, unaccompanied with a statement that there would be no longer a voluntary abatement of the rent, he was knowingly deceiving them, and that the natural effect of the deception was to obtain a higher price for the public house than it was worth.

I believe that the plaintiff's bid of £430 was considerably higher than what he would have offered if he had the knowledge which the auctioneer possessed; and than the real value of the premises.

The measure of damages is the difference between such real value and £430 . . .

¹· 14 AC 374.   ²· 9 AC 201.

Carbin *v* Sommerville [1933] IR 276

The plaintiff claimed to have entered into a contract to purchase a house from the defendant on the basis of a false misrepresentation that the house was free from damp and that the roof was in good condition. She then claimed rescission of the contract, return of the purchase money and damages for misrepresentation. Alternatively, she claimed damages for breach of warranty of the condition of the house.

The trial judge found that the defendant was asked if the house was dry and if the roof was adequate, and replied to each question that it was. He also found that neither statement was justified and that the plaintiff had entered the contract upon the truth of these statements. However he refused the relief claimed on the ground that fraud had not been proven.

FitzGibbon J.:

. . .

Now, that the house was neither dry nor free from damp, and that the roof was not perfect, as stated by the defendant, has been abundantly proved, but the question which we have to decide is whether it is so clear that the defendant knew his statement to be untrue (as the judge has found it was), or that he made it so recklessly without regard to its truth or falsehood, that the judge's findings that he was no more than 'unduly optimistic', that he was 'inclined to believe what he wanted to believe', and that 'his reticence on the question' which he was not asked, 'will not convict him of fraud', cannot stand.

. . .

'Early in 1928' he noticed cracks in the compo which he had put on in March, and late in June 1929, he treated them with waterex. In June 1929, he again repapered the house. More damp patches appeared in February or March 1930, in the dining-room and the kitchen, and the defendant then found several fresh cracks in the walls, which he 'supposed would be admitting damp into the house'. He then 'completely repapered' the dining-room and the kitchen. This occurred only five or six weeks before he described the house to the plaintiff as 'dry and free from damp'. His own case is that he did not so describe the house, and that he could not have so described it, because it would not have been honest to do so. . . .

. . . 'Was this house free from damp and dry?' The judge has found that this question was put; the defendant agrees that if the question had been put, honesty must have compelled him to point out, or tell the plaintiff of, the damp patches, and the judge has found that he answered the question with an unconditional and unqualified affirmative. To my mind this alone, having regard to the defendant's knowledge of the facts, suffices to establish the plaintiff's case that the misrepresentation was fraudulent, but the Chief Justice, in the course of the argument, has directed attention to an equally convincing proof of the defendant's lack of belief in the truth of the assertion that the house was 'free from damp'. He had repapered the house, in whole or in part, in consequence of patches of damp and discoloration appearing upon the walls, on no less than three occasions between June 1927, and March 1930. In February or March 1930 he applied black pitch paint on the *interior* walls of the house. This he admits was done to prevent 'the damp that was still in the walls' from discolouring the new paper. That damp was there, in spite of the cementing and waterexing of 1929, and the second application of waterex in 1930. Now, if the defendant applied pitch to the *interior* surface of a wall to prevent the new paper from destruction by damp, it is clear that he must have believed that the damp had penetrated, or would penetrate, from the outside through the wall, for it could not by any other means attack the paper on the inside surface, and if the defendant had believed that the outside surface of the wall was waterproof, there could be no necessity for coating the inside face with pitch to protect the paper from damp. To my mind his action, and his own explanation of his action, in applying pitch to the interior surface of the walls, demonstrates his knowledge that the walls were not free from the damp, which, indeed, he admits in his replies to many questions, was in the walls, and it was because of this knowledge that he said he could not honestly have described the house as dry and free from damp.

. . .

. . . It is perfectly clear that when the defendant answered the question in the affirmative, as the judge has found he did, he intended his answer to be taken in the sense in which the question was asked, and in the sense in which the judge has found the plaintiff did take it and act upon it, and so given, the misrepresentation was false and fraudulent.

If there be no other ground for denying the plaintiff's claim to the relief by way of rescission, the conclusions I have stated establish it, in accordance with the statement of the law by Blackburn J. in *Kennedy v Panama, etc., Mail Co.*:[1]

> It is enough to show that there was a *fraudulent* representation as to any part of that which induced the party to enter into the contract which he seeks to rescind; but where there has been an *innocent* misrepresentation or misapprehension, it does not authorise a rescission unless it is such as to show that there is a complete difference in substance between what was supposed to be, and what was, taken, so as to constitute a failure of consideration.

The plaintiff has contended that there was such 'a complete difference' in the present case, and that even if the defendant's representation that the house was dry and free from damp was innocent or inadvertent, she is still entitled to rescind her bargain upon the ground of 'a failure of consideration'. I do not agree with this contention. To sell a leaky house or a leaky ship on a fraudulent misrepresentation that it is sound entitles the party defrauded to rescind the contract, but if the misrepresentation be innocent there is not that difference in the subject matter of the sale which would entitle the party to be relieved of his bargain on the ground of defect of substance when there is really only an inferiority of quality. Any remedy the purchaser may have in such a case would sound in damages only.

We have not been referred to any decision of any court, or to any opinion of any reputable text-writer, to the effect that when a party to a contract has been induced to enter into it by fraudulent misrepresentation he loses his right to repudiate it on discovery of the fraud because the subject matter cannot be restored to the defendant in the identical condition in which it was at the date of the contract, where the alteration is due to the nature of the subject matter itself and cannot be attributed to any act of the plaintiff. In *Adam v Newbigging*[2] the House of Lords, Lords Halsbury, Watson, FitzGerald and Herschell, considered that the circumstance that the business, in which the plaintiff had been induced to become a partner by the misrepresentation of the defendants made without any fraud on their part, had become totally insolvent and worthless between 1 February 1883, the date of the contract, and November 1884, the date of the commencement of proceedings for rescission, did not disentitle the plaintiff to rescission and repayment of his capital although the defendants could not recover against him for money lent and goods sold by them to the partnership during the interval. It was held unanimously that the mere deterioration of the business, though it might have been anticipated if the plaintiff had known the actual state of affairs in the beginning of 1883, could not stand in the way of the plaintiff's claim for mutual restitution, and that was a case of innocent misrepresentation only. The present defendant sold the plaintiff a defective house, by fraudulent misrepresentation as to its condition. He will get back his own defective house, which has deteriorated since he sold it through its own inherent vice, and has not been depreciated by any act of the plaintiff, who has simply refrained from spending any more of her own money upon the defendant's house in a vain endeavour to make it what he contracted to sell her.

[1] LR 2 QB 580, p. 587.   [2] 13 AC 308.

Note

Statute law provides an array of statutory causes of action in relation to misrepresentations, these statutes commencing with the Merchandise Marks Act 1887, for example. This diverse body of law, some of which has been based on consumer protection legislation generated by the European Legislator, has been swept away by the Consumer Protection Act 2007, which both consolidates earlier legislation and transposes Directive 2005/29/EC. Of particular significance are sections 42 and 51, which seek to outlaw misleading commercial practices, including false, misleading or deceptive information or advertising in relation to products.

B. NEGLIGENT MISREPRESENTATION

The Governor and Company of the Bank of Ireland *v* Smith and Others
[1966] IR 646
(Facts on p. 300.)

Kenny J.:
. . .

The next contention was that the decision of the House of Lords in Hedley Byrne & Co. Ltd v Heller[1] had established that a person who relies on an innocent misrepresentation and suffers loss as a result is entitled to damages. The speeches in that case establish that, in some cases, a negligent misrepresentation made to anyone who, to the knowledge of the speaker or writer will rely on it and will be damaged if it is incorrect, gives a right to damages: they do not establish that every innocent misrepresentation gives such a right. . . .

. . . It was said that an auctioneer acting for a vendor should anticipate that any statements made by him about the property will be relied on by the purchaser and that he, therefore, owes a duty of care to the purchaser and is liable in damages to him if the statement was incorrect and was made carelessly. In my opinion, the decision in Hedley Byrne & Co. Ltd v Heller does not give any support to this startling proposition. It decides that, if a person seeks information from another in circumstances in which a reasonable man would know that his judgment is being relied on, the person giving the information must use reasonable care to ensure that his answer is correct, and if he does not do so, he is liable in damages: but the relationship between the person seeking the information and the person giving it, if not fiduciary or arising out of a contract for consideration, must be, to use the words of Lord Devlin, 'equivalent to contract', before any liability can arise. The basis of the decision in Hedley Byrne & Co. Ltd v Heller is, I think, contained in the speech of Lord Devlin when he said (at p. 528):

> I think, therefore, that there is ample authority to justify your Lordships in saying now that the categories of special relationships which may give rise to a duty to take care in word as well as in deed are not limited to contractual relationships or to relationships of fiduciary duty, but include also relationships which in the words of Lord Shaw in Nocton v Lord Ashburton[2] are 'equivalent to contract', that is, where there is an assumption of responsibility in circumstances in which, but for the absence of consideration, there would be a contract . . .

Even if an auctioneer's fees are paid by the purchaser (and in this case the vendors are liable for them), a contractual relationship between the vendors' auctioneers and the purchaser does not exist. The decision of Davitt P. in Securities Trust Ltd v Hugh Moore & Alexander Ltd[3] supports this conclusion. Moreover, the purchaser has not proved that Mr Mulcahy was negligent. He was told by an employee of Mr Smith that the lands had been undersown, he visited them on many occasions and the error which he made is one which could be made by the most careful of auctioneers. The claim in negligence against the vendors fails.

[1.] [1964] AC 465.   [2.] [1914] AC 932, 972.   [3.] [1964] IR 417.

Stafford v Mahony & Others [1980] ILRM 53

The plaintiff claimed to have entered into a contract on the basis of a misrepresentation by the defendants, a firm of auctioneers, as to the potential resale value of certain property purchased. The defendants denied making any representation to the plaintiff and stated that they had been acting exclusively for the plaintiff's brother, Mr James Stafford, prior to the signing of the contract.

Doyle J. in the High Court found that the evidence indicated that no representations had been made. However Doyle J. considered the legal situation which would have arisen had these representations actually been made:

. . .

Based upon the assumption that Mr Patrick Stafford did have discussions with Mr Mahony and Mr Palmer in the course of which he obtained some information amounting to representations, innocent but mistaken, which induced him to purchase the premises, [counsel for the plaintiff] directs a legal argument founded in the first instance upon the doctrine of innocent misrepresentation and its consequences. [Counsel] relied chiefly upon the doctrine as expounded by the Court of Appeal in England in *Esso Petroleum Co. Ltd v Mardon* [1976] QB 801. In this case the Court of Appeal purported to found their judgment upon the decision of the House of Lords in *Hedley Byrne & Co. Ltd v Heller*, the well known authority which expounded for the first time in a full way the question as to how far the duty to exercise care was imposed upon a person giving information or advice to another. It would, I think, be generally considered that the Court of Appeal in *Esso v Mardon* considerably extended the application of the principle which had been laid down in *Hedley Byrne*. The principle upon which this decision was based was summarised by Lord Denning M.R. at p. 820 as follows:

> It seems to me that *Hedley Byrne* . . . , properly understood, covers this particular proposition: if a man, who has or professes to have special knowledge or skill, makes a representation by virtue thereof to another—be it advice, information or opinion—with the intention of inducing him to enter into a contract with him, he is under a duty to use reasonable care to see that the representation is correct, and that the advice, information or opinion is reliable. If he negligently gives unsound advice or misleading information or expresses an erroneous opinion, and thereby induces the other side to enter into a contract with him, he is liable in damages.

Omrod L.J. at p. 287, after analysing the principles which he said underlay the decision in *Hedley Byrne*, stated:

> The parties were in the kind of relationship which is sufficient to give rise to a duty on the part of the plaintiffs. There is no magic in the phrase 'special relationship'; it means no more than a relationship the nature of which is such that one party, for a variety of possible reasons, would be regarded by the law as under a duty of care to the other. In this case the plaintiff had all the expertise, experience and authority of a large and efficient organisation carrying on the business of developing service stations to sell their petroleum through dealers who were expected to invest a substantial amount of capital in the business. . . . On the evidence they clearly assumed responsibility for the reliability of their own [estimated annual consumption].

Similar views were expressed by Shaw L.J. and it is difficult to avoid the suspicion that the views of these learned judges were to some extent coloured by the provisions of the English Misrepresentation Act of 1967 which was already law for some years at the date of the judgment but which had not been effective in 1963 at the date of the matters complained of by Mr Mardon the applicant.

Hedley Byrne is reported at [1964] AC 465. It is difficult to state compendiously the effect of this very important decision, but I think it may perhaps be summarised by adopting the words of Lord Devlin at p. 530. He is reported as saying:

> I shall therefore content myself with the proposition that wherever there is a relationship equivalent to contract, there is a duty of care. Such a relationship may be either general or particular. Examples of a general relationship are those of solicitor and client and of banker and customer. . . . There may well be others yet to

be established. Where there is a general relationship of this sort, it is unnecessary to do more than prove its existence and the duty follows. Where, as in the present case, what is relied on is a particular relationship created *ad hoc*, it will be necessary to examine the particular facts to see whether there is an express or implied undertaking of responsibility.

He goes on in the next sentence to state an aspect of the doctrine which appears important in considering the present case, namely; 'I regard this proposition as an application of the general conception of proximity'.

In the speech of Lord Morris there is to be found an analysis of *Derry v Peek* (1889) 14 App Cas 337, in the course of which he also referred to the speech of Lord Shaw in *Nocton v Lord Ashburton* [1914] AC 932, at p. 972:

. . . Once the relations of parties have been ascertained to be those in which a duty is laid upon one person of giving information or advice to another upon which that other is entitled to rely as the basis of a transaction, responsibility for error amounting to misrepresentation in any statement made will attach to the adviser or informer, although the information and advice have been given not fraudulently but in good faith.

Having discussed other speeches in *Derry v Peek*, Lord Morris went on to comment [1964] AC 465, at p. 502:

The enquiry in the present case, and in similar cases, becomes, therefore, an enquiry as to whether there was a relationship between the parties which created a duty and, if so, whether such duty included a duty of care.

Lord Morris continued:

I consider that it follows that it should not be regarded as settled that if someone possessed of a special skill undertakes, quite irrespective of contract, to apply that skill for the assistance of another person who relies upon such skill, a duty of care will arise.

He follows this with an observation which might be thought to be of assistance to the plaintiff in the present case:

Furthermore, if in a sphere in which a person is so placed that others could reasonably rely upon his judgment or his skill or upon his ability to make careful enquiry, a person takes upon himself to give information or advice to, or allow his information or advice to be passed on to, another person who, as he knows or should know, will place reliance upon it, then a duty of care will arise.

The force of this last observation, as I understand it, is that if advice had been given to Mr James Stafford which might reasonably have been expected to be passed on to or have come to the knowledge of his brother Mr Patrick Stafford and if Mr Patrick Stafford had placed reliance upon it, then the duty of care would have extended to him. The observation however clearly contemplates that there must be a person making the representation and another person to whom the representation is made or to whom it is likely to be conveyed.

In my view the application and extent of the doctrine of negligent although innocent misrepresentations giving rise to an action for damages have been correctly stated by Davitt P. in *Securities Trust Ltd v Hugh Moore and Alexander Ltd* [1964] IR 417. Having at p. 421 stated his view that, contrary to the narrow interpretation formerly given to *Derry v Peek*, the law now provided that an action for damages might be based on innocent, that is non-fraudulent, but negligent misrepresentation, the learned judge went on to consider the then recent decision of *Hedley Byrne*. He stated:

> The proposition that circumstances may create a relationship between two parties in which, if one seeks information from the other and is given it, that other is under a duty to take reasonable care to ensure that the information given is correct, has been accepted and applied in the case of *Hedley Byrne & Co. Ltd v Heller*, recently decided by the House of Lords.

Having considered the circumstances in the case which he was then deciding, under which Mr Kevin Anderson, the chairman and managing director of the plaintiff company, had sought information from the defendant company, the learned judge pointed out that Mr Anderson, who had made the request, was a shareholder but that the plaintiff company had not then been registered as owner of any shares in the defendant company. Davitt J. stated the plaintiff was entitled to the information and entitled to receive it personally *qua member*; he was not entitled to receive it *qua agent* of the plaintiff company, and he later went on to say:

> It seems to me that there was no relationship between the parties in this case [that is to say the plaintiff company and the defendant company] other than such as would exist between the defendant company and any person (other than Mr Anderson) who might chance to read the copy supplied to him; or, indeed, between that company and any members of the community at large, individual or corporate, who chanced to become aware of the last sentence in Article 155 of the defective reprint of the Memorandum of Articles.

This was the document which had given rise to the misrepresentation. The learned judge went on to say:

> It can hardly be seriously contended that the defendant company owed a duty to the world at large to take care to avoid mistakes and printers' errors in the reprint of their articles. In my opinion, counsel is correct in his submission that in this case the defendant company owed no duty to the plaintiff company to take care to ensure that the copy of the article supplied to Mr Anderson was a correct copy.

Adopting the principles thus laid down by Davitt P., I have come to the conclusion that in order to establish the liability for negligent or non-fraudulent misrepresentation giving rise to an action there must first of all be a person conveying the information or the representation relied upon; secondly, that there must be a person to whom that information is intended to be conveyed or to whom it might reasonably be expected that the information would be conveyed; thirdly, that the person must act upon such information or representation to his detriment so as to show that he is entitled to damages. It follows, I think, that if Mr James Stafford had been the plaintiff in the present case and had made out to the satisfaction of the court that misrepresentations had been made to him by the defendants or any member of the firm upon which he acted to his detriment relying upon their skill and experience, then he would have made out such a case. I do not think that this liability would extend to his brother Patrick, even if he had learned in the course of his various visits to the offices of the defendant firm the nature of the transaction which his brother James was conducting up to the date upon which the contract of sale was executed. . . .

Note

Subsequent Irish case-law has established that a negligent misstatement may be relied upon by persons who are 'proximate' to the misstatement, in the sense that they are included in a limited and identifiable class of person: Glencar Exploration plc v Mayo County Council (No. 2) [2002] IR 84; Wildgust v Bank of Ireland [2006] 2 ILRM28; Walsh v Jones Lang Lasalle [2007] IEHC 28.

C. INNOCENT MISREPRESENTATION

Connor v Potts [1897] 1 IR 534 (Ch.)

The plaintiff agreed to purchase land from the defendant for £5,500 calculated on the basis of 442 acres at £12 10s per acre. The plaintiff accepted the defendant's representation as to the total acreage involved. Later the area proved to be 67 acres less. The plaintiff sought specific performance to the extent of the real acreage.

V.C.:

. . . Fraudulent misrepresentation is not necessary for the plaintiff to establish, for a mistaken representation by the defendant of a matter that it was his duty to state correctly, and on the faith of which he knew the plaintiff acted, is sufficient, though he may himself have believed it to be true.

. . .

The general principle applicable to this case is well established that where a misrepresentation is made by a vendor as to a matter within his knowledge even though it may be founded upon an honest belief in the truth of what he states, and the purchaser has been misled by such misrepresentation, the purchaser is entitled to have the contract specifically performed so far as the vendor is able to do so, and to have compensation for the deficiency.

. . .

On the whole case I am of opinion that the plaintiff is entitled to judgment for the specific performance of the contract as to the portion of Knockcairn to which the defendant can show title, being 249 acres and the entire of Fourscore 126a. 2r. 10p., and that he is entitled to compensation for the 67 acres' deficiency of the acreage of Knockcairn . . .

Note

This case was referred to in Keating & Others v Bank of Ireland & Others [1983] ILRM 295 where it was held that if the purchasers of property were entitled to compensation for a misdescription, they were entitled to it out of the purchase money, and thus they could not be forced to close the sale until such time as the amount of compensation, if any, and therefore the amount of the balance of the purchase price, had been ascertained.

Doolan *v* Murray, Murray, Murray, Cheever, Aziz and Dun Laoghaire Corporation (HC) 21 December 1993, unrep.

The plaintiff purchased a mews house from the first and second defendants, aware that there was a right of way in favour of the third and fourth defendants. Prior to completion the vendors executed a deed which affirmed that the right of way was a pedestrian way only. Following completion the plaintiff discovered that the right of way was more extensive and that planning restrictions, of which the first and second defendants, as well as the plaintiff, had not known, prevented the plaintiff from carrying out improvements to her property. The third defendant, however, was aware of these restrictions. The plaintiff sought damages against the various defendants for misrepresentation.

Keane J.:
. . .

As to the liability that arises in law from a misrepresentation, whether innocent, negligent or fraudulent, and whether made by parties to a contract or made in other circumstances, the law in Ireland appears to be as follows. A fraudulent misrepresent-ation will unquestionably give rise to an action for damages for deceit. An innocent misrepresentation will not *in general* give rise to any action for damages, although it may afford grounds for rescission of a contract or a defence to an action for specific performance. There are, however, two broad categories of cases in which a person may be entitled to recover damages for an innocent misrepresentation. They are:

(a) Where a representation is made for the purpose of inducing a person to enter into a contract, and it actually induces him or her to act on it by entering into the contract;

(b) Where the representation is made negligently by a person owing a duty of care in relation to the making of such a statement to the person to whom the representation is made.

The representation in the first category of cases has been described in some of the English authorities as a 'collateral warranty' and that is the way in which it has been pleaded and relied on in the present case. The suggestion also appears to have been made that the 'warranty' is enforceable because it is a 'promise', presumably sup-ported by consideration in the form of a corresponding promise by the person to whom the representation is made to enter into the contract. (See, for example, the observations of Denning L.J. as he then was, in *Oscar Chess Ltd v Williams* [1957] 1 All ER 325 at p. 328). . . .

With those qualifications in mind, one can safely adopt the following statement of the law by Denning L.J., as he then was, in *Bentley (Dick) Productions Ltd v Harold Smith (Motors) Ltd* [1965] 1 WLR 623:

Looking at the cases once more, as we have done so often, it seems to me that if a representation is made in the course of dealings for a contract for the very purpose of inducing the other party to act on it, and it actually induces him to act upon it by entering into the contract, that is *prima facie* ground for inferring that the representation was intended as a warranty. It is not necessary to speak of it as being collateral. Suffice it that the representation was intended to be acted on and was in fact acted on.

It is also clear that the 'collateral warranty' principle may apply where the main contract is not between the plaintiff and the defendant, but between the plaintiff and a third party: see *Shanklin Pier Ltd v Detel Products Ltd* [1951] 2 KB 854.

As to the second category of cases, the cause of action, if any, here derives from the legal principle enunciated by the House of Lords in *Hedley Byrne and Co. Ltd v Heller* [1964] AC 465 and adopted by the High Court in *Securities Trust Ltd v Hugh Moore and Alexander Ltd,* [1964] IR 417 and *Bank of Ireland v Smith* [1966] IR 646. In the first of the Irish decisions, Davitt P. succinctly defined the context in which liability may arise as follows: 'Circumstances may create a relationship between two parties in which, if one seeks information from the other, and is given it, that other is under a duty to take reasonable care to ensure that the information is correct.'

The decision in *Hedley Byrne* had reversed in England the view of the majority of the Court of Appeal in *Candler v Crane Christmas and Co.* [1951] 2 KB 164 that no liability arose for purely economic loss (as contrasted with physical injury) caused by a negligent misstatement. Before *Hedley Byrne*, the generally accepted view was that such negligent misstatements causing economic loss did not come within the ambit of Lord Atkin's often quoted 'neighbour' principle in *Donoghue v Stevenson* [1932] AC 562, *viz.*:

> The rule that you are to love your neighbour becomes in law you must not injure your neighbour; and the lawyer's question, who is my neighbour? receives a restrictive reply. You must take reasonable care to avoid acts or omissions which you can reasonably foresee would be liable to injure your neighbour. Who, then, in law is my neighbour? The answer seems to be—persons who are so closely and directly affected by my act that I ought reasonably to have them in contemplation as being so affected when I am directing my mind to the acts or omissions which are called in question.

Some passages in the speeches in *Hedley Byrne* are important as specifying in more detail the circumstances which will create a duty in law to take care in relation to the making of statements. Lord Reid, having cited an extract from the speech of Lord Haldane in *Robinson v National Bank of Scotland* [1916] SC 154, says:

> This passage makes it clear that Lord Haldane did not think that a duty to take care must be limited to cases of fiduciary relationship in the narrow sense of relationships which had been recognised by the Court of Chancery as being of a fiduciary character. He speaks of other special relationships, and I can see no logical stopping place short of all those relationships where it is plain that the party seeking information or advice was trusting the other to exercise such a degree of care as the circumstances required, where it was reasonable for him to do that, and where the other gave the information or advice when he knew or ought to have known that the inquirer was relying on him. I say 'ought to have known' because in questions of negligence we now apply the objective standard of what the reasonable man would have done.

Lord Devlin puts the matter thus:

I think, therefore, that there is ample authority to justify Your Lordships in saying now that the categories of special relationships, which may give rise to a duty to take care in word as well as in deed, are not limited to contractual relationships or to relationships of fiduciary duty, but include also relationships which in the words of Lord Shaw in *Nocton v Lord Ashburton* are 'equivalent to contract' that is, where there is an assumption of responsibility in circumstances in which, but for the absence of consideration, there would be a contract. Where there is an express undertaking, an express warranty as distinct from a mere representation, there can be little difficulty. The difficulty arises in discerning those cases in which the undertaking is to be implied. In this respect the absence of consideration is not irrelevant. Payment for information or advice is very good evidence that it is being relied on and that the informer and adviser knows that it is. Where there is no consideration, it will be necessary to exercise greater care in distinguishing between social and professional relationships and between those which are of a contractual character and those which are not. It may often be material to consider whether the adviser is acting purely out of good nature or whether he is getting his reward in some indirect form.

It was urged in *Esso Petroleum Co. Ltd v Mardon* [1976] 2 All ER 5 that, where negotiations between two parties resulted in a contract between them, their rights and duties were governed by the law of contract and not by the law of tort and there was therefore no place in their relationship for *Hedley Byrne* which related solely to liability in tort. That view was rejected by the Court of Appeal. Lord Denning M.R., in the course of his judgment, said that: 'If a man, who has or professes to have special knowledge or skill, makes a representation by virtue thereof to another—be it advice, information or opinion—with the intention of inducing him to enter into a contract with him, he is under a duty to use reasonable care to see that the representation is correct, and that the advice, information or opinion is reliable.'

That statement of the law was cited, without apparent disapproval, by Doyle J. in *Stafford v Mahony Smith and Palmer* [1980] IRLM 53.

There remains the question as to whether, in considering either of these categories, mere silence can ever amount to an actionable misrepresentation or a negligent misstatement. In the case of parties to a contract, the authorities suggest that there are three categories of cases in which silence can amount to a misrepresentation giving rise to a cause of action. One of them, where a contract requires *uberrima fides*, does not arise in the present case. The others are where the silence distorts a positive representation and where a fiduciary relation exists between the contracting parties. I would adopt as a correct statement of the law in this jurisdiction the following statement in Cheshire, Fifoot and Furmston's *Law of Contract*, (12th ed.), 273:

> Silence upon some of the relevant factors may obviously distort a positive assertion. A party to a contract may be legally justified in remaining silent about some material fact, but if he ventures to make a representation upon the matter it must be a full and frank statement, and not a partial and fragmentary account that what is withheld makes that which is said absolutely false. A half truth may be in fact false because of what it leaves unsaid and although what a man actually says may be true in every detail, he is guilty of misrepresentation unless he tells the whole truth.

And at p. 308, dealing with the nature of the confidential relationship, the learned authors have this to say:

> Such a confidential relationship is deemed to exist between persons connected by certain recognised ties, such as parent and child, principal and agent, solicitor and

client, religious superior and inferior, and trustee and beneficiary. But the courts have always refused to confine this equitable jurisdiction to such familiar relations. They are prepared to interfere in a contract wherever one party deliberately and voluntarily places himself in such a position that it become his duty to act fairly and to have due regard to the interest of the other party.

These passages are concerned with the position of parties to a contract. It should not be assumed that they are applicable without qualification when one is considering liability for an alleged negligent misstatement. In the first place, while Lord Atkin's statement of the 'neighbour' principle expressly extends to omissions, the authorities both in England and other common law jurisdictions have reflected a reluctance to extend liability to cases of 'pure omissions'. Giving the judgment of the Court of Appeal in *Banque Financiere v Westgate Insurance Co.* [1989] 2 All ER 952, Slade L.J. said at p. 1009:

> The same reluctance on the part of the courts to give a remedy in tort for pure omission applies, perhaps even more so, when the omission is a failure to prevent economic harm . . . a corresponding distinction is drawn by the law of contract which in general imposes no liability by virtue of a failure to speak as opposed to a misrepresentation.

In the second place, as this citation suggests, the general principle of *caveat emptor*, based on it is on the recognition by the law that parties should be left free to determine their obligations to each other, is not to be eroded by the inappropriate invocation of tortious liability.

Where, however, a person elects to make a representation on a matter which is capable of being misleading because of its partial nature, there seems no reason why liability in tort for negligent misstatement should not arise, provided there was a duty to take care in relation to the making of the representation. Whether such a duty of care arose in the circumstances of the present case must be determined having regard to the legal principles laid down in *Hedley Byrne* and subsequently adopted in our courts.

Note

1. Keane J., in applying these principles to the facts before him, found the first two defendants and the fourth defendant had not made a fraudulent misrepresentation nor had the first two defendants made any pre-contractual warranties, negligent misstatements or breached covenants of quiet enjoyment. The third defendant was held liable under *Hedley Byrne*.
2. In *Carey v Independent Newspapers (Ireland) Ltd* (2005) 15 ELR 45, unrep. Gilligan J. held that when the plaintiff had been recruited by the editor of a newspaper, his failure to disclose that the working hours agreed between the plaintiff and the editor had been viewed with disquiet by the editor's immediate superiors constituted a negligent misrepresentation.

D. Misrepresentation by Conduct

Spice Girls Ltd v Aprilia World Service BV [2000] EMLR 478

The Spice Girls management entered into a sponsorship arrangement in March 1998, the March arrangement being finally agreed on 6 May 1998. Under the terms of this agreement Aprilia had rights to the persons 'currently comprising' the Spice Girls and rights to use the images of the Spice Girls for the period up to March 1999. Unknown to Aprilia, one member of the group had indicated her intention to leave the group but this information was not disclosed to Aprilia by the Spice Girls Management.

The performer in question, Geri Halliwell, left shortly after the 6 May agreement was signed. Aprilia alleged a misrepresentation by virtue of (i) the express term relating to Aprilia's rights extending to all performers 'currently comprising' the Spice Girls, and (ii) non-disclosure of Halliwell's intention to leave the group.

Arden J.:

[Counsel for Aprilia] places particular reliance on *Brown v Raphael* [1958] Ch. 636. This concerned the sale of an absolute reversion in a trust fund. The particulars stated that: 'Estate duty will be payable on the death of the annuitant who is believed to have no aggregable estate' and the name of the solicitors who prepared the particulars was given. The solicitors made the statement of belief honestly but they had no reasonable grounds for so believing. The solicitors were better equipped with information or the means of information than the purchaser. In those circumstances, the Court of Appeal, applying the earlier decision of the Court of Appeal in *Smith v Land House Property Corporation* (1884) 28 Ch. D 7 held that the statement of belief not merely implied that the solicitors held that belief, but also by implication that the solicitors knew facts which justified their opinion; that is that they had reasonable grounds for their belief.

The particular facts on which Lord Evershed M.R. relied in reaching his decision were the materiality to a purchaser of a reversion of a representation as to the impact of estate duty on the annuitant's death; and the fact that the name of the solicitors was added. Lord Evershed considered the effect of this language on the mind of a possible purchaser. He concluded that:

> . . . it would flow from the language used and would be intended to be understood by a reader of the particulars that persons who know the significance of this matter and who were experienced and competent to look into it were expressing a belief founded upon substantial and reasonable grounds.

Romer L.J. gave a concurring judgment; Ormerod L.J. agreed in the result.

In my judgment, however, *Brown v Raphael* does not assist Aprilia. In that case there was a statement of belief. The words 'currently comprising' in the preamble to the agreement do not constitute a statement of belief. Those words were literally true and signal the possibility of future changes in the line-up of the group. There is as I see it no representation in the agreement as to the preservation of the composition of the group. There is therefore no representation in the agreement which is falsified by the failure to disclose the stated intention of Ms Halliwell to leave the group. In those circumstances the words 'currently comprising' cannot in my judgment constitute a misrepresentation. . . .

Accordingly I now turn to the question whether participation in the commercial shoot amounted to a representation by conduct that SGL did not know and had no reasonable grounds to believe at or before the time of entry into the agreement that any of the Spice Girls had an existing declared intention to leave the group.

SGL knew the importance which Aprilia attached to having the right to endorse their products with images of the Spice Girls down to March 1999. Without those rights, Aprilia could not manufacture and sell the limited edition Spice Sonic scooter or use promotional literature for its products which used images of the Spice Girls. SGL knew the very considerable expense involved in the shoot. SGL did not consider what effect a change in the line-up would have on Aprilia and in my judgment SGL could not reasonably form the view that there would be no or no significant adverse affect. SGL would not be prevented from passing the information to Aprilia. It could have done so in the strictest confidence.

Given that the benefits of the commercial shoot could not be enjoyed by Aprilia if one of the Spice Girls left the group before March 1999, participation in the shoot in my judgment carried with a representation by conduct that SGL did not know, and had no reasonable ground to believe, that any of the Spice Girls had an existing declared intention to leave the group before that date. Nothing was done to correct that representation which was a continuing representation. It was on the facts found material to Aprilia's decision to enter into the agreement that none of the Spice Girls was intended to leave in the contract period. Accordingly, SGL had a duty to correct its misrepresentation. What I have said about the commercial shoot must equally apply to other promotional material depicting the five Spice Girls which was intended to be used at any time during the period of the agreement.

I next turn to the question whether the representations by conduct induced the agreement. This is a necessary requirement for an action in misrepresentation (see *Horsfall v Thomas* 9 (1852) 1 H. & C. 90 and see the Misrepresentation Act 1967, s. 2(1). . . . In certain limited circumstances, reliance can be inferred. In *Smith v Chadwick* (1884) 9 A.C. 187, Lord Blackburn stated:

> I think if it is proved that the defendants with a view to induce the plaintiff to enter a contract made a statement to the plaintiff of such a nature as would be likely to induce a person to enter into a contract, and it is proved that the plaintiff did enter into the contract, it is a fair inference of fact that he was induced to do so by the statement.

[The plaintiffs] gave evidence that Aprilia would not have entered into the agreement if it had been known that Ms Halliwell had declared an existing intention to leave the group in September 1998. This would have deprived Aprilia of the full benefits of the five girl promotional material, and I have no doubt that AWS would have consulted Aprilia's marketing department if it had been told of Ms Halliwell's intentions. Before the agreement was made, Aprilia incurred expenditure on the commercial shoot. I have held that SGL's participation in this carried with it an implied representation that SGL did not know and had no reasonable grounds to believe that any of the Spice Girls had an existing declared intention to leave the group and that this was a continuing representation which SGL had a duty to correct if it was falsified before Aprilia entered into the agreement. Given that Aprilia had to sign the agreement to get the right to use the commercial shoot (and that there was no other reason for it to sign the agreement except to get the rights thereunder), it seems to me that the court can infer that indirectly it was induced to enter the contract by the representation made to it when it made the shoot. The same would apply to other promotional material which constituted a representation by conduct. I am satisfied that SGL participated in the commercial shoot and provided logos, images and so on of the Spice Girls in order that Aprilia should sign the agreement. I am also satisfied that the representations by conduct were such as to be likely to induce a person to enter into the agreement. An inducement to enter into a contract need not of course be the sole inducement.

SECTION THREE—REMEDIES

A. Damages

As we have seen in the *Delany* case (p. 538 above) an entitlement to damages depends on establishing that the representation was made either fraudulently or negligently.

Sale of Goods and Supply of Services Act 1980 s. 45 (1)

45. (1) Where a person has entered into a contract after a misrepresentation has been made to him by another party thereto and as a result thereof he has suffered loss, then, if the person making the misrepresentation would be liable to damages in respect thereof had the misrepresentation been made fraudulently, that person shall be so liable notwithstanding that the misrepresentation was not made fraudulently, unless he proves that he had reasonable ground to believe and did believe up to the time the contract was made that the facts represented were true.

(2) Where a person has entered into a contract after a misrepresentation has been made to him otherwise than fraudulently, and he would be entitled, by reason of the misrepresentation, to rescind the contract, then, if it is claimed in any proceedings arising out of the contract that the contract ought to be or has been rescinded, the court may declare the contract subsisting and award damages in lieu of rescission, if of opinion that it would be equitable to do so, having regard to the nature of the misrepresentation and the loss that would be caused by it if the contract were upheld, as well as to the loss that rescission would cause to the other party.

(3) Damages may be awarded against a person under subsection (2) whether or not he is liable to damages under subsection (1), but where he is so liable any award under subsection (2) shall be taken into account in assessing his liability under subsection (1).

Phelps *v* White (1881) 5 LR (Ir.) 34

In the *Phelps v White* case (facts on p. 533 above) the Vice Chancellor noted that the case of fraudulent misrepresentation is an exception to the rule that relief is unavailable after completion of purchase:

. . . In every case where relief was refused on the ground that it was sought after the completion of the purchase, I find that the case of a fraudulent misrepresentation is stated to be an exception to the rule on which those decisions were founded. Malins V.C., in *Manson v Thacker*,[1] says, 'No doubt, if there has been a fraudulent misrepresentation on the part of the vendor, there may be compensation even after completion.' The fraudulent misrepresentation spoken of in those cases means a misrepresentation fraudulent in a legal sense, within the principles I have already stated, and does not necessarily involve moral fraud. The recent case of *Hart v Swaine*,[2] before Fry J., is a very clear authority for this proposition, and bears a close resemblance to the present case in every respect save one, which I shall afterwards consider. That was an action to set aside a sale after conveyance, on the ground of misrepresentation. Fry J. said, during the argument, that he saw no evidence of actual fraud on the part of the defendant, and that he had only made a mistake; but that, as the defendant had taken on himself to assert that the land was freehold, he was not at liberty to look into the state of his mind. The land there proved to be copyhold. In his judgment he said that the defendant took upon himself to assert that to be true which had turned out to be false, and made this assertion for the purpose of benefiting himself; and, that though he might have done this believing it to be true, he had, in the view of a court of law, committed a fraud. He quoted from the judgment of Maule J., in *Evans v Edmonds*,[3] a passage which it is unnecessary to repeat, and from that of Turner L.J., in *Rawlins v Wickham*,[4] the passage which I have already mentioned, and held that there had been a legal fraud committed by the defendant, which had resulted in a sale to the plaintiffs, and that he was bound by the authorities to give the plaintiffs the relief which they asked; and accordingly set aside the sale. If this misrepresentation authorised the setting aside the sale, it would at least equally entitle the purchaser to compensation, if he elected to hold his purchase. . . .

[1.] 7 ChD 620.   [3.] 13 CB 777, 786.
[2.] 7 ChD 42.   [4.] 3 De G. & J. 316, 317.

Pat O'Donnell & Co. Ltd v Truck and Machinery Sales Ltd [1997] 1 ILRM 466

The defendant was involved in the business of leasing and selling earth-moving equipment in Ireland and internationally. The plaintiff carried on business as a main dealer in heavy construction and engineering machinery manufactured by Volvo. In late 1989 and 1990, the defendant purchased from the plaintiff mechanical shovels manufactured by a company called Zettlemeyer. This machinery proved to be unreliable, and in May 1991 the defendant instituted High Court proceedings. In late 1991, the Volvo Group took over Zettlemeyer and launched a new model of mechanical shovel called the L150. In a compromise of the proceedings against Zettlemeyer, the defendant and the plaintiff in these proceedings came to an agreement in February 1992 whereby the plaintiff agreed to deliver to the defendant 20 Volvo L150 mechanical shovels. Eleven of these were in direct exchange for the Zettlemeyer shovels previously purchased, and nine were for a cash price of £100,000 per unit. In variation of the initial agreement the defendant later sought that two of the L150s be changed to the larger and more expensive L180 model. The defendant also insisted that tyres larger than the normal specification be fitted to the L150s.

The defendant exported eight of the new L150s to the Middle East as part of a large consignment of equipment intended for resale. Efforts to sell the equipment, and in particular the L150 mechanical shovels, to the Pakistan Army, caused conflict with local Volvo sales personnel. The Volvo representative decried the defendant's equipment to prospective customers, pointing out that the exported L150s had no oil bath filters, that they had been fitted with larger and unrecommended tyres making them 'sluggish', and that they were fitted with 'old' style axles.

In response, the defendant resolved to withhold payment for the two Volvo L180 shovels it had been supplied with by the plaintiff until it received some satisfaction for what had transpired in relation to the exported L150s in the Middle East. The plaintiff instituted proceedings against the defendant by way of summary summons for the unpaid purchase price of the two L180 shovels together with interest thereon. On 21 November 1995 judgment was granted in favour of the plaintiff, but a stay was ordered pending the determination of the counterclaim. By its defence and counterclaim, the defendant alleged that it had entered into the contract with the plaintiff on the basis that the Volvo L150 shovels that it was to be supplied with were the latest Volvo model, of the highest standard and comparable in every respect to the market leader in such machinery. The defendant claimed damages in respect of the alleged representation made by the plaintiff in respect of the L150 mechanical shovel, alleging (i) that it amounted to a warranty for the breach of which the defendant was entitled to damages, and (ii) that it also amounted to negligent or in the alternative statutory misrepresentation in breach of the plaintiff's duty of care. It was submitted by the plaintiff that the losses complained of by the defendant had been caused, in whole or in part, by the defendant's own insistence that larger tyres be fitted on the L150s, thereby diminishing the performance of the said equipment.

Moriarty J:

Following upon the decision of the House of Lords in *Hedley Byrne & Co. Ltd v Heller & Partners Ltd* [1964] AC 465, it was accepted by Davitt P. in *Securities Trust Ltd v Hugh Moore & Alexander Ltd* [1964] IR 417 that an action for negligent misrepresentation could succeed in this jurisdiction where a relationship between two parties was of such a nature that upon one seeking information from the other damage resulted from a breach of a duty to take reasonable care that the information furnished was correct. In *Doolan v. Murray*, High Court December 1993, Keane J. approved the dictum of Lord Denning MR in *Esso Petroleum Co. v Mardon* [1976] 2 All ER 5, to the effect that:

> If a man, who has or professes to have special knowledge or skill, makes a representation by virtue thereof to another—be it advice, information or opinion—with the intention of inducing him to enter into a contract with him, he is under a duty to use reasonable care to see that the representation is correct, and that the advice, information or opinion is reliable.

In setting forth a statutory entitlement to damages for non-fraudulent misrepresentation in 1980, the Oireachtas did not require that a duty of care should exist between representor and representee. By s. 45(1) of the Sale of Goods and Supply of Services Act 1980, it is provided that:

> Where a person has entered into a contract after a misrepresentation has been made to him by another party thereto and as a result thereof he has suffered loss, then, if the person making the misrepresentation would be liable for damages in respect thereof, had the misrepresentation been made fraudulently, that person shall be so liable notwithstanding that the misrepresentation was not made fraudulently, unless he proves that he had reasonable ground to believe and did believe up to the time the contract was made that the facts represented were true.

Having appraised the evidence on both sides, I am of the opinion that the counter-claimant is entitled to succeed in respect of misrepresentation both on a basis of negligent misrepresentation and statutory misrepresentation, but primarily in respect of the former.

Patently, Mr O'Donnell was under a duty of care in relation to the representations he made to [the defendant] with a view to inducing sales. He was a specialised and experienced dealer and up to 90% of his business was Volvo-produced, and he knew from previous dealings over dump trucks that Mr Mansfield was not a person who would exhaustively study vehicle specifications and he had, on his own evidence, assiduously canvassed [the defendant] as a large potential purchaser of L150s whilst further knowing of his difficulties regarding Zettlemeyer over whom Volvo had attained control.

Equally clearly, the recommendations made by Mr O'Donnell in relation to the L150 were instrumental in persuading him to enter into the agreement.

There remains an issue as to whether or not in law or in fact, in so far as the supply of L150s with larger wheels undoubtedly very significantly contributed to the losses complained of, Mr Mansfield should be held to have contributed towards any resultant misfortune that accrued. By s. 34(1) of the Civil Liability Act 1961, it is provided that:

Where, in any action brought by one party in respect of a wrong committed by any other person, it is proved that the damage suffered by the plaintiff was caused partly by the negligence or want of care of the plaintiff or of one for whose acts he is responsible (in this Part called contributory negligence), and partly by the wrong of the defendant, the damages recoverable in respect of the said wrong shall be reduced by such amount as the court thinks just and equitable having regard to the degrees of fault of the plaintiff and defendant.

'Wrong' is defined in s. 2 as:

Tort, breach of contract or breach of trust whether the act is committed by the person to whom the wrong is attributed or by one for whose acts he is responsible, and whether or not the act is also a crime, and whether or not the wrong is intentional.

These provisions expressly including breaches of contract as wrongs are more widely drafted than equivalent English legislation and appear to reflect the view of Professor Glanville Williams that contributory negligence should be extended to contract law and that, as argued by him at p. 215, of his work on *Joint Torts and Contributory Negligence* (1951), 'Contributory negligence is appropriate even where the contractual duty broken is a strict one.'

As recently as in *Lyons v. Thomas* [1986] IR 666, Murphy J. noted and applied the wide definition of wrong as aforesaid. Further in *Gran Gelato Ltd v. Richcliff (Group) Ltd* [1992] Ch 560, it was held that in principle the concept of contributory negligence applied to statutory misrepresentation under the Misrepresentation Act 1967, Nicholls VC holding that such a defence should be applicable in the context of statutory misrepresentation, no less than in respect of negligent misrepresentation founded upon the same representation.

In the light of the foregoing, I am of the view that contributory negligence is in principle applicable to a case such as the present counterclaim, although I would readily accept that in many commercial cases involving representations or contractual terms it may be deemed inappropriate. Should it be applied in this present instance? [The defendant's buyer] was an accomplished and experienced businessman who was able to recall in evidence that he had purchased £10 million worth of equipment in the Falkland Islands. He was well versed in the practicalities of mechanical shovels. He insisted on a relatively radical departure from the then standard specification for his own commercial reasons, in the knowledge that it must to some degree impact negatively upon performance, albeit not to the extent of a general sluggishness. It accordingly seems to me that when dealing with redress, some appropriate discounting on a basis of contributory negligence will require to be ordered.

Note

This case was overruled on the facts at [1998] 4 IR 191 but the Supreme Court endorsed Moriarty J's view of the relevant legal principles.

B. RESCISSION

where the contract is executed

There are certain situations in which the remedy of rescission may not be available to the injured party.

In *Seddon v North Eastern Salt* [1905] 1 Ch. 326 the court determined that an executed contract may only be set aside in equity where there has been equitable fraud.

This rule, however, is not confined to cases where land formed the subject matter of the contract.

Lecky *v* Walter [1914] 1 IR 378 (Ch.)

The plaintiff entered into a contract to purchase bonds of a Dutch oil company on the basis of the defendant's representation that they were secured by company property in the US. When this proved to be untrue the plaintiff sought to have the contract set aside.

O'Connor M.R.:

. . . I am satisfied from the plaintiff's evidence that the statement that the bonds were charged on the oil-fields was, if not the only inducement, a material inducement to purchase them.

I need not pause to establish the proposition that it is not necessary to prove that a particular representation was the sole cause of the transaction, and that it is enough that it constituted a material inducement. I have now come to the point when I consider it established that the plaintiff purchased the bonds from the defendant, and that he was induced to make the purchase by misrepresentation by the defendant's agent, which is equivalent to misrepresentation by the defendant himself. The purely legal question then arises, does this state of affairs give the plaintiff the right to set aside a transaction which has been in fact completed, and is not merely in the process of completion? It must be borne in mind that there is no allegation of fraudulent misrepresentation, and therefore the case is to be treated as one in which a *bona fide* mistake was made by the defendant.

. . . counsel for the defendant, contended that in such circumstances the plaintiff had no cause of action, and he relied upon the judgment of Lord Campbell in the House of Lords in *Wilde v Gibson*,[1] where he says:

My Lords, after the very attentive and anxious consideration which this case has received, I have come to the clear conclusion that the decree appealed against ought to be reversed; and I must say that in the court below the distinction between a bill for carrying into execution an executory contract, and a bill to set aside a conveyance that has been executed, has not been very distinctly borne in mind. With regard to the first: if there be, in any way whatever, misrepresentation or concealment, which is material to the purchaser, a court of equity will not compel him to complete the purchase; but where the conveyance has been executed, I apprehend, my Lords, that a court of equity will set aside the conveyance only on the ground of actual fraud. And there would be no safety for the transactions of mankind, if, upon a discovery being made at any distance of time of a material fact not disclosed to the purchaser, of which the vendor had merely constructive notice, a conveyance which had been executed could be set aside.

In *Brownlie v Campbell*,[2] Lord Selborne affirms the same principle. He says there:

Passing from the stage of correspondence and negotiation to the stage of written agreement, the purchaser takes upon himself the risk of errors. I assume them to be errors unconnected with fraud in the particulars, and when the conveyance takes place it is not, so far as I know, in either country the principle of equity that relief should afterwards be given against that conveyance, unless there be a case of fraud, or a case of misrepresentation amounting to fraud, by which the purchaser may have been deceived.

There appears to be no doubt that the law established by these cases is just as applicable to the sale of a chattel or a chose in action as to the sale of real property which is carried out by conveyance: *Seddon v The North Eastern Salt Co. Ltd.*[3]

How are these authorities met by the plaintiff's counsel? [Counsel] in reply admitted, as of course he was obliged to admit, that the authorities referred to were binding on this court, but argued that they only apply to cases in which the purchaser has got in substance what he contracted to buy, and have no application when he has got something substantially different; and he relies upon the judgment of Blackburn J. in *Kennedy v Panama, New Zealand, and Australian Mail Co.*,[4] and particularly on the passage quoted by Joyce J., in *Seddon v The North Eastern Salt Co. Ltd.*[3] Lord Blackburn, then Blackburn J., says at p. 587:

There is, however, a very important difference between cases where a contract may be rescinded on account of fraud, and those in which it may be rescinded on the ground that there is a difference in substance between the thing bargained for and that obtained. It is enough to show that there was fraudulent representation as to *any part* of that which induced the party to enter into the contract which he seeks to rescind; but where there has been an innocent misrepresentation or misapprehension, it does not authorise a rescission unless it is such as to show that there is a complete difference in substance between what was supposed to be and what was taken, so as to constitute a failure of consideration. For example, where a horse is bought under the belief that it is sound, if the purchaser was induced to buy by a fraudulent representation as to the horse's soundness, the contract may be rescinded. If he was induced by an honest misrepresentation as to its soundness, though it may be clear that both vendor and purchaser thought they were dealing about a sound horse and were in error, yet the purchaser must pay the whole price, unless there was a warranty; even if there was a warranty, he cannot return the horse and claim back the whole price, unless there was a condition to that effect in the contract.

Now, if I may so speak of such an eminent judge as Lord Blackburn, the proposition which he there lays down must commend itself, not only to all lawyers, but to all persons of sound judgment. If there is a complete difference in substance between the thing contracted for and the thing delivered, there is a complete failure of consideration, and the price may be recovered. But if the thing delivered is in substance what was contracted for, and the price is paid, the transaction stands, and the purchaser has no remedy unless there has been a warranty. I am speaking of course of cases in which there has been no fraud, and where any misrepresentation which has induced the contract was a wholly innocent misrepresentation. Lord Blackburn gives as an example the common case of a horse bought on the representation that it was sound. The purchaser has no remedy unless he has got a warranty; and why? Because he has got in substance what he contracted for, *viz.* a horse. The horse may be in fact unsound, but still it is a horse, even though a very inferior one; and there is not a complete failure of consideration.

There would, of course, be a complete difference in substance if some animal other than a horse had been delivered, if such a thing can be imagined. I will try to give an example nearer akin to the present case. If a man contracts to purchase mortgage debentures of a public company, and takes delivery of what he believes to be such, but what he afterwards discovers to be ordinary shares, he has not got in substance what he bargained for, but something quite different, one being a specifically secured liability of the company, the other being a share in the company's undertaking on which the liability is imposed. Here again there is a complete failure of consideration. In *Kennedy v Panama, New Zealand, and Australian Mail Co.*, the plaintiff sought to set aside the contract for taking shares in the company on the ground that it was induced by an untrue statement in the company's prospectus that the company had a contract with the government of New Zealand for an important monthly mail service. The statement was made quite innocently, and as the result of mistake. It was held that the plaintiff was not entitled to any relief, there having been no fraud, and he having got what he contracted for, *viz.* shares, although not so valuable as they would have been if the company had had the mail contract mentioned. Lord Blackburn, in his judgment, referred to two reported cases: *Gompertz v Barlett*[5] and *Gurney v Wormersley*,[6] in which the plaintiffs got relief on the ground that they did not get what they bargained for. In each case there was a sale of a bill of exchange: in one case the bill was a forgery; in the other the bill was void under the stamp laws. In neither case did the plaintiff get what he contracted for—a valid bill of exchange.

I think that these decisions make it easy to determine whether in the present case the plaintiff got in substance what he agreed to buy.

. . . He agreed to buy bonds and he has got bonds. They may be of little or no value, but they are bonds. It is not alleged that they are forgeries. Their validity is not in any way impeached. In substance, then, the plaintiff has got what he bargained for. . . .

. . .

. . . if the representation was part of the contract, there might have been a warranty which would give the plaintiff the right to relief. But a representation is not necessarily a warranty. It may be only an inducement, and such it appears to me to have been in the present case. I am, therefore, bound to hold that inasmuch as the contract was completed, and there was no fraud, the sale cannot be set aside, and the action must be dismissed.

---

1. 1 HLC 605, 632–3.
2. 5 AC 925, 937.
3. [1905] 1 Ch. 326.

4. LR 2 QB 580.
5. 2 E & B 849.
6. 4 E & B 133.

Note

S. 44(b) of the Sale of Goods and Supply of Services Act 1980 removes the rule in *Seddon v N.E. Salt* as an objection to the grant of rescission. However, because s. 43 makes s. 44 (b) applicable only to contracts of sale of goods, hire purchase, and supply of services, the rule is not abrogated in sale of real property transactions.

Rescission will not be available where the contract is affirmed

Lutton v Saville Tractors (Belfast) Ltd [1986] NI 327. (See this case in Chapter 18 especially at p. 963).

Note

Compare the *Lutton* decision to the case of *Thomas Dillon-Leetch v Maxwell Motors Ltd* [1984] ILRM 624. There the plaintiff bought a car from the defendant in May of 1981 following representations that the car was free from any defect and suitable for substantive journeys. Two months later the car manifested a significant defect in the braking system, which despite several attempts at repair recurred a second time during the following month. The plaintiff notified the defendant of the recurrence of the defect but did not return the car for further repair until November, having used the car in the interim period with a disconnected handbrake. Later the plaintiff wrote to the defendant stating that if the car failed again he would seek compensation. The car failed again the same month and the car was returned. Although the car was repaired the defendant failed to meet the plaintiff's proposals for compensation. Murphy J. held that as it would not be possible to restore parties to their pre-contractual positions rescission was not possible. He noted however that the defendants' unequivocal acceptance of the return of the car in November implied in the absence of any counter proposals by the defendant, that he had accepted the proposal of the plaintiff for the return of the car and payment of compensation.

Where there has been a delay in seeking relief

Delay in seeking rescission may prevent equitable relief. However, where fraud or oppression exists as a fact the courts are more lenient. In *O'Kelly and Wife v Glenny* (1846) 9 Ir Eq R 25 a delay of twelve years was held not to be fatal. There the plaintiff had been the victim of fraudulent misrepresentation.

In cases of innocent misrepresentation the courts may be less indulgent. See for example *Leaf v International Galleries* [1950] 2 KB 86.

Where third party rights are affected

Anderson v Ryan [1967] IR 34

Henchy J.:

In January 1965, an advertisement appeared in a Dublin evening paper for the sale of an Austin-Healey (Sprite) motor car. A Mr Edwin Davis saw it and, being interested in cars, he telephoned a number indicated in the advertisement. As a result, two men called to his house with the Sprite. It happened that Mr Davis had an Austin (Mini) motor car. The two men seemed to take a fancy to the Mini, as Mr Davis did to the Sprite, and the upshot of the negotiations was that it was agreed to exchange the Mini for the Sprite. The two men left with the Mini and Mr Davis found himself with the Sprite. No money had passed; it was a straight swop. The unfortunate part of the transaction was that, unknown to Mr Davis, the Sprite was a car that had been stolen in Northern Ireland. Within a week detectives descended upon him and took it away. Later a man pleaded guilty in the Dublin Circuit Court to fraudulently obtaining the Mini from Mr Davis by falsely pretending that he was the owner of the Sprite. Mr Davis eventually recovered the Mini and has since sold it.

In the meantime, someone approached the defendant in this action, who carries on business as a panel beater in Cork Street, Dublin, and indicated that he was prepared to sell the defendant a Mini for £200. It was, in fact, the Mini belonging to Mr Davis. The defendant was interested in the purchase but was not prepared to go through with it until he had obtained a purchaser to whom he could sell the car at a profit. The plaintiff, who is a garage owner in Bray, turned out to be such a person. He visited the defendant's premises, where the Mini happened to be, inspected the car, and agreed to buy it for £225 plus £22 for panel repairs to it, which the defendant agreed to do. The plaintiff, having made enquiries which showed that the car was not subject to a hire-purchase agreement, there and then, on 15 January 1965, made out a cheque in favour of the defendant for the sum of £244 10s 0d to cover the £225 for the Mini and also to cover an account that the plaintiff owed to the defendant for panel beating which had been previously done for the plaintiff by the defendant. The defendant lodged the cheque to his account on the following day. My impression from the evidence is that the defendant had no title to the Mini when that deal was made. But, later, on the same evening as he got the cheque from the plaintiff, the defendant gave a cheque for £200 for the car to someone who purported to be, but was not Mr Davis. The defendant proceeded to do the panel beating which he had arranged with the plaintiff to do.

A few days later the plaintiff called to the defendant's premises, paid the defendant the sum of £22 for the further panel beating, collected the registration book (which showed Mr Davis to be the owner) and took the Mini away. He then placed it on display in the forecourt of his garage in Bray as a second-hand car for sale. Once again the arm of the law reached out. Two detectives called and said that the Mini was the subject matter of criminal proceedings. They told the plaintiff that he would have to allow them to take it away and that if he did not give it to them they would return with a warrant. He let them take it away. That is the last he saw of the car or his £247. The plaintiff recovered judgment in the Circuit Court against the defendant for the sum of £247, and the defendant has appealed against that judgment.

. . .

In the present case, it is clear that, if the defendant was not the owner of the Mini at the time he sold it to the plaintiff, the plaintiff got nothing for his money and he would be entitled to recover the £247 as money paid upon a consideration that had wholly failed. Counsel for the plaintiff says that the car was sold on 15 January 1965, when the plaintiff inspected it, agreed on the price and gave a cheque for £244 10s 0d; and that the defendant then had no title.

. . .

The transaction between the plaintiff and the defendant on 15 January 1965, was no more than an agreement to sell. The property in the car did not pass. It was plainly the intention of the parties that the property would not pass until the panel beating had been done by the defendant and the balance of £22 had been paid; until that had happened the agreement to sell would not have merged into a sale.

. . .

. . . the central question is: 'Did the defendant have a good title to the car when he sold and delivered it to the plaintiff?' To decide this question one must go back to the circumstances under which the original owner, Mr Davis, parted with possession of the car. As I have said, he exchanged it for the Sprite. The inducement for him to do so was not alone the desirability to him of the exchange but also the representation by the other party that the Sprite was his property. That was a false and fraudulent representation as to an existing fact. The contract of exchange was, therefore, a voidable contract. Since Mr Davis intended to pass the ownership of the Mini, the person who got the car in exchange acquired a title to it, but it was a voidable title, that is, voidable at the option of Mr Davis. It would have been different if Mr Davis had parted with the Mini as a result of larceny by a trick, for then no title would have passed. Authority for the conclusion that what passed on the exchange was a voidable title is to be found in *Cundy v Lindsay;*[1] *Robin & Rambler Coaches, Ltd v Turner;*[2] *Central Newbury Car Auctions Ltd v Unity Finance Ltd*[3] and *Archbold on Criminal Pleading* (36th ed.) para. 1497.

There is no evidence that there was any intermediate sale of the Mini between the fraudulent exchange and the sale to the defendant. In fact, all the likelihood is that the car was sold to the defendant by or on behalf of the person who effected the fraudulent exchange. One looks then to see what title, if any, such person conveyed to the defendant. The answer is to be found in s. 23 of the Act, which is as follows: 'When the seller of goods has a voidable title thereto, but his title has not been avoided at the time of the sale, the buyer acquires a good title to the goods, provided he buys them in good faith and without notice of the seller's defect of title.' It is clear from the evidence that Mr Davis had not avoided the title of the person who sold the car to the defendant at the time to that sale, and it has not been suggested that the defendant bought otherwise than in good faith and without notice of the seller's defect of title. I am satisfied, therefore, that the defendant acquired a good title to the car and that he in turn passed a good title to the plaintiff. It is unfortunate that the plaintiff has been deprived of a car of which he was the rightful owner, but the fault for that does not lie with the defendant.

. . .

. . . I go no further than saying that no liability attaches to the defendant for the plaintiff's loss and that the plaintiff's claim must be dismissed.

[1] 3 App Cas 459, 464   [2] [1947] 2 All ER 284.   [3] [1957] 1 QB 371, 382.

Note

In *Crystal Palace* FC (2000) Ltd v Dowie [2007] EWHC 1392 (QB) the plaintiff football club employed the defendant as manager under a contract that provided that should he leave to join a premiership club he would pay compensation of £1 million to the plaintiff. The defendant falsely misrepresented that for family reasons he wished to terminate his contract and return to live in the North of England. The defendant also falsely intimated that he had not been approached by Charlton Athletic (then a premiership club). On the basis of these representations the plaintiff negotiated a settlement agreement terminating the defendant's contract of employment (including the £1 million compensation clause). A few days later the defendant was appointed to the job of manager of Charlton Athletic, a post he held for a short period of time. The defendant later took up employment as the manager of Coventry City FC. The plaintiff sought a rescission of the settlement agreement but Tugendhat J. declined to grant rescission on the basis that a third party interest, that of Coventry City FC, had intervened. Revival of the employment contract between the plaintiff and defendant was sought solely to reinstate the £1 million compensation clause, but on these facts Tugendhat J. said that 'practical justice' required the ordering of an inquiry into damages: 'practical justice does not require that the compensation clause be revived on its own, severed from all the other obligations the Employment Contract placed on Mr Dowie.'

C. ABATEMENT OF PRICE

If property is purchased for a given price and the quantity delivered is less than that promised, there can be an abatement or reduction in price, *pro rata*. See also article 7(2)(b) of the Consumer Goods Regulations (S.I. No. 11 of 2003).

D. EQUITABLE INDEMNITY

Costs contractually incurred under a contract can be recovered in equity, even if damages are not available. See *Whittington v Seale Hayne* (1890) 82 LT 49.

EXERCISES

1. Formulate a list of all the possible causes of action available when a pre-contractual statement turns out to be inaccurate. Formulate the claims in tort, contract and under statute.
2. Consider what remedies are available for each cause of action: damages, rescission (common law or in equity), abatement of price. Why is rectification not available as a remedy in respect of a misrepresentation?
3. Review the scope of the Consumer Protection Act 2007. Is similar legislation needed in the context of 'business-to-business' misrepresentations?

Chapter Eleven

Disclosure

INTRODUCTION

In the previous chapter we considered how verbal or written misstatements could be actionable. Liability in those cases depended on proof of a misstatement being made in breach of a contractual or tortious duty, the duty being either strict or based on some other standard such as reasonable care. There is no general duty to provide a full and frank explanation of all surrounding circumstances (e.g. that the car being offered for sale has been involved in an accident) that may influence a decision whether to contract or not. In an arms' length transaction, the seller and buyer, for example, are regarded as being of equal competence and if the buyer wants an assurance that the thing being offered meets the buyer's requirements the buyer should inspect the subject matter, seek to extract an express promise by way of warranty, or invoke whatever consumer protection or general statute law remedies there are at the buyer's disposal. Additional relief is possible through the law of mistake (see Chapter 9) but contractual mistake is difficult to invoke in this context.

However, fraudulent concealment, or misrepresentation in a pre-contractual context, have always been actionable, but the boundary between fraudulent concealment and non-disclosure is a difficult one to draw at times. The law relating to non-marine insurance contracts establishes a general duty of disclosure of all material circumstances: this duty is often explained away on the basis of the applicant being in the best position to know the material circumstances surrounding the liability being covered by the policy, and, because of this imbalance as between the parties, the duty is defended on the grounds of economic efficiency; the insured can more cheaply disclose material circumstances as against the insurer seeking to establish these circumstances.

However, in *Banque Keyser Ullman S.A. v Skandia (UK) Insurance Co.* [1990] 1 KB 665, the right to avoid a contract for non-disclosure was stated by the Court of Appeal to depend not on contract but upon underlying principles of equity. This is an important observation because it helps to explain a number of recent Irish cases which have readjusted the scope of the duty so as to require the insurer to show greater clarity and uniformity in relation to business activities.

As a general rule there is no liability for non-disclosure of material facts.

Smith *v* Hughes (1871) LR 6 QB 597
(Facts on p. 490.)

Cockburn C.J.:

. . .

I take the true rule to be, that where a specific article is offered for sale, without express warranty, or without circumstances from which the law will imply a warranty—as where, for instance, an article is ordered for a specific purpose—and the buyer has full opportunity of inspecting and forming his own judgment, if he chooses to act on his own judgment, the rule *caveat emptor* applies. If he gets the article he contracted to buy, and that article corresponds with what it was sold as, he gets all he is entitled to, and is bound by the contract. Here the defendant agreed to buy a specific parcel of oats. The oats were what they were sold as, namely, good oats according to the sample. The buyer persuaded himself they were old oats, when they were not so; but the seller neither said nor did anything to contribute to his deception. He has himself to blame. The question is not what a man of scrupulous morality or nice honour would do under such circumstances. The case put of the purchase of an estate, in which there is a mine under the surface, but the fact is unknown to the seller, is one in which a man of tender conscience or high honour would be unwilling to take advantage of the ignorance of the seller; but there can be no doubt that the contract for the sale of the estate would be binding.

SECTION ONE—EXCEPTIONS TO THE GENERAL RULE

A. Restrictive Covenants in the Sale of Leasehold Premises

Power *v* Barrett (1887) 19 LR (Ir) 450
The plaintiff held a leasehold interest in certain premises which he agreed to sell to the defendant, a chandler and oil merchant. The lease contained a covenant not to use the premises to carry on *inter alia* any 'dangerous, noxious, or offensive trade, business, or profession whatsoever'. The plaintiff did not disclose the existence of this covenant to the defendant. When the defendant discovered it he refused to complete and the plaintiff sued for specific performance.

V.C.:

. . .

The plaintiff was aware at the time of the negotiations, of the object and purpose of the defendant in agreeing to take the premises. He was perfectly aware of the nature of the business intended to be carried on there, namely, that of chandler and oil merchant, which implies the sale of all goods ordinarily sold and stored by a person engaged in such a trade. The defendant, accompanied by two friends, visited the premises in question, when a conversation arose involving knowledge by the plaintiff of the purpose of the defendant; and the parties then discussed the quantity of oil with which the vaults and stores could be filled. It is idle to contend that the sale and storing of petroleum or paraffin is not within the business of the defendant as an oil merchant. It was, therefore, well known to the plaintiff that the defendant required the premises for the purpose of storing quantities of this substance—whether 1000 barrels or 100 barrels is unimportant—and it is clear that on the occasion of the defendant's visit there was mention of the quantity of oil the premises could contain.

This being so, it was the duty of the plaintiff to inform the defendant of the existence of the restrictive clause in the lease—to inform him of the existence of every covenant which could reasonably be a prohibition against carrying on the trade for which the defendant desired to take the premises.

It is immaterial whether the plaintiff was himself actually aware of the extent, or even of the existence, of this covenant. It was his duty to be aware and to know of it. Lord St Leonards, in his work on *Vendors and Purchasers* (14th ed.), 214, quoting the case of *Flight v Barton*,[1] states the law on the subject. I take the law to be as there laid down, and that there is now no question that it is so—that if the purchaser state the object which he has in purchasing, and the seller is silent as to a covenant in the lease prohibiting or interfering with that object, his silence would be equivalent to a representation that there was no such prohibitory covenant, although he was not aware of the extent or operation of the covenant. I am of opinion that a vendor in the position of the plaintiff here is bound to know what covenants are in his lease, and that he is bound, moreover, to communicate such knowledge to an intending purchaser— provided such covenant can be reasonably interpreted as affecting the object which he is aware the purchaser has in view in purchasing the premises, and I think that the plaintiff has not fulfilled that obligation.

The plaintiff states he was not aware of the existence of this covenant. On this point, however, I entertain great doubt. I cannot understand why he should have paid a visit to the defendant, and inquired whether he was a manufacturer, unless he was aware of some restriction. The defendant says the plaintiff added a statement that the lease under which he held the premises contained a clause prohibiting the manufacture of certain articles. This is denied by the plaintiff, but I rather incline to believe the defendant's testimony on this point. Why should the plaintiff ask the defendant if he was a manufacturer, unless to avoid the consequences of not informing him of something which would interfere with his manufacture? I must assume the plaintiff to have been aware that the restriction in the lease was not confined to manufacture. It would be an extraordinary conclusion of law that the defendant is affected with constructive notice solely because he was informed that there was a lease, while the plaintiff should not be deemed to know the contents of that lease, under which he held, and which he was about to sell.

The plaintiff went farther than this; for the very fact that he made the inquiry as to whether the defendant was a manufacturer—even if there was no mention on that occasion by the plaintiff of a prohibition in the lease—was sufficient to induce the defendant to suppose that any such prohibition did not prevent anything but manufacturing. The plaintiff goes beyond mere silence, because his observations constituted an implied misrepresentation that there was no restriction except as to manufacturing.

. . .

. . . I must dismiss this action, with costs.

[1]· 3 My. & K. 282. 2M 2.

Note

Equity requires the vendor of property to disclose unusual defects in the title of the property.

B. Error in Advertisement

Sargent *v* Irish Multiwheel Ltd (1955) 21–22 Ir Jur Rep 42

The defendants advertised in the following terms: 'Among our large selection of new and secondhand cars, vans, and trucks, we have to offer: . . . Vans—1947 Austin 10 cwt. English-assembled van for sale, taxed for year £55.' The one van only was priced at £55 in the advertisement. The plaintiff saw the advertisement and approached the defendants. He asked to see 'some vans' for sale. The defendants showed him various vans, including one, and only one, priced at £55. The plaintiff believed this was the van advertised, but did not verify this fact with the defendants. The defendants admitted in evidence that in fact this was the same van. They knew it was Irish-assembled. They also knew that by an error it had been described in the advertisement as English-assembled. When negotiating with the plaintiff they did not mention that it was Irish-assembled, nor did the plaintiff say that he required an English-assembled van. The plaintiff purchased the van in the belief that it was English-assembled. He subsequently sold it and warranted it to the purchaser as English-assembled. In due course its country of assembly was discovered and the plaintiff was sued for breach of warranty. He suffered, as a result, loss and expense. The plaintiff failed to recover this loss and expense from the defendants in the District Court and appealed to the Circuit Court.

MacCarthy J.:

I have no hesitation in finding for the plaintiff in this case. The plaintiff came to the defendants and purchased from them a van in full reliance on a representation as to that van given in the defendants' advertisement. That representation was false, to the knowledge of the defendants. The defendants have said that the representation was made in error. It may be so. But once the plaintiff came to the defendants in consequence of their advertisement and was shown the subject of it, there was a duty on the defendants to warn the plaintiff of the error. They failed in this duty, and are liable to the plaintiff for the loss he suffered.

C. Animal Sales

Gill *v* McDowell [1903] IR 463
(Facts on p. 496.)

O'Brien L.C.J.:

. . .

I think also there is evidence of misrepresentation sufficient to sustain the action. It is perfectly notorious that a bad animal is often placed among good, so that the defects of the bad animal may, by association with the general lot, escape detection. In the case before us the animal of itself was calculated to give occasion to mistake; from one point of view it might be regarded as a heifer, and from another point of view it might be regarded as a bullock. It would, indeed, be hard to find anything more calculated of itself to deceive, and the defendant, well knowing that it was not a bullock or heifer, drove it into a fair where bullocks and heifers are sold, and deliberately put it into a category to which it did not belong, and to which he knew it did not belong. He associates it with a heifer and a bullock, makes it as one of a lot, and thereby the purchaser was, as a matter of fact, deceived, there being, I think, a tacit representation that this animal, standing in this cattle fair with a heifer and bullock, and offered for sale with them, was either a heifer and bullock. The plaintiff was, as a matter of fact, deceived; the defendant knew he was deceived. In my opinion there is some evidence that he was thrown off his guard by the action of the defendant.

Note

See also *Kennedy v Hennessy* (1906) 40 ILTR 84.

D. A DUTY TO SPEAK?

In *Gill v McDowell*, and some of the misrepresentation cases such as the *Spice Girls* case, considered in the previous chapter, the Court was able to find that the defendant's conduct distorted earlier statements and could thus constitute a misrepresentation. There are some instances of mistake where, in general, one party is aware that the other is under a mistaken belief, but because the mistake is self-induced, the contract remains binding. In the next case the House of Lords had to consider whether the plaintiff's misapprehension about the way in which a contractual venture would be performed, if known to the other party, could trigger a duty, in tort, to disabuse the mistaken party. This is an important case because the House dealt with this separately from the issue of negligent misrepresentation.

Hamilton and Others *v* Allied Domecq Plc (Scotland) [2007] UKHL 33

In this case Hamilton negotiated with the respondents with a view to concluding a share-subscription agreement under which the respondents would acquire an interest in a mineral water business. Hamilton negotiated with Beatty, who acted on behalf of the respondents. An essential part of the venture was the marketing strategy, Hamilton wanting the respondents to market the mineral water through 'off-sales' (supermarkets, etc.) and, more important, 'on-sales' (restaurants, bars). The agreement was concluded but the mineral water was only sold through off-sales, a factor that contributed to the failure of the business venture. The trial judge made no finding on whether Beatty was aware of Hamilton's belief that an off-sale and on-sale marketing strategy would be embarked upon from the onset. In the House of Lords Lord Rodger of Earlsferry said (in relation to the possible duty to speak, under *Banque Keyser Ullmann SA v Skardia UK Insurance Co.*) that even assuming Beatty knew or ought to have known that Hamilton regarded on-sales access to be essential, delictual liability for remaining silent would not necessarily follow. In a judgment, with which all four other Law Lords agreed, Lord Rodger found that there was no duty to speak, nor could the respondents be held to have made any actionable misrepresentation.

Lord Rodger:

22. Mr Clark [for Hamilton] accepted that something more than mere silence would usually be required to found a delictual claim for damages, but he argued that in certain circumstances a duty to speak would arise. In such cases a failure to speak would be negligent in law and a claim for damages could arise. For support, he pointed to the passage in the decision of the Court of Appeal in *Banque Keyser Ullmann SA v Skandia (UK) Insurance Co Ltd* [1990] 1 QB 665, 794H–795A where Slade L.J. said:

> We can see no sufficient reason on principle or authority why a failure to speak should not be capable of giving rise to liability in negligence under *Hedley Byrne* principles, provided that the two essential conditions are satisfied.

Slade L.J. had already identified the two essential conditions as being 'that there has been on the facts a voluntary assumption of responsibility in the relevant sense and reliance on that assumption.' He added, at p. 794E–F:

> These features may be much more difficult to infer in a case of mere silence than in a case of misrepresentation.

23. My Lords, the simple truth is that Mr Clark [for Hamilton] was unable to point to anything in the facts or evidence to show that, in this particular commercial negotiation, there had been any voluntary assumption of responsibility on the part of Mr Beatty. Nor have I been able to find any. In these circumstances the *Banque Keyser* decision does not provide a basis for holding that Mr Beatty was under a duty of care to tell Mr Hamilton about the defenders' distribution strategy if it differed from the one favoured by Mr Hamilton. Mr Clark did not suggest that such a duty could be founded on anything other than a voluntary assumption of responsibility. The alternative way of putting the pursuers' case must therefore be rejected. So, if they are to succeed, it can only be on the basis that there was a negligent misrepresentation by Mr Beatty.

SECTION TWO—CONTRACTS *Uberrimae Fidei*—INSURANCE CONTRACTS

A duty to disclose material facts exists in certain types of contract in which one of the parties is in a stronger position to know the truth of the statements made. Examples of these type of contracts include family settlements and insurance contracts.

A. DISCLOSURE OF A MATERIAL FACT

Chariot Inns Ltd v Assicurazioni Generali SPA and Coyle Hamilton Hamilton Phillips Ltd [1981] ILRM 173

Kenny J.:

...

... A contract of insurance requires the highest standard of accuracy, good faith, candour and disclosure by the insured when making a proposal for insurance to an insurance company. It has become usual for an insurance company to whom a proposal for insurance is made, to ask the proposed insured to answer a number of questions. Any misstatement in the answers given, when they relate to a material matter affecting the insurance, entitles the insurance company to avoid the policy and to repudiate liability if the event insured against happens. But the correct answering of any questions asked is not the entire obligation of the person seeking insurance; he is bound, in addition, to disclose to the insurance company every matter which is material to the risk against which he is seeking indemnity.

What then is to be regarded as material to the risk against which the insurance is sought? It is not what the person seeking insurance regards as material nor is it what the insurance company regards as material. It is a matter or circumstance which would reasonably influence the judgment of a prudent insurer in deciding whether he would take the risk and, if so, in determining the premium which he would demand. The standard by which materiality is to be determined is objective, not subjective. The matter has, in the last resort, to be determined by the court: the parties to the litigation may call experts in insurance matters as witnesses to give evidence of what they would have regarded as material but the question of materiality is not to be determined by such witnesses.

The generally accepted test of materiality in all forms of insurance against risks when property of any kind is involved is stated in s.18(2) of the Marine Insurance Act, 1906: 'Every circumstance is material which would influence the judgment of a prudent insurer in fixing the premium or determining whether he will take the risk'. Although this test is stated in an Act dealing with marine insurance, it has been accepted as a correct guide to the law in insurance against damage to property or goods of all types.

The rule to determine the materiality of a fact not disclosed to the insurers was expressed by Lord Justice MacKinnon with his customary pungency in *Zurich General Accident and Liability Insurance Co. Ltd v Morrison* [1942] 1 All ER 529 at 539:

> Under the general law of insurance an insurer can avoid a policy if he proves that there has been misrepresentation or concealment of a material fact by the insured. What is material is that which would influence the mind of a prudent insurer in deciding whether to accept the risk or fix the premium. If this be proved, it is not necessary further to prove that the mind of that actual insurer was so affected. In other words the insurer could not rebut the claim to avoid the policy because of a material misrepresentation by a plea that the particular insurer concerned was so stupid, ignorant or reckless that he could not exercise the judgment of a prudent insurer and was in fact unaffected by anything the insured had represented or concealed.

The statement of Samuels J. of the rules relating to the law about materiality of facts not disclosed in insurance law in *Mayne Nickless Ltd v Pegler* (1974) 1 NSWLR 228 has the authority of having been approved and followed by the Judicial Committee of the Privy Council in *Marene Knitting Mills Pty Ltd v Greater Pacific General Insurances Ltd* [1976] 2 Ll. LR 631:

> Accordingly I do not think that it is generally open to examine what the insurer would in fact have done had he had the information not disclosed. The question is whether that information would have been relevant to the exercise of the insurers' option to accept or reject the insurance proposed. It seems to me that the test of materiality is this: a fact is material if it would have reasonably affected the mind of a prudent insurer in determining whether he will accept the insurance, and if so, at what premium and on what conditions.

In January 1976, the plaintiffs ('Chariot')—whose directors and shareholders were Mr and Mrs Wootton—bought licensed premises at Ranelagh, Dublin. The directors decided to run the premises as a public house and also to have a cabaret entertainment. This made it necessary to build a larger room at the back. There were furnishings in the existing room at the back and as the extension could not be built without removing them, the directors decided to store them in 82 Lower Leeson Street. This latter premises was owned by Consolidated Investment Holdings Limited ('Consolidated') whose shares had been purchased by Mr Wootton and his business partner, Mr Mockler, but had been registered in the maiden names of their wives. Mr Wootton and Mr Mockler intended to use the premises as a hotel and discotheque and as Mr Wootton had been associated with a number of night clubs which had been prosecuted for breaches of the licensing laws, the directors expected considerable local opposition when their application for permission for a change of user was made if it became known that his wife or he were associated with Consolidated.

The insurance brokers acting for Mr Wootton were Coyle Hamilton Hamilton Phillips Ltd ('the brokers'), the second-named defendants. Mr Wootton had almost all his dealings with the brokers through Mr John Hart, an employee of theirs. The brokers placed the insurance on 82 Lower Leeson Street with the Sun Alliance and London Insurance Group and, in the policy, the premises were described and it was stated that the property was 'at present unoccupied'. When the directors of Chariot decided to store their furnishings in 82 Lower Leeson Street, Mr Hart advised them that further insurance cover on the furnishings was necessary. An endorsement on the policy in connection with the furnishings valuing them at £15,000, was made. As the premises at Lower Leeson Street were unoccupied, they were broken into by squatters almost nightly between November 1975 and the happening of the fire on 19 April 1976. These squatters lit fires and cooked there but left each morning before Mr Wootton arrived. The premises and Chariot's furnishings, which Consolidated held as bailees, were badly damaged. A claim for malicious damage was lodged with the local authority and was compromised by an agreed award of £55,000. Chariot was paid £8,000 by Consolidated who forwarded them a Sun Alliance cheque for this sum made out in favour of Chariot in respect of the furnishings. The claim by Consolidated against their insurance company was handled by Corcoran Insurances Ltd. Mr Mockler and Mr Wootton were so dissatisfied with the type of cover which the brokers had negotiated in connection with the Lower Leeson Street premises that they had changed their brokers and had given their business to Corcoran Insurances Ltd in December 1975.

When the plaintiffs bought the Chariot Inn, it was insured with the General Accident Insurance Co. Ltd ('the General Accident') and this policy was renewed subsequently. The principal in Corcoran Insurances Ltd advised Mr Wootton that a different and wider insurance cover was advisable in respect of the Chariot Inn, but when the General Accident were asked to quote for this, they increased the premium which they would require by 50 per cent. Mr Wootton was most reluctant to pay such a large increase and decided to get his brokers to ask for tenders for the insurance. The first-named defendants, who are an Italian insurance company, are represented and carry on business in the Republic of Ireland through their agents, International Underwriters Ltd and they sent in the lowest tender. Mr Hart had remained on friendly terms with Mr Wootton and frequently called to his premises. Chariot wanted cover against fire risk, employer's liability, liability to the public and loss of profits. Separate proposal forms for each type of insurance were sent out by the first-named defendants and Mr Hart got these. On 22 February 1978 Mr Hart called to Chariot's premises in Ranelagh with these proposal forms. They were issued by International Underwriters Ltd. One related to material damage. Mr Hart asked the questions necessary to fill in the answers to the questions and gave any other information required. It was not disputed by anyone during the trial that the handwriting in which the answers appeared was Mr Hart's. There was a discussion about the fire at Leeson Street and Mr Hart said that it was totally unnecessary to disclose this on the proposal forms because (as Mr Wootton said) 'we were dealing with a separate company and only had to show what was relevant to the Chariot Inn' (Question 167 first day). It is of importance that there is a question in this case as to who were the brokers who negotiated the policy with the first-named defendants and Mr Hart wrote in 'Coyle Hamilton'. In the form dealing with material damage this appeared:

MATERIAL DAMAGE
Give claims experience for loss over the last 5 years (i.e. date, nature of loss, amount paid or outstanding. Brief details of how loss occurred).
If none in any class say so.

The answer written in by Mr Hart was 'None'.

The first-named defendants subsequently issued policies to the plaintiffs in respect of the various forms of liability for which the plaintiffs sought insurance cover and in respect of indemnity against material loss. On 14 May 1978 a serious fire occurred at the plaintiffs premises which caused extensive damage. In June 1978, the first-named defendants repudiated liability because of the non-disclosure of the fire in Leeson Street. From the time of the fire, the first-named defendants suspected that Mr Wootton had set fire to the premises and stated during the hearing of the case that they would not have raised the issue of non-disclosure if they had not suspected that this was a case of arson.

When the first-named defendants repudiated liability, the plaintiffs brought this action against them claiming a declaration that the policy issued by them giving indemnity against material losses was valid and as against the brokers, damages for breach of contract and negligence.

. . .

Three experts on insurance business gave evidence. Their unanimous view was that the fire at Leeson Street and the damage to the plaintiffs' goods were matters that were material to the risk which the first-named defendants were asked to insure. Their opinions were not conclusive on this matter. The question whether any of these matters were material is essentially an inference from facts established by evidence. The circumstance that Mr Wootton was a director of Chariot and of Consolidated would not of itself make a fire on the premises owned by Consolidated a fact material to the risk undertaken by the first-named defendants when they insured Chariot against fire in the latters' premises.

I think, however, that it was material to the insurance effected by Chariot with the first-named defendants that goods belonging to Chariot were damaged by fire in premises owned by Consolidated. The answer to the query about claims made by Chariot for loss over the last five years was literally correct, but though Chariot had no claim against the insurance company which had issued a policy in respect of the Leeson Street premises, they were paid by Sun Alliance the sum negotiated in respect of the furnishings stored.

The circumstances in which the goods of Chariot were stored in the Leeson Street premises and the fact that Chariot ultimately got payment in respect of them were, in my view, matters which would reasonably have affected the judgment of a prudent insurer in deciding whether to take the risk or in fixing the premium, particularly as Mr Wootton was a director of and managed and controlled Chariot and Consolidated.

It was strenuously contended by counsel for the brokers that the onus of establishing that the matter not disclosed was material to the risk undertaken lay on the first-named defendants and that to discharge this onus, they had to establish that the matter not disclosed did affect, and not might have affected the judgment of the first-named defendants. I accept the first part of this proposition but not the second. It is necessary to establish that the fact not disclosed would have reasonably affected the judgment of a prudent insurer . . .

(Henchy and Griffin JJ. concurred.)

Note

This standard of disclosure has been substantially revised by the Supreme Court in the following two cases.

B. LIMITS

Aro Road and Land Vehicles Ltd *v* The Insurance Corporation of Ireland Ltd [1986] IR 403

The plaintiff agreed to sell and deliver goods to a company in Northern Ireland. The carriers organised insurance cover for the consignment. The only information sought by the underwriters was the names and addresses of the consignor and consignee and the nature and value of the goods. When the consignment was hijacked and lost, the defendants sought to repudiate liability on the basis that the plaintiff had failed to disclose the fact that Mr Mansfield, its managing director and principal shareholder, had been convicted of a number of offences involving dishonesty twenty years previously.

Carroll J. in the High Court applied the test for the duty of disclosure laid down in the *Chariot Inns* case, and accepted that a reasonable under-writer may have regarded the conviction as relevant to the risk.

Henchy J.:

. . .

I accept without question that it is a general principle of the law of insurance that a person seeking insurance, whether acting personally or through a limited company, is bound to disclose every circumstance within his knowledge which would have influenced the judgment of a reasonable and prudent insurer in fixing the premium or in deciding whether to take on the risk. Carroll J., while personally of opinion that Mr Mansfield's non-disclosure of his convictions and imprisonment was not material, deferred to the expert opinion given in the High Court (which she accepted and considered to transcend her personal opinion) that a reasonable and prudent underwriter would regard that matter as material and would have regarded its non-disclosure as a good reason for refusing to underwrite the risk. Accordingly, she held that the insurers were entitled to avoid the policies in question and to repudiate liability. On the assumption that full disclosure of all known material facts was obligatory, I consider that the judge's conclusion could not be interfered with by this court: see *Northern Bank Finance v Charlton* [1979] IR 149.

It emerged, however, in the course of the hearing of this appeal, that a particular aspect of the case was not adverted to, either in the pleadings or in the argument in the High Court. This was whether the circumstances of the case showed it to be an exception to the usual requirement of full disclosure.

...

Generally speaking, contracts of insurance are contracts *uberrimae fidei*, which means that utmost good faith must be shown by the person seeking the insurance. Not alone must that person answer to the best of his knowledge any question put to him in a proposal form, but, even when there is no proposal form, he is bound to divulge all matters within his knowledge which a reasonable and prudent insurer would consider material in deciding whether to underwrite the risk or to underwrite it on special terms.

That is the general rule. Like most general legal rules, however, it is subject to exceptions. For instance, the contract itself may expressly or by necessary implication exclude the requirement of full disclosure. It is for the parties to make their own bargain—subject to any relevant statutory requirements—and if the insurer shows himself to be prepared to underwrite the risk without requiring full disclosure, he cannot later avoid the contract and repudiate liability on the ground of non-disclosure.

An example of a contract of insurance which excludes full disclosure is where the circumstances are such as to preclude the possibility of full disclosure; or where the requirement of full disclosure would be so difficult, or so impractical, or so unreasonable, that the insurer must be held by his conduct to have ruled it out as a requirement. This is exemplified by many forms of what I may call 'over-the-counter insurance'. Because this case is concerned only with fire and theft cover, I am addressing myself only to property insurance. Many concerns, such as airlines, shipping companies and travel agents—acting as agents for an insurance company and usually under the umbrella of a master policy—are prepared to insure travellers or consignors of goods in respect of luggage or of goods consigned, in circumstances in which full disclosure is neither asked for nor could reasonably be given effect to. The time factor, if nothing else, would rule out the requirement of full disclosure in many instances: an air traveller who buys insurance of his luggage in an airport just before boarding an aeroplane could not be expected to have time to make disclosure of *all* material circumstances. Insurance sold in that way obviously implies a willingness on the part of the insurer to provide the cover asked for without requiring disclosure of all material circumstances. The question in this case is whether this insurance, which the judge has held was entered into by Mr Mansfield's company in good faith and without any intention to defraud, was attended by circumstances which show that the insurers are precluded from claiming that full disclosure was a prerequisite of a valid contract of insurance.

Consider the relevant circumstances. Mr Mansfield, through his company, was sold this insurance. He did not look for it. It was suggested by CIE. He was reluctant to take it out; he considered it a waste of money. CIE as agents for the insurers arranged the rates and filled in the relevant certificates of insurance. Once that was done, CIE were ready to transport the goods. They sought no further information from Mr Mansfield and apparently deemed none necessary. Before collecting and transporting the goods, they did not furnish the certificates of insurance to Mr Mansfield or his company. They did not even inform Mr Mansfield or his company of the identity of the insurers. It is conceded by counsel for the insurers that if Mr Mansfield was to make full disclosure he would have to make such inquiries as would bring the identity of the insurers to his knowledge—or alternatively to pass the relevant information to CIE as their agents. CIE as well as being the insurers' agents, were to be the carriers of the goods insured. Everything points to the conclusion that when, as carriers of the goods, they got the information necessary for their purposes as carriers, and then arranged insurance of the goods during transit, the insurance was for all practical purposes concluded, so that no further information could have thereafter been asked for.

The circumstances of this case seem to me to show that CIE, acting as agents for the insurers, accepted this insurance without expecting or requiring disclosure of *all* relevant circumstances. The informal, almost perfunctory, way in which CIE effected this insurance, their readiness to collect the premium and proceed to carry the goods to their destination as soon as they had ascertained the premium, showed a failure or unwillingness to give the insured company an opportunity to make full disclosure before the contract of insurance was concluded. The relevant circumstances indicate an indifference on the part of CIE as agents for the insurers as to matters such as the personal circumstances of the managing director of the insured company.

It may well be the law that even in a case such as this certain types of information may not be knowingly withheld by the insured, but this case calls only for an answer to the question whether in the circumstances of the case an innocent non-disclosure of an incident in the past life of the managing director of the insured company entitled the insurers to avoid the policy. In my opinion it did not. Insurers who allow agents such as shippers, carriers, airlines, travel agents and the like to insure on their behalf goods being carried, and to sell that insurance to virtually all and sundry who ask for it, with minimal formality or inquiry, and with no indication that full disclosure is to be made of any matter which the insurers may *ex post facto* deem to be material, cannot be held to contract subject to a condition that the insured must furnish *all* material information.

I would allow the plaintiff's appeal and remit the case to the High Court for the assessment of damages.

(Griffin J. concurred.)

McCarthy J.:

. . .

In my view, if the judgment of an insurer is such as to require disclosure of what he thinks is relevant but which a reasonable insured, if he thought of it at all, would not think relevant, then, in the absence of a question directed towards the disclosure of such a fact, the insurer, albeit prudent, cannot properly be held to be acting reasonably. A contract of insurance is a contract of the utmost good faith on both sides; the insured is bound to disclose every matter which might reasonably be thought to be material to the risk against which he is seeking indemnity; that test of reasonableness is an objective one not to be determined by the opinion of underwriter, broker or insurance agent, but by, and only by, the tribunal determining the issue. Whilst accepted standards of conduct and practice are of significance in determining issues of alleged professional negligence, they are not to be elevated into being an absolute shield against allegations of malpractice—see *O'Donovan v Cork County Council* [1967] IR 173 and *Roche v Peilow* [1985] IR 232. In disputes concerning professional competence, a profession is not to be permitted to be the final arbiter of standards of competence. In the instant case, the insurance profession is not to be permitted to dictate a binding definition of what is reasonable. The learned trial judge depended part of her judgment upon the decision of this court in *Chariot Inns v Assicurazioni Generali* [1981] IR 199. In his judgment, with which Henchy and Griffin JJ. agreed, Kenny J. stated at p. 225:

> A contract of insurance requires the highest standard of accuracy, good faith, candour and disclosure by the insured when making a proposal for insurance to an insurance company. It has become usual for an insurance company to whom a proposal for insurance is made to ask the proposed insured to answer a number of questions. Any misstatement in the answers given, when they relate to a material matter affecting the insurance, entitles the insurance company to avoid the policy and to

repudiate liability if the event insured against happens. But the correct answering of any questions asked is not the entire obligation of the person seeking insurance: he is bound, in addition, to disclose to the insurance company every matter which is material to the risk against which he is seeking indemnity.

What is to be regarded as material to the risk against which the insurance is sought? It is not what the person seeking insurance regards as material, nor is it what the insurance company regards as material. It is a matter of circumstance which would reasonably influence the judgment of a prudent insurer in deciding whether he would take the risk, and, if so, in determining the premium which he would demand. The standard by which materiality is to be determined is objective and not subjective. In the last resort the matter has to be determined by the court: the parties to the litigation may call experts in insurance matters as witnesses to give evidence of what they would have regarded as material, but the question of materiality is not to be determined by such witnesses.

These observations were made in a case in which there was a proposal form, there were questions asked by the insurer and, as this court held, there was a non-disclosure of a matter material to the risk. In the High Court (in *Chariot Inns*) Keane J., at p. 209, said:

> The most widely accepted test of materiality in all forms of insurance on property and goods appears to be that set out in s. 18, sub-s. 2, of the Marine Insurance Act, 1906, which is in the following terms:
>> 'Every circumstance is material which would influence the judgment of a prud-ent insurer in fixing the premium, or determining whether he will take the risk.'
>
> That test has been frequently stated to be applicable to non-marine insurance as well: see *Joel v Law Union & Crown Insurance Co.* and *March Cabaret v London Assurance*. Another test has sometimes been proposed, i.e. the test of whether a reasonable man in the position of the assured and with knowledge of the facts in dispute ought to have realised that they were material to the risk. But this test has been confined normally in its application to cases of life see *MacGillivray & Parkington on Insurance Law* (6th ed.) paras 749, 750. It was not suggested by any of the parties as the appropriate test in the present case and, accordingly, I propose to apply the test set out in s. 18, sub-s. 2 of the Act of 1906.

Kenny J. did not expressly advert to this proposition but it reflects the argument advanced by the plaintiff here touching on what the insured might consider relevant or material. Keane J., at p. 207, referred to the judgment of Fletcher Moulton L.J. in *Joel v Law Union & Crown Insurance Co.* [1908] 2 KB 863 at p. 892. There it was said: 'Over and above the two documents signed by the applicant, and in my opinion unaffected by them, there remained the common law obligation of disclosure of all knowledge pos-sessed by the applicant material to the risk about to be undertaken by the company, such materiality being a matter to be judged of by the jury and not by the court.' The same Lord Justice, at p. 885, had some critical comments to make on the practices on the part of insurance offices of requiring that the accuracy of the answers to the proposal form should be the basis of the contract. I point to this so as to emphasise that *Joel v Law Union & Crown Insurance Co.* [1908] 2 KB 863 was a case concerned with a proposal form and insurance effected on foot of it as was *Chariot Inns* [1981] IR 199. This is not such a case, but the test remains one of the utmost good faith. Yet, how does one depart from such a standard if reasonably and genuinely one does not consider some fact material; how much the less does one depart from such a standard when the failure to disclose is entirely due to a failure of recollection? Where there is no spur to the memory, where there is no proposal form with its presumably relevant questions, how can a failure of recollection lessen the quality of good faith? Good faith is not raised in its standard by being described as the utmost good faith; good faith requires candour and disclosure, not, I think, accuracy in itself, but a genuine effort to achieve the same using all reasonably available sources, a factor well illustrated by Fletcher Moulton L.J. at p. 885 of *Joel*. If the duty is one that requires disclosure by the insured of all material facts which are known to him, then it may well require an impossible level of performance. Is it reasonable of an underwriter to say: 'I expect disclosure of what I think is relevant or what I may think is relevant but which a reasonable proposer may not think of at all or, if he does, may not think is relevant'? The classic authority is the judgment of Lord Mansfield in *Carter v Boehm* (1766) 3 Burr. 1905 where, in terms free from exaggeration, he stated at p. 1911:

> The *reason* of the rule which obliges parties to disclose, is to prevent fraud and to encourage good faith. It is adapted to *such* facts as vary the nature of the contract; which one privately knows, and the other is ignorant of, and has no reason to suspect.
>
> The question therefore must always be 'Whether there was, under all the circumstances at the time the policy was underwritten, a *fair representation*; or a *concealment*; fraudulent, if *designed*; or, though not designed, *varying materially the object* of the policy, and *changing the risque* understood to be run.

If the determination of what is material were to lie with the insurer alone I do not know how the average citizen is to know what goes on in the insurer's mind, unless the insurer asks him by way of the questions in a proposal form or otherwise. I do not accept that he must seek out the proposed insurer and question him as to his reasonableness, his prudence, and what he considers material. The proposal form will ordinarily contain a wide ranging series of questions followed by an omnibus question as to any other matters that are material. In the instant case, if Mr Mansfield had ever had the opportunity of completing a proposal form, which, due to the convenient arrangement made between the insurers and CIE, he did not, there is no reason to think that he would have recounted petty convictions of about twenty years before the time. For the reasons I have sought to illustrate, in my view, the learned trial judge failed correctly to apply the very stringent test; in my judgment, the insurers failed to discharge the onus of proof that lay on them.

There is a second ground upon which, also, in my view the plaintiff is entitled to succeed. Without detracting from what I have said in respect of the general law of insurance, in my judgment, that law is materially affected by over-the-counter insurance such as found in cases of the present kind, in other forms of transit and in personal travel, including holiday insurance. If no questions are asked of the insured, then, in the absence of fraud, the insurer is not entitled to repudiate on grounds of non-disclosure. Fraud might arise in such an instance as where an intending traveller has been told of imminent risk of death and then takes out life insurance in a slot machine at an airport. Otherwise, the insured need but answer correctly the questions asked; these questions must be limited in kind and number; if the insurer were to have the opportunity of denying or loading the insurance one purpose of the transaction would be defeated. Expedition is the hallmark of this form of insurance. [Counsel for the defendant] suggested that the whole basis of insurance could be seriously damaged if there was any weakening in the rigidity and, I must add, the severity, of the principle he sought to support. The force of such an argument as a proposition of law is matched by the improbability of the event.

(Walsh and Hederman JJ. agreed.)

Notes

1. Is McCarthy J.'s reference to the reasonable insured compatible with Kenny J.'s test in the *Chariot Inns* case of the prudent underwriter?
2. See 'Contract Property Insurance—A Return to Utmost Good Faith by Both Sides' by R. Clark in (1987) 9 DULJ 117.

Keating *v* New Ireland Assurance Co. plc [1990] ILRM 110

The plaintiff and her husband entered a life assurance policy in June 1985. At a medical examination prior to entering the insurance policy, Mr Keating disclosed that he had undergone examination for what appeared to be a digestive ailment and he made available the names of the doctors who had treated him. Unknown to Mr Keating he had been diagnosed as suffering from angina at that time and the drugs he had been subsequently prescribed were to treat this condition. Later Mr Keating died as a result of the angina and the defendants sought to repudiate the plaintiff's claim on the basis *inter alia* of non-disclosure of a material fact.

McCarthy J.:

. . .

The insurer might well contend that the deceased *ought* to have known that there was some problem arising with his heart; the onus, however, of proving that he *did* know lies upon the insurer; it is not sufficient to prove that he *ought* to have known. The fact that the three doctors concerned *did* know does not impute knowledge to the deceased, to whom the medical examiner for the insurer (Dr Duffy), was enjoined by the examination form to give no information as to the result of the examination.

The insurers were not informed of these material facts; was it a non-disclosure? One cannot disclose what one does not know, albeit that this puts a premium on ignorance. It may well be that wilful ignorance would raise significant other issues; such is not the case here. If the proposer for life insurance has answered all the questions asked to the best of his ability and truthfully, his next-of-kin are not to be damnified because of his ignorance or obtuseness which may be sometimes due to a mental block on matters affecting one's health.

Support for this view is to be found in my judgment, with which Walsh and Hederman JJ. agreed, in *Aro Road and Land Vehicles Ltd v Insurance Corporation of Ireland Ltd* [1986] IR 403. In that case, as in this, reliance was placed on the observations of Kenny J. in *Chariot Inns v Assicurazioni Generali* [1981] IR 199. *Chariot Inns* was, like this, a proposal form case; the decision turned upon the determination of what is material; such is not the issue here. The *Aro Road and Land Vehicles Ltd* case was decided upon a preliminary point as to materiality and, accordingly, the expressed challenge to the reasonably prudent test as outlined in *Chariot Inns* did not arise.

Note

It should be noted that limits to the duty to disclose relate to other areas apart from situations where no proposal form exists. For example, if specific questions are asked in proposal forms this may waive the insurer's right to further disclosure.

Kelleher *v* Irish Life Assurance Co. Ltd (SC) [1993] 1 ILRM 643

A 'special promotional offer' was made available, and accepted by the plaintiff who assured her husband's life in 1985. This offer consisted of two documents, one being a general application form containing general questions concerning the health and history of the life assured such as 'Has the life suffered at any time from any illness, injury requiring medical or psychiatric attention?' Through these questions was drawn a line of cancellation indicating that these questions need not be answered in the special promotion. The second document, titled a 'special proposal' form, merely declared that the assured has not undergone medical treatment in the previous six months.

When Mr Kelleher died the defendant rejected the plaintiff's claim due to the non-disclosure of the fact that Mr Kelleher had received treatment for cancer in 1981. The High Court dismissed the plaintiff's claim against the defendant, and the plaintiff appealed.

Finlay C.J.:

. . .

. . . The learned trial judge in the course of his judgment held that the special promotional offer was obviating the necessity for producing medical evidence but that it did not obviate the obligation to make full disclosure, and that that was in fact underlined on the other document which was sent to persons availing of the special scheme. The ratio of his decision is to be found in a paragraph contained at p. 9 of the judgment which is as follows: 'In these circumstances it seems to me that there was no waiver by the defendants of the obligation which was on the plaintiff and on the person whose life was insured. There was no variation of the common law duty. There was a contractual duty to disclose which was stated in clear terms. In my view, the breach of that contractual duty entitles the defendants to repudiate liability.'

No challenge was made on the hearing of this appeal to the general proposition of the implied obligation on persons proposing insurance to disclose, first stated by Lord Mansfield in *Carter v Boehm* (1766) 3 Burr 1905, and subsequently confirmed and repeated in many decisions both in England and in Ireland.

The sole issue raised by the appellant on the hearing of this appeal is a submission that upon the true construction of the two forms of proposal and, in particular, upon the true construction of the special form of proposal that the policy which is based on the two forms of proposal must be read as excluding a requirement of full disclosure with regard to the medical history of the life assured from the years 1981 to 1985 and that in addition the terms of those documents exclude any implied obligation arising under the doctrine laid down in the case of *Carter v Boehm*.

This doctrine was recently dealt with by this court in the case of *Aro Road and Land Vehicles Ltd v* ICI [1986] IR 403. In that case, Henchy J. in the course of his judgment at p. 408 stated as follows:

Generally speaking contracts of insurance are contracts *uberrimae fidei*, which means that utmost good faith must be shown by the person seeking the insurance. Not alone must that person answer to the best of his knowledge any question put to him in a proposal form, but, even when there is no proposal form, he is bound to divulge all matters within his knowledge which a reasonable and prudent insurer would consider material in deciding whether to underwrite the risk or to underwrite it on special terms.

That is the general rule. Like most general legal rules, however, it is subject to exceptions. For instance, the contract itself may expressly or by necessary implication exclude the requirement of full disclosure. It is for the parties to make their own bargain—subject to any relevant statutory requirements—and if the insurer shows himself to be prepared to underwrite the risk without requiring full disclosure, he cannot later avoid the contract and repudiate liability on the ground of non-disclosure.

The appellant in this case says it comes precisely within the exception referred to in that portion of the judgment as being an instance where the contract itself formed on the two proposals, by necessary implication, excludes the requirement of full disclosure.

Special emphasis is placed upon the unambiguous statement contained under the heading 'Special Promotional Offer on Life Assurance and Disability Benefit' in the special proposal form, whereby the insurance company, in effect, guarantees that 'for any member who is under sixty years old and who *satisfactorily completed the declaration of health below* we can offer life cover of £80,000 *free of medical evidence* and annual disability benefit cover of £10,000 *per annum*.' (Emphasis added). This it is submitted is the clearest possible assertion that completion of 'the declaration of health below' is the sufficient entry for a person who also is a member of the organisation, namely, the IMO, and who is under sixty years of age. The 'declaration of health below', there referred to, I have set out in this judgment and it is one expressly confined to the work experience and the negativing of excessive absence through illness for a period of three months prior to the date of the signing of the form and the absence of taking or seeking medical treatment during six months prior to the signing of the form. Such an unequivocal statement, it is submitted, not only clearly excludes the ordinary doctrine of *uberrima fides* or the implied obligation to make full disclosure with regard to the risk, but also must be read as confining clause 6 of the provisions, privileges and conditions in the policy of assurance to misrepresentation or non-disclosure confined to the precise questions and periods raised in the declaration of health. This topic is dealt with as a matter of general principle in *MacGillivray and Parkington* (8th ed., 1988). There, having set out the possibility that the form of questions asked in a proposal form may make the applicant's duty to disclose more strict than the general duty arising under the doctrine laid down in *Carter v Boehm*, at para. 646 it is stated as follows:

It is more likely, however, that the questions asked will limit the duty of disclosure, in that, if questions are asked on particular subjects and the answers to them are warranted, it may be inferred that the insurer has waived his right to information, either on the same matters but outside the scope of the questions, or on matters kindred to the subject matter of the questions. Thus, if an insurer asks 'How many accidents have you had in the last three years?', it may well be implied that he does not want to know of accidents before that time, though these would still be material. If it were asked whether any of the proposer's parents, brothers or sisters had died of consumption or been afflicted with insanity, it might well be inferred that the insurer had waived similar information concerning more remote relatives, so that he could not avoid the policy for non-disclosure of an aunt's death of consumption or an uncle's insanity. Whether or not such waiver is present depends on a true construction of the proposal form, the test being would a reasonable man reading the proposal form be justified in thinking that the insurer had restricted his right to receive all material information, and consented to the omission of the particular information in issue?

This identical paragraph which was contained in an earlier edition of the text-book involved, is cited with full approval by Woolf J. (as he then was) in *Hair v The Prudential Assurance Co. Ltd* [1983] 2 Lloyd's Rep., 667, at p. 673 of his judgment. In applying that principle to the facts of that particular case, Woolf J. laid particular emphasis on the last sentence of the paragraph.

I too would accept this as an accurate statement of the principle of limitation of the obligation for disclosure arising from the particular form of questions. I would also be satisfied that the true and acid test must be as to whether a reasonable man reading the proposal form would conclude that the information over and above it which is in issue was not required.

Applying that test to the form of the special proposal form in this case, I have no doubt that a reasonable man reading that would assume that, provided he could truthfully answer the two questions, namely, his absence from work due to illness being confined to not more than two weeks in the previous three months, and the second question, as to his not having undergone, taken or sought medical treatment within six months, he would be entitled, having fulfilled the other necessary qualifications of being a member of the IMO under the age of sixty years, to the insurance.

In essence, the grounds on which the defendants now seek to avoid payment on this policy consist precisely of a non-disclosure by the life assured, Dr Kelleher, of his having sought and obtained medical treatment in the year 1981 and in succeeding years, but outside of the time of six months provided for in the declaration of health contained in the special proposal form.

Whilst it is not necessary to go outside the forms of the proposal themselves, it is not without importance that what was described as the 'special promotional offer' being offered by the assurance company after negotiation through the brokers to all the members of the Irish Medical Organisation constitutes a very sound and probable commercial manner in which to attract a very substantial quantity of new business by one single project. That fact constitutes a probable reason why the defendant should significantly limit the disclosure required from proposers for that insurance.

I would, therefore, allow this appeal, vary the order made in the High Court and enter judgment for the plaintiff for the sum of £80,000.

C. Basis of the Contract Clauses

Often insurance contracts contain a clause stating that the answers given in a proposal form and the making of full and honest disclosure are the basis of the contract and the policy is thus conditional upon full disclosure.

The Insurance Act 1936 ss 61–64

61. (1) Every proposal for an industrial assurance policy shall, unless

(a) such policy is proposed to be effected on the life and on behalf of a child under the age of sixteen years, or
(b) the person whose life is proposed to be assured under such policy is a person in whom the proposer has an insurable interest,

contain a declaration by the person whose life is proposed to be assured under such policy that such policy is proposed to be taken out by him and that the premiums thereon will be paid by him.

(2) Where the person whose life is proposed to be assured under an industrial assurance policy is a person in whom the proposer has an insurable interest, the proposal for such policy shall contain a statement of the nature of such interest.

(3) Every industrial assurance company which fails to comply with or to observe the foregoing provisions of this section shall be deemed to have failed to comply with the provisions of this Act and every collector or agent of such company who takes part or is concerned in such failure shall be guilty of an offence under this sub-section and shall be liable on summary conviction thereof to a fine not exceeding five pounds.

(4) Whenever a proposal for an industrial assurance policy contains a statement, which is not true in fact, that the person in respect of whose life such proposal has been made is not at the time of making such proposal a person on whose life any other policy has been issued by the industrial assurance company to which such proposal is made, and a policy of assurance on the life of such person is issued by such company in pursuance of such proposal, such company shall, notwithstanding that such statement is not true and that the truth of such statement is made a condition of such policy, not be relieved because such statement is not true from liability on foot of such policy.

(5) Whenever a proposal for an industrial assurance policy consists of a form or proposal filled in, wholly or partly, by a person employed by the industrial assurance company to which such proposal is made and a misstatement which is not fraudulent has been made in some material particular by the proposer and embodied in such proposal, the following provisions shall have effect, that is to say:

(a) where such proposal has been filled in wholly by any person so employed, such company shall not be entitled to question the validity of the policy founded on such proposal on the ground of such misstatement so made by the proposer and embodied in such proposal, and

(b) where such proposal has been filled in partly by any person so employed, such company shall not be entitled to question the validity of the policy founded on such proposal on the ground of such misstatement so made by the proposer and embodied in such proposal unless such statement occurs in some part of such proposal which has not been filled in by any person so employed.

(6) Where, but for the provisions of the next preceding sub-section of this section, the validity of a policy issued by an industrial assurance company could have been questioned on the grounds of a misstatement in the proposal for such policy relating to the state of health at the date of such proposal of the person upon whose life such policy is proposed to be taken out, nothing in the said next preceding sub-section shall prevent such question being raised by such company within two years from the date of issue of such policy.

(7) Notwithstanding the provisions of this section, whenever a proposal for a policy of industrial assurance which was effected before the commencement of this Part of this Act contains an incorrect statement of the age of the person whose life is assured under such policy, the industrial assurance company which issued such policy may so adjust the terms of the policy, or of any policy which may be issued in lieu thereof, that such terms shall conform to the terms which would have been applicable if the true age of such person had been inserted in such proposal, and accordingly no industrial assurance policy issued before the commencement of this Part of this Act shall be invalidated on the ground that the age of the person in respect of whose life such policy was issued was incorrectly stated in such policy or in the proposal for such policy.

62. (1) Every policy of industrial assurance issued after the commencement of this Part of this Act shall, subject to the provisions of this section, contain a copy of such of the provisions of this Act as shall from time to time be prescribed by orders made by the Minister under this sub-section.

(2) The Minister may, if he thinks fit, grant permission to an industrial assurance company to insert and every such company shall thereupon insert in every policy of industrial assurance effected by such company after the commencement of this Part of this Act a statement setting forth the effect of the provisions of this Act for the time being prescribed by order made under the next preceding sub-section of this section, and such insertion shall be in lieu of and be deemed to be a compliance with the obligation imposed on every such company by the said next preceding sub-section.

(3) Every industrial assurance company which, after the commencement of this Part of this Act, issues a policy of industrial assurance which does not comply with whichever of the foregoing sub-sections of this section is applicable to such company shall be deemed to have failed to comply with the provisions of this Act, and shall, without prejudice to the liability incurred in respect of such failure, either (at the election of the person who has paid the premiums due on foot of such policy) rectify such policy or pay to such person a sum equal to the amount of the premiums so paid, but such company shall not be liable further or otherwise to such person, and such premiums may be recovered by such person from such company in any court of competent jurisdiction.

63. (1) The Minister may, if and whenever he so thinks proper, by notice in writing left in the case of an industrial assurance company which is registered in Saorstát Eireann, at the registered office of such company in Saorstát Eireann, and in the case of an industrial assurance company which is not registered in Saorstát Eireann, at the principal office of such company in Saorstát Eireann, require such company to delete or amend any term, condition, question, or provision contained in any form of proposal for a policy of industrial assurance issued by such company on or after the date specified in that behalf in such notice.

(2) The Minister may, if and whenever he so thinks proper, by notice in writing left in the case of an industrial assurance company which is registered in Saorstát Eireann, at the registered office of such company in Saorstát Eireann, and in the case of an industrial assurance company which is not registered in Saorstát Eireann, at the principal office of such company in Saorstát Eireann, require such company to delete or amend any term, condition, or provision contained in any form of policy of industrial assurance proposed to be issued by such company on or after the date specified in that behalf in such notice.

(3) Every industrial assurance company to which a notice is given by the Minister under this section shall forthwith comply with such notice and, for that purpose, do all such things as such company is required by such notice to do.

(4) Nothing in this section shall authorise or empower the Minister to require an industrial assurance company to alter either the premium payable under or the sum assured by or the date of maturity of a policy of industrial assurance.

64. (1) Every policy of industrial assurance issued after the commencement of this Part of this Act shall be deemed to be made on the terms that the age, at the date of the issue of such policy, of the person in respect of whose life such policy is issued is admitted by the company issuing such policy to be the age stated in that behalf in such policy or, where such age is not dated in such policy, to be the age stated in that behalf in the proposal for such policy, and accordingly no industrial assurance policy shall be invalidated or questioned on the ground that the age of the person in respect of whose life such policy is issued is incorrectly stated in such policy or in the proposal for such policy.

(2) Whenever an industrial assurance company receives a proposal for a policy of industrial assurance and such proposal contains an incorrect statement of the age of the person whose life is thereby proposed to be assured, such company may, within twelve months after the date on which it receives such proposal, to adjust the terms of the policy issued or about to be issued in pursuance of such proposal as to make such terms conform to the terms applicable to the true age of such person.

(3) Where an industrial assurance company requires, as a condition precedent to the issue of an industrial assurance policy, for the age of the person in respect of whose life such policy is to be issued shall be verified by production of a certified copy of the entry of the birth of such person or other evidence, and such company defrays the cost of obtaining such certified copy or other evidence, such company may adjust the amount of the money payable by such company under such policy by deducting from such money the amount of the said cost so defrayed by such company, if, but only if, the proposal form contained a clause to the effect that the production of such certified copy or other evidence would be required as aforesaid and that the cost thereof, if defrayed by such company, would be deducted from the money payable by such company under such policy.

(4) Every registrar of births, every assistant registrar of births and every other person having the custody of a register of births shall, on an application being made to him by an industrial assurance company in such form and manner as may be approved by the Registrar-General of Births, Deaths and Marriages and on being paid by such company a fee not exceeding six pence for each certified copy, furnish to such company a certified copy of the entry of the birth of any person whose birth is registered in such register of births and in respect of whom a proposal for a policy of industrial assurance has been received or a policy of industrial assurance has been issued by such company.

(5) Every registrar of marriages, every deputy registrar of marriages and every other person having the custody of a register of marriages shall, on an application being made to him by an industrial assurance company in such form and manner as may be approved by the Registrar-General of Births, Deaths and Marriages used on being paid by such company a fee not exceeding one shilling for each certified copy, furnish to such company a certified copy of the entry of the marriage of any married woman or widow whose marriage is entered into such register and in respect of whom a proposal for a policy of industrial assurance has been approved or a policy of industrial assurance has been issued by such company.

In *Keenan v Shield Insurance Co.* [1987] IR 113 Blayney J. in the High Court noted that while at common law only a misstatement of a material fact would entitle an insurer to repudiate, the situation is different where the insured has expressly warranted the accuracy of his or her answers and agreed that they would be made the basis of the insurance contract. In such cases he said the following passage from *MacGillivray & Parkington* (7th ed.) para. 725 must be applied:

Blayney J.:

...

It has always been the law since Lord Mansfield's day that there must be strict and exact compliance with the obligation or statement which is warranted, so that, as he himself said in *Pawson v Watson* (1778) 2 Cowp. 785, 787, 'Nothing tantamount will do or answer the purpose.' It is, therefore, not open to the assured to say that the obligation has been substantially complied with, or that the answer he made to a question was more or less accurate. This rule is presumably related to the general doctrine that a warranty is independent of any question of materiality, since an assured who gave an answer which was false only in trifling detail, and contended that it was accurate, might in a sense be contending that the difference was not material or important to the insurers' calculations.

Note

See also *Farrell v South East Lancashire Insurance Co. Ltd* [1933] IR 36.

Brady v Irish National Insurance Co. Ltd [1986] IR 698

The plaintiff insured his boat under a policy which incorporated *inter alia* a warranty as to the purpose and intended use of the boat and a warranty that the vessel would be 'laid up' over the winter in a place of safety, dismantled, not fitted out or used for any purpose whatsoever other than dismantling, fitting out or customary overhauling. The plaintiff did not disclose his intention to use the boat to cook meals during the maintenance works. When the boat was damaged the defendants resisted the claim on the basis *inter alia* of non-disclosure of a material fact. The plaintiff's action seeking indemnification was dismissed in the High Court and he appealed to the Supreme Court.

Finlay C.J.:

...

The principle applicable to this interpretation is, I am satisfied, similar to the principle which would be applicable to the interpretation of a contract proffered by one person to another. District Judge Walter E. Hoffman in *The Cristie* [1975] 2 Lloyd's Rep. 100, dealing with an express warranty in a marine insurance policy, states at p. 106: 'As far as the vagueness claim is concerned, plaintiffs are quite correct in stating that if the warranty was vague it should be construed against the insurer.'

In this case the phrase contained in special warranty number (ii), 'customary overhauling' is not expanded or amplified by any further definition in the policy, nor is it a phrase which has any special legal meaning. It must, in my view, therefore, be interpreted against the insurer in the light of evidence as to what is customary in this context. In the course of his judgment the learned trial judge dealing admittedly with the provisions of s. 18 [Marine Insurance Act 1906], but on the same topic, stated as follows:

> A good deal of evidence was tendered for the purpose of establishing that owners of boats of the type damaged in the explosions, commonly lay them up for the winter, either on the hard or afloat, and spend much of their spare time getting the boats ready for the new season; that it is common practice in such circumstances for the galley to be used while works of overhaul and refurbishing are in progress,

and that this was well known to the boat-owning fraternity and to their insurers—a 'matter of common notoriety' to use the words of the Act. I am prepared to accept that there is and always has been a common practice of the type referred to.

This finding was, as I have already indicated, not only well founded, on the evidence, but inevitable from it, and indeed in examining the only witness called on behalf of the defendant in the High Court, counsel on behalf of the defendant, at Question 490, summarised what the effect of the plaintiff's evidence so far had been, in the following question: 'We have had evidence which I think is uncontrovertible that it is within the contemplation of people overhauling boats during the laying up period that the cooker will be used. Is the boat fit for such use if the geyser has been disconnected in the circumstances described?'

I can not see any conceivable distinction between what has been described by the learned trial judge as a common practice which is and always has been, in this context, and a custom. I, therefore, conclude that on the true construction of special warranty number (ii), having regard to the findings of the learned trial judge, the use of the galley was part of the customary overhaul and ancillary to it and not a failure exactly to comply with this special warranty. The ground, therefore, on which the learned trial judge found against the plaintiff must, in my view, fail.

Keating v New Ireland Assurance Co. plc [1990] ILRM 110
(Facts on p. 581.)

Walsh J.:

. . .

Insurers may stipulate for any warranty they please and if an assured undertakes that warranty, although it may be something not within his or her knowledge, he or she must abide the consequences. But when insurers intend that there is to be a warranty of that sort they must make it perfectly plain that such is their intention and they must use unequivocal language, such as persons with ordinary intelligence may without any difficulty understand. No such language is to be found in the proposal form in the present case. What has been sought to be established in the present case is that there was a warranty which amounted to a pure and absolute condition that the proposer was a good life irrespective of his knowledge of the subject. Therefore it would follow that because it subsequently transpired that the proposer had, although unknown to himself, such an impairment of his health as not to be a good life the contract would be void upon that fact being established. In a case where there is such a warranty or condition then nothing need be told but it must in subsequent litigation, if that question is raised, be proved that the life in fact was a good one. Even in such circumstances the life may be a good one even though it may be suffering from some particular infirmity. The question would be whether it was in a reasonably good state of health and was such that it could be insured on ordinary common terms.

A life insurance contract is in essence a wagering contract. In a life policy obviously it is not a wager that the assured would never die.

It is appropriate to recall the words of Lord Mansfield in *Ross v Bradshaw* (1761) 1 Wm Bl 312 that: ' . . . such a warranty could never mean that a man has not in him the seeds of some disorder. We are all born with the seed of mortality in us. A man, subject to the gout, is a life capable of being insured, if he has no sickness at the time to make it an unequal contract.'

If the present case had been one of warranty or pure condition then the insured would have taken it upon themselves to prove in the case of death that at the time the insurance was effected the parties were in such a good state of health as not to suffer from anything which was dangerous to life at the time of the insurance. If it was proved that he simply had some ailment which was troublesome or inconvenient but not a danger to his life then there would have been no breach of the warranty. In the present case the condition of angina was a danger to life but the policy was not written on the basis of a warranty. Therefore the insurers took the risk upon themselves and cannot avoid the policy unless they can prove that there was a misrepresentation fraudulent or innocent in some material circumstance.

In my view, that has not been established from the evidence and the policy therefore cannot be avoided.

McCarthy J.:

. . .

The legal basis
S. 2 of the policy reads:

> 1. Legal basis
> (a) The policy is conditional upon full and true disclosure having been made in the proposal and medical statement, if any, of all material facts of which the company ought to have been informed for the purposes of the contract of assurance.
> (b) The allocation of units to the policy shall not constitute the company or any other person a trustee of such units on behalf of the owner of the policy.

Accepting, as he does for the purpose of this part of the argument, that neither the deceased nor the plaintiff were aware of the heart condition, counsel for the insurer contends that on the true construction of the policy, combined with the proposal form, there was an absolute warranty by the deceased as to the state of his health; that his health was not as warranted and, accordingly, the insurer was entitled to repudiate liability under the policy. In short, he says, the deceased warranted the answer to be correct—it was not correct. It is argued that it is immaterial that the insured believed his health to be satisfactory save as to the stomach upset, if the fact was that he had a heart condition. He points to the declaration contained in the proposal form:

> We, the proposer/s and the life/lives proposed, have read the statements and answers written in this proposal and we declare that they are true and complete.
> I/we, the proposer/s, agree that they, together with the written statements and answers, if any, made or to be made by the life/lives proposed to the company's medical examiner in connection with the proposal and together also with this declaration, shall form the basis of the proposed contract between me/us and the company.
> I/we, the proposer/s, hereby apply for a policy subject to such privileges, terms and conditions as are contained in the policy ordinarily used by the company for a contract of the kind proposed.
> I, the life proposed and I, the second life proposed, hereby respectively consent to the company seeking information from any doctor who at any time has attended me and from any insurance office to which at any time a proposal of insurance of any kind on my life has been made and I authorise the giving of such information.

Such declarations and provisions are known as 'basis of the contract' clauses. The contention is that their effect in law is that all answers in the proposal form are incorporated into the contract as warranties and that, if any one of them is inaccurate, the insurer may repudiate the contract for breach of warranty without regard to the materiality of the particular answer to the risk (see *Thomson v Weems* (1884) 9 App Cas 671, 689). The corollary is that the fact that the insured may have answered the questions in good faith and to the best of his knowledge and belief is irrelevant if the answers are in fact inaccurate. It is not difficult to think of instances where a serious symptomless condition exists affecting the life expectancy of a proposer for insurance and is unknown and unknowable; yet if he were to die and it be discovered that such condition had existed at the time of the creation of the contract of insurance, the contract, it is said, is vitiated. In support of this argument, counsel for the insurer relied upon a wealth of authority as cited in *MacGillivray and Parkington* (8th ed.) at paras 732 and 737 and cited some of the authorities (*Duckett v Williams* (1834) 2 Cr & M 348, *McDonald v Law Union* (1874) LR 9 QB 328, *Thomson v Weems* (1884) 9 App Cas 671, *Reid & Co. v Employers Accident* [1898] SC (1031). In *Duckett v Williams* (1834) 2 Cr & M 348 an insurance company in proposing a re-insurance of its risk on a life policy stated in the proposal that it agreed that if any untrue answers were contained in the proposal or if the facts required to be set forth therein were not truly stated the insurance would become void. It was held that 'untrue' did not mean untrue to the knowledge of the party but simply 'inaccurate' without reference to his knowledge. But in *Joel v Law Union and Crown* [1908] 2 KB 863 at 886, Fletcher Moulton L.J. appeared to question this when he said:

> To make the accuracy of these answers a condition of the contract is a contractual act, and if there is the slightest doubt that the insurers have failed to make clear to the man on whom they have exercised their right of requiring full information that he is consenting thus to contract, we ought to refuse to regard the correctness of the answers given as being a condition of the validity of the policy. In other words, the insurers must prove by clear and express language the *animus contrahendi* on the part of the applicant; it will not be inferred from the fact that questions were answered, and that the party interrogated declared that his answers were true.

It was in the course of that judgment that Fletcher Moulton L.J. said at 885: 'Unfortunately the desire to make themselves (insurance companies) doubly secure has made them depart widely from this position by requiring the assured to agree that the accuracy, as well as the *bona fides*, of his answers to various questions put to him by them or on their behalf shall be a condition of the validity of the policy. . . . I wish I could adequately warn the public against such practices on the part of the insurance offices.'

In *Zurich General Insurance Co. v Morrison* [1942] 1 All ER 529 Lord Greene M.R. at 537 described such clauses as being traps for the insured. In *Anderson v Fitzgerald* (1853) 4 HL Cas 484 Lord St Leonards (the dual Lord Chancellor) was of opinion that to give effect to such a clause would render the policy not worth the paper upon which it was written and liable to produce a result whereby (at 514):

> No prudent man (would) effect a policy of insurance with any company without having an attorney at his elbow to tell him what the true construction of the document is.
> A policy ought to be so framed that he who runs can read. It ought to be framed with such deliberate care that no form of expression by which, on the one hand, the party assured can be cut, or by which, on the other, the company can be cheated shall be found upon the face of it. Nothing ought to be wanting in it, the absence of which may lead to such results.

Whilst acknowledging that parties are free, subject to legislative interference; to make such lawful contracts as they may wish, in my view there are certain clear principles that must be applied in construing a contract of insurance of the kind with which the court is presently concerned. Some of these may be stated as follows:

1. Parties of full age and competence are, subject to any statutory impediment, entitled to contract as they wish.

2. Whilst acknowledging the right of parties to express the pre-contract representations as being the basis of the contract, same must be read in the light of the actual terms of the contract subsequently executed. The contract, so to speak, takes over from the proposal.

3. If insurers desire to found the contract upon any particular warranty, it must be expressed in clear terms without any ambiguity.

4. If there is any ambiguity, it must be read against the persons who prepared it (see *Anderson v Fitzgerald* at 503, 507, 514 and *Thomson v Weems* at 682, 687).

5. Like any commercial contract, such a policy must be given a reasonable interpretation.

'The policy is conditional upon full and true disclosure' means that it is a condition of the policy that there has been full and true disclosure. Disclosure can, plainly, be only of matters within the knowledge of the person making the disclosure. What are to be disclosed are 'all material facts of which the company ought to have been informed for the purposes of the contract of assurance.' This must be construed as related to the questions asked in the proposal form and in the answers to the examining doctor. As the learned trial judge said in his observation of enviable brevity when dealing with this matter—'How can it be said that a person ought to disclose some fact which he does not know about?'

How is the proposer for life insurance to comply with the requirement of full and true disclosure in answer to questions in a proposal form and from the medical examiner of all material facts of which the company ought to have been informed, if he does not know of some fact of which the company might well say it ought to have been informed? To read s. 2 (the legal basis) as conveying a warranty that the proposer is accepting a contract on the basis that he has disclosed something of whose existence he was wholly ignorant is demonstrably an irrational interpretation. It is neither irrational nor inappropriate in seeking to find a reasonable interpretation of a commercial contract to pose the question as to how the casual onlooker or, indeed, the officious bystander, would react if told of the construction favoured by one party or another. I would think such an individual would react in more forceful terms than those used by Fletcher Moulton L.J. as I have quoted. An alternative test of reasonable interpretation may be to extend Lord St Leonards' observation thus. If the proposal form were to contain a statement by the proposer that the statements and answers written in the proposal together with the written statements and answers made to the company's medical examiner shall form the basis of the proposed contract 'even if they are untrue and incomplete for reasons of which I am wholly unaware', would there be any takers for such a policy?

In my judgment, upon a reasonable interpretation of what is called the legal basis of the policy, the insurer has failed to establish either material non-disclosure or a breach of warranty as alleged. . . .

SECTION THREE—FRAUD

Since the policy holder is under a duty to observe the utmost good faith in dealings with the insurers, a fraudulent claim will result in the invalidation of the contract, whether there is a condition to that effect or not.

The definition of 'fraud' for the purposes of an insurance contract differs slightly from the common-law definition.

Fagan *v* General Accident Fire and Life Assurance (HC) 19 February 1993, unrep.

The defendants issued a policy insuring the contents of the plaintiff's house. Following a fire the plaintiff put in a large claim in respect of his loss. The defendants attempted to repudiate the policy stating that the plaintiff's claim was grossly exaggerated and that the values set out in the claim, in respect of the individual items, were in many cases grossly inflated. Furthermore they noted that the explanations given by the plaintiff in respect of the existence and the value of many of the items were unsatisfactory and often contradictory. Certain claims were submitted for items which were subsequently withdrawn and were later admitted not to have been damaged or to have already been claimed under a different heading.

Murphy J.:

. . .

There was no dispute between counsel on behalf of the parties as to the nature of the duty of an insured in putting forward a claim on foot of a policy of insurance. Obviously the insured must refrain from making any statement which is fraudulent in any material respect and in that context 'a claim is false not only if it is deliberately invented but also if it is made recklessly, not caring whether it is true or false but only seeking to succeed in the claim' see *Lek and Mathews* 1927 29 LL LR 141 at 145. In addition, the duty to exercise the utmost good faith (upon which attention is more frequently focused at the stage when the assurance company is considering whether or not to accept the risk offered) continues throughout the relationship up to and including the making of a claim on foot of a policy. Mr Justice Hirst dealt with that aspect of the matter in *Black King Shipping Corp. and Massie* 1985 1 LL LR 437 at 512 in the following terms:

> Moreover, in the leading and now authoritative textbook, the law relating to fire insurance, by Baker Wellford and Otter-Barry (4th ed., 1948) the paragraph under the heading 'fraudulent claims' on p. 289 starts: 'Since it the duty of the assured to observe the utmost good faith in his dealings with the insurers throughout, the claim which he puts forward must be honestly made . . . .' However, in contrast to the pre-contract situation, the precise ambit of the duty in the claims context has not been developed by the authorities; indeed no case has been cited to me where it has been considered outside the fraud context in relation to claims. It must be right, I think, . . . to go so far as to hold that the duty in the claims sphere extends to culpable misrepresentation or non-disclosure.

The consequence of making a fraudulent claim is summarised in *MacGillivray and Parkington* (8th ed.) at para. 1926 in the following terms:

The law is, that a person who has made such a fraudulent claim could not be permitted to recover at all. The contract of insurance is one of perfect good faith on both sides, and it is most important that such good faith should be maintained. It is common practice to insert in fire policies conditions that they should be void in the event of a fraudulent claim; and there was such a condition in the present case. Such a condition is only in accordance with legal principle and sound policy. It would be dangerous to permit parties to practice such frauds, and then, notwithstanding their falsehood and fraud, to recover the real value of the goods consumed. And if there is wilful falsehood and fraud in claim, the insured forfeits all claim whatever upon the policy.

The author having quoted the foregoing passage from *Britton and Royal Insurance Co.* 1866 4F and F905 went on to say as follows: 'The clause is most frequently invoked where the assured includes a claim for goods which he either never had or disposed of before the fire. It may also be invoked where the assured makes a deliberate over-valuation of the stock . . .'

Attention was also directed to the decision of the Supreme Court in *Banco Ambrosiano and Ansbacher* [1987] ILRM 669. Counsel on behalf of the company referred to that judgment as authority for the proposition that the onus of proof in a case of fraud is no more and no less than the ordinary burden of proof in a civil action. Counsel on behalf of Mr Fagan drew attention to the remarks of Mr Justice Henchy in the same judgment to the effect that the inference of fraud must not be drawn lightly or without due regard to all the relevant circumstances (p. 702). Counsel on behalf of the company referred to the observations of the Official Referee in *Albian Mills and Hill* 1922 Lloyd's Rep. where (at p. 98) the Official Referee said in relation to a claim under a policy of insurance as follows:

What was the motive for making this claim in this way? Whether there was a motive or not is immaterial. It was made by the man who was trusted by the plaintiffs, and one cannot suppose that he did not know perfectly well what he was doing. I believe there was ample motive having regard to Mr Harry Simmons' position. I have come to the conclusion that the plea of fraud has been made out and therefore I have not gone into the question as to whether there was fraud in the prices charged.

. . .

The company has contended originally and proved in the course of the hearing that the insured has ascribed values or prices to a small but significant number of goods which were grossly excessive. Counsel for the insured emphasised the problems with which the insured was faced in compiling the various lists discussed in evidence. It was not surprising—counsel argued—that errors, even substantial errors, should arise with regard to the value or cost of a relatively small number of the goods in the circumstances. If such errors occurred or if, in the absence of specific information or appropriate documentation, the insured had claimed for figures which were excessive in the sense that they represented an extremely optimistic view of the value of the items in question, that would not, in my view, justify the company in repudiating liability on foot of the policy.

This was not a case in which an insured sought to correct or explain errors or to revise claims proved to be unsupportable. So far from it the insured and his family sought to justify as correct facts and figures which, in my view, were untrue.

. . .

In the circumstances it seems to me to have been established on the evidence as a whole that the insured, in breach of both his general and contractual obligations to the company, claimed a loss under the policy based on figures which were deliberately over-stated in the original claims and persisted in on the hearing of the action. In those circumstances it seems to me that the company is entitled to repudiate liability on foot of the policy issued by it and to have such declaration as may be necessary to give effect to that decision.

Orakpo v Barclays Insurance Services, Court of Appeal 29 March 1994, unrep.

The plaintiff claimed for damages for loss of rent from thirteen bedsitter flats caused by flooding, storms and vandalism. The insurance company defended as to liability claiming that the claim was fraudulent as only three of the flats had been occupied when the storm and flood damage occurred and only one when the vandalism occurred.

The first judge held that the claim was fraudulent with the result that all the benefit under the insurance policy was forfeited. Mr Orakpo appealed.

Hoffmann L.J.:

. . .

. . . In principle insurance is a contract of good faith. I do not see why the duty of good faith on the part of the assured should expire when the contract has been made. The reasons for requiring good faith continue to exist. Just as the nature of the risk will usually be within the peculiar knowledge of the insured, so will the circumstances of the casualty; it will rarely be within the knowledge of the insurance company. I think that the insurance company should be able to trust the assured to put forward a claim in good faith. Any fraud in making the claim goes to the root of the contract and entitles the insurer to be discharged. One should naturally not readily infer fraud from the fact that the insured has made a doubtful or even exaggerated claim. In cases where nothing is misrepresented or concealed, and the loss adjuster is in as good a position to form a view of the validity or value of the claim as the insured, it will be a legitimate reason that the assured was merely putting forward a starting figure for negotiation. But in cases in which fraud in the making of the claim has been averred and proved, I think it should discharge the insurer from all liability. It is true that an express term to this effect is commonly inserted into insurance policies and that there is no such term in this one. But in my view the direction to the jury by Willes J. in *Britton v The Royal Insurance Co.* [1866] F & F, is sufficient authority for holding that such a term is implied by law as one which, in the absence of contrary agreement, it would be reasonable to regard as forming part of a contract of insurance: see Lord Cross of Chelsea in *Liverpool City Council v Irwin* [1877] AC 239, 257 H to 258 A, 13 HLR 38; see also Hirst J. in The 'Litsian Pride', (*Black King Shipping Corp. and Wayang (Panama) SA v Massie*) [1985] 1 Lloyd's Rep. 437, 518.

Sir Roger Parker:

. . .

On what basis can an assured who asserts, for example, that he has been robbed of five fur coats and some valuable silver, when he has only been robbed of one fur and no silver, be allowed, when found out, to say, 'You must still pay me for the one of which I was truly robbed'? I can see none and every reason why he should not recover at all. Just as on inception the insurer has to a large extent to rely on what the assured tells him, so also is it so when a claim is made. In both cases there is therefore an incentive to honesty, if the assured knows that, if he is fraudulent, at least to a substantial extent, he will recover nothing, even if his claim is in part good. In my view, the law so provides. . . .

(The appeal was dismissed.)

SECTION FOUR—MATERIAL CIRCUMSTANCES IN MARINE INSURANCE CONTRACTS

Pan Atlantic Insurance Co. Ltd and Another *v* Pine Top Insurance Co. Ltd [1995] 1 AC 501

A 'material circumstance' in s. 18 of the Marine Insurance Act 1906 was one that would have an effect, not necessarily a decisive influence, on the mind of the prudent underwriter in deciding whether to accept the risk or as to the premium to be charged.

To avoid a contract for non-disclosure of a material circumstance he had to show that he had been induced by the non-disclosure to enter into the policy on the relevant terms.

The House of Lords (Lord Templeman and Lord Lloyd dissenting on the first point) dismissed an appeal by the plaintiffs, Pan Atlantic and Republic Insurance Co. acting on their own behalf and on behalf of all members of the Pan Atlantic Group Reinsurance Syndicate and/or the Pan Atlantic Reinsurance Group in 1982, from the Court of Appeal (Sir Donald Nicholls, Vice-Chancellor, Lord Justice Farquharson and Lord Justice Steyn) (*The Times* 8 March 1993; [1993] 1 Lloyd's Rep. 496), who had dismissed the plaintiffs' appeal from Mr Justice Waller ([1992] 1 Lloyd's Rep. 101) who had dismissed their claims in their action against the defendants, Pine Top.

S. 17 of the 1906 Act provides: 'A contract of insurance is a contract based on the utmost good faith, and, if the utmost good faith be not observed by either party, the contract may be avoided by the other party.'

S. 18 provides: '(1) . . . the assured must disclose to the insurer, before the contract is concluded, every material circumstance which is known to the assured. . . . If the assured fails to make such disclosure, the insurer may avoid the contract.

(2) Every circumstance is material which would influence the judgment of a prudent insurer in fixing the premium, or determining whether he will take the risk . . . '

Lord Mustill:

said that although the issues arose under a policy of non-marine insurance, it was convenient to state them by reference to the 1906 Act since it had been accepted in argument, and was laid down in several authorities, that in relevant respects the common law relating to the two types of insurance was the same and that the Act embodied a partial codification of the common law.

Between 1977 and 1982 Pan Atlantic had written a quantity of direct American liability insurance. Much of that was 'long-tail' business, in which a long time might elapse before claims matured. Such business could involve the insurer in disastrous losses. The present case was no exception.

For 1977 to 1979 Pan Atlantic's casualty account had been reinsured with other insurers for excess of loss above a certain figure. For 1980, 1981 and 1982 Pine Top had been the reinsurer.

Disputes had subsequently arisen in relation to all three years. Judgment had been given in favour of Pan Atlantic in an action under 1980 and 1981 contracts. The present appeal was concerned only with its claim under the 1982 contract.

The basis on which Pine Top sought to avoid the 1982 contract on the ground of non-disclosure was the presentation that had been made by Pan Atlantic's broker to Pine Top's underwriter of the loss record for the previous years.

As against the disclosed losses of US$235,768 for the underwriting year 1981 it was common ground that the true losses had been US$468,168, that Pan Atlantic had had information about those additional losses available before the slip had been signed on 13 January 1982 and that those losses had not been disclosed.

The judge had upheld Pine Top's defence based on the understatement of the losses for 1981.

Two questions of law arose:

First, in considering the materiality of a circumstance under ss 18(2) and 20(2) of the 1906 Act, did it have to be shown that full and accurate disclosure would have led the prudent underwriter to a different decision on accepting or rating the risk or was a lesser standard of impact on his mind sufficient, and, if so, what was that lesser standard?

Second, was the establishment of a material misrepresentation or non-disclosure sufficient to enable the underwriter to avoid the policy, or was it also necessary that the misrepresentation or non-disclosure had induced the making of the policy, either at all or on the terms on which it had been made? If the latter, where did the burden of proof lie?

Both the judge and the Court of Appeal had been bound by the previous decision of the Court of Appeal in *Container Transport International Inc. v Oceanus Mutual Underwriting Association (Bermuda) Ltd* [1984] 1 Lloyd's Rep 476, (the CTI case).

The judge had directed himself (at p. 103) that the law laid down in the CTI case was that:

> any circumstance is material . . . if it . . .'would have had an impact on the formation of his opinion and on his decision-making process'.
>
> That is to say, 'judgment' was equal to 'formation of opinion' rather than the 'final decision.'
>
> The case also made clear that the test in relation to non-disclosure or misrep-resentation was influence on the judgment of a 'prudent insurer' and that thus the right to avoid did not depend on whether the particular insurer was influenced as a fact in relation to determining the premium he charged or in his decision whether or not to take the risk.

In the Court of Appeal, the Vice-Chancellor (at p. 508), with the concurrence of his brethren, had expressed his unease at the consequence to which inadvertent non-disclosure had led, for the result was that the reinsurer had avoided all liability for his own bad bargain and, moreover, had done so even though full disclosure would have resulted not in his declining to take the risk but only in an increased premium.

Justice and fairness would suggest that, when the inadvertent non-disclosure had come to light, what had been required was an adjustment in the premium or, perhaps, in the amount of cover, but those were not options available under English law.

In substance, the present was an appeal against the decision in the CTI case. Lord Justice Steyn had said that it had proved to be a remarkably unpopular decision not only in the legal profession but also in the insurance markets.

The books and articles produced in argument all adopted a critical stance. Nevertheless, although the unanimous disapprobation of the CTI case was striking, equally striking was the lack of unanimity about what exactly was wrong with it.

As to materiality, the main thrust of Pan Atlantic's argument was that the expression in ss 18(2) and 20(2) of the 1906 Act called for the disclosure only of such circumstances as would, if disclosed to the hypothetical prudent underwriter, have caused him to decline the risk or charge an increased premium.

His Lordship could not accept that argument. In the first place, he could not find the suggested meaning in the Act. The legislature had not said 'decisively influence' or 'conclusively influence'. It had left 'influence' unadorned. It therefore bore its ordinary meaning.

'Influence the mind' was not the same as 'change the mind'. The expression in ss 18(2) and 20(2) clearly denoted an effect on the thought processes of the insurer in weighing up the risk, quite different from words that might have been used but had not been, such as 'influencing the insurer to take the risk'.

Treating the matter simply as one of statutory interpretation, his Lordship would feel little hesitation in rejecting the test of decisive influence.

Having considered decisions and writings before and after 1906, he considered that the House was free to interpret ss 18(2) and 20(2) as proposed.

As to inducement, the question was as to the need, or otherwise, for a causal connection between the misrepresentation or non-disclosure and the making of the insurance contract.

Ss 17, 18(1) and 20(1) said that the other party or the insurer 'may avoid the contract'. There was no mention of a connection between the wrongful dealing and the writing of the risk.

But for that, his Lordship doubted whether it would nowadays occur to anyone that it would be possible for the underwriter to escape liability even if the matter complained of had had no effect on his processes of thought.

How did it happen that the Act seemed to contemplate that once a material misrepresentation or non-disclosure was established the underwriter had an invariable right to avoid?

His Lordship could not accept the proposition that the omission of an express requirement of inducement had been due to an oversight by the draftsman unless he was forced to do so by want of any other explanations. The draftsman, Sir Mackenzie Chalmers, had been a most learned and careful scholar.

There appeared to be three reasons why the Act might have taken the form that it had:

First, the common law had not required inducement and had been correctly reproduced by the Act. Second, the common law had required inducement but the promoters of the Act had wished the law to be changed and Parliament had changed it. Third, the common law had required inducement and the Act, properly understood, was to the same effect.

To make a choice one had to look behind the Act to the developing history of marine insurance law, and for that, again, particular regard had to be paid to the scholarly writings, the older cases having practically nothing useful to say on the matter.

Having done so, his Lordship concluded that there was to be implied into the Act a requirement that neither a material misrepresentation nor a wrongful non-disclosure would entitle the underwriter to avoid the policy unless it had induced the making of the contract, using 'induced' in the sense in which it was used in the general law of contract. The contrary view expressed in the CTI case should not be upheld. His Lordship's conclusion held good also for non-marine insurance.

As to the facts, his Lordship agreed with Lord Lloyd that the misrepresentation by Pan Atlantic had been material and that the position regarding causation was so clear that the appeal could be decided in favour of Pine Top without the need for remittal to the judge.

Lord Lloyd (dissenting in part):

said that, taken as a whole, the phrase 'would influence the judgment of a prudent insurer' pointed to something more than what the prudent insurer would want to know, or take into account. At the very least it pointed to what the prudent insurer would perceive as increasing, or tending to increase, the risk.

If one analysed the phrase word for word, the ordinary meaning of 'influence' was to affect or alter.

'Judgment' in a legal or quasi-legal context was often used in the sense of a decision or determination. Lord Justice Kerr in the CTI case had considered (at p. 492) that it meant not the decision itself but the decision-making process, but his Lordship saw no reason to give it that meaning in the present context.

In a commercial context, 'judgment' was often used in the sense of 'assessment'.

A market assessment meant a judgment as to what the market was going to do, not the process by which a stockbroker arrived at that judgment. That was the sense in which 'judgment' was used in s. 18(2) of the 1906 Act.

His Lordship's provisional conclusion, before going to the authorities, was that to avoid a contract for non-disclosure it had to be shown that a prudent insurer, if he had known of the undisclosed fact, would either have declined the risk altogether or charged an increased premium.

Having considered the authorities, his Lordship's view was that they did not help greatly one way or the other but on balance were in favour of Pan Atlantic's argument.

As to inducement, there were two separate but closely related questions to ask: had the misrepresentation or non-disclosure induced the actual insurer to enter into the contract on the terms in question, and would the prudent insurer have entered into the contract on the same terms if he had known of the misrepresentation or non-disclosure immediately before the contract had been concluded?

If both questions were answered in favour of the insurer he would be entitled to avoid the contract, but not otherwise. On the facts, the judge's conclusions had to be accepted.

(Lord Templeman agreed with Lord Lloyd; Lord Goff agreed with Lord Mustill and Lord Slynn agreed with Lord Mustill.)

EXERCISES

Examine the 17 July 2007 *Consultation Paper on Insurance Contract Law*, published jointly by the English Law Commission and the Scottish Law Commission; a summary of the Consultation Paper is available at *www.lawcom.gov.uk/docs/cp* 182 summary pdj. The Consultation Paper makes a distinction between consumer insurance and business insurance and suggests significant adjustments to the law, such as the abolition of consumer's duty to volunteer information, replacing this with a duty to answer questions honestly and reasonably. Remedies would be based on misrepresentation with distinctions between types of misrepresentation being drawn. The abolition of fact warranties or basis of contract clauses is also proposed and significant adjustments to warranties and standard terms in insurance contracts are proposed.

Chapter Twelve

Capacity to Contract

Certain categories of person are deemed to lack the legal capacity to enter into binding contracts.

SECTION ONE—INFANTS

The Age of Majority Act 1985

2. (1) Where a person has not attained the age of twenty-one years prior to the commencement of this Act, he shall, subject to *section* 4, attain full age:

    (a) on such commencement if he has attained the age of eighteen years or is or has been married, or

    (b) after such commencement when he attains the age of eighteen years or, in case he married before attaining that age, upon his marriage.

(2) *Subsection* (1) applies for the purposes of any rule of law and, in the absence of a definition or of any indication of a contrary intention, for the construction of 'age of majority', 'full age', 'infancy', 'infant', 'minor', 'minority' and of other cognate words and expressions in

    (a) any statutory provision passed or made before, on or after the commencement of this Act, and

    (b) any deed, will, court order or other instrument (not being a statutory provision) made on or after such commencement.

Irish Current Law Statutes Annotated at 85/2–11 (Binchy)

It is arguably a policy of debatable merit that where, for example, an immature minor aged between sixteen and eighteen contracts a marriage voidable on the ground of incapacity to form a caring or considerate relationship, he or she should on that account lose minority status. The practical implications of this general question are reasonably significant. One of the main purposes of the legislation is to encourage banks, building societies and other businesses to enter into contracts with young people without fear of having the contracts later set aside because the young people were not of full age. If, in order to attain full age, a marriage must be neither void or voidable—a fact very difficult, if not impossible, for outsiders to determine—then the commercial institutions may be cautious about entering into contracts with persons under the age of eighteen who have married. This issue provokes consideration of a wider question, which has application even where the marriage is valid. To what extent will the statutory conferment of full age on a person of eighteen or younger guarantee that third parties may contract with that person with confidence that the contract may not be vitiated on the ground of undue influence, inequality of bargaining power or lack of mental capacity?

The purpose of the law of infants is to protect infants against their own lack of experience, while simultaneously protecting adults who unwittingly enter into contracts with infants. The general rule is that an infant is not bound by his or her contract. However, certain contracts with minors are valid. These include contracts for necessaries or for beneficial contracts of service. In addition, certain types of contract are binding on the minor until repudiated by the minor.

A. CONTRACTS THAT ARE BINDING ON THE MINOR

Contracts for Necessaries

The concept of a 'necessary' has been the subject of both judicial and legislative interpretation.

Sale of Goods Act 1893 section 2

Capacity to buy and sell is regulated by the general law concerning capacity to contract, and to transfer and acquire property:

Provided that where necessaries are sold and delivered to an infant, or minor, or to a person who by reason of mental incapacity or drunkenness is incompetent to contract, he must pay a reasonable price therefor.

Necessaries in this section mean goods suitable to the condition in life of such infant or minor or other person, and to his actual requirements at the time of the sale and delivery.

Note

The Irish Law Reform Commission *Report on Minors' Contracts* (LRC 15–1985) at Chapter 2 criticised the ambit of the category of necessaries as 'imprecise'.

Nash *v* Inman [1908] 2 KB 1

Cozens-Hardy M.R.:

The plaintiff sues for goods sold and delivered. The defendant pleads infancy. The plaintiff must then reply, 'The goods sold were necessaries within the meaning of the definition in s. 2 of the Sale of Goods Act, 1893.' It is not sufficient, in my view, for him to say, 'I have discharged the onus which rests upon me if I simply shew that the goods supplied were suitable to the condition in life of the infant at the time.' There is another branch of the definition which cannot be disregarded. Having shewn that the goods were suitable to the condition in life of the infant, he must then go on to shew that they were suitable to his actual requirements at the time of the sale and delivery. Unless he establishes that fact either by evidence adduced by himself or by cross-examination of the defendant's witnesses, as the case may be, in my opinion he has not discharged the burden which the law imposes upon him.

Skrine *v* Gordon (1875) 9 IR CL 479

Lawson J.:

The question argued before us was whether the learned baron was right in leaving the question to the jury; i.e. whether there was any evidence fit to be submitted to a jury that the hunter was a necessary article for an infant in the defendant's position . . . we consider that there was no evidence proper to be submitted to a jury to find that a hunter was a necessary for the defendant. *Ryder v Wombell* LR 4 Ex. 32 correctly lays down the principles applicable to this case. And we think that, as shown by that case, the question of 'necessaries', or 'not necessaries', is one of fact for the jury; but, like all other questions of fact, it should not be left to the jury by the judge unless there is evidence on which they can reasonably find in the affirmative. . . . Of course we all know that hunting is a good sport and a manly exercise, but still that only shows it is a sport, and luxuries or amusement are quite distinct from necessaries.

Consider:

Are luxurious items of utility, such as caviar, necessaries?

Beneficial Contracts of Service

As the cases below demonstrate, this exception depends on both a finding as to the nature of the contract, i.e. a contract of service or similar apprenticeship-type contract, and a finding as to the effect of the contract.

De Francesco *v* Barnum [1890] 45 ChD 430

Fry L.J.:

I approach this subject with the observation that it appears to me that the question is this, Is the contract for the benefit of the infant? Not, Is any one particular stipulation for the benefit of the infant? Because it is obvious that the contract of apprenticeship or the contract of labour must, like any other contract, contain some stipulations for the benefit of the one contracting party, and some for the benefit of the other. It is not because you can lay your hand on a particular stipulation which you may say is against the infant's benefit, that therefore the whole contract is not for the benefit of the infant. The court must look at the whole contract, having regard to the circumstances of the case, and determine, subject to any principles of law which may be ascertained by the cases, whether the contract is or is not beneficial. That appears to me to be in substance a question of fact.

Keays *v* The Great Southern Rly Co. [1941] IR 534

The plaintiff, a twelve-year-old girl, sued the defendant for injuries sustained as a result of the defendant's negligence. The defendant claimed that as the plaintiff was a holder of a 'school season ticket' issued at a reduced price, she was bound by the conditions applying to such tickets, one of which absolved the defendant from all liability for injuries caused by their negligence. Counsel for the plaintiff argued that as an infant she should not be bound by a contract which was not for her benefit. Counsel for the defendant argued that the contract considered as a whole was for her benefit as it allowed her get a better education than was available locally by travelling to the city at a cheap rate.

Hanna J.:

An important point is raised in this case, namely, that by reason of the contract that was made by the railway company with the plaintiff, she is disentitled to maintain any action for injuries received through the negligence of the company's servants. This matter has been decided forty-six years ago in Flower's case [1894] 2 QB 65, and that decision has been accepted as the law, both in this country and in England, for that long period. It is a clear enunciation by eminent judges that, in considering a contract of this kind made with an infant, the court has to peruse and consider the entire contract to decide whether it is for the benefit of the infant. . . . In this case, the benefit to the infant is to be carried for 6s 3d per month, but her common law rights are entirely wrested from her by the clauses in the contract, which prevent her from making a claim against the railway company for any injury she may sustain through any negligence on the part of the company, or the servants of the company. It goes even further: that, in the case of her death, her parents or representatives are prohibited by the terms of the contract from making a claim that might otherwise be sustainable. These conditions are contained in a large notice which is properly put up, both in Irish and English, somewhere in the booking office. . . .

I am of opinion that the contract in this case is very unfair to the infant because it deprives her of practically every common law right that she has against the railway company in respect of the negligence of themselves or their servants. For that reason, I think it is not for her benefit, and accordingly, her case must go to the jury on ordinary principles of law, namely, whether the servants of the company were guilty of negligence, and whether there was any negligence on the part of the plaintiff.

Harnedy v The National Greyhound Racing Co. Ltd IR [1944] 160

The plaintiff sued the defendant for damages for negligence or alternatively for breach of contract as a result of injuries sustained by her dog. The dog was injured during a race organised by the defendant as part of a greyhound auction. The plaintiff was nine years of age at the time of the accident

Geoghegan J.:

The terms of the contract are to be found on the face of the entry form, in the 'Conditions of Sale' printed on the back, and on the front cover of the catalogue prepared by the defendants for the purpose of the sale. The entry form declares that the defendants 'accept no responsibility for accidents or disease during trials or sales', and the catalogue contains a similar provision together with a notice stating that 'the National Greyhound Racing Co., Ltd, or the auctioneer accept no responsibility for loss or damage suffered or incurred whether from death, disease, accident or any other cause whatsoever to owners, trainers, or their charges during trials or sales.' The entry form and the catalogue constitute the contract. The effect of the contract, if binding on the infant plaintiff, is to relieve the company of all liability for negligence by its servants in connection with trials or sales of dogs held in pursuance of the contract. The comprehensiveness of the stipulation in the catalogue need not be stressed.

It follows that a person contracting with the defendants on this basis is deprived of certain rights which otherwise would be afforded to him by common law. Some of these rights might be of such a nature as to arise only in rare and unusual circumstances, but others might arise frequently. No doubt, an owner of a dog who sells the animal through the medium of the sales held by the defendants may obtain an enhanced price as compared with a sale by private negotiation or otherwise, but, in my opinion, the possible disadvantages from a legal standpoint flowing from the express terms of the contract to which I have adverted oblige me to disregard them as against this plaintiff, and to treat the special contract (taken as a whole) as one substantially to the detriment of the plaintiff. I must regard the sale as having been held on an open contract of employment affording no protection to the defendants against their common law liability for negligence. In arriving at this conclusion I have followed the decisions in *Keays v Great Southern Rly Co* [1941] IR 534 and *Flower v London and North Western Rly Co.* [1894] 2 QB 65. I have dealt with the law point relied upon by the defendants. No point was taken as to the authority of the plaintiff's father to offer for sale the plaintiff's dog.

Turning to the evidence before me I have come to the conclusion that, while in the conduct of their business generally the defendants and their servants did their work with skill, knowledge, and consideration for those with whom they were dealing, there was negligence in the present instance. It has been established that on the occasion in question the dogs were prematurely released by reason of a defect in the mechanism of the traps, thereby creating the danger that some of the dogs might be attacked and bitten by others. The premature opening of the door of the trap was the effective cause of the accident. This constitutes negligence on the part of the defendants, for which they are answerable to the plaintiff.

Proform Sports Management Ltd *v* Proactive Sports Management Ltd [2006] EWHC 2903

At the age of 15, Wayne Rooney entered into a player representation agreement with the claimants under which he appointed them to act as his agents and representatives. The defendants subsequently entered into a player representation agreement with Rooney and the claimants sued them *inter alia* for the tort of procuring a breach of their contract. The High Court had to determine whether the original contract was voidable on the grounds of Rooney's lack of capacity.

Judge Hodge Q.C.:

[Counsel for the defendants] submits that the law as to minors' contracts is correctly stated in *Chitty on Contracts*, 29th edn (2004), paras 8–004 to 8–005. Para 8–004 identifies the only contracts which are binding on the minor as contracts for necessaries. However, a diversity of meanings has been given to the word 'necessaries'. In one sense the term is confined to necessary goods and services supplied to the minor, but in another it extends to contracts for the minor's benefit and in particular to contracts of apprenticeship, education and service. Para 8–005 provides that, apart from contracts for necessaries and contracts of apprenticeship education and service, the general rule at common law is that a minor's contract is voidable at his option; i e not binding on the minor, but binding on the other party. As to other beneficial contracts, [Counsel for the defendants] relies on para 8–028:

> The principle that contracts beneficial to a minor are binding on him is not
> confined to contracts for necessaries and contracts of employment, apprenticeship

or education in a strict sense. It extends also to other contracts which in a broad sense may be treated as analogous to contracts of service, apprenticeship or education. So, for instance, a contract by a minor (who was a professional boxer) with the British Boxing Board of Control whereby he agreed to adhere to the rules of the board was held binding on him because he could not have earned his living as a boxer without entering into the agreement: see *Doyle v White City Stadium Ltd* [1935] 1 KB 110. Similarly, it has been held that an agreement between a minor and a publisher for the publication of the minor's biography which was to be written by a 'ghost writer', was binding on the minor: *Chaplin v Leslie Frewin (Publishers) Ltd* [1966] Ch 71. So also, a contract between a group of under-age musicians (known as 'The Kinks') whereby they appointed a company as their manager and agent, was held binding as analogous to a contract of employment.'—The authority cited is the first instance decision in *Denmark Productions Ltd v Boscobel Productions Ltd* (1967) 111 Sol J 715, reversed on other grounds by the *Court of Appeal* [1969] 1 QB 699. The footnote goes on to contrast that case and *Shears v Mendeloff* 30 TLR 342, where the contract contained oppressive terms and was void—'On the other hand there is no general principle to the effect that any contract beneficial to a minor is binding on him. So a minor's trading contracts are not binding on him, even if beneficial.'

Thus, two questions arise. First, whether the contract between Wayne Rooney and Proform falls within the class of contracts analogous to contracts for necessaries and contracts of employment, apprenticeship or education. Secondly, and only if the first question is answered in a positive sense, whether this particular contract was one which was beneficial to Wayne Rooney. [Counsel for the defendants] submits that a contract analogous to one of apprenticeship, education or employment is only enforceable against a minor if it is of benefit to him at the time when he enters into it. Where the contract contains terms, some of which are beneficial to him and others not, the question is whether, taken as a whole, the contract is to his advantage. The burden of showing benefit is always on the party seeking to uphold the contract. In his written skeleton argument [counsel for the defendant] poses the question whether the Proform agreement fell within the class of minors' contracts which were analogous to those of apprenticeship, education and service. He proposes a negative answer to that question. He says that Proform cannot show that the contract is so analogous. At the time when it was signed, Mr Rooney was already with a club, Everton, that was providing him with training. He had no need for any training from Proform. He submits that the Proform agreement makes no provision for training, education or instruction in any way. The absence of such provision was, he submits, the basis of the decision in *Shears v Mendeloff* 30 TLR 342 that the contract could not be construed as one for necessaries. *Shears v Mendeloff* was of course the case before Avory J, where a minor who was a professional boxer had appointed the plaintiff his sole manager on commission and agreed not to take any engagements under any other management without the plaintiff's consent for three years. Such a contract was held unenforceable against the infant, on the grounds that it was a trading contract, and also as one which could not be construed as being beneficial to him. [Counsel for the defendants] contrasts such a case with the decision in *Roberts v Gray* [1913] 1 KB 520, where the infant had entered into a contract to go on a tour as a professional billiard player. That contract was held to be one for necessaries and for his benefit. The Court of Appeal held the contract to be binding on him as a whole. [Counsel for the defendants] submits that the basis of the decision in that case was clearly that the contract could be construed as one for necessaries, because it was for teaching, instruction and employment. By contrast, he submits that the Proform agreement contains nothing which can be said to be analogous to instruction, education or training. Nor did the Proform agreement permit Mr Rooney to make a start as a footballer or enable him to earn a living. It is on that basis that he distinguishes the cases of *Chaplin v Leslie Frewin (Publishers) Ltd* [1966] Ch 71 and *Doyle v White City Stadium Ltd* [1935] 1 KB 110, which are authorities relied upon by [counsel for the claimant]. [Counsel for the defendants] submits that in those two cases the minor was enabled to earn a living by reason of a contract he entered into. That is not the position here. There was no payment being made to him. He was already contracted to Everton. That was all that he needed. He had no need of a contract to represent him as a professional footballer. He would on turning 17 be in a position to earn his living via a contract with Everton Football Club or any other club, and he had no need of an agreement with an agent to enable him to do so. Certainly he did not need to be bound to such an agent for two years. After all, he could not under the Football Association Rules sign a professional contract at the earliest until he was 17, assuming he was not then in full-time education; and he had no need of representation in his work as a professional footballer, as clause 1 of the Proform agreement stated.

[Counsel for the claimant] submits that the terms of the Proform contract speak for themselves. He relies upon the terms of Mr McIntosh's witness statement, which record that Proform was providing all the functions in respect of personal representation and management, advice and negotiation for the benefit of Wayne Rooney. That was intended to encompass all aspects of the services undertaken by the claimant for a player aged 17 years or under. He submits that the case falls squarely within the principle stated at para 8–028 of *Chitty*, that contracts beneficial to a minor, and which can thus be upheld, are not confined to contracts for necessaries and contracts of employment, apprenticeship or education in a strict sense. They extend also to other contracts which in a broad sense may be treated as analogous to contracts of service, apprenticeship or education. In any event, he submits that the defendants cannot establish—and the burden is upon them—that the claimant has no real prospect at trial of bringing the agreement within these principles. Whether the agreement is within the same must, he submits, be a mixed question of construction and fact.

I am conscious that on this issue I have . . . to be satisfied that the claimant has no real prospect of succeeding in establishing that the Proform agreement falls within the class of contracts analogous to those described as contracts for necessaries, contracts of employment, apprenticeship or education. Clearly Wayne Rooney's agreement with Everton Football Club would fall squarely within the class of contracts identified at para 8–028 of *Chitty*. However, it does seem to me that the same cannot be said of the Proform agreement. On the evidence, Mr Rooney was already engaged with Everton. Under the terms of the Football Association Rules, he could not enter into any contract of employment until he was 17, if then not in full-time education. Even if he entered into a contract with Everton when he was 17, that contract, if not for his benefit, would of course be voidable at his election. It does not seem to me that a contract in the terms of the Proform agreement, whereby Proform was to act as his executive agent and to carry out all the functions in respect of personal representation on behalf of his work as a professional football player, falls to be considered as analogous to the class of contracts considered at para 8–028 of *Chitty* . As I say, Mr Rooney was already with Everton on Mr McIntosh's own evidence. At this time, and indeed in 2002, Wayne Rooney only wanted to play for Everton; he did not wish to play for any other club. He was already doing so.

It does seem to me that the Proform agreement is much more analogous to the contract considered by Avory J. in *Shears v Mendeloff* 30 TLR 342 than it is to the class of contract considered in cases such as *Doyle v White City Stadium Ltd* [1935] 1 KB 110, *Chaplin v Leslie Frewin (Publishers) Ltd* [1966] Ch 71 and *Denmark Productions Ltd v Boscobel Productions Ltd* 111 Sol J 715 . As Mr Joffe submitted, music group mangers are very different from players' representatives. Music group managers organise matters that are essential to the very business of the musical artiste. Players' representatives do not undertake matters that are essential to the player's training or his livelihood. They do not enable the minor to earn a living or to advance his skills as a professional footballer. In my judgment, cases such as *Chaplin v Leslie Frewin (Publishers) Ltd* [1966] Ch 71 and *Doyle v White City Stadium Ltd* [1935] 1 KB 110 make it clear that the basis of the class of analogous contracts is that the minor is entitled to earn his living or to start to do so. It does not seem to me that the Proform agreement is analogous to such a contract. I say that particularly bearing in mind the fact that, under the Football Association Rules, no contract can be entered into by a player as young as Wayne Rooney then was. No contract could properly be entered into by him until a time less than two months before this representation agreement was due to expire; and even if entered into by Wayne Rooney at that time, it would have been voidable at his instance if not genuinely for his benefit. That would have continued to be so throughout the remaining short duration of the management and agency agreement. It seems to me that the Proform agreement is at one remove from the class of contract that has been treated in the authorities as being subject to the exception to the general voidability of minors' contracts, applicable where such a contract is for the minor's benefit. As para 8–028 of *Chitty* makes clear: 'A minor's trading contracts are not binding on him, even if beneficial.' It seems to me that this case falls within the general principle that merely because a contract is beneficial to a minor, if such is the case, it is not binding on him unless it falls within a particular category. So for those reasons, it seems to me that Counsel for the defendants] is correct in saying that the Proform agreement does not fall within the class of minors' contracts which are analogous to contracts of apprenticeship, education and service. On that footing, it is unnecessary for me to consider . . . whether the Proform agreement was for Mr Rooney's benefit.

Consider:

Would a contract entered into by a minor to employ an adult in the minor's plumbing business be valid?

B. CONTRACTS THAT ARE BINDING UNLESS AND UNTIL REPUDIATED BY A MINOR, GENERALLY DESCRIBED AS VOIDABLE CONTRACTS

Certain transactions which involve recuring obligations will be binding unless disaffirmed by the minor during or within a reasonable time after infancy. Examples include family settlements, insurance contracts, liability for share calls, contracts to enter partnerships and contracts concerning land. In *Paget v Paget* (1882) 11 LR (Ir.) 26, Law C. accepted the principle that 'if an infant, having executed a deed, repudiates it on attaining his majority, or within a reasonable time afterwards, the instrument thereupon becomes null and void *ab initio*, so far as he is concerned.' Thus in that case a minor who repudiated a re-settlement immediately upon learning that he had been a minor at the date of the re-settlement rendered the agreement void *ab initio*.

Stapleton *v* Prudential Assurance Co. Ltd (1928) 62 ILTR 56

A nineteen-year-old girl entered into a life assurance contract under a bona fide mistake as to the nature of its terms. She paid premiums until she was thirty, at which stage she sued the company for the return of her premiums. The Circuit Court Judge ordered that the premiums be returned.

Sullivan P.:

This was a continuing contract, and the plaintiff if she wished to repudiate it on attaining full age was bound to do so within a reasonable time. Even if she could now repudiate, it did not follow that the premiums should be returned to her. If she had died between 1916 and 1927, the company would have been bound to pay, so it could not be held that no consideration had passed during those years. Accordingly the Circuit Judge's decision should be reversed, but his Lordship hoped that the company might deal with the young lady in a way that the court could not order.

(O'Byrne J. agreed. The appeal was allowed with costs.)

Where a contract with recurring obligations is repudiated before or within a reasonable time of attaining majority, the future obligations which have yet to accrue need not be performed but the obligations which accrued before repudiation should be performed.

Blake *v* Concannon (1870) 4 IR CL 323

Pigot C.B.:

It appears to me now, upon a consideration of the grounds on which an infant is held to be liable where . . . his liability is established, if he does not waive or repudiate the tenancy and the land, that he ought to be held bound by that liability when it has been once attached to the payment of the rent which accrued while he has occupied, and before he has repudiated. He is not, in an action of debt for the rent, held liable upon the contract of tenancy alone. His liability arises from his occupation and enjoyment of the land, under the tenancy so created. If his liability arose from the contract alone, the repudiation of the contract, by annulling it, would annul its obligations, which would then exist only by reason of the contract. But the infant, though he can repudiate the contract of demise, and the tenancy under it, and can so revest the land in the landlord, cannot repudiate an occupation and enjoyment which are past, or restore to the landlord what he has lost by that occupation and enjoyment of the infant. The reason given by Justice Newton, in 21 Hen. 6, 31, b., lies at the root of the infant's liability: 'he has had a *quid pro quo*'. Though quaintly expressed, it is a reason sanctioned by common sense, and in accordance with plain justice. The infant owed the rent because he has an equivalent in the occupation and enjoyment of the lands. The authorities . . . appear to me sufficiently to indicate that, if the infant does not avoid the tenancy under which he occupies before the rent becomes due, the mere fact of infancy constitutes no defence. If, therefore, he continues so to occupy without repudiation, the landlord, on the accruing of the rent, has a vested right of suit against the infant for the rent which has so accrued.

C. Contracts Deemed Void by the Infants Relief Act 1874

The **Infants Relief Act 1874** regulates contracts for the repayment of money lent or to be lent to a minor, contracts for goods supplied or to be supplied to a minor and all accounts stated with minors. Sections 1 and 2 state as follows:

1. All contracts, whether by specialty or by simple contract, henceforth entered into by infants for the repayment of money lent or to be lent, or for goods supplied or to be supplied (other than contracts for necessaries), and all accounts stated with infants, shall be absolutely void: provided always that this enactment shall not invalidate any contract into which the infant may, by existing or future statute, or by the rule of common law or equity, enter, except such as now by law are voidable.
2. No action shall be brought whereby to charge any person upon any promise made after full age to pay any debt contracted during infancy, or upon any ratification made after full age of any promise or contract made during infancy, whether there shall or shall not be any new consideration for such promise or ratification after full age.

Treitel ('The Infants Relief Act 1874' 73 LQR 194) described it as 'a somewhat mysterious statute' and opined that 'no convincing reason has ever been advanced to explain exactly why it was passed'. He noted 'Its object may be gathered, in general terms, from the preamble: it is 'to amend the law as to the contracts of infants, and as to the ratification made by persons of full age of contracts made by them during infancy, and as to necessaries.' As regards the first section, this object has been largely, if not entirely, frustrated by the orthodox interpretation placed upon it. As regards the second section, the object has indeed been achieved, but the language of the section is such as to give rise to some unexpected and curious results.'

In *Nottingham Permanent Benefit Building Society v Thurstan* [1903] AC 6, a minor borrowed from the Building Society to purchase land and executed a mortgage to the Society. The mortgage was void as the promise to repay the law was ineffective under section 1 of the Infants Relief Act 1874, but the House of Lords held that the Society was entitled to stand in the shoes of the vendor and exercise the lien the latter would have over the property if he had not been paid. This principle was applied, albeit somewhat reluctantly, by the Majority of the Supreme Court of Victoria— Court of Appeal in *Horvath v Commonwealth Bank of Australia* [1999] 1 VR 643.

D. Reform

The **Irish Law Reform Commission Report on Minors' Contracts (1985) LRC 15** recommended adopting a restitutionary approach. It noted:

The restitutionary approach has been perceived by some lawyers as having several advantages. First, it will provide some degree of encouragement for adults to provide goods or services for minors. Although the adult will lose the chance of a profit in a case where the minor repudiates the contract, he will have a reasonable prospect of being restored (in part or in full) to the position he would have been in had he not made the contract.[1] It may be argued that, for responsible adults contemplating a contract with a minor, the prospect of a fair system of restitution will be a sufficient incentive to them to enter the contract, provided, of course, the independent commercial incentives are sufficient.

As against this it can be argued that it would be too narrow to regard contracts between adults and minors as necessarily isolated events. Commercial realities dictate otherwise. In many cases the adult (or business company) will not be contemplating making *a* contract with a minor, but will instead have to make a decision as to whether to contract with minors *as a class*. Whereas an adult contemplating a single contract with a minor might well be satisfied with the prospect of a restitutionary principle being applied if the minor seeks to resile from the contract, a large scale business concern might well be less enthusiastic where the risks are multiplied by the large number of possible contracts involved.

The second advantage to the restitutionary approach is that it goes a good way to ensuring that a minor may not, as he may under the present law, use the defence of minority as a means of wrongfully profiting at the expense of the adult.[2]

The third advantage of the restitutionary approach is that to some degree it resolves the problem where (under present law) a minor who repudiates a contract may be unable to recover money he has paid or the value of services he has rendered.

Of course, support for the introduction of the restitutionary principle as a general rule does not exclude the possibility of exceptions being made in the proposed legislation for specific categories of contract, where different rules may apply.

The restitutionary approach has not attracted universal support. The English Law Commission in its Working Paper No. 81, *Minors' Contracts*, published in 1982, criticised[3] the recommendations of the Latey Committee that had favoured the restitutionary approach.

One objection was that the Latey Committee had not put forward any detailed proposals or guidelines to be followed by the courts in determining the question of restitution. This of course is not, in itself, a fundamental objection to the restitutionary principle since it is possible for the legislation to include specific guidelines for the court—indeed the English Law Commission itself envisages and spells out possible detailed guidelines.

Another objection to the restitutionary principle is its uncertainty of application. The English Law Commission, in its examination of the Latey Committee's proposals, expressed this objection in the following terms:

The need for a relative degree of certainty in the law is, in our view, of very great importance. The law serves not only to solve disputes when they arise but also regulate conduct so as to avoid them. In order to avoid disputes the law must be reasonably certain in its application. If contracts are unenforceable against minors, that is, in most cases, the end of it. While such a rule may in some cases lead to unjust enrichment it also avoids much fruitless litigation. Those who know the law can take precautions against its abuse by unscrupulous minors. Potential abuse of the law or its procedures is not limited to minors; many adults avoid paying their just debts by refusing to pay and leaving the creditors to the expense of trying to trace them and of getting and enforcing a judgment. The best protection, as is widely known, is not to give credit to the untrustworthy.

Under the Latey Committee's proposals of a general duty to account, coupled with a relieving power in the court, the outcome of any case would be uncertain and this uncertainty would exist on several levels: on the valuation of the benefit conferred; on the question of whether the minor should be relieved of his liability to account; and, if so, on the extent to which such relief should go. These uncertainties would make out of court settlement less likely. The scheme might well cause some increase in litigation: and, in a large number of cases, there would be a need for legal aid on one or both sides.[4]

We appreciate the force of this argument but we consider that it overstates the problem. Obviously a rule of absolute enforceability 'avoids much fruitless litigation' but if the rule is not itself an entirely fair one[5] it seems to us that this factor should not be given much weight. So far as the likely volume of litigation is concerned, we do not consider that the existence of a judicial discretion would necessarily increase the incidence of litigation. It is of course, quite possible that, under the restitutionary principle, litigation would be threatened or commenced; we do not see this as necessarily a bad thing, and we do not consider that what the English Law Commission stigmatise as the 'uncertainties' of the restitutionary principle would make an out-of-court settlement significantly less likely than in the normal run of litigation.

Whether the restitutionary approach would leave the law in a more or less 'uncertain' condition is a matter of prediction on which there may be differing views[6] but we do not consider that a discretionary principle is to be dismissed on account of its very flexibility.

On balance we consider that the restitutionary principle affords the most satisfactory general approach for the proposed legislation to take. We consider that it best resolves the divergent policies of protecting minors against unscrupulous adults and the risks that their youthfulness and lack of experience involve, on the one hand, and of protecting the interests of adults who contract with minors in good faith, on the other. . . .

Summary of Recommendations

1. The legislation should introduce a general principle of restitution whereby a contract made by a minor with an adult party would be enforceable by the minor against the adult but unenforceable by the adult against him; the adult would, however, be entitled to apply to the court for compensation from the minor based on restitutionary rather than contractual principles.

2. The legislation should be drafted so as to enable the court in proceedings for restitution to grant to any party such relief by way of compensation or restitution of property or both as is proper, and, upon doing so, to discharge the parties from further obligations specified by the contract if it considers it proper to do so.

3. In making any order under these powers the court should have regard to:
   (a) the subject matter and nature of the contract;
   (b) where the contract relates (in part or entirely) to property, the nature and value of the property;
   (c) the age, mental capacity and general experience of the minor at the time of making the contract, and at the time of the hearing, respectively;
   (d) the specific experience and knowledge of the minor relative to the particular circumstances of the contract;
   (e) the respective economic circumstances of the parties, at the time of the making of the contract and at the time of the hearing, respectively;
   (f) the circumstances surrounding the making of the contract and, in particular, the reasonableness and fairness, or otherwise, of the conduct of each party relative thereto;
   (g) the extent and value of any actual benefit obtained by each party as a result of making the contract;
   (h) the amount, if any, of any benefit still retained by each party at the time of the hearing;

    (i)   the expenses or losses sustained and likely to be sustained by each party in the making and discharge of the contract;

    (j)   all other circumstances that appear to the court to be relevant.

4.   The legislation should not give any one of these factors greater weight than the others.

5.   The restitutionary principle should apply to both concluded transactions and to those that have not yet been concluded.

6.   The legislation should include a provision that, in exercising its discretion when applying the restitutionary principle in cases where the contract has been concluded, the court should have regard to the extent of the difficulties likely to result for the party who contracted with the minor from re-opening the contract.

7.   The legislation should provide that property passes in an unenforceable contract; a person who receives any property should not have to concern himself or herself as to whether the donor, grantor, vendor or lessor, as the case may be, derived the article from a minor; this should apply whether or not *bona fide* purchasers for value are involved. However, so far as the parties to the contract—the minor and adult (or other minor, as the case may be)—are concerned, the court should be free to make any order affecting title to the property (to the extent that either of them retains title) as it may consider proper, in its application of the restitutionary principle.

8.   The legislation should include specific provisions enabling the court, in applying the restitutionary principle, to have regard to whether the goods or services which were the subject matter of the contract were suitable to the condition in life of the minor and to his actual requirements at the time of the making of the contract, so far as the other party was, or could reasonably be, aware, having regard to the circumstances, including any information given by the minor on this question.

9.   Subject to recommendation 10, a contract of employment or for personal services should bind a minor if, taken as a whole, it is for his or her benefit.

10. Where the court finds that a contract, taken as a whole, is not for the minor's benefit, because it contains a particular term or terms, then, rather than being obliged to declare the contract unenforceable against the minor, the court should have power to strike out the term or terms in question, if severable from the rest of the contract. In exercising this power, the court should not be entitled to re-draft the contract, and the contract as enforced should be substantially the same as the original contract. The court should, moreover, take into account the interests of the employer before deciding to enforce the contract without the unduly onerous term or terms.

11. For the avoidance of doubt, the legislation should specifically provide that minority may be relevant in determining whether a covenant in restraint of trade is reasonable.

12. Minors' trading contracts should be governed by the restitutionary principle rather than treated in the same manner as employment contracts and contracts for personal services.

13. Contracts of loans to minors should continue to be void.

14. No action should be capable of being brought on a promise made after full age to pay any debt contracted during infancy.

15. A fresh promise after majority to pay a loan that is void in law, and any negotiable instrument given in respect of such a loan should be void and incapable of enforcement against a former minor.

16. Recommendations 13 to 15 should apply to all contracts of loans, including loans for necessaries.

17. Minors, once they come of age, should be free, if they wish, to ratify undertakings made during minority as well as to make new contracts with a fresh consideration with respect to such undertakings.
18. After a minor comes of age, a contract involving continuing obligations should become fully enforceable, with respect to obligations contracted and to be discharged by the parties whether before or after the minor comes of age.
19. The legislation should include a validation procedure, whereby approval may be obtained for a contract to which a minor is a party, and for the granting of contractual capacity (general or subject of limitations) to a minor.
20. Parents should not be given powers in respect of the validation procedure proposed in recommendation 19.
21. The courts should have jurisdiction to make an order validating contracts or granting contractual capacity. The District Court should have jurisdiction where the consideration of the contract or value of the property concerned does not exceed £2,500. The Circuit Court should have jurisdiction up to a value of £15,000; the High Court would have jurisdiction without monetary limit.
22. Any party to the contract should be permitted to apply to the court for an order for validation; but such application should be made only before the contract has been made or, if it has already been made, only when the contract contains a condition precedent that application for validation will be obtained.
23. As regards the considerations to be taken into account by the court in deciding whether or not to validate a proposed contract or confer contractual capacity (whether general or subject to limitations) the court should have regard to all the circumstances, but, without prejudice to the generality of this discretion, the court may take into account:

    (a) the age of the minor;
    (b) the nature, subject matter and terms of the contract;
    (c) the reasonable likelihood of performance of the contract by each of the parties to it;
    (d) the requirements of the minor, having regard to his particular circumstances;
    (e) the financial resources of the minor;
    (f) the wishes, where they can reasonably be ascertained, of the guardian or guardians of the minor.

24. Where a contract is made between minors, the law should not treat the minors as adults: the restitutionary principle should apply.
25. The legislation should retain the rule that a minor should not be exposed to an action in tort where this would amount to an indirect enforcement of an unenforceable contract.
26. The restitutionary principle should apply to cases of misrepresentation as to age.
27. A guarantor should not be relieved of liability in respect of a guarantee by reason only of the fact that the person in respect of whom the guarantee is given is a minor.
28. So far as the minor's relationship with the guarantor is concerned, the restitutionary principle should apply, whether or not the minor has entered into a binding contract.

[1.] Law Reform Commission of British Columbia, *Report on Minors' Contracts*, p. 49 (LRC 26–1976).
[2.] Ibid.

3. W.P. No. 81, paras 4.6–4.15.
4. Ibid., paras 4.12–4.13.
5. As the English Law Commission (para. 4.12) appeared willing to concede.
6. It is worthy of note that one commentator has commended the *Latey Report* as follows: 'The principal virtue of the recommendations is their simplicity and *the relative certainty which they would provide in the law*': Evans, 'The Need for Reform in the Law of Infants' Contracts—Some Comments on the Latey Report,' Auckland UL Rev 65 at 75 (1970) (emphasis added).

SECTION TWO—MENTAL INCAPACITY

Where a person seeks to take advantage of a person who is known to be mentally unsound by enforcing a contract against them, the Court will deem the person lacking in contractual capacity and the contract unenforceable. An exception will be made for necessaries.

In *Imperial Loan Co v Stone* [1892] 1 QB 599, Lord Esher M.R. stated that even where the person does not understand the transaction 'the contract is binding on him in every respect, whether it is executory or executed, unless he can prove further that the person with whom he contracted knew him to be so insane as not to be capable of understanding what he was about.' This was followed by the New Zealand Court of Appeal and Privy Council in *Hart v O'Connor* [1985] 3 WLR 214 where Lord Brightman stated 'in the opinion of their Lordships, the validity of a contract entered into by a lunatic who is ostensibly sane is to be judged by the same standards as a contract by a person of sound mind, and is not voidable by the lunatic or his representative by reason of "unfairness" unless such unfairness amounts to equitable fraud which would have enabled the complaining party to avoid the contract even if he had been sane.'

Notes

1. Compare this to *Hassard v Smith* (1872) 6 IR Eq 429 where Chatterton V.C. stated:

'The knowledge of the lunacy or incapacity . . . must be understood to mean not merely actual knowledge, but that which must be presumed, from circumstances known to the other contracting party, sufficient to lead any reasonable person to conclude that, at the time the contract was made, the person with whom he was dealing was of unsound mind.'

2. Where a person's lack of capacity renders them incapable of acting on their own behalf, they do not currently have the legal capacity to appoint an agent (*Drew v Nunn* (1879) 4 QBD 661).

Law Reform Commission Consultation Paper on Vulnerable Adults and the Law: Capacity (LRC CP 37-2005) [abridged footnotes]

Chapter 5 Capacity to Contract

(1) A Presumption of Capacity to Contract

5.34 The Commission believes that, rather than relying on the existing judicial test in *Hart v O'Connor* of whether the other party had reason to suspect that the person may lack capacity, the law relating to capacity to contract should be governed by a rebuttable legal presumption of capacity to contract. A presumption of capacity to contract is in line both with the general presumption of capacity and the functional approach to capacity which the Commission has embraced in this Consultation Paper. . . .

5.35 The effect would be that where a person rebutted the presumption of capacity to contract, the contract would be void rather than voidable. This would mean no longer deciding that a contract is voidable based on a test of whether a lack of capacity would have been reasonably apparent to the other party from the circumstances.

The Commission considers that any potential hardship to good faith suppliers who had no reason to suspect a lack of capacity would be considerably tempered by the addition of a revised 'necessaries rule' requiring persons lacking contractual capacity to pay a reasonable sum for goods and services supplied to them for daily living.Therefore it would generally only be where goods or services contracted for are out of the ordinary that the issue of capacity would need to receive real consideration. Furthermore, while not strictly concerned with capacity, the equitable doctrines concerning unconscionable bargains and undue influence may be of assistance in relation to contracts with vulnerable adults where the other party has abused a position of superior bargaining power.

5.36 The Commission envisages that a presumption of capacity to contract would be subsumed within the general statutory presumption of capacity which the Commission recommended in Chapter 3.

5.37 *The Commission recommends that a presumption of capacity to contract should form part of a statutory presumption of capacity.*

5.38 The onus would be on the party disputing contractual capacity to rebut the presumption of contractual capacity on the balance of probabilities. In the *Consultation Paper on Law and the Elderly* (LRC CP 23–2003), the Law Reform Commission recommended that the system of wardship be replaced by the appointment of a personal guardian or the making of one-off provision by means of an intervention or services order. A functional approach to capacity would mean that while the existence of a guardianship order, services order or intervention order could be adduced as supporting evidence of incapacity to contract, the making of such an order would not in itself be decisive of the issue.

(2) Adjudicating on Contractual Capacity

5.39 Building on the guardianship framework set out in the *Consultation Paper on Law and the Elderly*, the proposed capacity legislation could provide that any party to the contract, a personal guardian or other person connected with a party in respect of whom a lack of understanding is alleged85 could refer a contract to the Office of the Public Guardian. Where both sides agree a mediator could be appointed by the Public Guardian. If the matter is not resolved bymediation, the Public Guardian could be given power to examine the case and (a) declare that the transaction is binding on both parties; or (b) declare the transaction void and make any adjustment to the rights of the parties which it considers just having regard to the circumstances of the case. . . . Furthermore, in cases where a lack of contractual capacity is determined, empowering the Public Guardian with a broad discretion to impose a just solution would enable the difficult question of deciding how the loss should fall to be determined in as just a manner as possible in the particular circumstances of the case.

5.40 *The Commission recommends that the proposed capacity legislation should provide that a contract purportedly entered into by an adult whom it is alleged lacked contractual capacity may be referred to the Public Guardian by a party to the contract, a personal guardian or other person connected with a person in respect of whom it is alleged there was a lack of contractual capacity. The Commission further recommends that on such a contract being referred to it, the Public Guardian could, with the consent of the parties, refer the matter to mediation, or the Public Guardian could examine the matter. The Public Guardian should be given power to declare the contract binding on both parties or to declare the contract void for lack of capacity and to make any adjustment to the rights of the parties considered just in the circumstances. A decision of the Public Guardian could be appealed to the Circuit Court and such an appeal would involve a full rehearing of the matter.*

(3) The Necessaries Rule

5.41 The Commission is in favour of the retention of the necessaries rule as a mechanism for fairly dividing rights and duties between suppliers and consumers who lack full decision-making capacity in relation to the purchase of everyday goods and services. Nevertheless we are conscious that the application of the necessaries rule is, in some respects, not free from doubt. We are therefore of opinion that a reformulated provision should be incorporated in the capacity legislation proposed by this Consultation Paper. This would accord with the Council of Europe's recommendation that'[w]henever possible adults should be enabled to enter into legally effective transactions of an everyday nature.'(Council of Europe *Committee of Ministers Recommendation No. R99(4) on Principles Concerning the Legal Protection of Vulnerable Adults* (23 February 1999), Principle 3(4))

5.42 First, such provision should be expressed to apply to both goods and services. Secondly, in order to avoid any doubt in relation to executory contracts, we submit that the provision should be expressed to apply where goods or services have been supplied (it is envisaged that this would also cover partly executed contracts – where part delivery of goods or services has occurred). Thirdly, a statutory clarification of the application of the necessaries rule to adults without the capacity to enter into such contracts would also afford a useful opportunity to formulate such a rule in modern terminology which is more easily understood. 'Necessaries' could be defined in terms of goods and services supplied which are suitable to the person's reasonable living requirements but excluding goods and services which could be classed as luxury in nature.

5.43 *The Commission recommends that the proposed capacity legislation should provide that an adult who lacks the capacity to enter into a particular contract is nonetheless obliged to pay the supplier a reasonable amount for necessaries supplied.*

5.44 *'Necessaries' should be statutorily defined as goods and services supplied which are suitable to the person's reasonable living requirements but excluding goods and services which could be classed as luxury in nature.*

SECTION THREE—DRUNKARDS

A contract made with a person who is so intoxicated that he or she does not understand the transaction may be voidable if the other party is aware of this fact.

White *v* McCooey (HC) 26 April 1976, unrep.

The defendant sought to avoid a contract for the sale of a licensed premises on the grounds that at the time it was made he was so drunk that he was incapable of contracting. Also, he argued that whatever agreement was made was unfair because he was in an unequal bargaining position of which the other party took advantage.

Gannon J.:

Two issues of fact fall to be determined namely whether and to what extent the defendant was so intoxicated as to be incapable as he alleged, and whether this was known to the plaintiff at the time, and on these issues the onus of proof lies on the defendant.

Notes

1. Gannon J. also stated that the onus of proof lies on the defendant to prove that the transaction was unfair and unconscionable. On the evidence before the court, Gannon J. determined that the defendant had not discharged the onus of proof in respect of these issues.
2. Even if infancy, lunacy or drunkenness is not made out as a defence, the relative disparity in age as between the parties, the mental condition of the parties *vis-à-vis* each other, or proof of intoxication or a history of alcoholism, are pertinent factors in establishing the equitable defences of undue influence, unconscionable bargain or improvident transaction. These matters are considered in Chapter 14.

Consider:

Is a contract by a taxi driver to drive a drunk person home from a nightclub enforceable?

SECTION FOUR—COMPANIES

Companies, as legal persons, have capacity to enter contracts. The relevant question in many cases of corporate capacity is whether the company may enter into transactions that are *ultra vires*.

The Directors &c. of the Ashbury Rly Carriage and Iron Co. (Ltd) *v* Hector Riche (1875) LR 7 HL 653

Lord Cairns:

Your Lordships are well aware that this is the Act which put upon its present permanent footing the regulation of joint stock companies, and more especially of those joint stock companies which were to be authorised to trade with a limit to their liability.

The provisions under which that system of limiting liability was inaugurated, were provisions not merely, perhaps I might say not mainly, for the benefit of the shareholders for the time being in the company, but were enactments intended also to provide for the interests of two other very important bodies; in the first place, those who might become shareholders in succession to the persons who were shareholders for the time being; and secondly, the outside public, and more particularly those who might be creditors of companies of this kind. And I will ask your Lordships to observe, as I refer to some of the clauses, the marked and entire difference there is between the two documents which form the title deeds of companies of this description—I mean the memorandum of association on the one hand, and the articles of association on the other hand. With regard to the memorandum of association, your Lordships will find, as has often already been pointed out, although it appears somewhat to have been overlooked in the present case, that that is, as it were, the charter, and defines the limitation of the powers of a company to be established under the [Companies Act 1862]. With regard to the articles of association, those articles play a part subsidiary to the memorandum of association. They accept the memorandum of association as the charter of incoporation of the company, and so accepting it, the articles proceed to define the duties, the rights and the powers of the governing body as between themselves and the company at large, and the mode and form in which the business of the company is to be carried on, and the mode and form in which changes in the internal regulations of the company may from time to time be made. With regard, therefore, to the memorandum of associations, if you find anything which goes beyond that memorandum, or is not warranted by it, the question will arise whether that which is so done is *ultra vires*, not only of the directors of the company, but of the company itself. With regard to the articles of association, if you find anything which, still keeping within the memorandum of association, is a violation of the articles of associations, or in excess of them, the question will arise whether that is anything more than an act *extra vires* the directors, but *intra vires* the company. . ..

It appears to me that it would be perfectly fatal to the whole scheme of legislation to which I have referred, if you were to hold that, in the first place, directors might do that which even the whole company could not do, and that then, the shareholders finding out what had been done, could sanction, subsequently, what they could not antecedently have authorised.

The following provision provides some comfort to those entering into contracts with companies.

Companies Act 1963 section 8

(1) Any act or thing done by a company which if the company had been empowered to do the same would have been lawfully and effectively done, shall, notwithstanding that the company had no power to do such act or thing, be effective in favour of any

person relying on such act or thing who is not shown to have been actually aware, at the time when he so relied thereon, that such act or thing was not within the powers of the company, but any director or officer of the company who was responsible for the doing by the company of such act or thing shall be liable to the company for any loss or damage suffered by the company in consequence thereof.

(2) The court may, on the application of any member or holder of debentures of a company, restrain such company from doing any act or thing which the company has no power to do.

Northern Bank Finance Corp. Ltd *v* Bernard Quinn & Achates Investment Co. [1979] ILRM 221

A company guaranteed a bank loan made to the first defendant. When he defaulted on his payments, the bank called in the guarantee at which stage the company pleaded *ultra vires*. The bank sought to rely on s. 8 (1) of the Companies Act 1963 to validate the guarantee. The bank's solicitor possessed copies of the memorandum and articles and Keane J. decided that he probably read the memorandum but believed the guarantee to be *intra vires*.

Keane J.:

The question accordingly arises as to whether, in these circumstances, the bank were 'actually aware', within the meaning of s. 8 (1) of the lack of *vires*. [Counsel for the plaintiff] submitted that the language of s. 8 (1) clearly demonstrated that the onus of establishing actual knowledge within the meaning of the section is on the person who asserts that such knowledge existed and that, accordingly, the onus was on the company, to establish that the bank were 'actually aware' of the lack of *vires*. This may very well be so, but I do not think it is material to the issue which has to be resolved in the present case. . . . The only question that arises is as to whether, having regard to that evidence and the inferences, which, in my view, necessarily follow from it, the bank can be said to have been 'actually aware' of the lack of *vires*.

[Counsel for the plaintiff] submitted that actual, as distinguished from constructive, notice of the lack of *vires* was essential if a third party was to lose the protection of s. 8 (1). I accept that this is so: altogether apart from authority, the language used would suggest that what the legislature had in mind was actual and not constructive notice. Moreover, to interpret the section in any other way would be to frustrate its manifest object. While there is no authority of which counsel were aware or which I have been able to discover on the section, the mischief which it was designed to avoid is clear. Prior to the enactment of the section, all persons dealing with a company were deemed to have notice of the contents of the company's public documents, including its memorandum and articles. If a transaction was *ultra vires*, the other party to it, speaking generally, had no rights at all. The manifest injustice and inconvenience which followed from this rule is amply illustrated by the decision in re: John Beauforte Ltd (1953) Ch. 131, which was referred to in the argument.

But if constructive notice can still be relied on in answer to a party claiming the protection of this action, the protection in question would be, to a significant extent, eroded. It is clear, moreover, that the doctrine of constructive notice should not normally be applied to purely commercial transactions, such as the advancing of money. (See the observations of Mr Justice Kenny delivering the judgment of the Supreme Court in *Bank of Ireland Finance Ltd v Rockfield Ltd* 1976 No. 46 Sp: 28 July 1978, unrep.)

But while I am satisfied that the doctrine of constructive notice does not apply to the sub-section under consideration, this does not dispose of the matter. The bank, because of the knowledge of their agent, Mr O'Connell, which must be imputed to them, were aware of the objects of the company. There were no further *facts* of which they could be put on notice. But they failed to draw the appropriate inference from those facts, i.e. that the transaction was *ultra vires*. Counsel for the plaintiff] submits that, even accepting this to be so, this is not the actual knowledge which the section contemplates.

A great number of transactions are entered into every day by companies, public and private, without any of the parties looking at the memorandum in order to see whether the transaction in question is in fact authorised by the memorandum. I think it probable that, on the occasions when the memorandum is looked at before a transaction is entered into, it is normally because the company's solicitor or a solicitor for a third party wishes to satisfy himself that the proposed transaction is *intra vires* the memorandum. I think it is clear that the section was designed to ensure that, in the first category of cases, persons who had entered into transactions in good faith with the company without ever reading the memorandum and accordingly with no actual knowledge that the transaction was *ultra vires* were not to suffer. I can see no reason in logic or justice why the legislature should have intended to afford the same protection to persons who had actually read the memorandum and simply failed to appreciate the lack of *vires*. The maxim *ignorantia juris haud neminem excusat* may not be of universal application, but this is certainly one situation where it seems fair that it should apply. This is best illustrated by an example. The directors of a public company decide to invest the bulk of the company's resources in a disastrous property speculation as a result of which the company suffers enormous losses. The company in fact had no power to enter into any such transaction, but the vendors' solicitors, although furnished with the memorandum and articles, failed to appreciate this. If the submission advance on behalf of the bank in this case is well founded, it would mean that, in such circumstances, the innocent shareholders would be the victims rather than the vendors. There seems no reason why the consequences of the vendors' failure to appreciate the lack of *vires* should be visited on the heads of the blameless shareholders. I do not overlook the fact that the sub-section gives the company a remedy against any director or officer of the company who is responsible for the *ultra vires* act; but such a remedy may not necessarily enable the innocent shareholder to recoup all his losses.

It is interesting in this context to note that in the UK the Jenkins Committee recommended that even actual knowledge of the contents of the memorandum should not deprive a third party of his right to enforce a contract if he honestly and reasonably failed to appreciate that they precluded the company or its officers from entering into the contract. (See Cmnd. 1749, paras 35–42.) Writing in the early days of the operation of our Act, Mr Alexis Fitzgerald said of s. 8. 'The draughtsmen wisely reject the advice of the Jenkins Committee, which would have given contractual rights even to third parties with actual knowledge, where such a third party could prove he honestly and reasonably failed to appreciate the effect of the lack of power. Acceptance of this recommendation would have created uncertain and therefore bad law'. (1 Ir Jur 1). In England, the *ultra vires* rule was modified by 9(1) of the European Communities Act, 1972, and while the language of the section is different from that of s. 8 of our 1963 Act, the requirement being that the third party should have acted in good faith, it is interesting to note that the editors of *Palmer's Company Law* (22nd edn) take the view that it would not protect the third party in circumstances such as the present.

I am satisfied that, where a party is shown to have been actually aware of the contents of the memorandum but failed to appreciate that the company were not empowered thereby to enter into the transaction in issue, s. 8 (1) has no application. It follows that, in the present case, the bank cannot successfully rely on s. 8 (1).

European Communities (Companies) Regulations 1973 S.I. No. 163

6. (1) In favour of a person dealing with a company in good faith, any transaction entered into by any organ of the company, being its board of directors or any person registered under these regulations as a person authorised to bind the company, shall be deemed to be within the capacity of the company and any limitation of the powers of that board or person, whether imposed by the memorandum or articles of association or otherwise, may not be relied upon as against any person so dealing with the company.

(2) Any such person shall be presumed to have acted in good faith unless the contrary is proved.

(3) For the purpose of this regulation, the registration of a person authorised to bind the company shall be effected by delivering to the registrar of companies a notice giving the name and description of the person concerned.

General Scheme of the New Companies Bill

In May 2007, the Company Law Reform Group published the *Report on the Companies Consolidation and Reform Bill* and the *Heads of Bill*. This incorporates the recommendations of the Group published in its first and second reports. Pillar A deals with private companies and Pillar B with other forms such as plcs, companies limited by guarantee and designated activity companies.

Part A2 Head 20—Capacity of a private company limited by shares

(1) Subject to Subhead (2), notwithstanding anything contained in its constitution a company shall have, whether acting inside or outside of the State—
- (a) full and unlimited capacity to carry on and undertake any business or activity, do any act or enter into any transaction; and,
- (b) for the purposes of paragraph (a) of this subhead, full rights powers and privileges.

(2) Nothing in Subhead (1) shall relieve a company from any duty or obligation under any enactment or the general law.

Explanatory note

This is a new head which gives effect to the recommendation in the *First Report of the Company Law Review Group* that private companies limited by shares should be granted the legal capacity of a natural person with the consequent effect that the doctrine of ultra vires is disapplied from private companies. The head is modelled on Section 16(1) of the New Zealand Companies Act, 1993. The Review Group recognised that nearly 90 per cent of registered companies are private companies limited by shares and the majority of these were closely held companies. Accordingly, the Review Group believes that such companies should not be required to set out any objects or powers; such companies should be empowered with the capacity of a natural person. Thus, it recommended that, except where otherwise specifically required by a company's promoters, private companies limited by shares should have the legal capacity of a natural person.

Part A2 Head 21—Registered person

Where a company appoints any person (a 'registered person') as a person entitled to bind the company it shall notify the Registrar in the prescribed form.

Explanatory note

This is a new head. The concept is drawn from Regulation 6(3) of the EC (Companies) Regulations 1973 (although it is not a direct re-enactment).

Part A2 Head 22—Persons or bodies of persons authorised to bind a company

(1) For the purposes of any question whether a transaction fails to bind a company because of lack of authority on the part of the person exercising (or purporting to exercise) the company's powers, the board of directors of a company and any registered person shall be deemed to have authority to—

(a)   exercise any power of the company; and

(b)   authorise others to do so,

and this applies regardless of any limitations in the company's constitution on the board's authority or a registered person's authority, but subject to Subheads (4) and (6).

(2) Subhead (1) shall not be taken to prevent the exercise of a company's powers otherwise than by the board, a registered person or a person authorised by the board or by a registered person, where authority for that exercise exists.

(3) Subhead (1) does not affect a director's duties (including his duty to observe any limitations in the company's constitution on the board's authority), or his or any other person's liability (including the liability of a registered person) in respect of any breach of those duties.

(4) Where a company is purportedly a party to a transaction—

(a)   in connection with which the board of directors exceeded limitations in the company's constitution on their authority; and

(b)   to which a person falling within Subhead (5) is also a party,

Subhead (1) does not apply in favour of the party falling within Subhead (5).

(5) A person falls within this subhead if he is—

(a) a director or shadow director of the company or of its holding company; or

(b) a person connected with such a director; or

(c) a registered person; or

(d) a person connected with a registered person

and in this subhead, references to a person's being 'connected' with another person are to be read in accordance with Part A5, Head 2 [equivalent of Section 26 of the Companies Act, 1990, as amended by Section 76 of the Company Law Enforcement Act, 2001].

(6) Subhead (1) does not apply in relation to a power of the company which this Bill requires to be exercised otherwise than by the board.

(7) Without prejudice to Subhead (2), in determining any question whether a person had ostensible authority to exercise any of a company's powers in a given case, no reference may be made to the company's constitution.

(8) In this head, references to limitations in the company's constitution include references to limitations deriving from—

(a) a resolution of the company or of any class of members; or

(b) any agreement between the members of the company or of any class of members;

and 'transaction' includes any act or omission.

Explanatory note

This is a new head. The head sets out those persons who are authorised to bind a company and draws on the provision in the UK White Paper Modernising Company Law, July 2002 at 6.2 p 50.

Subhead (1) is a new provision aimed at enhancing clarity and certainty in relation to the issue of the authority of the Board of Directors to bind the company. It is similar to the current Model Article 80 of Part I of Table A of the First Schedule to the Companies Act 1963. Subheads (2), (3), (4), (5), (6), (7) and (8) are all new provisions which further elaborate on authority to bind the company.

Part A2 Head 23—Powers of Attorney

(1) A company may, by writing under its common seal, empower any person, either generally or in respect of any specified matters, as its attorney, to execute deeds or do any other matter on its behalf in any place whether inside or outside the State.

(2) A deed signed by such attorney on behalf of the company and under his seal shall bind the company and have the same effect as if it were under its common seal.

Explanatory note

This head is an amended re-enactment of Section 40 of the Companies Act 1963. Subhead (1) is an amended re-enactment of Section 40(1) of the Companies Act 1963. It was amended in accordance with the recommendation of the First Report of the Company Law Review Group that Section 40 should be amended to expressly declare that the power to appoint an attorney (i) is regardless of any provision in the constitution, and (ii) extends to acts done within the State.

A further amendment was also made whereby the words 'or to do any other matter' were added which extends the powers of the attorney to act on behalf of the company. Subhead (2) is a re-enactment of section 40(2) of the Companies Act 1963.

Part A2 Head 24—Form of contracts

(1) Contracts on behalf of a company may be made as follows—

(a) a contract which, if made between natural persons, would be by law required to be in writing and to be under seal, may be made on behalf of the company in writing under the common seal of the company;

(b) a contract which, if made between natural persons, would be by law required to be in writing, signed by the parties to be charged therewith, may be made on behalf of the company in writing, signed by any person acting under its authority, express or implied;

(c) a contract which if made between natural persons would by law be valid although made by parol only, and not reduced into writing may be made by parol on behalf of the company by any person acting under its authority, express or implied.

(2) A contract made according to this head shall bind the company and its successors and all other parties thereto.

(3) A contract made according to this head may be varied or discharged in the same manner in which it is authorised by this head to be made.

Explanatory note

This head is an amended re-enactment of Section 38 of the Companies Act 1963. Subhead (1) is a slightly amended re-enactment of Section 38(1) of the Companies Act 1963. The reference to 'private persons' has been replaced by a reference to 'natural persons'. Subheads (2) & (3) are re-enactments of Sections 38(2) & 38(3) of the Companies Act 1963 respectively.

Part B2 Head 8—Corporate capacity of a PLC

A PLC shall have the capacity to do any act or thing stated in the objects set out in its constitution.

Explanatory note

This head states that a PLC has capacity to do that which is in its objects in its constitution. The provisions in Group A that provide for unlimited capacity are disapplied in Head 2 of this Part.

Part B2 Head 9—Corporate capacity not limited by a PLC's constitution

(1) The validity of an act done by a PLC shall not be called into question on the ground of lack of capacity by reason of anything contained in the PLC's objects.

(2) A member of a PLC may bring proceedings to restrain the doing of an act which, but for Subhead (1), would be beyond the PLC's capacity) but no such proceedings shall lie in respect of any act to be done in fulfilment of a legal obligation arising from a previous act of the PLC.

(3) It remains the duty of the directors to observe any limitations on their powers flowing from the PLC's objects and action by the directors which, but for Subhead (1), would be beyond the PLC's capacity may only be ratified by the company by special resolution.

(4) A resolution ratifying such action shall not affect any liability incurred by the directors or any other person, relief from any such liability must be agreed to separately by special resolution.

(5) A party to a transaction with a PLC is not bound to enquire as to whether it is permitted by the PLC's objects.

Explanatory note

This head mitigates the effect of a PLC having an objects clause whilst contemporaneously furthering creditor (Subhead 1) and shareholder (Subhead 2) protection. The mitigation of the doctrine of *ultra vires* in Section 8 of the Companies Act, 1963 has been abandoned in favour of this formulation which is based on Section 35 of the UK's Companies Act 1985. Whilst persons dealing with a PLC that is acting ultra vires will not be prejudiced, the directors of a PLC can be held to account for causing a PLC to take such action. This will be in the form of an *in personam* action against the directors and not an *in rem* action that would set aside the validity of the *ultra vires* transaction. Furthermore, UK law is mirrored in Subhead (5) which ousts the doctrine of constructive notice by providing that a person is not bound to enquire as to whether an activity is *intra vires*. Provision is also made for the ratification of an act beyond the capacity of the company by special resolution. This reverses the common law position stated in *Ashbury Railway & Iron Co. v Riche* (1875) LR 7 HLC 653 where not even a unanimous agreement of the shareholders would suffice. Such ratification offers the other party greater assurance. Ratification validates the transaction whilst a separate special resolution is required to absolve the directors or any registered persons from any liability arising. The second special resolution absolves directors and registered persons. It also applies to '. . . any other persons'—this includes any third party who may be liable as a constructive trustee on the basis of either providing knowing assistance in a breach of trust (see *Royal Brunei Airlines V Tan* (1995) 3 All ER 97) or knowing receipt of trust finds applied in breach of duty (see BCCI *v Akindele* (2000) 4 All ER 221).

Part B2 Head 10—Corporate authority and the power of directors to bind a PLC

(1) In favour of a person dealing with a PLC in good faith, the power of the board of directors to bind the PLC, or authorise others to do so, or of any person registered with the Registrar for the purposes of Part A2, Head 21 [equivalent of Reg.6(3) S.I. 173 of 1973] as a person authorised to bind the PLC, shall be deemed to be free of

any limitation under the PLC's constitution.

(2) For the purposes of Subhead (1)—

   (a) a person 'deals with' a PLC if he is a party to any transaction or other act to which the PLC is a party;

   (b) a person shall not be regarded as acting in bad faith by reason only of his knowing that an act is beyond the powers of the persons referred to in Subhead (1) under the PLC's constitution; and

   (c) a person shall be presumed to have acted in good faith unless the contrary is proved.

(3) The references in Subheads (1) and (2) to limitations on the directors' powers or those of a person registered with the Registrar for the purposes of Part A2, Head 21 as a person authorised to bind the PLC under the PLC's constitution include limitations deriving—

   (a) from a resolution of the PLC in general meeting or a meeting of any class of shareholders; or

   (b) from any agreement between the members of the PLC or of any class of shareholders.

(4) Subhead (1) does not affect any right of a member of the PLC to bring proceedings to restrain the doing of an act which is beyond thepowers of the directors or of a person registered with the Registrar for the purposes of Part A2, Head 21 as a person authorised to bind the PLC, but no such proceedings shall lie in respect of an act to be done in fulfilment of a legal obligation arising from a previous act of the PLC.

(5) Subhead (1) does not affect any liability incurred by the directors, or any other person including a person registered with the Registrar for the purposes of Part A2, Head 21 as a person authorised to bind the PLC, by reason of such person or persons, exceeding their powers.

(6) A party to a transaction with a PLC is not bound to enquire as to whether there is any limitation on the powers of the board of directors to bind the PLC or authorise others to do so or on the powers of a person registered with the Registrar for the purposes of Part A2, Head 21 as a person authorised to bind the PLC.

Explanatory note

This new head seeks to protect persons dealing with a company who may be faced with the defence that the persons with whom they dealt did not have the authority to conclude such a transaction. Again, shareholders are protected and may injunct transactions which are beyond the powers of directors. As in the case of corporate capacity in Head 9, the doctrine of constructive notice is again displaced and persons are expressly stated to be under no duty to enquire as to limitations on the powers of directors or others.

Notwithstanding the difficulties that can be associated with the formulation 'in favour of a person dealing with a PLC in good faith', the notion of good faith has been retained.

[The provision for registering a person authorised to bind the company previously contained in Section 8 has been subsumed into Part A2, Head 21 with cross references incorporated into this head. Section 35 also refers to the board authorising other persons to do so.]

EXERCISES

1. Bill, a minor, is a rider on the Irish Olympic team. He enters into a contract to buy a showjumper. He subsequently claims that this is not a contract for a necessary. Is he correct?

2. Matt, a minor, rents an expensive apartment beside the university claiming that the one-hour commute to class is too exhausting. Is this a contract for a necessary?

3. Hannah receives a phone call from Ted's manager asking her if she will sell her car to Ted. Hannah agrees. Ted subsequently seeks to avoid the contract on the basis that he was intoxicated at the time he asked his manager to make the phone call. Advise Hannah.

4. Rick enters a contract with Wicklow Pig Rearers Ltd to sell it €500,000 worth of diamonds. The company then seek to avoid the contract claiming that it should have been obvious to Rick that the contract was *ultra vires* and could have had nothing to do with its main business. Advise Rick.

Chapter Thirteen

Duress

INTRODUCTION

The existence of equitable concepts such as undue influence and uncon-scionable bargain have been useful ways of counteracting improper bargain-ing practices and coercion. Similarly, the doctrine of consideration and in particular the rule about the adequacy of consideration being ultimately a matter for the judiciary has been an important, if covert, method of frustrating persons who exert their superior bargaining position to coerce a further advantage after the contract has been concluded.

However, the concept of duress being a distinct vitiating factor has, in historical terms, only a limited scope. Initially, duress was confined to cases of physical restraint in the form of coercion or personal restraint.

Lessee of Blackwood v Gregg (1831) Hayes 277

This was an action for ejectment brought on the equity side. A man of ninety two, having executed a will leaving property to the plaintiff, was abducted by the defendant who prevailed upon the old man to both execute a new will and sell lands to the plaintiff's confederate. One plea set up was duress or coercion by imprisonment. The Court of Exchequer held that a plea of coercion had been properly left before the jury by the trial judge.

Smith B.:

But if the old man's sudden abandonment of his own house, and his subsequent absence from it, are not open to the observations which I have been making; if they were acts, not voluntary, but the result of compulsion; then they become a part of the evidence of duress. Without them, there is evidence of this. Persons are refused access to him. This is without his knowledge; and consequently not *with*, probably, on the evidence, *against* his consent. Is this no *direct* evidence of the coercion of personal restraint. Does it involve no *presumptive* evidence of still further coercion and control? Would he too, who had not scrupled to spoliate, hesitate to intimidate or to coerce?

Barton v Armstrong [1975] 2 All ER 465

Armstrong, the chairman of a company, became involved with Barton, the managing director of Landmark, in a struggle for control of the company. Ultimately, a deed was executed under which Armstrong's interest in Landmark would be purchased for a total consideration of A$320,000. Barton executed the deed on behalf of Landmark. Barton later sought a declaration that as against him the deed was void because his signature had been obtained following threats made by Armstrong against Barton's life and members of his family. Lord Cross gave judgment for the majority of the Privy Council.

Lord Cross:
. . .

. . . It is hardly surprising that there is no direct authority on the point, for if A threatens B with death if he does not execute some document and B, who takes A's threats seriously, executes the document it can be only in the most unusual circumstances that there can be any doubt whether the threats operated to induce him to execute the document. But this is a most unusual case and the findings of fact made below do undoubtedly raise the question whether it was necessary for Barton in order to obtain relief to establish that he would not have executed the deed in question but for the threats. In answering this question in favour of Barton Jacobs J.A. relied both on a number of old common law authorities on the subject of 'duress' and also—by way of analogy—on later decisions in equity with regard to the avoidance of deeds on the ground of fraud. Their Lordships do not think that the common law authorities are of any real assistance for it seems most unlikely that the authors of the statements relied on had the sort of problem which has arisen here in mind at all. On the other hand they think that the conclusion to which Jacobs J.A. came was right and that it is supported by the equity decisions. The scope of common law duress was very limited and at a comparatively early date equity began to grant relief in cases where the disposition in question had been procured by the exercise of pressure which the Chancellor considered to be illegitimate—although it did not amount to common law duress. There was a parallel development in the field of dispositions induced by fraud. At common law the only remedy available to the man defrauded was an action for deceit but equity in the same period in which it was building up the doctrine of 'undue influence' came to entertain proceedings to set aside dispositions which had been obtained by fraud: see *Holdsworth's History of English Law*.[1] There is an obvious analogy between setting aside a disposition for duress or undue influence and setting it aside for fraud. In each case—to quote the words of Holmes J. in *Fairbanks v Snow*[2]—'the party has been subjected to an improper motive for action'. Again the similarity of the effect in law of *metus* and *dolus* in connection with dispositions of property is noted by Stair in his *Institutions of the Law of Scotland*.[3] Had Armstrong made a fraudulent misrepresentation to Barton for the purpose of inducing him to execute the deed of 17 January 1967 the answer to the problem which has arisen would have been clear. If it were established that Barton did not allow the representation to affect his judgment then he could not make it a ground for relief even though the representation was designed and known by Barton to be designed to affect his judgment. If on the other hand Barton relied on the misrepresentation Armstrong could not have defeated his claim to relief by showing that there were other more weighty causes which contributed to his decision to execute the deed, for in this field the court does not allow an examination into the relative importance of contributory causes. 'Once make out that there has been anything like deception, and no contract resting in any degree on that foundation can stand' (per Lord Cranworth L.J. in *Reynell v Sprye*;[4] see also the other cases referred to in Cheshire and Fifoot's *Law of Contract*[5]). Their Lordships think that the same rule should apply in cases of duress and that if Armstrong's threats were 'a' reason for Barton's executing the deed he is entitled to relief even though he might well have entered into the contract if Armstrong had uttered no threats to induce him to do so.

1. Vol. 38, p. 51.
2. (1887) 13 NE at 598.
3. Book IV, tit 40, 25.

4. (1852) 1 De G. M. & G. 660 at 708.
5. (8th ed., 1972) 250, 251.

(Lords Wilberforce and Simon of Glaisdale dissented on the facts.)

SECTION ONE—DURESS OF GOODS

Related to the law governing coercion by physical restraint or harm are the rules found in quasi-contract, or restitution. Where a person pays money, or an excess charge, in order to gain access to property, or perhaps a business opportunity, that should have been available as of right, or on other terms, then the money improperly extracted will be returnable.

These demands, often made under colour of office, are seen as improper, even if made *bona fide*, and made following a mistake, such as an incorrect interpretation of the law.

Great Southern & Western Rly *v* Robertson (1878) 2 LR (Ir) 548

Ball C.:

The appellant is a carrier who, under and in pursuance of a contract with the military authorities, conveyed upon the Great Southern and Western Railway (Ireland) public baggage stores and ammunition; and having been by the company charged in excess of the rate prescribed by the Act 7 & 8 Vict. c. 85, for the carriage of such goods, sues to recover back this excess. The Court of Exchequer determined that he could not succeed.

The statutable provisions relating to the charges for the carriage of goods of the character of those forwarded by the defendant will be found in the Acts 5 & 6 Vict. c. 55, and 7 & 8 Vict. c. 85. Both oblige soldiers, with their baggage, stores, ammunition, and other necessaries and things, to be carried by railways; but the first left the payment to be settled between the Secretary-at-War and the company; and the second substituted for this a fixed rate of 2d per ton per mile.

The case of *The Attorney General v Great Southern and Western Rly Co.*[1] decided that, in order to take advantage of the provisions of s. 12 of the second Act (that which regulates the charges by the company), it was not necessary that the public baggage, stores, &c., should be accompanied by the whole regiment or battalion to whom they appertained, as passengers at the same time upon the railway. This section, in its recitals from the previous statute, quotes the words, 'whenever it shall be necessary to move any of Her Majesty's officers or soldiers, with their baggage, stores &c.' and these words were held to be satisfied by any officers or soldiers accompanying the baggage, stores &c., the public baggage, stores &c., being theirs in the only sense in which what is public can be theirs, as having the present custody of it, whether designed for their use or not. I am by no means satisfied that the true construction of this section is not that the provision as to the rate of charge for carriage of public baggage, stores &c., is quite independent of the circumstance whether or not such baggage, stores &c., are accompanied by soldiers; but as the view taken in the case I have cited is that suggested in the pleadings and argument of the appeal before us, I also shall for my judgment adopt it.

The question before us is raised upon a demurrer and the pleadings preceding it. The carrier alleges that a necessity had arisen for moving upon the railway military forces, with their public baggage, stores &c.—a contract by him with the proper authorities for moving such baggage &c., at the rates provided by the Act; that officers and soldiers accompanied such baggage &c.; that the military forces were always ready and willing to give their assistance in loading and unloading such goods—that is, he avers in pleading all the various matters which, if the baggage, stores &c., were transmitted and accompanied only by military persons, can be suggested as conditions to the assertion of their rights to have the goods carried at the statutable rate—and then complains that, notwithstanding, the railway company exacted charges exceeding 2d per ton per mile. Upon the assumption of all the matters thus stated having occurred, which in the argument of a demurrer we must make—it seems uncontroverted that if there had been no contract between the military authorities and the carriers, and if the baggage, stores &c., had been solely in charge of officers and soldiers, the rate of charge for carriage would have been 2d per ton per mile.

Then did the fact of the interposition of a contract with the carrier alter the rate of charge, and if so can the carrier sue to recover for overcharge? The Court of Exchequer seem to me to have answered the first question in the affirmative, and the second in the negative. We have arrived at conclusions differing from theirs; but it must be observed that cases have been cited before us, and principles deduced from those cases, which do not seem to have been submitted for their consideration.

With respect to the first question, namely, whether the rate of charge was different because of the contract with the carrier—it is to be observed that a route or order from the proper military authorities was produced to the officer of the railway company; that no doubt or controversy, either at the time of transmission or since, has arisen as to the baggage &c., being public baggage &c.; and that it was accompanied by soldiers. Then why should the addition of a civilian to the soldiers, whether he were contractor or overseer, or attendant, make the baggage &c., less public baggage, or alter the rate for which as such public baggage &c., when accompanied by soldiers, it ought to be carried? The object was to diminish the cost to the nation of transmitting military stores &c., and this object may be attained alike whether they are in charge of soldiers and a contractor, or of soldiers only. We cannot doubt that the payment under a contract, upon the basis of the carrier having to pay railway companies only the statutable fares, would be less expensive to the War Department than it otherwise would be; indeed in the present instance it is pleaded that on the railway the carrier was to convey at these rates. In the case of *Read v Willan*[2] cited in argument, a contractor supplying horses for the artillery was held entitled to the benefit of the Billeting Act, which obliged dragoon horses to be fed without charge. I fail to see the distinction in principle between that and the present case.

Then, if the true rate was 2d per ton per mile, is not the appellant, who paid more, entitled to have the excess refunded? The very learned judge, who delivered the judgment of the Court of Exchequer now appealed from, adopts and approves of the *dictum* of Mr Justice Willes in *The Great Western Rly Co. v Sutton*,[3] as I do also, that when a man pays more than he is bound to do for the performance of a duty which the law says is owed to him for nothing, or for less than he has paid, there is a compulsion in respect of which he is entitled to recover the excess by action for money had and received. Mr Robertson, in order to have the goods conveyed to their destination, was obliged to pay the fares required by the officers of the railway company, and he is entitled to demand back the amount by which he overpaid them.

Smelter Corp. of Ireland *v* O'Driscoll (SC) 27 July 1977, unrep.

O'Higgins C.J.:

This is an appeal brought by the plaintiffs from the decision and judgment of Butler J. refusing their claim for specific performance of an agreement entered into by the defendant for the sale to them of 55 acres 0 roods 36 perches of land situate at Carrigrenan, Co. Cork. The plaintiff is a limited liability company formed for the purpose of establishing in Ireland a smelter or base metal reduction plant and in pursuance of this aim was at the time of the agreement sought to be enforced engaged in the acquisition of land as a suitable site for such a plant in the Little Island area of Cork. The defendant is the owner of the land the subject of the agreement but the negotiations in relation to the agreement were conducted on her behalf by her husband Michael O'Driscoll and later by her solicitor who has since died, also named Michael O'Driscoll. The agreement necessarily took the form of an option to purchase dated 25 November 1969 under which for the sum of £7,000 the plaintiffs were given for twelve months an option to purchase at a price to be determined by Mr Owen MacCarthy, the well known arbitrator to the Land Values Reference Committee, on an arbitration specially held for that purpose.

Provision was made for the extension of the option for a further period of six months on the payment of a further sum of £3,250 and there were other clauses not relevant to the issues raised in this appeal. It was provided that the option payments should in the event of the option being exercised be credited against the purchase money and if the option was not exercised for any of the three grounds set out in clause 9 then one half of such sums should be returned to the plaintiffs and in the meantime such one half should be secured on deposit. On 10 January 1970 Mr Owen MacCarthy determined in his arbitration award that the purchase price of the land should be at the rate of £1,500 per acre, making a purchase price of £82,857.50. By letter dated 23 November 1970 the plaintiffs took a second option for six months for the sum of £3,250 thereupon paid to the defendant's solicitors. A second option for six months was then purchased by the plaintiffs as a result of negotiations between the auctioneer acting for the plaintiffs, Mr Ahern, and the defendant's solicitor. The consideration for this option was also £3,250 but this sum was not to be credited against the purchase money should the plaintiffs exercise the option. At the expiration of this third option a fourth was negotiated as evidenced by a letter dated 24 November 1971 from the defendant's solicitor to the plaintiffs. This option was for a further six months for a nominal consideration but on the terms that the option monies paid under the original option should now be freed to the defendant and should not be credited against the purchase money in the event of the option being exercised. In effect this arrangement constituted the ground of a fresh option to purchase for a fixed price of £93,087.50 being £82,837.50 as fixed by Mr MacCarthy, plus the £10,250 paid in respect of the options under the agreement of 25 November 1967. By letter dated 15 May 1972 the plaintiffs purported to exercise this final option. The defendant being unwilling and refusing to complete, these proceedings were commenced by the plaintiffs seeking specific performance of the agreement to sell and associated relief.

The defendants' defence to the plaintiffs' claim is based on two main grounds. In the first place it is contended that the option or options to purchase were given by her, I quote from para. 3 of the defence: 'Subject to a condition precedent that a smelter plant, otherwise a base metal reduction plant, would be built on the said lands and that the said lands would be used for no other purpose, but the defendants do not propose to build or utilise a smelter plant or base metal reduction plant on the said lands and the said option has not been fulfilled and will not be fulfilled and the plaintiff is thereby debarred from exercising the said or any option.' It was further contended with regard to the option and I quote from para. 4 of the defence:

The same was obtained from the plaintiff under duress and coercion whereby the plaintiff caused or permitted a local authority to clearly give her to understand that if she did not sell the said lands or give an option under the same to the plaintiff for the purpose of a smelter plant or base metal reduction plant, then the said lands would be acquired by compulsory acquisition by the said local authority and given to the plaintiffs for the stated purpose, and the defendant believed that this threat would be carried out to her damage and it was further represented to the defendant that she had a national and patriotic duty to permit employment on a large scale to be afforded by the plaintiffs at the said smelter plant or base metal reduction plant and it was in those circumstances and only on the understanding and pre-condition, express or implied, as hereinbefore indicated, that the defendant afforded such option to the plaintiffs.

I now turn to the grounds relied on by the defendant for resisting the order for specific performance claimed in this case. I wish to say at once that I find no substance in the first ground of objection. In my view the purpose for which the plaintiffs sought to purchase lands or the use to which they intended to put them in no way affected the transaction entered into. I can see no basis for suggesting that the proposed acquisition of the defendant's lands depended on the smelter project proceeding.

The second objection must, however, be viewed in a different light. Specific performance is a discretionary remedy. The discretion to grant or refuse the relief must be exercised in a manner which is neither arbitrary nor capricious but which has regard to the essential fairness of the transaction involved. Here it is, in effect, suggested that the defendant was coerced or forced into granting the option or options to the plaintiffs by the threat of compulsory purchase. It does not seem to me on the evidence that a threat as such was ever used. At the same time it seems perfectly clear that the defendant was at a serious disadvantage. Mr O'Driscoll, the defendant's husband, who acted for her throughout the negotiations, believed that if there was not a voluntary sale there would be a compulsory acquisition of the lands. He so believed because he was told this by the plaintiffs' agent, Mr Ahern. It is quite clear that this view was repeated to him by his own solicitor, Mr Michael O'Driscoll, and on 9 October 1969 further corroboration was provided by those who came to see him representing the Cork County Council. Believing this to be the situation there was no real purpose in refusing to sell or to give an option once, as was suggested, the price was to be determined by an agreed arbitrator. To refuse in these circumstances meant acquisition anyway and the determination of the price by an arbitrator in whose appointment the defendant might have no say. It now transpires that the situation was not as was intimated to the defendant's husband, Michael O'Driscoll. It is now clear that at the time that these negotiations were proceeding the county council had no plans whatsoever to interfere by way of the compulsory acquisition of the defendant's lands. It is well established that the discretion to grant specific performance should not be exercised if the contract is not equal and fair. In this instance the defendant was under a fundamental misapprehension as to the true facts. This misapprehension was brought about by the plaintiffs' agent, Mr Ahern. While Mr Ahern acted *bona fide* this does not alter the situation which he created. He led the defendant's husband, Mr O'Driscoll, and his solicitor to believe that if the defendant did not agree to sell the lands would be acquired. It appears clear also that Mr Filer, the plaintiffs' managing director was aware of the true position so far as compulsory acquisition was concerned. It is to be noted that he had Mr Ahern's file of correspondence and should from this file have been aware of the incorrect picture which Mr Ahern had painted. Nevertheless Mr Filer allowed the negotiations to proceed. In these circumstances it appears to me that there was a fundamental unfairness in the transaction. The defendant agreed to sell believing she had no real option and the plaintiffs accepted her agreement to sell knowing that this was not so. In my view it would create a hardship and would be unjust to decree specific performance in this case. I agree with the decision of the learned trial judge. I would refuse specific performance but would order that all monies paid to the defendant by the plaintiffs be returned to the plaintiffs by the defendant.

SECTION TWO—SETTLEMENT OF DISPUTES AND CLAIMS

A. ABUSE OF PROCESS

Rourke *v* Mealy (1879) 13 ILTR 52
The defendant accepted a bill of exchange in favour of the plaintiff. The bill was dishonoured and the defendant pleaded that the bill had been given by the defendant in order to discontinue proceedings brought by the plaintiff alleging a forgery by a relative of the defendant, such proceedings being a matter of some shame to the family. The defence, as set out, was one of public policy rather than coercion.

Palles C.B.:

The second argument which pressed me was that, the plaintiff having threatened to resort to criminal proceedings, and thereby obtained the bill now sued on, he ought to be estopped from denying that without which his threat would have been unjustifiable and idle—*viz.* that the bill was a forgery. I fully appreciate the weight of this argument, and the pressure which may be exercised by unscrupulous holders of instruments alleged to be forged, who, by threats of prosecution, extort from the fears of criminals or others, contracts which otherwise would not be entered into. I see too the danger of permitting the validity of the contract to depend upon its being possible to prove guilt at a time after the contract has been performed, and the evidence of that guilt probably destroyed. But, upon full consideration, I think that this threat constituted part of a different line of defence—*viz.* that to which I adverted in the commencement of my judgment. If we had here a defence of duress or extortion relying upon the threat, and the circumstances under which it was made, as amounting to such pressure as rendered the contract unjust or inequitable, a different question would arise. We should then have to deal, not as we have here, with a matter of illegality alone. We should have to determine to what extent, if at all, the threat prevented the defendant from acting as a free agent; and I confess that in determining the effect which might reasonably be produced upon his mind by a statement of forgery, I should be slow to listen to a statement by the utterer of the threat that it was one for which there was no solid or reasonable foundation. If the defence here clearly showed that the plaintiff groundlessly had alleged or represented that the former bill was in fact forged, that the representation was made to the defendant, and that the defendant believed that allegation, and in consequence accepted the bill sued upon, it would take much more argument than I have yet heard to convince me that such a defence was bad. These allegations, however, are not in the defence here. It does not rely either upon estoppel or upon pressure. Its sole ground is that the contract was against public policy, and, for the reasons I have already stated, I have been coerced to arrive at the conclusion that it cannot be sustained.

Rogers *v* Louth County Council [1981] ILRM 144

Griffin J.:

In proceedings brought against the defendants in the Circuit Court for the County of Louth the plaintiff, who is the personal representative of James Murphy deceased, claims the return to her of the sum of £935.53 which it is alleged had been overpaid by her to the defendants in redeeming an annuity in respect of a cottage the property of the deceased at Rathnure, Co. Louth. The annuity was redeemed under and in pursuance of the provisions of s. 99 of the Housing Act, 1966.

James Murphy was, at the time of his death, the owner of the said cottage, which by a vesting order made under the Labourers Act, 1936, was vested in him in fee simple free from encumbrances but subject to an annuity of £19 10s *per annum* for the period of forty nine years from 2 April 1958, and to the statutory conditions, being those set out in s. 17 of the 1936 Act. In 1968, he was anxious to redeem the said annuity, and on 25 November 1968 his solicitors wrote to the defendants stating that their client 'wished to purchase the fee simple of his property. We would be obliged if you would let us have a note of the amount due'. The letter erroneously referred to the purchase of the fee simple; it was the purchase of the annuity which was intended. James Murphy died on 17 October 1968, and after some further correspondence the defendants wrote to the solicitors for the personal representatives of the deceased on 22 September 1969 stating that the amount required to redeem the outstanding annuity on the vested cottage would be £1,163. The personal representatives had some difficulty in raising that sum and the redemption was not concluded until 12 October 1972 when £1,163 was paid to the defendants. On 18 October 1972, the county council certified that the annuity had been redeemed in full.

As already stated, the redemption took place under s. 99 of the Housing Act, 1966. That section provides:

> An annuity at any time outstanding may, if the housing authority entitled to receive the annuity think fit, be redeemed by the person liable to pay the annuity by payment to the authority of such amount as may be approved by the Minister, and the premises, which but for this section would be subject to and charged with the payment of the annuity or the part, shall, on receipt by the authority of the amount so approved, stand freed and discharged from the payment of the annuity.

The minister therein referred to was the Minister for Local Government, now the Minister for the Environment. Under s. 100 where an annuity is redeemed under s. 99, all the provisions of the Act of 1936, including the statutory conditions, shall cease to apply in respect of the cottage.

The sum of £1,163, as being the redemption value of the annuity, was arrived at by the defendants in accordance with directions included at para. 147D of a circular No.H.5/67 issued by the Department for Local Government (as it then was) in 1967, requiring the redemption value of the annuity to be based not on the capitalised value of the annuity, but on the current market value of the cottage, due allowance being made for the number of years for which the annuity had been paid on the cottage. In *Meade v Cork County Council* (SC) 31 July 1974, unrep., this court decided that the method of assessment of the redemption value of an annuity assessed in accordance with para. 147D of the said circular was incorrect, the correct amount being the capitalised value of the annuity outstanding at the time when redemption took place. In the instant case, it is agreed that the redemption value of the annuity under s. 99 of the 1966 Act, in accordance with the principles laid down by this court in *Meade v Cork County Council*, is the sum of £227.47.

There was therefore an overpayment by the plaintiff of the sum of £935.53. After *Meade's* case had been decided, the plaintiff claimed the return of the sums so over-paid by her in respect of the redemption of the annuity, but the defendants refused to refund such overpayment.

The defendants having failed to repay the overpayments made by the plaintiff, these proceedings were instituted, and the defendants pleaded that the sum of £1,163 was paid by the plaintiff voluntarily and with full knowledge of the facts, and that if any sum had been overpaid by the plaintiff, it was paid under a mistake of law and is irrecoverable. When the matter came for hearing before the Circuit Court Judge, he referred to this court for determination the following questions:

1. Whether the defendants were entitled to require payment by the plaintiff of the sum actually paid in respect of redemption of the said annuity?
2. If the defendants were not entitled to require the said sum to be paid, whether the sum was paid by a mistake either of law or of fact?
3. If the said sum was paid by the plaintiff by mistake, whether the said sum or any part thereof is now recoverable?

As to the first question, having regard to the decision of this court in *Meade v Cork County Council*, counsel for the defendants very properly conceded that the county council were not entitled to require payment by the plaintiff of the sum of £1,163 and that, as stated earlier in this judgment, it was agreed that the sum of £227.47 was the correct redemption value of the annuity.

Likewise, in respect of the second question, the argument in this court proceeded on the basis that the mistake was not one of fact but of law. Both parties were agreed that the mistake was one of law; the defendants submitted that, as it was a voluntary payment, no sum was recoverable by the plaintiff, whilst the plaintiff submitted that whilst the mistake was one of law, it was one made by the defendants when they were in a privileged position with the right to withhold that privilege and that therefore the payment was not voluntary.

The real question therefore for determination is whether a payment made, in circumstances such as the present, in mistake of law is recoverable. The general rule is usually stated to be that where money is paid under the influence of a mistake, and the mistake is one of fact, an action will lie to recover it back; but that to entitle the plaintiff to recover, the mistake upon which he has acted must be one of fact, not of law. Thus in *Pollock on Contracts*, (13th ed.), edited by Professor Winfield, it is stated at p. 378 that 'money paid under a mistake of law cannot in any case be recovered'. Similar statements are to be found in many textbooks. However, the Judicial Committee of the Privy Council held in *Kiriri Cotton Co. Ltd v Dewani* [1960] 2 WLR 127 that a plaintiff may recover money paid on a mistake of law provided that he is not in *pari delicto* with the defendant in mistaking the law. Delivering the advice of the Privy Council, Lord Denning said at p. 133:

Nor is it correct to say that money paid under a mistake of law can never be recovered back. The true proposition is that money paid under a mistake of law, by itself and without more, cannot be recovered back. James L.J. pointed that out in *Rogers v Ingham*. If there is something more in addition to a mistake of law—if there is something in the defendant's conduct which shows that, of the two of them, he is the one primarily responsible for the mistake—then it may be recovered back. Thus, if as between the two of them the duty of observing the law is placed on the shoulders of the one rather than the other—it being imposed on him specially for the protection of the other—then they are not *in pari delicto* and the money can be recovered back; see *Browning v Morris*, by Lord Mansfield. Likewise, if the responsibility for the mistake lies more on the one than the other because he has misled the other when he ought to know better—then again they are not in *pari delicto* and the money can be recovered back.

This passage was cited with approval by Kenny J. in *Dolan v Neligan* [1967] IR 247, at 260. Again, even where there has been no mistake of fact, a plaintiff may still recover monies so paid in an action for money had and received upon proof that the monies were paid by him involuntarily, that is, as the result of some extortion, coercion or compulsion in the legal sense—see per Windeyer J. in *Mason v New South Wales*, 102 CLR 108, 139. He cannot recover if the payment was made voluntarily. A payment may be said to be voluntary, in this context, when the payer makes it deliberately with a knowledge of all relevant facts, and either being indifferent to whether or not he is liable in law, or knowing, or having reason to think, himself not liable, yet intending finally to close the transaction—see per Windeyer J. at p. 143. Whether the payment has been voluntary in this sense may also be deduced from the relationship of the parties. As Abott C.J. said in *Morgan v Palmer*, 2 B & C 729 at p. 734:

It has been well argued that the payment having been voluntary, it cannot be recovered back in an action for money had and received. I agree that such a consequence would have followed had the parties been on equal terms. But if one party has the power of saying to the other, 'That which you require shall not be done except upon the conditions I choose to impose', no person can contend that they stand upon anything like an equal footing.

In such a case, the payment is by no means to be considered to be voluntary—see per McTiernan J. in *Bell v Shire of Serpentine*, (1969) 121 CLR 137.

Applying these principles to the present case, the plaintiff is in my judgment entitled to recover the overpayment of £935.43 made by her. The payment of £1,163 made by the plaintiff was not 'voluntary' in the context aforesaid. The parties were not on equal terms; the defendants had the power, if they thought fit, to withhold permission for the redemption of the annuity; they were however prepared to allow the plaintiff to redeem it, but only on the conditions imposed by them, which included exacting a payment in excess of that permitted by the statute. The plaintiff was not in possession of all the relevant facts, and did not know, nor had she reason to think, that she was not liable to pay the sum demanded by the defendants for the redemption of the annuity. The defendants were in my view primarily responsible for the mistake and the parties were accordingly not in *pari delicto*.

I would accordingly answer the questions submitted by the learned Circuit Court Judge as follows: Question 1 No. Question 2 The sum paid was paid by a mistake of law. Question 3 Yes.

Kenny J.:

. . . The aphorism 'money paid under a mistake of fact may be recovered but money paid under a mistake of law cannot' is grossly inaccurate. It has the advantage of simplicity but the matter is much more complex than it suggests. I have no doubt that the excessive sum fixed by the county council for the redemption was caused by the circular sent by the Department of Local Government which was based on an entirely wrong interpretation of s. 99 and which was, therefore, a mistake of law. The recovery of a sum so paid is well dealt with in *Law of Restitution* by Goff J. and Professor Jones (2nd ed., 1978) ch. 4. It has also been dealt with in the case law; my judgment when I was a judge of the High Court in *Dolan v Neligan* [1967] IR 245 and the decision of the Privy Council in *Kiriri Cotton Co. Ltd v Ranchoddas* [1960] AC 192.

In the latter Lord Denning said:

> It is not correct to say that everyone is presumed to know the law. The true proposition is that no man can excuse himself from doing his duty by saying that he did not know the law on the matter. *Ignorantia juris neminem excusat*. Nor is it correct to say that money paid under a mistake of law can never be recovered back. The true proposition is that money paid under a mistake of law by itself and without more cannot be recovered back . . . If there is something more in addition to a mistake of law—if there is something in the defendant's conduct which shows that of the two of them, he is the one primarily responsible for the mistake,—then it may be recovered back . . . if the responsibility for the mistake lies more on the one than the other—because he has misled the other when he ought to know better—then again they are not *in pari delicto* and the money can be recovered back.

In the instant case the plaintiff's solicitor wrote to the defendants asking what was the redemption price of the annuity. The plaintiff's solicitor could not be expected to know the redemption price. He relied on the defendants to give him the correct figure. Nor could he be expected to anticipate the decision of the Supreme Court in *Meade's* case. It is important to bear in mind that the decision of the Supreme Court reversed that of a High Court Judge who thought that the excessive amount of the redemption price of an annuity could not be recovered back from the defendants in that case.

I have no doubt that the plaintiff is entitled to recover the £935.53 from the defendants.

The answers to the questions posed by the Circuit Court Judge should, in my opinion be: (i) The defendants were not entitled to require payment by the plaintiff of the sum actually paid in respect of the redemption of the annuity. (ii) The amount of the redemption price of the annuity was paid under a mistake of law. (iii) £935.53, part of the redemption price paid, is recoverable by the plaintiff as personal representative from the defendants.

(O'Higgins C.J. concurred.)

B. DURESS BY THREATENED BREACH OF CONTRACT.

In Re Hooper and Grass Contract [1949] VLR 269

Fullagar J.:

Vendor and purchaser summons issued under s. 49 of the Property Law Act 1928 at the instance of the purchaser. The contract was made on 27 January 1948, and the date provided for payment of balance of purchase money was, in the events which happened, 24 February 1948.

The question in issue relates to an irrigation charge imposed by a by-law made by the State Rivers and Water Supply Commission under s. 66 of the Water Act 1928. The total amount of the charge is £26 2s. The by-law was published in the Gazette of 29 October 1947, and it provided, in compliance with s. 66, that the charge was made and should be levied for the period beginning 1 September 1947, and ending 30 April 1948, and that it should be payable at specified places on 31 October 1947. By virtue of ss. 324 and 326 of the Water Act the irrigation charge in question became a charge on the land on the day when it became payable, i.e. 31 October 1947. Apart, therefore, from special provision in the contract, the vendor would be bound either to pay the amount himself, or to allow it in account on completion. See *Re Sneesby and Ades and Bowes' Contract*, [1919] VLR 497, at p. 504: the question which actually arose for decision in that case does not arise here. The contract, however, incorporates Table A of the Transfer of Land Act 1928, and clause 10 of Table A provides that all rates, taxes, assessments, fire insurance premiums and other outgoings in respect of the land shall be borne and paid by the purchaser as from the date on which he becomes entitled to possession and the same shall, if necessary, be apportioned between the vendor and purchaser. On the argument before me it was common ground that this clause applies to the irrigation charge in question, and I should think that it was clearly an outgoing in respect of the land. The purchaser, however, contended that the apportionment should be on the basis of time, while the vendor contended that it should be on the basis of water consumed. If the first contention were correct, then, the period for which the charge was imposed being from 1 September 1947, to 30 April 1948, the vendor would be responsible for £17 1s 10d. If the second contention were correct, then, since the vendor had used no water before the date of possession, the whole of the amount in question would fall on the purchaser.

I am clearly of opinion that the contention of the purchaser is correct. The first part of clause 10 of Table A makes it plain, I think, that the apportionment contemplated is to be made by reference to the time after the purchaser becomes entitled to possession. Nor is there, in my opinion, anything in the nature of a charge under the Water Act to take it outside the provision for apportionment in clause 10 or to support the view that it is apportionable on some other basis than a time basis. I need not refer in detail to the relevant provisions of the Act. It is true that under s. 66 the amount of the irrigation charge in respect of any land is arrived at by reference to the quantity of water apportioned to that land as a right in pursuance of ss. 56 and 61. But it has no relation to water used. It is payable in full if no water is used or more or less water than the quantity apportioned to the land as a right. More may be used under the last two paragraphs of s. 61, and, if more is used, it must be paid for at a rate per unit of volume fixed by by-law. The irrigation charge had nothing to do with water actually used, and I do not think that the vendor's contention can be supported.

The summons asks for a declaration and an order for payment by the vendor to the purchaser. The vendor, however, argues that I cannot make an order for payment, and that I should not therefore make a declaration of a right which cannot be enforced. This argument arises in this way. At the time of settlement the amount of the charges had not been paid, and the purchaser's solicitor sought to debit the vendor with this amount in making the various adjustments of rates etc., to arrive at the net amount payable by him. The vendor's solicitor refused to allow this to be done, and in a letter written on 1 March stated that the amount payable was £1,456 17s 4d, an amount which did not allow for a deduction of £17 1s 10d. He added that he was ready to settle if that amount was paid at once, and he added: 'Otherwise, as your client is now in default, he must suffer the penalties provided for in the contract and any other loss he may sustain.' Thereupon the sum of £1,456 17s 4d was paid under protest with an intimation that a vendor and purchaser summons would be issued. The summons was issued a few days later. The argument now is that the payment made was a voluntary payment and the amount thereof cannot be recovered as money had and received. Reliance was placed on *Donaldson v Gray*, [1920] VLR 379.

If no action would lie for the recovery of the sum in question, I do not think that I ought to make a declaration. Nothing more, however, appears from the report of *Donaldson v Gray* than that 'for the purposes of not delaying the settlement the purchaser's solicitors agreed under protest' to the vendor's demand. Cussen J. said, at p. 382: 'They agreed at the time, and they are not in a position to recover the money back.' He held that the mere fact of protest could not alter the position. I think that a good deal more appears in this case than appeared in *Donaldson v Gray*. There is a certain ambiguity—perhaps a studied ambiguity—about the letter of the vendor's solicitor, but the time for completion had passed, and the purchaser's solicitor certainly could not be blamed if he read that letter as a threat to cancel the contract if a sum in excess of what was really due were not paid. At least it purported to treat the purchaser as in default, and, in effect, while offering to waive the default if the purchaser paid the whole of the charge in question, threatened to exercise any remedy available for default if the purchaser did not pay the whole of that charge.

Now, time is expressly made of the essence of the contract in this case, and, if the purchaser were really in default, and the vendor demanded a price for refraining from taking any step which he was entitled to take on default, and the purchaser, rather than have any such step taken, paid the price, it would seem clear that he could not recover the price so paid as money had and received. The position would not be affected by his paying expressly 'under protest'. This was really, I think, in substance the position in *Smith v William Charlick Ltd*, (1924) 34 CLR 38. A says to B: 'I am not bound to do a certain thing. I will, however, do it if, but not unless, you pay me £10.' B says: 'I pay you the £10. The consequences of not paying it would be disastrous. But, though I pay it, I pay it under protest.' That is plainly, in my opinion, not this case. The due date for completion under the contract was 24 February 1948. A letter written by the vendor's solicitor on that date shows that the vendor was not insisting on completion on that precise date. He had waived the condition that time was of the essence, and he could not thereafter insist on completion by any definite date unless and until he had given a notice requiring the purchaser to pay on or before some reasonable date in the future. What the vendor was doing was not threatening to exercise a legal right unless he were paid a price for not exercising it: he was threatening to withhold that to which the other party was legally entitled unless he were paid a price which he had no right to receive. In such a case I think the true rule of law is that a payment under protest is not a voluntary payment, whatever the position may be where the payment is not made under protest. It makes no difference that the vendor honestly believed that he was legally entitled in any case to the price which he asked. In these cases there is very reasonably said to be a practical compulsion to pay a demand not justified by law. The following authorities, to which Mr Adam referred me are all, I think, relevant: *Fraser v Pendlebury*, [1861] 31 LJ CP 1, *Close v Phipps*, [1844] 7 M & G 586, *Atkinson v Denby*, [1862] 31 LJ Ex 362, *Ashmole v Wainwright*, [1842] 2 QB 837, *Green v Duckett*, [1883] 11 QBD 275, and *Knutson v The Bourkes Syndicate*, [1941] SCR (Can.) 419. The Canadian case is criticised in a note in Can B Rev, 19, p. 694, but I am much more impressed by the decision than by the criticism. Kerwin J., who delivered the judgment of himself and four other judges, cited, at p. 423, two very pertinent passages from the judgments of Bayley J. and Holroyd J. in *Shaw v Woodcock*, [1827] 7 B & C 73. Holroyd J. put it very shortly. He said, at p. 85: 'Upon the question whether a payment be voluntary or not, the law is quite clear. If a party making the payment is obliged to pay, in order to obtain possession of things to which he is entitled, the money so paid is not a voluntary, but a compulsory payment, and may be recovered back.'

Bayley J. also rejected the argument, which had been put, that the owner must be shown to be under an immediate pressing necessity of receiving his property.

In cases of this type the withholding of another's legal right is, I think, itself treated as a 'practical compulsion'. Cases like *Criterion Theatres Ltd v Melbourne & Metropolitan Board of Works*, [1945] VLR 267 seem to differ only in that the 'practical compulsion' takes a different form. In the *Criterion Theatres* case, the plaintiff, if the water had been cut off, would in all probability have suffered very serious damage through the deterioration or practical destruction of its racing track. Such cases may be described in the words of Lord Ellenborough C.J. in *Smith v Cuff*, [1817] 6 M & S 160, at p. 165, as cases where 'one holds the rod, and the other bows to it', or in the words of Cockburn C.J. in *Atkinson v Denby*, [1862] 31 LJ Ex 362, as cases 'where one person can dictate and the other has hardly any other alternative but to submit'.

Possibly in both classes of case the underlying basis on which the money paid, but not legally payable, is recoverable is that it was paid without consideration. This basis would not support the action if the payment was made voluntarily and with full knowledge of the facts. But payments made in certain circumstances are not treated by the law as being made voluntarily for the purposes of this principle. The manner in which the question whether the payment was 'voluntary' is discussed in the cases seems to suggest that the voluntary character of the payment will take it outside a general rule which would make it recoverable. The other possible analysis is that the money is paid under duress, a widely extended meaning being attached to the word 'duress'. But I think that there is really more to be said in favour of the former suggested analysis.

In *Donaldson v Gray*, [1920] VLR 379, the purchaser, although he paid or allowed in account sums for which the vendor was in law responsible, was held, I think, not to have proved enough to entitle him to maintain money had and received. I would regard it as a decision on particular facts: the 'practical compulsion', which was established in the cases cited above, was not established in *Donaldson v Gray* to the satisfaction of Cussen J. Those cases afford, to my mind, ample justification for holding here that the 'practical compulsion' is established.

The question asked by the summons is answered: Yes. It is apportionable in respect of time. Order that vendor pay to purchaser the sum of £17 1s 10d. Order that costs of summons be paid by vendor to purchaser.

Maskell v Horner [1915] 3 KB 106

Lord Reading C.J.:

From the year 1900 till 1912 the plaintiff carried on business at Spitalfields Market as a dealer in produce and the defendant throughout this period demanded and received payment by the plaintiff of market tolls on goods sold by the plaintiff in the market. It was decided by the Court of Appeal in *Attorney General v Horner* (No. 2)[1] that the defendant Horner was not entitled to demand tolls from the sellers, and it follows from this decision, which has not been and could not be challenged in this court, that the plaintiff was never under legal obligation to pay tolls to the defendant. The plaintiff having, during this period of years, paid a number of small sums of money as market tolls to the defendant, now sues to recover these sums as money had and received by the defendant to the use of the plaintiff. The action came for trial before Rowlatt J., who decided in favour of the defendant, and the plaintiff appeals to this court for a reversal of this judgment.

The question is whether the plaintiff made these payments in such circumstances as entitle him to recover them from the defendant in an action at law for money had and received.

. . .

Upon the second head of claim the plaintiff asserts that he paid the money not voluntarily but under the pressure of actual or threatened seizure of his goods, and that he is therefore entitled to recover it as money had and received. If the facts proved support this assertion the plaintiff would, in my opinion, be entitled to succeed in this action.

If a person with knowledge of the facts pays money, which he is not in law bound to pay, and in circumstances implying that he is paying it voluntarily to close the transaction, he cannot recover it. Such a payment is in law like a gift, and the transaction cannot be reopened. If a person pays money, which he is not bound to pay, under the compulsion of urgent and pressing necessity or of seizure, actual or threatened, of his goods he can recover it as money had and received. The money is paid not under duress in the strict sense of the term, as that implies duress of person, but under the pressure of seizure or detention of goods which is analogous to that of duress. Payment under such pressure establishes that the payment is not made voluntarily to close the transaction (per Lord Abinger C.B. and per Parke B. in *Atlee v Backhouse*[2]). The payment is made for the purpose of averting a threatened evil and is made not with the intention of giving up a right but under immediate necessity and with the intention of preserving the right to dispute the legality of the demand (per Tindal C.J. in *Valpy v Manley*[3]). There are numerous instances in the books of successful claims in this form of action to recover money paid to relieve goods from seizure. Other familiar instances are cases such as *Parker v Great Western Rly. Co.*,[4] where the money was paid to the railway company under protest in order to induce them to carry goods which they were refusing to carry except at rates in excess of those they were legally entitled to demand. These payments were made throughout a period of twelve months, always accompanied by the assertion that they were made under protest, and it was held that the plaintiffs were entitled to recover the excess payments as money had and received, on the ground that the payments were made under the compulsion of urgent and pressing necessity. That case was approved in *Great Western Rly. Co. v Sutton*,[5] when the judges were summoned to the House of Lords to give their opinion. Willes J., in stating his view of the law, said: 'When a man pays more than he is bound to do by law for the performance of a duty which the law says is owed to him for nothing, or for less than he had paid, there is a compulsion or concussion in respect of which he is entitled to recover the excess by *condictio indebiti*, or action for money had and received. This is every day's practice as to excess freight.' That is a clear and accurate statement in accordance with the views expressed by Blackburn J. in the same case and adopted by the House of Lords. It treats such claims made in this form of action as matters of ordinary practice and beyond discussion. (See also per Lord Chelmsford in *Lancashire and Yorkshire Rly. Co. v Gidlow*[6]).

[1.] [1913] 2 Ch. 140.   [3.] 1 CB 594, 602, 603.   [5.] LR 4 HL 226, 249.
[2.] 3 M & W 633, 646, 650.   [4.] 7 Man. & G. 253.   [6.] LR 7 HL 517, 527.

(Buckley L.J. concurred with Lord Reading. Pickford L.J. dissented.)

Note

In *Maskell v Horner*, Pickford L.J., while not doubting the principle, found that the plaintiff had not on the facts 'established' quasi-duress of goods. As we shall see, the inferences to be drawn from facts are highly problematical in this area.

The Australian and Canadian courts have developed a doctrine of practical compulsion by building on decisions such as *Maskell v Horner*: see Sutton, (1974) 20 McGill LJ 555. In England, Beatson's observations on the limited role afforded to duress ((1974) CLJ 97) in that jurisdiction provided an interesting contrast. However, judicial pronouncements on economic duress were not universally negative.

Ogilvie, 'Economic Duress, Inequality of Bargaining Power and Threatened Breach of Contract' (1981) 27 McGill LJ 289 at 296–9

. . .

Relying on *Rookes v Barnard*, Lord Denning M.R., in D. & C. *Builders v Rees* made some comments which until recently have been overlooked in the discussion of economic duress. In that well known case the plaintiffs were owed about £480 by the defendants and, to the knowledge of the defendants, were in desperate financial straits. Exploiting this knowledge, the defendants said that they could pay only £300, which the plaintiffs accepted, signing a receipt 'in completion of the account' at the insistence of Mrs Rees. The Court of Appeal held that the plaintiffs were entitled to recover the remaining £180 on two grounds: first, because there was no consideration for the settlement and, second, that there was no true accord because, as Lord Denning said, '[n]o person can insist on a settlement procured by intimidation'. This could be viewed as economic duress; moreover, D. & C. *Builders* could also be viewed as a case of two-party intimidation.

II. *Recent developments in England*

The significance of Lord Denning's remark was not lost on Kerr J. in *The Siboen and the Sibotre*, which is the fresh starting point for recent cases which recognise economic duress by threatened breach of contract. Two oil tankers were chartered in 1970 to Concord Petroleum Ltd, at the rate of £4.40 per ton per month on standard charterparties, for use in transporting oil from the Persian Gulf in the event that Concord was shut out from its Libyan supplies. The market slumped and Concord's parent company, Occidental Petroleum Inc., sought to renegotiate the rate, and they devised a scheme to give the owners the false impression that they had not substantial assets and had suffered great losses. Occidental threatened to repudiate the charter and allow Concord to go into liquidation if the rates were not lowered. The pressure on the owners was exacerbated by the fact that if the charterparties were repudiated the ships would have to be laid up because of the depressed market. The ships were mortgaged and the owners relied on the charterparties' income to repay the mortgages, as the charterers well knew. In such a squeeze the owners seemed to have no alternative but to concede the rate reduction. By mid-1973 the market was rising steeply again and the charterers were making huge profits. The owners asked them to revert to the original rate or the charterparties would be cancelled on the ground of coercion. The charterers declined to reinstate the original rate, the owners withdrew the ships and the charterers sued. The owners alleged that the renegotiated terms were void for misrepresentation or for duress, and Kerr J. held that the charterers were liable for fraudulent and innocent misrepresentation, but that the action in duress could not succeed.

The learned judge conceded that there was room for the development of the law in regard to contracts concluded under some form of compulsion not amounting to duress to the person, and stipulated the appropriate test:

. . . the court must in every case at least be satisfied that the consent of the other party was overborne by compulsion so as to deprive him of any *animus contrahendi*. This would depend on the facts of each case. One relevant factor would be whether the party relying on the duress made any protest at the time or shortly thereafter. Another would be to consider whether or not he treated the settlement as closing the transaction in question and as binding upon him, or whether he made it clear that he regarded the position as still open.

In the instant case Kerr, J. decided that there was neither sufficient coercion of the will nor protest, and that the owners had admitted that they regarded the agreement as binding, thus 'acting under great pressure, but only commercial pressure, and not under anything which could in law be regarded as a coercion of his will so as to vitiate his consent.'

This approach is unsatisfactory. Undoubtedly, it was convenient for the court that the threatened breach of contract took the form of fraudulent and innocent misrepresentations. But if there had been no misrepresentations would the charterers have escaped liability? Or would the judge have made an extra effort to find an alternative ground of liability? One would hope so. Here was a situation in which the owners were apparently under the greatest type of commercial pressure possible, submitting to the charterer's demands or risking insolvency, in the event that they proved unable to renegotiate the mortgages or find some other adequate solution. On the presumption that insolvency was the only alternative to submission (and the court's failure to probe the existence of alternatives should be noted), the owners could hardly be said not to have entered the agreement voluntarily. In this Kerr J. was quite right; there had indeed been a voluntary submission. But there always will be when the only alternatives available are worse. Thus it is questionable whether coercion of the will is a satisfactory criterion for distinguishing real economic duress from acceptable 'commercial pressure'. Indeed, there is coercion in *all* contracts: if I wish to purchase a loaf of bread I must pay its price, although I would much rather have the bread and the money in my pocket. The coercion here is a vital matter, yet in the absence of other factors it is most unlikely that courts would allow avoidance of the contract for economic duress. But even if coercion of the will is accepted as the key to the presence of economic duress, how is it to be distinguished from mere commercial pressure?

Kerr J. suggested several other relevant factors in the determination of the presence of economic duress, notably whether the victim protested or regarded the agreement as forever binding. The relevance of these factors is minimal. At the very least the victim might not be the 'protesting sort' or might consider protest superfluous. Moreover, a victim at the time of submission to duress is likely to consider himself fully bound and will only question the transaction later. The learned judge might have considered other factors, such as an initial inequality of bargaining power, or a subsequent inequality of bargaining power, the 'wrongfulness' of the coercive act, the adequacy of the consideration, the actual availability of other alternatives and the seriousness of the consequences to the victim of not submitting. These will be considered later.

Issues similar to those in *The Siboen and the Sibotre* were raised in *The Atlantic Baron*. A contract was agreed to between the plaintiffs and a South Korean shipbuilding company to build an oil tanker, 'The Atlantic Baron', for £30, 950,000. Article XI stated that the price was to be paid in five instalments and that the builders were to open a letter of credit to provide security for the repayment of the instalments in the event of their default. Ten months later the American dollar was devalued by ten per cent and the builders demanded a ten per cent increase in the purchase price in respect of the four instalments payable after the devaluation. The plaintiffs took legal advice and were told that the claim lacked foundation. Correspondence ensued with the plaintiffs noting that they too were adversely affected by the devaluation, yet had not increased freight rates under existing contracts; but to no avail. On 26 June 1973 the builders sent a telex requesting a final and decisive reply by 30 June; otherwise the contract would be terminated. The plaintiffs were caught because on 22 May they had concluded a three-year charterparty with Shell and could not get a substitute tanker. The builders were ignorant of this fact as well as of the fact that the plaintiffs would still be left with a handsome profit from the Shell contract after paying the ten per cent. They replied to the telex on 28 June 1973 that they would pay, 'in order to maintain an amicable relationship and without prejudice to our rights'. They asked that the letter of credit be increased accordingly and this was done. In an action to recover the ten per cent, the plaintiffs argued, first, that there was no additional consideration for the payments and, second, that the agreement was voidable because made involuntarily under economic duress. Mocatta J. held, though with some doubt, that there was consideration in the detriment to the builders in increasing the letter of credit, thus showing yet again that the courts can find consideration whenever it suits them. With respect to the second question, the learned judge opined that even when there was good consideration, where a threatened breach of contract had led to a further contract, that contract could be voidable for economic duress. Just what economic duress is, he did not decide. He did not have to because the plaintiff's subsequent failure to protest or litigate the transaction for almost two years was an affirmation of it; thus they were not entitled to claim a refund.

SECTION THREE—ECONOMIC DURESS AND INDUSTRIAL CONFLICT

The first decision of the House of Lords to establish economic duress was *Universe Tankships Inc. of Monrovia v International Transport Workers Federation* [1982] 2 WLR 803.

The decision was not universally welcomed.

Atiyah, 'Economic Duress and "The Overborne Will"' (1982) 98 LQR 197

Since 1976 there have been four English and one Privy Council decision recognising the existence in principle of the concept of 'economic duress' as furnishing a defence to an action on a contract, or as providing a ground for the recovery of money paid: *The Siboen and the Sibotre* [1976] 1 Lloyd's Rep. 293; *North Ocean Shipping Co. Ltd v Hyundai Construction (The Atlantic Baron)* [1979] QB 705; *Pao On v Lau Yiu* [1980] AC 614; *Universe Tankships of Monrovia Inc. v International Transport Workers' Federation* [1981] ICR 129; *Syros Shipping Co. S.A. v Elaghill Trading Co.* [1981] 3 All ER 189. It is true that in only two of these cases (*The Atlantic Baron* and the *Universe Tankships* case) was the court satisfied that economic duress had been made out on the facts, and that even in these two cases relief for economic duress was ultimately denied, in the first because the contract was held to have been affirmed by the innocent party, and in the other because the guilty party was a trade union entitled to rely on the 'trade dispute' statutory immunities. Nevertheless, it is clear that here is a growth area of the law of contract of considerable potential importance.

It is, therefore, particularly desirable that this new doctrine should start life on a sound conceptual basis and not be shunted into a blind alley for lack of adequate analysis. Yet, as a result of an oversight of monumental proportions, this latter fate appears at present to be a serious danger, because all five of these cases have attempted to justify, to a greater or lesser degree, the concept of economic duress by invoking the traditional theory that duress 'overbears the will' of the party subject to it. The purpose of this note is to draw the attention of the practising profession to the fact that all these five cases have overlooked a crucially important case decided by the House of Lords as recently as 1975, namely *Lynch v DPP of Northern Ireland* [1975] AC 653, which totally demolishes the theory that duress operates by 'overbearing the will' of the party subject to it.

The 'overborne will' theory has, of course, a long history in cases of common law duress as well as in many equitable cases of undue influence, so it is hardly surprising that it should be used by the courts to justify the new concept of economic duress, and (as stated above) it was so used, to some extent, in all five of the cases listed above. It will suffice here to refer to the discussion in the *Pao On* case as this contains the fullest analysis of the basis of the new doctrine of economic duress. It is unnecessary to refer to the facts except to mention that the context was a complex commercial transaction in which the defendant alleged that he had been induced to make the promise sued on as a result of threats to break other contractual obligations. Delivering the opinion of the Privy Council, Lord Scarman several times reiterated that economic (or indeed, any other form of) duress operated by overbearing the will of the person subject to it. 'Duress, whatever form it takes, is a coercion of the will so as to vitiate consent' (p. 635). Again, where commercial pressures were alleged to constitute economic coercion, the duress 'must be such that the victim must have entered the contract against his will, must have had no alternative course open to him . . .' (p. 636). Further, it must even be shown that the victim's act 'was not a voluntary act on his part' (p. 636).

This analysis, it is submitted, is totally inconsistent with the speeches in the House of Lords in *Lynch's* case, which does not appear to have been cited in any of the five cases mentioned above. *Lynch's* case was, of course, a decision on the criminal law, concerning the applicability of the defence of duress to a charge of murder, where the accused was charged as an accessory and not a principal. The defence was upheld by a majority of three to two; but all five members of the House discussed the theoretical basis of the defence of duress, some of them at considerable length, and all five of them agreed in rejection of the 'overborne will' theory. Thus Lord Morris of Borth-y-Gest accepts that a person subjected to duress has a moment of time to decide whether he will submit or not. If he submits, 'what is done will be done most unwillingly but intentionally' (p. 670). Lord Wilberforce says that the best opinion is that duress does not negative intention, but is superimposed on the other ingredients of the offence. *Coactus volui* sums up the combination: the victim completes the act and knows that he is doing so; but the addition of the element of duress prevents the law from treating what he has done as a crime' (p. 680). Lord Simon of Glaisdale, dissenting in the result, concurred on this point in the fullest analysis to be found in the speeches (or, indeed, anywhere else in English law) on the nature of the concept of duress. He stresses that 'an *intention* to bring about a consequence of an act can coexist with a *desire* that such consequence should not ensue' (p. 690). He distinguishes a case of 'true necessity' from a case of duress. In the former, there is no choice of action and the act is not a product of the will at all, and is not even an 'act' of the person constrained. But this is not the case with other (not 'true') cases of necessity, nor with cases of duress. 'In both [such] sets of circumstances there is power of choice between two alternatives, but one of the alternatives is so disagreeable that even serious infraction of the criminal law seems preferable. In both, the consequence of the act is intended, within any permissible definition of intention' (p. 692). At the end of his analysis, Lord Simon concludes by saying, 'I hope, indeed, to have demonstrated that duress is not inconsistent with act and will, the will being deflected, not destroyed . . . ' (p. 695). Similar passages are to be found in the speeches of Lord Kilbrandon (p. 703) and Lord Edmund-Davies (p. 709). It appears from the latter's speech that the 'overborne will' theory was actually adopted by the trial judge and fully canvassed in argument before the House of Lords.

Thus what we have here is an unanimous and authoritative rejection of the 'overborne will' theory, doubtless overlooked in the contract cases mentioned above because this was a criminal case. But any suggestion that these remarks are, for that reason, inapplicable in the law of contract is surely unacceptable. First, it is clear that in the passages referred to above, the Law Lords were not discussing a doctrine of peculiar application to the criminal law, but the very nature and meaning of the concept of duress. They were addressing themselves to fundamentally juristic questions involved in the meaning of concepts like intention, act, will and voluntary conduct—all concepts which are just as relevant in contract law as in the criminal law. Secondly, two of their lordships, Lord Wilberforce and Lord Simon, actually referred, if only *en passant*, to the analogy of contract law (see pp 680 and 695) to justify the views they were upholding in relation to the criminal law. In doing this, Lord Wilberforce and Lord Simon may well have been guilty of a certain disingenuousness having regard to the fact that the 'overborne will' theory has undoubtedly held the field in contract law for many years, but that does not alter the fact that these two, at least, showed clearly enough that they regarded the new analysis as applicable to the law of contract.

But even if the speeches in *Lynch's* case are not finally authoritative in the law of contract, it is nevertheless submitted that they ought to be followed, both because they are far more rationally persuasive than the 'overborne will' theory, and also because they are more consistent with the developing rules of the doctrine of economic duress. As to the first point it is difficult to disagree with the various speeches in *Lynch's* case which demonstrate the difficulties of the 'overborne will' theory. A victim of duress *does* normally know what he is doing, does choose to submit, and *does* intend to do so. Indeed, as has often been pointed out by American writers (see, e.g. Dawson, 'Economic Duress—An Essay in Perspective' (1947) 45 Michigan LR 253, 267) the more extreme the pressure, the more real is the consent of the victim. The victim of the modern mugger who surrenders his wallet with a knife at his throat certainly knows what he is doing, and intends to do it. (This analysis may cause difficulty for other aspects of the criminal law—e.g. the victim's voluntary surrender of his wallet is clearly not such a consent as to negative a charge of theft—but that need not be pursued here.)

In the second place, the 'overborne will' theory is internally inconsistent and contradictory, even as enounced in the *Pao On* case. I have already cited a passage from Lord Scarman's speech (on p. 636 of the report) in which the defence of duress is confined to those cases in which the victim 'had no alternative course open to him'. Yet it is clear that this cannot be taken literally because on the very same page Lord Scarman indicates that one of the factors to be considered in deciding whether economic duress has been established, is the *effectiveness* of the alternative remedies open to the victim. So it is clear that the defence may be available even where the victim does have alternative courses of action open to him; indeed, on the analysis in *Lynch's* case, the victim *always* has such alternatives open to him. Even the victim of the mugger may resist at the price of his own life, if he has the courage to do so (as the late Professor W. Friedmann had).

Thirdly, as pointed out by Lord Simon in *Lynch's* case, the 'overborne will' theory is difficult to reconcile with the now established rule that duress renders a contract voidable and not void. As Lord Simon also points out, the contrast is with the defence of *non est factum*. That is a case where there is a total lack of consent. No doubt it is possible to envisage rare cases of duress or even undue influence where the victim is reduced to such a stage of submission that he acts as though in a trance without knowing what he is doing, in which case a different analysis may be appropriate. But that is certainly not the ordinary case of duress, still less is such an analysis likely to be relevant in the commercial contexts in which economic duress is pleaded.

It may, of course, be argued that all this is a highly theoretical debate, or perhaps even that it is merely a terminological or conceptual debate without practical import-ance. Provided that the courts evolve, as they seem to be doing, subsidiary rules which are to be applied to determine if and when the victim's will is to be 'taken' to have been 'overborne', it may not matter what formula is used to describe the process. For myself, I would reject this argument, if only because it is desirable that rules should be formulated in a way which commands rational assent. A rule which declares that it only operates when a person has no choice, but then requires examination of the choices open to him, does not inspire confidence among rational beings. But there are also practical reasons for desiring that the 'overborne will' theory should now be consigned to the historical scrapheap. So long as the law is stated in terms of this theory, there is a real danger that the formula may be taken too literally by those whose business it is to apply the law—and it must be remembered that this includes arbitrators as well as solicitors and counsel advising their clients. In the *Syros Shipping* case, for instance, Lloyd J., in remitting the case to the arbitrator to reconsider (among other issues) a plea of economic duress, simply said that the decisions cited above appeared to establish 'that the question of duress turns on whether the commercial pressure exercised by one party on the other was such as to vitiate the other party's consent by coercion of his will' (p. 192). This seems a clear invitation to the arbitrator to treat the issue as one of fact, but if the issue is so treated, it is surely bound to divert attention into quite irrelevant inquiries into the psychological motivations of the party pleading duress.

Careful study of the cases referred to above will show that this is the wrong approach. Duress is clearly only partly a question of fact. Once it is appreciated that the victim of duress has chosen between evils, it becomes necessary to examine the nature and acceptability of the choice he was presented with. That clearly involves important questions of law, and cannot be treated as a pure question of fact. To treat the issue as one of fact diverts inquiry from the really vital issues in a case of economic duress, namely what sort of threats is it permissible to make, and when is it permissible for a victim of duress to reopen a question which has apparently been closed by his submission to the coercion.

It is much to be hoped that the next case to involve a plea of economic duress will see *Lynch's* case drawn to the attention of the court, and the law placed on a sounder theoretical footing.

Lord Wedderburn (1982) 45 MLR 556 was also critical of this new line of authority:

In 1976, there began a line of judgments in commercial cases which swept this old learning aside. They were attempts to introduce a new element of 'fairness' into some commercial bargains by judges insufficiently reckless (or courageous, according to taste) to go the whole hog and limit private enterprise by judicial reference to 'inequality of bargaining power'.[1] Instead, the Privy Council and Kerr J. introduced the more limited concept that has come to be known as 'economic duress'. This operates whenever 'the consent of the other party was overborne by compulsion so as to deprive him of any *animus contrahendi*'.[2] Mere 'commercial pressure' by itself is not enough (how could it be?). But any 'coercion of the will which vitiates consent' suffices.[3] While English judges

have not stretched the doctrine to the length of their American counterparts,[4] and
most of the cases in which the doctrine has been applied have involved duress by way
of acts wrongful in themselves,[5] judges have now stated the doctrine in wider terms.[6]
Economic duress turns upon whether 'the commercial pressure exercised by one party
on the other was such as to vitiate the other party's consent by coercion of his will.'[7]

Although approved by today's modish liberalism, this fashionable new doctrine
suffers, even in commercial law, from a number of profoundly unsatisfactory features.
First, as Professor Atiyah has amply demonstrated, its conceptual apparatus of the
'overborne will' is wrongheaded, 'internally inconsistent and contradictory.'[8] A victim
of this sort of duress does choose to submit. His remedy stems from the fact not that
he has no choice but that the alternatives left open to him were in the court's eyes
inadequate. And a contract induced by such duress is voidable (not void).[9]

Secondly, is there not something absurd in asking whether, for the purposes of our
commercial law, one large corporate trading entity has 'overborne the will' of another?
Indeed, lawyers should now no doubt be eagerly seeking out the *alter ego* in each such
corporation, the men whose (real) will must be 'coerced' before the corporate (fictional)
consent is vitiated.[10]

Thirdly, consent is vitiated where the court decides that the pressure is not
'legitimate'.[11] And illegitimate pressure may not involve (though it usually will involve)
an act unlawful in itself. 'Duress can of course exist even if the threat is one of lawful
action; whether it does so depends upon the nature of the demand.'[12] At this critical
point, 'economic duress' becomes a formidable and uncertain liability. It is not in itself
a tort. But if it is threatened or employed deliberately to injure, would the judges, if it
suited them, not treat it as such? Would a combination to impose 'economic duress'
not be treated (if need be) as a conspiracy to damage by unlawful means thereby
giving rise to liability in damages and an injunction? Is the liability for economic
duress (even if limited to restitution of benefits and rescission of contracts) not
broadly equivalent to a civil liability for intentional injury without combination—the
so-called wrong of '*Quinn v Leathem* without the conspiracy'?[13] Such a liability outflanks,
in part at least, the liberal decision in *Allen v Flood*,[14] long disliked by many judges for
having 'damned a stream of thought that . . . would have had a beneficial effect on the
law of tort.'[15] Paradoxically, though, these strands of judicial interventionism are being
woven into society at the very time when orthodox economic and political thinking is
moving in the opposite direction, towards the hegemony of 'market forces'. In claiming
more control over the fairness of commercial bargains through such instruments as
'economic duress', perhaps some judges have seen themselves as seeking to introduce
a countervailing factor to that trend in the interest of social or economic 'stability',
always the 'supreme law' for the judiciary.[16]

But whatever the general merits of the new 'economic duress' doctrine, its application to labour relations gives it a quite novel social function. Not that it is being
applied to employment in what might be considered the most obvious way. The
individual employment relationship is indeed based upon 'coercion'. The contract of
employment is a 'command in the guise of an agreement'; the employer 'fills in the
blank' constituted by the legal institution of 'contract'.[17] The individual worker who
accepts engagement rather than starve or who obeys an employer's orders rather than
be dismissed into unemployment[18] is not normally understood by lawyers to have
suffered from 'economic duress' (though his will may surely have been 'overborne').
Few judges are likely to understand their new doctrine to apply to such cases.

[1] As would Lord Denning M.R., *Lloyds Bank v Bundy* [1975] QB 326, 339.
[2] Per Kerr J. *The Siboen*, p. 336; *Barton v Armstrong* [1976] AC 104 (PC).

3. Per Lord Scarman *Pao On v Lau Yiu Long* [1980] AC 614, 635. On burden of proof see *Barton v Armstrong* [1976] AC 104.

4. See J. P. Dawson 'Economic Duress' (1947) 45 Michigan LR 253.

5. E.g. torts or threats to break contracts: *North Ocean Shipping Co. Ltd v Hyundai Construction Co. Ltd* [1979] QB 705; the *Universe Tankships* case [1982] 2 WLR 803 (inducing breach of contract).

6. See Lord Scarman, *Burmah Oil Ltd v Bank of England* [1980] AC 1090, 1140; *Pao On v Lau Yiu Long* [1980] AC 614, 635–636. 'As yet the cases do not answer the question whether a threatened breach of contract marks the boundaries of economic duress,' A. Evans [1981] JBL 188, 192; G. Treitel, op. cit. p. 307 states that 'legally wrongful conduct . . . is necessary to constitute duress'. See too P. Baker (1979) 95 LQR 475; J. Adams (1979) 42 MLR 557; J. Beatson [1974] CLJ 97 and (1976) 92 LQR 496.

7. Per Lloyd J. *Syros Shipping S.A. v Elaghill Trading Co.* [1981] 3 All ER 189, 192.

8. 'Economic Duress and the Overborne Will' (1982) 98 LQR 197, 201 (also pointing out the 'monumental oversight' of the reasoning in *Lynch v DPP Northern Ireland* [1975] AC 653, in the recent civil cases). Atiyah's criticism is especially applicable to the judgment of Parker J. who found as a *'question of fact'* that the loss to the shipowners was 'so potentially disastrous that they had no practical option but to submit' [1981] ICR 141.

9. Confirmed by Lord Diplock, *Universe Tankships* [1982] 2 WLR 812.

10. See: *The Lady Gwendolen* [1965] p. 294; *The Garden City, Financial Times,* 12 March 1982; *Bolton (Engineering) Ltd v Graham* [1957] 1 QB 159; *Lennard's Carrying Co. v Asiatic Petroleum* [1915] AC 705, 713; *Tesco Supermarkets Ltd v Nattrass* [1972] AC 153; *Thomson & Son v Deakin* [1952] Ch. 646; *Belmont Finance Corp. v Williams Furniture* [1979] Ch. 250; (No.2) [1980] 1 All ER 393.

11. Per Lord Diplock, *Universe Tankships* [1982] 2 WLR 813–814; per Lord Wilberforce, *Barton v Armstrong* [1976] AC 104, 121: 'the pressure must be one of a kind that the law does not regard as legitimate.'

12. Per Lord Scarman, ibid. at p. 829, citing *Thorne v M.T.A.* [1937] AC 797, 806; see too Goff and Jones, *The Law of Restitution,* p. 182.

13. Per Lord Devlin, *Rookes v Barnard* [1964] AC 1215–1216. But this is the same House of Lords which has recently restricted the ambit of the tort of conspiracy to use unlawful means; see *Lonrho Ltd v Shell Ltd* [1982] AC 173; and Clerk and Lindsell, *Torts* (15th ed., 1982) paras 15–06, 15–15, 15–20 and 15–23 (Wedderburn).

14. [1898] AC 1 (HL). Lord Brandon in *Universe Tankships* actually states that duress is 'actionable as a tort if it causes damage or loss' [1982] 2 WLR 828. But the orthodox view is that it is not a tort as such; see, e.g. Lord Diplock, ibid. at p. 814. Compare the progress of 'breach of confidence' towards the character of a liability in tort; Law Commission, *Breach of Confidence* (Cmnd. 8388 (1981)).

15. Lord Devlin, 'Samples of Lawmaking' 1962, p. 11.

16. J. A. G. Griffith, *The Politics of the Judiciary* (2nd ed., 1981) p. 235: see too, J. Clark and Wedderburn, Chap. 6, *Labour Law and Industrial Relations—Building on Kahn-Freund* (Wedderburn, R. Lewis and J. Clark, eds forthcoming, O.U.P.).

17. O. Kahn-Freund, Introduction to K. Renner *The Institutions of Private Law and their Social Functions* (1949), p. 28; cf. his *Labour and the Law* (2nd ed., 1977) p. 6: the employee's 'submission' and 'subordination' is 'concealed by that indispensable figment of the legal mind known as the "contract of employment".'

18. Cf. *Latter v Braddell* (1881) 50 LJQB 448; (1880) 50 LJCP 166 (order to submit to medical examination obeyed under protest; no threat of force, therefore no duress; it seems unlikely that judges today would reverse the finding on duress).

B. & S. Contracts and Design Ltd *v* Victor Green Publications Ltd [1984] ICR 419

Eveleigh L.J.:

In September 1978 the plaintiffs agreed to erect stands for the defendants at Olympia for an international fire, security and safety exhibition, which was to be open to the public from 23 April 1979 until 27 April 1979. The contract price was £11,731.50. The contract contained a *force majeure* clause in these terms: 'Every effort will be made to carry out any contract based on an estimate, but the due performance of it is subject to variation or cancellation owing to an act of God, war, strikes, civil commotions, work to rule or go-slow or overtime bans, lock-out, fire, flood, drought or any other cause beyond our control, or owing to our inability to procure materials or articles except at increased prices due to any of the foregoing causes.'

The plaintiffs had a subsidiary company in Wales. That company was in some financial difficulty and indeed at the end of 1978 had become insolvent. In February 1979 that company gave notice to its employees that there was a danger that they would have to close down the works and it was later indicated that the directors were contemplating closing down the works on 27 April 1979. In the event sixty days' notice was given to that work force, terminating on 27 April 1979.

The contract provided for the dismantling of the stands and that would take place perhaps on 27 but probably on 28 and perhaps 29 April. The plaintiffs decided to use the men who were threatened with redundancy in the subsidiary company and some eighteen of them were brought to Olympia to do the work, and they arrived on 12 April. In the meantime there had been some negotiations between the subsidiary and trade union officials, and of course the plaintiffs were concerned in controlling that situation. The workmen were demanding severance pay. They asked for sixty days' wages. They were not entitled to any severance pay, and at some stage the plaintiffs did indicate that they would be prepared to pay two weeks' wages *ex gratia*. When the men arrived on 12 April at Olympia they stopped work: they wanted their sixty days' severance pay. They were also annoyed at the fact that the plaintiffs intended to use other labour to dismantle the equipment.

News of the stoppage reached Mr Barnes, who was the director responsible for the exhibition on behalf of the defendants, and he discussed the matter with the plaintiffs' financial director, Mr Fenech, on 17 April. The men had for a short while resumed work in the interval, but on that day, 17, they stopped working again. On 13, 14, 15 and 16 there was no work because Olympia was closed for the Bank Holiday period. Mr Fenech told Mr Barnes that the workforce had stated that they would settle for twenty eight days' severance pay and Mr Barnes said that he would have to refer that to his board.

There came the moment when Mr Barnes, realising that the plaintiffs were short of money, in the sense that their cash flow was not good, offered Mr Fenech £4,500. He intended that offer to be an advance payment on the contract price. Mr Fenech apparently understood it as an offer over and above the contract price, and when Mr Fenech subsequently, on 18 April, spoke with Mr Barnes and said that the plaintiffs were prepared to pay £4,500 towards the severance pay and to accept Mr Barnes' offer of £4,500—which figures together would have amounted to a sum acceptable to the men, namely £9,000—it then became clear to Mr Fenech that Mr Barnes' offer had been an advance payment and not one over and above the contract price. Mr Fenech then said that it would be necessary for him to consult the managing director as to whether or not the plaintiffs would be prepared to pay £4,500 and accept the £4,500 from the defendants as an advance payment only. Later Mr Fenech told Mr Barnes that that offer was not acceptable and it was made clear during these discussions to Mr Barnes that the plaintiffs would not be able to carry out their obligations under the contract unless the men could be persuaded to stay at work. When Mr Fenech told Mr Barnes that his proposition was not acceptable Mr Barnes said, 'Well, you have me over a barrel' and he paid £4,500 to the plaintiffs.

The men were paid and the work was done. The plaintiffs sent in their bill and the defendants deducted £4,500 from the price and sent a cheque for the balance. The plaintiffs sued for £4,500, the remainder, as they regarded it, of the contract price. The defence was that the money had been paid under duress and consequently the defendants were entitled to claim back the sum of £4,500.

The matter came before Sir Douglas Frank QC, sitting as a deputy judge of the High Court, and he said [1982] ICR 654, 658:

> The realities of the situation were this: leaving aside the *force majeure* clause, the plaintiffs were under a contractual obligation to carry out this work for the contract sum. The plaintiffs were saying 'We are not going to carry out that work; we are going to repudiate that contract because we are not prepared to pay the additional £4,500 demanded by the men.' It is necessarily implicit in that attitude adopted by the plaintiffs that unless somebody—and who else but the defendants—paid off the men, they would not carry out the contract. If the work was not done, then the exhibition would go with what would have been disastrous consequences to the defendants and I would think to the exhibitors. As I see it, Mr Barnes really had no alternative but to agree to pay that money. That seems to me to be a clear case of duress and it does not need any authorities to support it. It speaks for itself.

He then considered the *force majeure* clause and concluded that it could not come to the rescue of the plaintiffs, and consequently he held that their intimation that they would not carry on with the work amounted to a breach of contract and therefore they had caused the defendants to pay the £4,500 unlawfully under duress.

The matters that have to be established in order to substantiate a claim for the return of money on the ground that it was paid under duress have been stated in a number of different ways. We have been referred to a number of cases and indeed we have been taken through the history of the common law on duress, so thoroughly set out in the judgment of Mocatta J. in *North Ocean Shipping Co. Ltd v Hyundai Construction Co. Ltd* [1979] QB 705. It is not necessary to consider these cases: for the purpose of my judgment all I require to read is a passage from the speech of Lord Diplock in *Universe Tankships Inc. of Monrovia v International Transport Workers Federation* [1982] ICR 262. He said, referring to the law on duress, at pp 272–273:

> The rationale is that his apparent consent was induced by pressure exercised upon him by that other party which the law does not regard as legitimate, with the consequence that the consent is treated in law as revocable unless approbated either expressly or by implication after the illegitimate pressure has ceased to operate on his mind. It is a rationale similar to that which underlies the avoidability of contracts entered into and the recovery of money exacted under colour of office, or under undue influence or in consequence of threats of physical duress.

It is not necessary to consider precisely the meaning of the word 'legitimate' in that context. For the purpose of this case it is sufficient to say that if the claimant has been influenced against his will to pay money under the threat of unlawful damage to his economic interest he will be entitled to claim that money back, and as I understand it that proposition was not dissented from.

In this case the plaintiffs say that there was no threat; that Mr Fenech was really stating the obvious, stating the factual situation, namely, that unless they could retain the workforce they would be unable to perform their contract. I have had some difficulty in deciding whether or not the evidence in this case did disclose a threat, but on a full reading of the evidence of Mr Fenech and Mr Barnes and the cross-examination of Mr Fenech I have come to the conclusion that the judge was right in the way in which he put it. There was here, as I understand the evidence, a veiled threat although there was no specific demand, and this conclusion is very much supported, as I see it, by Mr Barnes' reaction, which must have been apparent to Mr Fenech when Mr Barnes said, 'You have got me over a barrel.' On 18 April what was happening was this. Mr Fenech was in effect saying, 'We are not going on unless you are prepared to pay another £4,500 in addition to the contract price,' and it was clear at that stage that there was no other way for Mr Barnes to avoid the consequences that would ensue if the exhibition could not be held from his stands than by paying the £4,500 to secure the workforce. But, the plaintiffs now say, 'Even so, this was not an unlawful threat or a threat of unlawful action because seeing that there was a strike the strike clause— the *force majeure* clause—applied and the plaintiffs were entitled to take advantage of that clause and to cancel the contract, and so there was here no threat of unlawful action.' They also drew the court's attention to authorities on the obligations of a contracting party when a strike arose. They did so in the context of a contention that they were under an obligation to take steps to avoid the consequence of the strike, which they had not done. Mr Hodgson for the plaintiffs referred the court to *Bulman & Dickson v Fenwick & Co.* [1894] 1 QB 179, in which it was held that there was no obligation upon the charterers to change the order to the vessel to proceed to another port when the port that they had originally ordered was strike-bound. In the context of the present case I do not find it necessary to consider the effect of such a case as *Bulman & Dickson v Fenwick & Co.* on the law generally because we are concerned with the words of a specific clause. I would say in passing, however, that the *Bulman v Fenwick* case is to my mind to be regarded as one where it was shown to be impossible to carry out the contract as finally crystallised once the port had been ordered by the charterers. Be that as it may, as I have said, it is not necessary to go into that matter because we are concerned with the words of the particular clause, and that clause begins, 'Every effort will be made to carry out any contract,' and the question, to my mind, in this case is whether or not every effort was made to carry out that contract in the face of the strike. I will of course have regard to the argument that the contracting party is only required to make efforts that will be reasonable in the circumstances.

Well, what are the circumstances in this case? To pay what for the plaintiffs would have been an extra £4,500, or indeed to pay the whole of the £9,000, would in the circumstances of this case have been reasonable. It was a simple solution to the problem. Mr Hodgson has argued that if an employer is required to give in to the demands of the workmen in these cases where a strike clause is inserted in the contract, the clause would have no meaning; it would be valueless. But I do not say that an employer must in every case give in: I simply say that on the facts of this case the evidence shows that it would have been reasonable for the plaintiff to have done so. It might have been distasteful to some employers to pay the workforce in this situation, but I do not think that the plaintiffs can claim that it would have been obnoxious to them to do so. They were prepared to do so provided the defendants paid half the price. Furthermore, they would not be creating a rod for their own backs because the workmen were not in their immediate employment and the workmen were not workmen with whom they were intending to have any further dealings after 27 April, so they could not, by giving in, have fed an appetite that in the future was likely to make even greater demands upon them. That being so, it seems to me that the only objection which the plaintiffs had to this easy solution of the problem was the sum of £4,500. It does not appear from the evidence in this case that it was impossible for them to find £4,500 for indeed £4,500 was offered to them as an advance payment.

In those circumstances I have come to the conclusion that every effort was not made to perform this contract, and consequently reliance cannot be placed upon that *force majeure* clause. Having come to that conclusion there is no need for me to deal with other arguments that have been put forward by the defendants in this case, for example to the effect that the plaintiffs, by their conduct in employing workmen who were on the brink of dismissal, were bringing strike troubles upon themselves. In my judgment that does not arise.

I would dismiss the appeal.

Griffiths L.J.:

I agree. The law on economic pressure creating a situation which will be recognised as duress is in the course of development, and it is clear that many difficult decisions lie ahead of the courts. Many commercial contracts are varied during their currency because the parties are faced with changing circumstances during the performance of the contract, and it is certainly not on every occasion when one of the parties unwillingly agrees to a variation that the law would consider that he had acted by reason of duress. The cases will have to be examined in the light of their particular circumstances. But two recent decisions of the highest authority—the decision of the Privy Council in *Pao On v Lau Yiu Long* [1980] AC 614 and *Universe Tankships Inc. of Monrovia v International Transport Workers Federation* [1982] ICR 262—establish that a threatened breach of contract may impose such economic pressure that the law will recognise that a payment made as a result of the threatened breach is recoverable on the grounds of duress.

The facts of this case appear to me to be as follows. The plaintiffs intended to break their contract, subject to the effect of the *force majeure* clause, by allowing their workforce to walk off the job in circumstances in which they could not possibly replace it with another workforce. The defendants offered to advance the sum of £4,500 on the contract price, which would have enabled the plaintiffs to pay the men a sufficient extra sum of money to induce them to remain on the job. The plaintiffs refused this sum of money. There is no question that they refused to pay as a matter of principle. They refused to pay because they did not want to reduce the sum they would receive for the contract. They said to the defendants, 'If you will give us £4,500 we will complete the contract.' The defendants, faced with this demand, were in an impossible position. If they refused to hand over the sum of £4,500 they would not be able to erect the stands in this part of the exhibition, which would have clearly caused grave damage to their reputation and I would have thought might have exposed them to very heavy claims from the exhibitors who had leased space from them and hoped to use those stands in the ensuing exhibition. They seem to me to have been placed in the position envisaged by Lord Scarman in the Privy Council decision, *Pao On v Lau Yiu Long* [1980] AC 614, in which they were faced with no alternative course of action but to pay the sum demanded of them. It was submitted to us that there was no overt demand, but it was implicit in negotiations between the parties that the plaintiffs were putting the defendants into a corner and it was quite apparent to the defendants, by reason of the plaintiffs' conduct, that unless they handed over £4,500 the plaintiffs would walk off the job. This is, in my view, a situation in which the judge was fully entitled to find in the circumstances of this case that there was duress. As the defendants' director said, he was over a barrel, he had no alternative but to pay; he had no chance of going to any other source of labour to erect the stands. That being so, the only fall-back position for the plaintiffs was the *force majeure* clause. Clauses of this kind have to be construed upon the basis that those relying on them will have taken all reasonable efforts to avoid the effect of the various matters set out in the clause which entitle them to vary or cancel the contract: see *Bulman & Dickson v Fenwick & Co.* [1894] 1 QB 179, in the speech of Lord Esher M.R. at p. 185. Quite apart from that general principle this particular clause starts with the following wording: 'Every effort will be made to carry out any contract based on an estimate,' which is saying in express terms that which the law will imply when construing such a clause.

There is no doubt that the plaintiffs were faced with a strike situation and the question is, did they behave reasonably when faced with this situation? I, like Eveleigh L.J., am far from saying that whenever a contracting party with such a clause is faced with a strike situation he must give in to it in order to perform his contract. If that were the situation the clause would be absolutely worthless. But the special circumstances of this case, as I see it, are as follows. The plaintiffs were going to close down their subsidiary company; they had already dismissed the workforce and the men were working out their time. There is no question here of any ongoing industrial situation between the plaintiffs' subsidiary company and the workforce. There was no question of principle at stake; the plaintiffs were perfectly prepared to pay what the men were demanding save for the fact, they said, they did not have the money available. Well, then there came the offer of the defendants to make the money available by giving them an advance. In those circumstances I can see no reason why they should not have accepted the money and paid the workforce save their own immediate economic interests, and they chose not to do that but to put pressure on the defendants by refusing the offer and indicating that the only way out was for the defendants to hand over the £4,500 as a gift rather than as an advance.

I think that was thoroughly unreasonable behaviour, and that being so they are not entitled to rely upon the *force majeure* clause, and for these reasons I agree this appeal fails.

Atlas Express Ltd *v* Kafco (Importers and Distributors) Ltd [1989] NLJR 111

The facts:

In June 1986 the plaintiffs, a national road carrier, entered into a contract with the defendants, a small company which imported and distributed basketware to the retail trade, to deliver cartons of basketware to branches of Woolworths for the defendants. The plaintiffs' depot manager inspected the cartons, which were of different sizes, before the contract was entered into and estimated that each load would contain a minimum of 400 and possibly as many as 600 cartons and on that basis he agreed a rate of carriage of £1.10 per carton. In fact the first load contained only 200 cartons and the plaintiffs' depot manager told the defendants that the plaintiffs would not carry any more cartons unless the defendants agreed to pay a minimum of £440 per load. The defendants were heavily dependent on the Woolworths' contract and were unable at that time of the year to find an alternative carrier. The defendants accordingly agreed to the new terms on 18 November 1986 but later refused to pay the new rate. The plaintiffs brought an action to recover the amount owing under the new rate.

Tucker J.:

I find that when Mr Armiger [a director of the defendants] signed [the amended] agreement he did so unwillingly and under compulsion. He believed on reasonable grounds that it would be very difficult if not impossible to negotiate with another contractor. He did not regard the fact that he had signed the new agreement as binding the defendants to its terms. He had no bargaining power. He did not regard it as a genuine arms length renegotiation in which he had a free and equal say and, in my judgment, that view was fully justified.

In the words of his co-director, Mr Fox, he felt that he was 'over a barrel'. He tried in vain to contact Mr Hope [the plaintiffs' depot manager] but, as he said to Mr Armiger, they really had no option but to sign. I accept the evidence of Woolworths' manager, Mr Graham, that if the defendants had told them that they could not supply the goods, Woolworths would have sued them for loss of profit and would have ceased trading with them. I find that this was well known to the defendants' directors . . . The defendants made their position quite clear through their solicitors, who wrote to the plaintiffs on 2 March 1987, saying that the revised contract was signed under duress. This was three months before the plaintiffs commenced proceedings.

The issue which I have to determine is whether the defendants are bound by the agreement signed on their behalf on 18 November 1986. The defendants contend that they are not bound, for two reasons: first because the agreement was signed under duress; second because there was no consideration for it.

The first question raises a particularly interesting point of law: whether economic duress is a concept known to English law.

Economic duress must be distinguished from commercial pressure, which on any view is not sufficient to vitiate consent. The borderline between the two may in some cases be indistinct. But the authors of *Chitty on Contracts* and of *Goff and Jones on the Law of Restitution* appear to recognise that in appropriate cases economic duress may afford a defence, and in my judgment it does. It is clear to me that in a number of English cases judges have acknowledged the existence of this concept. Thus, in D & C *Builders Ltd v Rees* [1965] 3 All ER 837 at 841 Lord Denning M.R. said: 'No person can insist on a settlement procured by intimidation.' And in *Occidental Worldwide Investment Corp. v Skibs A/S Avanti (The 'Siboen' v The 'Sibotre')* [1976] Lloyd's Rep. 293 at 336 Kerr J. appeared to accept that economic duress could operate in appropriate circumstances. A similar conclusion was reached by Mocatta J. in *North Ocean Shipping Co. Ltd v Hyundai Construction Co. Ltd* [1978] 3 All ER 1170. In particular, there are passages in the judgment of Lord Scarman in *Pao On v Lau Yiu Long* [1979] 3 All ER 65 at 78–79 which clearly indicate the recognition of the concept . . .

A further case, which was not cited to me, was B & S *Contracts v V. G. Publications* (1984) ICR 419 at 423 where Eveleigh L.J. referred to the speech of Lord Diplock in another uncited case. *Universe Tankship Inc. of Monrovia v International Transport Workers Federation* [1982] 2 All ER 67 at 75–76: 'The rationale is that this apparent consent was induced by pressure exercised upon him by that other party which the law does not regard as legitimate with the consequence that the consent is treated in law as revocable unless approbated either expressly or by implication after the illegitimate pressure has ceased to operate on his mind.'

In commenting on this, Eveleigh L.J. said of the word 'legitimate': 'For the purpose of this case, it is sufficient to say that if the claimant has been influenced against his will to pay money under the threat of unlawful damage to his economic interest, he will be entitled to claim that money back . . .'

Reverting to the case before me, I find that the defendants' apparent consent to the agreement was induced by pressure which was illegitimate and I find that it was not approbated. In my judgment that pressure can properly be described as economic duress, which is a concept recognised by English law, and which in the circumstances of the present case vitiates the defendants' apparent consent to the agreement.

In any event, I find that there was no consideration for the new agreement. The plaintiffs were already obliged to deliver the defendants' goods at the rates agreed under the terms of the original agreement.

There was no consideration for the increased minimum charge of £440 per trailer.

Accordingly, I find that the plaintiffs' claim fails and there will be judgment for the defendants with costs.

Note

It is no longer an open question whether economic duress is a concept known to English law. In *Carrillion Construction Ltd v Felix* UK Ltd [2001] BLR 1, Dyson J. (as he then was) had occasion to apply his own dicta from DSND *Subsea Ltd v Petroleum Geo-Services* ASA [2000] BLR 530:

The ingredients of actionable duress are that there must be pressure, (a) whose practical effect is that there is compulsion on, or a lack of practical choice for, the victim, (b) which is illegitimate, and (c) which is a significant cause inducing the claimant to enter into the contract: see *Universal Tankships of Monrovia v* ITWF [1983] AC 336, 400B-E, and *The Evia Luck* [1992] 2 AC 152, 165G. In determining whether there has been illegitimate pressure, the court takes into account a range of factors. These include whether there has been an actual or threatened breach of contract; whether the person allegedly exerting the pressure has acted in good or bad faith; whether the victim had any realistic practical alternative but to submit to the pressure; whether the victim protested at the time; and whether he affirmed and sought to rely on the contract. These are all relevant factors. Illegitimate pressure must be distinguished from the rough and tumble of the pressure of normal commercial bargaining.

SECTION FOUR—AFFIRMATION OF THE CONTRACT AND RESCISSION

A. AFFIRMATION

Haines v Carter [2001] 2 NZLR 167

The Facts

Haines and Carter lived together from 1993 until their relationship broke up in 1999. During this time they had built considerable wealth held in various companies and in the form of shareholdings. They could not agree on how to carve up this property and they agreed on 'irregular' mediation mechanisms involving the use of friends and relatives. A mediation agreement was drawn up and signed on 11 March 1999. Some time later Haines argued that the agreement was not binding upon him because it was procured by threats, specifically a threat to bring Haines' business and financial affairs before the Revenue. The New Zealand High Court upheld the contract and ordered Haines to pay Carter $1.5 (NZ) plus interest and costs. Haines appealed to the New Zealand Court of Appeal where the judgment of McGrath, Doogue and Young JJ. was delivered by Young J.

Young J.:

The principles of duress derive in part from the old common law rules for the avoidance of deeds and parol contracts entered into under duress of the person (see for instance *Skeate v Beale* (1841) 11 Ad & El 983), and in part from the principles developed in respect of the common law claim for money had and received (for which duress of goods and other forms of pressure short of duress to the person sufficed, e.g. *Maskell v Horner* [1915] 3 KB 106). What is not so widely recognised is that the courts exercising equitable jurisdiction also developed principles according to which contracts obtained by what was sometimes described as duress, and in other cases, coercion or pressure, could be set aside, see for instance *Williams v Bayley* (1866) LR 1 HL 200.

Duress necessarily involves the illegitimate application of pressure by threats. The illegitimacy of the pressure may lie in the illegality of the actions threatened or, alternatively, may be associated with the illegitimacy of the particular threats in the context in which they were made.

It will be recalled that the pressure complained of by Mr Haines was said to consist of threats by Ms Carter to cause trouble for him with the Inland Revenue Department and the Haines group's bank. Threats to report a person to a law enforcement agency unless that person submits to a particular bargain is conduct which could amount to the crime of blackmail and is thus illegitimate. Threats to inflict gratuitous harm may also be an illegitimate form of pressure. So the pressure complained of by Mr Haines could amount to duress.

We have reservations whether there could be much in the complaint made by Mr Haines about the threats allegedly made by Ms Carter to cause trouble with the bank. Ms Carter customarily dealt with the bank. There was a significant overdraft problem and the bank knew that there had been variance between projections and actuality. Comments to this effect made by Ms Carter in a situation where it was her position that Mr Haines would have some practical difficulties dealing with the bank without her assistance, do not appear to be duress but simply statements of the obvious. We are, however, prepared to accept that there was an arguable case for the view that Ms Carter had made threats to sour the relationship between the Haines group and the Bank of New Zealand.

The more significant issue relates to the threats to cause trouble for Mr Haines with the Inland Revenue Department. Randerson J. accepted the possibility that threats, broadly as alleged by Mr Haines, had been made. He was right to do so on the evidence which we have reviewed.

The facts that threats capable of amounting to duress have been made in the course of the negotiating process does not, without more, mean that the bargain reached as a result of that process can be avoided for duress. Many of the cases indicate that a plea of duress is available only when there has been 'coercion of the will' or 'vitiation of consent', see for example the remarks of Lord Scarman in *Pao On v Lau Yiu Long* [1980] AC 614 at p. 635 and the cases reviewed by Tipping J. in *Shivas v Bank of New Zealand* [1990] 2 NZLR 327 at p. 342 et seq. Statements to this effect in the cases, however, do not mean that the party affected by duress must have been psychologically crippled by reason of pressure before relief can be available. As Lord Scarman put it in *Universe Tankships Inc.of Monrovia v International Transport Workers Federation* [1983] 1 AC 366 at p. 400:

> Compulsion is variously described in the authorities as coercion or the vitiation of consent. The classic case of duress is, however, not the lack of will to submit but the victim's intentional submission arising from the realisation that there is no other practical choice open to him.

The point Lord Scarman was making is, at least in part, a causation issue. At the very least, a party alleging duress must show that the duress alleged was at least an appreciable factor in influencing that party to enter into the bargain in question, see *Barton v Armstrong* [1976] AC 104. Further, the courts do look for a significant degree of actual coerciveness, a level of coerciveness which is sometimes described as having left the victim with no practical choice but to submit.

In this case, the judge did not address in a definitive way whether he considered that there was an arguable case for the view that the pressure complained of by Mr Haines had been an appreciable factor in inducing him to sign the agreement of 11 March 1999 and had been sufficiently coercive, in fact, to amount to duress. He was, at best for Mr Haines, very sceptical on these points. The judge decided the case in accordance with the principles of affirmation.

We are content to deal with this case on the same basis as the judge did—in other words, by reference to the issue of affirmation. We should say, however, that considerations associated with the affirmation evidence given by Ms Carter are closely connected to the question whether the threats alleged by Mr Haines had any significant impact on his decision to execute the agreement on 11 March 1999 and whether they were sufficiently coercive to be regarded as duress.

What is important in this context, is that in duress cases, the courts will not regard as affirmation (or as conduct precluding rescission) steps taken by the victim while still under the influence of pressure from the other party, see for instance the discussion in *North Ocean Shipping Co. Ltd v Hyundai Construction Co. Ltd* [1979] 1 QB 705. The argument for Mr Haines is that steps which he took to implement the agreement should not be regarded as affirmation because he was still, at the material time, acting under duress or, in any event, there is at least a reasonable argument available on the facts to this effect.

We are of the view that, on the evidence before the High Court, Ms Carter established that Mr Haines did not have an arguable defence based on duress. We say this for the following reasons:

1. The negotiation process, via mediation, proved an improbable context in which duress could be applied. Participating in this process were people familiar to Mr Haines whom he respected and trusted.
2. Even on Mr Haines' own evidence, he did not see the pressure as particularly coercive. He claims that his tax affairs are characterised by regularity and that the only effect of the threatened exposures would have been a deferral of what was thought to be a then imminent settlement of a dispute with the Inland Revenue Department which went back to 1991. We see no reason not to take him at his word.
3. We mention these factors because they point to the duress alleged by Mr Haines as involving a comparatively low level of actual coerciveness. In deference to the way in which the judge dealt with the case, we are prepared to assume, without holding, that it was arguably the case that the threats attributed to Ms Carter by Mr Haines amounted to duress and were an appreciable factor for Mr Haines in his decision to enter into the agreement. The low level of coerciveness alleged by Mr Haines, however, is material in relation to the affirmation question to which we now turn. . . .

Mr Haines, by his insistence on performance of those aspects of the agreement of 11 March 1999 which suited him while, at the same time, declining to comply with his financial obligations under that agreement to Ms Carter, must be treated as having affirmed the contract. He did not, prior to the first judgment, give evidence on oath explaining this conduct. Although we regard his affidavit in support of the recall application as too late to be relevant in terms of our consideration of the case, it is fair to say, that in our view, it does not really make sense when viewed against the detail of what happened in the relevant period.

So, in agreement with Randerson, we see no arguable defence based on duress given the undenied and unexplained affirmation evidence of Ms Carter. [An appeal to the Privy Council on a point of interpretation failed: [2002] UKPC 49.]

Techform Products Ltd *v* Wolda (2001) 206 DLR (4th) 171

Facts

The defendant worked as a mechanical engineer for the plaintiff between 1981 and 1989 as a full-time employee. In 1987 he was assigned the task of inventing a 'Dual Motion Deck Lid Hinge' for which a patent application was filed by the plaintiff. In 1989 he resigned as a full-time employee and thereafter signed a consultancy agreement with the plaintiff in relation to 'special projects'.

In late 1992, the defendant presented to the plaintiff a hinge that he had designed on his own time and without the knowledge of the plaintiff. Concerned that the defendant might seek royalty payments for the invention, the plaintiff prepared an Employee Technology Agreement (ETA) which it presented to the defendant for signature. The ETA provided that in consideration for his continued employment by the plaintiff, the defendant agreed to assign all rights to inventions that he conceived or made while employed by the plaintiff. Although the defendant did not want to sign the ETA, he did so because he thought that if he refused, his services would be terminated. He indicated to the plaintiff that he did not agree with the ETA and that it did not apply because he was not an employee. To indicate his protest, he inserted a question mark beside the word 'employee' on the ETA.

In 1996, the plaintiff assigned to the defendant the task of designing a Tailgate Hinge Mechanism. The defendant executed a declaration for a patent application but was not asked to assign his patent rights. In 1996, the defendant, on his own initiative, invented a new 3D Hinge design. The defendant billed the plaintiff for 1,000 hours of work, received the assistance of the plaintiff's employees in refining the design and used the plaintiff's patent attorneys to prepare a patent application.

After the defendant proposed that he be compensated for assigning the invention rights, the plaintiff terminated his employment and commenced an action for a declaration of ownership of the 3D Hinge and the Tailgate Hinge Mechanism. The defendant counterclaimed for a declaration of ownership of the 3D Hinge and for damages for breach of contract for failure to give the required notice of termination.

The trial judge held that it was an implied term of the consultancy agreement that when the plaintiff specifically assigned to the defendant the task of inventing a product, it belonged to the plaintiff. As the Tailgate Hinge Mechanism was specifically assigned, it belonged to the plaintiff. However, as the 3D Hinge was not specifically assigned, it belonged to the defendant. The trial judge further held that the ETA was not binding on the defendant because there was no consideration and was entered into as a result of duress.

Rosenberg J.A.:

This appeal concerns ownership of an invention. The respondent, an employee of and then independent consultant to the appellant company, invented a valuable type of trunk hinge. The appellant claims that it is the owner of this thing, which the respondent worked on while being paid by the appellant. Its claim is based principally on a written agreement. Sachs J. concluded that the appellant cannot rely on the agreement because there was no consideration and, in any event, it was signed under duress [reported 5 CPR (4th) 25, supplementary reasons 5 CPR (4th) 289]. I have concluded that the trial judge erred in law in both respects and that the appeal must be allowed.

Duress

Although she found there was no consideration, the trial judge went on to consider whether, in any event, the ETA was unenforceable because of duress. She found that it was and the appellant recognised that to succeed on this appeal, it must show that she erred. In her reasons, the trial judge referred to this court's decision in *Stott v Merit Investment Corp* [1988] 63 OR (2d) 545, 48 DLR (4th) 288, leave to appeal to SCC refused [1988], 63 OR (2d) x, 49 DLR (4th) viii, where it was held that not all economic pressure will constitute economic duress. As she said, '[i]t must be pressure that the law does not accept as legitimate and it must be applied to such an extent that the person to whom the pressure is directed has no choice but to submit' (at pp. 45–6 CPR). She also recognised that in determining the legitimacy of the pressure, 'one must consider the nature of the pressure and the nature of the demand the pressure is applied to support' (at p. 46 CPR). Unfortunately, although the trial judge then gave extensive attention to whether the respondent was deprived of choice, she never returned to the question of whether the pressure was legitimate. In my view, in failing to do so she erred in law.

In considering whether the respondent was deprived of choice, the trial judge reviewed the application of the four factors from *Pao On v Lau Yiu*, [1979] 3 All ER 65 (PC), namely:

(a) Did the party protest at the same time the contract was entered into?
(b) Was there an effective alternative course open to the party alleging coercion?
(c) Did the party receive independent legal advice?
(d) After entering into the contract did the party take steps to avoid it? (At p. 46 CPR.)

The trial judge found in favour of the respondent on all four factors. These were principally findings of fact, and while I have some misgivings about the trial judge's findings, especially in relation to the fourth factor, I am not persuaded that they are unreasonable. However, as McKinlay J.A. said in *Gordon v Roebuck* [1992], 9 OR (3d) 1 at 6, 92 DLR (4th) 670 (CA), that does not end the matter; in addition, 'one must determine whether the coercion exerted on the [party] was legitimate'. Since the trial judge did not consider this aspect of the case it falls to this court to do so.

In *Stott* at p. 563, Finlayson J.A. referred with approval to *Universe Tankships Inc. of Monrovia v International Transport Workers' Federation* [1982] 2 ALL ER 657 (HL), where it was held that in determining what is legitimate two matters may have to be considered. The first is the nature of the pressure and the second is the nature of the demand that the pressure is applied to support. There are a number of characteristics of this case that, in my view, require a finding that the pressure was not illegitimate.

First, the respondent was an independent contractor, not an employee. Admittedly Techform was the respondent's only client, but it seems to me that the company could have insisted on something like the ETA as a condition for renewing the consultancy agreement for the following year.

Second, it seems apparent that the company genuinely believed that it was entitled to ownership of inventions by its employees and consultants. This was the position taken by Mr Connelly with the respondent. The trial judge did not seem to disbelieve Mr Van den Heuvel's evidence that the ETA was an attempt to put in place a more formal method of safeguarding the confidentiality of new projects for Techform. In fact, the trial judge found that when Techform specifically assigned to the respondent the task of inventing a new product, Techform was entitled to claim ownership of that product. The trial judge found that this was an implied term when the respondent was an employee and was implied in the 1989 consultancy agreement.

As the trial judge noted, the law would appear to be that absent an express or implied agreement to the contrary, an employee or independent contractor owns inventions. In my view, that does not mean that Techform's request or demand that the respondent execute such an agreement was illegitimate. Techform was paying the respondent for his work on the various inventions. While the trial judge held that Techform did not expressly assign the concept of the 3D Hinge to the respondent, he was generally assigned to work on hinges. In my view, Techform's bona fide belief that it was the owner of the inventions tells strongly in favour of finding that the pressure was not illegitimate: CNT *Cash and Carry Ltd v Gallaher Ltd*, [1994] All ER 714 (CA) at 718.

Finally, in looking at the nature of the pressure, it is important that the respondent was not forced to sign the ETA on the spot. He took it away with him and had ample opportunity to obtain independent advice. Thereafter, he had many years to reconsider, obtain the benefit of legal advice, seek a revised agreement or repudiate the agreement. He did not do so since as he put it, 'Why would I [shackle] myself'. This lengthy passage of time tells strongly against there being illegitimate pressure: *Stott*, at p. 55.

For these reasons, it is my view that the pressure was legitimate and the trial judge erred in finding that the agreement was unenforceable on the basis of economic duress.

B. RESCISSION

In *Halpern v Halpern* (No. 2) [2007] EWCA Civ 291, the English Court of Appeal considered an important issue of principle: where duress is successfully pleaded by A against B, in an action where restitution is sought by A against B, is the fact that A cannot effect *restitutio in integrum* (e.g. A has consumed property transferred by B) a barrier to ordering restitution in favour of A? The Court of Appeal inclined towards the view that it should not matter whether the vitiating factor is duress or fraudulent misrepresentation, for example, and that the central issue is whether the rescinding claimant can make counter restitution, whether specifically or by way of a monetary equivalent, citing in particular *Erlanger v New Sombrero Phosphate Co* (1878) 3 App Cas 1218 at 1278 per Lord Blackburn, and *Hulton v Hulton* [1917] 1 KB 813.

Chapter Fourteen

Equitable Intervention

SECTION ONE—UNDUE INFLUENCE

The equitable doctrine of undue influence is intended to provide relief to persons who enter into transactions in circumstances where there are potential or actual grounds for suspecting that an abuse of position has taken place, or that improper pressure has been brought to bear upon one of the contracting parties.

A. THE PRESUMPTION

Kirwan v Cullen (1854) 2 Ir Ch R 322

A Catholic lady transferred property to the Archbishop of Dublin, under a trust instrument, the trustees including a priest who had previously been the lady's spiritual confessor. On her death her brother sought to have the transfer set aside.

Lord St Leonards L.C.:

I feel no doubt in this case that this petition cannot be sustained. In substance this petition is to recall, for the purpose of administration, a sum of £3000 stock, which now stands in the names of Archbishop Cullen and Dr Curtis, to whom it was transferred by Miss Kirwan in the year 1851, when she was still living. I said that the object of this suit is to recall this sum from these two gentlemen, for the purpose of administration, as part of the assets of Miss Clare Kirwan; and it is insisted that these respondents cannot retain it, on the ground that the donation to them was made in consequence of undue influence over the mind of the lady, the exercise of which was the probable cause of their obtaining the gift; and further, that even if no undue influence had caused the gift, it was made for purposes which the law does not recognise, and that being thus given to the respondents upon trusts which were void in their inception, Miss Kirwan had a resulting interest in it which passed to her administrator. As to the first point, I do not think it necessary to go through a detailed examination of the authorities to which the counsel referred; this case seems perfectly distinct from all of them. Here was a lady of full age and competent understanding, moving in the world, living with her family, who possessed a sum of money; this she transferred through the medium of a duly authorised agent, to the names of these gentlemen of high position in the church to which she belonged. We find the respondents not claiming any personal interest, admitting that they are mere trustees for the objects of Miss Kirwan's bounty, and that they are bound to carry out purposes not connected with themselves individually. We find the donation effected by Miss Kirwan through the intervention of a third person, whose name has been mentioned here, who was

662

admittedly without interest in the subject of the gift, and who never has received the smallest portion of it. I do not think it possible to contend that this can be classed with the cases in which donations and gifts have been held by this court to have been tainted by the fact that they were made to a person who was placed in a situation giving him power to exercise undue influence over the donor, with which other cases certainly conflict as to the extent to which they have gone. . . . none of them seem to me to interfere with the decision of this case, which is, I think, to be resolved into this question, whether, in fact, there is evidence to show that when this lady made this gift, any influence was exercised to induce her to do so? On that subject the petitioner's case is wholly without evidence. I do not say that we can at all wonder at this, for it is conceded by the respondents that the knowledge of the transaction was wholly confined to this lady herself, and the gentleman to whom she confided the arrange-ment of the business; but unquestionably there is no evidence to impeach the gift, beyond the broad circumstances of the case. Then, as I said, here is a lady of mature age and undoubted understanding, living with her sisters, making this gift more than a year before her death. She never complained of it to any one, not even to her sisters with whom she resided. It appears that some dividends on the sum were received by the trustees, and that she made no objection to the fact of their receiving them, but that some discussion arose as to the application: all these circumstances showing that she perfectly well knew of and approved of the transaction; and I must therefore say that I consider the case made by the petition entirely destitute of foundation. No doubt, the court would not have been satisfied unless some explanation had been given of this transfer, which in itself seems a little remarkable; but that has been fully given. We have here affidavits of Dr Curtis and Archbishop Cullen, which show that so far as they are concerned they were wholly without influence. Dr Cullen swears 'that he never saw the said Clare Kirwan, or had the slightest intimacy or acquaintance with her, or with any of her family, and did not know there was such a person until he was asked to become a trustee of the fund.'

   Dr Curtis seems to have had a more intimate acquaintance with this lady, he had filled the position of her spiritual adviser; but the relation between them had ceased two years before the transaction occurred, and she had been before this perfectly independent of him. Dr Curtis and Dr Cullen both swear that they had no knowledge of the transaction; Dr Curtis until he was informed by another person; Dr Cullen until he was told by Dr Curtis. Dr Curtis says that he declined to accept the burden of this trust alone, and that he suggested that Dr Cullen, the spiritual superior of himself and of all other members of his church in Ireland, should be associated with him in the trust. He also states that they had an interview with this lady after the transfer, in which it did not appear that she had any wish to retract from the arrangement. There is then the affidavit of a gentleman who intervened in the transaction, at least so far as procuring the assent of the trustees. He also was in the position of a person not taking any personal benefit from the transaction, and seems to have declined to be in any way concerned in it, beyond procuring these persons to act as trustees. His statement is not in any way controverted, and his evidence is so full, clear and creditable to him, that though on the whole it may not be absolutely necessary, I shall read some portion of it. . . . This is, I may say, the whole evidence in the case, and it is not controverted. There was not any other person to whom the facts were communicated, and therefore no other evidence could exist. I will not say that the case might not assume a very different aspect if this claim were made by Miss Kirwan in her lifetime, and if she were to make affidavits contradicting these; but here we have the uncontroverted evidence of persons who appear only to have intervened between this lady and the objects of her bounty, without taking any personal benefit. To apply to this case of doctrine of *Huguenin v Basely*,[1] and the other similar cases, would be to strain it much beyond its legitimate bounds. It is said that such a gift is most extraordinary in its amount as well as in its circumstances; but this lady appears to have been of an unusually charitable and pious disposition. She does seem to have denuded herself of much property, but she still retained a considerable amount, which may have been enough for her desires. She frequently visited this institution which she benefited, and she seems to have esteemed it highly. She saw the purposes to which her bounty was to be devoted, and being of a charitable and religious disposition, she may have come to the conclusion that those were purposes which she ought to sustain, and to which her property ought to be devoted. I do not mean in saying this to call in aid of this gift the opinion that the object was charitable in a legal point of view; I do not mean to decide that these were what are legally denominated charitable purposes; I merely mean to show the motive, acting as it did seem to act on the mind of a person who was perhaps, if that be possible, religious and charitable even to excess—who approved of the purposes of this community, and who in consequence devoted a large portion of her property to its support. It may be that, in the opinion of some persons, she pursued her purposes not wisely, but too well; but, sitting in this court, I cannot venture to set a limit to her bounty.

[1]   14 Ves 273.

The Queen (Proctor) *v* Hutton [1978] NI 139

Facts

Mrs Founds, an elderly lady, transferred funds into a bank account, in the joint name of Mrs Founds and Proctor the prosecutrix, one of ten legatees. The transfer was challenged as having been procured by undue influence. The Lord Chief Justice held that there was no evidence to show that a relationship of trust and confidence existed from which a presumption of undue influence over Mrs Founds by Proctor could arise; on the fact the exercise of undue influence was negatived. The executors of the estate of Mrs Founds appealed to the Northern Ireland Court of Appeal.

Jones L.J.:

The legal principles applicable to cases of this type are to be found in Hanbury and Maudsley's *Modern Equity* (10th ed.) 628 where it is stated:

> It is possible to divide the cases up into those, first, in which equity readily perceives the possibility of such influence, such as parent and child, guardian and ward, doctor and patient, religious adviser and pupil, and other situations where it is shown that a similar relationship of confidence existed, cases in which equity requires positive evidence that no undue influence was in fact exerted; and, secondly, those in which equity requires positive proof of influence having actually been exerted. But in all cases the question is whether a defendant has taken advantage of his position, or, *per contra*, has been assiduous not to do so. The question can only be answered in each case by a meticulous consideration of the facts.

The present case is said by the appellant to fall into the first of the above categories, because of the finding that there was a relationship of confidence and trust between Mrs Founds and the prosecutrix. It is of course dangerous to seek to compare the facts of one case with those of another but it is not dangerous to observe that the facts of

Tate v Williamson (1866) 1 Eq 528, to which the learned deputy referred at this stage of his judgment, were very markedly different from those of the present case—I need refer to no more than that the purchaser of the estate in that case had obtained a valuation from a mining engineer which was very material but which was not communicated to the vendor who died in Plymouth, aged twenty three, of *delerium tremens*. No doubt the prosecutrix did say in evidence before the learned deputy that Mrs Founds put great confidence in her. I am sure she did. After all the prosecutrix was the one person who had come half way across the world to assist, I might say rescue, her but I am satisfied that if the learned deputy was thereby inferring the existence of any trust and confidence placed by Mrs Founds in the prosecutrix in relation to the disposal of her property which could give any foundation to a suggestion of undue influence in relation thereto there was no evidence to support such an inference. Indeed, so far as Mrs Founds' property was concerned, the prosecutrix's suggestion that all the family should share or that the monies should not be put into a joint account was rejected by Mrs Founds. I feel that the finding of a relationship of trust and confidence in the learned deputy's decision is one that can be reviewed. It is not a finding of a primary fact but is more like a deduction from other facts or an expression of opinion, and in either case it is reviewable on the ground that there is no support for it, and that it is therefore erroneous in point of law, having regard to the decision read as a whole.

Now the presumption of undue influence may arise in two sorts of cases. The evidence may show a particular relationship, for example that of solicitor and client, trustee and *cestui que trust*, doctor and patient or religious adviser and pupil. Those cases or some of them, depending on the facts, may of themselves raise the presumption. Such examples, as regards undue influence, have much in common with the doctrine [. . . Jones L.J. said the key findings at trial were these:]

> From her (that is the prosecutrix's) demeanour and from the way in which she gave her evidence I formed the view that Mrs Proctor was a truthful and reliable witness, and, on the basis of her own evidence, I formed the view that when she went out to bring her aunt home from Philadelphia and when she gave her a home in Portadown, she was not concerned about what money her aunt might have or about what money she might receive from her aunt. I also formed the view that Mr [*sic* but I think the quotation should read 'Mrs'] Proctor is a kind, warm-hearted person, who went out to America and brought her aunt home out of feelings of kindness and sympathy for a lonely old lady, and not by reason of hope or desire of receiving or extracting a financial reward or benefit from her aunt. I think that this view of Mrs Proctor's feeling and motives is supported by the terms of the letters which she wrote home from Philadelphia and which are set out above. I further consider that this view is supported by the evidence of Mr Dennison that in the discussion in the bank between him and Mrs Founds as to whose name or names the money should be lodged in, Mrs Proctor did not intervene and adopted the attitude that it was for her aunt to decide what to do with the money.

Indeed, like the learned Lord Chief Justice, I regard that as a salient point and the key to the whole situation.

(McGonigal L.J. and O'Donnell J. concurred in dismissing the appeal.)

McGonigle *v* Black (HC) 14 November 1988, unrep.

Barr J.:

The relevant facts in this case are as follows: Edward McGonigle, deceased, (Mr McGonigle) formerly of Flemingstown, Convoy, Co. Donegal, died intestate on 1 October 1983. He lived for over twenty years with his uncle and aunt, Mr and Mrs James McClure, on a farm at Convoy then owned by Mr McClure which is the subject matter of these proceedings. The McClures had no children. Mr McGonigle helped in running the farm and seems to have been regarded by them as a son. Mr McClure died in 1978 and left the farm by will to Mr McGonigle subject to Mrs McClure's life interest. After the death of his uncle, Mr McGonigle ran the farm and continued to reside with his aunt. At that time the property comprised three holdings; the home farm of 36 acres, which also included an old dwelling house, and two separate holdings not far away of $9^1/_2$ acres and 6 acres respectively. The entire comprised good quality land which at all material times had a value in excess of £1,000 per acre. Some time after Mr McClure's death the dwelling house on the home farm became derelict and thereafter Mr McGonigle and his aunt vacated the premises and lived in a mobile home on the land. However, it appears that Mrs McClure was in poor health and was transferred to hospital in or about 1979 where she remained until she died in 1981. After his aunt entered hospital there was no one to keep house for Mr McGonigle and he was obliged to fend for himself. It is evident that he was unable to do so satisfactorily and the effective loss of his aunt caused him to develop a serious drink problem which became more acute as time went on.

I accept the evidence of Mr Thomas Morrow, senior partner in David Wilson and Co., solicitors. He had a long-standing connection with Mr and Mrs McClure for whom he had acted as solicitor. He had also acted for Mr McGonigle whom he had known for many years. He first noticed that the latter was addicted to alcohol in 1980. Thereafter he often saw him in town and he personally observed that Mr McGonigle's drink problem was becoming progressively worse in the following years. He was barred from local pubs. The primary reason was that when intoxicated he insisted on buying drinks for everyone because, it seems, the was lonely and was anxious to make friends.

The defendant is a married man aged thirty nine years who owns a farm of 26 acres where he resides with his wife and three young children. That property is about half a mile from the McGonigle farm. The defendant knew the latter for about fourteen or fifteen years and for most of that time he rented 20 acres of the McClure lands on conacre. It appears that a friendship developed between them and in the latter years of Mr McGonigle's life, after the departure of his aunt to hospital, they spent much time together. Mr McGonigle often had breakfast in the Black household and some-times other meals also.

Dr Brian Lavelle of Convoy gave evidence that he had been the McClure family doctor and had also known Mr McGonigle for many years. In April and May 1983, he treated him for a urinary tract infection. He did not return for further treatment as intended. Dr Lavelle was aware that Mr McGonigle had a drink problem but he was not consulted in that regard. Mr McGonigle died on 1 October 1983.

The plaintiff is thirty years of age and was a nephew of Mr McGonigle. He is married and lives about $2^1/_2$ miles from his uncle's mobile home. I accept his evidence that each Sunday evening he brought Mr McGonigle to see Mrs McClure in hospital until she died in July 1981. He described that his uncle came to his home occasionally for meals and that quite often he had drink taken on those occasions. He also confirmed that his uncle's alcoholism became more acute after Mrs McClure's death. At that time he used to visit his nephew two or three times a week with occasional gaps of a fortnight or so. He described that for some years Mr McGonigle had a urinary problem which caused him to wet himself involuntarily when he had drink taken and this hap-pened more frequently from 1981 when his health seemed to deteriorate. The mobile home was very well kept in Mrs McClure's time. Mr McGonigle continued to maintain it reasonably well during her life but after her death it became, as the plaintiff described, 'rougher and rougher'. On his death it was found to be in an appalling condition and it was evident that no one had attempted to clean the place for a long time.

Mr McGonigle was not entitled to social welfare benefits because of the amount of land owned by him. It appears that from time to time he bought and sold a few cattle (though probably not in the last year of his life). He was dependent on that activity and on conacre lettings for his livelihood. In his latter years his income from those sources was not sufficient to support his drinking habits, including his insistence on buying drink for others. He had an overdraft in the Bank of Ireland, Ballybofey, which amounted to £2,786.17 on 26 October 1982 when the account was closed. The defendant also had an account in the same branch.

The first land transaction between Mr McGonigle and the defendant was in or about December 1980. Mr Morrow gave evidence that in that month Mr McGonigle called to his office and told him that he had agreed to sell his 9½ acre holding to the defendant for £3,500. Mr Morrow informed his client that in his view the price was very cheap, but the vendor insisted that he wished to go on with the sale. A contract dated 9 December 1980 was duly drawn up and executed by the parties. £500 was paid to the vendor on signing the contract; £250 on completion and the balance of £2,750 was to be paid by three annual instalments, the last one being due in December, 1983.

Three months later, in March 1981 Mr Morrow received a message from V. P. McMullin and Son, solicitors for the defendant, to the effect that Mr McGonigle had agreed to sell his 6 acre holding to the defendant for £3,000. Shortly afterwards the vendor came to see Mr Morrow and he told him that the sale was for far less than the true value of the land. He (Mr Morrow) formed the opinion at that time that Mr McGonigle was under the influence of the defendant. It was evident that he was not looking after himself properly and that his drink problem was getting worse. He did not accept Mr Morrow's advice and insisted on proceeding with the sale of the 6 acres for £500 an acre—the going rate at that time being in the region of three times that amount.

On 24 June 1982 Mr McGonigle and the defendant came to see Mr Morrow in his office. The former was quite unsteady and incoherent. The defendant spoke for him and said that Mr McGonigle wished to give him the home farm of 36 acres (i.e. all of his remaining lands) as a gift. Mr McGonigle signified his consent but at the time was clearly unfit to transact business. Mr Morrow told him to come back when he was sober. He did not do so.

The defendant's account of his business dealings with Mr McGonigle was as follows: He said that the plaintiff asked him to buy the 9½ acre plot because he was short of money. He had said that he wanted £3,000 and would give the defendant three years to pay for it. In the following year he again approached the defendant and asked him to buy the 6 acre plot and said that he wanted £3,000 in his hand to buy cattle. This contract was duly completed and the entire purchase price was paid in one sum. The explanation given by the defendant as to the background to his purchase of the home farm from Mr McGonigle in July 1982 was that about two months earlier the latter had received a letter from the bank regarding repayment of his overdraft which was then in the region of £2,500. The defendant alleged that Mr McGonigle asked him would he buy the home farm on terms that he would pay off the bank and give the vendor £1,000 over and above the bank debt. The defendant stated that Mr McGonigle was aware that the farm was worth about £40,000 but stated that he wished to give him the lands. At that point both men went to Mr Morrow but it was not possible to transact business as Mr McGonigle had too much drink taken at the time. I do not accept the defendant's evidence as to how Mr McGonigle came to transfer the home farm to him and I also doubt his explanation of the other transactions. First of all, his version of the deal relating to the home farm does not accord with Mr Morrow's account of the meeting which he had with Mr McGonigle and the defendant on 24 June 1982. Mr Morrow was not told anything about the debt due by Mr McGonigle to the bank; that he was being pressed for payment or that the plaintiff had initiated the transaction by offering to sell the home farm to the defendant in return for clearance of the bank debt and a further payment of £1,000. On the contrary, the defendant's explanation at that time was simply that Mr McGonigle wished to make a gift to him of the home farm. Secondly, the defendant went on to state in evidence that he was told by Mr McGonigle that he would not go back to Mr Morrow but instead had decided to consult James Boyle and Co., solicitors, in the matter of the home farm deal. He denied specifically that Messrs McMullin and Son, his own solicitors, had advised him to bring Mr McGonigle to Boyle and Co.. This also is patently untrue. It is specifically pleaded in para. 11 of the defence that acting upon the advice of his solicitors the defendant had brought Mr McGonigle to the firm of James Boyle and Co. for independent legal advice. It also emerged from the evidence of Mr John Heverin, manager of the Bank of Ireland, Ballybofey, that Mr McGonigle had obtained an overdraft of £2,500 on 8 March 1982 for the purpose of buying stock and providing for living expenses. This loan was to be repaid out of the sale of stock in November 1982. In fact the account was closed in the previous month when the outstanding balance at that time was discharged by the defendant. Mr Heverin had no note of any letter having been sent to Mr McGonigle earlier that year regarding the overdraft, nor was there any need for the bank to write to him because the loan was not due for repayment until the following November. I am satisfied that Mr McGonigle did not receive any demand from the bank about repayment of his overdraft and that in the period May, June and July, 1982 he was unlikely to have been concerned about it.

Miss McCrory, solicitor, of James Boyle and Co., gave evidence which I also accept. She said that in or about the last week of June 1982 Mr McGonigle accompanied by the defendant came to her office. The former was obviously under the influence of drink and she sent them away without enquiring into their business. About three weeks later on 16 July they both returned to her office again. Mr McGonigle was sober on this occasion. He explained that he wanted to transfer his home farm to the defendant. The latter was asked to leave the room and the remainder of Miss McCrory's interview with Mr McGonigle took place in private. She ascertained that the title deeds of the property were being held in the Bank of Ireland, Ballybofey as security against an overdraft. She telephoned the bank and ascertained the acreage of the farm as Mr McGonigle was not sure of the precise acreage. He told her that the purchase price of the land was to be £1,000 in cash and the purchaser was to clear the vendor's overdraft which Miss McCrory had ascertained from the bank then amounted to the sum of £2,623. She advised Mr McGonigle that the purchase price was not a realistic value and that it should be in the region of £30,000 to £35,000. She went on to advise that if he sold the farm on the open market he could expect to obtain about £1,000 per acre for it. Despite that advice Mr McGonigle insisted that he wanted to transfer the farm to the defendant. He also told her that he had already received £500 from the purchaser as a deposit. Miss McCrory made a written attendance immediately after the interview. A transfer deed was made out. No consideration was shown because the debt to the bank was rising daily as interest mounted. She asked Mr McGonigle to sign the transfer document and he did so. She then held it in trust until the consideration was paid in full. The transaction was completed on 19 November 1982. She handed over the title deeds to Mr Brian O'Mahony of V. P. McMullin and Son and in exchange received the sum of £300 which was purported to be the balance of the purchase price over and above the clearance of the overdraft and sums already paid by the purchaser to the vendor. She was not informed by Mr McGonigle or anyone else that at the time of the transfer the defendant already owed £1,000 to the vendor on an earlier transaction; nor was she given any family history by her client or told that Mr Morrow had acted for him and for the McClures for many years. The only observation Mr McGonigle made to her by way of explanation for wishing to transfer his farm to the defendant was that the latter and his wife were the only people who had bothered about him. In fact this was not true as I am satisfied that the plaintiff and his wife had also taken an interest in Mr McGonigle and had endeavoured to help him from the time when his aunt had gone into hospital.

It is well settled that equity will set aside a contract where one party thereto has exercised undue influence over the other party as a result of which the latter has been induced to enter into an improvident transaction against his own interest. Certain relationships give rise to a presumption of undue influence and the onus is on the benefiting party to prove that none was exercised in fact. The catalogue of relationships which may give rise to that presumption is unlimited and in that regard I adopt with respect the following passage from the judgment of Lowry L.C.J. in R. (Proctor) v Hutton (No. 2) [1978] NI 139 at 147–8:

> The relationships which raise the presumption are left unlimited by definition, wide open for identification on the facts and in all the circumstances of each particular case as it arises . . . . it is a common but not necessary feature of the relationship that the person on whose part undue influence is alleged assumed a responsibility for advising the donor or even managing his property. There are certain relationships which are recognised as giving rise to the presumption, but there are also those which, upon a consideration of the particular facts, may raise the same presumption.

I am satisfied that for several years prior to his death Mr McGonigle had a serious drink problem which became progressively worse as time went on and caused a deterioration in his health and general well-being. He was a bachelor and it is evident that he was particularly dependent on his aunt, Mrs McClure, to provide a home for him and generally to look after him. It seems that, essentially, his problems date from the time when she went into hospital some two years before her death and he was obliged for the first time to fend for himself. It is clear that this was too much for him and that he took refuge in alcohol. It is evident that he was a lonely man who was anxious to please and to be liked by his associates.

The defendant lived nearby Mr McGonigle and had been taking land from him on conacre for many years. I am satisfied that after Mrs McClure's departure to hospital he built up a dominant relationship with Mr McGonigle, who was then vulnerable to exploitation, through frequent contact and by providing him with some home comforts, though it seems that his help did not extend to giving any assistance to Mr McGonigle in maintaining his dwelling in habitable condition. I am also satisfied that the nature of that relationship was such as to raise a presumption of undue influence exercised by the defendant over Mr McGonigle in the matter of the transfer of the home farm thus casting an onus on the former to establish that that transaction was not brought about by any such improper influence. I have taken into account also that, although frequent drunkenness does not constitute absolute incapacity, it does lead a court to examine with particular care any transaction which may have been influenced by over-indulgence in alcohol even though the person so affected may have been sober at the time when the particular contract was made. I have no doubt that the defendant has failed to satisfy the onus upon him of establishing that his acquisition of Mr McGonigle's family farm for a small fraction of its true value was not brought about by his undue influence over the vendor. The evidence of Miss McCrory falls far short of discharging that onus. It is also eminently likely that the defendant was instrumental in persuading Mr McGonigle to leave his long-standing solicitor, Mr Morrow, because he (the defendant) was well aware that the former would be very loath indeed to allow his client to sell his last remaining asset for hardly more than a pittance.

Mr McGonigle was not sober on the first occasion when brought to Miss McCrory by the defendant. I appreciate that he was sober at the time of the crucial second visit to James Boyle and Co., but, for whatever reason, he failed to instruct Miss McCrory sufficiently about his relationship with the defendant and other relevant matters to enable her to assess the situation adequately and fully advise him. In particular, she was not informed that the defendant already owed Mr McGonigle £1,000 on an earlier transaction; that he was in the final stage of acquiring all of the defendant's lands at a gross undervalue and that before bringing him to Miss McCrory for so called independent advice, Mr McGonigle had been encouraged to leave the solicitor who had been advising him and his family for forty years. I have no doubt that Miss McCrory behaved with complete propriety in this matter, but if she had been appraised of all the salient information, including the fact that the lands comprised in the proposed transfer constituted Mr McGonigle's last remaining asset, she might well have advised him differently and probably would have refused to accept his instructions.

I am satisfied that the purported acquisition by the defendant of Mr McGonigle's home farm was for the vendor a grossly improvident transaction which was brought about by undue influence persistently exercised by the defendant over Mr McGonigle who, because of a combination of bereavement, inability to cope, loneliness, alcoholism and ill-health, was vulnerable to manipulation and was so manipulated by the dependant to the vendor's obvious disadvantage. It follows, therefore, that the plaintiff, as personal representative of Edward McGonigle, deceased, is entitled to the following relief:

(a) A declaration that the defendant holds the property which is the subject matter of this action in trust for the plaintiff; and
(b) an order that the defendant shall vacate the said property and shall take all such steps as are necessary to enable the plaintiff to be registered as owner of the same in his capacity as administrator of the estate of the said deceased.
(c) There shall be an enquiry in the Circuit Court as to damages limited to £15,000.
(d) The plaintiff shall have liberty to make further application to the High Court in these proceedings, if necessary.

Scope of the Presumption

Gregg v Kidd [1956] IR 183

Budd J.:

In these proceedings the plaintiff seeks to set aside a deed of 28 September 1953, whereby George Gregg, since deceased, in consideration of his affection for his nephew, John George Kidd, transferred his farm, situate at Tinryland in County Carlow, to William Gregg Kidd to hold in trust for the settlor for his life and in remainder in trust for John George Kidd (usually known as Jack Kidd) in fee simple.

Some months prior to the execution of the deed the settlor had made his will, dated 20 March 1953, whereby he devised all his property to his brother, Richard, for life and after his death to his nephew, Mark Gregg, the plaintiff. He appointed Richard Gregg and Mark Gregg his executors. He died on 29 December 1953, being then about fifty nine years of age. Richard Gregg pre-deceased him, but Mark Gregg, as sole surviving executor, proved the will on 2 April 1954, and thereafter launched these proceedings.

The defendants are the trustee and beneficiary under the deed, respectively, and are both sons of Mrs Hannah Kidd, a sister of the settlor. She and her family reside at Bohermore, near Bagenalstown, where they have a farm. John George Kidd is a young man of about thirty years of age.

It is alleged by the plaintiff that at the time of the making of the deed the settlor was reduced by mental ill-health or physical and mental debility to a state of help-lessness and was at the time residing in the house of the defendants and their mother, Mrs Hannah Kidd, and under their care; that the deed was improvident and was thus executed when the parties were not on equal terms. The deceased, it is alleged, was not competent by reason of mental illness to comprehend the nature and effect of the settlement. It is also alleged that the deed was obtained by the undue influence brought to bear upon the deceased by the defendants or on their behalf by Mrs Hannah Kidd, Mr Dawson Miller or one or other of them. These allegations the defendants deny and claim that the deed constitutes a valid settlement.

George Gregg acquired the farm by a transfer from his brother, Richard, on 13 January 1928, subject to a charge in favour of Richard for £500. He occupied the lands there-after up to about a year before his death. In January 1953, he was living at Tinryland, but being in bad health he went to reside with his brother, Richard, in his house at Kilmeany and was also for a time with his sister, Mrs Miller, at Shamrock Lodge, Carlow. He returned later to Kilmeany, Richard's place, and while there he had a stroke on 26 February 1953, which paralysed his left side. From 26 February to 13 March 1953, he was in Carlow Infirmary. From then until 1 May 1953, he was in the Meath Hospital in Dublin under the care of Dr Mayne. While in the Meath Hospital George Gregg made the will I have already referred to. From the Meath Hospital he returned to Carlow and went to reside again with his sister Mrs Miller. She went to London on holidays at the end of May 1953, and on 27 May George Gregg was taken to Mrs Hannah Kidd's house at Bohermore. While he was there he had two further serious relapses, (probably strokes, but that is uncertain) one in the beginning, and another at the end, of June. He remained in his sister's, Mrs Kidd's, house until he died on 29 December 1953.

During the early part of his illness George Gregg was attended by Dr Seale who had known him for about thirty years. Dr Seale, in the course of his evidence, stated that when he had the stroke George Gregg's left side became paralysed and for a time he could not speak. He had improved somewhat in May. Dr Seale saw the patient for the last time on 11 August 1953, and I shall refer later to his evidence as to his condition then. As he did not see him after that date he could not say what his condition was at the date of the execution of the deed.

Dr Mayne found George Gregg suffering from the result of the stroke and widespread arteriosclerotic disease; his mental capacity was impaired and his reasoning capacities to some extent affected. Dr Mayne said that the progress of the disease from which he was suffering would as a rule be one of deterioration but there might be improvement. Another stroke would, as one would expect, make deterioration probable.

During the period from June to September certain events took place which throw considerable light on the circumstances leading up to the execution of the deed of 28 September 1953, and I wish to refer to certain portions of the evidence which I regard as relevant to the issues which I have to decide. It is apparent that some discussions with regard to the recompense of the Kidd family for looking after George Gregg went on early in June 1953, between the Kidd family and Mr Dawson Miller, George Gregg's brother-in-law. These culminated in a visit by Dawson Miller and Jack Kidd to Mr Jeffers, who had up to then acted as George Gregg's solicitor, on 15 June. The burden of what they had to say was that George Gregg was living with the Kidds and that some arrangement should be made for the transfer of George Gregg's farm to Mrs Kidd or one of her sons subject to the payment of £500 to Mark Gregg. It transpired, however, that George Gregg was then very ill and had not himself sent for Mr Jeffers. In fact George Gregg had not, it appeared, mentioned settling his affairs and the whole idea of the purported transfer had apparently originated with Mr Miller and the Kidd family. The suggestion was no doubt made because the Kidds had taken on themselves the onerous duty of looking after George Gregg and there is no doubt Mr Miller supported the idea. Mr Jeffers very properly said that unless George Gregg himself wished to see him he could not do anything. Since George Gregg was very ill Mr Jeffers added that Dr Seale would have to certify him fit for business before he would take his instructions. They left, saying that they would see Dr Seale and get him to go out to see George Gregg.

On 22 June Mrs Hannah Kidd herself called at Mr Jeffers' office. She told him that Dr Seale had seen George and said he was incapable of doing business. She pointed out the work and cost involved in looking after her brother and asked what could be done about the matter. Mr Jeffers' view was that the moneys coming from the lettings of George's farm should be utilised to meet the expenses. He offered to ask Chancellor Nelson, George Gregg's rector, to approach George to see if he would be satisfied with the suggestion. Mr Jeffers did not know the precise income of the farm, but considered it would be ample to recompense the Kidds.

Towards the end of June 1953, Dr Seale formed the view that George Gregg should be sent to Dublin for further treatment by Dr Mayne. He engaged a room for him at a nursing home. Mrs Miller called out to Bohermore on 28 June to take him in her car to Dublin, but he was not removed on that occasion, and I am satisfied that this was mainly owing to Mrs Kidd's attitude.

On 25 July Jack Kidd called on Mr Jeffers and informed him that George Gregg wanted to see Mr Dawson Miller and himself the following Monday 27 July, for the purpose of making a will. Jack Kidd said that George Gregg was now recovered and was perfect. That was, to say the least of it, an overstatement as to George Gregg's condition. It transpired during the interview that Mrs Kidd had a short time before been to see the Reverend Mr Willis, the rector of the parish in which she resided, to get him to approach George Gregg to make a will, but he had declined to interfere. Jack Kidd further said that Mrs Kidd had also been to see Chancellor Nelson with the same object, that the Chancellor had called to see George, but that George Gregg would not discuss matters with him. He added that Dawson Miller had a week before told George Gregg that he should give the place to the Kidds. George Gregg was, he said, unwilling to adopt a suggestion that he should go to live with Edie Gregg, the plaintiff's sister, and, when told that the plaintiff had been tidying up at Tinryland, said that he would have him thrown out on the road. George Gregg, he said, had told his mother that he wanted to make a will giving her and Mark Gregg some money.

As a result of the interview with Jack Kidd Mr Jeffers repaired to Bohermore on 27 July with Mr Dawson Miller. What transpired at the interview is of importance and I should say that I accept what Mr Jeffers said in this evidence as a correct account of what occurred on that occasion. From what George Gregg said to Mr Jeffers it was obvious that Mrs Kidd was anxious that George Gregg would make a will and that at that stage he was unwilling to do so. In fact he said that he was being rushed by his sister. Mr Jeffers was anxious that George Gregg should state his attitude in the presence of Mr Miller and Mrs Kidd. George Gregg did not wish to see Mr Miller but consented to see Mrs Kidd. He told her that he could make no arrangements because he could not think clearly. An argument ensued in the course of which Mrs Kidd stated that she could not keep him unless he made a will. She was insistent that he would have to make a will or get out. He stated that he wished to have his existing will destroyed but appeared at some stages not to recollect what was in it. He directed Mr Jeffers to state what was in it in Mrs Kidd's presence, which he did. He was distressed and worried by this interview, fearing he would have to leave the house, which he did not wish to do. Mr Jeffers explained to him that entirely apart from making a will he should make provision for his maintenance and for paying Mrs Kidd for looking after him. He agreed to give her £50 out of the money in the auctioneers' hands in respect of the grazing rents of his lands. Mr Jeffers informed Mrs Kidd of this but she refused the offer and insisted that a will should be made. On this being reported to George Gregg, he was again worried and felt he would have to leave. Before Mr Jeffers left he saw Mrs Kidd again, along with Mr Miller, and both insisted to him that George Gregg would have to make a will or be put out. Mr Miller added that he would not be able to stand being moved if he was put out. Mr Miller and Mrs Kidd then returned to George Gregg's room, and, when they came out, Mr Miller said that George had refused to make a will, and, from what they said to Mr Jeffers, it was clear to him that they had made it clear to George Gregg that he must take a will or get out. Mr Jeffers told them that a will made under undue influence would be invalid, but he says that no attention was paid to what he said, and he then left having pointed out that while Mrs Kidd was quite justified in seeking some arrangement to be made for George's maintenance, no one had the right to insist upon his making a will if he did not wish to do so. I have dealt in some detail with this interview because it indicates what the attitude and aims of Mrs Kidd were at that early stage. Strong pressure was being put on George Gregg to make a will at a time when he was in poor condition to resist, and that pressure was backed by a threat which was bound to have a strong affect on George Gregg's mind. I have no doubt that the will which Mrs Kidd wished him to make was one in favour of some one or other of the members of the Kidd family.

Mrs Kidd was not satisfied to allow things to remain as they were. Dr Gavin, who had not attended George Gregg before, was summoned to visit him. He saw him on 31 July and again on 3 and 11 August. On 31 July he found George suffering from residual haemoplegia. His blood pressure was raised; his left arm was not as strong as his right; his hearing was affected but that was put right. He explained his condition, but things would have to be dragged out of him, as the doctor put it. On 3 August he was satisfied that he was capable of looking after his affairs; but he had not known George Gregg when he was in good health and admitted that his opinion would have been affected if he had known of George Gregg's previously cheerful and voluble disposition. He was then quiet and difficult to get answers from and required to have things explained slowly to him.

Having again received information, this time from the Reverend Mr Willis, to the effect that George Gregg wished to make a will, Mr Jeffers again went to Bohermore on 11 August. Mr Willis had informed him that it was Jack Kidd who had asked him to phone and that he had said that Dr Gavin had certified George Gregg fit to make a will. Mr Jeffers brought Dr Seale with him so that he could have the benefit of Dr Seale's views, as George Gregg's medical attendant, as to his capacity to make a will. Dr Seale formed the view that George Gregg was not competent to make a will. The doctor found that certain answers George Gregg gave to his questions were not correct and that his mental condition had deteriorated since June. He just answered, 'yes' or 'no', to questions and made no effort to chat, which was quite different from his normal habits. He was clear intermittently, but not for long enough to know what he was doing. His view was that George Gregg could not understand or appreciate affairs of business and that he could not evaluate or resist suggestions made to him. The doctor thought he could be persuaded to do anything. He never saw George Gregg again nor was his assistance with regard to George Gregg's medical history sought after that date by any other doctor. He did not on that occasion put any question to George Gregg about the extent of his property or about his family or generally about his making a will as he thought there was no use in doing so.

To Mr Jeffers George Gregg also seemed to have deteriorated. Although normally cheerful and chatty, he had little to say. His answers were short, his speech was not very clear and he was inclined to ramble a little at times. He informed George Gregg that having regard to Dr Seale's view he could not make a will for him, but later asked him what he would do if he was able to make a will. He replied that he would give the place to his sister, Hannah, and her son, Jack Kidd. When he was asked whether he meant to give them the place jointly or one after the other he seemed incapable of understanding what Mr Jeffers meant and mumbled something that Mr Jeffers could not hear. He also said he would like to benefit Dick's little girl. He said her name was Edie, but later said the name was Markey, the name he usually used to refer to the plaintiff. According to Mr Jeffers he seemed very confused but made some remark about paying Mrs Kidd for looking after him.

Mrs Kidd asked Mr Jeffers why he could not make a will having regard to the views of Dr Mansfield, who had also seen George Gregg prior to that date. Mr Jeffers replied that Dr Seale had better knowledge of the case than Dr Mansfield. Mrs Kidd was again not satisfied. She went that same evening to see Dr Gavin, and, as a result, he went out to see George Gregg. He was satisfied that George Gregg wanted to make some change in his affairs and was capable of making that change and of determining what he wanted to do. He admitted that he was slow in his answers and that he took no steps to test their accuracy. He might have lingered on for two or three years, he thought.

On 12 August Mrs Kidd again came to Mr Jeffers' office and asked him whether George's will had been destroyed, a question Mr Jeffers declined to answer. She stated that Dr Gavin had been called in to see George Gregg on the previous night, after Dr Seale and Mr Jeffers had left, and had certified George Gregg fit to make a will and that George Gregg had said that Mr Jeffers had let him down in not making a will for him. Mr Jeffers pointed out that George Gregg could get another solicitor if he was not satisfied. He had no more dealings with the parties up to the time of George Gregg's death.

On 15 August Mrs Kidd wrote a letter to her sister, Mrs Miller. She states that she wrote that letter at the dictation of Chancellor Nelson, a suggestion that I do not believe. The letter reads:

> Dear Susan. I want you to get a bed ready for your brother George in Tinryland, or the only alternative a bed in the county hospital. I have done all in my capacity for him. I cannot continue any longer. Please let me have a reply immediately.
>
> Yours
> H. M. Kidd.

Ken Miller, Mrs Miller's son, was given this letter to take to Bohermore to read to his uncle. He did so. While Mrs Miller's action in sending the letter to her brother may be open to criticism, it is hardly to be suggested that Mrs Kidd did not intend her attitude to be made known to him. The letter was, of course, a great shock to George Gregg.

Early in September Mrs Kidd betook herself to consult Mr Cody, a solicitor practising in Bagenalstown. She had several interviews with him. Her object, Mr Cody understood, was to get something done about George's affairs and to have her position as regards his maintenance secured. She gave him certain information about George Gregg, told him she was looking after him, that he had had a stroke and was possessed of the farm. She was Mr Cody's source of information as to the background. Mr Cody did not keep a note of his attendances on Mrs Kidd and does not remember what exactly passed between them, but he recalled that Mrs Kidd had said that Mr Jeffers had refused to make a will for George Gregg on the advice of Dr Seale. Mr Cody gave Mrs Kidd certain advice. He anticipated litigation and suggested the advisability of having George Gregg examined by two doctors. Mr Cody had not up to this time been sent for or consulted by George Gregg himself.

In accordance with Mr Cody's advice Dr Mansfield and Dr Humphries examined George Gregg on 25 September. Dr Humphries did not know him before and was about ten minutes with him. He asked him some questions about simple every day affairs, which he answered apparently to the doctor's satisfaction. Dr Humphries came to the conclusion that he was capable of doing business and altering the settlement of his affairs by a procedure of question and answer. While his mental processes were somewhat impaired he thought he could make a simple will if matters were explained slowly to him. The doctor expressed the view that he did not think that George Gregg would be influenced by the views of others but it would seem to me that the doctor's lack of knowledge of the background put him in a poor position to form any such view after so short an interview. He thought from what he saw that George Gregg might have lingered on for three or four years.

Dr Mansfield had previously seen George Gregg on 4 June. He was uncertain then whether he had had a second stroke or not, but he had just previously become worse and had little use of his arm and leg on the left side. When he saw him again on 6 June he answered simple questions and was clear to that extent. He saw him later on 6 July and on 26 and 27 August but there was not much change in his condition. Mrs Kidd it was who asked Dr Mansfield to see George Gregg on 25 September, the object being to see if he was fit to make a will. He asked him about his farm and whom he wished to leave it to; he said he wished to leave it to one of the Kidd family. His answers were satisfactory and the doctor came to the conclusion he could make a simple will but that he was not capable of making a complicated disposition of a lot of property; he was incapable of continuing a long process of thought or of concentration. As to his general observations of the patient, he agreed that any change would be towards deterioration. The disorder of haemoplegia, he agreed, affects the brain processes and there may be periods of clarity followed by periods of confusion. He also thought that he might have lingered on a few years.

William Kidd having informed Mr Cody that George Gregg wished to settle his affairs and wanted him to go out, Mr Cody went to Bohermore on 26 September and saw the deceased. He spent from half an hour to three quarters of an hour with him. He said that George Gregg looked all right to him and that he could see nothing wrong with him. He was able to talk to Mr Cody who said that he understood he wished to settle his affairs. Mr Cody spoke to him of his previous will and its contents and about his farm. George Gregg answered such questions as he was asked satisfactorily but was slow to answer and generally confined his answer to the one word, 'yes'. George Gregg said that he wanted to leave the farm at Tinryland to Jack Kidd by deed. Mr Cody explained to George Gregg the two ways in which he could dispose of his property, by will or by deed. He pointed out the salient differences between a deed and a will and in particular that a will can be changed but that a deed cannot be altered. Mr Cody was satisfied that George Gregg understood what he was told. Before leaving the house Mr Cody told the Kidds of the instructions he had received and asked William Kidd if he would act as trustee, which he agreed to do.

On 28 September Mr Cody returned with the engrossment of a deed which he had prepared in the meantime. By it the farm was transferred to William Gregg Kidd upon trust for George Gregg for life and in remainder to the use of John George Kidd in fee simple. The deed was read over to George Gregg. Mr Cody explained its effect and asked George Gregg if he understood it. George Gregg said that he did and executed it, after which Mr Cody departed.

Mr Cody says that George Gregg was on that occasion as clear as on the previous day he saw him and as far as he could judge understood what he was saying to him and knew what he was doing. He had not had the benefit of the views of the doctors who had examined George Gregg just before. He relied on what he saw himself. He did not realise that George Gregg was permanently paralysed, nor did he consider how long he might possibly live. He said that he did not consider what position George Gregg would be in if he changed his mind. He did not at the time of taking instructions or drawing the deed know that pressure was being brought to bear on George Gregg; he only discovered that when the affidavit of discovery was filed by the plaintiffs, when presumably he had the advantage of reading Mr Jeffers' notes of his attendances on the parties. He was in no way on guard against the possibility that the Kidds might be influencing George Gregg nor did he apparently appreciate that George Gregg was in a position in which he would require protection. He did not give George Gregg any advice as to the possibility or desirability of inserting in the deed a clause of revocation or any provision that would provide for him being permitted to reside at Bohermore or binding the Kidds to care for him for the rest of his life, nor did he consider the desirability of making any provision compelling Jack Kidd to work the lands during his life. In short, he did not give any serious consideration to the possibility that the Kidds might fall out with George Gregg after the deed was executed nor what would happen to George Gregg if they did. He got a payment on account of the costs relative to drawing the deed from Jack Kidd and intended to furnish the bill of costs to Jack Kidd later on.

Voluntary gifts, made *inter vivos*, obtained by persons standing in a confidential, fiduciary, or other relation to the donor in which dominion may be exercised over him may, upon principles of general public policy, be set aside where there has been some improper conduct, overreaching or coercion exercised against the donor. The general principles are well stated in White and Tudor's *Leading Cases in Equity* in the notes appended to the case of *Huguenin v Basely*.[1] As Lord Cottenham states in *Dent v Bennett*:[2] 'The relief . . . stands upon a general principle, applying to all variety of relations in which dominion may be exercised by one person over another.' It applies of course where the gift is the result of influence expressly used by the donee and also 'where the relations between the donor and donee have at or shortly before the execution of the gift been such as to raise a presumption that the donee had influence over the donor. In such a case the court sets aside a voluntary gift, unless it is proved that in fact the gift was the spontaneous act of the donor acting under circumstances which enabled him to exercise an independent will and which justifies the court in holding that the gift was the result of a free exercise of the donor's will', per Cotton L.J. in *Allcard v Skinner*.[3]

The courts have never confined the application of the principle to any stated forms of relationship. To do so would fetter that wide jurisdiction to relieve against all manner of constructive fraud which courts administering equitable principles have always exercised. The principle has been exercised in the case of an improvident voluntary settlement by a younger sister in favour of an elder sister, who had obtained great ascendancy and influence over the younger sister, the younger sister not having the benefit of independent advice: *Harvey v Mount*.[4] In *Sharp v Leach*[5] a voluntary deed, under which a brother obtained an advantage from a sister who lived with him and consulted him about her affairs, was set aside. The improvidence of the transaction was held to cast the onus on the defendant to show that the deed emanated from the free will of the sister after it had been explained to her. Similarly in *Griffiths v Robins*,[6] an old lady, nearly blind, who reserving only a life estate to herself, made a deed of gift of all her property to her niece and her husband, on whose kindness and assistance she depended, was held entitled to have the deed set aside. The onus was held to be upon the recipients to establish that the deed was made of her own free will and effected through the intervention of some indifferent person.

The authorities cited leave no doubt that the principle can be extended to the relationship of brother and sister, where a sister has for one reason or another acquired an influence or dominion over a brother and uses that influence improperly for her own ends. Likewise it can be extended in similar circumstances to the relationship between uncle and nephew. The influence may arise or be acquired in many ways, such as through disparity of age or the mental or physical incapacity of the donor or, indeed, out of a mere dependence upon the kindness and assistance of another. To bring the principle into play it must be shown that the opportunity for the exercise of the influence or ascendancy on the donor existed, as where the parties reside together or meet frequently. While close family relationship creates a situation where influence is readily acquired, mere blood relationship is not sufficient of itself to call the principle into play; it must be shown that the actual relations between the parties give rise to a presumption of influence.

Although the exercise of undue influence is pleaded against the donee of the deed impugned, as well as against others, it is true to say that the evidence was mainly directed to establishing that influence had been obtained and exercised over the donor by Mrs Hannah Kidd, mother of the donee. There is in my mind no doubt that if it be shown that his deed was obtained by the undue influence of Mrs Hannah Kidd or as a result of her dominion of mind over her brother, improperly exercised to benefit a member of her family, this deed cannot stand. Indeed, it is only right to say that a contention to the contrary was never made by the advisers of the defendants. Although authority is scarcely required on the point, I recall the words of Lord Eldon in the first paragraph of his judgment in *Huguenin v Basely* where he says: 'I should regret that any doubt could be entertained, whether it is not competent to a court of equity to take away from third persons the benefits which they have derived from the fraud, imposition, or undue influence of others.' If the proper deductions from the evidence adduced are that Jack Kidd knew perfectly well that his mother had acquired influence over the donor and that they acted together in order to obtain some advantage from the donor, the grounds for interfering are all the stronger.

Some debate took place during the hearing as to where the onus of proof lay. In the case of a voluntary gift where the relations between the donor and donee are such as to raise a presumption that the donee had influence over the donor, the onus lies, in my view, on the donee to establish that the gift was the spontaneous act of the donor acting in circumstances which enabled him to exercise an independent will and that the gift was the result of a free exercise of the donor's will. This proposition I believe to be one well established. Authority will be found for it in the cases of *Allcard v Skinner*, *Sharp v Leach*, and *Griffiths v Robins*, already referred to, and also in the observations of Lord Romilly in *Cooke v Lamotte*.[7] If more modern authority is required it will be found in the judgment of Lord Hailsham in the comparatively recent case of *Inche Noriah v Shaik Allie Bin Omar*.[8] Where the relations between the donor and another person raise a presumption that that other person had influence over the donor and the evidence shows that that third party is both closely related to the donee and was closely associated in action and interest with the donee at the time of the events leading to the transaction, it would seem to me on principle that the onus in such circumstances must be likewise thrown on the donee to establish that the gift resulted from the free exercise of the donor's will.

The presumption may, of course, be rebutted either by showing that the donor has had competent independent advice and acted of his own free will or in some other way. As Lord Hailsham says, in *Inche Noriah v Shaik Allie Bin Omar*: 'The most obvious way to prove [that the gift was the result of the free exercise of independent will is to establish] that the gift was made after the nature and effect of the transaction had been fully explained to the donor by some independent and qualified person so completely as to satisfy the court that the donor was acting independently of any influence from the donee and with full appreciation of what he was doing.' If that method of rebutting the presumption is adopted, and it is not the only method open, the advice relied on must, in the words of Lord Hailsham, 'be given with a knowledge of all relevant circumstances and must be such as a competent and honest adviser would give if acting solely in the interests of the donor.' The nature of that advice naturally must vary with the circumstances of each particular case.

Although there is considerable difference of medical opinion as to George Gregg's mental and physical condition at the time when the deed was executed and during the period immediately preceding that event, I have formed these conclusions as to his health during the relevant period: he had had at least one stroke and two serious relapses; he was partially paralysed and virtually bedridden; he suffered from a condition the usual progress of which is one of deterioration; during the summer and autumn his reasoning faculties became impaired; at times his memory was intermittent and faulty and I believe that he could not concentrate for any appreciable length of time; he had periods of confusion of mind. In character he had formerly been voluble and cheerful but had changed to saying little and had become difficult to get answers from. I believe that his capacity to make rational decisions was, by the autumn, definitely impaired and that his capacity to resist influence and suggestions was very slight and easily overcome. At times, I think, he might have been fit to make a simple officious will or simple disposition of his property if uninfluenced and properly advised, but it would, in my view, have been difficult to discover just when he was in that condition and equally difficult to bring him to a full understanding of the transaction. Someone well acquainted with him would obviously be the best person to make the attempt, but even such a person would require to exercise care and patience in examining him before coming to a conclusion as to his capacity. Even if he could be shown to have had the capacity to bring a reasoning mind to bear on such a disposition there would still remain the formidable difficulty of ascertaining and ensuring that his mind was emancipated from the influence and dominion of others alleged to have existed.

The last above-mentioned matter brings me to a consideration of the relations between the donor, on the one hand, and the donee and his mother, Mrs Hannah Kidd, on the other hand, at and immediately before the execution of the deed. As far back as the end of May 1953, George Gregg had been moved to the Kidds' house and he had remained with them until his death. During most of that time he was a very sick man, only a wreck of his former self. He was during that period entirely dependent on the Kidd family for all the attention his helpless condition required. If and when he was fit for company and conversation it would naturally be members of that family whom he would generally see and he does not seem to have seen much of other members of his family from June onwards. I believe that he knew with more or less clarity, according to the varying state of his health, that he was then dependent on the Kidd family and that he was at times at least most apprehensive as to what would become of him were they to refuse to look after him any longer. In short, his circumstances and condition laid him open in a high degree to the influence of that family, more particularly to that of Mrs Hannah Kidd, having regard to her relationship to him and her position in the household. Mrs Kidd's character as revealed by her evidence and demeanour is not, in this connection, by any means irrelevant to what I am dealing with, and I should say that she struck me as a woman of forceful and determined character, who believed in having her own way without much regard to the views or advice of others.

Apart from these circumstances which I have mentioned, there is a considerable body of evidence as to the actual relations existing between George Gregg and his relatives, the Kidds, and of their attitude to him, to which I must briefly refer. Before doing so I should say that it must, in all fairness, be recognised that the Kidds acted with kindness in taking George Gregg into their house, having regard to his condition, and I see no reason to doubt that they treated him kindly and looked after him to the best of their ability. No one would suggest that it would have been unreasonable for Mrs Kidd to seek reasonable recompense for the onerous services she performed. Unfortunately, I regret to say that the evidence does not lead me to believe that the Kidds' motives were by any means solely altruistic and moreover I was forced to take an unfavourable view of the veracity of such members of the family as gave evidence before me in respect of a good deal of what they told me.

The evidence leads me to believe that from an early stage Mrs Kidd formed the view, shared by her son, Jack Kidd, that George Gregg's farm at Tinryland should go to the Kidds in return for looking after him. It does not matter, to my mind, whether the idea originated with Dawson Miller or Mrs Kidd herself or her son. The attempts to get George Gregg to make some further settlement of his affairs, other than that provided for in his existing will, indicated by the approaches of Mrs Kidd and Jack Kidd to Mr Jeffers and of Mrs Kidd to Mr Cody, all indicate their frame of mind. Likewise, the fact that they kept stressing that doctors other than Dr Seale thought George Gregg fit to transact business betrayed their anxiety to have something done and I am satisfied that what was aimed at was the making of some disposition of George Gregg's property in favour of Mrs Kidd or some of her family and not merely obtaining some reasonable recompense for her services.

The facts as proved are such as to lead me to the conclusion not only that the relations between George Gregg and his sister were such as to raise a presumption that she had influence over him, but that she was exercising that influence towards securing his farm for some one or other of her family. She was certainly using active pressure on 27 July 1953, and her subsequent activities lead me to believe that that pressure was not relaxed to the date on which the deed was executed; that influence was such, having regard to George Gregg's incapacity and circumstances, as to preclude the exercise by him of a free and independent judgment. The facts are sufficient to support a finding of the actual exercise of undue influence, but it is sufficient to say that the relations between the donor, on the one hand, and his sister and nephew, on the other, were such as to raise a presumption that the donee's mother had influence over the donor. I am satisfied that the donee was aware of this influence and acted in combination with his mother; the onus consequently lies on the defendants to establish that the gift resulted from the free exercise of the donor's will acting in circumstances which enabled him to exercise an independent will.

I conceive that a solicitor advising one in the circumstances of George Gregg is at least under the following obligations to his client. To begin with, he should apprise himself of the surrounding circumstances in so far as he reasonably can; if he does not do this he can never put himself in a position to advise his client fully and effectively. He would need to discover the nature of the donor's illness so as to be able to estimate in some reasonable degree the nature of his incapacity. He would need to know how far his reasoning capacity was affected and how far he was capable of comprehending the manner in which the proposed transaction would affect his own interests and his future and to what extent he was competent to come to a rational decision. Without knowing all that, he could not be said to have sufficient knowledge of his client to enable him to judge the nature of the advice he should give him and the degree of protection he would require. With the knowledge that he would have gained upon inquiry that the donor was incapacitated to some degree both mentally and physically and had been living for some time with the family of the proposed transferee, by one of whom the solicitor in this case had originally been consulted with a view to having something done about the donor's affairs, he ought then to have been put on his guard and he should, in my view, then endeavour to discover whether his client was subject to the influence of the donee or any member of his family and, if so, the extent of that influence. Having discovered the extent of the donor's incapacity he should make sure that he was capable of fully understanding the nature and results of a transaction such as that proposed. Without that capacity the transaction could not be proceeded with, but, assuming that the solicitor satisfies himself that it exists, he should then make sure that his client did thoroughly understand what he was doing and how it would affect him. He would need in this connection to consider very carefully whether the transaction was one for his benefit and, as I see it, this was a case that called for positive and definite advice, not mere explanation. The suggested transfer was, on the face of it, an improvident transaction. The plight of the donor demanded that he should be protected against himself. He should have been told clearly that the transaction was improvident, that it secured nothing for him in return for what he was giving, and that he was not only depriving himself of most of what he possessed, but also the means of securing his future comfort. He should have been advised against entering into the proposed transaction unless he was adequately and properly safeguarded. In particular, he should have been told that he might safeguard himself to a great degree by having a power of revocation inserted in the instrument. Before he could conscientiously advise his client to proceed with the transaction the solicitor would also need to satisfy himself that his intervention and advice had emancipated the donor from any adverse influence he lay under and that he was acting of his own free will.

Mr Cody was faced with an unenviable task of difficulty and delicacy when he was called upon to attend George Gregg in September 1953. It is easy to be wise after the event and I feel sure that Mr Cody would have acted differently had he appreciated what the real circumstances were. It may well be that he was to some extent misled and it is right to say the he was quite candid about the advice he gave. I must, however, consider whether such advice as he did give could have the results contended for by the defendants. While I am alive to the fact that it was Mrs Kidd, and not the donee, who had previously consulted him I have the gravest doubts whether Mr Cody could be properly described as an independent solicitor; but even assuming for the moment that he was, Mr Cody did not, I fear, appreciate the full extent of George Gregg's physical and mental incapacity. He had not known his client previously and was not in a position to judge how much he had deteriorated and I believe he did not appreciate the extent to which his reasoning power and ability to make rational decisions was affected. He did not sufficiently consider what effect the transaction would have on George Gregg's future nor what would happen should he fall out with the Kidds, nor did he consider in what way George Gregg might be safeguarded, nor did he, I believe, appreciate the entire improvidence of the transaction. It follows that he did not feel called upon to give, nor did he give, George Gregg any positive advice in the way of dissuading him from entering into the transaction as proposed nor did he advise George Gregg as to the various ways in which he might be safeguarded from the improvidence he contemplated nor urge him to adopt any suggestions calculated to safeguard him. In particular, he never brought to his notice the possibility of inserting a power of revocation in the deed nor did he urge on him the desirability of such a course, which I believe the circumstances called for. Furthermore, Mr Cody did not appreciate the true nature of the relations existing between the donor and Mrs Kidd and the donor and the donee, to a lesser degree. Deprived of that knowledge, he was never in a position to consider what advice and warning he should properly give to the donor and what steps he should take to make sure that the settlor was acting with a free and independent mind and was emancipated from the influence of his sister. As a result, no steps were taken to ensure that George Gregg acted independently and freed from the effects of his sister's influence. The advice received by the donor was not therefore sufficient to enable the donor to understand fully and properly the nature of the entire transaction nor such as to protect the donor against himself; nor was it sufficient to rebut the presumption, nor does it satisfy me that the gift was the spontaneous act of a donor who knew what he was doing.

1. 14 Ves 273.
2. 4 My & C 277.
3. 36 ChD 145, at p. 171.
4. 8 Beav 439.
5. 31 Beav 491.
6. 3 Madd 181.
7. 15 Beav 234.
8. [1929] AC 127.
9. 3 D J & S 487 at p. 491.
10. 8 Ch App 430.
11. 17 LRI 641.
12. [1900] 1 Ch. 243.

Notes

1. Recent English case-law involving transactions relating to family property are very instructive. In *Daniel v Drew* [2005] EWCA Civ 507 (see below, p. 693) an application to set aside an instrument retiring as a trustee of family property was set aside as between an 'insensitive and forceful nephew' and his 'vulnerable and elderly aunt' who, in the words of the Court of Appeal, had been 'cornered' into signing the retirement instrument. The Court of Appeal upheld the view of the trial judge that the case was one of actual undue influence and that, in such a context, the threat of future litigation was a factor that could be relevant to the inquiry into freedom of action by one of the parties.

2. In contrast, *Turkey v Awadh* [2005] EWCA Civ 382, is authority for the proposition that family arrangements are in a different category from commercial transactions, and the fact that the parties to a contract transferring real property have not sought to establish the value of the property does not of itself require the transaction to be explained: the presumption did not arise. Chadwick L. J. explained the current state of English law thus on the nature of the presumption:

The conditions which must be established in order to raise the evidential presumption are, first, facts which persuade the court that the party seeking to uphold the transaction (say, party A) was in a position to influence the will of the other party (party B) in relation to a transaction of the relevant nature. That requirement is often referred to as the need to establish a relationship of trust and confidence. The judge found that first condition to be satisfied in the present case; and again there is no challenge to that finding.

Second, facts must be established which persuade the court that the transaction in question is of such a nature that a person in the position of party B, acting in the way that such a person might ordinarily be expected to act, would not have entered into the transaction unless his or her will was overborne. As Lord Scott of Foscote put it in *Royal Bank of Scotland v Etridge* [2002] 2 AC 773 at page 854, paragraph 220, the transaction must be shown to be one which cannot be explained by reference to the ordinary motives by which people are accustomed to act.

B. COHABITING PARTIES—THE OLD LAW

Hargreave v Everard (1856) 6 Ir Ch R 678

In this case a woman living in adultery with a married man assigned some of her property to secure a debt contracted by him. She later sought to have the transaction set aside.

In giving his judgment Lord St Leonards could not disguise his distaste at the conduct of the parties but he went on to consider the plea of undue influence:

. . . The question which I am obliged to consider is merely whether the petitioner is entitled to claim the interposition of this court to set aside the deed?

That interposition has been sought upon grounds which have been acted on in many cases in this court; but, from the first opening of this petition, I have felt great difficulty in applying the doctrine established in such cases to the present one. Those cases will be found, on examination, wholly distinct from the case now before the court. In the case of parties between whom certain recognised and lawful relations exist, calculated to give a strong influence to the one over the mind of the other, the court interferes on high grounds of public policy; not so much in many cases, for the sake of remedying injustice in the particular case, as for the sake of the relation itself, and to secure that those relations may stand free from risk, so that no one need fear to enter upon them, and that trustees, parents and guardians, may be relieved from any temptation to seek their own advantage in the discharge of their duties. Protected by this principle, the parent intrusts his child to a guardian, with the firm conviction that that guardian will not be allowed to make his office the means of working on the fears or affections of the child, in his own favour. So likewise, property may be given to a child, whom the law intrusts to the guardianship of the parent, and the giver may be sure that the parent will not be allowed, by any abuse of power or influence, to obtain any portion of the gift. Nor is the protection confined to the case of infancy. In legal relations between adult persons, in those, for example, of physician and patient, clergyman and penitent, and so on from one lawful relation to another, the law recognises the relation, and guards it in a similar manner. But all these are lawful relations, and necessary to the community; and this court therefore endeavours to keep them in a pure atmosphere, and to make it certain that the influence which arises out of them shall not be used for any purpose connected with the acquisition of property. But when we come to consider the relation which is put forward as the ground of relief in the present case, I know of no law, no public policy, which seeks to encourage it, or intervenes to protect one of the parties to such a relation from the other. In the eye of the law, they stand isolated from one another: there is no legal or recognised relation between them from which influence will be presumed. That, of course, does not exclude the consideration of any facts which may be proved to have occurred, and which may in themselves be strong enough to induce the court to set aside a transaction which has taken place between the parties. But the case made must be apart from the consideration of any connection between the parties, and facts must be shown strong enough to demonstrate the necessity of the court interfering to protect the weaker against the stronger. I do not see how these cases of parent and child, and the like, can be applied, considering the reasons upon which the decisions in these cases were grounded. The rule they establish was introduced for the purpose of protecting and encouraging certain relations recognised by the law, and has no bearing upon such a connection as is disclosed in this case. Here there is no legal presumption of influence at one side or the other, and conjecture is not sufficient ground to rely upon; nor could we with any certainty conjecture at which side the influence exists. It is much more frequently the woman who influences the man, than the man who influences the woman; and the cases in our books as to wills are much more frequently of the former class than the latter. No doubt, the influence may be brought to bear on the woman; but that is a question of fact to be made out from all the circumstances of the case, and not to be reasoned out by inferences from the existence of the connection. It is said, however, that the court would at all events interpose as against Mr Thomas himself, the great delinquent in this case, if this suit was instituted against him alone, on behalf of this unhappy woman, to refuse a restitution of the gifts which she has made to him. I am not sure of that. True it may be, that this court would not assist him to enforce any claim arising out of such a transaction, but it does not necessarily follow that it would set aside a deed which she had executed for his benefit, or give her relief even as against him. As I said before, it is difficult to say what influence there is, apart from the intensity of affection, which must exist in these cases. The cases which we have every day upon the separate property of married women are expressly in point. We have constantly suits by creditors of the husband, to enforce securities which they have got from the wife upon her separate estate; but who ever heard of a petition by a wife, to be relieved from such an engagement, on the ground of its having been procured through her affection for her husband? It is plain therefore there is a distinction recognised, and which we ought to bear in mind, though it may be sometimes difficult to make, between the effects of intense affection, such as a person in the position of the petitioner here may perhaps be presumed to feel, and what the law calls undue influence.

But let us examine the particular circumstances of the case itself. Here is a lady, not in her very early youth, but of mature intelligence, evidently not devoid of knowledge of business, possessed of and managing considerable property, who, making a case in her petition of delusion and weakness, in her affidavit avows, almost with exultation, the part which she has borne in the abandonment by this gentleman of the objects of his legitimate affection. Certainly, comparing her petition with her affidavit, and bearing in mind the case made by that petition, one is struck by the nervous language she uses, and the strong and business-like manner in which she speaks. It turns out also that this deed, instead of being procured, as alleged, by a sudden demand pressed unduly upon her, was the result of long deliberation and discussion. It forms part of the means adopted by this lady to relieve Mr Thomas from the consequences of the legal proceedings against him. It follows up a security, which is not impeached, given by her for the purpose of freeing him from imprisonment; for she gave her bond with warrant of attorney to the Sheriff, on Mr Thomas' arrest, not a month before the present matter took place. The suit against Mr Thomas went on, and there can be no doubt that the public hearing of the cause would have been an undesirable event both for her and him. It is pretty clear that, under these circumstances, the means of compromising the matter were suggested by him, or his sister, or his friends. It is to be lamented that this lady did not find some professional adviser to manage her affairs; but I do not wonder that no one would wish to take them up, seeing them involved with such a person. But she did find one gentleman, who, on her application to him, did caution and warn her not to give this security; and it is quite plain, from what she states, that she had a strong inclination and will in the other direction, that she determined to carry out the compromise, and that she acted on that determination.

C. Married Persons and Cohabitees—The New Law

Barclays Bank plc v O'Brien [1993] 4 All ER 417

Browne-Wilkinson L.J.:

My Lords, in this appeal your Lordships for the first time have to consider a problem which has given rise to reported decisions of the Court of Appeal on no less than eleven occasions in the last eight years and which has led to a difference of judicial view. Shortly stated the question is whether a bank is entitled to enforce against a wife an obligation to secure a debt owed by her husband to the bank where the wife has been induced to stand as surety for her husband's debt by the undue influence or misrepresentation of the husband.

The facts

The facts of the present case are very fully set out in the judgment of Scott L.J. in the Court of Appeal ([1992] 4 All ER 983, [1993] QB 109). I will only state them in summary form. Mr and Mrs O'Brien were husband and wife. The matrimonial home, 151 Farnham Lane, Slough, was in their joint names subject to a mortgage of approximately £25,000 to a building society. Mr O'Brien was a chartered accountant and had an interest in a company, Heathrow Fabrications Ltd. The company's bank account was at the Woolwich branch of Barclays Bank. In the first three months of 1987 the company frequently exceeded its overdraft facility of £40,000 and a number of its cheques were dishonoured on presentation. In discussions in April 1981 between Mr O'Brien and the manager of the Woolwich branch, Mr Tucker, Mr O'Brien told Mr Tucker that he was remortgaging the matrimonial home; Mr Tucker made a note that Mrs O'Brien might be a problem. The overdraft limit was raised at that stage to £60,000 for one month. Even though no additional security was provided, by 15 June 1987 the company's overdraft had risen to £98,000 and its cheques were again being dishonoured.

On 22 June 1987 Mr O'Brien and Mr Tucker agreed (1) that the company's overdraft limit would be raised to £135,000 reducing to £120,000 after three weeks, (2) that Mr O'Brien would guarantee the company's indebtedness and (3) that Mr O'Brien's liability would be secured by a second charge on the matrimonial home.

The necessary security documents were prepared by the bank. They consisted of an unlimited guarantee by Mr O'Brien of the company's liability and a legal charge by both Mr and Mrs O'Brien of the matrimonial home to secure any liability of Mr O'Brien to the bank. Mr Tucker arranged for the documents, together with a side letter, to be sent to the Burnham branch of the bank for execution by Mr and Mrs O'Brien. In a covering memorandum Mr Tucker requested the Burnham branch to advise the O'Briens as to the current level of the facilities afforded to the bank (£107,000) and the projected increase to £135,000. The Burnham branch was also asked to ensure that the O'Briens were 'fully aware of the nature of the documentation to be signed and advised that if they are in any doubt they should contact their solicitors before signing'.

Unfortunately the Burnham branch did not follow Mr Tucker's instructions. On 1 July Mr O'Brien alone signed the guarantee and legal charge at the Burnham branch, the document simply being produced for signature and witnessed by a clerk. On the following day Mrs O'Brien went to the branch with her husband. There were produced for signature by Mrs O'Brien the legal charge on the matrimonial home together with a side letter, which reads:

> We hereby agree acknowledge and confirm as follows: (1) That we have each received from you a copy of the guarantee dated 3 July 1987 (a copy of which is attached hereto) under which Nicholas Edward O'Brien guarantees the payment and discharge of all moneys and liabilities now or hereafter due owing or incurred by Heathrow Fabrications Ltd to you. (2) That the liability of the said Nicholas Edward O'Brien to you pursuant to the said guarantee is and will be secured by the legal charge dated 3 July 1987 over the property described above made between (1) Nicholas Edward O'Brien (2) Nicholas Edward O'Brien and Bridget Mary O'Brien and (3) Barclays Bank Plc. (3) That you recommended that we should obtain independent legal advice before signing this letter.

In fact the Burnham branch gave Mrs O'Brien no explanation of the effect of the documents. No one suggested that she should take independent legal advice. She did not read the documents or the side letter. She simply signed the legal charge and side letter and her signature was witnessed by the clerk. She was not given a copy of the guarantee.

The company did not prosper and by October 1987 its indebtedness to the bank was over £154,000. In November 1987 demand was made against Mr O'Brien under his guarantee. When the demand was not met possession proceedings under the legal charge were brought by the bank against Mr and Mrs O'Brien. Mrs O'Brien seeks to defend these proceedings by alleging that she was induced to execute the legal charge on the matrimonial home by the undue influence of Mr O'Brien and by his misrepresentation. The trial judge, Judge Marder Q.C., and the Court of Appeal rejected the claim based on undue influence: on the appeal to this House the claim based on undue influence is not pursued. However, the judge did find that Mr O'Brien had falsely represented to Mrs O'Brien that the charge was to secure only £60,000 and that even this liability would be released in a short time when the house was remortgaged. On those findings of fact the trial judge granted an order for possession against Mrs O'Brien holding that the bank could not be held responsible for the misrepresentation made by Mr O'Brien.

The decision of the Court of Appeal

The Court of Appeal (Purchas, Butler-Sloss and Scott L.JJ.) reversed his decision. The leading judgment in the Court of Appeal was given by Scott L.J., who found that there were two lines of authority. One line would afford no special protection to married women: the rights of the creditor bank could only be adversely affected by the wrongful acts of the principal debtor, the husband, in procuring the surety's liability if the principal debtor was acting as the agent of the creditor in procuring the surety to join or the creditor had knowledge of the relevant facts. I will call this theory 'the agency theory'. The other line of authority (which I will call 'the special equity theory') detected by Scott L.J. considers that equity affords special protection to a protected class of surety, *viz.* those where the relationship between the debtor and the surety is such that influence by the debtor over the surety and reliance by the surety on the debtor are natural features of the relationship. In cases where a surety is one of this protected class, the surety obligation is unenforceable by the creditor bank if (1) the relationship between the debtor and the surety was known to the creditor, (2) the surety's consent was obtained by undue influence or by misrepresentation or without 'an adequate understanding of the nature and effect of the transaction' and (3) the creditor had failed to take reasonable steps to ensure that the surety had given a true and informed consent to the transaction. The Court of Appeal preferred the special equity principle. They held that the legal charge on the O'Briens' matrimonial home was not enforceable by the bank against Mrs O'Brien save to the extent of the £60,000 which she had thought she was agreeing to secure.

Policy considerations

The large number of cases of this type coming before the courts in recent years reflects the rapid changes in social attitudes and the distribution of wealth which have recently occurred. Wealth is now more widely spread. Moreover a high proportion of privately owned wealth is invested in the matrimonial home. Because of the recognition by society of the equality of the sexes, the majority of matrimonial homes are now in the joint names of both spouses. Therefore in order to raise finance for the business enterprises of one or other of the spouses, the jointly owned home has become a main source of security. The provision of such security requires the consent of both spouses.

In parallel with these financial developments, society's recognition of the equality of the sexes has led to a rejection of the concept that the wife is subservient to the husband in the management of the family's finances. A number of the authorities reflect an unwillingness in the court to perpetuate law based on this outmoded concept. Yet, as Scott L.J. in the Court of Appeal rightly points out, although the concept of the ignorant wife leaving all financial decisions to the husband is outmoded, the practice does not yet coincide with the ideal (see [1992] 4 All ER 983 at 1008, [1993] QB 109 at 139). In a substantial proportion of marriages it is still the husband who has the business experience and the wife is willing to follow his advice without bringing a truly independent mind and will to bear on financial decisions. The number of recent cases in this field shows that in practice many wives are still subjected to, and yield to, undue influence by their husbands. Such wives can reasonably look to the law for some protection when their husbands have abused the trust and confidence reposed in them.

On the other hand, it is important to keep a sense of balance in approaching these cases. It is easy to allow sympathy for the wife who is threatened with the loss of her home at the suit of a rich bank to obscure an important public interest, *viz.* the need to ensure that the wealth currently tied up in the matrimonial home does not become economically sterile. If the rights secured to wives by the law renders vulnerable loans granted on the security of matrimonial homes, institutions will be unwilling to accept such security, thereby reducing the flow of loan capital to business enterprises. It is therefore essential that a law designed to protect the vulnerable does not render the matrimonial home unacceptable as security to financial institutions.

With these policy considerations in mind I turn to consider the existing state of the law. The whole of the modern law is derived from the decision of the Privy Council in *Turnbull & Co. v Duval* [1902] AC 429 which, as I will seek to demonstrate, provides an uncertain foundation. Before considering that case however, I must consider the law of undue influence which (though not directly applicable in the present case) underlies both *Turnbull v Duval* and most of the later authorities.

Undue influence

A person who has been induced to enter into a transaction by the undue influence of another (the wrongdoer) is entitled to set that transaction aside as against the wrongdoer. Such undue influence is either actual or presumed. In *Bank of Credit and Commerce International SA v Aboody* (1988) [1992] 4 All ER 955 at 964, [1990] 1 QB 923 at 953 the Court of Appeal helpfully adopted the following classification.

Class 1: *actual undue influence.* In these cases it is necessary for the claimant to prove affirmatively that the wrongdoer exerted undue influence on the complainant to enter into the particular transaction which is impugned.

Class 2: *presumed undue influence.* In these cases the complainant only has to show, in the first instance, that there was a relationship of trust and confidence between the complainant and the wrongdoer of such a nature that it is fair to presume that the wrongdoer abused that relationship in procuring the complainant to enter into the impugned transaction. In class 2 cases therefore there is no need to produce evidence that actual undue influence was exerted in relation to the particular transaction impugned: once a confidential relationship has been proved, the burden then shifts to the wrongdoer to prove that the complainant entered into the impugned transaction freely, for example by showing that the complainant had independent advice. Such a confidential relationship can be established in two ways, *viz.*:

Class 2A. Certain relationships (for example solicitor and client, medical advisor and patient) as a matter of law raise the presumption that undue influence has been exercised.

Class 2B. Even if there is no relationship falling within class 2A, if the complainant proves the *de facto* existence of a relationship under which the complainant generally reposed trust and confidence in the wrongdoer, the existence of such relationship raises the presumption of undue influence. In a class 2B case therefore, in the absence of evidence disproving undue influence, the complainant will succeed in setting aside the impugned transaction merely by proof that the complainant reposed trust and confidence in the wrongdoer without having to prove that the wrongdoer exerted actual undue influence or otherwise abused such trust and confidence in relation to the particular transaction impugned.

As to dispositions by a wife in favour of her husband, the law for long remained in an unsettled state. In the nineteenth century some judges took the view that the relationship was such that it fell into class 2A, i.e. as a matter of law undue influence by the husband over the wife was presumed. It was not until the decisions in *Howes v Bishop* [1909] 2 KB 390 and *Bank of Montreal v Stuart* [1911] AC 120 that it was finally determined that the relationship of husband and wife did not as a matter of law raise a presumption of undue influence within class 2A. It is to be noted therefore that when *Turnbull v Duval* was decided in 1902 the question whether there was a class 2A presumption of undue influence as between husband and wife was still unresolved.

An *invalidating tendency*?

Although there is no class 2A presumption of undue influence as between husband and wife, it should be emphasised that in any particular case a wife may well be able to demonstrate that *de facto* she did leave decisions on financial affairs to her husband thereby bringing herself within class 2B, i.e. that the relationship between husband and wife in the particular case was such that the wife reposed confidence and trust in her husband in relation to their financial affairs and therefore undue influence is to be presumed. Thus, in those cases which still occur where the wife relies in all financial matters on her husband and simply does what he suggests, a presumption of undue influence within class 2B can be established solely from the proof of such trust and confidence without proof of actual undue influence.

In the appeal in CIBC *Mortgages plc v Pitt* [1993] 4 All ER 433 (judgment in which is to be given immediately after that in the present appeal) Mr Price Q.C. for the wife argued that in the case of transactions between husband and wife there was an 'invalidating tendency', i.e. although there was no class 2A presumption of undue influence, the courts were more ready to find that a husband had exercised undue influence over his wife than in other cases. Scott L.J. in the present case also referred to the law treating married women 'more tenderly' than others. This approach is based on dicta in early authorities. In *Grigby v Cox* (1750) 1 Ves Sen 517, 27 ER 1178 Lord Hardwicke L.C., whilst rejecting any presumption of undue influence, said that a court of equity 'will have more jealousy' over dispositions by a wife to a husband. In *Yerkey v Jones* (1939) 63 CLR 649 at 675 Dixon J. refers to this 'invalidating tendency'. He also refers (at 677) to the court recognising 'the opportunities which a wife's confidence in her husband gives him of unfairly or improperly procuring her to become surety'.

In my judgment this special tenderness of treatment afforded to wives by the courts is properly attributable to two factors. First, many cases may well fall into the class 2B category of undue influence because the wife demonstrates that she placed trust and confidence in her husband in relation to her financial affairs and therefore raises a presumption of undue influence. Second, the sexual and emotional ties between the parties provide a ready weapon for undue influence: a wife's true wishes can easily be overborne because of her fear of destroying or damaging the wider relationship between her and her husband if she opposes his wishes.

For myself, I accept that the risk of undue influence affecting a voluntary disposition by a wife in favour of a husband is greater than in the ordinary run of cases where no sexual or emotional ties affect the free exercise of the individual's will.

Undue influence, misrepresentation and third parties

Up to this point I have been considering the right of a claimant wife to set aside a transaction as against the wrongdoing husband when the transaction has been procured by his undue influence. But in surety cases the decisive question is whether the claimant wife can set aside the transaction, not against the wrongdoing husband, but against the creditor bank. Of course, if the wrongdoing husband is acting as agent for the creditor bank in obtaining the surety from the wife, the creditor will be fixed with the wrongdoing of its own agent and the surety contract can be set aside as against the creditor. Apart from this, if the creditor bank has notice, actual or constructive, of the undue influence exercised by the husband (and consequentially of the wife's equity to set aside the transaction) the creditor will take subject to that equity and the wife can set aside the transaction against the creditor (albeit a purchaser for value) as well as against the husband: see *Bainbrigge v Browne* (1881) 18 ChD 188 and BCCI *v Aboody* [1992] 4 All ER 955 at 980, [1990] 1 QB 923 at 973. Similarly, in cases such as the present where the wife has been induced to enter into the transaction by the husband's misrepresentation, her equity to set aside the transaction will be enforceable against the creditor if either the husband was acting as the creditor's agent or the creditor had actual or constructive notice.

In my judgment your Lordships should seek to restate the law in a form which is principled, reflects the current requirements of society and provides as much certainty as possible.

Conclusions

(a) Wives
My starting point is to clarify the basis of the law. Should wives (and perhaps others) be accorded special rights in relation to surety transactions by the recognition of a special equity applicable only to such persons engaged in such transactions? Or should they enjoy only the same protection as they would enjoy in relation to their

other dealings? In my judgment, the special equity theory should be rejected. First, I can find no basis in principle for affording special protection to a limited class in relation to one type of transaction only. Second, to require the creditor to prove knowledge and understanding by the wife in all cases is to reintroduce by the back door either a presumption of undue influence of class 2A (which has been decisively rejected) or the Romilly heresy (which has long been treated as bad law). Third, although Scott L.J. found that there were two lines of cases one of which supported the special equity theory, on analysis although many decisions are not inconsistent with that theory the only two cases which support it are *Yerkey v Jones* and the decision of the Court of Appeal in the present case. Finally, it is not necessary to have recourse to a special equity theory for the proper protection of the legitimate interests of wives as I will seek to show.

In my judgment, if the doctrine of notice is properly applied, there is no need for the introduction of a special equity in these types of cases. A wife who has been induced to stand as a surety for her husband's debts by his undue influence, misrepresentation or some other legal wrong has an equity as against him to set aside that transaction. Under the ordinary principles of equity, her right to set aside that transaction will be enforceable against third parties (e.g. against a creditor) if either the husband was acting as the third party's agent or the third party had actual or constructive notice of the facts giving rise to her equity. Although there may be cases where, without artificiality, it can properly be held that the husband was acting as the agent of the creditor in procuring the wife to stand as surety, such cases will be of very rare occurrence. The key to the problem is to identify the circumstances in which the creditor will be taken to have had notice of the wife's equity to set aside the transaction.

The doctrine of notice lies at the heart of equity. Given that there are two innocent parties, each enjoying rights, the earlier right prevails against the later right if the acquirer of the later right knows of the earlier rights (actual notice) or would have discovered it had he taken proper steps (constructive notice). In particular, if the party asserting that he takes free of the earlier rights of another knows of certain facts which put him on inquiry as to the possible existence of the rights of that other and he fails to make such inquiry or take such other steps as are reasonable to verify whether such earlier right does or does not exist, he will have constructive notice of the earlier right and take subject to it. Therefore where a wife has agreed to stand surety for her husband's debts as a result of undue influence or misrepresentation, the creditor will take subject to the wife's equity to set aside the transaction if the circumstances are such as to put the creditor on inquiry as to the circumstances in which she agreed to stand surety.

It is at this stage that, in my view, the 'invalidating tendency' or the law's 'tender treatment' of married women, becomes relevant. As I have said above in dealing with undue influence, this tenderness of the law towards married women is due to the fact that, even today, many wives repose confidence and trust in their husbands in relation to their financial affairs. This tenderness of the law is reflected by the fact that voluntary dispositions by the wife in favour of her husband are more likely to be set aside than other dispositions by her: a wife is more likely to establish presumed undue influence of class 2B by her husband than by others because, in practice, many wives do repose in their husbands trust and confidence in relation to their financial affairs. Moreover the informality of business dealings between spouses raises a substantial risk that the husband has not accurately stated to the wife the nature of the liability she is undertaking, i.e. he has misrepresented the position, albeit negligently.

Therefore, in my judgment a creditor is put on inquiry when a wife offers to stand surety for her husband's debts by the combination of two factors: (a) the transaction is on its face not to the financial advantage of the wife; and (b) there is a substantial risk in transactions of that kind that, in procuring the wife to act as surety, the husband has committed a legal or equitable wrong that entitles the wife to set aside the transaction.

It follows that, unless the creditor who is put on inquiry takes reasonable steps to satisfy himself that the wife's agreement to stand surety has been properly obtained, the creditor will have constructive notice of the wife's rights.

What, then are the reasonable steps which the creditor should take to ensure that it does not have constructive notice of the wife's rights, if any? Normally the reasonable steps necessary to avoid being fixed with constructive notice consist of making inquiry of the person who may have the earlier right (i.e. the wife) to see whether such right is asserted. It is plainly impossible to require of banks and other financial institutions that they should inquire of one spouse whether he or she has been unduly influenced or misled by the other. But in my judgment the creditor, in order to avoid being fixed with constructive notice, can reasonably be expected to take steps to bring home to the wife the risk she is running by standing as surety and to advise her to take independent advice. As to past transactions, it will depend on the facts of each case whether the steps taken by the creditor satisfy this test. However for the future in my judgment a creditor will have satisfied these requirements if it insists that the wife attend a private meeting (in the absence of the husband) with a representative of the creditor at which she is told of the extent of her liability as surety, warned of the risk she is running and urged to take independent legal advice. If these steps are taken in my judgment the creditor will have taken such reasonable steps as are necessary to preclude a subsequent claim that it had constructive notice of the wife's rights. I should make it clear that I have been considering the ordinary case where the creditor knows only that the wife is to stand surety for her husband's debts. I would not exclude exceptional cases where a creditor has knowledge of further facts which render the presence of undue influence not only possible but probable. In such cases, the creditor to be safe will have to insist that the wife is separately advised.

I am conscious that in treating the creditor as having constructive notice because of the risk of class 2B undue influence or misrepresentation by the husband I may be extending the law as stated by Fry J. in *Bainbrigge v Browne* (1881) 18 ChD 188 at 197 and the Court of Appeal in BCCI *v Aboody* [1992] 4 All ER 955 at 980, [1990] 1 QB 923 at 973. Those cases suggest that for a third party to be affected by constructive notice of presumed undue influence the third party must actually know of the circumstances which give rise to a presumption of undue influence. In contrast, my view is that the risk of class 2B undue influence or misrepresentation is sufficient to put the creditor on inquiry. But my statement accords with the principles of notice: if the known facts are such as to indicate the possibility of an adverse claim that is sufficient to put a third party on inquiry.

If the law is established as I have suggested, it will hold the balance fairly between on the one hand the vulnerability of the wife who relies implicitly on her husband and, on the other hand, the practical problems of financial institutions asked to accept a secured or unsecured surety obligation from the wife for her husband's debts. In the context of suretyship, the wife will not have any right to disown her obligations just because subsequently she proves that she did not fully understand the transaction: she will, as in all other areas of her affairs, be bound by her obligations unless her husband has, by misrepresentation, undue influence or other wrong, committed an actionable wrong against her. In the normal case, a financial institution will be able to lend with confidence in reliance on the wife's surety obligation provided that it warns her (in the absence of the husband) of the amount of her potential liability and of the risk of standing surety and advises her to take independent advice.

[Counsel] for the bank urged that this is to impose too heavy a burden on financial institutions. I am not impressed by this submission. The report by Professor Jack's Review Committee on *Banking Services: Law and Practice* (1989), (Cmnd. 622) recommended that prospective guarantors should be adequately warned of the legal effects and possible consequences of their guarantee and of the importance of receiving independent advice. Pursuant to this recommendation, the Code of Banking Practice (adopted by banks and building societies in March 1992) provides in para. 12.1 as follows:

> Banks and building societies will advise private individuals proposing to give them a guarantee or other security for another person's liabilities that: (i) by giving the guarantee or third party security he or she might become liable instead of or as well as that other person; (ii) he or she should seek independent legal advice before entering into the guarantee or third party security. Guarantees and other third party security forms will contain a clear and prominent notice to the above effect.

Thus good banking practice (which applies to all guarantees, not only those given by a wife) largely accords with what I consider the law should require when a wife is offered as surety. The only further substantial step required by law beyond that good practice is that the position should be explained by the bank to the wife in a personal interview. I regard this as being essential because a number of the decided cases show that written warnings are often not read and are sometimes intercepted by the husband. It does not seem to me that the requirement of a personal interview imposes such an additional administrative burden as to render the bank's position unworkable.

(b) *Other persons*
I have hitherto dealt only with the position where a wife stands surety for her husband's debts. But in my judgment the same principles are applicable to all other cases where there is an emotional relationship between cohabitees. The 'tenderness' shown by the law to married women is not based on the marriage ceremony but reflects the underlying risk of one cohabitee exploiting the emotional involvement and trust of the other. Now that unmarried cohabitation, whether heterosexual or homosexual, is widespread in our society, the law should recognise this. Legal wives are not the only group which are now exposed to the emotional pressure of cohabitation. Therefore if, but only if, the creditor is aware that the surety is cohabiting with the principal debtor, in my judgment the same principles should apply to them as apply to husband and wife.

In addition to the cases of cohabitees, the decision of the Court of Appeal in *Avon Finance Co. Ltd v Bridger* [1985] 2 All ER 281 shows (rightly in my view) that other relationships can give rise to a similar result. In that case a son, by means of misrepresentation, persuaded his elderly parents to stand surety for his debts. The surety obligation was held to be unenforceable by the creditor *inter alia* because to the bank's knowledge the parents trusted the son in their financial dealings. In my judgment that case was rightly decided: in a case where the creditor is aware that the surety reposes trust and confidence in the principal debtor in relation to his financial affairs, the creditor is put on inquiry in just the same way as it is in relation to husband and wife.

Summary
I can therefore summarise my views as follows. Where one cohabitee has entered into an obligation to stand as surety for the debts of the other cohabitee and the creditor is aware that they are cohabitees: (1) the surety obligation will be valid and enforceable by the creditor unless the suretyship was procured by the undue influence, misrepresentation or other legal wrong of the principal debtor; (2) if there has been undue

influence, misrepresentation or other legal wrong by the principal debtor, unless the creditor has taken reasonable steps to satisfy himself that the surety entered into the obligation freely and in knowledge of the true facts, the creditor will be unable to enforce the surety obligation because he will be fixed with constructive notice of the surety's right to set aside the transaction; (3) unless there are special exceptional circumstances, a creditor will have taken such reasonable steps to avoid being fixed with constructive notice if the creditor warns the surety (at a meeting not attended by the principal debtor) of the amount of her potential liability and of the risks involved and advises the surety to take independent legal advice.

I should make it clear that in referring to the husband's debts I include the debts of a company in which the husband (but not the wife) has a direct financial interest.

The decision of this case

Applying those principles to this case, to the knowledge of the bank Mr and Mrs O'Brien were man and wife. The bank took a surety obligation from Mrs O'Brien, secured on the matrimonial home, to secure the debts of a company in which Mr O'Brien was interested but in which Mrs O'Brien had no direct pecuniary interest. The bank should therefore have been put on inquiry as to the circumstances in which Mrs O'Brien had agreed to stand as surety for the debt of her husband. If the Burnham branch had properly carried out the instructions from Mr Tucker of the Woolwich branch, Mrs O'Brien would have been informed that she and the matrimonial home were potentially liable for the debts of a company which had an existing liability of £107,000 and which was to be afforded an overdraft facility of £135,000. If she had been told this, it would have counteracted Mr O'Brien's misrepresentation that the liability was limited to £60,000 and would last for only three weeks. In addition according to the side letter she would have been recommended to take independent legal advice.

Unfortunately Mr Tucker's instructions were not followed and to the knowledge of the bank (through the clerk at the Burnham branch) Mrs O'Brien signed the documents without any warning of the risks or any recommendation to take legal advice. In the circumstances the bank (having failed to take reasonable steps) is fixed with constructive notice of the wrongful misrepresentation made by Mr O'Brien to Mrs O'Brien. Mrs O'Brien is therefore entitled as against the bank to set aside the legal charge on the matrimonial home securing her husband's liability to the bank.

For these reasons I would dismiss the appeal with costs.

(Templeman, Lowry, Slynn of Hedley and Woolf L.JJ. agreed.)

Note

1. In CIBC *Mortgages plc v Pitt* [1993] 4 All ER 433, (mentioned by Lord Browne-Wilkinson in his judgment in *Barclays Bank plc v O'Brien* at p. 687 above) their Lordships found on the facts that a wife who had consented to remortgaging the family home under pressure from her husband, was the victim of undue influence. In such a case the wife is not required to prove that the transaction was manifestly disadvantageous to her, their Lordships reasoning that the victim of fraud may still plead the fraud even if the transaction is beneficial to that person. However, the House of Lords did not set the transaction aside *vis-à-vis* the bank because the person exercising undue influence was in no sense acting as the agent of the bank and the transaction itself was a normal banking transaction.

2. Post *O'Brien* case law in England and Scotland has been voluminous and efforts to provide consistent decisions have been unsuccessful. *Royal Bank of Scotland v Etridge* (No. 2) [2001] 4 All ER 449 afforded the House of Lords with an opportunity to revisit the *O'Brien* guidelines. In giving the leading judgment, Lord Nicholls of Birkenhead observed that the constructive notice process mapped out in *O'Brien* required a bank to observe guidelines which minimised the risk that one marital or quasi-marital partner may have exercised undue influence or fraud over the other. Notice is only visited upon the bank when the arrangement is one in which the bank finds that one partner offers to stand as surety for the debts of the other because the transaction has no benefit for the surety and because of the substantial risk that there has been a wrong committed by one partner over the other. The presence of either of these possibilities puts the bank on inquiry.

Lord Nicholls went on to specify the steps that the bank should take when put upon inquiry. The bank must take reasonable steps to ensure that the surety has had the practical implications of the transaction set out to him or her. This is best done by ensuring independent advice has been given and in this regard their Lordships stressed the need for the bank to be proactive in ensuring that the surety gets advice from the independent source nominated by the surety and that a direct response from the surety has been obtained by the bank prior to closure of the transaction. Very significantly, the surety should be made aware of the financial position vis-a-vis the bank and the debtor.

3. Irish case law on this matter is both indirect and in need of review. The leading case is *Northern Banking Co. v Carpenter* [1931] IR 268. In cases where the transaction involves taking securities in respect of business debts in the form of a charge over the family home, the Family Home Protection Act 1976 makes it very difficult for a lending institution to enforce such a security: see *Bank of Ireland v Smyth* [1995] 2 IR 459.

However, where the property is not a family home the question whether a wife can be liable for the business debts of her husband does raise the possibility of an *O'Brien*-type approach to issues of misrepresentation, duress or undue influence by the husband. It is significant that the High Court of Australia, in *Garcia v National Australia Bank Ltd* (1998) has rejected *O'Brien*, preferring instead to use the decision of Dixon J. in *Yerkey v Jones* (1939) which essentially requires a lender to personally advise the surety if the surety is the spouse of the debtor. See Gardner (1999) 115 LQR 1 and Stone (1999) 62 MLR 604. So far, the Supreme Court has refused to be drawn on this issue, confining its assessment of *O'Brien* as being a decision which is 'both relevant and helpful': see Murphy J. in *Bank of Nova Scotia v Hogan* [1997] 1 ILRM 407.

D. UNDUE INFLUENCE AS OF FACT

Daniel v Drew [2005] EWCA Civ 507

Lord Justice Ward:

Introduction

This is an unusual family dispute. Aged aunt alleges that her nephew procured her resignation from a family trust by undue influence. On 2 September 2004 His Hon. Judge Weeks Q.C. sitting as a deputy judge of the Chancery Division found for her and ordered that a memorandum signed by her dated 20 February 2002 and the deed of retirement made between her and her nephews dated 25 February 2002 be set aside. He gave the nephew permission to appeal.

The background facts in more detail

The case concerns Hyde Farm, a farm of some 116 acres near Fordingbridge in Hampshire. Mr and Mrs Spicer lived and farmed there for some fifty years until Mr Spicer died in 1969. He left the farm to his wife for life and then to his two daughters in equal shares. The daughters are the claimant, Mrs Irene Margaret Drew, whom, for convenience and I hope not discourteously, I shall sometimes call Aunt Margaret, and her elder sister, Mrs Muriel Daniel. At some later time Muriel gave her interest in the farm to her sons, the defendants, Nicholas and Jeremy Daniel. Since Mrs Spicer was elderly and incapable of looking after herself Mr and Mrs Drew went to live at Hyde Farm and maintained the farm for her until her death in 1982. Mr and Mrs Drew continued to farm the property rent free until 1987. Then Nicholas, as I shall refer to the appellant, took over.

On 23 February 1988 Mr and Mrs Drew, as surviving executors of the late Tom Spicer, assented to the vesting of Hyde Farm in Aunt Margaret, Nicholas and Jeremy on trust for sale to hold the net proceeds of sale as to half for Aunt Margaret and as to one quarter each for Nicholas and Jeremy. On 21 March 1988 the trustees of this Assent granted a yearly agricultural tenancy of Hyde Farm to Nicholas at a rent of £1 per annum fixed for five years to reflect the fact that Mr and Mrs Drew had been in rent-free occupation for the previous five years.

On 12 March 1990, Mrs Drew, now a widow, assigned her beneficial interest to her son Stephen. Thereafter she took no part in the business of Hyde Farm and her son, Stephen, acted as de facto trustee in her place. No one at first questioned his doing so: after all the sons had stepped into their mothers' places and may well have been content to deal with each other for the sensible reason that they were co-owners of the property.

Trouble arose when Nicholas's rent-free period expired and Stephen began to ask for rent. There were arguments about the farm falling into disrepair. Matters came to a head in May 1999 when Stephen served a notice on his cousin Nicholas asking for an arbitration as to rent. Nicholas disputed Stephen's authority to serve the notice and served his own notice requiring arbitration as to repairs.

Nicholas had begun to demand of Aunt Margaret that she attend meetings of the trustees but she was unwilling to attend to business matters which she told the judge made her legs ache.

Solicitors were instructed and a compromise was negotiated subject to contract under which Nicholas and Jeremy would buy out Stephen's interest and Aunt Margaret would retire as trustee. A deed of resignation and a deed of assignment were drafted by Messrs. Wilsons acting for Nicholas and Jeremy and sent on 7 December 2001 to Messrs. Burges Salmon acting for Stephen. On 5 February 2002 Burges Salmon told Wilsons that Stephen had decided, as he was entitled, not to sell his interest in Hyde Farm. As the judge remarked, 'Understandably Mr Nicholas Daniel felt frustrated by this turn of events'.

The events leading to Aunt Margaret's 'resignation'

Mrs Muriel Daniel regularly visited her sister on Wednesdays. She did so on Wednesday 20 February 2002 but unusually took her son Nicholas with her despite her knowing that Margaret would not have admitted Nicholas on his own because she refused to discuss business matters with him. Margaret did not deny Nicholas entry when he attended with his mother. They stayed for about twenty minutes.

The judge found that both Mrs Drew and Mrs Daniel were totally honest witnesses trying to tell the truth as they remembered it but he concluded:

> . . . Given their age [Aunt Margaret was 85 years old at the time of the trial] and the fact that the events occurred over two years ago, I do not think that their recollection is wholly reliable. Mrs Drew in particular, towards the end of her evidence, was showing signs of confusion.

As for Nicholas he said:

> I did not find him a completely credible witness.

The judge made these important findings:

> Mr Nicholas Daniel wanted to speak to his aunt about repairs to the farmhouse, and, knowing that his aunt did not wish to see him, he arranged for his mother to visit her first. He did talk to her about the repairs needed to the farmhouse, and he did remind her of her duties as trustee. I do not think that he shouted or threatened her, but he did say that if she did not accept her responsibility the matter would have to be resolved in court.
>
> Mrs Drew intensely disliked any form of confrontation. She was afraid of her nephew, and frightened by the prospect of court. As a way out, she told him, untruthfully, that she thought she had already resigned. Mr Nicholas Daniel seized on this, knowing that it was not true, and asked her to put it in writing. She was cornered and felt unable to refuse. He drafted a short statement of resignation and came back in the afternoon with Mr Panton [a neighbour of Nicholas] and she signed.

That document recorded:

> I Mrs I.M. Drew of The Firs Frogham hereby give notice that from this day the 20 February 2002 I resign as Trustee/Landlord of Hyde Farm Hyde Lane Stuckton Fordingbridge Hampshire.
> Signed I.M. Drew.
> Witnessed Steve Panton.

On the following Sunday Margaret told her good friend, Mrs Wort, that as Mrs Wort recalled it:

> Margaret told me that Nick said she would have to resign as a trustee of the farm if she refused to discuss farm matters with him, or he would take her to court. She also told me it had been a very unpleasant experience for her and that Nick threatened her with court action if she did not sign this document.

There was 'a striking disparity', for which there was 'little scope for genuine error', between Nicholas's first witness statement and the version he gave in his defence verified as true in his oral evidence about what happened next. The judge found that on the following Monday, 25 February, Nicholas told his solicitor at Wilsons that Aunt Margaret had signed this document. He was advised, however, that the resignation was invalid because it had to be done by deed and he was reminded that a draft deed of resignation had been prepared a few months previously. Nicholas asked the solicitors to email him a copy which they did. He printed it out and went back to his aunt the same day 25 February before lunch. The judge found this:

> Aware that if his cousin, Stephen, or Messrs Burges Salmon had an opportunity to advise Mrs Drew, the resignation would not proceed, Mr Daniel chose not to instruct Wilsons to send another draft to Burges Salmon but asked them to send a copy to himself instead. On the same day, he went to his aunt's cottage twice with the deed. On the first occasion, he was not admitted. On the second occasion he went with Mr Joint and was admitted on his own. He spoke to his aunt for a long time before Mr Gregory intervened.
>
> On his own account, Mrs Drew raised the question of Stephen being appointed trustee in her place. According to Nicholas:
>
> 'I then reminded her of what her solicitor, Mr Ricketts of Trethowans, had said to me on the telephone to the effect that the trust deed had apparently provided that in the event of Mrs Drew ceasing to be a trustee she would not be replaced as trustee, and that this provision had been put in the trust deed at Mrs Drew's own request.'
>
> Whatever Nicholas may have been told, that advice was incorrect. There was no provision in the assent preventing Stephen's appointment but, as continuing trustees, the other two would, of course, have been in a position to block it. Mrs Drew would therefore have been ill advised to resign without securing agreement as to her successor.

Mr Gregory was Margaret's next door neighbour living in the other half of a semi-detached pair of cottages. He is a retired civil servant and he and his wife, conscious of Margaret's frailty, 'keep an eye open for any unusual events such as unfamiliar vehicles parked outside her house.' He did not recognise the four-wheel drive vehicle outside the cottage nor the gentleman, Mr Joint, who was sitting in it. Mr Joint was there at Nicholas' request to witness Margaret signing the deed. He decided to investigate. The judge was most impressed by him. He gave evidence that:

> I was immediately aware of the tension in the room. Margaret was clearly very distressed, looking worried and uncomfortable and, from the redness around her eyes, I thought perhaps close to tears. Although Margaret was obviously upset, I felt I should not intrude in what seemed to be a family affair. I assessed the situation for a few moments and again asked Margaret if there was anything I could do for her. She declined and so I left the house rather worried on her behalf.

The judge continued:

> During the meeting Mr Gregory came in and found her distressed but because he thought he ought not to intervene in a family dispute he left. Mr Joint then came in, angry at being kept waiting, and Mrs Drew signed the deed against her better judgment. She undoubtedly knew what she was signing, and intended to sign.

However, the question for me is, as Lord Nicholls said: how was that intention procured and was it procured by unacceptable means?

The deed was a formal deed of retirement between Margaret 'the retiring trustee' and Nicholas and Jeremy 'the continuing trustees'. The retiring trustee declared that she wished to retire and be discharged from the trust of the Assent dated 23 February 1988 and the continuing trustees consented to such retirement and discharge and to the vesting in themselves alone of the property now comprised in the assent.

Mrs Drew was apparently very disturbed by these events and wrote a rather confused note on the back of an envelope a day or two later. She noted, among other things:

> If I didn't sign he said we should have to go to court about it. . . . Two very unsettled nights, I might say. . . . I told him on the Monday, you like taking people to court don't you, getting up in the witness box. . . .

Stephen came to visit his mother shortly thereafter. As the judge found:

> Mrs Drew told him what she had done and the balloon went up.

They tried to see Nicholas to obtain a copy of the document. Mrs Drew saw the doctor on emergency duty and he found her to be 'confused' though she was ordinarily in excellent health and an infrequent attendee at the doctor's surgery. At Stephen's instigation she issued the present proceedings seeking to set aside the deed of retirement dated 25 February 2002 although, as she accepted, she wants to retire from the trusts of the Assent.

The judge's directions as to the law.
He said that the relevant law was not in dispute and was contained in Lord Nicholls of Birkenhead's speech in *Royal Bank of Scotland v Etridge* (No. 2) [2002] 2 AC 773 and he quoted from paragraphs 6 to 12 inclusive. In this part of his speech Lord Nicholls had found it 'necessary to go back to first principles'. He explained in paragraph 6 that:

> Undue influence is one of the grounds of relief developed by the Courts of Equity as a court of conscience. The objective is to ensure that the influence of one party over another is not abused.

In paragraph 7 he explained how equity supplemented the common law which dealt narrowly with duress:

> Equity extended the reach of the law to other unacceptable forms of persuasion. The law will investigate the manner in which the intention to enter into the transaction was secured; 'how the intention was produced'; in the oft repeated words of Lord Eldon as long ago as 1807 (*Huguenin v Baseley* 14 Ves 273, 300). If the intention was produced by an unacceptable means the law will not permit the transaction to stand. The means used is regarded as an exercise of improper or 'undue' influence and hence unacceptable, whenever the consent thus procured ought not fairly to be treated as the expression of a person's free will. It is impossible to be more precise or definite. The circumstances in which one person acquires influence over another, and the manner in which influence may be exercised, vary too widely to permit of any more specific criterion.

In paragraph 8 he drew the distinction between 'overt acts of improper pressure or coercion such as unlawful threats' and the second form now commonly referred to as presumed undue influence which:

... arises out of the relationship between two persons where one has acquired over another a measure of influence, or ascendancy, of which the ascendant person then takes unfair advantage.

As he explained in paragraph 9:

Typically this occurs when one person places trust in another to look after his affairs and interests, and the latter betrays this trust by preferring his own interests.

In paragraph 11 he pointed out that:

The principle is not confined to cases of abuse of trust and confidence. It also includes, for instance, cases where a vulnerable person has been exploited. Indeed there is no single touchstone for determining whether the principle is applicable. Several expressions have been used in an endeavour to encapsulate the essence: trust and confidence, reliance, dependence or vulnerability on the one hand and ascendancy, domination or control on the other. None of these descriptions is perfect. None is all-embracing. Each has its proper place.

Judge Weeks, a very experienced judge, said this:

The reference to 'exploitation of the vulnerable' in paragraph 11 was made in the context of what used to be called 'presumed undue influence'. Although this is a case, if anything, of express undue influence, I think the reference is relevant because the exploitation of the vulnerable can be regarded as an example of unacceptable conduct where the consent procured ought not fairly to be treated as an expression of a person's free will.

The judge's conclusion
Having asked whether Margaret's intention had been procured by unacceptable means he decided:

Mrs Drew was, in my judgment, a vulnerable person, unversed in business, anxious to avoid confrontation and eager to comply. Nicholas Daniel was younger and according to his aunt did not show her the respect she thought he should. I have heard him give evidence. He has a keen appreciation of his own interests and scant regard for those of others. 'Unscrupulous' would be too harsh a description but he is, at the very least, insensitive. Again, in my view, 'aggressive' would probably be too harsh and 'forceful' might be a better description of his character.

He knew that if his aunt was given the chance to talk to her son or her solicitors the transaction would not proceed as he wished. He deliberately chose not to involve them, but to take advantage of his aunt's naiveté in business matters. In my judgment the means by which her signature was procured is unacceptable. Mrs Drew's consent, obtained in the circumstances that I have described ought not fairly to be treated as an expression of her free will.

[After holding that Judge Weeks had taken account of 'overt acts of improper pressure or coercion such as unlawful threats' as the core to express or actual undue influence, Ward L. J. went on to hold that the vulnerability of Aunt Margaret could feature as relevant to both presumed undue influence and express or actual undue influence. Ward L. J. went on to hold that in all instances of undue influence, a court of equity strives to protect people 'from being forced, tricked or mislead in any way by others into parting with their property'. Finally, Ward L. J. found that when Nicholas told Aunt Margaret that unless this was settled the dispute would have to go to court, such as statement was relevant as it would influence a vulnerable elderly person such as Aunt Margaret.]

Ward L. J. went on:

It remains for me to consider whether on the facts found by the judge there was evidence of overt acts of improper pressure or coercion or persuasive conduct. I am satisfied there was an abundance of evidence to justify that finding. Not least among the many facts of this case are these:

i)   Nicholas told Aunt Margaret at their first meeting on the twentieth that she should either attend the meetings of trustees or retire and that it was not right for her to do neither.

ii) When she said she had already retired he told her to put it in writing.

iii) He returned later that day with the home-made memorandum for her to sign.

iv) He returned on the twenty-fifth with the deed of retirement saying: 'I reminded her she had already signed a document confirming her retirement.'

v)   He told her if she ceased to be a trustee she could not be replaced by Stephen or by any independent party.

vi) The whole of this lengthy and distressing meeting on 25 February was capable of being viewed as coercive forcing her to do that which she did not truly desire to do.

The next question is whether that amounted to improper or undue influence and the unfair procurement of her consent. These factors demonstrate the impropriety of Nicholas's actions:

i)   When Aunt Margaret said she had already resigned, Nicholas seized upon the opportunity to obtain confirmation from her there and then, knowing that what she had said was not true.

ii) He opportunistically exploited the advantage thus presented to him of having her 'cornered'.

iii) He chose not to involve her solicitors or Stephen in order 'to take advantage of his Aunt's naiveté in business matters'.

iv) She was 'a vulnerable person, unversed in business, anxious to avoid confrontation and eager to comply'.

v)   He on the other hand had 'a keen appreciation of his own interests and scant regard for those of others.'

vi) His statement that she could not be replaced as a trustee was an active, and in my view, crucial misrepresentation that it was not open to her to insist on an acceptable successor as a condition of her retirement.

In those circumstances it is no surprise the judge should conclude that Mrs Drew's consent 'ought not fairly to be treated as an expression of her free will'.

This disposes of Mr Batstone's last complaint that the judge wrongly trespassed upon the legitimate give and take of discussion between adults and wrongly allowed Stephen's influence upon her to seek her escape from an act which upon proper analysis worked to her advantage because it brought a continuing liability as trustee to an early end. Mr Batstone seeks to bring this case within that category referred to by Lindley L.J. where the Courts of Equity repudiate any jurisdiction to set aside gifts 'on the ground of the folly, imprudence or want of foresight on the part of donors'. In my judgement this case falls squarely within that other category to which he referred where the court, as a court of conscience, does intervene 'to protect people from being forced, tricked or misled in any way by others into parting with their property'.

In my judgment Nicholas's actions were unconscionable and this appeal is wholly without merit. I would dismiss it.

[Lord Justice Buxton and Wilson J. agreed]

O'Flanagan v Ray-ger and Others (HC) 28 April 1983, unrep.

In this action the plaintiff sought to set aside a transaction entered into by his late father in relation to a company in which the late Mr O'Flanagan held shares, the plaintiff alleging that one of the defendants, a Mr Pope had exercised undue influence over the plaintiff's late father.

Costello J.:

. . .
. . . The equitable principles which the plaintiffs call in aid are well established. The cases where a plaintiff seeks to set aside a gift or other transaction on the ground that it was procured by undue influence have been divided into two classes; firstly, those in which it can be expressly proved that undue influence was exercised, in which circumstances the court intervenes on the principle that no one should be allowed to retain any benefit arising from his own fraud or wrongful act; secondly, those in which the relations between the donor and donee have at or shortly before the execution of a gift been such as to raise a presumption that the donor had influence over the donee. Then, the court intervenes, not on the ground that any wrongful act has in fact been committed by the donee but on the ground of public policy and to prevent the relations which existed between the parties and the influence arising therefrom being abused. The court will set aside the gift unless it is proved (and the onus is on the donee in such cases) that in fact the gift was the result of a free exercise of the donor's will (see *Allcard v Skinner* 36 ChD 145 at 171). The courts have not defined the degree of confidence and trust which must exist in a relationship before it can be said that a donee is in a position to exert undue influence. It has been long established that the relationship of parent and child, guardian and ward, doctor and patient, religious adviser and pupil are relationships which give rise to the presumption to which I have referred. But the categories are not closed and in *Gregg v Kidd* [1956] IR 183 Budd J.

held that the relationship raised the presumption to which I have referred in a case in which an uncle settled property on his nephew. Recently in England a majority of the Court of Appeal (in *Re Brocklehurst's Estate* [1978] 1 Ch. 21) took the view that the presumption did not arise from the relationship of friendship between an elderly man and a companion from a different class in the social structure, whilst in in *Re Craig* [1971] 1 Ch. 95 it was held that the relationship between an elderly man and his secretary gave rise to the presumption. The presumption does not arise in the case of Mills (see, *In the goods of Kavanagh, decd* 24 October 1978, unrep. in which I held that express undue influence was proved).

Just as the courts have declined to define the exact categories of relationship which will give rise to the presumption of undue influence so too they have declined to define exactly what undue influence is. The approach which courts of equity should adopt was suggested by Sir Samuel Romilly (a distinguished chancery lawyer and former Solicitor General) in one of the early leading cases on the matter (*Huguenin v Basely* (1807) 14 Ves 273), an approach which subsequently obtained judicial approval from Lord Cottendham in *Dent v Bennett* (4 My Cr 277) and from Byrne J., in *Cavendish v Strutt* (19 TLR 483). The passage to which I refer reads as follows:

> Where a gift is immoderate, bears no proportion to the circumstances of the giver, where no reason appears, or the reason given is falsified, and the giver is a weak man, liable to be imposed upon, this court will look upon such a gift with a very jealous eye, and very strictly examine the conduct of the person in whose favour it is made; and if it sees that any arts or stratagems, or any undue influence have been used— if it sees the least speck of imposition at the bottom, or that the donor is in such a situation with respect to the donee as may naturally give an influence over him—if there be the least scintilla of fraud, this court will and ought to interpose . . . (quoted in White and Tudor *Leading Cases in Equity* vol. I p. 216).

The plaintiffs do not reply solely on the equitable principles relating to undue influence. They claim in the alternative that the agreement of 15 March 1976 should be set aside on the ground that it is an unconscionable bargain. The principle relied on was stated by Lord Hatherley in a dissenting judgment in *O'Rourke v Bolingbroke* 2 App Cas 814, 823, a case dealing with a sale at undervalue by an expectant heir but which enunciated a principle of wider application. The passage reads as follows:

> It . . . appears that the principle on which equity originally proceeded to set aside such transactions was for the protection of family property; but this principle being once established, the court extended its aid to all cases in which the parties to a contract have not met upon equal terms. In ordinary cases each party to a bargain must take care of his own interest, and it will not be presumed that undue advantage or contrivance has been resorted to on either side; but in the case of expectant heirs or of persons under pressure without adequate protection and in the case of dealings with uneducated ignorant persons, the burden of showing the fairness of the transaction is thrown on the person who seeks to obtain the benefit of the contract.

This passage was quoted with approval by Gavan Duffy J. in *Grealish v Murphy* [1946] IR 35, a case in which the plaintiff was a mentally retarded adult but in which no undue influence was shown to have been exercised. The transaction which he entered into, however, was set aside on the ground that equity comes to the rescue in cases where the parties to a contract have not met on equal terms, the court holding that the deed was an improvident one and that the plaintiff's weakness of mind coupled with the inadequacy of the advice he obtained justified the intervention of the court in that case (see also *Fry v Lane* 10 ChD 312, at 322)

As the evidence relating to the relationship between the deceased and the defendant and the evidence relating to the allegation of undue influence are inextricably mixed I propose to examine the facts surrounding the making of the agreement of 15 March 1976 and then give my opinion as to whether or not the plaintiff has made out a case for the intervention of the court on the ground that undue influence was exercised by the defendant in relation to it.

Costello J. reviewed the evidence and summarised the material facts and continued:

I have the following observations to make on the agreement and the defendant's evidence in relation to it:

(a) I found the defendant's evidence unconvincing and must record my view that he was not telling the truth as to how the agreement came to be made. He failed to give any or any acceptable explanation as to why (a) he insisted on a 'private meeting' with the deceased or (b) why he and Mr O'Flanagan should agree that the surviving partner should be entitled to the entire of the company's assets. I am also quite satisfied that the defendant, contrary to what he stated in the course of his testimony, knew full well that Mr O'Flanagan had had two major operations for cancer.

(b) I do not accept (as pleaded in para. 8 of the defence) that the defendant in March 1976 wished to wind up the company and that he was prevailed upon by the deceased not to do so. I think it is much more probable that the defendant used the threat to wind up the company as a means for procuring the deceased's signature to the agreement and that he used the IOUs which the deceased had signed for the same purpose.

(c) The written agreement refers to the fact that each of the partners should receive a copy of it. No copy was ever found amongst the deceased's effects after his death and Mrs O'Flanagan knew nothing about the agreement until the reply to the notice for particulars in this action. I think it is reasonable to assume that the defendant did not give Mr O'Flanagan a copy of it.

(d) In March 1976 the deceased was a very sick man. He had undergone a very serious operation the previous November and a letter written by him on 10 March a couple of days before he met the defendant shows that he had been ill in bed and had been unable to attend a business appointment.

(e) The deceased was aware that he was terminally ill with cancer and must have realised that his chances of surviving Mr Pope were slight. He was not well off and notwithstanding this he was apparently agreeing that on his death the defendant and not his wife or any of his eight children would obtain the benefit of two valuable commercial properties. There is nothing to suggest that Mr O'Flanagan had not the normal love and affection which a husband and father has for his wife and children and no explanation has been forthcoming as to why he should fail to give expression to that love and affection and instead give what was virtually a gift of these properties to Mr Pope.

(f) After Mr O'Flanagan's death, as we will see, the defendant sought advice from his accountant as to his right to appoint a new director and issue the balance of the share capital to himself and a nominee. In doing so he did not show him the secret agreement of 15 March 1976. His failure to do so demonstrates a lack of confidence in its validity, which could only have arisen if it was tainted by some wrongdoing on his part.

Taking into account all the evidence in the case I think there is only one conclusion to be reached in relation to this agreement namely that the defendant must have used undue influence to procure it. The defendant has a strong and forceful personality and had obviously exercised considerable influence amounting to domination of the deceased on previous occasions. The deceased was infirm and ill when he signed it. The agreement was egregiously unfair to the deceased's wife and family. The mutual promises it contained were largely illusory in that both parties knew that it was highly probable that the deceased would predecease the defendant. Furthermore the lack of candour of the defendant raises very serious suspicions about the circumstances in which it came to be executed. It is unnecessary for me to decide whether the relationship which existed raises any presumption as to what happened. The evidence satisfies me that I should set the agreement aside.

Carroll v Carroll [2000] 1 ILRM 210

Barron J.:

I agree with the judgment delivered by Denham J. I would, however, like to deal with the issue of undue influence.

These were proceedings to set aside a voluntary conveyance from Thomas Carroll Senior to his son Thomas Carroll Junior dated 3 May 1990 whereby Thomas Carroll Senior transferred to his son his licensed premises with living accommodation situate at Burke Street, Fethard, Co. Tipperary.

These premises had been purchased by Thomas Carroll Senior in the year 1960. Thereafter they had comprised also the family home. The business was run by his wife Sadie. They had three children. Winifred was the eldest having been born in 1962. Next came Thomas Junior born in 1964, and the youngest Mary Jane born in 1968. Until 1974 Sadie Carroll ran the business with the help of a part-time barman. From 1974 there was a full-time barman. Unfortunately, Sadie Carroll died in June 1989. At that stage her husband was aged 78. He had never been seriously involved in the running of the business. After his wife's death Mary Jane stayed for six months helping to run the premises. When she left to take up a job in Dublin there was no one to run the business.

Thomas Junior was willing to take over the running of the business. However, he was basically a farmer and was involved in looking after farms for two of his uncles. Nevertheless he was anxious that his father should make arrangements for him to take over the running of the business. Although Mary Jane had gone to live in Dublin early in 1990 both she and her sister had always helped at weekends in the premises.

Thomas Carroll Senior executed a conveyance of the licensed premises to his son dated 3 May 1990 reserving to himself a right of residence in the premises. Thereafter the licensed premises continued to be run as before with the two daughters coming down at weekends and helping to run the business. Thomas Junior married in September 1993.

Unfortunately, he was killed in a motor accident on 17 January 1994. Some weeks after the plaintiffs learned for the first time that the document which had been executed in May 1990 was not as they had thought an arrangement whereby Thomas was entitled to run the business but in fact a conveyance of the entire property. They were surprised by this as it was a very close-knit family and their father had never told them that this is what he had done. On the contrary he had always assured them both before and after the execution of the transfer that they always had a home in the premises. The plaintiffs consulted a solicitor and ultimately the present proceedings were instituted in December 1994.

As found by the learned trial judge the circumstances in which the conveyance came to be executed were as follows. Thomas Junior was anxious that some arrangement should be come to with his father whereby he should run the business. He contacted Philip Joyce, a local solicitor, who was not in fact the family solicitor and told him of the proposed arrangement. Mr Joyce went to see Thomas Senior and obtained instructions from him. These instructions were to transfer the entire premises to his son. There was some doubt as to whether he wanted to reserve a right of residence only or a right of residence coupled with a right of maintenance. In the event Mr Joyce was informed by Thomas Junior that his father wanted a right of residence only. Mr Joyce then had two deeds engrossed, one reserving a right of residence, the other a right of residence and a right of maintenance, and went to see Thomas Senior. Thomas Senior said that he wanted only a right of residence and accordingly, the deed reserving this right only was executed by him. In both meetings the amount of time which Mr Joyce spent with Thomas Senior was approximately half an hour not all of which was devoted to the transaction in hand.

The case made to set aside the deed was that Mr Joyce was unaware of what assets Thomas Senior had nor was he aware of the family relationships. The evidence was also clear that the donor was old and infirm and devastated by the recent death of his wife. She had been some twenty-five years his junior. It was submitted that the presumption of undue influence arose and that there was no independent legal advice nor any independent advice of any sort given to Thomas Senior. It was also contended that the transaction was an improvident one since it transferred the entire of his estate without reserving to himself the means of living.

The case for the defendant who is the widow of Thomas Junior was to the effect that Thomas Senior was of sound mind and knew very well what he was doing. It was also submitted that he had available to him the independent legal advice of Mr Joyce, further since the plaintiffs did not allege improper conduct on the part of Thomas Junior this rebutted the presumption of undue influence. In relation to the plea that the gift was improvident it was submitted that he had alternative assets and that Thomas Junior provided consideration in that he took over the liabilities of the business.

Shanley J. before whom the matter came found for the plaintiffs on both grounds. As against this judgment the defendant has appealed. The essential grounds of appeal as set out on the notice of appeal are:

(1) the clarity and independence of mind of the donor;
(2) the availability of independent legal advice; and
(3) the admission on behalf of the plaintiffs that Thomas Junior had not exerted undue influence on his father.

At the hearing of the appeal counsel on behalf of the appellants accepted that the presumption of undue influence applied, but sought to rebut this by the admission by the plaintiffs that no improper influence had been exercised by their brother over their father. He relied in the main on the Northern Ireland case of R. (*Proctor*) v *Hutton* [1978] NI 139.

In that case the donor was the aunt of the donee. The aunt was aged eighty-five and had been living alone in Philadelphia. The niece brought her aunt home to live with her as one of the family. Unfortunately, her aunt died within a few weeks. Before her death she had opened a bank account in the joint names of herself and her niece, the money in the account to be paid to 'either or survivor'. The administrator of the aunt's estate contested the right of the niece to the monies in the account. In the course of the proceedings, the question arose whether the presumption of undue influence arose, and, if so, whether it had been rebutted. Dealing with this presumption Lowry L.C.J. said at p. 148:

> But rebuttable presumptions are rules of evidence. They arise only when the facts are not sufficiently known and operate only until the facts become known.

In the actual case he was satisfied that all the facts were known and that the gift should not be set aside. The relevant facts as found were and are referred to in the judgment of Lowry LCJ, at p. 145, as:

> From her demeanour and from the way in which she gave her evidence I formed the view that Mrs Proctor [the niece] was a truthful and reliable witness, and on the basis of her own evidence, I formed the view that when she went out to bring her aunt home from Philadelphia and when she gave her a home in Portadown, she was not concerned about what money her aunt might have or about what money she might receive from her aunt. I also formed the view that Mrs Proctor is a kind warm-hearted person who went out to America and brought her aunt home out of feelings of kindness and sympathy for a lonely old lady, and not by reason of hope or desire of receiving or extracting a financial reward of benefit from her aunt.

Having regard to the facts, Lowry L.C.J. said at p. 149:

> But proof of adequate independent advice is merely one way of establishing that the gift was 'the spontaneous act of the donor acting under circumstances which enabled him to exercise an independent will,' and on the rare occasions (such as the present) when it can be done, the simple and conclusive thing is to prove positively that the donee exercised no influence. When this proof is forthcoming (as in this case) *pari passu* with the evidence which is said to prove the relationship of trust and confidence, it is more accurate to say that the presumption never arises rather than to say that it has been rebutted.

I would agree that once the full facts are known, it is a matter for the court to determine whether there was or was not undue influence. In such case, the presumption really plays no part.

In reaching his conclusions Lowry L.C.J. was influenced by the decision of the English Court of Appeal in In *re Brocklehurst* [1978] Ch. 14. That was an unusual case on the facts. The owner of a large estate who on the evidence was reluctant to benefit his nearest relation leased the shooting rights over the estate to a garage proprietor in a totally different social position from that of the testator which had the effect of seriously depreciating its value. The court was satisfied from the evidence that the testator had intended to do what he did, probably as a halfway house between giving his relative the entire estate and none of it. Accordingly, it was held that although on the facts a presumption of undue influence might well have arisen the court was satisfied that the disposition was the free exercise of an independent will of the testator. At p. 152 Lowry L.C.J. referring to In *re Brocklehurst* says:

> At page 43E the Lord Justice draws attention to a feature with which the facts of this case have something in common and which, I suggest, conduces to a similar result: I refer to the availability, as opposed to the paucity, of evidence on the relevant issues. While the facts of the two cases are completely different, *Re Brocklehurst* furnishes a most useful reminder of the role played by the actual evidence. Remembering that presumed undue influence conveys the notion of the undue

influence which is alleged to arise from the relationship being actually exercised, even if not proved, it must, in order to count, be capable of affecting the relevant transaction. All the evidence points away from that possibility in the present case. And if the exercise of undue influence is negatived by evidence which is believed, there can be no presumption in favour of the donor or those claiming through her.

These two cases decide essentially that when all the facts are known surrounding the execution of the impugned document and these show that the donee exercised no influence over the donor then there is no ground to set the deed aside.

In the ordinary way, the person seeking to set aside a voluntary deed does not know all the circumstances surrounding the execution of the document. Accordingly, where the relationship between the donor and donee suggests that the deed might have been procured by undue influence, a presumption arises and the onus of rebutting it is placed upon the donee.

As Bridge L.J. said in In *re Brocklehurst's Estate* [1978] Ch. 14 at p. 43:

> . . . the presumption of undue influence, like other presumptions, is a tool of the lawyer's trade whose function it is to enable him to arrive at a just result by bridging a gap in the evidence at a point where, in the nature of the case, evidence is difficult or impossible to come by.

What has to be shown is that the gift was the spontaneous act of the donor acting under circumstances which enabled him to exercise an independent will and which justifies the court in holding that the gift was the result of a free exercise of the donor's will. See the judgment of Cotton L.J. in *Allcard v Skinner* (1887) 36 Ch. D. 145 at p. 171.

There is no one way in which the presumption may be rebutted. The usual way is to show that the donor had advice from someone who was independent and who was aware of all the relevant circumstances. But as can be seen from R. (*Proctor*) *v Hutton* it is equally good to show that all the relevant facts are before the court and that these show that the donor was not in any way influenced in what he did by the donee. The presumption is important when all the facts are not known. It cannot be rebutted until all the gaps in the evidence are filled and the evidence then denies the existence of any undue influence.

The present case is easily distinguished from R. (*Proctor*) *v Hutton* upon which counsel for the appellant relies. In the present case the donee was instrumental in instructing the solicitor who prepared the document and was present when it was executed. He told the solicitor what his father wanted. The evidence also shows that the latter did not realise what he had done since he continued to tell his daughters that there would always be a home for them in the premises. This evidence leaves a clear doubt as to whether the donor knew what he was doing and also as to what was his real intention.

It is important to realise that a presumption is a rule of evidence which shifts the burden of proof, and where the real intention of the testator cannot be determined the onus has not been discharged.

In the present case, the appellant relies essentially on three matters. The first is that the plaintiffs accept that their brother did not do anything improper. That alone is insufficient. As I have already indicated the evidence does not show clearly why the donor did what he did, that he knew what he was doing, and that it was the free exercise of his will.

The next basis upon which the appellant relies is the clarity and independence of mind of the donor. That may well be so, but it has no bearing on this case since it is not necessary to establish undue influence to establish that the donor was not mentally alert.

The final ground upon which the appellant relies is that the donor received independent legal advice from Mr Joyce. The question of advice by a solicitor was considered by Budd J. in *Gregg v Kidd* [1956] IR 183. At pp. 201 and 202 Budd J. approved certain principles from the judgment of Farwell J. in *Powell v Powell* [1900] Ch. 243. These were:

(1) A solicitor who acts for both parties cannot be independent of the donee in fact; and
(2) to satisfy the court that the donor was acting independently of any influence from the donee and with the full appreciation of what he was doing it should be established that the gift was made after the nature and effect of the transaction had been fully explained to the donor by some independent and qualified person. Further, the advice must be given with a knowledge of all relevant circumstances and must be such as a competent advisor would give if acting solely in the interests of the donor.

Accepting these principles, there can have been no independent advice given by Mr Joyce since at best he was acting for both parties. In any event his evidence was lacking in two important respects:

(1) He did not have knowledge of all the relevant circumstances; and
(2) he did not give advice, he merely set out to carry out the donor's instructions.

Even if he had been the donor's solicitor what he did would not have saved the transaction. As I have said before, a solicitor or other professional person does not fulfil his obligation to his client or patient by simply doing what he is asked or instructed to. He owes such a person a duty to exercise his professional skill and judgment and he does not fulfil that duty by blithely following instructions without stopping to consider whether to do so is appropriate. Having done so, he must then give advice as to whether or not what is required of him is proper. Here his duty was to advise the donor to obtain independent advice.

In the present case whatever independence Mr Joyce may have had has been destroyed by his acting in the present proceedings as solicitor to the personal representative of the donee.

In my view this was a case in which the presumption of undue influence arose to transfer the onus to the defendant, an onus which has not been discharged.

Denham J. (Lynch J. concurring):

Undue influence—decision
There are two classes of transactions which may be set aside on the grounds of undue influence. They were described by Cotton L.J. in *Allcard v Skinner* (1887) 36 Ch. D 145 at p. 171 as:

The question is—Does the case fall within the principles laid down by the decisions of the Court of Chancery in setting aside voluntary gifts executed by parties who at the time were under such influence as, in the opinion of the court, enabled the donor afterwards to set the gift aside? These decisions may be divided into two classes—first, where the court has been satisfied that the gift was the result of influence expressly used by the donee for the purpose; second, where the relations between the donor and donee have at or shortly before the execution of the gift been such as to raise a presumption that the donee had influence over the donor. In such a case the court sets aside the voluntary gift, unless it is proved that in fact the gift was the spontaneous act of the donor acting under circumstances which enabled him to exercise an independent will and which justifies the court in holding that the gift was the result of a free exercise of the donor's will. . . . In the second class of cases the court interferes, not on the ground that any wrongful act has in fact been committed by the donee, but on the ground of public policy, and to prevent the relations which existed between the parties and the influence arising therefrom being abused.

This case arises under the second class of case. Counsel for the appellant quite rightly accepted that this case falls into the latter category. He acknowledged that the relationship between Thomas Carroll Senior and Thomas Carroll Junior and the surrounding circumstances gave rise to the presumption of undue influence. . . .

In R. (*Proctor*) *v Hutton* [1978] NI 139 at p. 146 Lord Lowry described the different approaches to the different classes of undue influence. He stated:

When relying on 'express undue influence' the plaintiff must prove that an unfair advantage has been gained by an unconscientious use of power in the form of some unfair and improper conduct, some coercion from outside, some overreaching, some form of cheating. The undue influence which is presumed in the second class of case is influence of the same kind: the difference lies in not being able to prove its existence but, by virtue of the presumption, undue influence is deemed to have been exercised until its exercise is negatived on a balance of probabilities by evidence.

It is clear that what is at issue is whether the donee has taken advantage of his position or:

. . . been assiduous not to do so. The question can only be answered in each case by a meticulous consideration of the facts: Hanbury, *Modern Equity* (9th ed.), p. 652.

I am satisfied that this is the correct approach. In this case, the presumption existing, it was then necessary to conduct a careful analysis of the facts. On the facts it was a matter of determining if the donee, Thomas Carroll Junior, had taken advantage of his position or had been assiduous not to do so. This was not a case where the issue was whether Thomas Carroll Junior had taken advantage of his position expressly. Rather it was a case where in the circumstances assiduous care should have been taken not to take advantage of the position of Thomas Carroll Senior.

The learned trial judge conducted a painstaking analysis of the facts as has been set out fully in this judgment. I am satisfied that the appeal was argued on a mistaken approach to the law. The reason for the equitable law to protect Thomas Carroll Senior is one of public policy—to protect a frail person. As Cotton L.J. said in *Allcard v Skinner* at p. 171:

In the second class of cases the court interferes, not on the ground that any wrongful act has in fact been committed by the donee, but on the ground of public policy, and to prevent the relations which existed between the parties and the influence arising therefrom being abused.

Thus, the issue is whether on the facts and circumstances of the case the donee has rebutted the presumption of undue influence. The facts and circumstances of this case were fully considered and determined by the learned High Court Judge. In this case the donor was giving away practically his sole asset and the learned trial judge made careful findings of the fact about the transaction.

The conclusions reached in *Inche Noriah* are analogous on the law and facts to those found by the learned trial judge. In that case Lord Hailsham, describing amongst other matters the conduct of the lawyer Mr James Aitken, stated at p. 136:

> In the present case their Lordships do not doubt that Mr Aitken acted in good faith; but he seems to have received a good deal of information from the respondent; he was not made aware of the material fact that the property which was being given away constituted practically the whole estate of the donor, and he certainly does not seem to have brought home to her mind the consequences to herself of what she was doing, or the fact that she could more prudently, and equally effectively, have benefited the donee without undue risk to herself by retaining the property in her own possession during her life and bestowing it upon him by her will. In their Lordships' view the facts proved by the respondent are not sufficient to rebut the presumption of undue influence which is raised by the relationship proved to have been inexistence between the parties; and they regard it as most important from the point of view of public policy to maintain the rule of law which has been laid down and to insist that a gift made under circumstances which give rise to the presumption must be set aside unless the donee is able to satisfy the court of facts sufficient to rebut the presumption.

The learned trial judge reached a similar conclusion on the law in this case. I am satisfied that he was correct, it was not necessary to prove specific acts of undue influence by Thomas Carroll Junior. The evidence as a whole must be considered to see whether the presumption of undue influence has been rebutted. This was done most carefully by the learned trial judge. I would affirm his decision on this aspect of the appeal.

Improvidence of the transaction—decision

Thomas Carroll Senior was disposing of practically his only asset. At the time he was frail. He did not retain any right of maintenance or support. I have already analysed the nature of the legal advice he received and affirmed the decision that it was inadequate. In all the circumstances, as described above, it is clear that Thomas Carroll Senior was an unequal party. In *Grealish v Murphy* [1946] IR 35 at pp. 49–50 Gavin Duffy J. stated:

> The issue thus raised brings into play Lord Hatherley's cardinal principle (from which the exceptions are rare) that equity comes to the rescue whenever the parties to a contract have not met upon equal terms, see Lord Hatherley's judgment (dissenting on facts) in *O'Rourke v Bolingbroke* 2 App Cas. 814; the corollary is that the court must inquire whether a grantor, shown to be unequal to protecting himself, has had the protection which was his due by reason of his infirmity, and the infirmity may take various forms. The deed here was in law a transaction for value: *Colreavy v Colreavy* [1940] IR 71; however tenuous the value may have proved to be in fact, and, of course, a court must be very much slower to undo a transaction for value; but the fundamental principle to justify radical interference by the court is the identical principle, whether value be shown or not, and the recorded examples run from gifts and voluntary settlements (including an abortive marriage settlement) to assignments for a money consideration. The principle has been applied to improvident grants, whether the particular disadvantage entailing the need for protection to the grantor

were merely low station and surprise (though the grantor's rights were fully explained). *Evans v Llewellin* 1 Cox Eq Cas. 333; or youth and inexperience: *Prideaux v Lonsdale* 1 De GJ & S 433; *Everitt v Everitt* 10 Eq 405; or age and weak intellect, short of total incapacity, with no fiduciary relation and no 'arts of inducement' to condemn the grantee: *Longmate v Ledger* 2 Giff 157; *Anderson v Elsworth* 3 Giff 154. Even the exuberant or ill-considered disposition of feckless middle-aged women have had to yield to same principle: *Phillipson v Kerry* 32 Beav 628; *Wollaston v Tribe* 9 Eq 44.

He also concluded at p. 51:

> In my judgment, without any regard to any question of undue influence, upon Lord Hatherley's principle and the concurrent authorities the plaintiff by reason of his own weakness in mind, coupled with the deficiencies in the legal advice under which he acted and his unawareness, is entitled to have the improvident indenture of settlement, dated 24 October 1942, set aside and the Register of Freeholders rectified.

Whilst one might not agree with all of the classifications recognised by Gavan Duffy J. the legal principle is stated clearly and is applicable to this case.

In light of the evidence of the omissions in relation to the legal advice given, the fact that there was no evidence that the transfer was read over to Thomas Carroll Senior, his frail health, his lack of practically any other assets, his relationship with his daughters and all the circumstances, there was clear evidence upon which the learned trial judge could come to the determination, which he did, at p. 232, that:

> This in my view is a clear case where the equitable jurisdiction can and should be involved with a view to setting aside the transaction on the grounds of its improvidence.

I would affirm his conclusion.

Elton John and Others *v* James and Others [1991] FSR 397

The facts

The action concerned a series of publishing, recording and management agreements entered into by Elton John and his lyricist, Bernie Taupin, with DJM, beginning in 1967, when they were unknown and still minors.

The plaintiffs' primary claims were for the setting aside, on the ground of undue influence, of the publishing and recording agreements, the return of the copyrights in all compositions and recordings covered by the agreements and delivery up of all master recordings. The copyrights involved were of 144 compositions and 169 song recordings, the retail sales value of which probably exceeded £200 million. The plaintiffs conceded that the defendants should retain all sums received by them so far, save that they should account for (a) all sums wrongly retained by them by way of the sub-publishing agreements, (b) the difference between the royalty rates in the agreements being set aside and the best possible rates obtainable in the market, and (c) compound interest on the above. Alternatively, they claimed payment of substantial additional sums which they alleged ought to have been paid under the publishing agreements as mechanical royalties on original recordings, or the sums retained by the second defendant's sub-sidiaries in excess of the normal commercial sub-publishing rates.

Nicholls J.:

I turn to the plaintiffs' primary claim, to have the various recording and publishing agreements set aside on the basis that they were procured by undue influence. On the law I have the advantage of the recent authoritative exposition given by the House of Lords in the case of *National Westminster Bank Ltd v Morgan* [1985] 2 WLR 588,1 which concerned a claim by a wife that her signature to a mortgage of the matrimonial home in favour of a bank had been procured by the bank manager exercising undue influence over her. In the leading speech Lord Scarman (at pp 597–8) observed that the principle justifying the court in setting aside a transaction for undue influence was the need to protect one party from being victimised by the other. He quoted approvingly a passage from the judgment of Lord Shaw of Dunfermline in the Privy Council case of *Poosathurai v Kannappa Chettiar* LR 47 IA 1 on the subject of undue influence, which commenced with the sentence: 'It must be established that the person in a position of domination has used that position to obtain unfair advantage for himself, and so to cause injury to the person relying upon his authority or aid.' Lord Scarman then said (at p. 599):

> The wrongfulness of the transaction must, therefore, be shown: it must be one in which an unfair advantage has been taken of another. The doctrine is not limited to transactions of gift. A commercial relationship can become a relationship in which one party assumes a role of dominating influence over the other. In *Poosathurai's* case, LR 47 IA 1 the board recognised that a sale at an undervalue could be a transaction which a court could set aside as unconscionable if it was shown or could be presumed to have been procured by the exercise of undue influence. Similarly a relationship of banker and customer may become one in which the banker acquires a dominating influence. If he does and a manifestly disadvantageous transaction is proved, there would then be room for the court to presume that it resulted from the exercise of undue influence.

So, in short, and whatever be the precise form of words used, the substance of the two ingredients required before the court will set aside a transaction is, first, a relationship in which one person has a dominating influence over the other and, secondly, a manifestly disadvantageous transaction resulting from the exercise of that influence. In appropriate circumstances presumptions may be employed regarding either of the two ingredients: in appropriate circumstances the existence of a dominating influence may be presumed; the court may also, again in appropriate circumstances, presume that where a dominating influence exists, a manifestly disadvantageous transaction was the result of the exercise of undue influence.

This is all subject to the warning given by Lord Scarman at the conclusion of his speech (at p. 602):

> There is no precisely defined law setting limits to the equitable jurisdiction of a court to relieve against undue influence. This is the world of doctrine, not of neat and tidy rules. The courts of equity have developed a body of learning enabling relief to be granted where the law has to treat the transaction as unimpeachable unless it can be held to have been procured by undue influence. It is the unimpeachability at law of a disadvantageous transaction which is the starting point from which the court advances to consider whether the transaction is the product merely of one's own folly or of the undue influence exercised by another. A court in the exercise of this equitable jurisdiction is a court of conscience. Definition is a poor

instrument when used to determine whether a transaction is or is not unconscionable: this is a question which depends upon the particular facts of the case.

The defendants' case was that neither of the necessary ingredients existed in this
case regarding any of the agreements. Thus, for example, as to the 1967 publishing
agreement, DJM never acquired a dominating influence over Mr John or Mr Taupin, nor
was the transaction manifestly disadvantageous either at its inception or as it was
subsequently implemented. On whether Mr James (because he alone was the person
concerned for DJM) assumed a role of dominating influence, the gist of the defendants'
submission was that although DJM, like the banker in the *Morgan* case, was in a much
stronger bargaining position, the relationship of music publisher and would-be writers
did not *per se* give rise to a presumption of undue influence, and Mr James never crossed
the line which divides a normal business relationship from one of undue influence. Mr
James never sought to persuade or encourage the two individual plaintiffs to enter the
publishing agreement.

I shall consider the various agreements in turn, starting with the 1967 publishing
agreement. Under this the writers tied themselves exclusively to DJM for what would be
a period of six years if DJM exercised its option. DJM was entitled to obtain and retain for
all time the full copyright in all their works produced in that period (unless, as was
unlikely, DJM rejected any work as unsuitable) and to do so even if DJM never published
the work or works in question. In return for this, viewed in strict terms of legal obligations of DJM, the writers obtained precious little. They obtained a right to royalties.
The defendants claimed that the writers also obtained the benefit of an implied
obligation that DJM would use reasonable diligence to publish, promote and exploit
the compositions accepted, but even if this was so such an obligation was necessarily
so loose and imprecise that it would have afforded the writers little protection.

The defendants further claimed that under an oral contract made at the same time
as the written agreement DJM was obliged to pay Mr John and Mr Taupin £20 per week
between them during the currency of the 1967 publishing agreement as an advance on
royalties. Mr James' evidence was that he intended to commit himself to pay this sum
for the whole life of the agreement come what may. He explained that he suggested to
Mr John that the weekly payments should not be mentioned in the agreement, even
though they were to endure for its full term, because the sum might be increased from
time to time, in which event letters would have to be exchanged if the payments were
included in the written agreement. I am unable to accept Mr James' evidence on this. I
have no doubt that if, for example, the two writers had failed miserably to produce any
work of any potential and there was no realistic prospect of them earning any royalties
other than of a minimal amount and Mr James had wished not to continue with the
1967 publishing agreement, he would have considered himself free, after a reasonable
time and on giving reasonable notice, to discontinue the weekly payments long before
the end of the six year period (the renewal option was exercisable by the writers as well
as by the publisher). I am not satisfied that there was a binding contract beyond this.

It may be inherent in the nature of this type of publishing agreement that the
publisher's strictly legal obligations will be very limited. What Mr John and Mr Taupin
wanted was a foot in the door, the *entrée* to the popular music publishing world, and in
practice they obtained this by the 1967 publishing agreement. They were put on the
'books' of a leading publisher; they obtained the use of a studio; and they also obtained
the financial means enabling them to pursue their ambitions. The value of this to the
two young would-be writers is not to be underestimated. They were fortunate to have
found in Mr James a leading music publisher who was willing to encourage and support
them. But the agreement contained no provision for early termination or return of copy-

rights if, for example, successful publication was not achieved and the writers became aware of another publisher who had more confidence in their songs. Conversely, and more importantly, if, as was no doubt the hope in every case, the writers succeeded enormously, their entire output for six years was bound to DJM effectively for ever, whether published or not, and there was no provision for any increase in royalty rates.

Obviously it takes time for a new writer to succeed. Mr James' estimate was that on average between one and two years is needed before there is any success, if there is to be any. The publisher is entitled to a reasonable period to obtain a proper reward for taking on the new writers, paying the (comparatively modest) costs of making demonstration records, providing studio facilities, seeking to promote the works and, in this case, paying the writers their weekly retainer. But six years is an appreciable time in anyone's professional career, particularly at the threshold of so uncertain a career as that of pop music writer. I consider that to have tied these two young men to DJM in 1967 for six years on the terms in question represented an unacceptably hard bargain.

Did Mr Dick James assume a role of dominating influence? I consider that, brief though their acquaintance had been at this stage, he did. Once he had decided that the two young men, who like so many others were anxious to be signed by him, were worth pursuing and encouraging, he really took charge of the arrangements. At his request they assigned the copyright in the seventeen songs to Gralto Music Ltd, even though they were under no obligation to do so. And although, understandably after so many years, some obscurity now surrounds precisely what was said at the relevant meetings, and, indeed, it is uncertain how many meetings there were, what does emerge clearly is that Mr James did not regard himself as obliged to give Mr John or Mr Taupin, nor did he give them, a thorough explanation of the terms of the proposed agreement. In particular, he did not explain to them that, whatever might happen in practice, under the agreement all the songs they wrote over the next three years, or six years if DJM exercised its option, would belong to DJM for ever, regardless of how successful those songs might be and whether published or not, and that for those songs, again regardless of how successful they might be, they would be entitled to receive only the one fixed rate of royalties. When the typed form of agreement was produced, no one went through the four and a half pages, explaining the practical implications of the eighteen clauses. Mr John and Mr Taupin were young and inexperienced minors. They were very apprehensive at meeting such a giant in the music publishing industry, and they were very anxious to be taken on by him. No negotiation took place. They would have been disinclined to question the terms of any agreement Mr James put before them, the more so when he told them that the terms were the standard terms within the industry. They were, as must have been obvious to him, trusting and relying on him that the contractual terms were fair and reasonable. The formality of requiring parental signature in the circumstances of these two young men and their parents was not an adequate counterbalance to this. In my view it is clear that the reason why Mr John and Mr Taupin signed the agreement for such an onerously long period lies not only in their keenness to be signed by Mr James but also, and importantly, and this is partly why they were so keen, in the trust they reposed in him as a man of stature in the industry that he would treat them fairly.

My conclusion is that, in respect of the period for which the artists were bound and because of the circumstances in which the agreement was entered into, at its inception the 1967 publishing agreement was an unfair transaction (I prefer to use this expression rather than 'unconscionable transaction', but without intending any different meaning).

In stating this conclusion I wish to emphasise that there is no question of Mr James having sought consciously to obtain an unfair advantage. At the time he thought his normal terms for a publishing agreement were standard in the trade and therefore fair.

And if, contrary to what normally happened in the popular music business, these two young writers succeeded spectacularly, it would have been his intention to increase their royalty rates, as indeed in the event happened. But finding, as I do unhesitatingly, that in this transaction Mr James was acting in good faith does not in my view provide a complete answer to the undue influence claim. One can obtain an unfair advantage by the exercise of a dominating influence without intending to act unfairly.

I move on to 1971. The defendants placed considerable reliance on the termination of the existing publishing and recording agreements effected by the new agreements entered into in March and April 1971 as part of Mr John's and Mr Taupin's double employment schemes. For the defendants it was emphasised that in relation to the 1971 agreements the individual plaintiffs were advised by independent solicitors experienced in the field of entertainment agreements (and it is right to recognise that it was at Mr James' suggestion that Mr John first consulted solicitors). The 1971 agreements could not have been, and indeed were not alleged to have been, procured by undue influence.

I am unable to accept the defendants' argument on this. Berger Oliver were not instructed to consider whether the existing agreements were unfair or impeachable on any ground. Mr Oliver (who did not give evidence) seems, not surprisingly, to have proceeded on the footing that there were in existence valid contracts and that one of the parties had offered to vary the terms of one of those contracts. Mr Oliver took part in negotiations with Mr James concerning the proposed variations, and advised Mr John and Mr Taupin thereon, and his firm prepared the documents required for the tax mitigation scheme, reflecting therein the agreed variation. No one suggested that the defendants' rights under the existing contracts might be impeachable, and with the one exception of the improvement in the publishing royalty rates, the defendants stood on their rights under the existing agreements and the terms of those agreements were carried over into the new agreements. Thus the negotiations took place, and the independent advice was given, not against a background of Mr John and Mr Taupin being free or possibly being free from any existing obligations to the defendants, but against a background of the existing agreements upon which, with one exception, the defendants were standing firm. I do not see how such negotiations and advice, followed by the 1971 agreements, by themselves can have been operated to cure the taint attaching to the 1967 agreements. On the contrary, any existing taint was carried over and, subject to any complications arising from the difference in the parties to the 1971 agreements, insofar as the existing publishing and recording agreements were then still capable of being set aside on the ground that they were procured by undue influence, so also at their inception were the corresponding 1971 agreements.

Note

In this case Nicholls J. did not consider the issue of whether undue influence could be presumed, preferring instead to examine the status of the parties and the merits of the various transactions. For a recent case involving a presumption which played a pivotal role in the outcome of the case see *Wadlow v Samuel (p.k.a. Seal)* [2006] EWHC 1492 (Ch).

E. PROBLEMS OF PROOF—UPHOLDING THE TRANSACTION

McCormack v Bennett (HC) 2 July 1973, unrep.

Finlay J.:

The plaintiff Philomena McCormack brings this action as legal personal representative of her father James Seery to set aside and cancel an indenture of transfer dated 4 October 1967 executed by James Seery and for other relief. By that transfer James Seery transferred the lands of which he was then registered as full owner on folio no. 7790 of the County of Westmeath to the defendant Teresa Bennett subject to his life estate. The defendant is a sister of the plaintiff being another daughter of James Seery.

The grounds on which this deed is challenged as stated in the original pleadings were that it was improvident; that at the time of its execution the transferor had no independent advice and that he did not know or appreciate the consequences of the deed.

The proceedings were commenced by the late James Seery in his lifetime by a plenary summons dated 27 February 1970. A statement of claim purports to have been filed on his behalf on 9 March 1971 although he had in fact died on 22 May 1970. By order of 5 November 1971 the proceedings were continued in the name of the present plaintiff and an amended statement of claim was filed on 27 January 1972 which did not enlarge or amend the grounds already alleged for setting aside the deed.

By notice dated 15 June 1973 the plaintiff gave notice to the defendant of her intention to apply at the hearing of the action to amend the statement of claim by additional allegations of 1) undue influence by the defendant 2) the absence of a revocation clause in the deed 3) the absence of covenants on the part of the defendant to look after James Seery and to work the lands for his benefit and 4) the absence of covenants on the part of the defendant to look after James Seery's wife.

The case came on for hearing before me on 20 June and I allowed this amendment notwithstanding its extreme lateness upon the grounds that it was desirable that all issues between the parties should be tried and because I concluded that the defendant did not require any adjournment of the case to put herself in a position to meet these additional allegations.

Some of the facts of the case were agreed or admitted and some were in dispute. The facts as I find them to be are as follows:

James Seery was on 4 October 1967 when he executed this deed aged seventy nine years and his wife Mary who lived with him at that time was eighty. She died in November 1968.

James Seery was the registered owner of approximately 22 statute acres of land and a small house on it which I am satisfied was situated in an inaccessible place and probably had in the year 1967 a market value of approximately £1,500.

The lands were let by James Seery at that time at £80 per year and the only other income which he and his wife had were their social welfare benefits probably amounting though the figure was not clearly established to about £5,00.

Much of the disputed evidence concerned the mental and physical condition of James Seery and to some extent the condition of his wife. I am satisfied that Mary Seery was in October 1967 in extremely bad physical condition and that she was commencing to be affected by senility and as far as her condition is relevant to the issues in this case I am satisfied that she needed some sort of relatively constant attention from a person able in effect to give her unskilled nursing and that she also required from time to time skilled medical attention.

James Seery was I am satisfied at the time of this deed in 1967 suffering from no form of mental abnormality. He was suffering from the loss of the sight of one eye. Some evidence was given that he was hard of hearing but I am satisfied that this was not so and certainly was not to an extent which affected his capacity to hear people nor did he ever complain of it to Doctor Kelly. He had had a bowel complaint in 1963 and a perforated ulcer when he had been obliged to go to hospital and undergo an operation but I am satisfied that operation was a success and that he was not suffering from any particular form of physical disability which would impair his capacity to transact business. Doctor Kelly who was his constant medical attendant during the relevant period gave evidence that James Seery was of a nervous and fretful condition and that he was more anxious about his future and that of his wife than could be expected to be normal. Doctor Kelly expressed the view that it was not desirable for him to have to transact worrying business but I am satisfied that this view was expressed more in the light of the effect it might have on the health of James Seery than in the light of an expression of opinion by the doctor that he was unfit to carry out serious business. I am satisfied that he was very anxious about both his own future and that of his wife but I am not completely satisfied that this anxiety having regard to his wife's general condition which was extremely bad and to his own age and hers was necessarily abnormal or exaggerated.

James and Mary Seery had nine children consisting of one son and eight daughters. With the exception of the plaintiff Mrs McCormack who was though not constantly for long periods living at home all these children had departed for a considerable time from their home, one of them Hannah was a nun known in religion as Sister Xavier and the others were married. The son Patrick was married and settled in England. Two sisters the defendant Mrs Bennett and a Mrs Ann Seery were married and living close to where the deceased and his wife lived. Prior to the transactions of October 1967 James Seery had made two dispositions of his property by two successive wills. In the year 1956 he made a will leaving his property substantially to Mrs Seery and making minor provisions for some other members of the family after the lifetime of his wife. In the year 1963 he changed this will and made his substantial beneficiary his son Patrick. Some evidence was given that a dispute had arisen between the late James Seery and his daughter Mrs Ann Seery which led to the change of will. Mrs Ann Seery in evidence denied that such a dispute occurred and I am satisfied that it was not necessary or relevant for the purpose of the issues in this case to enquire further into that matter.

Two conflicting accounts are given by the plaintiff and defendant respectively with regard to the circumstances preceding the transactions of October 1967. The plaintiff in evidence said that the defendant was constantly urging the deceased James Seery to benefit her with the lands upon promises of looking after him and his wife. The defendant on the other hand stated in evidence that Patrick Seery the son of James having returned home on a holiday in the summer of 1967 pointed out to his father that he was not going to return to Ireland and could not look after his father and mother and suggested to him that he should instead give the lands to his daughter the defendant Mrs Bennett who was the logical and most likely person to look after himself and his wife. The defendant said in evidence that her brother Patrick told her about this conversation with her father and that subsequently her father came to her and asked her if he gave her over the place would she be prepared to take care of himself and his wife as long as they lived. She said that she would but that she would prefer to buy the place as after his death there might be arguments from the other members of the family. The defendant's account of this conversation then went on to say that they agreed a price of £300 that she knew that that was below the value of the place and that her father who also knew it was below the value of the place thought it was sufficient. The defendant admitted that it was she who suggested a sale rather than a transfer or voluntary gift of the lands.

I accept as being substantially accurate the account of the origin of this transaction given by the defendant and I reject the account given by the plaintiff, I am therefore satisfied as a matter of fact that the idea of a giving of the land to the defendant in some form originated with James Seery on the suggestion of his son Patrick and I am satisfied that Mrs Bennett did not exercise any influence over James Seery her father to induce him to enter into this transaction. I am satisfied that after this conversation James Seery brought the defendant Mrs Bennett into Mullingar on 26 September to visit Mr Kevin Wallace of the firm of N. J. Downes and Co.. I am quite satisfied on the evidence that it was James Seery who chose Mr Wallace as solicitor to transact this business and that he did so because he had previously done all his business including making his two wills with the firm of N. J. Downes and Co. and had made the will of 1963 specifically with Mr Kevin Wallace.

I have had evidence from Mr Kevin Wallace of the interview which then took place with James Seery and with Mrs Teresa Bennett present the whole time. I accept as being accurate and correct that account of that interview. Mr Wallace's recollection of what occurred is fortified by a full note which he took in the form of an attendance and which has been produced before me. In general it was Mr Seery who gave all the instructions and did all the discussion with Mr Wallace and Mrs Bennett made practically no intervention in the proceedings.

James Seery then instructed Mr Wallace that his daughter Mrs McCormack the plaintiff and his other daughter Mrs Ann Seery were kicking up a row and having given a full outline of the members of his family where they were and how they were situated he informed Mr Wallace that he wished to sell the farm outright to the defendant Mrs Bennett for the sum of £300,00. Mr Wallace advised Mr Seery strongly against this course, and urged him instead to make a will. I am satisfied that a considerable part of the time occupied in the attendance of Mr Wallace on Mr Seery which was approximately an hour and a half was taken up with a discussion in which Mr Wallace was urging upon Mr Seery the desirability of simply making a new will. Mr Seery was not content to make a new will only and was then informed by Mr Wallace of the alternative of making a deed retaining to himself a life interest in the lands and transferring them in remainder to the defendant Mrs Bennett. This alternative he James Seery I am satisfied specifically chose. Although there is no note of it in the attendance Mr Wallace told me in evidence and I accept it as being accurate that he informed Mr Seery of the possibility of inserting a revocation clause in this deed. He said however that he did not emphasise the desirability of a revocation clause largely as I understand his evidence because he had urged upon Mr Seery the even more easily revocable method of giving these lands by will to Mrs Bennett and that Mr Seery had definitely refused to adopt that course. Mr Wallace also I am satisfied made specific enquiry as to the position of James Seery's wife particularly if he were to die before her. Mr James Seery in reply indicated that his wife would not want for anything and in fact indicated that he placed a total reliance upon Mrs Bennett to look after her mother. At the conclusion of this interview Mr Wallace arranged that he would send out to Mr Seery addressed to him care of Mrs Bennett at his request a draft of the proposed deed. This was done and a deed in the simple form of a transfer of the remainder interest reserving a life interest to James Seery was sent in draft form to him. He returned to Mr Wallace's Office on 30 September 1967 accompanied again by Mrs Bennett. On this occasion James Seery demanded that he should in addition make a new will asserting that it was undesirable that he would have a will leaving the place to one member of the family and a deed transferring it to another. Mr Wallace took some care again to enquire from James Seery as to whether he was totally satisfied with the arrangement which he proposed to make and in particular to the position of his wife and having done so and James Seery appearing totally satisfied with it the deed was then executed and was subsequently dated 4 October 1967.

At no time during any of the discussions between James Seery and Mr Kevin Wallace did James Seery ever mention to Mr Wallace the fact that his proposal to transfer an interest in the lands to his daughter Mrs Bennett had originated in association with a promise requested by him and given by her that she would look after him and his wife to the end of their lives. Mr Wallace in evidence properly conceded that had he been aware of the existence of that sort of arrangement he would have had to take cognisance of it. The possibility in these circumstances of inserting into the deed covenants on the part of Mrs Bennett for the support and maintenance and care of James Seery and or his wife was never considered at any of the discussions in the solicitor's office.

Much of the evidence was concerned with events which occurred after the execution of this deed. Except in relation to a claim by the plaintiff against the defendant that she unlawfully trespassed on her father's land during his lifetime, the issues arising from this part of the evidence seem to me to be irrelevant to the question of the validity of the deed. If as is alleged by the plaintiff the defendant Mrs Bennett subsequent to the execution of this deed failed to fulfil the promise which she had given to look after her mother and father this would not of itself affect the validity of the deed. If on the other hand the deed is in fact invalid then no matter how much care Mrs Bennett bestowed on her mother and father after its execution it would not render it valid. Since the issues have been raised however and the allegations have been made I should say that in general I accept and prefer the account of these contentious issues given by Mrs Bennett than the account given by Mrs McCormack or by Sister Xavier. In particular I find it a fact that Mrs Bennett was in occupation of her father's land during his lifetime by his permission and under an arrangement to pay him for that occupation which she fulfilled.

It is necessary to summarise the above rather lengthy findings of fact in order to clarify the legal position as between the parties. The summary is as follows:

I find that this deed was not executed as a result of any undue influence on the part of Mrs Bennett. I find that James Seery had no mental or physical infirmity which prevented him from fully understanding the nature and consequences of this deed. I find that James Seery had the benefit of independent advice from the solicitor of his choice and that that was fully and carefully available to him. I find that the possibility of a clause of revocation was explained to James Seery and that the desirability of making a revocable disposition of his property was urged upon him. I find that the deed is on the face of it improvident in that James Seery disposed of the remainder interest in his only piece of property without any valuable consideration moving to him in respect of that disposition. I find that by reason of the failure of James Seery and or Mrs Bennett to inform Mr Wallace of the promises made by Mrs Bennett in respect of the care and maintenance of her father and mother that he was not aware of all the circumstances of the case when he was advising James Seery.

On these findings of fact I am satisfied that the legal position is as follows:

I accept and adopt as applicable to this case the reasoning of Mr Justice Budd in the case of *Gregg v Kidd* [1956] IR 183. In particular I would adopt and repeat the portion of his judgment at p. 196 [see above p. 588] where he says:

Where the relations between the donor and another person raise a presumption that that other person had influence over the donor and the evidence shows that the third party is both closely related to the donee and was closely associated in action and interest with the donee at the time of events leading to the transaction it would seem to be on principle that the onus in such circumstances must be likewise thrown on the donee to establish that the gift resulted from the free exercise of the donor's will. The presumption may of course be rebutted either by showing that the donor has had competent independent advice and acted of his own free will or in some other way.

As Lord Hailsham says in *Inche Noriah v Shaik Allie Bin Omar*:

The most obvious way to prove that the gift was the result of the free exercise of independent will is to establish that the gift was made after the nature and effect of the transaction had been fully explained to the donor by some independent and qualified person so completely as to satisfy the court that the donor was acting independently of any influence from the donee and with full appreciation of what he was doing.

If that method of rebutting the presumption is adopted and it is not the only method open the advice relied on must in the words of Lord Hailsham be given 'with a knowledge of all relevant circumstances and must be such as a competent and honest adviser would give if acting solely in the interests of the donor.'

The ignorance by Mr Wallace at the time when he was advising the late James Seery of the promises made by Mrs Bennett in respect of a transfer of the land meant that he was not a person with knowledge of all relevant circumstances. If to defend this deed and to discharge the onus which is in my view upon her the defendant must rely only on the independent advice of Mr Wallace she must therefore fail. However from the passage which I have quoted Mr Justice Budd was of this view and in this I am in full agreement with his judgment that the presence of full and satisfactory independent advice is not the only way of proving that a voluntary deed even though it may be on the face of it improvident resulted from the free exercise of the donor's will. I am satisfied that James Seery in October 1967 himself was particularly concerned to make an out and out transfer of these lands by deed to his daughter Mrs Bennett. I am satisfied that that idea for practical purposes originated with him and certainly did not originate with the defendant Mrs Bennett. His reason for making such a transfer instead of a will which would have been revocable was I am satisfied that he wanted a permanency and finality with regard to the disposition of his affairs. I think it is a reasonable inference from the evidence which I have heard that he was a sufficiently astute man to know that no form of bargain or commercial transaction concerned with his land was likely to secure for himself and his wife what they really needed and that was personal care and attention granted largely through affection and kindness by a member of their family. I believe therefore that James Seery when he executed this deed did so as an act entirely of his own free will and did so in the expectation and belief which was his own and not induced to them that by so doing he would secure or reinforce what he believed to be the affectionate attendance of his daughter for both himself and his wife. In these circumstances I conclude that there is evidence before me which I accept other than and in addition to the evidence of the independent advice which James Seery received before executing the deed which satisfies me that the deed was his own act and resulted from an exercise of his own free will. In these circumstances as I understand the legal principles applicable I must uphold this deed even though it may on the face of it appear improvident and even though events which occurred after its execution may have made James Seery in his lifetime dissatisfied with it. Having already concluded that there was no trespass on the life interest of James Seery in these lands I therefore dismiss this action.

Note

See also the judgments in the Supreme Court in *Carroll v Carroll* [2000] 1 ILRM 210 on the issue of upholding the transaction in the face of a presumption of undue influence.

SECTION TWO—UNCONSCIONABLE BARGAIN

SALES OF REVERSIONS

A general equitable jurisdiction to protect persons from their own weakness or vulnerability developed from early case-law which gave relief to the sons of the aristocracy who had dealt in their future property rights—e.g. by mortgaging or charging landed estates—in order to satisfy present needs or requirements. The jurisdiction expanded in order to protect the more feckless or underprivileged members of society.

Fry v Lane (1888) 90 ChD 312

Property was left to five 'poor persons in a humble position' in society. The defendant Lane induced them to sell the property to him, on less than favourable terms. Various actions were brought to set these transactions aside, *inter alia*, under 31 Vict. c.4. (The Sale of Reversions Act 1867).

Kay J.:

. . .

. . . Long before the passing of that Act it was settled that the court of chancery would relieve against a sale of or other dealing with a remainder or revision at an undervalue on that ground alone, and this even where the remainderman was of mature age and accustomed to business: *Wiseman v Beake;*[1] *Berkley-Freeman v Bishop;*[2] *Davis v Duke of Marlborough;*[3] *Earl of Portmore v Taylor;*[4] *Boothby v Boothby;*[5] *Foster v Roberts;*[6] *Beynon v Cook.*[7] In such cases it was held that the onus lay upon the purchaser to shew that he had given the 'fair' value as it was called in *Earl of Aldborough v Trye,*[8] or 'the market value': *Talbot v Staniforth.*[9]

By the 31 Vict. c. 4, reciting that it was expedient to amend the law as administered in courts of equity with respect to sales of reversions, it was enacted (by s. 1) that 'no purchase, made *bona fide* and without fraud or unfair dealing, of any reversionary interest in real or personal estate shall hereafter be opened or set aside merely on the ground of undervalue,' and by s. 2 the word 'purchase' in the Act is to include 'every kind of contract, conveyance, or assignment, under or by which any beneficial interest in any kind of property may be acquired.' This Act came into operation on 1 January 1868.

It is obvious that the words 'merely on the ground of undervalue' do not include the case of an undervalue so gross as to amount of itself to evidence of fraud, and in *Earl of Aylesford v Morris*[10] Lord Selborne said that this Act:

> leaves undervalue still a material element in cases in which it is not the sole equitable ground for relief. These changes of the law have in no degree whatever altered the *onus probandi* in those cases, which, according to the language of Lord Hardwicke, raise 'from the circumstances or conditions of the parties contracting—weakness on one side, usury on the other, or extortion, or advantage taken of that weakness'—a presumption of fraud. Fraud, does not here mean deceit or circumvention; it means an unconscientious use of the power arising out of these circumstances and conditions; and when the relative position of the parties is such as *prima facie* to raise this presumption, the transaction cannot stand unless the person claiming the benefit of it is able to repel the presumption by contrary evidence, proving it to have been in point of fact fair, just, and reasonable.

The most common case for the interference of a court of equity is that of an expectant heir, reversioner, or remainderman who is just of age, his youth being treated as an important circumstance. Another analogous case is where the vendor is a poor man with imperfect education, as in *Evans v Llewellin*;[11] *Haygarth v Wearing*.[12]

In the case of a poor man, in distress for money, a sale, even of property in possession, at an undervalue has been set aside in many cases, as in *Wood v Abrey*,[13] where the only professional person employed was the purchaser's attorney, and the price was one fourth of the value, Sir John Leach saying: 'A court of equity will inquire whether the parties really did meet on equal terms; and if it be found that the vendor was in distressed circumstances, and that advantage was taken of that distress, it will avoid the contract.' So in *Longmate v Ledger*[14] (which it seems, was affirmed on appeal),[15] where property in possession was sold for a price greatly below the value, and one solicitor acted for vendor and purchaser, and the vendor was a man advanced in years, and known to have been of a weak and eccentric disposition.

In *Clark v Malpas*,[16] an improvident sale of property in possession by a poor and illiterate man, the same solicitor being employed by both parties, was set aside. Again, the same thing was done in *Baker v Monk*,[17] where the vendor was an elderly woman in humble life, and the purchaser a substantial tradesman, whose solicitor carried out the transaction for both parties, the consideration being an annuity of 9s a week for the life of the vendor. In that case Turner L.J. distinguishes *Harrison v Guest*[18]—a case in which the transaction was allowed to stand—on the ground that there the offer came first from the vendor, and the purchaser advised him to take time to consider and to consult some one else about it, no such advice having been given by the vendor in *Baker v Monk*.

The result of the decisions is that where a purchase is made from a poor and ignorant man at a considerable undervalue, the vendor having no independent advice, a court of equity will set aside the transaction.

This will be done even in the case of property in possession, and *a fortiori* if the interest be reversionary.

The circumstances of poverty and ignorance of the vendor, and absence of independent advice, throw upon the purchaser, when the transaction is impeached, the onus of proving, in Lord Selborne's words, that the purchase was 'fair, just, and reasonable'.

Upon the evidence before me I cannot hesitate to conclude that the price of £170 in J. B. Fry's case and £270 in George Fry's case were both considerably below the real value. The property has been subjected to the costs of appointing new trustees, and also to part of the costs of an administration suit, and yet the net produce of one fifth share is £730. Managed in a more careful manner it might have produced more.

Both J. B. Fry and his brother George were poor, ignorant men, to whom the temptation of the immediate possession of £100 would be very great. Neither of them in the transaction of the sale of his share, was, in the word of Sir J. Leach, 'on equal terms' with the purchaser. Neither had independent advice. The solicitor who acted for both parties in each transaction seems from the *Law List*, to have been admitted in March 1877. In October 1878, at the time of completing the sale of J. B. Fry's share he had not been more than a year and a half on the roll. His inexperience probably in some degree accounts for his allowing himself to be put in the position of solicitor for both parties in such a case. I think in each transaction he must have been considering the purchaser's interest too much properly to guard that of the vendors. Nothing could be more obvious than to test the value by obtaining an offer from one or more of the leading offices in London, which deal in purchases of this kind. But, although when borrowing money for one of the beneficiaries, he did make some application to the Law Reversionary Society, he says it never occurred to him to do so when he had to effect a sale. He found it was easy to borrow £200 upon an interest of this kind before he completed the sale of J. B. Fry's share for £170. He does not seem even to have informed either of the vendors that one of the £250 legacies had been satisfied, and he allowed the sale by auction of William's share to proceed without correcting the inaccurate statement in the particulars that this legacy was still due, though he says that he informed the intending purchaser of William's share, that the legacy had been discharged. I regret that I must come to the conclusion that, though there was a semblance of bargaining by the solicitor in each case, he did not properly protect the vendors, but gave a great advantage to the purchasers, who had been former clients, and for whom he was then acting. The circumstances illustrate the wisdom and necessity of the rule that a poor, ignorant man, selling an interest of this kind, should have independent advice, and that a purchase from him at an undervalue should be set aside, if he has not.

1. 2 Vern 121.
2. 2 Atk 39.
3. 2 Sw 108, 143.
4. 4 Sim 182.
5. 1 Mac. & G. 604; SC 15 Beav 212.
6. 29 Beav 467.
7. Law Rep 10 Ch. 389.
8. 7 Cl. & F. 436, 456.
9. 1 J. & H. 484, 503.
10. Law Rep 8 Ch. 484, 490.
11. 1 Cox, 333.
12. Law Rep 12 Eq. 320.
13. 3 Madd. 417, 423.
14. 2 Giff. 157.
15. See 3 D. F. & J. 402.
16. 4 D. F. & J. 401.
17. 4 D. J. & S. 388.
18. 8 HLC 481.

Note

In *Slator v Nolan* (1877) 11 Ir Eq R 367, at 407–8 the jurisdiction was stated very broadly by Sullivan M.R.:

It is an idle thing to suppose that the relation of trustee *cestui que trust*, or guardian and ward, or attorney and client, or some other confidential relation, must exist to entitle a man to get aid in this court in setting aside an unconscionable transaction. I take the law of the court to be that if two persons—no matter whether a confidential relation exists between them or not—stand in such a relation to each other that one can take an undue advantage of the other, whether by reason of distress or recklessness or wildness or want of care and where the facts show that one party has taken undue advantage of the other, by reason of the circumstances I have mentioned—a transaction resting upon such unconscionable dealing will not be allowed to stand: and there are several cases which show, even where no confidential relation exist; that, where parties are not on equal terms, the party who gets a benefit cannot hold it without proving that everything has been right and fair and reasonable on his part.

Sometimes the position of weakness involves the combination of a number of circumstances. These could include illiteracy, old age, physical or mental illness, to name just a few. In *Rae v Joyce* (1892) 29 LR (Ir.) 500, the plaintiff entered into an unfavourable property mortgage while in severe financial need and in poor health as a result of a complicated pregnancy. Disparate socio-economic status is also a factor.

Kelly v Morrisroe (1919) 53 ILTR 145

Pim J.:

Two cases came before me on appeal from the decisions of the County Court Judge of Mayo. In the first case the plaintiff, Andrew J. Kelly, issued a civil bill for ejectment on the title against the defendants, Michael Morrisroe and Honoria Morrisroe, in respect of a plot of ground in Chapel Street, in the town of Swinford. The plaintiff claimed the premises by virtue of a deed of 23 May 1918, under which a woman called Mary Gaven, the owner-in-fee, granted and conveyed to him the estate in the premises for the sum of £25, subject to her right to the use during her lifetime, rent free, of a cottage on the said plot. Mary Gaven died on 14 June 1918. The County Court Judge gave a decree in ejectment for possession of the premises. In the second case (the matter of the case stated) the plaintiff, Michael Morrisroe, and the sole executor and universal legatee and devisee under the will of Mary Gaven (dated 12 June 1918, and proved on 16 August 1918), claimed to have the deed of 23 May 1918, rescinded and delivered up to be cancelled. The County Court Judge dismissed the equity civil bill with costs. The premises in respect of which the two civil bills were issued consist of a plot of ground upon which two cottages formerly stood, but one has for some years past been in ruins, and the other, in which Mary Gaven resided, is in a state of considerable dilapidation. The valuation of the whole plot is 10s. The engineers called on each side agreed in stating, and I find as a fact, that the substantial value of the plot is its site value, and that apart from the site it is not worth much. The plot is situated between the business premises of the plaintiff, Andrew J. Kelly, and of one, Martin Campbell, both of whom stated in their evidence before me that it would be of substantial value to them as a site. I am satisfied from the evidence, and I so find, that either Andrew J. Kelly or Martin Campbell would have been willing to give Mary Gaven a very much larger sum for the premises than £25 (Martin Campbell stated that he was ready to give £100). Apart from its value to either of these parties as a means of improving their business premises, it would not have been worth to a third person more than £25, if, indeed, so much. It was stated by Andrew J. Kelly that the first suggestion of a sale of the premises was made to him by Mary Gaven, that she asked £30 and a life interest in the cottage, and that he offered her £20. Evidence was given by Mr E. H. Dolphin, a baker and merchant in Swinford, a magistrate, and a former employer of Mary Gaven, that she came to him for advice as to the offer made to her, and that he suggested the sum of £25. Mr Dolphin's account of the negotiations before the sale was not seriously disputed, and I find it to be substantially correct, but I am not satisfied that the first suggestion of a sale came from Mary Gaven. On 22 May 1918, Andrew J. Kelly instructed Mr P. O'Connor, solicitor, of Swinford, to prepare a conveyance, and on 23 May the parties, with Mr Dolphin, called at Mr O'Connor's office. Mr O'Connor stated that he read over the conveyance to Mary Gaven and explained it to her, and that in his opinion she understood its nature and effect. He said she stated that she was expecting to get £30, but that Mr Kelly was only willing to give her £25. She then executed the conveyance and memorial, Mr O'Connor holding her hand to assist her in signing. The £25 was then paid by Mr Kelly, who also paid Mr O'Connor's costs and the stamp duty. I accept Mr O'Connor's evidence so far as it goes. Mr Kelly has almost completed an entrance to his premises on the portion of the premises sold to him, which was not covered by Mary Gaven's cottage. Mary Gaven never appears to have made any objection, and there was no evidence offered showing that she was at any time dissatisfied with her bargain. I am satisfied that Mary Gaven was not in the strict sense of the word insane, but she was between seventy and eighty years of age, evidently senile, very eccentric in her habits, and altogether mentally abnormal. I find as a fact that she understood that she was selling the premises for £25, subject to her life interest therein; but I also find as a fact that owing to age and mental weakness she was not capable of duly and properly judging the fairness of the offer made to her; that she was unaware that a larger—possibly a much larger—price might have been obtained owing to the value of the site to Messrs Campbell and Kelly, and to the competition between these two gentlemen; and that neither the plaintiff nor his solicitor gave her any information as to matters which she ought to have known. It was admitted that she had not any independent advice in the transaction, and I have no doubt that an independent solicitor would have succeeded in making a much better bargain on her behalf. I do not impute any intention of fraud either to Mr Kelly or to Mr O'Connor. They thought they were making a good bargain for Mr Kelly, that they had a right to do what they did, and I dare say they also thought the bargain was not a bad one for Mary Gaven. I reversed the decision of the County Court Judge on the grounds: (1) That Mary Gaven had no independent legal advice; (2) that she was very old, and evidently infirm of mind; (3) that the premises had a competitive site value, of which she was unaware, and concerning which the purchaser's solicitor would hardly be expected to inform her; (4) that no information as to the site value was given to her either by the plaintiff or by his solicitor, and that the premises were in consequence sold at a figure much below their real value. The question of law arising for the determination of the court is as follows: Are the above facts sufficient in law to justify the court in setting aside the deed of purchase at the suit of the executor and legatee of Mary Gaven?

Sir James Campbell L.C.:

In this case the learned judge has asked us the following question: 'Are the facts as set out in the case stated sufficient in law to justify the court in setting aside the deed of purchase at the suit of the executor and legatee of Mary Gaven?' Speaking for myself, the only conceivable difficulty that I would have is the suggestion made by Mr McCormack, that there was some evidence on which the judge might come to the determination he did, and therefore that we ought not to interfere. But that argument would really evade the object which Pim J. had in view in stating the case, otherwise he never would have stated it in the way in which he did. What he really meant in stating a case was, that he wished us to decide the question whether, in our view, the evidence was reasonably sufficient for setting aside the deed that has been impeached—in other words, did the evidence justify the conclusion that the deed must be set aside? The facts in the case are few, and are not disputed. An old lady was living alone in humble circumstances in this dilapidated cottage. She had no near relatives or dependants. She had two neighbours, Mr Kelly and Mr Campbell, but the latter had never had any negotiations with her up to the date of the impeached transaction: the only offer that was made to her came from Mr Kelly, and he offered her £20. The valuation of the place is 10s. It is a remarkable fact that there is no evidence that any individual whatever would give even a shilling for it except Mr Kelly or Mr Campbell. Be that as it may, she got this offer from Mr Kelly, and she went to her former employer, Mr Dolphin, in whom she trusted, and who lives in the same town—a man of position and respectability, and a justice of the peace. Here is what Pim J. says of him: 'Evidence was given by Mr E. H. Dolphin, a baker and merchant in Swinford, a magistrate, and a former employer of Mary Gaven, that she came to him for advice as to the offer made to her, and that he suggested the sum of £25. Mr Dolphin's account of the negotiations before the sale was not seriously disputed, and I find it to be substantially correct.' How is it possible, then, to say that this old lady was without advice, or the best possible advice? The learned judge does not say that this old lady was not capable of transacting business, but that she was eccentric in habits and mentally abnormal. It would have been a dangerous contention for the plaintiff to have put forward—that the old lady was not capable of transacting business, seeing that he claims as executor under a subsequent will. The judge merely says that she was eccentric and not normal, but we have all had experience of eccentric old ladies—eccentric in habits and eccentric in dress, but as cute as possible in money matters, and quite well able to understand the value of money and transact business, yet not mentally normal. Mr Kelly's offer having been accepted, he went to Mr O'Connor, solicitor, Swinford, and instructed him to prepare a conveyance, and on the next day the old lady, accompanied by Mr Dolphin, called at Mr O'Connor's office, and Mr O'Connor—whose evidence the judge accepts—read out and explained the deed to her, and swears she understood it. The judge finds that she understood that she was getting £25, but he says the place had a sort of fancy value owing to the competition for it between the two merchants, Mr Kelly and Mr Campbell. But, apart from Mr Campbell's offer of £100 in court, its fancy value up to that time was something between £20 or £30, and there is no evidence that it was of any value except to these two gentlemen, and even for its adventitious value at that date neither went above £25. It is said that because Mr Campbell stated in court that he would have given £100, that there was something in Mr Kelly's mind about Mr Campbell's anxiety to get the place, which should have been communicated to this old lady, but the price of £100 was apparently never suggested until after her death. There is no evidence upon which the judge could reasonably find that this deed could be set aside. This old lady had all the protection necessary: her former employer, whom she trusted, advised her in the matter, and was present when the deed was completed. It was a fair and honest transaction, and although the age of the old lady threw the onus on Mr Kelly of showing that he took no advantage, that onus has been discharged by him. There is no ground whatever for any imputation either against him or Mr O'Connor, and the validity of the deed cannot be impeached. Accordingly, the question put to us by the learned judge must be answered in the negative.

(Ronan and O'Connor L.JJ. concurred.)

The leading case is **Grealish v Murphy [1946] IR 35**

Gavan Duffy J.:

The plaintiff sues (1) to have an indenture of settlement of October 1942, set aside, either (a) as improvident, or (b) for his own mental infirmity and incapacity to understand the deed, coupled with undue influence by the defendant; (2) to assert his sole title to a sum of £2,000 standing at the National Bank, Galway, in the joint names of plaintiff and defendant; (3) to recover two sums of £500 and £645, as money improperly obtained or retained by the defendant from the plaintiff; and (4) to have an account taken. The defendant justifies his action under each head.

Peter Grealish, the plaintiff, is by way of being a farmer; he is a bachelor in the sixties; he is a man of a generous turn, but obstinate; he can hardly read and he signs as a marksman; he is afflicted with a worse than Boeotian headpiece and a very poor memory; a long life has not taught him sense. At the opening of the year 1942 this poor old victim of his circumstances was living under rather dismal conditions; Peter, for as Peter he is known, had a couple of labouring men sleeping under his roof, but otherwise lived alone on a remote farm and ranch of some 180 acres at Carnmore in the Oranmore district of the County of Galway, neglected by his relatives and almost bereft of friends; he was loaded with possessions, far above his modest wants and far beyond his modest capacity for management; moneys exceeding £5,500 lay to his credit on deposit at a bank in Galway, though considerable portions of this fortune were destined to be dissipated in the course of the year 1942; he had some cattle and his land had for many years brought him into frequent conflict with certain of his smaller neighbours, who were in the habit of taking conacre from him; he felt, as I surmise, that he could not by himself hope to hold his own in any considerable purchases or sales of cattle; he also owned a little farm a few miles away from Carnmore; and he needed, and realised that he needed, a reliable factotum as manager and as protector.

Peter had tried hard, and failed, to solve his problem; he had sought to marry first a cousin of his, then a niece, and finally another niece, to one, Thomas Fox, who had promised to bring in a marriage portion, payable to the plaintiff, first of £400, then of £1,000 and lastly of £500, and to look after Peter and his affairs, in exchange for a settlement of the big farm, as from Peter's death, on Fox and his bride, and their maintenance on the farm during Peter's life: Fox had eventually refused the first two ladies; the third deed had been executed on 3 December 1941; but a few weeks later the third lady had positively said 'No.'

Peter was bitterly disappointed, but he was not defeated. His family had known a family of Murphys, who lived as far away as Headford, and he resolved to invite one of the sons to step into the breach. Accordingly Thomas Murphy, the defendant, whom Peter had never seen, presented himself at Carnmore on 26 January 1942; Peter liked his looks and at once came to business; he admits that he promised to give Murphy the farm after his own (Peter's) death, if Murphy would in the meantime work the land for him. In view of that admission, borne out by Peter's later instructions to his own solicitor, I need not determine precisely how much further Peter's promises may have gone, though Murphy is much more explicit; his evidence is that Peter explained that he was boycotted and that his land had been forcibly seized and that he wished to put an end to the conacre holdings on his land and to have a man to manage and work the farm and live with him; he says that Peter went on to promise that, if Murphy would come, Peter would leave him the farm, buy him a new lorry and also, if he wished, a new car, settle on Murphy any sum of money he required and let him marry any girl he liked; Murphy says that Peter wanted to go to a solicitor the very next day to 'sign me over the farm.'

Murphy's reply, he says, was that he must see his own solicitor, Mr McDonagh, at Tuam, and he saw him on 27 January, and discovered the Fox settlement of the previous month; he returned at once to Carnmore, when Peter assured him that he had already given instructions for a suit to set that deed aside; they agreed, Murphy continues, to call on Mr Concannon, Peter's solicitor, at Galway on the following day; they did so, according to Murphy, and during that visit he and Peter agreed, in the presence of the solicitor and his clerk, Costello, that pending the setting aside of the Fox settlement, Murphy should manage for Peter Grealish, take him into town to buy and sell generally and do any business that Peter might ask him to do. This agreement of 28 January 1942, is decisive upon the onus of proof for any transaction prior to the impugned indenture of October 1942. This agreement is not corroborated; Peter is incapable of affirming or disputing it; Concannon denies it; Costello, called as a witness by Murphy, was asked nothing about it, and his answer, were it available, would have carried little weight; but, as against Murphy, I must accept his own evidence as proving at least that on some day at the outset of his dealings with Peter he undertook in consideration of Peter's promises, to act for him in business matters generally, pending the action against Fox. And during the time that elapsed before October 1942, when that action was heard, Murphy must have discovered beyond doubt, if he did not know from the first day, that Peter needed decidedly more protection than the ordinary western farmer and cattle dealer.

[Counsel for the defendant] pressed on me vigorously the view that Peter is merely a simple-minded and not a feeble-minded old man, but that is not the impression made on me by his performance as a witness; I must go with the medical evidence to the extent of classifying him among the mentally deficient, though I should not myself assimilate him to a child of twelve. I cannot measure his deficiency in scientific terms and I need say no more than this, that, as I appraise him, the brain, while it must have developed with time, has never since childhood attained the normal powers of an adult; and he is liable to be erratic, especially outside the daily routine of his life at home. The trial threw occasional side-lights on Peter's faculties; for instance, he can read the clock, but cannot tell the time; Murphy virtually admitted that Peter was unable to count £2,000 in £50, £10 and £5 notes; and, having made to Murphy in October 1942, an astounding present of, as Murphy says, £700, Peter was unable, as I must necessarily infer from the pleadings, to give his advisers in this action any instructions whatever on the matter, which came to light only through a question in Murphy's cross-examination by [counsel for the plaintiff] at the trial; I gather, moreover, that Peter had completely lost all trace of a further large sum of money, which he drew from the bank at the same time.

Murphy, who comes of farming stock, had been a road worker and he was a haulier in a small way, with a car and a lorry of his own, when Peter's proposal burst upon him and a bright vista suddenly opened out before his eyes. True, he was being asked to give up his freedom, he had no idea what sort of principal Peter would prove to be and he could not tell what stings he would have to endure from waspish neighbours. But he was only thirty two years of age and the possible difficulties may well have loomed dim in the dazzle of the glittering reward proffered by his glowing benefactor; the golden prospect was that he would be a rich man after a few years of not too arduous labour and surely he could well bear any little passing troubles that the venture might entail. Murphy accepted Peter's proposal, but did nothing at this time to rush the old man; I do not think he called on him again until the following March. Then he began to see him, as he says himself, about twice a week until June, and I see no reason to believe that his attentions slackened during the summer; he used to take Peter for shopping or business purposes to Galway by car; he drove him at different dates as far as Dublin and Limerick and to several fairs; he says he bought cattle for him to the value of £480 at Gort Fair in May, and early in October sold cattle for him at Tuam Fair, taking £530 net, and immediately afterwards bought cattle for him at Westport Fair. He was kind to Peter and that solicitude did not go unrewarded; Peter gave Murphy £450 towards a motor lorry in May 1942, and (at about the same time, I think, or earlier) £250 for a Chrysler car. In June Peter actually placed a sum of £2,000 in the joint names of himself and Murphy at the National Bank, in Galway, though not necessarily out of munificence towards Murphy and primarily, I think, as a strategic diversion to defeat the apprehended machinations of a rapacious Estate Duty Office.

In June 1942, the court adjourned the Fox action, and Peter, blaming Mr Concannon and chafing at the delay, entrusted his case to another solicitor, Dr Comyn of Loughrea. On 10 October 1942, the Circuit Court in Galway annulled the Fox deed on Peter's evidence, Fox not appearing, and on 13 October Peter gave the instructions upon which Dr Comyn drew the settlement that is the chief bone of contention in this action. The deed was executed on 20 October, and bears date 24 October 1942, and Peter, theretofore full owner of the Carnmore land, was registered as limited owner by reference to this document. The stamp duty puts the net value of the farm at some £1,000. The deed, in pursuance of the January agreement, gave Murphy a position at Carnmore equivalent to, but really better than, that of an adopted son.

On 30 October 1942, Peter drew out £1,900, standing on deposit in his own name at the Bank of Ireland in Galway, thus closing the account, which was distinct from the still subsisting joint account for £2,000 with the National Bank. There is some evidence that Peter, when taking the money out, alleged that he was buying a farm. Murphy avowed in cross-examination that Peter had given him £700 of this money and had lodged £1,000 out of the £1,900 in the National Bank (presumably at Galway). I understand that, until this admission by Murphy as to his £700, the whole sum drawn had vanished, and, unless the money has been discovered during the long vacation, the sum of £1,000 still has to be found. Murphy may be mistaken as to the precise bank, but his evidence of a bank lodgment is specific, and the mystery cannot be brushed aside as if a mere bagatelle were involved. I am not to be understood as throwing blame on Murphy for the loss of the money; I do not know who is to blame. This extraordinary disappearance of the money of an irresponsible old man calls, in my view, for close and persistent investigation, with the aid, if necessary, of the Gárda Síochána; but that matter is outside the purview of this action on the pleadings and the evidence.

Murphy says that he did not go to live at Carnmore in pursuance of the settlement until early in December 1942, when he lodged, hard by Peter's own house, with a Mrs Fahy; a young Fahy lived with Peter and worked for him. Local hostility had declared itself against Murphy as early as October, but, after his arrival, a quite unforeseen and particularly unpleasant series of attacks came from one of Peter's sisters, a bedlam, living some three miles away, who would descend in wrath upon Carnmore at intervals, giving tongue to loud maledictions upon the grabber of her brother's land. Murphy, I think actually went in fear of his life from some of the local roughs, a number of whom had stoned his car, and he found the onslaughts of the termagant almost equally hard to endure.

Early in January 1943, I find (in a conflict of evidence) that Murphy, as Peter says, told Peter that he must have money or he would leave; I find that Peter offered him £500 and that Murphy refused this sum and went off to Galway; and that Peter at once sent him an urgent message with an offer, if he would come back. Murphy's evidence, for which there is some corroboration, is that the messenger brought him an offer of £500 and of all Peter's cattle, and that Peter also promised to keep his sister away; so he returned and accepted the offer. I find that Murphy did return and come to terms with Peter, but, as his witness, the messenger, says 'I suppose he really meant to stay anyway'; my reading of the position is that Murphy knew that Peter was afraid of being beaten or killed, if deprived of Murphy's protection, and knew that Peter was sure to succumb to the demand for money, to prevent his desertion by Murphy. Murphy now says that he had not decided to abandon the undertaking, but he could not live there nor work the farm 'on account of the trouble', he did not like the place 'inside or outside', he was under police protection (in fact the Gárdaí had not yet come) and he wanted to go home to see his own people and to consult his solicitor. He admits having gone away, but denies having demanded money before he left. Peter (whose evidence here I do not accept) says that Murphy got the £500 before leaving and he denies having sent a messenger with an offer to bring him back. The fact that Murphy got the money is not in dispute. But I do not know where Peter got the £500; he says that he drew it from the Bank of Ireland, Murphy having driven him to Galway for the purpose; Murphy, as I follow him, says that Peter drew the money from the National Bank and paid him on 15 January 1943. But neither bank account shows any such drawing and no witness has suggested that the justly timorous owner kept any large sum of money at home.

On the night of 12 January 1943, a day or two after Murphy's return, shots were fired into Mrs Fahy's house; the incident was described by the police as 'an attempted murder on the house of Fahy'; young Fahy was afraid to work for Peter or live with him any more, though the other labourer stayed; Peter's house and Fahy's were kept under police protection for eighteen months thereafter, as was also Murphy's person on dark nights, while he remained at Carnmore.

On 10 March, Murphy sold on the land thirty nine head of cattle (Peter's alleged present to him), realising £643, for his own account. The deal was not carried out as openly as the circumstances required. I see no need to determine whether Peter had given Murphy the cattle or not; Peter vehemently denies the gift; but I think the probabilities are that Peter had regretted and repudiated his excessive liberality in a crisis and that Murphy felt uneasy about the whole discreditable affair. On 3 May Murphy fell ill and went home; he and Peter parted on good terms. But Murphy's amazing statement that, when leaving, he was 'under the impression' (*sic*!) that Peter knew that the cattle were gone, throws a nasty light on the rape of the cattle. On 28 May Murphy returned; Peter was angry and at once taxed him with having sold Peter's cattle surreptitiously. By this time Peter had another man, a relative, living in the house. Early in June Peter consulted Mr Conway, his present solicitor, with a view to taking action against Murphy. By 22 June Peter and Murphy were not on speaking terms and on that night Murphy was locked out by Peter and went five miles away for a bed, under police protection. At the end of June, Murphy, feeling that he was in effect supplanted by the new arrival, left Carnmore.

That is the story in outline. But the difficulty of ascertaining the facts has been prodigious. I could not depend much on Peter's memory, nor on the accuracy of either contestant; the other local witnesses did not impress me; and several witnesses who might have been called did not appear.

Let me now examine the making of the settlement which the plaintiff seeks to set aside. We have Peter's promise to Murphy at the very outset of their connection; that was a promise, according to Murphy, to 'leave me the farm' and 'settle any sum of money I wanted on me', and Peter had wished to go to a solicitor at once to 'sign me over the farm'. Then, according to Murphy, 'he used to say every time I would meet him that he had decided to leave the place to me and that the marriage settlement would be set aside.' And there is ample evidence (whatever the terms actually were in which Peter expressed himself to Murphy) that Peter was fuming with impatience to rid himself of his commitments to Fox, obviously in order to be free to conclude his arrangements with Murphy. There is evidence that Costello, Mr Concannon's clerk, who claims to have been an old friend of Peter's and was called as a witness for Murphy, in March 1942, definitely ascertained that Mr Concannon would have nothing to do with any settlement of the land by Grealish upon Murphy, and I cannot doubt that Costello made this fact known to Murphy, if not to Peter, who changed his solicitor in June 1942, as I have said. Costello lost his place in the Concannon office early in July. Peter paid several visits to Dr Comyn during the summer, always accompanied, I think by Murphy and by Costello; Costello's presence on these occasions is unexplained, but Peter clearly trusted him and afterwards rewarded him liberally for his miscellaneous services. According to Dr Comyn's recollection, Costello occasionally made some remarks on these occasions, but Peter did the talking, while Murphy 'never uttered a word', a singularly modest attitude for the heir-presumptive during the long wait from June to October; if this persistent silence is an example of western caution, it suggests tactical caution carried rather too far.

On 13 October 1942, three days after the court had set aside the Fox deed, Peter, duly accompanied by Murphy and Costello, called on Dr Comyn. In the outer office Peter intimated to the solicitor that he intended to 'take in' a man and Dr Comyn understood the man to be Murphy, whereupon Dr Comyn took Peter by himself upstairs and wrote down his instructions; he had no conversation at all with Murphy. If Murphy is to be believed (and there are limits to my credulity), Peter (who may fairly be said to have been living for this day) did not tell Murphy when he came down, that he had actually given the instructions; but Murphy did admit in cross-examination that Peter had said he was going in (that is, to Dr Comyn) in order to transfer the land to Murphy.

The effect of the detailed instructions, as taken down, was that, being old, delicate and unable to work his land without loss, Peter wished to take Murphy, who was not a relative, into his house as factotum and general worker and, while keeping a life interest, to transfer the big farm after his death to Murphy, who was to be supported and to live at Carnmore in the meantime; Peter meant to deal with the other farm and with his stock and moneys later. The instructions were read to Peter, who approved of them, and upon them Dr Comyn instructed counsel, verbally, as I understand, to settle the deed.

On 20 October the engrossment was read to Peter, who executed the deed as a marksman. The solicitor was acting for Peter alone; he was not told that Murphy had a solicitor of his own; Murphy had no adviser at all and had not been consulted in any way during the preparation of the settlement. Dr Comyn himself 'knew about the boycotting thoroughly well'; 'boycott' was counsel's term and it is right to say that the evidence, so far as it goes, suggests that the facts do not warrant so strong an expression to describe Peter's annoyances from his neighbours up to this time. Dr Comyn says that he explained Murphy's covenants to him and that Murphy also then executed the deed. Finally he 'told Peter, in the presence of Murphy, that, if Murphy did not comply with the covenants, he, Peter, knew where to find me.' He did not give Murphy any copy or duplicate of the deed. It is not suggested that Murphy made any claim to a money settlement.

The settlement purports to make Peter Grealish, as beneficial owner, assign the farm absolutely as from Peter's death to Thomas Murphy, his heirs and assigns, subject to a life interest in Peter; the land is expressly charged with a right for Murphy to reside in Peter's house and to be supported and maintained out of the land during Peter's life; Murphy for his part covenants with Peter, during Peter's life, without reward to reside in the house and work and manage the land and sow and harvest the crops and attend to and take proper care of all farm stock and implements and the buying and selling of stock and generally to perform all the farm work and the duties of a labourer as required by Peter and (a very important covenant) duly and properly to account for all moneys expended or received by him on behalf of Peter; and Murphy covenants to pay Peter £1 a week for every week in which he fails to reside with Peter and to indemnify Peter for any loss and expense incurred on the maintenance or wages of any person employed by Peter to perform any work that Murphy may fail to do.

Thus Peter executed an improvident settlement, surrendering irrevocably his own absolute title for a life interest in consideration of personal covenants, backed by no adequate sanction; the farm itself was hypothecated to secure the newcomer, beside whom Peter was a Croesus; and Peter was to be left for the remainder of his life very much at the mercy of a rather impecunious young man, who had no ties of blood and was still unproved as a friend. I think effective safeguards for Peter could have been devised, if there was to be a settlement, or alternatively Peter might have contracted to settle the property on Murphy by will, upon the lines suggested by *Coverdale v Eastwood*;[1] whatever plan was adopted, I think that suitable conditions could and should have been determined in negotiation between the solicitors for the parties, each of whom ought to have been separately represented. But these reflections are otiose, if the conclusive answer to Peter's present claim is that he was separately advised by an independent solicitor.

That contention deserves careful examination and I have examined it with great care. I am satisfied that Peter received from an experienced solicitor advice that was absolutely independent and I am satisfied that the draft deed was settled by very able counsel, upon instructions reflecting, of course, the state of mind and knowledge of the solicitor. Nevertheless, the question of Peter's actual understanding of the solemn document that he executed on 20 October 1942, is a question of first importance. Dr Comyn, who avows that he looked upon the settlement as a transaction similar to the three attempts which, as Peter told him, had broken down, says that he was absolutely satisfied that Peter understood the instructions he gave for the deed. I have no doubt that Peter did know that the deed would secure the land to Murphy at Peter's death and that he knew generally the undertakings that Murphy was giving in return; Peter showed his own understanding of the young man's obligations, when he formulated his grievance in his own words: 'He (Murphy) did not do anything about the agreement; he failed. . . . He was bound to look after me and buy and sell and give up the money—what he did not do.' But the trouble is that the solicitor, whose advice was essential to Peter, did not advise *en connaissance de cause* and that Peter's actual knowledge of what he was doing fell very short of the knowledge that the settlor ought to have had. That is the result in my mind of candid evidence from Dr Comyn himself and of inferences therefrom. Consequently the principle of *Harrison v Guest*[2] and *Coomber v Coomber*;[3] that a competent assignor, who knows what he is doing, must be held to his deed, does not apply here.

The evidence proves that the solicitor did not know all the material facts, that he did not give Peter a complete explanation of the nature and effect of the deed, and that the duty of illuminating Peter's benighted mind was more imperative and more formidable, if the task was possible, than the solicitor supposed.

First. Dr Comyn did not get the facts. He did not ascertain the total of Peter's property, nor the proportion between that total and the value of the farm at Carnmore; yet that was relevant and material information for an adviser. Still more important to be known was the fact that Peter had already placed £2,000 on deposit in the joint names of himself and Murphy, with Murphy's ready acquiescence, under the illusion, known to Murphy, that this device would ward off the imaginary terrors of Dublin Castle. Murphy, knowing Peter for what he was, could not assume that Peter had mentioned the episode, still less that he had given an accurate account of it; Murphy ought to have told the solicitor all about it, but he persisted in his curious policy of silence. Perhaps Murphy did not know positively how silly Peter's ruse was as a measure of defence, but he is intelligent enough, in my estimate of him, to have felt the transaction to be one of questionable virtue and of very dubious value, and, both for this reason and because he stood to gain a large sum of money from his pitiable patron, he ought to have spoken out at this juncture. Here was cogent evidence, had the solicitor and counsel known it, that Peter was and would be incapable of taking care of his own interests and that Peter and Murphy combined were and would be unequal to the burden of taking care of his property. Instead of favouring the projected settlement, as he did, Dr Comyn must have gone into the whole affair very much more warily, had he known. He did not know, because, by agreement or coincidence, each of the two men vitally concerned said nothing.

Secondly. Peter was not told and did not realise how gravely he was committing himself and jeopardising his own interest; he probably understood neither the immediate pledging of his favour to Murphy nor the effect of that charge; certainly the difference between the deed and a will was not explained to him, nor the fact that the settlement was to be irrevocable and his alienation irretrievable, no matter how badly Murphy might behave, no matter what untoward development might supervene; and he was certainly not a man to apprehend the risks, at least without the clearest and most insistent exposition of them. What precautions were taken in the deed against the vicissitudes of life? Murphy might have mismanaged the farm hopelessly, for all the solicitor could tell; or, for all he could tell, Murphy might have taken to drink or gone to the devil or married a shrew who would make Peter's life a torture; he might have become a bankrupt; he might have been sent to hospital for years, or been committed for some time to an asylum; he might even have been sentenced to imprisonment. Unlikely events, very unlikely? Perhaps, but why do I insure my house against fire, and how was the solicitor, a stranger to Murphy, to gauge the probabilities of an ensuing incapacity or incompetence? An act of God is always unlikely (before it happens) and the devil's action may often seem unlikely too. And if some such calamity had smitten Peter, the law might or might not have given him some costly redress. It was unlikely, perhaps very unlikely, that the young man would predecease the old; but how deplorable would Peter's position have been, if Murphy had died after a few months' work under the deed and perhaps twenty years before Peter himself! However, Peter's advisers had no more dark forebodings than their client. Clearly there were some important aspects of the deed far outside poor Peter's ken, when he scratched his rude mark upon the paper.

Thirdly. The solicitor quite erroneously considered and treated Peter as a normal member of the farming community; in fact I think he treated him as a man of high intelligence. Taking his client to be a competent judge of his own man, the solicitor, who just knew Murphy to be a farmer's son and no relative and Peter's dumb attendant, made no inquiries at all as to Murphy's antecedents, character, capacity or financial position; he assumed both the fitness of Murphy and the value of his covenants; he did not suspect how easily the young man might become master of the situation, nor how much he would be tempted to abuse his trust; and the deed reflects that kindly confidence; whether Dr Comyn seriously expected Murphy to keep accounts, I do not know. No need was felt to appoint trustees; perhaps they would have been hard to find, but, had the solicitor realised the settlor's weakness, he would have seen that Peter required and must have the protection for which trusts were invented. Unless there be a legal presumption of undue influence against Murphy, making other questions quite subordinate, I regard it as a matter of high importance that Peter's advisers in this particular transaction should have been equipped to advise him with a just appreciation of his mental debility and his special need of protection. They were not so equipped and Peter did not get the circumspect advice and protection so necessary to him.

Now, how is Murphy affected by any criticism reflecting upon the advice under which Peter acted? I have shown that Murphy's own conduct in the matter was not beyond reproach, but any impartial person will see that it is quite impossible to say that the deed was procured through Murphy's undue influence, even if he did his part during nearly nine months, as he naturally would, to keep the old man's ardour alive. Nor is this the familiar case in which the court, from the relation of the parties, must presume undue influence until disproved positively by the recipient of the bounty; Murphy had constituted himself Peter's interim confidential agent in January 1942, and had thus placed himself in a very delicate position, an exceptionally delicate position in view of Peter's mentality; but the undoubted fact is that some such transaction as that eventuating in the actual settlement had been expressly envisaged by the parties from the outset, before Murphy can have acquired any influence whatsoever; therefore I cannot fairly impute to him Peter's decision to put the business on a legal basis as soon as the way was made clear by the final elimination of the Fox interest, the only obstacle. And Murphy in no way interfered with the drafting of the deed in the particular form which it took.

Peter had intended all through to leave the property to Murphy and to bind himself to that effect, in return for the precious services to be rendered by the vigorous young man to the rather helpless old one. As from January 1942, Murphy had only to be kind to Peter, as he was, and to retain his goodwill, as he certainly did, in order to secure his reward from that eager benefactor.

Besides, the plan was not originated by Murphy, but by Peter, and by Peter alone. Murphy on his side had faced appreciable risks in accepting Peter's advances; and any picture of him as an adventurer, inveigling his witless victim into a trap in the October settlement, would be a caricature. Much as I blame Murphy for his reticence (partly perhaps through ignorance) as to the existence of his own solicitor and for his want of candour in suppressing the eccentric and disquieting £2,000 deposit in the joint names, I could not in common sense treat these faults as any evidence of undue influence in relation to the settlement on the facts; and, if Murphy throws doubt on the veracity of his own evidence concerning Peter's alleged original offer to settle money on him, by his failure to mention that important promise to Dr Comyn and his failure to call upon the solicitor to make good that promise in the deed, here again my criticism of Murphy as a witness is foreign to the issue of undue influence in fact and remote from any evidence that would raise a legal presumption of undue influence against Murphy, so far as the settlement is concerned.

The result is that the plaintiff's attempt to set aside the deed on the ground of undue influence, whether actual or presumptive, by Murphy cannot succeed, and, if the deed had to stand or fall upon that issue, there would be nothing more to say. But the position in law as I see it, upon the pleadings, is not so simple as that; there is another crucial matter to be determined.

Peter cannot avoid the deed for undue influence; but his claim is further based on the improvidence of the transaction and also he directly alleges (though in connection with the charge of undue influence) his own mental incapacity; I think I can reasonably read these averments together without calling for an amendment of his pleadings.

The issue thus raised brings into play Lord Hatherley's cardinal principle (from which the exceptions are rare) that equity comes to the rescue whenever the parties to a contract have not met upon equal terms, see Lord Hatherley's judgment (dissenting on facts) in *O'Rourke v Bolingbroke*;[4] the corollary is that the court must inquire whether a grantor, shown to be unequal to protecting himself, has had the protection which was his due by reason of his infirmity, and the infirmity may take various forms. The deed here was in law a transaction for value: *Colreavy v Colreavy*;[5] however tenuous the value may have proved to be in fact, and, of course, a court must be very much slower to undo a transaction for value; but the fundamental principle to justify radical interference by the court is the identical principle, whether value be shown or not, and the recorded examples run from gifts and voluntary settlements (including an abortive marriage settlement) to assignments for a money consideration. The principle has been applied to improvident grants, whether the particular disadvantage entailing the need for protection to the grantor were merely low station and surprise (though the grantor's rights were fully explained): *Evans v Llewellin*,[6] or youth and inexperience: *Prideaux v Londsdale*;[7] *Everitt v Everitt*,[8] or age and weak intellect, short of total incapacity, with no fiduciary relation and no 'arts of inducement' to condemn the grantee: *Longmate v Ledger*;[9] *Anderson v Elsworth*.[10] Even the exuberant or ill-considered dispositions of feckless middle-aged women have had to yield to the same principle: *Phillipson v Kerry*;[11] *Wollaston v Tribe*.[12]

The principle prevailed, when the deed was 'the most honest thing in the world' so far as the settlor and her solicitor were concerned: *Everitt v Everitt*, and though the evidence of the solicitor acting for the grantor was fully accepted: *Phillipson v Kerry*, and again where the deed had been prepared by the grantor's own solicitor, a man of honour, but the grantor, while fully understanding the benefit to accrue to the grantee, had not fully understood the effect of her deed as it affected her own interests: *Anderson v Elsworth*; in several other instances the inadequacy of the explanations given to the grantor has been a conspicuous, indeed a decisive, factor in the court's action against an improvident deed, the court either assuming: *Prideaux v Lonsdale*, or having direct evidence: *Phillipson v Kerry*; *Wollaston v Tribe*, to prove a serious lack of understanding. The least the court can demand is that an infirm grantor shall have known what he was doing. In the much more frequent, but analogous, instances of deeds attacked for undue influence the Judicial Committee has insisted that the donor must have had a complete explanation of the nature and effect of the transaction, from an adviser who himself knew all the relevant circumstances: *Inche Noriah v Shaik Allie Bin Omar*,[13] even where the adviser was selected by the donor: *Williams v Williams*,[14] and the same imperative requirement was stressed in a transaction for value by Isaacs J. upon a deed closely resembling the deed in this action in some aspects, but obtained by undue influence: *Watkins v Combes*.[15]

In my judgment, without any regard to any question of undue influence, upon Lord Hatherley's principle and the concurrent authorities the plaintiff by reason of his own weakness of mind, coupled with the deficiencies in the legal advice under which he acted and his unawareness, is entitled to have the improvident indenture of settlement, dated 24 October 1942, set aside and the Register of Freeholders rectified.

I may add that the balancing of equities is not complicated here by any plea of estoppel, nor have I on the evidence any reason to suppose that the defendant has suffered any prejudice worth mentioning through executing the settlement.

1. 15 Eq. 121.
2. 6 De G. M. & G. 424; 8 HLC 481.
3. [1911] 1 Ch. 723.
4. 2 AC 814, at p. 823.
5. [1940] IR 71.
6. 1 Cox, Eq Cas 333.
7. 1 de G. J. & S. 433.
8. 10 Eq. 405.
9. 2 Giff. 157.
10. 3 Giff. 154.
11. 32 Beav. 628.
12. 9 Eq. 44.
13. [1929] AC 127, 135.
14. [1937] 4 All ER 34, 83.
15. 30 CLR 180, 196–7.

Note

See also *Gregg v Kidd* (p. 670 above) where the same plea was raised.

Lydon v Coyne (1946) 12 Ir Jur Rep 64

O'Byrne J.:

This is an action to set aside a deed dated 25 January 1943, and made between Martin Lydon of the one part and Martin Coyne of the other part. Martin Lydon, the transferor, died within a few months, namely, on 10 April 1943, and the present proceedings have been brought by his widow, Bridget Lydon, who sues personally and as his personal representative.

Martin Lydon owned a very small farm of land in the neighbourhood of Tourmakeady. Early on the morning of 25 January 1943, Martin Coyne came to the offices of Messrs Michael Moran & Co., in Castlebar, and asked Mr Michael Moran to come out to Tourmakeady. Mr Moran arrived at Tourmakeady between 11 and 12 o'clock that morning. He had been told beforehand that the old man was making over his land; but when he got to the house it appeared that the matter was not so simple, and a very long discussion took place between the parties. I can appreciate the very great difficulty in which Mr Moran was placed, wishing to draw up the deed and finding that the parties had not come to any firm agreement. But solicitors must often protect parties against themselves.

The deed is technically not a voluntary deed by reason of two provisions therein. Firstly, there is the covenant to support the old couple, which is in the following terms: 'That he will support, clothe and maintain the said assignor and his said wife Bridget Lydon during their lives out of the rents and profits of the said lands.' It is to be noted that Bridget Lydon, who takes a benefit under the deed, is not a party to it. Secondly, there is a covenant by the assignee for payment of £100 in the following terms: 'The assignee hereby covenants with the assignor for the payment of the sum of £100 to the assignor by instalments on demand in writing by the assignor such instalments not to exceed the sum of £10 in any year.' That covenant, while technically sufficient, is in all the circumstances of this case quite illusory. I do not deal with the deed as a voluntary deed, but as one of a highly improvident character. In one respect it is quite unique; the *habendum* is worded as follows: 'To hold the same unto the assignee to the use of the assignor for his life and should Bridget Lydon wife of the assignor survive the assignor then and in such event to the use of said Bridget Lydon for her life and from and after the death of the assignor or the said Bridget Lydon or the death of the survivor of them then unto and to the use of the assignee his heirs executors administrators and assigns for all the estate right title term and interest of the assignor therein.'

It is clear to me that Lydon never intended parting with the dominion over his property during his lifetime, for he kept insisting that his name should be in the rent receipt, showing in this way his intention that he should remain the owner while he lived. The limitation in the *habendum* purports to be controlled and governed by a subsequent covenant by the assignee in the following terms: 'And the assignee hereby covenants with the assignor that he will reside in the dwelling house on the said lands and that he will manage and work the said lands in a good and husbandlike manner during the lifetime of the assignor and his said wife Bridget Lydon or the survivor of them . . . and the assignor hereby covenants with the assignee that he will allow the assignee to manage and to work the said lands during the lifetime of the assignor and during the lifetime of the said Bridget Lydon and the survivor of them and to retain the rents and profits of the said lands for his own use and benefit.' If (as I think is the fact) it was intended to reserve a life estate to the assignor, the terms of the deed with reference to the application of the rents and profits during the lifetime of the assignor are extremely peculiar. Apart from the peculiarity of form, it throws some light upon the value of the covenant to support, for this is enforceable only out of the rents and profits.

There is one question—the main question to which I must address myself—and it is whether the assignor understood the transaction into which he was entering. If this were a voluntary deed there would be an absolute onus upon the assignee to show that the transaction was the free and voluntary act of the assignor and that he understood the transaction. Owing to the circumstances of this case, the onus here is not so great. It seems to me that Mr Moran, though undoubtedly doing his best for all parties, must be looked upon as Coyne's solicitor. He had acted for him before; Coyne brought him out and paid his fees for drawing the deed. But, approaching the transaction in that way and having regard to the improvidence of the transaction and the difficulty of interpreting some of the clauses in the deed, can I be satisfied that the settlor understood the transaction? I am quite satisfied he did not understand it. I do not understand it myself nor can I see how effect can be given to some of its provisions. That being so, and having regard to the fact that the deed contained no power of revocation and that no independent advice was given, this assignment cannot be allowed to stand.

I see the difficulty of inserting a power of revocation in the circumstances of this case since it would probably have resulted in the transaction falling through, but, in my opinion, that would have been the lesser of two evils. I see the difficulty of getting independent advice having regard to the remoteness of the place where the settlor lived and the cost of getting a second solicitor out. I realise that Mr Moran did the best he could, but, making full allowance for these facts, I am of opinion that the deed cannot be allowed to stand and, accordingly, I shall declare that the defendant is a trustee of the lands for the plaintiff as personal representative of the settlor. I shall order a reconveyance of the lands and I shall direct the defendant to pay the plaintiff's costs.

SECTION THREE—UNCONSCIONABLE BARGAINS IN COMMERCIAL CONTRACTS

INTRODUCTION

One celebrated attempt to compel the English courts to recognise the general application of inequality of bargaining power as a general invalidating factor was made by Denning M.R., in the Court of Appeal in *Lloyds Bank v Bundy* [1974] 3 All ER 757. While the *ratio decidendi* of the case is a narrow one, turning upon the peculiar circumstances in which the bank was placed by its customer in this particular instance, Denning M.R. examined a diverse range of cases (e.g. *Fry v Lane*, *D. & C. Builders v Rees*, *Maskell v Horner*) and sought to extract the following general principle:

Gathering all together, I would suggest that through all these instances there runs a single thread. They rest on 'inequality of bargaining power'. By virtue of it, the English law gives relief to one who, without independent advice, enters into a contract on terms which are very unfair or transfers property for a consideration which is grossly inadequate, when his bargaining power is grievously impaired by reason of his own needs or desires, or by his own ignorance or infirmity, coupled with undue influences or pressures brought to bear on him by or for the benefit of the other. When I use the word 'undue' I do not mean to suggest that the principle depends on proof of any wrongdoing. The one who stipulates for an unfair advantage may be moved solely by his own self-interest, unconscious of the distress he is bringing to the other. I have also avoided any reference to the will of the one being 'dominated' or 'overcome' by the other. One who is in extreme need may knowingly consent to a most improvident bargain, solely to relieve the straits in which he finds himself. Again, I do not mean to suggest that every transaction is saved by independent advice. But the absence of it may be fatal.

Note

The breadth of this principle is such that it has not found favour with other members of the English judiciary, particularly the House of Lords: see Lord Scarman in *National Westminster Bank v Morgan* [1985] 1 All ER 821 at 829–30. Nor has it been supported in Northern Ireland, *McCrystal v O'Kane* [1986] NI 123.

The case has been more enthusiastically received in Canada and Australia. Indeed, these courts have utilised this general principle in a great number of cases. Three examples of the application of equitable principles in commercial cases are taken from non-English case-law.

A. Bank Guarantees

Commercial Bank of Australia *v* Amadio (1983) 151 CLR 447

Two elderly people of Italian origin who had emigrated to Australia gave a guarantee by way of mortgage to secure their son's business debts. The mortgage was not explained to them—their grasp of English was poor—and the bank was aware that they had been misinformed about the document. Gibbs C.J., Mason, Wilson and Deane JJ., set the transaction aside, the latter three judges on the grounds of unconscionability.

Mason J.:

I agree with Deane J.'s comprehensive statement of the facts and with his conclusion that the respondents are entitled to relief on the ground that the bank was guilty of unconscionable conduct in procuring the execution of the mortgage guarantee by the respondents.

Historically, courts have exercised jurisdiction to set aside contracts and other dealings on a variety of equitable grounds. They include fraud, misrepresentation, breach of fiduciary duty, undue influence and unconscionable conduct. In one sense they all constitute species of unconscionable conduct on the part of a party who stands to receive a benefit under a transaction which, in the eye of equity, cannot be enforced because to do so would be inconsistent with equity and good conscience. But relief on the ground of 'unconscionable conduct' is usually taken to refer to the class of case in which a party makes unconscientious use of his superior position or bargaining power to the detriment of a party who suffers from some special disability or is placed in some special situation of disadvantage, e.g. a catching bargain with an expectant heir or an unfair contract made by taking advantage of a person who is seriously affected by intoxicating drink. Although unconscionable conduct in this narrow sense bears some resemblance to the doctrine of undue influence, there is a difference between the two. In the latter the will of the innocent party is not independent and voluntary because it is overborne. In the former the will of the innocent party, even if independent and voluntary, is the result of the disadvantageous position in which he is placed and of the other party unconscientiously taking advantage of that position.

There is no reason for thinking that the two remedies are mutually exclusive in the sense that only one of them is available in a particular situation of the exclusion of the other. Relief on the ground of unconscionable conduct will be granted when unconscientious advantage is taken of an innocent party whose will is overborne so that it is not independent and voluntary, just as it will be granted when such advantage is taken of an innocent party who, though not deprived of an independent and voluntary will, is unable to make a worthwhile judgment as to what is in his best interest.

It goes almost without saying that it is impossible to describe definitively all the situations in which relief will be granted on the ground of unconscionable conduct. As Fullagar J. said in *Blomley v Ryan*:[1]

> The circumstances adversely affecting a party, which may induce a court of equity either to refuse its aid or to set a transaction aside, are of great variety and can hardly be satisfactorily classified. Among them are poverty or need of any kind, sickness, age, sex, infirmity of body or mind, drunkenness, illiteracy or lack of education, lack of assistance or explanation where assistance or explanation is necessary. The common characteristic seems to be that they have the effect of placing one party at a serious disadvantage *vis-à-vis* the other.

Likewise Kitto J.[2] spoke of it as 'a well known head of equity' which ' . . . applies whenever one party to a transaction is at a special disadvantage in dealing with the other party because illness, ignorance, inexperience, impaired faculties, financial need or other circumstances affect his ability to conserve his own interests, and the other party unconscientiously takes advantage of the opportunity thus placed in his hands.'

It is not to be thought that relief will be granted only in the particular situations mentioned by their Honours. It is made plain enough, especially by Fullagar J., that the situations mentioned are no more than particular exemplifications of an underlying general principle which may be invoked whenever one party by reason of some condition of circumstance is placed at a special disadvantage *vis-à-vis* another and unfair or unconscientious advantage is then taken of the opportunity thereby created. I qualify the word 'disadvantage' by the adjective 'special' in order to disavow any suggestion that the principle applies whenever there is some difference in the bargaining power of the parties and in order to emphasise that the disabling condition or circumstance is one which seriously affects the ability of the innocent party to make a judgment as to his own best interests, when the other party knows or ought to know of the existence of that condition or circumstance and of its effect on the innocent party.

Because times have changed new situations have arisen in which it may be appropriate to invoke the underlying principle. Take, for example, entry into a standard form of contract dictated by a party whose bargaining power is greatly superior, a relationship which was discussed by Lord Reid and Lord Diplock in A. *Schroeder Music Publishing Co. Ltd v Macaulay*.[3] See also *Clifford Davis Management Ltd v W.E.A Records Ltd*.[4] In situations of this kind it is necessary for the plaintiff who seeks relief to establish unconscionable conduct, namely that unconscientious advantage has been taken of his disabling condition or circumstances.

Of course the relationship between the present parties and the transaction into which they entered were by no means novel, viewed as a situation to which the general principle can apply. That the principle might justify the setting aside of a guarantee is established by decisions such as *Owen and Gutch v Homan*[5] and *Bank of Victoria Ltd v Mueller*.[6]

To say this involves no contradiction of the well entrenched proposition that a guarantee is not a contract *uberrimae fidei*, that is, a contract which of itself calls for full disclosure. However, it is accepted that the principal creditor is under a duty:

> . . . to disclose to the intending surety anything which has taken place between the bank and the principal debtor 'which was not naturally to be expected', or as it was put by Pollock M.R., in *Lloyds Bank Ltd. v Harrison*[7] cited in *Paget's Law of Banking*, (7th ed., 1966), 583 'the necessity for disclosure only goes to the extent of requiring it where there are some unusual features in the particular case relating to the particular account which is to be guaranteed.
> (*Goodwin v National Bank of Australasia Ltd*,[8] per Barwick C.J.).

It has been said that this duty to disclose does not require a bank to give information as to matters affecting the credit of the debtor or of any circumstances connected with the transaction in which he is about to engage which will render his position more hazardous (*Wythes v Labouchere*,[9] per Lord Chelmsford L.C.). No surety is entitled to assume that the debtor has not been overdrawing, the proper presumption being in most instances that he has been doing so and wishes to do so again (*London General Omnibus Co. Ltd v Holloway*[10]).

But the fact that a bank's duty to make disclosure to its intending surety, arising from the mere relationship between principal creditor and surety, is so limited has no bearing on the availability of equitable relief on the ground of unconscionable conduct. A bank, though not guilty of any breach of its limited duty to make disclosure to the intending surety, may nonetheless be considered to have engaged in unconscionable conduct in procuring the surety's entry into the contract of guarantee.

It is to be hoped that the respondents' amended statement of claim does not find its way into the precedent books. It leaves much to be desired. It alleges unconscionable conduct and alternatively undue influence on the part of the bank. It does not, as it might have done, allege undue influence on the part of the respondents' son Vincenzo, with notice on the part of the bank. The findings, and indeed the evidence, contradict or fail to support the alleged case of undue influence on the part of the bank. The critical issue then is whether, in accordance with the principle already explained, the respondents are entitled to relief on the ground of unconscionable conduct.

There are a number of factors which go to establish that there was a gross inequality of bargaining power between the bank and the respondents, so much so that the respondents stood in a position of special disadvantage *vis-à-vis* the bank in relation to the proposed mortgage guarantee. By way of contrast to the bank, the respondents' ability to judge whether entry into the transaction was in their own best interests, having due regard to their desire to assist their son, was sadly lacking. The situation of special disadvantage in which the respondents were placed was the outcome of their reliance on and their confidence in their son who, in order to serve his own interests, urged them to provide the mortgage guarantee which the bank required as a condition of increasing the approved overdraft limit of his company, V. Amadio Builders Pty. Ltd ('the company'), from $80,000 to $270,000 and misled them as to the financial position of the company. Their reliance on their son was due in no small degree to their infirmities—they were Italians of advanced years, aged seventy six and seventy one respectively, having a limited command of written English and no experience of business in the field or at the level in which their son and the company engaged. They believed that the company's business was a flourishing and prosperous enterprise, though temporarily in need of funds. In reality, as the bank well knew, the company was in a perilous financial condition.

In the weeks immediately preceding the execution of the mortgage guarantee the company was unable to pay its debts as they fell due. In this situation the bank had selectively paid cheques drawn by the company in favour of suppliers in order to ensure continuity in the supply of building materials, the company being a building contractor. In this period the bank had regularly and continuously dishonoured other cheques, the payment of which was not essential to the maintenance of the supply of building materials. In pursuing this course and in agreeing to an increase in the company's overdraft limit, the bank was substantially influenced by a special consideration. The company was a major customer of the bank, indeed the largest customer at the Glynde branch of the bank, and the company's continuation in business was advantageous to General Credits Ltd, a finance company and subsidiary of the bank. In fact the company built houses for a joint venture comprising General Credits Ltd and another company of Vincenzo's at cost plus ten per cent, this figure being designed to cover building costs and administration charges. It was not intended to yield a profit to the company. General Credits Ltd's share of the joint venture profits was sixty per cent. In addition it provided the bulk of the finance required for the joint venture's operations. The respondents, needless to say, were quite unaware of these circumstances.

The effect of the respondents' execution of the mortgage guarantee was disastrous for them though advantageous to the bank. The bank agreed to increase Vincenzo's overdraft limit in the light of his statement that the property comprising four shops which was the subject of the mortgage guarantee was valued in the vicinity of $200,000.
. . .

No doubt the respondents' age and lack of business experience played a part in their reliance on their son's judgment and in their failure to make any inquiries as to the financial position of the company and their failure to seek advice as to the probable or possible consequences of the transaction into which they entered. Their lack of command of English, especially written English, apart from contributing to their reliance on their son, had an additional importance. Vincenzo had informed them that the bank would present for signature a guarantee and very probably a security of some sort, though the precise nature of that security, i.e. mortgage or charge, was not specified. He had incorrectly said that the liability would be limited to a period of six months and to an amount of $50,000. Mr Virgo, the bank manager, in the conversation which took place immediately before execution, informed them that their liability under the instrument was unlimited in time, the question having been raised by Mr Amadio senior. Mr Virgo said nothing on the topic of unlimited liability because the respondents did not mention it.

The primary judge found that if Vincenzo 'had disabused his parents' minds of their confidence in him, his parents would not have helped him.' The correctness of this finding has not been challenged. Nor could it be for the simple reason that any rational person knowing the circumstances of the company at the time would not have executed the instrument which they signed.

In deciding whether the bank took unconscientious advantage of the position of disadvantage in which the respondents were placed, we must ask, first, what knowledge did the bank have of the respondents' situation?

Mr Virgo was aware that the respondents were Italians, that they were of advanced years and that they did not have a good command of English. He knew that Vincenzo had procured their agreement to sign the mortgage guarantee. He had no reason to think that they had received advice and guidance from anyone but their son. In cross-examination he conceded that he believed that Vincenzo had acted in the 'role of adviser/explainer' in relation to the transaction and referred to him as acting 'in his capacity as dominant member of the family'. Mr Virgo also knew that, in the light of the then financial condition of the company, it was vital to Vincenzo to secure his parents' signature to the mortgage guarantee so that the company could continue in business. It must have been obvious to Mr Virgo, as to anyone else having knowledge of the facts, that the transaction was improvident from the viewpoint of the respondents. In these circumstances it is inconceivable that the possibility did not occur to Mr Virgo that the respondents' entry into the transaction was due to their inability to make a judgment as to what was in their best interests, owing to their reliance on their son, whose interests would inevitably incline him to urge them to sign the instrument put forward by the bank.

Indeed, the inquiry by Mr Amadio senior as to the duration of the arrangement should have alerted Mr Virgo to the likelihood that Vincenzo had not adequately or accurately explained the intended transaction to them, let alone the possible or probable consequences which attended it.

Whether it be correct or incorrect to attribute to Mr Virgo knowledge of this possibility, the facts as known to him were such as to raise in the mind of any reasonable person a very real question as to the respondents' ability to make a judgment as to what was in their own best interests. In *Owen and Gutch v Homan*, Lord Cranworth L.C. said: '. . . it may safely be stated that if the dealings are such as fairly to lead a reasonable man to believe that fraud must have been used in order to obtain [the concurrence of the survey], he is bound to make inquiry, and cannot shelter himself under the plea that he was not called on to ask, and did not ask, any questions on the subject. In some cases wilful ignorance is not to be distinguished in its equitable consequences from knowledge.' The principle there stated applies with equal force to

Section 3: Unconscionable Bargains in Commerical Contracts

this case. The concept of fraud in equity is not limited to common law deceit; it extends to conduct of the kind engaged in by the respondents' son when he took advantage of the confidence and reliance reposed in him to induce his parents to enter into a transaction in order to serve his ends, thereby depriving them of the ability to make a judgment as to what is in their interests.

As we have seen, if A having actual knowledge that B occupies a situation of special disadvantage in relation to an intended transaction, so that B cannot make a judgment as to what is in his own interests, takes unfair advantage of his (A's) superior bargaining power or position by entering into that transaction, his conduct in so doing is unconscionable. And if, instead of having actual knowledge of that situation, A is aware of the possibility that that situation may exist or is aware of facts that would raise that possibility in the mind of any reasonable person, the result will be the same.

The knowledge of Mr Virgo was the knowledge of the bank.

1. (1956) 99 CLR 362, at p. 405.
2. (1956) 99 CLR, at p. 415.
3. [1974] 1 WLR 1308, at pp 1314–5, 1316; [1974] 3 All ER 616, at pp 622–3, 624.
4. [1975] 1 WLR 61, at pp 64–5; [1975] 1 All ER 237, at p. 240.
5. (1853) 14 HLC 997, at pp 1034–5 [10 ER 752, at p. 767].
6. [1925] VLR 642, at p. 649.
7. (1925) Unrep.
8. (1968) 117 CLR 173, at p. 175.
9. (1859) 3 De G. & J. 593, at p. 609.
10. [1912] 2 KB 72, at pp 83–4, 87. [44 ER 1397, at p. 1404].

Minister for Industrial Affairs *v* Civil Tech (1998) 70 SASR 394

This case involved a dispute relating to payments sought by an engineering contractor, Civil Tech, for additional works undertaken on behalf of the Minister, these additional works being necessary due to man-made obstacles that had to be removed from the sea bed before the main Construction work could commence.

The parties negotiated a deed of release under the terms of which Civil Tech were paid $343,000 (Australian). Threats to discontinue all payments have been made if the release was not signed and at the time of signature, on 14 February 1992, Civil Tech were in financial difficulties. An arbitrator found the deed of release was not binding and the Minister appealed to the Full Court of South Australia. The decision of the Full Court was given by Bleby J.

Unconscionability
The arbitrator found, in essence, that the respondence had been induced by the unconscionable conduct of the appellant to enter into the release dated 14 February 1992. In short, that unconscionable conduct consisted of a retraction from the agreement made on 12 April 1991 on the faith of which the respondent had proceeded to clear the obstructions, and the threats to terminate the contract unless the release was given, at a time when, as the appellant well knew, the respondent was financially extremely vulnerable. Furthermore, the release that the appellant required had the effect of discharging the appellant from all outstanding claims, not merely those relating to direct costs of and delays relaying to the removal of the obstructions.

As Mahoney J.A. observed in *Antonovic v Volker* (1986) 7 NSWLR 151 at 165, the principle of unconscionability is better described than defined. The authors of J W Carter and D J Harland, *Contract Law in Australia* (3rd ed., 1998) at p. 500 view it as a component of the court's general jurisdiction to grant relief in cases of equitable fraud. It is therefore not a principle which lends itself to detailed specification. However, substantial guidance can be obtained from what the High Court said of the topic in *Commercial Bank of Australia v Amadio* (1983) 151 CLR 447. Although Gibbs C.J. decided the matter on the basis of a misrepresentation he said (at 459):

> A transaction will be unconscientious within the meaning of the relevant equitable principles only if the party seeking to enforce the transaction has taken unfair advantage of his superior bargaining power, or of the position of disadvantage in which the other party was placed. The principle of equity applies 'whenever one party to a transaction is at a special disadvantage in dealing with the other party because illness, ignorance, inexperience, impaired faculties, financial need or other circumstances affect his ability to conserve his own interests, and the other party unconscientiously takes advantage of the opportunity thus placed in his hands': see *Blomley v Ryan* (1956) 99 CLR 362 at 415, per Kitto J., and (at 405–6) per Fullagar J.

Mason J. said (at 461):

> . . . relief on the ground of 'unconscionable conduct is usually taken to refer to the class of case in which a party makes unconscientious use of his superior position of bargaining power to the detriment of a party who suffers from some special disability or is placed in some special situation of disadvantage . . .

Relief on the ground of unconscionable conduct will be granted when unconscientious advantage is taken of an innocent party whose will is overborne so that it is not independent and voluntary, just as it will be granted when such advantage is taken of an innocent party who, though not deprived of an independent and voluntary will, is unable to make a worthwhile judgment as to what is in his best interest.

It goes almost without saying that it is impossible to describe definitively all the situations in which relief will be granted on the ground of unconscionable conduct. As Fullagar J. said in *Blomley v Ryan* (at 405):

> The circumstances adversely affecting a party, which may induce a court of equity either to refuse its aid or to set a transaction aside, are of great variety and can hardly be satisfactorily classified. Among them are poverty or need of any kind, sickness, age, sex, infirmity of body or mind, drunkenness, illiteracy or lack of education, lack of assistance or explanation where assistance or explanation is necessary. The common characteristic seems to be that they have the effect of placing one party at a serious disadvantage vis-a-vis the other.

Likewise Kitto J. (at 415) spoke of it as a 'well-known head of equity' which:

> . . . applies whenever one party to a transaction is at a special disadvantage in dealing with the other party because illness, ignorance, inexperience, impaired faculties, financial need or other circumstances affect his ability to conserve his own interests, and the other party unconscientiously takes advantage of the opportunity thus placed in his hands.

It is not to be thought that relief will be granted only in the particular situations mentioned by their Honours. It is made plain enough, especially by Fullagar J., that the situations mentioned are no more than particular exemplifications of an underlying general principle which may be invoked whenever one party by reason of some condition of (sic) circumstance is placed at a special disadvantage vis-a-vis another and unfair or unconscientious advantage is then taken of the opportunity thereby created.

Deane J., with whom Wilson J. agreed, said (at 474):

> The jurisdiction is long established as extending generally to circumstances in which (i) a party to a transaction was under a special disability in dealing with the other party with the consequence that there was an absence of any reasonable degree of equality between them and (ii) that disability was sufficiently evident to the stronger party to make it *prima facie* or 'unconscientious' that he procure, or accept, the weaker party's assent to the impugned transaction in the circumstances in which he procured or accepted it. Where such circumstances are shown to have existed, an onus is cast upon the stronger party to show that the transaction was fair, just and reasonable . . .

In my opinion it was open to the arbitrator to find that the respondent was lulled into a false sense of security by the 12 April 1991 agreement and by the variation order given in May and a part payment apparently made in pursuance of that agreement. There was no need to challenge the stated position of the appellant in that letter. It was open to him to find that there was an apparent change of heart by the appellant, which may, as a matter of law, have been in breach of the contract as varied, and that the appellant attempted to force a settlement at a time when the respondent was in no economic position to challenge the appellant's stated position but instead was threatened with termination of the contract.

Notes

1. It is generally recognised that English decisions are less willing to countenance a wide application for the unconscionable bargain doctrine. English judges are certainly suspicious of giving decisions like *Bundy* and *Amadio* a wide application. See for example *Portman Building Society v Dusangh* [2000] 2 All ER (Comm) 221 and *Kalsep Ltd v X Flow BV, The Times* 3 May 2001.
2. Nevertheless there are signs of a wider approach being adopted by some English judges.
3. Although the following case is often said to provide an exception to the general trend in *Barclays Bank v O'Brien* case law (see page 684) the decision of Millett L.J. is very important generally.

Credit Lyonnais *v* Burch [1997] 1 All ER 144

Millett LJ.:

This transaction cannot possibly stand.

This is sufficiently demonstrated by a recital of the principal facts. Mr Pelosi was the *alter ego* of his company. The company ran a small business and had an overdraft facility with its bank. The overdraft was operating within an agreed limit of £250,000. Mr Pelosi asked the bank to increase the limit of the facility to £270,000. The bank agreed but required additional security to be provided. So far the story is familiar, even commonplace. What follows, I hope, is not.

Mr Pelosi provided the bank with an unlimited all moneys guarantee given by Miss Burch at his request. She was a junior employee of the company employed at a modest wage. She was not a director of the company or shareholder in it. Her guarantee was supported by a second charge on her home, a small flat of suitably modest value, which was valued at £100,000 and was subject to a mortgage of £30,000. She understood that the guarantee and charge were unlimited in time and amount, but she had not taken independent legal advice.

No court of equity could allow such a transaction to stand. The facts which I have recited are sufficient to entitle Miss Burch to have the transaction set aside as against Mr Pelosi and the company. Every one of those facts was known to the bank when it accepted the security. The bank must accordingly be taken to have had notice of Miss Burch's equity, and must submit to the transaction being set aside against it also.

An eighteenth-century Lord Chancellor would have contented himself with saying as much. It is an extreme case. The transaction was not merely to the manifest disadvantage of Miss Burch; it was one which, in the traditional phrase, 'shocks the conscience of the court'. Miss Burch committed herself to a personal liability far beyond her slender means, risking the loss of her home and personal bankruptcy, and obtained nothing in return beyond a relatively small and possibly temporary increase in the overdraft facility available to her employer, a company in which she had no financial interest. The transaction gives rise to grave suspicion. It cries aloud for an explanation.

Miss Burch did not seek to have the transaction set aside as a harsh and unconscionable bargain. To do so she would have had to show not only that the terms of the transaction were harsh or oppressive, but that 'one of the parties to it has imposed the objectionable terms in a morally reprehensible manner, that is to say, in a way which affects his conscience' (see *Multiservice Bookbinding Ltd v. Marden* [1978] 2 All ER 489 at 502, [1979] Ch 84 at 110 per Browne-Wilkinson J. and *Alec Lobb (Garages) Ltd v Total Oil GB Ltd* [1983] 1 All ER 944 at 961, [1983] 1 WLR 87 at 95, where I pointed out that there must be some impropriety, both in the conduct of the stronger party and in the terms of the transaction itself, but added that 'the former may often be inferred from the latter in the absence of an innocent explanation').

In the present case, the bank did not obtain the guarantee directly from Miss Burch. It was provided to the bank by Mr Pelosi, who obtained it from Miss Burch by the exercise of undue influence. In such a context, the two equitable jurisdictions to set aside harsh and unconscionable bargains and to set aside transactions obtained by undue influence have many similarities. In either case it is necessary to show that the conscience of the party who seeks to uphold the transaction was affected by notice, actual or constructive, of the impropriety by which it was obtained by the intermediary, and in either case the court may in a proper case infer the presence of the impropriety from the terms of the transaction itself.

In saying this I do not dissent from the observations of Sir John Salmond in *Brusewitz v Brown* (1922) 42 NZLR 1106 at 1109–1110, where he said:

The mere fact that a transaction is based on an inadequate consideration or is otherwise improvident, unreasonable, or unjust is not in itself any ground on which this court can set it aside as invalid. Nor is such a circumstance in itself even a sufficient ground for a presumption that the transaction was the result of fraud, misrepresentation, mistake, or undue influence, so as to place the burden of supporting the transaction upon the person who profits by it. The law in general leaves every man at liberty to make such bargains as he pleases, and to dispose of his own property as he chooses. However improvident, unreasonable, or unjust such bargains or dispositions may be, they are binding on every party to them unless he can prove affirmatively the existence of one of the recognised invalidating circumstances, such as fraud or undue influence.'

But Sir John Salmond proceeded to describe an important exception:

Where there is not merely an absence or inadequacy of consideration for the transfer of property, but there also exists between the grantor and the grantee some special relation of confidence, control, domination, influence or other form of superiority, such as to render reasonable a presumption that the transaction was procured by the grantee by some unconscientious use of his power over the grantor, the law will make that presumption . . . . The commonest and most important instances of this presumption are those cases in which the relation between the parties is some recognised legal relationship of confidence, such as that existing between solicitor and client and between trustee and beneficiary. The rule, however, is not limited to any exclusive and defined list of recognised legal relations. It is quite general in its application. The question in each case is . . . did there exist between [the parties] such a relation of superiority on the one side and inferiority on the other (whatever the source or nature of that superiority or inferiority may be), and therefore such an opportunity and temptation for the unconscientious abuse of the power and influence so possessed by the superior party, as to justify the legal presumption that such an abuse actually took place and that the transaction was procured thereby?'

This is an early description of the threefold classification adopted by the Court of Appeal in *Bank of Credit and Commerce International SA v. Aboody* [1992] 4 All ER 955 at 964, [1990] 1 QB 923 at 953, which was approved by the House of Lords in *Barclay's Bank plc v. O'Brien* [1993] 4 All ER 417 at 423, [1994] 1 AC 180 at 189. This classifies cases of undue influence in three categories: class 1 where the complainant proves affirmatively that she was induced to enter into the transaction by the exercise of undue influence upon her; class 2a where she need prove, in the first instance, only the existence of a relationship between her and the wrongdoer of a kind which is sufficient in law to give rise to a rebuttable presumption that any transaction between them which is favourable to the wrongdoer has been obtained by the exercise of undue influence; and class 2b where she must prove the existence in fact of a relationship between her and the wrongdoer which, although not of a kind which falls within class 2a, was one under which the complainant was accustomed to repose trust and confidence in the wrongdoer, in which case the same rebuttable presumption arises. The difference between class 2a and class 2b is that in the former case there is an irrebuttable presumption of law that the relationship is one of trust and confidence; in the latter this must be proved as a fact. (I refer throughout for convenience to the complainant as a woman and the wrongdoer as a man, because that is the present case; but it is not of course always the case.)

In the present case, the only relationship between Mr Pelosi (and his company) on the one hand and Miss Burch on the other which has been proved (and of which the bank had any knowledge) was that of employer and junior employee. That is not a relationship within class 2a. At the same time, it is clearly one which is capable of developing into a relationship of trust and confidence with the attendant risk of abuse, particularly in the case of a small business where the parties are accustomed to work closely together.

Accordingly, it was for Miss Burch to prove that the relationship between her and Mr Pelosi had developed into a relationship of trust and confidence. Whether it had done so or not was a question of fact. While she had to prove this affirmatively, she did not have to prove it as a primary fact by direct evidence. It was sufficient for her to prove facts from which the existence of a relationship of trust and confidence could be inferred. In the present case, the excessively onerous nature of the transaction into which she was persuaded to enter, coupled with the fact that she did so at the request of, and after discussion with Mr Pelosi, is in my judgment, quite enough to justify the inference, which is really irresistible, that the relationship of employer and employee had ripened into something more and that there had come into existence between them a relationship of trust and confidence which he improperly exploited for his own benefit.

I do not accept the bank's submission that this conclusion is inconsistent with the authorities. I repeat that the mere fact that a transaction is improvident or manifestly disadvantageous to one party is not sufficient by itself to give rise to a presumption that it has been obtained by the exercise of undue influence; but where it is obtained by a party between whom and the complainant there is a relationship like that of employer and junior employee which is easily capable of developing into a relationship of trust and confidence, the nature of the transaction may be sufficient to justify the inference that such a development has taken place; and where the transaction is so extravagantly improvident that it is virtually inexplicable on any other basis, the inference will be readily drawn.

The bank submitted that in the absence of evidence that there was a sexual or emotional tie between Mr Pelosi and Miss Burch the facts were insufficient to justify the recorder's finding that there was a relationship of confidence between them; and that, in the absence of evidence that the bank was aware of such a tie between Mr Pelosi and Miss Burch, the facts known to the bank were insufficient to fix it with notice of the existence of a relationship of trust and confidence between them. I do not accept this. The presence of a sexual or emotional tie would at least make the transaction explicable. A wife might well consider (and be properly advised) that it was in her interest to provide a (suitably limited) guarantee of her husband's borrowings and to charge it on her interest in the matrimonial home, even if she had no legal interest in the company which owned the business. Her livelihood and that of her family would no doubt depend on the success of the business; and a refusal to entertain her husband's importunity might put at risk the marital relationship as well as the continued prosperity of herself and her family. Similar considerations would no doubt influence a cohabitee and her adviser.

But Miss Burch had no such incentive to induce her to enter into the transaction. No competent solicitor could possibly have advised her to enter into it. He would be bound to warn her against it in the strongest possible terms, and to have refrained from acting for her further if she had persisted in it against his advice (see *Powell v. Powell* [1900] 1 Ch 243 at 247).

The bank had actual notice of the facts from which the existence of a relationship of trust and confidence between Mr Pelosi and Miss Burch could be inferred. It knew that they were respectively employer and junior employee working in a small business, and should have 'appreciated that the possibility of influence exist[ed]' (see *Avon Finance Co. Ltd v Bridger* (1979) [1985] 2 All ER 281 at 288 per Brandon LJ.) It also knew that Miss Burch was neither a shareholder nor a director of the company and, so far as it knew, had no incentive to enter into the transaction, which was entirely for his benefit and to her detriment. This was sufficient to put the bank on inquiry. It probably appreciated this, or it would not have encouraged Miss Burch to take legal advice.

The bank submitted that it had discharged its duty to Miss Burch by urging her to obtain independent legal advice. This does not accurately reflect the legal position. The bank owed no duty to Miss Burch. If it urged Miss Burch to take independent legal advice, this was for its own protection. If it had not had cause to suspect that Miss Burch's agreement to enter into the transaction might have been improperly obtained, it would have had no need to encourage her to take legal advice. Since it did have cause to suspect it, it could not avoid the consequences unless two conditions were satisfied: (i) it must have taken reasonable steps to allay any such suspicion; and (ii) the result of the steps which it took must be such as would reasonably allay any such suspicion.

The bank urged Miss Burch to obtain independent legal advice. In a letter obviously written at the instance of Mr Pelosi and after consultation with him, she declined to do so. The bank had taken all reasonable steps open to it to allay any suspicion it might have had that Miss Burch's agreement to the transaction had been procured by the exercise of undue influence on the part of Mr Pelosi. But what followed could not reasonably have allayed any such suspicion; on the contrary, it should have confirmed it.

That is sufficient to dispose of this appeal, but I should not be taken to accept that it would necessarily have made any difference even if Miss Burch had entered into the transaction after taking independent legal advice. Such advice is neither always necessary nor always sufficient. It is not a panacea. The result does not depend mechanically on the presence or absence of legal advice. I think that there has been some misunderstanding of the role which the obtaining of independent legal advice plays in these cases.

It is first necessary to consider the position as between the complainant and the alleged wrongdoer. The alleged wrongdoer may seek to rebut the presumption that the transaction was obtained by undue influence by showing that the complainant had the benefit of independent legal advice before entering into it. It is well established that in such a case the court will examine the advice which was actually given. It is not sufficient that the solicitor has satisfied himself that the complainant understands the legal effect of the transaction and intends to enter into it. That may be a protection against mistake or misrepresentation; it is no protection against undue influence. As Lord Eldon LC said in *Huguenin v. Baseley* (1807) 14 Ves 273 at 300, [1803–13] All ER Rep 1 at 13: 'The question is, not, whether she knew what she was doing, had done, or proposed to do, but how the intention was produced . . .'

Accordingly, the presumption cannot be rebutted by evidence that the complainant understood what she was doing and intended to do it. The alleged wrongdoer can rebut the presumption only by showing that the complainant was either free from any undue influence on his part or had been placed, by the receipt of independent advice, in an equivalent position. That involves showing that she was advised as to the propriety of the transaction by an adviser fully informed of all the material facts (see *Powell v Powell, Brusewitz v Brown, Permanent Trustee Co of New South Wales Ltd v Bridgewater* [1936] 3 All ER 501 at 507 and *Bester v Perpetual Trustee Co. Ltd* [1970] 3 NSWLR 30 at 35–36).

Some of those cases were concerned with the equity to set aside a harsh and unconscionable bargain rather than one obtained by the exercise of undue influence, but the role of the independent adviser, while not identical, is not dissimilar. The solicitor may not be concerned to protect the complainant against herself, but he is concerned to protect her from the influence of the wrongdoer. The cases show that it is not sufficient that she should have received independent advice unless she has acted on that advice. If this were not so, the same influence that produced her desire to enter into the transaction would cause her to disregard any advice not to do so. They also show that the solicitor must not be content to satisfy himself that his client understands the transaction and wishes to carry it out. His duty is to satisfy himself that the transaction is one which his client could sensibly enter into if free from improper influence; and if he is not so satisfied to advise her not to enter into it, and to refuse to act further for her if she persists. He must advise his client that she is under no obligation to enter into the transaction at all and, if she still wishes to do so, that she is not necessarily bound to accept the terms of any document which has been put before her but (where this is appropriate) that he should ascertain on her behalf whether less onerous terms might be obtained.

It is next necessary to consider the position of the third party who has been put on enquiry of the possible existence of some impropriety and who wishes to avoid being fixed with constructive notice. One means of doing so is to ensure that the complainant obtains competent and independent legal advice before entering into the transaction. If she does so, and enters into the transaction nonetheless, the third party will usually escape the consequences of notice. This is because he is normally entitled to assume that the solicitor has discharged his duty and that the complainant has followed his advice. But he cannot make any such assumption if he knows or ought to know that it is false.

In the present case, the bank did not have actual notice of the exercise of undue influence, or even of the existence of a relationship of trust and confidence between Miss Burch and Mr Pelosi. It did not know for a fact that Miss Burch had no incentive to enter into the transaction. For all the bank knew, for example, the parties might be intending to set up home together and live off the profits of the company's business. It did not, therefore, know (as was the case) that no competent solicitor could possibly advise Miss Burch to guarantee the company's overdraft.

But it must have known that no competent solicitor could advise her to enter into a guarantee in the terms she did. He would be bound to inquire, of the bank if necessary, of the reason why it required additional security. Having discovered that it was to enable the limit of the company's overdraft to be increased from £250,000 to £270,000, he would be bound to advise Miss Burch that an unlimited guarantee was unnecessary and inappropriate for this purpose, and that, if she felt that she must accommodate Mr Pelosi's wishes, she should offer a limited guarantee with a limit of £20,000 or (better still) a guarantee of the company's liability in excess of £250,000 with a maximum of £270,000. The terms of Miss Burch's letters indicate that if she had been given appropriate advice of the alternatives which were legally available, she would have chosen one which was less onerous to her while still meeting the bank's ostensible requirements.

I do not, therefore, accept that a bank, in circumstances where it ought to appreciate the possibility that undue influence has been exercised, can escape the consequences by putting forward an unnecessarily onerous form of guarantee and relying on the failure of the guarantor's solicitor to advise her of the possibility of offering a guarantee on less onerous terms and more appropriate to the situation.

In the present case, the bank accepted an unlimited guarantee of her employer's indebtedness obtained by the employer from a junior employee with no incentive to give it; and who had, at the instance of her employer, declined to obtain legal advice, was known to be concerned at the unlimited nature of the obligation which she was undertaking, and was almost certainly unaware of the alternatives open to her. In my opinion, the transaction must be set aside and the appeal must be dismissed.

Note

Nourse and Swinton Thomas LJJ also dismissed the appeal and while each agreed with the reasons given by Millett LJ, neither of the Lords Justices discussed the unconscionability issue in detail.

B. INSURANCE SETTLEMENTS

Doan v Insurance Corporation of British Columbia (1987) 18 BCLR 286

Paris J.:

The plaintiff, Mr Doan, suffered a brain injury when struck down in a crosswalk by the defendant Bassey on 24 September 1982. The defendants' negligence is admitted.

The Insurance Corporation of British Columbia (ICBC) appointed Mr David Slessor to adjust the claim and he dealt directly with Mr and Mrs Doan.

On 12 August 1983 they signed a release settling their claim for a total of $60,000 including Pt. 7 benefits, loss of income, non-pecuniary damages and all other claims.

The brain damage suffered by Mr Doan left him incapacitated and the incapacitation has become progressively worse since the accident. Mrs Doan has had to quit her job to look after him.

[After finding that Doan was not independently represented, Paris J. relied on Slessor's advice and that Slessor was in a position of conflict of interest, Paris J. continued:]

The result was predictable. The bargain arrived at was clearly improvident and seriously so. At first Slessor offered the Doans $40,000 in full settlement. They declined. He then came back with an offer of $60,000 which they accepted. He told them that this was $20,000 more than they should be receiving. In fact, ICBC's own reserve estimate for the file at that time, as set out in Ex. 119, was in the neighbourhood of $110,000. The breakdown by ICBC of the settlement proceeds given by Slessor to the Doans allocated $30,000 for non-pecuniary damages. However, it is agreed by the parties that non-pecuniary damages should be fixed by the court at $140,000, assuming that there is no apportionment of those damages to some cause other than the motor vehicle accident.

Incidentally, I say parenthetically, in my view this is a fair assessment of those non-pecuniary damages.

I will deal in due course with the other aspects of the plaintiffs' claim to which they are entitled. Suffice it to say for the moment that they are very greatly out of proportion to what the settlement represented, particularly bearing in mind the pay-back which had to be made by the plaintiffs to the long term disability plan. And further, that the settlement included the Pt. 7 no fault benefits to which they were entitled as insured persons under the universal coverage aspect of the public motor vehicle insurance scheme in place in this province.

Finally, Slessor told Mrs Doan that she personally had no claim although, of course, he got her to sign the release.

In sum, by any of the three tests set out in the *Towers v Affleck*[1] and *Harry v Kreutziger*[2] cases, the test of unconscionable bargain is met and the release must be set aside.

[1] [1974] 1 WWR 714.   [2] (1978) 95 DLR (30) 231.

C. SALE OF REAL PROPERTY TO A COMMERCIAL DEVELOPER

Fusty v McLean Construction Ltd (1978) 6 Alberta LR (2d) 216

Rowbotham D.C.J.:

The plaintiff asks for rescission of a certain contract made between himself and the defendant and dated 30 May 1975, respecting the sale by the plaintiff to the defendant of a certain parcel of land described as lot 11, block 2, plan Drumheller 561JK.

The plaintiff came to Canada from Hungary in 1927 and despite the fact that he has been in Canada for fifty years has very great difficulty in understanding the English language let alone the details of a real estate transaction. He is now an old man and has recently suffered some illness and undergone several operations. Insofar as I could understand his testimony he said that he had a discussion with the agent of the defendant company in which he stated that if he returned to his native Hungary to live he would sell the land in question, on which his house is situated, to the defendant for the sum of $3,300. He delivered his duplicate certificate of title to the agent for the defendant, subsequently attended at the office of the solicitor for the defendant and signed several documents without receiving any independent advice and subsequently received the sum of $3,300. After the completion of the transaction he attempted to pay the taxes on his house as he described it and was informed that he would not be permitted to do so because it was no longer his house.

The value of the house and lot according to the witness Raymond Page of Page Agencies Drumheller Limited is between $11,000 and $13,000.

According to the testimony of Mr D. E. Harrison, the real estate agent involved, the defendant McLean Construction Ltd is, to use his words, 'the mother company of McLean Agencies', the real estate firm involved.

The plaintiff argues that this is a case where the doctrine of *Fry v Lane; Re Fry, Whittet and Bush* (1888), 40 ChD 312, should be applied. The doctrine is found in the judgment of Kay J. at p. 322 in these words:

> The result of the decisions is that where a purchase is made from a poor and ignorant man at a considerable undervalue, the vendor having no independent advice, a court of equity will set aside the transaction.
>
> This will be done even in the case of property in possession, and *a fortiori* if the interest be reversionary.
>
> The circumstances of poverty and ignorance of the vendor, and absence of independent advice, throw upon the purchase, when the transaction is impeached, the onus of proving, in Lord Selborne's words, that the purchase was fair, just and reasonable.

The plaintiff argues that the defendant has tendered no evidence to show that the purchase was fair, just and reasonable and I agree with him.

The plaintiff also cited *Earl of Aylesford v Morris* (1873) 8 Ch App 484, and *Butler v Miller* (1867) 1 IR Eq 195.

Fry v Lane was first followed in Canada in *Hrynyk v Hrynyk* 40 Man R 173, [1932] 1 WWR 82, [1932] 1 DLR 672 (CA). A seventy seven year old ignorant and apparently worn out man transferred his land to his son in consideration for a lease back to the father on the house and garden found on the same parcel of land for $1 consideration. The Manitoba Court of Appeal held (p. 84): 'I look on this as an improvident transaction, made practically without consideration and without advice, in favour of a person who had a duty at least to see that the transaction went no farther than was actually necessary. I think that on this ground and following the principles of equity jurisprudence in such a case the transaction cannot be allowed to stand.'

The Supreme Court of British Columbia in *Hnatuk v Chretian* (1960) 31 WWR 130 refused specific performance of an agreement for sale where the plaintiff had taken advantage of illiterate defendants who were in difficult financial circumstances.

The British Columbia Court of Appeal in *Morrison v Coast Finance Ltd* (1965) 54 WWR 257, 55 DLR (2d) 710, set aside a mortgage as an unconscionable transaction in circumstances where a seventy nine year old widow of meagre means granted a mortgage on her house and lot under unfavourable circumstances without any independent advice.

Davey J.A. set out the distinction between undue influence and unconscionable bargains at p. 259:

> The equitable principles relating to undue influence and relief against unconscionable bargains are closely related, but the doctrines are separate and distinct. The finding here against undue influence does not conclude the question whether the appellant is entitled to relief against an unconscionable transaction. A plea of undue influence attacks the sufficiency of consent; a plea that a bargain is unconscionable invokes relief against an unfair advantage gained by an unconscientious use of power by a stronger party against a weaker. On such a claim the material ingredients are proof of inequality in the position of the parties arising out of the ignorance, need or distress of the weaker, which left him in the power of the stronger, and proof of substantial unfairness of the bargain obtained by the stronger. On proof of those circumstances, it creates a presumption of fraud which the stronger must repeal by proving that the bargain was fair, just and reasonable: *Earl of Aylesford v Morris*, per Lord Selborne at p. 491, or perhaps by showing that no advantage was taken: See *Harrison v Guest* (1855), 6 De G. M. & G. 424 at 438, affirmed 8 HL Cas 481 at 492, 493, 11 ER 517. In *Fry v Lane; Re Fry, Whittet and Bush* Kay J. accurately stated the modern scope and application of the principle, and discussed the earlier authorities upon which it rests.

The Saskatchewan Court of Appeal in *Knupp v Bell* (1968), 67 DLR (2d) 256, refused to uphold an agreement for sale of land by an eighty five year old senile woman without any business experience at a value of approximately half of its market value.

Beck J. in *Anderson v Morgan* 11 Alta LR 526, [1917] 2 WWR 969, 34 DLR 728 (CA), concerning alleged misrepresentations made in negotiations resulting in an exchange of lands said at pp 971–72:

> It is not necessary that that relationship should arise by reason of a previous contractual or quasi-contractual relationship (per Lord Shaw [in *Nocton v Lord Ashburton*, [1914] AC 932] p. 971, but applies to such a case as *Waters v Donnelly* (1884), 9 OR 391, cited by my brother Walsh which holds that if two persons, no matter whether a confidential relationship exists between them or not, stand in such a relation to each other that one can take an undue advantage of the other, and advantage is taken, the transaction will not be allowed to stand.
>
> Boyd C. in *Waters v Donnelly*, at p. 401 says that the method of investigation is to determine first whether the parties were on equal terms; if not, and the transaction is one of purchase, and any matters requiring explanation arise, *then it lies on the purchaser* to show affirmatively that the price given was the value.

In view of the foregoing the contract between the plaintiff and the defendant is rescinded and the plaintiff shall have an order directing the Registrar of the South Alberta Land Registration District to cancel certificate of title 751060460 in the name of McLean Construction Ltd and issue a new certificate of title in the name of the plaintiff.

Because the plaintiff has remained in possession of the property he shall be responsible for the payment of property taxes during the period of time in question.

The plaintiff shall have costs of the action.

Chapter Fifteen

Privity of Contract

INTRODUCTION

The doctrine of privity of contract states that only a party to a contract may sue on or be bound by that contract (*Murphy and Others v Bower* (1868) IR 2 CL 506). This chapter will explore the nature and effect of the rule and the exceptions to it which have developed.

Viscount Haldane in the *Dunlop* case set out the modern doctrine, together with two of its main exceptions.

Dunlop Pneumatic Tyre Co. Ltd *v* Selfridge & Co. Ltd [1915] AC 847

Viscount Haldane L.C.:

My Lords, in the law of England certain principles are fundamental. One is that only a person who is a party to a contract can sue on it. Our law knows nothing of a *jus quaesitum tertio* arising by way of contract. Such a right may be conferred by property, as, for example, under a trust, but it cannot be conferred on a stranger to a contract as a right to enforce the contract *in personam*. A second principle is that if a person with whom a contract not under seal has been made is to be able to enforce it consideration must have been given by him to the promisor or to some other person at the promisor's request. . . . A third proposition is that a principal not named in the contract may sue upon it if the promisee really contracted as his agent. But again, in order to entitle him so to sue, he must have given consideration either personally or through the promisee, acting as his agent in giving it.

Consider:

What is the rationale for the doctrine of privity of contract?

SECTION ONE—CONSIDERATION AND PRIVITY

The doctrine of privity is very similar to the rule (noted in Chapter 3 at p. 140) that consideration must move from the promisee. In many cases, a claimant who is not a party to a contract will not have provided consideration to the promisor.

M.P. Furmston, 'Return to Dunlop v Selfridge?' (1960) 23 MLR 373.
(Footnotes abridged.)

The prevailing view is that the [rule that only a party to a contract may sue upon it and the rule that consideration must move from the promise] are separate, although in many circumstances they overlap. This seems to be one of the more unfortunate legacies of comparative law. When English lawyers discovered that continental systems of law which knew nothing of consideration nevertheless had the rule that a contract could only benefit and bind the parties, they assumed that this must be a fundamental characteristic of a contract and promptly transferred it to English law although the situation was already provided for. It has been felt necessary to justify this dichotomy by giving illustrations of cases where the two rules do not overlap. Thus it is said that if 'by the terms of a joint agreement, A promises B and C to pay C £100 if B will carry out work desired by A, C is a contracting party, but he cannot sue A, because B alone has given consideration for A's promise.' With respect, this view is not completely convincing. In English law a contract is not a mere promise but a promise supported by consideration, or, in modern rationalisation, a bargain. If A were to promise C to pay him £100 *simpliciter*, we should not say that there is a contract but that C cannot enforce it because he has not given consideration. We should simply say that there is no contract. To do otherwise is to deprive the word contract of any legal meaning. Similarly a promise to C to pay him £100 if B carries out work is not a contract but a mere gratuitous promise. It is not easy to see why when we do not describe a gratuitous promise to C as a contract, we should suddenly describe it as a contract, albeit one C cannot enforce, because B has bargained for and bought the same promise. If C is not a party to the bargain he is not a party to the contract.

A converse case is sometimes put. A promises B to pay C £100 if C does work. It is said that if C does the work he cannot recover because, although he has furnished consideration, he was not a party to the contract. This analysis again is not completely convincing. If C does the work in ignorance of the offer he would seem not to provide consideration, because although he has no doubt suffered a detriment, the detriment is not causally connected with the offer. This is clearly the case where there are only two parties. Thus, for example, in *Wigan v English and Scottish Law Life Assurance Assoc.* [1909] 1 Ch. 291 one Hackblock had a life assurance policy for £5,000 which was to be void if the assured died by his own hand 'but without prejudice to the *bona fide* interests of third parties based on valuable consideration.' He owed Wigan, who was pressing for payment, over £5,000 and executed an assignment to him of the policy, which was to be revealed in negotiations if necessary. In fact Wigan forebore without the assignment being revealed, and Parker J. held that there was no consideration because, although the assignment had been executed with the object of obtaining further time and further time had in fact been obtained, it had not been obtained in exchange for the assignment. The presence of a third party may obscure but should not confuse the issue. Even if C knew of the promise when he acted there would not strictly be consideration unless the offer was addressed to him. It might well be, however, that the court would infer from the express promise to B an implied offer to C of £100 for his doing the work—a unilateral contract.

There does not seem to be any binding authority against this view. . . . No doubt *obiter dicta* can be found which treat the principles as separate, notably those of Lord Haldane in *Dunlop v Selfridge* [1915] AC 847, but it does not appear that these remarks have ever had any practical effect. Indeed, if the above conditions are correct, the question is one which never can arise in practice. It is submitted, therefore, that there is no difference in the English law of simple contracts between the doctrine of privity of contract and the rule that consideration must move from the promisee.

Note

Paragraph 3.25 of the Irish Law Reform Commission *Report on Privity* (LRC 88–2008) recommended that 'provided the other requirements are met, a third party should be able to enforce the contract even though they have not provided any consideration. In other words, consideration need not move from the third party beneficiary. However, this would not affect the requirement of consideration in general, and the normal rules as to consideration should apply as between the promisor and promisee.' (See below at p. 788.)

Joint Promises

A difficulty arises in practice in the case of joint promises. Where such promises are made, only one of the promisee may in practice have provided consideration and yet both parties may claim to be parties to the contract.

McEvoy v The Belfast Banking Co. Ltd [1935] AC24

The appellant's father deposited £10,000 in the respondents' bank and received a deposit receipt in the following form: '£10,000 . . . Received from John McEvoy esq. And Mr Joseph McEvoy (a minor), Newry, the sum of ten thousand pounds sterling for credit in deposit account. Not transferable . . . Payable to either or the survivor. . . .' When the appellant's father died the executors were empowered under his will to hold the rest of his property in trust for the appellant until he was twenty five years old and to carry on the business. The £10,000 deposit was transferred to an account in the name of the executors. This money was gradually exhausted in meeting the expenses of the business. Ten years after the original contract and 4 years after attaining his majority, the appellant sued the bank to recover the sum on the grounds that it had been wrongfully and without his authority paid by the bank to the executors. The majority of the House of Lords rejected the appellant's claim on the basis that he was not a party to the contract. Lord Atkin took a different approach.

Lord Atkin:

The suggestion is that where A deposits a sum of money with his bank in the names of A and B, payable to A or B, if B comes to the bank with the deposit receipt he has no right to demand the money from the bank or to sue them if his demand is refused. The bank is entitled to demand proof that the money was in fact partly B's, or possibly that A had acted with B's actual authority. For the contract, it is said is between the bank and A alone. My Lords, to say this is to ignore the vital difference between a contract purporting to be made by A with the bank to pay A or B and a contract purporting to be made by A and B with the bank to pay A or B. In both cases of course payment to B would discharge the bank whether the bank contracted with A alone or with A and B. But the question is whether in the case put B has any rights against the bank if payment to him is refused. I have myself no doubt that in such a case B can sue the bank. The contract on the face of it purports to be made with A and B, and I think with them jointly and severally. A purports to make the contract on behalf of B as well as himself and the consideration supports such a contract. If A has actual authority from B to make such a contract, B is a party to the contract *ab initio*. If he has no actual authority then subject to the ordinary principles of ratification B can ratify the contract purporting to have been made on his behalf and his ratification relates back to the original formation of the contract. If no events had happened to preclude B from ratifying, then on compliance with the contract conditions, including notice and production of the deposit receipt, B would have the right to demand from the bank so much of the money as was due on the deposit account.

(On the facts, however, Lord Atkin opined that the son by his conduct indicted that he did not intend to ratify the contract and that he was content that the money should be applied as part of his father's estate. Lord Thankerton, while concurring with the majority, agreed with Lord Atkin that had the appellant been a party to the contract, it would not have been relevant that the consideration was provided by his father. This suggests that the rule of privity is distinct from that of consideration.)

Coulls v Bagot's Executor and Trustee Co. Ltd 119 CLR 460 (1967)

The respondent's late husband contracted to grant a licence to a quarrying company to quarry and remove stone from a quarry which he owned. The last paragraph of the contract stated: 'I authorise the above company to pay all moneys connected with this agreement to my wife, Doris Sophia Coulls and myself, Arthur Leopold Coulls as joint tenants (or tenants in common?) (the one which goes to living partner).' The contract was signed by both husband and wife. After his death, the executors of his estate claimed that his estate was entitled to the royalties. The majority of the High Court of Australia found that as the respondent was not a party to the agreement, the authorisation of a payment to her was revoked. In a dissenting judgment, Barwick C. J. found that the respondent and her husband were joint promiseees. Although the promise was not 'as between promisor and promise' gratuitous, he opined that as the respondent had not provided consideration the promise is only enforceable if both parties to the action enforce it.

Note

In 'Consideration and the Joint Promisee' [1978] CLJ 301, Coote argues that the joint promisee doctrine enunciated in *Coulls* was based on a misapprehension of what constitutes 'consideration' and of what constitutes a 'party' to a contract. He states that as a contract is a species of bargain, an essential condition of a contract is the reciprocal exchange of consideration between the parties. Thus only those who provide consideration can be parties. In the case of bilateral contracts, however, the consideration is not the payment by the promisee, but his initial acceptance of an obligation to pay. If this is accepted, Coote argues, it is easy to see how there can exist a series of cases where a person was held able to enforce a contract even though the contract price had been paid by someone else. He thus explains how, while a majority of their Lordships in *McEvoy v Belfast Banking Co.* rejected the son's claim because he was not a party to any contract with the bank it was quite possible in law for Lord Thankerton, while concurring with the majority, to agree with Lord Atkin that had the son been a party it would have been immaterial that the father had provided all the funds for the deposit. What could have made the son a party, Coote suggests, would have been an acceptance by him of an obligation to make or join in making the deposit, or even a mere acceptance by him, through his father, of the ordinary duties of a customer to the bank.

Consider:

What is involved in becoming a joint promisor?

Multipartite contracts

Finally, it should be noted that the courts may determine, on the facts, that a multipartite contract has been formed. In such a case, all claimants are parties to the contract and the rule of privity does not arise.

Fox v Higgins (1912) 46 ILTR 22

The plaintiff was appointed as a national school teacher by the current school manager. After a period of absence due to ill health, the plaintiff attempted to recommence work. When the new manager refused to allow him do so, the plaintiff sued for damages for breach of an implied contract. This contract was implied, *inter alia*, by the defendant having undertaken to observe the rules of the National Board of Education.

Gibson J.:

I think the question whether the manager has entered into an implied contract with the teacher is one which is full of difficulty. There is no authority on these rules or on analogous legislation, and the matter is one on which different judges might come to different conclusions. On this somewhat confused legislation the fair inference is that the national board, the manager, and the teacher are put together in a kind of triangular pact, and if the manager accepts the terms of the national board for the school, and undertakes for the teacher that he shall have the benefit of the national board rules, and if the teacher has signed a contact which would bind him, then the manager is bound, in my opinion, in the same way and to the same extent as if he had signed the contract. If he is bound that way, what is the plaintiff's measure of damages? He cannot be in a better position than if the defendant had signed the contract, and that would entitle him only to damages measured at the amount of his salary for three months. I shall, therefore, give him that amount, and nothing over and above it.

Note

Tripartite contracts such as these are, however, exceptional as may be seen in the case of *Halpin v Samuel Rothwell and United Dominions Trust (Ireland) Ltd* [1984] ILRM 613. There, the plaintiff purchased a lorry from the first defendant, who held the lorry under a hire-purchase contract with the second defendant. The plaintiff later sued both defendants for alleged breach of warranties as to the age of the lorry and as to the existence of certain liabilities and charges in respect of the lorry. The court dismissed the action against the second defendant. O'Hanlon J. in the High Court noted that at the time of the sale only the first defendant had title to the lorry, as he had paid all moneys due to the second defendant from funds provided by the plaintiff. Accordingly no privity existed between the plaintiff and the second defendant.

SECTION TWO—REMEDIES FOR THE THIRD PARTY

Recovery of Loss Occasioned by a Third Party

In considering the available remedies, it should be noted that the parties to a contract who are entitled to sue for breach may not have occasioned any loss. Often the loss will be sustained by the third party.

For example, A promises to pay B £10 if B gives C a book. If A pays B but B refuses to complete this contract, C will suffer a loss, yet only A can sue. In an action for breach A's damages will be measured by reference to his loss which in this case is minimal. An argument that A should be allowed to sue for C's loss was rejected by the House of Lords in *Woodar Investment Development Ltd v Wimpey Construction (UK) Ltd* [1980] 1 All ER 571.

In *Dunlop v Lambert* (1839) 6 CL & F 600 a carrier of goods by sea was held liable for substantial damages to the consignor with whom he had contracted for the carriage of goods on bill of lading terms, even though, when the loss occurred, property in the goods had passed to a third party, by whom the loss was therefore suffered. This case was subsequently followed in a second carriage case, *The Albazero* [1977] AC 774. The rule was then applied in the context of building contracts in *St Martin's Property Corporation v Sir Robert McAlpine* [1994] 1 AC 85, *Darlington BC v Wiltshier Northern Ltd* [1995] 1 WLR 68 and *Alfred McAlpine Construction Ltd v Panatown Ltd* [2001] 1 AC 518. In the latter case, the *St Martins* case and the *Darlington* BC case, were described as 'black hole' cases, 'that is to say if the employer under the building contract could not recover from the contractor the owner of the building would receive nothing and the contractor would effectively be relieved of liability for his breach'.

In the *St Martins* case, both a narrow and a broader grounds for the exception were discussed by the House of Lords. The majority adopted the former. This allows recovery by the promisee for the loss suffered by and for the benefit of the third party on the basis of the *Albazero* exception to the general rule that such damages are not recoverable. It assumes that the shipper and carrier must have assumed that the property in the goods might be transferred to a third party after the contract was formed and that the shipper must in law be treated as having made the contract of carriage for the benefit of such persons.The promise thus will be accountable to such a third party. By contrast, Lord Griffiths based his decision to award damages on the broader claim. This involves the promisee seeking to recover the loss which he personally has suffered 'because he ha[d] to spend money to give [the third party] the benefit of the bargain which the defendant had promised but failed to deliver'(at p. 97). In this case, the Court would have to be satisfied that the money had indeed been spent securing the intended benefit for the third party.

Alfred McAlpine Construction Ltd *v* Panatown Ltd (No. 1) [2001] 1 AC 518

Panatown Ltd entered into a building contract with Alfred McAlpine Construction Ltd ('McAlpine') for the development of property owned by Unex Investment Properties Ltd ('UIPL'), another subsidiary of Panatown's parent company. UIPL also entered into a 'duty of care' deed ('DCD') with McAlpine giving the former a direct remedy against McAlpine in the event of a failure by McAlpine to exercise reasonable care and skill in respect of any matter within the scope of McAlpine's responsibilities under the building contract. McAlpine's work was defective and Panatown estimated the cost of repairs at £40 million. Panatown launched arbitration proceedings against McAlpine claiming substantial damages. McAlpine claimed that Panatown had not suffered any loss and could not recover damages for loss incurred by a third party. Panatown sought to recover both for the narrow ground and the broad ground described above. A majority of the House of Lords held that Panatown could not recover for the loss sustained by UILP as the latter had its own right of action under the DCD. The majority also denied recovery under the broader ground because Panatown had not incurred any expenditure in making good the defects .

Lord Jauncey:

In the second place in the *The Albazero* [1977] AC 774 there were clear statements both in the Court of Appeal (Cairns L.J. at p. 803C, Ormerod L.J. at p. 823C) and in your Lordships' House that in an action of damages for breach of contract the plaintiff can only recover such damages as he has actually suffered. Lord Diplock, at p. 846G, referred to:

> . . . the general rule of English Law that apart from nominal damages a plaintiff can only recover in an action for breach of contract the actual loss he has himself sustained. (See also 845G.)

The existence of this general rule was again referred to by my noble and learned friend Lord Browne-Wilkinson in *St Martin's Property Corporation v Sir Robert McAlpine Ltd* [1994] 1 AC 85, 114G. . . .

The Narrow Ground
The starting point is the Scots case of *Dunlop v Lambert* 6 Cl. & F. 600, 3 Maclean & R. 663 which has been treated ever since by authoritative English textbook writers:

> . . . as authority for the broad proposition that the consignor may recover substantial damages against the ship owner if there is privity of contract between him and the carrier for the carriage of goods; although, if the goods are not his property or at his risk, he will be accountable to the true owner for the proceeds of his judgment.
> (*The Albazero* [1977] AC 774, 884D, *per* Lord Diplock.)

Scottish textbook writers have been less enthusiastic . . . . My noble and learned friend Lord Clyde in his powerful and detailed analysis of the case has already referred to Professor Gloag's comment. In the 10th ed. (1899) of *Bell's Principles*, para. 88; *Dunlop v Lambert*, among other cases, is cited as vouching the proposition that the risk is continued in the seller 'where there is an express or implied undertaking of the risk by the seller, as to deliver at a certain place.'
 Lord Diplock at p. 847E rationalised the rule in *Dunlop v Lambert* 6 Cl. & F. 600 as an application of the principle:

> . . . that in a commercial contract concerning goods where it is in the contemplation of the parties that the proprietary interests in the goods may be transferred from one owner to another after the contract has been entered into and before the breach which causes loss or damage to the goods, an original party to the contract, if such be the intention of them both, is to be treated in law as having entered into the contract for the benefit of all persons who have or may acquire an interest in the goods before they are lost or damaged, and is entitled to recover by way of damages for breach of contract the actual loss sustained by those for whose benefit the contract is entered into.

Although the rule in *Dunlop v Lambert*, as Lord Diplock described it, was held not to be applicable to the circumstances of *The Albazero* where the breach of a charterparty resulted in a total loss of cargo he refused to accept counsel's invitation to jettison it (847B) . . . [T]he so-called rule as Lord Diplock pointed out in *The Albazero* has become firmly established in English Law notwithstanding its exceedingly dubious parentage and I must proceed accordingly. I should, however, emphasise that throughout the proceedings in *Dunlop v Lambert* there was never any suggestion that the carrier could escape liability for any breach of contract resulting in the loss. The Inner House of the Court of Session concluded that at the time of the loss the puncheon was the property of and at the risk of the consignee who could have sued in terms of the contract. This House simply concluded that it should have been left to the jury to determine whether there was a special contract which modified the terms of the written contract so that the consignors rather than the consignee could sue. I would only add that I agree with my noble and learned friend Lord Clyde that rather more relevant to what has become the *Albazero* exception than *Dunlop v Lambert* was *Joseph v Knox* [1813] 3 Camp 320 in which Lord Ellenborough held that the plaintiffs who had shipped the goods and paid the freight were entitled to recover the value of the lost cargo which they would 'hold as trustees for the real owner.'
 The rule in *Dunlop v Lambert*, as expounded by Lord Diplock, was applied in *St Martins Property Corporation Ltd v Sir Robert McAlpine Ltd* [1994] 1 AC 85 to a case arising out of breach of a building contract whereby St Martins had contracted with McAlpine

for the multipurpose development of a site in Hammersmith. The contract contained a clause prohibiting the assignment of the contract by St Martins without the consent of McAlpine. Some seventeen months after the contract date St Martins assigned to another company in the group for full value their whole interest in the property without attempting to obtain the consent of McAlpine. After the practical completion of the works a serious defect was discovered which was remedied at a substantial cost paid for initially by St Martins who were later reimbursed by the assignee company. The defect was alleged to have resulted from a breach of contract occurring after the assignment. St Martins sued McAlpine who maintained that since St Martins had suffered no loss they were only entitled to nominal damages. In a speech with whose reasoning Lord Keith of Kinkel, Lord Bridge of Harwich and Lord Ackner agreed, Lord Browne-Wilkinson concluded that St Martins were entitled to recover substantial damages. At pp. 114G–115C he stated:

> In my judgment the present case falls within the rationale of the exceptions to the general rule that a plaintiff can only recover damages for his own loss. The contract was for a large development of property which, to the knowledge of both Corporation and McAlpine, was going to be occupied, and possibly purchased, by third parties and not by Corporation itself. Therefore it could be foreseen that damage caused by a breach would cause loss to a later owner and not merely to the original contracting party, Corporation. As in contracts for the carriage of goods by land, there would be no automatic vesting in the occupier or owners of the property for the time being who sustained the loss of any right of suit against McAlpine. On the contrary, McAlpine had specifically contracted that the rights of action under the building contract could not without McAlpine's consent be transferred to third parties who became owners or occupiers and might suffer loss. In such a case, it seems to me proper, as in the case of the carriage of goods by land, to treat the parties as having entered into the contract on the footing that Corporation would be entitled to enforce contractual rights for the benefit of those who suffered from defective performance but who, under the terms of the contract, could not acquire any right to hold McAlpine liable for breach. It is truly a case in which the rule provides 'a remedy where no other would be available to a person sustaining loss which under a rational legal system ought to be compensated by the person who has caused it.'

The reasoning of Lord Browne-Wilkinson (supra), was applied by the Court of Appeal in *Darlington Borough Council v Wiltshier Northern Ltd* [1995] 1 WLR 68, another building contract case in which a third party and not the employer under the contract who had no interest in the site had suffered the physical loss flowing from the breach.

The circumstances in the instant case differ from those in the *St Martins* case in as much as in the latter case the employer had an interest in the site at the date of the contract whereas Panatown had no such interest at that date or thereafter. I very much doubt whether this distinction is sufficient to remove the case from the ambit of Lord Browne-Wilkinson's reasoning. There are, however, certain other considerations to be examined.

In *The Albazero* [1997] AC 774, Lord Diplock pointed out that the rationale of the rule in *Dunlop v Lambert* did not extend to cases where there existed a separate contract of carriage between the person who actually suffered the loss and the carrier. . . . He subsequently stated:

> The complications, anomalies and injustices that might arise from the co-existence in different parties of rights of suit to recover, under separate contracts of carriage

which impose different obligations upon the parties to them, a loss which a party to one of those contracts alone has sustained, supply compelling reasons why the rule in *Dunlop v Lambert*, 6 Cl. & F. 600 should not be extended to cases where there are two contracts with the carrier covering the same carriage and under one of them there is privity of contract between the person who actually sustains the loss and the carrier by whose breach of that contract it was caused.

. . . The DCD in favour of UIPL was executed by McAlpine in pursuance of an obligation contained in the building contract. In these circumstances Mr Pollock for McAlpine argued that the *Dunlop v Lambert* rule had no application and the general rule that a plaintiff can only recover damages (other than nominal) for his own loss applied. Mr Friedman countered this by pointing out that the remedies available to UIPL under the DCD were different from and less effective than those available under the building contract. . . .

He also referred to an article by Mr I N Duncan Wallace QC in [1999] 15 Const. L.J. 245 in support of the proposition that the DCD could not properly be treated as the equivalent of the 'separate contract of carriage' referred to by Lord Diplock in *The Albazero* as an exception to the *Dunlop v Lambert* rule. Mr Friedman also urged upon your Lordships that the DCD was granted, not for the benefit of UIPL, but to enable that company to assign the benefit thereof to a future purchaser. Be that as it may there can be no doubt that UIPL were, and indeed are, entitled to sue McAlpine under the DCD and this cannot be ignored.

My Lords it is of course correct that the DCD is not co-terminous with the building contract but does that necessarily mean that the exception to the *Dunlop v Lambert* rule above referred to has no application? That rule provides a remedy where no other would be available for breach of a contract in circumstances where it is within the contemplation of contracting parties that breach by one is likely to cause loss to an identified or identifiable stranger to the contract, rather than to the other contracting party. It prevents the claim to damages falling into what Lord Keith of Kinkel in G.U.S. *Property Management Ltd v Littlewoods Mail Stores* 1982 SLT 533, 538 so graphically described as 'some legal black hole'. It must however, be remembered that the *Dunlop v Lambert* rule is an exception to the general rule that a party who has suffered no loss cannot recover substantial damages for breach. Neither in the speeches of Lord Diplock nor of Lord Browne-Wilkinson, to which I have referred, is it suggested that the *Dunlop v Lambert* rule will only be displaced by rights vested in a third party which are identical to those of the innocent contracting party, indeed Lord Diplock, *The Albazero* [1977] AC 774, 848C, considered that there were even stronger grounds for not applying the rule to cases where the two sets of contractual rights were different. What is important, as I see it, is that the third party should as a result of the main contract have the right to recover substantial damages for breach under his contract even if those damages may not be identical to those which would have been recovered under the main contract in the same circumstances. In such a situation the need for an exception to the general rule ceases to apply. I therefore conclude that in this case the general rule is not displaced by the rule in *Dunlop v Lambert* and that Mr Pollock's submissions are correct. I find support for this conclusion in an article by Professor Treitel 'Damages in Respect of a Third Party's Loss' (1998) 114 LQR 527, 533–4.

The Broader Ground
For the purposes of his argument Mr Friedman limited the application of the broader ground to contracts for the supply of services and defined it as recovery on the basis that the promisee suffers a loss if there is a breach of a contract to confer a benefit on

a third party. The promisee suffers that loss because he has not received the benefit of the bargain for which he contracted. Since Panatown had not received what they had contracted for, namely the construction of a building conform to contract, it followed that they had suffered loss, which was the cost of achieving that objective.

The basis for the foregoing proposition was the speech of Lord Griffiths in St *Martins Property Corporation Ltd v Sir Robert McAlpine Ltd* [1994] 1 AC 85, which it is necessary to look at in some detail. After referring to two defences advanced by McAlpine to the effect (1) that St Martins had no proprietary interest in the property when the breach occurred, and (2) that they had been reimbursed from within the group for the cost of repairs Lord Griffiths, continued at, p. 96F, in relation to the first defence:

> I cannot accept that in a contract of this nature, namely for work, labour and the supply of materials, the recovery of more than nominal damages for breach of contract is dependent upon the plaintiff having a proprietary interest in the subject matter of the contract at the date of breach.

Lord Griffiths instanced the case of a husband who was the sole earner contracting for the repair of the matrimonial home owned by his wife and having to pay a second builder to remedy the defects created by the first. He continued, at 96H:

> Is it to be said that the husband has suffered no damage because he does not own the property? Such a result would in my view be absurd and the answer is that the husband has suffered loss because he did not receive the bargain for which he had contracted with the first builder and the measure of damages is the cost of securing the performance of that bargain by completing the roof repairs properly by the second builder.

Lord Griffiths then gave a further similar example where the husband after contracting with the builder, on advice, transferred his house to his wife and defects appeared. In response to the argument that neither husband nor wife could recover damages he remarked that that would be so unjust a result that the law could not tolerate it. This comment was made with reference to a hypothetical situation in which if the husband had no right of action no one else had and the claim to damages would fall into Lord Keith's black hole.

Lord Griffiths considered McAlpine's argument that *The Albazero* [1977] AC 774 supported their argument that a contracting party suffered no loss if they did not have a proprietary interest in the property at the date of the breach and continued, at 97D:

> *The Albazero* was not concerned with money being paid to enable the bargain, i.e. the contract of carriage, to be fulfilled. The damages sought in *The Albazero* were claimed for the loss of the cargo, and as at the date of the breach the property in the cargo was vested in another with a right to sue it is readily understandable that the law should deny to the original party to the contract a right to recover damages for a loss of the cargo which had caused him no financial loss. In cases such as the present the person who places the contract has suffered financial loss because he has to spend money to give him the benefit of the bargain which the defendant had promised but failed to deliver. I therefore cannot accept that it is a condition of recovery in such cases that the plaintiff has a proprietary right in the subject matter of the contract at the date of breach.

Two matters emerge from that passage namely (1) that Lord Griffiths was contrasting a situation where the promisee (the consignor in *The Albazero*) had suffered no financial loss by the breach of contract and the case before him where St Martins had paid for the necessary repairs, and (2) that he clearly considered it to be of importance that a third party who had actually sustained the financial loss had a right to sue. I summarise Lord Griffith's position on the first defence as follows: Where A employs B to perform work on Whiteacre, which B performs defectively the fact that Whiteacre is owned by C who has no contractual rights against B is no bar to an action for damages by A provided that he has paid or intends to pay for the necessary remedial treatment. In relation to the second defence Lord Griffiths expressed the view that:

> . . . who actually pays for the repairs is no concern of the defendant who broke the contract. The court will of course wish to be satisfied that the repairs have been or are likely to be carried out . . .

I do not find it entirely easy to reconcile Lord Griffith's last observation with his reference to the promisee, St Martins, having suffered financial loss because they had to spend money. It is true that they did initially pay for the remedial work but they were reimbursed in full and cannot therefore be said to have suffered financial loss in the end of the day. Can it matter that they were reimbursed afterwards rather than being put in funds before they made payment? Lord Griffiths vouched his remarks about the second defence by reference to *Jones v Stroud District Council* [1986] 1 WLR 1141, in which the plaintiffs were unable to prove that they had paid for repair carried out to their building and rendered necessary by the defendants' negligence. In the *Jones* case Neill L.J., at p. 1150H, after referring to the general principle that a plaintiff who seeks to recover damages must prove that he has suffered loss continued:—'but if property belonging to him has been damaged to an extent which is proved and the court is satisfied that the property has been or will be repaired I do not consider that the court is further concerned with the question whether the owner has had to pay for repairs out of his own pocket or whether the funds have come from some other source.' Such a case must be distinguished from that where the defect is in the property of a third party and the cost is met by that party or someone other than the plaintiff. In the latter case it is the third party rather than the plaintiff who has suffered financial loss. Given the detailed reasoning of Lord Griffiths in relation to McAlpine's first defence which proceeded upon the footing that the plaintiff although not the proprietor of the subjects had incurred or would have to incur expenditure to remedy the defect I do not think that he can have intended his remarks on the second defence to be taken as authority for the proposition that a plaintiff who had neither incurred expenditure on a third party's property nor had any interest in so doing was nevertheless entitled to recover substantial damages for breach of contract by the contractor. Indeed his comments on *The Albazero* would suggest that a plaintiff should not recover substantial damages for breach of contract when he had suffered no financial loss and when the third party had an independent right of action against the promisor. This would appear to be how Lord Keith of Kinkel understood Lord Griffith's position because having expressed sympathy with the view that a building contractor in breach of his contract should not be relieved of liability to pay substantial damages merely by reason that the other contracting party had no proprietary interest in the works at the time of the breach continued at 95F:

> There is much force in the analysis that the party who contracted for the works to be done has suffered loss because he did not receive the performance he had

bargained for and in order to remedy that has been required to pay for the defects to be put right by another builder.

It was not mere lack of performance but lack of performance plus the requirement to incur expenditure by the promisee which impressed Lord Keith. In my view Mr Friedman's definition of the broader ground goes far beyond what Lord Griffiths said in St Martins and consequently is not supported by his speech in that case.

In *Darlington Borough Council v Wiltshier Northern Ltd* [1995] 1 WLR 68, where A entered into a contract with B for an erection of a building on C's land the Court of Appeal applied the narrow ground in *St Martins*. However, Steyn L.J. (as he then was) at p. 80E expressed his agreement with Lord Griffith's wider principle which he defined as where a builder fails to render the contractual service the employer suffers a loss of bargain or expectation of interest which loss can be recovered on the basis of what it would cost to remedy the defect. Steyn L.J. went on to express the view that 'in the field of building contracts, like sale of goods, it is no concern of the law what the plaintiff proposes to do with his damages,' thereby rejecting Lord Griffiths' qualification that the court would wish to be satisfied that the repairs have been or are likely to be carried out. *Darlington Borough Council v Wiltshier Northern Ltd* was a case in which the employer suffered no financial loss by reason of the contractors' breach and the third party, for whose benefit the works were to be carried out, had no independent right of action. On the reasoning of Steyn L.J. it would appear that the employer in such a case could recover the cost of effecting the necessary repairs and then put the money in his own pocket. This would be a particularly unattractive result and certainly not one which Lord Griffiths would have advocated. Indeed it would seem to raise very sharply the question of whether the employer had suffered any financial loss at all. . . . It is interesting that in *The Albazero* there was no suggestion in Lord Diplock's speech that a plaintiff had a right to recover on the broader ground, which would in that case have rendered unnecessary application of the rule in *Dunlop v Lambert*. Indeed, in refusing to jettison the rule Lord Diplock, at p. 847B said:

. . . there may still be occasional cases in which the rule would provide a remedy where no other would be available to a person sustaining loss which under a rational legal system ought to be compensated by the person who has caused it.

Had Lord Diplock thought that recovery under the broader ground was generally available there would have been little or no content for these observations. I accept, of course, that Mr Friedman in his submissions restricted the application of the broader ground to supply contracts but if the broader ground is to be accepted as a principle there seems little reason for restricting its application to one type of contract.

In *Woodar Investment Development Ltd v Wimpey Construction U.K. Ltd* [1977] 1 WLR 277, Wimpey agreed to buy land from Woodar for a sum of £850,000 of which £150,000 was to be paid to Transworld. A month later Wimpey sent a letter purporting to rescind the contract and Woodar sued for damages including the £150,000 payable to Transworld. This House, in allowing the appeal, held that Wimpey had not repudiated the contract but in view of the Court of Appeal's decision that Wimpey were liable in damages for the £150,000 made certain observations thereon. At p. 284A–D Lord Wilberforce referred to the proposition:

. . . that if Woodar made a contract for a sum of money to be paid to Transworld, Woodar can, without showing that it has itself suffered loss or that Woodar was agent or trustee for Transworld, sue for damages for non-payment of that sum. That would certainly not be an established rule of law. . . .

Lord Wilberforce later said, at p. 284C:

> Whether in a situation such as the present—viz where it is not shown that Woodar was agent or trustee for Transworld, or that Woodar itself sustained any loss, Woodar can recover any damages at all, or any but nominal damages, against Wimpey, and on what principle, is, in my opinion, a question of great doubt and difficulty—no doubt open in this House—but one on which I prefer to reserve my opinion.

Lord Salmon considered that the law in relation to damages of the kind under consideration was most unsatisfactory (at p. 291C). Lord Russell of Killowen would have concluded that in the absence of evidence to suggest that Woodar would suffer any damage from a failure by Wimpey to pay the £150,000 Woodar had established no more than nominal damages (at p. 293F). Lord Keith of Kinkel agreed with Lord Scarman, at p. 300G, that it was open to the House to declare that:

> . . . in the absence of evidence to show that he has suffered no loss, A, who has contracted for a payment to be made to C, may rely on the fact that he required the payment to be made as *prima facie* evidence that the promise for which he contracted was a benefit to him and that the measure of his loss in the event of non-payment is the benefit which he intended for C but which has not been received.

Lord Scarman pointed out that this was clearly a difficult question.

It is clear from the speeches in the Woodar case that none of their Lordships were aware of an existing principle such as the broader ground contended for by Mr Friedman. Lord Wilberforce and Lord Russell of Killowen were, to say the least, extremely doubtful whether such a principle could exist and certainly did not consider that mere loss of bargain or expectation *per se* with no resultant financial loss would justify substantial damages. Mr Friedman has not persuaded me otherwise.

My Lords there is a fundamental distinction between the narrow and broader grounds whether as examined by Lord Griffiths or as expounded by Mr Friedman. In the former the promisee seeks to recover the loss suffered by and for the benefit of the third party, and is accountable therefore to that party (*Joseph v Knox*, The Albazero 845–6). In the latter the promisee seeks to recover the loss which he personally has suffered. Given that the law is not generally concerned with what a plaintiff proposes to do with his damages one must ask what principle of law would require the promisee to hand over his damages to the third party. It was suggested that in applying the broader ground the court would only award substantial damages to the promisee if satisfied that he was likely to pass them on to the third party. John Cartwright in 'Damages, Third Parties and Common Sense' (1996) 10 JCL 244, 256 recognising the difficulty suggests that the court might require the promisee to give an appropriate undertaking on condition of allowing recovery. These suggestions, however, throw no light on the principle which dictates that thereafter the promisee should hand over the damages. Furthermore consequential loss resulting to the third party due to delay and resultant loss of profits would appear to be irrecoverable. Lord Griffiths in the St Martins case [1994] 1 AC 85, 97A referred to the husband's loss as being the cost of securing performance of the bargain with the first builder, namely the proper completion of the roof repairs. He did not require to consider consequential loss.

The *St Martins* case and *Darlington Borough Council v Wiltshier Northern Ltd* [1995] 1 WLR 68 were both what I may describe as 'black hole' cases, that is to say if the employer under the building contract could not recover from the contractor the owner of the building would receive nothing and the contractor would effectively be relieved of liability for his breach. The greater part of Lord Griffith's reasoning was directed to reject the proposition that entitlement to more than nominal damages was dependent upon the plaintiff having a proprietary interest in the subject matter. His examples predicated that the husband/employer required to pay for repairs rendered necessary by the breach. He did not require to address the situation where, as here, Panatown has neither spent money in entering into the contract nor intends to do so in remedying the breach and has therefore suffered no loss thereby. Had he had to do so I very much doubt whether he would have expressed the same views in relation thereto.

Since writing this speech, I have had the advantage of reading in draft the speech of my noble and learned friend Lord Goff of Chieveley. I respectfully agree with his rejection of the proposition that the employer under a building contract is unable to recover substantial damages for breach of the contract if the work in question is to be performed on land or buildings which are not his property. In such a case the employer's right to substantial damages will, in my view, depend upon whether he has made good or intends to make good the effects of the breach. . . . This produces a sensible result and avoids the recovery of an 'uncovenanted' profit by an employer who does not intend to take steps to remedy the breach.

However, there is a further matter to be considered in this case namely the DCD in favour of UIPL. This, in my view, is equally relevant to the broader as to the narrow ground. The former as does the latter seeks to find a rational way of avoiding the 'black hole'. What is the justification for allowing A to recover from B as his own a loss which is truly that of C when C has his own remedy against B? I would submit none. The complications and anomalies to which Lord Diplock referred in *The Albazero* [1977] AC 774, 848F as arising from two contracts of carriage for the same goods could arise equally if not more sharply were Panatown entitled to claim substantial damages on the broader ground. If Panatown have a claim for loss of expectation of interest measured by the cost of achieving what they contracted for and UIPL have a separate claim in relation to the same defects McAlpine cannot be mulcted twice over in damages. Panatown's claim for loss of expectation of interest can have only nominal value when UIPL has an enforceable claim and Panatown has no intention of taking steps to remedy the breach. Were it otherwise the great practical difficulties referred to by my noble and learned friend Lord Browne-Wilkinson at the end of his speech would arise. Lord Griffiths in a passage to which I have already referred ([1994] 1 AC 85, 97E) accepted that A should not have a remedy for loss of cargo which had caused him no financial loss when C had a direct right of action. It would be surprising if he had taken a different view of the position of Panatown and UIPL. I therefore consider that Panatown is not entitled to recover under Mr Friedman's broader ground not only because they have suffered no financial loss but also because UIPL have a direct right of action against McAlpine under the DCD. As I have come to the conclusion that neither the narrow nor the broader ground is applicable to the facts of this case I would allow the appeal.

Lord Browne-Wilkinson:

In my judgment the direct cause of action which UIPL has under the DCD is fatal to any claim to substantial damages made by Panatown against McAlpine based on the narrower ground. First, the principle in *The Albazero* [1977] AC 774 as applied to building contracts by the *St Martin's* case [1994] 1 AC 85 is based on the fact that it provides a remedy to the third party 'where no other would be available to a person sustaining loss which under a rational legal system ought to be compensated by the person who has caused it.': see *The Albazero*, at p. 847B and the *St Martin's* case, at p. 114G. If the contractual arrangements between the parties in fact provide the third party with a direct remedy against the wrongdoer the whole rationale of the rule disappears. Moreover, as I have said, both the decision in *The Albazero* case itself and dicta in the *St Martin's* case at p. 115F state that where the third party (C) has a direct claim against the builder (B) the promisee under the building contract (A) cannot claim for the third party's damage.

I turn now to the broader ground on which Lord Griffiths decided the *St Martin's* case. He held that the building contractor (B) was liable to the promisee (A) for more than nominal damages even though A did not own the land at the date of breach. He held in effect that by reason of the breach A had himself suffered damage, being the loss of the value to him of the performance of the contract. On this view even though A might not be legally liable to C to provide him with the benefit which the performance of the contract by B would have provided, A has lost his 'performance interest' and will therefore be entitled to substantial damages being, in Lord Griffiths' view, the cost to A of providing C with the benefit. In the *St Martin's* case Lord Keith of Kinkel, Lord Bridge of Harwich and I all expressed sympathy with Lord Griffiths' broader view. However, I declined to adopt the broader ground until the possible consequences of so doing had been examined by academic writers. That has now happened and no serious difficulties have been disclosed. However, there is a division of opinion as to whether the contracting party, A, is accountable to the third party, C, for the damages recovered or is bound to expend the damages on providing for C the benefit which B was supposed to provide. Lord Griffiths in the *St Martin's* case (at p. 97G) took that view. But as I understand them Lord Goff of Chieveley and Lord Millett in the present case (in agreement with Lord Steyn in *Darlington Borough Council v Wiltshier Northern Ltd* [1995] 1 WLR 68, 80H) would hold that, in the absence of the specific circumstances of the present case A, is not accountable to C for any damages recovered by A from B.

I will assume that the broader ground is sound in law and that in the ordinary case where the third party (C) has no direct cause of action against the building contractor (B) A can recover damages from B on the broader ground. Even on that assumption, in my judgment Panatown has no right to substantial damages in this case because UIPL (the owner of the land) has a direct cause of action under the DCD.

The essential feature of the broader ground is that the contracting party A, although not himself suffering the physical or pecuniary damage sustained by the third party C, has suffered his own damage being the loss of his performance interest, i.e. the failure to provide C with the benefit that B had contracted for C to receive. In my judgment it follows that the critical factor is to determine what interest A had in the provision of the service for the third party C. If, as in the present case, the whole contractual scheme was designed, *inter alia*, to give UPIL and its successors a legal remedy against McAlpine for failure to perform the building contract with due care, I cannot see that Panatown has suffered any damage to its performance interests: subject to any defence based on limitation of actions, the physical and pecuniary damage suffered by UPIL can be redressed by UPIL exercising its own cause of action against McAlpine. It is not clear to me why this has not occurred in the present case: but, subject to questions of limitation which were not explored, there is no reason even now why UPIL should not be bringing the proceedings against McAlpine. The fact that the DCD may have been primarily directed to ensuring that UPIL's successors in title should enjoy a remedy in tort against McAlpine is nothing to the point: the contractual provisions were directed to ensuring that UPIL and its successors in title did have the legal right to sue McAlpine direct. So long as UPIL enjoys this right Panatown has suffered no failure to satisfy its performance interest.

The theoretical objection to giving the contracting party A substantial damages for breach of the contract by B for failing to provide C with a benefit which C itself can enforce against B is further demonstrated by great practical difficulties which such a view would entail. Let me illustrate this by postulating a case where, before the breach occurred, UPIL had with consent assigned the benefit of the DCD to a purchaser of the site, X. What if Panatown itself was entitled to, and did, sue for and recover damages from McAlpine? Presumably McAlpine could not in addition be liable to X for breach of the DCD: yet Panatown would not be liable to account to X for the damages it had recovered from McAlpine. The result would therefore be another piece of legal nonsense: the party who had suffered real, tangible damage, X, could recover nothing but Panatown which had suffered no real loss could recover damages. Again, suppose that X agrees with McAlpine certain variations of McAlpine's liability under the building contract. What rights would Panatown then have against McAlpine? The Law Commission in its Report 'Privity of Contract: Contracts for the Benefit of Third Parties' (1996) (Law Com. No. 242) considered at length questions like these (see in particular paragraphs 11.14, 11.21 and 11.22) and many other problems such as set off and counter-claims. The Law Commission recommended that in certain defined circumstances third parties should be entitled to enforce the contract. But in the draft Bill annexed to the Report and in the Act of Parliament which enacted the recommendations, the Contract (Rights of Third Parties) Act 1999, specific statutory provisions were included to deal with the difficulties arising. Although both the Law Commission's Report (paragraphs 5.10 and 5.11) and sections 4 and 6(1) of the Act make it clear that the Act is not intended to discourage the courts from developing the rights of third parties when it is appropriate to do so, in my judgment there is little inducement in a case such as the present where a third party has himself the right to enforce the contract against the contract breaker, to extend the law so as to give both the promisee and the third party concurrent rights of enforcement.

For these reasons I would allow the appeal.

Lord Clyde:

It seems to me that a more realistic and practical solution is to permit the contracting party to recover damages for the loss which he and a third party has suffered, being duly accountable to them in respect of their actual loss, than to construct a theoretical loss in law on the part of the contracting party, for which he may be under no duty to account to anyone since it is to be seen as his own loss. The solution is required where the law will not tolerate a loss caused by a breach of contract to go uncompensated through an absence of privity between the party suffering the loss and the party causing it. In such a case, to avoid the legal black hole, the law will deem the innocent party to be claiming on behalf of himself and any others who have suffered loss. It does not matter that he is not the owner of the property affected, nor that he has not himself suffered any economic loss. He sues for all the loss which has been sustained and is accountable to the others to the extent of their particular losses. While it may be that there is no necessary right in the third party to compel the innocent employer to sue the contractor, in the many cases of the domestic or familial situation that consideration should not be a realistic problem. In the commercial field, in relation to the interests of such persons as remoter future proprietors who are not related to the original employer, it may be that a solution by way of collateral warranty would still be required. If there is an anxiety lest the exception would permit an employer to receive excessive damages, that should be set at rest by the recognition of the basic requirement for reasonableness which underlies the quantification of an award of damages.

The problem which has arisen in the present case is one which is most likely to arise in the context of the domestic affairs of a family group or the commercial affairs of a group of companies. How the members of such a group choose to arrange their own affairs among themselves should not be a matter of necessary concern to a third party who has undertaken to one of their number to perform services in which they all have some interest. It should not be a ground of escaping liability that the party who instructed the work should not be the one who sustained the loss or all of the loss which in whole or part has fallen on another member or members of the group. But the resolution of the problem in any particular case has to be reached in light of its own circumstances. In the present case the decision that Panatown should be the employer under the building contract although another company in the group owned the land was made in order to minimise charges of VAT. No doubt thought was given as to the mechanics to be adopted for the building project in order to achieve the course most advantageous to the group. Where for its own purposes a group of companies decides which of its members is to be the contracting party in a project which is of concern and interest to the whole group I should be reluctant to refuse an entitlement to sue on the contract on the ground simply that the member who entered the contract was not the party who suffered the loss on a breach of the contract. But whether such an entitlement is to be admitted must depend upon the arrangements which the group and its members have decided to make both among themselves and with the other party to the contract. In the present case there was a plain and deliberate course adopted whereby the company with the potential risk of loss was given a distinct entitlement directly to sue the contractor and the professional advisers. In the light of such a clear and deliberate course I do not consider that an exception can be admitted to the general rule that substantial damages can only be claimed by a party who has suffered substantial loss. I agree that the appeal should be allowed.

(Lord Goff and Lord Millett dissented.)

Consider:

If no DCD had existed in the Panatown case, what would have been the likely outcome of the case?

Note

In *Law of Contract* (11th edn, 2003) at pp. 598–602, Treitel notes that this decision leaves a number of issues open. Firstly, the effect of the case on the status of Lord Griffiths' 'broader ground' in the *St Martins* case. Treitel suggests that a promisee would not be allowed to recover where the third party had no contractual rights of his own against the promisor in respect of loss suffered by him in consequence of the defective services rendered under the contract unless either the condition stated by Lord Griffiths is satisfied i.e. 'the repairs had been or are likely to be carried out' or the employer has entered a separate contract with the owner undertaking liability in respect of the defects in the contractors work. Secondly, if the 'broader ground' is accepted for cases in which the third party has no contractual rights of his own, a problem arises as to its scope. Does the rationale apply to cases in which the breach consists of a simple failure or refusal to perform or to cases where the obligation which is not performed is one to do something other than render services? Thirdly, is it a requisite of the operation of the 'broader ground' that 'the repairs have been or are likely to be carried out'?

Specific Performance

An action by the promisee for specific performance may provide the third party with a remedy. This is a discretionary remedy and is useful where damages would not constitute an appropriate remedy.

Beswick v Beswick [1968] AC 58

Lord Reid:

My Lords, before 1962 the respondent's deceased husband carried on business as a coal merchant. By agreement of 14 March 1962, he assigned to his nephew, the appellant, the assets of the business and the appellant undertook first to pay to him £6 10s per week for the remainder of his life and then to pay to the respondent an annuity of £5 per week in the event of her husband's death. The husband died in November 1963. Thereupon, the appellant made one payment of £5 to the respondent but he refused to make any further payment to her. The respondent now sues for £175 arrears of the annuity and for an order for specific performance of the continuing obligation to pay the annuity . . .

It so happens that the respondent is administratrix of the estate of her deceased husband and she sues both in that capacity and in her personal capacity. So it is necessary to consider her rights in each capacity.

For clarity I think it best to begin by considering a simple case where, in consideration of a sale by A to B, B agrees to pay the price of £1,000 to a third party X. Then the first question appears to me to be whether the parties intended that X should receive the money simply as A's nominee so that he would hold the money for behoof of A and be accountable to him for it, or whether the parties intended that X should receive the money for his own behoof and be entitled to keep it. That appears to me to be a question of construction of the agreement read in light of all the circumstances which were known to the parties . . .

In the present case I think it clear that parties to the agreement intended that the respondent should receive the weekly sums of £5 in her own behoof and should not be accountable to her deceased husband's estate for them. Indeed the contrary was not argued. Reverting to my simple example the next question appears to me to be: Where the intention was that X should keep the £1,000 as his own, what is the nature of B's obligation and who is entitled to enforce it? It was not argued that the law of England regards B's obligation as a nullity, and I have not observed in any of the authorities any suggestion that it would be a nullity. . . .

Lord Denning's view, expressed in this case not for the first time, is that X could enforce this obligation. But the view more commonly held in recent times has been that such a contract confers no right on X and that X could not sue for the £1,000 . . .

What then is A's position? I assume that A has not made himself a trustee for X, because it was not argued in this appeal that any trust had been created. So, if X has no right, A can at any time grant a discharge to B or make some new contract with B. If there were a trust the position would be different. X would have an equitable right and A would be entitled and, indeed, bound to recover the money and account for it to X. And A would have no right to grant a discharge to B. If there is no trust and A wishes to enforce the obligation, how does he set about it? He cannot sue B for the £1,000 because under the contract the money is not payable to him, and, if the contract were performed according to its terms, he would never have any right to get the money. So he must seek to make B pay X.

The argument for the appellant is that A's only remedy is to sue B for damages for B's breach of contract in failing to pay the £1,000 to X. Then the appellant says that A can only recover nominal damages of 40s because the fact that X has not received the money will generally cause no loss to A. He admits that there may be cases where A would suffer damage if X did not receive the money but says that the present is not such a case.

Applying what I have said to the circumstances of the present case, the respondent in her personal capacity has no right to sue, but she has a right as administratrix of her husband's estate to require the appellant to perform his obligation under the agreement. He has refused to do so and he maintains that the respondent's only right is to sue him for damages for breach of his contract. If that were so, I shall assume that he is right in maintaining that the administratrix could then only recover nominal damages because his breach of contract has caused no loss to the estate of her deceased husband.

If that were the only remedy available the result would be grossly unjust. It would mean that the appellant keeps the business which he bought and for which he has only paid a small part of the price which he agreed to pay. He would avoid paying the rest of the price, the annuity to the respondent, by paying a mere 40s damages . . .

The respondent's second argument is that she is entitled in her capacity of administratrix of her deceased husband's estate to enforce the provision of the agreement for the benefit of herself in her personal capacity, and that a proper way of enforcing that provision is to order specific performance. That would produce a just result, and, unless there is some technical objection, I am of opinion that specific performance ought to be ordered.

Lord Pearce:

My Lords, if the annuity had been payable to a third party in the lifetime of Beswick senior and there had been default, he could have sued in respect of the breach. His administratrix is now entitled to stand in his shoes and to sue in respect of the breach which has occurred since his death.

It is argued that the estate can only recover nominal damages and that no other remedy is open, either to the estate or to the personal plaintiff. Such a result would be wholly repugnant to justice and commonsense. And if the argument were right it would show a very serious defect in the law.

In the first place, I do not accept the view that damages must be nominal. Lush L.J. in *Lloyd's v Harper*[1] said:

Then the next question which, no doubt, is a very important and substantial one, is, that Lloyd's, having sustained no damage themselves, could not recover for the losses sustained by third parties by reason of the default of Robert Henry Harper as an underwriter. That, to my mind, is a startling and alarming doctrine, and a novelty, because I consider it to be an established rule of law that where a contract is made with A for the benefit of B, A can sue on the contract for the benefit of B, and recover all that B could have recovered if the contract had been made with B himself.

(See also *Drimmie v Davies*.[2]) I agree with the comment of Windeyer J. in the case of *Coulls v Bagot's Executor and Trustee Co. Ltd*[3] in the High Court of Australia that the words of Lush L.J. cannot be accepted without qualification and regardless of context and also with his statement: 'I can see no reason why in such cases the damages which A would suffer upon B's breach of his contract to pay C $500 would be merely nominal: I think that in accordance with the ordinary rules for the assessment of damages for breach of contract they could be substantial. They would not necessarily be $500; they could I think be less or more.' In the present case I think that the damages, if assessed, must be substantial. It is not necessary, however, to consider the amount of damages more closely since this is a case in which, as the Court of Appeal rightly decided, the more appropriate remedy is that of specific performance.

The administratrix is entitled, if she so prefers, to enforce the agreement rather than accept its repudiation, and specific performance is more convenient than an action for arrears of payment followed by separate actions as each sum falls due. Moreover, damages for breach would be a less appropriate remedy since the parties to the agreement were intending an annuity for a widow; and a lump sum of damages does not accord with this. And if (contrary to my view) the argument that a derisory sum of damages is all that can be obtained be right, the remedy of damages in this case is manifestly useless.

The present case presents all the features which led the equity courts to apply their remedy of specific performance. The contract was for the sale of a business. The defendant could on his part clearly have obtained specific performance of it if Beswick senior or his administratrix had defaulted. Mutuality is a ground in favour of specific performance.

Moreover, the defendant on his side has received the whole benefit of the contract and it is a matter of conscience for the court to see that he now performs his part of it. Kay J. said in *Hart v Hart*[4]: '. . . when an agreement for valuable consideration . . . has been partially performed, the court ought to do its utmost to carry out that agreement by a decree for specific performance.'

What, then, is the obstacle to granting specific performance?

It is argued that since the widow personally had no rights which she personally could enforce the court will not make an order which will have the effect of enforcing those rights. I can find no principle to this effect. The condition as to payment of an annuity to the widow personally was valid. The estate (though not the widow personally) can enforce it. Why should the estate be barred from exercising its full contractual rights merely because in doing so it secures justice for the widow who, by a mechanical defect of our law, is unable to assert her own rights? Such a principle would be repugnant to justice and fulfil no other object than that of aiding the wrongdoer. I can find no ground on which such a principle should exist.

In *Hohler v Aston*[5] Sargant J. enforced a contract relating to the purchase of a house for the benefit of third parties. The third parties were joined as plaintiffs, but the relief was given to the plaintiff who had made the contract for their benefit: 'The third parties, of course, cannot themselves enforce a contract made for their benefit, but the person with whom the contract is made is entitled to enforce the contract.' In *Keenan v Handley*[6] the court enforced an agreement providing the benefit of an annuity in favour of a mother who was a party to the agreement and, after her death, to her child, who was not a party to it.

And in *Drimmie v Davies* the Court of Appeal in Ireland ordered specific performance of an agreement whereby annuities were provided for third parties. Holmes L.J. there said:

> In this case Davies, junior, covenanted for valuable consideration with Davies, senior, that in certain events he would pay certain annuities to the children of the latter. If such annuities had become payable in the life of the covenantee, and they were not paid, what legal obstacle would there be to his suing the covenantor? Indeed, I believe that it is admitted that such an action would lie, but that it would only result in nominal damages. A result more repugnant to justice, as well as to legal principle, I can hardly imagine. The defendant would thereby escape from paying what he had undertaken to pay by making an illusory payment never contemplated by either party. Well, if Davies, senior, would have been entitled to sue in his lifetime if the annuities were then payable, his executors would have the same right of action after his death. As I have already said, the question is elementary.

Recently in *Coulls v Bagot's Executor and Trustee Co. Ltd* the learned Chief Justice of Australia, Sir Garfield Barwick, in commenting on the report of the Court of Appeal's decision in the present case, said:

> I would myself, with great respect, agree with the conclusion that where A promises B for a consideration supplied by B to pay C that B may obtain specific perform- ance of A's promise, at least where the nature of the consideration given would have allowed the debtor to have obtained specific performance. I can see no reason whatever why A in those circumstances should not be bound to perform his promise. That C provided no part of the consideration seems to me irrelevant.

Windeyer J. in that case said:

> It seems to me that contracts to pay money or transfer property to a third person are always, or at all events very often, contracts for breach of which damages would be an inadequate remedy—all the more so if it be right (I do not think it is) that damages recoverable by the promisee are only nominal. Nominal or substantial, the question seems to be the same, for when specific relief is given in lieu of dam- ages it is is because the remedy, damages, cannot satisfy the demands of justice. 'The court,' said Lord Selbourne, 'gives specific performance instead of damages, only when it can by that means do more perfect and complete justice': *Wilson v Northampton and Banbury Junction Rly Co.*[7] Lord Erskine in *Alley v Deschamps*[8] said of the doctrine of specific performance: 'This court assumed the jurisdiction upon this simple principle; that the party had a legal right to the performance of the contract; to which right the courts of law, whose jurisdiction did not extend beyond damages, had not the means of giving effect.' Complete and perfect justice to a promisee may well require that a promisor perform his promise to pay money or transfer property to a third party. I see no reason why specific performance should not be had in such cases—but of course not where the promise was to render some personal service. There is no reason to-day for limiting by particular categories, rather than by general principle, the cases in which orders for specific performance will be made. The days are long past when the common law courts looked with jealousy upon what they thought was a usurpation by the Chancery court of their jurisdiction.

He continued later:

> It is, I think, a faulty analysis of legal obligations to say that the law treats the promisor as having a right to elect either to perform his promise or to pay damages. Rather, using one sentence from the passage from Lord Erskine's judgment which I have quoted above, the promisee has 'a legal right to the performance of the contract.' Moreover we are concerned with what Fullagar J. once called 'a system which has never regarded strict logic as its sole inspiration.' *Tatham v Huxtable*.[9]

I respectfully agree with these observations.

1. (1880) 16 ChD 290, 321, CA.
2. [1899] 1 IR 176.
3. (1967) 40 ALJR 471, 486.
4. 18 ChD 670, 685.
5. [1920] 2 Ch. 420.
6. 2 De G. J. & Sm. 283.
7. (1874) 9 Ch App 279, 284.
8. (1806) 13 Ves 225, 227–8.
9. (1950) 81 CLR 639, 649.

(Lords Hodson, Guest and Upjohn agreed that the respondent was entitled to a decree of specific performance.)

Note

For a critical comment on this case see Treitel, 'Specific Performance and Third Parties' (1967) 30 MLR 687.

SECTION THREE—EXCEPTIONS

A. Restrictive Covenants

The rule in *Tulk v Moxhay* (1848) 2 Ph. 774 states that the burden of a restrictive covenant will run with the land to which it relates, and thus may be enforced against successors in title, with the exception of a *bona fide* purchaser for value without notice of the covenant. This rule is based on the premise that the restrictive covenant concerns the preservation of the value of the land. (See Wylie, *Irish Land Law* (3rd edn) ch. 19 'Restrictive Covenants'). In *Whelan and Whelan v Cork Corporation* [1991] ILRM 19, Murphy J. accepted that when a lessee contemplates acquiring the interest of his immediate lessor with a view to relieving himself of the burden of covenants in the lease, he or she is put upon enquiry as to the existence and identity of third parties who might have the right to enforce covenants of a like effect as those contained in the lease.

Section 47 of the *Land and Conveyancing Law Reform Bill* 2006, which is currently before the Oireachtas, proposes to make freehold covenants, positive and negative, fully enforceable by and against successors in title.

Consider:

Why should contracts concerning land be afforded special treatment?

B. Irish Statutory Exceptions to the Privity Doctrine

In certain cases it has been enacted that a contract may be enforceable by a person who is not a party to the contract.

Married Women's Status Act 1957 s. 7 (1)–(3), s. 8 (1)–(2)

7. (1) This section applies to a policy of life assurance or endowment expressed to be for the benefit of, or by its express terms purporting to confer a benefit upon, the wife, husband or child of the insured.

(2) The policy shall create a trust in favour of the objects therein named.

(3) The moneys payable under the policy shall not, so long as any part of the trust remains unperformed, form part of the estate of the insured or be subject to his or her debts. . . .

8. (1) Where a contract (other than a contract to which s. 7 applies) is expressed to be for the benefit of, or by its express terms, purports to confer a benefit upon, a third person being the wife, husband or child of one of the contracting parties, it shall be enforceable by the third person in his or her own name as if he or she were a party to it.

(2) The right conferred on a third person by this section shall be subject to any defence that would have been valid between the parties to the contract.

Note

In *Ian Burke (a minor) v Dublin Corporation* [1991] IR 340 the Supreme Court noted that section 8(1)'is clearly restricted to contracts which are expressed to be for, or whose express terms confer benefits upon third persons.'

Road Traffic Act 1961 s. 76 (1)

76. (1) Where a person (in this section referred to as the claimant) claims to be entitled to recover from the owner of a mechanically propelled vehicle or from a person (other than the owner) using a mechanically propelled vehicle (in this section referred to as the user), or has in any court of justice (in proceedings of which the vehicle insurer or vehicle guarantor hereinafter mentioned had prior notification) recovered judgment against the owner or user for, a sum (whether liquidated or unliquidated) against the liability for which the owner or user is insured by an approved policy of insurance or by the payment of which, by the owner or user is guaranteed by an approved guarantee, the claimant may serve by registered post, on the vehicle insurer by whom the policy was issued, or on the vehicle insurer or the vehicle guarantor by whom the guarantee was issued, a notice in writing of the claim or judgment for the sum, and upon the service of the notice such of the following provisions as are applicable shall, subject to sub-s. (2) of this section, have effect:

(a) the insurer shall not after service of the notice pay to the owner or user in respect of the sum any greater amount than the amount (if any) which the owner or user has actually paid to the claimant in respect of the sum;

(b) where the claimant has so recovered judgment for the sum, or after service of the notice so recovers judgment for the sum or any part thereof, the insurer or guarantor shall pay to the claimant so much of the moneys (whether damages or costs) for which judgment was or is so recovered as the insurer or guarantor has insured or guaranteed and is not otherwise paid to the claimant, and the payment shall, as against the insured or principal debtor, be a valid payment under the policy or guarantee;

(c) where the claimant has so recovered judgment for the sum, or after service of the notice so recovers judgment for the sum or any part thereof, and has not recovered from the owner or user or such insurer or guarantor the whole amount of the judgment, the claimant may apply to the court in which he recovered against the insurer or guarantor, grant the application either in respect of the whole amount of the judgment or in respect of any specified part of that amount;

(d) where the claimant has not so recovered judgment for the sum, the claimant may apply to any court of competent jurisdiction in which he might institute proceedings for the recovery of the sum from the owner or user for leave to institute and prosecute those proceedings against the insurer or guarantor (as the case may be) in lieu of the owner or user, and the court, if satisfied that the owner or user is not in the State, or cannot be found or cannot be served with the process of the court, or that it is for any other reason just and equitable that the application and thereupon the claimant shall be entitled to institute and prosecute those proceedings against the insurer or guarantor any sum which he would be entitled to recover from the owner or user and the payment of which the insurer or guarantor has insured or guaranteed;

(e) the insurer or guarantor shall not, as a ground for refusing payment of moneys to the claimant or as a defence to proceedings by the claimant, rely on or plead any invalidity of the policy or guarantee arising from any fraud or any misrepresentation or false statement (whether fraudulent or innocent) to which the claimant was not a party or privy and which, if constituting a misdemeanour under this Part of this Act, was not the subject of a prosecution and conviction under the relevant section of this Act.

A number of exceptions exist in relation to consumer protection. For example, the Consumer Credit Act 1995 (section 80) and the Package Holidays and Travel Trade Act 1995 (section 2). One of the most frequently used is the Sale of Goods and Supply of Services Act 1980. Section 13 of that Act gives a cause of action in respect of persons who are injured whilst travelling in an unroadworthy vehicle which has been sold to a purchaser within the terms of the section.

Furthermore, certain legislative provisions provide for the assignment of contractual rights. For example the Policies of Assurance Act 1867 allows for the assignment of life assurance policies. The Supreme Court of Judicature (Ireland) Act 1877 provides for the assignment of debts and other legal choses in action.

C. TRUSTS

If A promises B to give C £50, C may be able to avoid the privity rule and enforce the contract, if equity will treat B as the trustee for C for the benefit of the contract. C will thus be entitled 'by way of property' to the benefit of the contract. C may thus sue on foot of the contract, although as the legal right vests in B, B would have to be joined as a party to the action. The following case indicates the court's willingness to imply the existence of a trust in order to give relief to third parties.

Drimmie v Davies [1899] 1 IR 176

A father and son entered into a partnership agreement which included a clause obliging the son to pay his brothers and sisters certain annuities in the event of the father dying during the continuance of the partnership. When the father died, the executors of the will, and the brothers and sisters sued to enforce payment of the annuities.

Chatterton V.C.:

The case therefore comes to this, whether any action can be brought by any one against the defendant for his breach of his contract. I say 'by any one', because both the daughters and sons of F. Davies, senior, as the beneficiaries, and his acting executors are joined as co-plaintiffs, the latter of course suing only for the benefit of the former.

The defendant's contention is based on the common law rule that in the case of contracts under seal no one can sue who is not a party to the deed. That rule is fully stated in the case of *Tweddle v Atkinson*,[1] namely, that a stranger to the contract, that is to say, a person who is not a party to the contract and from whom no consideration moved, cannot sue upon it. The test seems to be whether such a person could be sued upon the contract. Now here the daughters and sons were not parties to the contract, nor did any consideration move from them, nor could they be sued upon the contract. But this rule did not prevail in equity, and since the Judicature Act the rules in equity are to prevail in cases where such a conflict exists. The equitable rule was that the party to whose use or for whose benefit the contract had been entered into has a remedy in equity against the person with whom it was expressed to be made. The court deems the latter a trustee for the former, and would compel him to execute his trust according to the apparent intention of the contracting parties. In the case of *Page v Cox*,[2] which has much resemblance to the present case, an agreement was held to amount to a trust which, as stated by Wood V.C., may well be created, though there may be an absence of any expression in terms importing confidence, and a trust cannot be the less capable of being enforced, because it is founded on contract. It was sought to distinguish that case on the ground that there a trust was imposed to pay out of specific property, which, as I have stated, did not exist here, but it seems to me that as the contract here was such that, if the executors of the deceased partner had a right to sue on it, any money recovered by them must have been held by them in trust for the daughters and sons, there is sufficient to create an equity in favour of the beneficiaries. The case chiefly relied on by the defendant was that of the *Empress Engineering Co.*[3] where it was held that a contract made by the promoters of the company with third parties for payment of a sum of money, and which was in itself null and void, could not be made the subject of a claim against the company when formed by reason of its having been mentioned in the purchase deed as a charge subject to which the business was purchased by the company. The case was decided principally on the ground that the agreement with the third parties being in itself null and void was not capable of ratification, but certainly the learned judges who decided the appeal drew a distinction between cases where there was intended to be a charge in favour of the third party on specific property, and cases where there was a mere agreement to pay a sum of money to a third party. Jessel M.R., guards his decision by the observation that he was far from saying that there might not be agreements which may make the third party a *cestui que trust*.

In the case of *Lloyd's v Harper*[4] a question bearing on the principle applicable to such transactions was considered first by Fry J., and afterwards by the Court of Appeal, namely, whether a guarantee given by a father to Lloyd's Assocation on the admission of his son as an underwriter could be sued on by persons who had been underwritten by the son. Lloyd's were co-plaintiffs in the action with outside persons, not members of Lloyd's, who had been underwritten by the son. One of the questions raised was that Lloyd's not having sustained any damage, could only recover nominal damages for themselves, and could not recover for the losses sustained by third parties by reason of the default of the son as an underwriter. This contention was disallowed. As to it, Lush L.J. (p. 321), says 'To my mind it is a startling and an alarming doctrine, and a novelty, because I consider it to be an established rule of law that where a contract is made with A for the benefit of B, A can sue on the contract for the benefit of B, and recover all that B could have recovered if the contract had been made with B himself.' This principle shows that if the executors of F. Davies the elder, who are co-plaintiffs in this action, had sued alone, they could recover all that the defendant agreed with his father to pay, and of any sums so recovered they would of course be trustees for the daughters and sons.

In the case of *Murray v Flavell*[5] before North J., and afterwards on appeal, in which the decision in *Lloyd's v Harper* was referred to, the question arose as to the effect of partnership articles, in which it was provided that from the determination of the partnership the retiring partner or his widow should be entitled to receive out of the profits for a stated period an annuity; and it was contended that this was a mere bargain between the partners, and that no trust was created for the widow, and that she could not enforce an agreement to which she was not a party, and which was not communicated to her. The cases of *Gregory v Williams*;[6] *In re Empress Engineering Co.*; and *Lloyd's v Harper* were considered, and it was held both by North J. and the Court of Appeal that a valid trust for the widow was created by the articles.

The last case referred to, *Gandy v Gandy*,[7] is probably the most important. The action there was brought upon a deed of separation containing a covenant by the husband with trustees to maintain the children. The husband afterwards refused to maintain one of the children, and she sued the husband and the trustees to carry out the trusts of the deed. The husband raised an objection that the plaintiff was not competent to sue upon the deed, and that the only proper parties to sue were the trustees; and it was contended that the children were not parties to the deed, and that the consideration did not move from them. Bacon V.C. held that there was a relation of trustee and *cestui que trust* existing, and that as the trustees refused to sue, the *cestui que trust* could sue. From this the husband appealed, and the judgement of the Vice-Chancellor was reversed. Cotton L.J. stated the rule of law to be as follows:

> As a general rule, a contract cannot be enforced except by a party to the contract; and either of two persons contracting together can sue the other, if the other is guilty of a breach of or does not perform the obligations of that contract. But a third person—a person who is not a party to the contract—cannot do so. That rule, however, is subject to this exception: if the contract, although in form it is with A, is intended to secure a benefit to B, so that B is entitled to say he has a beneficial right as *cestui que trust* under that contract; then B would, in a court of equity, be allowed to insist upon and enforce the contract.

He considered the objection to the plaintiff suing as fatal to the action in its present form, but he allowed the case to stand over to see whether the plaintiff could induce the trustees to sue. Bowen L.J. concurred, and said that whatever may have been the common law doctrine, if the true intent and effect of the deed were to give to the children a beneficial right under it, that is to say, to give them a right to have the covenants performed, and to call upon the trustees to protect their rights and interests under it, then the children would be outside the common law doctrine, and would in a court of equity be allowed to enforce their rights under the deed, but the whole application of that doctrine depends upon its being made out that upon the true construction of the deed, it was a deed which gave the children such a beneficial right.

The case was allowed to stand over. The trustees refused to become plaintiffs. The statement of claim was amended by making the wife and her two eldest daughters co-plaintiffs, and the case came on again for hearing; and it was held that the wife was entitled to sue, for that the agreement was really one between the husband and wife, and the trustees were introduced merely to obviate the objection to the wife suing her husband, and that the case came within the authorities referred to, that where a covenant is entered into with one person for the benefit of another, then if the covenantee will not sue, the person beneficially interested may sue in equity. The case was accordingly heard on the merits and disposed of.

The difficulties raised in these cases do not arise here. In *Gandy v Gandy* it was not disputed that the trustees could sue, and again that the wife could sue, these being parties to the contract. Here we have the personal representatives of F. Davies, senior, who was a party to the contract, and the persons beneficially interested joined as co-plaintiffs suing the defendant. He it was who expressly bound himself to pay these annual sums, and his obligation was to his father, who is now represented by his executors. The defendant having got the full benefit of that contract, now inequitably declines to perform his part of it. Consequently it is not necessary to decide the question whether a fiduciary relation exists between the executors and the beneficiaries for the purpose of enabling the suit to be maintained by the latter. The executors of course admit that any moneys recovered by them from the defendant will be held by them for the benefit of the daughters and sons as provided by the deed.

There must be judgment for payment by the defendant to the executors of the sums due on foot of the arrears of the annuities, and for payment of the accruing gales to be applied by them in accordance with the terms of the 15th clause of the deed.

The decision was upheld by the Court of Appeal.

Holmes L.J.:

I decide this case on very simple—even elementary—grounds. The proposition affirmed in *Tweddle v Atkinson* is excellent law; but it has no application to the present case. In that case it was held that a contract by which a benefit was provided for a person not a party to it cannot be sued on by such person: but it contains no suggestion that the contract could not have been enforced by the person with whom it was made. In this case Davies, junior, covenanted for valuable consideration with Davies, senior, that in certain events he would pay certain annuities to the children of the latter. If such annuities had become payable in the life of the covenantee, and they were not paid, what legal obstacle would there be to his suing the covenantor? Indeed, I believe that it is admitted that such an action would lie, but that it would only result in nominal damages. A result more repugnant to justice, as well as to legal principle, I can hardly imagine. The defendant would thereby escape from paying what he had undertaken to pay by making an illusory payment never contemplated by either party. Well, if Davies, senior, would have been entitled to sue in his lifetime if the annuities were then payable, his executors would have the same right of action after his death. As I have already said, the question is elementary.

I desire to add that I am not to be understood as holding that in the circumstances of this case the children could not have maintained the action without the personal representatives. I see grounds resting on both authority and legal principle for thinking that *Tweddle v Atkinson* is distinguishable; but it is unnecessary to consider this.

1. 1 B & S 393.
2. 10 Ha. 163.
3. 16 ChD 125.
4. 16 ChD 290.
5. 25 ChD 89.
6. 3 Mer 582.
7. 30 ChD 57.

Note

In *Kenney v Employers' Liability Assurance Corp.* [1901] 1 IR 301, the same principle was applied and a trust was said to exist despite the strong opinion of Walker L.J. dissenting. Having referred to the cases of *Lloyd's v Harper*, *Drimmie v Davies*, *Gandy v Gandy*, *Tomlinson v Gill* and *re Empress Engineering Co.*, Walker L.J. continued:

Let us apply the tests furnished by the authorities to the case before the court—was it the object of intent or effect of the deed and bond, according to their true construction, to confer a beneficial right upon the mortgagor, or to make the mortgagees in any sense trustees for the mortgagor? . . . There is nothing from which it can be inferred that the benefit of the mortgagor was in any way in contemplation. The object of the mortgagee was solely to protect his own interest, and guard against the loss which, directly or indirectly, might fall upon him by putting a receiver in receipt of the rents, and this is natural, though the mortgagor and the mortgagor's estate were still between him and ultimate loss. The mortgagor indirectly gets a benefit from the due application of the rents, but it is not from his being a *cestui que trust*, or object of the bond or deed. If he was not a *cestui que trust*, the mortgagee cannot be a trustee for him, and therefore when the mortgagee was paid off, as he was before action, the mortgagor could recover nothing on that which was solely the security obtained by and held for the benefit of the mortgagee. I am of opinion that neither the mortgagor, or, on the facts, the mortgagee who was paid off, could separately maintain this action, and if that be so, they could not maintain it together.

The following case indicates that the courts now appear more reluctant to imply the existence of a trust unless it is clear that this was the intention of the parties. The Law Reform Commission Report 88–2008 describe this as an acknowledgment that the trust involves serious and often more far-reaching consequences than a contract.

Cadbury Ireland Ltd *v* Kerry Co-operative Creameries Ltd and Dairy Disposal Co. Ltd [1982] ILRM 77

The second defendant owned a number of creameries which supplied milk to the plaintiff. To encourage the plaintiff to expand its operations the second defendant, with the endorsement of the Minister for Agriculture, agreed to adequately supply the plaintiff in the event of their expansion. The plaintiff proceeded with expansion. When the second defendant was negotiating the sale of certain of its creameries to the first defendant, it emphasised that adequate milk supplies to the plaintiff would have to be ensured. In a subsequent agreement between the first and second defendants for the transfer, a clause was inserted ('clause 19') containing an undertaking by the first defendant to continue supplying the plaintiff, subject to price and total supply stipulations. The plaintiff was not however a party to this agreement. Later, when milk supplies were threatened, the plaintiff attempted to rely on this undertaking.

Barrington J.:

In my view clause 19 was inserted in the agreement by the second-named defendant for the benefit of the plaintiffs.

The plaintiffs accordingly maintain that, though not a party to the contract, they are entitled to sue upon clause 19 of it because the Dairy Disposal Co. Ltd is, in the circumstances of this case, a trustee of the benefit of that clause for the plaintiff company. They rely upon the principle laid down in *Lloyd's v Harper* (1880–1) 16 ChD 290 and in particular on the law as stated by Fry J., at 309: 'It appears to me from the cases which were cited in the course of the argument, especially *Tomlinson v Gill* Amb 330 and *Lamb v Vice* 6 M & W 467 that where a contract is made for the benefit and on behalf of a third person, there is an equity in that third person to sue on the contract, and the person who has entered into the contract may be treated as a trustee for the person for whose benefit it has been entered into.'

The principle that the parties to a contract can create a trust of contractual rights for the benefit of a third party and that that third party can himself enforce those rights, if his trustee does not enforce them for him, by suing the person placed under a duty to him by the contract and by joining his trustee as a co-defendant, is well established. It is discussed in *Anson on Contract* (1975 edn), 408 and on which the plaintiffs rely. It is also discussed in *Cheshire and Fifoot on Contract* (1976 edn), 440 and on which the defendants rely. The latter authors (at 442) quote Lord Wright as referring to the doctrine of a trust of contractual rights as 'a cumbrous fiction' and suggest that the courts are reluctant to extend it. A similar view is expressed in the *Halsbury* (4th edn) vol. 9 para. 341 and, in *Chitty on Contracts* (24th edn) vol. 1, 528 para. 1122, it is stated that the trust device has so far only been applied to promises to pay money or to transfer property. The passage continues: 'It is sometimes suggested that it might be applied to other kinds of promises, e.g. that an employer might hold the benefit of an exemption clause on trust for his employee. In view of the present judicial tendency to confine the trust device within narrow limits, it seems unlikely that such extensions will be made; though other techniques may be used for making the benefit of exemption clauses available to third parties.'

As previously stated, it seems clear to me, that in the present case the minister and the Dairy Disposal Co. Ltd intended to benefit Cadburys, not indeed because they wished to confer any favours on Cadburys, but because they wished, through the Cadbury factory at Rathmore, to advance their view of what the public interest required. One factor which makes the courts more ready to infer that the promisee in a contract is a trustee for the third party is that the promisee should have some contractual or fiduciary duty to the third party. In the present case there was certainly no fiduciary relationship between the Dairy Disposal Co. Ltd and the plaintiffs. It seems improbable that there was a contractual relationship between them. What there was was an undertaking given by the Dairy Disposal Co. Ltd to the plaintiffs with the knowledge and approval of the minister. The value of such an undertaking to the plaintiffs lay not so much in any legal sanction as in the fact that it committed the good faith of the public authority. This undoubtedly provided the motive for the Dairy Disposal Co. Ltd to attempt to protect the interest of the plaintiffs when they were selling creameries the produce of which was covered by the undertaking, but it does not necessarily follow that the Dairy Disposal Co. Ltd intended to, or did in fact, constitute itself a trustee of its rights under clause 19 for the benefit of the plaintiffs. The answer to this question depends, at least in part, on whether clause 19 in fact created legal rights which either the Dairy Disposal Co. Ltd or the plaintiffs can now enforce. . . .

It appears to me that the imprecision of the language in clause 19 is explained by the fact that the clause was concerned with policy considerations and that the draughtsman assumed that clause 19 would be supplemented by a bilateral agreement between the plaintiffs and the first-named defendants in which the precise rights and duties of both parties would be set out. Put another way one could say that clause 19 contemplated a further agreement between the plaintiffs and the first-named defendants to give it business efficacy. . . .

If the first-named defendants had any legal commitments to the plaintiffs under the provisions of clause 19 it appears to me that this was, at most, a commitment to enter into honest negotiations for a legal trading agreement to govern future relations between the parties. In the past the plaintiffs had the benefit of an undertaking which they had received from the Dairy Disposal Co. Ltd with the approval of the minister. The chief value of that undertaking appears to me to have been that, despite the fact that the Dairy Disposal Co. Ltd was in form a company incorporated under the Companies Acts, the undertaking committed the good faith of the public authorities. When, therefore, the Dairy Disposal Co. Ltd was selling its creameries and placing itself in a position where it could no longer fulfil its undertaking, it would have been appropriate for the plaintiffs to have entered into a properly binding legal agreement with the private body which was acquiring the creameries in order to protect the plaintiff's interests in the future.

They did not do so at the time and it appears to me that it is now too late for them to do so pursuant to the provisions of clause 19. Seven years have elapsed and, in the interval, conditions in the dairying industry have totally changed from those which prevailed at the end of 1973 and early 1974.

Moreover I do not believe that the concept of a trust of contractual rights for the benefit of a third party can be extended to cover a case as complex and unusual as the present one.

Notes

1. In *Inspector of Taxes' Association v The Minister for Public Service, Ireland and the Attorney General* [1986] ILRM 296 where Murphy J. had to decide whether the plaintiff staff association or its members could take advantage of a

conciliation and arbitration contract to which they were not parties, the *Cadbury* case was cited as support for the right of the plaintiffs to maintain an action.

2. The trust concept has been used in recent years to try to enable an employee to recover as against an insurance policy taken out by an employer when the employee has been injured in a work-related accident. These applications have generally been unsuccessful: see *Green v Russell* [1959] 2 QB 226, *Bradley v Eagle Star Insurance Co.* [1989] 1 All ER 961, and the decision of Morris J. in *McManus v Cable Management (Ireland) Ltd and Others* (HC) 8 July 1994, unrep.

SECTION FOUR—AGENCY

'It is certainly true, that when a contract is made by an agent, ostensibly acting as principal himself, or as agent for an undisclosed principal, the principal may assume the place of his agent, disclose himself, and sue upon the contract. But this assumes that there were both a principal and an agent when the contract was made.' per Vice-Chancellor Chatterton in *Sheppard v Murphy* (1867) 1 IR Eq 490.

Many of the cases in which reliance is placed on the agency exception to the privity rule involve contracts where third parties seek the protection of exemption or limitation clauses in contracts of carriage. The following three cases are examples.

Scruttons Ltd *v* Midland Silicones Ltd [1962] AC 446

A drum of chemicals was consigned to the respondents from America by ship under a bill of lading signed on behalf of the shipowners. The bill included a clause limiting the liability of the carrier for damage to $500. The appellants, a stevedoring company, were employed by the shipowners to discharge the ship at London port and deliver goods to the consignees. The contract between the appellants and the shipowners stated that the appellants should have 'such protection as is afforded by the terms . . . of the bills of lading'. The respondents were not aware of this contract. When the chemicals were damaged as a result of the appellants' negligence, the respondents sued the stevedores who attempted to rely on the bill of lading. The appellants argued inter alia that through the agency of the carrier they were brought into contractual relations with the shipper.

Lord Reid:

I can see a possibility of success of the agency argument if (first) the bill of lading makes it clear that the stevedore is intended to be protected by the provisions in it which limit liability, (secondly) the bill of lading makes it clear that the carrier, in addition to contracting for these provisions on his own behalf, is also contracting as agent for the stevedore that these provisions should apply to the stevedore, (thirdly) the carrier has authority from the stevedore to do that, or perhaps later ratification by the stevedore would suffice, and (fourthly) that any difficulties about consideration moving from the stevedore were overcome. And then to affect the consignee it would be necessary to show that the provisions of the Bills of Lading Act, 1855, apply.

But again there is nothing of that kind in the present case. I agree with your Lordships that 'carrier' in the bill of lading does not include stevedore, and if that is so I can find nothing in the bill of lading which states or even implies that the parties to it intended the limitation of liability to extend to stevedores. Even if it could be said that reasonable men in the shoes of these parties would have agreed that the stevedores should have this benefit that would not be enough to make this an implied term of the contract. And even if one could spell out of the bill of lading an intention to benefit the stevedores there is certainly nothing to indicate that the carrier was contracting as agent for the stevedores in addition to contracting on his own behalf. So it appears to me that the agency argument must fail.

New Zealand Shipping Co. Ltd *v* A.M. Satterthwaite & Co. Ltd (The Eurymedon) [1975] AC 154

The consignors contracted with a carrier to transport machinery from England to New Zealand. The contract provided that the liability of the carriers, their employees and agents and independent contractors would be limited. The defendant stevedores who were employed by the carrier, damaged the machinery through their negligence in unloading it. In an action for damages, the defendant sought to rely on the limitation clause in the carrier's contract.

Lord Wilberforce (gave the leading judgment for the majority):

The question in the appeal is whether the stevedore can take the benefit of the time limitation provision. The starting point, in discussion of this question, is provided by the House of Lords decision in *Midland Silicones Ltd v Scruttons Ltd* [1962] AC 446. There is no need to question or even to qualify that case in so far as it affirms the general proposition that a contract between two parties cannot be sued on by a third person even though the contract is expressed to be for his benefit . . . *Midland Silicones* left open the case where one of the parties contracts as agent for the third person: in particular Lord Reid's speech spelt out, in four propositions, the prerequisites for the validity of such an agency contract. There is of course nothing unique to this case in the conception of agency contracts: well known and common instances exist in the field of hire purchase, of bankers' commercial credits and other transactions. . . .

The question in this appeal is whether the contract satisfies these propositions.

Clause 1 of the bill of lading, whatever the defects in its drafting, is clear in its relevant terms. The carrier, on his own account, stipulates for certain exemptions and immunities: among these is that conferred by article III, rule 6, of the Hague Rules which discharges the carrier from all liability for loss or damage unless suit is brought within one year after delivery. In addition, to these stipulations on his own account, the carrier as agent for, *inter alios*, independent contractors stipulates for the same exemptions.

Much was made of the fact that the carrier also contracts as agent for numerous other persons; the relevance of this argument is not apparent. It cannot be disputed that among such independent contractors, for whom, as agent, the carrier contracted, is the appellant company which habitually acts as stevedore in New Zealand by

arrangement with the carrier and which is, moreover, the parent company of the carrier. The carrier was, indisputably, authorised by the appellant to contract as its agent for the purposes of clause 1. All of this is quite straightforward and was accepted by all the judges in New Zealand. The only question was, and is, the fourth question presented by Lord Reid, namely that of consideration.
. . .

It [the present contract] is one of carriage from Liverpool to Wellington. The carrier assumes an obligation to transport the goods and to discharge at the port of arrival. The goods are to be carried and discharged, so the transaction is inherently contractual. It is contemplated that a part of this contract, *viz.* discharge, may be performed by independent contractors—*viz.* the appellant. By clause 1 of the bill of lading the shipper agrees to exempt from liability the carrier, his servants and independent contractors in respect of the performance of this contract of carriage. Thus, if the carriage, including the discharge, is wholly carried out by the carrier, he is exempt. If part is carried out by him, and part by his servants, he and they are exempt. If part is carried out by him and part by an independent contractor, he and the independent contractor are exempt. The exemption is designed to cover the whole carriage from loading to discharge, by whomsoever it is performed: the performance attracts the exemption or immunity in favour of whoever the performer turns out to be. There is possibly more than one way of analysing this business transaction into the necessary components, that which their Lordships would accept is to say that the bill of lading brought into existence a bargain initially unilateral but capable of becoming mutual, between the shipper and the appellant, made through the carrier as agent. This became a full contract when the appellant performed services by discharging the goods. The performance of these services for the benefit of the shipper was the consideration for the agreement by the shipper that the appellant should have the benefit of the exemptions and limitations contained in the bill of lading. The conception of a 'unilateral' contract of this kind was recognised in *Great Northern Rly Co. v Witham* (1873) LR 9 CP 16 and is well established. This way of regarding the matter is very close to if not identical to that accepted by Beattie J. in the Supreme Court: he analysed the transaction as one of an offer open to acceptance by action such as was found in *Carlill v Carbolic Smoke Ball Co.* [1893] 1 QB 256. But whether one describes the shipper's promise to exempt as an offer to be accepted by performance or as a promise in exchange for an act seems in the present context to be a matter of semantics. The words of Bowen L.J. in *Carlill v Carbolic Smoke Ball Co.* at p. 268: 'why should not an offer be made to all the world which is to ripen into a contract with anybody who comes forward and performs the condition?' seem to bridge both conceptions: he certainly seems to draw no distinction between an offer which matures into a contract when accepted and a promise which matures into a contract after performance, and, though in some special contexts (such as in connection with the right to withdraw) some further refinements may be needed, either analysis may be equally valid. . . .

(Viscount Dilhorne and Lord Simon dissented.)

Notes

1. In this case, the Privy Council opined that consideration may quite well be provided by the appellant even though it was already under an obligation to discharge to the carrier. Lord Wilberforce stated 'An agreement to do an act which the promisor is under an existing obligation

to a third party to do, may quite well amount to valid consideration and does so in the present case: the promisee obtains the benefit of a direct obligation which he can enforce. This proposition is illustrated and supported by *Scotson v Pegg* (1861) 6 H & N 295 which their Lordships consider to be good law.'

2. The finding of a collateral contract between the cargo owner and the stevedore has been criticised. For example, Treitel notes that 'it is by no means unknown for contracts to come into existence by a process which cannot be strictly analysed in terms of offer and acceptance'. (Treitel 2003, 11th edn, p. 632)

Consider:

Was it relevant that the consignees had possession of the bill of lading in the *Eurymedon* case but not in the *Midland Silicones* case?

Hearne & Matchroom Boxing Ltd *v* Collins (HC) 3 February 1998 unrep.

The second plaintiff sought to enforce an agreement ('the bout agreement') which it had entered with the defendant a boxer, for the benefit of the first plaintiff, a boxing promoter, who managed and controlled the defendant. A management agreement already operated between the parties for a one year period commencing on 12 May 1994. Clause 4 of the bout agreement provided:

> the fighter agrees that should he defeat Chris Eubank and win the WBO Middleweight title then the fighter agrees to extend the management agreement dated 9 May 1994 with Barry Hearn for a period of one year as and from the termination date of his existing management contract.

O'Sullivan J.

This general defence is articulated by means of a number of specific arguments which include reference to the doctrine of privity of contract where it is stressed that the exceptions to the general principle that only parties to an agreement are entitled to enforce must be strictly applied. It is contended that the only party to the bout agreement was Matchroom Boxing and that it was clear that they were not acting as agent for Barry Hearn. In relation to this latter point reliance was placed on Eurymedon [1974] 1 All ER 1015 and in particular to an extract from the judgment of Lord Wilberforce at page 1018 which in turn referred to the leading case of Scruttons Limited v. Midland Silicones Limited [1962] AC 446. In the latter, however, Lord Reid had referred to the possibility of success of the agency argument if four conditions were satisfied, namely:

(a) that it was intended by the parties that the non-party would be protected;
(b) that it was clear that the contracting party was doing so as agent for the non-party;
(c) that the contracting party had authority so to do; and
(d) that any difficulties about consideration moving from the non-contracting party were overcome.

In my view these four conditions are satisfied in the bout agreement. It is clear that both parties were aware that only a human individual as distinct from a company could be a manager of a boxer. Clause 4 of the First Schedule to the bout agreement must be given some meaning and cannot be so interpreted or applied as to have no effect or no enforceability. That I think would be the result if the defendant's argument was correct. From this it follows, I think, that the parties to the bout agreement intended that Barry Hearn as a human individual would have the benefit and be under the obligations specified therein, and to that extent it was clear, in my view, that Matchroom Boxing was contracting as agent for Barry Hearn. The company clearly had authority, in my view, to do that. The consideration which moved from Barry Hearn as an individual was his undertaking to extend the management agreement and also of course to be bound by its terms and provide appropriate services to Stephen Collins thereunder.

It follows that Barry Hearn is entitled to sue on foot of the bout agreement and also that he is bound by any obligations arising thereunder for a year following the termination date of the management agreement. . . .

SECTION FIVE—REFORM

A. The UK Approach

In 1996, the UK Law Commission published a Report on Privity of Contract: Contracts for the Benefit of Third Parties (Law Com. No. 242 (1996)). It recommended reform of the rule of English law whereby a third party to a contract may not enforce it. The recommendations contained in the Report, with some amendments, were implemented by the House of Lords in the Contracts (Rights of Third Parties) Act 1999. Section 1 of this Act sets out the circumstances in which a third party would have the right to enforce a term of the contract.

Contracts (Rights of Third Parties) Act 1999

1. (1) Subject to the provisions of this Act, a person who is not a party to a contract (a 'third party') may in his own right enforce a term of the contract if:
    (a) the contract expressly provides that he may, or
    (b) Subject to subsection (2), the term purports to confer a benefit on him.
   (2) Subsection (1)(b) does not apply if on a proper construction of the contract it appears that the parties did not intend the term to be enforceable by the third party;.
   (3) The third party must be expressly identified in the contract by name, as a member of a class or as answering a particular description but need not be in existence when the contract is entered into.
   (4) This section does not confer a right on a third party to enforce a term of a contract otherwise than subject to and in accordance with any other relevant terms of the contract.
   (5) For the purpose of exercising his right to enforce a term of the contract, there shall be available to the third party any remedy that would have been available to him in an action for breach of contract if he had been a party to the contract (and the rules relating to damages, injunctions, specific performance and other relief shall apply accordingly).

(6) Where a term of a contract excludes or limits liability in relation to any matter references in this Act to the third party enforcing the term shall be construed as references to his availing himself of the exclusion or limitation.

(7) In this Act, in relation to a term of a contract which is enforceable by a third party:

'the promisor' means the party to the contract against whom the term is enforceable by the third party, and

'the promisee' means the party to the contract by whom the term is enforceable against the promisor.

Note

For commentary on the Contracts (Rights of Third Parties) Act 1999 see Kincaid (2000) 116 LQR 43 and Dean (2000) JBL 143.

B. IRELAND

Law Reform Commission Paper (88–2008)—Privity of Contract and Third Party Rights

Chapter 2–B The Need to Reform the Privity Rule [abridged footnotes]
(1) *The intentions of the contracting parties*
2.03 The privity rule can thwart the intentions of the contracting parties. As the law currently stands, a third party cannot enforce a contract made for their benefit, even if the contracting parties agreed that they should be able to do so. The refusal of the courts to give full effect to the contract could be said to undermine the principle of freedom of contract. . . . There is, however, no public policy reason why the courts should refuse to allow a third party to enforce a contract, or term of a contract, when the contracting parties intended for the third party to have this right. Rather, the contractual intention of the parties should be enforced in the most effective way possible by the courts.

(2) *The third party who suffers a loss cannot sue, while the contracting party who can sue has not suffered a loss*
2.04 The rule of privity can produce the bizarre result that the third party who suffers a loss cannot sue, while the contracting party who can sue has not suffered a loss, and thus may only be entitled to nominal damages.

2.06 Even if the promisee can obtain a remedy, the promisee may not wish to sue. It has been pointed out that 'the stress and strain of litigation and its cost will deter many promisees who might fervently want their contract enforced for the benefit of third parties' (Law Commission for England and Wales Privity of Contract: *Contracts for the Benefit of Third Parties* (Law Com No 242, 1996) at paragraph 3.4.). Also, in a situation where the promisee has died, their personal representatives may decide that it is not in the interests of the estate to bring an action.

(3) *The injustice to the third party*
2.07 Where a third party cannot sue for breach of contract, and the promisee is either unwilling to sue, or unable to obtain a remedy on behalf of the third party, it could cause injustice to the third party, who may have had a reasonable expectation that the

contract would be enforced. This injustice is particularly clear where the third party has relied on the contract to its detriment, but it is the view of the Commission that detrimental reliance should not be a prerequisite for the third party's right to enforce the contract, as injustice can also be seen simply where the third party has a reasonable expectation that a contract, or term of a contract, made for its benefit would be enforced.

(4) *The effect of the exceptions to the privity rule*

2.08 The privity rule is subject to a large number of common law and statutory exceptions. These exceptions have developed in a piecemeal fashion to deal with specific problems which were caused by the privity rule. Some of these exceptions are quite complex, and there are various difficulties associated with them. However, more fundamentally, it is clear that the current exceptions do not, and will not, cover every situation where an unjust or illogical result is caused by the privity rule. It could be argued that further specific exceptions could be created to deal with such situations, but it is the Commission's view, for reasons discussed below that this would not be an appropriate measure of reform. Rather, the non-comprehensive nature of an already long list of exceptions supports the need for a more general rule in favour of third party rights.

2.09 A further difficulty caused by the variety of exceptions to the rule is that it can be unclear whether the courts will apply the privity rule or an exception to the rule. . . .

2.11 The Commission is of the view that if a more general exception was created it would increase certainty . . .

(5) *Commercial inconvenience and expense*

2.12 Legal practitioners and others who draft contracts have developed methods of circumventing the privity rule, for example by using assignments and collateral warranties. It could thus be said that the rule of privity does not cause real difficulties in practice. However, a considerable amount of commercial inconvenience and unnecessary expense is still caused by the privity rule . . . . [the use of collateral warranties and end user licence agreements were cited as examples.] . . .

2.14 It is the Commission's view that many of the commercial contractual arrangements which are currently entered into could be simplified by the creation of a general exception to the privity rule which allows third parties to enforce contracts which are entered into for their benefit. Reforms could facilitate a different means of conducting transactions so that those who wish to enter into contracts for the benefit of third parties will be able to do so, in the knowledge that such contracts will be enforceable by the third parties . . .

(6) *The use of collateral warranties*

2.16 The use of collateral warranties is a particular example of the commercial inconvenience caused by the privity rule. . . . [C]ollateral warranties are used extensively in the construction industry to circumvent the privity rule. However, large, complex projects may require the individual drafting of hundreds of separate collateral warranties. The negotiation and signing of so many collateral warranties can be difficult and time-consuming, and can generate a lot of paperwork. This is all very costly, and it has been estimated that for a typical development scheme, about a third of the legal fees can be attributed to the cost of putting collateral warranties in place.

(7) Software licences

2.26 When a customer purchases a software programme from a retailer, either online or from a shop, the contract of sale is between the customer and the retailer, and not between the customer and the producer of the software.

Thus, if the producer of the software wishes to protect their interest in the software programme they must attempt to enter into a collateral copyright licence with the customer. However, if third party rights were generally enforceable, the software producer could rely on the licence agreement in the contract of sale between the retailer and customer. This has been the approach taken in other jurisdictions and it could be seen as a preferableway of managing software licences.

(8) Insurance contracts for the benefit of third parties

2.27 . . . [T]here are still a number of situations where the privity rule can operate to prevent a third party from enforcing an insurance contract. It is the view of the Commission that where this occurs it can be contrary to the intentions of the third parties and can cause an injustice.

2.28 For example, Section 7 of the *Married Women's Status Act* 1957 provides that a policy of life assurance which is expressed to be for the benefit of, or by its express terms purports to confer a benefit upon, the spouse or child of the insured, is enforceable by that spouse or child. However, this section only applies to give rights to the spouse and children of the insured and does not apply to give rights to relatives or to other cohabitants under a contract of insurance. Third parties who do not fall under the legislative exception would either have to rely on the good will of the insurance company or show that they come under an exception to the privity rule, for example by showing that a completely constituted trust was formed in their favour. It is the view of the Commission that this is unnecessarily complicated and uncertain. Third party beneficiaries of life insurance policies should be able to enforce the contract when the contracting parties intended for them to be able to do so.

2.31 A further difficulty that can arise regarding third parties and insurance contracts concerns the subrogation rights of insurers, that is, the right of insurers to take over all the rights of the insured with regard to the claim. For example, if a landlord takes out insurance to protect against damage to its property, such insurance may be of benefit to tenants living in the property. Despite this, if damage occurs, an insurer might use its right of subrogation to bring an action against the tenant if, for example, the damage was caused by the tenant's negligence or if the tenant was in breach of a covenant to repair. To avoid this situation the insurer may agree in the policy to waive its rights of subrogation against the tenant. However, because this agreement not to bring an action against the tenant is contained in the insurance policy, to which the tenant is a third party, it is not clear whether the tenant could rely on it if the insurer did in fact bring an action . . .

(9) Recovery in tort for economic loss

2.34 The development of a system of third party contractual rights would not hinder any future judicial development of a tort of economic loss, but it would facilitate a situation where parties could regulate for themselves their future financial rights, obligations and liabilities . . .

(10) Risk allocation and exemption clauses

2.37 [Referring to the four preconditions in *Scruttons Ltd v Midland Silicones Ltd*] In subsequent cases, courts have taken a wide interpretation of these requirements, and have been willing to allow third parties to rely on exemption clauses where to do so 'is to give effect to the clear intentions of a commercial document' [(*New Zealand Shipping Co Ltd v A M Satterthwaite & Co Ltd; The Eurymedon* [1975] AC 154 at 169, per Lord Wilberforce. See also *Port Jackson Stevedoring v Salmond & Spraggon (The New York Star)* [1980] 3 All ER 257)]. However, this approach has been described as a mere 'partial solution', which 'raises . . . more problems than it solves'. For example, it must be shown that the contractor was acting as the third party's agent in obtaining the limitation of liability. It has been argued that ensuring that this requirement is satisfied 'imposes additional transaction costs and may present special difficulties where the subcontractors are not identified at the time the head contract is entered into and hence cannot be said to have authorized the head contractor to act on their behalf.' [Trebilcock 'The Doctrine of Privity of Contract: Judicial Activism in the Supreme Court of Canada' (2007) 57 Univ of Toronto LJ 269 at 280]

2.38 The law in Ireland is unclear as to whether a third party could rely on an exemption clause which is intended to extend to them. Section 34(1)(b) of the *Civil Liability Act* 1961 provides that a defence 'arising under a contract' is available in respect of a negligence action, but it is unclear whether this refers to a defence in *any* contract, or merely a contract to which the defendant is privy.

2.39 Such uncertainty is undesirable, and instead it should be made clear that third parties can rely on exemption clauses which seek to shield them from liability, subject to the normal rules on the incorporation and construction of exemption clauses.

2.40 In modern commercial transactions, contracting parties use exemption clauses in order to allocate the risk of certain events. For example, if A hires B to store his goods, a clause in the contract between A and B may exclude B's liability to compensate A for in the event that the goods are damaged in storage. Hence, A takes the risk that he may suffer a loss. This will be reflected in the price of the contract between A and B: A will have to either insure against the risk of loss, or self-insure, and thus the price payable to B will be reduced. If A wants to enter into a contract with B under which he has a right of recourse to B if the goods are damaged, i.e. a contract where B takes the risk of damage to the goods, then the price payable to B will increase. Now imagine that A and B are aware that B intends to sub-contract the storage of the goods to a third party C, and an exclusion clause in the contract provides that the liability of B 'and its sub-contractors' is excluded if the goods are damaged in storage. Here, again, the parties would intend that A is to take the risk that he may suffer a loss, and again this would be reflected in a reduced contract price between A and B. However, if the privity rule prevents C from relying on this exclusion clause, A may be able to bring an action in tort against C for A's loss, even though A agreed that it would take the risk of this loss and that B and its subcontractors, C, would not be liable.

2.41 The problem has been summarised in the Canadian Supreme Court as follows:

[A]n application of the [privity rule] so as to prevent a third party from relying on a limitation of liability clause which was intended to benefit him or her frustrates sound commercial practice and justice. It does not respect allocations and assumptions of risk made by the parties to the contract and it ignores the practical realities of insurance coverage. In essence, it permits one party to make a unilateral modification to the contract by circumventing its provisions and the express or implied intention of the parties. In addition, it is inconsistent with the reasonable expectations of all the parties to the transaction, including the third party beneficiary who is made to support the entire burden of liability. [*London Drugs v Kuehne & Nagel International Ltd* [192] 3 SCR 299 at 423 per Iacobucci J.]

2.42 The problem described above is compounded by the fact that tort law has been extended so as to increase the potential liability in tort of third parties such as C to contracting parties such as A. However, such expansion 'has not been accompanied by a matching expansion of the ability to limit that liability through contract, creating a logical gap in the law that could be opportunistically exploited.' (Trebilcock 'The Doctrine of Privity of Contract: Judicial Activism in the Supreme Court of Canada' (2007) 57 Univ of Toronto LJ 269 at 291.)

2.43 In England, this problem was resolved by section 1(6) of the *Contracts (Rights of Third Parties) Act* 1999, which allows third parties to enforce a term of a contract which excludes or limits the liability of the third party, provided that was the intention of the parties.

2.44 The Supreme Court of Canada has taken a very wide approach to this issue, and has allowed third parties to rely on an exemption clause even when the clause did not expressly benefit them. In *Fraser River Pile & Dredge Ltd v Can Dive Services Ltd* [1999] 3 SCR 108 the Court said that such a third party could rely on such a clause provided two conditions were met:

   (a) The parties to the contract must intend to extend the benefit of the clause in question to the third party seeking to rely on the clause.

   (b) The activities performed by the third party seeking to rely on the contractual provision must be the very activities contemplated as coming within the scope of the contract, as determined by reference to the intention of the parties.

In that case, the third party successfully relied on a clause in an insurance contract in which the insurer waived its right of subrogation against the third party. The third party thus had a defence when the insurer attempted to exercise its subrogation rights against the third party by bringing an action in tort for the loss caused to the insured.

2.45 This is a sensible approach which allows the courts to give effect to the allocation of risk and the contractual arrangements entered into by the contracting parties. A contracting party who agrees to take on certain risks, or who has agreed that their rights to bring an action against a third party will be limited, should not be able to circumvent this agreement merely because it is the third party and not the contracting party who seeks to rely on it. To the extent that the law currently prevents third parties from relying on such clauses, it is clearly in need of reform . . .

(11) Comparative analysis

2.60 It is clear from this comparative analysis that Ireland is one of the few jurisdictions which does not provide for a general scheme of third party rights. Reform of the privity rule would thus bring Ireland into line with the law in most countries in the European Union (including the United Kingdom) and the law in the United States, Canada, Singapore and parts of Australia.

Chapter 4 Summary of Recommendations

4.01 The recommendations of the Commission may be summarised as follows:

4.02 The Commission recommends that the privity of contract rule should be reformed to allow third parties to enforce rights under contracts made for their benefit.

4.03 The Commission recommends that legislative reform of the rule of privity is more appropriate than judicial reform. The Commission also recommends that legislative reform of the privity rule should not constrain judicial development of third party rights.

4.04 The Commission recommends that legislative reform of the promisee's remedies should not form part of the proposals to reform the rule of privity. The Commission acknowledges that reform of the rule of privity should not prevent judicial development of the principles relating to the award of damages or specific performance.

4.05 The Commission recommends that reform of the privity rule should not be by the creation of further exceptions to the privity rule in specific instances.

4.06 The Commission recommends that the privity of contract rule should be reformed by means of detailed legislation.

4.07 The Commission recommends that a third party should be able to enforce a term of a contract when the term expressly confers a benefit on the third party. However, the third party should not be able to enforce the term if it appears on a proper construction of the contract that the contracting parties did not intend the term to be enforceable by the third party. The contract should be interpreted in accordance with the ordinary rules of contractual interpretation, but surrounding circumstances should only be taken into account if they are reasonably available to the third party.

4.08 The Commission recommends that a third party should be able to enforce a contract or a term of a contract when the contract expressly states that they may.

4.09 The Commission recommends that a third party should have the right to rely on a term of a contract which excludes or limits the liability of the third party, provided that was the intention of the parties. This is subject to the normal statutory and common law rules on the incorporation and construction of exemption clauses.

4.10 The Commission recommends that the third party should be identified in the contract either by name or by description. Such description should include being a member of a class or group of persons.

4.11 The Commission recommends that there should be an express provision that there is no requirement that the third party be in existence at the time of the formation of the contract. [Paragraph 3.24]

4.12 The Commission recommends that a third party should be able to enforce a term of a contract even though they have not provided consideration. The normal rules on consideration should apply to the promisor and promisee.

4.13 The Commission recommends that the contracting parties should not be able to cancel or vary the contract in such a way as to affect the rights of the third party once either contracting party is aware that the third party has assented to the contract, either by word or by conduct. After this point the contracting parties would need to obtain the consent of the third party to cancel or vary the contract. If this consent is not obtained, the variation or termination of the contract will not affect the rights of the third party, who may bring an action based on the terms of the contract which existed before the variation.

4.14 The Commission recommends that the contracting parties should remain free to include in the contract an express term providing for variation or termination of the contract.

4.15 The Commission recommends that there should be judicial discretion to authorise a cancellation or variation of the contract, on such terms as seem appropriate, when the third party's consent is necessary for such a cancellation or variation, but this cannot be obtained because the third party cannot reasonably be contacted or because they are mentally incapable of giving such consent.

4.16 The Commission recommends that there should be an express provision that there is no requirement that a third party be in existence at the time of assent by another third party.

4.17 The Commission recommends that where a contract jointly benefits multiple third parties, assent by each third party should be needed to crystallise that third party's rights, but it should be possible for one third party to assent on behalf of other third parties in an appropriate case.

4.18 The Commission recommends that the rights of the third party to enforce the contract or a term of the contract should be subject to the other terms and conditions of the contract.

4.19 The Commission recommends that the rights of the third party should be subject to the usual defences which would be available to the promisor if the promisee had taken the action, provided the defence arises out of or in connection with the contract in which the promise is contained.

4.20 The Commission recommends that the rights of the third party should be subject to any defence which would have been available if the third party had been a party to the contract, provided the defence arises out of or in connection with the contract in which the promise is contained.

4.21 The Commission recommends that the defences available to the promisor should include the defence of set-off. The promisor should be free to set-off, against the claim of the third party, any claim the promisor has against the promisee. However the promisor's claim cannot exceed the amount claimed by the third party and the promisor's claim must arise out of or in connection with the contract in which the promise to the third party is contained.

4.22 The Commission recommends that the promisor should be free to counterclaim against the third party where the promisor would in any event have had a right of action against the third party.

4.23 The Commission recommends that the third party who brings an action for breach of contract should be entitled to a full range of remedies, including damages and specific performance, subject to the normal rules governing such remedies.

4.24 The Commission recommends that, unless otherwise agreed by the parties, the promisee should retain the right to enforce the contract even if the contract is enforceable by the third party. There should be no order of priority between the promisee and third party.

4.25 The Commission recommends that although there should be no requirement that the promisee be joined as a party to the litigation when a third party sues to enforce a contract, in an appropriate case it should be possible for the third party to be joined as a party where the promisee sues, and for the promisee to be joined as a party when the third party sues.

4.26 The Commission recommends that once a promisor has fulfilled their duty to the third party, either wholly or partly, the promisor should to that extent be discharged from their duty to the promisee.

4.27 The Commission recommends that if the promisee has recovered substantial damages representing the third party's loss or the expense to the promisee of making good to the third party any default of the promisor, then, in any proceedings brought by the third party against the promisor, the court should reduce any award to the third party to such an extent as it thinks appropriate to take account of the sum recovered by the promisee.

4.28 The Commission recommends that that existing common law and statutory exceptions to the privity rule should be retained and that third parties should not be denied existing remedies available to them.

4.29 The Commission recommends that existing common law and statutory exceptions to the privity rule should be kept under review.

4.30 The Commission recommends that the proposed legislation should not at this time include a comprehensive codification of the existing common law and statutory exceptions to the privity rule. However, this recommendation should not preclude any such codification in the future.

4.31 The Commission recommends that the proposed legislation should not give any third party a right to enforce any contract of employment against an employee.

4.32 The Commission recommends that the proposed legislation should not apply to the contract formed between a company and its shareholders, and between individual shareholders, under section 25 of the Companies Act 1963. The Commission also recommends that the proposed legislation should not apply where the third party is a company which has not yet been incorporated.

4.33 The Commission recommends that the proposed legislation should not apply to a contract for the international carriage of goods by air, rail or road, where the contract is subject to the rules of an international transport convention.

4.34 The Commission recommends that the proposed legislation should not apply to a contract for the carriage of goods by sea, except that a third party can enforce an exclusion or limitation of liability in such a contract if they satisfy the test of enforceability.

4.35 The Commission recommends that the proposed legislation should confer no rights on a third party in the case of a contract on a bill of exchange, promissory note or other negotiable instrument.

4.36 The Commission recommends that the proposed legislation should not apply to documentary credits.

4.37 The Commission recommends that the third party's right of enforcement should not be extinguished merely because one of the contracting parties has become insolvent. The contracting parties may, if they wish, provide in the contract that they are not liable to the third party in the event of the insolvency of either of the contracting parties.

4.38 The Commission recommends that the proposed legislation should apply to contracts and deeds.

4.39 The Commission recommends that the proposed reforms should not affect the rule that to enforce an insurance contract a party must have a sufficient interest in the insurance policy. However, this should not preclude the possibility of the future reform of this rule.

4.40 The Commission recommends that the proposed reforms should apply where the third party is a consumer.

4.41 The Commission recommends that the conferring of additional rights on third party consumers should not form part of the proposed reform of privity of contract.

4.42 The Commission recommends that the legislation should be applicable to give third party rights against consumers, subject to existing consumer protection laws.

4.43 The Commission recommends that nothing in the proposed reforms should be taken to exclude the application of existing legislation affecting contracts, including the Unfair Terms in Consumer Contracts Regulations 1995 and the Sale of Goods and Supply of Services Act 1980.

4.44 The Commission recommends that if a third party wishes to enforce a term of the contract under the proposed legislation, and there is an express term of the contract providing that the third party is to enforce the term by arbitration, the third party should be bound by that express term and should be considered a party to the arbitration agreement as regards disputes between the third party and the promisor.

4.45 The Commission recommends that if a third party wishes to enforce a term of the contract under the proposed legislation, and there is an express term of the contract providing that the third party is to enforce the term in a particular jurisdiction, the third party should be bound by that express term. This is subject to the normal rules relating to jurisdiction clauses.

4.46 The Commission recommends that contracting parties should be able to expressly exclude or . . . contract out of the proposed legislation.

EXERCISES

1. William enters into a contract with his publisher who promises to pay fifty per cent of the royalties to Willam and fifty per cent to his wife Sarah. The publisher subsequently refuse to pay Sarah, arguing that she is not a party to the contract. Advise William and Sarah.

2. William enters into a contract with his publisher who promises to pay fifty per cent of the royalties to Willam and fifty per cent to his wife Sarah. If William subsequently separates from Sarah and argues that she cannot enforce the contract, what options remain open to Sarah?

3. Lola agrees to pay Leslie €4,000 immediately in return for Leslie agreeing to visit Lola's elderly mother every week and to run errands for her mother. After two visits, Leslie stops visiting. Advise Lola and her mother.

4. A contract between the consignee of goods and the carrier provides that the firm of stevedores who have been employed to unload the goods at the destination will have the benefit of a limitation of liability clause. The stevedores drop two crates in the sea during the unloading process and seek to rely on the limitation clause. Can they?

Chapter Sixteen

Illegality

INTRODUCTION

We have already seen instances where the courts will deny a contract the right to enforcement on a number of grounds. In Chapter 3 the doctrine of consideration, through the notion that consideration, 'must be something of value in the eyes of the law' (i.e. the judge) was shown to have denied enforceability to some exchanges which were not devoid of substance, while allowing enforceability to others when the content was less easy to identify: compare *O'Donnell v O'Sullivan* (p. 133 above), with *Williams v Roffey Bros & Nicholls (Contractors) Ltd* (p. 150 above). In both cases the judges alluded to principles of public policy as crucial elements in shaping consideration. Similarly, in Chapter 4, the policy issues presented by contracts as between husband and wife proved dispositive for Atkin L.J. in *Balfour v Balfour* (see p. 221 above). The entire development of pleas of economic duress (Chapter 13) points up how universal issues such as 'improper' pressure or unfair bargaining practices can be addressed by the judiciary, often covertly.

In this chapter we consider a substantial body of case-law in which the courts have denied the enforceability of certain contracts on overt grounds of public policy. The four main policy arguments which have been put forward to justify a doctrine of illegality are: (1) upholding the dignity of the Courts in not requiring them to inquire into the merits and demerits of the particular parties, (2) not allowing a plaintiff profit from his or her own wrongdoing, (3) deterrence, and (4) punishment. The policy values that the courts strive to defend are both various and shifting. Certainly, in relation to so-called common law illegality, many of the social institutions and policy considerations of the eighteenth and nineteenth centuries that shaped the law are increasingly under review. While contracts should not encourage the commission of crimes, if the thing done is no longer criminal (e.g. suicide under the Criminal Law (Suicide) Act 1993) should the courts strike down related contracts or review the law in the light of legislative developments? In the area of human relationships, the desire to uphold the institution of marriage is laudable, but in other legal jurisdictions there has been substantial acceptance of property-related agreements between cohabitees and resort to pre-cohabitation contracts is an increasingly common phenomenon. The *a priori* application of precedents from a different era or another social or moral culture is undesirable, and some judges are sensitive to these issues.

797

Where the source of the illegality is statutory—often a technical, regulatory or fiscal rule that lacks any moral imperative other than the fact that it is parliamentary in origin—the judges are more sensitive to the extreme result that follows from a declaration that any related contract is illegal. Public policy may be better served by enforcement of such a contract, rather than by denying the agreement legal force, and the judges are edging their way towards a more rational, if *ad hoc*, set of solutions, based upon a more generous use of the *in pari delicto* exceptions, the severance of clauses, and a balancing of equities. While this is more evident in statutory illegality cases, decisions like *Saunders v Edwards* [1987] 2 All ER 651, show that certain perceptible shifts in approach are possible across the board, thus causing us to recall Borrough J.'s dictum that public policy is 'a very unruly horse, and when once you get astride it you never know where it will carry you. It may lead you from the sound law', *Richardson v Mellish* (1824) 2 Bing. 229 at 252. However, other judges with a more pronounced taste for judicial activism have stressed the utility of public policy considerations e.g. Denning M.R. in *Enderby Town F.C. Ltd v The F.A. Ltd* [1971] Ch. 591 at 606.

SECTION ONE—ILLEGAL CONTRACTS AT COMMON LAW

A. CONTRACTS TO COMMIT A CRIME OR A TORT

Gray *v* Hibernian Insurance Co. Ltd (HC) 27 May 1993, unrep.

When a public house owned by the plaintiffs's husband ('the deceased') burned down, the deceased made a claim on foot of his insurance policy and also commenced proceedings for damages for malicious injury. The deceased was subsequently charged with arson but acquitted. However, his malicious injury application was dismissed as the Court in that case accepted that testimony from his 'accomplices' in the arson was probably truthful. The High Court was asked to determine whether the insurance contract was enforceable. The defendant argued that she was not entitled to succeed because the loss was caused by her husband's deliberate act.

Barron J.:

In [Beresford v Royal Insurance Co. Ltd [1938] 2 All ER 602] there was a policy of life assurance. It provided that if the life assured should die by his own hand whether sane or insane within one year from the commencement of the insurance the policy should be void as against any person claiming the amount thereby assured or any part thereof. In June 1934 he became insolvent. He had no means of repaying his creditors save with the insurance moneys. Just before the policy expired he shot himself. It was held in those circumstances that it would be contrary to public policy to allow the personal representative of the assured to recover under the policy. ...In the judgment of Lord Atkin he said at 607:

I think that the principle is that a man is not to be allowed to have recourse to a court of justice to claim a benefit from his crime, whether under a contract or under a gift. No doubt the rule pays regard to the fact that to hold otherwise would in some cases offer an inducement to crime, or remove a restraint to crime, and that its effect is to act as a deterrent to crime, but, apart from these considerations, the absolute rule is that the courts will not recognise the benefit accruing to a criminal on his crime.

In the event, the claim failed.

The issue of public policy was considered in R v National Insurance Commissioner Ex-parte Connor 1981 1 All ER 769. An application by a widow for a widow's allowances pursuant to the Social Security Acts was refused upon the basis that she had become a widow through her own intentional criminal act. She had been convicted of manslaughter of her husband and the court accepted that the verdict of the jury must have been based upon a belief that she had deliberately caused the act which caused his death. . . . In that case the court decided that as a matter of public policy that the widow was not entitled to the allowance she claimed.

The two submissions made on behalf of the defendant assumed an onus of proof upon the balance of probabilities. In my view, this is not so. The defence of illegality in relation to insurance law is a question of contract. Here, if the defendant had not admitted liability, it would have had to prove the deceased's involvement in the malicious damage as a matter of probability. Once that defence fails, the defendant is asking the court to deny to the plaintiff upon grounds of public policy the benefit of the cause of action which she has established. To succeed on this defence it must therefore establish that the deceased committed a crime. The issue arises in civil proceedings, but the defence is permitted only because to refuse it would be to allow an unconscionable result. In my view, that requires a heavier standard of proof than the balance of probabilities.

There are only two pieces of evidence which have been adduced upon this issue:
(1) the acquittal of the deceased upon the charge of arson; and
(2) the finding by the Circuit Court that the evidence of the accomplices was probably correct.

. . . The position accordingly is as follows. The accused was acquitted at his own trial when he was there to defend himself. The evidence of the accomplices was accepted on the probabilities when he was not there to defend himself. In my view, public policy could not require the court on such evidence to deny to his estate the benefits to which it is entitled by contract. To do so would neither be fair nor be seen to be fair. Whatever the onus of proof upon the defendant upon this issue, it could not be so low as to be satisfied by the evidence adduced. It is accordingly unnecessary to indicate the proper standard of proof nor the evidence by which it should be established.

Namlooze Venootschap De Faam v The Dorset Manufacturing Co. Ltd [1949] IR 203

The plaintiff, a Dutch company, sued the defendant, an Irish company, for the price of goods sold and delivered. The defendant claimed that such payment either in Dutch guilders or in sterling would constitute a breach of the currency regulations of Ireland which prohibited the export of foreign exchange and the making of payments to persons outside the State without ministerial permission. The permission obtained by the defendant was in respect of a lower figure than required and had in any case expired.

Dixon J.:

The goods in this case were sold and delivered while the Emergency Powers (Finance) (No. 7) Order 1941, was in force. I do not find that the contract, or several contracts, under which the goods were ordered was or were thereby made either void or illegal. One reason is that the prohibitions in article 3 of the order, although void, related rather to what might be a contemplated or possible sequel to the contract rather than its essential nature. Another, and perhaps stronger, reason is that I think the qualification in that article enabling any of the prohibited acts to be done with the permission of the Minister for Finance places the contract in the category dealt with in J. W. *Taylor & Co. v Landauer & Co.* [1940] 4 All ER 335, viz. as being a legal contract with an implied representation that, so far as permission of the minister might be necessary, such permission existed or would be applied for...

Whatever the terms of the court's order, the legal effect of it would be to put the plaintiffs in a position to secure payment of the amount in question and it would thus, even if indirectly, compel the defendants to do an act prohibited by the law for the time being in force. Put thus, I feel that on general principles it would be improper and contrary to public policy for the court to give judgment for the plaintiffs on their claim as now framed. There is persuasive authority for this view in a recent decision of the Court of Appeal in England in *Stockholms Enskilda Bank Aktiebolag v Schering Ltd.* [1941] 1 KB 424. There, the claim was for an instalment provided for in a contract entered into before the Trading with the Enemy Act, 1939, but falling due after the coming into operation of that Act, and it was held that such payment would, in the circumstances of the case, be for the benefit of an enemy and would also be a payment of money to or for the benefit of an enemy. The court accordingly dismissed the action, thereby implying that they considered that an order enabling the recovery of the instalment by the plaintiffs would amount to the same thing as a payment of it by the defendants.

As a statement of principles applicable to the present case, and allowing for the different circumstances of the two cases, I adopt the following passage from the judgment of Lord (then Sir Wilfred) Greene M.R., at 440–441:

> He is claiming payment of a sum of money, and he is claiming it at a time when the law of this country declares that the thing which he is asking for, namely, payment, is illegal, and the fact that illegality has struck what in its origin was a perfectly innocent and proper transaction is, it seems to me, an answer to the claim. It is true that, so far as anything in this Act of Parliament is concerned, the prohibition of payment is a temporary one. It only exists so long as the payee, or the person to receive the benefit, is an enemy. If and when he ceases to be an enemy, and in the absence of further legislation affecting his rights, he will, according to ordinary principles, be entitled to receive the benefit which was to flow to him under the machinery of these agreements. At the moment that benefit is prohibited, and it seems to me that that circumstance in this case is a defence to the action.

Notes

1. This decision was affirmed by the Supreme Court in *Fibretex (Société Personnes à Responsabilité Limitée) v Beleir Ltd* (1958) 89 ILTR 141, a case involving an action for goods sold and delivered. The court also noted in that case that when the controlling legislation lapsed or was revoked the plaintiff would be in a position to take action, and if successful, to have an order for payment.

2. In *Westpac Banking Corp. v Anthony Matthew Dempsey* [1993] 3 IR 331, the defendant appealed against an order of the Master to enforce a judgment against him, awarded in the English High Court, in respect of money owed to the plaintiffs. The plaintiffs were a London-based banking company. The money was owed on foot of a loan agreement which the defendant claimed was void due to non-compliance with the Exchange Control Act 1954. Having referred to both the *Fibretex* and the *Namlooze* cases Morris J. noted that the exchange control restrictions had been relaxed on a gradual basis and from 1 January 1992 all restrictions on residents in respect of guarantees had been removed. As a result he stated 'The payments necessary under such guarantees may now be effected. It appears to me that precisely the circumstances envisaged for the removal of such restrictions by the Supreme Court in *Fibretex* have in fact occurred.'

B. CONTRACTS PREJUDICIAL TO THE ADMINISTRATION OF JUSTICE

In Re Adam Boyd (1885) 15 LR (Ir.) 521

On the eve of bankruptcy, a grocer who was both a customer and a commission agent of Leathem and Howard, a wholesale grocery firm, provided security to the firm for moneys due to them. Evidence suggested that the firm had threatened to prosecute the grocer for embezzlement if security was not provided.

Sullivan C.:

The question arose whether what occurred between these gentlemen and the bankrupt amounted to an agreement to stifle a prosecution. Lord Justice FitzGibbon thinks that there was an agreement to stifle a prosecution; and that this being the consideration for the equitable mortgage, that mortgage fails as being founded on an illegal consideration. I cannot agree in this view. *Ward v Lloyd* 7 Sc. NR 499 is a most distinct authority that a threat of prosecution will not invalidate a security thereupon given, if there was no agreement to abandon the prosecution ultimately. I see no agreement here not to prosecute. The result is that this mortgage security stands according to the opinion of the majority of the court.

Nolan v Shiels (1926) 60 ILTR 143

The defendant gave the plaintiff a cheque for £50 in consideration of the plaintiff's abandonment of an intended prosecution against a third party for an indecent assault. When the cheque was dishonoured, the plaintiff sued.

Pigot K.C.:

Indecent assault is a statutory offence punishable with two years' imprisonment. Common assault is punishable with one year's imprisonment and was indictable at common law. There is a clear distinction between compromising an indictable misdemeanour and 'stifling' a prosecution in respect of such an offence. By the latter phrase is to be understood an agreement not to take or refusing to take any part in a prosecution of a criminal nature. Before the time of Blackstone it had become a common practice, in the course of a criminal trial for a misdemeanour, for the defendant after conviction 'to speak with the prosecutor', and as a result, in consideration of compensation agreed to be given to the latter, the penalty was frequently made a nominal one. In one case reported the imprisonment was reduced from six to three months. Notwithstanding the adverse comments of that learned writer against such a custom, I have no doubt that it had become (and still is) a recognised part of the procedure in criminal trials for misdemeanour if rarely practised. And it is in that sense that the compromising of prosecutions is to be read as being allowable in criminal cases. From the earliest times we read that to agree not to prosecute in a criminal case was illegal; that a promise to pay money for such a promise is an illegal consideration, and that such a contract is void. To constitute such illegality there must be reasonable grounds for believing that the offence had been actually committed and that each party must have entered on the agreement on that assumption: *Rourke v Mealy* 4 LR Ir 166. Is there any exception to this general rule? The words used by Wilmot C.J., in *Collins v Blantern* 2nd Wils. 341, giving the grounds and reason for this rule, are of general application, and would appear to cover the 'stifling' of any indictable prosecution. But as was admitted in argument in the Exchequer Chamber in the hearing on writ of error in *Keir v Leeman* 9 QB 371, exceptions to this general rule are to be found. And in the course of his judgment at p. 375, Tyndall C.J., says: 'It is said, indeed, that in the case of an assault he (that is, the injured party) may also undertake not to prosecute on behalf of the public. It may be so. But we are not disposed to extend this any further.' That was a case of riot, a crime of a more public nature than assault. The ground upon which it was supposed that an agreement might be made not to prosecute in such a case was that compensation to the prosecutor might be commensurate with the possible penalty. And no doubt the elements of common assault regarded as an offence at common law were essentially the same as those giving rise to the right for assault in a civil action. If such an exception to a well known and general principle is to be recognised as still in existence (and I doubt whether it is), I am of opinion that any distinction should be laid hold of to prevent an interference with the right of the public to have protection through the criminal law. Inasmuch as no civil action could be brought for an indecent assault as distinguished from an ordinary assault, as the penalty to be possibly awarded by the court is a higher one for one offence than for the other, therein differing again from actionable assault; as I consider that the exception (if any) is probably founded on an historical development of our law rather than on principle; and finally because I am of opinion that the old and sound rule of the law should be restricted in the interests of the public welfare, I decide that this agreement was founded on an illegal consideration, that the contract was void and that the action fails.

Polymer Developments Group Ltd *v* Tilialo [2002] 3 NZLR 258

Mr Tilialo's brother Mr Poloa stole money from his employer, Polymer, to meet his gambling debts. Mr Tilialo agreed to pay a sum of money by instalments to Polymer in consideration for Polymer agreeing not to institute criminal or civil proceedings against his brother. Mr Tilialo subsequently claimed that the agreement was illegal and unenforceable and sought the return of the money already paid.

Glazebrook J.:

[Having reviewed the English, Scottish and New Zealand case-law.] The conclusion, therefore, is that there are no really sensible distinctions that can be drawn between different types of contract to stifle prosecutions. There are some contracts to stifle prosecutions that are clearly contrary to public policy and it is difficult to see the freedom to contract could ever override the public interest involved in those cases. In other cases the public policy concerns may not be so strong but ... all such contracts should at least be scrutinised by the courts. Holding them to be illegal allows this. . . . It is true that in the New Zealand context there is a very limited role of private prosecutions and cl. 4 of the deed only prohibits private prosecutions. There may in this context, however, still be public policy issues involved—for example a concern to protect the innocent from extortion and to ensure the guilty do not achieve this result by way of a bribe. Even contracts not to institute private prosecutions should still therefore, under the principles set out above, be deemed illegal so that they can be scrutinised by the court and decisions as to relief can be made. It follows that Polymer's arguments fail on this head. . . .The deed is held to be an illegal contract as it contains an illegal term—that is it contains in cl. 4 an agreement not to commence a private prosecution. This means that the deed, in accordance with s. 6(1) of the Illegal Contracts Act, is of no effect.

Note

As the Court viewed both parties as victims of Mr Poloa's gambling addiction, relief was granted to Polymer under the Illegal Contracts Act 1970 by severing the reference to criminal proceedings in the deed and also by validation to the extent of the payments made and variation to reduce the sum owed by Mr Tilialo.

Consider:

Why are contracts to settle a civil action valid?

The next three cases look at a particular type of agreement—a champertous agreement. This involves an agreement by one person to finance another's litigation in return for a share of the proceeds where the financier has no genuine or substantial interest in the outcome. If there is no requirement that the financier receive a share, it is termed a maintenance agreement. The *Fraser* case below explains why such agreements are deemed to be contrary to public policy. The *McIntyre Estate* case indicates that this area of the law is dynamic as befits the changing concerns of public policy.

Fraser and Another v Buckle and Others [1996] 2 ILRM 34

The two plaintiffs, professional next-of-kin agents, informed the three defendants that they could be heirs to an estate in New Jersey. The name of the deceased though known to the plaintiffs was not mentioned at this stage. The defendants entered into contracts agreeing to give the plaintiffs a one third share of any sums they might subsequently inherit from the estate in return for which the plaintiffs agreed to disclose the identity of the deceased and to assist in the presentation of the defendants' claim. The plaintiffs performed their part of the agreement but the defendants refused to pay the agreed sum claiming that the agreements were unenforceable because they were champertous. In the High Court [1994] 1 ILRM 276, Costello J. held that the agreements were unenforceable because they were champertous and contrary to public policy. The plaintiffs appealed.

O'Flaherty J.:

The law of Ireland
I would uphold the trial judge's findings that the agreements were champertous and unenforceable in Irish law. . . . While it appears that some of the excesses of the feudal system were more rampant in England than in Ireland . . . and the result of some of which excesses called for much legislative and judicial intervention outlawing maintenance and champerty, nonetheless, the Irish common law developed in tandem with English law in condemning maintenance and champerty. [O'Flaherty J. referred to *Kenny v Browne* (1796) 3 Ridg PC 462 and *Littledale v Thompson* (1879) 4 LR (Ireland) 43 on this point]. In the High Court decision *McElroy v Flynn* [1991] ILRM 294, Blayney J. had to consider a similar agreement to those in debate here. Following *Rees v De Bernardy* [1896] 2 Ch 437, he reached the conclusion (at p. 297):

> . . . in the case before me I think the true agreement made by the defendants was one contrary to the policy of the law. I agree that a contract by a person to communicate information on terms of getting a share of any property that may thereby be recovered by the person to whom the information is to be given, and, nothing more, is not champerty or void: see *Sprye v Porter* (1856) 7 E & B 58. But if the arrangement come to is not merely that information shall be given, but also that the person who gives it and who is to share in what may be recovered shall himself recover the property or actively assist in the recovery of it by procuring evidence or similar means, then I think the arrangement is contrary to the policy of the law and void: see *Sprye v Porter* and also *Stanley v Jones* (1831) 7 Bing 369, where the agreement held void was one by Stanley to communicate information to enable the defendant to recover a sum of money and to use and exert his utmost influence and means for procuring such evidence as should be requisite to substantiate the claims of the defendant.

It is true that the law can and, indeed, on occasion should develop so as to ameliorate the strictness of an existing precept of the common law or, indeed, extend its advantages: *McKinlay v Minister for Defence* [1992] 2 IR 333. The American experience in regard to contingency fees is instructive as to how the law developed there in a particular direction. It should be remembered that in the United States costs do not follow the event as is generally the case in our system. So, instead of counsel and solicitors being prepared to put effort into litigation in the expectation that if—and only if—their side is successful they will get their fees and costs from the unsuccessful party, the American mode provides for a bargain to be made at the outset between the attorney and the client so that, if successful, the attorney will get a percentage of what is recovered in the suit. As far back as 1848 when New York enacted a regime of free enterprise for lawyers, the Field Code repealed the statutes regulating lawyers' fees thereby dealing the champerty restriction a major blow and contributing significantly to the legitimation of contingency fees. Subsequent revisions of the 1848 Act added language which provided that the compensation of attorneys was to be governed by agreement with the client 'which is not restrained by law'. This provision was afterwards adopted by several other states and, by the middle of the nineteenth century, it had become common for lawyers to assist in collection matters, with their payment based on a percentage of the amount collected by the client. The increase in the number of industrial accidents produced many working class plaintiffs with no means to pursue their claims. It appears that young lawyers, struggling to become established, discovered that the contingent fee retainer agreement enabled them to represent a greater number of clients, since more clients could 'afford' to hire them. Judicial acceptance accelerated as these developments took hold. There is a view in the United States that litigation is a form of political and even commercial speech, which is to be encouraged and protected rather than disfavoured. Fees which promote access to the legal system are seen as an expression of national policy favouring such access. The contingent fee is regarded as the cornerstone of 'people's law'; it is strongly supported by consumer organisations who regard it as the strongest weapon in the hands of consumers when they do battle with large corporations and other defendants with substantial resources. The contingency fee has been called 'the key to the courthouse door' for the poor and the middle class. However, it is right to point out that contingency fees in personal injury cases, certainly, are almost universally regulated by law and by court rule. The courts keep a wary eye on matters so that a plaintiff is never mulcted.

Further, as noted by Dr John Murray in his book *On Contracts* (3rd edn, 1990) at p. 522:

> Notwithstanding the decline of maintenance and champerty, an agreement that has an undue tendency to promote litigation for the benefit of the promoter rather than the litigant, or which is oppressive to the litigant, or which involves an abuse of legal proceedings, is more than likely to be deemed unenforceable.

Of course, as related by the trial judge, these heir-locator agreements are disapproved of in New Jersey as being void and unenforceable as well as being contrary to public policy; similar disapproval is evident in other states of the United States.

I am satisfied that the law on maintenance and champerty has not undergone any sea change in this jurisdiction since the last century and, indeed, s. 68(2) of the Solicitors (Amendment) Act 1994, makes it clear that solicitors are not entitled to charge percentage or contingency fees except in very restricted circumstances. Therefore, I would uphold the statement of the law contained in the *McElroy* decision, which followed *Rees v De Bernardy* and which in turn was followed by the High Court judge in the present case, as being correct.

English law

As already related, the trial judge was faced with opposing views on the applicable English law and, therefore, resolved the question as one of fact and held that *Rees v De Bernardy* represented the law of England and Wales. While one would always approach the enterprise of discovering other people's laws with due deference, when the law in question seems to be in a state of flux, one must, in addition, regard it as a risky business. It is clear, I think, that Lord Mustill in the course of his speech (in which he spoke for the House of Lords) in *Giles v Thompson* [1994] 1 AC 142 was presaging a very restricted future role for maintenance and champerty. At the outset of his speech he said the following (at p. 153):

My Lords, the crimes of maintenance and champerty are so old that their origins can no longer be traced, but their importance in medieval times is quite clear. The mechanisms of justice lacked the internal strength to resist the oppression of private individuals through suits fomented and sustained by unscrupulous men of power. Champerty was particularly vicious, since the purchase of a share in litigation presented an obvious temptation to the suborning of justices and witnesses and the exploitation of worthless claims which the defendant lacked the resources and influence to withstand. The fact that such conduct was treated as both criminal and tortious provided an invaluable external discipline to which, as the records show, recourse was often required. As the centuries passed the courts became stronger, their mechanisms more consistent and their participants more self-reliant. Abuses could be more easily detected and forestalled, and litigation more easily determined in accordance with the demands of justice, without recourse to separate proceedings against those who trafficked in litigation. In the most recent decades of the present century maintenance and champerty have become almost invisible in both their criminal and their tortious manifestations. In practice, they have maintained a living presence in only two respects. First, as the source of the rule, now in the course of attenuation, which forbids a solicitor from accepting payment for professional services on behalf of a plaintiff calculated as a proportion of the sum recovered from the defendant. Secondly, as the ground for denying recognition to the assignment of a 'bare right action'. The former survives nowadays, so far as it survives at all, largely as a rule of professional conduct, and the latter is in my opinion best treated as having achieved an independent life of its own.

Nonetheless, despite the apparent relegation of maintenance and champerty, it is the position that the heir-locator contracts stand condemned by the decision of *Rees v De Bernardy* and that decision has not been disapproved of to date. It is in that context, too, that the American experience is illuminating because while restrictions as regards attorneys' contingency fees have been relaxed there over the years, the bonds remain as regards heir-locator contracts.

The learned trial judge made a finding of fact on the applicable English law. It was submitted on behalf of the appellants that we could form our own view of what the English law on the subject was just as readily and as properly as the trial judge but, as with any other finding of fact, I hold that we must pay great respect to the finding of the trial judge. In any event, I find no cause to disagree with it and, therefore, I would uphold his finding as to what the English law on the matter is and the only change I would make, as I indicated earlier in my judgment, is that I would regard this as the prime consideration in resolving the matter in dispute in favour of the respondents. But that change marks a difference in emphasis rather than substance.

I would dismiss the appeal.

(Hamilton CJ. and Barrington J. concurring.)

Notes

1. The Supreme Court did not consider the question of whether the heir-locator would be entitled to recover reasonable remuneration on a restitutionary basis. See O'Dell [1994] *Restitution Law Review* 196.
2. In 'The Heir Locator's Lost Inheritance' (1997) 60 MLR 286, Capper criticises the Supreme Court for its failure to examine whether the dictates

of public policy really require heir-locator agreements to be void in the present age.

The boundary between champertous contracts and everyday agreements that are beneficial to both parties, indeed agreements that have been sanctioned in legislation, is a difficult one to draw. In *Grovewood Holding plc v James Capel & Co. Ltd* TLR [1994] 4 All ER 417 Lightman J. held that a company liquidator who sought to pursue a claim in negligence against a firm of stockbrokers that had allegedly provided negligent advice to the company could not do so by entering into an agreement with anonymous backers who would fund the litigation in return for one half of the recoveries in the action. Lightman J. distinguished between an acceptable course of action—an assignment of the cause of action, and an illegal one, namely sale of the fruits of a cause of action. The fact that the liquidator may have been acting *bona fide* in the interest of creditors could not, in Lightman J.'s view, outweigh the fact that Parliament had not created a broad exception to champerty in passing s. 436 and para. 6 of schedule 4 to the UK Insolvency Act 1986. Lightman J. thus granted a stay in the action against the stockbrokers on the basis that it constituted a continuing abuse of process which the court, as well as the defendants, had an interest in bringing to an end.

In *Stocznia Gdanska SA v Latvian Shipping Co.* (No. 2) [1999] 3 All ER 822, Toulson J. noted that:

It is clearly established that the mere possibility of a funder making some profit out of his agreement with the litigant beyond the amount of the funder's preceding loss does not mean that the agreement must therefore be regarded as champertous: see *Trendtex Trading Corp. v Crédit Suisse* [1982] AC 679] and *Brownton Ltd v Edward Moore Inbucon Ltd* ED & F Man Ltd v Edward Moore Inbucon Ltd [1985] 3 All ER 499. But if, looking at the agreement and the circumstances in which it was made, there is an obvious disproportionality between what the funder lost and what he is bargaining to receive, the court may conclude that the agreement savours of champerty, and the more striking the disproportionality, the greater the likelihood of the court doing so.

The Queen on the Application of Factortame and Others *v* Secretary of State for Transport [2002] 3 WLR 1104

The claimants were Anglo-Spanish fishing companies who were found by the European Court of Justice to have been unlawfully excluded from fishing in UK territorial waters and entitled to damages provided *inter alia* that the breach was 'sufficiently serious'. They entered into an agreement with Grant Thornton, an accountancy firm, to determine this loss for a fee of eight per cent of the final settlement received. While section 58 of the Courts and Legal Services Act 1990 provides for the enforceability of certain conditional fee agreements, the Secretary of State argued that this agreement was champertous and could not be enforced.

Lord Phillips:

A person is guilty of maintenance if he supports litigation in which he has no legitimate concern without just cause or excuse'—Chitty, 28th edn, vol. 1, 17–050. Champerty 'occurs when the person maintaining another stipulates for a share of the proceeds of the action or suit'—ibid. 17–054. Because the question of whether maintenance and champerty can be justified is one of public policy, the law must be kept under review as public policy changes. As Danckwerts L.J. observed in *Hill v Archbold* [1968] 1 QB 686 at 697:

> . . . the law of maintenance depends upon the question of public policy, and public policy . . . is not a fixed and immutable matter. It is a conception which, if it has any sense at all, must be alterable by the passage of time.

In *Trendtex Trading v Credit Suisse* [1980] 1 QB 629 at p. 663 Oliver L.J. remarked:

> There is, I think, a clear requirement of public policy that officers of the court should be inhibited from putting themselves in a position where their own interests may conflict with their duties to the court by agreement, for instance, of so called 'contingency fees'.

The introduction of conditional fees shows that even this requirement of public policy is no longer absolute. This case raises the question of whether the requirement extends to expert witnesses or others in a position to influence the conduct of litigation and, if it does, whether on the facts of the present case the agreements concluded by Grant Thornton can be justified.

In *Trepca Mines Ltd (No. 2)* [1963] 1 Ch. 199 at p. 219 Lord Denning M.R. observed:

> The reason why the common law condemns champerty is because of the abuses to which it may give rise. The common law fears that the champertous maintainer might be tempted, for his own personal gain, to inflame the damages, to suppress evidence, or even to suborn witnesses. These fears may be exaggerated, but, be that so or not, the law for centuries had declared champerty to be unlawful, and we cannot do otherwise than enforce the law; and I may observe that it has received statutory support, in the case of solicitors, in section 65 of the Solicitors Act 1957.

Where the law expressly restricts the circumstances in which agreements in support of litigation are lawful, this provides a powerful indication of the limits of public policy in analogous situations. Where this is not the case, then we believe one must today look at the facts of the particular case and consider whether those facts suggest that the agreement in question might tempt the allegedly champertous maintainer for his personal gain, to inflame the damages, to suppress evidence, to suborn witnesses or otherwise to undermine the ends of justice. In reaching this conclusion we have been particularly influenced by the approach of the Court of Appeal and the House of Lords in *Giles v Thompson.* . . . On [the] facts Lord Mustill held that it was appropriate to consider whether the mischief was established against which the public policy was directed. As to this, he observed at p. 161:

> It is sufficient to adopt the description of the policy underlying the former criminal and civil sanctions expressed by Fletcher Moulton L.J. in *British Cash and Parcel Conveyors Ltd v Lamson Store Service Co. Ltd* [1908] 1 KB 1006, 1014:

It is directed against wanton and officious intermeddling with the disputes of others in which the [maintainer] has no interest whatever, and where the assistance he renders to the one or the other party is without justification or excuse.

This was a description of maintenance. For champerty there must be added the notion of a division of the spoils.

. . . This decision abundantly supports the proposition that, in any individual case, it is necessary to look at the agreement under attack in order to see whether it tends to conflict with existing public policy that is directed to protecting the due administration of justice with particular regard to the interests of the defendant. This is a question that we have to address. In so doing we revert to the statement of Lord Mustill that 'the rule, now in the course of attenuation, which forbids a solicitor from accepting payment for professional services calculated as a proportion of the sum recovered from the defendant . . . survives nowadays, so far as it survives at all, largely as a rule of professional conduct'. With respect, this statement is not correct. The basis of the rule is statutory. It is now necessary to look at the relevant statutory provisions, not merely because Mr Friedman has submitted that they are indicative of public policy which extends beyond the confines of the statutory provisions, but because he has submitted that the most recent statute, which came into force after the events with which we are concerned, would have outlawed the 1998 agreements. If this is correct, it strongly supports his contention that those agreements were in conflict with public policy. . . . [T]he legislative intent was that the provisions of s. 58 of the [Courts and Legal Services Act 1990 as amended by the Access to Justice Act 1999] were intended to apply only to those who could be described as 'litigators', that is advocates and those conducting the litigation . . . More generally, however, s. 58 evidences a radical shift in the attitude of public policy to the practice of conducting litigation on terms that the obligation to pay fees will be contingent upon success. Whereas before this practice was outlawed, it is now permissible—subject to the requirements imposed by the section. These requirements do not appear designed to mitigate the mischief that had led to the banning of contingency fees—the undesirability of the interests of officers of the court conflicting with their duties to the court. Rather the requirements appear designed to protect the litigants concluding conditional fee agreements who, when the section was first enacted, were required to pay any 'uplift' out of their recoveries. Conditional fees are now permitted in order to give effect to another facet of public policy—the desirability of access to justice. Conditional fees are designed to ensure that those who do not have the resources to fund advocacy or litigation services should none the less be able to obtain these in support claims which appear to have merit. . . .

To give evidence on a contingency fee basis gives an expert, who would otherwise be independent, a significant financial interest in the outcome of the case. As a general proposition, such an interest is highly undesirable. In many cases the expert will be giving an authoritative opinion on issues that are critical to the outcome of the case. In such a situation the threat to his objectivity posed by a contingency fee agreement may carry greater dangers to the administration of justice than would the interest of an advocate or solicitor acting under a similar agreement. Accordingly, we consider that it will be in a very rare case indeed that the Court will be prepared to consent to an expert being instructed under a contingency fee agreement. In the present case Grant Thornton did not perform the role of expert witnesses. They were careful to retain for that purpose experts who were entirely independent. . . .

Did the 1998 Agreements put at risk the purity of justice?
In *Giles v Thompson* Lord Mustill applied the test of public policy identified by Fletcher Moulton L.J. in the British Cash case. That test is appropriate when considering those

who, in one way or another, support litigation in which they are concerned. It is not, however, really in point when considering agreements under which those who are playing a legitimate part in the process of litigation provide their services on a contingency fee basis. A solicitor who charges a contingency fee which does not satisfy the requirements of s. 58, can hardly be said to be guilty of 'wanton and officious intermeddling in the disputes of others . . . where the assistance he renders to one party or another is without justification of excuse'. The public policy in play in the present case is that which weighs against a person who is in a position to influence the outcome of litigation having an interest in that outcome.

For this reason, it does not seem to us that one point made on behalf of Grant Thornton advances their case to any significant extent. This was that they had an interest in intervening in the litigation because the payment of their outstanding accountancy fees was dependent upon the Claimants recovering damages in the litigation. In paragraph 114 of his judgment, the Costs Judge held:

> I am satisfied that the role of GT in this case was not of a 'wanton and officious intermeddler'. GT had an interest in assisting the TCS fast-track Claimants to recover damages out of which the Claimants had promised to pay their outstanding professional fees. That, it seems to me, is a legitimate interest.

We do not consider that this goes far toward answering the case made by the Minister. That case identified the objectionable features of the 1998 Agreements, first that they gave Grant Thornton an interest in the outcome of the litigation and secondly that they entitled Grant Thornton to a percentage of the amounts recovered. We shall consider each feature in turn.

An interest in the result of the litigation
Anyone who provided services to the Claimants in connection with their litigation could only expect to be paid out of recoveries in the litigation. The Claimants were heavily in debt and had no other resources from which to pay for assistance. Thus the reality was that, whoever provided the services, would have a financial interest in the result of the litigation. Whether the agreement under which the services were rendered recognised this fact or not made little difference in practice. This might have raised problems so far as procuring the services of expert witnesses was concerned. By funding the fees of the two experts, Grant Thornton avoided the possibility that they also might have had an interest in the result of the litigation which, for the reasons that we have given, would have been undesirable.

In *Hamilton v Al Fayed*, both Chadwick L.J. and Hale L.J. emphasised the importance that public policy attached to access to justice. This had overborne the previous absolute prohibition on lawyers agreeing to act for contingency fees. The same public policy considerations mitigate the criticism that there might otherwise have been of the agreements under which Grant Thornton provided their own services, and funded the services of the expert witnesses, on a contingency basis.

There is another matter which greatly reduces the significance of the fact that Grant Thornton were acting on a contingency fee basis. By the time that the 1998 Agreements were concluded, the Claimants had succeeded on the issue of liability. While it was possible that their victory might be reversed by the House of Lords, this was no more than a possibility. Mr Davies, with the benefit of legal advice, believed that, after the final decision of the European Court, recovery of damages by the Claimants was inevitable. The advice which he had received proved sound. Thus the contingency that the claims might fail was not great. Furthermore, and this is also highly material, Grant Thornton had no role at all to play in the final battle before the House of Lords on the issue of liability. The fact that they had an interest in its outcome posed no threat of any kind to the manner in which that battle was conducted. For all of these reasons we have concluded that public policy was not affronted by the fact that Grant Thornton agreed to act on terms that made their remuneration contingent upon the success of the proceedings. . . . We do not believe than any reasonable onlooker, or indeed the Minister, would seriously have suspected that the fact that they were to receive eight of the recoveries would tempt Grant Thornton to deviate from performing their duties in an honest manner...

The Costs Judge concluded that the 1998 Agreements lacked the characteristics that might have rendered them contrary to public policy under the vestigial remnants of the law of champerty. As we considered the evidence and heard the argument unfold we became increasingly convinced that he was correct. . . . The 1998 Agreements were not champertous.

McIntyre Estate *v* Ontario (Attorney General) [2002] 218 DLR (4th) 193

The Ontario Court of Appeal was considering a proposed contingency fee agreement between counsel and her client in a wrongful death action under which the counsel would be compensated with a percentage of damages plus full payment of costs awarded if action was successful. In his judgment, O'Connor A.C.J.O. stated that the common law was relevant to an understanding of the applicable Champerty Act 1897.

O'Connor A.C.J.O.:

Although the type of conduct that might constitute champerty and maintenance has evolved over time, the essential thrust of the two concepts has remained the same for at least two centuries. Maintenance is directed against those who, for an improper motive, often described as wanton or officious intermeddling, become involved with disputes (litigation) of others in which the maintainer has no interest whatsoever and where the assistance he or she renders to one or the other parties is without justification or excuse. Champerty is an egregious form of maintenance in which there is the added element that the maintainer shares in the profits of the litigation. Importantly, without maintenance there can be no champerty (citing inter alia *Giles v Thompson*) . . . The courts have made it clear that a person's motive is a proper consideration and, indeed, determinative of the question whether conduct or an arrangement constitutes maintenance or champerty. It is only when a person has an improper motive, which motive may include, but is not limited to, 'officious intermeddling' or 'stirring up strife', that a person will be found to be a maintainer. . . . The type of conduct that has been found to constitute champerty and maintenance has evolved over time so as to keep in step with the fundamental aim of protecting the administration of justice from abuse. . . .'

The English courts also routinely held that champerty and maintenance require the element of an improper motive (citing inter alia *Giles v Thompson* and *Trepca Mines Ltd.* (No. 2)) . . . In the same vein,the courts have allowed exceptions to what constitutes champerty or maintenance when there has been the presence of a justifying motive or excuse (citing inter alia Re *Trepca Mines Ltd.* (No. 2)) . . . The fundamental aim of the law of champerty and maintenance has always been to protect the administration of justice from abuse. However, over time, that which has been considered to be champerty and maintenance has evolved. As they have done with many other common law concepts, the courts have shaped the rules relating to champerty and maintenance to accommodate changing circumstances and the current requirements for the proper administration of justice (citing *Giles v Thompson*). . . .

There is reason to question whether the contingent nature of a fee agreement, by itself, is the significant threat to professional ethics that was feared at common law. It is interesting to note that while historically these concerns about the potential for abuse by lawyers or damage to the lawyer-client relationship were frequently expressed, there is little, if any, evidence to show that the fears were well-founded. Although the lack of evidence may be attributable to the fact that contingency fee agreements were considered to be illegal and therefore not broadly used, we do know that for years lawyers have acted in what they considered to be meritorious cases for clients of modest means with the realization, if not the express agreement, that they would only be paid in the event of success. . . . Lawyers acting in these 'informal' arrangements were no doubt subject to some of the same temptations as those who formally agreed to be paid only in the event of a success. However, there is no evidence to indicate that lawyers who have acted in informal arrangements of this nature have performed to a lower ethical standard than those who were paid regardless of outcome. In addition, we have the benefit of the experiences of the many jurisdictions that have enacted legislation permitting regulated contingency fee agreements. This court was not shown any evidence to show that lawyers in these jurisdictions, properly regulated, are more likely to engage in the types of abuse to the administration of justice that were once feared to be the result of contingency fee agreements. . . .

The important point to be drawn from the recent jurisprudence is that the common law regarding contingency fee agreements has begun to evolve so as to conform to the widely accepted modern public policy norms recognizing the significant advantages in permitting contingency fee agreements in some circumstances. It is not surprising that all courts have not, at a single point in time, accepted the shift in attitude in favour of these types of agreements. The development of the common law most often is an evolutionary and incremental process rather than the result of a single defining judgment. . . .

I am persuaded that the historic rationale for the absolute prohibition is no longer justified. The common law of champerty was developed to protect the administration of justice from abuse, one aspect of which involved the protection of vulnerable litigants. Within that broad framework, the courts historically held that contingency fee agreements were *per se* champertous. But, as examples from other jurisdictions amply demonstrate, the potential abuses that provided the rationale for the *per se* prohibition of contingency fee agreements can be addressed by an appropriate regulatory scheme governing the conduct of lawyers and the amount of lawyers fees. Currently, in Ontario the *Solicitors Act* provides a comprehensive process for reviewing and assessing the reasonableness of lawyers' accounts. The *Rules of Professional Conduct* contain a complete set of standards for regulating lawyers' ethical behaviour and the complaints and discipline process of the Law Society of Upper Canada provide accessible means by which those standards can be enforced. While many of the jurisdictions that have enacted legislation permitting contingency fee agreements have enacted specific regulations to govern their use, I am satisfied that the basic regulatory framework necessary to address potential abuses in the use of contingency fee agreements is presently in place in Ontario. I am also of the view that the advantages to the administration of justice from permitting properly regulated contingency fee agreements in the form of increased access to justice are compelling. Indeed, there is a strong case to be made that the continuation of a *per se* prohibition against contingency fee agreements actually tends to defeat the fundamental purpose underlying the law of champerty — the protection of the administration of justice and, in particular, the protection of vulnerable litigants. In my view, it is no longer necessary or desirable to deem contingency fee agreements *per se* champertous. Neither the contingent nature of a fee agreement, nor the fact that the lawyer's fees may be paid from the recovery in an action, without more, ought to constitute an improper motive or officious intermeddling for purposes of the law of champerty. I am comfortable that this conclusion is consistent with the reasonable evolution of the common law in this area of the law. Some courts already have reached similar conclusions.

. . . To be clear, I am not suggesting that contingency fee agreements can never be champertous. Rather, I conclude only that contingency fee agreements should no longer be considered *per se* champertous. The issue of whether a particular agreement is champertous will depend on the application of the common law elements of champerty to the circumstances of each case. A court confronted with an issue of champerty must look at the conduct of the parties involved, together with the propriety of the motive of an alleged champertor in order to determine if the requirements for champerty are present. When considering the propriety of the motive of a lawyer who enters into a contingency fee agreement, a court will be concerned with the nature and the amount of the fees to be paid to the lawyer in the event of success. One of the originating policies in forming the common law of champerty was the protection of vulnerable litigants. A fee agreement that so over-compensates a lawyer such that it is unreasonable or unfair to the client is an agreement with an improper purpose—i.e., taking advantage of the client. See *Thai Trading, supra*, at 788, 790. The applications judge in this case dealt with this concern as follows, at 157:

> The suggested compensation may or may not be fair and reasonable, depending upon the outcome of the litigation in light of the difficulty of the case, as well as the time and expenses incurred. Counsel should be well rewarded if the litigation is successful, for assuming the risk and costs of the litigation. The compensation however should not be a windfall resembling a lottery win.

I agree with these comments. The lawyers who drafted the agreement provided an example of the potential fees which totalled over $9,000,000. While the amount of the damages on which the example is based may or may not be realistic, the example does make the point that unacceptably large fees could become payable under the agreement. . . . [I]n my view, contingency fee agreements that provide for the payment of fees that are unreasonable or unfair are agreements that have an improper motive and come within the prohibition in the Act.

Note

This case was applied in *Operation 1 Inc. v Phillips* [2004] 248 DLR (4th) 349.

C. Agreements which Serve to Defraud the Revenue

Starling Securities Ltd *v* Francis Woods, Thomas Woods and Investment Holdings International Ltd (HC) 24 May 1977, unrep.

The plaintiff agreed to sell a hotel to the defendants for £215,000. The contract, however, only stated a price of £190,000. The desired effect of this was to reduce the defendant's stamp duty liability. Later, when the plaintiff sought specific performance of this contract, the defendant claimed *inter alia* that there was no sufficient memorandum to satisfy the Statute of Frauds and that the contract was illegal. The court found that there was a sufficient act of part performance to take the case out of the statute and then it proceeded to deal with the issue of illegality.

McWilliam J.:

With regard to the defence of illegality it is argued that, *prima facie*, there is nothing to show any illegality and that full duty could have been paid on a transaction completed in this manner and that, in any event, the defendants cannot rely on illegality without pleading it. . . . The only interpretation I can put on the very peculiar method adopted to conduct these transactions is that both parties were trying to conceal from the Revenue authorities the true nature of the transactions. Certainly no other possible explanation has been suggested to me. Accordingly, on these two authorities, it appears to me that I am not entitled to countenance such attempted frauds on the Revenue by enforcing the performance of the contracts at the instance of either party. The issue of illegality should certainly have been pleaded but, once the evidence of it has been properly introduced in respect to one issue in the case, namely, with regard to the sufficiency of the memorandum, I am not entitled to ignore it. . . .

Note

See also *Lewis v Squash Ireland* [1983] ILRM 363 at p. 961 (below at p. 841).

Haden *v* Sean Quinn Properties Ltd (HC) 6 December 1993, unrep.

The plaintiff was appointed general manager of a hotel in Cavan owned by the defendant. A basic salary of £22,000 was agreed and added to this was a sum of £6,000 non-taxable allowance to cover expenses. Eight months later the plaintiff was dismissed and sued for damages for breach of contract. On the evidence Barron J. found that the grounds for dismissal given by the defendant were spurious and that there was no legal justification for the plaintiff's dismissal. However, he then considered the legal status of the contract.

Barron J.:

In the course of his evidence the plaintiff said that this was never intended to cover expenses of which there were none but was to enable him to have an after-tax salary equal to that being received by him in England. . . . . . . I am satisfied that the plaintiff would not have come to the hotel for less than he was getting and that the device of expenses was for the benefit of the defendant. . . .The defendant is clearly in breach of contract in that the plaintiff's dismissal was wrongful. However, the contract itself was an illegal one. It contained a term designed to lessen the defendant's liability at the expense of the Revenue, something with which the plaintiff concurred. In *Napier v National Business Agency Ltd*, 1951 2 All ER 264 the facts were almost identical. Part of the plaintiff's salary purported to be in respect of expenses, which at best were only minimal. The plaintiff had claimed to have been dismissed wrongfully. He sued for damages. His claim was dismissed upon the ground that the contract was unlawful and so unenforceable. Sir Raymond Evershed said at 266:

> . . . it must surely be that, by making an agreement in that form the parties to it were doing that which they must be taken to know would be liable to defeat the proper claims of the Inland Revenue and to avoid altogether, or at least to postpone, the proper payment of income tax. If that is the right conclusion, it seems to me equally clear . . . that the agreement must be regarded as contrary to public policy. There is a strong legal obligation placed on all citizens to make true and faithful returns for tax purposes, and, if parties make an agreement which is designed to do the contrary, i.e. to mislead and to delay, it seems to me impossible for this court to enforce that contract at the suit of one party to it.

The learned judge then went on to consider whether or not the fraudulent part of the agreement could be severed and held that it could not. In my view that case would have been decided in the same way and upon the same grounds in this jurisdiction at that date. Notwithstanding the very great changes that have occurred in society in this country since then I do not believe that public policy on this issue would have changed in any way. The plaintiff allowed himself to agree to something which would benefit the defendant at the expense of the Revenue. Such an agreement is unenforceable and the plaintiff's claim must therefore fail.

D. AGREEMENTS WHICH SERVE TO CORRUPT PUBLIC OFFICIALS

The Lord Mayor, Aldermen, and Burgesses of Dublin *v* Michael Angelo Hayes (1876) 10 IRCL 226

Morris C.J.:

The defendant was City Marshal, and as such was Marshal of the Borough Court, and also Marshal of the Court of Conscience, and by the provisions of the Irish Statutes 26 Geo. 43, c. 3, and 28 Geo. 3, c. 49, as Marshal, he became Registrar of pawnbrokers, and received considerable fees much exceeding the salary he was appointed at by the plaintiffs. The arrangement the plaintiffs entered into with the defendant on his appointment and the bond entered into by him in compliance with the arrangement provides that he is to pay over all the fees and emoluments of his office to the treasurer of the plaintiffs. Such an arrangement, it has been admitted on the part of the plaintiffs during the argument, would be clearly illegal prior to the passing of the Municipal Corporations Act, 3 & 4 Vict. c. 108. It would be illegal as a bargain of an office of trust by which the plaintiffs who were appointing the defendant were to obtain a large benefit by the receipt of the fees of the office. . . .

Notes

1. See *Marlwood Commercial Inc v Viktor Kozeny and Others* [2006] EWHC 872 where the High Court noted that 'An English contract will also be held invalid on account of illegality if the real object and the intention of the parties necessitates them joining in an endeavour to perform in a foreign and friendly country some act which is illegal by the law of that country', in this case bribing an official.

2. In September 2003, Ireland ratified the OECD Convention on Combating Bribery of Foreign Public Officials in International Business Transactions.

E. CONTRACTS TENDING TO PROMOTE IMMORALITY

Pearce and Another *v* Brooks (1866) 1 Ex 213

The plaintiffs hired a carriage to the defendant knowing the latter to be a prostitute. When the carriage was returned damaged they attempted to sue her for unpaid fees and for the damage.

Pollock C.B.:

I have always considered it as settled law, that any person who contributes to the performance of an illegal act by supplying a thing with the knowledge that it is going to be used for that purpose, cannot recover the price of the thing so supplied. If, to create that incapacity, it was ever considered necessary that the price should be bargained or expected to be paid out of the fruits of the illegal act (which I do not stop to examine), that proposition has been overruled by the cases I have referred to, and has now ceased to be law. Nor can any distinction be made between an illegal and an immoral purpose; the rule which is applicable to the matter is, Ex *turpi causa non oritur actio*, and whether it is an immoral or an illegal purpose in which the plaintiff has participated, it comes equally within the terms of that maxim, and the effect is the same; no cause of action can arise out of either the one or the other. The rule of law was well settled in *Cannan v Bryce* 3 B & A 179. . . . If, therefore, this article was furnished to the defendant for the purpose of enabling her to make a display favourable to her immoral purposes, the plaintiffs can derive no cause of action from the bargain. . . . If evidence is given which is sufficient to satisfy the jury of the fact of the immoral purpose, and of the plaintiffs' knowledge of it, and that the article was required and furnished to facilitate that object, it is sufficient . . .

Martin B.:

I am of the same opinion. The real question is, whether sufficient has been found by the jury to make a legal defence to the action under the third plea. The plea states first the fact that the defendant was to the plaintiffs' knowledge a prostitute; second, that the brougham was furnished to enable her to exercise her immoral calling; third, that the plaintiffs expected to be paid out of the earnings of her prostitution. In my opinion the plea is good if the third averment be struck out; and if, therefore, there is evidence that the brougham was, to the knowledge of the plaintiffs, hired for the purpose of such display as would assist the defendant in her immoral occupation, the substance of the plea is proved, and the contract was illegal. When the rule was moved I did not clearly apprehend that the evidence went to that point; had I done so, I should not have concurred in granting it. It is now plain that enough was proved to support the verdict.

As to the case of *Cannan v Bryce*, I have a strong impression that it has been questioned to this extent, that if money is lent, the lender merely handing it over into the absolute control of the borrower, although he may have reason to suppose that it will be employed illegally, he will not be disentitled from recovering. But, no doubt, if it were part of the contract that the money should be so applied, the contract would be illegal.

Pollock C.B.:

I wish to add that I entirely agree with what has fallen from my brother Martin, as to the case of *Cannan v Bryce*. If a person lends money, but with a doubt in his mind whether it is to be actually applied to an illegal purpose, it will be a question for the jury whether he meant it to be so applied; but if it were advanced in such a way that it could not possibly be a bribe to an illegal purpose, and afterwards it was turned to that use, neither *Cannan v Bryce*, nor any other case, decides that his act would be illegal. The case cited rests on the fact that the money was borrowed with the very object of satisfying an illegal purpose.

Note

In contrast, in *Armhouse Lee Ltd v Chappel* (*The Times*, 7 August 1996), the Court of Appeal determined that no general moral code condemned the operation of telephone sex lines. As a result, a contract to advertise the services of the defendant's sex line service was held to be enforceable.

Consider:

Was it fair to make the plaintiff in the *Pearce* case liable for the damage and benefit the defendant by excusing her from liability to pay for the damage to the carriage?

Devine *v* Scott and Johnston (1931) 66 ILTR 107

The plaintiff let premises to the second defendant, the first defendant acting as a guarantor. The contract did not refer to the purposes for which the premises were to be used. At the date of this contract, the premises had been sub-let by a former tenant to the second defendant who was already carrying on therein an illegal bookmaking business. The plaintiff then sued the defendants to recover rent due.

Thompson J.:

Since the letting was to the knowledge of the plaintiff's agent for the purpose of carrying on the business of a ready-money bookmaker, such purpose being illegal, the rent payable under the agreement cannot be recovered. I am also of opinion that the letting must be treated as a whole, and that no rent can be recovered in respect of a portion of the premises which was not being used for illegal purposes. The civil bill must be dismissed with costs.

F. CONTRACTS TO TRADE WITH ENEMIES OF THE STATE

Ross Bros Ltd *v* Edward Shaw & Co. [1917] 2 IR 367

In October 1915 the plaintiff sued the defendant for failure to deliver Belgian yarn pursuant to two contracts made in March 1914. Due to the German invasion of Ghent the yarn was unavailable to the defendant.

Gibson J.:

The problem before us . . . relates to illegality or impossibility created by our own law in consequence of war. Taking the contract embodying the custom as meaning that the yarn was to be drafted from Belgium (where meanwhile the contract assumes it might be legitimately kept), in pursuance of notifications delivered by the buyers to the sellers, the price of each lot when delivered constituting a debt referable to the primary contract, what was the effect of the war and the occupation of Belgium on the contract and its fulfilment? The situation is not one where the inability to carry out the contract results from enemy blockade, or stoppage of trade routes, or destruction of a mail steamer carrying the order or of the cargo vessel returning. Suppose Belfast as well as Belgium was held by the enemy, could the plaintiffs serve a specification and insist that reasonable time was to be deemed to run at once? The delivery of each lot ordered would make a debt from plaintiffs to defendants, and from defendants to the Belgian companies. The constitution of these companies was not proved, nor is there any evidence of what is the Belgian law regulating them, whether they are local or created by the general law of the country, as is likely. The contracts to be performed as contemplated by the custom assumed as a tacit condition that delivery could, as regards our own law, be legally carried out from Belgium. Once Belgium became an enemy territory by reason of German occupation this was impossible.

. . . *Daimler Co. v Continental Tyre Co.*[1] shows that the companies, being under enemy control, could not have lawful business relations with Belfast. *Horlock v Beal*,[2] *Moss v Donohoe*,[3] and *Jager v Tolme & Runge*[4] also illustrate the effect of war on contracts. If import of goods from Belgium had been expressly prohibited by statute, would not such prohibition have made performance in the manner contemplated by the custom unlawful? Taking the custom as part of the contract terms, I am of opinion that when the writ was issued, on 31 January 1915, there was no enforceable cause of action. . . .

[1.] [1916] 1 AC 307.   [3.] 32 TLR 343.
[2.] [1916] 1 AC 496.   [4.] [1916] 1 KB 939.

Note

Gibson J. stated also that a contract for the sale and delivery 'as required' of particular goods of which the vendor is not producer must incorporate a trade custom that delivery need not be made until a reasonable time to enable the vendor to obtain the goods from the particular source from the receipt of the purchaser's specification.

G. Contracts that Breach Foreign Law

Stanhope *v* Hospitals Trust Ltd (No. 2) [1936] Ir J Rep 25

The plaintiff sold Irish sweepstakes tickets in Natal notwithstanding the fact that sweepstakes were illegal in Natal. He then posted the counter-foils to the defendant's Dublin office where the draw was to take place. When the tickets were not included in the draw, the plaintiff sued for damages for alleged breach of contract, negligence and consequent loss of reputation. The trial judge withdrew the case from the jury and dismissed the action on the ground that a court of law in this country will not lend its aid in enforcing a contract entered into expressly for an unlawful purpose.

Fitzgibbon J.:

In my opinion, the judgment for the defendants cannot stand. The learned trial judge based his direction upon the view taken by him that the whole cause of action was so tainted with illegality that the plaintiff cannot apply to the courts in this country to enforce any claim he may have for damages for breach of contract, or for negligence in the performance by the defendants of their contract with him. In the first place, one must see what the contract was before considering the question as to its illegality. In my opinion, the contract between the plaintiff and the defendants was contained in the offer by the latter, made upon the tickets issued by them and accepted by the plaintiff when he returned the counterfoils and the appropriate money, that they would put into the draw the counterfoils transmitted to them by him with the appropriate fee, and that such counterfoils would have their chance in a draw that was to take place on the result of the 'Grand National'. The contract seems to be created by the offer held out on the tickets, to be accepted by anyone who returns a counterfoil with the sum of 10s.

The plaintiff gave evidence from which the jury might have come to the conclusion—if that evidence should not be displaced by evidence to the contrary presented on the part of the defendants—that he returned a number of counterfoils with the appropriate sum of money, and that, through the negligence of the defendants, these counterfoils did not find their way into the drum, but of course the case was not heard to the end. It is quite possible that there might have been evidence produced by the defendants which would have negatived the receipt of the counterfoils by them, but all I can say is that on the plaintiff's evidence there was a case upon which it was open to the jury to find that the defendants received a number of counterfoils, and that, through their negligence, they did not find their way into the drum.

The contract was one which, to my mind, was to be performed in Dublin, and to be governed by the law of the place of performance, that is, the law of the Irish Free State, and I can find no evidence that the contract was illegal either by the law of this country or by the law of Natal. It was a contract entirely to be performed in Dublin—completed, possibly, by the posting, by the plaintiff in Natal, of the counterfoils and the appropriate money—but to be carried out in the Irish Free State where it was perfectly legal. In my opinion, therefore, the learned judge was not entitled to withdraw from the jury the issue whether there had been a breach of that contract, and to what damages, if any, the plaintiff had established his right in respect of that breach.

But the plaintiff has also claimed damages for a totally different thing, that is to say, damages occasioned to him by the loss of his trade as a professional seller of sweepstake tickets in Durban, a trade which the learned judge has decided was illegal by the law of the country in which it was carried on. I agree with the learned judge that the courts in this country will not allow themselves to be used for the purpose of establishing a claim for damages for the loss of an illegal business, and I think also that the judge has a duty, where the illegality appears either on the face of the pleadings or from the evidence, to take notice of it himself: *Gedge's* case; *North Western Salt Co. Ltd v Electrolytic Alkali Co. Ltd*. I do not think that the parties, even by agreement, could call upon the court, on an apparent illegality, to assist them to carry out an illegal transaction between themselves....

As to the question of breach of contract, I do not think that the trial judge was justified in withdrawing it from the jury. There was not, in my opinion, a claim for damages for breach of an illegal contract. The contract in question was with the Hospitals Trust to put the plaintiff's tickets into the drum, and his claim is for whatever damages he can get, if he succeeds. Therefore, I think the judgment ought to be set aside, and the case sent back for trial on the question whether the plaintiff is entitled to damages, and, if so, how much, for breach of contract to put his tickets into the drum, provided that he can prove to the satisfaction of the jury that he did in fact send the money and the tickets, and that the defendants received them and failed to put the counterfoils into the drum.

(Murnaghan J. agreed and Kennedy C.J., while agreeing with the main issues, felt that non-expert evidence as to foreign law should not be sufficient evidence of legality or illegality.)

H. New Heads of Public Policy

As noted, the policy values which the Courts seek to uphold are constantly changing. This leads to the possibility thus of Courts being asked to recognise new heads of public policy.

Consider:

What changes in public policy might be relevant in this context?

Taylor *v* Burgess [2002] NSWSC 676

In order to claim against his late father's estate, the plaintiff had to prove paternity. The defendant, the executor and principal beneficiary under the deceased's will, argued that the plaintiff's mother should be restrained from giving evidence of paternity. The deceased had entered an agreement with the plaintiff's mother prior to the plaintiff's birth denying paternity but agreeing to maintenance payments on condition that she 'at all times . . . refrain from making any allegations' against the deceased in respect of the child's paternity 'to any person whatsoever'. The Court found that as a matter of construction the agreement only precluded voluntary statements implicating the deceased in financial claims by the mother and would not preclude communication of facts relevant to the plaintiff's paternity by the mother to the plaintiff or in the proceedings at hand. However, Barrett J stated that in the event he was wrong he would consider the public policy implications of the agreement.

Barrett J.:

The next issue is that of public policy. The question is whether the relevant part of clause 4 must be regarded as unenforceable because of its inconsistency with public policy. On this, it can be said at once that a promise not to make allegations of paternity against a particular man in respect of a particular child (or, going further, not to disclose the fact that a particular man is, or is claimed to be, the father of a particular child) does not fall within any of the time honoured and established categories of contractual promises regarded by the law as contrary to public policy. This is not a case of a contract to commit a crime or to engage in fraud or to promote sexual immorality or a contract prejudicial to the administration of justice or to promote corruption in public life. These are the traditional and accepted heads of public policy. No issue under these traditional heads arises here. That, however, is not the end of the public policy question. It is necessary to consider whether there exists today a head of public policy that causes a contract not to disclose information relevant to a person's parentage to be offensive. The question is one which may legitimately be canvassed. As Sir Frederick Jordan observed in *Re Morris (deceased)* (1943) 43 SR(NSW) 35:

> From generation to generation ideas change as to what is necessary or injurious, so that 'public policy' is a variable thing. New heads of public policy come into being and old heads undergo modification.

The approach to be taken was described by Isaacs J. in *Wilkinson v Osborne* (1915) 21 CLR 89 in a passage approved by members of the High Court in *A v Hayden* (1984) 156 CLR 532, Isaacs J. said:

> The public policy which a Court is entitled to apply as a test of validity to a contract is in relation to some definite or governing principle which the community as a whole has already adopted either formally by law or tacitly in its general course of corporate life. The Court is not a legislator; it cannot initiate the principle; it can only state or formulate if it already exists. The Courts refuse to give effect to such a bargain, not for the sake of the defendant—indeed they do not fail to notice that his failure to abide by the agreement sometimes adds dishonesty to illegality—but for the sake of the community, who will be prejudiced if such a bargain were countenanced.

Society today places a high value on establishing parentage. The law has moved significantly beyond presumptions of parentage based on the traditional marriage relationship. It now positively facilitates the establishment of parentage. In this State, we have the Status of Children Act 1996 which vests in the court jurisdiction not only to make declarations of parentage, but also to order genetic testing to aid in the exercise of that jurisdiction. There are similar provisions at Federal level in the Family Law Act 1975. The policy underlying these measures has been the subject of judicial observations. [*G v H* (1994) 181 CLR 382 and *Director General Department of Community Services v A* (2000) NSWSC 1179 were then cited.]

The reasons for the high value placed on establishment of paternity are obvious enough. The law today rejects distinctions between the legitimate and illegitimate, so far as the status of children is concerned. This is clearly established by legislation. The civil rights of children born out of wedlock are, today, exactly the same as those of children born to married parents. There is not only a species of human right for any individual to know their true identity, subject only to statutory constraints, but also a need for matters going to the very root of society—matters regulating procreation in a civilized society—to be capable of being known.

I turn now to the related question of the purpose and effect of the statute under which the plaintiff brings his claim, that is the Family Provision Act. Like its predecessor, the Testator's Family Maintenance and Guardianship of Infants Act, the present Act has a purpose of providing for the proper maintenance of persons for whom a testator might be expected to have made provision and who, in the absence of such provision, might otherwise become a charge on the community. . . . There is a right for persons standing in particular relationships to a deceased to invoke the provisions of the Act and thereby to activate the court's discretion. There is a clear public policy that such matters should be allowed to come before the court unfettered by private contracts not to resort to the jurisdiction. So much was held in *Lieberman v Morris* itself. I regard the same public policy considerations as operating upon contractual stipulations precluding the giving of evidence relevant to the due pursuit of such proceedings. If a contract not to invoke the jurisdiction is objectionable on public policy grounds because inimical to the achievement of the social objectives of the legislation, so must a contract not to volunteer information be objectionable to the extent that its effect is to suppress evidence necessary to the pursuit of a claim under the legislation.There is thus a firm basis on which to find that a contract to keep secret information about a child's parentage, where that question is relevant to an issue properly brought before a court by the child in the context of the Family Provision Act, is today a contract which is, to that extent, contrary to public policy. As Campbell J. noted in AG *Australia Holdings*, not all contracts to keep facts secret are objectionable on public policy grounds because they have the result that it is a breach of contract to volunteer evidence. But where, as here, that result involves a matter upon which high value is placed in the interests of society going beyond the availability of evidence as such, a new and distinct public policy consideration intrudes. This is clearly so where a person institutes Family Provision Act proceedings in which their paternity is in issue and the evidence is that of a person's mother.

   I am prepared to hold, and do hold, that a contract is contrary to public policy and unenforceable to the extent that it purports to preclude a mother giving evidence about her child's paternity in proceedings instituted by the child under the Family Provision Act in respect of the estate of the child's supposed father.

Consider:

How did the defendant avoid the rule of privity of contract in seeking to enforce a contract between the deceased and the plaintiff's mother?

SECTION TWO—STATUTORY ILLEGALITY

Contracts may be invalidated by express or implied prohibitions in Acts of the Oireachtas or statutory instruments. In such cases, determining the effect of the statute on the contracts may not be straightforward. An important question to determine will be whether the statute intended to invalidate the contract itself. As the next case indicates, in answering this question, the ordinary canons of interpretation apply.

Gavin Low Ltd *v* Field [1942] IR 86

The plaintiffs sold a cow unfit for human consumption to the defendants. The Court was asked whether the contract was illegal on the basis of legislation authorising health inspectors to confiscate unfit animals exposed for sale and authorising Justices of the Peace to penalise the owners of such animals.

Sullivan C.J.:

The contract is illegal if it is prohibited either expressly by those sections or by implication arising from the imposition of a penalty on the parties with the intention of prohibiting the contract. No question of express prohibition of the contract arises in this case—admittedly there is none; but it is conceded by counsel for the plaintiffs that, if the effect of the sections be to impose a penalty on the plaintiffs for entering into the contract, then the object of the legislature in this case was to prohibit such a contract, and it is prohibited by implication, and is therefore illegal.

It was contended on behalf of the plaintiffs [inter alia] that the effect of these sections was to impose a penalty, not on the *sale* of animals or articles intended for human consumption and unfit for that purpose, but on the exposure for sale, or deposit for the purposes of sale or of preparation for sale, of such animals or articles; In support of the first branch of this argument we were referred to the case of *Bothamley v Jolly*[1] in which the Court of King's Bench in England—Reading C.J., Ridley, Darling, Avory and Rowlatt JJ.—held that the appellant, who had sold diseased meat but had not exposed it for sale, was not liable to conviction under the provisions of s. 117 of the Public Health Act 1875, as amended by s. 28 of the Public Health Acts Amendment Act 1890…The authority of *Bothamley v Jolly* was not challenged by counsel for the defendant, in fact [counsel] said that it was an authority in their favour. They did not contend that the sections in question expressly penalised the contract for sale of a diseased animal or of unsound articles of food, what they did contend was that, if a contract be made for the sale of such animal or article when it is exposed for sale, then the exposure for sale and the sale together form one transaction, the entire of which is vitiated by the illegal exposure. In support of their argument they relied on the object that the legislature had in view in enacting the sections in question, as stated by Lord Coleridge C.J. in *Blaker v Tillstone*[2]: 'The object of the Act is that people shall not be exposed to the danger of eating and drinking poison, that anything that is likely to injure life shall not be sold,' and restated, in terms practically identical, by the judges of the Court of Appeal in *Hobbs v Winchester Corporation*.[3] That object would, they submitted, be defeated if the vendor could recover the price of the 'poison' which the purchaser had been induced to buy by seeing it exposed for sale.

The argument based on the policy of the Act loses in my mind much of its force when it is admitted that the Act does not penalise the sale of diseased or unsound articles of food. In my opinion the defendant's counsel, in order to succeed, must satisfy the court that the contract for sale and the exposure for sale should be regarded as together constituting one unlawful transaction. Sir Frederick Pollock in his *Principles of Contract* (6th edn), 354–5 expresses the opinion that an agreement may be made void by its connection with an unlawful purpose, though subsequent to the execution of it. 'To have that effect, however,' he says, 'the connection must be something more than a mere conjunction of circumstances into which the unlawful transaction enters so that without it there would have been no occasion for the agreement. It must amount to a unity of design and purpose such that the agreement is really part and parcel of one entire unlawful scheme.' I accept that as a correct statement of a legal principle which is, I think, applicable in the present case. In the view that I take of the facts in this case the connection between the unlawful exposure and the sale does not amount to a unity of design and purpose such that the sale is part of one entire unlawful scheme.

I am, therefore, of opinion that the contract for sale between the plaintiff and the defendant was not an illegal contract, and that the cheque, upon which the plaintiff sues, was not given for an illegal consideration.

(Murnaghan J. and Geoghegan J. concurred.)

[1] [1915] 3 KB 415.
[2] [1894] 1 QB 335, at p. 347.
[3] [1910] 2 KB 471.

Note

Meredith J. dissenting held that the exposure for sale of the cow unfit for human consumption was impliedly prohibited on the basis that the legislature may seek to intervene and 'cut short action that may in the natural course of events lead to what is the real mischief aimed at—it may, in other words, seek to nip the mischief in the bud. Prohibition of the bud is then prohibition of the blossom. If exposure for sale is impliedly prohibited, then the sale on such exposure is also impliedly prohibited.' O'Byrne J. agreed.

St John Shipping Corp. *v* Joseph Rank Ltd [1957] 1 QB 267

The plaintiffs, ship owners, contracted to transport grain to the defendants in England. On arrival the ship was found to be overloaded contrary to the Merchant Shipping (Safety and Load Line Conventions) Act, 1932 and the master was prosecuted and fined. The defendants withheld a sum equivalent to the freight on overall additional cargo carried by which the ship was found to be overloaded. The plaintiffs sued for the unpaid portion. The defendants claimed that since the contract of carriage was performed in such a way as to infringe the Act, the plaintiffs permitted an illegality which prevented them from enforcing the contract at all.

Devlin J.:

. . . It is a misfortune for the defendants that the legal weapon which they are wielding is so much more potent than it need be to achieve their purpose. Believing, rightly or wrongly, that the plaintiffs have deliberately committed a serious infraction of the Act and one which has placed their property in jeopardy, the defendants wish to do no more than to take the profit out of the plaintiffs' dealing. But the principle which they invoke for this purpose cares not at all for the element of deliberation or for the gravity of the infraction, and does not adjust the penalty to the profits unjustifiably earned. The defendants cannot succeed unless they claim the right to retain the whole freight and to keep it whether the offence was accidental or deliberate, serious or trivial. The application of this principle to a case such as this is bound to lead to startling results. . . . A shipowner who accidentally overloads by a fraction of an inch will not be able to recover from any of the shippers or consignees a penny of the freight. There are numerous other illegalities which a ship might commit in the course of the voyage which would have the same effect. . . . Of course, as [counsel] says, one must not be deterred from enunciating the correct principle of law because it may have startling or even calamitous results. But I confess I approach the investigation of a legal proposition which has results of this character with a prejudice in favour of the idea that there may be a flaw in the argument somewhere.
    . . . There are two general principles. The first is that a contract which is entered into with the object of committing an illegal act is unenforceable. The application of this principle depends upon proof of the intent, at the time the contract was made, to break the law; if the intent is mutual the contract is not enforceable at all, and, if unilateral, it is unenforceable at the suit of the party who is proved to have it. This principle is not involved here. Whether or not the overloading was deliberate when it was done, there is no proof that it was contemplated when the contract of carriage was

made. The second principle is that the court will not enforce a contract which is expressly or impliedly prohibited by statute. If the contract is of this class it does not matter what the intent of the parties is; if the statute prohibits the contract, it is unenforceable whether the parties meant to break the law or not. A significant distinction between the two classes is this. In the former class you have only to look and see what acts the statute prohibits; it does not matter whether or not it prohibits a contract; if a contract is deliberately made to do a prohibited act, that contract will be unenforceable. In the latter class, you have to consider not what acts the statute prohibits, but what contracts it prohibits; but you are not concerned at all with the intent of the parties; if the parties enter into a prohibited contract, that contract is unenforceable.

[T]he question always is whether the statute meant to prohibit the contract which is sued upon. One of the tests commonly used, and frequently mentioned in the later cases, in order to ascertain the true meaning of the statute is to inquire whether or not the object of the statute was to protect the public or a class of persons, ... If in considering the effect of the statute the only inquiry that you have to make is whether an act is illegal, it cannot matter for whose benefit the statute was passed; the fact that the statute makes the act illegal is of itself enough. But if you are considering whether a contract not expressly prohibited by the Act is impliedly prohibited, such considerations are relevant in order to determine the scope of the statute. . . . The fundamental question is whether the statute means to prohibit the contract. The statute is to be construed in the ordinary way; one must have regard to all relevant considerations and no single consideration, however important, is conclusive.

Two questions are involved. The first—and the one which hitherto has usually settled the matter—is: does the statute mean to prohibit contracts at all? But if this be answered in the affirmative, then one must ask: does this contract belong to the class which the statute intends to prohibit? For example, a person is forbidden by statute from using an unlicensed vehicle on the highway. If one asks oneself whether there is in such an enactment an implied prohibition of all contracts for the use of unlicensed vehicles, the answer may well be that there is, and that contracts of hire would be unenforceable. But if one asks oneself whether there is an implied prohibition of contracts for the carriage of goods by unlicensed vehicles or for the repairing of unlicensed vehicles or for the garaging of unlicensed vehicles, the answer may well be different. The answer might be that collateral contracts of this sort are not within the ambit of the statute. . . .

In my judgment, contracts for the carriage of goods are not within the ambit of this statute at all. A court should not hold that any contract or class of contracts is prohibited by statute unless there is a clear implication, or 'necessary inference', as Parke B. put it, that the statute so intended [2 M & W 159]. If a contract has as its whole object the doing of the very act which the statute prohibits, it can be argued that you can hardly make sense of a statute which forbids an act and yet permits to be made a contract to do it; that is a clear implication. But unless you get a clear implication of that sort, I think that a court ought to be very slow to hold that a statute intends to interfere with the rights and remedies given by the ordinary law of contract. Caution in this respect is, I think, especially necessary in these times when so much of commercial life is governed by regulations of one sort or another, which may easily be broken without wicked intent. Persons who deliberately set out to break the law cannot expect to be aided in a court of justice, but it is a different matter when the law is unwittingly broken. To nullify a bargain in such circumstances frequently means that in a case—perhaps of such triviality that no authority would have felt it worthwhile to prosecute—a seller, because he cannot enforce his civil rights, may forfeit a sum vastly in excess of any penalty that a criminal court would impose; and the sum forfeited will not go into the public purse but into the pockets of someone who is lucky enough to pick up the windfall or astute enough to have contrived to get it. It is questionable how far this contributes to public morality. . . .

On [counsel for the defendants'] third point I take the law from the dictum in *Beresford v Royal Insurance Co. Ltd* [1938] AC 586 that was adopted and applied by Lord Atkin: 'no system of jurisprudence can with reason include amongst the rights which it enforces rights directly resulting to the person asserting them from the crime of that person.' I observe in the first place that in the Court of Appeal in the same case Lord Wright [1937] 2 KB 197 doubted whether this principle applied to all statutory offences. His doubt was referred to by Denning L.J. in *Marles v Philip Trant & Sons* [1954] 1 QB 29, which I have already cited. The distinction is much to the point here. The Act of 1932 imposes a penalty which is itself designed to deprive the offender of the benefits of his crime. It would be a curious thing if the operation could be performed twice—once by the criminal law and then again by the civil. It would be curious, too, if in a case in which the magistrates had thought fit to impose only a nominal fine, their decision could, in effect, be overridden in a civil action. But the question whether the rule applies to statutory offences is an important one which I do not wish to decide in the present case. The dicta of Lord Wright and Denning L.J. suggest that there are cases where its application would be morally unjustifiable; but it is not clear that they go as far as saying that the application would not be justified in law. I prefer, therefore, to deal with [counsel's] submission in another way.

The rights which cannot be enforced must be those 'directly resulting' from the crime. That means, I think, that for a right to money or to property to be unenforceable the property or money must be identifiable as something to which, but for the crime, the plaintiff would have had no right or title. That cannot be said in this case. The amount of the profit which the plaintiffs made from the crime, that is to say, the amount of freight which, but for the overloading, they could not have earned on this voyage, was, as I have said, £2,295. The quantity of cargo consigned to the defendants was approximately thirty five per cent of the whole and, therefore, even if it were permissible to treat the benefit as being divisible *pro rata* over the whole of the cargo, the amount embodied in the claim against the defendants would not be more than thirty five per cent of £2,300. That would not justify the withholding of £2,000. The fact is that the defendants and another cargo owner have between them withheld money, not on a basis that is proportionate to the claim against them, but so as to wipe out the improper profit on the whole of the cargo. . . .

The result is that there must be judgment for the plaintiffs for £2,000. . . .

Archibolds (Freightage) Ltd *v* S. Spanglett Ltd [1961] 1 QB 375

The defendant questioned the validity of a contract to transport goods when the carrier was not properly licensed. Under the Road Traffic Act 1933 the use of goods vehicles for carriage of goods without a licence was prohibited.

Pearce L.J.:
[Having referred to Devlin J.'s judgment in *St John Shipping Corp. v Rank* [1957] 1 QB 267 he continued:]

The object of the Road and Rail Traffic Act 1933 was not (in this connection) to interfere with the owner of goods or his facilities for transport, but to control those who provided the transport, with a view to promoting its efficiency. Transport of goods was not made illegal but the various licence holders were prohibited from encroaching on one another's territory, the intention of the Act being to provide an orderly and comprehensive service. Penalties were provided for those licence holders who went outside the bounds of their allotted spheres. These penalties apply to those using the vehicle but not to the goods owner. Though the latter could be convicted of aiding and abetting any breach, the restrictions were not aimed at him. Thus a contract of carriage was, in the sense used by Devlin J., 'collateral', and it was not impliedly forbidden by the statute.

This view is supported by common sense and convenience. If the other view were held it would have far-reaching effects. For instance, if a carrier induces me (who am in fact ignorant of any illegality) to entrust goods to him and negligently destroys them, he would only have to show that (though unknown to me) his licence had expired, or did not properly cover the transportation, or that he was uninsured, and I should then be without a remedy against him. Or, again, if I ride in a taxicab and the driver leaves me stranded in some deserted spot, he would only have to show that he was (though unknown to me) unlicensed or uninsured, and I should be without remedy. This appears to me an undesirable extension of the implications of a statute.

Lord Wright said in *Vita Food Products Inc. v Unus Shipping Co. Ltd*[1]: 'Each case has to be considered on its merits. Nor must it be forgotten that the rule by which contracts not expressly forbidden by statute or declared to be void are in proper cases nullified for disobedience to a statute is a rule of public policy only, and public policy understood in a wider sense may at times be better served by refusing to nullify a bargain save on serious and sufficient grounds.' If the court too readily implies that a contract is forbidden by statute, it takes it out of its own power (so far as that contract is concerned) to discriminate between guilt and innocence. But if the court makes no such implication, it still leaves itself with the general power, based on public policy, to hold those contracts unenforceable which are *ex facie* unlawful, and also to refuse its aid to guilty parties in respect of contracts which to the knowledge of both can only be performed by a contravention of the statute: see *Nash v Stevenson Transport Ltd*,[2] or which though apparently lawful are intended to be performed illegally or for an illegal purpose, for example, *Pearce v Brooks*.[3]

It is for the defendants to show that contracts by the owner for the carriage of goods are within the ambit of the implied prohibition of the Road and Rail Traffic Act 1933. In my judgment they have not done so.

[1]. [1939] AC 277, 293; 55 TLR 402;[1939] 1 All ER 513.
[2]. [1936] 2 KB 128; 52 TLR 331.
[3]. (1866) LR 1 Ex 213.

Note

In *Marrinan v O'Haran* (HC, 17 June 1971, unrep.) Pringle J. followed the *Archibolds (Freightage) Ltd* case.

The following three cases consider the consequences of a financial institution operating in breach of legislation. It is submitted that the latter adopts a more logical approach to the area.

Hortensius Ltd and Durack *v* Bishop and Others, Trustees of the Trustee Savings Bank, Dublin [1989] ILRM 294

The defendants purchased all the loans and the securities given thereon of the Royal Trust Bank when the latter ceased to carry on banking business. The consent of the Minister for Finance was obtained for this purchase. The portfolio included a loan secured by a mortgage on premises owned by the first plaintiff and a personal guarantee from the second plaintiff. The first plaintiff failed to meet its obligations under the loan agreement and proceedings were instituted seeking *inter alia* declarations that the sale of the debt and the assignment of the mortgage to the defendants was void and unlawful. They claimed that since s. 3 of the Trustee Savings Bank Act 1965 did not authorise the use of depositors' funds for the purchase of funds any consent given by the minister was *ultra vires* and void. The transaction thus fell to be considered under s. 15 of the Trustee Savings Bank Act 1863 which did not give the defendants power to purchase the Royal Trust Bank's portfolio.

Costello J.:

(1) The doctrine of *ultra vires* contracts is one which relates to the acts and contracts of public authorities and companies. As applied to companies it means that any contract made otherwise than in the exercise of powers conferred by the company's memorandum of association is void. But the bank in this case is not a company and s. 15 is a section which imposes a statutory duty on trustees and prohibits the use of funds otherwise than in accordance with that duty. The *ultra vires* doctrine does not apply in such circumstances. What was involved here was a contract entered into in breach of duty imposed by statute, not an *ultra vires* contract. The plaintiffs cannot therefore successfully claim that the contracts are unenforceable because they were *ultra vires* the trustees' powers.

(2) At common law the enforcement of certain contracts was regarded as being against public policy and such contracts were termed 'illegal'. Illegal contracts included those which tend to injure the public service, or pervert the course of justice, or abuse the legal process, or are contrary to good morals, or restrain trade. Also included are those whose objects are clearly illegal, so that a contract which cannot be performed without a breach of the criminal law is unenforceable at common law. But in this case we are concerned with a statutory provision which prohibits the trustees from entering into the contracts of 19 December 1983, not a provision which made illegal the objects of the contracts they entered into. It seems to me therefore that the plaintiffs cannot rely on the common law rules relating to the unenforceability of illegal contracts to justify the claims for relief made in this action.

(3) It remains then to consider whether on a true construction of the 1863 Act the contracts in suit are void and therefore unenforceable. Some statutes may expressly declare certain types of contract to be void and unenforceable (without declaring them to be illegal) as does s. 18 of the Gaming Act 1845 which provides that all agreements by way of wagering shall be null and void and which prohibits any action brought to recover a sum alleged to have been won on a wager. Others may prohibit the making of certain contracts and impose penalties for doing so but remain silent as to the civil rights of the parties to them; it is then a question of the construction of the statute as to whether the contract entered into between the parties is to be regarded as an illegal

one. But in this case the 1863 Act did not make illegal *contracts* for the purchase of loans—it prohibited the trustees *from entering into* such contracts, which is not the same thing. There is, it seems to me, an important distinction between a statutory provision which makes it illegal for a trustee to enter into certain types of contracts and a statutory provision which makes certain types of contract illegal. In the former case (which is what happened on 19 December 1983) what the courts have to consider is what are the legal consequences which flow from a contract entered into by trustees contrary to the statutory provisions by which their trust is governed, in the latter case (which is not this case) what the court would have to consider are the consequences of entering into a contract declared by statute to be an illegal one.

(4) I have no doubt that had the Royal Trust Bank attempted to resile from their agreement with the trustees and had the trustees claimed that it be specifically performed their claim would have failed because the courts of equity will not give relief to a trustee acting in breach of trust. But here we have a completed transaction. It is well established that if a trustee has, in breach of trust, converted trust property into some other form, the property into which it has been converted becomes subject to the trust (see Underhill *Law of Trusts and Trustees*, (1987 ed.), 751). And so if a trustee actually acquires any property in breach of trust his wrongful act does not render the transaction void. That seems to me the position in this case. The statute can properly be regarded as one regulating the manner in which the trustees of savings banks to which the Act applies are to manage the funds which come into their possession. Should they act contrary to its provisions then the law relating to breach of trust by trustees should apply. This means that the property in the choses in action assigned to the trustees and in the freehold and leasehold conveyed and assigned to them by the agreements of 19 December 1983 vested in the trustees notwithstanding their breach of trust. And it follows that they can enforce the rights they thus obtained against the plaintiffs. In reaching this conclusion I have not overlooked the argument advanced by [counsel] on their behalf based on the long established principles most recently illustrated in *Euro-Diam Ltd v Bathurst* [1988] 2 WLR 517. That was a case involving a consignment of diamonds to Germany which were there stolen and which resulted in proceedings to enforce a policy of insurance relating to them. A false value had been inserted in the invoice sent to the German consignee for the purpose of avoiding German import tax and the claim on foot of the policy of insurance was resisted on the ground *inter alia* that the contract of insurance was tainted by the illegality relating to the consignment contract and was therefore unenforceable. The law relating to a defence based on the maxim *ex turpi causa non oritur actio* was helpfully summarised by Kerr L.J. at 526–7. But for reasons already explained I do not think that this maxim is of any avail to the plaintiffs in the present case. In my view the plaintiffs could not resist a claim brought against them by the trustees on the ground that the illegality of the contracts of 19 December 1983 has so tainted the original contracts between the plaintiffs and Royal Trust Bank (Ireland) Ltd that the court would not allow the trustees to enforce them. For reasons already pointed out the contracts of 19 December 1983 were not themselves 'illegal' contracts, so that the doctrine of tainting does not arise. Furthermore public policy has never required that trustees should be deprived of the right to enforce propriety claims over property acquired in breach of trust. In my judgment therefore the contravention of s. 15 which occurred does not invalidate the transaction of 19 December 1983 and the trustees are entitled to enforce the rights they acquired in the agreement and mortgage of 6 July 1982.

I turn now to deal with the alternative final submission made on the trustees' behalf by [counsel]. He argues, and I think argues correctly, that even if the transaction of 19 December 1983 can be regarded as an illegal one, once property has been delivered under it the fact that by reason of the illegality the trustees could not originally have enforced the agreement does not mean that the property in the interests they acquired has not passed to them. I think the statement to this effect in *Chitty on Contracts* (25th edn) para. 1169 is correct and is borne out by the authorities. *Singh v Ali* [1960] AC 167 was a case dealing with the unlawful sale of a motor lorry. In the course of his judgment Lord Denning made some observations of a general nature (subsequently approved of in *Belvoir Finance Co. v Stapleton* [1971] 1 QB 210 at 219). 'Although the transaction between the plaintiff and the defendant was illegal', he said:

> nevertheless it was fully executed and carried out; and on that account it was effective to pass the property in the lorry to the plaintiff. . . . The reason is because the transferor, having fully achieved his unworthy end, cannot be allowed to turn around and repudiate the means by which he did it—he cannot throw over the transfer. And the transferee, having obtained the property, can assert this title to it against all the world, not because he has any merit of his own, but because there is no one who can assert a better title to it. The court does not confiscate the property because of the illegality. . . .

And as Chitty points out (in para. 1169) this principle also applies in the case of real property so that where a person takes a lease intending to use it for an immoral purpose he acquires an interest in the executed lease despite the intention to use it for the immoral purpose. I think it follows that even if the agreements of 19 December 1983 can be regarded as illegal contracts which the trustees could not have enforced against the Royal Trust Bank (Ireland) Ltd once the consideration provided in them has been paid, and the property referred to in them transferred to the trustees they are not void contracts. I think therefore the trustees now have a good title to the choses in action (including the debt due by the plaintiff company and the right to enforce the guarantee of the second-named plaintiff under the agreements of 6 July 1982) as well as to the properties transferred to them by the agreements (including the fee simple of No. 62 Clontarf Road, Dublin). This means that the trustees are entitled to enforce the rights they have acquired by virtue of these agreements against both plaintiffs.

The claims the plaintiffs have made in this action must fail. To avoid doubts I would propose to dismiss the claims having recited that the court is satisfied that the defendants have acquired a good title to the property real and personal referred to in the agreements of 19 December 1983 and that they are entitled to enforce the rights obtained by them against the plaintiffs. The order should also declare the trustees' entitlement to the moneys on deposit in the joint names of the parties' solicitors.

Yango Pastoral Co. Pty Ltd and Others *v* First Chicago Australia Ltd and Others (1978) 139 CLR 410

S. 8 of The Banking Act 1959 (Cth) prohibited a corporate body from carrying on banking business in Australia without authority. Despite the fact that First Chicago Australia Ltd did not possess the relevant authority, it made a loan to the first appellant which was secured by a mortgage incorporating a guarantee given by the other appellants. When the respondent sued for default in repayment, the appellants pleaded illegality.

Gibbs A.C.J.:

There are four main ways in which the enforceability of a contract may be affected by a statutory provision which renders particular conduct unlawful: (1) The contract may be to do something which the statute forbids; (2) The contract may be one which the statute expressly or impliedly prohibits; (3) The contract, although lawful on its face, may be made in order to effect a purpose which the statute renders unlawful; or (4) The contract, although lawful according to its own terms, may be performed in a manner which the statute prohibits.

In the present case we are not concerned with the first of these possible situations. Clearly s. 8 does not render it unlawful to borrow or lend money or to give and take a mortgage, supported by guarantees, to secure its repayment. The contract sued upon was therefore not to do anything which s. 8 forbids. The principal question in the case is whether s. 8, on its proper construction, prohibited the making or performance of the contract. As will be seen if that question is answered in the negative, it will not be possible to say that the contract cannot be enforced on the ground that it was made in order to effect an unlawful purpose or was performed in an unlawful manner.

It is often said that a contract expressly or impliedly prohibited by statute is void and unenforceable. That statement is true as a general rule, but for complete accuracy it needs qualification, because it is possible for a statute in terms to prohibit a contract and yet to provide, expressly or impliedly, that the contract will be valid and enforceable. However, cases are likely to be rare in which a statute prohibits a contract but nevertheless reveals an intention that it shall be valid and enforceable, and in most cases it is sufficient to say, as has been said in many cases of authority, that the test is whether the contract is prohibited by the statute. Where a statute imposes a penalty upon the making or performance of a contract, it is a question of construction whether the statute intends to prohibit the contract in this sense, that is, to render it void and unenforceable, or whether it intends only that the penalty for which it provides shall be inflicted if the contract is made or performed.

The question whether a statute, on its proper construction, intends to vitiate a contract made in breach of its provisions, is one which must be determined in accordance with the ordinary principles that govern the construction of statutes. 'The determining factor is the true effect and meaning of the statute' (St John Shipping Corp. v Joseph Rank Ltd[1]). 'One must have regard to the language used and to the scope and purpose of the statute.' (Archbolds Freightage Ltd. v S. Spanglett Ltd[2]). One consideration that has been regarded as important in a great many cases, ... is whether the object of the statute—or one of its objects—is the protection of the public. An antithesis is commonly suggested between an intention to protect the public and an intention simply to secure the revenue, and it is said that when the former intention appears the contract must be taken to be prohibited, whereas if the intention is only to protect the revenue the statute will not be construed as imposing a prohibition on contracts. The question whether the statute was passed for the protection of the public is one test of whether it was intended to vitiate a contract made in breach of its provisions, but I am with respect in full agreement with the views expressed in St John Shipping Corp. v Joseph Rank Ltd and Shaw v Groom[3] that it is not the only test. It would be contrary to reason and principle to allow one circumstance to override all other considerations in the interpretation of a statute. As Devlin J. said in St John Shipping Corp. v Joseph Rank Ltd: 'The fundamental question is whether the statute means to prohibit the contract. The statute is to be construed in the ordinary way: one must have regard to all relevant considerations and no single consideration, however important is conclusive.'

Mason J.:

The principle that a contract the making of which is expressly or impliedly prohibited by statute is illegal and void is one of long standing but it has always been recognised that the principle is necessarily subject to any contrary intention manifested by the statute. It is perhaps more accurate to say that the question whether a contract prohibited by statute is void is, like the associated question whether the statute prohibits the contract, a question of statutory construction and that the principle to which I have referred does no more than enunciate the ordinary rule which will be applied when the statute itself is silent upon the question. Primarily, then, it is a matter of construing the statute and in construing the statute the court will have regard not only to its language, which may or may not touch upon the question, but also to the scope and purpose of the statute for which inferences may be drawn as to the legislative intention regarding the extent and the effect of the prohibition which the statute contains.

The first question is: Does s. 8 expressly prohibit the making of a contract of loan? The question must, I think, be answered in the negative. . . .The next question is whether by implication, that is by way of necessary inference, such a prohibition can be discovered in the section. . . .Where, as here, a statute imposes a penalty for contravention of an express prohibition against carrying on a business without a licence or an authority and the business is carried on by entry into contracts, the question is whether the statute intends merely to penalise the person who contravenes the prohibition or whether it intends to go further and prohibit contracts the making of which constitute the carrying on of the business. In deciding this question the court will take into account the scope and purpose of the statute and the consequences of the suggested implication with a view to ascertaining whether it would conduce to, or frustrate, the object of the statute. . . .

In this context there is little to be said for the view that the statute intends to prohibit contracts made by unauthorised banks in the course of carrying on banking business. To do so would be to prejudice depositors, not to protect them. The implication of such a prohibition would deny to innocent depositors the right to recover moneys deposited unlawfully with persons carrying on banking business because *ex hypothesi* the prohibited contract would be illegal and void. To place the defendants' interpretation upon the statute would confer an extraordinary advantage on the wrongdoer in enabling it to resist repayment of moneys deposited with it. In this respect the advantage given to the wrongdoer might conceivably go some distance towards outweighing the punishment imposed upon it by way of penalty under s. 8.

It is not rational to suppose that the Parliament intended to inflict such dire consequences on innocent depositors. Nor is it rational to suppose that the Parliament intended to advantage innocent borrowers whilst penalising innocent depositors. Even less is it to be supposed that the Parliament intended to invalidate the wide range of commercial and other securities which are brought into existence in the course of carrying on a banking business and thereby to inflict loss on the many persons acquiring such securities. I therefore conclude that the purpose of the Act is adequately served by the imposition of the very heavy penalty which is prescribed for a contravention of s. 8 and that it does not prohibit and thereby invalidate contracts and transactions entered into in the course of carrying on banking business in breach of the section...

In my opinion the plaintiff is able to enforce the mortgage against the defendants in this case as the contract is not rendered void, either expressly or impliedly, by the

Act and considerations of public policy operate, in the circumstances, so as to make inapplicable the maxim *ex turpi causa non oritur actio.*

1. [1957] 1 QB 267, at 286.   2. [1961] 1 QB 374, at 390.
3. [1970] 2 QB 504, at 518.

Note

The *Yango Pastoral Co.* decision was relied upon by Leggatt J. in *Stewart v Oriental Fire and Marine Insurance Co. Ltd* [1984] 3 All ER 777. This latter case was, however, overruled in the case of *Phoenix General Insurance Co. of Greece SA v Administratia Asigurarilor de Stat* [1987] 2 All ER 125.

Phoenix General Insurance Co. of Greece SA *v* Administratia Asigurarilor de Stat [1987] 2 All ER 125

The plaintiffs were insurers authorised under the Insurance Companies Act 1974. In 1978 new regulations were introduced reclassifying the various categories of insurance. The plaintiffs entered into reinsurance contracts with the defendants, but when they submitted their claims, the defendants refused to pay claiming that the contracts were illegal due to the plaintiff's lack of authorisation. The Court of Appeal held that transitional provisions in the regulations provided the necessary authorisation. However it went on to consider what the position would have been if no authorisation existed.

Kerr L.J.:

(i) Where a statute prohibits both parties from concluding or performing a contract when both or either of them have no authority to do so, the contract is impliedly prohibited: see *Mahmoud and Ispahani's* case [1921] 2 KB 716, [1921] All ER Rep 217 and its analysis by Pearce L.J. in the *Archibolds* case [1961] 1 All ER 417, [1961] 1 QB 374 with which Devlin L.J. agreed.

(ii) But where a statute merely prohibits one party from entering into a contract without authority and/or imposes a penalty on him if he does so (i.e. a unilateral prohibition) it does not follow that the contract itself is impliedly prohibited so as to render it illegal and void. Whether or not the statute has this effect depends on considerations of public policy in the light of the mischief which the statute is designed to prevent, its language, scope and purpose, the consequences for the innocent party, and any other relevant considerations. . . .

(iii) The Insurance Companies Act 1974 only imposes a unilateral prohibition on unauthorised insurers. If this were merely to prohibit them from carrying on 'the business of effecting contracts of insurance' of a class for which they have no authority, then it would clearly be open to the court to hold that considerations of public policy preclude the implication that such contracts are prohibited and void. But unfortunately the unilateral prohibition is not limited to the business of 'effecting contracts of insurance' but extends to the business of 'carrying out contracts of insurance'. This is a form of statutory prohibition, albeit only unilateral, which is not covered by any authority. However, . . . I can see no convincing escape from the conclusion that this extension of the prohibition has the unfortunate effect that contracts made without authorisation are prohibited by necessary implication and therefore void. Since the statute prohibits the insurer from carrying out the contract (of which the most obvious example is paying claims), how can the insured require the insurer to do an act which is expressly forbidden by statute? And how can a court enforce a contract against an unauthorised insurer when Parliament has expressly prohibited him from carrying it out? In that situation there is simply no room for the introduction of considerations of public policy. As Parker J. said in the Bedford case [1984] 3 All ER 766 at 775, [1985] QB 966 at 986: ' . . . once it is concluded that on its true construction the Act prohibited both contract and performance, that is the public policy'.

(iv) It follows that, however reluctantly, I feel bound to agree with the analysis of Parker J. in the Bedford case and his conclusion that contracts of insurance made by unauthorised insurers are prohibited by the 1974 Act in the sense that they are illegal and void, and therefore unenforceable...

But, with all due respect, the reliance which Leggatt J. placed on the decision of the High Court of Australia in the Yango case appears to me to be untenable. The statutory prohibition in that case (s. 8 of the Banking Act 1959) merely prohibited a body corporate from carrying on any banking business without authority, and imposed a daily penalty for contravention. It made no reference whatever to any contracts concluded by persons carrying on banking business without authority. This was the main basis for the conclusion of the High Court, but it cannot have any direct application here. Furthermore, it was held that the contracts in question, a loan, mortgage and guarantee, were not central to the business of banking. But this would be an obviously impossible argument in relation to contracts of insurance in the context of insurance business.

Note

It was observed in this case that this decision was based very much on its own facts, most statutes leaving room for a more purposive approach.

The High Court of Australia's approach in *Yango* has been developed further in the next case.

Fitzgerald *v* F J Leonhardt Pty Ltd (1997) 189 CLR 215

A drilling company entered into a contract with the owner of property to drill three bores for water. When the drilling company sought payment under this contract, the owner alleged that the contract was illegal as the drilling work was not authorised as required by the Water Act, 1992. The Court considered whether as a matter of public policy the court should decline to enforce the contract because of its association with the illegal activity of the owner.

McHugh and Gummow JJ.:

The refusal of the courts in such a case to regard the contract as enforceable stems not from express or implied legislative prohibition but from the policy of the law, commonly called public policy.[1] Regard is to be had primarily to the scope and purpose of the statute to consider whether the legislative purpose will be fulfilled without regarding the contract as void and unenforceable.[2] . . .

This leaves the separate question of whether, as a matter of public policy, a court should refuse a person in the position of the respondent the aid of its process so as to enforce a contract in circumstances where, as performed, illegality has been demonstrated. The rule permitting a court to refuse its assistance to enforce a contract where to do so would be contrary to public policy is an ancient one. It was given expression by Lord Mansfield in *Holman v Johnson*[3] in these terms:

> The principle of public policy is this . . . No Court will lend its aid to a man who founds his cause of action upon an immoral or an illegal act.

Sometimes the principle is expressed as involving the refusal of a court to enforce a contract where the party seeking such enforcement is obliged to disclose an unlawful consideration in making out the claim.[4] Sometimes it is expressed in the language that courts will not enforce 'rights directly resulting to the person asserting them from the crime of that person'.[5] But behind the notion is something quite different from the foundation upon which the statutory construction objection rests. There, a court is simply giving effect to the expressed or imputed will of Parliament. When it comes to public policy, the court may inform itself by reference to what Parliament has declared to be illegal. However the fundamental rationale for withholding relief is one essentially of the court's self-regard. It will not (unless required to) lend its authority and assistance to a party seeking to invoke its process in connection with illegal or otherwise seriously reprehensible conduct. This was the 'question' which remained in Yango, after the statutory construction point in that case was disposed of favourably to the enforcement of the contract.[6] Mason J. explained the question thus:[7]

> The question therefore remains whether the court will allow the plaintiff to enforce the contract. The suggestion is that the court will not do so and that its refusal so to do is dictated by the principle ex turpi causa non oritur actio or by the more specific rule that the court will not enforce the contract at the suit of a party who has entered into a contract with the object of committing an illegal act. . . .

In saying this I am mindful that there could be a case where the facts disclose that the plaintiff stands to gain by enforcement of rights gained through an illegal activity far more than the prescribed penalty. This circumstance might provide a sufficient foundation for attributing a different intention to the legislature. It may be that the true basis of the principle is that the court will refuse to enforce a transaction with a fraudulent or immoral purpose.[8] On this basis the common law principle of ex turpi causa can be given an operation consistent with, though subordinate to, the statutory intention, denying relief in those cases where a plaintiff may otherwise evade the real consequences of a breach of a statutory prohibition. . . . Even more explicitly, Jacobs J.,[9] asked:

> [W]hether, if the contract was neither expressly or impliedly forbidden, nevertheless on grounds of public policy the courts would not enforce it if it could only be performed in contravention of a statute or was intended to be performed illegally or for an illegal purpose.

Now, it was said long ago, and has been repeated often since, that public policy 'is a very unruly horse'.[10] Whereas it affords a measure of discretion to the courts to lend, or deny, their authority according to notions of the propriety, or otherwise, of enforcing a contract said to be affected by illegality or reprehensibility, the principle is scarcely conducive to certainty and consistency. Clearly, these are desirable objectives so far as the law of contract is concerned. Although some older authority suggests the classification of cases of public policy in closed categories to which courts will always deny relief, more recent decisions support a principle of greater flexibility. Thus, it has been said that public policy is not to be viewed as a 'blunt, inflexible instrument'.[11] Nor is the concept static.[12] The decision of this Court in Yango rejects the proposition that any prohibited conduct, involved directly or indirectly in the performance of a contract sued upon, denies to the parties the facility of the process of the courts.[13] Whatever may be the position in England following the decision of the House of Lords in *Tinsley v Milligan*,[14] in Australia it must be accepted, from decisions of this Court,[15] that the rule against enforcement is not inflexible.

Clearly it should not be so. It would be absurd if a trivial breach of a statutory provision constituting illegality, connected in some way with a contract or contracting parties, could be held to justify the total withdrawal of the facilities of the courts.[16] It would be doubly absurd if the courts closed their doors to a party seeking to enforce its contractual rights without having regard to the degree of that party's transgression, the deliberateness or otherwise of its breach of the law and its state of mind generally relevant to the illegality. Similarly, it would be absurd if a court were permitted, or required, to consider the refusal of relief without careful regard to the relationship between the prohibited conduct and the impugned contract. Thus, different considerations may exist where the contractual rights being enforced arise directly from the illegality, as distinct from those which arise only incidentally or peripherally.[17] It is one thing for courts to respond with understandable disfavour and reluctance to attempts to involve them and their processes in an inappropriate and unseemly way effectively in the advancement of illegality and wrongdoing. It is another to invoke a broad rule of so-called 'public policy' which slams the doors of the court in the face of a person whose illegality may be minor, technical, innocent, lacking in seriousness and wholly incidental or peripheral to a contract which that person is seeking to enforce. Considerations such as these led McHugh J. in *Nelson v Nelson*[18] to explore the ways in which a broad judicial discretion to withhold relief, the grant of which would affront 'the public conscience', could be given greater certainty of content. His Honour suggested that such a sanction would have to be proportionate to the seriousness of the illegality involved and not disproportionate to the seriousness of the breach.[19] It would have to further the purpose of the statute and not impose a sanction for unlawful conduct beyond that which Parliament has expressly condoned.[20] McHugh J. proposed the following general propositions:[21]

> [C]ourts should not refuse to enforce legal or equitable rights simply because they arose out of or were associated with an unlawful purpose unless: (a) the statute discloses an intention that those rights should be unenforceable in all circumstances; or (b),(i) the sanction of refusing to enforce those rights is not disproportionate to the seriousness of the unlawful conduct; (ii) the imposition of the sanction is necessary, having regard to the terms of the statute, to protect its objects or policies; and (iii) the statute does not disclose an intention that the sanctions and remedies contained in the statute are to be the only legal consequences of a breach of the statute or the frustration of its policies. . . .

For a number of reasons I have concluded that this is not a case where it would be appropriate to treat the contract between the parties as unenforceable on public policy grounds. If the criteria mentioned by McHugh J. in Nelson[22] are applied, it has already been held that the Act did not disclose an intention that the respondent's rights should be unenforceable in all circumstances. To refuse to enforce those rights would be disproportionate to the seriousness of the unlawful conduct in question. This is, in part, because the duty to obtain the necessary permit rested on the appellant. According to the then administration of the Act, both the appellant and the respondent (and the authorities) thought they had done all that was required. It would be disproportionate to the respondent's unlawful conduct to deprive it almost entirely of recovery under the contract, although there was nothing illegal in the contract itself and the performance by the respondent would have been lawful if the appellant had secured the requisite permits. Against the background of the mistaken understanding about the meaning and operation of the Act, the imposition of such a sanction is not necessary to protect the objects or policies of the Act. Other sanctions exist to uphold those ends. The Act being silent on contracts, it is a preferable construction of its terms that, at least in circumstances such as the present, the parties should be able to enforce their legal rights in courts of law and should not be deprived of those rights under the rubric of unenforceability for public policy reasons any more than on the basis of the application to the contract of the suggested construction of the Act. . . .

The position would be quite different if what had been involved had been a specific agreement between the parties deliberately to breach the Act (e.g. by the use of unlicensed and neglectful drillers or the deliberate refusal to obtain any permit) or to perform the contract in a way clearly damaging to the scarce resource of ground water in the Territory. . . .

But that is not this case. On the contrary, were the Court to withhold relief to the respondent, it would result in a windfall gain to the appellant which was unmerited and itself would be an affront to the public conscience. The appellant, a property developer, would have gained three successful water bores for a pittance. The respondent would have been denied recovery precisely on the basis of the failure of the appellant (whose duty it was) to obtain in advance the requisite permits. I do not accept that the rule of public policy, invoked by the appellant, is as inflexible and harsh as to produce such an offensive result.[23] The appellant therefore fails on the public policy point.

1. *Yango Pastoral Co. Pty. Ltd. v First Chicago Australia Ltd* (1978) 139 CLR 410 at 429–30, 432–3; 21 ALR 585; *Nelson v Nelson* (1995) 184 CLR 538 at 551–2, 593, 611; 132 ALR 133.
2. *Yango Pastoral Co. Pty Ltd v First Chicago Australia Ltd* (1978) 139 CLR 410 at 434; 21 ALR 585.
3. (1775) 1 Cowp. 341.
4. *St John Shipping Corporation v Joseph Rank Ltd* [1957] 1 QB 267 at 291–292.
5. *Cleaver v Mutual Reserve Fund Life Association* [1892] 1 QB 147 at 256; cf 586 at 596–597; *St John Shipping Corporation v Joseph Rank Ltd* [1957] 1 QB 267 at 292–293.
6. *Yango Pastoral Company Pty Ltd v First Chicago Australia Ltd* (1978) 249 CLR 410 at 427; cf *Scott v Brown, Doering, McNab & Co.* [1892] 2 QB 724 at 728; cited by Windeyer J. in *Smith v Jenkins* (1970) 119 CLR at 412.
7. *Yango Pastoral Company Pty Ltd v First Chicago Australia Ltd* (1978) 249 CLR at 427, 429–430.
8. *Beresford v Royal Insurance Co. Ltd* [1937] 2 KB 197 at 220.
9. *Yango Pastoral Company Pty Ltd v First Chicago Australia Ltd* (1978) 249 CLR 410 at 433; see also at 434], drawing upon earlier authority [*Archbolds (Freightage) Ltd v S Spanglett Ltd* [1961] 1 QB 374.
10. *Richardson v Mellish* (1824) 2 Bing 229 at 252 [130 ER 294 at 303].

11. *Saunders v Edwards* [1987] 1 WLR 1116 at 1132; [1987] 2 All ER 651 at 664; discussed Starke, Seddon and Ellinghaus, *Cheshire and Fifoot's Law of Contract*, 6th Aust. edn (1992) at 456, fn 78; Stowe 'The "Unruly Horse" has Bolted; *Tinsley v Milligan*' (1994) 57 *Modern Law Review* 441 at 443.

12. *Gray v Barr* [1971] 2 QB 554 at 582, discussed Stowe 'The "Unruly Horse" has Bolted; *Tinsley v Milligan*' (1994) 57 *Modern Law Review* 441 at 443.

13. See Enonchong, 'Title Claims and Illegal Transactions', (1995) 111 *Law Quarterly Review* 135.

14. [1994] 1 AC 340.

15. *Yango Pastoral Company Pty Ltd v First Chicago Australia Ltd* (1978) 249 CLR 410; *Nelson v Nelson* (1995) 184 CLR 538.

16. *St John Shipping Corporation v Joseph Rank Ltd* [1957] 1 QB 267 at 280–281, 288–289 per Devlin J.: 'It may be questionable . . . whether public policy is well served by driving from the seat of judgment everyone who has been guilty of a minor transgression.'

17. *St John Shipping Corporation v Joseph Rank Ltd* [1957] 1 QB 267 at 284, 289–290.

18. (1995) 184 CLR 538.

19. (1995) 184 CLR 538 at 612–613.

20. (1995) 184 CLR 538 at 613.

21. (1995) 184 CLR 538 at 613.

22. (1995) 184 CLR 538.

23. *Yango Pastoral Company Pty Ltd v First Chicago Australia Ltd* (1978) 249 CLR 410 at 428.

Note

This case was distinguished in *Corradini and Another v O'Brien Lovrinov Crafter P/L* [2000] SASC 224 where a contract to design and supervise renovations to a house for the defendant was not deemed to be unenforceable despite the fact that the plaintiff failed to comply with building legislation prescribing certain formal requirements for building contracts. Doyle C.J. noted that 'the prohibition relates to the form of the contract, and not to what is done pursuant to the contract'. While it was accepted that the court will not often enforce a contract, the making of which is expressly or impliedly prohibited by statute, the Court held that to permit the contract to be enforced is not inconsistent with the legislation nor contrary to public policy.

SECTION THREE—THE CONSEQUENCES OF ILLEGALITY

The general principle adopted by the courts is that no person can claim any right or remedy whatsoever under an illegal transaction in which he or she has participated. The principle is expressed by the Latin maxim, 'Ex turpi causi no oritur actio'. In *Scott v Brown, Doering, McNab & Co.*1 (cited with approval in *McIlvenna and McIlvenna v Ferris and Green* [1955] IR 318) Lindley L.J. explained this maxim as follows:

This old and well known legal maxim is founded in good sense, and expresses a clear and well recognised legal principle, which is not confined to indictable offences. No court ought to enforce an illegal contract or allow itself to be made the instrument of enforcing obligations alleged to arise out of a contract or transaction which is illegal, if the illegality is duly brought to the notice of the court, and if the person invoking the aid of the court is himself implicated in the illegality. It matters not whether the defendant has pleaded the illegality or whether he has not. If the evidence adduced by the plaintiff proves the illegality the court ought not to assist him.

A. WHERE THE CONTRACT IS UNLAWFUL ON ITS FACE

The general rule is that where a contract which is unlawful on its face, i.e. obviously unlawful, there can be no recovery on the contract itself.

Gray v Cathcart (1899) 33 ILTR 35

Under the Belfast Corporation Acts it was a penal offence to occupy a house not provided with proper yard accommodation. Despite being ordered to leave his house for this reason by the local authority the plaintiff let the house to the defendant. The latter was informed of the local authority's orders. Later the plaintiff sued for the balance of rent due under the letting agreement.

Johnson J.:

Everyone commits a misdemeanour who does any act forbidden by a statute; accordingly when these parties entered into the agreement to occupy a house which had been condemned it was a contract to do that which the statute says that you could not do. It was a contract to do an illegal thing, and, though the parties might go through the form, yet such a contract is not binding, and cannot be sued upon.

James L. Murphy & Co. Ltd v Crean [1915] 1 IR 111

The defendant sought to trade as a publican from premises in Douglas Street. In order to acquire a licence, a practice had arisen that an applicant would acquire and then agree to extinguish an existing licence attached to another public house. The plaintiffs purchased a licence from a third party and gave the defendants authority to surrender it in return for the defendant giving the plaintiffs an exclusive right to supply beer and stout to the public house. As an ancillary part of this agreement, the defendant agreed to transfer the licence to any other house directed by them. Subsequently, the plaintiffs sought damages for breach of this agreement as a result of the supply at the public house of beer and stout manufactured by another brewery. The Court held that the contract was unenforceable.

Palles C.B.:

In my judgment it is clear that the effect of this agreement is to provide for the carrying on of the publican's trade under a document purporting to be a licence, but which in truth is waste paper—that is, to carry it on without a licence, with an obligation on the defendant, at the plaintiffs' request, to transfer the licence to any house directed by them. Such an agreement is, in my opinion, illegal and incapable of enforcement. If there had been any valuable consideration for it, it consists in assistance in procuring a void licence by producing a document to the licensing authority, and thereby persuading it to purport to transfer it without authority from one house to another house, and thus to procure a licence for such other house without an inquiry as to the number of public houses in the neighbourhood.

Thus I am of opinion that the illegality pervades the entire agreement, both consideration and promises. It appears on the face of the document, and consequently need not have been pleaded.

Notes

1. The leading English case is re *Mahmoud and Ispahani* [1921] 2 KB 716 where at page 729 Scrutton L. J. observed:

In my view the court is bound, once it knows that the contract is illegal, to take the objection and to refuse to enforce the contract, whether its knowledge comes from the statement of the party who was guilty of the illegality, or whether its knowledge comes from outside sources. The court does not sit to enforce illegal contracts. There is no question of estoppel; it is for the protection of the public that the court refuses to enforce such a contract.

2. This approach was reaffirmed in *Macklin and McDonald v Graecen and Co. Ltd* [1983] IR 61 (see p. 342 above).

B. WHERE THE CONTRACT IS LAWFUL ON ITS FACE BUT ONE PERSON INTENDS TO PERFORM UNLAWFULLY

Where the contract appears lawful on its face but one person intends to perform it unlawfully, the contract may be enforceable at the instance of the innocent party. As the cases after *Whitecross* evidence, a substantial number of employment contracts are challenged in the courts on grounds of illegality.

Whitecross Potatoes (International) Ltd *v* Coyle [1978] ILRM 31

The plaintiff bought potatoes for resale to food processors in England. The defendant, a Meath potato grower, agreed to sell potatoes to the plaintiff at a fixed price. In anticipation of future export restrictions between England and Ireland, clause 11 of the contract stated that if such controls were imposed the potatoes would be supplied from Northern Ireland. The plaintiff claimed that he had been informed that this would involve the defendant buying the requisite quantity of potatoes from contacts in the North. The defendant claimed that he had made it clear that the potatoes would be smuggled from Meath to the North to meet the order. When the defendant breached a term of the contract the plaintiff sued and the defendant sought to rely on the illegality.

Finlay P.:

I am satisfied that the legal principles applicable to this conflict of evidence are relatively straightforward. If this was a contract which, on the apparent intention of the parties at the time of its formation, could be and would be carried out in a legal fashion then even though one of the parties, namely the defendant, in reality intended to carry it out in an illegal fashion it is enforceable. If, on the other hand, the acknowledged and accepted intention of both the parties at the time of the formation of the contract was that in the event of this export or import control being imposed the contract would be carried out by a smuggling operation, it is unenforceable and is contrary to public policy and cannot be upheld by the court.

I have had the greatest possible difficulty in reaching a conclusion as to which of the two accounts of this transaction I should accept. I have ultimately come to the conclusion that the onus being on the defendant he has failed to discharge it and to establish to my satisfaction as a matter of probability that the agreed understanding between him and the plaintiff was that this contract should, in the event of a restriction on export, be carried out by a smuggling operation.

Lewis v Squash Ireland Ltd [1983] ILRM 363

The claimant was employed as managing director of the respondent company. His salary was £16,000 per annum, £2,000 of which was described as 'expenses' in the respondent's accounts. This figure actually represented a salary increase and was misdescribed in order to reduce the respondent's tax liability. When the claimant was dismissed he sued for unfair dismissal and the Employment Appeals Tribunal had to consider whether the contract of employment was tainted with illegality.

Determination
Did [the illegality] render the contract void? We do not hold the view that the illegality rendered the contract void, i.e. at law deemed to have no effect. In this case the contract as originally made was, as far as we are concerned, perfectly legal and continued as such until tainted by the later agreement.

Did it render the contract unenforceable?
In *Tomlinson v Dick Evans 'U' Drive Ltd* [1978] ICR 639–643 the employee received a £15.00 per week pay rise paid to the knowledge of employer and employee out of petty cash against 'bogus vouchers' for collection and delivery charges. On a claim for compensation for unfair dismissal and a redundancy payment, the industrial tribunal held that the payment was a fraud on the Revenue and, therefore, as the contract of employment was unenforceable, they dismissed the claim. She appealed and her appeal was dismissed by the Employment Appeal Tribunal (EAT). In its judgment the EAT said:

The reason why rights and obligations which arise from a contract which is illegal will not be enforced in the courts was expressed by Lord Mansfield as long ago as 1775 in *Holman v Johnson* (1775) 1 Cowp. 341, 343 to be founded on general principles of public policy. 'The principle of public policy is this: *ex dolo malo non oritur actio*'. A distinguished judge using the idiom of 1977 and borrowing from A. P. Herbert has expressed it in language more apt to be used amongst those concerned with this branch of the law as 'the dirty dog gets no dinner here'. We take it to be clear law that someone who tries to assert in the courts a right contained in an illegal contract will not succeed.

It is not suggested on this appeal that the industrial tribunal was wrong in finding that it had to do with a deliberate fraud on the Revenue. It is clear that both Mr Evans and the employee knew exactly what they were doing and that both were in it up to the neck. Both in their evidence were what it is kinder to call candid than shameless about it. No doubt there are cases in which a junior employee goes along with an employer's tax fraud knowing it to be dishonest in circumstances where more blame attaches to the employer than to him. But even in such cases the evil lies in the dishonesty in which the employee knowingly participated and the law leaves the balancing of the respective degrees of blame to the discretion of the Revenue in deciding who is to be subjected to penalties or prosecuted, and the criminal court which has to decide upon what sentence to inflict. There is, for good reason, no relaxation in the rule that the dishonest party to the swindle cannot recover upon the contract.

In *Newland v Simons and Willer (Hairdressers) Ltd* [1981] ICR 521 the EAT, in a fraud on the Revenue case, stated (May J. delivering the majority decision):

> In the view of the majority of this appeal tribunal, however, where both employer and employee knowingly commit an illegality by way of a fraud on the Revenue in the payment and receipt of the employee's remuneration under the contract of employment, which is an essential part of such a contract, then we think that there can be no doubt that this does turn it into a contract that is prohibited by statute or common law, and consequently the employee is precluded from enforcing any employment rights she might otherwise have against her employer. The incidence of income tax frauds both large and small is so rife that they cannot be brushed on one side and the blame for them laid only at the feet of the employers (at p. 530).

In Newland's case at 531, May J. stated that in the view of the majority the essential question is 'Has the employee knowingly been a party to a deception on the Revenue?' Adopting this question, the tribunal has decided that on a subjective test the answer is yes. It is public policy that the courts and this tribunal, should not lend themselves to the enforcement of contracts either illegal on their face or in which the intended performance of obligations thereunder was illegal to the knowledge of the party seeking to enforce the contract. . . . The tribunal considers that the contract herein is not enforceable at the suit of the claimant by virtue of public policy being set against such enforcement.

Can statutory rights be based on an illegal contract?
Although the contract in this case is unenforceable it is not, as stated, void and [counsel] submitted that the mere existence of the contract of employment is sufficient to establish that the claimant was an employee of the respondent and he, having the requisite qualifying service, had met the requirement of the Unfair Dismissals Act 1977, to the extent that the tribunal should and could review the dismissal in accordance with the Act, the onus being on the respondent to justify the dismissal. . . . [In *Newland v Simons and Willer Ltd*], the EAT considered the matter and stated:

> In the view of the majority of this appeal tribunal, the question whether the employee is in her turn in such circumstances also affected by the illegal performance of the

contract by the employers depends upon whether she was a party to or knew of her employer's illegality. If she did take part in or continued working knowing of the illegal mode of performance by her employers of her contract of employment then she too was affected by that illegality and cannot now rely upon the statutory rights to which she would otherwise be entitled under the relevant employment legislation (at 528). The tribunal considers that in order that an employee be able to have his claim dealt with under the Unfair Dismissals Act 1977, he must be an 'employee' at law. An employee is defined as a person who has entered into or works under a contract of employment. The existence of the contract, therefore, establishes the status of employee which status is essential to the existence of his rights under the Act. In the case of an illegal contract as in this case public policy renders it unenforceable. In our view an employee's statutory rights under the Unfair Dismissals Act 1977, are dependant on his holding his employment under a legal and enforceable contract of employment, which the claimant did not.

Note

Section 8(11) of the Unfair Dismissal Act 1977 (as amended in 1993) would now allow an employee to recover under his or her contract in such a case.

Consider:

Did the result in the *Lewis* case unjustly reward the respondent employer?

Hall *v* Woolston Hall Leisure Ltd [2001] 1 WLR 225

Hall was dismissed from her position as a chef by the defendant upon learning that she was pregnant. An Industrial Tribunal subsequently determined that the dismissal amounted to unlawful discrimination contrary to the Sex Discrimination Act 1975 which implemented the Equal Treatment Directive (Directive No. 76/207/EEC). As the Tribunal discovered that tax was not being paid by her employer on her full salary, it determined that the contract was tainted by illegality and thus unenforceable disentitling her to compensation for its breach.

Peter Gibson L.J.:

In two types of case it is well-established that illegality renders a contract unenforceable from the outset. One is where the contract is entered into with the intention of committing an illegal act; the other is where the contract is expressly or implicitly prohibited by statute (*St John Shipping Corp. v Joseph Rank Ltd* [1957] 1 QB, 267 at p. 283 per Devlin J.). In a third category of cases a party may be prevented from enforcing it. That is where a contract, lawful when made, is illegally performed and the party knowingly participated in that illegal performance. In *Ashmore, Benson Ltd v Dawson Ltd* [1973] 1 WLR 828, Lord Denning M.R. (at p. 833) said:

> Not only did [the plaintiff's transport manager] know of the illegality. He participated in it by sanctioning the loading of the vehicle with a load in excess of the regulations. That participation in the illegal performance of the contract debars [the plaintiff] from suing [the defendant] on it or suing [the defendant] for negligence.

So too Scarman L.J. (at p. 836):

> But knowledge by itself is not enough. There must be knowledge plus participation. . . . For those reasons I think the performance was illegal.

In the employment law field the test of knowledge plus participation has also been recognised for illegality to be a defence. . . . In cases where the contract of employment is neither entered into for an illegal purpose nor prohibited by statute, the illegal performance of the contract will not render the contract unenforceable unless in addition to knowledge of the facts which make the performance illegal the employee actively participates in the illegal performance. It is a question of fact in each case whether there has been a sufficient degree of participation by the employee. And as *Coral Leisure Group* ([1981] ICR 503) shows, even if the employee has in the course of his employment done illegal acts he may nevertheless be able subsequently to rely on his contract of employment to enforce his statutory rights. . . .

In the present case, the employment contract of Mrs Hall at its inception and on its variation when she successfully bargained for increased wages on her promotion was entirely lawful. It did not incorporate a term that adopted the subsequent illegality. When on performance of the varied contract by the Employer the illegality appeared in the form of the false payslip, Mrs Hall queried it. The obligation to pay PAYE and NIC rested on the Employer . . . There was no active participation by her in the illegality. With the aid of counsel we have considered whether Mrs. Hall herself was guilty of any illegality under the fiscal legislation, or at common law by reason of the offence of cheating the public revenue, but I have seen nothing that shows that she herself was guilty of any unlawful conduct. No benefit is shown to have been received by her from the Employer's failure to deduct tax and NIC and to account for the same to the Revenue. Her acquiescence in the Employer's conduct, which is the highest her involvement in the illegality can be put, no doubt reflects the reality that she could not compel the Employer to change its conduct. That acquiescence is in no way causally linked with her sex discrimination claim. In the circumstances it would seem to me to be deplorable if someone in the position of Mrs Hall were left by English law unable to enforce her statutory claim. I am glad to be able to reach the conclusion that that is not the law and that public policy does not so require.

(Mance L.J. and Moore-Bick J. agreeing.)

Note

In *Wheeler v Quality Deep Ltd* (*t/a Thai Royale Restaurant*) [2005] ICR 265, the Court of Appeal following *Hall* found the contract to have been legal as there was no proof of participation. Hooper L.J., however, noted that it was 'a very unusual case concerning as it does a foreign national working in this country in that language with limited knowledge of the English language and of the tax and national insurance provisions of this country. Had she not had that limited knowledge, she may well not have succeeded.'

Consider:

Is the decision in *Hall* consistent with the decision in *Lewis*?

The following case demonstrates the circumstances in which the Court is likely to find the contract to be so tainted by the illegality as to be unenforceable.

Vakante v Addey & Stanhope School [2005] 1 CMLR 3

The applicant, a Croatian national, commenced paid employment with the Addey and Stanhope School (the Respondent) on a teacher training scheme. As he was seeking asylum at this time, it was a criminal offence for him to take up paid employment. Furthermore, it is a criminal offence for someone to employ an asylum seeker who is precluded from taking up employment. Following his dismissal, he made a claim of race discrimination against the Respondent. An Employment Tribunal held that he was not prevented by illegality from making a claim of race discrimination. The respondent appealed to the Employment Appeals Tribunal which held that 'it seems in those circumstances manifest that both the inception and the performance of this contract were illegal.' However, it then preceded to analyse the claim further.

Mummery L. J.:

Complaints to the employment tribunal based on the statutory torts of unfair dismissal and discrimination are sometimes met with the defence that the proceedings are barred by the applicant's involvement in illegal conduct. . . . The application of the illegality doctrine in an all-or-nothing way, operating as a complete bar, is obviously open to criticism and has invited proposals that the court should be given a discretion to bar a claim, after taking specified relevant factors into account, or to reduce the damages recoverable by the claimant, depending on the seriousness of the illegal conduct and the degree of connection between the illegal conduct and the claim. There are also real difficulties in formulating, either in case law or in legislation, a comprehensive legal test which works satisfactorily for all torts, ranging, as they do, across a wide spectrum of human conduct, involving different legally protectable interests and multifarious factual situations. Different public policy consideration may be relevant to different kinds of claim. Claims for personal injury and occupiers' liability in the workplace may raise different policy considerations from claims for unfair dismissal or discrimination in employment. The Law Commission observed in its Consultation Paper No 160 (2001) that:

> 1.5 . . . the problems with the clarity of the current law . . . mean that it is difficult to predict an outcome or to explain the outcome in terms of the apparent rationale for the illegality defence, with the result that there is a risk of arbitrariness or possibly disproportionality. Arbitrary or disproportionate results could lead to conflict with the European Convention on Human Rights . . .
> 2.2 . . . it remains difficult to identify when a claim in tort will be barred on the basis of the defence of illegality: part of the difficulty stems from the wide variety of factual situations in which the illegal conduct may arise.'
> The topic was explored in detail in Hall. . . . In the leading judgment Peter Gibson L.J. laid down an approach for the employment tribunal to follow in sex discrimination cases. It is binding on this court. The tribunal purported to apply it to the facts of this case. The proper approach

'. . . should be to consider whether the applicant's claim arises out of or is so clearly connected or inextricably bound up or linked with the illegal conduct of the applicant that the court could not permit the applicant to recover compensation without appearing to condone that conduct.'

The strength of the *Hall* approach is that it is flexible. It enables the tribunal to avoid arbitrary and disproportionate outcomes and to reach sensible and just decisions in most cases. The proper application of the test should produce reasonably consistent and predictable results, more so, I am inclined to think, than would be the case if, in cases of illegal conduct involving the applicant, the tribunal were given a general statutory discretion, constrained by specific limiting factors. Although *Hall* uses some of the familiar language of legal and factual causation ('connection', 'link'), the test does not restrict the tribunal to a causation question. Matters of fact and degree have to be considered: the circumstances surrounding the applicant's claim and the illegal conduct, the nature and seriousness of the illegal conduct, the extent of the applicant's involvement in it and the character of the applicant's claim are all matters relevant to determining whether the claim is so 'inextricably bound up with' the applicant's illegal conduct that, by permitting the applicant to recover compensation, the tribunal might appear to condone the illegality. . . .

The employment tribunal held, and the appeal tribunal affirmed, that Mr Vakante is prevented from pursuing the complaints on the ground that they are 'so closely or clearly connected with or inextricably bound up with illegal conduct that no claim should lie' and that if the application were permitted to go forward to a hearing 'the tribunal would appear to be endorsing the illegal actions of the complainant.' . . . There is no doubt that there has been illegal conduct in the form of Mr Vakante's employment by the respondent. In breach of [the Immigration Act 1971] Mr Vakante obtained his employment with the respondent contrary to the terms of the Home Office's Standard Acknowledgement Letter sent to him in June 1992 when he applied for asylum. The letter must have been clear to Mr Vakante, who is an educated man able to read and speak English. [He did not endorse this letter as required when he subsequently applied for employment.] . . . He did not tick the box indicating that he needed a work permit. . . . Throughout the period when he was working for the respondent Mr Vakante also claimed and continued to receive state benefits. In doing so he made fraudulent statements about his employment status...

The application of the *Hall* approach to this case is comparatively straightforward. This case is clearly different from *Hall* and similar cases, in which (a) the illegal conduct was that of the employer in the performance of the contract and (b) the involvement of the applicant was one of awareness of the employer's illegal conduct and in deriving benefit from it. It is not a case where the applicant has been working in good faith in the belief that it was lawful for him to work. . . . As for the illegal conduct here (a) it was that of the applicant; (b) it was criminal; (c) it went far beyond the manner in which one party performed what was otherwise a lawful employment contract; (d) it went to the basic content of an employment situation-work; (e) the duty not to discriminate arises from an employment situation which, without a permit, was unlawful from top to bottom and from beginning to end. It was not a case of innocent oversight or an acceptable misunderstanding. Mr Vakante had been clearly informed in writing of the true position. Instead of making an application for a work permit, he obtained work with the respondent by making a false statement. Mr Vakante was solely responsible for his illegal conduct in working for the respondent and creating an unlawful situation, on which he had to rely in order to establish that there was a duty not to discriminate against him. I agree with the employment tribunal that the complaints by Mr Vakante of his discriminatory treatment in employment are so inextricably bound with the illegality of conduct in obtaining and continuing that employment with the respondent that, if it were to permit him to recover compensation for discrimination, the tribunal would appear to condone his illegal conduct.

C. RECOVERY OF BENEFITS CONFERRED

Where a contract has already been executed, the issue of enforcing the contract is no longer relevant and the *ex turpis* rule does not thus apply. In such a case, one of the parties may seek to recover benefits conferred under the contract. In such a case, the maxim '*In pari delicto potior est conditio possidentis*', becomes relevant. This means that where both parties are equally in fault, the condition of the possessor is better.

However, in many cases before the courts, the plaintiff will argue that he or she is not equally at fault and thus entitled to recover. This lack of fault may be attributed for example to mistake, fraud or, a claim that he or she is a member of the class which the statute which has been contravened was designed to protect. The next two cases provide examples of such claims. It should also be noted that where a party can identify an independent cause of action aside from the illegal contract, recovery will be allowed. This may be based on an action in conversion, a resulting trust (see *Tinsley* case on p. 849) or on *quantum meruit* (See *Mohamed* on p. 853).

Martin v Messrs Galbraith Ltd [1942] IR 37

The plaintiff, a bread server, sold goods supplied by the defendants from a horse and van. Despite the fact that the plaintiff was working for longer periods of time than allowed by s. 20(2) of the Shops (Conditions of Employment) Act 1938, rendering the defendant guilty of an offence under s. 20(11), the plaintiff claimed to be entitled to overtime payments under s. 20(6) of the Act.

Murnaghan J.:

The object of s. 20(6), was to give the employee overtime pay for the excess hours worked. This sub-section does not say expressly that overtime is only to be paid in respect of excess hours permitted by the Act, but, in my opinion, this result follows from the general rules of law. Parties to a contract, which produces illegality under a statute passed for the benefit of the public, cannot sue upon the contract unless the legislature has clearly given a right to sue. Overtime can only be legally worked by a person who is aged sixteen or upwards, and a young person who worked overtime illegally cannot, in my opinion, sue for it under s. 20(6). Similarly, where overtime is permitted, the employee can recover the statutory remuneration for the amount of the permitted overtime. In s. 20(6), the legislature enacts that the employer shall be deemed to have agreed to pay, and he cannot, in my opinion, be deemed to have made a contract which the statute declares to be illegal.

(Sullivan C.J. and Geoghegan J. agreed.)

O'Byrne J. (dissenting):

It was contended, on behalf of the defendants, that where a member of the staff is allowed to work for any hours in excess of those permitted by the section, the statutory contract to pay for overtime is unenforceable as regards such excessive hours. If this contention be well founded, the plaintiff could not, in any circumstances, recover overtime pay, under the section, for periods in excess of sixty hours in any week, or 216 hours in any four consecutive weeks, or 2,600 hours in any year. The basis of this contention, as I understand it, is that where a member of the staff is permitted to work beyond the limits aforesaid, the proprietor is guilty of an offence, in respect of which he may be convicted and penalised under s. 5, and it is alleged that he cannot, in addition, be compelled to pay as for overtime under s. 20. I must say that I can find, in the Act, no foundation for this contention. Sub-s. 6 seems to me to be quite clear, and I do not think it is in any way dependent upon a question as to whether or not an offence has been committed. The contention seems to me to be quite inconsistent with the sub-section as enacted. . . .

Further, I am of opinion that construing the section in the manner contended for, so far from giving effect to the intentions of the legislature, would tend to defeat such intentions. To allow a member of the staff to do shop work during periods in excess of those permitted by s. 20 is undoubtedly an offence, but it is an offence on the part of the proprietor and not on the part of the servant. Why, in such circumstances, should the latter be penalised by being prevented from recovering overtime pay in respect of such excessive work—particularly in view of the fact that one of the expressed intentions of the legislature was to make provision for ensuring the payment of wages at fair rates to employees?I consider that the sub-section is free from all ambiguity and that it should be so construed as to effectuate the object of the legislature and to give the fullest effect to the beneficial provisions of the Act.

Note

Clark argues that the majority judgment is too simplistic and that the Court should have asked whether the parties agreed at the outset that unlawful overtime would be worked and whether they were thus equally at fault (Clark, *Contract Law in Ireland* (5th edn), p. 397).

Sumner v Sumner (1935) 69 ILTR 101

In contemplation of divorce the plaintiff and defendant entered an agreement by which the plaintiff agreed to settle certain securities on the defendant and their infant child. This constituted an illegal agreement. Later a settlement setting out the trust conditions was made by the plaintiff on the defendant. The plaintiff then attempted to have the settlement set aside on the grounds of illegality.

Megaw J.:

[It states] in the *Laws of England*, vol. 7 p. 408 (old edition), *viz.*:

> The illegality of a contract may be set up by way of defence to an action on the contract, even if it does not appear on the face of the contract; but in order to obtain relief in equity by getting the contract set aside, the applicant must prove,

not only that the contract was illegal, but that he was induced to enter into it by pressure or undue influence.

It was clearly stated by Lindley L.J., in *Jones v Merionethshire Permanent Building Society*, [1892] 1 Ch. 173 at p. 182: 'A plaintiff is not entitled to relief in a court of equity on the ground of the illegality of his own conduct. In order to obtain relief in equity he must prove not only that the transaction is illegal but something more; he must prove either pressure or undue influence.'At common law the same principle was recognised. Lord Mansfield in *Holman v Johnston* 1 Cowp. 343 put it in this way:

> The principle of public policy is this: *ex dolo malo non oritur actio*. . . . No court will lend its aid to a man who founds his cause of action on an immoral or an illegal act. If from the plaintiff's own statement or otherwise the cause of action appear to arise *'ex turpi causa'*, or the transgression of a positive law of the country, then the court says he had no right to be assisted. It had been on that ground that the court went; not for the sake of the defendant but because they will not lend their aid to such a plaintiff. So, if the plaintiff and defendant were to change sides, and the defendant were to bring his action against the plaintiff, the latter would have the advantage of it; for when both are equally in fault *potior est conditio defendentis*.

That had been recognised in such cases as *Scott v Brown* [1892] 2 QB 724, and *Gedge v Royal Exchange Assurance Corp.* [1900] 2 QB 214.

There were two old maxims of equity which should not be left out of sight entirely. 'He who seeks equity must do equity' and 'He who comes into equity must come with clean hands.' The plaintiff did not comply with either of these maxims, but it was not necessary to investigate how much or little weight was to be attached to them. . . . The principle that, where property had been transferred by an instrument that was tainted with illegality, the estate should lie where it fell, had been recognised from the time of Lord Eldon. The doctrine was accepted in a case of *Gascoigne v Gascoigne* [1918] 1 KB 223, and in his opinion the principle there recognised was applicable to the present case. The plaintiff sought an equitable remedy, and his Lordship was of opinion that in the circumstances he had pointed out he was not entitled to succeed.

Tinsley v Milligan [1993] 3 All ER 65

The parties jointly purchased a house. The house was registered in the sole name of the appellant in order to allow the respondent make false claims for social welfare benefits. Two years later the parties quarrelled and the appellant left the house. She subsequently brought an action seeking possession of the house and asserting ownership. The respondent counterclaimed for an order for an order for sale and a declaration that the house was held by the appellant on trust for the parties in equal share. The Court of Appeal held that it had discretion to balance the illegality against the consequences of the rejecting the claim and felt that the latter would be unduly harsh. The House of Lords allowed the appeal, unanimously agreeing that it was not appropriate to apply the public conscience test. The majority of the House of Lords applied technical rules of equity to determine that the respondent's contribution to the purchase price meant that the appellant held half of the property on a resulting trust for her. She did not thus need to rely on any illegal agreement in making her claim. Lord Goff dissenting opined that where property was registered in the name of only one of the owners in order to conceal the other's interest for illegal or fraudulent purposes, neither law nor equity would assist in allowing the latter party establish an equitable interest in it.

Lord Browne-Wilkinson:

My Lords, I agree with the speech of my noble and learned friend Lord Goff of Chieveley that the consequences of being a party to an illegal transaction cannot depend, as the majority in the Court of Appeal held, on such an imponderable factor as the extent to which the public conscience would be affronted by recognising rights created by illegal transactions. However, I have the misfortune to disagree with him as to the correct principle to be applied in a case where equitable property rights are acquired as a result of an illegal transaction.

Neither at law nor in equity will the court enforce an illegal contract which has been partially, but not fully, performed. However, it does not follow that all acts done under a partially performed contract are of no effect. In particular it is now clearly established that at law (as opposed to in equity) property in goods or land can pass under, or pursuant to, such a contract. If so, the rights of the owner of the legal title thereby acquired will be enforced, provided that the plaintiff can establish such title without pleading or leading evidence of the illegality. It is said that the property lies where it falls, even though legal title to the property was acquired as a result of the property passing under the illegal contract itself. . . . The position at law is well illustrated by the decision in *Bowmakers Ltd v Barnet Instruments Ltd* [1944] 2 All ER 579, [1945] KB 65. In that case Barnet acquired three parcels of machine tools which had previously belonged to Smith. The transaction was carried through by three hire-purchase agreements under which Smith sold the goods to Bowmakers, who then hired them to Barnet. All three agreements were unlawful as being in breach of defence regulations: it is important to note that in the case of at least two of the parcels the illegality lay in the contract under which Bowmakers acquired the machine tools from Smith (see [1944] 2 All ER 579 at 581, [1945] KB 65 at 69). Bowmakers succeeded in an action for conversion against Barnet. Even though it appeared from the pleadings and the evidence that the contract under which Bowmakers acquired the goods was illegal, such contract was effective to pass the property in the goods to Bowmakers, who could therefore found their claim on the property right so acquired. . . . In my judgment to draw such distinctions between property rights enforceable at law and those which require the intervention of equity would be surprising. More than 100 years has elapsed since the fusion of the administration of law and equity. The reality of the matter is that, in 1993, English law has one single law of property made up of legal and equitable interests. Although for historical reasons legal estates and equitable estates have differing incidents, the person owning either type of estate has a right of property, a right in rem not merely a right in personam. If the law is that a party is entitled to enforce a property right acquired under an illegal transaction, in my judgment the same rule ought to apply to any property right so acquired, whether such right is legal or equitable.

. . . the fusion of the administration of law and equity has led the courts to adopt a single rule (applicable both at law and in equity) as to the circumstances in which the court will enforce property interests acquired in pursuance of an illegal transaction, *viz.* the Bowmaker rule (see *Bowmakers Ltd v Barnet Instruments Ltd* [1944] 2 All ER 579, [1945] KB 65). A party to an illegality can recover by virtue of a legal or equitable property interest if, but only if, he can establish his title without relying on his own illegality. . . . As applied in the present case, that principle would operate as follows. The respondent established a resulting trust by showing that she had contributed to the purchase price of the house and that there was a common understanding between her and the appellant that they owned the house equally. She had no need to allege or prove why the house was conveyed into the name of the appellant alone, since that fact was irrelevant to her claim: it was enough to show that the house was in fact vested in the appellant alone. The illegality only emerged at all because the appellant sought to raise it. Having proved these facts, the respondent had raised a presumption of resulting trust. There was no evidence to rebut that presumption. Therefore the respondent should succeed.

Note

Lord Goff in his judgment suggested that any reform in this area should be instituted by the legislature. Subsequently, the Law Commission Consultation Paper 154 (1999) Part V, s.4 stated, 'Following this rejection of the public conscience test by the House of Lords in *Tinsley v Mulligan*, any possibility of wholesale judicial reform appears blocked. Although the courts may further refine the application of the present rules to the particular case before them, in doing so they will have little opportunity to assess the structure of the illegality rules as a whole. Such tinkering at the edges is only likely to result in a body of case law that is ever more complex and uncertain.'

Kavanagh v Caulfield [2002] IEHC 67

The plaintiff sought specific performance of a contract for the sale of a house to her for an agreed consideration of £145,000. The defendant argued that if an agreement was reached it was illegal as it understated the correct purchase price. The agreement omitted an additional sum of £7,500 which the plaintiff agreed to pay to charity and which was not disclosed to the Revenue Commissioners.

Murphy J.:

In *Starling Securities Limited v Woods and Others*, unreported judgment of 24 May 1977, McWilliams J. refused an application for a specific performance on the basis of what the trial judge held to be an incomplete contract. The only interpretation he could put on the peculiar method adopted to conduct the transactions was that both parties were trying to conceal from the revenue authorities the true nature of the transactions. On the basis of *Millar v Klinski* [1945] TLR 85 and *Alexander v Rayson* [1936] 1 KB 169 he found he was not entitled to countenance such attempted frauds on the Revenue by enforcing the performance of contracts at the instance of either party. In *Whitecross Potatoes (International) Limited v Raymond Coyle* (1978) ILRM 31, judgment was given against the defendant for breach of contract on the basis that the onus of proving the illegality of the contract is on the party alleging it and that the defendant had not proved an illegal intention on the part of the plaintiffs. In *Curust Financial Services Limited and Another v Lowe-Lackwerk* [1994] 1 IR 450 at 467 Finlay C.J., with whom O'Flaherty and Egan JJ. agreed, held:

I accept that, the granting of an injunction being an equitable remedy, the court has a discretion, where it is satisfied that a person has come to be court, as is so frequently expressed, otherwise than 'with clean hands', by that fact alone to refuse the equitable relief of an injunction. It seems to me, however, that this phrase must of necessity involve an element of turpitude and cannot necessarily be equated with a mere breach of contract.

This reasoning echoes that of the House of Lords in *Tinsley v Mulligan* [1994] 1 AC 340 at 353 F, 354 F and 359 B per Lord Goff of Chieveley. The underlying principle is the so-called public conscience test. The court must weigh, or balance, the adverse consequences of granting relief against the adverse consequences of refusing relief. The ultimate decision calls for value judgment (see Nicholas L.J. in *Tinker v Tinker* [1970] 1 All ER 540.

Lord Goff referred to the basic principle of Lord Mansfield C.J. in *Holman v Johnson* [1775] 1 COWP. 341, 343:

The objection, that a contract is immoral or illegal as between plaintiff and defendant, sounds at all times very ill in the mouth of the defendant. It is not for his sake, however, that the objection is ever allowed: but it is founded in general principles of policy, which the defendant has the advantage of, contrary to real justice, as between him and the plaintiff, by accident, if I may say so. The principle of public policy is this: ex dolo malo non oritur actio. No court will then give aid to a man who founds his cause of action upon an immoral or an illegal act.

The court must look at the quality of the legality relied upon by the defendant. The court must also look at all the surrounding circumstances. Three questions need to be answered: First, whether there has been an illegality of which the court should take notice and, second, whether in the circumstances it would be an affront to the public conscience if by affording him the relief sought the court were seen to be indirectly assisting or encouraging a criminal act. Thirdly, the court must be satisfied that the contract has not been otherwise rendered ineffective. It is clear that the onus of proving illegality of a contract is, in this case, on the defendant. The defendant must prove an illegal intention on the part of the plaintiff. It seems to me from the agreed facts of the case that the request to pay money to an alleged charity did, indeed, induce the contract. It does not follow that that, in itself, rendered the contract illegal or unenforceable. It was the defendant who described the payee as a charity. While the cheque was given by the plaintiff's son to the defendant it was in the name of the charity. There is no evidence of an intention of the plaintiff to defraud. This was a contract which, on the apparent intention of the parties at the time of its formation, could be and would be carried out in a legal fashion. There does not seem to me to be evidence sufficient to prove that the plaintiff intended to carry it out in an illegal fashion. This is so despite the plea in defence by the defendant. Accordingly, I find that there is no illegality such as to render the contract unenforceable. Moreover, no conveyance resulted for an undervalued consideration such as would defraud the revenue in relation to stamp duty. If I am wrong in this finding it does not seem to me whatever unintentional irregularity there might have been is not such as to deprive the plaintiff of the right to enforce the contract if the contract still subsisted.

In relation to the relief of specific performance sought, which is an equitable remedy, the court has a discretion to refuse such relief where the applicant comes otherwise than 'with clean hands' that phrase must, of necessity, involve an element of turpitude. I can find no turpitude on the part of the plaintiff.

Mohamed v Alga & Co. (a Firm) [1999] 3 All ER 699

The plaintiff agreed to introduce Somali asylum-seekers to a firm of solicitors and to assist them in the preparation of clients' cases in return for a share of any fees received from the Legal Aid Board in respect of his clients. When the solicitors refused payment, the plaintiff sued for breach of contract, or alternatively, he claimed a reasonable price for work carried out at the solicitors' request. The solicitors claimed that the agreement was unenforceable as it contravened Rule 7 of the Solicitors' Practice Rules 1990, subordinate legislation made by the Law Society which prohibits solicitors from sharing fees or agreeing to do so. Lord Bingham of Cornhill held that the St John Shipping case did not aid the plaintiff as Rule 7 prohibits not only the act but also the contract to perform it. He then considered the plaintiff's quantum meruit claim.

Lord Bingham of Cornhill:

[T]he plaintiff is not seeking to recover any part of the consideration payable under the unlawful contract, but simply a reasonable reward for professional services rendered. I accept that as an accurate description of what on this limited basis the plaintiff is, in truth, seeking. It is furthermore in my judgment relevant that the parties are not in a situation in which their blameworthiness is equal. The defendant is a solicitors' firm and bound by the rules. It should reasonably be assumed to know what the rules are and to comply with them. If, in truth, it made the agreement as alleged, then it would seem very probable that it acted in knowing disregard of professional rules binding upon it. By contrast the plaintiff, on the assumption made (which I have no difficulty in accepting), was ignorant that there was any reason why the defendant should not make the agreement which he says was made. In other commercial fields, after all, such agreements are common.

(Otton and Walker LJJ. agreed.)

Law Commission Consultation Paper, Illegal Transactions: The Effect of Illegality on Contracts and Trusts No 154 (1999)

Part IX—Summary of Provisional Recommendations and Consultation Issues

(2) [The following provisional views were expressed:]

the proposed discretion should be structured so that the court should be required to take into account specific factors in reaching its decision; and that those factors should be: (1) the seriousness of the illegality involved; (2) the knowledge and intention of the plaintiff; (3) whether denying relief will act as a deterrent; (4) whether denying relief will further the purpose of the rule which renders the contract illegal; and (5) whether denying relief is proportionate to the illegality involved? . . .

. . . (a) a court should have a discretion to allow a party to withdraw from an illegal contract, and to have restitution of benefits conferred under it, where allowing the party to withdraw would reduce the likelihood of an illegal act being completed or an illegal purpose being accomplished: but that (b) to succeed in a withdrawal claim the plaintiff must first satisfy the court that the contract could not be enforced against him or her? . . .

. . . in deciding whether or not to allow a party to withdraw and have restitution a court should consider (i) whether the plaintiff genuinely repents of the illegality (albeit that this should not be a necessary condition for the exercise of the discretion); and (ii) the seriousness of the illegality? . . .

. . . our proposed statutory discretion in relation to: (a) contractual enforcement should apply to all contracts which in their formation, purpose or performance involve a legal wrong (other than a mere breach of the contract in question); (b) the reversal of unjust enrichment should apply to all contracts which are unenforceable for illegality; and (c) the recognition of contractually transferred or created property rights should apply to all contracts which in their formation, purpose or performance involve a legal wrong (other than a mere breach of the contract in question) or conduct which is otherwise contrary to public policy?

. . . (with the exception of the locus poenitentiae doctrine) illegality should continue to act only as a defence to claims for standard rights and remedies and that, in particular, the courts should not be specially empowered to apportion losses under illegal contracts?

SECTION FOUR—SEVERANCE

Where the illegality taints only part of the contract, the Courts have discretion to sever the illegal part. This may only be done, however, where the remainder of the agreement is capable of standing alone.

Sheehy *v* Sheehy [1901] 1 IR 239

An equity civil bill was brought to foreclose a £56 mortgage. Consideration for the mortgage included alcohol sold upon credit in violation of the Tippling Acts. The amount did not exceed £1. It was contended that this figure invalidated the entire transaction.

Fitzgibbon L.J.:

If giving credit is illegal, it follows that any security given for the amount of the illegal credit is equally illegal. But the question remains whether such illegality necessarily vitiates the entire security, where part only of the consideration is affected by it. If the prohibition be what I think it is, namely, only a prohibition to recover the amount of the credit, this indiscriminate result will not follow. The part of the consideration which is good is severable, and full effect is given to the prohibition by preventing the recovery of so much as consists of credit illegally given. . . . In my opinion, the plaintiff's claim, to the extent of the credit given for drink within the Tippling Acts, cannot be recovered; but those Acts vitiate or affect nothing more. In *Burnyeat v Hutchinson* 5 B & Ald. 241 the verdict was sustained for the amount of the tavern bill, omitting the charge for spiritous liquors. In my own experience, on County Court appeals, in actions for the price of goods, and upon promissory notes, including the price of drink, the practice has been to deduct the irrecoverable items and to give decrees for the rest, and I think that this case should be decided in the same way.

Furnival & Co. *v* O'Neill [1902] 2 IR 422

In 1879, following a creditor's composition, the defendant's husband and the plaintiff, one of his creditors, entered into a contract under which the latter was to receive a secret benefit. In 1890 the defendant's husband mortgaged certain property to the plaintiff to secure the repayment of his debt. The defendant later provided promissory notes to the plaintiff to secure the outstanding debt. The plaintiff then sued the defendant on foot of those notes.

Andrews J.:

I think it clear that the main and leading consideration for the agreement of 14 October 1879, without which it would not have been entered into, was the undertaking that the plaintiffs' debt of £215 8s should be paid in full, and that the main and loading object of the deed of 1880, without which it would not have been entered into, was to secure the carrying out of that agreement, which was plainly illegal as being contrary to the settled principle and policy of the law, applicable to composition arrangements with creditors as well as to bankruptcy, that no creditor shall be allowed to obtain for himself, without the assent of the other creditors, a preference and exclusive advantage over the others. . . . Now I do not think that it can be disputed that where there are several considerations, some illegal and bad, and some good, and several agreements are entered into in the same instrument, founded on all the considerations, all the agreements are void, because it is impossible to say that the illegal consideration did not enter into each agreement and was not the main consideration which induced it. It is, in my opinion, beyond doubt that the illegal agreement to pay the plaintiffs' debt in full was the main and operative foundation for the entire of the deed of 1880, without which that deed would not have been entered into at all, and it follows that the entire deed was and is void and incapable of enforcement by reason of the illegality to which it sought to give effect…The [Sheehy v Sheehy] decision does not affect this case, in which the main consideration was illegal as being against the principle and policy of the law.

Note

In the case of statutory illegality, Templeman J. noted in *Ailion v Spiekermann and Others* [1976] 1 Ch. 158 that:

Where there are legal and illegal elements in a contract which are capable of severance, the jurisdiction to enforce the legal elements will only be exercised in a proper case and if the severance is in accordance with the enforcement of the principles which induced Parliament to outlaw the elements which are illegal.

The case concerned an agreement to sell a lease for an illegal premium. In that case, it was also noted that the fact that the purchasers of the lease knew of the illegality at the outset is a powerful reason why they should not obtain any relief. However, Templeman J. continued by sting that 'the Rent Act is designed to protect persons in the position of the purchasers. They could not insist on the elimination from the draft contract of the illegal premium without losing the flat. They had no choice if they needed somewhere to live. They committed no offence.' An order of specific performance was granted to assign the lease without the illegal premium.

Lewis v Squash Ireland [1983] ILRM 363
[See facts on p. 841.]

Determination
[Counsel for the claimant] submitted that if the tribunal were to find that the agreement regarding the £2,000 was illegal and not enforceable that it could and should, in that event, be severed from the remainder of the claimant's contract of employment which was a normal contract of its type, legal as to its object and its performance. The tribunal accepts that it is mathematically possible to sever the illegal agreement from the remainder of the claimant's salary but we feel that the parties knowingly incorporated the illegal agreement into the contract through a vital term viz. the claimant's consideration (his salary/remuneration) and the illegality infected the whole of the claimant's consideration and through it the whole of the contract. The illegal term entered the contract by consent and became part of it. . . .

We find that the contract as existing at the time of the dismissal and from the time of the agreement regarding the £2,000 increase was a contract which was wholly tainted with the illegality as stated, and that the illegal arrangement could not be severed from the contract of employment as a whole, leaving, as [counsel] submitted, the other parts of the contract enforceable and thus, pro tanto, the claimant's claim before this tribunal.

Carney v Herbert and Others [1985] 1 AC 301

The plaintiffs agreed to sell shares in a company 'Airfoil' to the defendant. The purchase price was to be paid in instalments secured by a personal guarantee by the defendant and mortgages by a subsidiary of Airfoil. These mortgages were illegal under s. 67 of the Companies Act 1961 which prohibited the provision of security by a subsidiary in connection with the purchase of shares in its holding company. When the plaintiff sued the defendant under his guarantees the defendant claimed that the illegality of the mortgages tainted the whole contract rendering it unenforceable.

Lord Brightman:

Questions of severability are often difficult. There are not set rules which will decide all cases. As was said by Kitto J. in *Brooks v Burns Philp Trustee Co. Ltd* (1969) 121 CLR 432, 438, tests for deciding questions of severability that have been formulated as useful in particular cases are not always satisfactory for cases of other kinds. To some extent each case must depend on its own circumstances, and in particular on the nature of the illegality. . . There are . . . two matters to be considered where a contract contains an illegal term, first, whether as a matter of construction the lawful part of the contract can be severed from the unlawful part, thus enabling the plaintiff to sue on a promise unaffected by any illegality; secondly, whether, despite severability, there is a bar to enforceability arising out of the nature of the illegality. . . .

In the light of the law as it has been developed in Australia and England, and also in Scotland though their Lordships have not been referred to the Scottish case law, their Lordships feel no doubt in the instant case that the illegal provision of the debentures can be severed from the composite transaction, leaving the plaintiffs free to enforce the sale agreements against Ilerain and the guarantee against the defendant; and that the nature of the illegality is not such as to preclude the plaintiffs on the ground of public policy from enforcing their rights under those documents. . . .

The contract in the present case was basically one for the sale by the plaintiffs to the defendant or his nominated company of shares in Airfoil. The mortgages, like the guarantee, were ancillary to that contract for the sole purpose of ensuring the due performance of the contract by the purchaser. The defendant wanted only the shares in Airfoil. The plaintiffs wanted only the purchase money. It made no difference to the plaintiffs, or to the nature of the transaction, what security was provided so long as it was satisfactory security. The mortgage did not go to the heart of the transaction, and its elimination would leave unchanged the subject matter of the contract and the primary obligations of the vendors and the purchaser. The debenture is therefore capable of being severed from the remainder of the transaction, and its illegality does not taint the whole contract. There is no public policy objection to the enforcement of the contract from which the debenture has been divorced. . . . Subject to a caveat that it is undesirable, if not impossible, to lay down any principles which will cover all problems in this field, their Lordships venture to suggest that, as a general rule, where parties enter into a lawful contract of, for example, sale and purchase, and there is an ancillary provision which is illegal but exists for the exclusive benefit of the plaintiff, the court may and probably will, if the justice of the case so requires, and there is no public policy objection, permit the plaintiff if he so wishes to enforce the contract without the illegal provision.

SECTION FIVE—CONTRACTS VOID AT COMMON LAW

A. AGREEMENTS WHICH OUST THE JURISDICTION OF THE COURT

A clause which attempts to prevent access to the Courts would be void. However, an agreement as to arbitration is valid. As Lord O'Brien L.C.J. explained in *Gregg & Co v Fraser & Sons* [1906] 2 KB 545 such an arbitration agreement 'merely creates a condition precedent to the right to sue'. See also *Winterthur Swiss Insurance Co. v ICI* [1990] ILRM 159.

Scott v Avery (1856) 5 HL Cas 811

Lord Cranworth:

There is no doubt that where a right of action has accrued, parties cannot by contract say that there shall not be jurisdiction to enforce damages in respect of that right of action. Now this doctrine depends upon the general policy of the law, that parties cannot enter into a contract which gives rise to a right of an action for the breach of it, and then withdraw such a case from the jurisdiction of the ordinary tribunals. But surely there can be no principle or policy of the law which prevents parties from entering into such a contract as that no breach shall occur until after a reference has been made to arbitration. It appears to me that in such cases as that, the policy of the law is left untouched.

B. CONTRACTS WHICH SUBVERT THE SANCTITY OF MARRIAGE

Common law dictated that agreements which subverted the sanctity of marriage were contrary to public policy and should be struck down. Such agreements included marriage contracts, pre-nuptial agreements and co-habitation agreements. With the introduction of divorce, it might be argued that these principles are somewhat outdated.

Separation Agreements

MacMahon v MacMahon [1913] 1 IR 428

Palles CB:

Firstly, then, we must treat it as settled that a contract between husband and wife, made during cohabitation, for a future as distinguished from an immediate separation, is void and inoperative, as being contrary to the policy of the law in relation to marriage. . . .

The question in the present case [is] whether an agreement between husband and wife, who were then living separate and apart, providing for their living together again, with a provision for her to take effect only in the event of a future separation, [is] legal and enforceable . . . Can we say that the necessary tendency of the contract here, which, in fact, caused cohabitation for ten years, was to induce separation? At the time of the contract the parties were living apart. Their primary object was reconciliation, not separation. Assuming, as has been decided, that in a marriage contract future separation is not to be anticipated or provided for—but when separation has actually taken place, is the possibility of its recurrence to be ignored? Common experience, and the sense of mankind, show that it cannot be. When matrimonial offences have been committed, and condoned by subsequent cohabitation, the condoned offences are revived on the occurrence of a fresh matrimonial offence. Thus parties reconciled after separation are not in the same relative position as when they started at marriage. Taking human nature as it is, it seems to me to be reasonable in a case such as the present to foresee the possible recurrence of the cause, whatever it may have been, of the former separation, and to provide in reference to it, and that it is not contra bonos mores, nor contrary to any policy of the law, that a husband whose wife is returning to cohabitation after a separation should trust her by whose voluntary act the cohabitation is renewed to be the sole judge of the circumstances which should render it advisable that such cohabitation should cease. In my opinion, it is rather of the highest policy of the law that in such a case the parties shall be absolutely unfettered in their freedom of contract. The less fettered they are, the more likely will they be to arrive at an agreement; and arrival at an agreement for a reconciliation is a matter which the law ought to encourage. . . . Upon the whole, then, I have arrived at the clear conclusion that, as the law now stands, there is nothing in its policy which renders illegal a contract between husband and wife for reconciliation, although it contains a provision, such as we have here, entitling the wife to separate maintenance in the event of a future separation, although dependent solely on her own will.

Dalton v Dalton [1982] ILRM 418

An application was made to have a separation agreement made a rule of court under s. 8 of the Family Law (Maintenance of Spouses and Children)

Act 1976. The agreement contained a clause whereby the parties, both domiciled in Ireland agreed to obtain a divorce a vinculo outside the jurisdiction.

O'Hanlon J.:

Considerations of public policy require that the court should not lend its support to an agreement provided for the obtaining of a divorce vinculo by a husband and wife and this may well be the position even if the parties are domiciled elsewhere than in Ireland when the application is made or proposed to take up such foreign domicile in the future . . . I am of the opinion that to ask the court to make the agreement which has been concluded between the parties in the present case a rule of court is to ask the court to lend its support to a course of conduct which is contrary to public policy within its jurisdiction.

Notes

1. The legality of agreements to obtain a divorce would appear settled now as a result of the removal pursuant to the Fifteenth Amendment of the Constitution Act 1995 of the constitutional ban on divorce in Article 41.3.2 of the Constitution. A Court may now grant a dissolution of marriage where the following conditions are satisfied:

    i.   at the date of the institution of the proceedings, the spouses have lived apart from one another for a period of, or periods amounting to, at least four years during the previous five years,

    ii. there is no reasonable prospect of a reconciliation between the spouses,

    iii. such provision as the Court considers proper having regard to the circumstances exists or will be made for the spouses, any children of either or both of them and any other person prescribed by law, and

    iv. any further conditions prescribed by law are complied with.

The Family Law (Divorce) Act 1996 provides for the exercise by the Courts of the jurisdiction conferred by the Constitution in this regard.

2. Despite the removal of the constitutional ban on divorce in Ireland, a contract for a future separation may be deemed contrary to public policy. See H v H (1983) 127 SJ 578.

3. In the UK, the Prime Minister's family policy group has endorsed the principle of pre-nuptial contracts and officials are reported to be considering introducing legislation in this area (*The Times*, 18 May 1998).

Co-habitation Agreements

Ennis v Butterly [1997] 1 ILRM 28

The plaintiff initiated an action for damages against the defendant for breach of contract. Both parties are married to other persons. They cohabited with each other for almost eight years before their relationship broke down. A few months later the parties were reconciled. The defendant promised to marry the plaintiff as soon as possible. He asked her to discontinue her business and to live full-time at home as a wife, home-maker and housekeeper. In return, the defendant promised that the plaintiff would have her own current account, access to the defendant's credit card account and a shareholding in a company owned by the defendant.

Kelly J.:

The first relief which is sought in the amended Statement of Claim is damages for breach of contract. On an examination of the Statement of Claim, it appears to me that the only contract . . . which is pleaded is a twofold one. The first is an agreement to marry. The second is an agreement to live together as man and wife until such marriage would be possible. In consideration of that agreement, the plaintiff discontinued her business and lived as a full-time housewife and home-maker.

The defendant contends that this twofold claim in contract must fail.

As to the first, he relies upon the provisions of Section 1 of the Family Law Act of 1981 which abolished the action for breach of promise of marriage. In my view, that enactment is fatal to any claim which is asserted by the Plaintiff to derive from the breach by the defendant of an agreement to marry her. Indeed, even before the enactment of the 1981 Act, at common law it had been held in England that a promise by a married person to marry one who knew that person to be already married was unenforceable as being against public policy (see *Wilson v Carnley*, 1908 1 KB 729, *Spears v Hunt*, 1908 1 KB 720, *Siveyer v Allison*, 1935 KB 403). In the instant case, both the plaintiff and the defendant at all times knew that they were each married to someone else. Even before the enactment of the 1981 Act, their agreement to marry each other would have been unenforceable as a matter of public policy. Subsequent to the 1981 Act, there can be, in my view, no doubt but that the defendant is correct when he says that this part of the plaintiff's claim must fail.

The second contractual arrangement alleged by the plaintiff is set forth at paragraph 8 of the amended Statement of Claim. It is that, pending marriage, she would 'in the meantime, live with him as a wife might and, in particular, discontinue her own business and live at home as a full-time housewife and home-maker'. The defendant contends that an agreement to cohabit, whether pending a forthcoming marriage or not, can not give rise to enforceable rights. This is so whether the parties agree to live together pending a dissolution of existing marriages or not. It is said that the enforcement of such agreements would be contrary to the public policy of this State. It is furthermore said that the present claim in attempting to enforce this agreement by means of seeking damages for its breach is not actionable as a matter of Irish law. It is furthermore said that the plaintiff's proceedings are, in effect, a claim for 'palimony'.

This expression 'palimony' was much used by Mr McDowell in the course of argument but it was never defined nor was any authority opened on the topic. The *Oxford English Dictionary* defines it as a slang word of American origin formed by a blend of 'pal' and 'alimony' and denoting 'compensation claimed by the deserted party after the separation of a couple living together out of wedlock'. That it is truly a slang term appears to be borne out by the fact that amongst the, admittedly relatively few, textbooks on American family law available to me, I fail to find a single instance of the word being used. Historically, applications to seek enforcement of cohabitation contracts in the United States have been treated in much the same way as such claims in England. They were invariably rejected either on grounds of immorality or lack of consideration. Things changed somewhat with the decision of the Supreme Court of California in *Marvin v Marvin* (1976) 18 CAL 3D 660. That court concluded, *inter alia*:

> The courts should enforce express contracts between non-marital partners except to the extent that the contract is explicitly founded on the consideration of meretricious sexual services.
>
> In the absence of an express contract, the courts should enquire into the conduct of the parties to determine whether that conduct demonstrates an implied contract, agreement of partnership or joint venture, or some other tacit understanding between the parties. The courts may also employ the doctrine of quantum meruit, or equitable remedy such as constructive or resulting trusts, when warranted by the facts of the case.

This is the case which appears to have spawned the expression 'palimony'. Since the Marvin decision, some State courts have been willing to find implied contracts where no express contract existed. Others have trenchantly refused to go down that path. For example, the New York Court of Appeal in *Morone v Morone* (1980) 429 NYS 2D 592 said that:

> Finding an implied contract such as was recognised in *Marvin v Marvin* . . . to be conceptually so amorphous as practically to defy equitable enforcement, and inconsistent with the legislative policy enunciated in 1933 when common law marriages were abolished in New York, we decline to follow the Marvin lead.

It seems, therefore, that insofar as the jurisdiction where this concept finds its genesis is concerned, the existence of such a claim is by no means universally accepted. The position in England and Wales on the other hand appears to be crystal clear. In *Windeler v Whitehall* (1990) 2 FLR 505, Millett J. (as he then was) said:

> If this were California, this would be a claim for palimony, but it is England and it is not. English law recognises neither the term nor the obligation to which it gives effect. In this country a husband has a legal obligation to support his wife even if they are living apart. A man has no legal obligation to support his mistress even if they are living together . . . The courts possess neither a statutory nor an inherent jurisdiction to disturb existing rights of property on the termination of an extramarital relationship, however long established the relationship and however deserving the claimant.

In my view, the law in this country is no different and, if anything, would lean more strongly against such a concept having regard to the special position of marriage under the Constitution. Agreements by persons to cohabit have long been held to be unenforceable at common law as being injurious to morality and marriage. Mr McDowell relied on the decision in *Beaumont v Reeve* 8 QB 483 in support of his contention that it would be contrary to public policy to permit the enforcement of the present contract. Whatever may have been the public policy in England in 1846 when that case was decided, this case must be decided upon the public policy of this State. That is to be found in the first instance in the Constitution and, in particular, Article 41 thereof. In that Article, the State recognises the family as the natural primary and fundamental unit group of society and as a moral institution possessing inalienable and imprescriptible rights antecedent and superior to all positive law. The State pledges itself to guard with special care the institution of marriage, on which the family is founded and protect it against attack.

In the *State* (*Nicolaou*) *v An Bord Uchtala*, 1966 IR 567, Henchy J. said:

> For the State to award equal constitutional protection to the family founded on marriage and the 'family' founded on an extramarital union would in effect be a disregard of the pledge which the State gives in Article 41.3.1 to guard with special care the institution of marriage'. (p. 622)

In that case, the Supreme Court, per Walsh J., said it was:

> Quite clear . . . that the family referred to in Article 41 is the family which is founded on the institution of marriage and, in the context of the Article, marriage means valid marriage under the law for the time being in force in the State. (p. 643)

Given the special place of marriage and the family under the Irish Constitution, it appears to me that the public policy of this State ordains that non-marital cohabitation does not and cannot have the same constitutional status as marriage. Moreover, the State has pledged to guard with special care the institution of marriage. But does this mean that agreements, the consideration for which is cohabitation, are incapable of being enforced? In my view it does since otherwise the pledge on the part of the State, of which this court is one organ, to guard with special care the institution of marriage would be much diluted. To permit an express cohabitation contract (such as is pleaded here) to be enforced would give it a similar status in law as a marriage contract. It did not have such a status prior to the coming into effect of the Constitution, rather such contracts were regarded as illegal and unenforceable as a matter of public policy. Far from enhancing the position at law of such contracts the Constitution requires marriage to be guarded with special care. In my view, this reinforces the existing common law doctrines concerning the non-enforceability of cohabitation contracts. I am therefore of opinion that, as a matter of public policy, such agreements cannot be enforced. I am strengthened in this view by the fact that, notwithstanding the extensive reform of family law which has taken place in this country over the last 20 years, nowhere does one find any attempt on the part of the legislature to substantially enhance the legal position of, or to confer rights akin to those of married persons upon the parties to non-marital unions e.g. a right to maintenance. This absence of intervention on the part of the legislature suggests to me that it accepts that it would be contrary to public policy, as enunciated in the Constitution, to confer legal rights on persons in non-marital unions akin to those who are married.

In the present case, the amended Statement of Claim makes it clear that the consideration for the second contract was the living together of the plaintiff and the defendant with the plaintiff living with him 'as a wife might' and 'at home as a full-time housewife and home-maker'. In my view, the contract contended for here is unenforceable as a matter of public policy. Whether one calls it palimony or not, it is not capable of enforcement in this jurisdiction. If the plaintiff's claim is truly a palimony one (which I doubt), I am of opinion that Irish law recognises neither the term nor the obligation to which it gives effect. Consequently, it must be struck out. If it is not a palimony claim, it is clearly an attempt to enforce a contract the consideration for which is wifely services being rendered on the part of a mistress.

Such contracts were always regarded as illegal and unenforceable and remain so. A claim of this type arising out of such a relationship must, in my view, be struck out.

In coming to the conclusion above, I have not forgotten the two English authorities which were cited by Mr O'Loughlin on behalf of the plaintiff. They were *Eves v Eves* (1975) 3 All ER 768 and *Tanner v Tanner* (1975) 3 All ER 776. I do not think that these cases can be of assistance to the plaintiff. The Eves case was concerned with an equitable interest which was alleged to exist in respect of certain real property. No claim in equity is made in the instant proceedings. Such equitable claim as was once asserted has expressly been abandoned. The *Tanner* case involved a licence over a premises occupied by an unmarried cohabiting couple. The Court of Appeal, on the facts, implied the existence of a contractual licence. That case is far from the present one. No implied contract is pleaded here. This case involves a straightforward claim for damages for breach of an express contract the principal, if not the only, consideration for which was cohabitation. Even if an implied contract were contended for the consideration involved would still render it unenforceable on grounds of public policy. I hold that the claims for damages for breach of contract must, as matter of law, fail. They are struck out.

Note

Commenting on this case, the Irish Law Reform Commission *Consultation Paper on The Rights and Duties of Cohabitees* (LRC CP 32-2004) states:

3.23   The conventional wisdom is that this decision places an insurmountable barrier in the way of the enforcement of cohabitation agreements. We are of the view that as the facts of the case were unusual, not to say egregious, and that as the decision was directed only towards the rather extreme 'home made' cohabitation agreement concerned, the case should not be taken as support for the general proposition that all cohabitation agreements are necessarily void for public policy.

3.30   In the Commission's view, an agreement that is in no way premised on the parties cohabiting or engaging in sexual relations but which confines itself merely to regulating their financial and property arrangements would not be contrary to public policy. If the parties wish, the document may be executed by means of deed to remove all doubt that the parties' cohabitation or consortium is intended to form part of the agreement. Similarly, if the parties wish, the agreement may refer to the parties' cohabitation but care should be taken that this is expressed as a fact rather than as a condition of the contract. This has the added advantage of ensuring that the contract would not be struck down on the grounds of public policy on the basis that it restricts the ability of the parties to marry.

Pre-nuptial Agreements

A Study Group on Pre-nuptial Agreements established by the Department of Justice, Equality and Law Reform (2007) recommended that separate provision be made in both the Family Law Act 1995 and Family Law (Divorce) Act 1996 to provide that the courts be required to have regard to existing pre-nuptial agreements when making ancillary relief orders in judicial separation and divorce proceedings. The report makes recommendations on the formalities necessary for the proper making of pre-nuptial agreements so that parties making such agreements would be both fully informed and protected. The report also recommended the introduction of a statutory basis upon which a court may make financial provision for a surviving spouse who may be unfairly affected by the provisions of a pre-nuptial agreement on the death of the other spouse in certain circumstances, e.g. as a result of the passage of time or other intervening events.

Note

Contracts in restraint of trade will be considered in Chapter 17.

EXERCISES

1. Riley books a taxi to collect him outside the bank and take him to the airport. He then robs the bank and is caught by the Gardai waiting outside for his taxi, which is late. Can Riley sue the taxi company for breach of contract?

2. Larry and Bob enter into a contract in Dublin betting on the outcome of an illegal dog fight in Belfast. Bob loses the bet but refuses to pay. Is the contract enforceable?

3. Larry sees a notice in the paper looking for relatives of the deceased hermit Roland Gibbons who resided in Brisbane and has left an estate worth $5 million. Terry, an Australian, promises to organise Larry's trip to Australia and to help him deal with all the paperwork in return for a ten per cent share of the estate. Is this contract enforceable?

4. Kate enters into a contract with HighGrove Transport Ltd to collect all her books and transport them from the warehouse to her home. She agrees to pay the fifteen- year-old driver cash upon collection so that the transaction need not be declared as taxable income by HighGrove Transport Ltd. When the books are stolen en route, HighGrove Transport Ltd refuses to compensate her. It claims that the contract is void as a result of its illegality. Advise Kate.

5. Excell is a business supplying computer hardware. It employs Hilary as its managing director for a salary of €120,000 and it agrees to pay her €15,000 for 'her relocation expenses' from her previous job in London. As both parties are aware, Hilary worked for her previous employer on-line from her own home and thus no such expenses were incurred. The purpose of the payment is to make the contract more attractive to Hilary. Two months later, Hilary announces that she is pregnant and is subsequently dismissed. When she argues that her dismissal breached employee protection legislation, Excell claim the contract is void for illegality and thus the legislation is inapplicable.

6. Richard enters into a contract to by a pornographic video. Is this contract enforceable?

Chapter Seventeen

Restraint of Trade

INTRODUCTION

In the age of Queen Elizabeth all restraints of trade, whatever they were, general or partial, were thought to be contrary to public policy, and therefore void (*Colgate v Bacheler*[1]). In time, however, it was found that a rule so rigid and far reaching must seriously interfere with transactions of every day occurrence. Traders could hardly venture to let their shops out of their own hands; the purchaser of a business was at the mercy of the seller; every apprentice was a possible rival. So the rule was relaxed. . . .

. . .

The true view at the present time I think, is this: The public have an interest in every person's carrying on his trade freely: so has the individual. All interference with individual liberty of action in trading, and all restraints of trade of themselves, if there is nothing more, are contrary to public policy, and therefore void. That is the general rule. But there are exceptions: restraints of trade and interference with individual liberty of action may be justified by the special circumstances of a particular case. It is a sufficient justification, and indeed it is the only justification, if the restriction is reasonable—reasonable, that is, in reference to the interests of the parties concerned and reasonable in reference to the interests of the public, so framed and so guarded as to afford adequate protection to the party in whose favour it is imposed, while at the same time it is in no way injurious to the public. That, I think, is the fair result of all the authorities.

[1]. Cro Eliz 872.

Per Lord Macnaghten in *Nordenfelt v Maxim Nordenfelt Guns and Ammunition Co.* [1894] AC 535.

John Orr Ltd and Vescom B.V. v John Orr [1987] ILRM 702

Costello J.:

. . .

The principles of law to be applied in the issue are not in controversy and can be briefly stated. All restraints of trade in the absence of special justifying circumstances are contrary to public policy and are therefore void. A restraint may be justified if it is reasonable in the interests of the contracting parties and in the interests of the public. The onus of showing that a restraint is reasonable between the parties rests on the person alleging that it is so. Greater freedom of contract is allowable in a covenant entered into between the seller and the buyer of a business than in the case of one entered into between an employer and employee. A covenant against competition entered into by the seller of a business which is reasonably necessary to protect the business sold is valid and enforceable. A covenant by an employee not to compete

865

may also be valid and enforceable if it is reasonably necessary to protect some proprietary interest of the covenantee such as may exist in a trade connection or trade secrets. The courts may in certain circumstances enforce a covenant in restraint of trade even though taken as a whole the covenant exceeds what is reasonable, by the severance of the void parts from the valid parts.

The facts established at the hearing are as follows. John Orr Ltd was established by the defendant in 1971 and carried on a business in Navan, County Meath, manufacturing and selling upholstery fabrics and garment fabrics. It had two members, the defendant and a Mr Jerry Linscheid. In the early part of 1977 it was failing badly—indeed it was insolvent. In an endeavour to revitalise the company (an attempt which in the event proved eminently successful) an agreement was entered into on 11 March of that year (the 'share-transfer agreement') by which Vescom B.V. (a company registered in Holland) would purchase the business of John Orr Ltd and invest £50,000 in it. It did this by purchasing the shares in the company owned by the defendant and Mr Linscheid for a nominal sum. As part of the financial package then negotiated the Industrial Development Authority agreed to make grants to the company, Foir Teoranta agreed to make available certain financial facilities, and certain major creditors agreed to write off their debts. As a result of this agreement John Orr Ltd became a wholly owned subsidiary of Vescom B.V. The share transfer agreement also contained provisions for the future role of the defendant and Mr Linscheid in John Orr Ltd, requiring both to enter into service agreements with the company by which the defendant would be appointed as its commercial director and Mr Linscheid its technical director. The share transfer agreement also contained a clause, clause 6(c) which falls for consideration in these proceedings. It provided that until the expiry of one year from the determination of his service agreements the defendant should:

(i) not have any interest in any other firm or company nor be employed by, or act as representative or agent for any other person firm or company which manufactures or trades or markets similar or competing goods to those manufactured or traded or marketed by the company or by Vescom;
or
(ii) not solicit nor seek to obtain orders from nor interfere with nor endeavour to entice away any person firm or company which at any time within the period of twelve months ending with the termination of employment of Mr Orr or Mr Linscheid (as the case may require) were customers of or in the habit of dealing with the company or Vescom or any associated or subsidiary company.

The following points are to be noticed about the restraints on competition; (a) they are for a twelve month period; (b) they are world wide; (c) they apply to goods similar to and competing with goods manufactured by (i) John Orr Ltd and (ii) its parent company, Vescom B.V. As to the restraints on soliciting customers it is to be noted (a) that they, too, are to operate for a twelve month period; (b) they apply worldwide; and (c) they apply not only to customers of John Orr Ltd, but also to customers of Vescom B.V. and to customers of any subsidiary or associated companies of Vescom B.V.

The defendant also on 11 March 1977 entered into a service agreement with John Orr Ltd. This took the form of a letter sent to him by the company which he signed. This confirmed that the defendant was to be employed as commercial director of the company as from 11 March 1977 and that the appointment should continue until terminated by a six months notice given by either side. It contained a clause restricting the defendants' trading activities for a period of one year after termination in exactly the same terms as those of the share transfer agreement and a non-solicitation obligation in exactly similar terms.

The defendant took up his duties under the service agreement. The company prospered (sales expanding to £1.7m in 1984). But the defendant decided to resign in 1985 and his resignation, having been accepted, became effective from 31 October of that year, from which date the restraints began to run. Unknown to the plaintiffs the defendant had established in England a company called Rossbrae Ltd which began trading on 1 November 1985 in upholstery fabrics. Early this year the plaintiffs ascertained that Rossbrae Ltd was doing business with one of John Orr Ltd's most important customers in England and furthermore that the defendant had been visiting some of its most valuable customers in the US soliciting business for his new company. These proceedings followed shortly thereafter.

The reasonableness of the restraints imposed on the defendant is to be tested by reference to the commercial realities of the situation which existed when they were imposed, that is in the year 1977. So the question for determination is whether in that year it was reasonably necessary for the protection of Vescom's investment in John Orr Ltd to impose the restraints contained in the share-purchase agreement and whether it was reasonably necessary for the protection of John Orr Ltd's trade connections that it should impose the restraints contained in the service agreement. The business actually carried on by John Orr Ltd in that year is obviously of crucial importance. But what was in the reasonable contemplation of the parties for its future development is also relevant and some limited assistance on this aspect of the case can be obtained from evidence of what happened to the business in subsequent years.

The evidences show that:

(a) In 1977 John Orr Ltd manufactured and sold upholstery fabrics and garment fabrics, both of high quality and design. It did not then trade in wall coverings nor did the parties contemplate that it would ever do so. This was the product manufactured by Vescom B.V.

(b) In 1977, 36.7 per cent of the sales of John Orr Ltd were sales of garment fabrics and these were almost exclusively on the home market. Virtually all its production of upholstery fabrics was exported. But its export markets were limited in area. Of its total turnover 39.8 per cent was sold to five customers in the US. Outside North America it only traded in Europe, having three customers in the UK, three in Germany, and one in Holland, Switzerland, Belgium, Denmark, France and Italy. The one customer in Holland was Vescom B.V. and it was an important customer. The quantities sold in other European countries was insignificant. Its business was obviously heavily dependent on its trade connection with a small number of customers. In that year nearly eighty per cent of its total turnover was sold to ten customers (five of which, as I have already pointed out being in the US).

(c) Its export trade was carried out (apart from its sales to its parent company) by means of orders obtained from wholesale distributors. To obtain a distributor in a foreign country required a considerable amount of persuasion and active promotion of the company's products. When referring to 'customers' of John Orr Ltd the parties had particularly in mind these distributors rather than the ultimate purchasers of their products. Having agreed to act as a distributor the foreign wholesaler purchased a small quantity of the company's fabrics and endeavoured to obtain orders for them. In a given year the 'customers' of John Orr Ltd included those distributors who had agreed to distribute the company's fabrics even though no sale in fact took place. The ultimate purchasers of these fabrics were mainly institutions or large commercial undertakings rather than domestic users, and the market for them was a highly specialised one. But the company faced competition from manufacturers of upholstery fabrics of a different quality to theirs, such as producers of damask, and from manufacturers using different looms to those employed by John Orr Ltd.

(d) At the time of their agreements the parties contemplated that one of the benefits from them would be the trade connection established between John Orr Ltd and its new parent company. This benefit in fact materialised. In 1978 export total sales were £445,077 (compared to £302,895 in the previous year) but thirty five per cent of its total turnover was with the parent company. In 1978 it obtained one new customer in Norway, one in Sweden and one in Australia but the pattern of its trade remained the same as it had been in 1977. 42.3 per cent of the volume of goods sold were sold in North America (principally the US), 20.7 per cent on the home market, and thirty five per cent in Holland. Twelve customers took 84.2 per cent of the total volume of sales.

(e) In later years the trade in garment fabrics fell off so that by 1985 the company's business was exclusively in upholstery fabrics. It had in 1985 extended its trading and had one customer in Japan, Hong Kong and the Middle East, but in each case the quantity sold was very small. Nearly ninety per cent of its turnover comprised sales to eight customers and nearly fifty per cent of its business was to the US.

I have no doubt that in 1977 the parties hoped that the company's business would expand and that new markets would be entered. But there is no evidence to suggest that the parties had at that time any plans to develop it on a worldwide basis. North America and Europe were then the only areas in which the company's products were sold, sales in those areas being confined in the main to a small number of customers.

These findings lead me to the following conclusions on the enforceability of the restraint of trade clauses in the two contracts on 11 March 1977.

(1) *The non-solicitation clauses*

(a) I am quite satisfied that it was reasonably necessary for the protection of Vescom's investment in John Orr Ltd that it should require the defendant not to solicit the customers of John Orr Ltd for a period of twelve months after the termination of his service agreement with that company. But the protection of that investment did not require the defendant to agree not to solicit the customers of Vescom Ltd or its subsidiaries or associated companies because John Orr Ltd was not manufacturing or trading in wall coverings and had no intention of doing so. The plaintiffs' counsel submitted, a submission with which the defendant's counsel agreed, that the severance rule could be applied to this clause. I will therefore hold that in respect of the share-purchase agreement of 11 March 1977 clause 6(c)(ii) is valid and enforceable with the deletion of the words 'or Vescom or any associated or subsidiary company' at the end of the paragraph.

(b) I am also quite satisfied that it was reasonably necessary for the protection of the proprietary interest of John Orr Ltd in its trade connection with its customers that it should require the defendant not to solicit its customers for twelve months after the termination of his service agreement with the company. But the protection of that interest did not require that he would not solicit the customers of Vescom or its associates and subsidiaries. As in the case of the share-purchase agreement counsel agree that the severance rule can be applied to the service agreement. Accordingly I will declare that para. 7(II) of that agreement is enforceable with the deletion of the words 'or the parent company or any associated or subsidiary company' at the end of the paragraph. In neither case will there be any adverse effect on the public interest.

(2) *The non-competition clauses*

(a) it will be recalled that the share-purchase agreement restrained the defendant for one year after the termination of his service agreement from manufacturing or selling (either personally or through a company) goods manufactured or sold by the parent Dutch firm Vescom as well as goods manufactured or sold by John Orr Ltd. In 1977 John Orr Ltd manufactured and sold upholstery and garment fabrics and did not manufacture or trade in wall coverings, which were the goods manufactured by Vescom

B.V. It had no intention of entering the market in these goods. The range of goods subjected to the restraints in clause 6(c)(i) of the share-purchase agreement was therefore unreasonably wide as it was not necessary for the protection of Vescom's investment in John Orr Ltd that the defendant should be restrained from manufacturing or trading in wall coverings. The clause therefore imposes an excessive restraint.

It is also excessively restrictive for another reason. It prohibited the defendant from manufacturing or trading in upholstery fabrics in any part of the world during the limitation period. In 1977 the vast bulk of the business of John Orr Ltd was done with a limited number of customers in a limited number of countries. A restriction on the defendant which would prohibit him for one year after termination of his service contract from manufacturing or selling in the countries in which John Orr Ltd had customers could well have been justified as necessary to protect Vescom's investment in this case. Indeed, it might even have been possible to justify a wider restriction if it could have been shown that in 1977 John Orr Ltd had definite proposals for expanding into markets outside North America and Europe. But a blanket worldwide restraint based merely on the possibility that markets in other parts of the world might be entered by the company is to my mind an unreasonable one as it was not reasonably required for the protection of Vescom's investment in the company.

(b) Exactly the same considerations apply to the restrictions contained in clause 7(1) of the service agreement. The protection of the trade connection of John Orr Ltd did not require that the defendant should be restrained from manufacturing or trading in goods manufactured or sold by Vescom B.V. And the protection of its trade connections could be assured without prohibiting the defendant from manufacturing or selling upholstery fabrics in any part of the world.

The defendant's counsel had urged that if I found that the restraints imposed by clause 6(c)(i) of the share-purchase agreement and clause 7(1) of the service agreement were excessive and therefore unreasonable that the clauses were unenforceable because I could not apply the severance rule to them as to do so would amount to re-writing the parties' contracts. The plaintiffs' counsel forcibly submitted that the worldwide restraints in the two agreements were reasonable ones, but did not suggest that if I were to hold otherwise that the infirmities could be cured by severing the unenforceable parts. In these circumstances I must hold that these two clauses are unenforceable.

That brings me to the plaintiff's motion for an interlocutory injunction. In the light of my decision on the preliminary issue it follows that if the trial of this action takes place before 31 October 1986 the trial judge would grant an injunction, (damages being an inadequate remedy) limited in the way I have described, and would in addition decide whether any breaches of the enforceable part of the non-solicitation clauses had occurred and if so what damages resulted. This means that I do not consider the plaintiffs' claim to interlocutory relief by the principles established in *American Cyanamid Co. v Ethicon Ltd* [1975] AC 396 but rather on the basis that the plaintiffs' right to an injunction has in fact been established. Although the defendant through his counsel has offered to give an undertaking not to solicit I think that to avoid any doubts as to the parties' rights I should formally make an order. This will restrain until 31 October 1986 the defendant either personally or by means of Rossbrae Ltd or any other company or firm with which he may be associated either directly or indirectly from soliciting or seeking orders from or interfering with or endeavouring to entice away any person firm or company which were customers of John Orr Ltd or were in the habit of dealing with John Orr Ltd at any time within the period of twelve months ending 31 October 1986.

Murgitroyd and Co. v Purdy [2005] IEHC 159

The plaintiff company engaged the defendant, a qualified European patent agent, to work in its Dublin office on a three-year fixed term contract. At commencement the contract contained a non-competition clause which indicated that the defendant, upon termination of his contract, would not for twelve months thereafter carry on any business that would compete with the plaintiff's business. The clause precluded such an activity anywhere in the Republic of Ireland but did not prevent the defendant from taking up employment in a competing business. The defendant left the plaintiff's employment and commenced to provide services in the area of intellectual property under the name of Purdy and Associates, in breach of the non-competition clause. After holding that the clause remained in force after the defendant left the plaintiff's employment, Clarke J. went on to consider the defendant's arguments that the restraint was unenforceable because of its geographical scope and because it was a restraint on competition *per se*.

Clarke J.

The final issue which arises is as to the extent to which the non-competition clause may be said to be enforceable having regard to the well established principles concerning contracts in restraint of trade. A restraint on a person working or being engaged in one or more lines of business is by definition a restraint of trade. It is well settled that such a term will not be enforced by the courts unless it meets a twofold test:

    (a) it is reasonable as between the parties; and
    (b) it is consistent with the interests of the public.

McEllistrom v Ballymacelligot Co-op (1919) AC 548 at p. 562.
    In relation to the first test i.e. reasonableness *inter partes*, in the leading case of *Stenhouse (Australia) Ltd v Phillips* [1974] AC 311, Lord Wilberforce said:

> The proposition that an employer is not entitled to protection from mere competition by a former employee means that the employee is entitled to use to the full any personal skill or experience even if this has been acquired in the service of his employer: it is this freedom to use to the full a man's improving ability and talents which lies at the root of the policy of the law regarding this type of restraint. Leaving aside the case of misuse of trade secrets or confidential information . . . the employer's claim for protection must be based upon the identification of some advantage or asset inherent in the business which can properly be regarded as, in a general sense, his property, and which it would be unjust to allow the employee to appropriate for his own purposes, even though he, the employee, may have contributed to its creation.

The test seems to be, therefore, as to whether in all the circumstances of the case both the nature of the restriction and its extent is reasonable to protect the goodwill of the employer. Clearly certain clauses which preclude solicitation come within that definition provided that they are not excessively wide. In certain other cases clauses have been upheld which have prohibited employees setting up a similar business within a specified distance of an employer's establishment. See for example *Marian White Limited v Francis* (1972) 1 WLR 1423. But it is clear that the duration of the prohibition and the geographical scope of same are important matters to be considered having regard to the nature of the work in question and the structure of the business.

In Halsbury (4th edn), vol. 47, the authors note in para. 31 that where a business is carried on by a small number of people and with customers widely distributed, a very large area will be allowed and a wider restraint may be reasonable in a business carried on by agents or correspondence than in one necessitating constant attendance in person. For example, all of England was regarded as an acceptable area of restriction for an accountant in *Isitt & Anor. v Ganson* [1899] 43 Sol. Jo. 744.

Having heard the evidence presented on behalf of the plaintiff as to the nature of the business in Ireland I am satisfied that there are only 10 (or perhaps 11 if one includes the defendant) patent attorneys operating in Ireland and that they all operate from Dublin. No difficulty would appear to be encountered in servicing the demands of the Irish business from Dublin. In those circumstances it does not seem to me that a geographical restriction based upon the jurisdiction of the Irish state is unreasonable having regard to the way in which the business operates in Ireland.

Having regard to the specialised nature of the business I am also satisfied that a period of 12 months is not unreasonable.

However, it is also clear that a more restrictive view is taken of covenants by employees than is taken of covenants given on sale of a business. Covenants against competition by former employees are never reasonable as such. They may be upheld only where the employee might obtain such personal knowledge of, and influence over, the customers of his employer as would enable him, if competition were allowed, to take advantage of his employer's trade connection. *Kores Manufacturing Co. Ltd v Kolok Manufacturing Co. Ltd* [1959] Ch. 108.

In those circumstances I have come to the view that the prohibition in this case on all competition is too wide. A prohibition on dealing with (in addition to soliciting of) customers of the plaintiff would, in my view, have been reasonable and sufficient to meet any legitimate requirements of the plaintiff. The wider prohibition which restricts dealing with those who might be, but are not, such customers is excessive.

There may be types of business where it is not practical to distinguish between customers and non-customers. This is not one of them. On the evidence, the number of customers is small and identifiable. A prohibition on dealing with those identified customers would be sufficient to prevent the defendant taking advantage of the plaintiff's trade connections. The wider restriction which prohibits competing for business in which the plaintiff might have an interest but where the client was not an existing customer, could not be directed to that end but to the wider aim of restricting competition as such. As pointed out in *Kores* that is not a permissible end.

In those circumstances I must view the anti-competition clause as an unreasonable restraint of trade. On that basis I must determine the preliminary issue by finding that the anti-competition charge, while applicable, is unenforceable.

Notes

1. For a non-solicitation clause case see *European Paint Importers v O'Callaghan* [2005] IEHC 280.
2. Non-solicitation clauses are more readily enforceable than non-competition clauses because they represent an attempt to interfere with

the former employer's customer base, but because solicitation is more difficult to prove, former employers seek to insert non-competition clauses to deter competition, even though such a clause may have dubious value when tested in litigation.

Winnipeg Livestock Sales Ltd *v* Plewman et al (2000) 192 DLR (4th) 525

Scott C J M:—This appeal concerns the enforceability of a restrictive covenant entered into as part of a contract for personal services. The defendant Desmond Plewman (Plewman), an independent contractor, agreed with the plaintiff Winnipeg Livestock Sales Ltd (Winnipeg Livestock) that for a period of eighteen months following the termination of his services, he would not:

> . . . solicit business from or provide livestock auctioneering services to any person within the Province of Manitoba who is or is likely to be in competition with the Business . . .

The two essential issues on the appeal are:
(1) the reasonableness of the restrictive covenant; and
(2) the interpretation of its specific terms.
These are, of course, not separate and distinct issues, but interrelated questions.

Facts
The plaintiff is the largest livestock auction market in Manitoba. Plewman is a highly skilled and well-known auctioneer. The defendant Grunthal Livestock Auction Mart. Limited (Grunthal) is a direct competitor of Winnipeg Livestock.

Plewman was engaged by Winnipeg Livestock to provide auctioneering services between November 1990 and May 1994 when he left to provide similar services for a competitor. The competitor's business was unsuccessful and Plewman's services were again retained by Winnipeg Livestock in January 1995. It was at this time that Plewman entered into a lengthy contract which contained *inter alia* a restrictive covenant.

The agreement also provided that Plewman would not disclose any information he had acquired in relation to Winnipeg Livestock's business, 'or any secrets of Winnipeg Livestock'.

The agreement was amended from time to time—essentially to provide for additional compensation to Plewman; on each occasion the remainder of the terms and conditions in the original agreement were confirmed.

Plewman was the principal auctioneer at Winnipeg Livestock until 5 November 1999, at which time, having earlier provided three months' notice in accordance with the terms of the agreement, he purchased an interest in Grunthal and commenced work in competition with Winnipeg Livestock providing auctioneering and other services.

Evidence disclosed that Plewman had provided valuable services for Winnipeg Livestock, not only because of his skill as an auctioneer, but by virtue of his reputation. Thus, he was able to assist Winnipeg Livestock in marketing its services to producers and acquired extensive knowledge of Winnipeg Livestock's customers:

> Over the course of time, however, my responsibilities increased to include 'country work', industry jargon for soliciting business which, more particularly, involved travelling around the countryside visiting livestock producers at their

premises, valuing their cattle, giving market advice and encouraging them to market their cattle through the plaintiff.

The motions court judge, in extensive oral reasons, granted an interim injunction in favour of Winnipeg Livestock.

The leading authority in Canada is undoubtedly *Elsley v J. G. Collins Insurance Agencies Ltd*, [1978] 2 SCR 916, 83 DLR (3d) 1. In that case, the respondent (Collins) purchased the general insurance business of Elsley. By a supplemental agreement Elsley was employed as manager of the Collins operation. After seventeen years Elsley resigned and recommenced his own general insurance business. Elsley had entered into a specific non-competition covenant. Dickson J., as he then was, writing for the court, identified the 'critical question' as being whether the employer in seeking to protect 'his trade connection, overreached in the formulation' of the restrictive covenant.

He then went on to say (at pp. 925–6)

In assessing the reasonableness of the clause with reference to the interests of the parties, several questions must be asked. First, did Collins have a proprietary interest entitled to protection? The answer to this question must surely be in the affirmative. Shortly before the agreement for the employment of Elsley, Colins had paid Elsley some $46,000 for the general insurance trade connection of Elsley. By the agreement Elsley was placed in control, not only of that trade connection, but also the trade connection which Collins enjoyed prior to that time. Second, were the temporal or spatial features of the clause too broad? Some argument was directed to the court as to those aspects, but I am in entire agreement with the courts below that they are not open to successful challenge. The next and crucial question is whether the covenant is unenforceable as being against competition generally, and not limited to proscribing solicitation of clients of the former employer. In a conventional employer/employee situation the clause might well be held invalid for that reason. The fact that it could have been drafted in narrower terms would not have saved it, for as Viscount Haldane said in *Mason v Provident Clothing and Supply Co*, [[1913] AC 724 (HL(E))], p. 732, '. . . the question is not whether they could have made a valid agreement but whether the agreement actually made was valid.' Whether a restriction is reasonably required for the pro-tection of the covenantee can only be decided by considering the nature of the covenantee's business and the nature and character of the employment. Admittedly, an employer could not have a proprietary interest in people who were not actual or potential customers. Nevertheless, in exceptional cases, of which I think this is one, the nature of the employment may justify a covenant prohibiting an employee not only from soliciting customers, but also from establishing his own business or working for others so as to be likely to appropriate the employer's trade connection through his acquaintance with the employer's customers. This may indeed be the only effective covenant to protect the proprietary interest of the employer. A simple non-solicitation clause would not suffice.

The defendants argue that the restriction against the provision of auctioneering services—whether broadly interpreted as was done by the motions court judge or not—is neither reasonable between the parties, nor with reference to the public interest. This is because it is not required to protect Winnipeg Livestock's trade secrets, confidential information or trade connections. See *Herbert Morris Limited v Saxelby*, [1916] 1 AC 688 (HL(E)). Rather, the sole purpose of the covenant, the defendants say, is to prevent Plewman from acting as an auctioneer for a competitor of Winnipeg Livestock. The clause did not attempt to protect proprietary interest—its sole purpose is to prevent competition and is hence void.

The essential character of Plewman's engagement was as an auctioneer, although there were other persons who also conducted livestock auctions on behalf of Winnipeg Livestock. Thus, it is argued, the services of Plewman were not of such an exceptional nature as to justify a restrictive covenant, the real effect of which is to simply ban competition. the circumstances are not exceptional.

In replay, Winnipeg Livestock asserts that there is no restriction against Plewman acting as an auctioneer other than for livestock auction marts and that in all the circumstances, given the 'background history', the bargain is 'fair'. See *Jostens Canada Ltd v Genderfon* (1993) 1 CCEL (2d) 275 (Ont. Ct. (Gen. Div.)). At the least, the circumstances are exceptional since by virtue of Plewman's enormous reputation and lengthy association with Winnipeg Livestock, he in reality became the personification of the company.

Is the restrictive covenant reasonable? In *Elsey* at p. 924, Dickson J. drew a distinction between a restrictive covenant in an agreement for the sale of a business and the enforceability of a restrictive covenant in a contract of employment. In the latter, a covenant must be reasonable between the parties and with reference to the public interest. With respect to the former, it is subjected to less scrutiny.

The specific question in this case is whether the fact that Plewman was an independent contractor rather than an employee means that the 'more rigorous' approach set out in *Elsey* in inapplicable. In *Deacons (a firm) v Bridge*, [1984] 2 All ER 19, the Privy Council concluded that with respect to employment-like relationships (at p. 22):

> . . . a decision on whether the restrictions in this agreement are enforceable or not cannot be reached by attempting to place the agreement in any particular category, or by seeking for the category to which it is most closely analogous. The proper approach is that adopted by Lord Reid in the *Esso Petroleum* case [1967] All ER 699 at 709, [1968] AC 269 at 301, where he said:
>
> > I think it better to ascertain what were the legitimate interests of the appellants which they were entitled to protect, and then to see whether these restraints were more than adequate for that purpose.

See as well *Salloum v Thomas* (1986), 12 CPR (3d) 2512 (BCSC) and *Sacallis v Georgia Pacific Securities Corp.*, [1998] BCJ No. 2987 (QL) (Prov. Ct. (Civ. Div.)).

In *Dynamex Canada Inc. v Miller* (1998), 161 Nfld. & PEIR 97 (CA), Green J.A. for the court noted (at para. 38):

> It was argued in this case that this restrictive approach in employment situations should not apply, given the fact that the parties had agreed that the relationship was not of employer-employee but one of principal and independent contractor. I do not place much emphasis on these distinctions. Whether Miller was an employee or an independent contractor, he was, in the circumstances, a person who faced an imbalance of bargaining power. The policy of protecting against an imbalance power that applies in the employer-employee situation also applies here.

In my opinion, the rigorous 'reasonability test' is as applicable with respect to independent contractor relationships such as this as with employer-employee relationships.

In *Elsley* at p. 925, Dickson J., in assessing the reasonableness of the restrictive covenant, identified three principal questions which should be asked:

(1) Does the party seeking to enforce the covenant have a proprietary or legitimate interest entitled to protection?
(2) Are the temporal and spatial features of the covenant reasonable, or too broad?
(3) Does the covenant prevent competition generally, and if so, is this restriction reasonably required for the protection of the covenantee in the circumstances?

He noted that a restrictive covenant which prevents competition generally will usually be invalid in an employer-employee relationship but that in 'exceptional cases' the nature of the employment may justify a covenant prohibiting not only the solicitation of the employer's customers but also competition generally in the same field.

The second question identified by Dickson J. is not an issue in case. With respect to the first question, trade secrets, confidential information and customer lists have all been identified as being legitimate proprietary interests. See England, Christie & Christie's *Employment Law in Canada* 3rd ed. (looseleaf) (Butterworths, Toronto) at $11.35, *Maguire v Northland Drug Company Limited* [1935] SCR 412 at 416, [1935] 3 DLR 521, and *Herbert Morris Limited v Saxelby* at p. 702. Employers also have a legitimate proprietary interest in their 'trade connections' and their 'goodwill' (*Jiffy Foods Ltd v Chomski* [1973] 3 OR 955 at 958–9, 38 DLR (3d) 675 (Div. Ct.), *Fitch v Dewes*, [1921] 2 AC 158 (HL(E)) at 168, and *White (Marion) Ltd v Francis* [1972] 1 WLR 1423 (CA) at 1429, but as stated in *Routh v Jones* [1947] All ER 179 (Ch.D.) at 181, affirmed [1947] 1 All ER 758 (CA):

> In the absence of special circumstances, an employer has no such proprietary interest as entitles him to protection from the competition of his former servant *per se*, nor can a former servant be restrained from turning to account his own business or professional skill, although that skill was acquired while he was in the service of his former master.

In other words, even though Plewman has a great deal of skill as an auctioneer, Winnipeg Livestock has no proprietary interest in his professional skill and experience, even if they were acquired during his time working for Winnipeg Livestock. Thus, Winnipeg Livestock has the burden of establishing that it has a legitimate proprietary interest requiring protection. On this key question there is little evidence before the court. The record discloses that part of Plewman's job was to 'mingle with the . . . crowd' and to telephone customers and prospective customers about future prospects for the sale of livestock. It may seem reasonable to assume that Winnipeg Livestock has a legitimate proprietary interest in its customer connections; but there is no evidence to indicate that there is any significant degree of 'customer loyalty' in the business, as opposed to customers making choices based on other considerations such as cost, availability and the like.

There are numerous cases dealing with the issue of an employer's proprietary interest in customer loyalty and customer connections. See T.S. *Taylor Machinery Co. Ltd v Biggar* (1968) 2 DLR (3d) 281 (Man. CA), *American Building Maintenance Co. Ltd v Shandley* (1966), 58 DLR (2d) 525 (BCCA), and *Maguire v Northland Drug*. I conclude that from these cases and others to similar effect that an employer has no proprietary right *per se* to its customers but only in the protection of its own goodwill. These cases also confirm that a lack of loyalty among the employer's customers is a significant factor to consider when determining whether an employer has a legitimate proprietary interest and whether a general non-competition covenant (as opposed to a much more specific and limited non-solicitation covenant) will be reasonable. Winnipeg Livestock has not provided evidence to establish that it has a legitimate proprietary interest in its customer connections. This being so, the restrictive covenant is not reasonable.

While the answer to this question is decisive of the result on the appeal, I will deal with the third issue identified by Dickson J. in *Elsey*, namely, does the restrictive covenant prevent competition generally from Plewman and, if it does, are there exceptional circumstances? This requires that the wording of the restrictive covenant be examined in detail.

The defendants argue, and I agree, that the restrictive covenant can effectively be broken down into two components. Firstly, Plewman is prohibited from soliciting business from anyone in Manitoba who is or is likely to be in competition with Winnipeg Livestock. Plainly, this wording does not encompass producers since they are not competitors of Winnipeg Livestock. Winnipeg Livestock argues that this interpretation essentially emasculates the prohibition, because there would be no reason for Plewman to undertake the task of attempting to solicit business away from direct competitors. This may be so but it cannot detract from the fact that the words used—chosen by Winnipeg Livestock—restrict the prohibition to competitors of Winnipeg Livestock.

The second and far more problematic part of the restrictive covenant prevents Plewman from providing livestock auctioneering services to any person within Manitoba who is or is likely to be in competition with Winnipeg Livestock for a period of eighteen months. The covenant does not merely restrict Plewman from soliciting or auctioneering for clients of Winnipeg Livestock but 'to any other livestock auctioneering company' in Manitoba. In a nutshell, the covenant effectively prevents Plewman from acting as a livestock auctioneer in Manitoba for a period of eighteen months. Winnipeg Livestock does not insist upon preventing Plewman from acting as a manager of Grunthal, but does seek to prevent him from auctioneering, which is the essence of his professional expertise and reputation, in the same area as its own auctioneers operate. The covenant is deliberately written in such a way as to prevent such competition; plainly the covenant does 'prevent competition generally' (*Elsey*, point 3). Thus, in '[i] in the absence of special circumstances, an employer has no such proprietary interest as entitles him to protection from the competition of his former servant *per se*' (*Routh v Jones* at p. 181) and see *Elsey*.

As we have seen, a restrictive covenant which prevents general competition from an ex-employee may be held to be reasonable in the circumstances and upheld as valid. When such a covenant will be considered reasonable and what circumstances will qualify as 'exceptional' will differ from case to case. As Dickson J. warned in *Elsey* (at p. 923):

> The test of reasonableness can be applied, however, only in the peculiar circumstances of the particular case. Circumstances are of infinite variety. Other cases may help in enunciating broad general principles but are otherwise of little assistance.

Numerous cases both before and after *Elsey* have considered this question. In *Elsey* at p. 927, Dickson J. concluded that the facts there were exceptional citing with approval the following passage of Lord Parker in *Herbert Morris, Limited v Saxelby* (at p. 709):

> Whatever such covenants have been upheld it has been on the ground, not that the servant or apprentice would, by reason of his employment or training, obtain the skill and knowledge necessary to equip him as a possible competitor in the trade,

but that he might obtain such personal knowledge of and influence over the customers of his employer . . . as would enable him, if competition were allowed, to take advantage of his employer's trade connection . . .

In *Herbert Morris* the close customer relations which were the decisive factor in *Elsey* were not present, leading to a different result.

Other authorities have offered a gloss or refinement to this general principle. In *Fitch v Dewes*, the degree of acquaintance which the employee has with clients and the likelihood that the employee could undermine the employer's business if allowed to compete were important factors to consider. The court concluded that a person employed as a managing clerk in a solicitor's office acquired a special advantage which required such a restrictive covenant to protect. See generally to the same effect the pre-*Elsley* decisions of *White (Marion) Ltd v Francis; Stenhouse Australia Ltd v Phillips* [1974] 1 All ER 117 (PC), and *Campbell, Imrie and Shankland v Park* [1954] 2 DLR 170 (BCSC), which demonstrates that it is important, when considering such cases, to look at the general nature of the business with particular emphasis on the loyalty of the clients, evidence regarding the employee's actual relationship with clients, and the degree to which the clients might identify the employee with the business.

Post-*Elsley* decisions are to the same effect. In *Doerner v Bliss & Laughlin Industries Inc.* [1980] 2 SCR 865, 117 DLR (3d) 547, McIntyre J., for the court, restated the principle in *Elsey* as follows (at p. 873):

> It may be acceptable, however, where the purpose of the covenant is not to prohibit the employee from exploiting the skills he has acquired in his past employment, but to protect the former employer against competition where the scope and nature of the employee's work and his contact with clients and customers of his former employer is such that he could readily do harm to his employer.

This court summarised the matter thusly in *Friesen and Hamilton v McKague* (1992) 81 Man. R. (2d) 290, 96 DLR (4th) 341 (at para. 17):

> *Elsley* is still the leading case on the validity of clauses that proscribe a former employee from competing for customers of his former employer. It can now be said with confidence that where the nature of the employment will likely cause customers to perceive an individual employee as the personification of the company or employer, the employer has a proprietary interest in the preservation of those customers which merits protection against competition from that individual employee after his termination; see, for example, *Metropolitan Life Insurance Co. v Qually* (1985) 36 Man. R. (2d) 59 (QB) and *Sunsweet Fundraisers Inc. v Moldenhauer and Theissing* (1991) 98 Sask. R. 81; 40 CPR (3rd) 212 (QB).

Personal contact alone between the employee and clients of the business is not sufficient to constitute such exceptional circumstances. *Ernst & Young v Stuart.* (1993) 50 CPR (3d) 142 (BCSC).

Finally, see *Williams Restaurant Supply Ltd v Leadley* (1994) 96 Man. R. (2d) 211 (QB), *Cradle Pictures (Canada) Ltd v Penner* [1978] OJ No. 471 (QL (HC)) [reported 34 CPR (2d) 34] affirmed [1982] OJ No. 1566 (QL) (CA), *Cannon v Island Acoustics (Courtenay) Inc.* (1996) 69 CPR (3rd) 73 (BCSC) and *Phytoderm Inc. v Urwin* [1999] OJ NO. 383 (QL) (Gen. Div.) [summarised 85 ACWS (3d) 1074]. Typical of these cases is the statement of Low J. in *Phytoderm* (at para. 14):

In exceptional circumstances, where an employee falls into none of the foregoing categories, a restrictive covenant not to solicit clientele for such a period of time as is necessary to protect the legitimate interests of the employer may be enforced where the employee's knowledge of the needs, preferences and idiosyncrasies of the employer's clients and the employee's knowledge of the manner in which the employer meets those needs gives the employee an unfair competitive advantage when he goes out in competition with the employer in supplying the same services to the same clientele . . . Such an employee is always in a position to give better terms or enriched service because he is in a unique position to know what he must do to win the client. Where the covenanting employee is the person rendering services to the employer's client, there is a real likelihood that the client will wish to have the continuity of having the service provided by the same individual. This is not so in the supply of beauty products where every brand must win its place in the marketplace with its own mystique.

In summary, the authorities reveal that the following circumstances will generally be relevant in determining whether a case is an 'exceptional' one so that a general non-competition clause will be found to be reasonable:

1. The length of the service with the employer
   See: *Elsey*; *Williams Restaurant Supply*
2. The amount of personal service to clients
   See: *Elsey*; *Herbert Morris*; *Fitch v Dewes*; *White (Marion)*; *Friesen v McKague*; *Rapid-Med Plus Franchise Corp. v Elliott* (1991) 73 Man. R. (2d) 150 (CA); *Cradle Pictures*; *Williams Restaurant*; *Cannon*; *Phytoderm*
3. Whether the employee dealt with clients exclusively, or on a sustained or recurring basis
   See: *Elsey*; *White (Marion)*; *Campbell, Imrie*; *Friesen v McKague*; *Cradle Pictures*; *Cannon*
4. Whether the knowledge about the client which the employee gained was of a confidential nature, or involved an intimate knowledge of the client's particular needs, preferences or idiosyncrasies
   See: *Elsley*; *Fitch v Dewes*; *Campbell, Imrie*; *Cradle Pictures*; *Cannon*; *Phytoderm*
5. Whether the nature of the employee's work meant that the employee had influence over clients in the sense that the clients relied upon the employee's advice, or trusted the employee
   See: *Herbert Morris*; *Fitch v Dewes*; *Cradle Pictures*
6. If competition by the employee has already occurred, whether there is evidence that clients have switched their custom to him, especially without direct solicitation
   See: *Elsey*; *Campbell, Imrie*; *Ernst & Young v Stuart*
7. The nature of the business with respect to whether personal knowledge of the clients' confidential matters is required
   See: *Stenhouse Australia*; *Campbell, Imrie*
8. The nature of the business with respect to the strength of customer loyalty, how clients are 'won' and kept, and whether the clientele is a recurring one
   See: *Stenhouse Australia*; *Campbell, Imrie*; *Ernst & Young v Stuart*; *Cradle Pictures*; *Cannon*
9. The community involved and where there were clientele yet to be exploited by anyone
   See: *Friesen v McKague*; *Cradle Pictures*

Applying these factors to the circumstances before us, I have no difficulty in concluding that the circumstances do not justify Winnipeg Livestock's claim that it requires blanket protection prohibiting Plewman from personally engaging in auctioneering. There is no evidence indicating that Plewman acted for clients exclusively or that clients requested him and only him to do their auctioneering. While Plewman doubtless would gain knowledge of the livestock he was selling and the auctioneering needs of clients, there is no suggestion that this information is of a confidential nature. Although there was evidence that Plewman had conducted an auction for Grunthal, there was no evidence that the customers he acted for in that instance, or in any other instance, were clients of Winnipeg Livestock. No evidence was presented regarding customer loyalty or how clients were acquired and retained. There is virtually nothing to support Winnipeg Livestock's contention that there were exceptional circumstances.

Notes

1. While non-competition clauses may only be enforceable in 'exceptional' cases, there are situations where a court may hold that non-solicitation clauses and confidentiality clauses may be inadequate for the purpose of protecting the legitimate interests of the employer, particularly in cases where the employee is a senior manager with knowledge of key elements in the way in which the business is operated and the business strategy is formulated. The difficulty in determining whether information is confidential, is in the nature of a trade secret, or is otherwise protected without an express term, may actually justify the court in upholding the non-competition clause. See *Thomas v Farr plc* [2007] EWCA Civ 118.
2. The restraint of trade doctrine is also applicable to the rules that determine how members of an association are to conduct themselves vis-à-vis a trade or profession. Persons who must observe the terms set by a regulatory body often invoke the restraint of trade doctrine in the hope of removing some onerous or restrictive rule that impedes freedom of action.

Macken v O'Reilly and Others [1979] ILRM 79

O'Higgins C.J.:

This is an appeal brought by the defendants against the judgment and order of Hamilton J. in the High Court in which he declared that a certain resolution adopted by them was void, as being, contrary to public policy, an unreasonable restraint of trade. The plaintiff is a professional show jumper and horseman and is resident and domiciled within the country. The defendants are members of and constitute the Equestrian Federation of Ireland (hereinafter referred to as the federation) which is the body responsible for both national and international aspects of all equestrian sports in Ireland. The resolution which led to the initiation of these proceedings was passed at a meeting of the federation on 21 January 1978.

. . .

The effect of this resolution was to reiterate and repeat the consistent policy of the federation which was not to permit Irish competitors at international events to be mounted on other than Irish horses, but to make a special exception in favour of the plaintiff, who was then resident in Germany, in respect of those international events (C.A.s and C.I.s) at which competitors from the different countries could compete as individuals. The plaintiff, who is now again resident in Ireland and whose standing and reputation as a showjumper and horseman is among the highest in the world, complains that the decision incorporated in this resolution interferes with his freedom to earn his living and is a restraint of trade which cannot be justified as being reasonable. . . .

All interference with an individual's freedom of action in trading is *per se* contrary to public policy and, therefore, void. This general prohibition is subject to the exception that certain restraints may be justified. Restraints, restrictions or interferences are permitted if they are, in the circumstances obtaining, fair and reasonable. Whether what is complained of can be justified on this basis involves a careful examination of all the circumstances—the need for the restraint, the object sought to be attained, the interests sought to be protected and the general interest of the public. What is done or sought to be done must be established as being reasonable and necessary and on balance to serve the public interest. The fact that the body or group imposing the restraint has the power to do so does not of itself justify its imposition. Any arbitrary or unreasonable use of power by those who have control or authority over a particular trade or profession would come within the prohibition. In this case the fact that its constitution and the FEI regulations appear to authorise the federation to act as it did, does not of itself authorise what was done. The question is whether in all the circumstances the action taken by the federation can be said to be fair and reasonable and in the public interest.

The learned trial judge in holding that the federation acted within its powers in passing the resolution in question said as follows:

> The federation is, under its constitution, the body responsible for both the national and international aspects of all equestrian sports in Ireland which are recognised by the federation and has sole jurisdiction in respect of international and ultimate authority in respect of national equestrian affairs. As such a body, it has, in my opinion, an interest in ensuring that the Irish half-bred breeding industry is in a healthy and thriving condition so as to ensure a reasonable supply of suitable horses available for all equestrian sports and is entitled to endeavour to take steps to protect that industry. Being so satisfied, I consider that the policy of the federation and the resolutions giving effect thereto are *intra vires* the power of the federation. . . .

This view is amply supported by the evidence and as already indicated it is a view with which I entirely agree. The learned judge went on to say:

> There is nothing unreasonable and the interest of all parties including the public, probably require that the federation do everything possible to encourage Irish riders to ride Irish-bred horses in international competitions. . . .

Having expressed this view he rather surprisingly went on to hold that by reason of the policy being inflexible he regarded it as an unreasonable restraint of trade in relation to the plaintiff. He gave his reasons as follows:

> None of the other national federations affiliated to the FIE have such a policy or rule. I accept Mr Macken's evidence that there are not available to him at this point of time sufficient Irish-bred horses of the necessary quality to enable him to maintain his position as one of the world's leading showjumpers. I consider that a policy which has the effect of inhibiting his efforts to maintain such a position to be unjust and unfair and that if he fails to maintain that position the public will be deprived of a great deal of pleasure. Having regard to the worldwide reputation of Irish half-bred horses I do not consider that the interests of the industry require that such a policy be maintained by the federation with regard to individual riders participating in international showjumping competitions as individuals and not representing their country officially.

It seems to me that in this part of his judgment the learned trial judge was in error. Having already held that the federation's policy was reasonable in the interest of all parties including the public, he nevertheless concluded that in its application to the plaintiff it was unjust and unfair. A policy of restraint which is held to be reasonable, having regard to all interests affected, including the public, cannot, in my view, properly be described as being unjust and unfair simply because in its particular application to one individual an inconvenience or loss is experienced. The trial judge was also influenced by the rule or policy being regarded as inflexible. This, it seems to me, is of the essence of any rule or policy until it is altered or changed. Any policy or ruling of this kind must be regarded in the light of all the circumstances to test whether it is reasonable or not. The mere fact that those who advocate it to enforce it are insistent as to their views cannot make what is otherwise reasonable suddenly unreasonable. In addition, it seems to me that the trial judge disregarded entirely the undisputed evidence as to the effect a change of policy would have on the horse breeding industry and on equestrian sport in Ireland. This ought to have been considered as a balance to the harm or inconvenience caused to the plaintiff by adhering to the rule. Finally, in my view the trial judge misinterpreted the FEI regulations when he referred to individual riders in international showjumping competitions competing as individuals and not as representatives of their country. As I have already indicated, in my view, this is just not possible under the regulations which apply.

I take a different view on the evidence and facts established before the learned trial judge. I accept that the plaintiff has been, as the trial judge put it, 'inhibited in his efforts to maintain his position as one of the world's leading show jumpers' by reason of the federation's rule. He is engaged on the international showjumping circuit from March to December each year. He has not the time to school or bring on young horses. As he said in his evidence he is faced by the fact that 'the majority of quality young horses in Ireland are sold at a very early stage'. It would be easier for him while on the circuit to look around for what he described as 'a talented young horse with a lesser rider'. This would be a horse already trained for jumping that he could include in his string without too excessive a loss of time or undue effort being involved. If he were free to buy such a horse, irrespective of its breeding, his interests would be well served and he could continue on the international circuit without any cessation. This is quite understandable if only the plaintiff's position were to be considered. This, however, is not the case. Also to be considered are the interests of the public as represented by those concerned with the horsebreeding industry in Ireland and also the interests of those already engaged in showjumping in this country who are looking for recognition and advancement in international events. The evidence established beyond question that if the plaintiff were permitted to ride foreign-bred horses as an accredited Irish competitor at international events then all others who wished to do so would have to get the same permission. This process once started would, through sponsorship and money, affect the standing of the Irish horse breeding industry. It would also have the effect of depriving young riders at home, particularly those of limited means, of any reasonable opportunity of advancement. It seems to me that on balance the policy and ruling of the federation can be justified as being reasonable, necessary and fair, having regard to all the tests which should be applied. The need for the rule in the first instance and the object of maintaining it was and is to build up the Irish half-bred horse industry in the interests of equestrian sport generally in the country. It is the view of the federation fairly and reasonably held, that in doing so it is serving the interests of the generality of young riders of limited means and thereby serving the general interests of the public. It is not a new rule. It is as old as the federation itself. It has been accepted and complied with by all Irish riders over the years and was of course so accepted by the plaintiff himself until recently. It can be said fairly that the plaintiff is where he is today because this policy was in operation over the years. The fact that his very success as a showjumper on the world circuit makes the application of the rule to him, now, inconvenient and expensive is no basis for condemning it as being unreasonable and unfair.

In my view, therefore, the resolution and ruling of the federation although in restraint of trade is, in the circumstances, reasonable and fair.

(Griffin and Parke JJ. agreed.)

Note

The restraint of trade doctrine was the judicial response to contractual or market practices which sterilised or constrained the power of individuals, groups, or companies to trade in a free or open market. The desire to maintain the supply of essential commodities such as foodstuffs, allow skilled artisans to carry on their trade to the benefit of themselves and the public, and avoid the creation of monopolies and artificial markets, are all evident in the voluminous body of case-law that restraint of trade produced. The restraint of trade doctrine was readily applied to employment and sale of business restraints and to exclusive selling and buying agreements; in recent years the courts have tested trade and professional association restraints, showing that the boundaries of restraint of trade are never closed.

The existing state of the authorities suggests that Lord Macnaghten's observations in *Nordenfelt* are only approximate guides to the methodology to be used in testing the agreement in question. In *Esso v Harpers* (see p. 907 below) the House of Lords suggested that certain contractual arrangements (conveyancing ties, ordinary supply agreements) are outside the doctrine altogether so that most but not all agreements that are manifestly a restraint upon a person's freedom to trade are *prima facie* void. Once this is established the question turns to whether the tie can be justified as being in the public interest; is it reasonable as between the parties and is it reasonable *vis-à-vis* the public generally?

In fact, reasonableness *inter partes* tended to be the main issue by which enforceability was determined. Very few cases dealt with the public interest in an abstract or realistically economic sense, and the judges tended to adopt negative positions when arguments about the inflationary or market distorting effects of an agreement were presented e.g. Ungoed-Thomas J. in *Texaco Ltd v Mulberry Filling Station* [1972] 1 All ER 513, at 525–6. While it is doubtless understandable to expect judges to admit that the balancing of several conflicting economic or business decisions is best left to Parliament, such observations help to point up the fact that the common law doctrine could not adequately deal with more complex economic or distributive issues, and the Oireachtas has intervened, firstly, through legislative control of certain kinds of agreement, such as motor fuel solus agreements in 1972, and secondly, through the Competition Act 2002.

Restraint of trade will remain a relevant ground for invalidity and some agreements, particularly employment restraints, will tend to fall outside the legislation, thus making these restraints enforceable only if they pass through the common law doctrine.

The objectives of the **Competition Act 2002**, as set out in the explanatory memorandum, are to prohibit, by analogy with Articles 85 and 86 (old) of the EEC Treaty, the prevention, restriction or distortion of competition and the abuse of dominant positions:

S. 4. (1)

4. (1) Subject to the provisions of this section, all agreements between undertakings, decisions by associations of undertakings and concerted practices which have as their object or effect the prevention, restriction or distortion of competition in trade in any goods or services in the State or in any part of the State are prohibited and void, including in particular, without prejudice to the generality of this subsection, those which:

(a) directly or indirectly fix purchase or selling prices or any other trading conditions;
(b) limit or control production, markets, technical development or investment;
(c) share markets or sources of supply;
(d) apply dissimilar conditions to equivalent transactions with other trading parties thereby placing them at a competitive disadvantage;
(e) make the conclusion of contracts subject to acceptance by the other parties of supplementary obligations which by their nature or according to commercial usage have no connection with the subject of such contracts.

Note

If the Competition Act 2002 does not apply to a transaction, the common law position must be considered. See Lucey (2003) 25 DULJ 124.

SECTION ONE—COMMON LAW AND STATUTORY POSITIONS

A. EMPLOYMENT AND MANAGEMENT AGREEMENTS

Faccenda Chicken Ltd v Fowler and Others [1986] 1 All ER 617

Fowler was employed by the plaintiff, a poultry breeding and marketing company as its sales manager. Fresh chickens were sold from refrigerated vans which operated on certain routes within a defined area. Fowler left the plaintiff and set up his own business in the same area selling fresh chickens from refrigerated vans. Eight of the plaintiff's employees resigned and joined him in his business. Fowler's vans operated on the same routes and serviced similar customers to the plaintiff's. The plaintiff sued the defendants alleging breach of their employment contracts. The trial judge dismissed this action and the plaintiff appealed to the Court of Appeal.

Neill L.J.:

In these two appeals it will be necessary to consider the interaction of three separate legal concepts. (1) The duty of an employee during the period of his employment to act with good faith towards his employer; this duty is sometimes called the duty of fidelity. (2) The duty of an employee not to use or disclose after his employment has ceased any confidential information which he has obtained during his employment about his employer's affairs. (3) The *prima facie* right of any person to use and to exploit for the purpose of earning his living all the skill, experience and knowledge which he has at his disposal, including skill, experience and knowledge which he has acquired in the course of previous periods of employment.

. . .

Having considered the cases to which we were referred, we would venture to state these principles as follows.

(1) Where the parties are, or have been, linked by a contract of employment, the obligations of the employee are to be determined by the contract between him and his employer: cf *Vokes Ltd v Heather* (1945) 62 RPC 135 at 141.

(2) In the absence of any express term, the obligations of the employee in respect of the use and disclosure of information are the subject of implied terms.

(3) While the employee remains in the employment of the employer the obligations are included in the implied term which imposes a duty of good faith or fidelity on the employee. For the purpose of the present appeal it is not necessary to consider the precise limits of this implied term, but it may be noted: (a) that the extent of the duty of good faith will vary according to the nature of the contract (see *Vokes Ltd v Heather*); (b) that the duty of good faith will be broken if an employee makes or copies a list of the customers of the employer for use after his employment ends or deliberately memorises such a list, even though, except in special circumstances, there is no general restriction on an ex-employee canvassing or doing business with customers of his former employer (see *Robb v Green* [1895] 2 QB 315, [1895–9] All ER Rep 1053 and *Wessex Dairies Ltd v Smith* [1935] 2 KB 80, [1935] All ER Rep 75).

(4) The implied term which imposes an obligation on the employee as to his conduct after the determination of the employment is more restricted in its scope than that which imposes a general duty of good faith. It is clear that the obligation not to use or disclose information may cover secret processes of manufacture such as chemical formulae (see *Amber Size and Chemical Co. Ltd v Menzel* [1913] 2 Ch. 239), or designs or special methods of construction (see *Reid Sigrist Ltd v Moss Mechanism Ltd* (1932) 49 RPC 461), and other information which is of a sufficiently high degree of confidentiality as to amount to a trade secret.

The obligation does not extend, however, to cover all information which is given to or acquired by the employee while in his employment, and in particular may not cover information which is only 'confidential' in the sense that an unauthorised disclosure of such information to a third party while the employment subsisted would be a clear breach of the duty of good faith.

This distinction is clearly set out in the judgment of Cross J. in *Printers and Finishers Ltd v Holloway* [1964] 3 All ER 731, [1965] 1 WLR 1, where he had to consider whether an ex-employee should be restrained by injunction from making use of his recollection of the contents of certain written printing instructions which had been made available to him when he was working in his former employers' flock printing factory. In his judgment, delivered on 29 April 1964 (not reported on this point in the WLR), Cross J. said ([1964] 3 All ER 731 at 738n):

> In this connection one must bear in mind that not all information which is given to a servant in confidence and which it would be a breach of his duty for him to disclose to another person during his employment is a trade secret which he can be prevented from using for his own advantage after the employment is over, even though he has entered into no express covenant with regard to the matter in hand. For example, the printing instructions were handed to [the first defendant] to be

used by him during his employment exclusively for the plaintiffs' benefit. It would have been a breach of duty on his part to divulge any of the contents to a stranger while he was employed, but many of these instructions are not really 'trade secrets' at all. [The first defendant] was not, indeed, entitled to take a copy of the instructions away with him; but insofar as the instructions cannot be called 'trade secrets' and he carried them in his head, he is entitled to use them for his own benefit or the benefit of any future employer.

The same distinction is to be found in E. *Worsley & Co. Ltd v Cooper* [1939] 1 All ER 290, where it was held that the defendant was entitled, after he had ceased to be employed, to make use of his knowledge of the source of the paper supplied to his previous employer. In our view it is quite plain that this knowledge was nevertheless 'confidential' in the sense that it would have been a breach of the duty of good faith for the employee, while the employment subsisted, to have used it for his own purposes or to have disclosed it to a competitor of his employer.

(5) In order to determine whether any particular item of information falls within the implied term so as to prevent its use or disclosure by an employee after his employment has ceased, it is necessary to consider all the circumstances of the case. We are satisfied that the following matters are among those to which attention must be paid. (a) The nature of the employment. Thus employment in a capacity where 'confidential' material is habitually handled may impose a high obligation of confidentiality because the employee can be expected to realise its sensitive nature to a greater extent than if he were employed in a capacity where such material reaches him only occasionally or incidentally. (b) The nature of the information itself. In our judgment the information will only be protected if it can properly be classed as a trade secret or as material which, while not properly to be described as a trade secret, is in all the circumstances of such a highly confidential nature as to require the same protection as a trade secret *eo nomine*. The restrictive covenant cases demonstrate that a covenant will not be upheld on the basis of the status of the information which might be disclosed by the former employee if he is not restrained unless it can be regarded as a trade secret or the equivalent of a trade secret: see for example *Herbert Morris Ltd v Saxelby* [1916] 1 AC 688 at 710, [1916–17] All ER Rep 305 at 317 per Lord Parker and *Littlewoods Organisation Ltd v Harris* [1978] 1 All ER 1026 at 1037, [1977] 1 WLR 1472 at 1484 per Megaw L.J.

We must therefore express our respectful disagreement with the passage in Goulding J.'s judgment where he suggested that an employer can protect the use of information in his second category, even though it does not include either a trade secret or its equivalent by means of a restrictive covenant (see [1985] 1 All ER 724 at 731). As Lord Parker made clear in *Herbert Morris Ltd v Saxelby* [1916] 1 AC 688 at 709, [1916–17] All ER Rep 305 at 317, in a passage to which counsel for Faccenda Chicken Ltd drew our attention, a restrictive covenant will not be enforced unless the protection sought is reasonably necessary to protect a trade secret or to prevent some personal influence over customers being abused in order to entice them away.

In our view the circumstances in which a restrictive covenant would be appropriate and could be successfully invoked emerge very clearly from the words used by Cross J. in *Printers and Finishers Ltd v Holloway* [1964] 3 All ER 731 at 736, [1965] 1 WLR 1 at 6 (in a passage quoted later in his judgment by Goulding J. (see [1985] 1 All ER 724 at 732–3):

> If [the managing director] is right in thinking that there are features in his process which can fairly be regarded as trade secrets and which his employees will inevitably carry away with them in their heads, then the proper way for the plaintiffs to protect themselves would be by exacting covenants from their employees restricting their

field of activity after they have left their employment, not by asking the court to extend the general equitable doctrine to prevent breaking confidence beyond all reasonable bounds.

It is clearly impossible to provide a list of matters which will qualify as trade secrets or their equivalent. Secret processes of manufacture provide obvious examples, but innumerable other pieces of information are *capable* of being trade secrets, though the secrecy of some information may be only short-lived. In addition, the fact that the circulation of certain information is restricted to a limited number of individuals may throw light on the status of the information and its degree of confidentiality. (c) Whether the employer impressed on the employee the confidentiality of the information. Thus, though an employer cannot prevent the use or disclosure *merely* by telling the employee that certain information is confidential, the attitude of the employer towards the information provides evidence which may assist in determining whether or not the information can properly be regarded as a trade secret. It is to be observed that in E. *Worsley & Co. Ltd v Cooper* [1939] 1 All ER 290 at 307 Morton J. attached significance to the fact that no warning had been given to the defendant that 'the source from which the paper came was to be treated as confidential'. (d) Whether the relevant information can be easily isolated from other information which the employee is free to use or disclose. In *Printers and Finishers Ltd v Holloway* [1964] 3 All ER 731 at 736, [1965] 1 WLR 1 at 6 Cross J. considered the protection which might be afforded the information which had been memorised by an ex-employee. He put on one side the memorising of a formula or a list of customers or what had been said (obviously in confidence) at a particular meeting, and continued:

> The employee might well not realise that the feature or expedient in question was in fact peculiar to his late employer's process and factory; but even if he did such knowledge is not readily separable from his general knowledge of the flock printing process and his acquired skill in manipulating a flock printing plant, and I do not think that any man of average intelligence and honesty would think that there was anything improper in his putting his memory of particular features of his late employer's plant at the disposal of his new employer.

For our part we would not regard the separability of the information in question as being conclusive, but the fact that the alleged 'confidential' information is part of a package and that the remainder of the package is not confidential is likely to throw light on whether the information in question is really a trade secret.

These then are the principles of law which we consider to be applicable to a case such as the present one. We would wish to leave open, however, for further examination on some other occasion the question whether additional protection should be afforded to an employer where the former employee is not seeking to earn his living by making use of the body of skill, knowledge and experience which he has acquired in the course of his career, but is merely selling to a third party information which he acquired in confidence in the course of his former employment.

We turn now to the facts of the instant case. It will be remembered that the case of Faccenda Chicken Ltd was that Mr Fowler and the other defendants were in breach of an implied term of their contracts of employment in using or disclosing the sales information that they had acquired while in the employment of Faccenda Chicken Ltd or, alternatively, that they were in breach of this implied term by using or disclosing their knowledge of the prices charged by Faccenda Chicken Ltd to individual customers. It will also be remembered that the sales information contained five elements: the names and addresses of customers; the most convenient routes to be taken to reach the individual customers; the usual requirements of individual customers; the days of the week and the times of day when deliveries were made to individual customers; and the prices charged to individual customers.

Counsel for Faccenda Chicken Ltd was prepared to concede that, if these pieces of information were looked at separately, some of them did not constitute confidential information at all. Thus he accepted that Mr Fowler and the other defendants were entitled to make use of any recollection they might have of the names and addresses of Faccenda Chicken Ltd customers as well as of the most convenient routes by which the premises of such customers could be reached. Moreover, we did not understand him to argue otherwise than rather faintly that Mr Fowler and the other defendants would have been in breach of contract if they had merely made use of their knowledge of the usual requirements of Faccenda Chicken Ltd customers or of the times when deliveries were made to them.

The central plank of the argument of counsel for Faccenda Chicken Ltd was that any information about the prices charged to individual Faccenda Chicken Ltd customers was confidential, and that, as this information about prices formed part of the package of sales information, the package taken as a whole was confidential too. It is therefore necessary to consider the information about prices more closely. It seems clear that, apart from the fact that the three main groups of customers, butchers, chains of shops and catering establishments, were charged slightly different prices, there were a number of individual variations inside these groups to take account, no doubt, of such matters as the size of the orders placed and the length of time that the traders concerned had been customers. It was this information, submitted counsel for Faccenda Chicken Ltd, which was confidential.

Counsel relied in particular on the following passage in the judgment of Goulding J. ([1985] 1 All ER 724 at 727): 'I find that an experienced salesman quickly acquires a good idea of the prices obtained by his employer's competitors, but usually such knowledge is only approximate; and in this field accurate information is valuable, because a difference of even a penny a pound may be important.' He also relied on the references to the confidentiality of prices in the three authorities which we have already mentioned.

We find ourselves unable to accept the submissions of counsel for Faccenda Chicken Ltd either as to the information about prices or as to the sales information as a whole. We can well appreciate that in certain circumstances information about prices can be invested with a sufficient degree of confidentiality to render that information a trade secret or its equivalent. The price put forward in a tender document is an obvious example. But there may be many other cases where the circumstances show that a price or prices are matters of great importance and highly confidential.

Information about the price to be charged for a new model of a car or some other product or about the prices negotiated, for example, for various grades of oil in a highly competitive market in which it is known that prices are to be kept secret from competitors occur to us as providing possible further instances of information which is entitled to protection as having the requisite degree of confidentiality.

But in the present case the following factors appear to us to lead to the clear conclusion that neither the information about prices nor the sales information as a whole had the degree of confidentiality necessary to support Faccenda Chicken Ltd's case. We would list these factors as follows: (1) the sales information contained some material which Faccenda Chicken Ltd conceded was not confidential if looked at in isolation; (2) the information about the prices was not clearly severable from the rest of the sales information; (3) neither the sales information in general, nor the information about the prices in particular, though of some value to a competitor, could reasonably be regarded as plainly secret or sensitive; (4) the sales information, includ-ing the information about prices, was necessarily acquired by the defendants in order that they could do their work. Moreover, as the judge observed in the course of his judgment, each salesman could quickly commit the whole of the sales information relating to his own area to memory; (5) the sales information was generally known among the van drivers who were employees, as were the secretaries, at quite junior level. This was not a case where the relevant information was restricted to senior management or to confidential staff; (6) there was no evidence that Faccenda Chicken Ltd had ever given any express instructions that the sales information or the inform-ation about prices was to be treated as confidential.

We are satisfied that, in the light of all the matters set out by the judge in his judgment, neither the sales information as a whole nor the information about prices looked at by itself fell within the class of confidential information which an employee is bound by an implied term of his contract of employment or otherwise not to use or disclose after his employment has come to an end.

Accordingly these appeals must be dismissed.

Notes

1. Where the evidence indicates that solicitation has actually occurred in breach of a non solicitation covenant an injunction is likely to issue because of the continuing losses to the plaintiff: *European Paint Importers v O'Callaghan* [2005] IEHC 280.

2. An employee who undertakes preparatory acts while still in employment (canvassing, taking lists of customers) will be held to have breached the implied duty to render faithful service to the employer: *Hivac v Park Royal etc. Instruments* [1946] Ch 169. However, a decision by an employee to compete with his/her current employer is not a breach of that duty, and unless the employee is also subject to a fiduciary duty, e.g. *Item Software (UK) v Fassihi* [2003] IRLR 769, preparatory work that does not exploit the property or information vested in the employer will not breach the implied common law obligation: *Helmet Integrated Systems Ltd v Tunnard* [2006] EWCA Civ 1735. Tunnard, a salesman, formulated a design for equipment that, if successful, would be a product that would compete with those of his employer. Tunnard was not employed as a designer, nor did he use his employer's resources. His preparatory acts could not be described as 'competitor activity' during his employment as a salesman.

Dawnay, Day & Co. *v* D'Alphen [1998] ICR 1068

Evans L.J. (Wasdaard, Nourse L.JJ. concurring.)

History
The following summary is taken, largely verbatim, from the admirable judgment of Robert Walker J. I would be glad to quote the whole of the relevant passages in extenso, but for present purposes it is unnecessary to do so. The managers each gave evidence at the hearing. The judge described them as 'intelligent, shrewd and ambitious individuals.' Their skills and experience lie in the European bond-broking business. Their success as employees of Euro Suisse led them to seek a business

partner with capital to invest, so that they could establish a new business of their own. They were hopeful that all or most of the personnel on the French and Belgian desks at Euro Suisse would decide to move en bloc with them. They were introduced to directors of Dawnay Day which specialised in joint ventures, especially in the area of financial services. Seven meetings took place in December 1991 and January 1992 where the proposed joint venture was discussed and negotiated in great detail. Dawnay Day took legal advice, and two managers, Mr Johnston and Mr D'Alphen had done so previously, in October 1991. Miss Parkman received informal advice from a solicitor before the negotiations were concluded, although initially in her affidavit evidence she said that she had not. The judge was satisfied that they were all in a position to obtain further independent advice, had they wished to do so.

The plaintiffs' evidence was that the terms of the restrictive covenants were gone through during the negotiations, and the judge accepted this. The managers said that they had no recollection of this being done. The judge said, ante p. 1087A:

> They did not however deny that those events occurred. Although it is sometimes credible for witnesses to forget discussions and negotiations (and even very important discussions and negotiations) after five years, I do find the managers' apparent amnesia very surprising and almost incredible. They had made a dramatic departure from Euro Suisse and there was a threat of legal action against them.

I would add, although without the benefit which the judge had of seeing the managers give evidence, that, if the discussion of these terms made little or no impression upon them, that can only have been because they did not contemplate that they would wish to leave or compete with the proposed new business, which they could not start. except as a joint venture with Dawnay Day which was providing the whole of the capital, at any time during the foreseeable future. If that is the correct explanation, then it casts some light on the nature of the joint venture upon which they embarked.

All parties recognised the fact that bond-broking of this sort is a team operation. Its success depends not only on skilled individuals but also upon establishing and maintaining the loyalty of a team, which means that leadership skills are also a premium. During the negotiations with Dawnay Day, the managers introduced the existing Euro Suisse teams to them, and in the event the French desk personnel did all come over. The Belgian desk did not, but it folded soon afterwards as a result of personnel moving elsewhere. The vital importance of team spirit and of leadership thus was graphically demonstrated.

Also important is the connection with clients. The judge said this:

> All the evidence supported the general proposition that the client connection is very important to an inter-dealer broker, and has a large influence on his success. The client is in this situation not a particular house (such as Morgan Stanley, Paris, J.P. Morgan, Paris or Salomon Brothers (London) but a particular individual (or small group of individuals) dealing in bonds of a particular type. No substantial house would deal exclusively through one single broker. The business is offered around, and ultimately each of the two principals (between whom the broker is an intermediary) is interested in competent and (in terms of rates of commission and discounts) economical service. Nevertheless, the personal relationship is important, and is generally understood by the market as being important.

The heads of agreement having been signed on 30 January 1992, both parties (meaning Dawnay Day and the managers) prepared for their parts in the joint venture scheme. The joint venture company was formed. Dawnay Day took 150 £1 shares through its subsidiary, Wilcourt Investments Ltd ('Wilcourt'), the second plaintiff, and the managers took 50 £1 shares each. This was the only financial investment the managers made. The plaintiffs provided capital of £350,000 for equipment and working capital and a further £300,000 to satisfy the capital adequacy requirements of the Securities and Futures Authority. These sums were secured in part by the issue of redeemable preference shares in Dawnay Securities and partly by subordinated loans. Premises were obtained (part of Dawnay Day's existing premises at 15, Grosvenor Gardens, London, (SW1), and the necessary equipment was installed. The managers gave one month's notice on 28 February 1992 to terminate their employment with Euro Suisse, and on 1 April 1992 they started working for the new business, though their service agreements with Dawnay Securities were not signed until June.

It was intended from the start that the business would expand into fresh areas or 'desks,' though always dealing with European bonds. The business prospered and the financial rewards for the managers were substantial. During the four-year period from 1992 to 1996 each of them received about £300,000 in salary and more than £600,000 in dividends which were net of tax credits (over £800,000 gross). The plaintiffs, through Wilcourt, have received the same dividends, although their total capital investment has proved to be about £1,165,000. As to the 1996 value of the business, there was evidence which suggested that this was in excess of £7m.

The three managers, although they have ceased to be employees of Dawnay Securities and have entered into agreements for their present or future employment by its competitor, Cantor, remain its directors and owners of one-half of the shares. The other three directors are nominees of Dawnay Day, and so currently the board is in deadlock. It is accepted by the defendants that in these circumstances Dawnay Day is entitled to bring proceedings in the name of Dawnay Securities under the service agreements, to which Dawnay Day itself is not a party.

(1) The principal issue is whether Dawnay Day is able to enforce the covenants against competition and solicitation of customers in clause 9.1 of the heads of agreement, which were expressed to continue for a one-year period from the termination of the manager's employment with Dawnay Securities. It is not suggested that the one-year period would be unreasonable or that the covenants could not be enforced, if the covenants were made with Dawnay Securities and if Dawnay Securities was claiming under them. The managers' submission is that Dawnay Day has no legitimate or lawful interest in enforcing the covenants in the circumstances of this case. Dawnay Day was, if it is submitted, no more than an investor in and a creditor of the business which is owned and carried on by Dawnay Securities.

Legitimate interest
Mr Elias submits on behalf of the managers that the only reported cases where anti-competition and anti-solicitation covenants have been enforced are those where the covenant was necessary to protect the interests of a business, meaning either its goodwill or specific confidential information which it owned, and where the plaintiff, i.e. the covenantee, was the owner of the business, as distinct from being merely an investor in it. Thus, he submits, where the business is owned by a company, a shareholder in the company cannot enforce such a covenant against its employees or ex-employees, however much it might be in his financial interest to do so. Nor can a person who has provided capital for or otherwise invested in the business do so, unless he has a proprietary interest in the business itself, as distinct from the rights of a creditor against its owner. Here the goodwill is owned by Dawnay Securities, which was not a party to the heads of agreement, and Dawnay Day has no interest of a kind which has been recognised by the courts.

Mr Grabiner makes what are essentially two submissions for the plaintiffs. First, he submits, the correct approach is for the court to consider the substance and not merely the form of these transactions. So regarded, Dawnay Day as the managers' joint venturer (I avoid the term 'partner,' for reasons which will appear below), under the heads of agreement between them dated 30 January 1992, does have a clear commercial interest which should be recognised and regarded as legitimate, even if it is not identical with any that has been recognised in any of the reported cases. Secondly, again having regard to the substance of the matter, Dawnay Day does have a recognisable interest in the goodwill of the joint venture business, notwithstanding that the chosen vehicle for developing and owning the business was a jointly-owned limited company, and therefore an independent legal person.

The judge held that Dawnay Day does have a legitimate interest, which enables it to enforce the covenants. He reached his conclusion partly by reference to the concept of partnership. He said, ante pp. 1092H–1093C:

> Had the business of Dawnay Securities been owned by the joint venturers as partners in the full sense, each partner would plainly have had a legitimate interest in restraining competition by an outgoing partner (once the business had become established with its own goodwill, as the venturers reasonably expected). . . . In this case Dawnay Day and the managers decided to proceed through the medium of a company incorporated with the privilege of limited liability . . .

This reference is criticised by Mr Elias because the heads of agreement provide expressly by clause 12(c): 'Nothing in this agreement shall constitute a partnership between any of the parties.' Therefore, he submits, the partnership analogy proves nothing. This was not a partnership, and nothing is gained by supposing that it was.

In my judgment, clause 12(c) is relevant in the present context only because it prevents the importation of any terms, statutory or otherwise, which might be implied or incorporated if the venture was held to be a partnership in law. No such term, however, is relied on. Without any such implication, the court has to consider the legal consequences of what was created in fact. That was a joint venture business to be carried on by a jointly-owned limited company. In deciding what the legal consequences were, it may or may not be possible to derive some assistance from the partnership analogy, if and to the extent that the analogy exists. But the fact that the arrangement was expressly declared not to be a partnership has no greater relevance than the negative factor referred to above.

So the question can be reformulated thus: Does a joint venturer (who is not a partner) have a sufficient interest to be permitted to enforce anti-competition and anti-solicitation covenants against his fellow joint venturer, when the business is to be developed and carried on by a jointly-owned company? There is no doubt as to the basic common law rule. This was stated by Sir Christopher Slade, giving the leading judgment of the Court of Appeal in *Office Angels Ltd v Rainer-Thomas* [1991] IRLR 214, 217:

(1) If the court is to uphold the validity of any covenant in restraint of trade, the covenantee must show that the covenant is both reasonable in the interests of the contracting parties and reasonable in the interests of the public: see for example *Herbert Morris Ltd v Saxelby* [1916] AC 688, 707 per Lord Parker of Waddington.

(2) A distinction is, however, to be drawn between (a) a covenant against competition entered into by a vendor with the purchaser of the goodwill of a business, which will be upheld as necessary to protect the subject matter of

the sale, provided that it is confined to the area within which competition on the part of the vendor would be likely to injure the purchaser in the enjoyment of the goodwill he has bought, and (b) a covenant between master and servant designed to prevent competition by the servant with the master after the termination of his contract of service: (see for example *Kores Manufacturing Co. Ltd v Kolok Manufacturing Ltd* [1959] Ch. 109, 118 per Jenkins L.J.).

In a later paragraph, he said, at p. 217:

> As Lord Parker stressed in *Herbert Morris Ltd v Saxelby*, at p. 7078, for any covenant in restraint of trade to be treated as reasonable in the interests of the parties, 'it must afford *no more than* adequate protection to the benefit of the party in whose favour it is imposed.' (Lord Parker's emphasis.)

The first question is whether as a matter of law such covenants can never be upheld outside the established categories of vendor/purchaser (of a business) and master/servant cases. I am sure that this is not the law, nor does Mr Elias contend otherwise. The House of Lords so held in *Esso Petroleum Co. Ltd v Harper's Garage (Stourport) Ltd* [1968] AC 269, and the speeches are replete with references to the need to state and apply the principles broadly. For example, Lord Wilberforce, at p. 331:

> The common law has often (if sometimes unconsciously) thrived on ambiguity and it would be mistaken, even if it were possible, to try to crystallise the rules of this, or any, aspect of public policy into neat propositions. The doctrine of restraint of trade is one to be applied to factual situations with a broad and flexible rule of reason.

Moreover, there are recent authorities which have underlined the need for such an approach. In *Stenhouse Australia Ltd v Phillips* [1974] AC 391, an employment case, the need for the covenantee to show that the restraining covenant was necessary for the protection of some legitimate interest of his own was stated thus, in the judgment of the Privy Council delivered by Lord Wilberforce, at p. 400:

> Leaving aside the cause of misuse of trade secrets or confidential information . . . the employer's claim for protection must be based upon the identification of some advantage or asset inherent in the business which can properly be regarded as, in a general sense, his property, and which it would be unjust to allow the employee to appropriate for his own purposes, even though he, the employee, may have contributed to its creation.

In that case, the business of insurance broking was carried on by the plaintiff company through its subsidiaries. It was submitted that the plaintiff had no separate interest of its own. The submission failed, at p. 404:

> The subsidiary companies were merely agencies or instrumentalities through which the appellant company directed its integrated business. Not only did the appellant company have a real interest in protecting the businesses of the subsidiaries, but the real interest of so doing was that of the appellant company.

That clearly was different from the relationship between Dawnay Day and Dawnay Securities, which is not a subsidiary, though it bears what might be regarded as a 'group' name, in the present case.

In two more recent cases, the covenants formed part of a transaction which involved both the sale of a business and the relationship of employer and employee. This occurs, for example, when the purchaser of the business retains the services of the vendor after the business has changed hands. In both cases it was submitted that the court should decide into which of the two categories the transaction and therefore the covenant should be placed, so as to know whether the more stringent test of reasonableness which is appropriate in employer/employee cases should be applied. Both Millett J. in *Allied Dunbar (Frank Weisinger) Ltd v Weisinger* [1988] IRLR 60 and Harman J. in *Systems Reliability Holdings plc v Smith* [1990] IRLR 377 held that it was wrong and unnecessary to categorise the cases strictly in this way. The question is one of substance, not of form (per Millet J. at p. 64), and the court has always 'to try and apply the test of reasonableness to the facts and circumstances of the particular case' (per Herman J. at p. 382). These judgments were followed by Robert Walker J. in the present case, and in my judgment he was right to do so.

The same approach was adopted by the Court of Appeal in *Office Angels Ltd v Rainer-Thomas* [1991] IRLR 214. The plaintiffs had employed the defendants in their employment agency. They maintained a pool of temporary workers which enabled them to supply their clients with temporary rather than permanent employees, when that was required. It was argued that their connection with the temporary workers was not a legitimate interest which they were entitled to protect at law. The argument was rejected by Sir Christopher Slade, at p. 219:

> In principle, I can see no reason why the plaintiff's trade connection with its pool of temporary workers should not in law be capable of protection by a restriction no greater than is reasonably necessary for such purpose.

In my judgment, far from confining the circumstances in which covenants in restraint of trade may be enforced to certain categories of case, and defining those categories strictly, the courts have moved in the opposite direction. The established categories are not rigid, and they are not exclusive. Rather, the covenant may be enforced when the covenantee has a legitimate interest, of whatever kind, to protect, and when the covenant is no wider than is necessary to protect that interest.

When the heads of agreement were entered into, the joint venture company was not yet formed. Each party depended on the other's proposed contribution for the development of the business which they set out jointly to create. Dawnay Day's undertaking to make the capital contribution, and certainly the contribution after it was made, gave Dawnay Day, a clear commercial interest in safeguarding itself against competition from the managers, individually or collectively, for the agreed periods set out in clause 9. The fact that the interest was 'commercial' does not mean that it was not lawful. In my judgment, the judge was correct to describe it as an interest 'of a proprietary nature' which falls within the established principle that 'a proprietary or quasi-proprietary interest' is entitled to protection, where and to the extent that protection is reasonably necessary: see *Chitty on Contracts*, 27th ed. (1994), vol. I, para. 16–75, p. 820. I would also be prepared to say more generally that Dawnay Day had a clear commercial interest in the success of the joint venture, by reason of its contribution to it, and that, whether or not the interest can be classified as proprietary or quasi-proprietary, Dawnay Day is entitled to claim protection for that interest in the form of the covenants which it now seeks to enforce. That further issue, however, does not arise for decision in the present case.

Note

The decision in *Wadlow v Samuel (p.k.a. Seal)* [2006] EWHC 1492(QB) is to similar effect. The artist known as Seal sought to invoke the restraint of trade doctrine to set aside a publishing and management contract, a publishing agreement, and a subsequent dispute settlement agreement. Even though the effect of these contracts was to require Seal to continue to pay his former manager royalties based upon sales of pre-termination recordings, without a sliding scale or 'sunset' clause, Gray J. felt that a contract which simply requires the payment of money is not an appropriate area for the restraint of trade doctrine to enter, and the fact that the agreement made it more difficult for Seal to employ a new manager (because of reduced profitability) did not constitute a restraint of trade.

Panayiotou and Others *v* Sony Music Entertainment (UK) Ltd TLR, 30 June 1994

Parker J. said that George Michael was claiming against the Sony Group that the agreement in 1988 for the delivery of eight albums of records over a period of time was void and unenforceable because it was an unreasonable restraint of trade and was in any event rendered void by article 85(2) of the EEC Treaty, directed at maintaining freedom of competition within the common market. Parker J. continued.

Restraint of trade

On the restraint of trade issue it had to be borne in mind that the 1988 agreement was a renegotiation of an agreement made in 1984; that by 1988 George Michael was already an established artist and that the essence of the renegotiation was a substantial improvement in the financial terms in exchange for additional albums.

In any event, his Lordship concluded that it was not open to the plaintiff to challenge the 1988 agreement on the ground of restraint of trade because:

1 There was a public interest in enforcing agreements reached by way of compromise of disputes. The 1984 agreement was such a compromise and as the 1988 agreement was a renegotiation of the 1984 agreement, the same applied.

2 It would be unjust to Sony if the 1988 agreement were treated as unenforceable or void because: (i) George Michael at all times had expert legal advice from Russels and was well aware of the doctrine of restraint of trade; (ii) Sony had agreed to bring forward dates of various payments for tax reasons; (iii) There was a further renegotiation in 1990 improving the plaintiff's terms; (iv) George Michael made a request for payment in advance in 1992 for a third album.

3 By requesting the advance for the third album when he knew it was open to him to challenge the 1988 agreement on the ground of restraint of trade, George Michael affirmed the 1988 agreement and he could not now resile from that affirmation.

Article 85

On the article 85 issue, it was necessary to consider the general European approach to the rules on competition. The need was for a broad and flexible approach, paying attention to substance rather than form (*Nungesser v Commission* (Case 2588/78) ([1982] ECR 2015)) and considering an agreement in its legal, economic and commercial context rather than applying a set of *a priori* principles.

That broad approach generally meant the need for a detailed investigation and analysis of the surrounding facts as the basis for a consideration of whether the agreement in question contravened the competition rules.

It should be said, however, that certain factors, the so-called rule of reason, the *de minimis* rule, and intellectual property rights, limited to some degree the scope for the application of article 85.

A further point was that where an agreement was said to contravene the competition rules, the particular aspect of competition said to be affected had to be identified: *Italian Flat Glass* (Cases T–68/69 and T–77/78/89) (1992) 5 CMLR 302, 342).

Also, the effect of an agreement for the purposes of article 85 had to be judged by reference to the competition which would occur in its absence: *Petrofina SA v Commission* (Case T–2/89)([1991] 2 ECR 1087).

As to the application to those rules to the 1988 agreement, it was said for George Michael, *inter alia*:

1 The effect of the agreement on trade between member states was that it prevented him from producing recordings in the field of pop music for other record companies in other member states;

2 It had the requisite effect on the end-product market in that it affected the flow of trade in records of his work since trade in his records was undertaken by Sony and not by some other record company;

3 Those actual or potential effects were appreciable, not *de minimis*, given the status and size of Sony and the fact that George Michael was a highly successful recording artist whose records had achieved substantial sales;

4 It was a fact that the 1988 agreement formed part of a network of similar agreements, that is, agreements between other recording artists and other artists.

It was an essential feature of George Michael's case that the market should be a Community wide market and not merely a national or domestic market since a national or domestic market would not attract article 85: *Hugin Kassaregister AB v Commission* (Case 22/78) ([1979] ECR 1869); yet, on the restraint of trade issue, it was said that there was a lack of evidence to indicate that UK recording artists signed with non-UK record companies, let alone with record companies from member states.

Indeed, the evidence before his Lordship was to the effect that the market for the services of UK recording artists in the pop field was a purely national and domestic market limited territorially to the UK.

It was unfortunate that the article 85 issue was not specifically addressed in evidence.

On the evidence before his Lordship however, he could only conclude that there was no Community wide market for the services of UK recording artists in the field of popular music since it was only in exceptional cases that UK recording artists signed to a non-UK record company.

Thus, so far as George Michael was concerned, in 1982 and again in 1984, the relevant market for his services was the UK market, consisting of UK record companies.

It followed that for the purposes of article 85(1), the 1988 agreement did not affect trade between member states at the raw material end of the chain of supply, that is, the market for George Michael's recording services.

The result therefore was that both George Michael's claims would be dismissed.

B. Competition Authority Decisions

Competition Authority; Employment Agreements and The Competition Act, Iris Oifigiuil 18 September 1992, 632–3

The Competition Authority has received numerous requests regarding the position of employment contracts or agreements between employers and employees under the Competition Act. Since this indicates that many employment contracts may include non-competition clauses, the Authority considers that it would be useful to give some indication of its views regarding such agreements. The Authority points out that the interpretation of the provisions of the Competition Act is ultimately a matter for the courts.

The prohibition in s. 4 (1) of the Competition Act relates to agreements between undertakings, decisions of associations of undertakings and concerted practices. Clearly most employers are undertakings. The Authority does not consider, however, that employees as such are undertakings within the meaning of the Act. Employees normally act on behalf of an undertaking and do not, therefore, constitute an undertaking themselves. This view is in accord with that expressed by the European Court of Justice in the *Suiker Unie* case, which involved article 85 (1) of the Treaty of Rome, upon which s. 4 (1) is based. The court indicated that employees should be regarded as an integral part of the undertaking which empowered them and were not therefore undertakings themselves. The view that employees are not undertakings was endorsed in a written answer to the European Parliament by the European Commission in relation to professional soccer players which stated that: 'individuals participating in professional sports normally do so as employees of a club on the basis of an employment contract and as such are not undertakings.'[1]

Although there is a difference between Irish and EC legislation, in that the Irish Act defines an undertaking as being engaged for gain, the Authority believes that employees as such should not be regarded as undertakings under s. 4 on the basis of the reasoning advanced by the Court of Justice in the *Suiker Unie* case.

As it does not consider that employees are undertakings, the Authority believes that an agreement between an employer and an employee is not an agreement between undertakings and is not therefore within the scope of s. 4 (1). It follows also that an employment agreement as such is not notifiable to the Authority, as ss 7 (1) and (2) of the Act only provide for the notification of agreements of a kind described in s. 4 (1).

The position changes, however, once an employee leaves an employer and seeks to set up his or her own business. They would then be regarded as an undertaking. This view is in accord with EC treatment of such cases. As Van Bael and Bellis point out: 'Employees are normally acting on behalf of an undertaking and therefore do not constitute an undertaking themselves. However, from the moment an employee pursues his own economic interests, and where they are different from his employer's interests, he might well become an undertaking within the sense of article 85.'[2]

At this stage the Authority would regard the agreement as an agreement between undertakings which could then be notified. If the former employer were to seek to enforce a non-competition clause in an employment contract in respect of an employee who had left and was seeking to establish his or her own business, the Authority believes that this would represent a restriction of competition within the meaning of s. 4 (1). While such an agreement between one individual and an employer may not have a substantial impact on competition, the existence of such agreements in many sectors of the economy means that their combined effect would be to greatly restrict competition. The Authority therefore believes that it would be difficult for such an agreement to satisfy the requirements specified for the grant of a licence in s. 4 (2) of the Act.

Should an employee in addition own or control the undertaking, the view of the Authority, expressed in several decisions, is that the individual can then be regarded as an undertaking.[3]

[1.] Written question no. 2391/83, OJ 1984 C222/21, 23 August 1984.

2. I. Van Bael and J. F. Bellis, *Competition Law of the* EEC, (2nd ed.), CCH Editions Ltd, 1990, point 206.
3. Notification nos CA/9/91 *Nallen/O'Toole* (*Belmullet*), decision of 2 April 1992, CA/9/91 ACT/*Kindle*, decision of 4 September 1992 and CA/1/92 *Budget Travel/Phil Fortune*, decision of 14 September 1992.

Note

It must be remembered that it is the function of the courts to interpret the provisions of the Competition Acts, and thus, the notices and decisions of the authority are subject to review by the courts. After the 2002 Amendments the decisions of the Authority no longer bind the parties and direct recourse to the ordinary courts is the anticipated means of resolving issues of Irish Competition Law. See Lucey (2003) 25 DULJ 124.

C. Employee or Undertaking?

Competition Authority Decision No. 9 Budget Travel/Phil Fortune (CA/ 1/92) 14 September 1992

An agreement for the sale by Budget Travel Ltd of their shares in Budget Travel Schools Abroad Ltd (hereinafter referred to as BTSA) to Phil Fortune, a former employee of BTSA, was notified to the Competition Authority on 17 January 1992 for the purposes of obtaining a licence under s. 4 (2) of the Competition Act 1991.

. . .

The agreement for the sale and purchase of BTSA was made on 7 November 1991. Under the agreement, Budget Travel Ltd agreed to sell BTSA to Phil Fortune and to accept a number of restrictions on their future activity in the market for group tours. Specifically, Budget Travel Ltd gave undertakings in clause 13(b) of the agreement not to:

  (i) For a period of two years from completion be directly or indirectly interested or concerned in or assist in carrying on any business, undertaking, company or firm actively marketing, promoting, or selling, tours or holidays catering for school or academic institutions, *provided always* that nothing in this clause shall prevent the vendor from accepting group bookings from school and other academic institutions for holidays the nature of which the vendor presently promotes, or
  (ii) For a period of *four years* from completion either on their own or each of their own account or on behalf of any person, firm or company solicit the employment of or enter into partnership with or appoint as consultant any person who is at completion or who has within the six months prior to completion [been] an officer or employee of the company or,
  (iii) At *any time* hereafter make use of or disclose or divulge to any third party any *information* of a secret or *confidential* nature relating to the business of the company.

. . .

Assessment

(b) *The undertakings and the agreement*

19. The Authority is concerned with an agreement between Phil Fortune and Budget Travel Ltd. S. 3(1) of the Competition Act defines an undertaking as 'a person being an individual, a body corporate or an unincorporated body of persons engaged for gain in the production, supply or distribution of goods or the provision of a service'.

20. Budget Travel Ltd is a subsidiary of the UK publicly quoted Granada group. It acts as a tour operator on the Irish market and is clearly an undertaking within the meaning of s. 3 of the Act. Prior to this agreement Budget Travel Ltd was the owner of BTSA.

21. Phil Fortune, a former employee of BTSA, has bought the company from Budget Travel Ltd. S. 3 of the Act explicitly states that individuals may come within the definition of undertakings if they are 'engaged for gain in the production, supply or distribution of goods or the provision of a service'.

22. The Competition Authority has decided in previous cases that individuals who either own or control a business are undertakings for the purposes of the Act[1] provided they are engaged for gain in the production, supply and distribution of goods and services through the firms which they control.

23. In this respect the Authority has followed the approach taken by the European Commission which has ruled in a number of cases under article 85(1) of the Treaty of Rome, on which s. 4(1) of the Act is based, that individuals can be undertakings in certain circumstances. In the *Nutricia* case the Commission decided, and the European Court of Justice agreed, that individuals were undertakings by virtue of their being the future proprietors of a business.[2] This ruling is of particular relevance to the present agreement as Phil Fortune became the owner of BTSA under the agreement.

24. For the reasons detailed above, Budget Travel Ltd and Phil Fortune are considered to be undertakings within the meaning of s. 4(1) of the Act. The present arrangements constitute an agreement between undertakings which applies within the State as both parties to the agreement operate within the State.

. . .

The Authority has given its views on non-competition clauses in *Nallen/O'Toole* and a number of other decisions. In these cases the Authority took the view that some restraint on the business activities of the vendors may be necessary to ensure the adequate transfer of the goodwill of the business concerned. The Authority decided that the restraint must be limited in terms of its scope, duration and geographical coverage to that which is necessary to fully secure that transfer of the goodwill. Provided this is the case, then such a restraint does not restrict competition in the market in question. In this respect the Authority has followed the views of the EC Commission in respect of similar agreements under article 85(1) which have been endorsed by the European Court of Justice.

29. The Authority accepts that in the present case some restriction on Budget Travel competing in the relevant market is necessary to secure the complete transfer of the goodwill of BTSA. The issue therefore is whether the restrictions in the notified agreement are limited to what is necessary to secure the transfer of the goodwill.

Clause 13(b)(i)

30. In clause 13(b)(i), Budget Travel Ltd have undertaken not to become involved in the relevant market for a period of two years. The Authority has indicated in previous decisions that it would normally regard a time limit of two years as being adequate for the transfer of goodwill. This clause, does not, therefore, offend against s. 4(1) of the Act by virtue of its duration.

31. On the question of the geographical scope of the non-competition clause in 13 (b) (i), no specific geographical area to which it applies is specified.

32. The European Commission ruled in the *Nutricia* case that: 'The geographical scope of a non-competition clause also has to be limited to the extent which is objectively necessary to achieve the aforementioned goal. As a rule, it should therefore only cover the markets where the products concerned were manufactured or sold at the time of the agreements.'

33. The Authority took a similar view in the *Nallen/O'Toole* and ACT/*Kindle* cases. In the latter case, no specific geographical area was mentioned in the restrictive clauses. This was found to be acceptable by the Authority given that, prior to the agreement, Kindle was operating on a worldwide basis.

34. It has been argued that Budget could compete directly with BTSA by establishing a company either in Northern Ireland or England and retaining sales persons on a commission or other basis. Accordingly, the application of the non-competition clause in 13(b)(i) was not limited to the Irish market. The Authority accepts the validity of this argument and does not consider that this restriction offends against s. 4(1) of the Act.

35. In relation to the scope of the clause, Budget Travel Ltd are required not to compete in the market for group tours which is the market in which BTSA was involved at the time of the agreement. Therefore, the scope of the restriction does not restrain the vendors from being active in any market outside of the one served by BTSA. It is evident that the scope of the restriction does not go beyond what is necessary for the transfer of the goodwill and does not offend against s. 4(1) of the Act.

Clause 13(*b*)(*ii*)

36. This clause prevents Budget Travel Ltd from soliciting into employment, entering into partnership with or appointing as consultants employees of BTSA for a period of four years.

37. The justification advanced for the restriction was that it was essential for BTSA to 'retain its qualified and trained staff, who constituted one of its principal assets', and that it was 'essential to the preservation of the transferred worth of the undertaking'.

38. There is little doubt that BTSA employees who have worked in this area over a number of years have become familiar with the various facets of the business and will be efficient in dealing with them. However, this knowledge does not constitute technical know-how as defined by the Authority in ACT/*Kindle*. Accordingly, it is the Authority's view that the expertise of the employees of BTSA represents primarily part of the goodwill of the company.

39. In principle, there is nothing wrong with preventing the vendors from soliciting the services of BTSA employees for a period of time. Such a restriction ensures that the goodwill of the company being purchased is transferred.[3] In this case, however, the original clause may have gone beyond what was required to secure the transfer of the goodwill of BTSA because of its duration. Phil Fortune has agreed to accept a lesser period of three years. The Authority believes that, given the fact that personal contacts are quite important in this business, Ms Fortune, despite her background in the business, will need some time to establish a reputation for the newly managed entity,

and that the restriction on Budget Travel competing in the group tour market is for only two years, the three years duration now proposed for this clause is acceptable and does not offend against s. 4(1).

Clause 13(b)(iii)

40. This clause prevents Budget Travel Ltd from using, disclosing or divulging information of a secret or confidential nature about BTSA. The restriction is not limited in terms of its duration.

41. In advancing a case to support this clause a distinction was made by Phil Fortune between business information in the public domain and other business information such as profits, margins, turnover, overheads and other financial matters not in the public domain. The intention is to prevent the disclosure and use of the latter type of information. Phil Fortune's main argument in relation to this clause was that it was essential to 'transfer the entire worth of the company'.

42. Confidential business information may constitute an important part of the value of the transferred undertaking. The use of such information may confer a competitive advantage on the vendor. Nonetheless, the value of the type of confidential business information referred to in this case will be eroded over time. Eventually, it will be worthless and restrictions on its disclosure or use will become meaningless.

43. The Authority is concerned, however, that such a clause should not be used to impede any possible re-entry into the market by Budget once the two year non-competition clause in 13(b)(i) has expired. In particular, the Authority would be concerned that the effect of this could be to prevent Budget using its knowledge of the market for group tours if they decided to engage in that market in the future. The Authority accepts Phil Fortune's undertaking not to 'use or attempt to use this clause in any manner which would prevent the vendor re-entering the market after the period provided by clause (b)(i) has expired'. In the light of this undertaking the Authority considers that this clause does not offend against s. 4(1) of the Act.

[1.] Notification Nos CA/8/91—*Nallen/O'Toole* (Belmullet), decision of 2 April 1992 and CA/9/91—*ACT/Kindle*, decision of 4 September 1992.
[2.] *Nutricia/De Rooij* and *Nutricia/Zuid Hollandse Conservenfabriek* (83/670/EEC, OJ L 376, 31 December 1983, p. 22), on appeal *Remia BV and Others v European Commission*, Case 42/84, [1985] ECR 2545.
[3.] The Authority took a similar view in *Woodchester Bank/UDT Bank*.

Note

In Competition Authority decision No. 24, *Cambridge/Imari* (CA/8/92E), 21 June 1993 an individual was regarded as an 'undertaking' by virtue of the fact that he was a part owner and managing director of a company, exercising 'considerable *de facto* control over the business'. The Authority noted that he was thus 'engaged for gain in the provision of services'.

Competition Authority Decision No. 13 Peter Mark/Majella Stapleton (CA/1011/92E) 18 February 1993

This decision concerns a contract of employment between Peter Mark and Ms Majella Stapleton, who is now a former employee of Peter Mark. The arrangements were notified to the Competition Authority on 30 September 1992 under s. 7 of Competition Act 1991 for the purpose of obtaining a certificate under s. 4(4) or, in the event of a refusal by the Authority to issue a certificate, a licence under s. 4(2).

...

Assessment
The agreement

The contract of employment between Peter Mark and their former employee, Majella Stapleton, was made on 16 July 1990 on commencement of her employment with Peter Mark. The relevant clauses in the notified agreement in these proceedings are clauses 4, 5 and 6 which provide as follows:

Clause 4: The employee upon ceasing employment with the employer shall not take up employment with any competitor of the employer nor commence business in competition with the employer within a radius of one mile of Peter Mark, Wine Street, Sligo for the term of six months from the date that such employment ceases.

Clause 5: As and from the termination of the employment the employee shall not canvas, circularise or solicit business from the employer's customers using the name Peter Mark.

Clause 6: In the event that the restraint provisions in this contract are modified by any court, then such provisions as are considered reasonable by such court shall apply in lieu of the foregoing provisions.

...

Peter Mark

16. Peter Mark, an unlimited company and subsidiary of Glenberg, is a body corporate engaged in the provision of hairdressing and hairstyling services for gain and is therefore an undertaking within the meaning of the Act.

Majella Stapleton

17. The Competition Authority in its Notice on Employee Agreements and the Competition Act outlined its views on the employee as an undertaking and on agreements between employers and employees.

18. In its decision in the *Aga Khan* case[2] the Authority indicated that it: 'had also taken the view that the provisions of ss 4(1), 4(4), 7(1) and 7(2) taken together, imply that an agreement may be notified, and a certificate requested, where the parties are in some doubt as to whether that agreement would offend against s. 4(1), but not otherwise. In the Authority's view, there must be reasonable grounds for such doubts.'

19. In the Notice on Employee Agreements it was further indicated by the Authority that once an employee leaves an employer and seeks to set up his or her own business they would then be regarded as an undertaking. The Authority, however, did not

deal directly with the question of an employee taking up employment with another employer in the notice. It was also noted that Van Bael & Bellis, had, in the context of Article 85, stated: 'However, from the moment an employee pursues his own economic interests, and where they are different from his employer's interests, he might well become an undertaking within the sense of Article 85.'[3]

20. Ms Stapleton's solicitors have claimed that she is an undertaking within the meaning of the Competition Act because she profits from an increase in the business of her employer through the payment of a commission. For these reasons the Authority believes that there was reasonable doubt in this instance, and it has considered the notified agreement in the context of the Competition Act 1991.

21. Majella Stapleton was employed by Peter Mark from July 1990 to September 1992 as a stylist. She left Peter Mark to take up employment in a competing hairdressing salon. Her position with Peter Mark was solely that of an employee. Her position with her new employer is also solely that of an employee. She had or has no ownership or control in her previous or present employment. The fact that Ms Stapleton is paid partly on a commission basis and, as a result, benefits directly from any increase in business, is not sufficient to establish, in the Authority's view, that she is an undertaking by virtue of pursuing her own economic interests. Accordingly, in the Authority's view she was not and is not an undertaking under s. 3(1) of the Competition Act 1991.

22. The position would of course be wholly different if Ms Stapleton were seeking to set up her own business. As the notified agreement is, therefore, not an agreement between undertakings the arguments submitted by Ms Stapleton's solicitor in support of a certificate or a licence in relation to clauses 4, 5 and 6 need not be considered by the Authority.

The decision

23. This decision applies solely to the contract of employment between Peter Mark and Ms Majella Stapleton, dated 16 July 1990. In the opinion of the Authority, that contract does not constitute an 'agreement between undertakings' for the purposes of the Competition Act 1991 because one of the contracting parties, Ms Stapleton, was not at any material time an 'undertaking' within the meaning of the Act. Accordingly, the agreement, not being 'of a kind described in s. 4(1)', falls outside the scope of s. 7 of the Act and the Authority refuses to grant a certificate or a licence under the Act.

[1] Written question No. 2391/83, OJ 1984 C222/21, 23 August 1984.
[2] Notification Nos CA/673/92E—*Thoroughbred Promotion and Development Co. Ltd/Grenfell Ltd* and CA/674/92E—*Bertram and Diana Firestone/His Highness Karim Aga Khan*.
[3] I. Van Bael and J. F. Bellis, *Competition Law of the EEC*, (2nd ed.), CCH Editions Ltd, 1990, point 206.

Helsby v Oliver [1999] INZLR 77

Cartwright J.:

The appellant seeks to overturn the judgment given in the District Court in proceedings in which she unsuccessfully claimed the breach of a contract between the parties.

The facts

By an agreement for sale and purchase dated 26 April 1995, the respondents agreed to sell a hairdressing salon in Takapuna to the appellant. The first respondent had owned and operated the business for eighteen years. The second respondent was her business partner. The appellant paid $30,000 for the business, of which $4,757 was for assets and $25,243 for goodwill.

The sale and purchase agreement was on the New Zealand Law Society standard form which contains a standard vendor's restraint of trade clause in the following terms:

> In consideration of the purchase price the vendor hereby agrees with the purchaser that the vendor will not during the vendor's restraint of trade period either directly or indirectly carry on or be interested either alone or in partnership with or as manager, agent, director, shareholder or employee of any other person in any business similar to that hereby sold within [a 5 km] radius from the premises.

The restraint of trade period was for three years from the possession date, 15 May 1995.

The sale and purchase agreement was conditional upon the landlords of the salon premises signing a deed of assignment of lease. This condition was fulfilled before settlement on 15 May 1995. The deed that was executed also contained a covenant in restraint of trade which was in the following terms:

> The Assignor hereby covenants with the Assignee that the Assignor will not, without the prior written consent of the Assignee, either alone or jointly with or as director, manager, agent or servant of any other person directly or indirectly carry on or be concerned in or interested in any business similar to that heretofore carried on by the assignor on the premises for a period of three years from 15 May 1995 within a radius of five kilometres from the premises, nor shall the Assignor permit [her] name to be used in carrying on or in connection with any business within the said period and radius, nor supply or solicit any of the existing customers of the said business.

The events leading to the appellant bringing the proceedings in the District Court are these. Following settlement of the sale of the business the first respondent continued to work at the salon in Takapuna for approximately eight months as an employee of the appellant. After she left, she went to work at a salon in Ponsonby situated more than 5 km from the appellant's salon in Takapuna. A large number of persons who had been clients of the first respondent stopped going to the salon in Takapuna and began having their hair done by the first respondent in Ponsonby. The 'supply' of these customers was admitted by the first respondent. The appellant claimed that the actions of the first respondent breached the covenant in restraint of trade contained in the deed, and that this caused loss to her business in Takapuna. By s. 67 of the Property Law Act 1952 the second respondent is jointly liable for the breach of the covenant.

The Judge in the District Court found for the respondents. The appellant appeals that decision.

Is the restraint of trade clause in the deed reasonable?

To be enforceable a covenant in restraint of trade must be shown to be reasonable both in the interests of the parties and in the public interest. The onus of justifying a covenant in restraint of trade as reasonable rests with the covenantee, in this case the appellant.

The law has developed guidelines where the circumstances involve the sale of a business, including goodwill. A covenant intended to protect the goodwill of a purchased business will be regarded more favourably than a covenant limiting the freedom of a former employee after the contract of service has ended (*Brown v Brown* [1980] 1 NZLR 484 (CA); *Bridge v Deacons* (A Firm) [1984] AC 705 (PC)). In general, the higher the price that is attributable to goodwill, the slower the court will be to release the covenantor from his or her side of the bargain (*Brown v Brown*).

There is however a difficulty in the present instance. The clause in question was included in a deed. At the time the deed was signed, the price for the business, including the goodwill, had already been agreed to. The respondents signed the document and they agree they are bound by it. The law states however, that in cases such as this, the inclusion of a restraint of trade clause is justified, or made reasonable, because it aims to protect goodwill for which the purchaser has paid (*Bridge v Deacons*). In this sense, the courts have viewed goodwill payments as a 'purchase' of a covenant in restraint of trade (see, for example, *Brown v Brown*). From the cases, it seems that the 'price' paid for the covenant is the most significant factor in the assessment of reasonableness—the higher the price paid for the covenant, the wider the covenant will be permitted to be. In this case no payment whatsoever was made as a result of making the deed. Obviously this does not mean that the deed was invalid; consideration is not an essential element of a deed. But does it mean that, at least on this ground, there is now no justification for the covenant in the deed restraining the respondent from trading.

The present case does not fit exactly into the category in which a person sells a business and, in return for the goodwill payment, accepts a limitation on his or her right to compete. The amount paid for goodwill in this case cannot therefore be the predominant justification for the clause. Nor do the facts fit the category in which restrictions are imposed by contract on former employees.

The Privy Council in *Bridge v Deacons* considered the approach to be taken in a case such as the present, where the facts are not able to be placed in a particular category. *Deacons* concerned the enforcement of a covenant in restraint of trade against a former partner of a law firm. The Board adopted the approach of Lord Reid in *Esso Petroleum Co. Ltd v Harper's Garage (Stourport) Ltd* [1968] AC 269 at p. 301. The approach which I have applied to this case, is to ascertain what were the covenantee's (the appellant's) legitimate interests which she was entitled to protect and were the restraints imposed more than necessary for that purpose. On this approach, the burden on the appellant to prove reasonableness is heavier than if the $25,000 paid for goodwill under the sale and purchase agreement could be taken as the predominant justification for the clause.

First then, what were the legitimate interests of the appellant which she was entitled to protect? The business sold by the respondents to the appellant was a hairdressing salon in Takapuna. The first respondent, in partnership with the second respondent, had owned and operated the business for eighteen years. The last eight of those years the business operated from the premises purchased by the appellant.

The business therefore had a well-established location and customer base. The District Court judge commented at p. 10:

I must have judicial notice as a husband of more than three decades and a father of three adult daughters of the special relationship women have with their hair stylist and the ability of the stylist to 'take' the customer to some other venue!

The relationship between a hairdresser and his or her clients is not a special gender-specific one, and is not one for which judicial notice may be taken. It is no different from relationships developed in other professions and trades, where a professional or tradesperson's personality and skill play a significant role in developing a relationship of trust and loyalty with clients. A number of the first respondent's clients may well have developed a relationship of trust with her and have wished to 'follow' her. It is precisely for this reason that someone in the appellant's position would be legitimately interested in not allowing this to happen. The appellant would wish to capitalise on the existing customers' loyalty to and familiarity with the salon itself, and at least to have a chance to develop a relationship with those customers herself. If you like, the appellant had a legitimate interest in securing a chance to compete for those customers. She would still have to compete in the market generally, but she would want to eliminate the need to compete against well-established loyalties to her predecessor.

It seems to be established law that persons are entitled to bind themselves not to act in future for a particular group of persons (see *Bridge v Deacons* at pp. 719–720). I therefore consider that the appellant's desire to stop the first respondent from supplying customers who were on the books of the business when it was sold was a legitimate interest which the appellant was entitled to protect.

The next question for me to consider is whether the restraints imposed went further than was necessary in the circumstances to protect those interests. There are generally three components to a restraint of trade clause. Whether a restraint is reasonable in the circumstances will depend on whether the cumulative effect of the components is acceptable. The first component is the scope of the clause, that is, what activities it seeks to restrict. The relevant portion of this clause restricts supply and/or solicitation, but only in respect of people who were customers of the business at the time it was sold. The evidence suggests that there were about 194 such people. The second component is the geographical area to which the clause applies. This clause has no geographical limitation whatsoever so is as broad in this respect as it is possible to be. The third component is the duration of the clause. In this case the clause will endure only as long as the lease. The evidence suggested that this was about five to six years.

Obviously each restraint of trade case will turn very much on its specific combination of components. I have however found several cases useful. The comment of Richardson J. in *Brown v Brown* at pp. 494–5 is a good starting point. He said that:

> . . . a severe restriction might be acceptable, if for a limited period, and a longer term might be reasonable because of the limited area or scope of the agreement.

In the present case the clause in question has no geographical limitation, but applies only to a very limited number of people, for a limited time.

In *Bridge v Deacons* the covenant in restraint of trade purported to prevent a solicitor from acting for any person who was at the time of the solicitor's ceasing to be a partner, or had been during the three years prior thereto, a client of the partnership. This restriction applied for five years and covered the whole of Hong Kong. Notably, the clause prevented the solicitor from acting not only for persons for whom he had acted personally, but also from acting for anyone who had been a client of the firm. In this sense that clause was much wider than the clause in the present case. The duration of the clause in *Deacons* was similar. As the clause applied to the whole of Hong Kong for practical purposes it would have made very little difference if there had been no geographical limitation at all. I therefore also consider that the geographical limitations in the two cases are similar.

The Privy Council upheld the clause in *Deacons*. The judgment is persuasive for two particular reasons. First, the clause in that case was wider than the clause in the present case. Secondly, it was also a case in which there existed an argument that inadequacy of consideration told against the reasonableness of the restriction.

Counsel for the appellant referred me to the English Court of Appeal decision in *Rannie v Irvine* (1844) 7 Man & G 969. It was an influential feature of that case that the restraint of trade clause restricted the defendant from trading with only a very limited number of persons whose names were well known to him at the time he entered into the contract. This is a consideration which is also relevant in the present case. The scope of the present clause is fairly narrow—provided she is outside the 5 km radius, the first respondent can cut the hair of anyone in the world other than the hair of the 194 original customers of the business she sold.

These cases would seem to support the appellant's contention that the covenant in restraint of trade is reasonable. As in *Deacons*, I must however consider the argument that the lack of consideration for the restrictions contained in the clause renders those restrictions unreasonable. In the absence of consideration in the deed itself the starting point is that the parties signed the deed and are therefore bound by the restraint clause, provided the clause is reasonable. The lack of payment for the restrictions contained in the clause does not mean the clause is unreasonable. Rather it means that the 'consideration' factor cannot assist to prove reasonableness in this case. This is a disadvantage to the appellant as it makes proving reasonableness more difficult. The standard of proof required becomes closer to that in employment cases where the courts have taken a much stricter approach to covenants in restraint of trade.

A further consideration, which might also support the court taking a stricter approach than in some of the cases discussed previously, is that the court is no longer faced with the common law position of either upholding a clause or deciding that it is inservable and void. Section 8 of the Illegal Contracts Act 1970 allows the court to modify any term that is unreasonable.

In this context it is helpful to consider a case which involved the modification of a covenant in restraint of trade in the employment context. In H & R *Block Ltd v Sanott* [1976] 1 NZLR 213 the court considered a restraint against a former employee of an income tax return preparation business. The clause in that case restricted the employee from competition for a period of five years over an area of twenty-five miles. Somers J. held that the clause was unreasonable as to term and area. The scope of the clause was wider than in the present case, as the covenantor was restricted from acting generally, not just from acting for persons who had been clients of the business.

That case also contains some general comments which seem relevant to the present case. Somers J., adapting a statement made by Parker L.J. in *Herbert Morris Ltd v Saxelby* [1916] 1 AC 688 at p. 709, said that a covenant against competition generally is invalid but a covenant against what is in effect competition may be valid on the grounds, *inter alia*, that an employee's personal knowledge and influence over the employer's customers would enable him or her, if competition were permitted, to take advantage of the employer's trade connection. This supports my finding that the appellant had a legitimate interest in preventing the first respondent from taking advantage of her personal knowledge and influence over the customers of the business.

Although it has been recognised that covenants in restraint of trade are in the public interest because they assist in the sale and purchase of business the public interest is not a significant factor in this decision. What I consider this case to turn on is whether the clause in the deed goes further than is necessary to protect the appellant's legitimate interests. I have already considered the nature of these interests. In my opinion the clause in restraint of trade should go no further than to allow the appellant to enjoy the established reputation of the business for as long as it takes to give her the chance to prove her own skill. As I have said, I do not believe she would have this chance if she had to compete directly with the first respondent for customers.

I have therefore concluded that the appellant is entitled to succeed in her appeal. The restraint against supplying or soliciting existing customers however, requires some modification. The period which must be read as terminating at the conclusion of the lease has elements of uncertainty; it is different from the term in the first two parts of the clause in the deed and in the agreement for sale and purchase, and requires knowledge of the actual date of the expiry of the lease for enforcement purposes. It is also longer than is necessary for its purpose. A total of three years from the date of possession, namely 15 May 1995 appears equitable in all the circumstances. The clause is therefore now spent and nothing is to be gained in rewriting it further to modify the geographical limitation.

However, in view of the finding I make that the respondents breached the restraint of trade by supplying customers for its duration it follows that the geographical limitation to 5 km does not assist them. For the purposes of fixing damages the prohibition on supply should be read as if it had no geographical limitation.

Damages

In the District Court the appellant was unsuccessful in her claim for breach of the restraint of trade. As a result, the court did not consider the issue of damages. It is therefore necessary to remit that question to the District Court for damages. It is therefore necessary to remit that question to the District Court for its assessment and determination. Given the costs to the parties, it may be that they can settle that issue without further court intervention. If so, that may be a material matter for my consideration in fixing the costs on appeal. I therefore:

1. Allow the appeal.
2. Remit the question of damages to the District Court.

SECTION TWO—EXCLUSIVE DEALING ARRANGEMENTS INCLUDING SOLUS AGREEMENTS

Esso Petroleum Co. Ltd *v* Harpers Garage (Stourport) Ltd [1968] AC 269

The respondent company which owned two service stations entered a typical 'solus' agreement with Esso, the appellant. This involved the respondent agreeing to purchase from the appellant the whole of its requirements of motor fuel for resale at its service stations, accepting a resale price maintenance clause, agreeing to operate the relevant service stations in accordance with the Esso dealer co-operation plan, which included a provision that the service station should be kept open at all reasonable hours for the Esso petrol and oil, and finally, agreeing that, before completing any sale or transfer of the relevant service station, the respondent would notify Esso and procure the intended successor to assume the respondent's obligations under the agreement. The agreement in respect of Mustow Green station was for a period of four years and five months and the agreement in respect of Corner station was for twenty one years. The appellant had a mortgage over the latter station to secure a loan made to the respondent. Subsequently the appellant sought injunctions restraining the respondents from buying or selling fuels other than those of the appellants at their stations. The Court of Appeal held that the agreement was in restraint of trade and unenforceable and Esso appealed to the House of Lords.

Lord Reid:

. . .

If a contract is within the class of contracts in restraint of trade the law which applies to it is quite different from the law which applies to contracts generally. In general unless a contract is vitiated by duress, fraud or mistake its terms will be enforced though unreasonable or even harsh and unconscionable, but here a term in restraint of trade will not be enforced unless it is reasonable. And in the ordinary case the court will not remake a contract: unless in the special case where the contract is severable, it will not strike out one provision as unenforceable and enforce the rest. But here the party who has been paid for agreeing to the restraint may be unjustly enriched if the court holds the restraint to be too wide to be enforceable and is unable to adjust the consideration given by the other party.

It is much too late now to say that this rather anomalous doctrine of restraint of trade can be confined to the two classes of case to which it was originally applied. But the cases outside these two classes afford little guidance as to the circumstances in which it should be applied. In some it has been assumed that the doctrine applies and the controversy has been whether the restraint was reasonable. And in others where one might have expected the point to be taken it was not taken, perhaps because counsel thought that there was no chance of the court holding that the restraint was too wide to be reasonable.

. . .

The main argument submitted for the appellant on this matter was that restraint of trade means a personal restraint and does not apply to a restraint on the use of a particular piece of land. Otherwise, it was said, every covenant running with the land which prevents its use for all or for some trading purposes would be a covenant on restraint of trade and therefore unenforceable unless it could be shown to be reasonable and for the protection of some legitimate interest. It was said that the present agreement only prevents the sale of petrol from other suppliers on the site of the Mustow Green garage: It leaves the respondents free to trade anywhere else in any way they choose. But in many cases a trader trading at a particular place does not have the resources to enable him to begin trading elsewhere as well, and if he did he might find it difficult to find another suitable garage for sale or to get planning permission to open a new filling station on another site. As the whole doctrine of restraint of trade is based on public policy its application ought to depend less on legal niceties or theoretical possibilities than on the practical effect of a restraint in hampering that freedom which it is the policy of the law to protect.

It is true that it would be an innovation to hold that ordinary negative covenants preventing the use of a particular site for trading of all kinds or of a particular kind are within the scope of the doctrine of restraint of trade. I do not think they are. Restraint of trade appears to me to imply that a man contracts to give up some freedom which otherwise he would have had. A person buying or leasing land had no previous right to be there at all, let alone trade there, and when he takes possession of that land subject to a negative restrictive covenant he gives up no right or freedom which he previously had. I think that the 'tied house' cases might be explained in this way, apart from *Biggs v Hoddinott*,[1] where the owner of a freehouse had agreed to a tie in favour of a brewer who had lent him money. Restraint of trade was not pleaded. If it had been, the restraint would probably have been held to be reasonable. But there is some difficulty if a restraint in a lease not merely prevents the person who takes possession of the land under the lease from doing certain things there, but also obliges him to act in a particular way. In the present case the respondents before they made this agreement were entitled to use this land in any lawful way they chose, and by making this agreement they agreed to restrict their right by giving up their right to sell there petrol not supplied by the appellants.

In my view this agreement is within the scope of the doctrine of restraint of trade as it had been developed in English law. Not only have the respondents agreed negatively not to sell other petrol but they have agreed positively to keep this garage open for the sale of the appellants' petrol at all reasonable hours throughout the period of the tie. It was argued that this was merely regulating the respondent's trading and rather promoting than restraining his trade. But regulating a person's existing trade may be a greater restraint than prohibiting him from engaging in a new trade. And a contract to take one's whole supply from one source may be much more hampering than a contract to sell one's whole output to one buyer. I would not attempt to define the dividing line between contracts which are and contracts which are not in restraint of trade, but in my view this contract must be held to be in restraint of trade. So it is necessary to consider whether its provisions can be justified.

But before considering this question I must deal briefly with the other agreement tying the Corner Garage for twenty one years. The rebate and other advantages to the respondents were similar to those in the Mustow Green agreement but in addition the appellants made a loan of £7,000 to the respondents to enable them to improve their garage and this loan was to be repaid over the twenty one years of the tie. In security they took a mortgage of this garage. The agreement provided that the loan should not be paid off earlier than at the dates stipulated. But the respondents now tender the unpaid balance of the loan and they say that the appellants have no interest to refuse to accept repayment now, except in order to maintain the tie for the full twenty one years.

The appellants argue that the fact that there is a mortgage excludes any application of the doctrine of restraint of trade. But I agree with your Lordships in rejecting that argument. I am prepared to assume that, if the respondents had not offered to repay the loan so far as it is still outstanding, the appellants would have been entitled to retain the tie. But, as they have tendered repayment, I do not think that the existence of the loan and the mortgage puts the appellants in any stronger position to maintain the tie than they would have been in if the original agreements had permitted repayment at an earlier date. The appellants must show that in the circumstances when the agreement was made a tie for twenty one years was justifiable.

It is now generally accepted that a provision in a contract which is to be regarded as in restraint of trade must be justified if it is to be enforceable, and that the law on this matter was correctly stated by Lord Macnaghten in the *Nordenfelt* case.[2]
. . .

So in every case it is necessary to consider first whether the restraint went farther than to afford adequate protection to the party in whose favour it was granted, secondly whether it can be justified as being in the interests of the party restrained, and, thirdly, whether it must be held contrary to the public interest. I find it difficult to agree with the way in which the court has in some cases treated the interests of the party restrained. Surely it can never be in the interest of a person to agree to suffer a restraint unless he gets some compensating advantage, direct or indirect. And Lord Macnaghten said: ' . . . of course the quantum of consideration may enter into the question of the reasonableness of the contract'.

. . .

The Court of Appeal held that these ties were for unreasonably long periods. They thought that, if for any reason the respondents ceased to sell the appellants' petrol, the appellants could have found other suitable outlets in the neighbourhood within two or three years. I do not think that that is the right test. In the first place there was no evidence about this and I do not think that it would be practicable to apply this test in practice. It might happen that when the respondents ceased to sell their petrol, the appellants would find such an alternative outlet in a very short time. But, looking to the fact that well over ninety per cent of existing filling stations are tied and that there may be great difficulty in opening a new filling station, it might take a very long time to find an alternative. Any estimate of how long it might take to find suitable alternatives for the respondents' filling stations could be little better than guesswork.

I do not think that the appellants' interest can be regarded so narrowly. They are not so much concerned with any particular outlet as with maintaining a stable system of distribution throughout the country so as to enable their business to be run efficiently end economically. In my view there is sufficient material to justify a decision that ties of less than five years were insufficient, in the circumstances of the trade when these agreements were made, to afford adequate protection to the appellants' legitimate interests. And if that is so I cannot find anything in the details of the Mustow Green agreement which would indicate that it is unreasonable. It is true that if some of the provisions were operated by the appellants in a manner which would be commercially unreasonable they might put the respondents in difficulties. But I think that a court must have regard to the fact that the appellants must act in such a way that they will be able to obtain renewals of the great majority of their very numerous ties, some of which will come to an end almost every week. If in such circumstances a garage owner chooses to rely on the commercial probity and good sense of the producer, I do not think that a court should hold his agreement unreasonable because it is legally capable of some misuse. I would therefore allow the appeal as regards the Mustow Green agreement.

But the Corner Garage agreement involves much more difficulty. Taking first the legitimate interests of the appellants, a new argument was submitted to your Lordships that, apart from any question of security for their loan, it would be unfair to the appellants if the respondents, having used the appellants' money to build up their business, were entitled after a comparatively short time to be free to seek better terms from a competing producer. But there is no material on which I can assess the strength of this argument and I do not find myself in a position to determine whether it has any validity. A tie for twenty one years stretches far beyond any period for which developments are reasonably foreseeable. Restrictions on the garage owner which might seem tolerable and reasonable in reasonably foreseeable conditions might come to have a very different effect in quite different conditions: the public interest comes in here more strongly. And, apart from a case where he gets a loan, a garage owner appears to get no greater advantage from a twenty year tie than he gets from a five year tie. So I would think that there must at least be some clearly established advantage to the producing company—something to show that a shorter period would not be adequate—before so long a period could be justified. But in this case there is no evidence to prove anything of the kind. And the other material which I have thought it right to consider does not appear to me to assist the appellant here. I would therefore dismiss the appeal as regards the Corner Garage agreement.

[1] [1898] 2 Ch. 307; 14 TLR 504, CA.   [2] [1894] AC 535, 565.

Note

Esso injunction stops filling station from selling other brands
(From *The Irish Times*, 19 April 2005.)
Esso Ireland Limited has secured an interim High Court order restraining the sale of
any brand of motor fuel other than Esso brands at a Co. Mayo filling station.

The order is against Ian Clarke, company director of Ridgepool Village, Ballina, and
relates to the Clarke and Doherty filling station, Dillon Terrace, Ballina, which is also
restrained from selling or offering for sale any of the contents of the fuel tanks on the
premises.

James Philips, senior counsel for Esso Ireland Limited, also secured an injunction
against a second defendant, McCormack Fuels Limited, from selling or supplying
motor fuel to Ian Clarke at the filling station during the term of his contract with Esso
Ireland Limited.

In an affidavit, Eugene Treacy, Esso area manager, said Mr Clarke had entered into
an agreement providing that Esso sell him his total requirements of motor fuels for
resale for a period of five years from September 1st, 2002, and not to sell motor fuels
supplied by others except with the written consent of the oil company.

It had come to Esso's attention that Mr Clarke may have been purchasing motor
fuel from a third party and selling it at his station in breach of the agreement with the
oil company.

About March 29th last, an Esso agent had observed a petrol tanker from
McCormack Fuels Ltd, Sligo, arriving on the forecourt of Clarke's service station.

The driver of the vehicle delivered fuel from the lorry into the underground tanks on
the premises. The delivery took about 45 minutes.

Mr Treacy said he has a subsequent telephone conversation with Mr Clarke in
which Mr Clarke contended he could not afford to purchase the Esso product,
claiming it was too expensive.

Mr Treacy added that Esso had provided substantial money towards the cost of
capital improvements to the service station concerned.

In the case of Irish solus agreements, these were regulated under the
old fair trade legislation (Restrictive Practices Act 1972) which struck down
restraints that lasted for longer than ten years. However, these agreements
are now open to more general scrutiny by the Authority.

Competition Authority Decision No. 4 Esso Solus and Related Agreements (CA/11–13/92) 25 June 1992

Notification was made with a request for a licence under s. 4 of the Competition Act
1991 by Esso Ireland Ltd on 19 December 1991 in respect of the standard Esso solus
agreement with independent dealers, and its dealer loan equipment and dealer loan
agreements, and its deed of charge/mortgage.

. . .

The facts:

This decision concerns the standard Esso solus agreement, which provides for the
exclusive purchase by an independent dealer of Esso motor fuels for resale, for a maximum period of ten years, and the following related agreements:

– the dealer loan equipment agreement, which relates to the provision of service
  station equipment on loan to the dealer;

- the dealer loan agreement, which is used when an interest-bearing loan is made available to the dealer for redevelopment of the outlet; and
- the deed of charge/mortgage, which is used to provide security for the loan to the dealer.

Each notified agreement is a standard agreement which Esso employs with the dealers in its independent dealer network throughout the State. While each independent dealer is a party to the solus agreement, not all dealers are party to the other three agreements.

...

48. In the opinion of the Authority, the solus and related agreements notified by Esso fulfil the conditions provided for in s. 4(2).

49. Solus agreements in the motor fuels sector differ from other exclusive purchase agreements in that the supplier confers on the reseller special commercial or financial advantages by contributing to his financing, granting him a loan on favourable terms, and providing him with equipment, while the reseller enters into a long-term exclusive purchasing obligation which is accompanied by a ban on dealing in competing products and the supplier agrees to supply the reseller's total requirements of motor fuels.

50. The solus agreements produce an appreciable improvement in distribution in which consumers are allowed a fair share of the resulting benefit. The commercial and financial advantages conferred by the supplier on the retailer make it significantly easier to establish, modernise, maintain and operate service stations. A high level of investment is needed to provide adequate facilities and to meet safety standards, and Esso has invested heavily in its company-owned stations. Independent dealers would have insufficient resources for the necessary investment without substantial support from the supplier, otherwise company stations would become dominant. They are able to provide a range of services which they would otherwise be unable to offer. The exclusive purchasing obligation and the ban on dealing in competing products imposed on the reseller encourage the reseller to devote all the resources at his disposal to the sale of motor fuels, while retaining his independence and freedom to run the business as he sees fit. Solus agreements lead to durable co-operation between the parties, allowing them to improve or maintain the quality of the motor fuels and of the services to the customer and the sales efforts of the reseller. The investment by the supplier ensures security of supply by providing assured outlets for its product, and retailers are guaranteed regular supplies. This allows long-term planning of sales and consequently a cost-effective organisation of production and distribution. The costs of distributing motor fuels to a limited number of exclusive outlets which purchase in large quantities are lower than delivering smaller volumes to a large number of outlets selling two or more brands at the one service station. The pressure of competition between different brands of motor fuel obliges the undertakings involved to determine the number and characteristics of service stations in accordance with the wishes of consumers.

51. The solus agreement includes a clause extending the exclusive purchasing requirements to include the sale of motor fuels by the dealer at any premises within a one mile radius of the designated service station. The Authority accepts that competition in the sale of motor fuels is a fairly localised phenomenon. Motorists do not tend to travel any great distance to buy at a cheaper price, since the cost of so doing would soon eliminate any savings made. The dedication of the dealer to maximising sales of Esso motor fuels at the designated outlet would be likely to be adversely affected if he

were permitted to sell another brand at a station owned or operated by himself within one mile of the designated station. Without such a requirement, the improvement in distribution would not be secured. The dealer is free, however, to sell competing motor fuels outside the one mile radius.

52. Consumers benefit from these improvements especially because they are ensured supplies of motor fuel of satisfactory quality while being able to choose between different brands of motor fuel. The solus system leads to more efficient distribution and to better facilities and services at dealer stations, to the benefit of consumers. They have a choice between stations offering differing degrees and types of service. The system should ensure both intra-brand and inter-brand competition, including price competition.

53. The advantages produced by solus agreements cannot be achieved to the same extent and with the same degree of certainty in any other way. The exclusive purchasing obligation on the reseller and the non-competition clause imposed on him are essential components of such agreements and are indispensable for the attainment of these advantages. These obligations are confined to the purchase of motor fuels for resale, and do not extend to other products. The limitation of the period of the exclusive agreement to ten years is sufficient to produce the advantages, while maintaining the reseller's commercial freedom to change supplier and to ensure access to the retail level of distribution on the part of other suppliers. Any shorter period would substantially lessen the incentive for suppliers to invest in dealer outlets, to the detriment of dealers and consumers. This is especially so in the State, where the average throughput in petrol stations is only about one quarter of the EC average.

54. There are large numbers of Esso solus, company and non-solus outlets, and there are many other outlets of these types which sell motor fuels under other brand names. There is a high degree of competition between outlets, both intra-brand and inter-brand, and, with the removal of price control, there is scope for price competition, in particular, since solus and non-solus dealers are free to determine their own selling prices. While the long-term nature of the exclusive supply contracts limits the possibilities for a new entrant to secure outlets, all dealers are free to change their supplier at the expiry of the contract, and this does occur, and agreements are expiring on a continuous basis. In addition, a new supplier entrant would be likely to want the security offered by long-term solus agreements before making the sizeable investment necessary to enter the market in the first place. There is thus no possibility of the undertakings being afforded the possibility of eliminating competition for a substantial part of the products in question.

55. It will be apparent that, in its assessment, the Authority has had regard to EC Regulation No. 1984/83, which exempts certain exclusive purchasing agreements, including service station agreements, from the prohibition of article 85(1) of the Treaty of Rome.
. . .

The Authority therefore grants a licence under s. 4(2) in respect of each of the notified Esso agreements. . . .

Note

See also Motor Fuels Decision No. 25, continued in force under s. 4 (3) of the Competition Act 2002 as an Authority declaration.

SECTION THREE—FRANCHISE AGREEMENTS AND POST-TERMINATION RESTRAINTS

Vendo plc *v* Adams [2002] NI 95

Girvan J.:

In the amended writ of summons in this action brought by Vendo plc (Vendo) against Mervyn Adams (the defendant) Vendo seeks an injunction effectively to prevent the defendant from engaging in any business in competition with Vendo in two geographical areas and from soliciting or canvassing or dealing with or endeavouring to entice away from the plaintiff any customers. It also claims damages for loss suffered by Vendo in relation to alleged breaches of agreements dated 10 November 1995 and 29 September 2000. These two agreements constituted so-called franchise agreements containing competition restrictions on the defendant in the event of their termination.

Vendo originally provided a truck washing service to large commercial vehicle fleet operators employing staff directly to do that work. In the late 1980s it decided to move from the direct provision of such services to the operation of a franchise business. As a franchisor it enters into franchise agreements with franchisees who take on responsibility for the provision of the vehicle washing services in specified geographical areas. Vendo provides centralised functions in relation to the franchise network including the identification of customers, the building up of a database identifying customers and potential customers, marketing, advertising and the provision of a centralised system of accountancy, together with the provision of materials such as detergents and assistance with the acquisition of cleaning equipment and vehicles. The franchisor provides franchisees with training, technical and quality control manuals.

The franchise agreements

In consideration of the payment of the initial franchise fee of £11,500, the accountancy services fees and management services fees and subject to the obligations on the part of the franchisee set out in the agreement the franchisor granted the franchisee the right to use Vendo's services trademark, trade name, copyright and designs and the right to carry on the franchise business within the specified territory for the term of five years in accordance with Vendo's 'method' as defined in the agreement. The franchise had a right of renewal. Under the agreement the franchisor undertook various obligations set out in cl. 6 and 7. These included a guarantee that the franchisee would have a minimum take of £100 per week during the first three months, an obligation on the part of the franchisor to assist the franchisee with the business launch by telephoning and/or visiting 500 or so prospective customers on behalf of the franchisee and an obligation as far as possible to negotiate and obtain from suppliers at competitive rates appropriate supplies. Clause 8 set out the obligations of the franchise. Clause 11 set out the provisions relating to termination.

The relevant positions which have arisen in the context of the present application are to be found in cl. 11 relating to the consequences of termination. On the expiry or other termination of the agreement the franchisee undertook to immediately cease carrying on the business, to procure the transfer of the telephone numbers of the business to such person as the franchisor directed or to discontinue use of such telephone numbers should the franchisor so direct, to destroy all stationery used in the business, to return all publicity promotion and advertising material and to return all originals and copies of all documents and information in any form containing or covering in any part of the intellectual property. Clause 11.3 provided:

11.3.1 For a period of 18 months after expiry or termination of this agreement howsoever caused the franchisee covenants and undertakes not to engage directly or indirectly in any capacity in any business venture in competition with the business or likely to damage the goodwill of the business in the territory.

11.3.2 For the period of 18 months after expiry or termination of this agreement howsoever cause the franchisee covenants and undertakes not to solicit canvas or deal with or endeavour to entice away from the business or the franchisor any current customers or customers who have been customers of the business within 2 years of the date of the expiry or termination of this agreement.

11.3.3 For a period of 9 months after the expiry or termination of this agreement howsoever caused the franchisee undertakes not to employ any employees who were employed in the business by the franchisee or by the franchisor or any other representative of the franchisor at the date of the expiry or termination of this agreement.

Under cl. 3.6 of the agreement the franchise was to expire on 10 November 2000.

From 20 July 2000 onwards for a period the defendant appeared to indicate a desire to renew the franchise agreement for the Lisburn area for a further five years. As it turned out there was no renewal effected and in consequence the franchise in respect of the Lisburn area came to an end having run its course and not having been renewed.

The Lisburn agreement was assigned to the defendant on 21 April 1997 and it is not in dispute that as a result of the assignment of the franchise agreement the defendant became bound by the terms of the franchise agreement including the provisions of cl. 11.

The defendant entered into a franchise agreement in respect of the Belfast area on 29 September 2000. That agreement was subject to the same terms and conditions as applied in relation to the Lisburn franchise. The initial franchise fee in the case of the Belfast agreement was £9,500.

On 10 April 2001 the defendant's legal representatives wrote a letter setting out a number of alleged complaints in relation to the franchise agreements, for example that the franchisor was charging excessive prices for the detergents provided on foot of the arrangements and that parts and equipment were being priced by the franchisor at a price considerably above what would have been available in the open market in Northern Ireland.

For the purposes of the present proceedings the parties have agreed that the Belfast agreement should be treated as terminated as from 10 April 2001. It is further agreed that if the restraint of trade provisions are reasonable the defendant will abide by the restrictions for the eighteen months from 10 April 2001 in relation to the Belfast territory. In the case of the Lisburn agreement the eighteen months would run from the date upon which the Lisburn branch's agreement came to an end by effluxion of time.

Mr Lavery QC on behalf of Vendo argued that Vendo's operation constitutes a specialist business in the transport sector commanding a substantial reputation. It is the only truck cleaning company which operates on a nationwide basis through a national network of franchises. A restrictive covenant in a franchise agreement is closer to a restrictive covenant affecting the sale of property and goodwill than to an agreement between employer and employee. Any covenant contained in such a franchise agreement needs to satisfy a far less stringent test of reasonableness than is required in an employer/employee case. There is potential for the franchisee to take unfair advantage of the considerable involvement made by the franchisor by way of training, providing equipment and product marketing, funding, accounting facilities and access to a very significant customer base. The franchisor cannot realistically re-let the franchise to a successor while the defendant is trading competitively. The defendant with his knowledge of the plaintiff's pricing structure and client base would allow him to undercut an incoming franchise and take advantage of his personal contact and relationship with previous customers. Failure to be able to enforce a reasonable restrictive clause would effectively make the running of any franchise business impossible as franchisees could simply withdraw and not renew their agreement and the defendant would not be able to find a franchise to come in and take over.

Mr Orr QC on behalf of the defendant contended that the eighteen-month period contained in the relevant clauses was too long a period for a restraint imposed on an outgoing franchisee. He referred in particular to Commission Regulation (EEC) 4087/88 of 13 November 1998 which introduced a block exemption for franchising agreements under former art. 85 of the EC Treaty (now art. 81 EC) and which appeared to indicate that the maximum reasonable period for a restraint in respect of an outgoing franchisee would be twelve months. A franchisee may be held to that obligation after termination of the agreement for a reasonable period which would not exceed twelve months in the territory where he has operated as a franchisee.

There is a limited number of decided cases relating to restraints of trade provisions in franchise agreements. The first reported case on which the issue arose is *Budget Rent a Car International Inc.v Mamos Slough Ltd* (1977) 121 Sol Jo 374. In that case the plaintiffs operated a worldwide car hire franchise business through local companies who provided the capital, premises and cars and paid the plaintiffs ten per cent of the gross takings and £400 for advertising, instructions and other services. There was a restraint provision precluding the defendant from engaging in such a business for 180 days after termination. Refusing an interlocutory injunction Lord Denning M.R. said that a franchise agreement was very different from an agreement by the owner of a business. The Court of Appeal held that there was a serious question to be tried and the balance of convenience was against the granting of an interlocutory injunction.

In *Kall-Kwik Printing* (UK) *Ltd v Rush* [1996] FSR 114 the plaintiff operated a franchise system for printing and copying services under which the plaintiff gave training and assistance to the franchisees and licensed them to use the name Kall-Kwik. The defendant was the plaintiff's franchisee of premises in Southend-on-Sea under a 1983 franchise agreement. In 1995 the plaintiff discovered the defendant had set up a parallel business in competition under the name Print Centre and was actively diverting customers from the franchise business to the parallel business. The defendant having realised that the plaintiff had discovered what was going on terminated the agreement and closed the franchised premises without giving the required six months' notice. The plaintiff sought to rely on a restraint of trade provision which prevented the defendant from competing for two years within a ten-mile radius of the site of the franchise premises. The defendant argued that the period and the area of the restraint was too wide. Judge Cooke sitting as a judge of the Chancery Division observed that one way of looking at a franchise agreement was that it was a form of lease of goodwill for a term of years with an obligation as it were to re-transfer the goodwill to the franchise or at the end of the term. To that extent the obligation was more akin to a goodwill case than to an employer-employee case. The court held that the plaintiff's business was the business of granting franchises. The interest to be protected was the interest in respect of that particular franchise business against unfair competition. The court considered two years was not an unreasonable period in which to allow a new franchisee in effect a clear run to provide the necessary and appropriate break from the previous activity. In that case the franchise also contained a covenant on the part of the franchisee not to interfere with, solicit or entice any of the customers or former customers of the business with the intent that they or any of them cease to patronise the business of the franchisor or direct their customers elsewhere. In relation to that covenant the court expressed the view that that was a covenant which left on its own as a method of protecting the plaintiff's interest ran into real practical problems. To police that in any real sense except by purely incidental discovery seemed to the court to be virtually impossible. The judge could see why other methods of restraint were needed.

In an earlier case of *Kall-Kwik Printing* (UK) *Limited v Bell* [1994] FSR 684 the relevant restraint was for the period of eighteen months and the area of restraint was a 1,700 metre radius of the relevant franchise premises. Harman J. in an interlocutory application held the restraint valid.

In *Dyno-Rod plc v Reeve* [1998] FSR 148 the plaintiff ran a drainage service business organised on a franchise basis the first defendant was a franchise. The plaintiff discovered that he and his wife had been covertly operating a parallel business in breach of a restrictive covenant in the franchise agreement. There was a restraint covenant providing that for one year following termination the defendant should not have any involvement in any business in competition or conflict with the plaintiff's business within the former franchise territory. Neuberger J. accepted the analysis in *Kall-Kwik Printing* (UK) *Ltd v Rush* [1996] FSR 114 that a franchise agreement could best be seen as a lease of the franchisor's goodwill and was closer to the vendor-purchaser type of case than to the employer-employee type. Any covenant in it needed to satisfy a far less stringent test of reasonableness than was required in an employer-employee case. In that case the period and area of restraint was considered to be reasonable.

The European and Competition Act dimensions
Since Mr Orr called in aid the provisions of Commission Regulation (EEC) 4087/88 of 13 November 1998 it is necessary to consider the context of the Commission Regulations and their current status. It is also necessary to consider the impact of the Competition Act 1998.

In *Pronuptia de Paris GmbH v Pronuptia de Paris Irmgard Schillgalis* (Case 161/84) [1986] ECR 353 the Court of Justice of the European Communities had to rule on questions of Community law effecting franchise agreements. The opinion of the Advocate General (Van Themaat) provides an illuminating insight into the nature, history and development of franchising arrangements. The court heard a system of franchise agreements relating to the distribution of goods which allowed the franchisor to derive financial benefit from a set of business methods and a reputation of business name does not of itself interfere with competition. The compatibility of such a franchise agreement with art. 85(1) of the EC Treaty (now art. 81 EC) could not be assessed in the abstract but depended on the provisions contained within the agreement in its overall context.

The court thus ruled that reasonable restraints are perfectly legitimate and not of themselves anti-competitive for the purposes of art. 81.

The *Pronuptia* decision on art. 81 is not directly relevant in the present case because art. 81 is dealing with matters affecting inter-state trade. The impugned provisions must have an 'influence, direct or indirect, actual or potential, on the pattern of trade between member states, such as might prejudice the realisation of the aim of a single market in all the member states' (see *Remia* BV v EC Commission (Case 42/84) [1985] ECR 2545 at 2572, para. 22). The impact of the Vendo franchising set up on inter-state trade must be minimal. The only aspect of the plaintiff's business which may affect inter-state trade is its requirement that franchisees acquire materials through Vendo. However, a criterion for the application of art. 81(1) is that the agreement must have an 'appreciable' effect on competition (see *Béguelin Import Co. v GL Import Export* SA (Case 22/71) [1971] ECR 949). The Commission considers that agreements between small and medium sized undertakings are rarely capable of appreciably affecting trade between member states or of appreciably restricting competition within the meaning of art. 81(1). Small and medium sized undertakings are defined as undertakings with a turnover of up to £27m and 250 employees. Vendo's turnover is such that it is well within that category. It follows that art. 81 is not engaged in this case. Regulation 4087/88 was a block exemption applied to franchise agreements falling within art. 81 and specified restrictions which may not be included in franchise agreements if these are to benefit from the block exemption granted by the Regulation. Under art. 1 it was declared that art. 85(1) of the EC Treaty (now art. 81 EC) should not apply to franchise agreements to which two undertakings are parties including one or more of the restrictions listed in art. 2. Article 3 also provides that art. 1 applies notwithstanding the presence of an obligation not to engage directly or indirectly in any similar business in a territory where it would be in competition with a member of the franchised network including the franchisor for a reasonable period which may not exceed one year in the territory where he has exploited the franchise. That regulation was due to expire on 31 December 1991. The current European Union regulation is Commission Regulation (EC) 2790/99. It covers 'vertical agreements' as defined by art. 2 thereof and this would include a franchise agreement. It contained similar provisions in relation to the post-termination restraints permissible in relation to vertical agreement. It contained the provisions of Regulation 4087/88 until 31 May 2000.

It is not necessary to expatiate on these Community provisions since the relevant franchise agreements do not infringe art. 81 and thus no question of any need for exemption under a block exemption arises.

Mr Orr QC relied on the provisions in the Regulations as showing that if a maximum period of twelve months is appropriate in relation to franchises falling within the block exemptions then twelve months is the maximum reasonable period in other similar agreements not falling strictly within the exemption or art. 81. However, what is deemed to be reasonable in an agreement potentially falling with art. 81 because it has the undesirable potential to affect inter-state trade is not determinative of what is reasonable in a contract which has no impact on inter-state trade. That falls to be determined in the application of ordinary domestic law principles.

Nor does the Competition Act 1998 assist the defendant in this regard. Section 2 applies in the domestic context provisions similar to art. 81 EC. Section 60(1) provides that the purpose of that section is to ensure that so far as is possible, having regard to any relevant differences between the provisions concerned, questions arising under Pt 1 (including s. 2) in relation to competition within the United Kingdom are dealt with in a manner which is consistent with the treatment of corresponding questions arising in Community law in relation to competition within the Community. Section 60(2) provides that the court must act with a view to securing consistency between the principles applied to domestic and to Community competition issues.

Even if the Vendo franchise network agreements taken together could be said to appreciably affect trade within the United Kingdom (which seems to be very doubtful in view of the turnover) there is a block exemption under the Competition Act, namely the Competition Act 1998 (Land and Vertical Agreements Exclusion) Order 2000, SI 200/320, which provides that the Ch. 1 prohibitions in Pt 1 of the 1998 Act do not apply to an agreement to the extent that it is a vertical agreement. A franchise agreement falls within the definition of a vertical agreement and in the result there is nothing in the Competition Act which impliedly imports into domestic law a twelve-month maximum on post-termination restraints in a franchise agreement.

Determination of the issues

The reasonableness of the post-termination restraints contained in these franchise agreements must be viewed in the overall context of the agreements, the nature of the business and the nature of the relationship between the franchisor and the franchisee and regard must be had to both the duration and the area of the restraint. Clause 13.3.1 prohibits competition for eighteen months in the defined territory. Clause 13.3.2 is more specific and prohibits for eighteen months the soliciting of or dealing with customers or past customers of the business.

In each of the agreements the territory is an extensive area covering individually large economically active and populated areas in Northern Ireland. Within each territory there is a large pool of potential customers (identified as concerns having three or more commercial vehicles). Under the agreements the franchisee is carrying on a vehicle washing business on a relatively small scale and he could not possibly serve the whole of the pool of potential customers within the area. Clearly the franchisor has a legitimate interest to protect and will want to be able to find a successor franchisee who will be able to run a commercially successful franchise business (thereby maximising the profit of the franchisor). The very extensive area covered by the defined territory in each case provides a sufficient pool for any incoming franchisee to run a prosperous franchise even with fair competition from a previous franchisee. This case differs from the case of a franchisee operating from a fixed set of premises set in a particular narrow location and serving a passing and fluctuating customer base localised in that area served by those premises. The franchisee in the present case has to travel round servicing a number of customers which by the nature of the business must be a limited number at any one time. To prevent the franchisee carrying on vehicle washing services within the franchised territory would deprive the defendant effectively of earning a livelihood in a field where he has acquired an expertise. In this connection this type of service franchise arrangement differs somewhat from franchise agreements relating to the supply of goods.

Even if one could divorce the question of the period of restraint from the area of the restraint the period of eighteen months in my view goes beyond what is a reasonable period particularly if cl. 11.3.1 can be meaningfully enforced. The first question is how long the franchisor reasonably requires to be protected in order to be able to bring in a franchisee who will be able to utilise the goodwill of the franchise business to enable the franchisee to develop the franchise for the economic benefit of the franchisee and franchisor. Having regard to the nature of the business and the area to be protected in my view eighteen months would be excessive. Accordingly I do not consider that cl. 11.3.1. can be enforced by injunction.

Clause 11.3.2 gives rise to different issues. The existing customer base represents a valuable asset to Vendo and represents the core of the franchisor's goodwill to be passed on to an incoming successor franchisee. Vendo as the franchisor would have great difficulties in finding a willing franchisee prepared to take over a franchise when the outgoing franchisee is taking the existing customers with him or threatening to do so. The franchisor's goodwill would have little value to the incoming franchisee. A clause such as cl. 11.3.2 represents a legitimate provision provided that the period of restraint is reasonable. Such a clause is also a meaningful and enforceable clause. Although Judge Cook in *Kall-Kwik v Rush* had doubts about the capacity of a plaintiff to enforce a non-solicitation clause, the covenant in that case did not include a restraint on *dealing* with existing or past customers. Here a breach of clause could be easily established in the case of the defendant dealing with a customer. In relation to the period of restraint it is necessary to bear in mind that it may take the plaintiff some months to find an incoming franchisee. Eighteen months does not appear to me to be an excessive or unreasonable period in all the circumstances nor is it unreasonable to extend the restraint to customers who have been customers within two years of the date of the expiry or termination of the agreement having regard to the nature of this business.

In the result I will grant an injunction to give effect to the provisions of cl. 11.3.2. I will hear counsel on the question of costs.

SECTION FOUR—SEVERANCE

Skerry, Wynne and Skerry's College (Ireland) Ltd *v* Moles (1907) 42 ILTR 46

In August 1904, the defendant entered the employment of the plaintiffs, Skerry and Wynne, as a teacher of shorthand, &c. On 12 October 1904, he signed an agreement with them, of which the following was the material clause:

> 2. In consideration of the said engagement, the said Joseph A. Moles shall not, during a period of three years, to be computed from the date on which the said J. A. Moles shall cease to be employed by the said G. E. Skerry and A. E. Wynne, carry on or engage in the business of teacher of shorthand, typewriting, and general business training, or in any or either of the said businesses, either as principal or assistant, in Dublin, Belfast, or Cork, or within a radius of 7 miles from the academy or place of business of the said G. E. Skerry and A. E. Wynne in any of the said cities. And if the said J. A. Moles shall so carry on or engage in such business, either as principal or assistant, he shall pay to the said G. E. Skerry and A. E. Wynne, or the survivor of them, the sum of £20 for every month during which or any part of which he shall so carry on or engage in the said business as and for liquidated damages.

The plaintiffs claimed: (1) An injunction restraining the defendant from carrying on business in Dublin, Belfast, or Cork, or within a radius of 7 miles from the academy or place of business of the plaintiffs in any of the said cities, in breach of the said agreement. (2) Damages for breach of the said agreement; and in the alternative (3) a declaration that, under the said agreement, the defendant was bound to pay either to the plaintiff company, or to the said Skerry and Wynne, the sum of £20 by way of liquidated damages for each month during which he had carried on business in Dublin, Belfast, &c., for three years from the date on which he left the plaintiffs' employment.

Barton J.:

. . . .

The contract of employment was limited to Skerry's Academy in Belfast, but the restrictive clause extended also to Dublin and Cork. I have no difficulty in saying that the clause was unreasonable *qua* Dublin and Cork, but reasonable *qua* Belfast, and that it is a case in which the reasonable part is severable from the unreasonable part.

. . .

I think that the injunction can and ought to be granted so far as the City of Belfast is concerned.

Mulligan *v* Corr [1925] 1 IR 170

The plaintiff, a solicitor sought an injunction to prevent the defendant, a former clerk, from practising as a solicitor within a radius of 30 miles from the towns of Ballina, and Charlestown or within 20 miles of Ballaghadereen in breach of an agreement entered into by him when taken into employment six years previously. The plaintiff had an office in Ballina and a branch office in Charlestown. The trial judge held that the restriction was severable as regards each area defined, and granted an injunction restraining the defendant from practising as a solicitor within 30 miles of Ballina. The defendant appealed.

Fitzgibbon J.:

. . .

The principles of law applicable to covenants of this description in restraint of trade may be regarded as now finally settled; the only difficulty is to ascertain the facts to which they are to be applied.

The restriction imposed must not be greater than is reasonably required for the protection of the convenantee. If it exceed in area or duration the limits which the court considers reasonable it is void. The question of reasonableness is one of law for the court to decide. A restriction though unlimited as to space may be reasonable if confined to a period of reasonable duration. All these points were settled by the *Nordenfelt* case[1] some thirty years ago, and the converse of the last proposition, *viz.*: that a restriction, though unlimited in point of time, was valid if limited to a reasonable area, was decided by the House of Lords in 1921 in the case of *Fitch v Dewes*,[2] which was, like this, an action brought by a solicitor to restrain a former clerk from practising as a solicitor within a radius of 7 miles of the Town Hall of Tamworth, in breach of an agreement entered into by him, when taken into employment as managing clerk ten years previously. The area in that case was smaller than this, but it included a thickly populated district and portions of four English counties, Stafford, Warwick, Leicester, and Derby.

The first question we have to decide is the true construction of the covenant in the present case. The defendant has contended that it prohibits him from practising within three separate circles, one having Ballina as its centre with a radius of 30 miles, another of like radius having Charlestown as its centre, and a third with a radius of 20 miles and Ballaghadereen as its centre, and maps marked by an engineer with these three circles have been given in evidence, and that this is the true construction has not been disputed by the plaintiff and was decided by Meredith J. It is not clear that this is the true interpretation of the clause, and I think the maps rather support a different construction, based on grammatical considerations, for it will be seen that the Ballaghadereen circle falls entirely within the Charlestown circle, and the prohibition relating to it was therefore wholly unnecessary. In case of ambiguity, a contract should receive an interpretation which will give some effect to every provision in it, if such a construction is reasonably practicable, and by construing the restriction regarding Ballina and Charlestown as prohibiting practice at any place within 30 miles of *both* towns, there will be a considerable area left to be included by the Ballaghadereen circle, comprising such important places as Carrick-on-Shannon, Castlerea, Boyle, and Dromahaire. Assuming the construction placed upon the agreement by the parties to be correct, does the restriction exceed that which was reasonably necessary for the protection of the plaintiff? He had not been long in practice, but he had good connections and might reasonably expect, before the defendant would be out of his indentures, to build up a fair business, which he was entitled to protect against the possibility that his managing clerk, with all the knowledge acquired in the plaintiff's service of the plaintiff's clients and their affairs, might set up, as he has done, in opposition to his former employer.

In my opinion, however, the area which the plaintiff endeavoured to protect was too large. It was certainly so if it included the two 30-mile circles. They covered three county Assize towns, practically the whole of Mayo, more than half of Sligo, a large part of Roscommon, and portions of Galway and Leitrim. That appears to us to go far beyond anything which the plaintiff could reasonably require for his protection. Even the more limited area which I believe to be covered by the clause is, in my opinion, excessive. The plaintiff does not appear to have done much business in Ballaghadereen or its vicinity, and it was suggested at the bar by his counsel that the reason for including Ballaghadereen in the agreement was that if he did not make good in Ballina he might go to the other side of the county and work Ballaghadereen alone or in connection with Charlestown. If this were so, a restriction imposed to protect a business which was not in fact being worked and might never be set up at all was quite unreasonable.

Having come to the conclusion that the agreement cannot in any view of its construction be upheld in its entirety, questions arise whether it can be divided, and, if so, whether any fraction of it can be supported as reasonable.

As to the former, this restrictive covenant falls in our opinion within the principle of decisions such as *Mallan v May*,[3] the case of a dentist's assistant; *Green v Price*,[4] the case of the perfumery business; *Davies v Lowen*,[5] the case of the carrier's clerk; and if, by eliminating part which appears to be void, we can leave a valid and effective contract remaining, such a course is lawful, though the court cannot make a new covenant or mould one which is already complete in itself so as to create a different restriction which would be reasonable in the opinion of the court. I confess that my own opinion has fluctuated during the argument (which was ably conducted on both sides), and since; but after very careful consideration, we have come to the unanimous conclusion that it is not reasonable for the plaintiff, though practising and having offices both in Ballina and Charlestown, to insist that his managing clerk should not practise or set up a business in any place which was within a distance so great as 30 miles from both or either of those towns. Even the more restricted area includes the town of Sligo, and although that part of County Sligo which is served by Ballina or Charlestown, each of which actually touches the county border, might fairly be the subject of a protective clause, we cannot hold that it is necessary for the fair protection of the plaintiff that the defendant should be precluded from practising in the capital of the adjoining county, a restriction which would in effect have debarred him from taking business at the Assizes from any part of the County Sligo, and would exclude him from all that portion of County Sligo which lies outside the 30-mile circle, but whose inhabitants resort to Sligo for legal advice. There is no possible construction of this agreement which would not include the town of Sligo in the prohibited area, and the Ballina circle, which was adopted by Meredith J., would include Westport, as well as Claremorris and Ballyhaunis, none of which is shown to be in any real competition with Ballina for legal affairs so far as the plaintiff is concerned. It is to be regretted that the plaintiff did not give fuller information as to his own business, and, in our opinion, having regard to the fact that, notwithstanding a dictum to the contrary of the Earl of Birkenhead, the onus appears to be upon the plaintiff to establish the reasonableness of the restriction imposed, we have come to the conclusion that it is not reasonable or necessary for the protection of the plaintiff's business that the defendant should be restrained from practising as a solicitor at any place within 30 miles of Ballina and Charlestown or of either of those towns.

1. [1894] AC 535.   3. 11 M & W 652.   5. 64 LT 655.
2. [1921] 2 AC 158.   4. 13 M & W 695; 16 M & W 346.

Note

Although Fitzgibbon J. delivered the judgment of the Court, Kennedy C.J. added his observations concerning the defendant's 'inauspicious beginning' to his career. He noted 'every man who appreciates the standards of conduct and of honour which are required of the members of that profession required by its privileges and the great trusts confided to it, must be shocked by the defendant's first invitation of public confidence.'

ECI European Chemical Industries Ltd v Bell [1981] ILRM 345

McWilliam J.:

The plaintiff manufactures mastic sealants and similar products at Castleblayney, County Monaghan. The defendant, who had previously been in employment as a qualified chemist dealing with somewhat similar products for a period of seven years or so, was employed by the plaintiff from 3 January 1980, under an agreement in writing which provided that his employment could be terminated by either party on giving three months' notice in writing.

By letter dated 27 March 1981, the defendant gave notice of termination of his employment on 26 June 1981. His object in leaving the employment of the plaintiff is to take up employment with ACS Teoranta in County Galway, a firm which manufactures products similar to those of the plaintiff. ACS Teoranta is a subsidiary or an associate of an American company. The plaintiff is a subsidiary or an associate of a German company. It is probable that the parent or associated companies have business interests in various parts of the world.

The contract of employment of the defendant contains the following clauses:

17. Upon the termination of his employment for any cause or by any means whatsoever the employee shall not for a period of two years thereafter:
(b) undertake to carry on alone or in partnership nor be employed or interested directly or indirectly in any capacity whatsoever in any trade or business of a nature similar to or competing or calculated to compete with any business or businesses carried on by the company or by any of its subsidiaries or associated companies at the date of such termination PROVIDED THAT this restriction shall not extend to any country in which neither the company nor any of its subsidiary or associated companies has or shall have established a place of business or in which neither the company nor any of its subsidiaries or associated companies carried on business at the time of such termination.
18. In the event that any covenant or provision herein shall be determined to be void or unenforceable in whole or in part by reason of the area, duration or type or scope of service covered by the said covenant then the said covenant shall be given effect to in its reduced form as may be decided by any court of competent jurisdiction. The employee hereby acknowledges and agrees that the restriction contained in this agreement is valid and reasonable.

Immediately after his employment with the plaintiff, the defendant was sent to Germany for a period of seven months for training in the plaintiff's processes, products and 'know-how'. The defendant agrees that he there learned the plaintiff's manufacturing techniques, testing techniques, production processes and some trade secrets.

It appears that, until recently, ACS Teoranta purchased supplies of mastik sealants from the plaintiff but that in January of this year, it entered into an agreement with a German company to produce similar material in Galway and has purchased a machine of a kind used by the plaintiff for the production of such material.

. . .

The case presented on behalf of the defendant is that this is a contract in restraint of trade, that the plaintiff has not got a reasonable interest to be protected by the agreement, that the restraint is unreasonable with regard to the geographical area of the restraint and that it is unreasonable with regard to the length of the period of restraint. The argument necessitates the submission that, even on an interlocutory application, there is an onus on the plaintiff to establish the reasonableness of the restraint in each of these respects, that this has not been done and that the plaintiff is, therefore, not entitled to succeed on this application.

Having regard to this approach to the case and the arguments which have been addressed to me I feel I ought to consider the doctrine of restraints of trade and its application by the courts.

The relevant clauses in the agreement are clearly in restraint of trade and this has not been contested on behalf of the plaintiff. A long line of cases from *Nordenfelt v Maxim Nordenfelt Guns and Ammunition Co. Ltd* (1894) AC 535 to *Greig v Insoles* [1978] 1 WLR 303 appears to establish that a contract in restraint of trade is contrary to public policy and void or unenforceable unless the restraint reasonably protects a valid interest of the person in whose favour it is imposed, is not unreasonable with regard to the person restrained and is not unreasonable as being injurious to the public interest.

On the affidavits before me, I am satisfied, notwithstanding the arguments to the contrary on behalf of the defendant, that there is *prima facie*, a valid interest of the plaintiff to be protected, that is to say, the protection of trade secrets, testing techniques and production processes which have come to the knowledge of the defendant. Certainly I cannot accept that there is not, at least, a serious issue to be tried in this respect.

A more substantial objection on behalf of the defendant is that the clause is unreasonable both because it is too wide in the area of its application geographically and as making the period of restraint too long. I was addressed at some length as to the power of the court to modify the agreement should it be considered to be unreasonable in its present form.

The most recent case to which I was referred is that of *Littlewoods Organisation v Harris* [1977] 1 WLR 1472. It has been discussed on behalf of both parties but I find some aspects difficult to follow. It seems to me that the majority of the court of Appeal, Lord Denning M.R. and Megaw L.J., formed the opinion, contrary to the view expressed in the case of *Commercial Plastics v Vincent* [1965] 1 QB 623; [1964] 3 WLR 820, that the court is entitled to ignore the literal meaning of such a covenant and construe it with regard to the surrounding circumstances existing at the time when the covenant was entered into. See Megaw L.J. at 1489, or that the clause should be interpreted as limited to the reasonable objects which the parties to the agreement sought to achieve, see Lord Denning at 1483.

It seems to me that a point to be determined is whether a covenant which can be construed as being too wide in some respects and therefore unreasonable in those respects is wholly void in all respects or whether, although including unreasonable provisions which will not be enforced, reasonable provisions which are contained in it may be enforced. This is an aspect discussed by Lord Denning in a different form at pp 1481–2 of *Littlewoods* case. He said, at 1482, 'It has often been said that a covenant in restraint of trade is not to be rendered invalid simply by putting forward unlikely or improbable contingencies in which it might operate unreasonably . . . If such an unlikely or unusual event should happen, the court would not enforce it so as to work an injustice.' The conclusion of the Court of Appeal in the case of *Commercial Plastics v Vincent* was that the covenant, being too wide, had to be ruled out and declared void although the actual relief sought was held to be reasonable and proper to be granted. See Pearson L.J. at 832 of the WLR. The same view was taken by Browne L.J. in his dissenting judgment in the *Littlewoods* case. He said at p. 1491 'It seems to me that if the clause is read literally it is much too wide and is void and unenforceable.' This was also the view of the Court of Appeal in the case of *Gledhow Autoparts v Delaney* [1965] 1 WLR 1366. Sellers L.J. said at 1371:

> The injunction for which the plaintiffs asked and which they received is admittedly less than clause 6 in its terms would have permitted as regards area, that is, places where the defendant had operated. But when, as is the defendant's contention, the clause is said to be unenforceable because it is in restraint of trade, it must be construed as it stands and not to the extent that the employer seeks to enforce it. The modified request may reveal an apprehension as to the full effect of the clause. Whether this clause is, as the judge held, enforceable and not in restraint of trade, or whether it is too wide and not to be invoked, is a question of law and has to be decided on the authorities.

Diplock L.J., said at 1377

> The defendant was in fact employed for over six years by the plaintiffs and no doubt became a valuable servant and acquired considerable knowledge of and personal relation with the plaintiff's customers. It is natural in these circumstances to tend to look at what in fact happened under the agreement. But the question of the validity of a covenant in restraint of trade has to be determined at the date at which the agreement was entered into and has to be determined in the light of what may happen under the agreement, although what may happen may cover many possibilities which in the event did not happen. A covenant of this kind is invalid *ab initio* or valid *ab initio*. There cannot be some moment at which it passes from the class of invalid to that of valid covenants.

These two statements are very clear and are difficult to reconcile with some of the views expressed in the *Littlewoods* case.

At the same time, doubts have been cast on the correctness of this strict view and it might be considered that a court of equity is entitled to consider the effect of the contract as the circumstances come before it so as to avoid working an injustice. The entire doctrine that contracts in restraints of trade are void or unenforceable is based on the proposition that such contracts are contrary to public policy or, as was said in a very old case, 'against the benefit of the Commonwealth'. Can it be said that it is of any advantage to public policy or refuse relief which is held to be reasonable and proper to be granted, as in the *Commercial Plastics* case?

In the case of *McEllistrim v Ballymacelligott Co-operative Agricultural & Dairy Society* [1919] AC 548; 53 ILTR 121, Viscount Finlay at 128 of ILTR adopted a statement of James V.C. in the case of *Leather Cloth Co. v Lorsont* (1869) LR 9 Eq, 345 at 353. It is:

> All the cases when they come to be examined seem to establish this principle— that all restraints upon trade are bad as being in violation of public policy unless they are natural, and not unreasonable for the protection of the parties dealing legally with some subject matter of contract. The principle is this—public policy

requires that every man shall be at liberty to work for himself, and shall not be at liberty to deprive himself or the State of his labour, skill or talent by any contract that he enters into. On the other hand, public policy requires that when a man has, by skill or other means, obtained something which he wants to sell, he should be at liberty to sell it in the most advantageous way in the market; and in order to enable him to sell it advantageously in the market, it is necessary that he should be able to preclude himself from entering into competition with the purchaser. In such a case the same public policy that enables him to do that does not restrain him from alienating that which he wants to alienate and, therefore, enables him to enter into any stipulation, however restrictive it is, provided that restriction, in the judgment of the court, is not unreasonable having regard to the subject matter of the contract.

I have considered these matters at some length because the present application has been met to a large extent on the basis that it should be refused on the ground that the covenant is void and the plaintiff cannot succeed in its action. I am not satisfied about this as there seems to be a number of arguments open to the plaintiff and it would be improper for me on an interlocutory application to decide the main issue in the case without hearing the evidence which may be adduced and having a full argument on the various aspects to which I have referred. All I have to do on an interlocutory application is to decide whether the plaintiff has established a *prima facie* case in the sense that there is a serious question to be tried and, if so, what is the balance of convenience to the parties between granting and refusing an injunction.

From the facts which are before me and the review which I have made of the decisions, I am satisfied that there is a serious issue to be tried. On the question of the balance of convenience, it seems to me that the defendant can be adequately compensated in damages if he is successful in his defence and that an undertaking by the plaintiff to pay such damages will be met, whereas damages would not be an adequate remedy for the plaintiff and it is doubtful whether any damages could be recovered from the defendant if the plaintiff were to be successful. Accordingly, I am of opinion that the *status quo* should be preserved and that I should grant the interlocutory injunction sought.

Note

Severance is provided for under s. 4 (6) and (7) of the Competition Act 2002:

4. (6) The prohibition in sub-s. (1) shall not prevent the court, in exercising any jurisdiction conferred on it by this Act concerning an agreement, decision or concerted practice which contravenes that prohibition and which creates or, but for this Act, would have created legal relations between the parties thereto, from applying, where appropriate, any relevant rules of law as to the *severance* of those terms of that agreement, decision or concerted practice which contravene that prohibition from those which do not.

(7) In respect of an agreement, decision or concerted practice such as is referred to in sub-s. (6) a court of competent jurisdiction may make such order as to recovery, restitution or otherwise between the parties to such agreement, decision or concerted practice as may in all the circumstances seem just, having regard in particular to any consideration or benefit given or received by such parties on foot thereof.

See 'How Severance by Courts might save Offending Articles' 2 *Competition* 153 (*Competition Press*).

Chapter Eighteen

Discharge of Contractual Obligations

INTRODUCTION

This section examines four different circumstances in which a party to a contract may be discharged from their contractual obligations. The usual manner in which a party ceases to have any obligations under a contract is by performing them. Contracts may also be discharged by express agreement where the parties agree not to be bound by an existing contract. Thirdly, a breach may occur where, without lawful excuse, a party fails to or refuses to perform their obligations under a contract. Certain types of breach may be sufficiently serious as to entitle the innocent party to treat the contract as at an end. Finally, where the contractual obligations are rendered impossible to perform, the contract will be frustrated and both parties will be discharged from their obligations under the contract from that time onwards.

SECTION ONE—PERFORMANCE

In order to discharge a contract by performance, exact performance according to the specific terms of the contract must be established. As the next case illustrates, this can produce harsh results.

Cutter v Powell (1795) 6 TR 320

The plaintiff's husband was employed as second mate on a ship to sail from Jamaica to Liverpool for a gross sum of 30 guineas. When he died on route, the plaintiff sued to recover a proportionate part of the wages on a *quantum meruit* basis.

Lord Kenyon C.J.:

That where the parties have come to an express contract none can be implied has prevailed so long as to be reduced to an axiom in the law. Here the defendant expressly promised to pay the intestate 30 guineas, provided he proceeded, continued and did his duty as second mate in the ship from Jamaica to Liverpool; and the accompanying circumstances disclosed in the case are that the common rate of wages is £4 per month, when the party is paid in proportion to the time he serves: and that this voyage is generally performed in two months. Therefore if there had been no contract between these parties, all that the intestate could have recovered on a *quantum meruit* for the voyage would have been £8; whereas here the defendant contracted to pay thirty guineas provided the mate continued to do his duty as mate during the whole voyage, in which case the latter would have received nearly four times as much as if he were paid for the number of months he served. He stipulated to receive the larger sum if the whole duty were performed, and nothing unless the whole of that duty were performed: it was a kind of insurance.

(Ashurst, Grose and Lawrence JJ. concurred.)

In the above case, the contract to serve on the ship was viewed as an 'entire contract', i.e. performance must be carried out in its entirety before the other party makes payment under the contract. Building contracts, such as those the subject of the next case, are frequently viewed as entire.

Callan *v* Marum (1871) 5 IRCL 315

The plaintiff sued the defendant for repair work executed on the defendant's house and materials provided. The defendant claimed that the plaintiff failed to execute the work according to the terms of a special contract. He pleaded that 'no work was done or material provided . . . as alleged'.

Whiteside C.J.:

I now come to the argument, which was founded on the common counts. It is not to be forgotten that the contract was to build a house for a specific sum of money to be paid on the completion of the building, if no instalments had, under certificates from the architect, and according to the agreement, been paid during the progress of the work. I take it to be clear that in such a case the contract is entire and indivisible, and that the employer is not bound to pay for half, or quarter of a house; for the court and jury can have no right to apportion that which the parties themselves have treated as entire. If the agreement had been, that the builder was to be paid for work and labour and materials provided by measure and value, he might then have demanded payment from time to time, as the work proceeded and after it had been duly measured; *Williams v Fitzmaurice*;[1] but that would be a different contract to the one relied on by the present plaintiff. And I am of opinion that the principle laid down by Ashurst J. in *Cutter v Powell*,[2] applies to this case. These cases are a complete answer to the argument that the general question of work and labour ought to have been left to the jury, who could have made the necessary deductions on the ground that the work had not been completed conformably to the contract. The question then that arises upon the common counts is this, can the plaintiff, under the common count for work done and materials provided, recover for work done in part performance of a written contract, which, when the action was brought was open, unrescinded, and unperformed? I believe the law is quite settled that he can not: *Hulle v Heightman*.[3] On the same principle proceeded, the decision in *Ellis v Hamlen*,[4] the application of which to the present case cannot be disputed; and no case has been cited in which *Ellis v Hamlen* is impugned or questioned. I have always thought that it was almost an axiom in the law, and the proposition is certainly so stated by the text books, that in order to maintain an action for work and labour the plaintiff must prove a performance of the work according to the terms of the contract; or, if he has deviated from these terms, he must show that the defendant acquiesced in such deviation. See *Add. Cont.* (6th edn), 388, where the substance of *Ellis v Hamlen* is stated as an authority, and as binding as if fresh from the legal mint. In the *Books of Evidence* also the case is given as good law; and Mr Starkie, in his excellent work, quotes with approval the well known judgment of Le Blanc J., in *Basten v Butter*,[5] deciding that if a man contracts with another to build him a house for a certain sum, the stipulated work must be done according to the contract. I am, therefore, of opinion that *Ellis v Hamlen* is a well decided case, and that so far as it applies to the facts of the principal case, it is decisive against the plaintiff. The pleadings and arguments in *Munro v Butt*[6] were very similar to those in the principal case, with this important exception, however, that in *Munro v Butt*, the facts were much more favourable for the plaintiff's contention; because, in that case a great deal—the whole as the plaintiff alleged—of the work had been done, and the defendant had actually taken possession of the house. The surveyor, however, refused to give the certificate, the obtaining of which was to be a condition precedent to the plaintiff's right to recover, on the ground that the work had been incompletely or imperfectly performed, yet in this case, also, it was held that the plaintiff could not recover for work and labour generally, because there was a written contract for the work open, and unrescinded, nor on the count upon the contract, because it was not in the terms performed. From the judgment in this case we perceive, with what firmness the principles of the law were applied to the facts of the case before the court. The builder who had contracted to build two houses according to a plan and specification, and who built them not according to the agreement, and of inferior materials, was not allowed to recover one shilling upon his special contract, because he had not performed it according to its terms; and the argument that he might so recover upon the common count for work and labour and material, because he had violated the specific written contract, the only contract assented to by the other party, was refuted and rejected. The decision in *Munro v Butt* I hold to be an excellent precedent, and to be clearly applicable to one portion of this case. The principle so well laid down in *Munro v Butt*, and the case itself, are directly affirmed in the Exchequer Chamber, and in an instructive judgment delivered by Blackburn J. in *Appleby v Myers*.[7]

1. 3 H & N 844.	5. 7 East 479.
2. 6 TR 320; 2 Sm LCL.	6. 8 E & B 738.
3. 2 East 145.	7. LR 2 CP 651; SC sub. nom.
4. 3 Taunt 52.	*Appleby v Myers*, 36 LJN SCP 331.

(The majority of the court decided that a new trial should be ordered due to the defendant's failure to make a special plea alleging that the work was done under a special contract.)

In *Sumpter v Hedge* [1898] 1 QB 673, Smith L.J. stated 'The Law is that, where there is a contract to do work for a lump sum, until the work is completed the price of it cannot be recovered.' The Courts are typically reluctant to depart from this presumption. In the same case Collins L. J. noted, 'There are cases in which, though the plaintiff has abandoned the performance of a contract, it is possible for him to raise the inference of a new contract to pay for the work done on a quantum meruit from the defendant's having taken the benefit of that work, but, in order that may be done, the circumstances must be such as to give an option to take or not to take the benefit of the work alone. It is only where the circumstances are such as to give that option that there is any evidence on which to ground the inference of a new contract'.

Consider:

What is the rationale of the rule in *Sumpter v Hedge*?

Coughlan *v* Moloney (1905) 39 ILTR 153

The plaintiff agreed to build a house for the defendants for £200, the house to be completed before Christmas 1902. There was no provision for payment by instalments but £83 had been so paid prior to the action. The work was not completed by Christmas and the following October the defendants asked the plaintiff to estimate a value for the work done so that the matter could be wound up. In November the defendants took possession of the site, denying the plaintiff access. The plaintiff sued for the balance due under the contract or alternatively for *quantum meruit*.

Palles L.C.B. (King's Bench Division):

Now, first, I wish to put out of consideration a contract which is plainly implied by law under the circumstances of this case. Christmas, 1902, was the date of performance. Plainly, after that date the plaintiff continued to perform work, and plainly either at the request or with the consent of the defendants, so there is ground for implying a contract to pay for this performance after the date fixed for completion. There is no evidence as to whether this implied contract was a contract in the terms of the old contract. It was an implied contract to do the work within a reasonable time. Taking it that the plaintiff sues on this implied contract under his *indebitatus* count, the answer to it is that the work was not completed within a reasonable time, or at all, and, consequently, on this contract he would not be entitled to recover. Ultimately, the question comes to what were the plaintiff's rights in reference, not to the mere taking over and entering upon this building by the defendants, but to the circumstances under which it was so entered. Evidence was given of two letters asking the plaintiff to furnish particulars of the work that he had done, and for an estimate of its value, in order that the matter should be finally wound up. I do not say that if the terms of these letters had been assented to by the plaintiff that there would not have been a complete contract to pay on a *quantum meruit*. But, then, there was no assent to those terms by the plaintiff, and, on the contrary, it is clear that from that time and always he has been insisting on his right to recover on the special contract. The plaintiff's right to recover upon this *quantum meruit* depended on a state of facts which it would have been impossible for the jury to have found. I am clear that the view of counsel was that they were entitled to recover on a *quantum meruit*, based not upon any contract found by the jury, but upon the fact that possession was taken up of the work by the defendants—that they retained the benefit of it—and that under the circumstances the plaintiff was entitled to recover the full value of his work. That proposition, stated nakedly, is simply that *Munro v Butt* 8 E & B 738, and cases of that description, are not law. It is going upon the principle applicable to chattels, that if a certain thing is done, not in performance of a contract, but under circumstances under which the defendant is able to obtain benefit from it, and if the defendant accepts and avails himself of it, then the plaintiff is able to recover on a *quantum meruit*. The decision in *Munro v Butt* is that this principle does not apply to a house on a man's land, because there is no possibility of rejecting the benefit of what has been done, unless he destroys the house built on it. Again, it was argued that if there was nothing more than the mere taking up of possession—that is, if the possession was availed of, and the house improved, that would render the defendant liable. I am of opinion that it cannot. I do not go into the question of hardship. *Cutter v Powell* 2 SLC 1 is always apt to work hardship, but I think that this application should be refused with costs, . . .

(The Court of Appeal confirmed this principle.)

Walker L.J:

The only question is that of the *quantum meruit*. The defendants were, by the findings of the jury, justified in serving notice and taking up possession. To enable the plaintiff to recover, something more than the defendants merely taking the benefit of the work done upon the land, is necessary, from which a new contract may be inferred. There is no evidence of such a kind here. The most favourable case for the plaintiff would be that possession was taken up on the terms that he should be paid on a *quantum meruit*. But terms mean terms agreed upon on both sides. The acts of the plaintiff show that he never adopted this view. The principle of *Munro v Butt* is quite applicable to this case.

Notes

1. In 'In Defence of *Sumpter v Hedge*' (2002) 118 LQR 569, McFarlane and Stevens argue in support of the general rule applied in *Sumpter v Hedge* [1898] 1 QB 673 that a party in breach cannot claim for the value of services rendered or the value of goods supplied under a contract unless he has accrued contractual entitlement to be paid. The authors suggest that the part performance of an entire obligation should not by itself entitle the performer to payment. Even where the breach confers a benefit on the other party by the part performance of an entire obligation, there is nothing unjust about such enrichment.
2. If one party's failure to perform their obligations is caused by some act or default of the other party *quantum meruit* may be available. See *Arterial Drainage Co. Ltd v Rathangan River Drainage Board* (1880) 6 LR (Ir.) 513.
3. Certain contracts may be deemed to be divisible in that they contain separate obligations which may be performed individually. In *Verolme Cork Dockyard Ltd v Shannon Atlantic Fisheries Ltd* 31 July 1978, unrep. Finlay P. in the High Court found that it was a term of a contract made between the plaintiffs and the defendants for the repair of a ship, that a substantial payment on account would be made by the defendants when a reasonably high proportion of the work had been carried out. The judge decided this despite the fact that the request for a payment on account did not precisely comply with the power to make such a request reserved in the printed conditions supplied by the plaintiffs. The defence argument that no payment was due until completion of the entire of the repairs was not accepted.

Consider:

On what basis can it be determined that obligations are entire or divisible?

A. SUBSTANTIAL PERFORMANCE

In order to afford some relief against the harsh results produced by the entire contract rule, the courts have developed a doctrine of substantial performance. This allows the party who has substantially performed his or her obligations under the contract to seek payment of the contract price less an amount to remedy the outstanding defects.

Kincora Builders Ltd *v* Cronin (HC) 5 March 1973, unrep.

The plaintiffs, a firm of builders, contracted to build a house for the defendant. Upon visiting the site the defendant noticed that the walls and ceilings were not insulated as stipulated in the contract. The defendant agreed to accept a sum of £350 in satisfaction of the failure of the plaintiffs to complete the insulation work on the walls but claimed to have received no settlement for failure to insulate the ceiling. The plaintiffs sued for the sum of £6,000, the balance due on foot of the contract. The defendant claimed that the house was never completed in accordance with the contract and counterclaimed for damages for breach of contract.

Pringle J.:

[Counsel for the plaintiffs] submitted that, as the contract had been *substantially* completed, his clients were entitled to insist on the completion of the contract, subject to whatever deductions the defendant was entitled to for defective work (if any). He referred to the case of *Bolton v Mahadeva* [1972] 1 WLR 1009, in which the Court of Appeal in England dealt with the question of the circumstances under which a building contractor who has entered into a lump sum contract, can recover anything on foot thereof, if the contract has not been completely performed. The court reviewed the authorities, and in particular distinguished an earlier decision of the Court of Appeal in the case of H. *Dakin & Co. v Lee* [1916] 1KB 566, which had been followed in the case of *Hoenig v Isaacs* [1952] 2 All ER 176.

In *Dakin's* case the plaintiffs had agreed to carry out certain repairs to the defendant's house for the sum of £264 and the plaintiffs claimed that sum and a sum for extras. The defendant, who had gone back into the house after the plaintiffs' workmen had left, disputed her liability to pay any part of the contract sum on the ground that the contract had not been fulfilled in three respects, (1) the concrete which was to be placed under a part of one of the side walls of the house which was to be underpinned was to be of the depth of 4 feet and it was in fact only done to a depth of 2 feet, (2) columns of hollow iron, 5 inches in diameter were to be used to support a certain bay window, whereas the columns supplied were of solid iron 4 inches in diameter, and (3) the joists over the bay window were to be cleated at the angles and bolted to caps and to each other and this was not done. The official referee found as a fact that the contract had not been fulfilled in the three instances mentioned, and he held that the plaintiffs were therefore not entitled to recover any part of the contract price, or of the amount claimed for extras, but he allowed £70 for the additional work. This decision was reversed by Ridley and Sankey JJ. in the Kings Bench Division and their decision was upheld by the Court of Appeal. The Master of the Rolls, Lord Cozens-Hardy, said in his judgment, after dealing with the deviations from the contract:

> In these circumstances it has been argued before us that, in a contract of this kind to do work for a lump sum, the defect in some of the items of the specification, or the failure to do every item in the specification, puts an end to the whole contract and prevents the builders from making any claim upon it: and therefore, where there is no ground for presuming any fresh contract, he cannot obtain any payment. The matter has been treated in the argument as though the omission to do every item perfectly was an abandonment of the contract. That seems to me, with great respect, to be absolutely and entirely wrong. An illustration of the abandonment of a contract which was given from one of the authorities was that of a builder who, when he had half finished the work, said to the employer 'I cannot finish it because I have no money' and left the job undone at that stage. That is an abandonment of the contract and prevents the builder, therefore from making any claim, unless there be some circumstances leading to a different conclusion. But to say that a builder cannot recover from a building owner merely because some item of the work has been done negligently, or inefficiently, or improperly, is a proposition which I should not listen to, unless compelled by a decision of the House of Lords. Take a contract for a lump sum to decorate a house: the contract provides that there shall be three coats of oil paint, but in one of the rooms only two coats of paint are put on, can anybody seriously say that, under these circumstances, the building owner could go and occupy the house and take the benefit of all the decorations which had been done in the other rooms without paying a penny for all the work done by the builder just because two coats of paint had been put on in one room where there ought to have been three? I regard the present case as one of negligence and bad workmanship and not as a case where there has been an omission of any one of the items in the specification. The builders thought apparently, as they have sworn, that they had done all that was intended to be done in reference to the contract: and I suppose that the defects are due to carelessness on the part of some of the workmen or of the foreman: but the existence of these defects does not amount to a refusal by them to perform part of the contract: it simply shows negligence in the way they have done the work.

Lord Justice Pickford in his judgment said:

Certainly I have not the slightest wish to differ from the view that, if a man agrees to do a certain amount of work for a lump sum and only does part of it, he cannot sue for the lump sum, but I cannot accept the proposition that, if a man agrees to do a certain amount of work for a lump sum, every breach which he makes of that contract by doing his work badly, or by omitting some small portion of it, is an abandonment of the contract, or is only a performance of part of the contract so that he cannot be paid his lump sum.

Lord Justice Warrington agreed with these judgments.

In *Bolton's* case the plaintiff agreed to install a combined heating and domestic hot water system in the defendant's house at a cost of £560. It was proved that there were certain defects in the work done by the plaintiff, the main being that the heating system did not heat adequately and gave out fumes, and to cure these defects would cost £174. The Court of Appeal, reversing the decision of the County Court Judge, held that the plaintiff had not substantially completed his contract and that he was therefore not entitled to recover the contract price. Lord Justice Cairns in his judgment said, at 1011: 'The main question in the case is whether the defects in workmanship found by the judge to be such as to cost £174 to repair—that is between one third and one quarter of the contract price—were of such a character and amount that the plaintiff could not be said to have substantially performed his contract. That is in my view clearly the legal principle which has to be applied in this case.' Again, at 1013, he said 'In considering whether there was substantial performance, I am of opinion that it is relevant to take into account both the nature of the defects and the proportion between the cost of rectifying them and the contract price. It would be wrong to say that the contractor is only entitled to payment if the defects are so trifling as to be covered by the *de minimis* rule.'

Lord Justice Sachs in his judgment at 1015 said:

> So far as the law is concerned, I would merely add that it seems to me to be compactly and accurately stated in *Cheshire and Fifoot's Law of Contract* (7th edn 1969), 492 in the following terms: . . . 'the present rule is that, so long as there is a substantial performance, the contractor is entitled to the stipulated price, subject only to a cross-action of counterclaim for the omissions or defects in 'execution', and to cross action or counterclaim I would of course add 'set off'.' The converse however is equally correct—if there is not a substantial compliance the contractor cannot recover. It is upon the application of that converse rule that the plaintiff's case here fails. This rule does not now work hardly on a contractor, if only he is prepared to remedy the defects before seeking to resort to litigation to recover the lump sum. It is entirely the fault of the contractor in this instant case that he has placed himself in a difficulty by his refusal on 4 December 1969 to remedy the defects of which complaint was being made.

Applying the principles of law laid down in these cases, with which I agree, to the facts of this case, I am satisfied that, while the cost of installing the insulation in the ceiling of the attic would be a very small figure compared with the contract price, the position is materially different from that which existed in *Dakin's* case in that the plaintiffs, owing no doubt to what I have held to be an erroneous interpretation of what had been agreed in regard to the payment of the £350, have up to the present time refused to do this work which was clearly part of their contract. There has therefore been a refusal by the plaintiffs to carry out part of their contract, and this amounts in law to an abandonment of their contract, which would have disentitled them to payment of the balance of the contract price until they did this work. I should also say that no question arises here as to the defendant having entered into possession and obtained any benefit from the work which has been done, as was the case in *Dakin's* case.

Note

See Anthony Beck, 'The Doctrine of Substantial Performance: Conditions and Conditions Precedent' (1975) 38 MLR 413.

Law Commission Report No. 121 (1983)
(Footnotes abridged.)

. . .

2.25 The principal justification of the present law as it applies to entire contracts is that 'it holds men to their contracts'.[1] The contractor who has agreed to do a job for an all-in price, to be paid when the work is completed, may not then insist on payments on account; much less may he break the contract by leaving the work half-finished and recover payment for what he has done. By refusing him redress except as provided by the contract the law gives him an incentive to complete the job. It may be argued that this incentive would be greatly reduced if he were to be entitled to payment, otherwise than under the contract, in respect of benefits conferred by partial performance.

2.26 The present law may also be justified on the basis that the drastic consequences for the contractor who fails to complete the work to be done under the contract place the other party in a strong bargaining position. It may be argued that this encourages the settlement of disputes in favour of the party not in breach of contract and that in consequence the removal of the hardship that the present law may cause to some could result in more serious and more general hardship to others whom the law now benefits. Finally the present law, whatever its defects, has the merit of being reasonably certain and therefore may be said to have the desirable effect of discouraging litigation.

2.27 However, although both parties may intend that the innocent party should not have to pay any amount in respect of a benefit obtained by him as a result of partial performance of the contract by the party in breach, it is arguable that such a result has a penal flavour and that accordingly it should not lightly be assumed that the parties so intend. The mere postponement of payment of a lump sum by one party until after the other party has completely performed is a normal provision and it is arguable that it should not have such penal overtones.

2.28 In our working paper[2] we considered that this type of provision should not *by itself* preclude the party in breach from recovering an amount which reflects any enrichment which the innocent party has obtained as a result of having had a benefit conferred upon him under the contract by the partial performance. It was this aspect of the present law that in our view constituted a mischief.

. . .

2.29 In considering whether the present law should be retained we have taken into account another factor, namely that in the great majority of contracts, involving substantial sums of money, there will be provision for stage payments. It might therefore be argued that any change in the present law would, in general, only affect contracts between jobbing builders and householders and that in such cases the bargaining position of the parties makes undesirable any such change. However, a number of points may be made in this regard.

2.30 The first point is that, in our view, the mischief we have identified in the present law may arise even in relation to contracts involving substantial sums of money. Not all such contracts will provide for stage payments and even where the parties have made such provision, they will not always have considered or provided for the situation where a stage is not completed. The second point is that many lump sum contracts between householders and jobbing builders involve not insignificant sums—contracts of this type involving several thousand pounds are far from unknown. Accordingly, the mischief which we have identified in the present law may well arise when considerable sums are at stake.

2.31 The final point concerns the bargaining position of the householder and his jobbing builder. Although any alteration in the present law will weaken the bargaining position of the householder, the extent of any such weakening should not be exaggerated. The householder is entitled not only to damages for losses caused by the failure to complete but also to damages for inconvenience.[3] This latter entitlement is a recent development in the law which has occurred since the rule relating to entire contracts was established. In the light of his entitlement to damages in respect of both loss and inconvenience the householder will be in a position where his claim in damages may well exceed whatever the builder is entitled to. Accordingly, any change in the present law which would entitle the builder to make a claim in respect of the work he has done would, in effect, only entitle him to recover money from the householder where the latter has received a significant benefit which exceeds the loss which he has suffered as a result of the breach.

2.32 We considered the justification of the present law but we think that it loses some of its force in view of the fact that the mischief which we have identified is not that the parties can require complete performance before any counter-performance is due, but that under the present law they may, and usually will, be held to have done so merely by providing for postponement of payment. In our view the present law leads to a result which was not necessarily the one which the parties in all cases would have contemplated as flowing from their agreement solely by reason of the postponement of payment.

2.33 Accordingly we consider that our provisional conclusion was correct and recommend that a new remedy should be provided for the party in breach (including, of course, his assignees) where he or a third party acting on his behalf has conferred a benefit on the innocent party by his incomplete or defective performance of an entire contract. We recommend that this new remedy should apply whether the consideration to be furnished by one party for the completion of something to be done by the other consists in promising to pay a sum of money or in promising either to do some other act or to forbear from doing something.

Note of Dissent

I have the misfortune to differ from my colleagues both as regards the principal policy conclusion reached in this report and as to the manner of its implementation. In almost all contracts of any substance today under which one party promises to carry out certain work in return for a consideration to be given by the other, the contract will make provision for stage payments of one sort or another. The facts of modern economic life have demonstrated that payments on account while the work proceeds are a necessity. Both printed and specially prepared contracts will therefore, in almost every case, provide for such payments. Where a written contract does not provide for such payments, the reason may well be that the parties intended that payment would be due if, but only if, the contractor finished the work. The so-called mischief which the report is intended to correct is therefore likely only to exist in relation to small, informal contracts of which the normal example will be a contract between a householder and a jobbing builder to carry out a particular item of work. Experience has shown that it is all too common for such builders not to complete one job of work before moving on to the next. The effect of the report is to remove from the householder almost the only effective sanction he has against the builder not completing the job. In short, he is prevented from saying with any legal effect, 'Unless you come back and finish the job, I shan't pay you a penny'. In my view, the disadvantages in practice of the recommendations contained in the report outweigh the advantages to be gained from the search for theoretically perfect justice between the parties. If the report's recommendations are implemented, the jobbing builder can leave the site and, when the irate and exasperated householder finally brings the contract to an end, send in a bill for the work done up to the time when he abandoned the site. It will then be for the householder to dispute the amount and calculate his counterclaim for damages. To put the burden on the householder in this manner is, in my view, to put him in a disadvantageous position where he negotiates from a position of weakness. It must not be forgotten that it is the builder who has broken the contract, not the householder, and that the contract is one under which the parties agreed that payment would be by lump sum only when the work was done.

(*Signed* Brian Davenport)

1. *Munro v Butt* (1858) E & B 735, 754, per Lord Campbell C.J.
2. Working Paper No. 65, para. 21.
3. *Rawlings v Rentokil Laboratories* [1972] EGD 744.

There have been certain statutory modifications of the entire contract rule.

Sale of Goods Act 1893 ss 30 and 31

30. (1) Where the seller delivers to the buyer a quantity of goods less than he contracted to sell, the buyer may reject them, but if the buyer accepts the goods so delivered he must pay for them at the contract rate.

(2) Where the seller delivers to the buyer a quantity of goods larger than he contracted to sell, the buyer may accept the goods included in the contract and reject the rest, or he may reject the whole. If the buyer accepts the whole of the goods so delivered he must pay for them at the contract rate.

(3) Where the seller delivers to the buyer the goods he contracted to sell mixed with goods of a different description not included in the contract, the buyer may accept the goods which are in accordance with the contract and reject the rest, or he may reject the whole.

(4) The provisions of this section are subject to any usage of trade, special agreement, or course of dealing between the parties.

31. (1) Unless otherwise agreed, the buyer of goods is not bound to accept delivery thereof by instalments.

(2) Where there is a contract for the sale of goods to be delivered by stated instalments, which are to be separately paid for, and the seller makes defective deliveries in respect of one or more instalments, or the buyer neglects or refuses to take delivery of or pay for one or more instalments, it is a question in each case depending on the terms of the contract and the circumstances of the case, whether the breach of contract is a repudiation of the whole contract or whether it is a severable breach giving rise to a claim for compensation but not to a right to treat the whole contract as repudiated.

Apportionment Act 1870 ss 2 and 3

2. From and after the passing of this Act all rents, annuities, dividends, and other periodical payments in the nature of income (whether reserved or made payable under an instrument in writing or otherwise) shall, like interest on money lent, be considered as accruing from day to day, and shall be apportionable in respect of time accordingly.

3. The apportioned part of any such rent, annuity, dividend, or other payment shall be payable or recoverable in the case of a continuing rent, annuity, or other such payment when the entire portion of which such apportioned part shall form part shall become due and payable, and not before, and in the case of a rent, annuity, or other such payment determined by re-entry, death, or otherwise when the next entire portion of the same would have been payable if the same had not so determined, and not before.

Note

This Act was applied in the case of *Treacy v Corcoran* (1874) IR 8 CL 40 to award the plaintiff who had resigned from his employment in the middle of a half year, an apportioned part of that half year's salary.

B. TIME OF PERFORMANCE

The time of performance may be deemed to be 'of the essence of the contract'. In such a case failure to perform on time may result in a discharge of the contract.

Sepia Ltd and Opel Ltd *v* M. & P. Hanlon Ltd and Another (HC) 23 January 1979, unrep.

The defendants agreed to sell two parcels of land to the plaintiffs. Block A was the subject of a contract which expressly fixed the closing date and expressly made time of the essence. The agreement was subject to the plaintiff's obtaining planning permission. In the events which occured the closing date in respect of both contracts became 31 December 1976. By notice of 7 April 1977 the defendants called on the plaintiffs to close both sales within three months, and made time the essence of the contract. As the sales were not closed, the defendants claimed to be entitled to retain the money paid by the plaintiffs on the signing of the two contracts.

Costello J.:

In the first contract the parties had expressly made time of the essence of the contract when they provided that the sale was to be closed on 1 May 1975. Condition 11 relating to planning permission must be interpreted in the light of the necessity strictly to observe the date set for closing. The result is, in my opinion, that if the plaintiffs had failed to obtain planning permission by 1 May 1975 and if the closing date was not extended by mutual agreement then the defendants were entitled to treat the contract as at an end if the plaintiffs refused to complete—the absence of planning permission would not have excused the non-performance by the plaintiffs of the contract.

The second contract of 16 May did not make time of the essence of the contract in relation to the sale of Block B and when it amended the closing date of the first contract it did not provide that in respect of the new closing date time was to be of the essence of the contract. In addition it will be observed that the two sales were to be closed simultaneously. It was not, in my opinion, the intention of the parties that time was to be the essence of the first contract but not of the second contract. The result was that two possible closing dates in respect of both sales were agreed to but time was not made the essence of the contract in respect of either sale.

The second sale was not made subject to planning permission being obtained but the first sale remained subject to special condition 11. The result of the amendment of the first contract was that if the plaintiffs were in default in closing the sales on either of the dates specified then the vendors could serve a notice making time the essence of the contract and fixing a reasonable time for their completion. If time was made the essence of the contract and the period for completion given a reasonable one then the position at the expiration of the notice would be this. If planning permission had then been obtained the plaintiffs were bound to complete both sales. If planning permission had not been obtained then the plaintiffs could waive this provision of the contract (for reasons given in the next succeeding contract) and complete both sales. If however the plaintiffs did not waive special condition 11 then the first contract would come to an end at the expiration of the notice (the condition relating to planning permission not having been complied with) (see *Smith v Butler* [1900] 1 QB 694; *Aberfoyle Plantation Ltd v Cheng* [1960] AC 115). Alternatively, the plaintiffs' refusal to complete would amount to a repudiation of the contract entitling the defendants to treat it as at an end. In either case, the defendant would be entitled to retain the non-refundable deposit of £30,000. As to the second contract (which was not expressly subject to a condition relating to planning permission) the plaintiffs' failure to complete at the expiration of the notice would entitle the defendants to treat this contract as at an end and to retain the non-refundable deposit of £20,000.

The evidence satisfies me that the clause in the first contract relating to planning permission had been inserted for the exclusive benefit of the plaintiffs. This means that it could be waived by them. The principle that a condition inserted exclusively for the benefit of one party can be waived by that party is referred to in *Heron Garage Properties Ltd v Moss* [1974] 1 WLR 148. The plaintiffs therefore could have waived condition 11 if they wished to close the sale in the absence of planning permission.

The two contracts remained separate and independent contracts notwithstanding the provision that they were to be closed simultaneously. In certain events the parties might have been under an obligation to complete one but not the other. In the events that have happened, however, a single notice fixing a date for the simultaneous closing of the two contracts was permissible. ...

Reasonableness of the notice
The legal principles to be applied in this case are clear and well established. If a stipulation as to time is not of the essence of a contract then when one party has been guilty of undue delay the other may give notice requiring the contract to be performed within a reasonable time specified in the notice. In considering the reasonableness of the time so limited the court will consider not merely what remains to be done at the date of the notice but all the circumstances of the case, including the previous delay of the purchaser and the attitude of the vendor to it. If the notice is a reasonable one

the vendor may at its expiration treat the contract as at an end if the purchaser refuses to complete (see *Stikney v Keeble* [1915] AC 386; and *Ajit v Sammy* [1967] 1 AC 255). In this case there was without any doubt undue delay on the part of the plaintiffs after 31 December 1976. In the previous July the plaintiffs had intimated that they were not prepared to close and on 7 September they had been made aware that their request for an extension of time had been refused. By 7 April 1977 three months had expired from the contractual closing date and the plaintiffs had by this time made it perfectly clear that they were not going to close the sale for an indefinite period (if at all). In these circumstances the defendants became entitled to serve a notice specifying a closing date and making time the essence of the contract. The real issue in the case, however, is whether the length of time given by the notice of 7 April was a reasonable one. I have come to the conclusion that in all the circumstances of this case, the notice given was in fact a reasonable one.

Notes

1. In *O'Connor v. Coady* [2005] 1 ILRM 256 (see p. 320) Geoghegan J., referring to *Sepia*, stated 'I do not think that Costello J.'s words should be interpreted as his having expressed any view as to whether in the case of a conditional contract, if the condition fails there is a self-executing termination of the contract or on the other hand if one of the parties has to indicate that he or she is treating it as at an end.'
2. See *Shawton Engineering Ltd v DGP International Ltd (t/a Design Group Partnership)* [2006] BLR 1 for a similar finding.

Crean v Drinan [1983] ILRM 82

The plaintiff entered into a contract to purchase a public house from the defendant. The closing date was to be 4 May 1979. Clause 2 provided that the contract was subject to the defendant obtaining an assignment of any outstanding third party interest in the property on or before the closing date. In the event of the deed of sale not being executed the deposit was to be returned. As the assignment was not available by the agreed date, the plaintiff decided not to proceed with the sale and sought the return of his deposit.

Barrington J.:

[Counsel for the plaintiff] relies principally upon the decision in *Aberfoyle Plantations Ltd v Cheng* [1959] 3 All ER 910. In that case, which was a decision of the Privy Council, the court drew a distinction between the flexibility which courts of equity have adopted in the past in relation to the closing date in contracts for the sale of land and the rigidity which courts have adopted toward dates fixed by conditions on which the very existence of the contract depends. The court adopted with approval a passage from the judgment of Maugham J. in *Re Sandwell Park Colliery Co.; Field v The Company* [1929] 1 Ch. 277 in which he stated at 282:

> Courts of equity, in dealing with actions for specific performance relating to land, have been accustomed to give effect to the real intention, rather than to the precise words, fixing the date for completion. The effect is that a clause fixing a date for

completion is equivalent to a clause stating that completion shall be on that date or within a reasonable time thereafter. But there is no ground for a similar construction in the case of a condition upon which the validity of the contract as one for sale depends. The distinction is obvious. In the first case both parties are bound and a moderate delay in completion is thought not to injure either. In the latter, the very existence of the mutual obligations is dependent upon the performance of the condition. The purchasers do not know in the first instance if their purchase money will ever be required. In general, and in the present case, there is no promise or undertaking by the vendor that the condition will be fulfilled. Equity has, I think never applied its liberal views as to time to such a condition. If a date is mentioned, the condition must be exactly complied with. If a date is not mentioned, the condition must be fulfilled within a reasonable time; there is no difference between the views of law and equity in considering what is a reasonable time, and the uncertain position of the purchasers must be borne in mind.

In *Aberfoyle Plantations v Cheng* the Privy Council having referred to the overriding rule that the meaning of a contract is to be found in the intention of the parties as expressed in, or to be implied from, the language they have used, went on to adopt 'as warranted by authority and manifestly reasonable in themselves' the following general principles of interpretation:

i. Where a conditional contract of sale fixes the date for the completion of the sale then the condition must be fulfilled by that date;
ii. Where a conditional contract of sale fixes no date for completion of the sale, then the condition must be fulfilled within a reasonable time;
iii. Where a conditional contract of sale fixes (whether specifically or by reference to the date fixed for completion) the date by which the condition is to be fulfilled, then the date so fixed must be strictly adhered to, and the time allowed is not to be extended by reference to equitable principles.

McWilliam J. appears to have adopted this third principle in *Maloney v Elf Investments Ltd* (HC) 1979 No. 295Sp 7 December 1979. The condition under discussion in that case provided that the 'sale is subject to the purchasers getting full planning permission before 31 July 1978'. Discussing this condition McWilliam J. says:

This can only mean that the contract is only to be enforceable if the permission is obtained by that date. Certainly no other meaning has been suggested to me. But it has been argued on behalf of the defendant that time was not, in this respect, made the essence of the contract and that a reasonable time ought to be allowed to obtain the permission by analogy to the principle that time for completing a contract is regarded in equity as the date fixed for completion or a reasonable time thereafter unless time has been made of the essence of the contract in this respect.

I was referred to conditions 4 and 28 of the general conditions in the contract. Condition 4 is the normal condition relating to payment of interest should the purchase not be completed on or before the closing date and condition 28 is the normal condition providing for service of notice to complete within twenty eight days save where the special conditions provide that time should be made of the essence of the contract in respect of the closing date. I do not consider that these conditions give me any assistance and I was not referred to any authority in support of the proposition that a reasonable time ought to be allowed for the performance of the condition. I have however, been referred on behalf of the plaintiff to the case of *Aberfoyle Plantations Ltd v Cheng* [1959] 3 WLR 1011 in which this proposition was rejected and Lord Jenkins said, at 1016: '(iii) Where a conditional contract of sale fixes . . . the date by which the condition is to be fulfilled, then the date so fixed must be strictly adhered to, and the time allowed is not to be extended by reference to any equitable principles.'

I was concerned by the fact that special condition no. 2 in the present case refers in terms not to '4 May 1979' but to 'closing date'.

However this matter appears to be covered by the passage in parenthesis in the third principle set out in the passage quoted above from the decision in *Aberfoyle Plantations v Cheng*. That principle is to the effect that where a conditional contract of sale fixes (whether specifically or by reference to the date fixed for completion) the date by which the condition is to be fulfilled, then the date so fixed must be strictly adhered to. . . .

     . . .

     [Counsel for the defendant] submitted that special condition no. 2 is not a condition precedent to the validity of the contract as a contract for sale. . . .

     . . .

He relied on *Property & Bloodstock Ltd v Emerton* [1967] 2 All ER 839. In that case the clause provided that the sale was subject to the vendor's obtaining the consent of the landlords to the assignment of the lease to the purchaser. The date fixed by the contract for completion of the sale was 24 October 1966. By that date the vendor had not in fact obtained the consent of the landlord but Ungoed-Thomas J., distinguishing *Aberfoyle Plantations Ltd v Cheng* held that the obtaining of the consent of the landlord was not a condition precedent to the validity of the contract but was a matter of title to be attended to before completion.

In a passage of the report Ungoed-Thomas J. states at 848: 'If what the agreement provides for is that title and not the creation of a contract of sale is subject to that consent being obtained, then that consent has to be forthcoming by the date at which title has to be established, normally actual completion.'

It appears to me that the decision in *Property & Bloodstock Ltd v Emerton* turned upon the actual wording of the contract in that case and upon the fact that the matter at issue was one of title only. It may well be in the present case that the matter at issue was also one of title, but it was a matter which [the plaintiff's solicitor], for legitimate reasons of his own, saw fit to make the subject matter of a special condition in the contract. The contract is expressed to be subject to the performance of that condition and in the event of the deed referred to not being executed the special condition itself provides that 'the purchaser shall be refunded his deposit but without interest, costs or compensation of any kind.' . . .

Consider:

Are there any types of contract where time will automatically be presumed to be of the essence?

SECTION TWO—AGREEMENT

A contract may be rescinded or varied by subsequent agreement

A. Rescission

Rescission involves releasing the parties from their obligations under the contract. For a contract to be terminated by mutual agreement ('accord'), consideration ('satisfaction') must be present. In an executory contract consideration is provided by the parties yielding up their rights against the other. However, if the contract has been executed by one of the parties rescission will be effective only if additional consideration is provided.

B. Variation

A variation involves altering a certain term or terms of the contract. Consideration will be required for a variation to be effective. In *McQuaid v Lynam* [1955] IR 564 (see p. 258 above), Kenny J. discussed the situations in which a variation would have to comply with s. 2 of the Statute of Frauds 1695.

C. Waiver

If a party to a contract requests and is granted some degree of forebearance, the contractual obligation remains unchanged. (As the obligation continues to exist, this waiver need not be evidenced in writing. This differs thus from a variation where the terms of the agreement are altered and thus the variation must be evidenced in writing.) Under this principle, the person who waives his or her rights under the contract may be prevented from later trying to insist on performance in accordance with the strict terms of the contract.

A party to a contract may only unilaterally waive a term of the contract if the term is one which relates to his or her exclusive benefit. This point is demonstrated by the next case.

McKillop and Another *v* McMullan [1979] NI 85

The defendant entered into a contract to sell land to the plaintiffs. Under this contract the defendant was entitled to a right of way over a road which the plaintiffs were to construct on part of the land. The contract was signed subject to the plaintiffs obtaining planning permission for the construction of the road. The stated completion date of 17 June 1974 passed and the defendant continued to enquire as to the existence of planning permission. He rejected the plaintiffs' suggestions that the planning condition be deleted from the contract. Finally, on 13 November 1975, the defendant without prior warning returned the deposit and notified the plaintiffs that he regarded the contract as no longer binding due to the non-fulfilment of the planning permission condition. Shortly afterwards permission was obtained and the plaintiffs sought specific performance of the contract.

Murray J.:

For the plaintiffs [counsel] put forward two main submissions:

   (1) that the planning condition was inserted for the sole and exclusive benefit of the plaintiffs and that they could and did unilaterally waive it; but

   (2) in the alternative, that if it could not be treated as waived, time was not of the essence of the contract in relation to the planning condition, and a reasonable period of notice to make it so would have been necessary on the part of the defendant before he became entitled to say that the failure to fulfil the condition had rendered the contract void.

      . . .

For the defendant [counsel] submitted:

   (1) that a distinction had to be drawn between the effect of a time stipulation in relation to the completion of an unconditional contract of sale, and a time stipulation related to the fulfilment of a condition precedent to the taking effect of a contract of sale;

   (2) that whereas equity might treat a provision saying that completion was to take place on a certain date as meaning on the date or within a reasonable time thereafter, it treated a time stipulation in relation to the fulfilment of a condition precedent as absolute, subject only to the operation of the doctrines of waiver and estoppel;

   (3) that in the present case it was a condition precedent to the parties being bound respectively to sell and buy, that by the completion date, *viz*. 17 June 1974, the planning condition should be fulfilled and

   (4) that at any time after 17 June 1974—the planning condition being then unfulfilled—it was open to the defendant without prior notice to the plaintiffs to declare the contract at an end for non-fulfilment of the condition precedent.

      . . .

I now come to my decision in the case.

In my view [counsel's] first submission on behalf of the plaintiffs, *viz*. that the planning condition is a stipulation incorporated in the contract for the exclusive benefit of the plaintiffs—and therefore waivable unilaterally by them—is quite unsustainable. On the face of the contract the defendant is entitled to a right of way with or without vehicles over the access road, and to suggest that it would not be of benefit to him to have a road lawfully and properly constructed in accordance with a valid planning permission does not bear a moment's examination: from the judgment of Brightman J. in *Heron Garage Properties v Moss* [1974] 1 WLR 148, it appears that in determining whether a stipulation is for the exclusive benefit of one party so as to be waivable unilaterally by him, it must be obviously so on the face of the contract.

It is my view that [counsel for the defendant] is correct and [counsel for the plaintiff] not so in the analysis of the legal situation created by the planning condition and the completion date condition. The planning condition created a condition precedent to the coming into existence of an effective and enforceable contract of sale, and on the basis of the principles enunciated in *Aberfoyle Plantations v Cheng* [1960] AC 115 I regard the contract, *as originally made between the parties*, as requiring the fulfilment of that condition by 17 June 1974, the completion date. (In passing I comment that in his opening the plaintiff's counsel suggested that 17 June 1974, was not the correct date for completion, but there was nothing in the evidence to bear this out and in my view that date must be taken as the originally agreed date.) It follows that if on 17 June 1974, the defendant had said to the plaintiffs—'You have now failed to obtain the necessary planning permission in accordance with the planning condition and the contract is therefore null and void' he (the defendant) would have been entitled in law to take up that attitude. In fact, of course, he did nothing of the kind and as late as 17 June 1975—exactly one year later—we find the defendant's solicitors writing: 'Our client insists that the contract be performed as it is written.' The inference is irresistible, and [counsel for the defendant] did not really try to resist it, that the defendant had waived the original failure of the plaintiffs to fulfil the planning condition, but basing himself on *Barclay v Messenger* (1874) 43 LJ Eq 449 [counsel] said it was only a qualified waiver. I think he is right about this. The defendant by not insisting on avoiding the contract on 17 June 1974, did not thereby lose his right to insist on a fulfilment of the planning condition as a condition precedent to the taking effect of the sale contract. However, the crucial question in this: what date was to be substituted for 17 June 1974, as the date by which the condition precedent had to be fulfilled? There was no difficulty about this in *Barclay v Messenger* because another specific date was substituted for the original date in the contract and the substituted date was taken by the court to be the relevant date. In this case no specified date was substituted. What then was the position? [Counsel] says that at any time after 17 June 1974, the defendant was entitled *without warning* to say to the plaintiffs—'I will wait no longer: you have not obtained the planning permission and the contract is void'—as he purported to do by his solicitors' letter of 13 November 1975. My opinion is that such a course of action was not open to the defendant. Clearly he was entitled to fix a new date for the fulfilment of the condition precedent, but in my judgment the principles of equity required him to give the plaintiffs reasonable notice of that date so that they had at least an opportunity of fulfilling the condition in time. I think this reasoning applies with particular force when one considers that even after a year—as I have pointed out—the defendant showed no sign whatever of calling the contract off for the non-fulfilment of the planning condition. I do not overlook the defendant's solicitors' letter of 7 July 1975, in which no doubt the solicitors made a distinctly frosty comment on the delay, but there is not in that letter a word of warning that the defendant is going to rely on the non-fulfilment of the condition precedent.

In the result I hold that the letter of 13 November 1975, was ineffective to avoid the contract and since the plaintiffs fulfilled the planning condition by obtaining the necessary planning permission on or about 26 November 1975, the contract of sale became effective and enforceable on that date. In case there should be any doubt about the matter I must say expressly that in my view the obtaining of the permission dated 25 November 1975, is a complete compliance with the planning condition, notwithstanding that the Roads Act consent—which of course is not referred to in the planning condition—had not, and still has not, been obtained.

Having regard to the basis upon which I have decided the case I will give leave at this late stage to the plaintiffs to amend their reply to plead a waiver by the defendant of the plaintiffs' original failure to fulfil the planning condition. In essence the point is a legal one arising on the correspondence and I am satisfied that no injustice will be done to the defendant by giving the plaintiffs leave to amend.

In the result the plaintiffs succeed in the action and I will decree specific performance of the contract.

Notes

1. In *Walmsley v Acid Jazz Records Ltd* [2001] ECDR 4, the plaintiff created a piece of music by using excerpts of other musicians' records and granted an exclusive licence of the copyright to the defendant, a recording company. When he sought royalties on record sales, the defendant

claimed that he had breached contractual warranties that he had secured copyright licenses from the other musicians. The plaintiff argued that he had acted in reliance on assurances from the defendant that it would approach the copyright owners for permission and that these assurances gave rise to a waiver of the strict terms of the agreement. The Court found that assurances by the defendant's employees acting under the apparent or ostensible authority of the defendant's manager and in-house legal adviser clearly indicated that the plaintiff was not responsible for obtaining copyright and that it would be inequitable to allow A to rely on the strict legal terms of the agreement. Etherton J. stated that '*Brikom Investments Ltd v Carr* [1979] 1 QB 467 . . . is authority that those findings of fact are sufficient to raise an estoppel or (if not strictly promissory estoppel) an equity precluding Acid Jazz from now relying upon the strict wording of the Agreement in relation to copyright infringement.'

2. In 'Resurrecting The Doctrine of Common Law Forbearance' (2007) 123 LQR 286, Phipps challenges the view that the principal doctrine by reference to which contractual modifications can be rendered enforceable is estoppel. She argues that the doctrine of common law forbearance or waiver has been unjustifiably relegated to a marginal, indeed non-existent, role whereas in reality the doctrine:

> (a) provides for the enforcement of promises to modify the 'manner of performance' of contracts, which refers to promises by which one party undertakes to hold in abeyance certain of his strict rights; (b) is suspensory in nature and thereby revocable by either party upon the giving of reasonable notice, following which the contractual position, adjusted to take account of the delay in performance occasioned by the forbearance, will reassert itself; and (c) does not effect a change to the terms of the contract in respect of which it is made but, rather, operates merely to modify the manner in which those terms can be enforced. To enforce a contract whose performance has been modified by a forbearance is not to sue on the forbearance but on the original contract, and the forbearance is therefore capable of being utilised by either the forbearer or the forbearee to complete that cause of action.'

3. See also Tony Dugdale and David Yates, 'Variation, Waiver and Estoppel —A re-Appraisal' (1976) 39 MLR 680.

Consider:

What is the difference between waiver and estoppel?

SECTION THREE—BREACH

Not every breach will allow the injured party treat themselves as discharged from their obligations. As we noted in Chapter 6, certain breaches may allow only a claim for damages but the injured party may still have to proceed with their contractual obligations. This section considers three circumstances in which the injured party may be entitled to treat the contract as at an end.

A. REPUDIATORY BREACH

A repudiatory breach involves one of the parties to a contract unilaterally indicating his or her intentions not to fulfil obligations due under the contract. The breach may involve an express refusal as in the following three Irish cases or it may involve be deduced by the Court from the circumstances of the case. In *Decro-Wall International v Practitioners in Marketing* [1971] 2 All ER 216, Salmon L. J. stated:

. . . breach of contract may be of such a nature as to amount to repudiation and give the innocent party the right (if he desires to exercise it) to be relieved from any further performance of the contract, or the breach may entitle the innocent party only to damages. How is the legal consequence of a breach to be ascertained? Primarily from the terms of the contract itself. The contract may state expressly or by necessary implication that the breach of one of its terms will go to the root of the contract and accordingly amount to repudiation. Where it does not do so, the courts must look at the practical results of the breach in order to decide whether or not it does go to the root of the contract.

Leeson v North British Oil and Candle Co. (1874) 8 IRCL 309

Whiteside C.J.:

A contract is to be regarded in reference to its subject matter. In this instance it was for the sale of a certain quantity of oil which was to be delivered by the defendants to persons named by the plaintiff in the orders sent by him from time to time. For a while the contract was kept, and the orders of the plaintiff were duly executed by the defendants, but after a time the defendants became irregular in the delivery of the oil. The plaintiff thereupon complained to their agent, who advised him to write direct to the manager in Glasgow. He did so, and subsequently the agent to whom he showed the letter he had received in reply pointedly informed him that the defendants had no oil to give him. It has been contended that, notwithstanding this announcement by the agent of the defendants, the plaintiff should have continued as before to send his orders for oil pursuant to the contract, and that having failed to do so, he is not entitled to retain his verdict. We are of opinion that he was quite justified in accepting the statement made by the defendants' agent, and in acting upon it, and that he was not any longer bound by the contract.

It has been argued that although the defendants may have been at the time this statement was made incapable of supplying the oil, yet that their inability might have been merely temporary, and that it might have passed away altogether in a short time. Their contract was, however, to deliver whenever the plaintiff transmitted an order. It does not appear that there was any particular time fixed until the arrival of which they could not be required to deliver, so that the argument which has been suggested does not apply. . . .

Robb & Co. v James and Clarke & Son (1881) 15 ILTR 59

The defendants auctioned certain drapery goods. The terms of the sale required that the goods purchased be removed within twenty four hours of the auction, and paid for prior to removal. The plaintiffs were declared the purchasers but they refused to pay the full price or to remove the goods within the set time. The defendants rescinded the contract and resold the goods to another person. The plaintiffs sued for breach of contract. The trial judge directed a verdict for the defendants.

May C.J.:

On their pleadings it is admitted that the plaintiffs absolutely refused to perform the most essential term of the contract, *viz.* to pay for and remove the goods of which they had been declared the purchasers. It is well established that, under such circumstances, the seller may treat the contract as abandoned by the purchaser, and may detain and resell the goods.[1] The law confers this right on the seller wholly independently of any consent of the purchaser.[2] And we, therefore, think that the replication affords no answer to the plea, and that the demurrer must be sustained.

[1] See Ex *parte Hunter*, 6 Ves. jun. 94; *Bowles v Rogers*, ibid. 954, n. (a), Cook's BL 146; Ex *parte Lord Seaforth*, 19 Ves. 235, 1 Rose, 106; Ex *parte Gyde*, 1 Glyn & Jam. 323; *Hope v Booth*, 1 B & Ad 498

[2] And it seems that, even in the absence of express stipulation, the first purchaser would be responsible for loss occurring, although he did not consent to the second sale: M'*Clean v Dunn*, 1 M & P 761, 4 Bing. 722.

Athlone (No. 2) Rural District Council *v* A.G. Campbell & Son (1912) 47 ILTR 142

Viscount Haldane L.C.:

My Lords, the litigation out of which this appeal and cross-appeal arise relates to a matter connected with two artesian wells which were made in the district of the appellants, who are a district council. The wells were constructed by contractors who had experience in making such wells, and the question is whether the contractors are now entitled to payment. . . .

. . .

. . . the contract contains a clause on which this question arises—'In consideration of the sums in the said tender and supplemental tender mentioned the contractors (that is to say, the respondents in this appeal) will upon and subject to the conditions hereinafter contained do all things necessary and execute and complete all work necessary to put down artesian wells and erect pumps in the said townlands of Famore, Kilmore, Ballyforan, Ballybrogan, and Bredagh, until a copious supply of water shall have been obtained to the satisfaction of the engineer to the council.' Then there are clauses which provide that 'immediately on the perfection of this agreement the contractors shall begin the works at the places in the townlands where pointed out by the engineer of the council, and shall regularly proceed with the said works, and shall complete' them within eight months from the date of the agreement subject to certain provisions for extension of time. No question turns here upon time being of the essence of the contract. The general view taken in the courts below was that time was not of the essence of the contract, and I see no reason to dissent from that view. Then there are other stipulations which enable the engineer to make an extension of time, and which provide that 'the works shall be completed to the satisfaction of the engineer to the council, and in accordance with the said tender and supplemental tender and these conditions, and the contractors shall be entitled to payment under the certificate of the engineer that the said works have been so completed.' I need read no more of the contract for the present purpose. My Lords, the respondents, who are contractors, set to work, and proceeded to bore at the well at Bredagh. The correspondence shows that they made progress, and that they got certain results which in their early stages were encouraging. The first document to which I wish to refer is a telegram of 21 April, which is from Carlton, the foreman of the respondents, to the respondents themselves. It appears from that telegram, and from a previous telegram, that the supply of water, which at first had promised well, had begun to run short. Then the respondents telegraphed to the appellants for 'engineer's instructions'. On that the engineer wrote a letter of 24 April to the clerk of the appellant council, in which he says: 'I went twice to Bredagh, where they said a sufficient supply was got, and on both occasions well gave out.' Then there is a meeting of the council of 8 May, at which a report was read from the engineer, stating the depth of various wells, and 'that the men have left Rackins and Bredagh as if they had given up hopes of finding water, and that he thought the safest thing the council could do would be to stop them going any further.' Then there is an order of the council, at a subsequent meeting on 22 May. The council orders 'that the engineer be instructed to stop the contractors at wells when he considers that a sufficient supply of water has been obtained for the needs of the district, and that the time of testing do not exceed twelve hours.'

Then on 23 May the engineer gives to the contractors certain instructions. My Lords, before I read those instructions, upon which a good deal turns, I wish to state what, in my view, was the position of the contractors. The contractors were mere licensees; they had no title to go upon the land, they had no right to continue to bore excepting by the permission of the appellants. No doubt, if the appellants had improperly withheld their permission it might have amounted to a breach of the contract, as preventing the respondents from earning money due to them, and they might have sued upon the contract for damages, but they had no right or title of any kind to bore except so far as the appellants gave them permission, accordingly the letter of 23 May, which I am now about to read, must be construed in that light. It is said that it was not a letter written by the engineer as such. That does not matter; it purports to have been written, and was written, on behalf of the council, and it affects very materially the right to bore. The letter says: 'Please send on two permanent pumps—one for Cornaseer and one for Bredagh—as I am satisfied there is a sufficient supply of water at both places.' Now, my Lords, that meant, and could only have meant, and it was taken to mean, that they were not to dig any deeper, but were to put in pumps for the well as dug to that depth.

Now, before I pass to the next material document, I will refer to what happened in the meantime. The appellants, being apparently satisfied with what they had done, the respondents put in the pumps—and the pumps were put in by 27 July. The respondents were uneasy about the money which was due to them, and they issued their writ the next day. My Lords, the action which they then commenced turned out most unfortunately for the respondents. It was decided against them on the ground that they had not got the engineer's certificate. The court said that without the engineer's certificate they were entitled to nothing, and their action was dismissed on the simple ground that they had not made out any case for payment.

That action was commenced, as I have said, on 28 July, and it proceeded, and judgment was given in it considerably later—in January. Meantime, of course, very little was done. There was a meeting of the appellant council on 21 August, at which the engineer reported as to Bredagh: 'There being no water, I cannot certify till a supply is obtained' apparently regarding the matter as to Bredagh as still continuing. Again, on

21 September, the clerk of the council writes to the contractors: 'The engineer reports that the supply of water at Bredagh pump has given out.'

My Lords, I only refer to these documents because they bear upon the contention which has been pressed upon us. It has been said that the issue of the writ in July by the contractors put an end to the contract, and that it became impossible to regard the contract as being a subsisting contract after that time.

With that contention, my Lords, I am quite unable to agree. The position when the writ was issued on 28 July was this—that the contract was still a subsisting contract in so far as the certificate had yet to be given (or withheld) under it, and payment had to be made to the contractors. The contractors had been told that they were to dig no further, and were to put in pumps on the well as sunk to that depth, and they had done so, and, for the time at any rate they had done all that they had to do under the contract. It might be that the result of further tests would involve their doing something more; but as matters stood there was for the moment nothing for the contractors to do. The next step remained to be taken by the appellants. It may be that the action was a totally misconceived action. That could not, in my opinion, affect the rights of the respondents under the contract. I see no ground at all for the contention, or for the view which has been taken in the King's Bench Division, that the action put an end to the contract, and made it impossible to say that the contract was any longer subsisting.

My Lords, in that state of things, the judgment of Mr Justice Wright in the first action was given, as I have said, in January, and the effect of it was that the respondents failed to obtain their money. Then they appear to have considered what they ought to do, and in February—obviously acting upon advice—they wrote, through their solicitors, to the appellants to say that they 'were willing to do all things necessary under the contract, . . . to complete the work at the defendants' expense, and to obtain the certificate necessary to entitle them to payment'; and they asked for definite instructions in writing as to what the council required them to do. The reply to that letter from the appellants was: 'The plaintiffs have utterly failed to carry out their contract, and at a time nearly five months after the time limited they have done no more than sink a well which is not in accordance with their tender, and which is producing no water, and no work has been done at it since the late action was brought. Under these circumstances, the defendants are advised that they are entitled to regard the contract as at an end, and will so treat it.' Thereupon the writ in the present action was issued.

Now, my Lords, the course of the second and present action, brought after that letter has been this: It was tried before Mr Justice Wright, sitting without a jury, who took evidence. Then his judgment, which was a judgment for the appellants, went to the King's Bench Division, and there Mr Justice Gibson and the Chief Baron gave judgment, affirming the judgment of Mr Justice Wright, and they did so on the ground which I have indicated, and which has been the main basis of the argument here. I have already stated that I cannot agree with the view which they took. The different view which I have indicated as being my own was taken by the Court of Appeal, which consisted of the Lord Chancellor, Lord Justice Holmes, and Lord Justice Cherry. The judgment of the Court of Appeal was delivered by Lord Justice Holmes. That learned judge held that the first action did not amount to a repudiation, or, rather, he dealt very little with that action, but he held that what took place in July and May, in the summer of 1909, did not put an end to the contract or amount to a repudiation on the part of the respondents; that the letter which I have read directing the putting in of the pumps when a certain depth had been sunk, amounted to a direction to the respondents to stop digging any deeper, and that, consequently, they were in a position in which, although they had failed in the first action for want of the certificate, they got entirely new rights when the repudiation by the appellants took place in February; and he held that that repudiation was a repudiation which was, under the circumstances, improper and unjustified, and entitled the respondents to sue either upon the contract for damages, which he measured, and there is no question raised as to the measure which he laid down, by their expenditure, amounting to £256, upon the works, or on a *quantum meruit*, which would have come to the same thing.

My Lords, that being the judgment of the Court of Appeal, I find myself in substantial agreement with it.

(Lord Atkinson and Lord Shaw of Dunfermaline agreed; Lord Ashbourne dissented.)

Notes

1. In *Stocznia Gdanska SA v Latvian Shipping Company & Others* (No. 2) [2002] 2 Lloyd's Rep. 436, the issue of repudiation was considered. Latreefers, a subsidiary of Latvian Shipping Company ordered the construction of six reefer vessels from the Gdansk Shipyards (the 'Yard') with each vessel covered by a separate contract. Payment was agreed to be by instalment, the first payable upon contracting. Although the Yard had laid the keels for the first two vessels, Latreefers defaulted in making the second payment. In consequence, none of the six vessels were built. The Yard exercised its contractual rights to terminate the first two contracts serving recission notices. It then gave keel laying notices appropriating the same keels to the second and third contract and purporting to terminate them for non-payment and then to do the same for the last two contracts. When this appropriation was held to be illegal, the question arose whether the latter four contracts had been repudiated by Latreefers' anticipatory breach or by the Yard's notices. The Court of Appeal held that when Latreefers failed to pay the keel laying instalment and had been notified of rescission under a contractual clause, that constituted a breach of contract and amounted to an actual repudiatory breach of the first two contracts. However its failure to pay the next instalment was not repudiatory until non-payment occurred beyond the contractually allowed time or the parties had agreed to regard continued non-payment as repudiatory. The Court also determined that there had been no affirmation of the contracts by the Yard, but that if there had been, there would have been continuing repudiation after affirmation.

Rix L. J. stated:

[T]here is of course a middle ground between acceptance of repudiation and affirmation of the contract, and that is the period when the innocent party is making up his mind what to do. If he does nothing for too long, there may come a time when the law will treat him as having affirmed. If he maintains the contract in being for the moment, while reserving his right to treat it as repudiated if his contract partner persists in his repudiation, then he has not yet elected. As long as the contract remains alive, the innocent party runs the risk that a merely anticipatory repudiatory breach, a thing 'writ in water' until acceptance can be overtaken by another event which prejudices the innocent party's rights under the contract - such as frustration or even his own breach. He also runs the risk, if that is the right word, that the party in repudiation will resume performance of the contract and thus end any continuing right in the innocent party to elect to accept the former repudiation as terminating the contract.

2. It should also be noted that the repudiatory breach may also occur before the performance is due. This ' anticipatory breach' allows the innocent party to treat himself or herself discharged from obligations which are not yet due for performance (see *Leeson v North British Oil and Candle Company* (1874) 8 IRCL 309.)

B. FUNDAMENTAL BREACH

A fundamental breach is 'a breach which goes to the root of a contract' (per Lord Denning in *Karsales* (*Harrow*) *Ltd v Wallis* [1956] 1 WLR 936). What amounts to a fundamental breach will depend on the facts and circumstances of each case. Compare the outcomes of the following two cases.

Continental Oil Co. of Ireland Ltd *v* Thomas Moynihan (Trading as Cobh Motor Works) and National Oil Co. of Ireland Ltd (1977) 111 ILTR 5

Kenny J.:

In November 1972 the Minister for Industry and Commerce allowed the petrol companies to increase their wholesale price to dealers by a halfpenny. There is price control of the wholesale price at which petrol may be sold to dealers but there is none on the retail price. When the minister gave this permission, the plaintiffs offered their dealers a choice of either increasing their price to the public by a $1/2$p a gallon and then the plaintiffs would charge them this extra amount on the wholesale price or keeping their price to the public at the amount it was before and, in that event, the plaintiffs would pay them a publicity allowance of $1/4$p per gallon which was to be deducted from the price of the petrol paid by the dealer. Though called a publicity allowance, the effect of this offer was that the dealers who did not increase their price to the public would be getting their petrol at $1/4$p per gallon less than those who did. The result for those who decided that they would not increase the price to the public was a further reduction in the profit margin. Mr Moynihan was determined that he would not accept this reduction and that he would continue to sell petrol at the former price and so, when he received his bills after 27 November, he deducted $1/2$p per gallon from the price. Mr Moynihan was then interviewed by Mr Morgan, the dealer representative of the plaintiff company. Mr Morgan told him that as he had not increased his price to the public, the price to him of petrol supplied by the plaintiffs would be increased by $1/4$p per gallon and that this would be carried out by giving him a credit note for the excess charged. Mr Moynihan was not prepared to accept this suggestion: he wanted petrol supplied to him at the price which was in force before 27 November and was not prepared to pay more. The plaintiffs therefore discontinued supplies to Mr Moynihan. . . .

The next argument was that the plaintiffs had committed a fundamental breach of contract because they sold petrol to Mr Moynihan at the higher price after 27 November and it was said that the breach was so fundamental that it entitled Mr Moynihan to repudiate the contract. In the invoices which were sent to Mr Moynihan after 27 November he was charged an additional 1/2p per gallon but I accept the evidence of Mr Morgan that he offered Mr Moynihan a credit note for petrol supplied after 27 November in respect of 1/4p of a gallon and that the plaintiffs are prepared to supply Mr Moynihan with petrol at the lower price if he does not increase the price which he charged to the public before 27 November. The plaintiffs call the 1/4p per gallon a publicity allowance but I think it is in fact a reduction in price. They may be committing a breach of the order of 1961 but Mr Moynihan cannot call this in aid when they are prepared to supply him at the lower price. Even if the charging of two prices was a breach of the agreement of 1970, it is not so fundamental that it would entitle Mr Moynihan to repudiate the contract. A person who relies on fundamental breach as a ground for discharging him from a contract must establish that the breach shows that the other party does not intend to be bound by the contract.

Dundalk Shopping Centre Ltd *v* Roof Spray Ltd (HC) 21 March 1979, unrep.

The defendants contracted to supply and execute a waterproof application and finish to the roof of the plaintiff's shopping centre. Work commenced in late September and despite the fact that the estimate suggested completion in under four weeks, by mid-November the roof was still unfinished. The spraying which had taken place proved totally useless and damaged the roof. The plaintiffs thus repudiated the contract, claiming damages on the basis that the work was not carried out in a professional manner and was not of merchantable quality. They engaged the services of another roofing contractor who laid an asphalt roof.

Finlay P.:

I am satisfied that this repudiation of the contract was justified and that the defendants had by that time failed in a fundamental term of the contract namely to provide an effective waterproofing of this roof within a reasonable time. On the evidence before me that failure was, it is clear, due to the fact that they never succeeded in applying the spray in appropriate weather conditions and was probably also contributed to by the manner in which the spray was applied. There is considerable evidence that it must have been applied in a loose and almost scattered fashion whereas the system required careful close spraying. Evidence of the meteorological conditions applicable during the period from about 20 October to the first week in November was made available to me during the hearing and it is clear that had the defendants been there with sufficient number of men and in sufficient time on each day that there were conditions which, according to their own specifications, would have led to a successful application of the spray and its setting before further weather intervened to spoil it. I therefore conclude that the plaintiffs are entitled to damages for breach of the contract by the defendants and that the defendants are not entitled to any damages by way of counterclaim for any breach by the plaintiffs of their contract with them the plaintiffs being entitled, in my view of the facts, to repudiate the contract when they did.

Note

In *House of Spring Gardens Ltd and Others v Point Blank Ltd and Others* [1985] IR 611 the defendants entered a licensing agreement with the plaintiffs to manufacture bulletproof vests designed by the latter. Subsequently the defendants commenced to manufacture a similar product and the plaintiffs sued for infringement of copyright and breach of contract. The Supreme Court affirmed the High Court's finding that a repudiatory breach of contract had occured. Evidence indicated that the defendants had attempted to defraud the plaintiffs by suppressing information and dissimilating the origins of their product. Compare this to the case of *Ultraframe (UK) Ltd v Tailored Roofing Systems Ltd* [2004] 2 All ER (Comm) 692. The appellant entered into an exclusive supply contract with the respondent under which it agreed to purchase roofing components exclusively from the respondent at a discounted price, subject to twelve months' notice of termination. It subsequently discovered that the respondent was inducing its customers to deal directly with it and claimed that the contract was subject to an implied term that the respondent would not act in a way that was prejudicial to the appellant's business. He claimed thus that the respondent was in repudiatory breach of the supply contract. The Court of Appeal held that there was no express term in the contract to prevent the respondent approaching the appellant's customers or offering them discounts and the implied term was not required on the basis of business efficacy and in any event would not have prevented U undercutting T during the notice period.

In the following case, the Court considered how a delay in performing the contract might amount to a repudiatory breach.

Taylor *v* Smyth, Kape Investments Ltd, Calla Associates Ltd and Northern Bank Ltd [1990] ILRM 377

As part of an agreement to compromise a legal dispute the plaintiff, an owner and lessor of premises agreed to sell his fee simple interest to the first defendant. The contract provided that the plaintiff would consent as lessor to the assignment of the leasehold interest and would waive all claims to arrears of rent. The sale was to be completed before 15 July 1980. On 16 September 1980 the first defendant purported to rescind the contract for sale and the plaintiff sued for breach of contract.

Lardner J.:

Firstly, was there unreasonable delay by Mr Taylor? Before he was in a position to complete there were at least two matters to be resolved, namely securing a withdrawal by his brother Thomas Taylor of his claim to an interest in the property and of the *lis pendens* he had registered against it and securing a settlement of Barclays Bank's claim as judgment mortgagee against the property. I think as a matter of probability that Mr Taylor was not in a position to complete until the beginning of December 1980. I conclude that having regard to what was required to be done after 20 June 1980 to effect performance of the contract for sale this was an unreasonable delay in all the circumstances.

The next question is whether this unreasonable delay in regard to the completion of the sale of the freehold entitled Mr Smyth, Kape Investments Ltd and Calder Investments Ltd to treat the agreement for sale as repudiated. . . .

. . . In my judgment the agreement for sale of the freehold is not severable from the other terms of the consent.

It was not contended by any of the defendants that the unreasonable delay of the plaintiff in completing the sale of the freehold should by itself properly be regarded as a repudiation of the entire consent. The first and second defendants have indeed asserted the continued existence of other terms of the settlement. So the question of the repudiation of the consent considered as an entire agreement does not arise. Nonetheless perhaps I should state my view in relation to the effect which the plaintiff's delay could be regarded as having. It seems to me that the correct principle to be applied in determining whether delay by one party in performing an obligation under a contract, where, as in this case, the contract must be considered entire but there are a number of heterogeneous obligations to be performed, entitles another party to treat it as a repudiation, is to consider the effect of the breach upon the contract as a whole and whether the effect of the delay (here in completing the sale of the freehold) deprived the innocent parties of substantially the whole benefit of the contract. See the observations of Diplock L.J. in *Hong Kong Fir Shipping Co. Ltd v Kawasaki Kisen Kaisha Ltd* [1962] 2 QB 26. If it has this effect the innocent parties in addition to any remedy in damages would be entitled to be discharged from any further obligation. But if the breach does not have this effect, its consequences can be remedied only by an award of damages. One of the matters urged on behalf of Kape Investments Ltd was that in September and October 1980 the delay in completing the sale of the freehold had put the licence attached to the hotel at risk and that this threatened the value of Kape's security. I am not satisfied that during these two months the position in regard to the licence had significantly deteriorated from what it had been since 1975. It certainly does not seem to me to justify Mr Smyth or Kape Investments Ltd treating the contract for sale as repudiated.

Having regard to the nature of the consent, that it was intended to settle the 1975 action and all other pending proceedings between the parties, that there were a number of terms whose performance was effected and achieved by the agreement to them of the relevant parties, (e.g. the plaintiff's agreement to waive all claims for arrears of rent), that there was at least one other term—the plaintiff giving his consent as lessor to the assignment of the leasehold interest—which was separately performed by the plaintiff, I am unable to conclude that the defendants were, as a result of the plaintiff's delay in completing the sale of the freehold, deprived of substantially the entire benefit of the consent agreement. Consequently they were not entitled to treat the consent agreement as having been repudiated.

Note

In *Peregrine Systems Ltd v Steria Ltd* [2005] EWCA Civ 239, the Court of Appeal examined the circumstances of the case to determine whether a repudiatory breach had occurred. On 29 March 2002, Peregrine granted Steria perpetual, non-exclusive licences to use certain software packages. On 5 February 2003, Steria terminated the agreement *inter alia* on the grounds of repudiatory breaches of contract by Peregrine. It argued that there was an implied term in the contract requiring Peregine to complete implementation within a reasonable time. Examining all the relevant documents and construing the contract the Court held that Peregrine had not contracted to complete implementation of the software but merely to provide £200,000 worth of services, as required by Steria. Peregrine had provided services to that value and no breach arose.

The next two cases demonstrate that the same principles will apply to a fundamental breach of an employment contract.

Industrial Yarns Ltd *v* Greene and Manley [1984] ILRM 15

Costello J.:

If there is no contractual power (express or implied) in the contract of employment to suspend the operation of the contract for a limited period then by ceasing to employ an employee and refusing to pay him wages the employer has been guilty of a serious breach of contract amounting to a repudiation of it. At common law that repudiation would not automatically bring the contract of employment to an end; the employee is free to accept that the repudiation has terminated the contract or not to do so (see: *Gunton v Richmond-upon-Thames London Borough Council* [1980] 3 WLR 714 for a recent view on the effect of an employer's repudiation of the contract of employment). If he accepts the repudiation of the contract then there has been a constructive dismissal of the employee at common law and the contract has been terminated by the employer. But if the employee responds to the employers' lay-off notice and adopts the lay-off procedures (instead of immediately accepting the employer's repudiation of the contract) and it is shown that the statutory condition for their initiation by the employer did not exist, then it seems, the employee is entitled to treat the repudiation of the contract (which occurred when the cesser of employment began) as having terminated the contract of employment, and to base his claim for redundancy payment on that fact. The tribunal was, therefore, in my view correct in its opinion that an employee can properly assert that an employer who ceases to employ him, and who cannot show that the cesser will not be permanent has terminated his contract of employment.

Cantor Fitzgerald International *v* Callaghan and others [1999] 2 All ER 411

The defendants were ex-employees of the plaintiff who argued that their employment contracts had been repudiated by the plaintiff in its failure or refusal to comply with agreed arrangements in relation to their salary packages and their consequent tax liabilities.

Judge L.J.:

In my judgment the question whether non-payment of agreed wages, or interference by an employer with a salary package, is or is not fundamental to the continued existence of a contract of employment, depends on the critical distinction to be drawn between an employer's failure to pay, or delay in paying, agreed remuneration, and his deliberate refusal to do so. Where the failure or delay constitutes a breach of contract, depending on the circumstances, this may represent no more than a temporary fault in the employer's technology, an accounting error or simple mistake, or illness, or accident, or unexpected events (see e.g. *Adams v Charles Zub Associates Ltd* [1978] IRLR 551). If so it would be open to the court to conclude that the breach did not go to the root of the contract. On the other hand if the failure or delay in payment were repeated and persistent, perhaps also unexplained, the court might be driven to conclude that the breach or breaches were indeed repudiatory.

Where however an employer unilaterally reduces his employee's pay, or diminishes the value of his salary package, the entire foundation of the contract of employment is undermined. Therefore an emphatic denial by the employer of his obligation to pay the agreed salary or wage, or a determined resolution not to comply with his contractual obligations in relation to pay and remuneration, will normally be regarded as repudiatory. . . .

I very much doubt whether *de minimis* has any relevance in this field. If the amount at stake is very small, and the circumstances justifying a minimal reduction are explained to the employee, then the likelihood is that he would be prepared to accept new terms by way of mutual variation of the original contract. However an apparently slight change imposed on a reluctant employee by economic pressure exercised by the employer should not be confused with a consensual variation, and in such circumstances an employee would be entitled to treat the contract of employment as discharged by the employer's breach.

In the present case the amount in issue was not in the context of the overall package very great, although the sums at stake were not trivial. However the refusal to pay was deliberate and determined, motivated by a desire improperly to pressurise the defendants into harder work. The decision wholly undermined the contract of employment and constituted a repudiatory breach.

In examining the facts in order to determine whether a fundamental breach has occurred, a question arises as to whether the innocent party can rely on grounds which were unknown to him at the time of termination in order to claim fundamental breach. This is considered in the following case.

Hearn and Matchroom Boxing Ltd *v* Collins (HC) 3 February 1998 unrep.

The High Court was asked *inter alia* to determine whether the conduct of Mr Hearn, the defendant's manager, constituted a repudiation of his management agreement with the defendant, a boxer. The conduct in question involved firstly, a series of correspondence between Mr Hearn and the World Boxing Organisation and secondly, Mr Hearn's conduct at a purse bid ceremony in relation to a proposed boxing match between the defendant and Chris Eubank.

O'Sullivan J.:

I think it is important to clarify the different legal consequences which arise where there have been breaches of an agreement as distinct from fundamental breaches. This matter is dealt with by O'Keeffe J., as he then was, in *Carvill v Irish Industrial Bank Limited* [1968] IR 325 at p. 345 as follows:

In principle it is difficult to understand how an act can be relied upon to justify dismissal unless it is known at the time of dismissal. It must be conceded that there can be some breaches of contract so fundamental as to show that the contract is entirely repudiated by the party committing them, and that such an act might be relied upon in an action for wrongful dismissal, not as justifying the dismissal, but as supporting a plea that the dismissed servant had himself put an end to the contract. Where the act is not of so fundamental a character but would warrant the dismissal of the servant at the option of the employer, it appears to me to be quite illogical to say that an employer may be heard to say that he dismissed his servant on a ground unknown to him at the actual time of dismissal.

Subsequently in *Glover v BLN Limited* [1973] IR 388 Walsh J. observed (page 426) as follows:

Furthermore, as was settled by this court in *Carvill v Irish Industrial Bank Limited* an employer in defending an action by an employee for wrongful summary dismissal, cannot rely upon misconduct which was not known by the employer at the time of the dismissal. I would add that the misconduct, if known but not in fact used as a ground for dismissal at the time, cannot be relied upon afterwards in an effort to justify the dismissal.

A distinction emerges from these passages between breaches and fundamental breaches.

If a fundamental breach comes to light after the dismissal it may still be relied upon by the employer to make a claim not that this subsequently known ground was relied upon as a reason for or otherwise justified the dismissal, but rather that the contract at the time of the dismissal had already been repudiated....

It will be recalled that Barry Hearn considered himself Stephen Collins' manager up to 13 October 1995 when the 30 days notice, which he served, pursuant to clause 6 of the management agreement expired. In any event the letter dated 6 June 1995 terminating what was therein described as the prior agreement was stamped and received by the plaintiffs on 9 June.

This correspondence comprises a series of letters from Barry Hearn to Francisco Valcarcel then President of the WBO. In the first, dated 7 June 1995 Barry Hearn raises a doubt as to whether Frank Warren really intended to promote the Collins Eubank rematch before 31 July as stipulated at the purse bid ceremony in New York on 29 May. He suggested that 'Mr Warren will ignore the orders of the WBO and instigate either a medical delay or some other reason . . .'. This suggestion carried with it the inference that Stephen Collins would be a party to an instigated medical reason for post-ponement of the fight in breach of the arrangement specified. The letter presses strongly for the right to have Chris Eubank fight for an interim championship '. . . on 29 July, with the winner going on to fight Steve Collins for the official title on a 50/50 basis'. This request, if it had been carried out, would have meant that Stephen Collins' entitlement to a 75% share of the purse as champion, would have been reduced to a 50% share. The letter did, indeed, acknowledge that if Frank Warren was not in a position to promote the fight then his deposit should be distributed to the champion and the challenger in accordance with the WBO rules.

The second letter in the series is dated 13 June 1995—coincidentally the date on which Barry Hearn wrote to Stephen Collins stating that he was staggered at the contents of Stephen Collins' letter to him of 6 June 1995 and writing 'to formally advise you that I do not accept your termination of our agreement and in an attempt that you will reconsider your position after you have had a time to reflect further on the matter'.

On the same day he wrote a letter to Mr Valcarcel noting that it would come as no surprise 'that Steve Collins has pulled out of his planned defence against Chris Eubank on the grounds of illness'. In the course of the letter he writes:

> Before a delay in this contest can be allowed, surely we must insist on a reputable doctor's certificate outlining details of the illness that Collins is suffering from. It is eight weeks before the fight, so one assumes that it must be quite a serious illness!

The request for an interim championship fight for Chris Eubank is repeated, this time supported by reference to precedent with a repetition of the suggestion that the winner would fight Steve Collins once again 'obviously on a 50/50 basis'.

The next letter is dated 15 June 1995 and commences:

> Dear Francisco,
> I have heard now that Steve Collins has an injured finger (!) and will not be able to train for two weeks and therefore promoter Frank Warren wishes to postpone the fight until September.

The earlier requests are repeated, the finger injury is criticised as a valid reason for postponing the contest when Barry Hearn points that '*an injured finger does not stop a fighter running, skipping and generally keeping himself 100% fit—it purely prevents him from sparring*'. He further writes:

> We all know, I believe that this is just an excuse and that Frank Warren has been unable to come up with a venue that can stage the fight within the WBO time scale and clearly he does not want to lose his deposit, hence Mr Collins' very serious injury to his finger!

A later paragraph refers to '*these ridiculous excuses*'. The letter is insistent upon a decision on the interim championship proposal and points out:

> Time is of course of the essence and bearing in mind the poor excuse of Steve Collins' finger injury, I hope the WBO will now fax me to confirm that Chris Eubank may fight an interim world championship on July 29th . . .

A second letter of the same date emphasises that Mr Eubank will face serious financial loss '. . . *due to the non-performance of Mr Warren of not promoting the Eubank/Collins fight under the deadline . . .*'

The next letter dated 19 June 1995 emphasises the *huge* financial losses and includes the following:

> Steve Collins' injury to his finger is laughable and I trust you will give us the opportunity now to keep this title active in line with past practice . . .

A further letter of 20 June emphasises that the purse bid was conditional on the fight taking place before 31 July and reiterates that there is a precedent within the WBO rules for previous interim championships when a mandatory fight cannot take place by the prescribed date. '*I trust again that we will maintain consistency in our decisions by ordering another interim championship prior to the end of July*'.

The last letter in the series is dated 26 June by which time an arrangement had been worked out. This letter seeks written confirmation of what is described as the:

. . . following compromise agreement in respect of Chris Eubank and Steve Collins'
mandatory title fight:

1. WBO will agree to Chris Eubank having a 10 round non-title fight on the 29th
   July against Jose Ingacio Barreutabena of Spain.
2. Barreutabena will be installed in the WBO ratings in July at number 4—to
   replace Frankie Liles, who has been included in the WBO rankings, but it is in
   fact the WBA super middleweight champion.
3. Should for any reason Frank Warren the promoter announce that the Eubank/
   Collins fight will not take place prior to 9 September 1995 then the
   Barreutabena/Eubank contest will be recognised as an interim title fight under
   the WBO rules.

The explanation given by Barry Hearn in evidence for the foregoing correspondence
was that he was acting as manager for Mr Eubank who was pressing him on a daily
basis to arrange an interim fight given that the Collins/Eubank rematch was going to
be postponed; that any criticism of Stephen Collins could not damage the latter's
position which was protected under the WBO rules which provided that once a
medical certificate had been furnished the title holder could not be stripped of his
title unless he failed to defend it within 180 days; that the entire correspondence was
tactical and aimed at achieving the result which was actually achieved namely that
Chris Eubank got a fight before the Collins/Eubank rematch. Steve Collins remained
champion entitled to his full purse on that rematch and Frank Warren remained
promoter. Barry Hearn explained in evidence that at the time he did not know the date
(subsequently established as 9 September) selected for the Collins/Eubank rematch
and he also agreed that he had no contact with Steve Collins at the time (despite
several attempts by him) so that his assertion that the finger injury (later clarified by
Steve Collins in evidence in this case as an injury to his knuckle) was based purely on
the information that he derived from newspaper reports.

I am unable to accept that this explanation given by Barry Hearn in evidence in this
trial represents the whole truth. I am asked by the author of these letters to reject their
plain, insistent and repeated meaning in favour of an explanation which leaves me
unconvinced. I accept that Barry Hearn's purpose in writing this correspondence was
to achieve a benefit for Chris Eubank, whom he also managed at this time. I consider
that he was motivated by hostility against Frank Warren, who had succeeded, despite
his best efforts to put an obstacle in his way, in winning the promotion of the
Collins/Eubank rematch at the purse bid ceremony in New York on the 29th May
thereby taking over one of his fighters as he has himself put it. On the face of it, this
correspondence seeks to damage Steve Collins in two fundamental ways, namely by
interfering with his 75% share entitlement to the Collins/Eubank rematch purse and
secondly, by suggesting that he was a party to a phoney medical excuse in order to
achieve a postponement of that rematch. I have been furnished with a copy of the
WBO rules and I do not accept Barry Hearn's claim that Stephen Collins' position as
title holder was absolutely impregnable under those rules once a medical certificate
had been furnished. Rule 8 refers to a champion being justifiably disabled but
specifies that 'such disability has to be proven to and accepted by the world championship's
committee'. I do not accept it as clear beyond argument, as Barry Hearn contended, that
the WBO could not accede to the various suggestions put forward in the Valcarcel
correspondence to the detriment of Steve Collins.

My conclusion is that if Barry Hearn was at that time under any obligation as
manager to Steve Collins, this correspondence comprises fundamental breach of such
obligation.

It was put to Barry Hearn in cross-examination on the third day of the hearing that he attended the purse bid ceremony in New York on 29 May 1995 in relation to the Collins/Eubank rematch, and that he addressed the presiding officer making various highly critical remarks about Sports Network and Mr Frank Warren. Barry Hearn's initial reply was:

No. I'm afraid I don't (remember). It doesn't mean to say I didn't make them. I just don't recall them.

Further on in evidence it was suggested to him that he spent close to half an hour damnifying Sports Network and Mr Warren in particular, that his remarks reflected on the integrity of Mr Warren and that he suggested that he should not be permitted to bid. He was asked did he recall any of that and he said '*No, but it doesn't surprise me.*' Barry Hearn went on to specify that if a company is registered and they have paid a sanction fee then despite his personal feelings about Sports Network '*I don't see it's possible to stop them bidding.*' It was put to him that he did his best to stop them, to which he replied '*It would be a futile exercise. You can't stop the bidding. I may have done my best to certainly criticise them, as I would have done for effectively, in my view, taking away one of my fighters when he was under contract.*' Later in evidence he accepted again, that he had been highly critical of Sports Network and Frank Warren, but claimed that it wasn't a 'long damning'.

In evidence Stephen Collins claimed that if this attack had succeeded in preventing Sports Network from bidding or being accepted it would have ruined everything for him and deprived him of the £1.2 million purse. Barry Hearn claims on the other hand that he could not prevent Sports Network from bidding or being accepted and that the attack was a futile exercise.

Once again I think this is not the whole truth. Barry Hearn acknowledges that he attended the purse bid ceremony as manager of Chris Eubank and Stephen Collins. It is accepted generally that a fighter's 'pay-day' comes if and when he wins a title which establishes him as a champion entitled to 75% (or 80%) of the purse involved in defending his title for as long as he remains champion. I cannot see how his manager, with an acknowledged obligation to do his best to achieve optimum earnings for his fighter, can justifiably attend a purse bid ceremony and launch an attack on the credibility of this substantial bidder and even go as far as suggesting that he should not be allowed to bid.

I do not consider that Barry Hearn spent his time engaged in exercises which he can subsequently describe as futile. He has asked me to accept that the attack on Frank Warren and Sports Network was futile. If so, why did he travel to New York in order to launch it? He has asked me to accept that the Valcarcel correspondence means something completely and wholly different to what it plainly and repeatedly says. In both instances my impression is that Barry Hearn was engaged in an attack on and an attempt to damage his rival Frank Warren and Sports Network and that he permitted himself in so doing to endanger the fundamental interests of his fighter Steve Collins, whether this was his primary objective or merely an ancillary by-product. Whatever the entire truth of the matter, I am satisfied that the attack made by Barry Hearn on Frank Warren and Sports Network at the purse bid ceremony in New York on 29 May 1995 constituted a fundamental breach of his obligations to Steve Collins because it was diametrically opposed to his acknowledged obligation to achieve the best possible financial outcome for Steve Collins. I do not accept that this attack was futile and the fact that it did not succeed in preventing Sports Network from bidding and being accepted as a bidder does not, to my mind, mean that the attack itself may now be regarded as innocent or excusable. On the contrary, in my view, it was a fundamental breach of Barry Hearn's obligation to Stephen Collins. It follows that no management fees could become owing to the Plaintiffs arising out of the Collins/Eubank rematch.

C. Breach of a Condition

Breach of a condition will entitle the injured party to repudiate the contract. (See Chapter 6, p. 308.) As noted above, however, this right may be waived by the injured party or in certain circumstances lost.

Sale of Goods Act 1893 s. 11:

11. (1) Where a contract of sale is subject to any condition to be fulfilled by the seller, the buyer may waive the condition, or may elect to treat the breach of such condition as a breach of warranty, and not as a ground for treating the contract as repudiated.

(2) Whether a stipulation in a contract of sale is a condition, the breach of which may give rise to a right to treat the contract as repudiated, or a warranty, the breach of which may give rise to a claim for damages but not to a right to reject the goods and treat the contract as repudiated depends in each case on the construction of the contract. A stipulation may be a condition, though called a warranty in the contract.

(3) Where a contract of sale is not severable, and the buyer has accepted the goods, or part thereof, the breach of any condition to be fulfilled by the seller can only be treated as a breach of warranty, and not as a ground for rejecting the goods and treating the contract as repudiated, unless, there be a term of the contract, express or implied, to that effect.

(4) Nothing in this section shall affect the case of any condition or warranty, fulfilment of which is excused by law by reason of impossibility or otherwise.

D. Election

Where a breach has occurred that allows the innocent party treat himself or herself as discharged from their obligations, the contract does not automatically come to an end. In such circumstances, the innocent party may elect to terminate the contract or to affirm the contract. Where the former option is chosen, the following two cases demonstrate that prompt action is required

An Bord Iascaigh Mhara *v* Scallan (HC) 8 May 1973, unrep.

The plaintiffs agreed pursuant to a hire purchase agreement to supply the defendant with a boat with a 'dog clutch' fitted to the engine for winch hydraulic pump drive. The boat which was delivered did not possess a clutch. However, the defendant accepted delivery as he was informed by the boat's builder that a dog-clutch was not necessary.

Pringle J.:

The evidence satisfies me that, for the purpose of efficient lobster fishing and trawling, the hydraulic winch was the most important part of the equipment, and I am also satisfied that at no time did the winch on this boat operate satisfactorily and the boat was not therefore reasonably fit for the purpose for which it was hired and the plaintiffs were guilty of a breach of the statutory condition under s. 9 (2) of the Act. The effect of a breach of this condition was dealt with by Mr Justice Davitt, the then President of the High Court, in the case of *Butterly v United Dominions Trust (Commercial) Ltd* [1963] IR 56, at 62, where he said:

> The only question remaining is the main one, whether the plaintiff was entitled to repudiate the contract. He was always of course entitled to terminate the hiring under the provisions of clause 8, but, quite apart from that, he would be entitled to repudiate, as soon as he discovered that the car was useless for the purpose for which he required it, and that the condition implied in s. 9 (2) had been broken. The principles which apply to the matter of repudiation under the Sale of Goods Act have no application in the case of a contract under the Hire-Purchase Act. In the case of the Sale of Goods Act, once the goods have been accepted and the property has passed to the buyer, he cannot repudiate and he is confined to the remedy by way of action for damages. The Hire-Purchase Act is entirely different and, having regard to the submissions on the point made by [counsel] on behalf of the defendants and by [counsel] on behalf of the plaintiff, it would appear to be common case that the hirer can repudiate within a reasonable time of becoming aware of a breach of a condition which would entitle him to repudiate.

In the present case therefore the defendant was entitled to repudiate the contract within a reasonable time of becoming aware that the boat was not reasonably fit for the purposes for which it was required. In the early stages, when attempts were being made by the plaintiffs to remedy the defects in the winch, and even though these attempts were unsuccessful, it was reasonable, in my opinion, for the defendant to delay repudiating the contract, but after about November 1967, when it was clear that the winch had still not sufficient power, the defendant not only did not repudiate the contract, but went on using the boat for another year and it was not until October 1968, that he notified the plaintiffs, through Mr Howlin, that he was abandoning the boat and that the plaintiffs could do what they liked with it. It was then in my opinion too late for him to repudiate the contract and require the plaintiffs to return the deposit, as claimed. He had clearly approbated the contract and could only rely on his claim for damages for breach of contract. . . .

Lutton *v* Saville Tractors (Belfast) Ltd and Another [1986] NI 327

The plaintiff purchased a secondhand car from the first defendant. The sales representative incorrectly assured him that the car was in good repair and had not sustained any accidental damage. A full service and three month warranty was provided. The plaintiff never found the car satisfactory and returned it constantly with lists of complaints. Finally, two months after purchase, after the plaintiff had done between 3,000 and 4,000 miles, the plaintiff notified the first defendant of his desire to return the car and obtain a refund. When the first defendant refused, the plaintiff sought to rescind the contract and sued for damages.

Carswell J.:

It is not established that Mr Lutton knew of the accident damage at any time up to his final attempt to get rid of the car. He accordingly cannot be said to have affirmed the contract with knowledge of the facts which gave him a right to rescind because of the misrepresentation that the car had not sustained any accident damage.

On the issue of the misrepresentation about the condition of the car the defendants point to the fact that the plaintiff kept the car for a period approaching two months and drove some 3,000 to 4,000 miles before finally attempting to return it. In *Farnworth Finance Facilities Ltd v Attryde* it was held that the purchaser of a new motor cycle which developed a number of serious defects had not affirmed the contract, which in that case was one of hire-purchase, by attempting over a period of over four months to have the defects put right, using the machine a good deal in the process. He did not elect to accept it until the defects were remedied, which they never were, and the final breakdown showed the plaintiff conclusively that it could not be relied on. The plaintiff relies upon this case in support of the proposition that his use of the car for a period did not amount to affirmation.

Before I reach a conclusion on the issue of affirmation, I should for the sake of completeness look at that of acceptance under the Sale of Goods Act 1979. By virtue of s. 11(4), where the buyer has accepted the goods, the breach of a condition to be fulfilled by the seller can only be treated as a breach of warranty, and not as a ground for rejecting the goods and treating the contract as repudiated. This express statutory provision accordingly dispenses with the need to consider affirmation in the case of breach of condition, for that issue is replaced by that of acceptance. The circumstances in which a buyer is regarded as having accepted the goods are set out in s. 35(1) of the 1979 Act: 'The buyer is deemed to have accepted the goods when he intimates to the seller that he has accepted them, or (except where s. 34 above otherwise provides) when the goods have been delivered to him and he does any act in relation to them which is inconsistent with the ownership of the seller, or when after the lapse of a reasonable time he retains the goods without intimating to the seller that he has rejected them.' The third part of the subsection is the material one here, and the issue is whether after the lapse of a reasonable time the plaintiff retained the car without intimating to Saville Motors that he had rejected it.

Reported decisions have varied to a marked extent in their approach to deciding on acceptance by a buyer. In some of them courts have held that the right of rejection is lost speedily where goods are in daily use, and this normally means days rather than months: see Atiyah, *The Sale of Goods* (5th edn), 402. On the other hand, there is a trend of thought, accepted by the Law Commission in its Working Paper No. 85, that time taken up while goods are being repaired should not count as part of the reasonable time during which the buyer must reject the goods. A possible avenue of approach is by the concept that the seller's attempts to cure defects constitutes acquiescence in the buyer's holding off final acceptance: see *Benjamin's Sale of Goods* (2nd edn), para. 925.

Some support for this type of approach may be found in the Canadian case-law. In *Burroughs Business Machines Ltd v Feed-Rite Mills (1962) Ltd* [1973] 42 DLR 3d 303, affd. on appeal 64 DLR 3d 767, an accounting machine supplied by the plaintiff proved defective. It was held that the defendant's efforts in co-operating with the plaintiff in an attempt to make the equipment work could not be used to negate the absence of acceptance as a matter of law. A *fortiori*, they would hardly constitute affirmation of the contract. In two cases concerning the sale of new cars, *Lightburn v Belmont Sales Ltd* [1969] 6 DLR 3d 692 and *Finlay v Metro Toyota Ltd* [1977] 82 DLR 3d 440, the purchasers used them for several months each and drove them for several thousand miles. In each case it was held that the buyer had not accepted the car within the meaning of a provision similar to that contained in our Sale of Goods Act. In the former case Ruttan J. said: 'He was endeavouring to give it a reasonable chance to perform, and I do not agree that delay in finally repudiating his contract can be attributed to that period of time or the mileage that was covered. He was not acting as a capricious buyer who had repented the purchase and sought to get out of his contract at an early time on a frivolous basis.'

This description would in my view apply aptly to Mr Lutton. He sensibly enough took the car back several times to try to have the defects cured, but eventually, in his own words, he was 'sick of having problems with the car'. He attempted to return the car, but the service manager would not accept it. His solicitors sent a letter of repudiation, and when the car broke down again the plaintiff washed his hands of it and attempted to return the keys and tax book to Saville Motors. On these facts I consider that the plaintiff did not at any time so act that he must be taken to have accepted the goods. I also hold that he did not by keeping the car for a period affirm the contract and lose his right of rescission.

Note

See also *Thomas Dillon-Leetch v Maxwell Motors Ltd* [1984] ILRM 624 (p. 563 above).

SECTION FOUR—FRUSTRATION

The traditional view was that contractual obligations were absolute, and the fact that performance may be difficult or even impossible was no excuse at common law. This traditional view was questioned in *Taylor v Caldwell* (1863) 3 B & S 826. This case concerned an agreement entered into by the plaintiffs and defendants whereby the defendants agreed to allow the plaintiffs have use of a music hall and gardens on four days for the purpose of giving a series of four grand concerts and day and night fetes. The plaintiffs agreed to pay £100 for each day. Prior to the day of the first concert, the hall was destroyed by fire and it proved impossible to hold the concerts as intended. The court held that the destruction of the hall discharged the contract.

The doctrine of frustration provides relief for the parties where contractual obligations are no longer capable of being performed as a result of unforeseeable circumstances which are beyond the control of either party. Unlike breach, the effect of the doctrine is to discharge the contract automatically.

A. Theoretical Basis of Frustration

The theoretical basis of the doctrine has been the subject of much judicial debate and controversy. In *Taylor v Caldwell* Blackburn J. stated:

There seems no doubt that where there is a positive contract to do a thing, not in itself unlawful, the contractor must perform it or pay damages for not doing it, although in consequence of unforeseen accidents, the performance of his contract has become unexpectedly burthensome or even impossible. The law is so laid down in 1 Roll Abr 450, Condition (G), and in the note to *Walton v Waterhouse*, and is recognised as the general rule by all the judges in the much discussed case of *Hall v Wright*. But this rule is only applicable when the contract is positive and absolute, and not subject to any condition either express or implied: and there are authorities which, as we think, establish the principle that where, from the nature of the contract, it appears that the parties must from the beginning have known that it could not be fulfilled unless when the time for the fulfilment of the contract arrived some particular specified thing continued to exist, so that, when entering into the contract, they must have contemplated such continuing existence as the foundation of what was to be done; there, in the absence of any express or implied warranty that the thing shall exist, the contract is not to be construed as a positive contract, but as subject to an implied condition that the parties shall be excused in case, before breach, performance becomes impossible from the perishing of the thing without default of the contractor.

The notion of an implied condition was accepted in *Cummings v Stewart* (No. 2) [1913] 1 IR 95 where O'Connor M.R. quoted the above extract from *Taylor v Caldwell*. In that case, the plaintiff, a patentee of improvements for making reinforced concrete, granted the right to work the patents to the defendant licensee in return for royalty payments. When the patents lapsed due to the plaintiff's non-payment of the renewal fees, the defendant refused to pay the plaintiff royalties.

O'Connor M.R. stated:

It is manifest that the parties contracted on the basis that at least three patents should continue to be existing patents during the whole term of the licence. Owing to the conduct of the plaintiff, two, or at least one, of the patents were lost, with the result that a substantial part of the subject matter of the contract was destroyed, and the contract, in a substantial part, became impossible of performance, and ceased to be binding.

The same concept was used to explain the doctrine in *Gamble v The Accident Assurance Company* (1896) IR 4 CL 204.

However, the modern tendency has been to move away from this dependence of implied terms and explain it on the basis of the true construction of the contract. Where frustration is allowed, performance of the contract following the frustrating event would be 'radically different'. This approach was adopted by Lord Radcliffe in *Davis Contractors Ltd v Fareham* UDC [1956] All ER 145. His Lordship explained as follows:

[T]here is something of a logical difficulty in seeing how the parties could even impliedly have provided for something which *ex hypothesi* they neither expected nor foresaw; and the ascription of frustration to an implied term of the contract has been criticised as obscuring the true action of the court which consists in applying an objective rule of the law of contract to the contractual obligations that the parties have imposed upon themselves. . . . So perhaps it would be simpler to say at the outset that frustration occurs whenever the law recognises that without default of either party a contractual obligation has become incapable of being performed because the circumstances in which performance is called for would render it a thing radically different from that which was undertaken by the contract.

A third theory was referred to by Kenny J. in *Browne v Mulligan, Gallagher and Others* (SC) 23 November 1997, unrep., as follows:

The third theory—associated with Lord Wright—is that where the dispute between the parties arises from an event which they never thought of, the court imposes the solution that in the circumstances is just and reasonable (Lord Wright's *Legal Essays and Addresses*, 258 and *Denny Mott and Dickson Ltd v Fraser and Co. Ltd* [1944] AC 265 at 275).'

Consider:

What are the problems associated with explaining the doctrine on each of these three bases?

B. FRUSTRATION OF PURPOSE

Impossibility to perform occurs in a wide array of circumstances. These include cases where the subject matter of the contract is destroyed or is unavailable, where performance in the manner specified is impossible, where there is a supervening illegality or upon the non-occurrence of an event central to the contract. In the latter case, it becomes necessary to distinguish between a situation where the event amounts to the object of the contract and a situation where it merely amounts to the motive for entering the contract.

Krell *v* Henry [1903] 2 KB 740

The defendant agreed to hire from the plaintiff some rooms overlooking Pall Mall in London in order to view the coronation of King Edward VII. When the coronation was cancelled the defendant denied that he was liable to pay the agreed rent on the basis that there was a total failure of consideration for the contract.

Vaughan Williams L. J.:

The real question in this case is the extent of the application in English law of the principle of the Roman law which has been adopted and acted on in many English decisions, and notably in *Taylor v Caldwell*.

. . . English law applies the principle not only to cases where the performance of the contract becomes impossible by the cessation of existence of the thing which is the subject matter of the contract, but also to cases where the event which renders the contract incapable of performance is the cessation or non-existence of an express condition or state of things, going to the root of the contract, and essential to its performance. It is said, on the one side, that the specified thing, state of things, or condition the continued existence of which is necessary for the fulfilment of the contract, so that the parties entering into the contract must have contemplated the continued existence of that thing, condition, or state of things as the foundation of what was to be done under the contract, is limited to things which are either the subject matter of the contract, or a condition or state of things, present or anticipated, which are expressly mentioned in the contract. But, on the other side, it is said that the condition or state of things need not be expressly specified, but that it is sufficient if such condition or state of things clearly appears by extrinsic evidence to have been assumed by the parties to be the foundation or basis of the contract and the event which causes the impossibility is of such a character that it cannot reasonably be supposed to have been in the contemplation of the contracting parties when the contract was made. In such a case the contracting parties will not be held bound by general words which, though large enough to include, were not used with reference to a possibility of a particular event rendering performance of the contract impossible.

I do not think that the principle of the civil law as introduced into the English law is limited to cases in which the event causing the impossibility of performance is the destruction or non-existence of some thing which is the subject matter of the contract or of some condition or state of things expressly specified as a condition of it. I think that you first have to ascertain, not necessarily from the terms of the contract, but if necessary from necessary inferences, drawn from surrounding circumstances recognised by both contracting parties, what is the substance of the contract, and then to ask the question whether that substantial contract needs for its foundation the assumption of the existence of a particular state of things. If it does, this will limit the operation of the general words, and in such case if the contract becomes impossible of performance by reason of the non-existence of the state of things assumed by both contracting parties, as the foundation of the contract, there will be no breach of the contract thus limited.

What are the facts of the present case? The contract is contained in two letters of 20 June 1902, which passed between the defendant and the plaintiff's agent, Mr Cecil Bisgood. These letters do not mention the coronation, but speak merely of the taking of Mr Krell's chambers, or, rather, of the use of them, in the daytime of 26 and 27 June 1902, for the sum of £75, £25 then paid, balance £50 to be paid on the 24th. But the affidavits, which by agreement between the parties are to be taken as stating the facts of the case, show that the plaintiff exhibited on his premises, third floor, 56A, Pall Mall, an announcement to the effect that windows to view the royal coronation processions were to be let, and that the defendant was induced by that announcement to apply to the housekeeper on the premises, who said that the owner was willing to let the suite of rooms for the purpose of seeing the royal procession for both days, but not nights, of 26 and 27 June. In my judgment, the use of the rooms was let and taken for the purpose of seeing the royal processions. It was not a demise of the rooms or even an agreement to let and take the rooms. It was a licence to use rooms for a particular purpose and none other. And in my judgment the taking place of those processions on the days proclaimed along the proclaimed route, which passed 56A, Pall Mall, was regarded by both contracting parties as the foundation of the contract. I think that it cannot reasonably be supposed to have been in the contemplation of the contracting parties, when the contract was made, that the coronation would not be held on the proclaimed days, or the processions not take place on those days along the proclaimed route; and I think that the words imposing on the defendant the obligation to accept and pay for the use of the rooms for the named days, although general and unconditional, were not used with reference to the possibility of the particular contingency which afterwards occurred...

Each case must be judged by its own circumstances. In each case one must ask oneself, first: What, having regard to all the circumstances, was the foundation of the contract?; secondly: Was the performance of the contract prevented?; and thirdly: Was the event which prevented the performance of the contract of such a character that it cannot reasonably be said to have been in the contemplation of the parties at the date of the contract? If all these questions are answered in the affirmative (as I think they should be in this case), I think both parties are discharged from further performance of the contract. I think that the coronation processions were the foundation of this contract, and that the non-happening of them prevented the performance of the contract . . .

It is not essential to the application of the principle of *Taylor v Caldwell* that the direct subject of the contract should perish or fail to be in existence at the date of performance of the contract. It is sufficient if a state of things or condition expressed in the contract and essential to its performance perishes or fails to be in existence at that time.

Note

This case should be compared to *Herne Bay Steam Boat Co. v Hutton* |1903| 2 KB 683 where a contract to hire a boat for two days for the stated purpose of viewing the naval review and for a day's cruise around the fleet was not deemed frustrated by the cancellation of the naval review. Vaughan Williams L. J. stated that it was not clear that the naval review was contemplated by both parties as the foundation of the contract.

Browne *v* Mulligan, Gallagher and Others (SC) 23 November 1977 unrep.

Kenny J.:

The expression 'the contract is frustrated' so commonly used today is misleading: the doctrine relates, not to the contract but to the events or transactions which are the basis of the contract. It is these which make performance of the contracts impossible. This aspect of the doctrine was explained by Lord Wright in the *Constantine Line v Imperial Smelting Corp.* |1942| AC 154:

> In more recent days, the phrase more commonly used is 'frustration of the contract' or more shortly 'frustration'. 'Frustration of the contract' however is an elliptical expression. The fuller and more accurate phrase is 'frustration of the adventure or of the commercial or practical purpose of the contract'. The change in language corresponds to a wider conception of impossibility, which has extended the rule beyond contracts which depend on the existence, at the relevant time of a specific object. . . . to cases when the essential object does indeed exist, but its condition has by some casualty been so changed as to be not available for the purposes of the contract, either at the contract date or if no date is fixed, within any time consistent with the commercial or practical adventure.

In *McGuill v Aer Lingus Teoranta and United Airlines Incorporated* (HC) 3 October 1983, unrep. (discussed below at p. 977), McWilliam J. insisted that 'The circumstances alleged to occasion frustration should be strictly scrutinised and the doctrine is not to be lightly applied.' The following three cases indicate that the Courts take this advice seriously. For a contract to be frustrated, performance must be rendered impossible by the frustrating event not merely harder or less lucrative (*Tsakiroglou v Noblee and Throl* [1961] 2 All ER 179).

William Neville and Sons Ltd *v* Guardian Builders Ltd [1990] ILRM 601

The defendant owned property in Dublin which was land-locked. Between this land and the public road was a small strip of land owned by Dublin County Council. The defendant agreed terms with the County Council for the acquisition of land. The plaintiff and the defendant entered into an agreement whereby the defendant gave the plaintiff a licence to develop the site. Subsequently a problem arose with the County Council as to the location of exits and the defendant refused to proceed with the purchase. The plaintiff instituted proceedings seeking specific performance of the licence agreement and damages. The defendant claimed that the contract had been frustrated.

Murphy J.:

What an analysis of the agreement and the circumstances in which it was executed shows is that the site which the parties agreed to develop was at the date of the contract effectively landlocked, that is to say, that the site was surrounded by land over which neither the plaintiffs nor the defendants had the right to pass and repass for the purpose of developing the site or granting similar rights-of-way to purchasers of the houses erected by them. No change took place in that objective situation between the date of the contract and the institution of the proceedings. However it seems to me clear beyond debate that both parties recognising this objective fact necessarily believed or assumed that the Dublin County Council as the owners of the crucial strip of land would facilitate the development and in that way enable the contract to be performed. The change that took place between the date of the contract and the time for its performance was the frustration of this expectation. In that sense the present case has something in common with the coronation cases and particularly *Krell v Henry* [1903] 2 KB 740. When the courts were satisfied that the foundation of the contract was the intention of the hirer to view the coronation procession and that the contract of hiring was entered into in the common expectation that the procession would take place on the date fixed for the hiring the cancellation of the procession was held to frustrate the contract. Of course it has long been recognised that care must be taken to ensure that a particular event was the purpose of the contract otherwise the alteration of a programme would not strike at the foundation of the contract (see *Herne Bay Steam Boat Co. v Hutton* [1903] 2 KB 683).

    The argument for frustration in the present case is in many respects far stronger than that which succeeded in *Krell v Henry* because here the change in expectation did not defeat the purpose of the agreement but effectively the only means of performing it short of requiring one or other of the parties to do something not merely different from what he had agreed to do but something which he had not agreed to do at all.

    . . . . In these circumstances I have concluded somewhat regretfully that the plaintiffs' claim must be dismissed.

The plaintiff appealed to the Supreme Court.

Blayney J.:

When one looks at these facts it is in my opinion impossible to say that the performance of this contract was frustrated. No event supervened which significantly changed the nature of Guardian's obligation to provide access to the licence plot which involved constructing the access road. When Guardian entered into the licence agreement, it had the informal agreement of 10 March 1984 with the county council which, if implemented, would have enabled it to construct the road. And in fact, under the terms of the agreement, it had an obligation to do so since it was a condition of the agreement that it would construct the road within twelve months of obtaining planning permission for its office development from the Dun Laoghaire Borough, and this had been obtained on 16 September 1986. And when this agreement went off, the county council showed its willingness to enter in to a new agreement in September 1988. Furthermore, it is quite clear from the evidence of the county council's witnesses that the county council wanted this access road built. The only unexpected problem that Guardian had was the county council insisting that the position of the exit from the Parkes Hotel car park to the access road should not be altered, but this could not by any means be termed a supervening event which significantly changed the nature of Guardian's obligation under the licence agreement. It made it more onerous, but that was all.

I am satisfied, therefore, that the defence of frustration fails, and that having been the only defence which was raised against Neville's claim for specific performance, I would allow this appeal and direct specific performance of the licence agreement.

(Finlay CJ and Denham J. concurred.)

Sullivan v Southern Health Board (HC) 29 July 1993, unrep.

The plaintiff, a consultant physician in the defendants' hospital, sued for breach of his contract of employment. He claimed that the defendants had failed to make reasonable resources or staff available to him requiring him to work excess hours for lower remuneration than agreed. The defendants claimed *inter alia* that the contract was rendered frustated and impossible to perform due to the refusal of the Minister for Health and the Comhairle na hOispideal to provide them with the necessary funds or necessary staff.

Keane J.:

It is clear, in my view, that a body such as the defendants cannot enter into contractual obligations with another person in the knowledge that they are dependent on the co-operation of a third party—in this case the minister and the comhairle—in implementing them and then repudiate responsibility for the consequences to the other contracting party because of the refusal of the third party to co-operate. That was also the view taken by Lardner J. in *Staunton v St Laurence's Hospital and Others* with which I respectfully agree.

Nor can the defendants escape liability by relying on the doctrines of frustration of contract and impossibility of performance. It is, of course, always open to a defendant to plead that the contract for the breach of which he is now asked to pay damages is not the contract into which he originally entered.

[Referring to Lord Radcliffe in *Davis Contractors Ltd v Fareham* UDC ([1956] AC 696) he continued:]

That is not this case. Here the contract, its underlying basis and the legal context in which it was entered into all remained the same. There is thus no ground which relieves the defendants from the legal consequences of their breach of the contract.

(Although an appeal to the Supreme Court was allowed (30 July 1997 unrep.), the issue of frustration was not considered.)

Note

Consider the case of Li *Ching Wing v Xuan Yi Xiong* [2004] 1 HKC 353. The plaintiff rented a flat in Kowloon for two years beginning 1 August 2002. In March 2003, a number of neighbours were infected with SARS and, to avoid being infected, the defendant moved out of the premises on 29 March 2003. On 31 March 2003, the Department of Health ordered the flats be evacuated for ten days. Although the plaintiff returned after this period, on 24 April 2003 he sent a letter to the plaintiff to terminate the tenancy agreement. In defence to an action for breach of contract, he claimed *inter alia* that the tenancy agreement was frustrated by the making of the isolation order due to SARS.

The District Court asked 'what relation does the likely period of interruption bear to the outstanding period for performance?' In relation to leases, it held that an event which caused an interruption in the unexpected use of the premises would not frustrate the lease, unless the interruption was expected to last for the unexpired term of the lease, or, at least, for the unexpired term. On the facts, the isolation order lasted for ten days and was quite insignificant a period in terms of the overall use of the premises for a term of two years. While the outbreak of SARS was an unforeseen event, such a supervening event did not significantly change the nature of the outstanding contractual rights or obligations from what the parties could reasonably have contemplated at the time of the execution of the tenancy agreement. Interestingly, the Court stated *obiter* that the genuine fear of tenants living in the flats as to whether their homes were safe did not provide them with legal justification to terminate their tenancy agreements and to hold otherwise might also be unfair to the landlords, as they had to bear with all the consequences arising from the outbreak, an event that was beyond their control.

Zuphen *v* Kelly Technical Services (Ireland) Ltd [2000] IEHC 117

In September 1999, the defendant recruitment company recruited the plaintiffs, South African technicians, for one year intending to use them to carry out work on behalf of Eircom plc. While the defendant's contract with Eircom gave no entitlement to any level of work, the defendant believed work would be available until March 2000. In December 1999, this work was no longer available and after finding only short-term work for the plaintiffs with British Telecom, the defendant claimed that the defendant's employment contracts were frustrated.

Kelly J.:

The plaintiffs submit that the theoretical basis for the doctrine of frustration is disputed. There are contradictory Irish authorities providing alternative explanations as between the implied contract theory and/or the true construction theory (*Cummings v Stewart* (No. 2) [1913] IR 95 and *Mulligan v Browne* (High Court, Kenny J. unreported, 9 July 1976)).

Notwithstanding the uncertainty as to its theoretical basis, the doctrine itself is straightforward. A contract may be discharged on the grounds of frustration when something occurs after the formation of the contract which renders it impossible to fulfil the contract or transforms the obligation to perform into a radically different obligation from that undertaken at the moment of entry into the contract. The doctrine is subject to the limitation that the frustrating circumstances must arise without fault of either party (*Maritime National Fish Limited v Ocean Trawlers* [1935] AC 5 24 and *Constantine Line v Imperial Smelting Corporation* [1941] 2 All ER 165).

The plaintiffs submit that the doctrine of frustration can never be applied in order to discharge a party to a contract from performing its contractual obligations in circumstances where it may be extremely difficult or even impossible to do so. In *Leeson v North Bristol Oil and Candle Limited* [1974] 8 IR CL 309, it was held that the fact that the defendants could not obtain paraffin from their own supplier because of a strike did not excuse their failure to supply the plaintiff. In *Paradine v Jane* [1647] Aleyn 26, the plaintiff had let lands to the defendant under the terms of a lease which required the lessee to pay rent on a quarterly basis. The lessees were ejected from possession by armed force, the lands then being occupied by the military during the English Civil War. In an action for arrears of rent, the lessee pleaded that the circumstances excused non-payment of rent. However, this plea was rejected and a distinction was drawn between a general duty imposed by law upon a lessee and a duty undertaken by way of contract. In respect of duty taken on by way of contract the Court stated that:

> When the party by his own conduct creates a duty or a charge upon himself he is bound to make it good, if he may, notwithstanding any accident by inevitable necessity because he might have provided against it by his contract.

The plaintiff submits that the defendants could have included the term in this contract specifically dealing with the situation which would arise if the Eircom work was no longer available. They did not do so under the section dealing with termination of contract. However, if such a term had been included the plaintiffs would not have accepted such a precarious and unguaranteed offer of employment.

Besides the requirement in relation to provision against a third party not providing work, an element of mutuality is necessary.

The advertisements and the letter of offer and letter containing the contract did not expressly or impliedly provide that the agreement would be terminated should Eircom work not be available.

The fact that the defendants had been able to provide work for thirty-nine of the plaintiffs who remained in Ireland disproves the contention that the contracts of employment entered into could not be fulfilled should the Eircom work no longer be available.

The plaintiffs submit that the Courts do not allow the doctrine of frustration to apply where increased costs or a limited amount of work make it impossible for one party to perform the contract without incurring serious financial losses and refer to *Clarke: Contract Law in Ireland*, 3rd edn, 425:

It would be undesirable for a business man to agree to perform a contract for a fixed amount and permit him to seek relief through the doctrine of frustration if, during performance, unanticipated difficulties arise.

Reference was also made to *Revell v Hussey* [1813] 2 Ball and B 280 and *Davis Contractors v Fareham* UDC [1956] AC 696.

The plaintiffs contend that the cessation of Eircom work was not unforeseen or unexpected and referred to paragraph 2.1 of the contract whereby work would be allocated 'as the need arises' by the head of outsourcing or his duly authorised representative. Moreover, paragraph 2.2 provides a forecast and projection of work that would be required on the 'best estimates of anticipated demand for the services as required and are therefore provided for information only and no commitment as to the level of business eventually awarded during the term of the contract is to be inferred, either in its entirety or the relative size or category of work.'

Counsel for the plaintiffs also referred to *Neville & Sons Limited v Guardian Builders Limited* [1995] 1 ILRM 1 where the Supreme Court held that frustration of a contract takes place when a supervening event occurs without the default of either party and for which the contract makes no sufficient provision. The event must so significantly change the nature of the outstanding contractual rights and obligations from what the parties could reasonably have contemplated at the time of the contract's execution that it would be unjust to hold them to its terms in the new circumstances.

The plaintiffs submit that the failure of Eircom to continue to provide work has not significantly changed the contractual rights entered into by the parties who remain employees of the defendants. Some are continuing to work while others are available for work. They say that the defendants do not wish to continue paying the plaintiffs money for work which is not as abundant as they thought would be the case. Frustration in this circumstance would provide an alternative to redundancy in which an employer would have no liability or responsibility to the employee. . . .

The defendants' case is that at all material times the contracting of the plaintiffs for the carrying out of work on their behalf was in the context of doing work on behalf of Eircom plc; and when Eircom indicated to the defendants in late December 1999 that no further work was available for the first named defendants to carry out, the contract was effectively terminated from that point onwards. . . . counsel for the defendants referred to the origin of the doctrine in the old case of *Taylor v Caldwell* (1863) 3 B. & S. 826. There a contract for a musical performance was discharged by frustration of the contract when the intended music hall venue was destroyed by fire. Counsel mentioned that while there are a number of academic theories as to the basis of the doctrine, the approach of the Courts to commercial arrangements between parties are more instructive. Where events arise which effectively change the basis for the performing of a contract so that what is in place is a materially different contract from that which is originally envisaged by the parties the Courts will alleviate the harshness of the contractual obligation by treating the original contract as being frustrated if its original purpose and intention cannot be met by virtue of outside circumstances with no wrong on the part of the contracting parties. The opposite extremes of the interpretation of the doctrine are to be found in the 'Coronation cases' of *Krell v Henry* (1903) 2 KB 740 and *Heron Bay Steamboat Co. v Hutton* (1903) 2 KB 683. It is submitted by the defendants that the cancellation of the Eircom contract effectively gave rise to a situation analogous to that in *Krell* where the procession which was to be viewed from particular rooms was no longer to take place rather than in *Heron Bay* where the hirers had at least the benefit of a trip around the port.

64. The defendants also referred to *Neville v Guardian Builders* (1990) ILRM 601 and (1995) 1 LLRM 1 . . . net position as emerges from the Neville case is as follows . . . and echoes Lord Radcliffe in *Davis Contractors v Farnham* UDC [1956] AC 696 at 778/9:

> A contract will be deemed to be frustrated whenever the law recognises without the default of either party a contractual obligation has become incapable of being performed because the circumstances in which it is called for would render it a thing radically different from that which was undertaken by the contract.

The defendants say that in the present case Eircom were limited under the terms of their contractual arrangement with the defendants to terminate the contract only for a stipulated breach. The contract between the plaintiffs and the defendants as reflected in the letter of 27 September 1999 and any of the surrounding documents did not provide for a *'force majeure'*: in fact the contracts did not provide as to what had to happen in the event that what apparently was the basis or cornerstone of the contract was to be removed.

In the initial advertising for the contract which is sought to be enforced by the plaintiffs herein it was specifically indicated that work was to be carried out 'At a large telecommunications company in Ireland'. The document of 17 September 1999 to the plaintiffs specifically indicated that the offer was for a twelve-month contract 'Working on . . . the Eircom network'. . . . The document went on specifically to indicate that an orientation course would be required to meet the requirements of Eircom representatives as to sufficiency of competence on the part of the plaintiffs. These matters were echoed in the letter of 27 September 1999 which the plaintiffs contend comprises the contract of obligation on the part of the defendants. Again reference was made to a twelve-month contract working on a particular aspect of the Eircom network (indicating that Eircom is Ireland's national telecommunications company). The document indicated that the contract could be terminated by the defendants only in the event that the plaintiffs fail to meet Eircom accreditation within a fixed period of time and specifically also requires that a good working relationship will be needed with the Eircom staff. The work permit available for the plaintiffs was only for work in Ireland. The only work in Ireland with the defendants was to work on the Eircom contract. The contract between the plaintiffs and the defendants never envisaged the plaintiffs being paid for not doing any work. Accordingly it is the contention of the defendants that once their was no work available on the Eircom contract, they had no other work available and the defendants were not obliged to pay the plaintiffs for doing no work. All of the present plaintiffs were required to attend training programmes which were relevant only to the aspect of the Eircom contract which was subsequently cancelled by Eircom. In these circumstances it is the contention of the defendants that the contract was discharged by frustration and without any wrongdoing or fault on the part of the defendants.

Applying the *Neville* criteria to the facts of the present situation counsel for the defendants submitted that all of the considerations determined in the *Neville* case to give rise to an effective application of the doctrine of discharge by frustration were met:

(a) There was no default on either the part of the plaintiffs or the defendants.
(b) The contract has become incapable of being performed. Eircom have ceased requiring the defendants to carry out the relevant work for them and therefore the defendants have no work for the plaintiffs with Eircom or on the relevant aspect of the Eircom network.

(c) What is now involved in continuing with the contractual obligation is to put in place a contract which is radically different from that which was intended between the parties.

. . . The issue before the Court is whether the contracts entered into on 17 September 1999 . . . and the several plaintiffs was frustrated by the termination of work by Eircom in January, 2000. . . . It is significant that the letter of 27 September 1999 was conditional only on being available for work in Dublin on 29 October 1999, or earlier as arranged, and not being refused a work permit by the Department. There was no condition about availability of work. Such a condition could have been inserted as would be provided in an engineering subcontract and could have been provided for in a carefully drafted contract of employment. The contract would be terminated by the employee on giving one month's notice at any time and could be terminated by the defendant companies where the employee had not passed the accreditation course within three attempts or had unsatisfactorily performed his duties. There is no evidence of either eventuality. Indeed, it is clear that it is not a matter of termination that is before the Court by of frustration of the contract without fault. . . . The basis of the doctrine of frustration would appear from the authorities is that there is a supervening event which must be so unexpected and beyond the contemplation of the parties, even as a possibility, that neither party can be said to have accepted the risk of the event taking place when contracting.

The clear evidence of Mr O'Flaherty [the defendant's financial director] was, while there was no form of commitment from Eircom, he did not feel it improper to rely on Eircom and felt able to make a judgment call. The general agreement of the defendant companies with Eircom as to work being 'allocated as the need arises' points to the possibility of such work not arising. It was certainly not so unexpected as to be beyond the contemplation of the parties, even as a possibility. Mr Raymond Kelly [a director of the defendant]. believed that Eircom intended to upgrade all exchanges and that, accordingly, the defendant companies made a commercial judgment accordingly.

The memorandum of 30 September 1999 related to a meeting between the first named defendant and Eircom. Mr Martin Cooper of Eircom did not describe it as a contract document but as a reflection of what was discussed. It seems to me that it was on the basis of this document that the defendant companies proceeded. Indeed, Mr Cooper agreed that the memo gave an indication that there was work even if there was no contractual commitment. Significantly, however, [the defendant] had sent letters to prospective employees with draft terms and conditions before that date. The clear evidence was that, notwithstanding the non-finalisation of the contract with Eircom, the defendant companies sought to engage technicians on one-year contracts. The defendants were aware in making a commercial judgment call that this was conditional on work being available. The Court must accordingly on a general impression of what the rule in relation to frustration requires. It is for that reason that special importance is necessarily to the occurrence of an unexpected event that, as it were, changes the face of things. It seems to me that this is not the case. It is not hardship or inconvenience or a material loss itself which calls the principles of frustration into play. There must have been such a change in the significance of the obligation that the thing undertaken would, if performed, be a different thing from that contracted for. Moreover, it does not seem to me that the contract had become entirely incapable of being performed. Indeed, the defendant companies, in order to mitigate loss or damage, have obtained work for some of the workers concerned. Indeed, the very commendable attempt by the defendant companies to procure such work for the technicians they had employed is to my mind an indication that a contractual relationship survived which would be inconsistent with the contract being frustrated...

Furthermore, I am satisfied from the evidence given by the four plaintiffs that they would not have entered into the contracts had there been a condition that the contract could be terminated if work were not available.... In the circumstances and for the foregoing reasons it does not seem to me that the contract was frustrated by the loss of the specific Eircom contract.

C. UNFORESEEN EVENTS

Where the parties have anticipated the frustrating event as a serious possibility, they will not subsequently be able to rely on the doctrine of frustration.

McGuill v Aer Lingus Teoranta and United Airlines Incorporated (HC) 3 October 1983, unrep.

In the summer of 1978, the plaintiff entered into negotiations with United Airlines to carry a tour group of 234 members of the Vintners' Federation from New York to San Francisco and from there to Hawaii and back from Hawaii to New York via Los Angeles and Las Vegas. A contract was signed in November 1978. Due to labour disputes with their employees, United Airlines could not carry them and the plaintiff had to enter into alternative arrangements with other carriers at a considerably increased expenditure. When the plaintiff sued for breach of contract, United Airlines claimed *inter alia* that the contract had been fruatrated.

McWilliam J.

I was referred to a number of authorities on the question of frustration. They were: *Davis Contractors Ltd v Fareham* UDC (1956) 3 WLR 37; *Pioneer Shipping Ltd v B.T.P. Tioxide Ltd* (1981) 3 WLR 292; *Paradine v Jane* (1647) Aleyn 26; *The Penelope* (1928) p. 180. I was also referred to *Halsbury*, (4th ed.), vol. 9 and to *Chitty on Contracts* ch. 23. Although it was not referred to during the hearing I note the following passage in *Chitty* (24th edn), para. 1417. 'If one party foresaw the risk but the other did not, it will be difficult for the former to claim that the occurrence of that risk frustrates the contract.' The reference given is to *Walton Harvey Ltd v Walker & Homfrays* |1931| 1 Ch. 274. I have also considered this report.

From these authorities, the following principles appear to apply when considering a claim that a contract has been frustrated.

1. A party may bind himself by an absolute contract to perform something which subsequently becomes impossible.
2. Frustration occurs when, without default of either party, a contractual obligation has become incapable of being performed.
3. The circumstances alleged to occasion frustration should be strictly scrutinised and the doctrine is not to be lightly applied.
4. Where the circumstances alleged to cause the frustration have arisen from the act or default of one of the parties, that party cannot rely on the doctrine.
5. All the circumstances of the contract should also be strictly scrutinised.

6. The event must be an unexpected event.
7. If one party anticipated or should have anticipated the possibility of the event which is alleged to cause the frustration and did not incorporate a clause in the contract to deal with it, he should not be permitted to rely on the happening of the event as causing frustration.

It does not appear, from the authorities to which I have been referred, what principle is to apply in considering frustration of a contract in circumstances such as the present so as to establish when a contract comes to an end. No evidence was tendered on behalf of United to indicate that United claimed at any particular time that the contract had come to an end and no submission was made as to the time of the termination of the contract. The suggestion on behalf of United seems to be that, once the parties became aware of the strike, a new agreement must be implied that the contract would continue until it was clear that the strike would not be settled in time to enable United to carry the group. Although the decision in the *Pioneer Shipping* case appears to support this proposition to some extent, I am not satisfied that such a proposition should be extended to the circumstances of the present case.

A significant circumstance in the present case is the fact, stated by two witnesses for United, that there had been a 'cooling-off' period of sixty days in operation prior to the strike being declared and taking effect. This must have been within the knowledge of United at all times during that period, that is to say, from 30 January 1979. It can hardly be suggested that there had not been some threat of industrial action before the 'cooling-off' period started to run and that, whatever the dispute was about, there had not previously been negotiations in progress between United and their employees. At no time was any communication about these circumstances made to the plaintiff and I conclude that this was because United felt that, if the plaintiff were made aware of the possibility of a strike, he might try to get another airline to carry the group. In my opinion this means that United, being aware of the threat or possibility of a strike, and the evidence is that United had had a somewhat similar strike a few years previously, but being anxious to obtain the business, took the risk of entering into the contract without including a provision to safeguard its position in the event of a strike taking place. Under these circumstances I am of opinion that United is not entitled to succeed on its defence that the contract was frustrated.

Consider:

Could United have argued that they confidently expected to resolve their industrial relations issues and that the strike was thus not foreseeable?

The doctrine of frustration will not normally operate to discharge a contract where the event which is alleged to give rise to the frustration is provided for by a term of the contract.

Browne *v* Mulligan, Gallagher and Others (SC) 23 November 1977, unrep.

In August 1958, the defendants, governors of a hospital in Donegal appointed the plaintiff as physician to the hospital. The appointment was stated to be terminable if insufficient funds were available to enable the hospital to continue in operation. In February 1974, the hospital closed due to lack of funds and the plaintiff's employment was terminated by the governors. The plaintiff sought compensation. The defendants argued that the contract had been frustrated by the closure of the hospital. The Supreme Court rejected this claim on the basis that the event was anticipated.

Kenny J.:

The event on which reliance is placed as terminating the contract must be unanticipated by the parties and so not mentioned in the contract. If it is dealt with in the contract, then it was within the contemplation of the parties and the doctrine cannot apply. 'Equally, if the terms of the agreement show that the parties contemplated the possibility of such an intervening circumstance arising, frustration does not occur' (per Viscount Simon in *Cricklewood Pty Trust Ltd v Leightons Investment Trust Ltd* [1945] 1 All ER 252 at 255). The contract dealt with the closing down of the hospital when there were not sufficient funds available to allow it to continue in operation. This is the event which happened and the parties provided in the contract for its effect on the plaintiff's position. The order of 11 February 1974 was a recognition of the impossibility of carrying on the hospital.

Even where the frustrating event is in existence at the time the contract is made, it may still be viewed by the courts as unforeseeable.

Gamerco SA *v* ICM/Fair Warning (Agency) Ltd [1995] 1 WLR 1226

The plaintiffs, Spanish pop concert promoters, agreed to promote a rock concert involving the defendant group Guns 'N Roses, at the Vicente Calderon Stadium in Madrid on 4 July 1992. On 30 June, engineers reported that the stadium was constructed with high alumina cement ('HAC') could not be safely used until further investigations had been carried out. On 1 July the authorities banned all use of the stadium and the permit issued to the plaintiffs to hold the event was revoked. As no alternative venue could be found, the concert was cancelled. The plaintiffs sought to recover $412,500 paid to the defendants on account and the defendants counter-claimed for damages for breach of contract by the plaintiffs in failing to secure the permit.

Garland J.:

The plaintiffs accept that there must be an implied term to give the contract commercial efficacy that the promoter would obtain such approvals, permits, licences etc. as might be required to enable the contract to be performed. [Counsel for the plaintiffs] submitted that such an implication would be 'to use all reasonable endeavours'. It would not be necessary to require absolute obligation, e.g. 'to obtain and at all times thereafter to ensure that there were in force all such approvals, permits, licences, and certificates, as may at any time be required etc.' In my view the proper implication would be to use all reasonable endeavours.

[Counsel for the defendants] submitted, . . . the group's obligation was simply to be ready, willing and able to perform in Madrid. . . . the thrust of his argument was that so long as the group was prepared to perform in Madrid there was no frustration and the plaintiffs were in breach of an express or an implied term to obtain a permit which remained valid for the day of the event. I do not consider these submissions tenable. The contract was to appear and actually to give a performance at the Vicente Calderon starting at 22.30 and lasting 90 minutes. This could not be done, not because a permit was revoked but because the stadium had been found to be unsafe. In any event it was impossible for the defendants to perform their side of the bargain; they could not appear in the stadium any more than the plaintiffs could perform their obligations to erect the stage, the roof and generally to prepare the venue.

A corollary of [Counsel for the defendant's] argument was that the plaintiffs had agreed to take all the commercial risks, whereas the defendants would collect US£1.1m even if very few tickets were sold. If the next step was that they had accepted the risk of the stadium becoming unavailable it is not a permissible step. The plaintiffs did not either expressly, or as a matter of construction, accept the risk of a concert not taking place due to events outside their control and not contemplated by either party. The contract became both physically and legally incapable of performance: there was no force majeure or catastrophe clause, not any provisions similar to those in some engineering contracts allocating the risks should the work become physically or legally impossible of performance. The parties made their own arrangements about insurance but there were no contractual obligations to insure—familiar enough provisions in many contracts.

The law

It is convenient to take as a statement of the law passages from the judgment of Bingham LJ. in J. *Lauritzen AS v Wijsmuller BV* [1990] 1 Lloyd's Rep 1, 8:

> The classical statement of the modern law is that of Lord Ratcliffe in *Davis Contractors Ltd v Fareham Urban District Council* [1956] AC 696, 729:
>
>> 'frustration occurs whenever the law recognises that without default of either party a contractual obligation has become incapable of being performed because the circumstances in which performance is called for would render it a thing radically different from that which was undertaken by the contract. *Non haec in foedera veni*. It was not this that I promised to do. ' As Lord Reid observed in the same case, at p. 721: 'there is no need to consider what the parties thought or how they or reasonable men in their shoes would have dealt with the new situation if they had foreseen it. The question is whether the contract which they did make is, on its true construction, wide enough to apply to the new situation: if it is not, then it is at an end.' Certain propositions, established by the highest authority, are not open to question: 1. The doctrine of frustration was evolved to mitigate the rigour of the common law's insistence on literal performance of absolute promises . . . The object of the doctrine was to give effect to the demands of justice, to achieve a just and reasonable result, to do what is reasonable and fair, as an expedient to escape from injustice where such would result from enforcement of a contract in its literal terms after a significant change in circumstances . . . 2. Since the effect of frustration is to kill the contract and to discharge the parties from further liability under it, the doctrine is not to be lightly invoked, must be kept within very narrow limits and ought not to be extended . . . 3. Frustration brings the contract to an end forthwith, without more and automatically . . . 4. The essence of frustration is that it should not be due to the act or election of the party seeking to rely on it . . . 5. A frustrating event must take place without blame or fault on the side of the party seeking to rely on it . . .'

[Counsel for the defendants] took me to a number of well known authorities. *Taylor v Caldwell* (1863) 3 B & S 826 he submitted might be applicable between the plaintiffs and the owners of the stadium, the dangerous state being arguably analogous to destruction by fire, but not as between the plaintiffs and the defendants. The basis for his submission came back to his formulation of the defendants' obligation which was simply to be willing to perform in Madrid. Neither of the coronation cases are, in my view, helpful—*Krell v Henry* [1903] 2 KB 740 and *Herne Bay Steam Boat Co. v Hutton* [1903] 2 KB 683—these were 'foundation of the contract' cases turning on their particular facts, as was *London and Northern Estates Co v Schlesinger* [1916] 1 KB 20. [Counsel for the defendants] placed reliance on a passage from Lord Wright in *Maritime National Fish Ltd v Ocean Trawlers Ltd* [1935] AC 524. This was an 'election of the plaintiff' case where the charterer of five trawlers had obtained the necessary licences for three, which he nominated, and then claimed that the charter in respect of one of the others had been frustrated. It was perhaps surprising that the case reached the Privy Council but Lord Wright, referring to criticism of *Krell v Henry* [1903] 2 KB 740, said [1935] AC 524, 529:

> The authority is certainly not one to be extended: it is particularly difficult to apply where, as in the present case, the possibility of the event relied on as constituting a frustration of the adventure (here the failure to obtain a licence) was known to both parties when the contract was made, but the contract entered into was absolute in terms so far as concerned that known possibility. It may be asked whether in such cases there is any reason to throw the loss on those who have undertaken to place the thing or service for which the contract provides at the other parties' disposal and are able and willing to do so.

He then goes on to comment that, where the parties might have inserted an express condition dealing with the eventuality that has arisen, the court should be very reluctant to interfere. I do not think that this citation of authorities assists [Counsel for the defendants]: in fact the service or thing which the contract provided was the use of the stadium in which the defendants had undertaken to perform. But, again, [Counsel for the defendants] was returning to his 'able and willing' argument.

I am in no doubt whatsoever that this contract was frustrated when, due to the discovery of HAC in the construction of the stadium, its use was banned pending further investigations and the permit for its use was revoked.

D. SELF-INDUCED FRUSTRATION

Parties to a contract may not rely on frustration which is self-induced as a ground for discharging their obligations under the contract. As McWilliam J noted in *McGuill v Aer Lingus Teoranta and United Airlines Incorporated* (HC) 3 October 1983, unrep. (see above at p. 977) 'where the circumstances alleged to cause the frustration have arisen from the act or default of one of the parties, that party cannot rely on the doctrine'. The actions of the persons seeking to rely on the doctrine of frustration in the following two cases were sufficient to deny them the benefit of the doctrine.

Achilles Herman and Others *v* The Owners and Master of the S.S. 'Vicia' [1942] IR 305

The plaintiffs were hired for a voyage from the US to Britain and back again. The ship's Finnish owners obtained a British ship's permit for the period from August 1940 to February 1941. This permit protected the vessel from British seizure. Although the permit had expired at the time the plaintiffs were hired it was not renewed. The British Ministry of Shipping assured the defendants that all facilities required would be provided. When the ship arrived in Dublin the plaintiffs were informed that the ship had no papers to proceed in Britain. They were discharged and subsequently they sued for breach of contract. The defendants pleaded frustration.

Hanna J.:

Now, on these facts can I come to the conclusion that there was what is known in law as frustration of the seamen's contract, and, if there was frustration, are the seamen still entitled to the cost of repatriation? These are difficult and unusual questions to be decided.

What is frustration? In the case of *Joseph Constantine S.S. Line Ltd v Imperial Smelting Corp. Ltd*[1] various definitions are given of frustration—incidental to the main question involved in that case—namely, upon whom the burden of proof lies. In that case, the ship in question, the 'Kingswood', was chartered to agents of the respondents in a voyage with ores from Port Pirie in South Australia to Europe. Before she became an 'arrived ship' at Port Pirie, there was a severe explosion in the neighbourhood of her auxiliary boiler, causing such damage that she could not perform her charterparty. As the headnote says, that was 'a destruction of the essential subject matter of the contract so as to frustrate the commercial object of the adventure.' In that respect the case differs from the one under consideration. As there was no negligence or default found with either party, it was held to discharge all liability under the charter. At 29, Viscount Simon L.C. says that 'when 'frustration' in the legal sense occurs, it does not merely provide one party with a defence in an action brought by the other. It kills the contract itself and discharges both parties automatically. The plaintiff sues for breach at a past date and the defendant pleads that at that date no contract existed.' He further says that frustration depends on the terms of the contract and the surrounding circumstances of each case, as some kinds of impossibility may not discharge the contract at all.

Lord Maugham says, at 31, that 'frustration is based on the presumed common intention of the parties,' and he also states that the legal rights already accrued are unaffected.

At 35–36, Lord Wright, while recognising frustration by the destruction of the subject matter, gives a wider conception of impossibility and says:

> Another illustration is where the actual object still exists and is available, but the object of the contract as contemplated by both parties was its employment for a particular purpose, which has become impossible, as in the coronation cases. In these and similar cases, where there is not in the strict sense impossibility by some casual happening, there has been so vital a change in the circumstances as to defeat the contract. . . . The common object of the parties is frustrated. The contract has perished, *quoad* any rights or liabilities subsequent to the change.

He then cites passages from the judgment in *Paradine v Jane;*[2] and from the judgments in *Hirji Mulji v Cheong Yue S.S. Co.;*[3] *Couturier v Hastie;*[4] and *Dahl v Nelson, Donkin & Co.,*[5] and then he says: 'I have quoted these statements of law to emphasise that the court is exercising its powers, when it decides that a contract is frustrated, in order to achieve a result which is just and reasonable.'

The converse proposition is that it is not to be held to be frustrated unless it is just and reasonable.

Lord Porter, in the same case, seems to give a larger interpretation to frustration, where he says, at 40: 'Frustration is the term now in common use in cases in which the performance of a contract becomes impossible because its subject matter has ceased to be available for the purpose for which both parties intended it to be used.' He points out that in that case no question arises as to the extension of the doctrine to a case where the subject matter of the contract is not itself destroyed but the underlying purpose alone has been frustrated.

On these principles I am of opinion that the evidence on the part of the owners is not sufficient to justify a finding of frustration of the seamen's contracts. Adopting the words of Lord Wright, I decline to hold that it would be just and reasonable under the circumstances to decide that the seaman's contracts had been frustrated. The vessel had gone from Lisbon to Tampa without a convoy and was not interfered with. She sailed for thirteen days alone in the Atlantic without a convoy and without a proper warrant. I can find no case similar in facts to this, where it has been alleged, or held to be, a frustration for the owners of the vessel, apart from any hostile act of an enemy, to be unwilling to send her to sea on account of the risks and perils of war, with possible interception or seizure. It seems to me that the vessel could have reasonably reached Cardiff to obtain bunkers as she had the undertaking of the British Ministry of Shipping to give her facilities to a port in the UK. As Lord Sumner described the rule in *Hirji Mulji v Cheong Yue S.S. Co.* at 510: 'The rule as to frustration is to reconcile justice with the absolute contract. The seamen's contract was in this case an absolute contract. If the contingency was known to the parties as something which might happen and they did not provide for it, the contract ought to stand.'

Upon this point of the implied term in the contract, in the case of *Emanuel v La Compagnie Fermière,*[6] Lord Esher says: 'A term which was not actually contained in a written contract could not be implied unless the court came to a clear conclusion that both parties must have intended that term to be implied. It was not enough that both parties should have contemplated that a certain state of circumstances would exist. The court must be satisfied that the party against whom the implied term was to be enforced intended to bind himself that that state of circumstances should exist.' A similar principle is stated by Viscount Simon L.C. in the case of *Luxor Ltd v Cooper,*[7] and in *Jacob Marcus & Co. v Crédit Lyonnais*[8] Bowen L.J. said: 'One of the incidents which the English law attaches to a contract is that . . . a person who expressly contracts absolutely to do a thing not naturally impossible, is not excused for non-performance because of being prevented by *vis major.*' And in the case of *Larrinaga & Co. v Société Franco-Américaine des Phosphates,*[9] Lord Sumner said: 'If the appellants' own ships were under requisition, they could have fulfilled their contract with other ships, of which they might be able to obtain the disposition.' Applying that principle to this case the agents here might have made arrangements to take the seamen back to America in other vessels, but they did not do so and relied upon frustration.

This case is obviously different on the facts from any other, and the critical point is the British shipping warrant. I am not satisfied that all the four plaintiffs had information as to the British shipping warrant having expired, or that the captain did not renew it. The captain knew, and it would have been his duty to anticipate, that if he did not get it renewed to the UK while in Charleston, or Halifax, or Sydney, there might be some difficulty in Dublin, and, therefore, he should have included in the conditions of the contract the rights of the crew on the kind of frustration which actually occurred as well as frustration by 'torpedo, mine or loss'. As he did not, I find as a fact that the alleged frustration in Dublin, if the British shipping warrant was necessary and the letter from the British Ministry of Shipping insufficient, was due to the neglect of the captain who was responsible to the owners. If the full British warrant was not absolutely necessary and the letter from the British Ministry of Shipping sufficient, then there was no frustration in the Port of Dublin as it would have carried the vessel to Cardiff.

For these reasons I am of opinion, when the case is carefully analysed, that in the Port of Dublin there was no ground for concluding that there was impossibility of performance. . . .

1. 165 LTR 27; [1942] AC 154.	6. [1889] WN 151.
2. Aleyn, 26, at 27.	7. [1941] 1 All ER 33, at 40.
3. [1926] AC 497, at 510.	8. 12 QBD 589, at 603
4. 5 HLC 673, at 681.	9. 92 LJKB 455, at 463.
5. 6 AC 38, at 59.	

Consider:

What is the rationale for the principle that the frustrating event should not result from one of the parties' deliberate actions or omissions?

Byrne *v* The Limerick Steamship Co. Ltd [1946] IR 138

On 3 February the plaintiff was hired as part of a crew for one of the defendant's ships. As the ship was to call at a British port the crew list had to be approved by the British Permit Office in Dublin. When the plaintiff's permit was refused, he was discharged and a substitute hired. The plaintiff sued for breach of contract.

Overend J.:

The defendants pleaded that, by reason of the refusal of the permit, performance of the contract was frustrated and the contract was determined. . . .

Now, assuming, as I do, that it was impossible, from a practical point of view to undertake this voyage save under the aegis and with the facilities afforded by the British, yet the defendants have proved nothing amounting to frustration on 3 February, as of which date the rights of the parties must be determined. Where an essential licence or permission is refused, the defendants must prove that they have taken all reasonable steps to have such refusal withdrawn: *Bakubhai & Ambalal v South Australian Farmers' Co-operative Union of Adelaide.*[1]

Byrne has been given an excellent character and there is no evidence that the refusal of a permit would have been continued had it been questioned, or that he would have been refused permission to sail on any of the subsequent voyages contemplated by the Articles. . . .

In F. A. *Tamplin Steamship Co. Ltd v Anglo-Mexican Petroleum Products Co. Ltd*,[2] the ship— a tanker—was chartered by the respondents on a time charter for sixty months from 4 December 1912 to 4 December 1917. The ship was requisitioned by the British government early in December 1914, and before her release was again requisitioned in February 1915. She was still under requisition at the date of the hearing in July 1916, having meantime been structurally altered to carry troops. The owners claimed that the charter had been determined. The judge of first instance, the Court of Appeal, and the majority of the House of Lords all held there had been no frustration. Lord Parker in his speech (pp 425–8) emphasises the difficulty of applying this principle of frustration in the case of a time charter in which no definite commercial adventure is contemplated, and especially where the contract is already partly performed.

In *Barras v Aberdeen Steam Trawling and Fishing Co.*[3] a seaman was employed on a running agreement for six months fishing in the North Sea. On the trawler's first return she collided with another and had to be docked for some days for repairs, the seaman being paid off. Four members of the court (Viscount Buckmaster L.C. and Lords Warrington, Russell, and Macmillan) clearly expressed the view that there was no frustration of the contract. The reasoning mentioned seems to me to apply with equal force in the present case.

It has been frequently stressed that frustration operates automatically to determine the entire contract and does not depend on the volition, or even the knowledge, of the parties: *Joseph Constantine Steamship Line Ltd v Imperial Smelting Corp. Ltd;*[4] *Hirji Mulji v Cheong Yue Steamship Co. Ltd;*[5] *Cricklewood Pty and Investment Trust Ltd v Leighton's Investment Trust Ltd;*[6] *Maritime National Fish Ltd v Ocean Trawlers Ltd.*[7]

In my opinion Byrne's contract with the defendant company was not determined by frustration, but by his discharge by the captain on 3 February.

1. 69 Lloyd's Rep. 138.
2. [1916] 2 AC 397.
3. [1933] AC 402, at 413, 439, 443, 448.
4. [1942] AC 154.
5. [1926] AC 497.
6. [1945] AC 221.
7. [1935] AC 524.

(The plaintiff was deemed to be entitled to one month's wages as compensation for the discharge.)

The following case indicates that the Court will examine carefully the frustrating event in order to determine whether it was caused by self-induced frustration.

F.C. Sheppard & Co. Ltd v Jerrom [1986] 3 All ER 589

An apprentice under a four-year training service agreement was convicted of affray and sentenced to borstal training, while less than halfway through his apprenticeship. He was sentenced for an indeterminate period of between six months and two years. Upon his release six months later his employer refused to re-hire him. His employer appealed from the decisions of an industrial tribunal and the Employment Appeal Tribunal that they had repudiated his contract and that the dismissal was thus unfair. In this case, somewhat unusually, the apprentice was seeking to rely on his own default to establish his right to claim unfair dismissal on the grounds that the contract was still valid.

Lawton L.J.:

. . . The first question is whether what happened was capable in law of frustrating the contract. The second is whether it did frustrate it; this is a question of fact (see *Pioneer Shipping Ltd v B.T.P. Tioxide Ltd, The Nema* [1981] 2 All ER 1030 at 1047, [1982] AC 724 at 752 per Lord Roskill)...

As to the first of these questions, there was an event, namely the sentence of borstal training, which was not foreseen or provided for by the parties at the time of contracting. It was a question of fact, to which I shall return later, whether it rendered the performance of the contract radically different from what the parties had contemplated when they entered into it. What has to be decided is whether the outside event and its consequences in relation to the performance of the contract occurred without either the fault or default of either party to it. I have based this dissection of the problem on the speech of Lord Barandon in *Paal Wilson & Co A/S v Partenreederei Hannah Blumenthal, The Hannah Blumenthal* [1983] 1 All ER 34 at 44, [1983] 1 AC 854 at 909.

There was no fault or default on the part of the employers. They were alleging that because of the unforeseen outside event the contract had been frustrated. If it had been, there had been no dismissal as defined in s. 55 of the [Employment Protection (Consolidation) Act 1978] . The oddity of this case is that the apprentice, for his own purposes, is seeking to allege that he was in default so as to keep in being a contract which the employers would otherwise have been able to say had been terminated by operation of law. Through his counsel he has submitted, relying on *Universal Cargo Carriers Corp. v Citati* [1957] 2 All ER 70, [1957] 2 QB 401, that his conduct, resulting as it did in a sentence of borstal training, amounted to a repudiation of the contract which the employers did not accept until January 1982. It seems to me that the apprentice is seeking to rely on his own default, if in law it should be regarded as such, to establish his right to claim for unfair dismissal.

This is the opposite of what happened in two of the leading cases dealing with the consequences of default in relation to the frustration of contracts, namely *Maritime National Fish Ltd v Ocean Trawlers Ltd* [1935] AC 524, [1935] All ER Rep 86 and *Mertens v Home Freeholds Co.* [1921] 2 KB 526, [1921] All ER Rep 372. In each of these cases the plaintiff had sought to enforce the contract and the defendants had pleaded frustration because of change of circumstances. It was adjudged in both cases that these pleas failed because the defendants' own acts had caused or contributed to what had made performance impossible. The frustration which the two defendants had sought to rely on were self-induced and in consequence in law there had been no frustrations. In the *Maritime National Fish Ltd* case the act had been an election; in the *Mertens* case, reprehensible conduct which could fairly be described as a default. As Lord Brandon commented in the *Paal Wilson & Co.* case ' . . . the courts have never defined with precision the meaning of the expression 'default' in this context.' This case does call for this court to decide whether the apprentice's conduct resulting in a sentence of borstal training was a default which prevented the contract from being frustrated.

The classic formulation of the concept of 'self-induced frustration' is to be found in the speech of Lord Sumner in *Bank Line Ltd v Arthur Capel & Co.* [1919] AC 435 at 452 when he said: 'I think it is now well settled that the principle of frustration of an adventure assumes that the frustration arises without blame or fault on either side. Reliance cannot be placed on a self-induced frustration; indeed, such conduct might give the other party the option to treat the contract as repudiated.'

In *Joseph Constantine Steamship Line Ltd v Imperial Smelting Corp. Ltd, The Kingswood* [1941] 2 All ER 165, [1942] AC 154 the House of Lords had to adjudge whether in a claim by charterers against shipowners for damages for failure to load a cargo when the shipowners pleaded that the contract had been frustrated by an explosion, for which no cause was ascertained, they had to prove that it had not been caused by their act or default. Their Lordships adjudged that they did not have to do so. At the end of his speech 'For purposes of clearness, and to avoid possible misunderstanding hereafter' Viscount Simon L.C. said:

> . . . I do not think that the ambit of 'default' as an element disabling the plea of frustration to prevail has as yet been precisely and finally determined. 'Self-induced' frustration, as illustrated by the two decided cases already quoted [that is the *Maritime National Fish Ltd* and *Mertens* cases], involves deliberate choice, and those cases amount to saying that a man cannot ask to be excused by reason of frustration if he has purposely so acted as to bring it about. 'Default' is a much wider term, and in many commercial cases dealing with frustration is treated as equivalent to negligence. Yet in cases of frustration of another class, arising in connection with a contract for personal performance, it has not, I think, been laid down that, if the personal incapacity is due to want or care, the plea fails. Some day it may have to be finally determined whether a *prima donna* is excused by complete loss of voice from an executory contract to sing if it is proved that her condition was caused by her carelessness in not changing her wet clothes after being out in the rain. The implied term in such a case may turn out to be that the fact of super-vening physical incapacity dissolves the contract without inquiring further into its cause, provided, of course, that it has not been deliberately induced in order to get out of the engagement.

The apprentice's criminal conduct was deliberate but it did not by itself have any consequences on the performance of his contract. What affected performance was his sentence of borstal training, which was the act of the judge and which he would have avoided if he could have done so. It cannot be said, I think, that the concept of 'self-induced frustration' can be applied to this case. What can be said, however, is that when the apprentice acted in the criminal way he did he was recklessly putting at risk his ability to perform his contract. He should have appreciated that if he joined in an affray he might lose his liberty. I doubt, however, whether as a matter of contract he had impliedly agreed with his employers that outside working hours he would never behave in a way which might interrupt for a substantial period his ability to go to work.

Lord Wright, in the same case [*Constantine*], after having referred to some of the undecided aspects of the law relating to frustration, said:

> The appeal can, I think, be decided according to the generally accepted view that frustration involves as one of its elements absence of fault, by applying the ordinary rules as to onus of proof. If frustration is viewed, as I think it can be, as analogous to an exception, since it is generally relied upon as a defence to a claim for failure to perform a contract, the same rule will properly be applied to it as to the ordinary type of exceptions. The defence may be rebutted by proof of fault, but the onus of proving fault will rest on the plaintiff. This is merely to apply the familiar rule which is applied, for instance, where a carrier by sea relies on the exception of perils of the seas. If the goods owner then desires to rebut that *prima facie* defence on the ground of negligence or other fault on the part of the shipowner, it rests on the goods owner to establish the negligence or fault.

This line of reasoning was discussed by Lord Porter. He queried whether an accidental injury to a contractor preventing performance would be regarded as caused by his default.

In the absence of any binding, or even persuasive, authority dealing with this problem I approach it in this way. The employers wanted to establish that the contract had been frustrated. They had to prove that there had been some outside event which rendered performance of the contract radically different from what the parties had contemplated when they made it. They proved an outside event which had occurred because of the sentence which the judge had imposed. They claimed that performance would have been radically different. The apprentice did not suggest that they had been at fault. In my judgment the apprentice should not be allowed to plead his own 'default' in order to establish his right to claim compensation for unfair dismissal.

In my judgment the principle of law is that he who asserts that the performance of a contract had been frustrated must prove not only the two essential elements to which Lord Brandon referred but that the outside event or extraneous change of situation was not caused by any default on his part. If the party against whom frustration is asserted can by way of answer rely on his own misconduct, injustice results, as is shown by the following example which was discussed in argument. A butler is convicted of stealing his employer's silver and is sentenced to two years' imprisonment. If this is no more than repudiatory conduct on his part and his employer does not tell him either expressly or by implication (see *London Transport Executive v Clarke* [1981] ICR 355) that he has been dismissed, he could claim on release from prison that he was still employed as a butler. Such a contention would surprise the employer, but perhaps not his solicitors.

The only decision of this court which deals with the effect of a custodial sentence on a contract of employment, *Hare v Murphy Bros Ltd* [1974] 3 All ER 940, was decided before the decision of this court in *London Transport Executive v Clarke*. In *Hare*'s case [1973] ICR 331 the National Industrial Relations Court had adjudged that the employee's criminal conduct which had resulted in his being sentenced to twelve months' imprisonment amounted to a breach of his contract of employment of so serious a nature that it constituted a unilateral repudiation of that contract at the date when he was convicted and sentenced. That made it impossible for him to claim unfair dismissal because at that date the Industrial Relations Act 1971 was not in force. The National Industrial Relations Court has said that the sentence was not an event frustrating the contract of employment because it had been brought about by the employee's own conduct. In this court the employee submitted that the contract had not been determined until his repudiatory conduct by being sent to prison had been accepted by his employers, which, he submitted, was within time for the purpose of claiming that he had been unfairly dismissed. Lord Denning M.R., who delivered the leading judgment, said that he could not accept that by becoming involved in a brawl the employee had been in breach of contract. He thought that the sentence of imprisonment was a frustrating event which brought his contract of employment to an end. Stephenson L.J. thought that the contract had been brought to an end in one of four ways, but he did not find it necessary to say which was the appropriate label to apply. I was a member of the court. I agreed that the appeal should be dismissed on what I called the 'common sense of the situation', which was not an example of sound legal reasoning. Since it is not clear on what grounds the court as such decided *Hare*'s case I do not regard it as a binding authority. In my opinion this court can reconsider the problem of the effect of a custodial sentence on a contract of employment. In my judgment such a sentence is capable in law of frustrating the contract.

The next question is whether on the facts of this case the sentence of borstal training did frustrate the contract. In my judgment it did. The parties must have contemplated that four years' training was necessary for producing a qualified plumber. The passing of the sentence meant that there was going to be a substantial break in the period of training, probably thirty nine weeks, possibly six months but also possibly more than thirty nine weeks. At the end of the contract period the apprentice was not going to be as well trained as the parties had contemplated he would be.

Much time was spent in this court discussing whether the apprentice's conduct, resulting as it did in his being sentenced to borstal training, was repudiatory of the contract. He broke no term of it. His conduct can only be said to be repudiatory on the grounds set out by Devlin J. in *Universal Cargo Carriers Corp. v Citati* [1957] 2 All ER 70 at 84, [1957] 2 QB 401 at 436. Even if that case states the law relating to commercial contracts correctly (and I make no comment on that) I doubt whether the principle it establishes applies to contracts of personal service. The apprentice's criminal conduct itself would have had no effect on his performance of it had he not been arrested, convicted and sentenced. The sentence was a consequence of the disorderly conduct; probably a foreseeable one; but not an inevitable one. . . .

I would allow the appeal.

(Mustill and Balcombe L.JJ. agreed.)

Note

In *The Queen in right of Newfoundland et al v Wells* 177 DLR 73, the Government of Newfoundland employed the respondent as Commissioner (Consumer Representative) but four years later enacted legislation abolishing this position and claimed the employment contract was frustrated. The Supreme Court of Canada rejected this claim on the basis of the principle that self-induced frustration does not excuse non-performance. It refused to accept the argument that the separation of powers between the legislative and executive branches meant that the frustration was not 'self'-induced noting that 'the same 'directing minds', namely the executive, were responsible for both the respondent's appointment and its termination'.

E. EMPLOYMENT CONTRACTS

Frustration may operate to discharge a party's obligations under a contract of employment.

Flynn *v* Great Northern Rly Co. (Ireland) Ltd (1953) 89 ILTR 46

The plaintiff, an employee of the defendant company, was injured as a result of an accident at work on 30 July 1947. The court had to decide *inter alia* whether the plaintiff's contract of services was frustrated due to his incapacity.

Budd J.:

The first ground relied on is that, whether properly dismissed or not, Flynn's contract of service is in any event at an end because of the nature of his incapacity, which it is alleged was such as to frustrate the contract.

Dr Bouchier Hayes said that he formed the opinion in October 1947, that Flynn was not then fit for work on the foot-plate. He made a report to that effect dated 16 October 1947. From 1947 to the present date he said there was no prospect of Flynn being able to work as a fireman on the foot-plate and that he had formed the opinion that it was undesirable that he should ever work on the foot-plate again. Dr Bouchier Hayes' view is that there was no period between 1947 and the present time when Flynn was fit for work on the foot-plate and he has in fact done no work since 30 July 1947, a period of nearly six years. He has suffered during that period from a number of serious complaints, and, from what Dr Bouchier Hayes said, and having regard to the nature of his condition and the record of his incapacity, my view is that in all human probability Flynn will not be fit to work on the foot-plate again and that he is permanently incapacitated for such service. Having regard to Flynn's history and condition my view is that prior to 16 October 1947, Flynn had become permanently incapacitated in the physical sense from performing his duties on the foot-plate.

The precise result of the illness of a servant on a contract of service is not always easy to determine. From a perusal of the cases it would seem that in law the illness or physical incapacity of the servant will determine the contract if it is of such a nature as to frustrate the business object of the engagement. In *Poussard v Spiers* 1 QBD 410, an opera singer was engaged to sing in an opera for three months, provided the opera ran so long. The plaintiff was unable to sing on the first night through illness, which was serious and of uncertain duration. It was held that the failure on the plaintiff's part went to the root of the matter and discharged the contract. The result was different in *Storey v Fulham Steel Works* 24 TLR 89, where six months illness, after two years service in a five years engagement, was held not to determine the contract. Lord Alverstone, however, in that case adopted what was said in *Jackson v Union Marine Insurance* Co. by Baron Bramwell as a correct statement of the law, namely, that if the illness was such as to put an end in the business sense to their business engagement and would frustrate the object of that engagement, then the employer could dismiss its servant and no action would lie against him. What Lord Alverstone said seems to indicate the necessity of the master giving notice before the contract is terminated, but that point was not at issue in the case. Lord Campbell used words in *Cuckson v Stone* 1 E & E 248 which would also seem to indicate that notice would be necessary where he says at 257 that, if the plaintiff in that case had by illness become permanently incapacitated to act in the capacity of a brewer, the defendant might in the view of the court have determined the contract. Again, Lord Atkinson in *Price v Guest Keen and Nettlefolds* [1918] AC 760 said that illness might be of such a permanent character that it would justify dismissal, thereby implying that notice was necessary, but again in neither of these cases was that precise point in issue. On the other hand, Scrutton L.J., in *Warburton v Co-operative Wholesale Society, Ltd* [1917] 1 KB 663, said that under the decided cases a servant incapacitated by illness and in the absence of notice does not cease to be employed unless the illness is such as seriously to interfere with or frustrate the business purpose of the contract, thereby implying that in such case notice is unnecessary. From the words used by Blackburn J., delivering the judgment of the court in *Poussard v Spiers* 'that the failure on the plaintiff's part went to the root of the matter and discharged the defendant' and from the nature of the decision it would appear that the court in that case did not regard notice as necessary, but it is right to bear in mind that the engagement was to commence on a specific date and was of a very particular nature. Of recent years as a result, no doubt, of cases arising from war conditions, the doctrine of frustration has received more detailed consideration. In *Denny Mott and Dickson Ltd v Fraser* [1944] AC 265, Lord Wright at 274 points out that where there is frustration a dissolution of the contract occurs automatically. Overend J., in *Byrne v*

Limerick Steamship Co. Ltd [1946] IR 138, 80 ILTR 142, also accepted the view that frustration operates automatically to determine the entire contract and does not depend upon the volition of the parties or even on their knowledge. It is right to add that he decided that the contract in that case had not been determined by frustration. If frustration is the test, there does not in principle seem to be any reason why a master should have to give notice to terminate a contract, already frustrated, and my view, therefore, is that notice is unnecessary.

It would seem to be a question of fact to be determined in each case as to whether or not the illness is of such a kind and duration, or likely duration, as to frustrate the business object of the contract, and I must consider what the true position is in this case, having regard to the nature of Flynn's illness or incapacity, and the nature of his contract. I have determined that he was a weekly wage earner whose contract was subject to be determined by a week's notice. He is a manual worker but without him and men of his grade the engines of the company cannot be properly manned and the service maintained. His incapacity is, I am satisfied, now permanent for work as a fireman. His incapacity on 16 October 1947, was such that it was the doctor's view, communicated to the company, that it would be undesirable that he should ever again resume duty as a fireman on the foot-plate, a view that has been amply substantiated by subsequent events. I am satisfied that in all the circumstances his incapacity was such at that time as to frustrate the business object of the engagement. I have come to the conclusion, therefore, that I ought to find in accordance with the defendant's alternative plea that Flynn was permanently incapacitated on 16 October 1947, to perform his duties as a fireman on the foot-plate and, his incapacity being such at the time as to frustrate the business object of the engagement, his contract, accordingly, then terminated. . . .

Donegal County Council *v* Langan. Employment Appeals Tribunal Case No. UD143/89

The determination of the tribunal was as follows:

The employer is appealing the recommendation of the Rights Commissioner, who found that the employee was unfairly dismissed.

The employee, a general operative, commenced employment with the employer in May 1974. On 27 June 1985, he became incapacitated for work, certified as suffering from lumbar pain.

He was still absent on sick leave and submitting medical certificates when he was informed by the employer in a letter dated 21 April 1988 that 'the council does not intend to re-employ you and it will therefore, not be necessary for you to submit any further medical certificates'.

The employee accepted this letter as a dismissal and we hold that he was entitled to do so. In July 1988, he was medically certified as fit to resume his employment by his own medical adviser. After he had served a claim for unfair claim dismissal on the employer he was requested to attend Dr David St C. Baird FRCS, Consultant Orthopaedic Surgeon in Derry, for medical examination. This he duly did and Dr Baird, in his report, stated 'I would feel that he is fit enough to carry out manual work'.

The employer is contesting that his contract of employment had become frustrated by illness.

The doctrine of frustration has been used very selectively and only in cases where the event relied on, renders all further performance of an employment contract impossible. In most cases a defence of fair dismissal because of sickness is entered. Such is not the case here. The general 'impossible to perform' test applies. There may be an event (e.g. a crippling accident) so dramatic and shattering that everyone concerned will realise immediately that to all intents and purposes the contract must be regarded as at an end. Or there may be an event, where an employee becomes incapacitated by an incurable disease, or an illness or accident, the course and outcome of which, is uncertain. It may be a long process before one is able to say whether the event is such as to bring about the frustration of the contract and that it is no longer possible to regard the contract as still subsisting. Among the matters to be taken into account in deciding whether the contract is frustrated are:

(i) the length of the previous employment.

(ii) how long it has been expected that the employment would last.

(iii) the nature of the job.

(iv) the nature, length and effect of the illness or disabling event.

(v) the need of the employer for the work to be done.

(vi) whether wages have continued to be paid.

(vii) the actions of the employer in relation to the employment.

(viii) whether consideration was given to retaining the employee on the books if not in employment.

(ix) whether the employer discussed with the employee and his trade union the employee's problems and prospects.

(x) whether adequate medical investigation was carried out, (e.g. employers should ask their own or their employee's doctor for reports to establish the real medical facts and if there is conflicting medical evidence, to seek an independent source).

(xi) whether, in all the circumstances a reasonable employer could be expected to wait any longer.

It was clear from the evidence that the employee was not a key worker. Apart from the initial twelve weeks of his absence he was not paid during his period of absence. There was no consultation with either the employee or his trade union and no medical investigation was carried out prior to termination of his employment. We are at a loss to know why the employer waited until some eleven months after the termination of the employment before requesting the employee to attend for medical examination. His own medical adviser had certified him fit for full duties, some three months after the termination of his employment. In a case of frustration it is not necessary that the employers should take steps to end the employment for the whole point of frustration is that it operates automatically to discharge the contract as a result of the event bringing it about. Proving frustration can be a difficult task and employers are more likely to succeed when there is clear evidence that there is little prospect of recovery. Where there is prospect of recovery, a lengthy absence does not necessarily frustrate the contract.

We find, that the employer has failed to prove that the employee's contract was frustrated by illness and the fact that he was medically certified as fit to resume his employment within some three months after the termination of his employment was not a factor in our finding. Even if the employer had contended that the employee was fairly dismissed because of his prolonged absence, we would find that the dismissal was unfair on procedural grounds. Accordingly we uphold the recommendation of the Rights Commissioner that the employee was unfairly dismissed.

Accordingly we determine that the employee should be reinstated in accordance with s. 7 (1)(a) of the Unfair Dismissals Act 1977.

EXERCISES

1. Dan wishes to sail his yacht from Athens to Dublin. He employs Rita and Ron as part of an eight-person crew to operate the boat for the duration of the voyage. He agrees to pay them a fee of €2,000 each for this. When the boat docks in Marseilles halfway through the journey, Rita disembarks and does not return. When Ron complains about this, Dan promises to give Rita's fee to Ron when the boat gets to Dublin, telling him that 'we will all have to pull together and work harder now that Rita has let us down'. However, when the boat arrives in Dublin Dan refuses to pay Ron the extra €2,000. Rita then phones Dan demanding to be paid €1,000 for her completed work. Advise Dan.

2. Ellen enters a three-month contract with Pam to act as her personal assistant on a tour of China. One month into the contract, Ellen informs Pam that she misses home to much and 'may need to leave'. Is Pam entitled to treat this as a repudiatory breach? Would your answer be different if Ellen informs Pam of her concerns that she might be homesick before they depart for China?

3. Liz is employed under a two-year contract. Her boss Gerry becomes irritated with her tedious jokes and dismisses her. He then discovers that she has been engaged in defrauding the company. He claims that her actions amount to a repudiation of the contract. She claims in turn that by dismissing her he has breached the contract.

4. If a vendor of a 'new' car delivers a car which he has been driving for the last month, has he breached a fundamental term of the sales contract?

5. Liz operates a secretarial agency. She agrees to supply temporary secretaries to Mulratty Finance Ltd within two hours of being notified that such staff are needed. On this basis, Mulratty Finance Ltd pay her a fixed amount per month, in addition to a fee based upon supply of individual secretaries. Liz has a similar arrangement with Martin Solicitors in relation to legal secretaries. Six months later, Mulratty Finance Ltd call upon Liz for the first time and request a temporary secretary. Liz explains that due to labour shortages she cannot supply anyone at present. Similarly, on the first occasion that Martin Solicitors seek a legal secretary, Liz explains that her legal secretaries have just declared a strike as she has reduced their pay. Liz claims that the two contracts are frustrated. Advise Mulratty Finance Ltd and Martin Solicitors.

6. Kate enters into a contract with Kevin to lease his warehouse for ten years. Kate uses the warehouse to store merchandise for sale in her bookshop. Five years into the lease, the local authority closes the street, giving only pedestrian access to the warehouse for twenty months. Although the local authority had announced to the public its intention to undertake drainage improvements on the road, it was never clear whether sufficient funds would be available to undertake this task, when work would start, what the scale of the improvements would be and whether full or partial road closure would be required. Kate claims that the contract is frustrated.

7. Ailish hires Hughes Ltd, a firm of building contractors, to develop a site in Cork and agrees to pay it €400,000. As a result of labour shortages, Hughes Ltd discover that the cost to them of doing the job is €800,000. The finance director informs the managing director of Hughes Ltd that if they complete the job the company will be bankrupt. Is the contract frustrated?

Chapter Nineteen

Damages

INTRODUCTION

A contracting party who is confronted by an actual or threatened breach of contract may seek a number of remedies, often in pleadings which stress that it is for the judge to select the most appropriate relief in the instant case. These remedies include a declaratory judgment in which the rights of the parties are clarified by the court, an injunction of some kind, specific performance of the contract, or an order that any profits made as a result of wrongdoing be estimated and paid to the victim of the breach of contract. However, many of these remedies may not be available for any number of reasons, and in such a case damages may be awarded as an alternative remedy. It is necessary to emphasise that in most cases the plaintiff's only realistic remedy will be damages and that the plaintiff may actually only seek this remedy. It is possible however for the plaintiff to use the rules which determine the way in which damages will be assessed, in order to maximise the plaintiff's prospects of obtaining compensation, so a clear understanding of the principles and rules which govern the assessment of damages is an important skill for any lawyer to acquire.

SECTION ONE—REASONS FOR THE AWARD OF DAMAGES FOLLOWING ON A BREACH OF CONTRACT

Robinson v Harman (1848) 1 Ex 850

This was an action which arose out of an agreement to grant a lease in favour of the plaintiff, for an annual rent of £110, the lease to run for twenty years. The plaintiff had entered into a good bargain, the leased premises being worth more than £110 per year. When the defendant failed to execute the lease the plaintiff sued. His costs in wasted solicitor's fees were £15 12s 8d but the jury awarded the plaintiff £200 damages. The defendant appealed against this award.

Parke B.:

. . . what damages is the plaintiff entitled to recover? The rule of the common law is, that where a party sustains a loss by reason of a breach of contract, he is, so far as money can do it, to be placed in the same situation, with respect to damages, as if the contract had been performed. The case of *Flureau v Thornhill*[1] qualified that rule of the common law. It was there held, that contracts for the sale of real estate are merely on condition that the vendor has a good title; so that, when a person contracts to sell real property, there is an implied understanding that, if he fail to make a good title, the only damages recoverable are the expenses which the vendee may be put to in investigating the title. The present case comes within the rule of the common law, and I am unable to distinguish it from *Hopkins v Grazebrook*.[2]

Alderson B.:

I am of the same opinion. The damages have been assessed according to the general rule of law, that where a person makes a contract and breaks it, he must pay the whole damage sustained. Upon that general rule an exception was engrafted by the case of *Flureau v Thornhill*, and upon that exception the case of *Hopkins v Grazebrook* engrafted another exception. This case comes within the latter, by which the old common law rule has been restored. Therefore the defendant, having undertaken to grant a valid lease, not having any colour of title, must pay the loss which the plaintiff has sustained by not having that for which he contracted.

Platt B.:

Upon general principle I cannot distinguish this case from *Hopkins v Grazebrook*.

[1.] 2 Wm. Bl. 1078.   [2.] 6 B. & C. 31.

Note

In this case a modern court would classify the £15 12s 8d as reliance loss with the £200 being expectation loss.

It is necessary to stress that the compensatory principle does not of itself identify the basic measure of damages. As we shall see both contract and tort damages are compensatory but different results follow depending on the cause of action. It is essential to distinguish possible measures of compensation from specific heads of loss. The 'exception' referred to in *Robinson v Harman* is considered below, the rule in *Bain v Fothergill* on p. 1067.

A. The Reliance Interest in Contract Damages

Fuller & Purdue (1936) 46 Yale LJ 52, 53–7 (Footnotes omitted.)

The Purposes Pursued in Awarding Contract Damages

It is convenient to distinguish three principal purposes which may be pursued in awarding contract damages. These purposes, and the situations in which they become appropriate, may be stated briefly as follows:

First, the plaintiff has in reliance on the promise of the defendant conferred some value on the defendant. The defendant fails to perform his promise. The court may force the defendant to disgorge the value he received from the plaintiff. The object here may be termed the prevention of gain by the defaulting promisor at the expense of the promisee, more briefly, the prevention of unjust enrichment. The interest protected may be called the *restitution interest*. For our present purposes it is quite immaterial how the suit in such a case be classified, whether as contractual or quasi-contractual, whether as a suit to enforce the contract or as a suit based upon a rescission of the contract. These questions relate to the superstructure of the law, not to the basic policies with which we are concerned.

Secondly, the plaintiff has in reliance on the promise of the defendant changed his position. For example, the buyer under a contract for the sale of land has incurred expense in the investigation of the seller's title, or has neglected the opportunity to enter other contracts. We may award damages to the plaintiff for the purpose of undoing the harm which his reliance on the defendant's promise has caused him. Our object is to put him in as good a position as he was in before the promise was made. The interest protected in this case may be called the *reliance interest*.

Thirdly, without insisting on reliance by the promisee or enrichment of the promisor, we may seek to give the promisee the value of the expectancy which the promise created. We may in a suit for specific performance actually compel the defendant to render the promised performance to the plaintiff, or, in a suit for damages, we may make the defendant pay the money value of this performance. Here our object is to put the plaintiff in as good a position as he would have occupied had the defendant performed his promise. The interest protected in this case we may call the *expectation interest*.

It will be observed that what we have called the *restitution interest* unites two elements: (1) reliance by the promisee, (2) a resultant gain to the promisor. It may for some purposes be necessary to separate these elements. In some cases a defaulting promisor may after his breach be left with an unjust gain which was not taken from the promisee (a third party furnished the consideration), or which was not the result of reliance by the promisee (the promisor violated a promise not to appropriate the promisee's goods). Even in those cases where the promisor's gain results from the promisee's reliance it may happen that damages will be assessed somewhat differently, depending on whether we take the promisor's gain or the promisee's loss as the standard of measurement. Generally, however, . . . gain by the promisor will be accompanied by a corresponding and, so far as its legal measurement is concerned, identical loss to the promisee, so that for our purposes the most workable classification is one which presupposes in the restitution interest a correlation of promisor's gain and promisee's loss. If, as we shall assume, the gain involved in the restitution interest results from and is identical with the plaintiff's loss through reliance, then the restitution interest is merely a special case of the reliance interest; all of the cases coming under the restitution interest will be covered by the reliance interest, and the reliance interest will be broader than the restitution interest only to the extent that it includes cases where the plaintiff has relied on the defendant's promise without enriching the defendant.

B. THE PLAINTIFF'S LOSS

British Westinghouse Electric and Manufacturing Co. Ltd v Underground Electric Rlys of London Ltd [1912] AC 673

The appellants, British Westinghouse, supplied turbines to the respondents. The turbines failed to perform to the standard set by the contract and the respondents replaced these turbines with a rival product that proved much more efficient than the British Westinghouse turbines. Indeed, in an arbitration the arbitrator found, (1) that purchase of the replacement turbines was a reasonable and prudent course for the respondents to take in mitigating their losses, and (2) that even if the original turbines had complied with the contract, there would have still been a pecuniary advantage to the respondent in replacing the British Westinghouse machines. The arbitrator, the Divisional Court, the High Court and the Court of Appeal nevertheless held that the respondents could recover the cost of the substituted turbines as part of their damages. British Westinghouse appealed to the House of Lords.

Viscount Haldane:

. . .

. . . I think that there are certain broad principles which are quite well settled. The first is that, as far as possible, he who has proved a breach of a bargain to supply what he contracted to get is to be placed, as far as money can do it, in as good a situation as if the contract had been performed.

The fundamental basis is thus compensation for pecuniary loss naturally flowing from the breach; but this first principle is qualified by a second, which imposes on a plaintiff the duty of taking all reasonable steps to mitigate the loss consequent on the breach, and debars him from claiming any part of the damage which is due to his neglect to take such steps. In the words of James L.J. in *Dunkirk Colliery Co. v Lever*,[1] 'The person who has broken the contract is not to be exposed to additional cost by reason of the plaintiffs not doing what they ought to have done as reasonable men, and the plaintiffs not being under any obligation to do anything otherwise than in the ordinary course of business.'

As James L.J. indicates, this second principle does not impose on the plaintiff an obligation to take any step which a reasonable and prudent man would not ordinarily take in the course of his business. But when in the course of his business he has taken action arising out of the transaction, which action has diminished his loss, the effect in actual diminution of the loss he has suffered may be taken into account even though there was no duty on him to act.

Staniforth v Lyall[2] illustrates this rule. In that case the defendants had chartered a ship to New Zealand, where they were to load her, or by an agent there to give the plaintiff, the owner, notice that they abandoned the adventure, in which case they were to pay £500. The ship went to New Zealand, but found neither agent nor cargo there, and the captain chose to make a circuitous voyage home by way of Batavia. This voyage, after making every allowance for increased expense and loss of time, was more profitable than the original venture to New Zealand would have been. The Court of Common Pleas decided that the action was to be viewed as one for a breach of contract to put the cargo on board the plaintiff's vessel for which the plaintiff was entitled to recover all the damages he had incurred, but that he was bound to bring into account, in ascertaining the damages arising from the breach, the advantages which had accrued to him because of the course which he had chosen to adopt.

I think that this decision illustrates a principle which has been recognized in other cases, that, provided the course taken to protect himself by the plaintiff in such an action was one which a reasonable and prudent person might in the ordinary conduct of business properly have taken, and in fact did take whether bound to or not, a jury or an arbitrator may properly look at the whole of the facts and ascertain the result in estimating the quantum of damage.

Recent illustrations of the way in which this principle has been applied, and the facts have been allowed to speak for themselves, are to be found in the decisions of the Judicial Committee of the Privy Council in *Eric County Natural Gas and Fuel Co. v Carroll*[3] and *Wertheim v Chicoutimi Pulp Co.*[4] The subsequent transaction, if to be taken into account, must be one arising out of the consequences of the breach and in the ordinary course of business. This distinguishes such cases from a quite different class illustrated by *Bradburn v Great Western Rly Co.*,[5] where it was held that, in an action for injuries caused by the defendants' negligence, a sum received by the plaintiff on a policy for insurance against accident could not be taken into account in reduction of damages. The reason of the decision was that it was not the accident, but a contract wholly independent of the relation between the plaintiff and the defendant, which gave the plaintiff his advantage. Again, it has been held that, in an action for delay in discharging a ship of the plaintiffs' whereby they lost their passengers whom they had contracted to carry, the damages ought not to be reduced by reason of the same persons taking passage in another vessel belonging to the plaintiffs: *Jebsen v East and West India Dock Co.*,[6] a case in which what was relied on as mitigation did not arise out of the transactions the subject matter of the contract.

The cases as to the measure of damages for breach of a covenant by a lessee to deliver up the demised premises in repair illustrate yet another class of authorities in which the qualifying rule has been excluded. In *Joyner v Weeks*[7] the lessor had made a lease to another lessee by way of anticipation, to commence from the expiration of the term of this lease, and the new lessee had made no claim to be reimbursed the cost which he had incurred in repairing after the expiration of the demised lease. Wright J. held that the true test was the amount of diminution in value to the lessor, not exceeding the cost of doing the repairs. The Court of Appeal, including Lord Esher and Fry L.J., took a different view. They thought that there had been a constant practice of laying down the measure of damages as being the cost of putting into repair, and that in the particular class of cases with which they were dealing it was a highly convenient rule which ought not to be disturbed. Any other measure appeared to involve complicated inquiries. Moreover, the arrangement between the lessor and the new lessee was *res inter alios acta* with which the original lessee had nothing to do and which he was not entitled to set up.

I think the principle which applies here is that which makes it right for the jury or arbitrator to look at what actually happened, and to balance loss and gain. The transaction was not *res inter alios acta*, but one in which the person whose contract was broken took a reasonable and prudent course quite naturally arising out of the circumstances in which he was placed by the breach. Apart from the breach of contract, the lapse of time had rendered the appellants' machines obsolete, and men of business would be doing the only thing they could properly do in replacing them with new and up-to-date machines.

[1] (1878) 9 ChD 20, at p. 25.	[5] LR 10 Ex 1.
[2] 7 Bing. 169.	[6] LR 10 CP 300.
[3] [1911] AC 105.	[7] [1891] 2 QB 31.
[4] [1911] AC 301.	

(Lords Ashbourne, Macnaghten and Atkinson concurred.)

Note

In *J. P. Morgan Chase Bank v Springwell Navigation Corporation* [2006] EWCA Civ 161, the Court of Appeal was asked to consider whether a double recovery situation existed. Springwell charged J. P. Morgan Chase Bank (Chase) with managing its investment portfolio, which was directed at generating sufficient funds to replace vessels used in a family shipping business. Chase allegedly caused losses of US$280 with the result that, instead of buying at least twenty new vessels, only two new vessels were obtained.

This had a negative impact on profits that would have been made via shipping activities (shipping losses). Chase contended that the shipping losses claim should be struck out because in order to secure the shipping profits Springwell would have had to divest itself of the portfolio. Chase argued that compensation for the portfolio losses would constitute adequate compensation, but the Court of Appeal found in favour of Springwell. Buxton L.J. wrote:

Cullinane v British 'Rema' Manufacturing [1954] 1 QB 292 is a much discussed, but perhaps less frequently cited, decision in which this court had to disentangle a claim for breach of warranty of performance of equipment that was based partly on expenditure wasted in installation, and partly on loss of the profits that would have been achieved if the machine had performed as warranted. Evershed M.R. pointed out that a claim for the whole of the capital loss and expenses, thus putting the plaintiff in the same position as if he had never made the contract at all, would be inconsistent with, alternatively wholly overlapped with, a claim for the profits that would have been made had the machine been available for use. Those were, in effect, two different ways of expressing in financial terms the damage caused by the breach of warranty. The claimant can chose which of the two measures to adopt, but as they are alternative measures of quantifying the same loss cannot assert both: see per Lord Denning MR in *Anglia Television v Reed* [1972] 1 QB 60 at pp 63H–64A. But our case is different. The shipping losses spring from Springwell's inability to make investments that, on its pleaded case, would have *increased* the value to it of the portfolio. They are therefore not, or at least not wholly, a form of quantification in money terms of the damage to the portfolio, but an additional head of loss caused to Springwell by its being deprived of the ability to use the portfolio.

Lord Justice Wall (concurring, with Jonathan Parker L. J.),

I also agree that this appeal should be dismissed. Mr Hapgood's principal argument was that Springwell would never have had both a restored portfolio and the shipping profits. By claiming both, Mr. Hapgood argued, Springwell was; (a) advancing claims on a mutually inconsistent basis; and (b) seeking to obtain double recovery.

I am unable to accept that submission. On Springwell's case, had all gone according to plan, it would have used the portfolio to purchase the ships which would then have made the profits. Chase's actions, by reducing the value of the portfolio, had deprived it of the capacity to purchase the ships and to earn profits from them. On this argument, I think it properly arguable that the measure of damage is (1) the loss of value of the portfolio; and (2) the loss of the shipping profits which would have followed from the purchase of the ships.

Hussey and Another *v* Eels [1990] 1 All ER 449

Mustill L.J.:

...

For many years until the beginning of 1984 the defendants had lived in a bungalow in Farnham, Surrey. The nature of the underlying ground was such that the building suffered from subsidence. At the end of 1983 the defendants commenced negotiations for the sale of the bungalow to the plaintiffs, whose solicitor served the customary inquiries before contract. Additional inquiry 5 read as follows: 'Please confirm to the vendor's

knowledge that the property has not been subject to the following matters . . . . (c) subsidence.' The response was: 'Confirmed'. In due course the transaction went ahead,
and on 7 February 1984 the purchase and sale was completed at a price of £53,250.

The judge has found that the untrue statement given on the defendants' behalf in
the response to additional inquiry 5 was made negligently, and that the plaintiffs
relied on this statement when deciding to purchase the bungalow.

Resuming the story, it was not long before the plaintiffs discovered that there was
something badly wrong with the house. They had wanted to carry out a roof conversion but their builder advised them of the subsidence, and they formed the view that
they could not live there without measures to stabilise the foundations. This would
have required them to vacate the house for two or three months, and to pay a sum
estimated at £17,000 as the cost of necessary work. They did not have sufficient money
to permit this to be done, so they decided to build another residence in the existing
garden. Accordingly, within a few months of the purchase they made a planning
application to erect another building. This was refused on 9 August 1984, essentially
on the ground that this would lead to overcrowding. A second application was refused
five months later. The plaintiffs then reformulated their application, so as to permit
the erection of one new bungalow and one new chalet bungalow, after the demolition
of the existing bungalow. This time the application was successful, permission being
granted on 18 August 1986. The plaintiffs then set about finding buyers for the land
with planning permission, and by October 1986 they had sold it to developers for a
price of £76,094.47. The purchasers were going to pull down the bungalow and build
on the land, so the question of repair was no longer relevant.

Meanwhile in January 1986 the plaintiffs had commenced their action in the High
Court; it was subsequently transferred to the County Court. In its original and amended
form that statement of claim contained no particulars of damage. These were, however,
requested and in response the plaintiffs pleaded as follows:

> The value of the freehold land and bungalow known as Oakwood had it not suffered
> from subsidence is £80,000. The plaintiffs in an attempt to mitigate their loss have
> managed to sell the bungalow and land for a gross sale price of £78,500.
>   The cost of the sale is £1,905.53. The cost of removal from the premises is £500.
> The net price obtainable for the bungalow and land by the plaintiffs is therefore
> £76,094.47. The net loss in value of the land to the plaintiffs is therefore £3,905.53.

The plaintiffs have adopted this course of action in preference to having remedial
work carried out on the premises to remedy the damage caused by the said subsidence
which would have cost in excess of £17,000.

Seventeen months later, on 12 July 1988, the plaintiffs amended the particulars to
increase the sound value of the land and bungalow to £90,000 and hence the 'net loss
in value' to £13,905.53. All this happened before the grant of planning permission and
the sale to the developers.

The trial began on 7 November 1988. On the first day the plaintiffs' counsel (who
had not pleaded either the first or the amended set of particulars) applied to reamend
so as to add the following paragraph: 'Alternatively the plaintiffs' claim is for the
difference between the price paid of £53,250 and the actual market value of the
property at the date of completion namely £36,250, the difference representing the
cost of carrying out repairs to the property to remedy the subsidence.' In addition, the
amendment deleted the second of the paragraphs from which I have quoted. There is
an unfortunate difference of recollection about whether the amendment also involved
the deletion of the first paragraph. The appeal bundle prepared on behalf of the plain-

tiffs contains a document purporting to be the reamended particulars, which the judge gave leave to serve on the second day of the trial; these do not show any deletion of the first paragraph, but counsel maintained that this is a later copying error. On the other hand, counsel for the defendants recalls that the reamended pleading never showed this paragraph as deleted. We cannot resolve this dispute. Three things are however clear. (1) For the eighteen months leading up to the trial the plaintiffs had been advancing a case based on the proposition that they had sold to developers in mitigation of damage. (2) By the end of the trial (as the judge's notes disclose) the plaintiffs were contending that the proper measure of damage was '£17,000, being the difference between the sound value of the property, less the price paid'. (3) Counsel were agreed that this would indeed have been the proper measure of damage on the hypothesis that the plaintiffs had remained in occupation. The sole question on damages was whether the effect of the resale at a price much greater than had been paid was to nullify this *prima facie* right of recovery. The judge answered this question in the affirmative. After concluding in favour of the plaintiffs on damages he continued (according to counsel's agreed note):

> However the matter does not end there due to a vitally important mitigation point. I am persuaded by counsel for the defendants that this is a classic *Westinghouse* case. [Counsel] also referred me to the case of *Bellingham v Dhillon* [1973] 1 All ER 20, [1973] QB 304. Damages accrue on the date of completion: the tortious measure applies. I do not think, having considered Lord Denning M.R.'s judgment in *Perry v Sidney Phillips & Son* (a firm) [1982] 3 All ER 705, [1982] 1 WLR 1297, that these principles are affected or excluded. I am bound to hold that the windfall accruing to the plaintiffs wipes out by far the loss that follows. Thus, despite what I have found about the subsidence, the defendants succeed.

In the course of his argument in support of the notion thus briefly conveyed by the judge, counsel for the defendants advanced two distinct propositions. (1) The plaintiffs owed a duty towards the defendants to mitigate the loss resulting from their purchase of the house in reliance on the misrepresentation; the sale to the developers was a performance of this duty; the result of this mitigation was to be taken into account in computing the loss. (2) Whether the resale was a mitigation or not, the fact is that when the plaintiffs' dealings are regarded as a whole it can be seen that they have suffered no loss. Very often it happens that no distinction need be drawn between these two ways of approaching the problem: they raise the same issues of fact and lead to the same conclusion, and are often treated together under the same heading of 'mitigation'. Nevertheless, I believe that counsel for the defendants was right to recognise the distinction when advancing his clients' case.

The first argument depends on proof that the plaintiffs were under a duty to resell the house in mitigation. Counsel for the plaintiffs takes the initial point that there can never be a question of mitigating a loss which has already crystallised, and that the loss has crystallised here in terms of the conventional measure of damage for an unsatisfactory purchase made in reliance on an actionable misrepresentation by the vendor. I feel some reservations about this proposition. It is true that the question of a duty to mitigate tends most often to arise in the context of a continuing loss. Thus, for example, where a plaintiff is suffering a loss of business profits which will go on until he does something to stop it, then if there is something which he could reasonably do, and yet he fails to do it, the damages are computed as if the loss had come to an end; conversely, if he does take action to prevent further loss, all the consequences of his act are brought into account. It is also true that superficially the proposition of counsel for the plaintiffs does appear at first sight to gain support from the cases on failure to perform contracts for the supply of goods or services for which there is an available market, where the courts have tended to proceed directly to a conventional measure of damage without investigating what the injured party has actually done after the breach. (I say 'at first sight' because these conventional measures of damages depend on the fiction that the innocent party has gone into the market to sell against the defaulting buyer, or to buy in against the defaulting seller. The loss is therefore crystallised, not in terms of the immediate consequences of the breach, but of a deemed mitigation.) Nevertheless, I would not be prepared without a very full review of the authorities to underwrite a generalisation such as counsel for the plaintiffs proposes, especially in the field of damages, where broad statements of principle tend to be unreliable. (Indeed I believe that R. *Pagnan & Flli v Corbisa Industrial Agropacuaria Ltd* [1971] 1 All ER 165, [1970] 1 WLR 1306 shows the generalisation to be unsound.) This is of no moment here, however, because whatever the true state of the law it is to my mind clear that the defendants' first argument fails at the outset. The breach compelled the plaintiffs to choose between (a) continuing to live in the bungalow despite its serious faults, (b) repairing the bungalow or (c) selling the bungalow and land and going to live elsewhere. If the plaintiffs had chosen to pursue either of the first two options it is inconceivable that they would have been held to be in breach of any obligations towards the defendants; their recovery of the estimated or actual cost of repair (as reflecting the difference between the true market value and the price) would have followed as a matter of course. Given therefore that alternatives (a) and (b) were legitimate, the proposition that the plaintiffs were under a duty to spend more than two years in applications for planning permission, and that having obtained it were under a further duty to move out of the house in which they had hoped to live and to buy somewhere else, all for the benefit of the defendants who had by their actionable wrong put them into this dilemma need only be stated to be rejected, and the rest of the argument falls with it.

The alternative proposition is more formidable. Before considering its legal aspects the assertion that the plaintiffs made a profit out of the transaction needs to be examined. In one sense of course it is right, since the plaintiffs ultimately sold the property for twice what they had paid for it. This is however misleading, for it ignores the general rise in the housing market in the interval between purchase and resale, and it also terminates the analysis halfway through. The plaintiffs were not property speculators but residents; their object in reselling was not to realise a profit, but to rid themselves of an uninhabitable house so that they could acquire another. What they actually did do after the sale to the developers was never explored at the trial, nor is it possible on the judge's findings to arrive at an assessment of the cost of buying a comparable bungalow into which they could have moved after the resale. If one of the experts was right, and the comparator would have cost about £80,000 then over the whole run of transactions the plaintiffs would have broken even. But if the other expert's figure of £90,000 is preferred the plaintiffs would have made a substantial loss, for which on any view they ought to be compensated.

Thus, if the right approach in law is to look at the plaintiffs' position at the end of a chain of transactions consisting of purchase, resale and fresh purchase, the case will have to be returned to the County Court for a further investigation of the figures.

Is this the right approach in law? Undoubtedly, the starting point is *British Westinghouse Electric and Manufacturing Co. Ltd v Underground Electric Rlys Co. of London Ltd* [1912] AC 673, [1911–13] All ER Rep 63.

. . .

It will be seen that the decision in the *Westinghouse* case had two aspects. First, the conclusion that the benefits derived from the purchase of superior machinery should be set against the two elements of loss. In retrospect it is hard to see how the contrary could have been maintained. The purchase amounted to mitigation in the narrower sense, designed to put a stop to the continuing loss. To compensate the respondents for the cost of replacement while ignoring the additional benefits which this replacement had brought would have been a palpable injustice.

The second aspect of the decision concerned the element of over-mitigation introduced by the fact that the respondents had bought equipment with a greater output than before, presumably at greater cost than if exactly equivalent replacements had been obtained. Again, once it was found that the purchase had been reasonably made the conclusion in favour of the appellants now seems inevitable, given that the act which constituted the mitigation and the act which was said to constitute the over-mitigation were in the event the same. Thus, there was no question of the case being concerned with a chain of disconnected transactions, and so I cannot follow the judge in treating the present case as directly governed by the *Westinghouse* case.
. . .

I have dealt with the authorities at some length, because it was said that in one direction or another they provided a direct solution to the present problem. For the reasons already stated, I do not see them in this light. Ultimately, as with so many disputes about damages, the issue is primarily one of fact. Did the negligence which caused the damage also cause the profit, if profit there was? I do not think so. It is true that in one sense there was a causal link between the inducement of the purchase by misrepresentation and the sale two and a half years later, for the sale represented a choice of one of the options with which the plaintiffs had been presented by the defendants' wrongful act. But only in that sense. To my mind the reality of the situation is that the plaintiffs bought the house to live in, and did live in it for a substantial period. It was only after two years that the possibility of selling the land and moving elsewhere was explored, and six months later still that this possibility came to fruition. It seems to me that when the plaintiffs unlocked the development value of their land they did so for their own benefit, and not as part of a continuous transaction of which the purchase of land and bungalow was the inception.

Accordingly, although I acknowledge that the plaintiffs had until the start of the trial persisted in a claim which was inconsistent with the one which they introduced by reamendment, I consider that in fact and law their second thoughts were correct, and that the proper measure of damages here is the difference between the contract price and the market value of the property in its unsound condition. I would therefore allow the appeal.

(Farquharson L.J. and Sir Michael Kerr agreed.)

Note

In this case the Court of Appeal gave damages of £17,000, being the difference between the contract price of £53, 250 and the actual market value of the property, £36,250. This is sometimes described as the reinstatement value. Once the Court of Appeal held that no duty to mitigate (in either sense) arose it was unlikely that the plaintiffs would be content with the net loss in value measure of £3,905.53.

If no loss is shown then damages may be nominal.

Baker Perkins Ltd and C. J. O'Dowd Ltd (HC) 13 April 1989, unrep.

Blayney J.:

This case involves a claim and counterclaim arising out of two contracts for the supply of bakery equipment entered into on the 13 September 1982.

The plaintiffs are an English company specialising in the manufacture of plant for bakeries. The defendant is a company carrying on a bakery business in Kinsale, County Cork. In March 1982 the defendant ordered orally from the plaintiffs certain plant of which the main item was a convertoradiant (CVR) oven. The price was UK£250,000. The plant was to be manufactured and ready for dispatch in October 1982. The terms of the contract were formalised on 13 September 1982 when both parties signed a document entitled an 'Order Confirmation' which was the standard form of contract used by the plaintiffs. The substantive part of this document provided as follows: 'This contract is subject to the seller's general conditions of sale which are printed overleaf. The seller shall sell and the customer shall purchase the goods described in the order confirmation on the terms and conditions stated therein'.

The plant was ready for dispatch in October 1982 but was not sent as the defendant had not been able to arrange finance. This continued to be the position in the following year. At a meeting between representatives of the parties in Peterborough on 17 February 1984 the price of £250,000 was by agreement increased to £300,000 to compensate the plaintiffs for interest and storage charges which had been incurred, and on 26 March 1984 the plaintiffs wrote to the defendant suggesting *inter alia* that they should agree to the contract being subject to cancellation if the £300,000 sterling was not received by 9 April. The defendant agreed to this. The money was not received by the date mentioned, and finally by letter dated 10 July 1984 the plaintiffs wrote saying they had to accept that the contract was cancelled. Their solicitor then wrote claiming cancellation charges and on 10 January 1985 these proceedings were issued.

The defendant claimed in its defence that the contract had been conditional on its being able to obtain finance and that, as this condition had not been satisfied, the contract automatically came to an end. In the course of the hearing, however, counsel for the defendant abandoned this defence so that insofar as the plaintiffs' claim is concerned the sole issue is what damages, if any, the plaintiffs are entitled to recover. As this issue is wholly separate from the defendant's counterclaim I propose to deal with it before taking up the latter.

In their statement of claim the plaintiffs claimed the following heads of damage:

1. Interest charges pursuant to clause 10 of the general conditions of sale which form part of the contract.
2. Loss of profits.
3. Storage charges.

. . .

The clause which is applicable in assessing the plaintiffs' damages is in my opinion subclause (iv) of clause 10: 'The measure of damages shall be any loss or expense of any nature incurred by seller arising out of disposal of the goods.'

I accept the submission of counsel for the defendant that it is the measure of damages specified in the contract that is to be applied rather than that set out in s. 50(3) of the English Sale of Goods Act 1979—this being the relevant Act, as the general conditions provide in clause 15 that 'the contract shall in all respects operate and be construed in accordance with English law.' There was no real dispute in regard to this. Counsel for the plaintiffs accepted that where the parties had agreed on the measure of damages he could not contend for a different measure.

Damages may only be given, accordingly, in respect of any loss or expense of which it can be said that it arose 'out of the disposal of the goods'. The question is whether the loss of profits and the storage charges up to the date of the termination of the contract fall into this category.

In my opinion they do not. The loss of profit claimed is the profit that the plaintiffs would have made if the defendant had completed the contract. It seems to me that this loss resulted from the defendant's refusal to pay for the goods and did not arise out of the disposal of the goods. In refusing to pay for the goods, the defendant deprived the plaintiffs of their profit. So the plaintiffs' loss was suffered at that stage which at the latest occurred on 10 July 1984 when the plaintiffs terminated the contract by reason of the defendant's breach. And it was only then that the question of the disposal of the goods arose. But the loss of profit, having already been suffered, could not have arisen out of that disposal. It preceded it and was caused by the plaintiffs' breach of contract.

As regards the storage charges, what are in question here are the charges up to 10 July 1984, when the contract was terminated. I will deal later with charges which arose after that date. It seems to me that those which arose before it were incurred in connection with the performance of the contract by the plaintiffs and did not arise out of the contract by the plaintiffs and did not arise out of the disposal of the plant. The plant had to be stored by the plaintiffs so that it would be available to be dispatched to the defendant when the latter had procured the necessary finance to pay for it. So the storage was necessitated by the plaintiffs' obligation to perform its part of the contract. The charges arose out of this obligation and were unconnected with the disposal of the plant after the contract had come to an end. Accordingly they did not arise out of that disposal.

Counsel for the defendant submitted that the plaintiffs had suffered no loss or expense whatsoever arising out of the disposal of the plant. In particular he submitted that on the resale to East Midlands Co-Op the plaintiffs had made a profit and so there was no question of their having suffered a loss in respect of which they would be entitled to damages. It seems to me that this latter submission is correct. The evidence in regard to the disposal of the plant which was the subject matter of the contract was that it was sold to the East-Midlands Co-Op together with other plant on 5 October 1984 for a total consideration of UK£585,900. The part of the consideration referable to the defendant's plant exceeded by £60,359 the original purchase price of £250,000 which the defendant had agreed to pay. Whether or not there was a loss on the resale hinges on what the defendant would have had to pay to complete the purchase in July 1984, in other words, on what the price would have been at that time. This is the figure which has to be compared with what the plaintiffs obtained from the East Midlands Co-Op.

While the original purchase price was £250,000, this was, by agreement, increased to £300,000 at a meeting in Peterborough between Mr Harold Jackson, the plaintiffs' sales manager, and Mr Charles O'Dowd, the defendant's managing director. This agreement was referred to by Mr Jackson in a letter to the defendant of 26 March 1984 and was confirmed by a telex of 4 April 1984 from Mr O'Dowd to Mr Jackson. In that letter Mr Jackson suggested 'that we agree to regard this contract as being subject to cancellation should we not receive the UK£300,000 payment by 9 April 1984—in other words should your current financing investigations prove to be unsuccessful'. It is clear from this that had Mr O'Dowd been able to obtain the finance in time, the amount he would have needed to complete the contract before 9 April 1984 would have been £300,000. So the figure for the purchase price would have been the same then as was agreed on 17 February 1984. Would this still have been the position in July? This depends upon whether the plaintiffs would have claimed interest on the purchase money between April and July.

Clause 11 of the general conditions in the contract, provides that interest at the rate of two per cent per month shall be payable by the buyer on the written demand of the seller where any payment is not made on the due date. On 11 May 1984, Mr J. M. Hicks, the plaintiffs' bakery division accountant, wrote to Mr Kidney, who was the defendant's financial adviser at the time, and amongst other things he pointed out 'that further storage and interest costs are accruing since our meeting in Peterborough when we agreed that the sterling payment should be made on 9 April 1984'. That put the defendant on notice that the plaintiffs might exercise their right to demand interest if the defendant succeeded in getting the necessary finance to complete. But it is still an open question as to whether they would have exercised their right in this respect. There was no evidence that further interest would in fact have been demanded so there is nothing to support a finding that it is probable that this would have been done. Furthermore, since the plaintiffs had been waiting since December 1982 for payment I think it very likely that if the defendant had been able to come up with £300,000 at any time between May and July 1984 the plaintiffs would have been prepared to accept that sum in full discharge and would not have insisted on interest. And in that case the deal would have been concluded at the figure of £300,000. It follows that since the plaintiffs were able to dispose of the plant to East Midlands Co-Op at a figure in excess of this they did not, insofar as the resale price was concerned, suffer any loss arising out of the disposal of the plant.

The position in regard to the storage charges is different. The plant clearly had to be stored pending its disposal. So the storage charges after 10 July 1984 did arise out of the disposal. But in my opinion such charges must be confined to the warehousing charges. They could not include the hire of the six trailers on which the plant had been loaded in July 1983 in expectation of its being delivered to the defendant and on which it had remained up to July 1984. It was not necessary to keep it loaded on trailers while awaiting resale. All that was required was that it should be warehoused. The evidence was that the cost of warehousing was £16 per trailer per week. There were six trailers, so the weekly cost was UK£96. The sale to East Midlands Co-Op was on 5 October 1984, so the plant would have had to be warehoused for approximately thirteen weeks. This gives a total charge of UK£1,248. To this must be added interest at eleven per cent from the middle of October 1984 to 21 January 1989 and at eight per cent from that date to 10 March 1989 which I calculate comes to £597. So the total due for principal and interest is UK£1,845.

To this must be added the cost of the circulating table which was delivered to the defendant and not paid for. It cost UK£5,234. And interest under the Courts Act up to 7 March 1989 comes to £2,660.84 giving a total of £7,894.84.

When this is added to the amount due for the storage charges, the final figure to which the plaintiffs are entitled on their claim is £9,739.84 and there will be judgment for them for this amount.

(The defendants' counterclaim was dismissed.)

C. WHICH HEAD OF LOSS?

It is generally accepted that the plaintiff may select which head of loss the plaintiff is to be compensated for. If the contract was breached at a preliminary stage, or the venture never came to fruition, this may give the plaintiff the opportunity to recover all costs incurred following on from the breach. The question, what follows from the breach, is an interesting one.

Anglia Television Ltd v Reed [1972] 1 QB 60

Lord Denning M.R.:

Anglia Television Ltd, the plaintiffs, were minded in 1968 to make a film of a play for television entitled 'The Man in the Wood'. It portrayed an American man married to an English woman. The American has an adventure in an English wood. The film was to last for ninety minutes. Anglia Television made many arrangements in advance. They arranged for a place where the play was to be filmed. They employed a director, a designer and a stage manager, and so forth. They involved themselves in much expense. All this was done before they got the leading man. They required a strong actor capable of holding the play together. He was to be on the scene the whole time. Anglia Television eventually found the man. He was Mr Robert Reed, the defendant, an American who has a very high reputation as an actor. He was very suitable for this part. By telephone conversation on 30 August 1968, it was agreed by Mr Reed through his agent that he would come to England and be available between 9 September and 11 October 1968, to rehearse and play in this film. He was to get a performance fee of £1,050, living expenses of £100 a week, his first class fares to and from the US and so forth. It was all subject to the permit of the Ministry of Labour for him to come here. That was duly given on 12 September 1968. So the contract was concluded. But unfortunately there was some muddle with the bookings. It appears that Mr Reed's agents had already booked him in America for some other play. So on 3 September 1968, the agent said that Mr Reed would not come to England to perform in this play. He repudiated his contract. Anglia Television tried hard to find a substitute but could not do so. So on 11 September they accepted his repudiation. They abandoned the proposed film. They gave notice to the people whom they had engaged and so forth.

Anglia Television then sued Mr Reed for damages. He did not dispute his liability, but a question arose as to the damages. Anglia Television do not claim their profit. They cannot say what their profit would have been on this contract if Mr Reed had come here and performed it. So, instead of claim for loss of profits, they claim for the wasted expenditure. They had incurred the director's fees, the designer's fees, the stage manager's and assistant manager's fees, and so on. It comes in all to £2,750. Anglia Television say that all that money was wasted because Mr Reed did not perform his contract.

Mr Reed's advisers take a point of law. They submit that Anglia Television cannot recover for expenditure incurred *before* the contract was concluded with Mr Reed. They can only recover the expenditure *after* the contract was concluded. They say that the expenditure *after* the contract was only £854.65, and that is all that Anglia Television can recover.

The master rejected that contention: he held that Anglia Television could recover the whole £2,750; and now Mr Reed appeals to this court.

[Counsel], for Mr Reed, has referred us to the recent case of *Perestrello & Companhia Limitada v United Paint Co. Ltd*, *The Times*, 16 April 1969, in which Thesiger J. quoted the words of Tindal C.J. in *Hodges v Earl of Litchfield* (1835) 1 Bing. NC 492, at 498: 'The expenses preliminary to the contract ought not to be allowed. The party enters into them for his own benefit at a time when it is uncertain whether there will be any contract or not.' Thesiger J. applied those words, saying: 'In my judgment pre-contract expenditure, though thrown away, is not recoverable.'

I cannot accept the proposition as stated. It seems to me that a plaintiff in such a case as this has an election: he can either claim for loss of profits; or for his wasted expenditure. But he must elect between them. He cannot claim both. If he has not suffered any loss of profits—or if he cannot prove what his profits would have been—he can claim in the alternative the expenditure which has been thrown away, that is, wasted, by reason of the breach. That is shown by *Cullinane v British 'Rema' Manufacturing Co. Ltd* [1954] 1 QB 292, 303, 308.

If the plaintiff claims the wasted expenditure, he is not limited to the expenditure incurred *after* the contract was concluded. He can claim also the expenditure incurred *before* the contract, provided that it was such as would reasonably be in the contemplation of the parties as likely to be wasted if the contract was broken. Applying that principle here, it is plain that, when Mr Reed entered into this contract, he must have known perfectly well that much expenditure had already been incurred on director's fees and the like. He must have contemplated—or, at any rate, it is reasonably to be imputed to him—that if he broke his contract, all that expenditure would be wasted, whether or not it was incurred before or after the contract. He must pay damages for all the expenditure so wasted and thrown away. This view is supported by the recent decision of Brightman J. in *Lloyd v Stanbury* [1971] 1 WLR 535. There was a contract for the sale of land. In anticipation of the contract—and before it was concluded—the purchaser went to much expense in moving a caravan to the site and in getting his furniture there. The seller afterwards entered into a contract to sell the land to the purchaser, but afterwards broke his contract. The land had not increased in value, so the purchaser could not claim for any loss of profit. But Brightman J. held, at 547, that he could recover the cost of moving the caravan and furniture, because it was 'within the contemplation of the parties when the contract was signed.' That decision is in accord with the correct principle, namely, that wasted expenditure can be recovered when it is wasted by reason of the defendant's breach of contract. It is true that, if the defendant had never entered into the contract, he would not be liable, and the expenditure would have been incurred by the plaintiff without redress; but, the defendant having made his contract and broken it, it does not lie in his mouth to say he is not liable, when it was because of his breach that the expenditure has been wasted.

I think the master was quite right and this appeal should be dismissed.

(Phillimore and Megaw L.JJ. agreed.)

Note

However, this principle of choice is subject to the overriding requirement that the breach of contract must occasion the plaintiff's loss.

Bowlay Logging *v* Domtar Ltd (1978) 87 DLR (3d) 325

Domtar Ltd were under a contractual obligation to provide logging trucks to allow Bowlay Logging transport the logs it felled to its sawmill. Eventually the Bowlay Logging operation closed down. Bowlay Logging sought damages for breach of contract by Domtar Ltd in failing to provide a sufficient number of trucks.

Berger J.:

...

This brings me to the issue of damages. Bowlay's claim is not for loss of profits, but for compensation for expenditures made in part performance. Bowlay is not in a position to claim damages for loss of profits, because it cannot prove that if it had gone on to complete the contract it would have made any money. Bowlay, since it cannot prove any loss of profits, is seeking to recover its losses for actual outlay. These came to $232,905. The payments received from Domtar for deliveries of logs came to $108,128.57. Bowlay's claim is for the balance, $124,776.43.

While it is true that the parties contemplated that the contract might be renewed on an annual basis, I think Bowlay's claim for damages must be limited to damages in respect of Bowlay's losses on Timber Sale No. A03518. Any claim based on the loss of expected profits on future timber sales would be too uncertain and remote. In any event, Bowlay has limited its claim to compensation for expenditures made in part performance. It has not advanced any claim for loss of profits.

The cases say that a plaintiff can sue for expenses incurred in part performance of a contract when the contract has been ended by breach. In *Cullinane v British 'Rema' Manufacturing Co. Ltd* [1954] 1 QB 292, Lord Evershed said at 303:

> As a matter of principle also, it seems to me that a person who has obtained a machine, such as the plaintiff obtained, being a machine which was mechanically in exact accordance with the order given but which was unable to perform a particular function which it was warranted to perform, may adopt one of two courses. He may say, when he discovers its incapacity, that it was not what he wanted, that it is quite useless to him, and he may claim to recover the capital cost he has incurred, deducting anything he can obtain by disposing of the material that he got. A claim of that kind puts the plaintiff in the same position as though he had never made the contract at all. In other words, he is back where he started; and, if it were shown that the profit-earning capacity was in fact very small, the plaintiff would probably elect so to base his claim. But, alternatively, where the warranty in question relates to performance, he may, in my judgment, make his claim on the basis of the profit which he has lost because the machine as delivered fell short in its performance of that which it was warranted to do.

See also *McRae et al. v Commonwealth Disposals Com'n et al.* (1951) 84 CLR 377.

In *Anglia Television Ltd v Reed* [1972] 1 QB 60, Lord Denning M.R., held that a plaintiff had the right to sue for expenditures made in part performance. He said, at 64: 'If he has not suffered any loss of profits—or if he cannot prove what his profits would have been—he can claim in the alternative the expenditure which has been thrown away, that is, wasted, by reason of the breach. That is shown by *Cullinane v British 'Rema' Manufacturing Co. Ltd* [1954] 1 QB 292, 303, 308.'

But Domtar has raised an issue not reached by these cases. [Counsel for the defendant] says that even if there was a breach of contract Domtar is not bound to compensate Bowlay for its expenses—at any rate certainly not the full measure of those expenses—because the operation was losing money. If it had continued it would have lost more money. Domtar says that in fact Bowlay's losses on full performance would have exceeded its losses in expenses 'thrown away'. It is said that in these circumstances Bowlay cannot recover any damages.

May a claim for expenses made in part performance be sustained where the defendant shows that the plaintiff was engaged in a losing operation and, even if there had been no breach and the contract had been fully performed, would inevitably have suffered a loss on the contract? Should the defendant be entitled to have the losses that would have been incurred deducted from the plaintiff's claim for compensation for expenses made in part performance? What if the plaintiff's losses, in the event the contract had been fully performed, would have exceeded the claim for expenses? To what extent should the plaintiff be entitled to recover in such a case?

McGregor on Damages (13th edn, 1972), 28–9, commenting on the *Anglia* case, said:

> This decision however does not cover the case where the plaintiff has made a bad bargain, and it is still an open question whether in such circumstances he should be allowed to opt for the alternative measure. The argument on the one side is that he should not be entitled to more than the normal measure would give him; the argument on the other is that a defendant in breach should not be entitled to object to a claim for the alternative measure even though not dictated by law or by the difficulties of proof.

Mr Shaw says that the plaintiff should be entitled to recover all of its expenses by way of outlay, and that no deduction should be made even if the plaintiff would have suffered a net loss if the contract had been fully performed. He relies on a judgment of the US Supreme Court: *United States v Behan* (1884) 110 US 338. Mr Justice Bradley, speaking for the court, said, at 345–6:

> When a party injured by the stoppage of a contract elects to rescind it, then, it is true, he cannot recover any damages for a breach of the contract, either for outlay or for loss of profits; he recovers the value of his services actually performed as upon a *quantum meruit*. There is then no question of losses or profits. But when he elects to go for damages for the breach of the contract, the first and most obvious damage to be shown is, the amount which he has been induced to expend on the faith of the contract, including a fair allowance for his own time and services. If he chooses to go further and claims for the loss of anticipated profits, he may do so, subject to the rules of law as to the character of profits which may be thus claimed. It does not lie, however, in the mouth of the party who has voluntarily and wrong-fully put an end to the contract, to say that the party injured has not been damaged at least to the amount of what he has been induced fairly and in good faith to lay out and expend (including his own services), after making allowance for the value of materials on hand; at least it does not lie in the mouth of the party in fault to say this, unless he can show that the expenses of the party injured have been extrav-agant, and unnecessary for the purposes of carrying out the contract.

If it is only 'extravagant and unnecessary expenses' that the defendant may insist be deducted from the plaintiff's claim, then what about expenses legitimately incurred, but in an unprofitable venture? The implication in the *Behan* case is that the defendant may not have them deducted from the plaintiff's claim for compensation for expenses. Mr Justice Bradley went on at 346–7: '. . . the party who voluntarily and wrongfully put an end to a contract and prevents the other party from performing it, is estopped from denying that the injured party has not been damaged to the extent of his actual loss and outlay fairly incurred.' The *Behan* case was decided in the last century. It has been rejected in the US in this century.

Professor L. L. Fuller and W. R. Perdue Jr., writing in 'Reliance Interest in Contract Damages', 46 Yale LJ 52 (1937), concluded that the principle enunciated in the *Behan* case compromised the basic notion of *restitutio in integrum*. They urged, at 79, that the law ought to reflect the following proposition: 'We will not in a suit for reimbursement for losses incurred in reliance on a contract knowingly put the plaintiff in a better position than he would have occupied had the contract been fully performed.' In L. *Albert & Son v Armstrong Rubber Co.* (1949) 178 F. 2d 182 (USCA, 2nd Cir.), Chief Justice Learned Hand, speaking for the Court of Appeals, Second Circuit, held that on a claim for compensation for expenses in part performance the defendant was entitled to deduct whatever he can prove the plaintiff would have lost if the contract had been fully performed. Chief Justice Learned Hand expressed his concurrence with the formula laid down by Professor Fuller: see also Re Yeager Co. (1963) 227 F. Supp. 92 (DC Ohio).

It has been said by the US Circuit Court of Appeals in Dade County, Florida v Palmer & Baker Engineers Inc. (1965) 339 F. 2d 208 (USCA, 5th Cir.), that where the defendant alleges that full performance by the plaintiff would have resulted in a net loss to the plaintiff, the burden of proof is on the defendant. Accepting then that the onus is on the defendant, what has the defendant been able to prove in the case at bar?

Mr Dunn, a chartered accountant called by Domtar, prepared a list of expenses of the Bowlay logging operation. The list is not complete. But Mr Dunn says that when the revenues of the operation are measured against the expenses, whether on a cash basis or an accrual basis, there is no footing on which the operation could have been regarded as a profitable one. I think he is right about this. The losses would have been very high. Bowlay was entitled to $15 per cunit from Domtar. Mr Dunn said that expenses stood at $114,000 on 31 July 1972; On 15 October 1972, they came to $186,434.79. Given that the actual cut by Bowlay came to 8,029.56 cunits, Bowlay's actual cost of production per cunit came to $22.94.

Then there is the evidence of Greg Lay. On 26 July he made an analysis of Bowlay's costs. His diary reveals that Bowlay's costs were running at $19 per cunit. Lay said that to operate at a profit Bowlay had to deliver fifteen loads of hot and cold wood a day. He said that they would have to keep hauling fifteen loads a day until 30 November (hauling could continue until then) to supply 10,000 cunits as required by the contract. Of course they never did haul fifteen loads a day, even before the diminution in the supply of trucks. And Bowlay says that its total outlay came to $232,905.

The law of contract compensates a plaintiff for damages resulting from the defendant's breach; it does not compensate a plaintiff for damages resulting from his making a bad bargain. Where it can be seen that the plaintiff would have incurred a loss on the contract as a whole, the expenses he has incurred are losses flowing from entering into the contract, not losses flowing from the defendant's breach. In these circumstances, the true consequence of the defendant's breach is that the plaintiff is released from his obligation to complete the contract—or in other words, he is saved from incurring further losses.

If the law of contract were to move from compensating for the consequences of breach to compensating for the consequences of entering into contracts, the law would run contrary to the normal expectations of the world of commerce. The burden of risk would be shifted from the plaintiff to the defendant. The defendant would become the insurer of the plaintiff's enterprise. Moreover, the amount of the damages would increase not in relation to the gravity or consequences of the breach but in relation to the inefficiency with which the plaintiff carried out the contract. The greater his expenses owing to inefficiency, the greater the damages.

The fundamental principle upon which damages are measured under the law of contract is restitutio in integrum. The principle contended for here by the plaintiff would entail the award of damages not to compensate the plaintiff but to punish the defendant. So it has been argued that a defendant ought to be able to insist that the plaintiff's damages should not include any losses that would have been incurred if the contract had been fully performed. According to Treitel, Law of Contract, (3rd ed., 1970), at 798: 'It is uncertain whether the plaintiff can recover his entire expenses if those exceed the benefit which he would have derived from the contract, had there been no breach.' Ogus, in The Law of Damages (1973), has said at 347 that, 'it is not yet clear whether English law imposes this limitation'.

The tendency in American law is to impose such a limitation. And I think Canadian law ought to impose it too.

The onus is on the defendant. But the onus has been met. The only conclusion that I can reach on the evidence is that if the plaintiff had fully performed the contract its losses would have continued at the rate that the figures show they were running at up to the time when the logging operation was closed down.

Notes

1. *Bowlay Logging v Domtar Ltd* was followed by the English Court of Appeal in *C & P Haulage (a firm) v Middleton* [1983] 3 All ER 94. Here, a tenant who had been unlawfully evicted from commercial premises by his landlord unsuccessfully sued for expenditure incurred in improving those premises. In fact, following his unlawful eviction his local council allowed him to run his business from his own residential garage, thus saving him the rental due if the leased premises had been available to him. In awarding nominal damages of £10 Ackner L.J. said of *Bowlay Logging*:

. . . In my judgment, the approach of Berger J. is the correct one. It is not the function of the courts where there is a breach of contract knowingly, as this would be the case, to put the plaintiff in a better financial position than if the contract had been properly performed. In this case the appellant, if he was right in his claim, would indeed be in a better position because, as I have already indicated, had the contract been lawfully determined, as it could have been in the middle of December, there would have been no question of his recovering these expenses.

2. The onus of proof lies upon the defendant to show that the plaintiff's business venture was such that the plaintiff would not have led to recovery of the expenditure incurred by the plaintiff. If the defendant does not satisfy the court of this the plaintiff will be able to recover wasted expenditure: *CCC Films (London) Ltd v Impact Quadrant Films Ltd* [1984] 3 WLR 245.

Ruxley Electronics and Construction Ltd v Forsyth [1995] 3 All ER 268

Forsyth contracted with Ruxley and another company to have a swimming pool built in his garden. The contract stipulated that the pool was to be built to a depth of 7 ft 6 in at its maximum depth. On completion it was found to be 6 ft deep at its maximum. This was accepted to be a breach of contract by the builders. An action for monies due was brought by the builders; Forsyth counter-claimed but recovered only £2,500 at the trial for loss of amenity. The Court of Appeal reversed the trial judge on the issue of quantum, holding that it would have not been unreasonable to award Forsyth the monies necessary to demolish the pool and replace it with one that met the specification. This was estimated to be the sum of £21,560. The House of Lords had to consider the appropriate award to make in a case of this kind. The three possibilities were (1) loss of amenity, (2) diminution of value to the plaintiff in financial terms, (3) replacement costs (so called cost of cure).

The leading judgment was given by Lord Jauncey of Tullichettle, the House of Lords reversing the Court of Appeal and reinstating the decision of the trial judge.

Lord Jauncey of Tullichettle:

My Lords, the respondent entered into a contract with the appellant for the construction by them of a swimming pool at his house in Kent. The contract provided for the pool having a maximum depth of 7 ft 6 in but, as built, its maximum depth was only 6 ft. The respondent sought to recover as damages for breach of contract the cost of demolition of the existing pool and construction of a new one of the required depth. The trial judge made the following findings which are relevant to this appeal: (1) the pool as constructed was perfectly safe to dive into; (2) there was no evidence that the shortfall in depth had decreased the value of the pool; (3) the only practicable method of achieving a pool of the required depth would be to demolish the existing pool and reconstruct a new one at a cost of £21,560; (4) he was not satisfied that the respondent intended to build a new pool at such a cost; (5) in addition such cost would be wholly disproportionate to the disadvantage of having a pool of a depth of only 6 ft as opposed to 7 ft 6 in and it would therefore be unreasonable to carry out the works; and (6) that the respondent was entitled to damages for loss of amenity in the sum of £2,500.

The Court of Appeal by a majority (Staughton and Mann LJ.; Dillon LJ. Dissenting) ([1994]) 3 All ER 801, [1994] 1 WLR 650) allowed the appeal, holding that the only way in which the respondent could achieve his contractual objective was by reconstructing the pool at a cost of £21,560 which was accordingly a reasonable venture.

The general principles applicable to the measure of damages for breach of contract are not in doubt. In a very well-known passage Parke B in *Robinson v Harman* (1848) 1 Exch 850 at 855, [1843–60] All ER Rep 383 at 385 said:

> The next question is: What damages is the plaintiff entitled to recover? The rule of the common law is that where a party sustains a loss by reason of a breach of contract, he is, so far as money can do it, to be placed in the same situation, with respect to damages, as if the contract had been performed.

In *British Westinghouse Electric and Manufacturing Co. Ltd v Underground Electric Railways Co of London Ltd* [1912] AC 673 at 688–689, [1911–13] All ER Rep 63 at 69 Viscount Haldane LC. said:

> The quantum of damage is a question of fact, and the only guidance the law can give is to lay down general principles which afford at times but scanty assistance in dealing with particular cases . . . Subject to these observations I think that there are certain broad principles which are quite well settled. The first is that, as far as possible, he who has proved a breach of a bargain to supply what he contracted to get is to be placed, as far as money can do it, in as good a situation as if the contract had been performed. The fundamental basis is thus compensation for pecuniary loss naturally flowing from the breach; but this first principle is qualified by a second, which imposes on a plaintiff the duty of taking all reasonable steps to mitigate the loss consequent on the breach . . .

More recently, in what is generally accepted as the leading authority on the measure of damages for defective building work, Lord Cohen in *East Ham BC v Bernard Sunley & Sons Ltd* [1965] 3 All ER 619 at 630, [1966] AC 406 at 434–435 said:

> . . . the learned editors of Hudson's *Building and Engineering Contracts* (8th edn, 1959) say, at p. 319, that there are in fact three possible bases of assessing damages,

namely, (a) the cost of reinstatement; (b) the difference in cost to the builder of the actual work done and work specified; or (c) the diminution in value of the work due to the breach of contract. They go on (ibid.): "There is no doubt that wherever it is reasonable for the employer to insist upon reinstatement the courts will treat the cost of reinstatement as the measure of damage." In the present case it could not be disputed that it was reasonable for the employers to insist on reinstatement and in these circumstances it necessarily follows that on the question of damage the trial judge arrived at the right conclusion.'

Lord Upjohn likewise stated that in a case of defective building work reinstatement was the normal measure of damages (see [1965] 3 All ER 619 at 637, [1966] AC 406 at 445).

Mr McGuire QC for the appellant argued that the cost of reinstatement was only allowable where (1) the employer intended as a matter of probability to rebuild if damages were awarded, and (2) that it was reasonable as between him and the contractor so to do. Since the judge had found against the respondent on both these matters the appeal should be allowed. Mr Jacob on the other hand maintained that reasonableness only arose at the stage when a real loss had been established to exist and that where that loss could only be met by damages assessed on one basis there was no room for consideration of reasonableness. Such was the case where a particular personal preference was part of the contractual objective—a situation which did not allow damages to be assessed on a diminution of value basis.

I start with the question of reasonableness in the context of reinstatement. There is a considerable body of authority dealing with this matter. Lord Cohen in the passage in *East Ham BC v Bernard Sunley & Sons Ltd* quoted above referred to the reasonableness of insisting on reinstatement. In *Imodco Ltd v Wimpey Major Projects Ltd* (1987) 40 BLR 1 at 19 Glidewell LJ. stated that the cost of work to put pipes in the position contracted for would be recoverable if there was an intention to carry out the work and if it was reasonable so to do. In *Minscombe Properties Ltd v Sir Alfred McAlpine & Sons Ltd* (1986) 2 Const LJ 303 at 309 O'Connor LJ. applied the test of reasonableness in determining whether the cost of reinstatement of land to its contracted for condition should be recoverable as damages. In *Radford v De Froberville* [1978] 1 All ER 33 at 54, [1977] 1 WLR 1262 at 1283 Oliver J. said:

> In the instant case, the plaintiff says in evidence that he wishes to carry out the work on his own land and there are, as it seems to me, three questions that I have to answer. First, am I satisfied on the evidence that the plaintiff has a genuine and serious intention of doing the work? Secondly, is the carrying out of the work on his own land a reasonable thing for the plaintiff to do? Thirdly, does it make any difference that the plaintiff is not personally in occupation of the land but desires to do the work for the benefit of his tenants?

In *C R Taylor (Wholesale) Ltd v Hepworths Ltd* [1977] 2 All ER 784 at 791, [1977] 1 WLR 659 at 667 May J. referred with approval to a statement in *McGregor On Damages* (13th edn, 1972) paras 1059–1061 that in deciding between diminution in value and cost of reinstatement the appropriate test was the reasonableness of the plaintiff's desire to reinstate the property and remarked that the damages to be awarded were to be reasonable as between plaintiff and defendant. He concluded that in the case before him to award the notional cost of reinstatement would be unreasonable since it would put the plaintiffs in a far better financial position than they would have been before the fire occurred (see [1977] 2 All ER 784 at 794, [1977] 1 WLR 659 at 670). In *McGregor* (15th edn, 1988) para. 1092, after a reference to the cost of reinstatement being the normal measure of damages in a case of defective building, it is stated:

If, however, the cost of remedying the defect is disproportionate to the end to be attained, the damages fall to be measured by the value of the building had it been built as required by the contract less its value as it stands.

In *Bellgrove v Eldridge* (1954) 90 CLR 613 at 617–618 the High Court of Australia in a judgment of the court, after referring with approval to the rule stated in *Hudson on Building Contracts* (7th edn, 1946) p. 343 stated that —

> The measure of the damages recoverable by the building owner for the breach of a building contract is . . . the difference between the contract price of the work or building contracted for and the cost of making the work or building conform to the contract . . .

and referring to a number of cases supporting this proposition, continued:

> In none of these cases is anything more done than that work which is required to achieve conformity and the cost of the work, whether it be necessary to replace only a small part, or a substantial part, or, indeed, the whole of the building is, subject to the qualification which we have already mentioned and to which we shall refer, together with any appropriate consequential damages, the extent of the building owner's loss. The qualification, however, to which this rule is subject is that, not only must the work undertaken be necessary to produce conformity, but that also, it must be a reasonable course to adopt.

A similar approach to reasonableness was adopted by Cardozo J. delivering the judgment of the majority of the Court of Appeals of New York in *Jacob & Youngs Inc. v Kent* (1921) 230 NY 239 at 244–245.

Damages are designed to compensate for an established loss and not to provide a gratuitous benefit to the aggrieved party, from which it follows that the reasonableness of an award of damages is to be linked directly to the loss sustained. If it is unreasonable in a particular case to award the cost of reinstatement it must be because the loss sustained does not extend to the need to reinstate. A failure to achieve the precise contractual objective does not necessarily result in the loss which is occasioned by a total failure. This was recognised by the High Court of Australia in the passage in *Bellgrove v Eldridge* cited above where it was stated that the cost of reinstatement work subject to the qualification of reasonableness was the extent of the loss, thereby treating reasonableness as a factor to be considered in determining what was that loss rather than, as the respondents argued, merely a factor in determining which of two alternative remedies were appropriate for a loss once established. Further support for this view is to be found in the following passage in the judgment of Megarry V-C in *Tito v Waddell (No 2)* [1977] 3 All ER 129 at 316, [1977] Ch 106 at 332:

> *Per contra*, if the plaintiff has suffered little or no monetary loss in the reduction of value of his land, and he has no intention of applying any damages towards carrying out the work contracted for, or its equivalent, I cannot see why he should recover the cost of doing work which will never be done. It would be a mere pretence to say that this cost was a loss and so should be recoverable as damages.

I take the example suggested during argument by my noble and learned friend Lord Bridge of Harwich. A man contracts for the building of a house and specifies that one of the lower courses of brick should be blue. The builder uses yellow brick instead. In all other respects the house conforms to the contractual specification. To replace the yellow bricks with blue would involve extensive demolition and reconstruction at a very large cost. It would clearly be unreasonable to award to the owner the cost of reconstructing because his loss was not the necessary cost of reconstruction of his house, which was entirely adequate for its design purpose, but merely the lack of aesthetic pleasure which he might have derived from the sight of blue bricks. Thus in the present appeal the respondent has acquired a perfectly serviceable swimming pool, albeit one lacking the specified depth. His loss is thus not the lack of a usable pool with consequent need to construct a new one. Indeed were he to receive the cost of building a new one and retain the existing one he would have recovered not compensation for loss but a very substantial gratuitous benefit, something which damages are not intended to provide.

What constitutes the aggrieved party's loss is in every case a question of fact and degree. Where the contract breaker has entirely failed to achieve the contractual objective it may not be difficult to conclude that the loss is the necessary cost of achieving that objective. Thus if a building is constructed so defectively that it is of no use for its designed purpose the owner may have little difficulty in establishing that his loss is the necessary cost of reconstructing. Furthermore, in taking reasonableness into account in determining the extent of loss it is reasonableness in relation to the particular contract and not at large. Accordingly, if I contracted for the erection of a folly in my garden which shortly thereafter suffered a total collapse it would be irrelevant to the determination of my loss to argue that the erection of such a folly which contributed nothing to the value of my house was a crazy thing to do. As Oliver J. said in *Radford v De Froberville* [1978] 1 All ER 33 at 42, [1977] 1 WLR 1262 at 1270:

> If he contracts for the supply of that which he thinks serves his interests, be they commercial, aesthetic or merely eccentric, then if that which is contracted for is not supplied by the other contracting party I do not see why, in principle, he should not be compensated by being provided with the cost of supplying it through someone else or in a different way, subject to the proviso, of course, that he is seeking compensation for a genuine loss and not merely using a technical breach to secure an uncovenanted profit.

However, where the contractual objective has been achieved to a substantial extent the position may be very different.

It was submitted that where the objective of a building contract involved satisfaction of a personal preference the only measure of damages available for a breach involving failure to achieve such satisfaction was the cost of reinstatement. In my view this is not the case. Personal preference may well be a factor in reasonableness and hence in determining what loss has been suffered but it cannot *per se* be determinative of what that loss is.

My Lords, the trial judge found that it would be unreasonable to incur the cost of demolishing the existing pool and building a new and deeper one. In so doing he implicitly recognised that the respondent's loss did not extend to the cost of reinstatement. He was, in my view, entirely justified in reaching that conclusion. It therefore follows that the appeal must be allowed.

It only remains to mention two further matters. The appellant argued that the cost of reinstatement should only be allowed as damages where there was shown to be an intention on the part of the aggrieved party to carry out the work. Having already decided that the appeal should be allowed I no longer find it necessary to reach a conclusion on this matter. However, I should emphasise that in the normal case the court has no concern with the use to which a plaintiff puts an award of damages for a loss which has been established. Thus, irreparable damage to an article as a result of a breach of contract will entitle the owner to recover the value of the article irrespective of whether he intends to replace it with a similar one or to spend the money on something else. Intention, or lack of it, to reinstate can have relevance only to reasonableness and hence to the extent of the loss which has been sustained. Once that loss has been established intention as to the subsequent use of the damages ceases to be relevant.

The second matter relates to the award of £2,500 for loss of amenity made by the trial judge. The respondent argued that he erred in law in making such award. However, as the appellant did not challenge it, I find it unnecessary to express any opinion on the matter.

Note

1. Even 'cost of cure' claims require difficult decisions to be made by a plaintiff. In *Leahy v Rawson* and others (HC) 14 January 2003, unrep. the plaintiff sought damages for breach of contract in respect of building work undertaken by the defendants. The work resulted in a botched house extension and the central issue was the basis upon which the damages could be awarded. The plaintiff sought the cost of demolition and construction. O'Sullivan J. proceeded to find that under *Munelly v Calcon* [1978] IR 387 damages awarded are to be such as are reasonable as between the plaintiff and the defendant. O'Sullivan J. calculated that the cost of repair as well as diminuation in value, damages in form of loss of business as a bed and breakfast, damages for inconvenience, and items of special damage, could provide an alternative basis of assessment. However, because the demolition and rebuild basis of assessment was less than this alternative approach (£96,000 as distinct from 98,645) an award of the euro equivalent of £96,000 was awarded (€121,894.85). In the Supreme Court, in an unreported decision for which there is no written judgement, the Supreme Court apparently endorsed O'Sullivan J.'s demolition and rebuild measure of compensation, but the Supreme Court deducted €20,000 relating to loss of earnings as a bed and breakfast establishment (perhaps for non-compliance with either limb in *Hadley v Baxerdale*). See *The Irish Times*: '€100,000 for woman over "botched" extension' (*Irish Times*, 30 November 2006).

2. For a recent case on quantum relating to the purchase of property following upon a negligent misstatement see *Walsh v Jones Lang Lasalle Ltd* [2007] IEHC 28.

SECTION TWO—ASSESSMENT OF DAMAGES AS GUESSWORK

In some instances the plaintiff may not have incurred any wasted expend-iture, or the plaintiff may not wish to return the property purchased and seek the return of the price. If there is a breach of contract which results in a loss of expectation the assessment of damages may be intuitive rather than a precise arithmetical exercise.

Hawkins v Rodgers (1950) 85 ILTR 1L8

Dixon J.:
. . .

The plaintiff was a person interested in horse-racing and the breeding of racehorses, while the defendant was, and had been for a good many years, a breeder and trainer of racehorses. The partnership between them commenced about 1943 and continued until 1949, when, by a letter from his solicitor, dated 28 May 1949, the plaintiff purported to terminate the partnership. For some weeks previously there had been what each party described as a 'coolness' between them. The evidence made it clear that the partnership was considered and treated as having been dissolved in or about the date of receipt of the letter referred to. There was never any written partnership agreement nor any arrangement as to the length of notice of dissolution necessary, and accordingly, his Lordship would be prepared, if necessary, to hold the letter effectual for its declared purposes.

By the time the partnership came to be dissolved, its assets comprised a considerable number of horses, including foals, yearlings, racehorses in training, brood mares and one stallion. During its currency the activities of the partnership included the buying and selling of horses, and their breeding, training and racing. So far as the training and racing of horses were concerned the defendant was the active partner. He trained the horses, and made the entries and other arrangements with regard to racing them; he had authority to act on behalf of the plaintiff in these matters. Horses were generally entered in the defendant's name as owner. The partnership was never registered with the racing authorities. The expenses in respect of all partnership horses were borne equally, while the profits were also equally divided.

In the letter of 28 May 1949, already referred to, the plaintiff withdrew from the defendant all authority to act on his behalf in connection with partnership property, and requested an agreement that the horses be sold by public auction. Subsequently there were conversations between the defendant and the plaintiff's solicitor, Mr Dunne; these were mainly concerned with the time, place and mode of sale of the horses. The accounts of those conversations given in evidence to his Lordship differed substantially in only one important matter, a finding on which was necessary for the purpose of his Lordship's decision between the parties.

It was with the sale of one particular horse, belonging to the partnership, that his Lordship was concerned. The animal in question was a thoroughbred filly, foaled in 1947, to a mare bought that year, in foal, as partnership property; and it was not disputed that the filly was partnership property. She was registered with the Turf Club in the name of 'Lonely Maid'. The importance of this animal, and the source of the present dispute, lay in the fact that, at the time of the sale, she had been entered for three important races, known in racing phraseology as 'classics'. In the same phraseology entries for races are known as 'engagements' and his Lordship would so refer to them. The three classics were the Curragh Foal Plate, to be run in July 1949, the Irish 1,000 Guineas to be run in May 1950, and the Irish Oaks to be run in July 1950. The value of those engagements would, of course, depend on whether the horse had a reasonable prospect of winning, or doing well in, any or all of the races. The prize money involved in those three races was very substantial. The entries were all made by the defendant in his own name, the plaintiff being debited in accounts between them with half the entry fees that had been paid. In the case of each of the races, there were dates subsequent to the original entry at each of which, under the condition of the race, further fees (called 'forfeits') became payable if the entry of the horse for the particular race was not cancelled or struck out of that race.

At the auction which took place at the Phoenix Park on 25 June, the plaintiff became the purchaser of 'Lonely Maid'. He bid for and bought her through Mr Prendergast who had become the trainer for horses of the plaintiff which had previously been with the defendant, and whom the plaintiff had also appointed his agent in racing matters. The defendant also bid at the auction through an agent; and these two agents appeared to have been the only bidders. Both parties were present but took no part in the auction, although each had had a conversation with the auctioneer prior to the auction.

The foundation of the plaintiff's claim was that he bought the horse with its engagements. A few days after the sale, on 29 June 1949, the defendant, without consulting either the plaintiff or Mr Prendergast, struck the horse out of all engagements in his name. That action prevented the plaintiff from running the horse in any of the important races already mentioned, and he claimed that he thereby lost a reasonable chance of securing prize money in any of those races, and in addition the enhanced value that a good performance in any of those races would have given her. He claimed that the defendant's action in striking the horse out of the engagements was a breach of contract or a breach of trust on his part, and was also malicious, in the sense not merely of ill-will, but also of being deliberately intended to injure him.

. . .

His Lordship reviewed in detail the evidence given of the conversations that took place between the defendant and the plaintiff's solicitor, prior to the auction, concerning the mode of sale of the partnership horses. He had no hesitation in accepting Mr Dunne's account as not only probable but accurate. The position, therefore, was that he was satisfied that there was an agreement between the partners to sell 'Lonely Maid' with her engagements, a list of such engagements to be supplied to the auctioneer at the auctions; and he thought that the letter from Mr Dunne to the Phoenix Park authority should have conveyed that the intention was to sell the horse with her engagements. The auctioneer was furnished with the relevant correspondence but one could readily understand his silence on the question of the engagements at the auction when, although he spoke to each partner shortly before the auction, neither made any reference to engagements and nobody at any time tendered him a list of the engagements. From the point of view of the actual purchaser, the plaintiff, his Lordship was satisfied that there was no doubt in his mind but that he was buying the engagements with the horse; and he was also satisfied that that was the state of mind of the plaintiff's agent.

The outstanding event was, that a few days after the sale 'Lonely Maid' was struck out of all engagements in the name of the defendant, which, in effect, put her out of all her engagements. This was done by the defendant on a form known as a 'Nomination circular' dealing with the entry and striking out of horses, used by trainers and owners and sent periodically to the Turf Club. The defendant explained in evidence that he was completing that form for that particular week on the day previous to the twenty ninth and, having looked up a publication known as 'Races to come', to see if any forfeits were falling due, he saw that 'Lonely Maid' was entered for the Curragh Foal Plate and that it then came to his mind that she might be entered for other races and he looked this up and found it was so. Thereupon he decided to strike her out of all engagements in his name, and did so. The explanation offered by the defendant for his action was that in so doing he was merely following his invariable practice of striking out every horse he sold, lest he should become liable for forfeits in respect of animals in which he had ceased to have any interest.

Commenting on that suggestion his Lordship stated that the question was whether or not the occasion in question was an example of the general practice. The proposition could only apply where it was clear that the horse had been sold without engagements, or, if not, where the striking out was in accordance with the new owner's wishes.

. . .

His Lordship said that on the evidence before him he did not accept the defendant's explanation of his action in striking out 'Lonely Maid's' engagements. He referred to the fact that the total extent of the forfeits that could have become payable after the sale to the plaintiff was £39 in respect of all the engagements; he found it impossible to believe that the defendant was seriously perturbed by that liability, either immediate or prospective, or that the more rational alternative of ascertaining the views of his partner or of Mr Prendergast to whom at least he knew the horse had been knocked down, did not occur to him. If it occurred to him, as his Lordship felt sure it must have, why did he reject it?

. . .

That there was loss to the plaintiff he had no doubt, but the assessment of its amount was a matter of difficulty for the reason that it was not a matter of certainty but of probability. The damage was alleged to consist in the loss of one or more of the amounts payable as prize money in the three engagements, with the further loss of the enhanced value of the animal if it had done well in any of those races. Such loss clearly depended on a contingency, the second branch of it on a double contingency. The case of *Chaplin v Hicks* [1911] 2 KB 786, seemed to be authority for the view that the fact of such loss depending on such contingencies did not disentitle the plaintiff to damages, but only rendered their assessment more difficult.

On all the evidence, and having regard to the value of the stakes in the three races in question, and to the ability of the filly as proved by her subsequent performances, his Lordship assessed damages at £750 and gave judgment for that amount.

O'Keeffe *v* Ryanair Holdings plc [2003] 1 ILRM 14

For the full facts of this case see above at page 131. After finding that Ryanair's 'free flights for life' 1988 promotion was the subject of a binding contract and that it had been breached by the defendant, Kelly J. considered the issue of how damages were to be assessed:

Kelly J.:

Damages
The plaintiff is entitled to damages for breach of her contract. She is entitled to damages for her inability to utilise the entitlement from the date of the breach in 1997 to date. She is also entitled to the capital value of her entitlement into the future. I will deal with each of these heads of damage separately.

Loss to date
The plaintiffs use of her entitlement has on any view of it been modest. Her family circumstances at present with two young children aged four and two respectively mean that she is not in a position to make any more extensive use of the facility than has been the case to date. Accordingly, I conclude that I ought to fix the number of journeys which she is likely to have made since 1997 to date as four per annum. That would be four round trips for herself and one other person.

I have had substantial evidence, argument and debate over the value to be attributed to each of these trips. The plaintiff's actuary went into the defendant's website, extracted a range of prices which were available for one-way flights and averaged them out as being €112 per flight. The defendants say that is not the appropriate way of approaching the matter and they have put in evidence returns which they have made to the Unites States regulatory authorities. Those returns demonstrate that the average passenger fare is of an altogether lower figure namely of the order of €55–€60 per one-way trip. But these are averages and do not necessarily reflect the actual loss.

For the purposes of the loss to date I think it reasonable to assume an average fare of €150 per round trip (€75 per flight one way) giving a loss of €600 per annum to the plaintiff for herself and a further €600 in respect of her nominated companion. That amounts to a total loss of €1,200 per annum, for the last five years giving a loss of €6,000 to date.

In addition, following *Jarvis v Swan Tours Ltd* [1973] 1 All ER 71, I think she is also entitled to be compensated for the disappointment, frustration and upset that was suffered by her in respect of the holiday weekend in October 1997 arising from the unpleasant and shabby treatment which she suffered on that occasion. I will therefore award an additional €1,500 to deal with that. That gives an award of €7,500 for loss to date.

The future

The first task which I must undertake is to make what I believe to be a reasonable assessment of the number of trips that are likely to be taken by the plaintiff and her nominated companion over the remainder of her life. I think it likely that the plaintiff's use will continue at the rate of four per annum, until her children become older. I have little doubt but that at that stage, as she said herself, her use will increase and I think as a matter of probability, substantially. In addition the routes being flown by the defendant are continually increasing and that is likely to be the case in future. Weekend trips to close locations will increase as will holidays to places further afield. If, as she hopes, she purchases a premises abroad then even greater use will be made of the entitlement. As she gets into old age use of it will decrease. Taking one thing with another therefore, I have come to the conclusion that an allowance of ten trips per annum would not in the circumstances be unreasonable.

I accept the defendant's evidence that in recent times airline prices have tended to reduce and that that is likely to continue for some time into the future. I do not accept that a stage will be reached where the cost will be zero and the defendant will be making its money solely from ancillary services.

I have already indicated how the plaintiff's actuary acquired his average of £112 per flight (one way). The defendant adduced evidence of returns which it has made to its United States regulatory authorities of the average passenger fare over the years. These figures are on the basis of a one-way trip and over the past eleven years demonstrate an average fare of as little as €48.38 to as much as €60.09. Those figures are of course averages and therefore may not necessarily represent the actual loss which the plaintiff would be likely to incur in any one year. In the circumstances it seems to me to be not unreasonable to take a figure of €60 per one-way trip as being the appropriate sum on which to make the calculation. The round trip would therefore be €120 and that of course must be doubled to take account of the loss of the trip of the plaintiff's companion. That gives an annual loss of €2,400 which then has to be capitalised.

I have had evidence from actuaries on both sides giving me the benefit of their views of capital value on different figures and having regard to the tax status of the plaintiff. Their evidence does not of course take into account unforeseen possibilities concerning both the plaintiff and the defendant. I must make allowance for them as best I can (*Reddy v Bates* [1983] IR 141; [1984] ILRM 197). I hold that inflation will apply to future ticket prices and whilst therefore there will be a reduction in net cost, inflation will to some extent offset that. In these circumstances I have come to the conclusion having regard to all of the evidence that the appropriate sum to be awarded to the plaintiff in respect of future loss is the sum of €60,000.

To that must be added the €7,500 for loss to date giving a grand total of €67,500.

McGregor on Damages (15th edn) London: Sweet & Maxwell, 1988, 469–70 (Footnotes omitted.)

Is the measure of damages in contract and tort the same? This is a question frequently posed. Sometimes it is said that it is, sometimes that it is not. Before any clear answer can be found it is necessary to break down this omnibus question, for the term 'measure of damages' may refer to a number of things.

The clearest and undoubted distinctions between contract and tort lie in the exceptional cases where damages are not given strictly on the principle of awarding compensation. On the one hand since liquidated damages can only result from agreement, they apply to contract and cannot in the nature of things refer to tort. On the other hand exemplary damages, though now explicitly confined to three categories of case, continue to be awarded only in tort and have not spread to contract. Further, nominal damages have application to all contracts but only to some torts.

Turning to the case of compensatory damages, which is much more important because it represents the norm, there is at the very start a basic, though somewhat latent, distinction between contract and tort. This distinction is in the general rule which is the starting point for resolving all problems as to measure of damages. The distinction is latent because the leading formulation of the general rule is sufficiently wide to cover contract and tort equally: this formulation is that the plaintiff is entitled to be put into the same position, as far as money can do it, as he would have been in had the wrong not been committed. In contract, however, the wrong consists not in the making but in the breaking of the contract and therefore the plaintiff is entitled to be put into the position he would have been in if the contract had never been broken, or in other words, if the contract had been performed. The plaintiff is entitled to recover damages for the loss of his bargain. In tort, on the other hand, no question of loss of bargain can arise: the plaintiff is not complaining of failure to implement a promise but of failure to leave him alone. The measure of damages in tort is therefore to be assessed on the basis of restoring as far as possible the *status quo ante*. This distinction does not stand out in the great majority of cases since contract and tort have such widely different areas of application, but in cases involving misrepresentations there is an overlap of contract and tort which is instructive in this connection. Where the plaintiff has been induced to enter into a contract by a misrepresentation of fact on the defendant's part, then if the representation constitutes a term of the contract, whether condition or warranty, he can sue for breach of contract and, in claiming for loss of his bargain, is entitled to such damages as will put him into the position he would have been in had the misrepresentation been true. If, however, the representation does not constitute a term of the contract, then, although the plaintiff may be entitled to rescind on the ground of misrepresentation, there is no breach of contract for which he can get damages, and his only common law action for damages can be in tort, in deceit if the misrepresentation has been fraudulently made, in negligence where it has been carelessly made. It is sometimes assumed that if the plaintiff can show fraud he is in as good a position as far as damages are concerned as if he had been able to sue for breach of contract on the ground that the representation was a term of the contract. This is fallacious, for the proper measure of damages in deceit—a measure adopted in the late nineteenth century and now firmly established by the Court of Appeal in *Doyle v Olby* (*Ironmongers*)—is to put the plaintiff in the position he would have been in, not if the representation had been true, but if the representation had never been made. This is a more restrictive rule: the action in tort does not take into account the loss of a bargain. Conversely, cases of breach of warranty of authority are sometimes regarded as in effect giving damages for innocent misrepresentation. That this is not the proper view is shown by the fact that it has been consistently decided in the cases, of which *Re National Coffee Palace Co., ex p. Panmure* is perhaps the most important, that the measure of damages is based upon putting the plaintiff in the position he would have been in, not if the representation had never been made, but if the representation had been true.

A. MEASURES OF COMPENSATION

Sale of Goods Act 1893 ss 50 and 51

Part V. Actions for Breach of the Contract

Remedies of the Seller

50. (1) Where the buyer wrongfully neglects or refuses to accept and pay for the goods, the seller may maintain an action against him for damages for non-acceptance.

(2) The measure of damages is the estimated loss directly and naturally resulting, in the ordinary course of events, from the buyer's breach of contract.

(3) Where there is an available market for the goods in question the measure of damages is *prima facie* to be ascertained by the difference between the contract price and the market or current price at the time or times when the goods ought to have been accepted or, if no time was fixed for acceptance, then at the time of the refusal to accept.

Remedies of the Buyer

51. (1) Where the seller wrongfully neglects or refuses to deliver the goods to the buyer, the buyer may maintain an action against the seller for damages for non-delivery.

(2) The measure of damages is the estimated loss directly and naturally resulting, in the ordinary course of events, from the seller's breach of contract.

(3) Where there is an available market for the goods in question the measure of damages is *prima facie* to be ascertained by the difference between the contract price and the market or current price of the goods at the time or times when they ought to have been delivered, or, if no time was fixed, then at the time of the refusal to deliver.

Macauley & Cullen v Horgan [1925] 2 IR 6

In this case the defendant was held to be in breach of a contract to deliver wool, the contract being concluded by correspondence on 26 October 1923.

Sullivan P.:

. . .

I hold that a reasonable time for delivery had elapsed by 5 December, and that the wool should have been delivered on or before that date. I further hold that the refusal or neglect of defendant to answer the plaintiffs' letters of 5 December and 18 December amounted to a refusal by the defendant to perform his contract, one month prior to his receipt of the letter of 18 January 1924, from the plaintiffs' solicitors.

The measure of damages is prescribed by s. 51 of the Sale of Goods Act 1893. That section provides that where the seller wrongfully neglects or refuses to deliver the goods to the buyer, the buyer may maintain an action against the seller for damages for non-delivery (sub-s. (1)). The measure of damages is the estimated loss directly and naturally resulting, in the ordinary course of events, from the seller's breach of contract (sub-s. (2)). And then sub-s. (3) provides: 'Where there is an available market for the goods in question the measure of damages is *prima facie* to be ascertained by the difference between the contract price and the market or current price of the goods at the time or times when they ought to have been delivered, or, if no time was fixed, then at the time of the refusal to deliver.' The section, it will be seen, states two alternative dates for ascertaining the measure of damages, namely, 'when the goods ought to have been delivered,' or, if no time was fixed, then 'the time of the refusal to deliver.'

I have held that the conduct of the defendant in not answering the letters of the plaintiffs amounted to a refusal to deliver, that before the end of December there had been a refusal by the defendant to deliver the wool to the plaintiffs, and that the plaintiffs were not entitled to wait until the end of January before accepting such refusal. Accordingly, the next question is, was there an available market for the goods in question, and, if so, what was the difference between the market price and the contract price at that time? There was no evidence as to the existence of an available market for wool at Cahirciveen where delivery was contracted for, but, having regard to the previous dealings between the parties and the inter-communication between Cahirciveen and Dublin, I think that the market price at Cahirciveen may, for the purposes of the measure of damages, be taken to be the market price at Dublin, less the cost of carriage, and, accordingly, I hold that the plaintiffs can rely on the market price in Dublin. I think that *Wertheim v Chicoutimi Pulp Co.*[1] justifies me in so holding and in accepting evidence of the Dublin price.

Accordingly, the next question is, what was the Dublin price at the end of December? [His Lordship then dealt with the figures given in evidence as to the price of such wool in Dublin at the end of December, and held that the price then was £100 in excess of the price contracted for, and continued:]

Accordingly, I hold that the price of wool in Dublin at the end of December was £100 over that contracted for, and from this I deduct £50 for the cost of carriage to Dublin, and I therefore assess damages at £50.

[1.] [1911] AC 301.

Golden Strait Corporation *v* Nippon Yusen Kubishka Kaisha [2007] UKHL 12

By a time charterparty dated 10 July 1998 GSC chartered their tanker, *Golden Victory*, to NYKK for seven years. On 14 December 2001, the charterers repudiated the charter by redelivering the vessel to GSC, the owners; at this time the charter had nearly four years to run. There was an available market for the rehire of the vessel at this time. The owners sought damages which the charterers resisted in an arbitration. The arbitrator found that the vessel should have been redelivered under the contract by 6 December 2005, and the owners sought damages for repudiatory breach for the period between acceptance of the repudiation, 17 December 2001, and 6 December 2005. The charterers sought to rely on clause 33 in the charterparty, this clause providing a right of termination should war break out, the charterers indicating that they would have exercised this right in March 2003 when the second Gulf War commenced. The arbitrator took the view that, judged on 17 December 2001, 'a reasonably well-informed person' would have held that large-scale hostilities involving the UK, the USA and Iraq was not inevitable, or even probably likely to happen, but merely a possibility. The Arbitrator nevertheless felt bound by precedent (in particular, the *Mihalis Angelos*, and the *Seaflower*) to hold that he was bound to take account of subsequent events, namely, the probable frustration of the contract by war, to limit damages to the period 17 December 2001 to 20 March 2003. The Arbitrator, the Commercial Court and Court of Appeal found for the charterers. In the House of Lords the House divided by 3:2 in favour of dismissing the owner's appeal. In his dissenting judgement Lord Bingham of Cornhill explained the law thus:

Principle

The repudiation of a contract by one party ('the repudiator'), if accepted by the other ('the injured party'), brings the contract to an end and releases both parties from their primary obligations under the contract. The injured party is thereupon entitled to recover damages against the repudiator to compensate him for such financial loss as the repudiator's breach has caused him to suffer. This is elementary law.

The damages recoverable by the injured party are such sum as will put him in the same financial position as if the contract had been performed. This is the compensatory principle which has long been recognised as the governing principle in contract. Counsel for the charterers cited certain classical authorities to make good this proposition, but it has been enunciated and applied times without number and is not in doubt. It does not, however, resolve the question whether the injured party's loss is to be assessed as of the date when he suffers the loss, or shortly thereafter, in the light of what is then known, or at a later date when the assessment happens to be made, in the light of such later events as may then be known.

An injured party such as the owners may not, generally speaking, recover damages against a repudiator such as the charterers for loss which he could reasonably have avoided by taking reasonable commercial steps to mitigate his loss. Thus where, as here, there is an available market for the chartering of vessels, the injured party's loss will be calculated on the assumption that he has, on or within a reasonable time of accepting the repudiation, taken reasonable commercial steps to obtain alternative employment for the vessel for the best consideration reasonably obtainable. This is the ordinary rule whether in fact the injured party acts in that way or, for whatever reason, does not. The actual facts are ordinarily irrelevant. The rationale of the rule is one of simple commercial fairness. The injured party owes no duty to the repudiator, but fairness requires that he should not ordinarily be permitted to rely on his own unreasonable and uncommercial conduct to increase the loss falling on the repudiator. I take this summary to reflect the ruling of Robert Goff J in *Koch Marine Inc v D'Amica Società di Navigazione ARL* (*The 'Elena D'Amico'*) [1980] 1 Lloyd's Rep 75. That case concerned the measure of damages recoverable by a charterer for breach of a time charter during its currency by an owner. While taking care to avoid laying down an inflexible or invariable rule, the judge held (p. 89, col. 2) that if, at the date of breach, there is an available market, the normal measure of damages will be the difference between the contract rate and the market rate for chartering in a substitute ship for the balance of the charter period. An analogy was drawn with section 51(3) of the Sale of Goods Act 1893. Neither party challenged this decision, which has always been regarded as authoritative. It does however assume that the injured party knows, or can ascertain, what the balance of the charter period is.

It is a general, but not an invariable, rule of English law that damages for breach of contract are assessed as at the date of breach. Authority for this familiar proposition may be found in *Jamal v Moolla Dawood Sons & Co* [1916] AC 175, 179: *Miliangos v George Frank (Textiles) Ltd.* [1976] AC 443, 468; *Johnson v Agnew* [1980] AC 367, 400–401; *Dodd Properties (Kent) Ltd v Canterbury City Council* [1980] 1 WLR 433, 450-451, 454–455, 457; *County Personnel (Employment Agency) Ltd. v Alan R. Pulver & Co.* [1987] 1 WLR 916, 925–926; *Chitty on Contracts*, 29th edn (2004), vol. 1, para. 26–057; Professor S. M. Waddams, 'The Date for the Assessment of Damages' (1981), 97 LQR 445, 446. The Sale of Goods Acts of 1893 and 1979 both give effect to this prima facie rule in section 51(3) of the respective Acts in the case of refusal or neglect by a seller to deliver goods to a buyer where there is an available market.

The argument

While not, I think, challenging the general correctness of the principles last stated, the charterers dispute their applicability to the present case. Their first ground for doing so is in reliance on what, from the name of the case in which this principle has been most clearly articulated, has sometimes been called 'the *Bwllfa* principle'. It is that where the court making an assessment of damages has knowledge of what actually happened it need not speculate about what might have happened but should base itself on the known facts. In non-judicial discourse the point has been made that you need not gaze into the crystal ball when you can read the book. I have, for my part, no doubt that this is in many contexts a sound approach in law as in life, and it is true that the principle has been judicially invoked in a number of cases. But these cases bear little, if any, resemblance to the present. In *Bwllfa and Merthyr Dare Steam Collieries (1891) Limited v Pontypridd Waterworks Company* [1903] AC 426 a coalowner claimed statutory compensation against a water undertaking which had, pursuant to statutory authority, prevented him mining his coal over a period during which the price of coal had risen. The question was whether the coal should be valued as at the beginning of the period or at its value during the currency of the period. The coalowner was entitled to 'full compensation' and the House upheld the latter measure. In doing so, it was at pains to distinguish the case from one of sale or property transfer: see Lord Halsbury LC, pp 428-429; Lord Macnaghten, p 431; Lord Robertson, p 432. *In re Bradberry* [1943] Ch 35, where the principle was invoked, concerned the valuation of an annuity in the course of administering an estate. The claim in *Carslogie Steamship Co. Ltd v Royal Norwegian Government* [1952] AC 292 was a claim by shipowners for loss of time during repairs of damage caused by a collision. After the collision the ship had suffered heavy weather damage, which required the ship to be detained for repair of that damage. It was common ground that the ship would have been detained for the same period if the collision had never occurred (p 313). In *In Re Thoars Deceased* ([2002] EWHC 2416(Ch), unreported, 15 November 2002) the principle was invoked in the course of deciding whether a policy of life insurance had been transferred at an undervalue within the meaning of section 339 of the Insolvency Act 1986. The principle was again invoked in *McKinnon v E Survey Ltd* ([2003] EWHC 475 (Ch), unreported, 14 January 2003), a claim against negligent surveyors in which the court was asked to assume, for purposes of a preliminary issue, that the property had not been the subject of movement at the date of valuation and had not been subject to movement since, but that it would not have been possible to establish these facts until after the purchase of the property. In *Aitchison v Gordon Durham & Company Limited* (unreported, 30 June 1995) the Court of Appeal applied the principle where a joint venture agreement to develop land had been broken and the court took account of what actually happened to decide what the claimant's profit would have been. I do not think it necessary to discuss these cases, since it is clear that in some contexts the court may properly take account of later events. None of these cases involved repudiation of a commercial contract where there was an available market.

The charterers further submit that even if, as a general rule, damages for breach of contract (or tort, often treated as falling within the same rule) are assessed as at the date of the breach or the tort, the court has shown itself willing to depart from this rule where it judges it necessary or just to do so in order to give effect to the compensatory principle. I accept that this is so. But it is necessary to consider the cases in which the court departs from the general rule. Some are personal injury claims, of which *Curwen v James* [1963] 1 WLR 748 and *Murphy v Stone-Wallwork (Charlton) Ltd* [1969] 1 WLR 1023 may serve as examples. *Dudarec v Andrews* [2006] EWCA Civ 256, [2006] 1 WLR 3002 was in form a negligence claim against solicitors, but damages were sought for the loss of a chance of success in a personal injuries action struck out for want of prosecution seven years earlier, and the issue was similar to that in a personal injuries action. It is unnecessary to consider the extent to which, in the light of *Baker v Willoughby* [1970] AC 467 and *Jobling v Associated Dairies Ltd* [1982] AC 794, the breach date principle applies to the assessment of personal injury damages in tort. The court has also departed from the general rule in cases where, on particular facts, it was held to be reasonable for the injured party to defer taking steps to mitigate his loss and so reasonable to defer the assessment of damage. *Radford v De Froberville* [1977] 1 WLR 1262 and *Dodd Properties (Kent) Ltd v Canterbury City Council* [1980] 1 WLR 433 are examples. In both cases the general rule was acknowledged and reasons given for departing from it. *County Personnel (Employment Agency) Ltd v Alan Pulver & Co.* [1987] 1 WLR 916 was a claim against solicitors whose negligent advice had saddled the plaintiffs with a ruinous underlease, from which the plaintiffs had had to buy themselves out. The ordinary diminution in value measure of damage was held to be wholly inapt on the particular facts. Again, reasons were given for departing from the normal rule. In *Miliangos v George Frank (Textiles) Ltd.* [1976] AC 443 the effect of inflation led the House to sanction a departure from the rule that losses sustained in a foreign currency must be converted into sterling at the date of breach. The plaintiff in *Re-Source America International Ltd v Platt Site Services Ltd* [2005] EWCA Civ 97, [2005] 2 Lloyd's Rep 50 was bailee of spools used to carry optic fibre cables which it was to refurbish. The spools were destroyed by fire. It was held to be entitled to recover the cost of replacing the spools, subject to a deduction based on the saved cost of refurbishment. The Court of Appeal took account of what happened after the fire. It was expressly found (para 5) that there was no available market in used spools, so the plaintiff could not have mitigated its loss by replacing them. *Sally Wertheim v Chicoutimi Pulp Company* [1911] AC 301, cited by the charterers, was not a case of non-delivery or refusal to deliver, but of delayed delivery. The goods, although delivered late, were received and there was no accepted repudiation. The case would not have fallen under section 51(3) of the 1893 Act. The buyer made a claim for damages, based on the difference between the market price at the place of delivery when the goods should have been delivered and the market price there when the goods were in fact delivered. It was apparent on the figures that this claim, if successful, would have yielded the plaintiff a much larger profit than if the contract had not been broken, and he was compensated for his actual loss. None of these cases, as is evident, involves the accepted repudiation of a commercial contract such as a charterparty. It is necessary to consider some cases more similar to the present case to which the House was referred.

Considerable attention has been paid to the decision of the Court of Appeal (Lord Denning MR, Edmund Davies and Megaw LJJ) in *Maredelanto Compania Naviera SA v Bergbau-Handel GmbH* ('*The Mihalis Angelos*') [1971] 1 QB 164. The case concerned a voyage charterparty by which the ship was fixed to sail to Haiphong and there load a cargo for delivery in Europe. In the charterparty dated 25 May 1965 the owners stated that the ship was 'expected ready to load under this charter about July 1, 1965'. The charterparty also provided, in the first sentence of the cancelling clause, 'Should the vessel not be ready to load (whether in berth or not) on or before July 20, 1965, charterers have the option of cancelling this contract, such option to be declared, if demanded, at least 48 hours before vessel's expected arrival at port of loading'. On 17 July 1965 the ship was at Hong Kong still discharging cargo from her previous voyage. It was physically impossible for her to finish discharging and reach Haiphong by 20 July. The charterers gave notice cancelling the charter. The owners treated this as a repudiation and claimed damages, which were the subject of arbitration and of an appeal to Mocatta J. On further appeal, there were three issues. The first was whether the 'expected readiness' clause was a condition of which the owners were in breach, entitling the charterers to terminate the charter contract. All three members of the court decided this issue in favour of the charterers and against the owners. The second issue was whether (if the answer to the first issue was wrong) the charterers had repudiated the contract by cancelling on 17 July, three days before the specified 20 July deadline. Lord Denning held that they had not, but Edmund Davies and Megaw LJJ held that they had. The third issue was as to the damage suffered by the owners, on the assumption that the charterers' premature cancellation had been a repudiation. Lord Denning, in agreement with the arbitrators, who were themselves agreed, held that they had suffered no damage (p. 197):

> Seeing that the charterers would, beyond doubt, have cancelled, I am clearly of opinion that the shipowners suffered no loss: and would be entitled at most to nominal damages.

Edmund Davies L.J. agreed (p. 202):

> One must look at the contract as a whole, and if it is clear that the innocent party has lost nothing, he should recover no more than nominal damages for the loss of his right to have the whole contract completed.

Megaw L.J. (at pp. 209–210) stated:

> In my view, where there is an anticipatory breach of contract, the breach is the repudiation once it has been accepted, and the other party is entitled to recover by way of damages the true value of the contractual rights which he has thereby lost; subject to his duty to mitigate. If the contractual rights which he has lost were capable by the terms of the contract of being rendered either less valuable or valueless in certain events, and if it can be shown that those events were, at the date of acceptance of the repudiation, predestined to happen, then in my view the damages which he can recover are not more than the true value, if any, of the rights which he has lost, having regard to those predestined events.

It is evident that all members of the court were viewing the case as from the date of acceptance of the repudiation (although only Megaw L.J. said so in terms). They were not taking account of later events. They were recognising, as was obvious on the facts as found, that the value of the contractual right which the owners had lost, as of the date of acceptance of the repudiation, was nil because the charter was bound to be lawfully cancelled three days later.

Conclusion

The thrust of the charterers' argument was that the owners would be unfairly over-compensated if they were to recover as damages sums which, with the benefit of hindsight, it is now known that they would not have received had there been no accepted repudiation by the charterers. There are, in my opinion, several answers to this. The first is that contracts are made to be performed, not broken. It may prove disadvantageous to break a contract instead of performing it. The second is that if, on their repudiation being accepted, the charterers had promptly honoured their secondary obligation to pay damages, the transaction would have been settled well before the Second Gulf War became a reality. The third is that the owners were, as the arbitrator held (see para. 7 above), entitled to be compensated for the value of what they had lost on the date it was lost, and it could not be doubted that what the owners lost at that date was a charterparty with slightly less than four years to run. This was a clear and, in my opinion, crucial finding, but it was not mentioned in either of the judgements below, nor is it mentioned by any of my noble and learned friends in the majority. On the arbitrator's finding, it was marketable on that basis. I can readily accept that the value of a contract in the market may be reduced if terminable on an event which the market judges to be likely but not certain, but that was not what the arbitrator found to be the fact in this case. There is, with respect to those who think otherwise, nothing artificial in this approach. If a party is compensated for the value of what he has lost at the time when he loses it, and its value is at that time for any reason depressed, he is fairly compensated. That does not cease to be so because adventitious later events reveal that the market at that time was depressed by the apprehension of risks that did not eventuate. A party is not, after all, obliged to accept a repudiation: he can, if he chooses, keep the contract alive, for better or worse. By describing the prospect of war in December 2001 as 'merely a possibility', the expression twice used by the arbitrator in paragraph 59 of his reasons, the arbitrator can only have meant that it was seen as an outside chance, not affecting the marketable value of the charter at that time.

There is, however, a further answer which I, in common with the arbitrator, consider to be of great importance. He acknowledged the force of arguments advanced by the owners based on certainty ('generally important in commercial affairs'), finality ('the alternative being a running assessment of the state of play so far as the likelihood of some interruption to the contract is concerned'), settlement ('otherwise the position will remain fluid'), consistency ('the idea that a party's accrued rights can be changed by subsequent events is objectionable in principle') and coherence ('the date of repudiation is the date on which rights and damages are assessed'). The judge was not greatly impressed by the charterers' argument along these lines, observing (paras 13, 35) that although certainty is a real and beneficial target, it is not easily achieved, and the charterparty contained within it the commercial uncertainty of the war clause.

The importance of certainty and predictability in commercial transactions has been a constant theme of English commercial law at any rate since the judgment of Lord Mansfield CJ in *Vallejo v Wheeler* (1774) 1 Cowp 143, 153, and has been strongly asserted in recent years in cases such as *Scandinavian Trading Tanker Co. AB v Flota Petrolera Ecuatoriana* ('*The Scaptrade*') [1983] QB 529, 540–541, [1983] 2 AC 694, 703–704; *Homburg Houtimport BV v Agrosin Private Ltd* [2003] UKHL 12, [2004] 1 AC 715, 738; *Jindal Iron and Steel Co Ltd. v Islamic Solidarity Shipping Co. Jordan Inc.* ('*The Jordan II*') [2004] UKHL 49,

[2005] 1 WLR 1363, 1370. Professor Sir Guenter Treitel QC read the Court of Appeal's judgment as appearing to impair this quality of certainty ('Assessment of Damages for Wrongful Repudiation', (2007) 123 LQR 9–18) and I respectfully share his concern.

For these reasons and those given by my noble and learned friend Lord Walker of Gestingthorpe, with which I wholly agree, I would, for my part, have allowed the owners' appeal.

Lord Scott of Foscote (Lords Carswell and Brown of Eaton-under-Heywood concurring).

Two important matters that have, or may have, a bearing on the answer to the question are now common ground. First, it is common ground that, if the charterparty had still been on foot when, in March 2003, hostilities between the USA and the UK on one side and Iraq on the other side began, the Charterers would have exercised their clause 33 right to terminate the charterparty. Second, it is common ground that as at 17 December 2001 the chance that any hostilities triggering the clause 33 right of termination would break out was no more than a possibility and certainly not a probability.

My Lords, the answer to the question at issue must depend on principles of the law of contract. It is true that the context in this case is a charterparty, a commercial contract. But the contractual principles of the common law relating to the assessment of damages are no different for charterparties, or for commercial contracts in general, than for contracts which do not bear that description. The fundamental principle governing the quantum of damages for breach of contract is long established and not in dispute. The damages should compensate the victim of the breach for the loss of his contractual bargain. The principle was succinctly stated by Parke B in *Robinson v Harman* 1 Ex 850 at 855 and remains as valid now as it was then.

> The rule of the common law is, that where a party sustains a loss by reason of a breach of contract, he is, so far as money can do it, to be placed in the same situation, with respect to damages, as if the contract had been performed.

If the contract is a contract for performance over a period, whether for the performance of personal services, or for supply of goods, or, as here, a time charter, the assessment of damages for breach must proceed on the same principle, namely, the victim of the breach should be placed, so far as damages can do it, in the position he would have been in had the contract been performed.

If a contract for performance over a period has come to an end by reason of a repudiatory breach but might, if it had remained on foot, have terminated early on the occurrence of a particular event, the chance of that event happening must, it is agreed, be taken into account in an assessment of the damages payable for the breach. And if it is certain that the event will happen, the damages must be assessed on that footing. In *The Mihalis Angelos* [1971] 1 QB 164, Megaw L.J. referred to events 'predestined to happen'. He said, at p.210, that:

> . . . if it can be shown that those events were, at the date of acceptance of the repudiation, predestined to happen, then . . . the damages which [the claimant] can recover are not more than the true value, if any, of the rights which he has lost, having regard to those predestined events.

Another way of putting the point being made by Megaw L.J. is that the claimant is entitled to the benefit, expressed in money, of the contractual rights he has lost, but not to the benefit of more valuable contractual rights than those he has lost. In *Wertheim v Chicoutimi Pulp Co.* [1911] AC 301, Lord Atkinson referred, at 307, to:

> . . . the general intention of the law that, in giving damages for breach of contract, the party complaining should, so far as it can be done by money, be placed in the same position as he would have been in if the contract had been performed

and, in relation to a claim by a purchaser for damages for late delivery of goods where the purchaser had, after the late delivery, sold the goods for a higher price than that prevailing in the market on the date of delivery, observed, at 308, that:

> . . . the loss he sustains must be measured by that price, unless he is, against all justice, to be permitted to make a profit by the breach of contract, be compensated for a loss he never suffered, and be put, as far as money can do it, not in the same position in which he would have been if the contract had been performed, but in a much better position.

The result contended for by the appellant in the present case is, to my mind, similar to that contemplated by Lord Atkinson in the passage last cited. If the charterparty had not been repudiated and had remained on foot, it would have been terminated by the Charterers in or shortly after March 2003 when the Second Gulf War triggered the clause 33 termination option. But the Owners are claiming damages up to 6 December 2005 on the footing, now known to be false, that the charterparty would have continued until then. It is contended that because the Charterers' repudiation and its acceptance by the Owners preceded the March 2003 event, the rule requiring damages for breach of contract to be assessed at the date of breach requires that event to be ignored.

That contention, in my opinion, attributes to the assessment of damages at the date of breach rule an inflexibility which is inconsistent both with principle and with the authorities. The underlying principle is that the victim of a breach of contract is entitled to damages representing the value of the contractual benefit to which he was entitled but of which he has been deprived. He is entitled to be put in the same position, so far as money can do it, as if the contract had been performed. The assessment at the date of breach rule can usually achieve that result. But not always. In *Miliangos v Frank (Textiles) Ltd.* [1976] AC 443 Lord Wilberforce at 468 referred to 'the general rule' that damages for breach of contract are assessed as at the date of breach but went on to observe that:

> . . . It is for the courts, or for arbitrators, to work out a solution in each case best adapted to giving the injured plaintiff that amount in damages which will most fairly compensate him for the wrong which he has suffered . . .

and, when considering the date at which a foreign money obligation should be converted into sterling, chose the date that 'gets nearest to securing to the creditor exactly what he bargained for'. If a money award of damages for breach of contract provides to the creditor a lesser or a greater benefit than the creditor bargained for, the award fails, in either case, to provide a just result.

In *Dodd Properties v Canterbury City Council* [1980] 1 WLR 433, Megaw L.J., commenting on the 'general rule' to which Lord Wilberforce had referred in the *Miliangos* case, said, at 451, that it was 'clear' that the general rule was 'subject to many exceptions and qualifications'. In *County Personnel Ltd. v Alan R Pulver & Co.* [1987] 1 WLR 916, Bingham

LJ, as my noble and learned friend then was, said at 926 that the general rule that damages were assessed at the date of the breach 'should not be mechanistically applied in circumstances where assessment at another date may more accurately reflect the overriding compensatory rule.' In *Lavarack v Woods of Colchester Ltd* [1967] 1 QB 278, the Court of Appeal held that damages for wrongful dismissal could not confer on an employee extra benefits that the contract did not oblige the employer to confer and Diplock L.J. (as he then was) said at 294, that:

> . . . the first task of the assessor of damages is to estimate as best he can what the plaintiff would have gained in money or money's worth if the defendant had fulfilled his legal obligations and had done no more. Where there is an anticipatory breach by wrongful repudiation, this can at best be an estimate, whatever the date of the hearing. It involves assuming that what has not occurred and never will occur has occurred or will occur, i.e. that the defendant has since the breach performed his legal obligations under the contract and, if the estimate is made before the contract would otherwise have come to an end, that he will continue to perform his legal obligations thereunder until the due date of its termination. But the assumption to be made is that the defendant has performed or will perform his legal obligations under his contract with the plaintiff and nothing more.

This passage was cited and applied by Waller L.J. in giving his judgment, concurred in by Roch and Ward LJJ, in *North Sea Energy Holdings NV v Petroleum Authority of Thailand* [1999] 1 Lloyd's Rep 483 at 494/5.

The assessment at the date of breach rule is particularly apt to cater for cases where a contract for the sale of goods in respect of which there is a market has been repudiated. The loss caused by the breach to the seller or the buyer, as the case may be, can be measured by the difference between the contract price and the market price at the time of the breach. The seller can re-sell his goods in the market. The buyer can buy substitute goods in the market. Thereby the loss caused by the breach can be fixed. But even here some period must usually be allowed to enable the necessary arrangements for the substitute sale or purchase to be made (see e.g. *Kaines v Österreichische* [1993] 2 Lloyd's Rep 1). The relevant market price for the purpose of assessing the quantum of the recoverable loss will be the market price at the expiration of that period.

In cases, however, where the contract for sale of goods is not simply a contract for a one-off sale, but is a contract for the supply of goods over some specified period, the application of the general rule may not be in the least apt. Take the case of a three year contract for the supply of goods and a repudiatory breach of the contract at the end of the first year. The breach is accepted and damages are claimed but before the assessment of the damages an event occurs that, if it had occurred while the contract was still on foot, would have been a frustrating event terminating the contract, e.g. legislation prohibiting any sale of the goods. The contractual benefit of which the victim of the breach of contract had been deprived by the breach would not have extended beyond the date of the frustrating event. So on what principled basis could the victim claim compensation attributable to a loss of contractual benefit after that date? Any rule that required damages attributable to that period to be paid would be inconsistent with the overriding compensatory principle on which awards of contractual damages ought to be based.

The arguments of the Owners offend the compensatory principle. They are seeking compensation exceeding the value of the contractual benefits of which they were deprived. Their case requires the assessor to speculate about what might happen over the period 17 December 2001 to 6 December 2005 regarding the occurrence of a clause 33 event and to shut his eyes to the actual happening of a clause 33 event in March 2003. The argued justification for thus offending the compensatory principle is that priority should be given to the so-called principle of certainty. My Lords there is, in my opinion, no such principle. Certainty is a desideratum and a very important one, particularly in commercial contracts. But it is not a principle and must give way to principle. Otherwise incoherence of principle is the likely result. The achievement of certainty in relation to commercial contracts depends, I would suggest, on firm and settled principles of the law of contract rather than on the tailoring of principle in order to frustrate tactics of delay to which many litigants in many areas of litigation are wont to resort. Be that as it may, the compensatory principle that must underlie awards of contractual damages is, in my opinion, clear and requires the appeal in the case to be dismissed. I wish also to express my agreement with the reasons given by my noble and learned friends Lord Carswell and Lord Brown of Eaton-under-Heywood for coming to the same conclusion.

Note

It is difficult to see how the majority judgement will do anything other than encourage parties to a contract to prolong settlement discussions or arbitration proceedings in the hope that some supervening event might come along to minimise the flow of damages. Lord Carswell said that this danger can be averted by courts and arbitrators who have 'the ability to prevent such abuse if application is made to them to proceed with dispatch' (paragraph 67). How realistic is this response?

B. So-called 'Lost Volume Sales' Cases

W. L. Thompson Ltd *v* Robinson (Gunmakers) Ltd [1955] Ch. 177

The defendant company refused to accept delivery of a Vanguard motor car which they had contracted to buy from the plaintiffs, who were dealers in motor cars. The Vanguard motor car was readily available and the retail selling price was fixed by the manufacturers.

The plaintiffs mitigated their damage by returning the vehicle to their suppliers, who took it back, but the plaintiffs contended that they were nevertheless entitled to damages amounting to £61, the loss of profit on the repudiated sale. The defendants, relying on s. 50 (3) of the Sale of Goods Act 1893, contended that the plaintiffs' loss was only nominal:

Upjohn J. held for the plaintiffs:

Apart altogether from authority and statute it would seem to me on the facts which I have to consider to be quite plain that the plaintiffs' loss in this case is the loss of their bargain. They have sold one Vanguard less than they otherwise would. The plaintiffs, as the defendants must have known, are in business as dealers in motor cars and make their profit in buying and selling motor cars, and what they have lost is their profit on the sale of this Vanguard. There is no authority exactly in point in this country, although it seems to me that the principle to be applied is a clear one. It is to be found in In re Vic Mill Ltd.[1]

---

[1]. [1913] 1 Ch. 465.

C. EMPLOYMENT CONTRACTS CONCERNING LIABILITY IN CONTRACT AND TORT AND QUANTUM OF DAMAGES

Carey v Independent Newspapers (Ireland) Ltd (HC) (2005) 15 ELR 45

The plaintiff who had left her employment with *Ireland on Sunday* to become a political correspondent of the *Evening Herald* was summarily dismissed from her employment without cause. A fuller statement of the facts is at p. 303. In an action for damages she established liability via wrongful dismissal, breach of contractual warranty, liability in tort for misrepresentation by silence, and negligent misstatement. Gilligan J. addressed the issue of the basis of assessing damages where concurrent liabilities are established in contract and tort.

Gilligan J.:

An action for wrongful dismissal in an action for breach of contract: in essence, the breach complained of in such an action is that the plaintiff's employment has not been terminated in accordance with his/her contract or, where no such procedures exist, that the contract has not been terminated in accordance with fair procedures and the common law. The normal measure of damages in a wrongful dismissal action is the amount of salary the employee would have earned had he/she been allowed to remain working for the balance of his contract, or for the period for which notice of termination should have been given in accordance with the contract. The same principle applies where no notice period as such has been incorporated into the contract: in such cases the common law implies a term into the contract that the employee may only be dismissed on giving reasonable notice and damages will be confined to the measure of the salary the plaintiff would have earned for the period of notice found reasonable in all the circumstances by the court. This has been the rule since *Addis v Gramophone Co. Ltd* [1909] AC 488.

However, the plaintiff has also made separate claims for breach of warranty and/or negligent misrepresentation/misstatement. The basis of awarding damages in these two contexts differs considerably from the attenuated scope of awarding damages in wrongful dismissal claims *per se* and is potentially far more remunerative: accordingly; it is necessary to outline the basis upon which the court will award damages in these contexts in some detail.

The common law courts have drawn a firm distinction between contract and tort in terms of awarding the damages upon a finding of liability.

In tort, the plaintiff is entitled to be put in the same position, as far as money can do so, as he would have been in had the tort not been committed. This has been established since *Livingstone v Rawyards Coal Co.* (1880) 5 App. Cas. 25 at 39, per Lord Blackburn. This principle is the basis of awarding damages in tort in Irish law: subject to the application of the test of remoteness of damages laid down in *Hadley v Baxendale*, the general purpose of an award of damages in a tort claim is to place the plaintiff in the same position as they had been before the commission of the tort in question: damages cannot be awarded for loss of bargain. In *Foley v Thermocement Products Ltd* (1954) 90 ILTR 92 at 98, the Supreme Court referred to *restitutio in integrum* as 'the underlying principle by which courts are guided in awarding damages.'

In contract, however, the compensatable wrong consists not in the making but in the breach of the contract and accordingly the plaintiff is entitled to be placed in the position he would have been had the contract been performed. In other words, the plaintiff is entitled to recover damages for loss of bargain.

Experience has shown that the distinction between the principles upon which contract damages and tort damages are awarded outlined above tends to blur in cases involving misrepresentations of fact inducing entrance into contractual relations, which is the type of case at issue in the present proceedings: in such cases there is inevitable scope for pleading that the representation was a term of the contract entered into and that the misrepresentation leading to the non-observance of contractual obligations is an actionable tort. Where a plaintiff has been induced to enter into a contract by a misrepresentation of fact on the part of a defendant or his agent, if the representation forms part of the concluded contract (whether the representation constitutes a condition or a warranty is immaterial in this context), the plaintiff may sue for breach of contract and loss of bargain, which entitles the plaintiff to be placed in the same position as he/she would have been had the representation of fact been true and obligations consequent upon the representation been performed by the defendant. However, if the representation is not a term of the contract, there is by definition no breach of contract and the plaintiff's only remedy will lie in tort: the plaintiff will have a remedy in deceit where the misrepresentation is fraudulently made, and there will be a remedy in negligent misrepresentation where the misrepresentation was made negligently in the context of a duty of care owed by the representor to the plaintiff.

This vital distinction is established in Irish law. O'Hanlon J. contrasted the basis upon which damages for misrepresentation in tort are awarded and the basis upon which damages for breach of warranty are awarded in *McAnarney v Hanrahan* [1993] 3 IR 492 at 498 as follows:

> What now falls for consideration is the correct way in which damages should be assessed in a case of negligent misrepresentation. Damages in such cases are assessed by analogy with claims for damages for deceit. Where damages are claimed for fraudulent misrepresentation then they are assessed so as to put the plaintiff in the position he would have been in if the representation had not been made to him. This is different to the case where damages are being assessed on the basis that the warranty was true. So, in the case of a sale of shares induced by fraudulent misrepresentation the normal measure of damages is the purchase price of the shares less their actual value at the time of acquisition (see McGregor, *Damages*, 15th ed., paras. 17.18, 17.24 and 19.39) and in a case like the present one, where a plaintiff has been induced to enter into a contract for the purchase of land by a misrepresentation negligently made, the normal measure of damages is the price paid for the land less its actual value at the time of sale.

O'Hanlon J. followed his approach in *McAnarney v Hanrahan* in *Donnellan v Dungoyne Ltd* [1995] 1 ILRM 388.

In this case, the plaintiff has made claims for breach of contract (at paragraph 5 of her Statement of Claim) and negligent misrepresentation (at paragraph 6 of her Statement of Claim). Applying the analysis above, if the plaintiff is entitled to succeed in her claim for negligent misrepresentation, the damages she is entitled to will be assessed on the assumption that she would not have left her position as political correspondent with *Ireland on Sunday* but for the misrepresentation that she would be permitted to work from home from 7 a.m. until the first edition deadline and thereafter would work from the Dáil for the remainder of the working day. In short, the plaintiff will not be entitled to damages based on the remuneration she would have earned had her contractual obligations with the *Evening Herald* been met.

If it is found that the representation with which the plaintiff takes most significant issue, i.e. that she would be allowed to work from home until the first edition deadline, is a term of the contract entered into by her and the defendant and that such term has been breached, the plaintiff will be entitled to damages awarded on the basis that the defendant would have observed the contract: in other words, the plaintiff will be entitled to damages based on the net pay she would have earned had the defendant allowed her to remain in her position with the *Evening Herald*. . . .

Approaching the matter from first principles, the boundaries of contract and tort actions suggest that there is no conceptual objection to imposing liability in both contract and tort provided the facts as found meet the criteria of liability of the type of tort and contract action taken. Going back to first principles, the obvious condition precedent to an action for breach of contract is the existence of a contractual obligation: an action in tort has never required a contractual relationship between the parties, although the circumstances of a contractual obligation may give rise to a duty of care in tort over and above the normal 'duty of care' (so to speak) to observe the terms of the agreement in the contractual context. To take the causes of action in tort and contract at issue in the present proceedings, it is not a requirement of an action for negligent misrepresentation that the parties enter into the contract, even if this is the effect of the representation. Secondly—again going back to the first principles—in order to bring an action for negligent misrepresentation, it must be proved that the party making the representation owed a duty of care to the representee (*Hedley Byrne v Heller* [1964] AC 465: see the first instance decision of *O'Donnell v Truck and Machinery Sales* [1997] 1 ILRM 466 at 473, per Moriarty J. His decision was overturned on the facts by the Supreme Court but the court did not question Moriarty J.'s interpretation of the law.) For an action for breach of warranty, the existence of the warranty as a contractual obligation is the only condition precedent to the finding of a compensatable breach: no duty of care of the standard required in tort is required.

The Irish courts have accepted that a defendant may be liable in both contract and tort: the law does not require a plaintiff to elect between the remedies and he may plead either or both. In *Kennedy v Allied Irish Banks plc* [1998] 2 IR 48 at p. 56 Hamilton C.J. stated:

> . . . where a duty of care exists, whether such duty is tortious or created by contract, the claimant is entitled to take advantage of the remedy which is most advantageous to him subject only to ascertaining whether the tortious duty is so inconsistent with the applicable contract that, in accordance with ordinary principle the parties must be taken to have agreed that the tortious remedy is to be limited or excluded. . . .

Note

Gilligan J. found that the plaintiff had been able to establish that it was a fundamental term of her contract of employment that she be able to work from home in the mornings and that the defendants were liable for breach of warranty. Also, the editor was held to have been in breach of his duty of care to avoid making a negligent misrepresentation and that the editor's failure to disclose that these working arrangements did not find favour with other senior managers prevented the plaintiff from fully appreciating her employment position. Gilligan J. went on:

> My findings bring about a situation where I have to assess damages both for breach of warranty and for negligent misrepresentation. I am satisfied following the judgment of Hamilton C.J. in *Kennedy v Allied Irish Banks plc* [1998] 2 IR 48 at p. 56, that the claimant in these proceedings is entitled to take advantage of the remedy which is most advantageous to her, subject only to ascertaining whether the tortious duty is so inconsistent with the applicable contract that in accordance with ordinary principles the parties must be taken to have agreed that the tortious remedy is to be limited or excluded. In the particular circumstances of this case I am satisfied that the plaintiff is entitled to seek damages for concurrent remedies both in respect of breach of warranty and negligent misrepresentation.
>
> I am further satisfied following the decision of O'Hanlon J. in *McAnarney v Hanrahan* [1993] 3 IR at 498 that damages to which the plaintiff is entitled for negligent misrepresentation are to be assessed on the basis that the plaintiff would not have left her position as political correspondent with *Ireland on Sunday* but for the misrepresentation and these damages will be based on the plaintiff's net loss of earnings and dependent on the remuneration she would have earned if she had remained on with *Ireland on Sunday*.
>
> Insofar as the plaintiff is entitled to damages for breach of warranty, she is entitled to damages based on net loss of earnings and dependent on the remuneration she would have earned had she remained on in her position at the *Evening Herald*.
>
> In assessing the appropriate level of damages for negligent misrepresentation, and breach of warranty I conclude that the appropriate measure is two years' net loss of earnings less the net remuneration as earned by the plaintiff from alternative sources during this period.
>
> Insofar as there is an element of dispute as regards the appropriate taxation levels relating to the plaintiff's earnings I propose to rely on the figures as produced by Mr Russell because from the taxation perspective he has been for a number of years the plaintiff's accountant and has been responsible for her tax returns and I consider it probable that he is more familiar with the taxation situation than the person who produced the figures on behalf of the defendants.
>
> Furthermore while I accept that on or about the 24th day of March 2000 the plaintiff's salary was reduced by the exclusion of the fifth day due to the intervention of the trade union the plaintiff's contract with the defendants was for a salary of IR£45,000 and having regard to the unusual circumstances that brought about the change I propose for the purpose of assessing damages herein to disregard that change of circumstances and to rely on the original contract.
>
> The plaintiff is entitled to six months' notice of termination of her employment with the *Evening Herald* or, alternatively, six months' net pay in lieu thereof, which I calculate to be a sum of €18,637.06.
>
> In respect of the plaintiff's claim for negligent misrepresentation, I assess damages in the sum of €33,227.61 being two years' net loss of earnings from the plaintiff's position with *Ireland on Sunday* less remuneration derived from alternative sources.
>
> In respect of the plaintiff's claim for damages for breach of warranty, I assess damages in the sum of €52,266.00 being two years' net loss of earnings from the plaintiff's position with the *Evening Herald* less remuneration derived from alternative sources.
>
> Accordingly, while the plaintiff is entitled to succeed in her claim as against the defendants under a number of headings, she is not entitled to recover damages

under all of the headings because the claim arises out of the same set of circumstances and cause of action. The plaintiff is only entitled to recover damages under one heading of claim but she is entitled to recover damages from her optimum position which in the particular circumstances is in respect of her claim for breach of warranty and accordingly I award the plaintiff €52,266.00 damages.

SECTION THREE—NON-COMPENSATORY DAMAGES

Exemplary Damages

In *Rookes v Barnard* [1964] 2 WLR 269 the House of Lords indicated that an award of damages should not in general be utilised to punish a wrongdoer. The Supreme Court in subsequent cases has endorsed *Rookes v Barnard*.

Garvey v Ireland An Taoiseach and Others (HC) 19 December 1980, unrep.

McWilliam J.:

The plaintiff became a member of the Garda Siochana in 1939 and rose through the ranks until he was appointed Commissioner of the force on 1 September 1975. He then had the expectation of continuing as Commissioner until his retirement in February 1980. The government purported to remove him from office on 19 January 1978. It has been held by the Supreme Court that the circumstances of his purported removal from office, with which I am not now concerned, were such that his appointment was not validly terminated.

He resigned his position in May 1979, having then only about nine months to go before reaching the retiring age. Although he was deprived of all his functions and ceased to have any authority in the force, it is accepted by the defendants that he was entitled to his salary as Commissioner from 20 January 1978, until 15 May 1979, and the sum of £11,309, the accumulated arrears of salary, was paid to him on 23 May 1979, in respect of this period.

The matter comes before me now to decide whether the plaintiff is entitled to damages for his wrongful removal from office and, if so, what is the measure of those damages.

Damages appear to me to be conveniently grouped under three headings: (1) Special damage, which includes all pecuniary loss caused by a wrongful act. (2) General damages, which, where appropriate include recompense for such things as physical suffering, injury to reputation, consequential loss, etc. (3) Exemplary damages, which may, in certain circumstances, be awarded for the aggravated nature of the wrongful act. The plaintiff makes his claim under each head.

Although the appointment of the plaintiff as Commissioner did not create the relationship of master and servant between the government and the plaintiff, it seems to me that the offer and acceptance of the appointment must have been accompanied by some form of implied agreement that the plaintiff would receive pay in accordance with the provisions of s. 12 of the Police Forces Amalgamation Act 1925, for so long as he should hold his appointment. The relevant orders made under this section have not been opened to me but it appears to be accepted that the plaintiff was entitled to be paid fortnightly. After his purported removal from office the plaintiff was not paid anything until 23 May 1979. It seems to me that the plaintiff did suffer loss by not receiving his salary at the proper times because either he had to borrow money at interest to replace his salary or he was deprived of the opportunity of using the money by investment or otherwise so as to make a profit. The only evidence as to this was given by an accountant who gave evidence on behalf of the plaintiff and calculated this loss at the sum of £1,298.11. I am of opinion that the plaintiff is entitled to recover this sum under this heading.

Under the second heading, the plaintiff claims general damages for loss of job satisfaction, loss of opportunity for preparing for his retirement, invasion of privacy due to the public interest in his removal from office, injury to his health and general distress aggravated by the effect the events had upon his family.

The case of *Cox v Phillips Industries Ltd* [1976] 1 WLR 638 is very strongly relied upon on behalf of the plaintiff. In this case it was held that vexation, frustration and distress caused by being relegated to a position of lesser responsibility in his firm in breach of his contract of employment which led to a plaintiff's ill-health was a matter which could be compensated in damages where the effects of the wrongful conduct by the employers must have been within the contemplation of the parties.

The case of *Addis v Gramophone Co. Ltd* [1909] AC 488 was equally strongly relied upon on behalf of the defendants. This case was somewhat similar to the present in that the plaintiff was given six months notice but was not permitted to discharge his duties as manager during that period. Lord Loreburn said, at 490, 'To my mind it signifies nothing in the present case whether the claim is to be treated as for wrongful dismissal or not. In any case there was a breach of contract in not allowing the plaintiff to discharge his duties as manager, and the damages are exactly the same in either view.' At 491 he said 'If there be a dismissal without notice the employer must pay an indemnity; but that indemnity cannot include compensation either for the injured feelings of the servant, or for the loss he may sustain from the fact that his having been dismissed itself makes it more difficult to obtain employment.' It is right to point out that in the *Addis* case, no question of a breakdown in health was alleged and the distinction drawn in the judgments was between what I have called special damage and exemplary damages. It was held that a claim for exemplary damages could not be sustained but it was emphasised that, where a claim is made for breach of contract whether of a contract of employment or otherwise, circumstances of malice, fraud, defamation or violence which might sustain an action of tort cannot be taken into consideration.

I accept the decision in this case. Accordingly, unless some injury was occasioned to the plaintiff as a result of the wrongful removal from office of the plaintiff which could reasonably have been foreseen by the defendants, I am of opinion that he is not entitled to any general damages under this heading. In this connection I am not satisfied that there was any injury to the health of the plaintiff in the normally accepted sense. In addition all the other matters of which he complains would have been applicable to a greater or lesser extent had he been lawfully removed from office and cannot be solely attributable to the unlawful nature of his removal.

Finally, the plaintiff claims to be entitled to exemplary damages and the statement of Lord Devlin in *Rookes v Barnard* [1964] 2 WLR 269 at 328 is relied upon. This statement is 'that there are certain categories of cases in which an award of exemplary damages can serve a useful purpose in vindicating the strength of the law and thus affording a practical justification for admitting into the civil law a principle which logically ought to belong to the criminal. The first category is oppressive, arbitrary or unconstitutional action by the servants of government.' As that case was not dealing with actions by servants of government, this statement was not elaborated. It was, however, very fully discussed in the case of *Broome v Cassell & Co.* [1972] 2 WLR 645 and

I am satisfied from the judgments in that case that I should award what I have described as exemplary damages to the plaintiff but that these must be related to the injury which the plaintiff has suffered by reason of the arbitrary and oppressive conduct of the government. Having regard to my view that similar injury would, to a large extent, have been sustained by the plaintiff had he been lawfully removed from office I will award £500 on this part of the claim.

Note

In *Conway v* INTO [1991] ILRM 497 the Supreme Court ruled that exemplary and punitive damages are to be considered as the same thing. Such damages are properly awardable in the case of a breach of a constitutional right. However, such damages are not automatically awarded. The relationship between various civil law causes of action and exemplary damages has recently been considered by the English Court of Appeal (see [1993] 1 All ER 609). Law Commission Working Paper No. 132 (1993) has canvassed extensive reform of the law relating to exemplary damages in England. The Law Reform Commission in a Consultation Paper on Aggravated, Exemplary and Restitutionary Damages (LRC, April 1998) undertook a helpful review of relevant case-law and took the provisional view that exemplary damages should not be extended into contract. This conclusion was adopted in the Final Report (LRC 60–2000).

R. Clark 'Unjust enrichment as a non-compensatory principle justifying the award of damages' (1978) 29 NILQ 129

Damages and Unjust Enrichment

As is well known the House of Lords in *Rookes v Barnard*[1] considered those situations in which the award of punitive or exemplary damages may be permissible as a means of punishing a wrongdoer or depriving him of any pecuniary advantage he may obtain from his misconduct. Lord Devlin outlined three such categories: firstly, instances of arbitrary or unconstitutional action by servants of the government; secondly, instances where the defendant has calculated that a profit he may make by an act of wrongdoing will exceed the compensation payable to any person injured by that unlawful act; and thirdly, where statutory authority exists for such an award. The Law Lords asserted that apart from such cases damages should be assessed on compensatory principles. This cardinal principle of law is necessary lest the fundamental distinction between the functions of the criminal and civil law becomes confused.

In a recent decision the President of the Irish High Court, Mr Justice Finlay, has indicated that those guidelines are not authoritative within the Republic of Ireland. While the present writer concedes that the fact that English precedents run contrary to such a stance is not sufficient reason to doubt the soundness of Mr Justice Finlay's reasoning in this case, it is submitted that general aspects of the judgment in *Hickey and Co. Ltd v Roches Stores (Dublin) Ltd*[2] are difficult to reconcile with both legal principle and current authority.

The defendants, Roches Stores (Dublin) Ltd, owned a large drapery shop in Dublin and were in association with other Roches Stores in Limerick and Cork. In 1969 they entered into an agreement with Hickeys, a drapery company, under the terms of which Hickeys were to be allowed to sell fashion fabrics in the defendant company's Dublin store. The agreement provided certain procedures to be applicable when either party sought to terminate it. If either party terminated with good cause no compensation was to be payable. However, where one party unilaterally terminated the agreement, whilst it was functioning satisfactorily, compensation was to be payable by the party terminating. A proviso to the clause gave Roches Stores in such a situation the power to terminate the agreement and avoid the obligation to pay compensation, provided they tendered six months' notice to Hickeys and gave an undertaking that Roches Stores would not sell fashion fabrics for a further period of twelve months following expiry of that notice.

Although the commercial venture was successful and profitable to both parties, Roches Stores, some two years later, terminated the agreement in circumstances which an arbitrator later found to be unjustifiable. Further, the notice given, less than two months, clearly did not satisfy the proviso therefore rendering it incumbent upon Roches Stores to pay compensation for termination. More seriously, perhaps, Roches Stores began immediately to sell fashion fabrics in all three of their stores. The Dublin store was thus in direct competition with Hickeys who had left the Dublin premises and found an alternative location nearby.

The sole issue before Finlay P. in the High Court related to the principles that were to apply in calculating the damages payable by Roches to Hickeys. Roches Stores conceded that they were in breach of the obligation to give six months' notice of intention to terminate, and that they had failed to give an undertaking not to sell fashion fabrics for a further twelve months but submitted that damages were to be estimated solely by reference to profits Hickeys would have made had the contract not been terminated in breach of the agreed procedure and to any loss to Hickeys caused by Roches Stores competing in fashion drapery until the date upon which the restraint covenant, had notice been given, would have expired.

Hickeys, however, contended that they were entitled to recover damages not simply for their own loss of profit but were also to be awarded the value of the business carried on by Roches Stores during the post-breach period. In addition, a sum in accordance with the goodwill built up by Roches Stores, with the assistance of the plaintiffs, was to be recoverable. In short, Hickeys were contending that two factors other than their own economic loss were relevant: the profits made by the wrongdoer subsequent to breach that were only possible because of his breach and also the benefits accruing to the defendants from performance by the plaintiffs. The task of Finlay P. was to determine which, if either, of these rival modes of assessment was to be applicable and, in particular, whether the conduct of a party in breach and the benefits he obtains from the contract broken are relevant in assessing damages. Put in these terms the judgment of Finlay P. is of great importance for Irish commercial lawyers and of interest in other jurisdictions.

After examining the facts Finlay P. found that the defendants had broken the agreement because of a decision taken at executive level that the defendants should develop their own retail business in fashion drapery. Finlay P. advanced the following propositions that were to determine the issues before him.

Firstly, 'assessment of damages in tort and in breach of contract should have as its purpose the putting back of the injured party, insofar as money can do so, to the position in which he would have been had the wrong not been committed.' With the greatest respect to the learned judge, such a proposition seems inaccurate. The courts have long recognised that damages in contract have a different function, that is, to put the party in the position he would have been in but for the breach, rather than to restore him to the *status quo ante*, which is the function of an award of damages in tort. These alternative theoretical starting points can have important practical consequences. Finlay P. continued: 'There are exceptions both in cases of tort and in cases of breach of contract some of which may be different for each particular cause of action and some of which are the same.'

However, 'Where a wrongdoer calculated and intended by his wrongdoing to achieve and has in that way acted *male fide* then irrespective of whether the form of his wrongdoing constitutes a tort or a breach of contract the court should, in assessing damages, look not only at the loss suffered by the injured party but also to the profit or gain unjustly or wrongfully obtained by the wrongdoer.'

If, after considering the quantum of the damages calculated by reference to the innocent party's loss, the wrongdoer would still obtain a profit then damages should be assessed so as to deprive him of that profit. On the facts before him Finlay P. was unable to apply the principle outlined above because no allegation of *mala fides* had been made against the defendants. This suggests that *mala fides* should be expressly pleaded for it is clear that Roches deliberately acted in bad faith by terminating the agreement and therefore would have satisfied such a test.

Nevertheless, the court did not accept the defendants' submissions on the extent of their liability. An additional head of damage, the loss the plaintiffs must have suffered because of the competition presented by the defendants operating a business which the plaintiffs had helped develop, was to be considered and compensated for by an award of aggravated damages. This dictum of Finlay P. is not (as would appear at first sight) an application of Lord Devlin's second category mentioned at the beginning of this article. Lord Devlin indicated that exemplary damages are the result of a calculation on the part of the wrongdoer that he will make a profit in excess of compensation payable to the plaintiff. Finlay P.'s judgment is based upon a wider calculation by the wrongdoer. The difference between the two approaches can be illustrated by reference to a situation where a party to a contract calculates that he will profit by breaking an existing contract with A and negotiating a similar contract with B. Falling market prices may render this an attractive economic proposition.

If the anticipated profit does not materialise, according to Finlay P., non-compensatory damages are irrecoverable and, presumably, damages in excess of any profit made cannot be awarded. Under Lord Devlin's second category (assuming that such a calculation is permissible in an action in contract) exemplary damages are recoverable because the essential issue is the calculation made at the time of breach rather than profits actually made. It, therefore, appears that in *Hickey* the assessment is based upon principles of unjust enrichment rather than exemplary or punitive damages, which seems curious given that *Rookes v Barnard*, heavily relied on by Finlay P., is an authority on the award of punitive or exemplary damages in tort.

Finlay P. acknowledged that he was well aware that he was extending non-compensatory principles of assessment into areas of contract when the scope of such factors in the law of tort is uncertain within the Irish Republic. This principle of unjust enrichment was immediately qualified by the learned judge, reflecting the essential difference between contract and tort, that is, the possibility of contractual obligations being created and limited by agreement. In a passage not free from ambiguity he stated that: '. . . where an action lies in contract only, the necessity to create certainty as to the obligations which may arise from the contract and from breach thereof make it necessary to confine, in cases where the element of *male fides* has not occurred, damages to the loss suffered by the injured party even though such restriction may result in a profit to the wrongdoer.'

Finlay P. left open the possibility that the parties to a contract may covenant to the effect that if one breaches the contract damages are to be assessed by reference to both the loss of the injured party and the profits made by the other. This, of course, is simply another application of the principle of freedom of contract. Nevertheless, the possibility of contracting parties drafting such a clause seems to be both unlikely and fraught with difficulty; may not a court faced with such a provision strike it down as a penalty clause, for, by definition, such a term would not be a genuine pre-estimate of the loss suffered by one party.

A further difficulty caused by the conceptual differences between the law of torts and contract, may attach to the converse position to that considered by the court. How would a court deal with the situation where one party wilfully breaks a contract because he calculates that he may profit from such a breach and that contract contains a clause which, on its true construction, limits the damages that are to be recoverable even in cases where one party deliberately and cynically breaks the agreement? Would a substantive rule of law apply so as to defeat such a clause? The courts would be faced with the clear intent of the parties and to award damages greater than those expressly provided for would once again flout freedom of contract as a means of allocating risk between parties contracting at arm's length.

The decision in *Hickey* itself indicates that the principles advanced therein will be largely superfluous. Exemplary damages and the principle of unjust enrichment may well be necessary in limited instances in order to display to a *tortfeasor* that his conduct is socially unacceptable. Where, however, an action in contract lies and the loss is entirely economic—a head of damage not extensively covered in tort—then ordinary principles of assessment may be able to produce a satisfactory result. In most situations (and the eventual result in the *Hickey* case bears this out) a breach of contract will have some effect upon the other contracting party. By concentrating on assessing the loss suffered by the innocent party and awarding aggravated damages accordingly, the plaintiff will be compensated and the defendant forced to disgorge his ill-gotten gains without having to extend what amount to quasi-criminal remedies into the law of contract.

[1.] [1964] AC 1129.   [2.] (HC) 14 July 1976, unrep.

Note

There are no Irish cases in which the court has actually applied this principle of assessment. the most recent case in which the *Hickey* decision was considered is *Vavasour v O'Reilly and Windsor Motors Ltd.* [2005] IEHC 16. The plaintiff was party to a motor vehicle franchise agreement that was to run for three years, the plaintiff having an option to extend his participation in the venture for a further year. Approximately fifteen months into the agreement the other parties excluded the plaintiff from participating in the franchise. The plaintiff was held entitled to fifty per cent of the profits denied to him for the four-year period and he was awarded damages for loss of opportunity to participate in a profit earning venture for the rest of the period in which the agreement operated (with a forty per cent discount in recognition of the 'significant risk' that the plaintiff may not have continued to participate in the venture after year four, applying *Philip v Ryan* [2004] IESC 105). *Vavasour* also advanced a claim to damages under *Hickey*, Clarke J. clearly distinguishing *Hickey* damages as being 'additional' damages, as distinct from compensatory damages. After noting that the arrangement between the parties involved a 50/50 division of profits and that the defendant O'Reilly had been found liable in damages, Clarke J. held the *Hickey* case had no application:

It is also necessary for me to deal with the contention made by the plaintiff that he should be entitled to additional damages based upon what he contends were the *mala fides* of the defendants . . . In that regard he referred me to *Hickey v Roches Stores*, an unreported judgment of Finlay P. delivered on 14 July 1976. That case is concerned with the circumstances in which it may be appropriate to approach the question of damages on the basis of calculating the gain which the wrongdoer made rather than the loss suffered by the plaintiff. It is obviously only relevant in cases where there is a difference between those two sums such that the wrongdoer gains more by his breach than the plaintiff has actually suffered by the wrongdoing. On the facts of this case it does not seem to me that that principle has any relevance. The agreement between the parties (which I have held has been breached by Mr O'Reilly) was that Mr O'Reilly would procure that 50% of the profits attributable to the franchise should be paid to the plaintiff. What Mr O'Reilly gained by his breach was, therefore, exactly the same as the plaintiff lost, i.e. 50% of the net profits. While there may be some debate between the parties as to how those profits should be calculated (to which I will return), nonetheless in principle, and on the facts of this case, there does not appear to be any difference between the gain achieved by the breach and the loss suffered as a result therefrom.

The English Courts have in the meantime been pushing the boundaries which traditionally limit the award of damages to the compensatory principle. *Hickey* speaks of damages being awarded where a defendant has acted *mala fides*, in bad faith, whereas English courts have concentrated on 'gain-based' awards, seeking to require a defendant to disgorge the ill-gotten gains secured by tortious conduct or breach of contract or a restrictive covenant. While the equitable remedy of an account of profits has been recognised as a remedy for breach of confidence, or infringement of other kinds of personal property right (often due to a statute making an account of profits available to a plaintiff, e.g. Trade Marks Act 1996, s. 18(2)), the availability of such reliefs arising out of a breach of contract is less well established. In cases where a restrictive covenant relating to land, or an intellectual property right, has been infringed, the plaintiff being unable to establish economic loss, the English courts in a long line of cases have awarded damages based upon the argument that the plaintiff is entitled to the amount the plaintiff would have charged in order to licence the defendant to utilise the property, even though, on the facts, no licence would have been granted: *Wrotham Park Estate Co. Ltd v Parkside Homes Ltd* [1974] IWLR 798. The English Courts engaged in a long and ultimately futile exercise in categorising such awards as being compensatory or gains-based. In *Attorney General v Blake* [2001] 1 AC 268 the House of Lords affirmed the view that *Wrotham Park* damages were essentially compensatory, disapproving of the contrary view expressed in *Surrey County Council v Bredero Homes Ltd* [1993] 1 WLR 1361.

While many of these cases involve the question whether damages may be awarded in addition to, or in lieu of injunctive relief, there is a strong line of authority that holds that not only may damages be awarded by reference to the benefit gained by the wrongdoer, the law may recognise that in exceptional cases 'an account of profits may be the most appropriate remedy for breach of contract': Lord Nicholls in *Attorney General v Blake* [2001] 1 AC 268 at 284–5; Chadwick L.J. in WWF – *World Wide Fund for Nature v World Wrestling Federation Entertainment Inc.* [2007] EWCA Civ 286. Indeed, Chadwick L.J. in this later case stated *obiter* that *Wrotham Park* damages should be available even where an injunction is neither sought nor obtainable, on the basis that *Wrotham Park* damages are available at common law and not under Lord Cairns' Act.

While the Report of the Law Reform Commission, in its 2000 Report *Aggravated, Exemplary and Restitutionary Damages* (LRC 60) now looks rather dated in the light of subsequent English developments, it should be noted that the Law Reform Commission indicated that damages for equitable wrongs should be available on compensatory principles (and even exemplary damages) if case-law from other jurisdictions were followed (para. 4.01), and that the Law Reform Commission approved of the award of restitutionary damages under *Hickey*, suggesting that the development of this area should be left to the common law (para. 6.48).

SECTION FOUR—REMOTENESS OF DAMAGE

Hadley v Baxendale (1854) 9 Ex 341

The plaintiffs were millers in the city of Gloucester. The crank shaft of the steam engine that operated the mill broke and the plaintiffs engaged the defendants to transport the broken shaft to Greenwich to have a replacement made. However, the defendants negligently failed to deliver the shaft expeditiously and the mill was stopped for five days more than would have been the case if delivery had taken place in accordance with the contract.

One crucial issue of fact that was resolved at the trial was whether the plaintiffs had told the defendants that the mill had ceased to function because of the broken crank shaft. The headnote states that before Crampton J. the plaintiffs proved that their employee had told the defendants that the mill was stopped. The jury awarded damages of £50. The defendants appealed and while a new trial was ordered Alderson B. indicated the principles that should govern remoteness of damages in contract.

Alderson B.:
. . .

Now we think the proper rule in such a case as the present is this: Where two parties have made a contract which one of them has broken, the damages which the other party ought to receive in respect of such breach of contract should be such as may fairly and reasonably be considered either arising naturally, i.e. according to the usual course of things, from such breach of contract itself, or such as may reasonably be supposed to have been in the contemplation of both parties, at the time they made the contract, as the probable result of the breach of it. Now, if the special circumstances under which the contract was actually made were communicated by the plaintiffs to the defendants, and thus known to both parties, the damages resulting from the breach of such a contract, which they would reasonably contemplate, would be the amount of injury which would ordinarily follow from a breach of contract under these special circumstances so known and communicated. But, on the other hand, if these special circumstances were wholly unknown to the party breaking the contract, he, at the most, could only be supposed to have had in his contemplation the amount of injury which would arise generally, and in the great multitude of cases not affected by any special circumstances, from such a breach of contract. For, had the special circumstances been known, the parties might have specially provided for the breach of contract by special terms as to the damages in that case; and of this advantage it would be very unjust to deprive them. Now the above principles are those by which we think the jury ought to be guided in estimating the damages arising out of any breach of contract. It is said, that other cases such as breaches of contract in the non-payment of money, or in the not making a good title to land, are to be treated as exceptions from this, and as governed by a conventional rule. But as, in such cases, both parties must be supposed to be cognisant of that well known rule, these cases may, we think, be more properly classed under the rule above enunciated as to cases under known special circumstances, because there both parties may reasonably be presumed to contemplate the estimation of the amount of damages according to the conventional rule. Now, in the present case, if we are to apply the principles above laid down, we find that the only circumstances here communicated by the plaintiffs to the defendants at the time the contract was made, were, that the article to be carried was the broken shaft of a mill, and that the plaintiffs were the millers of that mill. But how do these circumstances shew reasonably that the profits of the mill must be stopped by an unreasonable delay in the delivery of the broken shaft by the carrier to the third person? Suppose the plaintiffs had another shaft in their possession put up or putting up at the time, and that they only wished to send back the broken shaft to the engineer who made it; it is clear that this would be quite consistent with the above circumstances, and yet the unreasonable delay in the delivery would have no effect upon the intermediate profits of the mill. Or, again, suppose that, at the time of the delivery to the carrier, the machinery of the mill had been in other respects defective, then, also, the same results would follow. Here it is true that the shaft was actually sent back to serve as a model for a new one, and that the want of a new one was the only cause of the stoppage of the mill, and that the loss of profits really arose from not sending down the new shaft in proper time, and that this arose from the delay in delivering the broken one to serve as a model. But it is obvious that, in the great multitude of cases of millers sending off broken shafts to third persons by a carrier under ordinary circumstances, such consequences would not, in all probability, have occurred; and these special circumstances were here never communicated by the plaintiffs to the defendants. It follows, therefore, that the loss of profits here cannot reasonably be considered such a consequence of the breach of contract as could have been fairly and reasonably contemplated by both the parties when they made this contract. For such loss would neither have flowed naturally from the breach of this contract in the great multitude of such cases occurring under ordinary circumstances, nor were the special circumstances, which, perhaps, would have made it a reasonable and natural consequence of such breach of contract, communicated to or known by the defendants. The judge ought, therefore, to have told the jury, that, upon the facts then before them, they ought not to take the loss of profits into consideration at all in estimating the damages. There must therefore be a new trial in this case.

Note

On the factual issue of whether the stoppage of the mill had been communicated see *Danzig* (1975) 4 JLS 249 and the judgment of the Court of Appeal in *Victoria Laundry (Windsor) Ltd v Newman Industries Ltd* [1949] 2 KB 528 (see p. 1053 below).

The application of Hadley v Baxendale

A. The first limb of the Remoteness Test

Wilson *v* Dunville (1879) 6 LR (Ir.) 210

Palles C.B.:

This is an action for damages for breach of a contract for the sale of distillery grains. We held on a former argument,[1] that under the circumstances of the sale, the contract implied was (not that the grains were fit for cattle-feeding, but) that the thing sold reasonably answered the description of grains. The plaintiff bought the substance in question for the purpose, known to the defendants, of applying it to a use which was proved to be *an* ordinary (if it were not its *only* ordinary) use, cattle-feeding. This substance, but not to the knowledge of the defendants, contained an admixture of fine particles of lead to such an extent that (according to the finding of the jury, which is not in this respect quarrelled with), it did not reasonably answer the description of grains. It was used in feeding the plaintiff's cattle, several of which were poisoned by the lead and died. The question is, was the value of the cattle an element which the jury were entitled to take into consideration in assessing damages?

Now, the breach of contract was, that the grains contained an admixture of lead to an extent which prevented them answering the description. The usual course was, that this substance which was sold as grains should be used for feeding cattle; it was so used, and the natural result of that use was that the cattle were poisoned. Under such circumstances I confess that, from the moment I heard the case opened, I thought it essentially unarguable. The circumstances demonstrated that the loss of the cattle might fairly and reasonably be considered as arising, according to the usual course of things, from the breach of contract itself: *Hadley v Baxendale*.[2]

The argument of [counsel], as I understood it, was this: The breach alleged was, that the thing sold did not reasonably answer the description of grains. That might be true, and still the grains might not contain an admixture of lead, or be otherwise poisonous; therefore, the death of the cattle could not have been in the contemplation of the parties at the time of the contract as the probable result of the breach of it.

It is admitted that, if the contract were particular instead of general, if it had been that the substance did not contain lead or poisonous matter the result would have been different; but it is argued that, in such a case any breach would have involved the existence of poison, and that injury by poison should, therefore, be taken to have been within the contemplation of the parties. This reasoning, it is suggested, was the *ratio decidendi* of *Smith v Green*.[3] It might be sufficient in answer to this argument to say, that in the present case there is evidence that those acting for the defendants knew there were some unusual substances in the thing sold; and that there might be risk in its use for cattle-feeding unless caution were used.

But, for myself, I desire to base my judgment upon broader grounds. I think that the mode in which the case was left to the jury was right, irrespective of the evidence that the defendants contemplated risk. In my opinion the defendants' argument applies to the breach of contract considerations applicable only to the consequences of the breach, not to the breach itself. For the purpose of rendering a defendant responsible for damages which in the ordinary course of things flow from a particular breach, it is unnecessary that the actual breach of contract which ensued should have been within the contemplation of the parties. For anything which amounts to a breach of contract, whether foreseen or unforeseen, the party who breaks the contract is responsible. In the present case the delivery of poison as food did not cease to be the defendants' act because of any want of knowledge in them of the nature of the thing delivered. Nor was the plaintiff by reason of the absence of knowledge in them the less entitled to act upon their contract that the thing sold was grains, or the less damnified by its being in fact poison. It is because the consequences of the defendants' acts are not themselves necessarily the acts of the defendants, that the liability for consequences is limited. If those consequences result solely from the act in question, and an usual state of things, they are the ordinary and usual consequences of that act, and the defendants are liable.

If the consequences flow not from the defendants' act alone, or from the defendants' act operating upon an usual state of things, but from that act and an exceptional state of circumstances, then a question of much difficulty (and one as to which the cases are not wholly consistent) would arise as to the effect on the defendants' liability of their knowledge, at the time of the contract, of such exceptional circumstances. Upon the discussion of this latter question, as to which alone many of the cases cited were material, I do not propose to enter. It has no application here. The loss of the cattle did not arise from exceptional circumstances, but was a natural result of the ordinary use of the substance sold to the plaintiff as grains. The motion to reduce the damages must be refused with costs.

[1.] *Wilson v Dunville* 4 LR (Ir) 249.   [2.] 9 Ex 341.   [3.] 1 CP Div 92.

(Fitzgerald and Dowse BB. concurred.)

Stock *v* Urey [1951] NI 71

The plaintiff purchased a motor car from the defendant for £35 and later sold it to one Eakin for £58 10s. While the car was in the possession of Eakin it was seized by the customs authorities as having been illegally imported into Northern Ireland. Eakin paid to the customs authorities the sum of £68 3s 2d, the amount due in respect of duty and tax, in order to regain possession of the car. Eakin sued the plaintiff for the sum of £68 3s 2d as damages for breach of the implied warranty for quiet possession and of the implied condition, treated as a warranty, that the seller had the right to sell the car. Eakin was awarded the full amount claimed and costs, and the plaintiff paid £86 13s 10d on foot of the decree. The plaintiff then sued the defendant to recover that sum from the defendants as damages for the breach of the implied warranty and condition on the sale of the car to the plaintiff. The defendant contended that since Eakin might have abandoned the car and then sued for the purchase price which he had paid for it, the sum of £68 3s 2d, being in excess of that price, could not be regarded as the reasonable measure of the damage 'directly and naturally resulting' from the breaches alleged. The acting County Court Judge gave a decree for the full amount claimed and the defendant now appealed.

Curran J.:

The claim by Eakin against Stock was based upon breach of warranty and breach of condition. The claim by Stock against Urey is on the same basis. The legal basis for the claim is to be found in ss 12 and 53 of the Sale of Goods Act 1893. S. 12(1) provides for an implied *condition* on the part of the seller that he has a right to sell the goods. Since Eakin retained the motor car and sued for damages it would appear that the implied condition has been treated as a warranty. Accordingly, the claim is, in substance, for damages for breach of warranty under two heads, (1) breach of condition (treated as a warranty) that the seller had a right to sell, and (2) breach of warranty under s. 12 (2) of the Sale of Goods Act 1893, that the buyer shall have and enjoy quiet possession of the goods. Mr Agnew contends that Eakin need not have paid the £68 3s 2d to the customs authorities. He might have let the car go and have sued Stock for the price he paid him, namely, £58 10s 0d. S. 53(2) provides that the measure of damages for breach of warranty is the estimated loss directly and naturally resulting, in the ordinary course of events, from the breach of warranty.

As I see it, the purchaser was warranted quiet enjoyment—in order to secure that quiet enjoyment he had to pay the duty to the customs authorities. That payment, in my view, directly and naturally resulted from the breach of warranty.

Mr Agnew has contended that the payment to the customs authorities was in excess of the actual value of the car and was not 'reasonable and natural'. Undoubtedly, the seizure of the car was an unusual occurrence and there is substance in the contention that it was not reasonably foreseeable by the defendant—assuming that he had no knowledge of the illegal importation of the car from Eire. The substance of the breach of warranty is, however, that the car had been illegally imported and was liable to seizure. Accordingly, s. 53(2), in my opinion, must be read in this way, 'the estimated loss directly and naturally resulting in the ordinary course of events'—from a breach of warranty for quiet enjoyment, such breach being based upon a liability to seizure for illegal importation. What 'directly and naturally results in the ordinary course of events' from a breach of warranty must depend, in my view, on the nature of the grounds upon which the warranty for quiet enjoyment is impeached—in this case liability to seizure for illegal importation. From the breach of warranty, based upon this liability to seizure, the payment made to prevent such seizure and to protect the purchaser's quiet enjoyment, in my opinion, was reasonable and natural, and directly and naturally resulted, in the ordinary course of events, from the breach of warranty. Whether the amount paid was greater or less than the actual value of the car cannot, in my view affect the matter. I accordingly affirm the decree.

B. The Second Limb of the Remoteness Test

Waller *v* Midland Great Western Rly (1879) 4 LR (Ir.) 376
The plaintiff wished to send some horses to an auction sale. The railway company failed to provide horse-boxes, thereby requiring the plaintiff to send the horses by road. The horses arrived at the sale in a distressed state and were sold for less than they would have fetched if they had made the journey without mishap. Damages were awarded to the plaintiff: the railway company appealed.

Morris C.J.:

The damages awarded by the jury on the reference to the Master of the Queen's Bench Division were the entire amount claimed by the plaintiff, *viz.* £200, and were awarded as damages for the lameness and injury of the horses, as appears by the Master's notes. The defendants have contended that the damages should be nominal, or in the alternative that the inquiry had should be set aside and a new inquiry directed.

Adopting as a principle the rule as to damages laid down in *Hadley v Baxendale*,[1] *viz.* that the damages should be such as arose, according to the usual course of things, from the breach of contract, or such as reasonably might be supposed to have been in the contemplation of the parties at the time they made the contract, how does it apply to this case?

The plaintiff, I assume, adopted a reasonable alternative in sending his horses by road, when the defendants could not supply horse-boxes, nor undertake to do so in time, as he wanted his horses to reach Sewell's on the Wednesday night, in order to show them, as is usual, on the day prior to the auction. His manager, Patrick Johnston, who was in charge of the horses, and who made the decision to go to Dublin by road, states in his evidence that he did not expect lameness or injury to the horses there-from, and that he did not expect they would be unfit for the journey, and attributes their injury to their being in soft condition, as it turned out they were; that one of the horses became lame, and the rest were injured, by the journey; and that they were unfit to make the journey—why? because they had been from 6 April, the end of the hunting season, or eighteen days, in soft condition as to feeding, *viz.* fed on oats, bran, linseed cake and seed cake. Now, applying any reasonable principle, why should the defendants be amerced in damages to the amount of the loss accruing to the plaintiff by reason of the mistaken conclusion of the plaintiff's manager, that the horses could make the journey by road to Dublin without injury? Would that be usual or natural damage; or would it be in the contemplation of the parties at the time they made the contract? The plaintiff appears to me to be in a dilemma: either his horses were fit to make the journey or they were not. If they were fit, nothing to the extent of these con-sequences of lameness and injuries could have occurred to them; if these consequences did occur, why then they must have been in an unfit and exceptional condition, and susceptible to injury to an extraordinary degree—when for such exceptional suscep-tibility the defendants would not be liable in damages.

I am of opinion that the damages, the natural or direct result of the breach of con-tract, or which the parties could have ever contemplated at the time of the contract, or that any reasonable rule on the subject could support, would be the deterioration that horses that were fit to make the journey would experience in doing so. That might be, and I should say would be, more than nominal damages, and would be analogous to the damages for inconvenience to which the plaintiff was held entitled in *Hobbs v The London & South Western Rly Co.*[2]

The result is that we reverse the judgment of the Queen's Bench Division, which decides that the plaintiff should retain his verdict for £200, and we direct that the inquiry had should be set aside, and a new inquiry had; and as neither party has succeeded to the full extent contended for, the plaintiff is seeking to retain his full verdict, and the defendants in seeking to enter the verdict for nominal damages only, let each party abide his own costs of this appeal and of the motion in the Queen's Bench Division.

Fitzgibbon L.J.:

The injuries resulting from breaches of contract may be of infinite variety, and con-nected in infinite degrees and closeness or remoteness with the breaches from which they spring.

It is impossible to hold those who break contracts answerable for all consequences, however remote, unexpected or serious; and hence, in each case it must be decided whether the damage which has arisen is so closely connected with the breach as to make it just and reasonable to hold the person in default liable to make compensation for it. This question of remoteness of damage should be decided by the court, and not by the jury; and, though the general principle of decision may be easily stated, its application must depend upon the special circumstances of the particular case. Where the principle has been applied it is for the jury to measure the amount. The general principle is, that the person breaking his contract must answer for the necessary, natural, or probable consequences of his default, and for those which ought to have been within the reasonable contemplation of both parties when making their contract, as likely to arise from its breach. These are not separate definitions: it is presumed that every necessary natural and probable result was contemplated by the parties. But if the injured party wishes to go beyond presumption, he may prove that any specified result was, in fact, contemplated as likely to arise from a breach of the particular contract.

To recover compensation, however, for extraordinary damage, he must show that the defendant ought to have contemplated, or did in fact contemplate it, as likely to arise, and undertook, expressly or by implication, in case of breach, to answer for it.

The Court of Queen's Bench held that the injury sustained in this case was a natural and probable consequence of the breach, and also was, or ought to have been, contemplated by the parties as likely to arise.

I am quite unable to agree with this decision; it seems to me to rest on a confusion of the enforced journey which the horses took, and which was a probable or perhaps a necessary consequence of the failure to send them by train, with the lameness and other serious injury, and the depreciation at a particular sale, which followed from that journey, and for which it is conceded that the jury have compensated the plaintiff.

That these serious injuries were not in fact contemplated is proved by the plaintiff's steward, who was in charge of the horses, and who swore that he did not expect that they would be injured, and, therefore, we have only to consider whether damage to the amount of £200 was the natural necessary or probable consequence of the journey which was undertaken.

Common experience and common sense are opposed to the conclusion that such an amount of injury is the natural or probable consequence of sending ordinary horses such a distance; and if, with a view to an immediate sale, or from the condition of the animals, or from any other circumstances, it was impossible to bring these horses to Dublin by road on the evening in question, without such serious injury, the plaintiff was bound either to have adopted some other mode of transit, or to have taken more time or greater precautions; and not having done so, he cannot look to the defendants to compensate him for the unexpected and exceptional loss which he sustained. I can see no escape from the dilemma pointed out by my Lord Chief Justice, that if lameness, and injury, and depreciation to the extent of £200, was the natural or probable consequence of taking these fifteen horses, in their then condition, 26 miles by road, it was not reasonable so to take them. But if the injury sustained was not the natural or probable consequence of the journey, it was not within the scope of the defendants' liability.

I agree with [counsel] that the question resolves itself into this: 'Was it reasonable, under the circumstances, to take the horses to Dublin by road?' The answer is, 'It was not, if such serious injury was the natural or probable result of so taking them.' If we were to allow the plaintiff to recover damages to the average amount of £13 6s 8d, or 10s per mile for each horse, as compensation for having to send his horses a journey of 26 miles, we should either compel the defendants to pay for an unexpected, unnecessary, and improbable amount of injury, or we should disregard the limitation well expressed in *Le Blanche v London & North Western Rly Co.*,[3] and hold the plaintiff entitled to fulfil the broken contract for himself unreasonably, extravagantly, and oppressively.

The assessment made cannot stand, but it does not follow by any means that the measure of damages is nominal. Nor do I think they are to be measured by hypothetical expenses or damages consequential on other possible courses of action which the plaintiff did not adopt, and was, in my judgment, not bound to adopt. Where a defendant, by his breach of contract, forces a plaintiff to select some one course of several, I think he must answer for the natural and probable consequences of the course chosen, if the choice be a reasonable one, though some other might possibly have turned out more fortunately; and, just as Mr and Mrs Hobbs were held entitled to recover compensation for their fatigue and inconvenience, but not for the exceptionally injurious consequences of their walk, I think the plaintiff here is entitled to recover compensation for the time and labour of both men and horses expended upon the road, with reasonable compensation for the fatigue, inconvenience, and depreciation which would naturally arise from such a journey when undertaken by horses in ordinary condition; but not for lameness or extraordinary injury caused by the exceptional state of the horses, nor for depreciation, measured not by any alteration in their permanent intrinsic value, but by offering them for sale while footsore and temporarily out of condition. A jury alone can fix the amount to be assessed on this principle; and if the railway company, who very unjustifiably broke their contract, and undoubtedly thereby caused very serious loss to the plaintiff, will not now agree to name a reasonable sum, which they may measure more liberally on escaping further litigation, we can only reverse the decision of the Queen's Bench Division, and direct a new inquiry.

1. 1 CP Div. 286. 2. 9 Ex 341. 3. LR 10 QB 111.

C. Remoteness of Damage—Terminology

Victoria Laundry (Windsor) Ltd *v* Newman Industries Ltd [1949] 2 KB 528

The plaintiffs, a limited company, carrying on a business as launderers and dyers at Windsor, were in January 1946, minded to expand their business, and to that end required a boiler of much greater capacity than the one they then possessed, which was of a capacity of 1,500–1,600 lbs evaporation per hour. Seeing an advertisement by the defendants on 17 January 1946, of two 'vertical Cochran boilers of 8,000 lb per hour capacity heavy steaming', the plaintiffs negotiated for the purchase of one of them, and by 26 April had concluded a contract for its purchase at a price of £2,150, loaded free on transport at Harpenden, where it was installed in the premises of the defendants. The defendants knew that the plaintiffs were launderers and dyers, and wanted the boiler for use in their business. Also, during the negotiations the plaintiffs by letter expressed their intention to 'put it into use in the shortest possible space of time.' Arrangements were made by the plaintiffs with the defendants to take delivery at Harpenden on 5 June, and the plaintiffs on that date sent a lorry to Harpenden to take delivery, but it was then ascertained that four days earlier the third parties, who had been employed by the defendants to dismantle the boiler, had allowed it to fall on its side and sustain damage. The plaintiffs refused to take delivery unless the damage was made good and ultimately the defendants agreed to arrange for the necessary repairs. The plaintiffs did not receive delivery of the boiler until 8 November 1946, and in the present action they claimed damages for breach of contract and sought to include in the damages loss of business profits during the period from 5 June to 8 November 1946.

Streatfeild J. gave judgment for the plaintiffs against the defendants for £110 damages under certain minor heads, but held that they were not entitled to include in their measure of damages loss of business profits during the period of delay. The boiler, he said, was not a whole plant capable of being used by itself as a profit-making machine. Only the entire plant, including the vats, was a profit-making machine. The defendants were supplying the plaintiffs with only a part, the function of which they did not know, of that plant. The case fell, in his opinion, within the second rule in *Hadley v Baxendale*[1] and the defendants were not liable for the loss of profits because the special object for which the plaintiffs were acquiring the boiler had not been drawn to the defendants' attention.

Asquith L.J.:

. . .

The ground of the learned judge's decision, which we consider more fully later, may be summarised as follows: He took the view that the loss of profit claimed was due to special circumstances and therefore recoverable, if at all, only under the second rule in *Hadley v Baxendale* and not recoverable in this case because such special circumstances were not at the time of the contract communicated to the defendants. He also attached much significance to the fact that the object supplied was not a self-sufficient profit-making article, but part of a larger profit-making whole, and cited in this connexion the cases of *Portman v Middleton*[2] and *British Columbia Sawmills v Nettleship*.[3] Before commenting on the learned judge's reasoning, we must refer to some of the authorities.

The authorities on recovery of loss of profits as a head of damage are not easy to reconcile. At one end of the scale stand cases where there has been non-delivery or delayed delivery of what is on the face of it obviously a profit-earning chattel: for instance, a merchant or passenger ship: see *Fletcher v Tayleur*,[4] *In re Trent and Humber Co., ex parte Cambrian Steam Packet Co.*;[5] or some essential part of such a ship; for instance, a propeller in *Wilson v General Ironscrew Co.*,[6] or engines, *Saint Line v Richardson*.[7] In such cases loss of profit has rarely been refused. A second and intermediate class of case in which loss of profit has often been awarded is where ordinary mercantile goods have been sold to a merchant with knowledge by the vendor that the purchaser wanted them for resale; at all events, where there was no market in which the purchaser could buy similar goods against the contract on the seller's default, see, for instance, *Borries v Hutchinson*.[8] At the other end of the scale are cases where the defendant is not a vendor of the goods, but a carrier, see, for instance, *Hadley v Baxendale* and *Gee v Lancashire and Yorkshire Rly*.[9] In such cases the courts have been slow to allow loss of profit as an item of damage. This was not, it would seem, because a different principle applies in such cases, but because the application of the same principle leads to different results. A carrier commonly knows less than a seller about the purposes for which the buyer or consignee needs the goods, or about other 'special circumstances' which may cause exceptional loss if due delivery is withheld.

Three of the authorities call for more detailed examination. First comes *Hadley v Baxendale* itself. Familiar though it is, we should first recall the memorable sentence in which the main principles laid down in this case are enshrined:

> Where two parties have made a contract which one of them has broken, the damages which the other party ought to receive in respect of such breach of contract should be such as may fairly and reasonably be considered as either arising naturally, i.e. according to the usual course of things, from such breach of contract itself, or such as may reasonably be supposed to have been in the contemplation of both parties, at the time they made the contract, as the probable result of the breach of it.

The limb of this sentence prefaced by 'either' embodies the so-called 'first' rule; that prefaced by 'or' the 'second'. In considering the meaning and application of these rules, it is essential to bear clearly in mind the facts on which *Hadley v Baxendale* proceeded. The head-note is definitely misleading in so far as it says that the defendant's clerk, who attended at the office, was told that the mill was stopped and that the shaft must be delivered immediately. The same allegation figures in the statement of facts which are said on p. 344 to have 'appeared' at the trial before Crompton J. If the Court of Exchequer had accepted these facts as established, the court must, one would suppose, have decided the case the other way round; must, that is, have held the damage claimed was recoverable under the second rule. But it is reasonably plain from Alderson B.'s judgment that the court rejected this evidence, for on p. 355 he says: 'We find that the only circumstances here communicated by the plaintiffs to the defendants at the time when the contract was made were that the article to be carried was the broken shaft of a mill and that the plaintiffs were the millers of that mill,' and it is on this basis of fact that he proceeds to ask, 'How do these circumstances show reasonably that the profits of the mill must be stopped by an unreasonable delay in the delivery of the broken shaft by the carrier to the third person?'

British Columbia Sawmills v Nettleship annexes to the principle laid down in *Hadley v Baxendale* a rider to the effect that where knowledge of special circumstances is relied on as enhancing the damage recoverable that knowledge must have been brought home to the defendant at the time of the contract and in such circumstances that the defendant impliedly undertook to bear any special loss referable to a breach in those special circumstances. The knowledge which was lacking in that case on the part of the defendant was knowledge that the particular box of machinery negligently lost by the defendants was one without which the rest of the machinery could not be put together and would therefore be useless.

Cory v Thames Ironworks Co.[10]—a case strongly relied on by the plaintiffs—presented the peculiarity that the parties contemplated respectively different profit-making uses of the chattel sold by the defendant to the plaintiff. It was the hull of a boom derrick, and was delivered late. The plaintiffs were coal merchants, and the obvious use, and that to which the defendants believed it was to be put, was that of a coal store. The plaintiffs, on the other hand, the buyers, in fact intended to use it for transhipping coals from colliers to barges, a quite unprecedented use for a chattel of this kind, one quite unsuspected by the sellers and one calculated to yield much higher profits. The case accordingly decides, *inter alia*, what is the measure of damage recoverable when the parties are not *ad idem* in their contemplation of the use for which the article is needed. It was decided that in such a case no loss was recoverable beyond what would have resulted if the intended use had been that reasonably within the contemplation of the defendants, which in that case was the 'obvious' use. This special complicating factor, the divergence between the knowledge and contemplation of the parties respectively, has somewhat obscured that general importance of the decision, which is in effect that the facts of the case brought it within the first rule of *Hadley v Baxendale* and enabled the plaintiff to recover loss of such profits as would have arisen from the normal and obvious use of the article. The 'natural consequence', said Blackburn J., of not delivering the derrick was that £420 representing those normal profits was lost. Cockburn C.J., interposing during the argument, made the significant observation: 'No doubt in order to recover damage arising from a special purpose the buyer must have communicated the special purpose to the seller; but there is one thing which must always be in the knowledge of both parties, which is that the thing is bought for the purpose of being in some way or other profitably applied.' This observation is apposite to the present case. These three cases have on many occasions been approved by the House of Lords without any material qualification.

What propositions applicable to the present case emerge from the authorities as a whole, including those analysed above? We think they include the following:

(1) It is well settled that the governing purpose of damages is to put the party whose rights have been violated in the same position, so far as money can do so, as if his rights had been observed: (*Sally Wertheim v Chicoutimi Pulp Co.*[11]). This purpose, if

relentlessly pursued, would provide him with a complete indemnity for all loss *de facto* resulting from a particular breach, however improbable, however unpredictable. This, in contract at least, is recognised as too harsh a rule. Hence,

(2) In cases of breach of contract the aggrieved party is only entitled to recover such part of the loss actually resulting as was at the time of the contract reasonably foreseeable as liable to result from the breach.

(3) What was at that time reasonably so foreseeable depends on the knowledge then possessed by the parties or, at all events, by the party who later commits the breach.

(4) For this purpose, knowledge 'possessed' is of two kinds; one imputed, the other actual. Everyone, as a reasonable person, is taken to know the 'ordinary course of things' and consequently what loss is liable to result from a breach of contract in that ordinary course. This is the subject matter of the 'first rule' in *Hadley v Baxendale*. But to this knowledge, which a contract breaker is assumed to possess whether he actually possesses it or not, there may have to be added in a particular case knowledge which he actually possesses, of special circumstances outside the 'ordinary course of things', of such a kind that a breach in those special circumstances would be liable to cause more loss. Such a case attracts the operation of the 'second rule' so as to make additional loss also recoverable.

(5) In order to make the contract breaker liable under either rule it is not necessary that he should actually have asked himself what loss is liable to result from a breach. As has often been pointed out, parties at the time of contracting contemplate not the breach of the contract, but its performance. It suffices that, if he had considered the question, he would as a reasonable man have concluded that the loss in question was liable to result (see certain observations of Lord du Parcq in the recent case of A/B *Karlshamns Oljefabriker v Monarch Steamship Co. Ltd*[12]).

(6) Nor, finally, to make a particular loss recoverable, need it be proved that upon a given state of knowledge the defendant could, as a reasonable man, foresee that a breach must necessarily result in that loss. It is enough if he could foresee it was likely so to result. It is indeed enough, to borrow from the language of Lord du Parcq in the same case, at 158, if the loss (or some factor without which it would not have occurred) is a 'serious possibility' or a 'real danger'. For short, we have used the word 'liable' to result. Possibly the colloquialism 'on the cards' indicates the shade of meaning with some approach to accuracy.

If these, indeed, are the principles applicable, what is the effect of their application to the facts of this case? We have, at the beginning of this judgment, summarised the main relevant facts. The defendants were an engineering company supplying a boiler to a laundry. We reject the submission for the defendants that an engineering company knows no more than the plain man about boilers or the purposes to which they are commonly put by different classes of purchasers, including laundries. The defendant company were not, it is true, manufacturers of this boiler or dealers in boilers, but they gave a highly technical and comprehensive description of this boiler to the plaintiffs by letter of 19 January 1946, and offered both to dismantle the boiler at Harpenden and to re-erect it on the plaintiffs' premises. Of the uses or purposes to which boilers are put, they would clearly know more than the uninstructed layman. Again, they knew they were supplying the boiler to a company carrying on the business of laundrymen and dyers, for use in that business. The obvious use of a boiler, in such a business, is surely to boil water for the purpose of washing or dyeing. A laundry might conceivably buy a boiler for some other purpose; for instance, to work radiators or warm bath water for the comfort of its employees or directors, or to use for research, or to exhibit in a museum. All these purposes are possible, but the first is the obvious purpose which, in the case of a laundry, leaps to the average eye. If the purpose then be to wash or dye, why does the company want to wash or dye, unless for purposes of business advantage, in which term we, for the purposes of the rest of this judgment, include maintenance or increase of profit, or reduction of loss? (We shall speak henceforward not of loss of profit, but of 'loss of business'.) No commercial concern commonly purchases for the purposes of its business a very large and expensive structure like this—a boiler 19 feet high and costing over £2,000—with any other motive, and no supplier, let alone an engineering company, which has promised delivery of such an article by a particular date, with knowledge that it was to be put into use immediately on delivery, can reasonably contend that it could not foresee that loss of business (in the sense indicated above) would be liable to result to the purchaser from a long delay in the delivery thereof. The suggestion that, for all the supplier knew, the boiler might have been needed simply as a 'stand-by', to be used in a possibly distant future, is gratuitous and was plainly negatived by the terms of the letter of 26 April 1946.

Since we are differing from a carefully reasoned judgment, we think it due to the learned judge to indicate the grounds of our dissent. In that judgment, after stressing the fact that the defendants were not manufacturers of this boiler or of any boiler (a fact which is indisputable), nor (what is disputable) people possessing any special knowledge not common to the general public of boilers or laundries as possible users thereof, he goes on to say:

> That is the general principle and I think that the principle running through the cases is this—and to this extent I agree with [counsel for the plaintiffs]—that if there is nothing unusual, if it is a normal user of the plant, then it may well be that the parties must be taken to contemplate that the loss of profits may result from non-delivery, or the delay in delivery, of the particular article. On the other hand, if there are, as I think there are here, special circumstances, I do not think that the defendants are liable for loss of profits unless these special circumstances were drawn to their notice. In looking at the cases, I think there is a distinction as [counsel for the defendants] has pointed out and insists upon, between the supply of the part of the profit-making machine, as against the profit-making machine itself.

Then, after referring to *Portman v Middleton*, he continues:

> It is to be observed that not only must the circumstances be known to the supplier, but they must be such that the object must be taken to have been within the contemplation of both parties. I do not think that on the facts of the case as I have heard them, and upon the admissions, it can be said that it was within the contemplation of the supplier, namely, the defendants, that any delay in the delivery of this boiler was going to lead necessarily to loss of profits. There was nothing that I know of in the evidence to indicate how it was to be used or whether delivery of it by a particular day would necessarily be vital to the earning of these profits. I agree with the propositions of [counsel for the defendants] that it was no part of the contract, and it cannot be taken to have been the basis of the contract, that the laundry would be unable to work if there was a delay in the delivery of the boiler, or that the laundry was extending its business, or that it had any special contracts which they could fulfil only by getting delivery of this boiler. In my view, therefore, this case falls within the second rule of *Hadley v Baxendale* under which they are not liable for the payment of damages for loss of profits unless there is evidence before the court—which there is not—that the special object of this boiler was drawn to

their attention and that they contracted upon the basis that delay in the delivery of the boiler would make them liable to payment of loss of profits.

The answer to this reasoning has largely been anticipated in what has been said above, but we would wish to add: First, that the learned judge appears to infer that because certain 'special circumstances' were, in his view, not 'drawn to the notice of' the defendants and therefore, in his view, the operation of the 'second rule' was excluded, ergo nothing in respect of loss of business can be recovered under the 'first rule'. This inference is, in our view, no more justified in the present case than it was in the case of *Cory v Thames Ironworks Co.* Secondly, that while it is not wholly clear what were the 'special circumstances' on the non-communication of which the learned judge relied, it would seem that they were, or included, the following: (a) the 'circumstance' that delay in delivering the boiler was going to lead 'necessarily' to loss of profits. But the true criterion is surely not what was bound 'necessarily' to result, but what was likely or liable to do so, and we think that it was amply conveyed to the defendants by what was communicated to them (plus what was patent without express communication) that delay in delivery was likely to lead to 'loss of business'; (b) the 'circumstance' that the plaintiffs needed the boiler 'to extend their business'. It was surely not necessary for the defendants to be specifically informed of this, as a precondition of being liable for loss of business. Reasonable persons in the shoes of the defendants must be taken to foresee without any express intimation, that a laundry which, at a time when there was a famine of laundry facilities, was paying £2,000 odd for plant and intended at such a time to put such plant 'into use' immediately, would be likely to suffer in pocket from five months' delay in delivery of the plant in question, whether they intended by means of it to extend their business, or merely to maintain it, or to reduce a loss; (c) the 'circumstance' that the plaintiffs had the assured expectation of special contracts, which they could only fulfil by securing punctual delivery of the boiler. Here, no doubt, the learned judge had in mind the particularly lucrative dyeing contracts to which the plaintiffs looked forward and which they mention in para. 10 of the statement of claim. We agree that in order that the plaintiffs should recover specifically and as such the profits expected on these contracts, the defendants would have had to know, at the time of their agreement with the plaintiffs, of the prospect and terms of such contracts. We also agree that they did not in fact know these things. It does not, however, follow that the plaintiffs are precluded from recovering some general (and perhaps conjectural) sum for loss of business in respect of dyeing contracts to be reasonably expected, any more than in respect of laundering contracts to be reasonably expected.

Thirdly, the other point on which Streatfeild J. largely based his judgment was that there is a critical difference between the measure of damages applicable when the defendant defaults in supplying a self-contained profit-earning whole and when he defaults in supplying a part of that whole. In our view, there is no intrinsic magic, in this connection, in the whole as against a part. The fact that a part only is involved is only significant in so far as it bears on the capacity of the supplier to foresee the consequences of non-delivery. If it is clear from the nature of the part (or the supplier of it is informed) that its non-delivery will have the same effect as non-delivery of the whole, his liability will be the same as if he had defaulted in delivering the whole. The cases of *Hadley v Baxendale*, *British Columbia Sawmills v Nettleship* and *Portman v Middleton*, which were so strongly relied on for the defence and by the learned judge, were all cases in which, through want of a part, catastrophic results ensued, in that a whole concern was paralysed or sterilised; a mill stopped, a complex of machinery unable to be assembled, a threshing machine unable to be delivered in time for the harvest and therefore useless. In all three cases the defendants were absolved from liability to compensate the plaintiffs for the resulting loss of business, not because what they had failed to deliver was a part, but because there had been nothing to convey to them that want of that part would stultify the whole business of the person for whose benefit the part was contracted for. There is no resemblance between these cases and the present, in which, while there was no question of a total stoppage resulting from non-delivery, yet there was ample means of knowledge on the part of the defendants that business loss of some sort would be likely to result to the plaintiffs from the defendants' default in performing their contract.

We are therefore of opinion that the appeal should be allowed and the issue referred to an official referee as to what damage, if any, is recoverable in addition to the £110 awarded by the learned trial judge. The official referee would assess those damages in consonance with the findings in this judgment as to what the defendants knew or must be taken to have known at the material time, either party to be at liberty to call evidence as to the quantum of the damage in dispute.

1. (1854) 9 Ex 341
2. 4 CB (NS) 322.
3. LR 3 CP 499.
4. (1855) 17 CB 21.
5. (1868) LR 6 Eq 396.
6. (1878) 47 LJ (QB) 23.

7. [1940] 2 KB 99.
8. (1865) 18 CB (NS) 445.
9. 6 H & N 211.
10. LR 3 QB 181, 187.
11. [1911] AC 301.
12. [1949] AC 196.

Notes

1. In *Koufos v Czarnikow* (*The Heron* II) [1969] 1 AC 350 at 388–9. Lord Reid had this to say about Asquith L.J.'s judgment in *Victoria Laundry*:

. . . The plaintiffs bought a large boiler from the defendants and the defendants were aware of the general nature of the plaintiffs' business and of the plaintiffs' intention to put the boiler into use as soon as possible. Delivery of the boiler was delayed in breach of contract and the plaintiffs claimed as damages loss of profit caused by the delay. A large part of the profits claimed would have resulted from some specially lucrative contracts which the plaintiffs could have completed if they had had the boiler: that was rightly disallowed because the defendants had no knowledge of these contracts. But Asquith L.J. then said: 'It does not, however, follow that the plaintiffs are precluded from recovering some general (and perhaps conjectural) sum for loss of business in respect of dyeing contracts to be reasonably expected, any more than in respect of laundering contracts to be reasonably expected.'[1]

It appears to me that this was well justified on the earlier authorities. It was certainly not unlikely on the information which the defendants had when making the contract that delay in delivering the boiler would result in loss of business: indeed it would seem that that was more than an even chance. And there was nothing new in holding that damages should be estimated on a conjectural basis. This House had approved of that as early as 1813 in *Hall v Ross*.[2]

But what is said to create a 'landmark' is the statement of principles by Asquith L.J.[3] This does to some extent go beyond the older authorities and insofar as it does so I do not agree with it. In para. (2) it is said that the plaintiff is entitled to recover 'such part of the loss actually resulting as was at the time of the contract reasonably foreseeable as liable to result from the breach.' To bring in reasonable foreseeability appears to me to be confusing measure of damages in contract with measure of damages in tort. A great many extremely unlikely results are reasonably foreseeable: it is true that Lord Asquith may have meant foreseeable as a likely result, and if that is all he meant I would not object further than to say that I think that the phrase is liable to be misunderstood. For the same reason I would take exception to the phrase 'liable to result' in para. (5). Liable is a very vague word but I think that one would usually say that when a person foresees a very improbable result he foresees that it is liable to happen.

[1.] [1949] 2 KB 528, 543.   [2.] (1813) 1 Dow. 201, HL.   [3.] [1949] 2 KB 528, 539, 540.

2. In *Scheps v Fine Art Logistic Ltd* [2007] EWHC 541(QB) the plaintiff purchased a sculpture in June 2004 for US $35,000. The art work was bailed with the defendants but it was lost and, in all likelihood, thrown into a skip. The court found that at this time the sculpture was worth much more, around £135,000. The plaintiff was also held to be entitled to damages reflecting the increased value of the sculpture in the period between breach of contract (September 2004) and the date of judgement (March 2007). This figure by way of consequential damages was estimated at £219,375. Teare J. held that the sharp rise in value of the works of the sculptor, Anish Kapoor, was not too remote, rejecting an argument that this increase in value could be compared to the particularly lucrative dyeing contracts that were too remote in *Victoria Laundry*.

Lee and Donoghoe *v* Rowan (HC) 17 November 1981, unrep.

The plaintiffs agreed to construct a drying shed for the defendant, a farmer, for £10,500. The work was not carried out satisfactorily and the defendant resisted the plaintiff's *quantum meruit* claim and counterclaimed for £2,000, being the cost of getting another contractor to provide similar facilities over and above the (unpaid) contract price of £10,500. The defendant also sought compensation for loss of profit resulting from the entire loss of the potato harvest due to non-completion of the drying shed. Costello J. held the plaintiffs entitled to £1,291.63 being the value of work completed and accepted by the defendant. The learned judge went on to consider the defendant's counterclaim.

Costello J.:

. . .

The rule relating to damages for breach of contract has been stated in the well known case of *Hadley v Baxendale* (9 Ex at 354) as follows:

> Where two parties have made a contract which one of them has broken, the damages which the other party ought to receive in respect of such breach of contract should be such as may fairly and reasonably be considered either arising naturally, i.e according to the usual course of things from such breach of contract itself, or such as may reasonably be supposed to have been in the contemplation of the parties, at the time they made the contract, as the probable result of the breach of it.

It seems to me that under the first branch of this rule will fall the defendant's claim arising from the extra building costs amounting to £2,000. Such loss, in my opinion, may fairly and reasonably be considered as arising according to the usual course of things from the plaintiffs' breach of contract. The remainder of the defendant's loss is sustainable, if at all, under the second branch of the rule. Under this branch I must decide what damages may reasonably be supposed to have been in the contemplation of the parties at the time they made the contract as the probable result of its breach. In this connection, the plaintiffs of course knew that the defendant was growing a substantial amount of vegetables for drying and storage in the building they were erecting for him. They were not, however, aware of the exact acreage sown by the defendant but this does not, I think, affect their liability. In view of their knowledge of the trade I think the plaintiffs would have known that if they broke their contract in May 1977 so that the defendant would have to erect a new building in place of the plaintiffs' unfinished one it would have been highly probable that the new building would not be completed in time to take the produce of the 1977 harvest. But I do not think that either party could have contemplated that the effect of a breach of contract would have been the loss of the defendant's entire crop. This unfortunate result arose not only because of the defendant's inability to have the work completed in time by a new contractor but also because of the shortage in the country of adequate storage and drying facilities. The defendant has not established to my satisfaction that at the time the contract was made the plaintiffs were aware that such a shortage would arise in 1977 and that as a result the defendant would be unable to dry and store his crop. The plaintiffs could not have contemplated that all the defendant's sowing and cultivating costs would be thrown away and so I do not think that the claim for this loss is sustainable. But the plaintiffs would have contemplated that some loss of profits would result in a breach of contract on their behalf as the defendant would be put to expense in hiring alternative storage and extra transport charges in putting his crop into store. The defendant was not able to help me as to the storage charges which he would have incurred in 1977/78 and I have not been supplied with any figures as to what the possible transport charges would be. The assessment of damages, therefore, must be to a considerable extent conjecture. Based on the total marketing costs which have been proved I think that a figure of £10 per ton would be a reasonable estimate of the extra cost to which I have referred. It seems to me, therefore, that the claim for loss of profits should be limited to the sum of £9,240 being the extra transport and storage costs of 300 tons of onions and 644 tons of potatoes, costs which the parties would have contemplated as arising from the breach by the plaintiffs in May 1977, of their contract.

The total damages to which the defendant is entitled are £11,240. He is entitled to set off this sum against the plaintiffs' claim of £1,291 and recover on the counterclaims the balance, namely, the sum of £9,949.

The plaintiffs' claim will therefore be dismissed with no order as to costs. There will be judgment on the counterclaim amounting to £9,949 with costs.

Kemp v Intasun (1987) 2 FTLR 234

Kerr L.J.:

On 2 February 1984 Mrs Kemp and her daughter called at Thomas Cook to choose a summer holiday.

There was a conversation with one of the assistants in which Mrs Kemp referred to the fact that her husband suffered from asthma. She said he could not be there because he was ill, and that because of his health special insurance was required.

It was decided they should choose a holiday at a hotel called America 1 at Calas de Mallorca. The relevant booking form and an insurance proposal form were taken away by Mrs Kemp.

By 29 February the Kemps had completed the booking form and returned it, and it was accepted by Intasun. Accordingly by that date the contract was concluded between the Kemps and Intasun on the terms of the booking note.

The booking note had a space for 'special requests', but nothing was inserted in it.

The first thirty hours of the holiday proved disastrous. The America 1 was full up, and the family was taken to a Spanish hotel called Las Chihuahuas, which was of nothing like the same quality.

They were taken to a room in the staff quarters. It had a broken window filled with bricks, glass on the floor, and it was filthy and very dusty. The toilet had no door and the shower did not work. There were two single beds, and a portable bed which they could not operate.

The room's dusty and dirty condition had a particular effect on Mr Kemp's asthma. He had an attack which caused him and his family considerable distress. He suffered from it throughout the thirty hours spent in that insalubrious room, and continued to be affected for several days.

Mr Kemp sued Intasun on behalf of himself and his family.

Judge Lee awarded £1,000 for breach of Intasun's contractual obligations. He divided the award into two parts. The first part was £400 for inconvenience, discomfort, loss of enjoyment and disappointment. That was not appealed.

The second part was £800 for the consequences of Mr Kemp's having suffered an asthma attack due to the state of the alternative accommodation. Intasun challenged that as a consequence which was too remote to be recoverable.

The judge had said that to succeed on this point Mr Kemp must prove that Intasun 'had knowledge of his asthma and associated problems.' He found that asthma was sufficiently uncommon to be not normally in the contemplation of Intasun—'it would, however, be sufficient if the defendant's agent was told.'

Once Intasun had knowledge, he said, the circumstances in which it came to know were irrelevant, as was the purpose for which the information was given.

He held that knowledge was attributable to Intasun.

The relevant test was not formulated entirely accurately or completely when the judge said that Mr Kemp must prove that Intasun 'had knowledge of his asthma and associated problems.'

Intasun was responsible for all the consequences which it could reasonably have contemplated as liable to flow from its breach of contract (see *Koufos v Czarnikow* [1969] 1 AC 350).

It was clear that the foreseeable consequences of a breach of contract of this kind would always include distress, discomfort, disappointment. For that the £400 was awarded.

But the responsibility of a tour operator did not necessarily stop there. He must also accept liability for any other consequences which should have been in the reasonable contemplation of the parties if they flowed naturally from his breach and caused additional foreseeable loss or damage.

The issue really was whether Intasun should have reasonably contemplated that the conditions in a room provided by way of alternative accommodation, might foreseeably be injurious to Mr Kemp's health.

The answer was in the negative. Mrs Kemp answered the question frankly in evidence when she said that had her husband not been susceptible 'we'd have had an unpleasant thirty hours or so, but no more.'

That must be read in the context of the judge's unchallenged finding that asthma was not sufficiently common to be in Intasun's reasonable contemplation and foreseeable.

Mrs Kemp's evidence was that her conversation in Cook's was casual and not part of the booking arrangements. The judge was in error in attributing any contractual consequences to that casual conversation.

At the time of the conversation Thomas Cook was not the agent of Intasun, let alone for the purpose of receiving or passing on the content of the conversation. Whether it became its agent at a later stage and for what purpose it was unnecessary to decide.

The circumstances in which Mrs Kemp's remarks were made and the position which Thomas Cook then occupied entirely precluded the court from holding that the limited knowledge about Mr Kemp's state of health which a Thomas Cook assistant happened to acquire casually, had any consequence for Intasun's contractual obligations.

The £800 was not awarded for any consequence which flowed in the ordinary course of events from Intasun's breach.

The appeal would be allowed and the award of £800 struck out.

Lord Justice Parker agreeing said that he could not accept that a casual conversation in February was sufficient to bring the asthma attack within the contemplation of the parties, even if knowledge of it were imputed to Intasun.

Seven Seas Properties Ltd v El Assa and Another (No. 2) [1993] 3 All ER 577

In this case Gavin Lightman Q.C., sitting as a deputy judge of the English High Court, undertook an inquiry into damages payable by the vendors of real property arising out of the vendor's failure to complete the contract of sale. Al-Essa owned properties in London that they wished to sell. The properties were in need of refurbishment and through Willets, a sales agent, they agreed to sell the property to Seven Seas for £1.5 million. Seven Seas arranged an immediate resale to Grangeville, not informing Al-Essa of this fact because Seven Seas knew that if Al-Essa were aware that there was a higher market for the unfurbished flats Al-Essa would not have proceeded to sell to Seven Seas. The sale price in the contract between Seven Seas and Grangeville was £1.635 million. Were damages for loss of bargain recoverable under Hadley v Baxendale?

Gavin Lightman Q.C.:

. . .

The decision on this application whether these claims should be upheld turns on the application to the facts of this case of the rule in Hadley v Baxendale (1854) 9 Ex 341, [1843–60] All ER Rep 461. The two branches of this rule were stated by Lord Upjohn in Koufos v Czarnikow Ltd (The Heron II) [1967] 3 All ER 686 at 715, [1969] 1 AC 350 at 421 as follows: '1. Damages should be such as may naturally and usually arise from the breach, or 2. Damages should be such as in the special circumstances of the case known to both parties may be reasonably supposed to have been in the contemplation of the parties, as the result of a breach, assuming the parties to have applied their minds to the contingency of there being such a breach.'

The plaintiffs do not in their pleadings claim that the damages sought fall within the first branch. Indeed, I invited [counsel for the plaintiffs], if he so wished, to apply to amend to invoke this head but he declined. He has, no doubt quite properly, nailed his flag to the second branch. [Counsel] does not contend that at the date of the plaintiffs' contract the defendants actually knew of any intention on the part of the plaintiffs to enter into a contract of resale, but he contends that in the special circumstances of this case known to the defendants there may reasonably be supposed to have been in their contemplation that the plaintiffs would or might enter into such a contract and that if they did so the result of the defendants' breach of contract was liable, indeed likely, to put the plaintiffs in breach of such contract of resale and would occasion to the plaintiffs such damages as were indeed occasioned in this case. The special circumstances relied on are, first of all, the character of the premises, namely a block of flats ripe for refurbishment; secondly, the character of likely interested purchasers who have been called by at least one witness 'property professionals', persons who may be expected to buy in order to turn the property to account as opportunity might arise and to resell quickly if the price available was right; thirdly, the buoyant state of the property market for this kind of property at the time of the contract with both rising property prices and in many cases rapid returns and resales.

I accept that the evidence establishes these special circumstances. Indeed, they are not materially, if at all, in dispute. A more contentious issue relates to the probability or likely quick return or resale by the purchasers of this property after the marketing by Willetts at the price of £1.5m. It was common ground that the purchaser should be expected to purchase for the purpose of refurbishment and subsequent sale of the flats after refurbishment. Mr Duncan, the plaintiffs' expert, expressed the view that none-theless there was a chance, which he estimated at ten per cent, that such a purchaser might yet seek and achieve such a quick return as the plaintiffs in fact achieved. On the other hand, the defendants' expert, Mr Hutchinson, firmly expressed the view that after the extensive marketing by Willetts and the achievement of the optimum price a resale by the plaintiffs within the ten week completion period was highly unlikely and the shortest period within which a resale could reasonably be expected was six to nine months. [Counsel for the plaintiffs], in his address to me, cautioned me about accepting Mr Duncan's (his own expert's) opinion on the percentage chance as a spot assessment off the cuff in his oral evidence rather than a careful, considered judgment. His purpose was to persuade me to treat his expert's assessment as too low. Mr Duncan on at least two occasions in his oral evidence gave this percentage assessment and I cannot see how in particular in the light of the careful and considered evidence of Mr Hutchinson, who plainly thought the assessment of ten per cent was over-generous, I can evaluate the odds above ten per cent. Indeed, in the light of the caution with which perhaps I should view Mr Duncan's spot assessment and the unequivocal considered views of Mr Hutchinson, I think I should conclude that a reasonable assessment of the prospects of an early resale contract, and certainly prior to the contractual completion date, were somewhat below ten per cent.

I turn now to the law. The relevant legal principles appear to me to be as follows. First of all, under the first head of the rule in *Hadley v Baxendale* a plaintiff is entitled to recover all damages which may fairly and reasonably be considered as arising naturally, i.e. according to the usual course of things, from the breach of contract. In the case of a breach by a vendor under a contract for sale, losses occasioned to the purchaser under and by reason of the existence of a sub-contract entered into by him will not without more fall within this head. The court will not take into account the existence of such sub-contract whether to increase or decrease the award of damages and the same principle applies whether the contract is for the sale of goods or the sale of land: see *Brading v McNeill* [1946] Ch. 145. No doubt it is for this reason that the plaintiffs in this case quite properly disavow any reliance on the first head and rely solely on the second head of the rule.

Secondly, a plaintiff is entitled to recover by way of damages all loss which at the date of contract the defaulting party was on notice might be occasioned by the breach such that he may fairly be held, in entering into his contract, to have accepted the risk. A party of this purpose is on notice of facts (i) which were actually known by him, (ii) which were known by his agent and which it was his agent's duty to communicate to him, and (iii) which he should reasonably have deduced from (i) and (ii). He will only be held to have accepted the risk if he was on notice of the purpose and intent of the plaintiff in entering into the contract with him and the consequent exposure of the plaintiff to the risk of damage of the character in question in the event of the defendant's breach: see *Treitel on Contract* (8th ed., 1991), 860–862 and the cases cited and in particular *Finlay & Co. Ltd v NV Kwik Hoo Tong* HM [1929] 1 KB 400, [1928] All ER Rep 110. This is only just, for a party to a contract should not be exposed to risks of liability going beyond the first branch of the rule but arising out of the special susceptibility to damage of the plaintiff unless he has had the opportunity to make an informed decision whether or not by entering into the contract to accept such risk, and whether to negotiate some exclusion from such liability.

Third, applying these principles to a claim by a plaintiff to recover from a defendant vendor losses arising under a sub-contract, the plaintiff must establish that the defendant was on notice of the existence at the date of the contract of the purpose and intent on the part of the vendor to enter into the sub-contract and that its fulfilment depended on the performance by the defendant of his contractual obligations to the plaintiff. It is not sufficient for the plaintiff to establish that the conclusion of a sub-contract was an available option: consider *Diamond v Campbell-Jones* [1960] 1 All ER 583, [1961] Ch. 22. He must show that he or the circumstances 'signalised' (in the language of *Cheshire and Fifoot on Contract* (11th ed., 1986), 588 such to be his purpose or intent in entering into the contract with the defendant. If such notice or acceptance of risk is established, the plaintiff is entitled to recover loss of profit in respect of such sub-contract and an indemnity in respect of liabilities arising from breach: see *Household Machines Ltd v Cosmos Exporters* [1946] 2 All ER 622, [1947] KB 217.

Applying those principles to the facts of this case, it is quite clear that neither the defendants nor their agent knew of any intention on the part of the plaintiffs to enter into any such contract as the first Grangeville contract. Indeed, quite deliberately the plaintiffs kept this from them and encouraged their naturally held view that their intent was refurbishment. Nor can I see how the special circumstances relied on signalised any such intent or purpose. At best such circumstances indicated that such an early sale was a possibility, but even then only a somewhat remote possibility, a possibility not greater than, and in my view, probably somewhat short of ten per cent.

In these circumstances the plaintiffs' claim based on the second limb of *Hadley v Baxendale* must fail. The defendants were not on notice of the first Grangeville contract and accordingly any loss in respect of such contract arising from the defendants' default under the plaintiffs' contract was not within their contemplation as required by the second limb. I should add that even if, contrary to my view, it was not necessary for the plaintiffs to establish that the defendants were on notice and it was sufficient that objectively the losses in question were liable to occur, the likelihood of such occurrence on the facts of this case were very limited indeed and certainly beyond any reasonable contemplation of the defendants: consider *Transworld Oil Ltd v North Bay Shipping Corp., The Rio Claro* [1987] 2 Lloyd's Rep. 173. Reaching this conclusion, as [counsel for the plaintiffs] conceded in argument, all his claims must fail. I should perhaps add that if I had held that the first Grangeville contract fell within the contemplation of the defendants at the date of the plaintiffs' contract, whilst I would have awarded the plaintiffs the sum claimed for loss of profit I would have awarded nothing more. The alleged losses on resale would have been irrecoverable in the absence of any allegation in the pleadings and evidence that the price on resale was the best price reasonably obtainable. Indeed, there are reasons to doubt whether this was the case and whether the sale at this price may have been designed to appease Grangeville. The sum claimed in respect of the compromise likewise I would have rejected, for it is neither pleaded nor proved that the settlement was a reasonable one to enter into. The onus was on the plaintiffs to do this if they were to seek to recover this sum from the defendants: see *Biggin Co. Ltd v Permanite Ltd* [1951] 2 All ER 191, [1951] 2 KB 314. It is not sufficient for the plaintiffs merely to plead the compromise without any explanation as to how the figure was made up or arrived at or any evidence as to how or why or on what advice it was entered into. The settlement appears to me on its face to place far too high a premium on the possible claim by Grangeville for damages for loss of bargain, a claim which could only succeed if the House of Lords were persuaded to overrule the rule in *Bain v Fothergill*. Whatever the prospects at the time of the case of *Sharneyford Supplies Ltd v Edge (Barrington Black Austin & Co. (a firm), third party)* [1987] 1 All ER 588, [1987] Ch. 305, that is to say 14 October 1986, when the Court of Appeal attacked the injustice of the rule and gave leave to appeal to the House of Lords to enable the House of Lords to review that decision, the situation had critically changed after the passing of the 1989 Act. The possibility that the House of Lords would grant leave to appeal after the new legislation, which is deliberately not retrospective, and after the refusal to leave to appeal on the leap-frog application, appear to me to have been remote indeed. My doubts about the compromise are reinforced by the apparent deliberate choice not to involve the defendants in the decision despite the apparent intent to claim an indemnity from them. As to the claim for recovery of the legal costs, assuming that it could be established that the costs of defending the Grangeville action were paid, I would have felt the need for evidence explaining the course taken in respect of that action and in particular the advice (if any) taken regarding whether there should be a payment into court. In respect of the compromise, involving as it did the plaintiffs forgoing any prospect of recovery of the costs of the action, I would wish to have known how much was due in reimbursement to the plaintiffs under orders for costs against Grangeville (for example in respect of the hearing before Hirst J.). I am given no details. I cannot think that a bare claim to have paid a figure in respect of costs is enough to found any claim.

For the reasons which I have given, I hold therefore that the claims made by the plaintiffs should be dismissed and I so direct.

Note

The most important recent remoteness case is a Court of Appeal decision handed down in September 2007. In *The Achilleas* [2007] EWCA Civ 901 a ship demised on a time charter was late in being redelivered by eight days. Daily rate of hire was $16,700 so the 'overrun' damages were $158,301. Owner had let the vessel on a rising market and the new charterers renegotiated down the daily rate from $39,500 to $31,500, using a cancellation right to level this concession from the owners. Damages were thus either $158,301 (overrun) or $1.3 million (late delivery). No previous English case had dealt with this issues of damages for late redelivery and the application of *Hadley v Baxendale* (1854) 9 Exch. 341 was central. The owners and charterers knew that it was a hazard of late redelivery that the vessel might trigger a cancellation date for her next fixture. This was not unusual but was a consequence that the parties might well have in contemplation. Rapid variations in rates were market knowledge. Further, should the vessel be late in taking up its follow-on engagement, some renegotiation downwards on the previously agreed rate of hire might be necessary. The loss therefore could legitimately be treated as 'arising naturally, i.e. according to the usual course of things from such breach of contract itself'. Both the trial judge and the Court of Appeal rejected the view that the second limb required to be satisfied. The Court of Appeal endorsed the view that a follow-on fixture by a shipowner is rather like the resale of goods by a merchant buyer. Loss of profit measures in sale of goods cases were followed, particularly the view that if goods which are unique or made to special order are delivered late, lost profits may well be recoverable, following *Kwei Tek Chao v British Traders Shippers Ltd* [1954] 2QB459. The argument that damages for late redelivery should be limited to the overrun period unless the owners can show that they gave the charterers follow-on information is both undesirable and un-commercial. It is undesirable because it puts the owners at the mercy of the opportunities offered to charterers on a rising market for 'spot' engagements and still only leave charterers liable for the market rate. Limiting damages to the overrun period is also un-commercial because if the charterers need to know more than they already know, i.e. that upon redelivery the vessel will already have been committed to onward engagements, this will be too high a standard and the silence of the owner will not be enough to put the charterer on notice.

The Court of Appeal affirmed the view that modern communications and co-operation between the parties 'ought to make a dangerous mishap an unusual event'. The Court of Appeal resisted the argument that the measure of damages in late redelivery should be the 'overrun measure' simply because it was the standard measure for overrun cases and was therefore likely to lead to consistency, certainty and simplicity of application. The agrument that liability might be too wide, where a very long charter was the follow-on engagement, was rejected on the basis that cases like *Victoria Laundry* already accommodated instances of abnormally high claims to future profits.

D. THE RULE IN BAIN V FOTHERGILL

J. O'Driscoll 'A Note on the Rule in *Bain v Fothergill*' (1975) 10 Ir Jur (NS) 203 (Footnotes abridged.)

Where a party fails to perform his contract, the injured party is to be placed, so far as money can do it, in the same position as he would have been in had the contract been performed. This is the principle established in the case of *Robinson v Harman*.[1]

The damages which the injured party ought to receive in respect of the breach of contract should be such as may fairly and reasonably be considered to arise naturally, i.e. according to the usual course of things, from such breach of contract itself, or such as may reasonably be supposed to have been in the contemplation of both parties, at the time they made the contract, as the probable result of the breach of it. This is the now well established rule in *Hadley v Baxendale*, a decision of the Court of Exchequer in 1854.[2]

Where a seller or lessor of land fails to complete the contract through a defect in his title, the purchaser cannot claim damages for the loss of his bargain, but is restricted to recovery of his deposit and his expenses in investigating title. This, broadly, is the rule in *Bain v Fothergill*, a decision of the House of Lords in 1874.[3] The decision, consequently, came after both *Hadley v Baxendale* and *Robinson v Harman*.

Whilst the principle of law is now known as the rule in *Bain v Fothergill*, an examination of the judgments in the case make it clear, however, that the House of Lords was following what it considered to have been decided by *Flureau v Thornhill*[4] in 1776. As is pointed out later, the judgment in *Flureau v Thornhill* is unsatisfactory in that no attempt to provide a rationale for the rule was provided. Further, the question of the principles behind the proper measure of damages does not appear to have been properly tackled until *Hadley v Baxendale*, some eighty years after *Flureau v Thornhill*.

It is now well settled that the rule in *Hadley v Baxendale* failed to remove the principle that was understood to have been laid down in *Flureau v Thornhill*. As we will see later, the rationale of *Bain v Fothergill* and what is considered to have been the true rationale of *Flureau v Thornhill* was the difficulty which existed at that time of showing title to land in England.

The facts in *Bain v Fothergill* were as follows. Fothergill having contracted for the purchase of a mine, held under an agreement for a lease with a clause against assignment without licence, entered into possession, and, without taking any assignment, agreed to sell to Bain. At the date of this sub-contract, Fothergill was aware that the assent of the lessors was necessary to complete his title but did not anticipate any difficulty in obtaining it and treated the matter as unimportant, and did not mention it to Bain. Subsequently, the lessors, having first verbally promised their assent, withdrew it and the sale to Bain fell through. In an action by Bain for non-performance of the contract, the House of Lords, affirming the decision of the Court of Exchequer, held that Bain could only recover the expenses which he had incurred, not damages for the loss of his bargain.

The extracts from the judgments set out in the headnote impart the sense of the decision. There appears first this extract from the speech of Lord Chelmsford:

> The rule laid down in *Flureau v Thornhill* as to the limits within which damages may be recovered upon the breach of a contract for the sale of real estate must be taken to be without exception. If the person enters into a contract for the sale of real estate, knowing that he has no title to it, nor any means of acquiring it, the purchaser cannot, in an action for breach of the contract, recover damages beyond the expenses he has incurred. Any other damages must be the subject of an action for deceit.

The law report editor then adds this extract from the speech of Lord Hatherley: 'A contract for sale of real estate is very different from a contract for the sale of a chattel. In the former the purchaser knows that there must, with all the complications of our law, be an uncertainty as to making out a good title; in the latter the vendor must know what his right to the chattel is.'

The judges in *Bain v Fothergill* clearly considered that the principle enunciated in *Flureau v Thornhill* was now well established in law, but were critical of both the reasoning or lack of reasoning and the report itself. Mr Justice Denman was among the judges summoned to advise the House of Lords, and he stated:

> It may be admitted that the case of *Flureau v Thornhill* is not a wholly satisfactory case. The report is meagre, and the judgments unargumentative; but the case cannot truly be said to be founded on no principle. . . . For example, in *Robinson v*

Harman, Parke B., in speaking of *Flureau v Thornhill*, says, 'It was there held that contracts for the sale of real estate are merely on condition that the vendor has a good title' (adopting the judgment of Blackstone J.), and then adds, 'so that when a person contracts to sell real property there is an implied understanding that if he fails to make good title the only damages recoverable are the expenses which the vendor may be put to in investigating the title.

Lord Chelmsford, in referring to the decision in *Flureau v Thornhill*, stated: 'Lord Chief Justice De Grey merely laid down the rule, without giving any reason for it. But Mr Justice Blackstone said this: "These contracts are merely upon condition frequently expressed, but always implied, that the vendor had a good title."'

Later in his speech, Lord Chelmsford continued:

There is, perhaps, some difficulty in ascertaining the exact grounds of the judgment in *Flureau v Thornhill*; but, in addition to those which have been previously assigned, it seems to me that the following consideration may be suggested as in some degree supporting the correctness of the decision: 'The fancied goodness of the bargain' must be a matter of a purely speculative character, and in most cases would probably be very difficult to determine, in consequence of the conflicting opinions likely to be formed upon the subject; and even if it could be proved to have been a beneficial purchase, the loss of the pecuniary advantage to be derived from a resale appears to me to be a consequence too remote from the breach of the contract.

To describe 'the fancied goodness of the bargain' as of a purely speculative character and difficult to determine would clearly not be accepted in modern times. Neither, is it submitted, would the proposition that the loss of the pecuniary advantage to be derived from a resale was too remote. Indeed, the pecuniary advantage is very frequently a primary consideration when parties have entered into an agreement for the sale of lands.

Some Irish cases

In *Kelly v Duffy*[5] the vendor agreed with the purchaser for the sale of certain leasehold premises and the purchaser paid a deposit on his purchase money. At the date of the agreement, the vendor had no interest in the premises agreed to be sold. The vendor died without having completed his contract. The purchaser sued the vendor's personal representative for specific performance and damages, and it was held that the action, being founded upon breach of contract and not upon fraud or deceit, the damages award in lieu of specific performance must be confined to the loss occasioned to the purchaser by the vendor's failure to complete; the rule in *Bain v Fothergill* applied. O'Connor M.R., in his judgment, commented on the unsatisfactory nature of the report of *Flureau v Thornhill*. Yet, he continued, unsatisfactory as the decision might be, it was then too late to question it; it was settled law. Mr Justice Denman had described it in *Bain v Fothergill* 'as a part of the law of the land binding upon all Courts of Justice, and only to be altered, if at all, by legislation'. The concern of O'Connor M.R. was solely as to whether the facts in the case came within the rule in *Bain v Fothergill*, and he held that they did. The Master of the Rolls next considered a celebrated passage in the judgment of Lindley M.R. in *Day v Singleton*:[6] 'The only reason which can be assigned for deciding that he [Day] is entitled to more is that the rule which limits his damages in the first case, is itself an anomalous rule based upon and justified by difficulties in shewing a good title to real property in this country, but one which ought not to be extended to cases in which the reasons on which it is based do not apply.'

Of this, O'Connor M.R. remarked: 'I do not know what is meant by an anomalous rule of law. A rule is either good or bad. If it is good, as founded on some principles, it can't be called anomalous. If it is bad, it ought not to be followed.'

It seems to this writer that O'Connor M.R. failed to grasp the essential nature of the rule and certainly failed to grasp the argument of Lindley M.R. referred to, and decided *Kelly v Duffy* in blinkers, once he had established that the fact fitted the rule. He did not consider the rationale for the rule itself.

In *McDonnell v McGuinness*[7] it was held by the Supreme Court, where a right of dower was subsisting in the lands, that the vendor had, without fraud, been unable to make title; in consequence, the purchaser was entitled only to interest on his deposit, together with the costs and expenses actually incurred by him in investigating title, and was not entitled to damages for the loss of his bargain. The court specifically applied the rule in *Bain v Fothergill*, adding that, if wilful default had been proved, it would not have been.

1. (1848) 1 Ex 850, at 855.
2. (1854) 9 Ex 341.
3. (1874) LR 7 HL 158.
4. (1776) 2 Wm. Bl. 1078.
5. [1922] 1 IR 62.
6. [1899] 2 Ch. 320.
7. [1939] IR 223.

The Law Reform Commission, in its *Report on Land Law and Conveyancing Law*: (1) *General Proposals* (LRC 30-1989) commented on the Rule in *Bain v Fothergill* and recommended that it be abolished by statute (paragraphs 30–32). This course of action was again endorsed in LRC Consultation paper 34-2004, paragraphs 576–579 and again in the *Report on the Reform and Modernisation of Land Law and Conveyancing Law* (LRC 74-2005). Accordingly, section 51 of the Land and Conveyancing Law Reform Bill 2006 (as introduced) provides 'The rule of law restricting damages recoverable for breaches of contract occasioned by defects in title to land (known as the Rule in *Bain v Fothergill*) is abolished),' vis-à-vis contracts made after commencement of the section.

The 2006 Bill is due to be enacted during 2008.

E. Remoteness of Damage and Actions in Fraud

Spice Girls Ltd *v* Aprilia World Service BV (No. 2) [2001] EMLR at 181

Arden J.:

As I stated in my earlier judgment, under the Misrepresentation Act 1967, s. 2(1), damages are calculated on the basis of fraud (*Royscot v Rogerson* [1991] 2 QB 297). Section 2(1) [S.45(1) of the Sale of Goods and Supply of Services Act 1980] states:

> Where a person has entered into a contract after a misrepresentation has been made to him by another party thereto and as a result thereof he has suffered loss, then, if the person making the misrepresentation would be liable to damages in respect thereof had the misrepresentation been made fraudulently, that person shall be so liable notwithstanding the misrepresentation was not made fraudulently, unless he proves that he had reasonable grounds to believe and did believe up to the time the contract was made that the facts represented there were true.

Moreover, the purpose of the award of damages is to compensate AWS for its loss, directly flowing from entering into the agreement, not to place it in the position in which it would have been if the misrepresentation had not been made (see for example, *East v Maurer* [1991] 1 WLR 461). Where damages are awarded for fraudulent misrepresentation, the measure of damages is reparation for all loss directly caused, whether or not foreseeable and including consequential loss (*Smith New Court Ltd v Scrimgeour Vickers* [1997] AC 254). By virtue of section 2(1), this measures applies also to damages under that section, even though the wrong relied on was not fraudulent. Furthermore the basis on which damages are to be awarded in this action is that AWS is entitled to be compensated for its loss on the basis that an agreement would not have been made.

SECTION FIVE—BANKER AND CUSTOMER CASES

Kinlen v Ulster Bank [1928] IR 171

In this case the plaintiff had a current account credit balance with the defendant bank. He tried to withdraw moneys within this balance but the bank manager refused to allow the plaintiff to do this. The plaintiff even resorted to drawing cheques on the account but these cheques were refused. At trial of the action substantial damages of £250 were awarded. The bank appealed.

Kennedy C.J.:

. . .

The questions for consideration arise out of the relationship of banker and customer in respect of what we all know as a 'current account'. The principles governing that relationship have been gradually defined during the past century in a series of judicial decisions in England. We have not been referred to any decision of the courts in Ireland touching the subject. No difference, however, in banking usage and practice as to current accounts in the two countries has been brought to our notice, and we may take it that the same governing legal principles apply to current accounts in both countries in the existing state of the law. They may be collected, so far as they have been stated up to the present time, in a group of early cases, namely: *Marzetti v Williams;*[1] *Pott v Clegg;*[2] *Foley v Hill;*[3] and *Rolin v Steward;*[4] and in a recent review of the authorities by the English Court of Appeal in *Joachimson v Swiss Bank Corp.*[5]

When a person desires to open a current account at a bank he pays a sum of money into the bank. The common expression that he '*lodges money* in bank' is somewhat misleading as to the nature of the transaction. The legal relation which thereupon arises is that of debtor or creditor. It is not the fiduciary relation of *cestui que trust* and trustee, nor the relation of principal and agent. The money paid in is no longer the money of the customer. It has been, as it were, lent to the bank, and the customer has, in lieu of it, a common law debt due to him by the bank, and recoverable by an action for money lent. But it is not merely a simple loan. Certain terms as to repayment are (apart from any special contract) implied from the relationship of customer and banker. These include, on the part of the banker, a promise to repay the money on demand made during banking hours at the branch of the bank at which the account is standing, and a promise to repay the money against the cheque or written order of the customer presented at the branch during business hours.

It follows that if the customer's account be in funds, the failure of the banker to comply with the customer's own demand for repayment or to honour his cheques, in either case up to the amount standing to credit of the account, entitles the customer to at least nominal damages for breach of contract. The matter is carried a stage further by the authorities, for it has long been settled law that if a banker wrongfully dishonours the cheque of a customer who is a trader, the customer is entitled to substantial, and not merely nominal, damages, without proof of special damage. There does not appear to be any positive decision directly negativing the like right of a non-trader in the same circumstances. Nor have we been referred to, and I do not know of, any decision directly on the question which precisely defines the damages to which a customer is entitled for non-compliance with his demand for repayment of his balance to himself.

. . .

The real position, then, may be shortly stated, and it is right to say that it is fully covered by the statement of claim as pleaded. The plaintiff had a current account with the defendant bank, with a balance standing to his credit. Admittedly now (for the attempt to make another case failed at the trial, and was not pursued here) there was no special contract affecting the credit balance. It was, therefore, subject to the ordinary contract of banker and customer. Admittedly, the customer on several occasions personally, in business hours, at the branch where the account was kept, demanded payment of sums within the limits of the amount of his credit balance, and, as found by the jury, tendered on three occasions cheque forms filled up in writing answering the purpose of demands in writing and receipts. Admittedly, his demands were wrongfully refused, and wholly untenable grounds of excuse were put forward by the bank through their manager. The plaintiff is clearly entitled to nominal damages, at least, in respect of each of these several breaches of contract. The question is whether he is entitled to substantial damages (apart from special damage), as the learned trial judge directed the jury, or to special damages.

The rule as to damages in the case of the dishonouring of a trader's cheque, to which I have referred, was invoked by plaintiff's counsel. Now the right of a trader to substantial damages, without proof of special damage for the wrongful dishonouring of his cheque, is really founded upon the implication of defamation—of slander of the trader in the way of his trade and credit. The bank represents him to the holder, payee, or indorsee of the cheque, as having committed a fraud in drawing upon a bank where he has no assets, or as having made a false statement as to a fact within his own knowledge, or the bank may be taken as conveying an imputation of the trader-customer's insolvency. Hence, in such cases the jury is properly directed not to limit their verdict to nominal damages, but to give substantial, though temperate and reasonable, damages for the injury caused to the plaintiff: *Rolin v Steward*. This is one of the anomalous cases of damages for breach of contract analogous to the case of breach of promise of marriage. The learned trial judge in his direction to the jury on the question of damages was certainly following the lines of the trader's cheque cases. His emphasis on the defamatory element demonstrates this.

In my opinion, the principle applied to cases of dishonoured traders' cheques has no application to the facts of the present case. A demand made personally by a customer upon his banker for payment is a two-party transaction. The refusal of payment cannot give rise to the implication of defamation of the customer to a third party, which necessarily arises when a trader's cheque, drawn or endorsed in favour of a third party, is presented by the holder and dishonoured by the banker.

. . .

The plaintiff has relied on two matters for the purpose of aggravating the damages to which he is entitled. In the first place, he said that the bank manager not only refused him the money to which he was entitled, but refused it contemptuously, and with contumely. Indeed, I have no doubt that the plaintiff was very badly treated indeed by the bank. In the second place, he urged that by reason of the first refusal he was subjected to great humiliation in raising money to pay his workmen. He had to pawn some of his personal belongings to raise part of the money, and he had to borrow part of it from a friend. These matters were greatly pressed upon us, and they evoke much sympathy with the plaintiff, but they are not matters which can be considered as elements of damages. It is very clearly settled, both in this country and in England, and affirmed in many cases, that in actions for breach of contract damages may not be given for such matters as disappointment of mind, humiliation, vexation, or the like, nor may exemplary or vindictive damages be awarded. See *Breen v Cooper*;[6] *Hamlin v Great Northern Rly*;[7] *Addis v Gramophone Co. Ltd.*[8] I am not now, of course, referring to the three recognised anomalies—actions for breaches of promise of marriage, actions for dishonouring traders' cheques, and a special class of actions for failure by a vendor to make title.

In the case of a breach of a simple contract to pay money, the law in this country, settled by a long line of authorities, is that the measure of damages is a reasonable compensation for non-performance of the contract, and that the amount of such compensation is to be arrived at by allowing interest on the money (which may vary in amount). See *Fletcher v Tayleur*;[9] *British Columbia Sawmill Co. v Nettleship*;[10] *Prehn v Royal Bank of Liverpool*;[11] *Wallis v Smith*;[12] *In re English Bank of the River Plate, ex parte Bank of Brazil*;[13] *South African Territories v Wallington*;[14] *Parker v Dickie*.[15]

I think, however, that there is no doubt that the courts are not bound to apply the measure I have just stated to the case of a special contract; as, for instance, where the money is to be paid for a special purpose known to the debtor, and injurious consequences of a particular character flow naturally from the non-payment: *Mackenzie v Corballis*.[16]

Now the relation of banker and customer in respect of a current account rests upon a special contract, to the special terms of which I have already referred. The due and unfailing performance of that contract on the part of the banker is, as he knows, vital to the ordinary daily life of his customers in our modern social organisation. The customer relies on his credit balance being at his instant call for innumerable purposes—commercial, domestic, social—constantly pressing upon him. The banker knows that if the credit balance is withheld from the customer when he demands payment, inevitably the customer must immediately procure an equivalent amount of money from some other source—probably by borrowing at interest. But the customer may fail to obtain a loan, or the delay may be such that injurious consequences naturally flow from the banker's default—a judgment may be marked against the customer, he may be evicted, his goods may be taken in execution, he may lose the benefit of a valuable contract, in a variety of ways he may suffer grievous loss and damage as the direct result of the banker's refusing him payment of his credit balance on his demand, a result which in the nature of things cannot but be within the banker's contemplation.

In my opinion, a customer is entitled to recover from his banker by way of damages for wrongfully refusing payment of a demand not exceeding the amount of the customer's credit balance on his current account—in the first place, the amount which he must pay for interest upon a loan of the amount of his demand during such time as payment is withheld by the banker. In the second place, the customer is, in my opinion, entitled, if he pleads and proves that he has suffered special damage flowing naturally in the circumstances from the banker's breach of contract, to recover special damages.

. . .

The measure of damages then to which the plaintiff is in my opinion entitled is only the amount of the interest which he should pay to procure the loan of a sum equivalent to his demand, payment whereof was wrongfully refused, during the period while payment was so withheld. The rate of such interest would necessarily be larger in the case of a poor man, without security, such as the plaintiff is. Strictly speaking, it should I think be calculated only on the first demand of £25. He would be entitled to nominal damages, and no more, for the dishonouring of the fourth, the test, cheque.

1. 1 B & Ad 415.
2. 16 M & W 321.
3. 2 H of L Cas 28.
4. 14 CB 595.
5. [1921] 3 KB 110.
6. IR 3 CL 621.
7. 1 H & N 408.
8. [1909] AC 488, per Lord Atkinson, at 495, 496.
9. 17 CB 21, per Willes J., at 29.
10. LR 3 CP 499 per Bovill C.J., at 506.
11. LR 5 Ex 92.
12. 21 ChD 243, per Jessel M.R., at 257.
13. [1893] 2 Ch. 438, per Chitty J., at 446.
14. [1897] 1 QB 692, per Chitty L.J., at 696.
15. 4 LR (Ir) 244, per Lawson J., at 248.
16. 40 ILTR 28.

Kpohraror v Woolwich Building Society [1996] 4 All ER 119

The plaintiff converted a building society savings account into a current account. During this process he described himself on the application form as a self-employed exporter/importer. In breach of his contract the defendant building society dishonoured a cheque drawn in favour of a company with whom the plaintiff was doing business. The plaintiff sought damages, *inter alia*, for the injury done to the plaintiff's credit by reason of the dishonour of the cheque and the reason given for this to the third party.

Evans LJ. gave the leading judgment for the Court of Appeal:

As will appear below, the issue in my view is whether a person who is not 'a trader' for the purposes of the common law rule—and it is not at all clear what the limits of that category are—can recover substantial rather than nominal damages for loss of business reputation when his cheque is wrongly dishonoured by the bank. A subsidiary question is how much the measure of damages is affected by the extent of the bank's knowledge of its customer and of the purposes for which he uses his account.

I will start with the authorities which establish that a 'trader' is entitled to recover substantial, rather than nominal, damages for loss of business reputation without proof of actual damage. This was recognised and applied, although in a different context, by the House of Lords in *Wilson v United Counties Bank Ltd* [1920] AC 102 Lord Birkenhead LC said:

The objection was taken by the defendants that this finding of the jury cannot be supported without proof of special damage. In deciding this point, I do not lay down a rule of general law, but I deal with the exceptional language of an exceptional contract. The defendants undertook for consideration to sustain the credit of the trading customer. On principle the case seems to me to belong to that very special class of cases in which a banker, though his customer's account is in funds, nevertheless dishonours his cheque. The *ratio decidendi* in such cases is that the refusal to meet the cheque, under such circumstances, is so obviously injurious to the credit of a trader that the latter can recover, without allegation of special damage, reasonable compensation for the injury done to his credit. The leading case upon this point is that of *Rolin v Steward* ((1854) 14 CB 595). The direction of Lord Campbell to the jury has been generally accepted and treated as an accurate statement of the law. If it be held that there is an irrebuttable presumption that the dishonour of a trader customer's cheque in the events supposed is injurious to him and may be compensated by other than nominal damages, the conclusion would appear to follow almost *a fortiori* that such damages may be given where the defendant has expressly contracted to sustain the financial credit of a trading customer and has committed a breach of his agreement.' (See [1920] AC 102 at 112.)

Two passages should be quoted from *Rolin v Steward* (1854) 14 CB 595, 139 ER 245. Lord Campbell CJ. directed the jury to give 'not nominal, nor excessive, but reasonable and temperate damages' (see 14 CB 595 at 605, 139 ER 245 at 249). In the Court of Common Pleas, Williams J. said that —

when . . . the [customer] is a trader . . . the jury, in estimating the damages, may take into their consideration the natural and necessary consequences which must result to the [customer] from the [bank's] breach of contract: just as in the case of an action for a slander of a person in the way of his trade, or in the case of an imputation of insolvency on a trader, the action lies without proof of special damage.' (See (1854) 14 CB 595 at 607.)

The rule so stated made it necessary to consider in every case whether or not the plaintiff was a trader. In Australia in 1884 a farmer was not (see *Bank of New South Wales v Milvain* 10 VLR 3). In England, in 1940, a bookmaker was (see *Davidson v Barclay's Bank Ltd* [1940] 1 All ER 316), but it is an open question whether professionals such as solicitors and accountants who are 'akin to businessmen' are within the rule.

It is abundantly clear, in my judgment, that history has changed the social factors which moulded the rule in the nineteenth century. It is not only a tradesman of whom it can be said that the refusal to meet his cheque is 'so obviously injurious to [his] credit' that he should 'recover, without allegation of special damage, reasonable compensation for the injury done to his credit' (see [1920] AC 102 at 112, per Lord Birkenhead LC). The credit rating of individuals is as important for their personal transactions, including mortgages and hire-purchase as well as banking facilities, as it is for those who are engaged in trade, and it is notorious that central registers are now kept. I would have no hesitation in holding that what is in effect a presumption of some damage arises in every case, in so far as this is a presumption of fact.

So the question becomes, whether the authorities compel the conclusion as a matter of law that the presumption cannot extend beyond the category of trader. In my judgment, they do not. The most directly relevant are *Gibbons v Westminster Bank Ltd* [1939] 3 All ER 577, and *Rae v Yorkshire Bank plc* [1988] BTLC 35. In the former case, Lawrence J. regarded the presumption in favour of a trader as one of four exceptions to the general rule that the plaintiff in a claim for damages for breach of contract cannot recover substantial damages in the absence of proof that some actual damage has been suffered, and he felt unable to extend the exception to non-traders (see *Addis v Gramophone Co. Ltd* [1909] AC 488 at 495, per Lord Atkinson). He said:

The authorities which have been cited to me all lay down that a trader is entitled to recover substantial damages without pleading and proving actual damage for the dishonour of his cheque, but it has never been held that that exception to the general rule as to the measure of damages for breach of contract extends to any one who is not a trader. (See [1939] 3 All ER 577 at 579.)

In *Rae v Yorkshire Bank plc* the plaintiff's claim was for damages for 'inconvenience and humiliation' (see [1988] BTLC 35 at 37). Parker LJ., with whom O'Connor LJ. agreed, cited *Bliss v South East Thames Regional Health Authority* [1987] ICR 700, where Dillon LJ held that the general rule laid down in *Addis v Gramophone Co. Ltd* is that —

> where damages fall to be assessed for breach of contract rather than in tort it is not permissible to award general damages for frustration, mental distress, injured feelings or annoyance occasioned by the breach. (See [1987] ICR 700 at 717–718.)

Dillon LJ. also noted a further exception to the general rule which is now permitted 'where the contract which has been broken was itself a contract to provide peace of mind or freedom from distress' (see [1987] ICR 700 at 718). Parker LJ. continued ([1988] BTLC 35 at 37): 'That authority, and *Gibbons*, are two of many which in my view make Mr Rae's an appeal which must inevitably fail.' Clearly, the judgment in *Rae v Yorkshire Bank plc* was based primarily in the application of the law as stated by Dillon LJ. to the facts of that case, where the claim was for 'inconvenience and humiliation' (only). That is a different kind of damage from loss of reputation or credit, unless 'humiliation' is intended to include such injury in the eyes of third parties, but that point was not taken in *Rae*'s case because the kinds of damage referred to by Dillon LJ. all refer to the injured feelings of the plaintiff himself.

The trial judge in *Rae* had referred to *Gibbons* and said (see [1988] BTLC 35 at 36): 'It is clear that Mr Rae was not a trader and that in those circumstances, damages are purely nominal.' Apart from the passing reference to *Gibbons* in the passage already quoted, the 'trader' rule, or exception, was not considered in the judgments in the Court of Appeal.

In these circumstances, neither *Rae* nor *Gibbons* itself is binding authority which precludes this court from considering whether a bank's customer who is not a trader is precluded from recovering substantial damages for injury to his reputation or credit, unless special damage is alleged and proved. The trader exception itself recognises, as does the general rule regarding the recovery of damages for tort, that his is a kind of injury recognised by law. If the trader is an exception to the general rules regarding damages for breach of contract, then the explanation may lie in the tortious analogy with damages for injury to business credit. In *Addis v Gramophone Co. Ltd* Lord Atkinson did not refer to any 'trader' rule, but generally to 'actions against a banker for refusing to pay a customer's cheque when he has in his hands funds of the customer's to meet it' (see [1909] Ac 488 at 495). *McGregor* deals with the rule as applying only to traders but also states generally that 'loss by injury to credit and reputation caused by the defendants' failure to honour the plaintiff's drafts may be presumed' (see paras 1222, 1785). (Damages for loss of reputation *simpliciter* are excluded, whether in contract or for torts other than defamation (see *Joyce v Sengupta* [1993] 1 All ER 897).

Moreover, if the exception is a presumption of fact then it is open to the court, in my judgment, to hold that changing social circumstances should cause the presumption to be reviewed and if necessary expanded in order to take those changes into account.

For these reasons, I would reject the defendants' allegation by way of cross-appeal that the master was wrong to award more than a nominal sum by way of general damages. I should, however, also refer to their contention that the master was wrong to do so when the defendants denied that they had knowledge of the fact that he was a trader. In none of the reported cases where a trader has succeeded in recovering substantial damages has the bank's knowledge been in issue. The master decided this effectively as a preliminary issue. The defendants wished to call as a witness their employee who dealt with the plaintiff when he converted his savings account into a current account in June 1991. She would have denied, as her affidavit evidence indicated, that he told her that the account would be used for trading purposes. So the master gave 'part 1' of his judgment holding that substantial damages could be awarded even where the bank had no knowledge 'actual or implied of the plaintiff's status as a trader and the use of his account'. If the trader 'exception' is good law then I doubt whether this can be correct, if only because it offends against the basic requirement of both parts of the rule in Hadley v Baxendale which is that the test of remoteness and therefore of the right to recover a particular head of damage depends upon the state of the defendant's knowledge of the likely, or 'not unlikely' (see *The Heron* II, *Koufos v C Czarnikow Ltd* [1967] 3 All ER 686), consequences of his breach, whether 'in the usual course of things' because of what the defendant is taken to have known or by reason of his actual knowledge of special facts. But it is unnecessary to express a concluded view, because the evidence is that the plaintiff described himself in the application form as a part-time self-employed 'exporter/importer' although clearly on a modest scale. This evidence is not and cannot be disputed and it is sufficient in my judgment to fix the defendants with knowledge that that was the self-styled description of the plaintiff for the purposes of the contract between them with regard to the current account. To this extent, it was a question of 'status' and the defendants knew what that status was. If it is objected that they should also have knowledge that the account was to be used for trading purposes, then this is a further refinement of the trader exception—the dishonour of a personal cheque could be no less harmful to the trader's credit than of one drawn on a trading account, perhaps even more so—and an additional reason why in my judgment, the exception or rule should not be confined as the defendants say that it should.

. . .

SECTION SIX—DAMAGES FOR PHYSICAL DISCOMFORT AND INCONVENIENCE CAUSED BY BREACH OF CONTRACT

Hobbs *v* London and South Western Rly (1875) 10 QBD 111

Cockburn C.J.:

. . .

The facts are simple. The plaintiffs took tickets to be conveyed from the Wimbledon station of the defendants' railway to Hampton Court. It so happened that the train did not go to Hampton Court, and the plaintiffs were taken on to Esher Station, which increased the distance which they would have to go from the railway station to their home by two or three miles.

Damages were asked for upon two grounds: first, for the inconvenience that the husband and wife, with their two children, sustained by having to go this distance, the night happening to be a wet night; in the second place, damages were asked by reason of the wife, from her exposure to the wet on that night, getting a bad cold and being ill in health, the consequence of which was that some expense was incurred in medical attendance upon her. We think these two heads of damage must be kept distinct, and I propose to deal with them as distinct subjects.

With regard to the first, there can be no doubt whatever upon the facts that the plaintiffs were put to personal inconvenience: they had to walk late at night, after twelve o'clock, a considerable distance, the wife suffered fatigue from it, and they had to carry their children, or to get them along with great difficulty the children being fatigued and exhausted; and there is no doubt that there was personal inconvenience suffered by the party on that occasion, and that inconvenience was the immediate consequence and result of the breach of contract on the part of the defendants. The plaintiffs did their best to diminish the inconvenience to themselves by having recourse to such means as they hoped to find at hand; they tried to get into an inn, which they were unable to do; they tried to get a conveyance; they were informed none was to be had; and they had no alternative but to walk; and therefore it was from no default of their part, and it cannot be doubted that the inconvenience was the immediate and necessary consequence of the breach of the defendants' contract to convey them to Hampton Court. Now inasmuch as there was manifest personal inconvenience, I am at a loss to see why that inconvenience should not be compensated by damages in such an action as this. It has been endeavoured to be argued, upon principle and upon authority, that this was a kind of damage which could not be supported; and attempts were also made to satisfy us that this supposed inconvenience was more or less imaginary, and would depend upon the strength and constitution of the parties, and various other circumstances; and that it is not to be taken that a walk of so many additional miles would be a thing that a person would dislike or suffer inconvenience from; and that there may be circumstances under which a walk of several miles, so far from being matter of inconvenience, would be just the contrary. All that depends on the actual facts of each individual case; and if the jury are satisfied that in the particular instance personal inconvenience or suffering has been occasioned, and that it had been occasioned as the immediate effect of the breach of the contract, I can see no reasonable principle why that should not be compensated for. The case of *Hamlin v Great Northern Rly Co.*[1] was cited as an authority to shew that for personal inconvenience damages ought not to be awarded. That case appears to me to fall far short of any such proposition. It merely seems to amount to this: that where a party, by not being able to get to a place which he would otherwise have arrived at in time to meet persons with whom he had appointments, has sustained pecuniary loss, that is too remote to be made the subject of damages in an action upon a breach of contract. That may be perfectly true, because, as in every one of the instances cited, you would have to go into the question whether there was a loss arising from the breach of contract, before you could assess that loss. And, after all, if the true principle be laid down in *Hadley v Baxendale*,[2] the damage must be something which is in the contemplation of the parties as likely to result from a breach of contract; and it is impossible that a company who undertake to carry a passenger to a place of destination can have in their minds all the circumstances which may result from the passenger being detained on the journey. As far as the case of *Hamlin v Great Northern Rly Co.* goes, I am far from saying it was a wrong decision; but it did not decide that personal inconvenience, however serious, was not to be taken into account as a subject matter of damage in a breach of contract of a carrier to convey a person to a particular destination. If it did, I should not follow that authority; but I do not think it applicable to this case at all. I think there is no authority that personal inconvenience, where it is sufficiently serious, should not be the subject of damages to be recovered in an action of this kind. Therefore, on the first head, the £8, I think the verdict ought to stand.

With regard to the second head of damage, the case assumes a very different aspect. I see very great difficulty indeed in coming to any other conclusion than that the £20 is not recoverable; and when we are asked to lay down some principle as a guiding rule in all such cases, I quite agree with my brother Blackburn in the infinite difficulty there would be in attempting to lay down any principle or rule which shall cover all such cases; but I think that the nearest approach to anything like a fixed rule is this: That to entitle a person to damages by reason of a breach of contract, the injury for which compensation is asked should be one that may be fairly taken to have been contemplated by the parties as the possible result of the breach of contract. Therefore you must have something immediately flowing out of the breach of contract complained of, something immediately connected with it, and not merely connected with it through a series of causes intervening between the immediate consequence of the breach of contract and the damage or injury complained of. To illustrate that I cannot take a better case than the one now before us: Suppose that a passenger is put out at a wrong station on a wet night and obliged to walk a considerable distance in the rain, catching a violent cold which ends in a fever, and the passenger is laid up for a couple of months, and loses through this illness the offer of an employment which would have brought him a handsome salary. No one, I think, who understood the law, would say that the loss so occasioned is so connected with the breach of contract as that the carrier breaking the contract could be held liable. Here, I think, it cannot be said the catching cold by the plaintiff's wife is the immediate and necessary effect of the breach of contract, or was one which could be fairly said to have been in the contemplation of the parties. As my brother Blackburn points out, so far as the inconvenience of the walk home is concerned, that must be taken to be reasonably within the contemplation of the parties; because, if a carrier engages to put a person down at a given place, and does not put him down there, but puts him down somewhere else, it must be in the contemplation of everybody that the passenger put down at the wrong place must get to the place of his destination somehow or other. If there are means of conveyance for getting there, he may take those means and make the company responsible for the expense; but if there are no means, I take it to be law that the carrier must compensate him for the personal inconvenience which the absence of those means has necessitated. That flows out of the breach of contract so immediately that the damage resulting must be admitted to be fair subject matter of damages. But in this case the wife's cold and its consequences cannot stand upon the same footing as the personal inconvenience arising from the additional distance which the plaintiffs had to go. It is an effect of the breach of contract in a certain sense, but removed one stage; it is not the primary but the secondary consequence of it; and if in such a case the party recovered damages by reason of the cold caught incidentally on that foot journey, it would be necessary, on the principle so applied, to hold that in the two cases which have been put in the course of the discussion, the party aggrieved would be equally entitled to recover. And yet the moment the cases are stated, everybody would agree that, according to our law, the parties are not entitled to recover.

(Blackburn J. concurred.)

Mellor J.:

I am entirely of the same opinion. I quite agree with my brother Parry, that for the mere inconvenience, such as annoyance and loss of temper, or vexation, or for being disappointed in a particular thing which you have set your mind upon, without real physical inconvenience resulting, you cannot recover damages. That is purely sentimental, and not a case where the word inconvenience, as I here use it, would apply. But I must say, if it is a fact that you arrived at a place where you did not intend to go to, where you are placed, by reason of the breach of contract of the carriers, at a considerable distance from your destination, the case may be otherwise. It is admitted that if there be a carriage you may hire it and ride home and charge the expense to the defendants. The reason why you may hire a carriage and charge the expense to the company is with the view simply of mitigating the inconvenience to which you would otherwise be subject; so that where the inconvenience is real and substantial arising from being obliged to walk home, I cannot see why that should not be capable of being assessed as damages in respect of inconvenience.

[1.] 1 H & N 408; 26 LJ (Ex) 20.   [2.] 9 Ex 341; 23 LJ (Ex) 179.

Note

The rule about physical discomfort also applies in sale of real property or house construction contracts. *Murphy v Quality Homes* (HC) 22 June 1976, unrep.

Contracts for the carriage of persons to places of entertainment are also covered: *French v West Clare Rly Co.* (1897) 31 ILT 140. The plaintiff recovered £10 damages when a train transporting him to a concert failed to arrive on time, thereby causing him to miss the event.

In relation to the possibility of damages for distress caused by breach of a commercial contract see *Lennon and Others v Talbot Ireland* (see p. 1110 below).

Jarvis v Swans Tours [1973] 1 All ER 71

Lord Denning M.R.:

The plaintiff, Mr Jarvis, is a solicitor employed by a local authority at Barking. In 1969 he was minded to go for Christmas to Switzerland. He was looking forward to a ski-ing holiday. It is his one fortnight's holiday in the year. He prefers it in the winter rather than in the summer.

Mr Jarvis read a brochure issued by Swans Tours Ltd. He was much attracted by the description of Mörlialp, Giswil, Central Switzerland. I will not read the whole of it, but just pick out some of the principal attractions:

> House Party Centre with special resident host . . . Mörlialp is a most wonderful little resort on a sunny plateau . . . Up there you will find yourself in the midst of beautiful alpine scenery, which in winter becomes a wonderland of sun, snow and ice, with a wide variety of fine ski-runs, a skating-rink and an exhilarating toboggan run . . . Why did we choose the Hotel Krone . . . mainly and most of all, because of the *Gemütlichkeit* and friendly welcome you will receive from Herr and Frau Weibel . . . The Hotel Krone has its own Alphütte Bar which will be open several evenings a week . . . No doubt you will be in for a great time, when you book this houseparty holiday . . . Mr Weibel, the charming owner, speaks English.

On the same page, in a special yellow box, it was said: 'Swans Houseparty in Mörlialp. All these Houseparty arrangements are included in the price of your holiday. Welcome party on arrival. Afternoon tea and cake for seven days. Swiss Dinner by candlelight.

Fondue-party. Yodler evening. Chali farewell party in the Alphütte Bar. Service of representative.' Alongside on the same page there was a special note about ski-packs: 'Hire of Skis, Sticks and Boots . . . twelve days £11.10.'

In August 1969, on the faith of that brochure, Mr Jarvis booked a fifteen day holiday, with ski-pack. The total charge was £63.45, including Christmas supplement. He was to fly from Gatwick to Zurich on 20 December 1969 and return on 3 January 1970.

The plaintiff went on the holiday, but he was very disappointed. He was a man of about thirty five and he expected to be one of a houseparty of some thirty or so people. Instead, he found there were only thirteen during the first week. In the second week there was no houseparty at all. He was the only person there. Mr Weibel could not speak English. So there was Mr Jarvis, in the second week, in this hotel with no houseparty at all, and no one could speak English, except himself. He was very disappointed, too, with the ski-ing. It was some distance away at Giswil. There were no ordinary length skis. There were only mini-skis, about 3 feet long. So he did not get his ski-ing as he wanted to. In the second week he did get some longer skis for a couple of days, but then, because of the boots, his feet got rubbed and he could not continue even with the long skis. So his ski-ing holiday, from his point of view, was pretty well ruined.

There were many other matters, too. They appear trivial when they are set down in writing, but I have no doubt they loomed large in Mr Jarvis' mind, when coupled with the other disappointments. He did not have the nice Swiss cakes which he was hoping for. The only cakes for tea were potato crisps and little dry nutcakes. The yodler evening consisted of one man from the locality who came in his working clothes for a little while, and sang four or five songs very quickly. The Alphütte Bar was an unoccupied annex which was only open one evening. There was a representative, Mrs Storr, there during the first week, but she was not there during the second week. The matter was summed up by the learned judge: ' . . . during the first week he got a holiday in Switzerland which was to some extent inferior . . . and, as to the second week he got a holiday which was very largely inferior [to what he was led to expect].'

What is the legal position? I think that the statements in the brochure were representations or warranties. The breaches of them give Mr Jarvis a right to damages. It is not necessary to decide whether they were representations or warranties; because, since the Misrepresentation Act 1967, there is a remedy in damages for misrepresentation as well as for breach of warranty.

The one question in the case is: what is the amount of damages? The judge seems to have taken the difference in value between what he paid for and what he got. He said that he intended to give 'the difference between the two values and no other damages' under any other head. He thought that Mr Jarvis had got half of what he paid for. So the judge gave him half the amount which he had paid, namely, £31.72. Mr Jarvis appeals to this court. He says that the damages ought to have been much more.

There is one point I must mention first. Counsel together made a very good note of the judge's judgment. They agreed it. It is very clear and intelligible. It shows plainly enough the ground of the judge's decision; but, by an oversight, it was not submitted to the judge, as it should have been; see *Bruen v Bruce*.[1] In some circumstances we should send it back to the judge for his comments. But I do not think we need do so here. The judge received the notice of appeal and made notes for our consideration. I do not think he would have wished to add to them. We will, therefore, decide the case on the material before us.

What is the right way of assessing damages? It has often been said that on a breach of contract damages cannot be given for mental distress. Thus in *Hamlin v Great Northern Rly Co.*[2] Pollock C.B. said that damages cannot be given 'for the disappointment of mind occasioned by the breach of contract'. And in *Hobbs v London & South*

Western Rly Co.[3] Mellor J. said that: ' . . . for the mere inconvenience, such as annoyance and loss of temper, or vexation, or for being disappointed in a particular thing which you have set your mind upon, without real physical inconvenience resulting, you cannot recover damages.' The courts in those days only allowed the plaintiff to recover damages if he suffered physical inconvenience, such as, having to walk five miles home, as in *Hobbs'* case; or to live in an overcrowded house: see *Bailey v Bullock.*[4]

I think that those limitations are out of date. In a proper case damages for mental distress can be recovered in contract, just as damages for shock can be recovered in tort. One such case is a contract for a holiday, or any other contract to provide entertainment and enjoyment. If the contracting party breaks his contract, damages can be given for the disappointment, the distress, the upset and frustration caused by the breach. I know that it is difficult to assess in terms of money, but it is more difficult than the assessment which the courts have to make every day in personal injury cases for loss of amenities. Take the present case. Mr Jarvis has only a fortnight's holiday in the year. He books it far ahead, and looks forward to it all that time. He ought to be compensated for the loss of it.

A good illustration was given by Edmund Davies L.J. in the course of the argument. He put the case of a man who has taken a ticket for Glyndbourne. It is the only night on which he can get there. He hires a car to take him. The car does not turn up. His damages are not limited to the mere cost of the ticket. He is entitled to general damages for the disappointment he has suffered and the loss of the entertainment which he should have had. Here, Mr Jarvis's fortnight's winter holiday has been a grave disappointment. It is true that he was conveyed to Switzerland and back and had meals and bed in the hotel. But that is not what he went for. He went to enjoy himself with all the facilities which the defendants said he would have. He is entitled to damages for the lack of those facilities, and for his loss of enjoyment.

A similar case occurred in 1951. It was *Stedman v Swan's Tours.*[5] A holidaymaker was awarded damages because he did not get the bedroom and the accommodation which he was promised. The County Court Judge awarded him £13 15s. This court increased it to £50.

I think the judge was in error in taking the sum paid for the holiday, £63.45, and halving it. The right measure of damages is to compensate him for the loss of entertainment and enjoyment which he was promised, and which he did not get. Looking at the matter quite broadly, I think the damages in this case should be the sum of £125. I would allow the appeal accordingly.

(Stephenson L.J. agreed.)
Edmund Davies L.J.:

Some of the observations of Mellor J. in the 100 year old case of *Hobbs v London & South Western Rly Co.* call today for reconsideration. I must not be taken to accept that, under modern conditions and having regard to the developments which have taken place in the law of contract since that decision was given, it is right to say, as the learned judge did, that: ' . . . for the mere inconvenience, such as annoyance and loss of temper, or vexation, or for being disappointed in a particular thing which you have set your mind upon, without real physical inconvenience resulting, you cannot recover damages. That is purely sentimental, and not a case where the word inconvenience, as I here use it, would apply.' On the contrary, there is authority for saying that even inconvenience that is not strictly physical may be a proper element in the assessment of damages. In *Griffiths v Evans,*[6] in the course of a dissenting judgment where a solicitor was being sued for negligence in wrongly advising a plaintiff as to his right to sue his employers at common law, Denning L.J. said that the damages should be assessed: 'by taking into account the inconvenience and expense to which [the plaintiff] will be put in suing the employers and the risk of failure.'

Be that as it may, Mellor J. was dealing with a contract of carriage and the undertaking of the railway company was entirely different from that of the defendants in the present case. These travel agents made clear by their lavishly illustrated brochure with its ecstatic text that what they were contracting to provide was not merely air, travel, hotel accommodation and meals of a certain standard. To quote the assurance which they gave regarding the Mörlialp House Party Centre, 'No doubt you will be in for a great time, when you book this houseparty holiday'. The result was that they did not limit themselves to the obligation to ensure that an air passage was booked, that hotel accommodation was reserved, that food was provided and that these items would measure up to the standards they themselves set up. They went further than that. They assured and undertook to provide a holiday of a certain quality, with *Gemütlichkeit* (that is to say, geniality, comfort and cosiness) as its overall characteristics, and 'a great time', the enjoyable outcome which would surely result to all but the most determined misanthrope.

If in such circumstances travel agents fail to provide a holiday of the contracted quality, they are liable in damages. In assessing those damages the court is not, in my judgment, restricted by the £63.45 paid by the client for his holiday. Nor is it confined to matters of physical inconvenience and discomfort.

1. [1959] 2 All ER 375, [1959] 1 WLR 684
2. (1856) 1 H & N 408 at 411
3. (1875) LR 10 QB 111 at 122, [1874–80] All ER Rep 458 at 463
4. [1950] 2 All ER 1167
5. (1951) 95 Sol J 727
6. [1953] 2 All ER 1364, [1953] 1 WLR 1424

Note

This line of authority has taken root in Ireland also, as this extract from *The Irish Independent* 28 February 1985 illustrates.

A Dublin housewife was hospitalised suffering from food poisoning and exhaustion after she returned from a Spanish holiday, the Dublin District Court heard yesterday.

Mrs Patricia Hynes and her husband Michael, of Blanchardstown, were awarded £300 plus costs after they sued Happy Holidays Ltd, Blanchardstown.

They claimed that facilities and accommodation in Malaga were 'deplorably inadequate' and that they suffered severe inconvenience and disruption.

Mrs Hynes said she wanted to come home a few days after she arrived. The blankets were dirty and the floors full of dust. She added that she was hospitalised suffering from food poisoning and exhaustion after she returned.

Mr Hynes said he booked the holiday last April. He paid £650.

During the holiday in May, his son had to sleep on a mattress on the floor, while he and his wife slept in two single beds. They made a bed for their daughter out of cushions. He gave examples of facilities which were not as described in the brochure.

Mr Freddie Greehan of Happy Holidays said the family had only paid for three people. Their youngest child, an infant, had travelled free. The apartment block was used every week by about fifty people and he had few complaints.

Awarding damages and costs, Justice Liam McMenamin said any reasonable person reading the brochure would assume they were entitled to fourteen days' comfort in hygienic surroundings. This was not so, he said. He added that the courts must protect consumers.

More recently, *The Irish Times* of 17 May 2006 reports a typical case in which the District Court, exercising jurisdiction as a Small Claims Court, has allowed damages awards for either distress, physical discomfort, injury, misrepresentation or loss of amenity arising out of package holidays that go badly wrong. Under the headline, 'Family awarded compensation for holiday ordeal', the newspaper reports that the Furlong family were subjected to 'a litany' of problems such as a three and an half-hour flight delay, construction work going on in the early hours around the pool, physical injury through broken glass being left around the pool area, as well as rowdy parties in the complex. Damages to the maximum financial limit of €1,269 were awarded. In *Scaife v Falcon Leisure Group* [2007] IESC 57 the Supreme Court has held that hotel proprietors, both at common law and under the Package Holiday Directive, owe a duty to exercise reasonable care and skill vis-à-vis facilities to be provided, and that if these obligations are not met the consumer is entitled to sue the organiser of the holiday.

Dinnegan *v* Ryan (HC) 13 May 2002, unrep.

Facts

Mr Dinnegan engaged Mr Ryan, a publican, to provide food and drink for a small informal wedding reception. When the wedding party arrived at the public house Mr Ryan refused to serve the party, causing considerable distress and humiliation to Mr and Mrs Dinnegan who had just been married earlier that day. Murray J. held that Mr Ryan was in breach of contract and went on to consider the award of damages to both Mr Dinnegan and Mrs Dinnegan.

Murray J.:

Damages for breach of contract
As regards damages I think it should first be noted that the contract was broader than the simple provision of sandwiches and cocktail sausages. This was no bread and butter business contract where the purely commercial value of the transaction is the sole or primary subject of the contract. It was a contract not only to provide food and a bar service but also to provide a place which would be an occasion for the enjoyment and celebration of the wedding day of the plaintiffs to be shared in by their family and friends. It was a contract intended to ensure that the plaintiffs could mark and bring to a close a momentous day in their lives in the comfort of Downs Inn.

The loss sustained by the plaintiffs arising from the breach of contract was not just disappointment at losing the advantages which might accrue from a successfully completed commercial transaction. The loss which they sustained, was the denial to the plaintiffs of the occasion for enjoyment and happiness to be shared with their family and friends. That was the essence of the contract. For that loss they are entitled to compensation. The degree of that loss was undoubtedly exacerbated by the manner in which the contract was breached, namely, without forewarning and at the last minute when they arrived in the public house. This meant that instead of their wedding day ending on a memorable and high note, it was plunged to the depths of humiliation, shock and disappointment, which not only brought it to a distressing end but engraved a permanent blotch on the memory of what should always have been a day of good memories. Given the nature and purpose of the contract, the loss in this regard which the plaintiff sustained was reasonably foreseeable and, moreover, flows directly from its breach. Damages are intended to be compensatory. In the circumstances of this case I am satisfied that the plaintiffs are entitled to be compensated for the fact that they were wrongfully and in breach of contract deprived of their happy occasion to celebrate their wedding day and suffered the distress and disappointment which is inevitably a direct consequence of the breach of such a contract. The law and practice of the courts in awarding damages for breach of this type of contract has evolved in recent decades (see for example *Contract Law in Ireland*, Robert Clark, 4th edition at 479) stimulated to a significant extent by the decision of the English Court of Appeal in *Jarvis v Swan Tours Ltd* [1973] 1 AER 71. In *Johnson v Longleat Properties (Dublin) Ltd* (unrep. High Court, 19 May 1976 and noted in 13 IR. Jur. 186, 1978). McMahon J. stated:

> It appears to me that in principle damages may be awarded for inconvenience or loss of enjoyment when these are within the presumed contemplation of the parties as likely to result from the breach of contract. That will usually be the case in contracts to provide entertainment or enjoyment. . . .

On the evidence, both Mr Dinnegan and Mrs Dinnegan suffered not only humiliation in front of their friends, but a great deal of personal distress that this particular day should be spoilt in such a shocking, uncaring and arbitrary manner. I accept the evidence that they were emotionally devastated, that Mrs Dinnegan was tearful for many hours afterwards and that although they had the option of seeking out some other hostelry to get together for a least a drink, they were so distressed that they really did not have the heart in them to do so. Mrs Dinnegan was so upset that she visited her father's grave for solace. In my view they are both entitled to significant damages against the defendants. I would not differentiate between the plaintiffs on the question of damages and therefore I award €6,000 damages to Mr Dinnegan the first named plaintiff and €6,000 damages to Mrs Dinnegan the second named plaintiff. Accordingly there will be a decree of €12,000 damages for the plaintiffs against the defendants.

Note

The *Irish Times* of 2 March 1995 contains an account of a Circuit Court case under the heading, '£13,000 award for wedding day miss'.

What happened on a Dublin woman's wedding day would rival a low-grade comedy film, a judge said yesterday.

Recalling evidence of Ms Lisa Burke's undignified arrival at Clogher Road Church, Crumlin, squashed into a two-seater sportscar with her father and a driver, Judge Cyril Kelly awarded her £13,000 damages.

He said he would make no apportionment as to how the money might be divided between Lisa and her husband, Mr John Burke, of Willow Drive, Greenpark, Clondalkin.

The couple sued David Kenny Studios of Crumlin Road, Dolphin's Barn, for breach of contract and negligence arising from let-downs on their wedding day on 30 August 30 1991.

She and her husband told the court that they had hired David Kenny Studios to look after the limousines and the photography. A white Rolls-Royce never turned up to collect the bride at her home as her husband-to-be, John, thought he was 'going to be left stranded at the altar'.

Ms Burke told the court that she was taken on the seven-mile journey to the church in a friend's white two-seater sports car, holding up the hoops of her wedding gown to save it from being destroyed. Her father was squashed into the back.

As a result, the wedding ceremony started 40 minutes late and had to be rushed to facilitate two other couples literally queuing up to get married after the initial delays.

Judge Kelly said he had heard psychiatric evidence of Ms Burke's suffering since the wedding. She could not look at the video or picture albums and had left the court while he had watched a video of the wedding.

After hearing that David Kenny, owner of the studios, was 'not a man of means', Judge Kelly ordered that the Burkes be paid their award within 14 days.

Farley v Skinner [2001] 4 All ER 801

Lord Steyn:

My Lords, the central question is whether a buyer who employed a surveyor to investigate whether a property in the countryside was seriously affected by aircraft noise may in principle recover non-pecuniary damages against the surveyor for the latter's negligent failure to discover that the property was so affected. The trial judge answered this question in the affirmative. A two-member Court of Appeal disagreed on it. The point was then re-argued before a three-member Court of Appeal ((2000) 73 Con LR 70). By a majority the Court of Appeal reversed the decision of the trial judge and ruled that there was no right to recover non-pecuniary damages in such cases. The second Court of Appeal was deluged with authorities. So was the House on the present appeal. The hearings of what was a comparatively simple case took up an exorbitant amount of time. This circumstance underlines the importance, in the quest for coherent and just solutions in such cases, of simple and practical rules.

Riverside House, aircraft noise and the surveyor
In 1990 the plaintiff, a successful businessman, contemplated retirement. He owned a flat in London, a house in Brighton and a property overseas. He wanted to buy a gracious country residence. He became interested in a beautiful property known as Riverside House in the village of Blackboys in Sussex which was situated some fifteen miles from Gatwick International Airport. The property is in the heart of the countryside. There is a stream running through the middle of it. The property has a croquet lawn, tennis court, orchard, paddock and swimming pool. Although the attractive house required modernisation and refurbishment, it appeared to ideal for the plaintiff. There was, however, one question mark over the transaction. For the plaintiff a property offering peace and tranquility was the raison d'être of the proposed purchase. He wanted to be reasonably sure that the property was not seriously affected by aircraft noise.

The plaintiff engaged as his surveyor the defendant, who had been in practice as a sole practitioner for some years. The surveyor had to investigate the usual matters expected of a surveyor who inspects a property. In addition the plaintiff also specifically asked the surveyor to investigate, amongst other things whether the property would be affected by aircraft noise. The plaintiff told the surveyor that he did not want a property on a flight path. The surveyor accepted these instructions.

On 17 December 1990 the surveyor sent his report to the plaintiff. From the plaintiff's point of view it was a satisfactory report. About aircraft noise the surveyor reported:

> You have also asked whether you felt the property might be affected by aircraft noise, but we were not conscious of this during the time of our inspection, and think it unlikely that the property will suffer greatly from such noise, although some planes will inevitably cross the area, depending on the direction of the wind and the positioning of the flight paths.

Comforted by this reassuring report the plaintiff decided to buy the property. The purchase price was £420,000 (which included £45,000 for chattels). The purchase was completed in 28 February 1991.

In the next few months the plaintiff caused the house to be modernised and refurbished at a total cost of about £125,000. During this period he was unaware that there was a significant problem associated with aircraft noise. On 13 June 1991 the plaintiff and his partner (who had a 32.7% beneficial interest) moved in. Since 1991 they had lived there three to four days a week for seven to nine months of the year.

After he moved in the plaintiff quickly discovered that the property was indeed affected by aircraft noise. In fact, the property was not far away from a navigation beacon (the Mayfield Stack) and at certain busy times, especially in the morning, the early evening, and at weekends, aircraft waiting to land at Gatwick would be stacked up maintaining a spiral course around the beacon until there was a landing slot at the airport. Aircraft frequently passed directly over, or nearly over, the position of the house. The impact of aircraft noise on the tranquility of the property was marked. The property was undoubtedly affected by aircraft noise.

It is common ground that the plaintiff's enjoyment of the property was diminished by aircraft noise at those times when he was enjoying the amenities of the property outdoors and aircraft were stacked up, maintaining their spiral course around the beacon, waiting for a landing slot at the airport. Nevertheless, after initial vacillation, the plaintiff decided not to sell the property and he does not presently intend to do so.

The principal claim was one for a diminution of value of the property by reason of the negative effect of aircraft noise. The judge found that the purchase price coincided with the open market value of the property after taking into account aircraft noise. He accordingly dismissed the principal claim. There is also no challenge to this part of the judgment at first instance.

The judge then had to consider the plaintiff's claim for non-pecuniary damage. He accepted the evidence of a sound expert. The report of this expert summarised the general effect of the aircraft noise on Riverside House as follows:

> On a subjective basis, the aircraft noise, with its particular character, is out of keeping with the nature of the area around the house. The grounds are in a very beautiful setting with many specimen trees and with a stream running through the middle. The outlook is also very beautiful. Essentially, this house and garden are in the heart of the countryside. The noise from the aircraft, flying overhead, represents a very significant intrusion into the peace of this setting . . . It is the opinion of the author that the aircraft noise represents a very significant nuisance to anyone trying to enjoy the amenity of the grounds at Riverside House.

The judge approached the claim in accordance with the law as stated in *Watts v Morrow* [1991] 4 All ER 937, [1991] 1 WLR 1421. He upheld the plaintiff's claim:

Here I think one must bear in mind that this was a specific contract dealing, iter alia, with noise so far as the defendant is concerned, and I was impressed by the account that Mr Farley gave of a number of matters. Firstly, he is particularly vulnerable because he has a habit, practice, of being an early riser and of wishing, when clement weather conditions prevail as even in this country [they] occasionally do, to sit outside on his terrace, or wherever, and enjoy the delightful gardens, the pool and the other amenities which is made pretty intolerable, he says, and I accept from his point of view between, say, the hours of 6 o'clock and 8 o'clock in the morning which is the time when he would be minded to do this. Likewise, pre-dinner drinks are not made the better for the evening activity in the sky not far away. That he is not a man, if I may say so, with excessive susceptibilities is shown by the fact that he did his best to grit his teeth and put up with it but, as he ultimately said, 'Why should I when I had endeavoured to cover this particular point in the instructions that I had given to a professional man whom I had paid to do this?' He finds it a confounded nuisance, and this is a matter that, of course, he will be stuck with. It is not a case of something like drains or dry rot or what have you that he can do anything about. Short of buying Gatwick and closing it down, this is a matter that will continue. (My emphasis.)

For what he described as the discomfort that had been sustained by the plaintiff the judge awarded £10,000.

Immediately after this judgment was given counsel for the defendant invited the judge to deal specifically with one of his arguments, viz. that the plaintiff's claim must be rejected because he had decided not to move house. The judge dealt with this point as follows:

Bingham L.J. said in *Watts v Morrow* [1991] 4 All ER 937 at 959, [1991] 1 WLR 1421 at 1445: 'If, on learning of the defects which should have been but were not reported, a purchaser decides (for whatever reason) to retain the house and not move out and sell, I would question whether any loss he thereafter suffers, at least in the ordinary case, can be laid at the door of the contract-breaker.' Dealing with that, in my judgment this is not an ordinary case because if you look how matters worked out, Mr Farley, not knowing at the time of the defect of which he should have been informed, on my judgment, thereafter incurred vast expense in altering the house to get it to a much higher standard. I think the sum of £100,000-odd was mentioned. It was a very large sum. It seems to me, he not learning of the matters which I find in my judgment in this case until much later than he incurred that expense, it seems to me it would be putting too high a burden to say that he should then have decided to move and to get away from the nuisance, if I may so describe it. That nuisance being, for obvious reasons, not one that one can do anything about. It is not a structural defect that can be remedied, and that therefore he made the best of a bad job and stayed. I think in my judgment with the greatest deference, what Bingham L.J. was saying was, in my view *obiter*. He should not be penalised for not having done that. Thank you for reminding me of that matter.

The judge's decision on the claim for non-pecuniary damages therefore stood. The judgments in the Court of Appeal and the arguments before the House took as their starting point the propositions enunciated by Bingham L.J. in *Watts v Morrow*. In that case the Court of Appeal had to consider a claim for damages for distress and inconvenience by a buyer of a house against his surveyor who had negligently failed to report defects in the house. Bingham L.J. observed:

(1) A contract-breaker is not in general liable for any distress, frustration, anxiety, displeasure, vexation, tension or aggravation which his breach of contract may cause to the innocent party. This rule is not, I think founded on the assumption that such reactions are not foreseeable, which they surely are or may be, but on considerations of policy. (2) But the rule is not absolute. Where the very object of a contract is to provide pleasure, relaxation, peace of mind from molestation, damages will be awarded if the fruit of the contract is not provided or if the contrary result is procured instead. If the law did not cater for this exceptional category of case it would be defective. A contract to survey the condition of a house for a prospective purchaser does not, however, fall within this exceptional category. (3) In cases not falling within this exceptional category, damages are in my view recoverable for physical inconvenience and discomfort caused by the breach and mental suffering directly related to that inconvenience and discomfort. If those effects are foreseeably suffered during a period which defects are repaired I am prepared to accept that they sound in damages even though the costs of the repairs is not recoverable as such. But I also agree that awards should be restrained, and that the awards in this case far exceeded a reasonable award for the injury shown to have been suffered. (See [1991] 4 All ER 937 at 959–960, [1991] 1 WLR 1421 at 1445; numbering introduced by me.)

As Stuart-Smith L.J. (at 76–81) pointed out in the present case, the propositions of Bingham L.J. have been cited and applied.

But useful as the observations of Bingham L.J. undoubtedly are, they were never intended to state more than broad principles.

Recovery of non-pecuniary damages
The examination of the issues can now proceed from a secure foothold. In the law of obligations the rules governing the recovery of compensation necessarily distinguish between different kinds of harm. In tort the requirement of reasonable foreseeability is a sufficient touchstone of liability for causing death or physical injury: it is an inadequate tool for the disposal of claims in respect of psychiatric injury. Tort law approaches compensation for physical damage and pure economic loss differently. In contract law distinctions are made about the kind of harm which resulted from the breach of contract. The general principle is that compensation is only awarded for financial loss resulting from the breach of contract (*Livingstone v Rawyards Coal Co.* (1880) 5 APP Cas. 25 at 39 per Lord Blackburn). In the words of Bingham L.J. in *Watts v Morrow* [1991] 4 All ER 937 at 959, [1991] 1 WLR 1421 at 1445, as a matter of legal policy 'a contract-breaker is not in *general* liable for any distress, frustration, anxiety, displeasure, vexation, tension or aggravation which his breach of contract may cause to the innocent party' (my emphasis). There are, however, limited exceptions to this rule. One such exception is damages for pain, suffering and loss of amenities caused to an individual by a breach of contract (see *McGregor on Damages* (16th ed. 1997) 56–7 (para. 96). It is not material in the present case. But the two exceptions mentioned by Bingham L.J., namely where the very object of the contract is to provide pleasure (proposition (2)) and recovery for physical inconvenience caused by the breach (proposition (3)), are pertinent. The scope of these exceptions is in issue in the present case. It is, however, correct, as counsel for the surveyor submitted, that the entitlement to damages for mental distress caused by a breach of contract is not established by mere foreseeability: the right to recovery is dependent on the case falling fairly within the principles governing the special exceptions. So far there is no real disagreement between the parties.

The very object of the contract: the framework

I reverse the order in which the Court of Appeal considered the two issues. I do so because the issue whether the present case falls within the exceptional category governing cases where the very object of the contract is to give pleasure, and so forth, focuses directly on the terms actually agreed between the parties. It is concerned with the reasonable expectations of the parties under the specific terms of the contract. Logically, it must be considered first.

It is necessary to examine the case on a correct characterisation of the plaintiff's claim. Stuart-Smith L.J. thought ((2000) 73 Con LR 70 at 79) that the obligation undertaken by the surveyor was 'one relatively minor aspect of the overall instructions'. What Stuart-Smith and Mummery L.JJ. would have decided if they had approached it on the basis that the obligation was a major or important part of the contract between the plaintiff and the surveyor is not clear. But the Court of Appeal's characterisation of the case was not correct. The plaintiff made it crystal clear to the surveyor that the impact of aircraft noise was a matter of importance to him. Unless he obtained reassuring information from the surveyor he would not have bought the property. That is the tenor of the evidence. It is also what the judge found. The case must be approached on the basis that the surveyor's obligation to investigate aircraft noise was a major or important part of the contract between him and the plaintiff. It is also important to note that, unlike in *Addis v Gramophone Co. Ltd* [1909] AC 488, [1908–10] All ER Rep 1, the plaintiff's claim is not for injured feelings caused by the breach of contract. Rather it is a claim for damages flowing from the surveyor's failure to investigate and report, thereby depriving the buyer of the chance of making an informed choice whether or not to buy resulting in mental distress and disappointment.

The broader legal context of *Watts v Morrow* must be borne in mind. The exceptional category of cases where the very object of a contract is to provide pleasure, relaxation, peace of mind or freedom from molestation is not the product of Victorian contract theory but the result of evolutionary developments in case law from the 1970s. Several decided cases informed the description given by Bingham L.J. of this category. The first was the decision of the sheriff court in *Diesen v Samson* 1971 SLT (Sh Ct) 49. A photographer failed to turn up at a wedding, thereby leaving the couple without a photographic record of an important and happy day. The bride was awarded damages for her distress and disappointment. In the celebrated case of *Jarvis v Swans Tours Ltd* [1973] 1 All ER 71, [1973] QB 233, the plaintiff recovered damages for mental distress flowing from a disastrous holiday resulting from a travel agent's negligent representations (compare also *Jackson v Horizon Holidays Ltd* [1975] 3 All ER 92, [1975] 1 WLR 1468). In *Heywood v Wellers (a firm)* [1976] 1 All ER 300, [1976] QB 446, the plaintiff instructed solicitors to bring proceedings to restrain a man from molesting her. The solicitors negligently failed to take appropriate action with the result that the molestation continued. The Court of Appeal allowed the plaintiff damages for mental distress and upset. While apparently not cited in *Watts v Morrow*, *Jackson v Chrysler Acceptances Ltd* [1978] RTR 474 was decided before *Watts v Morrow*. In the *Chrysler Acceptances* case the claim was for damages in respect of a motor car which did not meet the implied condition of merchantability in s. 14 of the Sale of Goods Act 1893. The buyer communicated to the seller that one of his reasons for buying the car was a forthcoming touring holiday in France. Problems with the car spoilt the holiday. The disappointment of a spoilt holiday was a substantial element in the award sanctioned by the Court of Appeal.

The very object of the contract: the arguments against the plaintiff's claim

Counsel for the surveyor advanced three separate arguments each of which he said was sufficient to defeat the plaintiff's claim. First, he submitted that even if a major or important part of the contract was to give pleasure, relaxation and peace of mind, that was not enough. It is an indispensable requirement that the object of the entire contract must be of this type. Secondly, he submitted that the exceptional category does not extend to a breach of a contractual duty of care, even if imposed to secure pleasure, relaxation and piece of mind. It only covers cases where the promiser guarantees achievement of such an object. Thirdly, he submitted that by not moving out of Riverside House the plaintiff forfeited any right to recover non-pecuniary damages.

The first argument fastened onto a narrow reading of the words 'the very object of [the] contract' as employed by Bingham L.J. in *Watts v Morrow* [1991] 4 All ER 937 at 960, [1991] 1 WLR 1421 at 1445. Cases where a major or important part of the contract was to secure pleasure, relaxation and peace of mind were not under consideration in *Watts v Morrow*. It is difficult to see what the principled justification for such a limitation might be. After all, in 1978 the Court of Appeal allowed such a claim in the *Chrysler Acceptances* case in circumstances where a spoiled holiday was only one object of the contract. Counsel was, however, assisted by the decision of the Court of Appeal in *Knott v Bolton* (1995) 45 Con LR 127 which in the present case the Court of Appeal treated as binding on it. In *Knott's* case an architect was asked to design a wide staircase for a gallery and impressive entrance hall. He failed to do so. The plaintiff spent money in improving the staircase to some extent and he recovered the cost of the changes. The plaintiff also claimed damages for disappointment and distress in the lack of an impressive staircase. In agreement with the trial judge the Court of Appeal disallowed this part of his claim. Reliance was placed on the dicta of Bingham L.J. in *Watts v Morrow* [1991] 4 All ER 937 at 959–60, [1991] 1 WLR 1421 at 1445.

Interpreting the dicta of Bingham L.J. in *Watts v Morrow* narrowly, the Court of Appeal in Knott's case ruled that the central object of the contract was to design a house, not to provide pleasure to the occupiers of the house. It is important, however, to note that the *Knott's* case was decided a few months before the decision of the House in the *Ruxley Electronics* case. In any event, the technicality of the reasoning in Knott's case, and therefore in the Court of Appeal judgments in the present case, is apparent. It is obvious, and conceded, that if an architect is employed only to design a staircase, or a surveyor is employed only to investigate aircraft noise, the breach of such a distinct obligation may result in an award of non-pecuniary damages. Logically the same must be the case if the architect or surveyor, apart from entering into a general retainer, concludes a separate contract, separately remunerated, in respect of the design of a staircase or the investigation of aircraft noise. If this is so the distinction drawn in Knott's case and in the present case is a matter of form and not substance. David Capper 'Damages for Distress and Disappointment—The Limits of *Watts v Morrow*' (2000) 116 LQR 553 at 556 has persuasively argued:

A ruling that intangible interests only qualify for legal protection where they are the 'very object of the contract' is tantamount to a ruling that contracts where these interests are merely important, but not the central object of the contract, are in part unenforceable. It is very difficult to see what policy objection there can be to parties to a contract agreeing that these interests are to be protected via contracts where the central object is something else. If the defendant is unwilling to accept this responsibility he or she can say so and either no contract will be made or one will be made but including a disclaimer.

There is no reason in principle or policy why the scope of recovered in the exceptional category should depend on the object of the contract as ascertained from all its constituent parts. It is sufficient if a major or important object of the contract is to give pleasure, relaxation or peace of mind. In my view *Knott's* case was wrongly decided and should be overruled. To the extent that the majority in the Court of Appeal relied on *Knott's* case their decision was wrong.

That brings me to the second issue, namely whether the plaintiff's claim is barred by reason of the fact that the surveyor undertook an obligation to exercise reasonable care and did not guarantee the achievement of a result. This was the basis upon which Hale L.J. after the first hearing in the Court of Appeal thought that the claim should be disallowed. This reasoning was adopted by the second Court of Appeal and formed an essential part of the reasoning of the majority. This was the basis on which they distinguished the *Ruxley Electronics* case. Against the broad sweep of differently framed contractual undertakings, and the central purpose of contract law in promoting the observance of contractual promises, I am satisfied that this distinction ought not to prevail. It is certainly not rooted in precedent. I would not accept the suggestion that it has the pedigree of an observation of Ralph Gibson L.J. in *Watts v Morrow* [1991] 4 All ER 937 at 956–7, [1991] 1 WLR 1421 at 1442: his emphasis appears to have been on the fact that the contract did not serve to provide peace of mind, and so forth. As far as I am aware the distinction was first articulated in the present case. In any event, I would reject it. I fully accept, of course, that contractual guarantees of performance and promises to exercise reasonable care are fundamentally different. The former may sometimes give greater protection than the latter. Proving breach of an obligation of reasonable care may be more difficult than proving breach of a guarantee. On the other hand, a party may in practice be willing to settle for the relative reassurance offered by the obligation of reasonable care undertaken by a professional man. But why should this difference between an absolute and elative contractual promise require a distinction in respect of the recovery of non-pecuniary damages? Take the example of a travel agent who is consulted by a couple who are looking for a golfing holiday in France. Why should it make a difference in respect of the recoverability of non-pecuniary damages for a spoiled holiday whether the travel agent gives a guarantee that there is a golf course very near the hotel, represents that to be the case, or negligently advises that all hotels of the particular chain of hotels are situated next to the golf courses? If the nearest is in fact fifty miles away a breach may be established. It may spoil the holiday for the couple. It is difficult to see why in principle only those plaintiffs who negotiate guarantees may recover non-pecuniary damages for a breach of contract. It is a singularly unattractive result that a professional man, who undertakes a specific obligation to exercise reasonable care to investigate a matter judged and communicated to be important by his customer, can in Lord Mustill's words in the *Ruxley Electronics* case [1995] 3 All ER 268 at 277, [1996] AC 344 at 360: '. . . please himself whether or not to comply with the wishes of the promise which, as embodied in the contract, formed part of the consideration for the price.' If that were the law it would be seriously deficient. I am satisfied that it is not the law. In my view the distinction drawn by Hale L.J. and by the majority in the Court of Appeal between contractual guarantees and obligations of reasonable care is unsound.

The final argument was that by failing to move out the plaintiff forfeited a right to claim non-pecuniary damages. This argument was not advanced in the Court of Appeal. It will be recalled that the judge found as a fact that the plaintiff had acted reasonably in making 'the best of a bad job'. The plaintiff's decision also avoided a larger claim against the surveyor. It was never explained on what legal principle the plaintiff's decision not to move out divested him of a claim for non-pecuniary damages. Reference was made to a passage in the judgment of Bingham L.J. in *Watts v Morrow* [1991] 4 All ER 937 at 959, [1991] 1 WLR 1421 at 1445. Examination showed, however, that the observation, speculative as it was, did not relate to the claim for non-pecuniary damages (see the criticism of Professor MP Furmston 'Damages— Diminution in Value or Cost of Repair?—Damages for Distress' (1993) 6 JCL 64 at 65). The third argument must also be rejected.

While the dicta of Bingham L.J. are of continuing usefulness as a starting point, it will be necessary to read them subject to the three points on which I have rejected the submissions made on behalf of the surveyor.

In the surveyor's written case it was submitted that the award of £10,000 was excessive. It was certainly high. Given that the plaintiff is stuck indefinitely with a position which he sought to avoid by the terms of his contract with the surveyor I am not prepared to interfere with the judge's evaluation on the special facts of the case. On the other hand, I have to say that the size of the award appears to be at the very top end of what could possibly be regarded as appropriate damages. Like Bingham L.J. in *Watts v Morrow* [1001] 4 All ER 937 at 960, [1991] 1 WLR 1421 at 1445 I consider that awards in this area should be restrained and modest. It is important that logical and beneficial developments in this corner of the law should not contribute to the creation of a society bent on litigation.

Conclusion
In agreement with the reasoning of Clarke L.J. I would therefore hold that the decision of the majority in the Court of Appeal was wrong. I would also reject the subsidiary written agreement of counsel for the surveyor that the plaintiff was not entitled to his costs at trial.

Inconvenience and discomfort
It is strictly unnecessary to discuss the question whether the judge's decision can be justified on the ground that the breach of contract resulted in inconvenience and discomfort. It is, however, appropriate that I indicate my view. The judge has a great deal of evidence on aircraft noise at Riverside House. It is conceded that noise can produce a physical reaction and can, depending on its intensity and the circumstances, constitute a nuisance. Noise from aircraft is exempted from the statutory nuisance system and in general no action lies in common law nuisance by reason only of the flight of aircraft over a property (see s. 6(1) of the Civil Aviation Act 1982 and McCracken, Jones, Pereira and Payne *Statutory Nuisance* (2001) para. 10.33). The existence of the legislation shows that aircraft noise could arguably constitute a nuisance. In any event, aircraft noise is capable of causing inconvenience and discomfort within the meaning of Bingham L.J.'s relevant proposition. It is a matter of degree whether the case passes the threshold. It is sufficient to say that I have not been persuaded that the judge's decision on this point was not open to him on the evidence which he accepted. For this further reason, in general agreement with Clarke L.J., I would rule that the decision of the Court of Appeal was wrong.

Disposal
I would allow the appeal and restore the judge's decision.

Lord Browne-Wilkinson, Lord Clyde, Lord Scott and Lord Hutton delivered concurring judgments.

Note

In *Ruxley Electronics* damages for 'loss of amenity' were modest, some £2,500. In *South Parklands Hockey and Tennis Centre Inc. v Brown Falconer Group Property Ltd* [2004] SASC 81 the defendants installed a playing surface for hockey and tennis in 1994–1995. Soil movement made the surface erratic in terms of bounce and ball movement. The evidence indicated that it was reasonable for the plaintiff to wait until the soils below the surface 'settled down', a situation that was reached in 2003, before replacement work would continue. General damages for disturbance and inconvenience, including having to put up with erratic ball movement in the sum of Aus$30,000 were awarded.

SECTION SEVEN—THE IMPORTANCE OF FREEDOM TO SUE IN CONTRACT

McAnarney & McAnarney v Hanrahan and T. E. Potterton Ltd [1994] 1 ILRM 210

Costello J.:

The facts

Nearly nine years ago, on 4 December 1984 and again on 21 December 1984, conversations took place between the plaintiffs and Mr Hanrahan (the first-named defendant). At that time Mr Hanrahan was an auctioneer in the employment of the second-named defendant. The conversation related to the possibility that the plaintiffs might purchase a residential licensed premises in Athboy, County Meath. Not surprisingly recollections are infirm about what was said and a clash of evidence has resulted. Liability in this case depends entirely on which version of the evidence I accept and I should begin this judgment by giving my conclusions on this point.

I think that the recollections of the plaintiffs and their solicitor, Mr Binchy, are more accurate than that of Mr Hanrahan and Mr Potterton (the principal in the defendant firm) and their version of events finds support in the contemporary correspondence. My conclusions on the evidence are therefore as follows:

1. In December 1984 the defendant firm held an auction for the sale of a licensed premises situated in Athboy, County Meath which was then known as 'Farrells' or 'the Central Bar'. It was a small two-storey premises with living accommodation. The premises were held under a lease dated 31 July 1959 for a term of thirty one years from 13 November 1958 at a yearly rent of £80. Thus there was a serious infirmity in the title—the lease would expire within about five years, but under the existing law the lessee would have been entitled to a renewal on expiration, but at the market (and therefore greatly increased) rent then prevailing.

2. The plaintiffs were most anxious to buy the premises, partly as a residence for their family, (for they were then living with Mrs McAnarney's mother at the time with their four young children) and partly as a business venture. The premises were offered for sale without any accounts as to turnover or profitability. Before attending the auction the plaintiffs had obtained particulars of the premises and a promise of financial

accommodation for £35,000 from a financial institution. They also had approximately £8,000–£10,000 available to add from property in Northern Ireland.

3. The plaintiffs were late for the auction on 4 December 1984, arriving with their solicitor, Mr Binchy, at the offices of the defendant firm when the auction was over. They were brought into the offices by Mr Hanrahan who told them that there had been a bid at the auction of £54,000 and that the property had then been withdrawn. In fact this information was not true—there had been no such bid at the auction. He asked them to bid £55,000. The plaintiffs said that they would be prepared to make an offer of £55,000 if they could get an increase in their loan facilities. In the course of conversation leading up to this offer Mr Hanrahan referred to the short remaining term of the lease. He informed them that there had been negotiations with the ground landlords about the purchase of the freehold and he told the plaintiffs and Mr Binchy not to worry as the freehold could be purchased for £3,000 or perhaps less. This was not true— there had been no negotiations about the purchase of the freehold and the landlords had not at that time or any time previously been asked to indicate the price at which the freehold could be purchased. Mr Hanrahan was basing his statements on the fact that the principal of the firm, Mr Potterton, had previously negotiated with the landlords in respect of other premises and had done so on terms he considered favourable.

4. The representations were made by Mr Hanrahan, and not by Mr Potterton. He made them for the purpose of inducing the plaintiffs to purchase the premises. Whilst the plaintiffs undoubtedly were anxious to purchase the premises I think that the information concerning the purchase of the freehold materially induced their final decision to purchase at a price higher than that which they originally were prepared to bid.

5. The plaintiffs failed to obtain an increase in their financial accommodation. They could only make an offer of £50,000, which the defendant firm accepted. On 21 December 1984 the plaintiffs again returned to Athboy and signed a proposal to purchase. The agreed price for the premises was £45,000 and £5,000 for the furniture and fittings. Prior to signing the proposal form Mr Hanrahan again assured the plaintiffs that they could probably purchase the freehold for £3,000.

6. The contract for sale is dated 8 January 1985. It contained no contractual obligation on the vendor in relation to the freehold.

7. The plaintiffs duly went into occupation. They paid the contract price of £45,000 but not the sum of £5,000 (which was left outstanding on a promissory note). They made no effort to purchase the freehold as they were not in a financial position to do so. They got into serious financial difficulties after about eighteen months and in 1986 they then decided to attempt to sell the property. For this purpose they were advised to purchase the freehold. They then discovered that the landlords' price for the freehold was £40,000. In 1988 they instructed their solicitors to write claiming damages against the defendants. Shortly afterwards these proceedings were instituted.

The law

The plaintiffs do not maintain a claim for damages for deceit—their claim is for damages for negligence. It is claimed that Mr Hanrahan owed a duty of care to them and that this duty was breached and in support they rely on the principle established in *Hedley Byrne and Co. Ltd v Heller & Partners Ltd* [1964] AC 465. It is important to bear in mind that this is not a case in which a party to a contract (or his agent) has made a negligent misstatement to another—it is a case of an auctioneer acting for a vendor making a statement to a proposed purchaser. The question for determination is whether in the particular circumstances the auctioneer owed a duty of care to the purchasers. As pointed out in *Hedley Byrne* by Lord Morris at 502–3: 'If, in a sphere in which a person is so placed that others could reasonably rely upon his judgment or his skill or upon his ability to make careful enquiry, a person takes it upon himself to give information or advice to, or allows his information or advice to be passed on to, another person who, as he knows or should know, would place reliance upon it, then a duty of care will arise.'

Here Mr Hanrahan took upon himself responsibility for giving his opinion about the purchase of the freehold. He should have known that the plaintiffs would place reliance on what he told them, particularly as he expressly stated that negotiations had already taken place with the landlords. In my opinion a special relationship thus arose between Mr Hanrahan and the plaintiffs which imposed on him the duty of care in giving the information. He breached that duty in that before making the statement he took no care to see what price the landlords would require for their interest. This case is different to that of *Bank of Ireland v Smith* [1966] IR 646 in which Kenny J. held that no duty of care towards prospective purchasers was imposed on an auctioneer when placing an advertisement which contained misleading information. In this case the particular circumstances of the negotiations and the express assumption of responsibility to which I have referred created a special relationship which was absent in the circumstances which Kenny J. was considering.

It follows, therefore, that if the plaintiffs can establish loss arising from the negligent misstatement that damages are recoverable against Mr Hanrahan personally and against his employers, the second-named defendants, who are vicariously liable for his negligence.

Damages

The plaintiff claims damages under three headings (a) £27,000 being the difference between the represented price of the freehold and its eventual cost, (b) £15,000 spent on refurbishing the premises and (c) general damages for mental distress.

As to (a) the facts relevant to this claim are as follows. The plaintiffs took no step to purchase the freehold after they obtained the assignment of the lease because they were in no financial position to do so. Out of the business takings they raised £15,000 needed for refurbishing the premises but they had not enough cash available to meet the commitment to pay the £5,000 due on the promissory note (this sum was never, in fact, paid). The business was carried on successfully only for a limited period of about eighteen months—thereafter it failed virtually completely and in 1986 the plaintiffs decided to sell the premises. When enquiries were made they found that the landlords were looking for £40,000 for their interest in the premises, a sum which the plaintiffs had no possibility of paying. They remained in the premises and paid no rent after the lease expired and were unable to make any payments to their bankers and eventually they owed them £61,000 approximately. After these proceedings were instituted in 1988 the plaintiffs remained in possession but by 1991 their fortunes changed. The bankers agreed to write down their debt to £21,000, and the plaintiffs were able to negotiate the purchase of the freehold in May 1991 for £30,000 and able to sell the premises with the benefit of the freehold in October 1991 for £80,000. Thus they were able eventually to make a substantial profit on the transaction.

What now falls for consideration is the correct way in which damages should be assessed in a case of negligent misrepresentation.

Damages in such cases are assessed by analogy with claims for damages for deceit. Where damages are claimed for fraudulent misrepresentation then they are assessed so as to put the plaintiff in the position he would have been in if the representation had not been made to him. This is different to the case where damages are being assessed in the case of a claim based on breach of warranty—then damages are assessed on the basis that the warranty was true. So, in the case of a sale of shares induced by fraudulent misrepresentation the normal measure of damages is the purchase price of the shares less their actual value at the time of acquisition (see *McGregor on Damages*, (15th ed.) paras 1718, 1724 and 1939) and in a case like the present one, where a plaintiff has been induced to enter into a contract for the purchase of land by a misrepresentation negligently made the normal measure of damages is the price paid for the land less its actual value at the time of sale. This means that damages are not assessed on the basis as urged on the plaintiff's behalf that he lost a bargain for the purchase of the freehold at £3,000 and should be compensated by a payment of £27,000, being the difference between the price of the freehold (£30,000) and the sum referred to in the misrepresentation. Instead, damages must be assessed on the difference between the price actually paid for the premises (£45,000) and the actual market value of the premises (that is the premises with the infirm title to which I have referred) at the time of sale.

In cases where a client sues his own solicitor or valuer for damages for advice negligently given in relation to the purchase of property the principle which I am applying in this case is also applied. *Ford v White & Co.* [1964] 1 WLR 885 is an example of the operation of this measure of damages. That was a case in which the plaintiff had negotiated for the purchase of land. The land was subject to a restriction on its development and the offered price reflected this fact. The plaintiff's solicitors, however, negligently advised the plaintiffs that the land was not so restricted and acting on that advice the plaintiffs purchased it at the price originally asked. In an action for damages for negligence against his solicitors the plaintiffs contended that the plaintiffs were entitled to be placed in the same position as if the property were indeed free from building restrictions and claimed that the measure of damages was the difference between the market value at the date of the sale subject to restrictions and its market value free from those restrictions. This argument was rejected and the court held that the proper measure of damages was the difference between the market value and the price actually paid. In that case, as the plaintiff had acquired property equal in value to the price paid for it, they had suffered no damage.

The onus is on the plaintiffs to prove their loss. They have adduced no expert evidence of the market value of the premises at the date of sale and the evidence of the auctioneer, Mr Heffernan called on their behalf, was directed to a different aspect of the case. As I do not accept that there were any genuine bids at the auction I cannot rely on the evidence of what happened at the auction to establish the market value of the premises. There was, however, some evidence on which this fact could be established with reasonable accuracy. Before the auction and before any misrepresentation had been made a financial institution was prepared to lend £35,000 to the plaintiffs on the existing (defective) title. It is notorious that financial institutions do not lend 100 per cent of the value of premises in circumstances like the present case and so it follows that the value placed on the premises by the financial institution must have been in excess of the sum to be lent. The plaintiffs' evidence was to the effect that they had out of their own resources a limited sum available to add to the money to be borrowed. Whilst precise evidence of their intended offer has not been forthcoming it appears to me to have been in the region of £45,000 all-in as this was the limit of the finances available to them when the sale actually took place. In this case, I think I can reasonably take the price the plaintiffs were prepared to pay before the misrepresentation as representing the market value. This was a sum of £45,000 which included fixtures and fittings and as these were valued at £5,000 it seems to me that the market value of the premises was approximately £40,000. The plaintiffs' loss under this heading is therefore £5,000, being the difference between the market value of the premises at the date of sale and the sum they actually paid for it.

In addition the plaintiffs have claimed £15,000 special damages being the cost of refurbishing the premises after they took possession of them. This sum was certainly spent but I do not think that it is recoverable as damages from the defendants as it was a sum which would have been spent in any event on the premises and is not a loss which had flowed from the negligent act complained of.

Finally, general damages for mental distress have also been claimed. Compensation for injury to feelings may be included in cases of fraud (see *Doyle v Olby (Ironmongers) Ltd* [1969] 1 QB 158, 170) and in principle in suitable cases I think that damages for negligent misrepresentation in respect of mental distress caused to the plaintiff could be assessed. In the present case, however, I do not think that the distress caused by the defendants' wrongdoing can be measured in any meaningful way and I do not think that the justice of the case requires damages to be increased under this heading.

There will therefore be a decree for £5,000.

Mahmud and Malik *v* BCCI [1998] AC 20
The facts can be found on p. 377 above.

Lord Nicholls of Birkenhead:
. . .

Remedies: (2) damages

Can an employee recover damages for breach of the trust and confidence term when he first learns of the breach after he has left the employment? The answer to this question is inextricably linked with one aspect of the decision in *Addis v Gramophone Co. Ltd* [1909] AC 488.

At first sight it seems almost a contradiction in terms that an employee can suffer recoverable loss if he first learns of the trust-destroying conduct after the employment contract has already ended for other reasons. But of the many forms which trust-destroying conduct may take, some may have continuing adverse financial effects on an employee even after his employment has ceased. In such a case the fact that the employee only learned of the employer's conduct after the employment had ended ought not, in principle, to be a bar to recovery. If it were otherwise, an employer who conceals a breach would be better placed than an employer who does not.

Premature termination losses

This proposition calls for elaboration. The starting point is to note that the purpose of the trust and confidence implied term is to facilitate the proper functioning of the contract. If the employer commits a breach of the term, and in consequence the contract comes to an end prematurely, the employee loses the benefits he should have received had the contract run its course until it expired or was duly terminated. In addition to financial benefits such as salary and commission and pension rights, the losses caused by the premature termination of the contract ('the premature termination losses') may include other promised benefits, for instance, a course of training, or publicity for an actor or pop star. Prima facie, and subject always to established principles of mitigation and so forth, the dismissed employee can recover damages to compensate him for these promised benefits lost to him in consequence of the premature termination of the contract.

It follows that premature termination losses cannot be attributable to a breach of the trust and confidence term if the contract is terminated for other reasons, for instance, for redundancy or if the employee leaves of his own volition. Since the trust destroying conduct did not bring about the premature termination of the contract, *ex hypothesi* the employee did not sustain any loss of pay and so forth by reason of the breach of the trust and confidence term. That is the position in the present case.

Continuing financial losses

Exceptionally, however, the losses suffered by an employee as a result of a breach of the trust and confidence term may not consist of, or be confined to, loss of pay and other premature termination losses. Leaving aside injured feelings and anxiety, which are not the basis of the claim in the present case, an employee may find himself worse off financially than when he entered into the contract. The most obvious example is conduct, in breach of the trust and confidence term, which prejudicially affects an employee's future employment prospects. The conduct may diminish the employee's attractiveness to future employers.

The loss in the present case is of this character. BCCI promised, in an implied term, not to conduct a dishonest or corrupt business. The promised benefit was employment by an honest employer. This benefit did not materialise. Proof that Mr Mahmud and Mr Malik were handicapped in the labour market in consequence of BCCI's corruption may not be easy, but that is an assumed fact for the purpose of this preliminary issue.

There is here an important point of principle. Are financial losses of this character, which I shall call 'continuing financial losses', recoverable for breach of the trust and confidence term? This is the crucial point in the present appeals. In my view, if it was reasonably foreseeable that a particular type of loss of this character was a serious possibility, and loss of this type is sustained in consequence of a breach, then in principle damages in respect of the loss should be recoverable.

In the present case the agreed facts make no assumption, either way, about whether the applicants' handicap in the labour market was reasonably foreseeable by the bank. On this there must be scope for argument. I would not regard the absence of this necessary ingredient from the assumed facts as a sufficient reason for refusing to permit the former employees' claims to proceed further.

The contrary argument of principle is that since the purpose of the trust and confidence term is to preserve the employment relationship and to enable that relationship to prosper and continue, the losses recoverable for breach should be confined to those flowing from the premature termination of the relationship. Thus, a breach of the term should not be regarded as giving rise to recoverable losses beyond those I have described as premature termination losses. In this way, the measure of damages would be commensurate with, and not go beyond, the scope of the protection the trust and confidence term is intended to provide for the employee.

This is an unacceptably narrow evaluation of the trust and confidence term. Employers may be under no common law obligation, through the medium of an implied contractual term of general application, to take steps to improve their employees' future job prospects. But failure to improve is one thing, positively to damage is another. Employment, and job prospects, are matters of vital concern to most people. Jobs of all descriptions are less secure than formerly, people change jobs more frequently, and the job market is not always buoyant. Everyone knows this. An employment contract creates a close personal relationship, where there is often a disparity of power between the parties. Frequently the employee is vulnerable. Although the underlying purpose of the trust and confidence term is to protect the employment relationship, there can be nothing unfairly onerous or unreasonable in requiring an employer who breaches the trust and confidence term to be liable if he thereby causes continuing financial loss of a nature that was reasonably foreseeable. Employers must take care not to damage their employees' future employment prospects, by harsh and oppressive behaviour or by any other form of conduct which is unacceptable today as falling below the standards set by the implied trust and confidence term.

This approach brings one face to face with the decision in the wrongful dismissal case of *Addis v Gramophone Co. Ltd* [1909] AC 488. It does so, because the measure of damages recoverable for breach of the trust and confidence term cannot be decided without having some regard to a comparable question which arises regarding the measure of damages recoverable for wrongful dismissal. An employee may elect to treat a sufficiently serious breach of the trust and confidence term as discharging him from the contract and, hence, as a constructive dismissal. The damages in such a case ought, in principle, to be the same as they would be if the employer had expressly dismissed the employee. The employee should be no better off, or worse off, in the two situations. In principle, so far as the recoverability of continuing financial losses are concerned, there is no basis for distinguishing (a) wrongful dismissal following a breach of the trust and confidence term, (b) constructive dismissal following a breach of the trust and confidence term, and (c) a breach of the trust and confidence term which only becomes known after the contract has ended for other reasons. The present case is in the last category, but a principled answer cannot be given for cases in this category without considering the other two categories from which it is indistinguishable.

Addis v Gramophone Co. Ltd.

Against this background I turn to the much discussed case of *Addis v Gramophone Co. Ltd* [1909] AC 488. Mr Addis, it will be recalled, was wrongfully and contumeliously dismissed from his post as the defendant's manager in Calcutta. At trial he was awarded damages exceeding the amount of his salary for the period of notice to which he was entitled. The case is generally regarded as having decided, echoing the words of Lord Loreburn LC, at p. 491, that an employee cannot recover damages for the manner in which the wrongful dismissal took place, for injured feelings or for any loss he may sustain from the fact that his having been dismissed of itself makes it more difficult for him to obtain fresh employment. In particular, *Addis*'s case is generally understood to have decided that any loss suffered by the adverse impact on the employee's chances of obtaining alternative employment is to be excluded from an assessment of damages for wrongful dismissal: see, for instance, *O'Laoire v Jackel International Ltd* (No. 2) [1991] ICR 718, 730–731, following earlier authorities; in Canada, the decision of the Supreme Court in *Vorvis v Insurance Corporation of British Columbia* (1989) 58 DLR (4th) 193, 205; and, in New Zealand, *Vivian v Coca-Cola Export Corporation* [1984] 2 NZLR 289, 292; *Whelan v Waitaki Meats Ltd* [1991] 2 NZLR 74, where Gallen J. disagreed with the decision in *Addis*'s case, and *Brandt v Nixdorf Computer Ltd* [1991] 3 NZLR 750.

For present purposes I am not concerned with the exclusion of damages for injured feelings. The present case is concerned only with financial loss. The report of the facts in *Addis*'s case is sketchy. Whether Mr Addis sought to prove that the manner of his dismissal caused him financial loss over and above his premature termination losses is not clear beyond a peradventure. If he did, it is surprising that their Lordships did not address this important feature more specifically. Instead there are references to injured feelings, the fact of dismissal of itself, aggravated damages, exemplary damages amounting to damages for defamation, damages being compensatory and not punitive, and the irrelevance of motive. The dissenting speech of Lord Collins was based on competence to award exemplary or vindictive damages.

However, Lord Loreburn LC's observations were framed in quite general terms, and he expressly disagreed with the suggestion of Lord Coleridge CJ. in *Maw v Jones* (1890) 25 QBD 107, 108, to the effect that an assessment of damages might take into account the greater difficulty which an apprentice dismissed with a slur on his character might have in obtaining other employment. Similarly general observations were made by Lord James of Hereford, Lord Atkinson, Lord Gorell and Lord Shaw of Dunfermline.

In my view these observations cannot be read as precluding the recovery of damages where the manner of dismissal involved a breach of the trust and confidence term and this caused financial loss. *Addis v Gramophone Co. Ltd* was decided in the days before this implied term was adumbrated. Now that this term exists and is normally implied in every contract of employment, damages for its breach should be assessed in accordance with ordinary contractual principles. This is as much true if the breach occurs before or in connection with dismissal as at any other time.

. . .

Breach of contract and reputation

I must now turn to two submissions made concerning injury to reputation. The liquidators submitted that injury to reputation is protected by the law of defamation. The boundaries set by the tort of defamation are not to be side-stepped by allowing a claim in contract that would not succeed in defamation: see *Lonhro plc v Fayed* (No. 5) [1993] 1 WLR 1489, 1496, *per* Dillon LJ. Here, it was submitted, a claim in defamation would not succeed: the bank made no defamatory statements, either referring to the applicants or at all. This submission is misconceived.

I agree that the cause of action known to the law in respect of injury to reputation is the tort of defamation. With certain exceptions this tort provides a remedy, where the necessary ingredients are present, whether or not the injury to a person's reputation causes financial loss. No proof of actual damage is necessary, and damages are at large. If, as a result of the injury to his reputation the plaintiff does in fact suffer financial loss, this may be recoverable in a defamation action as 'special damage'.

All this is commonplace. It by no means follows, however, that financial loss which may be recoverable as special damage in a defamation action is irrecoverable as damages for breach of contract. If a breach of contract gives rise to financial loss which on ordinary principles would be recoverable as damages for breach of contract, those damages do not cease to be recoverable because they might also be recoverable in a defamation action. There can be no justification for artificially excising from the damages recoverable for breach of contract that part of the financial loss which might or might not be the subject of a successful claim in defamation. Hallett J. summarised the position in *Foaminol Laboratories Ltd v British Artid Plastics Ltd* [1941] 2 All ER 393, 399–400:

> a claim for mere loss of reputation is the proper subject of an action for defamation, and cannot ordinarily be sustained by means of any other form of action . . . However . . . if pecuniary loss can be established, the mere fact that the pecuniary loss is brought about by the loss of reputation caused by a breach of contract is not sufficient to preclude the plaintiffs from recovering in respect of that pecuniary loss.

Furthermore, the fact that the breach of contract injures the plaintiff's reputation in circumstances where no claim for defamation would lie is not, by itself, a reason for excluding from the damages recoverable for breach of contract compensation for financial loss which on ordinary principles would be recoverable. An award of damages for breach of contract has a different objective: compensation for financial loss suffered by a breach of contract, not compensation for injury to reputation.

Sometimes, in practice, the distinction between damage to reputation and financial loss can become blurred. Damage to the reputation of professional persons, or persons carrying on a business, frequently causes financial loss. None the less, the distinction is fundamentally sound, and when awarding damages for breach of contract courts take care to confine the damages to their proper ambit: making good financial loss. In *Herbert Clayton and Jack Waller Ltd v Oliver* [1930] AC 209, 220, when considering an award of damages to an actor who should have been billed to appear at the London Hippodrome, Lord Buckmaster regarded loss of publicity rather than loss of reputation as the preferable expression. In *Aerial Advertising Co. v Batchelors Peas Ltd (Manchester)* [1938] 2 All ER 788, 796–797, where aerial advertising ('Eat Batchelors Peas') took place during Armistice Day services, Atkinson J. was careful to confine damages to the financial loss flowing from public boycotting of the defendant's goods and to exclude damages for loss of reputation. Lord Denning MR drew the same distinction in *G.K.N. Centrax Gears Ltd v Matbro Ltd* [1976] 2 Lloyd's Rep. 555, 573.

Breach of contract and existing reputation

The second submission concerning reputation was that the appellants' claims for damages to their existing reputations is barred by the decision of the Court of Appeal in *Withers v General Theatre Corporation Ltd* [1933] 2 KB 536.

There is an acute conflict between this decision and the earlier decision, also of the Court of Appeal, in *Marbe v George Edwardes (Daly's Theatre) Ltd* [1928] 1 KB 269. In *Marbe*'s case clear views were expressed that when assessing damages for loss flowing from a failure to provide promised publicity, the loss may include loss to existing reputation: see Bankes LJ., at p. 281, and Atkin LJ., at p. 288. In the *Withers* case equally clear views were firmly stated to the contrary by all three members of the court: see Scrutton LJ., at p. 547, Greer LJ., at p. 554, and Romer LJ., at p. 556. I have to say that, faced with the embarrassing necessity to choose, I prefer the views expressed in *Marbe*. They accord better with principle. Loss of promised publicity might cause an actor financial loss, for two reasons: first, through loss of opportunity to enhance his professional reputation and, secondly, his absence from the theatre scene might actually damage his existing professional reputation. If as a matter of fact an actor does suffer financial loss under both heads, and that is a question of evidence, I can see no reason why the law should deny recovery of damages in respect of the second head of loss.

Conclusion

For these reasons I would allow these appeals. The agreed set of assumed facts discloses a good cause of action. Unlike the courts below, this House is not bound by the observations in *Addis v Gramophone Co. Ltd* [1909] AC 488 regarding irrecoverability of loss flowing from the manner of dismissal, or by the decision in *Withers v General Theatre Corporation Ltd* [1933] 2 KB 536.

. . .

Note

The failure of the House of Lords to overrule *Addis v Gramophone Co. Ltd* [1909] AC 488 has been regretted by a number of commentators. *Addis* simply fails to address the issue of what heads of loss can be said to follow from the manner of dismissal and the fact that *Addis* survives can lead to some unfortunate decisions. Irish courts have recognised both the implied term (*Berber v Dunnes Stores* [2006] IEHC 327) and the availability of stigma damages (*Cronin v eircom Ltd* [2006] IEHC 380) although in the latter case because the contract of employment was not terminated Laffoy J. held that this head of damage 'does not arise'. *Addis* has not been followed in New Zealand: *Stuart v Armourguard Security Ltd* [1996] 1 NZLR 484.

Johnson v Unisys Ltd [2001] 2 All ER 801, at 823

In this case Johnson sought damages in a wrongful dismissal action for distress and subsequent physical and emotional damage caused by the manner of his dismissal. The House of Lords declined to hold that the contract contained an implied term, which would provide a cause of action. Lord Millett also explained why he would not allow this case to come within the exceptions to *Addis v Gramophone Co. Ltd* and the other Law Lords delivered judgments to the same effect.

Lord Millett:

My Lords,
I have had the advantage of reading in draft the speech of my noble and learned friend Lord Hoffmann, with which I am in full agreement. I add some words of my own in order to explain why I consider that the present is not an appropriate occasion in which to revisit the decision of your Lordship's House in *Addis v Gramophone Co. Ltd* [1909] AC 488, [1908–10] All RE Rep 1.

That case established the principle that damages are awarded for breach of contract and not for the manner of the breach; accordingly nothing can be recovered for mental distress, anxiety, injury to feelings or (so it is said) damage to reputation. The case was concerned with a contract of employment and the actual decision was that damages for wrongful dismissal are limited to compensation for the financial loss arising from the premature determination of the contract where proper notice of dismissal has not been given: they cannot include compensation for the employee's injured feelings because he has been dismissed in an offensive and humiliating manner. The principle, however, is not limited to contracts of employment but is of general application in the law of contract.

The supposed rule that damages are not recoverable for financial loss arising from injury to reputation (or in a case of wrongful dismissal for making it more difficult for the plaintiff to find employment) is not easy to defend and may no longer be the law after *Malik v Bank of Credit and Commerce International SA (in liq)*, *Mahmud v Bank of Credit and Commerce International SA (in liq)* [1997] 3 All ER 1, [1998] AC 20. My noble and learned friend Lord Steyn has argued powerfully that it never was the law, being derived from a faulty headnote which misrepresented the true *ratio decidendi* of the case. Subject to this caveat, however, the general rule would seem to be a sound one, at least in relation to ordinary commercial contracts entered into by both parties with a view of profit. In such cases non-pecuniary loss such as mental suffering consequent on breach is not within the contemplation of the parties and is accordingly too remote. The ordinary feelings of anxiety, frustration and disappointment caused by any breach of contract are also excluded, but seemingly for the opposite reason: they are so commonly a consequence of a breach of contract that the parties must be regarded not only as having foreseen it but as having agreed to take the risk of its occurrence; see Teitel *The Law of Contract* (10th ed., 1999) p. 923. Contracts which are not purely commercial but which have as their object the provision of enjoyment, comfort, peace of mind or other non-pecuniary personal or family benefits (as in *Jarvis v Swan Tours Ltd* [1973] 1 All ER 71, [1973] QB 233 and similar cases) are usually treated as exceptions to the general rule, though in truth they would seem to fall outside its rationale. Such injury is not only within the contemplation of the parties but is the direct result of the breach itself and not the manner of the breach. Indeed the avoidance of just such non-pecuniary injury can be said to be a principal object of the contract.

In *Addis's* case the House of Lords treated a contract of employment as an ordinary commercial contract terminable at will by either party provided only sufficient notice was given in accordance with the terms of the contract. This was the classical approach to such contracts which the House of Lords was content to confirm more than half a century later. In *Ridge v Baldwin* [1963] 2 All ER 66 at 71, [1964] AC 46 at 65 Lord Reid observed that an employer can terminate the contract of employment at any time and for any reason or for none. It follows that the question whether damages are recoverable does not depend on whether the employer had a good reason for dismissing the employee, or had heard him in his own defence, or had acted fairly towards him: it depends on whether the dismissal was in breach of contract. In *Malloch v Aberdeen Corp* [1971] 2 All ER 1278 at 1282, [1971] 1 WLR 1578 at 1581 Lord Reid restated the position:

> At common law a master is not bound to hear his servant before he dismisses him. He can act unreasonably or capriciously if he so chooses but the dismissal is valid. The servant has no remedy unless the dismissal is in breach of contract and then the servant's only remedy is damages for breach of contract.

The common law, which is premised on party autonomy, treated the employer and the employee as free and equal parties to the contract of employment. Each had the right, granted by the contract itself, to bring the contract to an end in accordance with its terms. But by 1971 there was a widespread feeling, shared by both sides of industry, that the legal position was unsatisfactory. In reality there was no comparison between the consequences for an employer if the employee terminated his employment and the consequences for an employee if he was dismissed. Many people build their lives round their jobs and plan their future in the expectation that they will continue. For many workers dismissal is a disaster. In 1964 the government announced that it would discuss with representatives of employers and trade unions the provision of procedures to give employees effective safeguards against arbitrary dismissal. In 1968 the Royal Commission on Trade Unions and Employers' Associations under the chairmanship of Lord Donovan reported that it was urgently necessary for employees to be given better protection against unfair dismissal and recommended the establishment of statutory machinery to achieve this.

The recommendations of the Royal Commission were given effect by the Industrial Relations Act 1971. This left the common law and the contract of employment itself unaffected. It did not import implied terms into the contract. Instead it created a new statutory right not to be unfairly dismissed, enforceable in the newly established National Industrial Relations Court. The 1971 Act was replaced by the Employment Rights Act 1996. The National Industrial Relations Court was short-lived and the jurisdiction in respect of unfair dismissal has for many years been exercised by industrial tribunals (now known as employment tribunals). These consist of a legally qualified chairman sitting with two lay members, one being a representative of the trade unions and the other of employers.

For the first time the 1971 Act enabled an employee to challenge his employer's conduct in exercising his legal rights on the ground that it was unreasonable. The Act contained elaborate provisions which defined the concept and scope of unfair dismissal and provided for compensation to be awarded or reinstatement or re-engagement to be ordered. It set an upper limit to the amount of compensation which could be awarded, which has since been increased from time to time, and allowed the tribunal to reduce the amount of an award if it considered that the employee had caused or contributed to his own dismissal. It provided for an upper age limit and a qualifying period of employment (which has since been reduced but not abrogated) thereby excluding certain categories of employees from its scope altogether.

During the past thirty years an extensive jurisprudence has been developed in relation to unfair dismissal. Employers have responded to the existence of the statutory right, as the Royal Commission intended that they should, by introducing elaborate procedures of complaint and warning before eventual dismissal which, whether or not contractually binding, are designed to ensure that employees are not unfairly dismissed. Since the right not to be unfairly dismissed is a statutory right which is not derived from contract, however it is still open to an employee to claim that he has been unfairly dismissed even if his employer has faithfully complied with the contractual procedures.

Section 205 of the 1996 Act provides that some claims under the Act (including a claim in respect of unfair dismissal) must be brought by way of complaint to an industrial tribunal and not otherwise. This is a new provision made necessary because the 1996 Act (unlike its predecessor) gives industrial tribunals a limited jurisdiction in respect of some common law claims. The 1971 Act did not expressly provide that the jurisdiction of the industrial tribunals was exclusive, but it did not need to. It was clearly predicated on the existing state of the law as established in *Addis's* case and confirmed in *Malloch's* case. There would have been no point (for example) in excluding certain categories of employee from obtaining compensation for unfair dismissal if they could obtain a remedy by way of damages at common law; or for enabling the industrial tribunal to reduce the amount of compensation by reference to the employee's own conduct if the employee could obtain damages at common law without any such reduction. Prior to 1996, therefore, the jurisdiction of the industrial tribunals to award compensation for unfair dismissal was exclusive in practice, not because it was made so by statute, but because it was premissed on the absence of a corresponding remedy at common law.

But the common law does not stand still. It is in a state of continuous judicial development in order to reflect the changing perceptions of the community. Contracts of employment are no longer regarded as purely commercial contracts entered into between free and equal agents. It is generally recognised today that 'work is one of the defining features of people's lives'; that 'loss of one's job is always a traumatic event'; and that it can be 'especially devastating' when dismissal is accompanied by bad faith: see *Wallace v United Grain Growers Ltd* [1997] 152 DLR (4th) 1 at 33 per Iacobucci J. This change of perception is, of course, partly due to the creation by Parliament of the statutory right not to be unfairly dismissed. If this right had not existed, however, it is possible that the courts would have fashioned a similar remedy at common law, though they would have proceeded by implying appropriate terms into the contract of employment. It would have been a major step to subject the employer's right to terminate the relationship on proper notice to an obligation not to exercise the right in bad faith, and a still greater step to subject it to an obligation not to exercise it without reasonable cause (a difficult distinction, but one drawn by McLachlin J. in *Wallace's* case (at 44)). Even so, these are steps which in the absence of the statutory right, the courts might have been prepared to take, though there would have been a powerful argument for leaving the reform to Parliament. If the courts had taken the steps themselves, they could have awarded common law damages for unfair dismissal consistently with *Addis's* case, because such damages would be awarded for the breach of an implied but independently actionable term (as in *Malik's* case) and not for wrongful dismissal. But the courts would have been faced with the difficult task of distinguishing between the mental distress and other non-pecuniary injury consequent upon the unfairness of the dismissal (for which the employer would be liable) and the similar injury consequent upon the dismissal itself (for which he would not). In practice, he would probably have been reduced to awarding conventional sums by way of general damages much as the industrial tribunals do.

I agree with Lord Hoffman that it would not have been appropriate to found the right on the implied term of trust and confidence which is now generally imported into the contract of employment. This is usually expressed as an obligation binding on both parties not to do anything which would damage or destroy the relationship of trust and confidence which should exist between them. But this is an inherent feature of the relationship of employer and employee which does not survive the ending of the relationship. The implied obligation cannot sensibly be used to extend the relationship beyond its agreed duration. Moreover, manipulating it for such a purpose would be unrealistic. An employer who summarily dismisses an employee usually does so because, rightly or wrongly, he no longer has any trust or confidence in him, and the real issue is: whose fault is that? That is why reinstatement or re-engagement is effected in only a tiny proportion of the cases that come before the industrial tribunals.

Note

Johnson v Unisys has been followed in *Orr v Zomax Ltd* [2004] IEHC 47. Even though Gilligan J. in *Carey v Independent Newspapers (Ireland) Ltd* (2005) 15 ELR 45 August 2003, unrep.) indicated that in a wrongful dismissal action the decision in *Addis* directs that the damages recoverable are the salary that would have been earned in the notice period, and that no compensation for the stressful or humiliating circumstances surrounding the dismissal, general damages for depression have been awarded in *Dooley v Great Southern Hotels Ltd* [2001] ELR 340. Gilligan J.'s succinct summary of the existing state of English law is of interest.

Subsequent case-law such as *Maher v Jabil Global Services Ltd* [2005] 16 ELR 233 and *Berber v Dunnes Stores* [2006] IEHC 327 allow damages to be recoverable for clinical depression caused by an employer's breach of duty during the currency of the contract, but *Carroll v Dublin Bus* [2005] IEHC 278 holds that, absent evidence of a clinical medical condition being created by the breach of contract, general damages for frustration, stress or injured feelings are not recoverable. Despite *Johnson v Unisys Ltd*, which has been approved by the High Court in *Orr v Zomax Ltd* [2004] IEHC 47, it has been held by the House of Lords that if an employee has a cause of action for breach of contract (e.g. treatment during the currency of the employment contract such as improper disciplinary proceedings or suspension) that cause of action may be relied upon even if the employment contract is terminated and proceedings for unfair dismissal are brought, a situation that causes duplication of proceedings, difficulties of causation and quantum and other strange results. 'An employer may be better off dismissing an employee than suspending him,' per Lord Nicholls in *Eastwood v Magnox Electric* [2004] UKHL 35. Somewhat hesitantly, this line of authority has been endorsed in Ireland: *Quigley v Complex Tooling and Moulding* [2005] IEHC 71; *Berber v Dunnes Stores* [2006] IEHC 327.

SECTION EIGHT—MITIGATION OF DAMAGE

McGregor on Damages (15th ed.) ch. 7

Various Meanings of the Term 'Mitigation'

The expression 'mitigation of damage' is an umbrella term applied, in the books and in the cases, to a number of matters, some of which are related and some of which are completely unconnected. Surprisingly, in view of the importance of the subject these differences have not been fully analysed in English law; yet it is vital to an understanding of the issues to separate the various meanings of the term.

(1) *Principal meaning: the three rules as to the avoiding of the consequences of a wrong*

The principal meaning of the term 'mitigation', with which alone this chapter deals, concerns the avoiding of the consequences of a wrong, whether tort or breach of contract, and forms probably the only exact use of the term. Even if the subsidiary or residual meanings enumerated below cannot strictly be called incorrect, it would be well if the use of the term 'mitigation' in connection with them was qualified, if not completely discarded, as matters are only confused by employing one term to describe disparate concepts.

The principal meaning itself comprises three different, although closely interrelated, rules. This analysis into three rules, although clearly implicit in the cases, is one which has not formerly been given explicit statement in English law. It is submitted that such a division lends clarity to a difficult topic. The three rules are these.

(1) The first and most important rule is that the plaintiff must take all reasonable steps to mitigate the loss to him consequent upon the defendant's wrong and cannot recover damages for any such loss which he could thus have avoided but has failed, through unreasonable action or inaction, to avoid. Put shortly, the plaintiff cannot recover for avoidable loss.

(2) The second rule is the corollary of the first and is that, where the plaintiff does take reasonable steps to mitigate the loss to him consequent upon the defendant's wrong, he can recover for loss incurred in so doing; this is so even though the resulting damage is in the event greater than it would have been had the mitigating steps not been taken. Put shortly, the plaintiff can recover for loss incurred in reasonable attempts to avoid loss.

(3) The third rule is that, where the plaintiff does take steps to mitigate the loss to him consequent upon the defendant's wrong and these steps are successful, the defendant is entitled to the benefit accruing from the plaintiff's action and is liable

only for the loss as lessened; this is so even though the plaintiff would not have been debarred under the first rule from recovering the whole loss, which would have accrued in the absence of his successful mitigating steps, by reason of these steps not being ones which were required of him under the first rule. Put shortly, the plaintiff cannot recover for avoided loss.

Note

Sometimes the opportunity to mitigate loss occasioned by breach of contract may result from an offer made by the party in breach.

Payzu Ltd *v* Saunders [1919] 2 KB 580

McCardie J.:

By a contract in writing dated 9 November 1917, the defendant, who was a dealer in silk, agreed to sell to the plaintiffs 200 pieces of crêpe de chine at 4s 6d a yard and 200 pieces at 5s 11d a yard, 'delivery as required January to September 1918; conditions 2.5 per cent. One month,' which meant that payment for goods delivered up to the twentieth day of any month should be made on the twentieth day of the following month, subject to 2.5 per cent discount. At the request of the plaintiffs the defendant delivered, in November 1917, a certain quantity of the goods under the contract, the price of which amounted to £76, less 2.5 per cent discount. On 21 December the plaintiffs drew a cheque in favour of the defendant in payment of these goods, but the cheque was never received by the defendant. Early in January 1918, the defendant telephoned to the plaintiffs asking why she had not received a cheque. The plaintiffs then drew another cheque, but owing to a delay in obtaining the signature of one of the plaintiffs' directors, this cheque was not sent to the defendant until 16 January. On that day the plaintiffs gave an order by telephone for further deliveries under the contract. The defendant in the belief, which was in fact erroneous, that the plaintiffs' financial position was such that they could not have met the cheque which they alleged had been drawn in December, wrote to the plaintiffs on 16 January refusing to make any further deliveries under the contract unless the plaintiffs paid cash with each order. The plaintiffs refused to do this, and after some further correspondence brought this action claiming damages for breach of contract. The damages claimed were the difference between the market prices in the middle of February 1918, and the contract prices of the two classes of goods, the difference alleged being respectively 1s 3d and 1s 4d a yard.

. . .

Bankes L.J.:

At the trial of this case the defendant, the present respondent, raised two points: first, that she had committed no breach of the contract of sale, and secondly that, if there was a breach, yet she had offered and was always ready and willing to supply the pieces of silk, the subject of the contract, at the contract price for cash; that it was unreasonable on the part of the appellants not to accept that offer, and that therefore they cannot claim damages beyond what they would have lost by paying cash with each order instead of having a month's credit and a discount of 2.5 per cent. We must take it that this was the offer made by the respondent. The case was fought and the learned judge has given judgment upon that footing. It is true that the correspondence suggests that the respondent was at one time claiming an increased price. But in this court it must be taken that the offer was to supply the contract goods at the contract price except that payment was to be by cash instead of being on credit.

In these circumstances the only question is whether the appellants can establish that as matter of law they were not bound to consider any offer made by the respondent because of the attitude she had taken up. Upon this point McCardie J. referred to *British Westinghouse Electric and Manufacturing Co. v Underground Electric Rlys Co. of London,*[1] where Lord Haldane L.C. said:

> The fundamental basis is thus compensation for pecuniary loss naturally flowing from the breach; but this first principle is qualified by a second, which imposes on a plaintiff the duty of taking all reasonable steps to mitigate the loss consequent on the breach, and debars him from claiming any part of the damage which is due to his neglect to take such steps. In the words of James L.J. in *Dunkirk Colliery Co. v Lever*[2]: 'What the plaintiffs are entitled to is the full amount of the damage which they have really sustained by a breach of the contract. The person who has broken the contract not being exposed to additional cost by reason of the plaintiffs not doing what they ought to have done as reasonable men, and the plaintiffs not being under any obligation to do anything otherwise than in the ordinary course of business.

It is plain that the question what is reasonable for a person to do in mitigation of his damages cannot be a question of law but must be one of fact in the circumstances of each particular case. There may be cases where as matter of fact it would be unreasonable to expect a plaintiff to consider any offer made in view of the treatment he has received from the defendant. If he had been rendering personal services and had been dismissed after being accused in presence of others of being a thief, and if after that his employer had offered to take him back into his service, most persons would think he was justified in refusing the offer, and that it would be unreasonable to ask him in this way to mitigate the damages in an action of wrongful dismissal. But that is not to state a principle of law, but a conclusion of fact to be arrived at on a consideration of all the circumstances of the case. [Counsel for the plaintiffs] complained that the respondent had treated his clients so badly that it would be unreasonable to expect them to listen to any proposition she might make. I do not agree. In my view each party was ready to accuse the other of conduct unworthy of a high commercial reputation, and there was nothing to justify the appellants in refusing to consider the respondent's offer. I think the learned judge came to a proper conclusion on the facts, and that the appeal must be dismissed.

Scrutton L.J.:

I am of the same opinion. Whether it be more correct to say that a plaintiff must minimise his damages, or to say that he can recover no more than he would have suffered if he had acted reasonably, because any further damages do not reasonably follow from the defendant's breach, the result is the same. The plaintiff must take 'all reasonable steps to mitigate the loss consequent on the breach', and this principle 'debars him from claiming any part of the damage which is due to his neglect to take such steps': *British Westinghouse Electric and Manufacturing Co. v Underground Electric Rlys Co. of London,* per Lord Haldane L.C. [counsel for the plaintiffs] has contended that in considering what steps should be taken to mitigate the damage all contractual relations with the party in default must be excluded. That is contrary to my experience. In certain cases of personal service it may be unreasonable to expect a plaintiff to consider an offer from the other party who has grossly injured him; but in commercial contracts it is generally reasonable to accept an offer from the party in default. However, it is always a question of fact. About the law there is no difficulty.

1. [1912] AC 673, 689.   2. (1878) 9 ChD 20, 25.

(Eve J. agreed.)

Lennon and Others *v* Talbot Ireland Ltd (HC), 20 December 1985, unrep.

Keane J.:

In these proceedings, the plaintiffs claim damages in respect of what they say was the wrongful termination by the defendants of certain agreements entered into by the plaintiffs with the defendants.

The background to the dispute is as follows. Each of the plaintiffs had entered into main dealership agreements at various times with the defendants in respect of private and commercial vehicles imported by them and distributed throughout the Republic of Ireland. The defendants notified the plaintiffs by letter dated 5 October 1984, that with effect from 2 November 1984 the Talbot range would be distributed in the Republic of Ireland by the Gowan Group. The plaintiffs contend in these proceedings that this letter constituted an unlawful termination by the defendants of the agreements and claim compensation for damage which they allege they have sustained as a result. While a defence was delivered in the proceedings denying liability, it was conceded shortly before the case came on for hearing that the agreements had been wrongfully terminated by the defendants. This concession was, however, withdrawn almost immediately before the hearing in respect of the sixth-named defendants, Gleeson Brothers Motor Engineers Ltd (who are referred to in this judgment as 'Gleesons'). None of the agreements contained any provision for termination, but it was agreed by the parties that six months' notice would have been reasonable in the case of an agreement such as this. In respect of the plaintiffs other than Gleesons, the case accordingly became an assessment of damages only.

Gleesons wrote to the defendants on 29 November 1984 saying that they thought it was essential for them to continue getting supplies from the Gowan Group, as it was not possible for them to suspend operations in mid-stream. [Counsel for the defendants] submitted that in writing such a letter, Gleesons had acquiesced in the assignment by Talbot of their liability under the dealership agreements to the Gowan Group. This letter was, however, written after the defendants had by their letter of 5 October wrongfully terminated each of the dealership agreements and represented no more than an attempt by Gleesons to mitigate the loss arising from that wrongful termination. It follows, in my view, that they also are entitled to damages for the wrongful termination of the agreement.

While it will be necessary at a later stage to consider the position of the plaintiffs individually, since their circumstances differed significantly from one another, there are also features common to all the claims which can be conveniently considered at the outset.

All the plaintiffs claimed that, as a result of the wrongful termination by the defendants of the dealership agreements, they had lost profits that they would other-wise have earned on the sale of vehicles and spare parts, the carrying out of repair work and the provision of spare parts and repair work to which the customers were entitled under 'warranties'. The defendants contended that, even if such losses had been established, they were effectively the result of the plaintiffs' negligent failure to mitigate their loss by entering into new dealership arrangements with the Gowan Group under which they would have been entitled to a continued supply of Talbot vehicles and spare parts. The plaintiffs for their part said that it was unreasonable to expect them to enter into new agreements with the Gowan Group in order to ensure themselves a continuing supply of Talbot vehicles and parts. They claimed that the arrangements with the Gowan Group would be significantly different in the following respects:

(1) The defendants were manufacturers, whereas the Gowan Group were not. It was said that this would put the plaintiffs in the invidious position of depending for their supplies of vehicles and spare parts on a firm which was in direct competition with them rather than a manufacturer such as the defendants who could be relied on not to discriminate between the individual dealers and had never done so in the past.
(2) The plaintiffs had established a relationship of trust and confidence with the defendants, which did not exist between them and the Gowan Group.
(3) The plaintiffs were afforded the valuable facility by the defendants of free stocking of vehicles until they were sold. It was said that the Gowan Group, by contrast, required to be paid cash for vehicles as they were supplied to the dealer except in the case of models which were not selling particularly well.
(4) In the case of those dealers who were limited companies, the Gowan Group required the directors to enter into personal guarantees, whereas no such requirement had been imposed upon the dealers by the defendants.
(5) The Gowan Group were engaged in the export of vehicles from the Republic of Ireland in competition with some of the plaintiffs.

While some of these matters were in dispute during the hearing, there was and could be no dispute as to the first. It was beyond controversy that the Gowan Group were in a different position from the defendants: they were distributors of vehicles and not manufacturers. It is obvious that their interests as distributors would not necessarily coincide with those of the plaintiffs and it is not surprising that the plaintiffs were concerned that their interests might suffer under the new dispensation.

[Counsel for the defendants] relied on the decisions in *Payzu v Saunders* [1919] 2 KB 581 and *Houndsditch Warehouse Co. Ltd v Waltex* [1944] KB 579 as establishing that where the defendant is in breach of contract but gives the plaintiff an opportunity to mitigate his loss, the plaintiff refuses that offer at his peril, because if the court should subsequently determine that it was a reasonable offer the plaintiff is then confined to such losses as he suffered up to the date of the offer. But these decisions do not assist the defendants in circumstances such as arose in the present case where the new arrangement proposed was significantly different from the existing arrangement in a way which could only be detrimental to the plaintiffs. In the words of Lord Macmillan in *Banco de Portugal v Waterlow & Sons Ltd* [1932] AC 452 at 506:

> Where the sufferer from a breach of contract finds himself in consequence of that breach placed in a position of embarrassment, the measures which he may be driven to adopt in order to extricate himself ought not to be weighed in nice scales at the instance of the party whose breach of contract has occasioned the difficulty. It is often easy after an emergency has passed to criticise the steps which have been taken to meet it, but such criticism does not come well from those who have themselves created the emergency. The law is satisfied if the party placed in a difficult situation by reason of the breach of a duty owed to him has acted reasonably in the adoption of remedial measures, and he will not be held disentitled to recover the cost of such measures merely because the party in breach can suggest that other measures less burdensome to him might have been taken.

I am satisfied that the refusal of the plaintiffs, other than the sixth-named plaintiffs, to enter into arrangements with the Gowan Group did not constitute an unreasonable refusal by the plaintiffs to mitigate the loss flowing from the defendants' admitted breach.

The plaintiffs are entitled to the damages which might fairly and reasonably be considered as arising naturally from the breach or might reasonably be supposed to have been in the contemplation of both parties at the time of the agreements as the probable result of the breach. It was agreed that in the present case this meant that the plaintiffs were entitled to such damages as would restore them to the position that they would have been in had the appropriate length of notice been given.

SECTION NINE—PENALTY CLAUSES AND LIQUIDATED DAMAGES

Treitel, G. H. Remedies for Breach of Contract, Oxford: Clarendon, 1988, 212–3. (Footnotes omitted.)

Purposes of penalty clauses

One purpose of penalty clauses is to fix in advance the damages payable in the event of default. That is in itself a perfectly legitimate and indeed laudable purpose. It obviates the often difficult tasks of assessing the aggrieved party's loss and of determining how much of that loss is legally recoverable. A clause which serves this purpose may even be advantageous from the point of view of the defaulting party in enabling him with some degree of certainty to know in advance what his liability will be in the event of default.

A second object of penalty clauses is precisely to limit a defaulting party's liability; and this is true in spite of the fact that penalty clauses are distinct in their legal nature from limitation clauses. This second object of penalty clauses is not always achieved; we shall see that in many legal systems liability is not necessarily limited to the amount of the payment stipulated.

A third object of penalty clauses is to provide a means of pressure on the debtor so as to coerce him into performing his principal undertaking. Indeed, in France penalty clauses have been described as a sort of *astreinte*, an analogy which is particularly apt where the penalty clause provides for a series of payments for each designated period of delay. It is obvious that the use of penalty clauses for this purpose is a potential source of abuse in that it may enable the creditor to exert an amount of pressure on the debtor which a particular legal system regards as excessive. It may at the same time enable the creditor to recover a sum of money which manifestly and very considerably exceeds the amount of his loss; and there is a natural reluctance on the part of the courts to make awards which drastically cut across the rules of law which determine the assessment of damages.

Such considerations have led to restrictions on the enforceability of penalty clauses in many legal systems: as a Scottish judge has said, 'the law will not let people punish each other.' This represents the attitude of Anglo-American law in which certain kinds of penalty clauses are wholly invalid, and indeed are sometimes said to be contrary to 'public policy' or to be 'unlawful' contracts; it is also the basis of the rule adopted in German law, in French law (since 1975) and in certain other systems by which the courts have power to reduce the amount of a disproportionately high penalty. These solutions are of course open to the objection that they tend to subvert the first and legitimate purpose of penalty clauses; and this purpose is best served by the general principle (which formerly prevailed in France and is still found in Belgium) of giving literal effect to penalty clauses. What is at stake here is the perennial conflict between certainty and justice; and in fact some degree of compromise is to be found in all the legal systems under consideration.

A. AGREED DAMAGES AND PENALTY CLAUSES

Dunlop Pneumatic Tyre Co. *v* New Garage and Motor Co. [1915] AC 79

Lord Dunedin:

My Lords, the appellants, through an agent, entered into a contract with the respondents under which they supplied them with their goods, which consisted mainly of motor tyre covers and tubes. By this contract, in respect of certain concessions as to discounts, the respondents bound themselves not to do several things, which may be shortly set forth as follows: not to tamper with the manufacturers' marks; not to sell to any private customer or co-operative society at prices less than the current price list issued by the Dunlop company; not to supply to persons whose supplies the Dunlop company had decided to suspend; not to exhibit or to export without the Dunlop company's assent. Finally, the agreement concluded (clause 5), 'We agree to pay the Dunlop Pneumatic Tyre Co. Ltd the sum of £5 for each and every tyre, cover or tube sold or offered in breach of this agreement, as and by way of liquidated damages and not as a penalty.'

The appellants, having discovered that the respondents had sold covers and tubes at under the current list price, raised action and demanded damages. The case was tried and the breach in fact held proved. An inquiry was directed before the master as to damages. The master inquired, and assessed the damages at £250, adding this explanation: 'I find that it was left open to me to decide whether the £5 fixed in the agreement was penalty or liquidated damages. I find that it was liquidated damages.'

The respondents appealed to the Court of Appeal, when the majority of that court, Vaughan Williams and Swinfen Eady L.JJ., held, Kennedy L.J. dissenting, that the said sum of £5 was a penalty, and entered judgment for the plaintiffs the sum of £2 as nominal damages. Appeal from that decision is now before your Lordships' House.

My Lords, we had the benefit of a full and satisfactory argument, and a citation of the very numerous cases which have been decided on this branch of the law. The matter has been handled, and at no distant date, in the courts of highest resort. I particularly refer to the *Clydebank* case[1] in your Lordships' House and the cases of *Public Works Commissioner v Hills*[2] and *Webster v Bosanquet*[3] in the Privy Council. In both of these cases many of the previous cases were considered. In view of that fact, and of the number of the authorities available, I do not think it advisable to attempt any detailed review of the various cases, but I shall content myself with stating succinctly the various propositions which I think are deducible from the decisions which rank as authoritative:

1. Though the parties to a contract who use the words 'penalty' or 'liquidated damages' may *prima facie* be supposed to mean what they say, yet the expression used is not conclusive. The court must find out whether the payment stipulated is in truth a penalty or liquidated damages. This doctrine may be said to be found *passim* in nearly every case.

2. The essence of a penalty is a payment of money stipulated as *in terrorem* of the offending party; the essence of liquidated damages is a genuine covenanted pre-estimate of damage (*Clydebank Engineering and Shipbuilding Co. v Don Jose Ramos Yzquierdo y Castaneda*).

3. The question whether a sum stipulated is penalty or liquidated damages is a question of construction to be decided upon the terms and inherent circumstances of

each particular contract, judged of as at the time of the making of the contract, not as at the time of the breach (*Public Works Commissioner v Hills* and *Webster v Bosanquet*).

4. To assist this task of construction various tests have been suggested, which if applicable to the case under consideration may prove helpful, or even conclusive. Such are:

(a) It will be held to be penalty if the sum stipulated for is extravagant and unconscionable in amount in comparison with the greatest loss that could conceivably be proved to have followed from the breach. (Illustration given by Lord Halsbury in *Clydebank* case.)

(b) It will be held to be a penalty if the breach consists only in not paying a sum of money, and the sum stipulated is a sum greater than the sum which ought to have been paid (*Kemble v Farren*[4]). This though one of the most ancient instances is truly a corollary to the last test. Whether it had its historical origin in the doctrine of the common law that when A promised to pay B a sum of money on a certain day and did not do so, B could only recover the sum with, in certain cases, interest, but could never recover further damages for non-timeous payment, or whether it was a survival of the time when equity reformed unconscionable bargains merely because they were unconscionable,—a subject which much exercised Jessel M.R. in *Wallis v Smith*[5]—is probably more interesting than material.

(c) There is a presumption (but no more) that it is penalty when 'a single lump sum is made payable by way of compensation, on the occurrence of one or more or all of several events, some of which may occasion serious and others but trifling damage' (Lord Watson in *Lord Elphinstone v Monkland Iron and Coal Co.*[6]).

On the other hand:

(d) It is no obstacle to the sum stipulated being a genuine pre-estimate of damage, that the consequences of the breach are such as to make precise pre-estimation almost an impossibility. On the contrary, that is just the situation when it is probable that pre-estimated damage was the true bargain between the parties (*Clydebank* case, Lord Halsbury; *Webster v Bosanquet*, Lord Mersey).

Turning now to the facts of the case, it is evident that the damage apprehended by the appellants owing to the breaking of the agreement was an indirect and not a direct damage. So long as they got their price from the respondents for each article sold, it could not matter to them directly what the respondents did with it. Indirectly it did. Accordingly, the agreement is headed 'Price Maintenance Agreement', and the way in which the appellants would be damaged if prices were cut is clearly explained in evidence by Mr Baisley, and no successful attempt is made to controvert that evidence. But though damage as a whole from such a practice would be certain, yet damage from any one sale would be impossible to forecast. It is just, therefore, one of those cases where it seems quite reasonable for parties to contract that they should estimate that damage at a certain figure, and provided that figure is not extravagant there would seem no reason to suspect that it is not truly a bargain to assess damages, but rather a penalty to be held *in terrorem*.

The argument of the respondents was really based on two heads. They overpressed, in my judgment, the dictum of Lord Watson in *Lord Elphinstone's* case, reading it as if he had said that the matter was conclusive, instead of saying, as he did, that it raised a presumption, and they relied strongly on the case of *Willson v Love*.[7]

Now, in the first place, I have considerable doubt whether the stipulated payment here can fairly be said to deal with breaches, 'some of which'—I am quoting Lord Watson's words—'may occasion serious and others but trifling damage.' As a mere matter of construction, I doubt whether clause 5 applies to anything but sales below price. But I will assume that it does. Nonetheless the mischief, as I have already pointed out, is an indirect mischief, and I see no data on which, as a matter of construction, I could settle in my own mind that the indirect damage from selling a cover would differ in magnitude from the indirect damage from selling a tube; or that the indirect damage from a cutting-price sale would differ from the indirect damage from supply at a full price to a hostile, because prohibited, agent. You cannot weigh such things in a chemical balance. The character of the agricultural land which was ruined by slag heaps in *Elphinstone's* case was not all the same, but no objection was raised by Lord Watson to applying an overhead rate per acre, the sum not being in itself unconscionable.

I think *Elphinstone's* case, or rather the dicta in it, do go this length, that if there are various breaches to which one indiscriminate sum to be paid in breach is applied, then the strength of the chain must be taken at its weakest link. If you can clearly see that the loss on one particular breach could never amount to the stipulated sum, then you may come to the conclusion that the sum is penalty. But further than this it does not go; so, for the reasons already stated, I do not think the present case forms an instance of what I have just expressed.

As regards *Willson's* case, I do not think it material to consider whether it was well decided on the facts. For it was decided on the view of the facts that the manurial value of straw and of hay were known ascertainable quantities as at the time of the bargain, and radically different, so that the damage resulting from the want of one could never be the same as the damage resulting from the want of the other.

Added to that, the parties there had said 'penalty', and the effort was to make out that that really meant liquidated damages; and lastly, if my view of the facts in the present case is correct, then Rigby L.J. would have agreed with me, for the last words of his judgment are as follows:

> On the other hand it is stated that, when the damages caused by a breach of contract are incapable of being ascertained, the sum made by the contract payable on such a breach is to be regarded as liquidated damages. The question arises, What is meant in this statement by the expression 'incapable of being ascertained'? In their proper sense the words appear to refer to a case where no rule or measure of damages is available for the guidance of a jury as to the amount of the damages, and a judge would have to tell them they must fix the amount as best they can.

To arrive at the indirect damage in this case, supposing no sum had been stipulated, that is just what a judge would, in my opinion, have had to do.

I move your Lordships that the appeal be allowed.

1. [1905] AC 6.
2. [1906] AC 368.
3. [1912] AC 394.
4. 6 Bing. 141.
5. 21 ChD 243.
6. (1886) 11 App Cas 332.
7. [1896] 1 QB 626.

Note

While penalty clauses are normally found to exist where the party in breach of contract is required to pay a sum of money upon breach, it has been recognised that where non-monetary obligations arise following a breach of contract, the law relating to penalties may still be invoked. In *Ringrow Pty Ltd v BT Australia Pty Ltd* [2005] HCA 71, R purchased a filling station from BP, the transaction involving a five-year solus tie in favour of BP. In breach of this agreement R took petroleum products from another supplier. The transaction included a provision that gave BP an option to purchase back the property upon breach of contract by R. Under the option agreement the price was to be fixed by a valuer but the valuer was not to make an allowance for goodwill and the option clause was cumulative in the sense that the contract also contained a liquidated damage clause (which was not challenged by R). The High Court of Australia held that the option provision was not extravagant or unconscionable, particularly in the light of evidence that goodwill in this context was unlikely to be of any value. In this case the High Court of Australia adopted a very traditional view of the law relating to penalties and this approach stands in stark contrast to the more recent commercial purpose approach canvassed in the English courts and discussed below.

Bradshaw *v* Lemon [1929] NI 159

Andrews L.J. (Best L.J. concurring):

In this case the plaintiff appeals from that portion of an order of the Lord Chief Justice made on 30 January 1929, by which he held that a rent of £50 sued for in paras 5 and 6 of the statement of claim was in the nature of a penalty, and that the plaintiff was therefore only entitled to such damages as he could prove. These damages the Lord Chief Justice measured at the sum of one shilling, and for this sum he, accordingly, gave judgment with costs of suit. The plaintiff asks that the judgment be set aside, and that judgment be entered for him for the sum of £369 15s, or, alternatively, that a new trial be ordered.

The only questions argued before us were whether the learned Lord Chief Justice was right in holding that the said rent of £50 was in the nature of a penalty; and, if he was correct in so holding, whether the damages of one shilling which he awarded were inadequate.

By lease, dated 9 September 1919, the plaintiff demised to the defendants certain premises situate in the town of Enniskillen consisting of a shop, dwelling house, yard and out offices, which were then in the occupation of the defendants for the term of twelve years from 1 November 1918, at the rent of £100, payable quarterly in every year. The lease contained the usual provisions for distress and re-entry, and a covenant by the defendants for payment of the rent, rates and taxes. Then followed a further covenant by the defendants that, owing to dilapidations caused during the defendants' present tenancy, they would within two years put the demised premises into a state of thorough repair according to the estimate of Mr Harvey at a cost of at least £420 16s 9d; and a proviso that if the works included in the estimate should not be completely finished within two years the said rent of £100 should be increased by the annual sum of £50, and during the residue of the term or so long as the said works should be unfinished the annual sum of £150 should be the rent reserved. Next followed covenants by the defendants for insurance, for the execution of sanitary works, for painting the cement on the front and gable of the premises, for keeping the premises in repair, and also against using any part of the front of the house as a bill posting hoarding, and against carrying on offensive trades in the premises. These covenants and provisions are followed by the clause with which alone we are directly concerned in this appeal, and which, by reason of its importance, I shall set out verbatim, namely:

. . . that on breach of any of these covenants or any part thereof this present demise shall be utterly null and void to all intents and purposes as if the same had never been made or that otherwise at the election of the lessor the lessees shall forfeit and pay unto the lessor from the time of the breach of any of these covenants or any part thereof a further additional yearly rent or sum of £50 sterling, to be paid quarterly as the said other rent and to be recovered by action of debt, distress or otherwise as the said hereby reserved yearly rent is recoverable anything herein contained to the contrary in anywise notwithstanding.

The construction of this covenant is a matter of some difficulty. I agree with [counsel for the plaintiff] that this additional rent of £50 is payable quarterly, as this is expressly provided, but I look in vain for any words similar to those contained in the covenant for payment of the first mentioned rent of £50, which would make the liability for this rent terminate if and when the breach of covenant were remedied; and it is difficult to imply words of limited duration in regard to the second rent which are expressed in regard to the first. Were it necessary, therefore, to decide the point I would not, as at present advised, be prepared to hold with [counsel's] contention that liability for this second rent of £50 could be determined at any time by remedying the breach and paying the sum of £12 10s as the then current quarter's instalment of such additional rent. It is unnecessary, however, to express any concluded opinion on the point, as there are other features of the liability for this rent which satisfy me that the Lord Chief Justice was perfectly right in holding that it was penal in character, and that the £50 must not be regarded as in the nature of liquidated damages.

In the first place, it is to be observed that on breach of any covenant the lessor is given an alternative remedy. He is entitled to elect whether the demise should be 'utterly null and void to all intents and purposes'—a right against which, no doubt, a court of equity would in a proper case grant relief under s. 14 of the Conveyancing Act 1881, yet one which is obviously penal in character. In these circumstances it would not be unreasonable to suppose that the alternative right—the additional rent of £50—was likewise penal. The view that it is such is in my opinion also supported, though not determined, by the expression that the lessees should 'forfeit and pay' this rent to the lessor—the significance of the use of this word *'forfeit'* is referred to by Lord Dunedin in *Public Works Commissioner v Hills*,[1] in which (at 375) he says that the word 'forfeited' is 'peculiarly appropriate to penalty, and not to liquidated damages.'

It is necessary, however, to consider briefly, so far as applicable, the general principles upon which the courts act in determining whether a named sum is to be regarded as a penalty or as liquidated damages. These principles have been enunciated so frequently during the last quarter of a century in both the House of Lords and the Privy Council that there can be no longer any doubt in regard to them. Amongst these cases may be cited *Clydebank Engineering & Shipbuilding Co. Ltd v Don Jose Ramos Yzquierdo y Castaneda*,[2] *Public Works Commissioner v Hills*, *Webster v Bosanquet*,[3] and *Dunlop Pneumatic Tyre Co. Ltd v New Garage & Motor Co. Ltd.*[4] From these cases it is clear that the essence of a penalty is a payment *in terrorem*, whilst the essence of liquidated damages is a genuine covenanted pre-estimate of damage. Hence if the sum stipulated for is extravagant and unconscionable in amount in comparison with the greatest amount of damage which could have possibly been in the contemplation of the parties when they made the contract, it is a penalty. The mere fact, however, that precise pre-estimation of damage is almost an impossibility is not a reason for a named sum being regarded as a penalty. On the contrary, it is just in such a case, where precise proof of damage would be difficult or complex, that the parties may reasonably be said to have intended the sum which they named to be a pre-estimate which would avoid all such difficulties of proof. Again, there is a presumption (though one which is rebuttable) that when a single indiscriminate lump sum is made payable by way of compensation on the occurrence of one or more or all of several events, some of which may occasion serious and others but trifling damage, such sum is a penalty; and the strength of the chain must be tested on its weakest link, so that if it be clearly established that the loss on one particular breach could never possibly amount to the stipulated sum, it must be regarded as a penalty. On the other hand, if, though there be several stipulations of varying degrees of importance, the damage likely to accrue from each is the same in kind, and the same agreed sum could be properly construed as a fair and reasonable pre-estimate of probable damage, the named sum would be held to be in the nature of liquidated damages. Enormous disparity of the sum to any conceivable loss will point one way; while the fact of the payment being in terms proportionate to the loss will point the other.

When I apply these principles to the facts of the present case I have no hesitation in holding that this additional rent of £50, imposed in respect of breaches of covenant of varying importance and different in kind, must be regarded as fixed *in terrorem* to compel the lessee's obedience to the covenants in the lease, and, therefore, in the nature of a penalty; for such a sum would in my opinion be 'disproportionate to', and 'wholly extravagant and unconscionable' in comparison with any damage which the parties could possibly have contemplated as resulting from the breach of such covenants, as, for example, the covenants to paint the cement, or not to use any part of the front of the house as a bill-posting hoarding.

In these circumstances it was in my opinion the duty of the learned Lord Chief Justice to assess as damages the actual loss which in his opinion the plaintiff sustained by the breach of covenant established by the evidence.

1. [1906] AC 368.   3. [1912] AC 394.
2. [1905] AC 6.   4. [1915] AC 79.

(Best L.J. agreed.)

Irish Telephone Rentals Ltd *v* Irish Civil Service Building Society [1992] 2 IR 525

The plaintiff rented out to the defendant a telephone installation for use in its head office. The system proved unfit for its purpose and was replaced by another system. This system, while far from problem free, was held by Costello J. not to be such as to justify repudiation of the contract by the defendant. The plaintiff sought damages for wrongful termination under clause 11 of the contract.

Costello J.:

. . .

What falls therefore now for consideration is whether the plaintiff is entitled to an award under clause 11 or whether this clause, as the defendant contends, is a penalty clause and therefore unenforceable. If it is then I must assess damages according to common law principles.

Clause 11 provides as follows:

If the subscriber [that is, the defendant] shall repudiate this contract and the company [that is, the plaintiff] shall accept such repudiation so as to terminate this contract the company may thereupon remove the installation and the subscriber shall pay to the company all payments then accrued and also a sum equal to the present value on a 5 per cent basis of the remaining rentals that would have been payable under this contract if not so terminated less an allowance of 25 per cent to cover the estimated cost of maintenance and value of recovered material. The said sums shall be payable as liquidated damages it being an agreed estimate of the loss the company would suffer.

I have the following comments to make on this clause.

(1) The estimate of the plaintiff's loss arising from premature termination is based on the gross rents outstanding for the unexpired term of the contract. However, the clause accepts, and correctly accepts, that the plaintiff is not entitled to the full amount of these rents. It also accepts that whatever may be the figure for the agreed loss which the plaintiff may suffer that figure should be discounted because instead of receiving the balance of the rents in instalments over the years an accelerated payment of the rent will be made to the plaintiffs. The discount in clause 11 is 5 per cent. Whilst the defendant readily accepts the principle of discounting it is urged that the sum estimated for the plaintiff's loss should be discounted at a higher rate.

(2) The figure for the gross rent is to be reduced, according to clause 11, by a further 25 per cent of the discounted rent because (a) the plaintiff will have been saved maintenance costs during the unexpired term and (b) an allowance should be given for the value of the installations recovered. The plaintiff's evidence is that the 25 per cent deduction was calculated by allowing a figure of 5 per cent of the discounted gross rent as the percentage attributable to maintenance charges and 20 per cent of the discounted gross rent as the percentage attributable to the value of the returned installations.

(3) It will be observed that the formula is based on a deduction from the gross amount of the outstanding rent of a sum equivalent to 28.7 per cent of the gross rent (25 per cent of 5 per cent of the gross rents) in respect of the estimated cost of maintenance and the estimated value of the recovered installations. The clause was attempting to make an estimate of what the plaintiff would lose by the contract's premature termination. As the correct measure of the plaintiff's loss on premature termination at any point of time during the life of the contract is the profit it would have earned in the outstanding period of the contract's life the formula in clause 11 can only be correct if it produces a figure which approximates to that profit. It follows, therefore that this clause can be shown to be a correct estimate of the plaintiff's loss if in every case of premature termination the profit thereby lost is 71.25 per cent of the gross rental then outstanding.

(4) Clause 11 is a standard clause. All the plaintiff's hiring contracts contain this estimate of the loss suffered on each of the plaintiff's contracts should they be prematurely terminated. The defendant has submitted that the sum calculated in accordance with the condition does not represent a genuine pre-estimate of the actual loss which the plaintiff sustained as a result of the wrongful repudiation of the hiring agreement but is a penalty clause which the court should not enforce. The courts have evolved various rules for considering whether a stipulated sum is a penalty or a genuine pre-estimate. That which is relevant to the present case is that stated by Lord Dunedin in *Dunlop Pneumatic Tyre Co. Ltd v New Garage and Motor Co. Ltd* [1915] AC 79 at 87: 'It will be held to be a penalty if the sum stipulated for is extravagant and unconscionable in amount in comparison with the greatest loss that could conceivably be proved to have followed from the breach.'

The application of this principle is to be seen in the majority decision of the Court of Appeal in England in *Robophone Facilities Ltd v Blank* [1966] 1 WLR 1428 in which the court considered a contract for the hiring of a telephone-answering machine for a seven year period which was repudiated before the hiring began. The hiring agreement contained a clause which made provision in the event of premature termination for the payment of agreed liquidated damages equal to 50 per cent of the total of the rentals due. In deciding that the sum of 50 per cent was a genuine pre-estimate of loss and not a penalty Lord Diplock examined what would be recoverable by way of damage assessed on common law principles and concluded that because 50 per cent of the gross rent would not produce a figure which was 'extravagantly greater' than those damages the clause was enforceable.

Before considering in greater detail the operation in this case of clause 11 I should give some more detail of how the plaintiff's claim is made up.

The plaintiff has calculated that there were nine full years of the agreement to run from the date of termination. The annual rent at that time (which had been increased over the years pursuant to the rent revision clause) was then £1,438.16. This annual rent was discounted over a nine year period by 5 per cent giving a discounted figure of £10,222.15. There was added to this one quarter's rent unpaid in 1988 (that is, £359.51) giving a total of £10,581.69. A figure of 25 per cent of this sum was then calculated, that is a sum of £2,645.42. This was deducted from the sum of £10,581.69 giving a figure of £7,936.27. It is to be noted that the gross rent for the unexpired nine year period of the hiring was £13,043.62 according to these calculations.

I have come to the conclusion that the formula contained in clause 11 does not produce a liquidated sum that can properly be regarded as a genuine pre-estimate made at the date of the contract of the loss which the plaintiff would suffer should the contract be prematurely determined and that it is in reality a penalty and therefore unenforceable. My reasons are as follows:

(a) In estimating the plaintiff's loss clause 11 correctly allows a deduction from the gross rents of the sums saved in maintenance charges. But the evidence establishes that the 5 per cent figure is an estimate not of all the maintenance charges which would have been incurred had the contract run its course but only an estimate of the cost of materials used in maintenance and expenses such as daily allowance, petrol and the travelling expenses of maintenance staff. The wages of the maintainence staff are excluded. Support for this approach is claimed by the plaintiff from an unreported judgment of the High Court in England (the transcript of which was made available) in *Telephone Rentals Ltd* (the plaintiff's English parent company) *v Photophone Ltd* delivered 8 February 1957. I do not think that this approach is correct and, with respect, I cannot follow that judgment to which I was referred. In estimating the loss which the plaintiff would suffer the draftsman of clause 11 should have attempted to estimate the net profit which the plaintiff would have earned had the contract been performed. This net profit should have been calculated by deducting the actual total costs of maintenance and not only a proportion of those costs. It seems to me that this error produces an estimate very much in excess of the plaintiff's actual loss and cannot be regarded as a genuine pre-estimate of that loss.

(b) The clause makes no allowance for other deductions which in my judgment should have been made from the gross rent figure. The evidence establishes that when originally fixing the rent under the contract the plaintiff took into account not only the likely maintenance charges but also finance charges, administrative costs and engineering costs. Any genuine calculation of the actual loss likely to be suffered from premature termination should make an allowance for these charges as otherwise the plaintiff would receive more than the profit it would have made had the contract run its course.

. . .

lations. It is to be borne in mind that the hiring was to last for twelve years and that there was a rent variation clause.

(d) The result of the operation of the formula is to award a liquidated sum equal to 71.25 per cent of the gross rent, less 5 per cent for accelerated payment. This predicates a net profit of 71.25 per cent had the contract not been terminated. This is quite an enormous net profit. Whilst the onus is on the party who alleges that a clause in a contract is a penalty and not a genuine pre-estimate of the loss which would be suffered by premature termination I think the onus is discharged once the clause in question is based on the assumption that this is an estimate of the profit the plaintiff lost.

The plaintiff has not produced its profit and loss account and so I do not know what it shows. But I am entitled to apply the knowledge of financial affairs which is available to every reader of the daily press from which companies' net profits as a percentage of their turnover is shown for an extensive range of different classes of businesses. These, of course, vary widely. In the retail trade a net profit of 10 per cent of turnover is an average figure. In some manufacturing companies it may be considerably less or considerably more. A net profit of 71 per cent of turnover would be a staggeringly large one in any business and in the absence of proof that this is what the plaintiff earned I am driven to the conclusion that the estimate of loss contained in clause 11 is not a genuine pre-estimate but is a penalty.

I cannot therefore allow the plaintiff's claim based on clause 11 and must assess damages based on the actual loss I think the plaintiff suffered.

Note

The distinction between a clause that is operative on breach by a hirer, as distinct from the exercise of a termination right, is generally overlooked with the law of penalties being applied in both instances. This is a pro-consumer approach.

In *Volkswagen Financial Services* (UK) *v Ramage* (9 May 2007), an English County Court decision, a hire contract provided that, upon early termination, the hirer would pay 'as compensation or agreed damages, the total amount of rental (thirty-six months) less amount of rental paid. This clause was held to be a penalty. No account was taken of the benefit of early return of a profit-earning chattel, and certain savings to the owner under the agreement (breakdown service), as well as the fact that there was no effort to estimate the loss in any genuine way. This is a similar process of reasoning to that demonstrated by Costello J. in *Irish Telephone Rentals*.

B. A New Approach in the English Courts

Case-law in England in the 1990s has led to reassessment of the the *Dunlop* case with the result that freely negotiated provisions are less likely to be struck down as penalties. Perhaps the most important dicta are two observations of Coleman J. in _Lordsville Finance plc v Bank of Zambia_ [1996] QB 752 and on eby Lord Woolf in _Philips Hong Kong Ltd v AG of Hong Kong_ (1993) 61 BLR 49. These are, respectively:

- Whether a clause is a penalty is a matter of construction to be resolved by asking, was the predominate contractual function behind the clause to deter a party from breaking the contract or compensate the innocent party upon breach. That the clause is a deterrent rather than compensatory can be deduced by comparing the amount payable on breach as distinct from the loss occasioned by breach.
- Certain clauses may appear to be deterrent in nature (e.g. a clause that increases the consideration payable in an executory contract upon breach), but will not be struck down 'if the increase can be explained as commercially justifiable provided it's dominant purpose was not to deter any party from breach'.
- The court should not set too stringent a standard, and bear in mind that 'what the parties have agreed should normally be upheld. Any other approach will lead to undesirable uncertainty especially in commercial contracts' (Lord Woolf).

Of the four Tests set out by Lord Dunedin, factor (a) has to an extent been recast as requiring the court to compare the amount payable under the clause with that which would have been payable if the claim were brought at common law. But it has been said that it does not follow that the clause will be a penalty if there is discrepancy between these amounts: the issue should be judged 'in the round' as befits 'a broad and general question'. This is particularly the case in certain kinds of contract where the traditional learning on penalty clauses does not readily fit, such as employment contracts, although in cases such as _Girand UK v Smith_ [2002] IRLR 763 the English High Court had no difficulty in using the Dunedin tests to strike down a clause as a penalty.

In the area of employment law the decision of the English Court of Appeal, in _Murray v Leisureplay Plc_ [2005] EWCA Civ 963 bring together these new approaches. Murray was the chief executive of a financial services company that sought to acquire other financial institutions. Murray was himself involved in other businesses and was engaged to work for three days a week. His draft contract provided that upon wrongful termination of his contract, he was to be given up to three years' salary, although this was later revised down to require one year's compensation. Murray was dismissed with seven and a half weeks' notice and claimed to be entitled to pocket both the salary paid during that seven and a half weeks, plus one year's salary under the liquidated damages clause. Leisureplay claimed that the clause was a penalty: in particular Leisureplay pointed out that under the clause Murray had no obligation to mitigate his loss and, given his other business interests, it was likely on breach that Murray would find employment elsewhere.

The comparison between the stipulated sum and the sums recoverable in a common law action resulted in the stipulated sum being more favourable to Murray, but this did not mean the sum was a penalty. The sum need not be an accurate statement of loss. Buxton L.J. said the contract terms were generous but not unconscionable.

On the 'broader' issue of what the agreement sought to do, Buxton L.J. took judicial notice of the fact that a company in this area would need to offer a package that gave 'generous reassurance' against the eventuality of dismissal. The contract contained restrictions against Murray working in a competing environment after departure. The clause precluded any right to claim arrears of pension contribution. The contract injected certainty and averted possible disputes and unwanted publicity. The mitigation point was met by remarking that *at the time of contract* it was by no means clear that Murray would get other employment and the absence of any statement in the contract vis-à-vis duty to mitigate was intended to avoid disputes about whether Murray was acting reasonably. On the *in terrorem* point, the Court of Appeal stressed that Murray had no interest in deterring breach but, objectively, the clause was there to compensate for the loss to other business interests that followed from his employment with Leisureplay. Note also:

- Strong emphasis was placed on the need for contracts to be upheld – *pacta sunt servanda*
- The onus rests on the party seeking to invalidate the clause to show the clause is a penalty
- As long as dominant purpose is not to deter, commercial justification for the clause will be respected, especially in cases like this where there is considerable parity of bargaining power.

This approach has also been applied in construction contracts: CFW *Architects (a firm) v Cowlin Construction Ltd* [2006] EWHC (TCC)6, as well as in employment agency contracts such as *Euro London Appointments Ltd v Claessens International Ltd* [2006] EWCA Civ 385.

Note

In *Philips Hong Kong v AG of Hong Kong* (1993) 61 BLR 41 the Privy Council held that a clause is not a penalty if it seeks to impose different penalties for breach, even if such a clause contains a minimum amount by way of liquidated and ascertained damages, regardless of the extent to which the actual performance falls short of the contracted standard.

C. THE RULE IN RELATION TO PENALTIES CAN BE AVOIDED BY CAREFUL DRAFTING

Lombard North Central plc *v* Butterworth [1987] 1 All ER 267

Mustill L.J.:

The respondent plaintiffs are a finance company. The defendant appellant is an accountant. The defendant wished to buy a computer to improve his business, and enlisted the help of the plaintiffs. They purchased a particular model, and then entered into an agreement of hiring whereby they agreed to lease the computer to the defendant for a period of five years. There was to be an initial payment of £584.05 and nineteen subsequent instalments of the same amount, payable at intervals of three months. In addition, VAT was to be paid.

The hiring agreement contained the following material provisions:

> *The lessee . . . agrees . . .*
>
> 2. (a) to pay to the lessor: (i) punctually and without previous demand the rentals set out in part 3 of the schedule together with VAT thereon punctual payment of each which shall be of the essence of this lease . . .
>
> 5. *In the event that* (a) the lessee shall (i) make default in the due and punctual payment of any of the rentals or of any sum of money payable to the lessor hereunder or any part thereof . . . then upon the happening of such event . . . the lessor's consent to the lessee's possession of the goods shall determine forthwith without any notice being given by the lessor, and the lessor may terminate this lease either by notice in writing, or by taking possession of the goods . . .
>
> 6. *In the event* that the lessor's consent to the lessee's possession of the goods shall be determined under clause 5 hereof (a) the lessee shall pay forthwith to the lessor: (1) all arrears of rentals; and (ii) all further rental which would but for the determination of the lessor's consent to the lessee's possession of the goods have fallen due to the end of the fixed period of this lease less a discount thereon for accelerated payment at the rate of 5 per cent per annum; and (iii) damages for any breach of this lease and all expenses and costs incurred by the lessor in retaking possession of the goods and/or enforcing the lessor's rights under this lease together with such VAT as shall be legally payable thereon; (b) the lessor shall be entitled to exercise any one or more of the rights and remedies provided for in clause 5 and sub-clause (a) of this clause and the determination of the lessor's consent to the lessee's possession of the goods shall not affect or prejudice such rights and remedies and the lessee shall be and remain liable to perform all outstanding liabilities under this lease notwithstanding that the lessor may have taken possession of the goods and/or exercised one or more of the rights and remedies of the lessor. (c) Any right or remedy to which the lessor is or may become entitled under this lease or in consequence of the lessee's conduct may be enforced from time to time separately or concurrently with any other right or remedy given by this lease or now or hereafter provided for or arising by operation of law so that such rights and remedies are not exclusive of the other or others of them but are cumulative.

The letting under this agreement did not go well. The instalments were due to be paid by direct debit. The first two were effected satisfactorily but the third was twice recalled by the bank and remained unpaid for a period of four months. The fourth was paid two weeks late. The fifth was two months late. The sixth was paid on time, but was recalled by the bank. It was paid again one month later, and again recalled by the bank. Two weeks later the plaintiffs lost patience and sent to the defendant a letter in the following terms:

> We regret that in spite of our previous reminders you are still in arrear with your payments. Please take notice that pursuant to the terms of the lease our consent to

your possession of the goods is now withdrawn and you are required to make them available for collection. Your liability under the terms of the lease will not cease upon the return of these goods as we are entitled to call upon you to make payment of the balance of the rentals due under the remaining period of the lease. If payment of the arrears has been made within the last seven days please ignore this notice.

Subsequently, the plaintiffs recovered possession of the computer and sold it. The instrument fetched very little by comparison with its purchase price, and the net proceeds of sale were only £172.85.

On 18 May 1984 the plaintiffs commenced the present action by specially indorsed writ. The material parts read:

4. Pursuant to clause 5 of the said lease agreement the plaintiff terminated its consent to the defendant's possession of the said computer and printer by a notice in writing dated the 20th day of December 1982 and by virtue of the defendant's default under the said lease agreement the same has been determined.

5. Pursuant to clause 6 of the said lease agreement and by virtue of the determination of consent to possession pursuant to clause 5 thereof the plaintiff is entitled to claim (a) all of his rentals (b) all further rentals which would have been payable had the lease agreement continued for the full period and (c) damages for breach of the lease agreement.

6. The plaintiff has recovered possession of the said computer and printer in accordance with its entitlement to do so under clause 5 of the said lease agreement and the net proceeds of sale amounted to £172.85. Calculating the amounts due to the plaintiff the defendant will be given credit for this sum and an allowance will be made for accelerated receipt of the payment due under the said lease agreement as provided in clause 6 thereof.

7. The defendant has failed to pay the sums referred to in para. 5 hereof and the plaintiff is entitled under the lease of alternatively as damages for breach of the lease, the sum of £6,869.97.

The sum of £6,869.97 was arrived at by adding the amount of the unpaid instalment and VAT, and the thirteen rentals due after termination, and then giving credit for the net proceeds of sale and an allowance of £1,221.49 for accelerated receipt. The pleading concluded with claims of £6,869.97 under para. 7, interest and 'damages for breach of contract'.

The reason why I am impelled to hold that the plaintiffs' contentions are well founded can most conveniently be set out in a series of propositions. (1) Where a breach goes to the root of the contract, the injured party may elect to put an end to the contract. Thereupon both sides are relieved from those obligations which remain unperformed. (2) If he does so elect, the injured party is entitled to compensation for (a) any breaches which occurred before the contract was terminated and (b) the loss of his opportunity to receive performance of the promisor's outstanding obligations. (3) Certain categories of obligation, often called conditions, have the property that any breach of them is treated as going to the root of the contract. On the occurrence of any breach of condition, the injured party can elect to terminate and claim damages, whatever the gravity of the breach. (4) It is possible to express provision in the contract to make a term a condition, even if it would not be so in the absence of such a provision. (5) A stipulation that time is of the essence, in relation to a particular contractual term, denotes that timely performance is a condition of the contract. The consequence is that delay in performance is treated as going to the root of the contract, without

regard to the magnitude of the breach. (6) It follows that where a promisor fails to give timely performance of an obligation in respect of which time is expressly stated to be of the essence, the injured party may elect to terminate and recover damages in respect of the promisor's outstanding obligations, without regard to the magnitude of the breach. (7) A term of the contract prescribing what damages are to be recoverable when a contract is terminated for a breach of condition is open to being struck down as a penalty, if it is not a genuine covenanted pre-estimate of the damage, in the same way as a clause which prescribes the measure for any other type of breach. No doubt the position is the same where the clause is ranked as a condition by virtue of an express provision in the contract. (8) A clause expressly assigning a particular obligation to the category of condition is not a clause which purports to fix the damages for breaches of the obligation, and is not subject to the law governing penalty clauses. (9) Thus, although in the present case clause 6 is to be struck down as a penalty, clause 2(a)(i) remains enforceable. The plaintiffs were entitled to terminate the contract independently of clause 5, and to recover damages for loss of the future instalments. This loss was correctly computed by the master. These bare propositions call for comment. . .
. . .

. . . The seventh is uncontroversial, and I would add only the rider that when deciding on the penal nature of a clause which prescribes a measure of recovery for damages resulting from a termination founded on a breach of condition, the comparison should be with the common law measure, namely with the loss to the promisee resulting from the loss of his bargain. If the contract permits him to treat the contract as repudiated, the fact that the breach is comparatively minor should in my view play no part in the equation.

I believe that the real controversy in the present case centres on the eighth proposition. I will repeat it. A clause expressly assigning a particular obligation to the category of condition is not a clause which purports to fix the damages for breach of the obligation, and is not subject to the law governing penalty clauses. I acknowledge, of course, that by promoting a term into the category where all breaches are ranked as breaches of condition, the parties indirectly bring about a situation where, for breaches which are relatively small, the injured party is enabled to recover damages as on the loss of the bargain, whereas without the stipulation his measure of recovery would be different. But I am unable to accept that this permits the court to strike down as a penalty the clause which brings about this promotion. To do so would be to reverse the current of more than 100 years' doctrine, which permits the parties to treat as a condition something which would not otherwise be so. I am not prepared to take this step.

For these reasons I conclude that the plaintiffs are entitled to retain the damages which the master has awarded. This is not a result which I view with much satisfaction, partly because the plaintiffs have achieved by one means a result which the law of penalties might have prevented them from achieving by another and partly because if the line of argument under clause 2 had been developed from the outset, the defendant . . .

(Nicholls and Lawton, L.JJ. gave judgments to like effect.)

Note

When the contract is drafted so as to label obligations to be conditions precedent rather than provisions that trigger payment obligations, the natural reluctance of the courts to extend the law relating to penalties, viewed in the light of the dominant contractual purpose test, may be expected to operate so as to exclude the law on penalties. However, conditions subsequent may not always have this effect: CML *Group plc v Zhang* [2006] EWCA Civ 408.

EXERCISES

1. John leaves a roll of film to be developed with his local chemist. When he returns to collect his prints, he is informed that the film was accidentally exposed to sunlight and that the images have been lost. John informs the chemist that the film contained images of the Loch Ness monster and that John had sold the rights to the *Daily Blagg* for €2 million. Can John recover €2 million from the chemist?

2. Edna has agreed to buy a first edition of *Ulysses* for €20,000 from Bertie. Bertie had told Edna the book is worth €30,000, but that Bertie will take €20,000 for a quick sale. Just before delivery is due to take place, Bertie sells the book to Martin for €25,000. Edna has not paid any of the price to Bertie. Advise Edna on what damages, if any, she is entitled to in contract and tort.

3. Sam contracts to have his garden landscaped by Audrey. Sam returns from holiday to find that Audrey, inspired by an award-winning Chelsea Flowershow garden, has departed dramatically from the agreed design. Audrey has planted shrubs (not in the design) which emit high levels of pollen. Sam is forced to cancel his daughter's wedding (set in the landscaped garden) because he and his daughter suffer from hay fever. The cancellation causes great distress to Sam and his daughter, who seek your advice on damages.